FAUST'S METROPOLIS

FAUST'S METROPOLIS

A HISTORY OF BERLIN

ALEXANDRA RICHIE

HarperCollins*Publishers*

HarperCollins*Publishers*
77–85 Fulham Palace Road
Hammersmith, London W6 8JB

Published by HarperCollins*Publishers* 1998
1 3 5 7 9 8 6 4 2

A catalogue record for this book is
available from the British Library

ISBN 0 00 215896 5

Set in Postscript Minion by
Rowland Phototypesetting Limited
Bury St Edmunds, Suffolk

Printed in England by Clays Ltd, St Ives plc

For Władysław Bartoszewski

PREFACE

From the moment I first set foot in the city as a young student I became fascinated by Berlin. Like Faust, Berlin can be said to have two spirits in the same breast; it is both a terrible and a wonderful city, a place which has created and destroyed and whose name is both acclaimed and blackened. It is not without reason that Berlin has been called everything from the 'symbol of German destiny' to the 'city of the twenty-first century'. Above all, it is a place where history could not and still cannot be hidden away.

When I first went to live there Berlin was the ultimate border city, representing nothing less than the Cold War division between the 'Communist' and the 'Free' world. It was a capital city and a strange backwater, a centre and a borderland at the same time. The revolution which erupted in 1989 and led to the destruction of the Berlin Wall made it once again the focus of world attention. As I watched the Wall being reduced to rubble I realised that the dramatic changes would raise very disturbing questions about Berlin's role in Germany and its function as a symbol in the creation of German identity. Now more than ever it is imperative for us to be aware of the triumphs and the mistakes of its past, as the decisions made in Berlin in years to come will affect us all.

I have tried to write a book that addresses the city's crucial role in world events. It is not a local history, although it has elements of this, but is a history of Germany – even of Europe, including the often-neglected east – as seen through the 'prism' of Berlin. The book is meant for the general reader. Much of the material is known and its claim to originality lies more in the selection and presentation of information than in new discoveries. I have tried to avoid specialist language and the narrow categories of contemporary historiography, choosing instead to weave various aspects of cultural, social and economic history together with more conventional military or diplomatic approaches into a comprehensive whole. With the exception of the introduction, which brings the story up to date, the book follows a broad chronological framework. Although I cover all periods of Berlin's past, the emphasis is clearly on the city in the twentieth century, its role in the First World War, in the Holocaust, in the creation of modernist culture, in the identity of post-Cold War Europe – in numerous crucial events of the recent past.

Many people have helped me in the writing of this book. It evolved from the D.Phil which I wrote at St Antony's College, Oxford, and I would like to thank the Warden of St. Antony's, Lord Dahrendorf, and the Fellows of the College, particularly those at the European Studies Centre who have done so much to support my research. I would like to thank the President of Wolfson College, Sir David Smith, and the Fellows of the College for granting me a fellowship and providing the wonderful haven in which I was able to work. Timothy Garton Ash has been a great source of inspiration and I am most grateful to him for recommending me to HarperCollins. I would also like to thank Michael Burleigh for first suggesting Berlin as a topic, and Warren Magnusson and Raymond Klibansky for their help. I am most grateful to the late Sir Isaiah Berlin for persuading me to write history; it is not too much to say that his words changed the course of my life.

HarperCollins has been everything an author could hope for. Michael Fishwick has been an exemplary editor and has patiently guided this project from the beginning; Rebecca Lloyd was not only highly professional but also great fun to work with; both have become friends. I am grateful, too, to Helen Ellis, Stuart Proffitt, Kate Parrish, Annie Robertson, Phyllis Richardson, Sophie Nelson for copy-editing, Phil Lewis for the picture lay-out, Jon Gilkes for cartography and the many others who have contributed to the book.

Literally hundreds of Berliners let me into their lives and helped me to understand their city. Some selflessly showed me their neighbourhoods and took me into their homes; some assisted me in the search for sources, guided me through the archives and answered seemingly endless questions with characteristic good humour. I am particularly indebted to those East Berliners who befriended me before 1989, when such contact put them at considerable risk, and to the 'rubble ladies' who spoke of their post-1945 experiences with candour and courage. I would also like to thank the Boston Consulting Group, and in particular Barry Jones, John Lindquist and Charbel Ackermann, for giving me the opportunity to glimpse at first hand the economic transformation of East Germany after 1989.

I was enormously touched that Gordon Craig, that most respected of German historians and a man whose work I have long admired, took the time to read the manuscript and send comments and corrections, and I thank him for his very kind words. Thanks also to Peter Gay for reading so much and for his very helpful comments, to Harold James for reading the book and sending his very reassuring and insightful remarks, to Norman Naimark for reading the post-war chapters, to Thomas DaCosta Kaufmann for his detailed corrections of the early chapters and to Robert Conquest for, amongst other things, shedding light on the realities of 1930s Berlin. I would also like to thank James Sheehan, Fritz Stern, Max Hastings, Sir Michael Howard and Charles Maier for their comments, advice, and kind words of encouragement.

The writing of this book would have been much less enjoyable without the contributions of my dear friends Victoria Joffe, Levin von Trott zu Solz, Erik Svendson, Marlene Apmann, Stephen Pettyfer, James Allison, Margaret Craig and Serguisz Michalski. I am grateful to the many members of my extraordinary extended family around the globe who have done so much, and I owe a special debt to my father-in-law, Wladyslaw Bartoszewski, and to Andrew Ciechanowiecki, not least for their insights into German-Polish history. Above all, I would like to thank my father, Karl-Wilhelm, who, through his love and knowledge of German culture first awakened my passion for our shared heritage; my mother, Heather, whose unconditional love made this possible, and my brother, Fraser, with whom I shared my first Berlin adventures and so much besides. Finally, I have dedicated this book to my beloved husband, Wladyslaw Bartoszewski, whose tolerance, kindness and compassion know no limits and without whom the book would simply never have come to fruition. My gratitude is beyond words.

CONTENTS

MAPS AND ILLUSTRATIONS

LIST OF MAPS

LIST OF ILLUSTRATIONS

xi

Napoleon enters Berlin through the Brandenburg Gate (© Archiv für Kunst
    und Geschichte, Berlin)
'German Michael once again gives everything of himself' (© Bildarchiv
    Preussischer Kulturbesitz)
Berliners on the barricades (© Bildarchiv Preussischer Kulturbesitz)
Borsig's iron foundry (© Bildarchiv Preussischer Kulturbesitz)
The 'true Berliner' (© Bildarchiv Preussischer Kulturbesitz)
Young Silesian farm labourers (© Ullstein)
The Hochbahn, 1902 (© Ullstein)
'Who calls for a butcher?' (© Bildarchiv Preussischer Kulturbesitz)
The Prussian Garde in Versailles, 1871 (© Bildarchiv Preussischer
    Kulturbesitz)
Frederick William in the Schlosspark at Charlottenburg (© Bildarchiv
    Preussischer Kulturbesitz)
The Siegesallee (© Bildarchiv Preussischer Kulturbesitz)
Statues of William I, Johann II and Otto II (© Bildarchiv Preussischer
    Kulturbesitz)
Poster for the Berlin Secession (© Bildarchiv Preussischer Kulturbesitz)
Bismarck leaving Berlin from the Lehrter Bahnhof (© Bildarchiv
    Preussischer Kulturbesitz)
The Berlin Library, 1925 (© Bildarchiv Preussischer Kulturbesitz)

pp. 388–389

Poster for the Flotten Schauspiele (© Bildarchiv Preussischer Kulturbesitz)
A young woman putting flowers in the buttonhole of a recruit (© Ullstein)
A concert in the tower of the Berlin Rathaus (© Ullstein)
Berlin's first casualty list (© Ullstein)
Elephants of Hagenbeck's circus used to draw coal (© Ullstein)
War-wounded in the Moabit hospital, Christmas, 1918 (© Bildarchiv
    Preussischer Kulturbesitz)
The Russian delegation on its way to sign the Treaty of Brest-Litovsk
    (© Bildarchiv Preussischer Kulturbesitz)
Frontline troops returning to Berlin, 1918 (© Bildarchiv Preussischer
    Kulturbesitz)
Revolutionary troops before the Brandenburg Gate (© Ullstein)
Karl Radek (© Bildarchiv Preussischer Kulturbesitz)
The murdered Karl Liebknecht (© Ullstein)
The leaders of the Spartacus Uprising (© Ullstein)
Artistic festival at Der Sturm, 1923 (© Bildarchiv Preussischer Kulturbesitz)

INTRODUCTION

FAUST: Yes, one great thing did tempt me, one.
    You guess at it!

MEPHISTOPHELES: That's quickly done.
    I'd choose a typical metropolis,
    At centre, bourgeois stomach's gruesome bliss,
    Tight crooked alleys, pointed gables, mullions,
    Crabbed market stalls of roots and scallions . . .
    Then boulevards and spacious squares
    To flaunt aristocratic airs;
    And lastly, with no gate to stop them,
    The suburbs sprawl ad infinitum.

(Goethe, *Faust*, Part Two, Act IV)

AT THE END OF GOETHE'S *FAUST* Mephistopheles takes his charge to the top of a great mountain and tempts him one last time. 'You have surveyed the kingdoms of this world and all their glory,' he says to Faust and asks him if his 'insatiable appetite' would not be fulfilled by a life in the heart of the metropolis. He offers him a teeming city where he could explore streets bustling with 'activity and stench', through crowds of men and women who run back and forth like ants whose nest has been kicked in. It is not a flattering picture; nor is it surprising that Goethe equates 'the metropolis' with the Devil's world. The city in *Faust* is a mythical place, but it could well have been based on Berlin – which Goethe loathed. He visited only once, in May 1778, and apart from those he saw on his Italian journeys it was the only big city – certainly the only German 'metropolis' – that he ever experienced. When he arrived Frederick the Great was preparing for one of his campaigns and Goethe was overwhelmed by the 'thousands upon thousands of people' who filled the streets in 'preparation of their sacrifice'. He found the grandiose buildings overbearing, and the crowds and the noise and the brashness of the place oppressive: 'one doesn't get very far with politeness in Berlin', he snorted, 'because such an audacious race of men lives there that one has to have a sharp tongue in order to keep oneself afloat.' He summed up Berlin in a single word: 'crude'.[1]

Goethe was certainly not the only one to comment on Berlin's raw edges.

Like the metropolis in *Faust* it has always been a rather shabby place – it is neither an ancient gem like Rome, nor an exquisite beauty like Prague, nor a geographical marvel like Rio. It was formed not by the gentle, cultured hand which made Dresden or Venice but was wrenched from the unpromising landscape by sheer hard work and determination. The city was built by its coarse inhabitants and its immigrants, and it became powerful not because of some Romantic destiny but because of its armies and its work ethic, its railroads and its belching smokestacks, its commerce and industry and its often harsh *Realpolitik*. The longing to make something out of the flat, windswept landscape is still reflected in the remnants of Berlin's grimy brick slums, in its ground-breaking industrial architecture, in its heavy imperial buildings, even in its rusting memorials to the gods of war – now embarrassing reminders of a belligerent past. Berlin is no beauty, to be sure, but for those captivated by her she does have a strange, rough magic; an endearing resilient spirit that is hard to define. In *Streets in Berlin and Elsewhere* Siegfried Kracauer, another admirer, wrote: 'Before my window the city condenses into an image that is as wondrous as the spectacle of nature. This landscape is artless Berlin. Unintentionally she speaks out her contradictions – her toughness, her openness, her co-existence, her splendour.' Kracauer is right – Berlin is special not as a result of any carefully placed statues or magnificent buildings, but because of an unintended ugly beauty which surrounds the old ochre *Hinterhöfe* or tenements in Moabit or the unpretentious local *Kneipen* with their menus of pea soup and *Bockwurst* and beer, or the extravagant nineteenth-century villas in Zehlendorf or the little fountain in Friedrichshain with its carved frogs and turtles. It is a sprawling city with an ever-changing landscape from the wealthy Tiergarten to the desolate anonymity of Hellersdorf; from the imposing Mitte to the old citadel at Spandau, one of the best-preserved Italian Renaissance fortresses in Europe.[2]

It is impossible to escape the ghosts of history which hover above the Reichstag and over Göring's intact Air Ministry and around the Brandenburg Gate. They waft around the remnants of the great brick and iron railway stations and the pieces of the Wall being ground to gravel on disused wasteland on the outskirts of the city; they linger in the pungent, mustard-coloured hallways of the monstrous East German housing projects and in the remnants of the *Hinterhof* cellars where, during the last century, the poor workers died of typhus and cholera. History is in the Landwehr Canal into which Rosa Luxemburg's body was dumped in 1919, in Schinkel's beautifully proportioned buildings and in the rubble mountains of 'Mont Klamott' and the Teufelsberg, the latter built on the ruins of Speer's Technical University. Ghosts watch the shores of Berlin's lovely lakes: the peaceful Grunewaldsee, so beautifully painted in Walter Leistikow's 1895 work of the same name; or the Wannsee with its little sailboats and pretty aspects, the site of Heinrich von Kleist's suicide in 1811 after writing the poem *On the Morning of my Death*, and of the conference which formalized the Final Solution.[3]

But above all history is in the empty spaces – in the broad, windswept fields and vacant lots which still stretch across the centre of town, where one can still find pieces of wrought iron or porcelain from long-forgotten staircases or dinner services. History is there in the single houses which stand alone – all that is left of a row, or perhaps even an entire street – their awkwardness emphasized by the 1970s murals peeling from the huge, beige fire walls. History twines through the branches of the trees which follow abandoned streets and along rusty tram tracks which lead nowhere and lingers on the piece of ground where Spandau Prison once stood. In Berlin the wounds of a troubled past are still painfully open, the scars still fresh.

Many have tried to capture this strange, incomplete city, this unfinished metropolis. It has been filmed and written about in hundreds of works, the subject of a thousand paintings. Ernst Toller and Sergei Diaghilev and Arnold Schoenberg loved it; Goethe and Lessing and Heinrich Heine were infuriated by it; Theodor Fontane and Alfred Döblin saw through it. Paunchy, cocky Berliners were the main subjects of Heinrich Zille's witty sketches; weary, grey-faced workers inhabit Baluschek's moving portrayals of the slums; self-confident Wilhelmine ladies dazzle us from Menzel's warm portraits of the Kaiser's court; its hardness is captured in the faces of prostitutes leering from the works of Georg Grosz and Otto Dix, and its very history is encapsulated in Meidner's apocalyptic visions which exploded across his canvases and foretold the end of innocence in the twentieth century. Berlin (disguised as London) is the star of Brecht and Weill's *Threepenny Opera* and of Isherwood's *Goodbye to Berlin* and the film *Cabaret*; it is captured in the *Berlin Diaries* of Marie Vassiltchikov and William Shirer and in films like Wim Wenders's *Der Himmel über Berlin* or Walter Ruttmann's *Sinfonie der Grossstadt* or Michail Tchiaureli's 1949 *The Fall of Berlin* with its score by Dmitri Shostakovich. Now a new group of hopefuls have taken up where Döblin left off and Berlin has become the main character of novels from Botho Strauss's *Die Feheler des Kopisten* and Matthias Zschokke's *Der dicke Dichter* to Bodo Morshäuser's *Gezielte Blicke* and Jakob Arjouni's *Magic Hoffmann*.

All these works offer tantalizing glimpses of Berlin but none can truly capture the essence of a place whose identity is based not on stability but on change. Berlin can appear solid and secure at one moment, but its history has shown the dangers of taking the image for granted. It is a volatile place, and many have found to their cost that the veneer of normality can vanish as quickly as yellow Mark Brandenburg sand slips through the fingers. Berliners themselves have rarely appreciated their own unique qualities and have spent much of their history striving to emulate – or dominate – Paris or London or Moscow, or boasting that they have more bridges than Venice, or that they are the Athens or the Chicago on the Spree. Berlin is a city which has never been at ease with itself.

It is in its portrayal of constant striving without counting the cost that the legend of *Faust* can serve as a metaphor for the history of Berlin. With Mephistopheles at his side Faust embarks on a terrible journey of discovery, meeting vile witches and the griffins and sphinxes of antiquity, being thrilled by the science and art and politics of the world, and murdering and burning those who stand in his way. Berlin, too, has undertaken an extraordinary journey, and its persistent quest for change has left it either – as now – cautiously searching for a role, or indulging in overweening arrogance and aggression. Its chameleon tendency to follow each new great ideology or leader, or to lurch maniacally from one grand political vision to another, has left a mesmerizing but often tragic legacy.

'So it is, when long-held hopes aspire', Goethe's Faust cries, 'fulfilment's door stands open wide when suddenly, from eternal depths inside, an over-powering flame roars to confound us.' Berlin is no stranger to this fire. No other city on earth has had such a turbulent history; no other capital has repeatedly become so powerful and then fallen so low. Its early years were marked by waves of immigration and population shifts – Burgundians, Wends, missionary Christians all left their mark on the little trading town in the Mark Brandenburg. Its rise began in earnest with the coming of the Hohenzollern dynasty which, after the gruesome deprivations of the Thirty Years War, led Prussia's relentless drive for great power status through the creation of a stable economy and, more to the point, a formidable army – the 'army with a state'. But the path was not a smooth one and Berlin seesawed between triumphalism and defeat, one moment revelling in the spoils of Frederick the Great's victory in the Seven Years War, the next licking its wounds as the humiliated vassal occupied by Napoleon. Berlin's drive for prestige was fulfilled when it became the capital of Bismarck's united Germany in 1871, when the *parvenu*, 'upstart' city took on the world and became a dynamic industrial powerhouse. But this too was shattered in the slaughter of the First World War, a bloodbath largely provoked by Berlin's leaders which led to the deaths in the trenches of 350,000 of its young men. The city emerged from war a mere shadow of its former self, racked by civil strife and targeted both by Lenin as the key to the world revolution, and by Hitler as the key to the German one. The extraordinary burst of creativity for which the Weimar Republic is remembered was not enough to prevent both left and right from turning its streets into a bloody battleground. Hitler's victory led to another convulsion, and all that Weimar had stood for was swept aside. Many of Berlin's greatest artists, writers, directors, architects and actors – men and women who touched every aspect of twentieth-century culture – fled or were murdered after 1933. Nevertheless, most Berliners dedicated themselves energetically to the Nazi cause with only a few brave individuals risking their lives to resist the downward spiral into criminality and mass murder. The shadow cast by Hitler's 'Germania' was dark indeed – it was Berlin, after all, which prompted Elias Canetti to write in 1943 that he could no longer look at a map as 'the names of cities reek of burnt flesh'.[4] Throughout its history Berlin has seemed to contain, in Nietzsche's words, something that 'is hostile to life and destructive . . . a hidden will to death'.[5] As early as 1907 the Berlin critic Maximilian Harden wrote in *Die Krisis* that Berlin held the seeds of its own destruction; it was already famous for its tendency 'to suffer more than other cities in an endless parade of grisly disappointments'.[6]

The city has a violent past, but the 'misery thesis' of the post-war period which taught that Luther begot Frederick begot Bismarck begot Hitler, or that the Prussian capital was the ultimate source of all that was evil in German history, was simplistic at best and overshadowed its great cultural, political and economic contributions to Europe's heritage. The poetry and music written to celebrate the end of the Thirty Years War, the tolerance enshrined in the Edict of Potsdam which granted asylum to the persecuted Huguenots of France, the Enlightenment of Nicolai and Mendelssohn and the salons of Rahel Levin and Henriette Hertz also have their place in Berlin's history. The city was a focus for the arts: Carl Maria von Weber's *Der Freischütz* was premièred in Berlin, as was Alban Berg's *Wozzeck*; indeed the first ever performance of fragments of Part I of Goethe's *Faust* took place there in 1819.[7] Nineteenth-century Berlin might have been the most militaristic city in Europe, but its university and its myriad institutes and museums and societies also made it one of the greatest centres of intellectual life; if Berlin was the city of von Roon and von Moltke it also belonged to Hegel and Virchow, Schinkel and Fontane. And it was then that a tough new breed of businessmen – Rathenau, Borsig, Bleichröder, Ullstein and Siemens – began to invent and invest and industrialize, transforming nineteenth-century Berlin from a struggling manufacturing centre into the mightiest industrial city in Europe. Industry attracted immigrants, and 'Red Berlin' grew exponentially, from 170,000 in 1800 to 4 million in just over a century, becoming the focal point of the new working-class movement soon to sweep the world. Lenin, Marx, Luxemburg and Liebknecht, Bebel and Radek all spent time there, plotting the Communist revolution to be carried out by disgruntled workers rising up in the factories and slums. At the same time Berlin became an unlikely centre for those modernists who dared to defy the Kaiser's bizarre pronouncements on art; the new Freie deutsche Bühne staged plays by Ibsen and Hauptmann while the Berlin Secession displayed the works

of Max Liebermann and Käthe Kollwitz and Edvard Munch. And then, in
the 1920s, Berlin became a magnet for the most innovative spirits of the age,
home to architects and members of the Bauhaus such as Mies van der Rohe,
Walter Gropius, Moholy-Nagy and Wassily Kandinsky, artists from Otto Dix
and Georg Grosz to Christian Schad, directors like Fritz Lang and Josef
von Sternberg and Billy Wilder, actors such as Josephine Baker, Marlene
Dietrich and Greta Garbo; musicians including Wilhelm Furtwängler, Otto
Klemperer and Arnold Schoenberg; and writers like Heinrich Mann, Gerhart
Hauptmann and Stefan Zweig, Carl Zuckmayer and Alfred Döblin. For a brief
shimmering moment these men and women made Berlin the undisputed
capital of twentieth-century culture. The Nazis destroyed all that and the city
has never recovered; nor did it recover from the demise of its once thriving
Jewish community. Most of Berlin's 170,000 Jews – a third of all Jews in
Germany – were forced to flee, or were murdered.

Defeated by the Allies in 1945 and occupied by the rapacious Soviet army,
Berlin turned its back on history and 'began again' at *Stunde Null* – Zero
Hour. The Cold War brought division between the world's two dominant and
opposing ideologies, and the sector boundary became the place where the
'Communist east' and the 'capitalist west' confronted each other, bringing
with them the constant threat of nuclear war. With the erection of the Wall
in 1961 the city was divided, each half with its own identity and culture yet
linked by a common past which everyone wanted to forget. In 1989 the grim,
Stasi-ridden GDR collapsed, and Berlin was once again unified and was later
named the capital of a united Germany. Now a new city is rising from the
vast building sites at the Potsdamer Platz and the Alexanderplatz and the
Spreebogen. Great promises are being made for this 'symbol of the new Germany', the 'capital of *Mitteleuropa*', the 'heart of Europe'. But how accurate
will such predictions be?

When Berlin was named the capital of a united Germany in 1871 the
optimism was unbridled. Pages of newsprint were dedicated to 'the phenomenon that is Berlin': a 1900 guide entitled *Berlin für Kenner* (Berlin for Con-
noisseurs) called it 'the most glorious city in the world', 'the capital of the
German Reich and the Kingdom of Prussia, Residence of the German Emperor
and the Kings of Prussia, Seat of the German Reichstag and Prussian Landtag'.
Greater Berlin, it said, had 'a population of 3,019,887', a 'garrison of 23,000
men'; it was the 'cleanest city in the world', it contained 'as much railway
track as lay between Frankfurt and Berlin', it collected 'over 89 million marks
in taxes' and had '362 million marks in savings in its banks' – even its mayor
had written a masterpiece, the (now forgotten) *Green Chicken*.[8] By the turn
of the century the optimism seemed justified. As Berlin approached the year
1900 it claimed to be the 'richest city in Europe' and the 'metropolis of

intelligence'. In an 1899 survey published in the *Berliner illustrirte Zeitung* Berliners declared that the most important event in the past hundred years of world history had been the unification of Germany – which had in turn led to the creation of its new capital.[9] Berlin, it was said, was destined to be the most important place on earth, which would hold the key to history 'economically, culturally, politically'. But twenty years after the ebullient predictions the city was suffering war, defeat and revolution. The term 'capital city' became a curse as Berlin was transformed into the doomed capital of Weimar, then the criminal capital of the 'Thousand Year Reich', and then the illegal capital of the GDR. It has not been a very promising record.

Today Berlin stands on the threshold of another centenary and its new status is a *fait accompli*; on 31 August 1990 Germans signed the Unification Treaty naming Berlin as 'Capital of United Germany'; on 20 June 1991, after a fierce debate, the Bundestag voted by 337 to 320 to move the capital back to Berlin; on 25 August 1992 Helmut Kohl signed the Capital Agreement, followed on 10 March 1994 by the Berlin/Bonn Act, which enshrined the move of the German parliament (the Bundestag) and the federal government (the Bundesregierung) to Berlin. The Chancellery of the Federal President had already moved by January 1994, and the rest are to be transferred in the course of 1999. Berlin will soon house Germany's most important ministries, including Foreign Affairs, the Interior, Justice and Finance and Economics, as well as Transport, Labour and Social Affairs, the Family and Regional Planning. Berlin will be the political capital; only a handful of offices will remain in the administrative capital, Bonn.[10] Like Faust, Berlin has been given another chance.

The new Berlin visionaries are not daunted by the failures of the past. On the contrary, they are keen to prove that Berlin has changed and that its present aspirations are peaceful and democratic. Berlin, say its supporters, now has a 'new role' in Germany and in Europe, a new place in the world. Its construction will be based on its past excellence – the so-called 'critical reconstruction' of the architectural historian Dieter Hoffmann-Axthelm – and incorporated into Hans Stimmann's extensive street plans.[11] An official guide to the city, with a foreword by the mayor, Eberhard Diepgen, spelled this out:

> Berlin has a future again. Our city is the biggest in Germany and will soon have a population of 4 million people ... developing into a metropolis of science and culture, of the media and of business. The universities and research institutes, the opera houses, theatres, museums and libraries are just as much attractions to our city as its colourful neighbourhoods and the charming landscape of woods and lakes surrounding it.

The Berlin Wall and the Iron Curtain which divided the whole of Europe have also made Berlin 'an attractive location for business again . . . Important companies are setting up new offices in the city or intensifying their involvement here. Building is going on all over the city . . . The construction means hope for the future. A new city is growing, carefully merging with the old buildings which have been handed down to us.'[12] A visitor who last stood at the Wall in 1989 will find the centre virtually unrecognizable. Ironically, however, this is not the first time Berliners have passed over this same ground and marvelled at the construction sites.

Only a hundred years ago Berliners were making the very same comments about the very same squares and intersections and boulevards. Georg Hermann, the Berlin writer who died in Auschwitz in 1943, remarked in 1896 that 'only five, ten, twenty years ago nothing but windswept fields and willow trees stood . . . on these very sites which are now covered with asphalt and litter'; in 1914 Paul Scheerbart wrote of the shiny glass buildings rising from the sand, structures which were to create a 'new milieu' in Berlin and which would 'bring us a new culture'; Maximilian Harden noted in 1901 that old Berlin was being completely 'walled in' and 'bricked up' in the rush to redevelop the city centre; and in his 1888 novel *Wer ist der Stärkere?* Conrad Alberti described the huge construction site near the Potsdamer Platz, marvelling at the number of cranes and workmen and piles of earth to be found there. Later, in the 1930s, Berliners watched and wondered as Albert Speer and Hitler ordered buildings and streets to be blown up to clear the way for the North–South Axis in their bid to create Germania, the capital of the Third Reich; after the war, Berliners watched again as many of the last vestiges of the historic city were removed during the post-war building boom. In 1961 the reconstruction was hindered by the sudden erection of the Wall, leaving what was the very heart of Berlin a desolate no man's land. Today those areas are finally, in the new Berlin jargon, being 'knitted together' into the new capital of the 'Berlin Republic'.[13]

On a cold grey day in 1996 I stopped in at the Red Rathaus, Berlin's old city hall, to see a display of the new architectural plans for the city. The dingy trappings of East German culture had been replaced by West German chrome-and-white displays. In the centre of the room stood a broad platform the size of two billiard tables covered with a gigantic relief map. A young man in designer jeans and designer glasses and a designer haircut was standing under the halogen lights gesticulating at a group of rather shy Berliners and explaining what their new city was going to look like. He pointed at the model with a long chrome stick: 'The white represents Berlin as it *is*,' he said; 'the cream represents Berlin *as it will be*.' Sure enough, great swathes of the map, from Rummelsburg to Marzahn and from Karow Nord to the Falkenberg

Garden City, were daubed in cream-coloured paint. The man continued his lecture: there were already over 150 architects from eleven countries and over 250,000 other specialists and consultants and contractors working on the reconstruction of the city; an entirely new government quarter on the Spree-bogen was being built to a design by the Berlin architect Axel Schultes; Günter Behnisch and Manfred Sabatke had designed a new Academy of Arts, Check-point Charlie was being turned into an American business centre, Alex-anderplatz would soon be ringed in by a network of new highrise buildings – a 'People's Space' – designed by Hans Kollhoff and Helga Timmermann, although the GDR 'time clock' would remain. And that was not all. The Potsdamer Platz, the Friedrichstrasse, the old Schloss, the Spittelmarkt, the Spreeinsel, the Spandau Wasserstadt, the Lindencorse, the Stock Exchange and a dozen other sites were to be transformed. Pariser Platz, the historical central entrance to Berlin, would once again house the American, British and French embassies; the Hotel Adlon was being rebuilt and was soon to reopen – had we seen the advertising hoardings around the building site listing all the famous people who had stayed there?[14] So many memories were evoked by the names and places on the map – the site of the first Academy of Sciences where Leibniz had taught; the hotel in which Bismarck and Disraeli had cemented their friendship, the balcony from which the Kaiser had promised his troops that they would be 'home by Christmas' in 1914 and where Liebknecht had declared the 'free Socialist Republic of Germany' four years later. There were the many places still chillingly associated with the National Socialists, from Hitler's bunker and the Reichsbank to the three train stations from which Jews were deported; there was Karlshorst, where Keitel surrendered to the Allies on 8 May 1945, later the Berlin headquarters of the NKVD; there was the long path where the Wall had snaked its oppressive way through the heart of the city; there were the airfields built during the Berlin blockade of 1949. But the young man made no mention of history; indeed, the buildings and squares and spaces were clearly to be treated as if they were quite new. The former Reichsbank was simply the 'future seat of the Foreign Office', Göring's Reich Air Ministry had taken on a fresh identity as the seat of the 'Federal Ministry of Finance', the Neue Wache, which had served as everything from Berlin's First World War memorial to the GDR's shrine to the 'Victims of Fascism' had now become the 'Central Memorial of the Federal Republic of Germany for the Victims of War and Tyranny'; the Bendlerblock, built in 1914 as the Reich Navy Office and seat of the General Staff, was now the 'second domicile of the Federal Ministry of Defence'; the gigantic Stalinallee, where the 1953 Uprising had begun, was merely a street requiring 'DM750 million' worth of repairs. For the young man with the map – and for many others keen to promote the new capital – Berlin is a great *tabula rasa*, an architect's dream.

The chameleon city is busy reinventing itself for the third time this century.

The amount of work already undertaken by the late 1990s would have astounded even the nineteenth-century commentators; the sheer number of cranes – which have been decorated, photographed and even synchronized to move up and down to music – is staggering. Berlin is presently a DM 50 billion construction zone filled with piles of earth and iron girders and cement trucks and arc lights and populated with Polish and Irish labourers (locals are too expensive). By August 1997 30 million tons of gravel had been poured, 70 million cubic feet of water pumped out for foundations, road and rail tunnels, and 17,411 trees had been planted – even the river Spree had been temporarily redirected to allow for the work near the Reichstag. The budget signed on 30 June 1994 provided DM 2.8 billion merely to move the parliament while an estimated DM 20 billion has been earmarked for the improvement of the transportation and communications infrastructure. 'Berlin, the City' has become the greatest millennium project in Europe. Local kiosks, bookshops and tourist stands are stuffed with brightly coloured maps which extol the virtues of the 'new Berlin'; one sells the ultimate guide to *Pläne und Kräne* (Plans and Cranes); another advertises *Der Tagespiegel* under a picture of a construction site with the caption: '*Berlin ist kaum zu fassen*' (Berlin is difficult to get a grip on); a nearby billboard promotes one of the many construction-site tours, this one sponsored by Deutsche Bahn: 'When a city gets a new suspension bridge then it is time to go on the *Architektour*. Berlin, bestir yourself. Don't miss it.'[15] The Reichstag, wrapped in silver foil in 1995 by Christo to the delight of Berliners, is getting a new dome designed by the British architect Sir Norman Foster, who enthuses: 'If you look at what has happened in Berlin since unification, it is miraculous. It is faster and more precipitous than anyone's wildest dreams.'[16] The precocious architect of Berlin's new Jewish Museum, Daniel Libeskind, believes the city will become the 'exemplary spiritual capital of the twenty-first century, as it once was the apocalyptic symbol of the twentieth-century demise'.[17] The architect of the Spreebogen, who was careful not to appear to be following Albert Speer's plans for the same area, calls his design 'very simple in its reserve . . . in keeping with the hardness of the city and its fate'. The Potsdamer Platz, once curiously touted as the 'busiest intersection in Europe', was by 1997 the centre of the largest private-sector construction project in German history: nineteen new buildings on seventeen prime acres, including headquarters for Daimler-Benz and Sony Europe, will provide 1.1 million square feet of floor space.[18] A Sony representative calls his building 'an important landmark' which 'represents how we see the future'; the Daimler-Benz spokesman Dr Klaus Mangold promises that his will capture the 'dynamic, the fascination and the vitality of this city . . . at the most extraordinary place in Europe, the Potsdamer Platz';

Libeskind calls Potsdamer Platz the place 'where East–West, centre–periphery division can overcome the conflicts which were born, witnessed and died in this very place'.[19] Coca-Cola has already invested DM100 million in Berlin, Kodak has moved back to its old plant in East Berlin, and over 200 other American firms are represented there. On 1 June 1993 the first Berlin edition of *Die Welt* was published, a German 'Silicon Valley' is being built in Adlershof on the site of the former East German Academy of Sciences, while a CIS (Commonwealth of Independent States) International Trade Centre will 'turn Berlin into the European financial centre for the CIS in Europe'; there are already over 100 institutions in Berlin with east–west business links, in part promoted by the early work of the Treuhand which oversaw privatization of eastern businesses after the collapse of the GDR. In 1994 the Berlin Banking Company was created; it has already become Germany's sixth largest banking organization, and by 1996 Berlin housed 145 banks, sixty-two of which were foreign. Berliners hope that their Stock Exchange will take off under the slogan 'investment in Berlin is investment for all of Germany' and they look forward to the creation by the year 2000 of 200,000 new jobs in banking, the service sector and other professions.

The entire infrastructure of the city, from communications to sewage disposal, is being rebuilt. Trains, which brought the city its nineteenth-century prosperity, are to be improved; DM40 billion is to be spent on replacing obsolete stock, reopening abandoned routes and renovating old stations, while the Deutsche Bahn has earmarked DM20 billion for improvements to the network. The first ICE express train left Berlin Lichtenberg for Munich on 21 May 1993. The Lehrter Bahnhof will be Berlin's main railway station, although six other important stations will be rebuilt or improved in the so-called 'Mushroom Plan'; the Deutsche Bahn estimates that around 400 trains a day will move through Berlin by 2002; the massive new Lehrter Bahnhof alone is expected to process 240,000 travellers a day, and local transportation networks from the S-Bahn to the trams, from the U-Bahn to roads and bicycle paths are being improved to carry over one billion people per year. Water transport along the canals will grow by an estimated 85 per cent by 2010; the airports of Tegel, Tempelhof and Schönefeld, already stretched to capacity with their 10 million passengers a year, are to be replaced by the new 'Berlin-Brandenburg International' in 2010, by which time air traffic is expected to double.

Other institutions are being reorganized, unified or rebuilt. The 150,000 students at the Free University, the Technical University and Humboldt University can now transfer from one to another and Berlin's academic reputation is beginning to recover after the dismal days of the 1960s and 1970s; 250 other research institutions are now located in Berlin, including the famous

Wissenschaftszentrum Berlin für Sozialforschung (Central Academy for Social Research) and the Max Planck Society, which moved its legal base there in 1993. Berlin is presently trying to co-ordinate its three opera houses, its 150 theatres and concert halls, its 170 museums and collections, its 300 public and private galleries, its 250 public libraries and the dozens of other centres which were often replicated on each side of the Wall. But, as the brochures hastily point out, with everything from the Philharmonic Orchestra and the Schaubühne to the Film Festival Berlin is already an 'international metropolis of culture'.[20] Berliners have no doubt that the city is destined for greatness; by 2000 'Berlin will have more residents than Hamburg, Munich and Cologne together'; it will have created '2 million more jobs by 2010'; Greater Berlin, already six times the size of Paris in area with 4.2 million inhabitants, is 'expected to reach 6 million in the next century'; it will be 'the largest urban centre between the Atlantic and the Urals, a centre of commerce, culture, politics'. Willy Brandt's words are repeated like a mantra: Berlin is the '*Schicksalstadt der Deutschen*' – the city of German destiny.

The claims for Berlin are great, and it is true that what has been accomplished since 1989 is amazing by any standards. But a kind of desperation has crept into some of the slogans and statistics as Berliners struggle to maintain the enthusiasm at a time when the true costs of unification and the transferring of the capital have started to bite. Germany went through a bad patch in the late 1990s and the mood was edgy, with *Ossis* complaining of everything from high unemployment to the loss of the old benefits of the GDR and *Wessis* bickering about high taxes and the huge amounts of cash being siphoned off for the east. Even now the move from Bonn has become a sore point for some; Germans from Bremen to Leipzig to Erfurt complain that too much money is being spent in Berlin, while Frankfurt fears for its role as Germany's main financial centre, Munich fears for its industry, Hamburg for its trade, and Bonn for its loss of status as capital. Germany as a whole is trying to work out how to reconcile the desire for a world-class centralized metropolis with the idea of a federal Germany which proved so successful after 1945. Some Germans even refer to the notion of a 'capital city' as an obsolete nineteenth-century concept and point in horror to places like Mexico City, the most polluted place in the world with its 25 million inhabitants and a subway which carries more people every day than Berlin's entire population. As one Green activist put it to me in 1991, 'We say *no* to this capital of smog.' Berlin has suffered other disappointments – the hoped-for merger between the two provinces of Berlin-Brandenburg which would have greatly improved both economies was rejected in a 1996 referendum; the city was turned down as the site of the 2000 Olympics; and the government is moving when Berlin – one of the poorest of the federal *Länder* – is practically broke.[21] The price of unity – from the decision to exchange the East German Mark with the Deutschmark on a one-to-one basis to the monetary requirements of a backward ex-GDR – has led to much unhappiness amongst East Germans; indeed, the birthrate there fell by 60 per cent between 1989 and 1992. Their plight was not helped by crass westerners who had never visited the GDR and certainly had no notion of what it meant to live in a police state, but who felt justified in treating *Ossis* with barely concealed disdain or, as one woman told me, like 'children who haven't yet learned to read'. Mutual antagonism is still strong in Berlin, with western Germans seeing the *Ossis* as '*undankbar, kryptokommunistisch und völlig unproduktiv*' – ungrateful, crypto-Communist and totally unproductive. For their part the *Ossis* consider the West Berliners to be '*elitär, egoistisch und faul*' – elitist, egotistical and lazy.[22] Jürgen Kocka noted recently that 'the transfer of the West German order to the former East German states has worked relatively well on the constitutional, legal, and institutional level. However, it has met with stiff resistance and has not progressed far on the level of social relations, political culture and everyday life.'[23]

But sympathy for citizens of the former GDR can go too far. Their Berlin is being transformed beyond recognition largely by western money: the dreariness of a decade ago has been replaced by buzzing and colourful streets and shops and the sense of freedom there is quite new. Whatever they now say about their 'camaraderie' or the marvellous child-care benefits of days gone by the GDR was virtually bankrupt by 1989, kept alive only by Soviet muscle and by East German minders like Erich Honecker and Erich Mielke and Markus Wolf. The 'benefits' were paid for by crime and oppression; even Wolf admits that selling 'dissidents' was the state's biggest hard-currency earner. The end of the GDR is something to be celebrated, not mourned.

Even without the enormous financial and psychological costs of reunification, Berlin would find it difficult to convince all Germans that the move is a good idea. The much-favoured Spreebogen architect Axel Schultes complained in 1997 that 'Berlin is stumbling into an almost too precipitous future. The euphoria of beginning is overshadowed by the feeling of being late ... the fear of making mistakes, fear of taking risks, fear of loss of identity.' Schultes even quoted Theodor Fontane, who said of the reconstruction of Berlin in the 1870s: 'the city is growing, but the botching continues'.[24] Dr Wolfgang Schäuble implored Germans to back the new capital, emphasizing that although the move might be expensive or cause disruption 'it is not about the work place, moving or travel costs, or regional politics or structural politics. All those things are important, but in reality it is about the future of Germany. That is the decisive factor.'[25] Even so, in a 1993 opinion poll only 51 per cent of Germans said that they thought of Berlin as their capital.[26] Berliners clearly have much to do if they are to win over their fellow Germans. But they can at least take cold comfort from one thing – Berlin has been here before.

It is difficult to believe it now, but Berlin was not much more popular in Germany when it was first named capital in 1871. For many it has always been something of an 'unloved' capital, a place which arouses resentment or blame as much as respect or admiration. This has been brought about by German history itself. The country does not have a tradition of a grand capital and the choice of Berlin was made above all by the politics of 'blood and iron'.

'In the beginning, there was Paris ' – or so said nineteenth-century Frenchmen. From the time of Clovis it has been accepted that Paris is an expression of France's political sovereignty – so much so that those who sought to undermine it always moved the capital – Charlemagne to Aix-la-Chapelle, Marshal Pétain to Vichy. Berlin holds a very different place in German history. Goethe once complained that whereas the French could boast proudly that 'Paris is France', his countrymen 'have not even a region of which one could say: "Here is Germany!"' Walter Benjamin named Paris, not his native Berlin, as the capital of the nineteenth century.[27] Throughout the Middle Ages the Holy Roman Emperor moved from place to place and although German lands contained numerous beautiful princely cities there was never an obvious equivalent to London or Paris. At least not until Bismarck. The decision to name Berlin as capital in 1871 was immensely popular in the city itself but many other Germans resented the choice – it was 'too Prussian', 'too showy', 'too militaristic', 'too Protestant', 'too pompous', 'too new'. An article entitled 'The Voice of Germany', which appeared in *Die Grenzbogen* in 1892 to mark Berlin's twentieth anniversary as capital, was typical:

> In the last days of the old year the Berlin newspapers have once again been given the opportunity to pontificate dithyrambically about the Reich capital. The newspapers carefully explain to those in the dumb provinces ... how Berlin has truly become the head and heart of Germany, and that in all political, social, artistic and literary questions Berlin's judgement is to be known as the 'voice of Germany' ... But as long as we still have cities like Cologne, Stuttgart, Munich and Leipzig, Berlin will never have the right to bear the German tradition and spirit.

It concluded with the words: 'there is no place as unloved in all Germany as the capital Berlin', which was nothing but 'a dreadful mixture of Warsaw and Paris'.[28]

Such attacks continued after 1900 even when Berlin was at its most successful. Now it was called a 'Babel', a 'gigantic slum', a 'hotbed of radical-ism'. In *Der Hungerpastor* Wilhelm Raabe decries its moral laxity; others called it the 'tomb of Germanism'.[29] Berlin was attacked by the new breed of *völkisch* nationalists who had watched in horror as the city reached a population of 4 million in 1920 and for whom it lacked any sense of tradition; the fact that reformers like Ernst Dronke lauded its ability to destroy class barriers or Heinrich Mann praised the *Menschenwerkstatt* which would 'hasten demo-cratization' only made it seem more dangerous. What was a 'Berliner' anyway, they asked suspiciously, if not a mere immigrant from the east? And, in a way, they were right. As Heinz Knoblock pointed out in his book *Herbert-Baum-Strasse 43*: 'There are philosophers buried in Weissensee, linguists, famous jurists and architects, historians and religious scholars, the Asian specialist Huth, the publisher S. Fischer, the philosopher Hermann Cohen. No one in the ranks of honour was born in Berlin. They came from Poland, Hungary, Silesia, Moravia, Galicia and Ukraine, but also from Baden and Bavaria, Riga and Magdeburg.'[30] And because Berlin was always changing and growing it never really had a chance to develop an identity. It remained the 'unfinished capital in the middle of an unfinished nation'. Princess Blücher saw it as a new city, 'built up in the midst of a dull sandy plain by a patient, hard-working people who have no traditions of culture and style to carry on, but are more or less at the beginning of their history.'[31] Even Walther Rathenau quipped that he was not certain if there were just 'no Berliners left, or if they simply haven't appeared yet', concluding that 'I believe most Berliners are from Posen and the rest are from Breslau.'[32] By 1912 one fifth of the population were immigrants, grist for the mill of those who saw Berlin as 'too cosmopoli-tan' or 'too eastern' or 'too Jewish', or just 'too foreign'. The defeat in 1918, the Spartacus Uprising and the slow, violent death of the Weimar Republic on its streets did little for the city's reputation. Hitler might have turned his Germania into a popular capital for an adoring local public had he succeeded in creating his Thousand Year Reich, but his demise in the *Götterdämmerung* of April 1945 and the subsequent attempts by Germans to dissociate themselves from anything to do with Nazism worked against Berlin.

The divided and disgraced city was in no position to resume its role as capital after the war. The East Germans tried to exploit its old status by illegally naming it capital of the GDR in 1949 but it did little good. By the time Berlin was being considered in 1989 the very fact that it had last served as a capital to Hitler's murderous regime made people nervous. Many western Germans had come to believe that the nation could only be true to itself if it was 'federal', with an insignificant city like Bonn at its head. Germany, they argued, should be united not by a strong centralized capital, but by other things like language or culture or the Deutschmark. Berlin's post-war reputation did not help; ex-East Berlin was seen as the evil capital of the GDR crawling with former Stasi agents and government hacks while western Berlin retained its reputation as a centre for drug addicts and anti-nuclear activists and 'artists' who resented the loss of their subsidized lives in the shadow of the Wall. The journalist Felix Huby said recently that his friends from Stuttgart not only believe that German culture 'begins in Palermo and ends in Tauberbischofs-heim'; they think that Berlin is 'godless, cultureless and for the last forty years has taken paid leave from capitalism'.[33] The city's image is not helped by the fact that far from rejoicing at their good fortune many Berliners spend time demonstrating against it: the number of protests mounted there rose from 1,008 in 1996 to 2,070 in 1997.

Even the notion of creating an 'instant capital' is fraught with problems; Berlin is still trying to re-create itself rather than allowing a natural evolution. I was born in the 1960s, and yet I have already lived in three quite different Berlins – East Berlin, West Berlin and the new united capital. The city changes identities like a snake sloughing its skin. It is impossible to imagine New York or London undergoing even one of the great convulsions which have racked Berlin in the past century. The political upheaval itself has been bad enough, but more worrying is the way in which Berliners have responded to it, leading outsiders to suspect that whatever Berliners are today, the status quo might not last for long. It is not enough simply to declare that the city will be the 'workshop of German unity' or that it 'marks Germany's coming of age' or that 'with its historical and cultural *Ausstrahlungskraft*' (radiating power) it will make German democracy 'better and more stable' than the mere 'political decision-making centre of Bonn'.[34] It may seem unfair, but Berlin will have to work hard to prove to the world that this 'democratic phase' is not merely another passing trend.

While the domestic problems of unification and of the move to Berlin occupy the Germans, the rest of the world is watching and waiting to discover what this new 'Berlin Republic' will do elsewhere. Policy-makers in Washington, Moscow and Paris, in London, Tokyo or Beijing, do not much care whether ex-Stasi members have had their rent increased or if former West Berlin artists lose their subsidies. What they do care about is the international arena. There is a great question mark hanging over Germany: Will the move from Bonn to Berlin signal a fundamental shift in German foreign policy? Will Berlin continue to behave like Bonn, or will the geographical move mean a change in Germany's overall perspective on international affairs? Will Germany continue its pursuit of supra-national goals, or will the new capital create a new kind of German national pride – a new and more clearly defined national identity? And if so, what will this new Germany look like? Will it continue on its present course, or will it once again begin to assert itself in

Europe? Will some of the old arrogance and the old resentments be rekindled, or will it remember the lessons of the past? These questions are of the utmost importance, as the decisions taken in the new German capital will affect us all. We can only hope that it continues in the footsteps of its predecessor.

Bonn was one of the greatest success stories of the twentieth century, perhaps of all German history. Established in 1949 under the auspices of the western Allies, it guided West Germany as it grew from a shattered, disgraced and divided ruin into a prosperous, stable country. It helped to prove to a sceptical post-war world that the Germans could indeed be trusted to govern themselves peacefully and democratically.

From the beginning the United States was Bonn's most important ally. American and West German interests complemented one another during the Cold War and as the US tried to retain its influence over western Europe and keep the Soviets at bay, the Federal Republic worked hard to be accepted into the western community and became a loyal member of NATO in 1955. Germany also joined that other child of the Cold War, the Western European Union, which was based from the beginning on the relationship between France and Germany – and in particular on the remarkable friendship between General de Gaulle and Konrad Adenauer. It too was a symbiotic relationship. France's military contribution to the Second World War was minimal; even so it was given a chunk of territory to administer, including a slice of Berlin. It became wealthy in part by hitching itself to the German economic boom, but although its status in Europe was maintained it had become increasingly dependent on Germany. In the 1980s France chose to socialize further rather than introducing difficult reforms, leaving it economically vulnerable. This would have mattered less had borders remained as they were. But in 1989 the Europe it had known for nearly half a century melted away.

When the Berlin Wall fell all the assumptions of the previous forty years were thrown into confusion. The Soviets' loss of control over central Europe saw the end of the clearly defined bloc around which West German and western European foreign policy had revolved, and free countries like Poland, the Czech Republic, Slovakia, Latvia, Lithuania, Estonia, Hungary, Ukraine and others emerged from the once homogeneous Soviet zone, all with diverse interests and all at different stages of economic and political development. Suddenly everything was much more complicated, and much more volatile. West German foreign policy based on *Ostpolitik*, which had so gently prodded at the Russian bear for a few foreign policy scraps, and *Genscherism*, which had so carefully balanced West Germany between the superpowers, suddenly lost its *raison d'être*.

France was worried about German unity. It feared, as one French talk-show host put it, that the 'uncontrollable German totalitarian tendency' might yet rear its ugly head: 'the shadow of *Faust* darkens the old continent again'.[35] Worse still, far from having a European alliance based on a Franco-German partnership it looked increasingly as if Germany would look to the east. André François-Poncet's quip was repeated frequently: 'We all know that the Germans, whenever they join forces with the Russians, are soon afterwards on the outskirts of Paris.'[36] The answer was the Maastricht Treaty, the treaty meant to tie Germany to France before it could look elsewhere. In the words of one French newspaper Maastricht was 'the Treaty of Versailles without war' whose foremost aim was 'to get rid of the German mark'.[37]

The French had reason to be nervous. The newly unified Germany was daunting. In a matter of months quiet West Germany had become a nation of 80 million people, the biggest and most powerful in the European Union and, despite its somewhat sclerotic and over-regulated economy, one of the wealthiest and most influential in the world. France had to face the fact that it was, and would always remain, less influential in Europe than a united Germany. It was only the Maastricht Treaty which made the new order bearable for France: the expansion of German interests to the east was to be exchanged for one thing – the adoption of the single European currency and the demise of the Deutschmark.[38]

As long as Helmut Kohl remains Chancellor it is likely that the German–French relationship will go on much as before even after the move to Berlin. Both countries seem to be willing to overcome all obstacles to achieve their goals; in 1997 Helmut Kohl even tried to fudge the value of Germany's gold reserves in order to meet the Maastricht criteria. In any other country the idea of performing such financial gymnastics to give away one's own extraordinary currency would be unthinkable but it is likely that by 1999 the new capital of Berlin will be part of a different European monetary system. The reasons for this also lie in a kind of mutual blackmail: if France needs Germany, Germany also needs France.

'Germany is our Fatherland,' goes Helmut Kohl's slogan, 'but Europe is our future.'[39] The phrase is loaded with meaning. Whatever claims they may make about the 'grace of late birth' separating them from the Nazi past Helmut Kohl and his generation are very much products of the Second World War and their thinking is shaped both by the conflict and by the shattered world which they grew up in after 1945. Kohl – who first saw decimated Berlin in 1947 at the age of seventeen – genuinely believes that the European Union will stifle aggressive nationalism and will prevent another war. He is also aware that Germany's membership in the European Union helps to quell fears about German nationalism while at the same time disguising Germany's own ambitions under the colours of the blue star-spangled flag. There is no doubt that it was useful for Germany to be able to refer to the European Union when it struggled to unify after November 1989, particularly when articles began to appear in the foreign press accusing Germany of trying to create a 'Fourth Reich'.[40] The Germans do not want to lose their 'European identity' – at least not yet – because they are unsure of their own national identity and because they are too insecure to voice their own national ambitions. That is why the endless pictures of Berlin's Brandenburg Gate that appeared after unification showed it topped by the European, not the German flag. But in a way the French were right. If the move to Berlin symbolizes anything it is Germany's shift to the east.

Berlin's location alone will not determine its future foreign policy, but it will play a role. The old cultural and economic ties which made Bonn so accessible to Paris are already working in reverse for Berlin. In the old West Germany the only eastern city which mattered was Moscow. The smaller Warsaw Pact countries were all but ignored and even the GDR was pressured into German–German agreements via Moscow. All that changed in 1989. Suddenly 'the east' was on the doorstep: the Czech Republic is a mere two-hour drive from Berlin; Poland is less than an hour away.

Unlike Bonn Berlin has few historic ties with the west but has traditionally always looked to the east, either for commerce or for conquest. Its ancestral hinterland was in Pomerania and Silesia and East Prussia, and Berlin itself was built up largely by labourers from East Elbian regions – in 1911 1,046,162 people moved there from German lands (including German-held Poland) and 97,683 from the Russian empire; in the same year only 11,070 came from France. Trade links with the east have always been strong: by the early 1930s 30 per cent of both Hungarian and Czech trade was with Germany.[41] Even before the collapse of the Wall West Germany had been trading with eastern bloc countries; after 1989 it signed bilateral trade agreements with most east and central European countries and quickly established Goethe Institutes throughout the region. True, the West Germans initially treated the three key central European states as little more than a 'threefold *cordon sanitaire*', a 'buffer zone' against surprise attacks from Russia, against Chernobyl-like disasters, and above all against economic migrants from the former USSR.[42] But that view has already changed. Today airports, hotels and business centres in Budapest or Gdańsk or Prague are packed with German businessmen making deals and discussing strategies for the future; the roads in the Mark Brandenburg are filled with Polish cars heading to and from the border and Polish highways are in turn populated by speedy Germans in their Mercedes and Porsches heading to Poznań or Cracow or Warsaw. According to Bundesbank figures of June 1996 Germany's trade with central Europe has overtaken trade with the United States and has already reached 80 per cent of its total trade with France. And attitudes between the once hostile nations are changing too.

In 1995 Václav Havel called Germany 'a part of our destiny, our inspiration as well as our pain ... some regard Germany as our greatest hope, others as our greatest peril', but despite deep misgivings on both sides the Czechs and Germans signed a treaty of reconciliation in January 1997.[43] But the most extraordinary change has taken place between Poland and Germany. Thanks to the work of people like the ex-Prime Minister Tadeusz Mazowiecki, Senator Stanisław Stomma and ex-Foreign Minister Władysław Bartoszewski, who is a friend of Helmut Kohl, these once implacable enemies have begun to heal the terrible scars not only of the Second World War, but of centuries of hostility. Cultural events like the 1997 exhibition outlining the historic links between Poland and Saxony organized by the erudite head of Warsaw Castle, Andrzej Rottermund, and held both in Germany and Poland would have been unthinkable a decade ago.[44] In a 1997 survey the pollster Lena Kolarska-Bobinska revealed that 77 per cent of Polish businessmen and women liked working with Germans – only 58 per cent liked working with Americans; 74 per cent desired Germans as political partners – 67 per cent cited Americans. And it has been the government of Helmut Kohl which has striven to usher Poland, the Czech Republic and Hungary into NATO, and which has pushed for their EU membership as early as 2005. As he put it in 1994, 'It is of vital importance for Germany that Poland becomes part of the European Union,' and this aim has been extended to other countries in the region.[45] The effort has not gone unnoticed. Central and eastern Europeans have not forgotten their recent past, but Germans have rarely been so popular east of the Oder–Neisse.

It is in Bonn's and will continue to be in Berlin's self-interest to promote stability in central Europe. Any disaster there, whether military, political or economic, will have an immediate impact on Germany which would be all the more acutely felt in Berlin. Furthermore, as the most influential player in the region the new capital will enhance Germany's claim that it deserves a greater role in international affairs, including a seat on the UN Security Council. Since 1989 Germany's priority has been to create a western-oriented Europe stretching as far to the east of the Polish border as possible. Berlin's claims that it is already a vital link, a 'bridge between east and west' take on a new meaning when seen in this context; the city seeks to become both the 'future capital of the European community' and the capital of *Schaukelpolitik* – the 'fulcrum politics' between east and west. As a working paper prepared by the CDU (Christian Democratic Union) in November 1994 put it, Germany will be the 'pivotal power in Europe, involved in an eternal balancing act between east and west, seeking to reconcile and integrate. It will do so with one hand still tied behind its back. For it will still be loath to lead, and merely seek to react to the initiatives of others.'[46]

So far this malleable German foreign policy has been a success. The nation was fortunate that unification took place during a period of relative stability and peace. True, its first foray into international politics in the form of the hasty recognition of Croatia and Slovenia proved to be a disaster, but since then there have been no other major crises.[47] The United States remains a close and trusted ally. Unlike the French or the British, the Americans were positive about German unity from the beginning; it was George Bush who overruled other western leaders and advocated reunification, while Bill Clinton has let it be known that Helmut Kohl is his key ally on the continent. As if to give credence to this strong bond Henry Kissinger said in 1994, 'I consider Kohl one of the seminal leaders of our period. He has been a guarantee of Germany's Atlantic and European orientation and a shield against the national-istic or romantic temptations from which his people have suffered through much of modern history.'[48] Kohl, now the longest ever serving German Chancellor, has not been nicknamed the 'Bismarck of the Twentieth Century' without reason. Furthermore the Americans have assumed Germany's historic role of supporting Russia, leaving Germany free to pursue its interests in central Europe and in the west. It seems that Berlin's first years as capital will be marked by a delicate balancing act between the United States, western Europe, east central Europe, Russia and other regions. But what will happen after Helmut Kohl's departure? What will the situation be in five or ten years' time? And what kind of legacy will Berlin look back on when it celebrates its first centenary as capital of the 'Berlin Republic'?

Konrad Adenauer referred to any attempts to deviate from the western liberal democratic tradition as 'experiments' which were to be avoided at all costs. The strength of post-war Germany resulted from its strict adherence to the Anglo-American model of government, which was nurtured in the new Federal Republic by the western Allies. It resulted in a democracy which was stable precisely because concern for the political, economic and general well-being of its citizens was put before self-aggrandizement or aggressive wars. Berlin owes a great deal to the United States, from its rescue during the blockade to support over the reunification of Germany. One hopes that Berlin will continue to look westward, retaining the United States as its primary ally, and will not succumb to the cheap anti-Americanism which permeated West Berlin in the 1970s and 1980s. Given the crucial role played by President Bush it is pathetic to see the likes of Willy Brandt's widow Brigitte Seebacher-Brandt, Heinrich Lummer, Klaus Rainer Röhl (at one time a Communist married to a Red Army Faction terrorist leader) and others of the so-called 'generation of 1989', or the members of the 'New Right' attack the United States and portray the 'Bonn Republic' as a rather unfortunate episode which destroyed German national pride or made the Germans 'too western'.[49] The road away from the United States is the road to disaster.

Germans today have been told to suppress their national ambitions in favour of the European Union, but it is stretching the bounds of credibility to think that united Germans are any more loyal to faceless Brussels bureaucrats than East Germans were to the Soviet representatives of the 'Communist International'. Germans cannot rely solely on a supra-national identity, or indeed on vague notions of regional identity or *Heimat* for a stable future; they must accept that they have, and need, a national identity. Stability does not result from the signing of treaties and contracts alone, it also comes from the creation of a culture which people actually believe in. The utopian visions and political Romanticism of Berlin's past have caused chaos; the dreamy environmentalists, the radical relativists of 1968, the neo-Nazis, the self-pitying ex-Communists of the GDR, the anti-American '1989 generation' and the New Right who want so desperately to forget the terrible lessons of Germany's history all pose their own kind of danger. The only way to prevent these, or indeed some other radical force from taking hold in the new Germany is to stop pretending that Brussels is a substitute for history, and to create a national framework in which the vast majority of people can find some measure of financial, political and spiritual security; in short, to form a nation which its citizens believe in and want to protect. The surest way to prevent radicalism in a future Berlin is to nurture and support the capital as the seat of a sound, stable, democratic government which will reflect the values espoused by Bonn, values which were so clearly rejected by the GDR's Berlin. Helmut Kohl's notion that without European integration or the single currency there will be another war is bizarre; it implies that he does not really trust his own citizens or the democracy of which they are now so rightly proud.

If Berlin may eventually re-evaluate its dependence on the European Union the same is true of its ties with the east. Berlin will always be involved in central Europe but there is still a danger of falling back into the old stereotypes and prejudices which lie deep in German culture. Eminent politicians, journalists and academics continue to justify Germany's violent past by calling it the vulnerable '*Land der Mitte*', ignoring the fact that other countries in 'the middle' have avoided such a fate. They speak of '*Polnische Wirtschaft*', dismissing Poles as incapable of working to 'higher' German standards despite the fact that the Polish economy grew faster than any other in Europe in the 1990s.[50] Lingering resentments resurface against Poles and Czechs for the loss of the eastern territories with no thought as to how they came to be lost in the first place, and countries like Ukraine are referred to as mere 'buffer states' between possibly troublesome Russia and the west. Berliners tactlessly proclaim themselves the 'capital of central Europe'. As Adam Krzemiński, the editor of the Polish weekly *Polityka*, has pointed out: 'In Vilna they will tell you that you are in the very centre of Europe, in Ukraine they will take you to the

Carpathians and show you a granite phallus erected by the Habsburgs. It has a German inscription which states that this is the centre of Europe. In Bohemia you will hear that the centre is near Prague and in Poland that it is near Łódz.' Berliners are still extraordinarily ignorant about countries to the east; as the novelist Hans Magnus Enzensberger has put it, some members in the Berlin Senate clearly do not possess a map of Europe as they 'persist in their belief that Milan is closer to Berlin than Warsaw'.[51] The new relationships between these countries are still very fragile, as witnessed by the ugly accusations hurled between Germany, the Czech Republic and Poland across the Oder during the terrible floods of 1997. Berlin will not counter the historic fears about Germany – particularly the accusation that it is achieving with the chequebook what it failed to do with tanks; or, put another way, that it is pursuing Hitler's ends by peaceful means – merely by declaring that it has changed or by explaining that it has only good intentions. Only time and experience will show that it is worthy of the trust of other nations. Nothing in central Europe can be taken for granted.

This blinkered vision of central Europe also extends further east – to Russia. Germany has consistently been brought to the brink of tragedy because it was seduced by Russian power, by Russian strength, even by the Russian 'soul'. From Frederick the Great to Bismarck, from Weimar to Rapallo and from the Ribbentrop–Molotov Pact to Ostpolitik, Berlin's foreign policy has too often been based on the notion that its ties with Russia are more important than its ties with the little countries in between; indeed, central Europeans are said by some Germans to be suffering from what they consider to be an irrational 'Rapallo complex'. But the failing has persisted over the centuries. Berlin now claims that it has always acted as a 'bridge between east and west'; in reality it has often been a bridge between 'east and east', between autocratic Berlin and autocratic Russia over territory conveniently divided between the two great powers; countries like Poland and Czechoslovakia have traditionally been more western oriented than Prussia. As Henry Kissinger put it with reference to West Germany's attempt to establish links with Moscow in the early 1970s, 'A free-wheeling, powerful Germany trying to maneuver between East and West, whatever its ideology, [poses] the classic challenge to the equilibrium for Europe.'[52] Berlin has always experienced short-term gains when allying itself with Russia at the expense of these central European nations, but in the long term the relationship has proved dangerous indeed.

At the moment, however, such dilemmas seem far away. Russia is stable and Berlin will no doubt continue to improve relations with Moscow as well as with Warsaw, Prague, Budapest, Kiev and other capitals, keen, as one recent article put it, to 'prepare itself to become the third centre of world politics after Washington and Moscow'.[53] The city has inherited one of the most enviable legacies imaginable. It is at the helm of a peaceful democracy. It is a close ally of the Americans and NATO, and of the countries of the European Union; it is on good terms with Russia and on better terms with central European countries like Poland than it has been for centuries. It is difficult to think of anything else Bonn could have done to give the new German capital a more positive start. But if Berlin's history tells us anything it is that the future is unpredictable. Problems never resurface in the form one expects, but they resurface nevertheless. Berlin could not have been more prosperous or apparently stable in 1900, but a mere fourteen years later it was shattered by the First World War. A century before that Europe seemed unassailable, only to find itself convulsed by the French Revolution and the Napoleonic Wars. The fact that German unification was achieved without violence was a political miracle, but experience shows that disruption often emerges later and in unexpected ways. A closer look beneath the positive slogans and forced optimism surrounding the new 'Berlin Republic' reveals an unsettled, insecure Germany which is undergoing a crisis of identity. *Les incertitudes allemandes* have in the past tended to lead Germans into a strange, inward-looking Romanticism. One way of trying to guess at the future, and above all to learn from the mistakes made by others, is to study the past.

Berlin is a city of myth, of legend, and of the deliberate manipulation of history. Some myths have become integral parts of the city's identity, like the notion of the 'true Berliner' who, according to a typical 1990s handbook, is 'loud and jovial, cheeky and insolent, sentimental and crude, unstyled and indulgent'. This 'character' is in fact a nineteenth-century creation. Another local stereotype is the notion of '*Berliner Unwille*', which claims that Berliners have always been defiant, politically independent people who resisted their rulers. This particular myth was popularized by the democratic historian Adolph Streckfuss, who reminded Berliners of a long-forgotten medieval skirmish against an early ruler in an attempt to motivate them to rise up and demand liberal reforms from the Hohenzollern King Frederick William IV. But after the failure of the 1848 revolution they grumbled, complained, met in their coffee houses and wrote pamphlets, and yet did nothing.[54] But if *Berliner Unwille* was a myth Berlin conformity was not; a disappointed Lenin would later say that it was impossible to stage a revolution in a city in which the mob refused to disobey the KEEP OFF THE GRASS signs.

The equally compelling stereotypes created by outsiders are persistently countered by Berliners. The city may be accused of being the focus of Romantic German nationalism, but Berliners point to the legacy of Nikolai and Mendelssohn, to the Enlightenment and to their 'tradition of tolerance'. Nearly 4 per cent of Germans may claim to dislike Berlin because it was the centre of Prussian militarism, but Berliners argue that the people themselves hated the officers who strutted about in their midst. It may be depicted as the decadent and irresponsible capital of the Golden Twenties, but Berliners point to the profound contribution made to European culture by those who worked there. It may be damned by over 10 per cent of Germans because it was the centre of Nazism, but Berliners retort that all German cities contained Nazis and that theirs was the centre of anti-Nazi resistance. Although more than 7 per cent of Germans still see it as the tainted ex-capital of the GDR Berliners point to their Cold War struggle for democratic freedom and their role in the airlift and the 1953 Uprising.[55]

There are grains of truth in each of these stereotypes; many are harmless. But in Berlin the revision of history to suit current political needs has long been more extreme and more damaging than elsewhere. From the beginning German historiography was political; indeed historical philosophy was first developed there as a reaction to the French Revolution. Berlin was the city of Ranke, the great historian who claimed that he wrote about events as they 'really happened' but who nevertheless devoted his energies to the value-laden areas of diplomacy and the military. Berlin was also home to the historians of the Prussian School – of Sybel and Droysen and Treitschke – who were keen to prove that their interpretation of Hegel was correct: namely that Prussia's domination over the rest of Germany was justified; that Berlin's rise to power had been inevitable and that the Kaiser's expansionist aims in the years before the First World War were legitimate. They ignored Hegel's own gloomy warning that governments and people 'have never learned anything from history'.[56] Attempts to counter these views were unsuccessful; the liberal historian Theodor Mommsen criticized Bismarck and Treitschke to no avail, and Jacob Burckhardt, who warned of the dire consequences of the blind pursuit of national power, eventually left Berlin for the relative freedom of Switzerland.[57] The 'Borrussian' view helped to stabilize Bismarck's Reich, but it left a tainted legacy, and the promotion of the *Machtstaat* did not end with defeat in 1918. Imperial myths were quickly replaced by Weimar ones and then by carefully manufactured Nazi ones, which included the vicious lies that Germany had been 'stabbed in the back' in 1918, that Berlin was the home of the 'November criminals' and, quoting Treitschke in a context he had never intended, that 'the Jews are our misfortune'.[58]

The overlap between history and politics has persisted in a unique manner in Germany and in Berlin.[59] Historiography during the Cold War was largely determined by politics. This was particularly true of the GDR, where German history, including the Second World War, was rewritten as propaganda to justify post-war Soviet policies.

The GDR was created by Stalin in 1949 out of Soviet-occupied Germany. From the very beginning, and in marked contrast to the Federal Republic, it was an oppressive police state which suspended basic rights from free elections to free speech. When its citizens began to leave *en masse* the regime built a wall, transforming the state into a gigantic prison. East Germany became Moscow's most obedient ally, retaining many of the worst aspects of Stalinism long after they had been abandoned elsewhere; it also spent a disproportionate amount of its resources on recruiting and spying on its own citizens and creating a falsified history to justify the repressive regime. I first visited the GDR in 1981 and travelled there frequently until its demise in 1989. Every aspect of life was shaped by its approach to the past: I was allowed to live there in 1985 because it was Johann Sebastian Bach's 300th anniversary; the East Germans were keen to 'claim' the composer as their own and I was given permission to enter not as a 'historian', but because I could fortunately prove that I was also a musician. The attempt to claim 'good Germans' like Bach was typical; Beethoven was considered 'East German' even though he had been born in Bonn, while people like the SS leader Reinhard Heydrich was labelled a 'West German' although he had been born in Halle. I lived in East Berlin in 1987 in order to observe the 750th Anniversary celebrations. Again I was able to stay because I showed interest in an official event; I did not admit that my main reason for being there was to gather material for my Oxford D.Phil on the political manipulation of history – this would no doubt have led to my expulsion. The Wall fell in 1989, but it was obvious to anyone who had lived in East Germany that many young people clearly believed in at least some of the fabrications which they had been taught for so long. These ranged from the mundane – in which minor events were hailed as great milestones on the road to the inevitable creation of the 'peasants' and workers' state' – to the ludicrous – that the entire population of the GDR was made up of 'Communist resistance fighters' who had helped the Red Army to liberate Germany, that all Nazis had fled to the Federal Republic in 1945, and that individuals like Hitler had played a relatively unimportant role in the creation of the Third Reich.[60]

When the Wall fell there was an immediate sense that this poisonous heritage should be exposed. It was a time of great hope and optimism in Germany and in Berlin. Old history textbooks were thrown out, hard-line East German teachers were barred from schools, official museum displays were changed and the history of both Soviet and East German crimes against its citizens was investigated – in November 1990, for example, a library dedicated to the victims of Stalinism was opened on the Hausvogteiplatz with the support of prominent ex-GDR activists, including Bärbel Bohley, Lew Kopelew and Jürgen Fuchs. But the mood did not last. East Berlin was the very core of the old GDR. It was the centre of government, of the Stasi and of the party. Every seventh East Berliner had been employed by the state and around 100,000 people were members of the SED elite, ranging from high-ranking security personnel to top party functionaries. It was they who had profited from the old regime with their subsidized flats, their access to western goods and their exercise of power. Suddenly a number of eastern Germans began to reject the new western orientation and to hanker after lost days of prestige and influence in the cosy world of the SED or the Stasi. Self-examination has never been a strong feature of old, corrupt and criminal elites. Only two years after the collapse of the state some began to call for a return to the 'values of the old GDR' and the defunct state was presented as a wonderful place which had cared for its people and given them fulfilling lives. A growing number of ex-GDR citizens began to exhibit those destructive traits which have plagued Berlin in the past: self-pity, sentimentality and a tendency to gloss over the worst aspects of their history.

The group which has led this movement was none other than the heir to the SED – the East German Communist Party – known as the Party of Democratic Socialism or PDS and headed by the East German lawyer Gregor Gysi. The PDS gained the support of much of the old GDR elite, in particular those who were unable to launch themselves in new western careers, but it also played on the alienation and bitterness felt by many ordinary citizens struggling to find a way in the capitalist world, exploiting this misery for its own political gain. It has been highly successful. Rather than hearing about the SED's crimes and abuses of power a visitor to eastern Germany in the late 1990s might well be told about the wonderful Shangri-La that was East Berlin. Those westerners who question this version are told that they 'could not know' because they 'had not lived in the GDR'. Those who *did* live in the GDR tend not to be so easily swayed, but it is troubling to meet so many people who now long for their 'good old days'. This has also had political repercussions. In the 1994 elections an amazing one third of eastern Berliners voted for the PDS.[61]

This so-called '*Ostalgia*' – nostalgia for the east – has become the new scourge of Berlin, turning the city into a battleground over the history of the GDR. It has already had an effect on post-Wall planning and reconstruction: bitter arguments have erupted over what to do with that symbol of the old regime, the Palast der Republik on Unter den Linden.

It is a plain rectangular structure with square, copper-coloured glass windows and white walls and lies in the midst of the few remaining old buildings in the heart of Berlin. It is a perfect symbol of the GDR, epitomizing the lack of creativity, the dearth of compassion and the insensitivity to the past which characterized the bankrupt regime; indeed it stands on the site of the former palace which was blown up for ideological reasons by Walter Ulbricht in 1950. The Palast also represented the powerlessness of East German citizens: it was built as a 'people's palace' open to all ordinary citizens in order to show them that they were participants in the running of 'their' state. In reality, however, ordinary people had no access to power at all – indeed they rarely saw their leaders except on carefully staged ceremonial occasions, and political activity was forbidden unless specifically sanctioned by the SED. When the Wall fell it was understood that the Palast would be demolished and that some sort of building recapturing the proportions and facade of the old palace would go up on this historic spot; supporters of this idea had a life-sized mock-up of the old building painted on to vast canvas sheets and erected them at the site in 1993. But then *Ostalgia* struck. Suddenly the Palast der Republik was called a 'monument' to the people of the GDR; some easterners began to reminisce about how much they had enjoyed visits to concerts or speech days or exhibitions in the 1970s and 1980s. In 1995 the decision to remove this building was reversed.

The question of what to do with the Palast der Republik is an aesthetic problem rather than a political one; East Berlin is filled with eyesores built by the former regime but nobody is suggesting that these should all be ripped down. The palace is controversial not so much because it is an ugly ex-GDR government building – there are plenty of those – but rather because of where it is; if it had been built far from the site of the historic palace few would question its right to stay. The debate is troubling only in that it demonstrates a lingering nostalgia for a regime which does not deserve the loyalty of its people. But *Ostalgia* is having an effect on other aspects of history.

In 1989 it seemed that the destruction of the huge 63-foot-high statue of Lenin in the former East Berlin district of Lichtenberg was a foregone conclusion. The enormous red granite sculpture by the Soviet artist Nikolai Tompsky was typical of those which had sprouted all over the Warsaw Pact countries after 1945 – enormous, oppressive, heroic, and detested symbols of Soviet oppression. These statues were amongst the first things to be vandalized or torn down in the aftermath of the revolutions in central Europe – except in East Berlin. Indeed, Berlin's Lenin became a rallying point for those keen to salvage the reputation of the ex-GDR. For this noisy minority Lenin no longer represented tyranny but was the 'symbol of history' which 'reflected GDR traditions' and whose removal would be an 'affront to the *Ossis*'. One group calling itself the Initiative politische Denkmäler advocated the preservation of all monuments, while members of the Green Party and the PDS introduced a resolution in the municipal parliament calling for the destruction of the old Victory Column in the Tiergarten if Lenin was taken down. This glib comparison between the monument honouring Bismarck's unification of

Germany and a statue of a man responsible for the murder of millions of people was simply staggering. East Berlin earned the dubious distinction of being the only non-CIS capital which actually wanted to preserve the symbol of its enslavement. In the end a suitable compromise was reached. The statue was taken apart piece by piece and laid to rest in a Berlin gravel pit, but it was not destroyed.

The controversy over Lenin was a mere taste of what was to come. The next statue to be championed was the enormous Ernst Thälmann in Prenzlauer Berg, complete with flag and clenched fist and a heater in the nose to prevent snow from piling up in winter. This time the arguments for its preservation came directly from the misleading pages of official GDR history textbooks.

Ernst Thälmann was one of the great heroes of the GDR. Every school child learned that he was chairman of the German Communist Party between 1925 and 1933; every museum of modern history recounted how he was arrested and killed by the Nazis, and how he was the very model of an 'anti-Fascist resistance fighter'. There is no doubt that Thälmann suffered terribly under the Nazis and for that he deserves universal sympathy. But East Germans had not been taught the other side of his story.

Ernst Thälmann was also the man responsible for the forced Stalinization of the German Communist Party in the 1920s. It was he who brought the KPD under Moscow's direct control, it was he who supervised the eviction of all its opponents, and it was he who on Stalin's direct orders broke all links with the Social Democrats – who were labelled 'Social Fascists' – in 1928. Thälmann then did something which alone might have provoked the removal of his statue. Rather than join with the moderate left, whom he still saw as the 'greatest threat to the revolution', he actually allied himself with the Nazis who were, in his words, 'merely an extreme form of the doomed bourgeois order'; he even put Hitler's popularity down to his sexual appeal to German women. Thälmann proceeded to lead a relentless attack on the legitimate Weimar government, one minute standing up in the Reichstag along with Hermann Göring and others to harangue its leaders, the next co-operating with the Nazis in the transport strike of November 1932. In short, Thälmann was directly involved in bringing to power the very people who would destroy him. He is no German hero. The statue is not merely an ugly remnant of Soviet-German Communism; it supports a deliberately doctored version of history and glorifies a man who helped to destroy the Weimar democracy. Nevertheless, thanks to pressure from the *Ostalgia* movement, it will remain in place in the new German capital.[62]

It would be absurd to remove everything created by the GDR during its forty-year history and in March 1992 the Berlin government established an independent commission, largely made up of ex-East Germans, to study such monuments and to recommend what should be done with them. From the beginning the body faced noisy protests from those who now objected to the removal of any piece of the 'GDR heritage' no matter how appalling its symbolism, but it has nevertheless made wise and informed decisions. Most structures are to be retained out of historical interest – there is little harm in the large wall murals of workers and peasants, the paintings of tractors in the fields, the statues of long-forgotten Communist artists or writers clutching their paintbrushes along with tool kits and sheaves of wheat.[63] The Marx–Engels statue erected in 1985 near the Alexanderplatz is seen by most easterners as inoffensive and will stay, and the Soviet war memorials by the Brandenburg Gate, at Schönholz and at Treptow Park which contain mass graves of the thousands of Red Army soldiers who died in the Battle for Berlin are rightly being protected.[64] Some controversial figures, including Rosa Luxemburg and Karl Liebknecht, are to keep their street signs although the GDR 'hero' Georgi Dimitroff was removed because, irrespective of his performance at the Reichstag Trial, he was Stalin's representative in Bulgaria and was responsible for the forced Sovietization of that country. Streets named after ex-Communist leaders from Wilhelm Pieck to Ho Chi Minh have also been changed. The guidelines are simple: those monuments which were built by the regime, which were meant overtly to glorify it, and which would still be considered a rallying point for those who hanker after the old GDR are to be removed – Lenin, Dzerzhinsky and Ulbricht included. It is not appropriate simply to equate East Germany with the Nazi regime, but to have retained Pieck or Dimitroff would have been rather like keeping heroic statues of Göring or the Horst-Wessel-Strasse after 1945 merely out of 'historical interest'. The Allies were right to blow the enormous swastikas off old Nazi buildings even if they retained the structures themselves.

The conflicts over official GDR monuments are merely one manifestation of the deep divisions which exist not only between different groups of eastern Germans, but also between the two halves of the city. Berlin will have to deal with many scars left over from the GDR regime – not least the 'Wall in the Head' phenomenon, in which the physical divisions are destroyed but the spiritual ones remain – in addition to the totally different approaches to culture, education and history experienced by two groups of Germans for half a century.[65] But more important than debates over the Thälmann statue or the Palast der Republik is the question of how the most reprehensible aspects of the GDR should be remembered in the new Germany.

Many East Germans were stunned in 1989 to discover the extent to which they had been controlled, manipulated and impoverished by their own regime. The anger and sense of resentment amongst ordinary people grew as they began to uncover the truth about those who had created and maintained this

grim system for so long, and the tens of thousands who had willingly co-
operated by spying on friends, neighbours and colleagues. As the Wall was
dismantled activists broke into the Stasi headquarters and began to examine
the documents there and as the extent of spying was revealed it became
painfully clear that Berliners had not lost their eagerness – so evident during
the Nazi period – to inform on one another in the 'interest of state security'.

The revelations about the Stasi prompted the unprecedented opening of
the files to all those people who appear in them and in 1991 a law was passed
regulating their use. Today the records, which fill five miles of shelves, are
kept in the former archive for the Ministry for State Security in the Normannenstrasse – known locally as the Gauck Authority after the East German
clergyman who heads it.[66] By 1997 over 1 million people had applied to read
their personal files while nearly 2 million employers had asked for the vetting
or 'Gaucking' of potential colleagues to see if they had collaborated with the
Stasi. There have no doubt been painful revelations, unfair dismissals and
abuses of the information contained in the files but exposure of the past was
essential. Not only have the victims been able to find out the truth about what
was done to them; those who made the conscious decision to spy in order to
further their careers or obtain a car or travel abroad have also been unmasked.
The opening of the files has helped to lay bare the terrible human cost of this
deceit.

The Stasi files alone represent a powerful counter-argument to those
Ostalgia advocates now trying to present the GDR as a harmless, bureaucratic
and rather dull state. The files also record how security personnel committed
brutal murders and imprisoned people without trial; it is now known that
nearly 1 per cent of the population of the GDR, at least 100,000 people, died
at the hands of the state.[67] According to one former prisoner, Gunter Toepfer,
people are now referring to the GDR as a place with plenty of kindergarten
places and cheap train fares; it was in fact 'a state which accepted death and
extermination. Yet there has been a *de facto* amnesty.' And, as David Rose
and Anthony Glees have pointed out, thousands of those still free in East
Berlin were 'responsible for abductions, torture, and medical experiments on
children'.[68] Some courageous individuals like Harald Strunz have tried to help
those who suffered under the regime; after being imprisoned by the East
German government Strunz set up the League of Victims of Stalinism to help
those who had been falsely accused of crimes. Gauck himself insists that rather
than taking the easy path of nostalgia East Germans must confront difficult
truths: 'There can be no peace without confronting the past with honesty and
maturity.'[69] Many Berliners argue that the Stasi headquarters should be kept
open; that the Stasi security prison at Hohenschönhausen – the former meat
factory where helpless prisoners were tortured in the dank 'U-boat' cells –

should be turned into a museum; and that the remnants of the Wall – now all but gone from the city centre – should be preserved so that future generations can see what this incredible structure actually looked like.[70]

Their task may prove difficult. None of the torturers who worked at Hohenschönhausen Prison has been brought to justice; indeed one former prisoner recently came across his erstwhile tormenter while trying to buy an insurance policy in western Berlin. In a 1994 opinion poll 57 per cent of former East Germans advocated closing the Stasi files.[71] At the end of 1997 the federal police unit or Zerv, which is made up of 270 detectives charged with investigating Stasi crimes, shut down. On 1 January 1998 the statute of limitations comes into force, making it impossible to bring prosecutions for any offence except murder committed in the old East Germany. Manfred Kittlaus, Zerv's chief, has said that after that date 'The majority of human rights violations will be beyond the law. The perpetrators will soon be free to walk down Unter den Linden with impunity.'[72] Many decent eastern Germans who resisted the regime felt betrayed when such brilliant self-publicists as Markus Wolf, who ruined innocent lives by recruiting women as 'honey trap spies', or Erich Mielke, who ordered the torture of civilians for having 'dangerous' religious beliefs, or Margot Honecker, who had the babies of politically 'dubious' parents stolen and given to good military couples, or Erich Honecker, who built the Wall, were all allowed to go free. Many believed that these people should have been brought to justice; once again, they felt, the spirit of the law in Germany had been trampled by the letter of the law. (It was some consolation that on 25 August 1997 Erich Honecker's successor, Egon Krenz, was sentenced to six years' imprisonment.) One way to integrate those who suffered under the Communist regime is to continue to fight the siren voices of those trying to rewrite its history, while supporting people like Gauck who reveal the truth about the oppressive nature of East Germany.[73]

It is not surprising that the GDR was a grim place. How could it be otherwise, given that it was the product of the two most evil dictatorships in European history: the Third Reich and Stalin's Soviet Union. It was a vassal of the Soviet Union, but it also retained many of the worst features of the previous regime. The crimes committed by the GDR were not remotely of the same magnitude as those committed by the Nazis, but the two regimes were joined by history and there were frightening continuities between them, not least that they employed similar propaganda methods and block warden systems to police entire districts of Berlin.[74] Despite, or rather because of the Nazi legacy East Germans learned virtually nothing about the Third Reich; hence they feel no responsibility for it, and are for the most part still unaware of the links between Nazism and the regime under which they lived. This history should be documented in the new capital city, for understanding the

Nazi period is one of the keys to understanding what happened in East Berlin under the GDR. But the need to face the Nazi past goes much deeper than that. The legacy of the years 1933 to 1945 still presents enormous problems for Berlin as a whole, and it is not an exaggeration to say that the way in which its citizens face the past will help to shape both the future of the capital and the very identity of the new Germany. And the rest of the world will be watching.

In an article written in July 1997 the British historian Andrew Roberts commented that in the preceding week he had come across a number of references both to Nazi Germany and the Second World War: the Swiss Bankers Association had published a list of accounts thought to contain gold belonging to Nazi victims; there were calls for Monaco and the Vatican to 'come clean about the extent of their wartime financial relations with the Nazis'; there was a 'row at Harvard over whether the new chair in Holocaust studies should be filled by Daniel Goldhagen, the controversial author of *Hitler's Willing Executioners*; while in Germany Volker Rühe swore to prosecute the soldiers of the 571 Mountain Combat Battalion who 'made a video nasty of explicit viciousness and depravity during training which disgusted many Germans and evoked memories of war-time atrocities'; the Nuremberg city council was criticized for giving an honorary citizenship to Karl Diehl, aged ninety, whose company had used slave labour to build concentration camps and produce armaments in the war; and the sacking of Amnon Barzel, the Israeli curator of Berlin's Jewish Museum, was denounced by the board of Berlin's Jewish community as 'bearing a tragic comparison with the dark times between 1933 and 1938'. As Roberts put it, 'For those who thought that the celebrations marking the 50th anniversary of VE-Day somehow might have drawn a line under the Second World War, the events of last week must have been a grave disappointment. They prove how the scars of Hitler's war are far from healed, and that the echoes of 1939–45 will stay with us long after the last veteran has gone off to join his comrades.' Roberts was right – the Second World War is not going to go away.[75]

In purely physical terms it is impossible to escape the evidence of Nazism in Berlin, the more so now that the Wall has been removed, exposing and drawing attention to artefacts long hidden or forgotten. Reminders of this history are everywhere: in the tunnels which planners must take account of when developing new buildings; in the segments of Goebbels's Propaganda Ministry which, contrary to popular belief, was not completely destroyed and is still in use; in the huge column of concrete hidden behind a few scrubby bushes, all that is left of Speer's attempt to test the foundations of the huge dome for Germania; in the East–West Axis, now the Strasse des 17 Juni, still lit by Speer's prominent streetlamps. The reconstruction of Berlin is throwing up long-lost reminders of the conflict: on 15 September 1994 one of 15,000 war-time bombs exploded at a construction site killing three people and blowing a huge hole in the side of a building; the remains of Goebbels' bunker and Hitler's Chancellery bunker have been exposed, and construction workers frequently come across the skeletons of those who died in the Battle for Berlin.[76] This is one German city in which the *Aufarbeitung der Geschichte*, the working through of history, cannot be put aside. Questions about how to 'come to terms with' the Nazi past permeate virtually every aspect of the city's new role, including its suitability as the new German capital.

The history of Nazi criminality has been a source of controversy in Germany since 1945. Attempts to address the involvement of ordinary Germans in the form of the Allied *Fragebogen* – the de-Nazification procedure – or in the Nuremberg Trials were quickly forgotten after the war as most Germans tried to drew a veil over their past in the *Stunde Null* or Zero Hour of 1945. The advent of the Cold War was a boon to all those keen to hide their involvement in the old regime; moreover, both the western Allies and the Soviets made extensive use of NSDAP members in the rebuilding of their respective Germanys. Historiography was written to reflect the new Cold War world. Russia's captive East Germans were taught a highly fictitious version of history which included the bizarre notion that all *Hitlerfascisten* had moved to the west in 1945 and that all those who remained were innocent of any involvement in the Third Reich. West Germans did produce some interesting work, particularly Friedrich Meinecke's *Die deutsche Katastrophe*, which hinted at the historical roots of Nazism, but most popular histories encouraged the view that the entire period had been an aberration during which the nation had been led to ruin by the demonic Hitler – a view which conveniently allowed most people to forget their own support of the regime. Most West Germans looked to the future and poured their energy into the *Wirtschafts-wunder* – the economic miracle. The East Germans continued to peddle their ludicrous version of history right up until 1989. But this was not possible in the west.

The world of the 1950s was preoccupied with the Cold War and there was little discussion of Nazi crime in general and the mass murder of European Jews in particular; this was true even in Israel, where many survivors felt unable to talk about their experiences. The situation began to change in the 1960s, particularly after the Adolf Eichmann trial in 1961. Eichmann was the SS officer who had headed the Jewish Evacuation Department of the Gestapo; amongst many other things he had taken personal charge of transports from Moravia and had even run Auschwitz for a short time in order to learn about the 'problems' of the operation first hand. The trial was immaculately conducted in Israel by the Chief Prosecutor, Gideon Hausner, and it was televised. Eichmann did not deny his role in the Holocaust; indeed he could be seen talking with indifference – even pride – about the fact that he had helped to kill millions of human beings. Although the Eichmann trial aroused interest amongst people in the rest of the world most Germans ignored it and continued to try to 'put the past behind them'.[77] Few German universities offered courses on twentieth-century history and none taught about the Nazi period; parents refused to discuss the Second World War with their children, and it seemed that the past would remain firmly hidden away. West German scholars continued to carry out important research but few concentrated on Nazi crimes or on the Holocaust, preferring to debate various theories of totalitarianism or to study the leadership structure of the Third Reich or the military history of the war. The general public were first prompted to confront the most criminal aspects of their history not by schools or universities, but by the media. Above all, it was the screening of the American mini-series *Holocaust* in January 1979 – which coincided with yet another attempt by Germans to extend the statute of limitations for war crimes and crimes against humanity – which finally brought the horror of what had happened into people's living rooms. History had not gone away after all.[78]

The film was a milestone in post-war West Germany because it took the study of the Holocaust out of the specialist academic realm and made it an issue of national debate. More research was carried out and some understanding developed as to how and why these crimes had been committed. It was ironic that it took a Hollywood film – and not a particularly good one – to provoke such a response, and there were problems with the approach.[79] Rather than reflect upon its significance to all Germans, including themselves, many of the younger generation veered towards a blanket condemnation of all who had lived under National Socialism: most knew very little about the complexities of Nazi history and made little attempt to learn how and why the Nazis had come to power, or to find out what it had been like to live under a dictatorship, or to differentiate between, say, an SS camp commander and a young Wehrmacht soldier stationed in Norway. And, as few older Germans had actually been directly engaged in the act of killing Jews, they in turn dismissed these shrill accusations of 'collective guilt' as ill-informed and irrelevant, ignoring their own often substantial contributions to the maintenance of the criminal regime. Many who had lived through the war years still failed to see that even if they had not actually carried out the first Zyklon-B test in Auschwitz or experimented on the bodies of camp prisoners, they had helped to maintain the system which had made these crimes possible.

The study of the Holocaust and the Nazi period continued in West Germany during the late 1970s and early 1980s and a great deal of original research was carried out. West Germany became unique in its attempts to confront its history and to atone for its crimes, and it won respect in the international community.[80] Nevertheless, debates over how to approach this history became increasingly politicized and were bound up with questions about German national identity. Very generally, those on the left tended to argue that the Holocaust was unique, that it could never be put into a historical context, while more conservative historians argued that the crimes of other nations were also terrible and that Germans must stop thinking that they were uniquely evil so that they could begin to build a normal nation. The debate intensified in the 1980s in response to the *Tendenzwende*, a shift to the right represented by Helmut Kohl's electoral success. Kohl provoked controversy through his ill-judged 1985 visit with President Reagan to the Bitburg cemetery, where Waffen-SS men were buried. This in turn fuelled the *Historikerstreit* – the historians' debate – which focused on how Germans should approach the Nazi past. This debate was sparked off by an article published in the *Frankfurter allgemeine Zeitung* by Ernst Nolte in June 1986 in which he argued that the mass murder of the Jews should be put into a broader historical context and that the Final Solution had perhaps been an 'asiatic deed' modelled on Bolshevik crimes to which the Nazis had added only the technology of gassing.[81] The article was hastily rebutted by Jürgen Habermas in *Die Zeit*, and the exchange set off a flurry of argument and counter-argument about whether Nazi crimes were unique or whether they were comparable to other national atrocities, in particular the Stalinist Terror. The debate produced little new research and quickly degenerated into bitter personal attacks between rival groups, prompting Gordon Craig to dub it 'the war of the historians'.[82] The arguments were tempered somewhat by Richard von Weizsäcker's moving and courageous speech as Federal President on the fortieth anniversary of the German surrender in 1945. Weizsäcker renounced the notion of 'collective guilt' but acknowledged the 'historical consequences' of the Third Reich and maintained that Germans could not 'come to terms with the past' because that implied ignoring the moral burdens of history. Indeed, he argued, only by facing and accepting the past could Germans look forward to any credible future.[83]

When I worked in both East and West Berlin in the 1980s – in particular during the 750th Anniversary celebrations in 1987 – I was always struck by the extraordinary contrast between West Berlin, with its vast range of debate and discussion, and the GDR, where nobody was permitted to deviate from the official line. The contrast alone was a powerful argument in favour of the West German system, and of the attempt to be open about the past. Nevertheless, although discussion about Nazi crimes had become widespread amongst historians and journalists and writers and film makers, there were many ordinary people who resented it. The members of the 'Active Museum' who created the first exhibition at the former Gestapo headquarters did so in the face of unpleasant protests from members of the general public; those who put up signs marking infamous landmarks such as the site of Freisler's People's Court had to repair them when they were repeatedly knocked down; members of the Neue Gesellschaft für Bildende Kunst who displayed and discussed Nazi art at the *Inszenierung der Macht* exhibition carried on in spite of the death threats they received for 'stirring up the past'.[84]

The controversies about how to come to terms with this history after reunification remain unresolved, but although interest was still strong amongst the educated elite it had become clear by the 1990s that many ordinary people were tired of seeing their nation in terms of this terrible history and wished to look to the future. Some claimed that too much attention was being paid to the Holocaust, and that it was time to draw a line under the past. Young West Germans born after the war may have felt remorse at what their forefathers had done but many now echoed Helmut Kohl's claim that the 'grace of late birth' absolved them of guilt. The desire to draw a line was reflected in a *Der Spiegel* survey of January 1992 commemorating the Wannsee Conference. Two-thirds of Germans stated that they wanted less discussion about the persecution of the Jews. Far more worrying, however, was the result which showed that 32 per cent of those polled believed that the Jews were themselves partly to blame for being 'hated and persecuted'.[85]

There is another reworking of the *Faust* legend which takes place in the city of Berlin. This one was written in 1936 by Thomas Mann's son Klaus, who committed suicide in Cannes in 1949. It is entitled *Mephisto – Roman einer Karriere*, and was made into the extraordinary film *Mephisto* by István Szabó in 1981.[86] A true story, it recounts the career of Mann's brother-in-law, the actor Gustav Gründgens, who went to Berlin in 1928 and remained until 1945, becoming the head of the Deutsches Theater and then the Staatliches Schauspielhaus under the Nazis. During those years he became one of the best-known actors in Germany. He was most famous for his production of Goethe's *Faust*, and for his own performances in the role of Mephistopheles.

Klaus Mann's story is also a metaphor for Berlin, and for all the people who sold their souls for the fame and fortune, security and success afforded by the new regime. Mann mocks the poet Gottfried Benn – 'Pelz' – and André Germain – 'Pierre Larue' – who remained in Berlin to further their careers, but he reserves his venom for the main character, Gustav Gründgens – 'Hendrik Höfgen'. Like Gründgens, Höfgen is initially a supporter of left-wing experimental productions but his attempt to found a workers' theatre founders and he gradually finds an audience amongst the new Nazi elite. Slowly, steadily, they court him, and his blinding ego coupled with his burning hunger for success at any price make him useful to them. It is they who arrange for ever more productions and new directorships, rewarding him with even greater honours and power. But each time he is asked to do something in return. Höfgen is expected to rid the theatre of 'undesirable elements', or to abandon his black mistress, or to divorce his wife now living in exile, or to make propaganda speeches extolling the virtues of the 'new German *Kultur*'. One evening, shortly after Höfgen has asked 'the general' if one of his friends might be spared, he is taken to the great Olympic stadium. The general barks an order. Höfgen is pushed on to the field and the general watches as glaring white spotlights are turned on him. Höfgen tries to hide but the intense lights follow him; he races to the centre of the vast arena but he cannot escape; he turns and tries to shield his eyes, but the piercing glare is too bright. Finally, in despair, he looks up and whispers: 'What do they want from me? I am only an actor.'

Klaus Mann's *Mephisto* is the story of the seductive power of evil. His Faust does not sign a dramatic pact with the Devil but relinquishes his soul slowly, gradually, almost imperceptibly. Like so many Berliners caught in the Nazi net Höfgen is not an inherently evil man – he is talented, hard working, even loyal up to a point. But he wants to be better off, he longs for power and security and influence. Many of those who worked for the Nazis were, like Höfgen, ordinary people who were just 'doing their job', just signing the paper or stamping the file, part of a long, efficient but often anonymous chain of command in which those German traits – order and discipline and efficiency – so often seen as virtues became its worst vices. Nazism was made up not only of the Himmlers and Heydrichs, the SS camp guards and the Einsatzgruppen commanders; it also functioned because of those minute acts of betrayal, those imperceptible moments of cowardice – looking the other way when someone was being beaten, refusing to enter a shop daubed with the Star of David. The warning of *Mephisto* is that a person makes his moral choice much earlier than he thinks – it is already too late when a single person has been hounded out of his office for being of the 'wrong race'; it is already too late if someone is kicked to death in a cellar because he holds political views which do not conform with those of 'the people'; it is already too late if a child is removed from the classroom for being Jewish, or if someone is turned in and perhaps executed for listening to an 'enemy' broadcast. Berliners continued down this road between 1933 and 1945, carrying on doggedly until the city lay in ruins around them and millions of innocent people had been murdered.

Berlin is itself a testimony to the insidious nature of evil; a warning of the power of *Mephisto*. And the evil was everywhere in Berlin between 1933 and 1945. How many people realize that in 1943 there were over fifty key Gestapo and SS offices in the city centre, not to mention the hundreds of other government and related offices? How many have walked past number

98/99 Wilmersdorfer Strasse and realized that it was at one time the central SS Personnel Office; or past Unter den Eichen 126–135, which was the site of the SS Economic and Administration Office; or past the Hedemannstrasse 24, which was the SS Race and Settlement Office, or the Knesebeckstrasse 43, which housed the Office of the SS-Reichdoctors? How many people have passed Meinekestrasse 10, once the SS Gruppe IVB, responsible for the political control of churches, sects and Jews, or the Kurfürstenstrasse 115/116, once the site of Referat IVB4 – better known as Adolf Eichmann's division of Judenangelegenheiten (Jewish Affairs)? How many have walked over the former Schlossstrasse 1, now at the centre of the palace debate, knowing that they are on the site of the central SS training school? How many shoppers have strolled down the bustling Kurfürstendamm past numbers 140–143 and realized that it once housed a warren of offices dealing with everything from 'saboteurs' in the occupied territories to the protection of German *Volkstum*?[87]

Attempts to commemorate this aspect of Berlin history have often reflected contemporary politics. West Berlin's first monument to the Second World War was created in 1952 at the former Plötzensee Prison. It was here that 2,500 people, mainly German nationals (including many resistance fighters involved in the 1944 plot), were hanged or guillotined, and the site was dedicated to all victims of Fascism.[88] A short time later a memorial was erected at the Bendlerblock, where Stauffenberg was shot after the failed 1944 assassination attempt. It was dedicated to the German resistance.[89] These monuments were important, but the choice of location and the choice of 'victim' echoed the post-war West German tendency to concentrate on the fate of the 'good' Germans – the 1944 plotters – to the exclusion of others. This choice of 'victim' was mirrored in East Berlin in the re-dedication of Schinkel's Neue Wache with an eternal flame in memory of the 'victims of Fascism', which in East German iconography meant their largely fictitious 'Communist resistance fighters'. It did not mention victims in Poland, Russia, the Netherlands or Greece; nor did it mention the gypsies or the Jews.

The Neue Wache has already served as the Kaiser's guardhouse, as a war memorial for the Weimar Republic, as a memorial for the Nazis and as a shrine for East Germans guarded until 1989 by goose-stepping soldiers. In 1993 it was renamed the 'Central Memorial of the Federal Republic of Germany for the Victims of War and Tyranny' and the long inscription now commemorates resistance fighters, homosexuals, Jews, gypsies, soldiers who fell on the front, people killed in the bombing raids – indeed all those who were victims of war and terror. It reflects Helmut Kohl's view that there is a 'community of victims', all of whom should be remembered together.

It is right for Germans to have a place to mourn all those who died tragically during the Second World War; however, the idea of a 'community of victims' glosses over one very important aspect of the Nazi past: it implies that a young man who was forced into the army against his will and then died on the front can be compared to a young man killed in Auschwitz, or that a Berlinerin who met her death in a bombing raid can be compared to a young Russian woman burned to death in a barn in 1942. There is a difference between those who were victims of the 'horrors of war' and those who were specifically targeted, hunted down and murdered by the Nazis themselves – not only victims of war, but victims of the Germans as well.

The central memorial to 'all victims of Fascism', which includes those killed by the Nazis, implies that Berliners had as little responsibility for their own suffering in the war as, say, those who eked out an existence in the camps; that Berliners were victims too. But Berlin was not Auschwitz or Maidanek or Stutthof or Kulmhof, nor was it Leningrad or Minsk or Amsterdam or Warsaw. Innocent people were hunted down by the Nazis in Berlin, to be sure, but they were in the minority in this city of 4 million people. Berlin was the centre of the Third Reich; here the worst crimes ever committed by Germans were discussed, ordered, codified, registered, approved. For every Berlin resistance fighter, for every Berlin Jew deported to Auschwitz, there were dozens of members of the Gestapo or the SS; dozens who worked in the laboratories or the railway offices or the bureaucracy or the corrupt courts, oiling the wheels and allowing the brittle edifice to function right until the bitter end. In *Henry IV* Part 2 Shakespeare says that 'There is a history in all men's lives' – a history, hidden since 1945, which can best be addressed in Berlin.

The most successful attempt to do this so far is the *Topographie des Terrors*, which started as a temporary exhibition on the site of Gestapo headquarters in 1987 and which is to become a permanent installation in Berlin. The site has a chilling history. It became the headquarters of the Geheime Staatspolizei – the Gestapo – in 1933. In 1934 Heinrich Himmler moved the SS headquarters to the Hotel Prinz Albrecht next door and shortly afterwards the building behind was leased to the SS Security Service, the Sicherheitsdienst (SD) headed by Reinhard Heydrich. In 1939 the Gestapo, the criminal police and the SD were united in the Reichssicherheitshauptamt (the Reich Main Security Office), headed by Heydrich and officially headquartered at Prinz-Albrecht-Strasse 8.[90] This accumulation of power made it the centre of the terror both in Germany and abroad. The site was damaged during the war and blown up in 1949; it was due to have a road built over it until 1981, when the architectural historian Dieter Hoffmann-Axthelm recommended that the area be preserved. In 1983 a group calling itself the 'Active Museum of Fascism and Resistance in Berlin' dedicated to confronting the Nazi past began to excavate the site. Part of the cellar complex was cleared and a temporary exhibition created, which included details of the orders issued from there, the prisoners who had been brought there, the people executed there. It explained the system of terror which had extended out from the buildings until it oppressed almost all of Europe, but it was concerned both with those in command and their victims. It remains a thoughtful presentation and has attracted many visitors – although its director Herr Lutz said that of the 1 million people who came in 1993, half were foreigners.[91]

Many Berliners, like the members of the Active Museum, feel that the city could use more initiatives and memorials of this kind. Rather than being demolished or covered up, they argue, the Nazi past should be exposed, demystified and scrutinized; rather than concentrating only on victims Berlin must, as Gerhard Schoenberner put it, counter the portrayal of the Gestapo or the SS as 'people from Mars who attacked and invaded a peaceful Germany'.[92] It has been suggested that instead of being destroyed, the Chancellery bunker, which is about to disappear for ever under the new Federal Representative Offices, might be turned into a museum in the mode of the *Topographie des Terrors*. Alfred Kernd'l, former head of the Municipal Archaeology Office, lobbied to save a bunker covered with paintings created by SS men during their fight to defend Hitler in April 1945, arguing that it was a truly amazing phenomenon: even as bombs rained down on them and as their capital city went up in flames, some soldiers were still able to paint pictures of the invasion of England.[93] The future of the paintings has not yet been decided, but it is likely that they will be destroyed – ostensibly for fear that they will become neo-Nazi monuments.

Berlin is now being rebuilt as the capital of a new Germany, and it would be ludicrous to preserve all artefacts from the Nazi period; the city centre would be little more than a windswept wasteland. Nevertheless, the argument that none of these things can be saved because they might become neo-Nazi shrines is both insulting to Berliners and worrying to all Europeans, implying as it does that the authorities see Fascism lurking just behind Berlin's new facade. Hitler's Wolfschanze bunker complex in the former East Prussia is open to the public, but far from becoming a neo-Nazi shrine it exposes the ghastly mentality of the men who hid in these cramped, dingy buildings to plot the deaths of innocent people. It is a powerful reminder of an abhorrent regime.

The debate about the preservation of such artefacts is linked to the question of how the Holocaust itself should be commemorated in Berlin. Apart from a few minor sites set up in the west before 1989 no separate memorial has yet been created in memory of the Jews who were murdered between 1933 and 1945. Historians, planners and politicians alike have tried to address this issue and in 1995 a competition was held for the development of a five-acre site near the Brandenburg Gate for which DM16 million had been set aside. There were 527 entries ranging from gigantic boxcars to monstrous sculptures of ovens, but on 17 March 1995 the chairman of the jury, president of the Berlin-Brandenburg Academy of Arts Walter Jens, awarded the first prize to a design in the form of a huge slab the size of two football fields to be inscribed with the names of over 4 million known Jewish victims, a design also favoured by the television talk-show host Lea Rosh, who funded a group known as 'Perspective Berlin' which campaigned for the monument. The project was criticized by many Berliners on the grounds of its enormous size, and was eventually vetoed by Helmut Kohl. A second competition was held in 1997 and a new monument is set to be inaugurated on 20 January, 1999, the 56th anniversary of the Wannsee Conference. Those making the choice of what to build on the site took over a decade to decide, precisely because they were faced with the terrible question of how Berlin can appropriately pay tribute to people whose deaths were ordered from its very core.[94] And Berliners were responsible.[95] On 16 October 1941 Hans Frank, who presided over the General Gouvernement in Poland, reported on a recent discussion with his superiors about how to deal with the Jews under his jurisdiction: 'We were told in Berlin, "Why all this bother? We can do nothing with [the Jews] either in the Ostland or in the Reichskommissariat. So liquidate them yourselves." '[96]

The creation of a memorial in Berlin is contentious partly because of where the actual killing took place. The murder of Europe's Jews was directed from Berlin, but there were no killing centres in Germany itself. Unlike concentration camps such as Bergen-Belsen or Dachau or Sachsenhausen, the extermination camps were located some distance away. Kulmhof (Chelmno), where 360,000 people were killed and three people survived, was located in western Poland. Belzec, where 600,000 people died and two survived, Sobibór, where 250,000 people died and sixty-four survived, and Treblinka, where over 870,000 people died and fewer than seventy survived, were all located in eastern Poland.[97] Around 1 million Jews and 270,000 non-Jewish Poles were killed in Auschwitz, in southern Poland. The thousands of Jews who survived Auschwitz did so only because it had a dual function both as an extermination camp (Birkenau) and a concentration/slave labour camp. This relatively 'high' survival rate came about because some Jews were selected to be worked to death rather than gassed upon arrival. This is one of the reasons why Auschwitz has become something of a symbol for the Holocaust – there were simply no witnesses left to tell of what had happened elsewhere.[98] If one counts only the number of Jews murdered in the first four extermination camps listed, and excludes those killed in Auschwitz, it would be tantamount to murdering over half Berlin's 1939 population – more than 2 million people. The survivors could easily fit into an average Berlin apartment.

Because so few non-Jewish Germans were interned in the extermination camps, and because so few people survived, the mass murder of Jews has entered German memory as something of a figurative rather than a literal experience. As James Young has put it,

> had it not been for the massive, last-ditch evacuations of Jewish prisoners from death camps in Poland ... the mass murder might have remained a foreign phenomenon altogether. German experience of the prisoners' plight in the camps was limited largely to either helping Jewish neighbours or watching quietly as they disappeared, guarding the camps or being forced by Allied soldiers to march through them after liberation. As a result, what we call Holocaust memorials in Germany tend to be highly stylized when remembering the Jews.[99]

Nowhere is this better demonstrated than in West Berlin's existing memorial to the camps.

As one approaches the pretty Wittenberg Platz U-Bahn station one sees a sign which looks rather like a bus timetable. There is another nearby. As one comes closer one sees that it is not a timetable but rather a list of twelve concentration and extermination camps headed by the words PLACES OF TERROR THAT WE SHOULD NEVER FORGET. The signs were erected in 1967 and they are astounding in their inadequacy.[100] They show why so many felt Berlin needed a central monument to the Holocaust, however controversial it might be. On another level, independent groups have recently set up a number of other more convincing memorials on historic sites, such as the projection of the names of deported Jews on to a blank wall near the building in which they once lived in Steglitz, or the imaginative description of the history of the Sonnenallee slave labour camp located next to an ordinary playing field in Neukölln.[101] There is a new interest in other sites as well; the siding at Grunewald train station, one of the points from which 36,000 Berlin Jews were deported, is to be preserved; there is to be a plaque there and another at the Putlitzstrasse station. There is now a sculpture and plaque at the Tiergarten 4 site next to the Philharmonie, where the euthanasia pro-gramme was devised. Another place in Berlin dedicated to remembrance is Daniel Libeskind's Jewish Museum, an annex to the Berlin Museum. The structure has been built in the form of a distressed Star of David with a space in the centre, creating a void into which one can look, but cannot enter. The museum will show the long history of Berlin's Jewish citizens; how they were crucial to its prosperity, its culture and its identity. It will also show what the loss of so many Berliners − Jewish Berliners − meant to a city in which they had played such an important role. In 1992 the villa at Am Grossen Wannsee 56−58, the site of the Wannsee Conference of 20 January 1942, was finally turned into a Holocaust Memorial Centre, and signs were put up both at the Jewish retirement home in Grosse Hamburger Strasse and at the site of the Levetzowstrasse synagogue.[102] It is important that Berlin should preserve such places for the future and continue to fight against people like those who spray-painted the headstones in the Weissensee Jewish cemetery or who on 25 August 1992 fire-bombed Sachsenhausen – a camp just outside Berlin in which 100,000 people died.[103]

The clock can never be turned back, and the lives taken or ruined because of the orders issued from Berlin cannot now be saved. But something good can come of this history. More than anywhere else in the world Berlin can contribute to an understanding of the Holocaust and of the other crimes committed by Nazi Germany by exposing the insidious nature of evil. Visitors should be encouraged to understand how it crept into the city slowly, into hearts and minds, into cafés and *Hinterhöfe* and side streets and entire districts. So many of those who worked in Berlin were not for the most part inhuman monsters but ordinary people who made the wrong choices. Berliners should not try to draw a *Schlussstrich*, a line under the past, or repress it, or turn it into a mere tool of contemporary party politics, or counter it with proof of the terrible crimes committed by other dictators. In the end, only the victims can forgive the perpetrators; all Berliners can do is to try to be worthy of forgiveness both by remembering the past, and by trying to build the kind of society in which such things cannot happen again. Those who claim that the past does not matter, or that such things will never be repeated need only look across the old death strip towards the building which contains the Stasi files in the ex-GDR and remind themselves of the thousands of people who so very recently once again put personal gain above human decency. Nazi crimes did not happen just because a handful of criminals deemed they should; they were also possible because of the tiny steps taken by millions of people who helped to maintain these systems of repression and terror either by working within them, or by informing on people, or by simply ignoring what was happening and refusing to take responsibility for it. Berliners should face up to the curse of *Mephisto* which permeates their city's past.

The politicized debates over Germany's history have intensified with reunification. Conservative historians continue to accuse their left-wing colleagues of seeing the past only in relation to the Holocaust while those on the left accuse conservatives of trying to relativize history: to many assume that one cannot do both – that one cannot appreciate Berlin's extraordinary history while at the same time working to understand its role as the capital of the Third Reich.

Berlin is an incredible city. It has a long and varied history and its people have created marvels in the fields of art and culture, technology and research, commerce and industry. Its past is filled with moments of beauty, of tolerance, of astounding creativity, of great suffering and great poignancy. Berlin was the centre of the Third Reich, but it has also been many other things. Rather than dismissing their entire past because of what happened between 1933 and 1945 Berliners should be encouraged both to learn about what went so terribly wrong, and to trace those things which were good or noble or creative in their heritage, whether in the eighteenth-century traditions of religious tolerance or in the reforms introduced by vom Stein; whether in the spirit exhibited during the Berlin blockade when the city became the focal point of the Cold War, or in the lessons of the tragic 1953 Uprising or in the courage shown when the Wall was built in 1961. For the first time in decades all Berliners are in a position to choose which values they wish to emulate. A clear view of history can offer them the insights they need to make this choice. It can also warn them of the likely consequences if they refuse to take responsibility for their actions. Berliners cannot afford to fall back on stereotypes or sentimental myths and legends about their past. Rather than alluding to kitschy images of the Golden Twenties they could perhaps ask themselves why Marlene Dietrich's grave is still regularly defaced; rather than claiming that Berlin was traditionally a city of immigrants they might protect its minorities from increasingly frequent attacks; rather than trying to remove the Soviet war memorial at Treptow they might ask why so little is known about the war-time treatment of Russian prisoners, 3 million of whom were killed by the Nazis.[104] Rather than merely commemorating the July 1944 plotters now featured in hundreds of books, museums, memorials and street signs they might question why these honourable men and women are still legally considered 'traitors to Germany' and have not yet been pardoned by a 'grateful nation'.[105] Rather than complain about how much is written about the concentration camps they might ask how it was that in 1991 Ravensbrück, only 35 miles from Berlin, barely escaped being transformed into a shopping mall and car park.[106]

There is no doubt that a proud German national identity will emerge again, whether in ten years or in fifty. The key is not to prevent it from happening, which is impossible, but to try to ensure that it does not once again become a destructive force. German nationalism could explode in a kind of resentful frenzy sometime in the future if people are repeatedly told that they have no right to be proud of any aspects of their past; the new Germany should applaud its impressive achievements as one of the great nations of Europe, while remaining mindful of its failures. History provides a guide which warns against the worst elements of the German national identity – xenophobia, anti-Semitism and political Romanticism. Berlin is already reeling from a host of social problems ranging from high youth unemployment, rifts between easterners and westerners, an influx of economic migrants, a growing drug problem and the arrival of various mafias dealing in everything from prostitution to the smuggling of nuclear material – problems from which Berlin was largely sheltered until 1989.[107] An understanding of the past might encourage people to face these complex issues head on, whatever their political views, rather than blaming easy scapegoats like 'foreigners' or 'politicians' or 'asylum-seekers'.

History cannot be used to determine contemporary policies, but it can remind people why it is important to strive for certain goals. Germany's history demonstrates some of the worst alternatives and the recent benefits of the maintenance of a self-confident, humanitarian, western, liberal-democratic state. Hopefully this will encourage the new Berlin to continue to build on Bonn's legacy, nurturing the kinds of institutions and values of which Germans can be proud. The frank acknowledgement and discussion of history can help to build the moral, intellectual, political and spiritual strength of the new capital. As Richard von Weizsäcker put it, young Germans 'are not responsible for what happened over forty years ago. But they are responsible for the historical consequences . . . We must help younger people to understand why it is vital to keep memories alive.'[108]

The monumental reconstruction now taking place in the city should not become an excuse to re-invent the past yet again. Berlin cannot build an identity out of nothing. It has tried many times before, and has always failed precisely because there is always continuity between one era and another. Social, political, religious, cultural and other values and ideals lie deeply embedded in a nation's psyche. Identity can be influenced by politicians and historians and architects, but it cannot be created by them; it is fluid, intangible, mercurial, and it is the product of a thousand factors. Social engineering does not work, and attempts to rip down and build again, to create a 'new city' from scratch, to put glass and asphalt over a troubled legacy smacks of totalitarianism, of Hitler's Germania, of *Stunde Null*. It ignores the complexity and continuity of a living, breathing city, and it distorts the importance of both the failures and the successes of the past.

Schiller once said that the world's history is also the world's judgement, and Berliners will continue to come up against the dilemmas posed by their difficult past. The history of Berlin will not 'pass away', and the more its citizens learn from the past and accept its consequences the more it will win the world's respect, and the more stable and the more successful it will be as a capital. It is Mephistopheles who, in Act IV of *Faust*, carefully explains that history should be forgotten; that 'there is no room either in the world or in human memory to preserve the past indefinitely'. One hopes that the new Berlin will choose instead to live by Voltaire's dictum: 'we owe respect to the living; to the dead only truth.'[109]

I

History, Myth, and the Birth of Berlin

Set him down here close at hand –
to find new life in this land
of myth and legend . . .

(Goethe, *Faust*, Part II, Act 2)

STENDHAL ONCE SAID OF BERLIN: 'What could have possessed people to found a city in the middle of all this sand?' He was not the only visitor to wonder at Berlin's curious location, its *parvenu* style, its seeming lack of roots. August Endell said it was a place of 'dreary desolation', and even the German nationalist historian Heinrich von Treitschke remarked that the Germans were the only people to have achieved greatness without having built a great capital.[1] In his famous work *Berlin: Ein Stadtschicksal* Karl Scheffler contrasted Berlin with other European capitals, those glorious places which 'are the centres of a country, are rich and beautiful cities, harmoniously developed organisms of history'. Berlin, on the other hand, developed 'artificially, under all kinds of difficulties, and had to adapt to unfavourable circumstances'. It was a 'colonial city' made up of the dispossessed and uprooted. And, when one views the gigantic building sites and new developments covering the latest incarnation of Berlin, Scheffler's words seem even more appropriate today than when he wrote them nearly a century ago: 'Berlin is a city that never is, but is always in the process of becoming.'[2]

Geography does not make history but it does influence it, and Berlin's location seems to embody its erratic, insouciant nature. It is striking precisely because, unlike Paris or Rome or Istanbul, Berlin seems to have come from nowhere, wrenched from the sandy soil by some hidden force. One looks in vain for great rivers or lakes, for ports or mountains, for natural riches or fortifications, and as one approaches there is precious little to suggest the presence of one of Europe's great cities. Instead, Berlin lies in a long sweeping plain dotted with pine forests, marshes and swamps which stretch out until cut by the Oder in the east and the Elbe in the west. The land south and east extends down into wooded base moraine with small hills, chains of lakes and

1

streams created by the distortions and deposits of the last Ice Age. This area, known as the Mark Brandenburg, covers an area of around a quarter of a million square kilometres and forms part of the great Grodno–Warsaw–Berlin depression. The German capital lies in the centre of this strangely inhospitable land, exposed as it is to the cold winds from the east.[3] It is clear both from the dearth of natural features and from the vast network of rail tracks, old industrial slums, roads and factories that Berlin was made into a formidable powerhouse not by nature, but by the industry and the politics of man.

The exposed position has made Berlin, like Warsaw and Moscow, subject to endless migrations and wars. Tacitus defined the Germani as people who inhabit the dense forests between the 'Rhine and the Vistula' and claimed that they were a 'pure' race who had lived there since time immemorial. He was wrong. These plains dwellers were – and are – the product of countless population shifts which have occurred over millennia. Berlin history made a mockery of notions of German racial purity which became so popular in the nineteenth and early twentieth centuries. Nor were migrations a product of the industrial age; in Berlin the pattern was set in prehistoric times.

From the very beginning the region was populated by successive waves of different peoples and cultures. Humans reached the Berlin area around 55,000 BC, but settlements were first formed at the end of the last Ice Age, around 20,000 BC, when hunter-gatherers followed migrating animals north to the area around the river Spree. The earliest farms with their small enclosures of domesticated cows and pigs appeared as late as 4000 BC; one still lies buried under the famous Weimar horseshoe housing estate, the Britzer Hufeisensied-lung. The last of the Stone Age peoples represented the *Kugelamphoren Kultur* and moved into areas from Tegel to Rixdorf and even on to the present Museum Island around 2000 BC, leaving glimpses of their artistic prowess in the beautiful pottery deposited at sacred religious sites. They too disappeared with the coming of the Bronze Age, which saw a succession of different groups in districts from Spandau to Steglitz. The most successful of these were the 'Lausitzer' people, who by 1300 had reached the substantial population of 1,000 people. But they, too, would disappear around 700 BC, when the climate began to cool, and were replaced by the Germanic 'Jastorf' people whose weapons, tools and utensils are dotted throughout the soil from Spandau to Mahlsdorf. A site on the Hauptstrasse in Schöneberg contains the remains of horses and the cooked bones of domesticated animals including pigs and sheep, but most incredible are the finds of inlaid bronze jewellery with twisted threads of silver as delicate and beautiful as any found at Celtic sites of the same period.[4] But despite the fact that people had lived in the Berlin area since the last Ice Age it was the next group, the Germanic 'Semnonen' of the first century BC, who would later be referred to as 'original Berliners'. This was in part because the Semnonen were the first to appear on the pages of recorded history. They were described not by the Germans, who were illiterate, but by the Romans.

Berlin's history was shaped by an event which did not take place. The area was never conquered by the Romans. Unlike Paris or London or Cologne or Trier, Berlin would not be able to boast of its imperial heritage nor look to *romanitas*, with its ideals of government and architecture and use of Latin by the educated elite, and it was this which contributed to Berlin's later lack of self-confidence. The Romans were not ignorant of the peoples beyond the Elbe, but except for one brief foray into the area they did not attempt to conquer the region. This momentous decision changed the destiny of the city.

It is not known what the Germanic tribes thought of the Romans who edged up to the river Elbe around the time of the birth of Christ, but for their part the Romans viewed these frightening tribesmen with a mixture of awe and contempt. Julius Caesar had incorporated the river Rhine into the empire by 31 BC but had refused to allow expansion further east; not only did he believe that the dark forests were home to fearful beasts and magical creatures like unicorns, but he and other Romans considered the Germans to be too barbaric to be absorbed into the empire. General Velleius was typical when he dismissed them as 'wild creatures' incapable of learning arts or laws, or said that they resembled human beings only in that they could speak. It was Julius Caesar's adopted son Augustus who decided to capture the land east of the Rhine and to push the boundary of the empire up to the Elbe. In a campaign led by Augustus' stepsons Nero Drusus and Tiberius Roman troops reached the mysterious river bank in 3 BC. The legate L. Domitius Ahenobarbus actually crossed the water to meet some of the tribesmen in order to conclude *amicitia* or treaties of peace.[5] Despite this success Augustus forbade his armies to cross the Elbe. This decision was apparently sanctioned by the gods, for it was said that when Tiberius' brother Drusus approached the water a horrible giantess had appeared and warned him to go back as he had only a short time to live. Drusus retreated and died a few days later, convincing his companions that they had in fact seen a deity.[6] Shortly afterwards, in AD 9, Varus was ambushed in the Teutoberg forest. In one of the worst routs in Roman history three legions were massacred by Arminius, the chief of the Cherusci tribe, who came to be known in Germany as the legendary Hermann. The Romans lost control of the territory between the Rhine and the Elbe, and only a handful of traders dared brave the dangers of the 'Amber Road' which led up to the Baltic Sea. Those who returned continued to fascinate Rome with their tales of the strange religious rituals and the fierce tribesmen to be found in the land beyond the Elbe.

The forests of the north remained unconquered, but they were nevertheless the subject of much popular literature in Rome. The Teutons were mentioned in classical sources as early as 400 BC and the word 'German' was first used by Posidonus in 90 BC.[7] Caesar wrote about the Teutons in his *Gallic War*; Livy devoted his 104th book of histories to them; Pliny the Elder followed with his now lost work *German Wars* and in *Naturalis Historia*; and both Cassius Dio and Velleius Paterculus described aspects of the German campaigns in their histories of Rome.[8] But by far the best known and most influential account was written in AD 98 by Cornelius Tacitus. It is called *De origine et situ Germanorum* or *Germania*.[9]

Tacitus had not been to Germany but had lived along the Roman frontier, had read contemporary works about the region and had talked to the soldiers and traders who had travelled there. His account is an intriguing mixture of fact and fiction. Tacitus also seems to have had a definite moral or political purpose in mind when writing the book. *Germania* was published in the reign of the Emperor Trajan, who had served in the German provinces.[10] In some passages it appears that Tacitus is trying to warn the Romans not to be complacent about the Germans, and to show them that if the Teutons should ever combine their skill in battle with Roman discipline they would be invincible. If Rome does nothing or continues to degenerate, he argues, and if the Germans should ever organize against them the empire will be lost: 'Long I pray may foreign nations persist, if not in loving us, at least in hating one another.'[11] Apart from this political warning and despite the historical inaccuracies *Germania* was the first systematic attempt to describe the land on the edge of the civilized Roman world, beyond the Albis or Elbe which, he laments, was 'well known and much talked of in earlier days, but [is] now a mere name'.[12] Tacitus was also the first to shed some light on the Elbe German Semnonen, the people who lived in the region around what is now the city of Berlin.

Tacitus' descriptions of the Semnonen, with their topknots and their warlike appearance, are particularly vivid. For him, an author with republican sympathies, the very structure of their tribes was a model of good government. Each was a state in itself with no permanent central government and no king; the supreme authority was found in the assembly of all free men who met at intervals at a *Thing* or *Moot*, where chiefs were chosen to decide on specific questions of war and justice. The chiefs themselves possessed great wealth and had large retinues made up mostly of family members. According to Tacitus, chastity was highly regarded, as were family loyalty and ferocity in battle; wives even accompanied their husbands to war. He did note, however, that during peacetime the men were lazy, gluttonous gamblers, and drunkards capable of acts of appalling brutality. They were also deeply religious and at a set time 'deputations from all the tribes of the same stock would gather in a grove hallowed by the auguries of their ancestors and by immemorial law'. The sacrifice of a human victim in the name of all 'marks the grisly opening of their savage ritual'. The meeting place in a sacred grove in the forest is 'the centre of their whole religion . . . the cradle of the race and the dwelling-place of the supreme god to whom all things are subject and obedient'.[13] Tacitus talks of tree and horse worship; gods included Ziu, who was probably derived from Zeus and later ousted by Odin, while the goddess of mother earth was Nerthus.[14] A number of her shrines, situated near water, have been found in the Berlin area – including at spring in Spandau, which was found filled with the remains of birds, and in Neukölln, which was littered with the skeletons of dogs and other animals. The sacrifice of horses was also important to the Semnonen, as were gifts made to lesser deities – wooden carvings, pots of fat and hazelnuts.

Archaeological remains have verified many of Tacitus' claims. We know that the villages were small and that freemen had their own long houses of wood-post construction with the cracks filled and covered in lime for protection against the elements and vermin. The houses had a hearth and a stable under a gable roof and families lived together with their animals. Arable land was divided into sectors and the ploughing and sowing was done in common. Remains of an industrial area were found in the Donaustrasse in Neukölln which consisted of wells and three lime kilns; there were even facilities for smelting iron.[15] Even so, the Germanic tribes were not sophisticated compared to their Roman cousins: agriculture was primitive, and instead of enlarging their resources by cutting down the forests and cultivating new areas they preferred to conquer the nearest fertile land for themselves, a practice which was particularly common on the provincial borders. By the second century AD ever more Teutons were clamouring to get inside the empire. The population of Europe had begun to shift once again.

When Tacitus was writing *Germania* Teutonic tribes extended deep into eastern Europe, past present-day Poland and into Ukraine. Had Europe been more stable the Semnonen might well have remained in place and become the forebears of present-day Berliners. But, as Tacitus had warned, the Teutons were set to invade Rome itself. In the middle of the second century the German Marcomanni tribe suddenly surged across the Danube into Italy. They were held back with difficulty by the Emperor Marcus Aurelius but fifty years later the Goths conquered present-day Romania and spread throughout the Balkans into Asia Minor, while the Alamanni broke through the Roman *Limes* and moved to the Rhine and the Danube. The Berlin area was affected in turn around AD 180 when the Elbe German Semnonen suddenly packed up and moved to the south-west, eventually settling by the river Main. They were replaced around AD 260 by the Burgundians, who moved from the Danish island of Bornholm (Borgundarholmr) and whose remains have been found in the Berlin-Rudow area.

Up until this point the movement of peoples towards Rome had been deflected by a series of strong emperors who managed to protect the old imperial boundaries, but in 375 the Teutons attacked once again. This time the onslaught was unstoppable. The Germanic tribes were no longer moving of their own free will but were being forced west by one of the most ferocious charges in European history, the attack of the Huns. The 'movement of the peoples', or the *Völkerwanderungzeit*, had begun in earnest, and the migrations destroyed the old ethnic make-up of the European continent for ever.[16]

It was Kipling who said:

> For all we have and are,
> For all our children's fate,
> Stand up and take the war,
> The Hun is at the gate!

The word 'Hun' still conjures up horrifying images in the minds of Europeans. During the First World War the name was given to the Germans accused of murdering babies in Belgium; in the Second the young soldier Alexander Solzhenitsyn, horrified by the carnage meted out by the Soviets during their conquest of East Prussia in 1945, likened the Red Army to the mongol hordes. Nobody knows why these people suddenly left the steppes north of the Aral Sea and swept into Europe in the fourth century – perhaps there had been a change in the climate like that which prompted the Vikings to raid with such restless energy – but when the Roman Ammianus Marcellinus asked them where they were born and where they came from he reported that 'they cannot tell you'. Their unstoppable expansion into Europe was one of the most gory in history. Romans wrote of their hideous features, which they believed to be the result of self-mutilation; all referred to their masterful horsemanship and deadly archery, but above all it was the pleasure they were reported to take when butchering their victims which left a lasting reputation for ruthlessness and barbarism.

As the Hun advanced westwards the Goths were driven to take refuge in the Roman Empire. Teutons surged over the frontier; in 406 the Vandals attacked southern Gaul and Spain and then moved on to Africa; the Burgundians, who had for a time settled around Berlin, now moved westwards.[17] The Berlin area had become a part of the Hunnic confederacy by 420; indeed a grave was found in Neukölln-Berlin in which a warrior lies buried beside his horse according to their custom. The Burgundians from Berlin were not yet safe; in 436 the Hun caught up with them in Worms and drove them on to the Rhône valley, where they gave their name to Burgundy. In 450 Attila the Hun moved his forces across Germany with such brutality and violence that it was said no grass would grow where his horse had stepped. Then, on the eve of the campaign of 453, fate intervened. On the drunken night of his wedding to the beautiful German Ildiko (called Kriemhild in legend) Attila had a stroke and died and his kingdom was destroyed. The battles did yield one cultural treasure, namely an epic which tells the story of the battle between the Burgundian King Gundahar and Attila the Hun. It was called the *Nibelungenlied* (the Burgundians are the Nibelungs) and became the basis for Wagner's cyclical *Bühnenfestspiel, Der Ring des Nibelungen*.

By the time of Attila's death the old integrity of Europe had already been shattered and thousands of restless people were on the move. The sixth-century emperor Justinian tried to keep the empire together but the barbarian invasions did not stop; the gradual decline of Rome and cross-fertilization of Roman and barbarian culture and customs continued.[18] In the north the Slavs, who had lived around the eastern Carpathian mountains since perhaps 2000 BC, began to migrate westward.[19] It was they who now moved into the area around Berlin.

The Slavs were the latest newcomers to the lands which would later be known as Poland and Germany; by the seventh century they had spread over most of eastern Europe from the Baltic to the Peloponnese and had crossed the Oder into the Elbe-Saale region and into what is now Germany. The border between Germans and Slavs was later confirmed in the 843 Treaty of Verdun: it ran along the river Elbe and down a boundary which cut north-west from Dresden to Magdeburg, past Hamburg and up to the North Sea.[20] The Slavs founded a number of cities along the border, including old Lübeck, Meissen and Leipzig, whose name was derived from the Slav word *lipsk* or linden tree.

As the Slavs moved towards the Berlin area they found a vast, depopulated land with only a few Germans remaining scattered in small settlements. These stragglers were not massacred; on the contrary, archaeological evidence in over forty sites in Barnim and Teltow shows that the remaining Germans were assimilated into the new communities and that the Slavs even adopted some of the old Germanic place names like the river 'Havel' and the 'Müggelsee', which survive to this day.[21] The great Theodor Fontane was one of the few nineteenth-century Germans to acknowledge Berlin's debt to this much maligned people, and in the third part of the *Wanderungen durch die Mark Brandenburg* describes how the myriad lakes, streams and hills of the Berlin area which end in '-itz' like Wandlitz, '-ick' as in Glienicke and '-ow' like

Teltow had in fact been named by the Slavs.[22] Nineteenth-century Germans would have been shocked to learn that the capital was not named after the noble 'bear', but was old Elbe-Slav *brl*, meaning 'swamp' or 'marsh'.[23] But long before Berlin existed there were dozens of Slavic settlements within the present city limits: Gatow and Glienicke, Steglitz and Marzahn were Slavic; Pankow was named for the Slavic word *pania*, meaning 'flat moor'; pottery shards confirm the existence of a Slavic radial village in Babelsberg; Lützow (Charlottenburg) was founded in the fifth century, and even nearby Potsdam began as a Slavic stronghold. But by far the most important settlements for the future of Berlin were two gigantic fortresses which now lie only a U-Bahn ride away from one another on either side of the city, but which at one time represented the borders of two great territories: Köpenick to the south-east, and Spandau to the north-west.

If nineteenth- and early twentieth-century Germans admitted the presence of the Slavs at all they tended to dismiss them as coarse and unsophisticated – all they had built there was seen as uncivilized compared with superior Germanic culture. This was ahistorical, and had more to do with contemporary German politics than with ancient history. In reality the Slavic fortresses of Spandau and Köpenick were not only highly developed; they created an infrastructure which would prove crucial to the development of Berlin itself.

Each fortress represented the boundary of a great Slavic principality and although the Slavs were collectively referred to by the Latin term *Venedi* – the Wends – there were two distinct groups in the regions.[24] Those who had settled on the river Havel were known as the Hevellians, rulers of the *provintia heveldun*. Their headquarters were at Brannabor (Brandenburg) but their second town was at Spandau, which was built in the 750s and which already contained around 250 people by the end of the century. The Slavs who settled around the Spree were known as the Sprewans and their province was called the *provintia Zpriauuani*; they were based around Mittenwalde and founded the villages of Mahlsdorf, Kaulsdorf, Pankow and Treptow. Their capital was Köpenick, itself founded on an old Neolithic site. The name was derived from the Slavic word for 'settlement on an earth hill' and, although protected by the Spree, the fort had a commanding view over the area. In 825 it was fortified with high oval wooden walls of about fifty metres in length complete with towers and palisades and gates.[25]

The first written evidence of such fortresses dates from the records of a 798 expedition by a Frisian fleet under Charlemagne which made its way up the tributaries of the Havel and saw typical Havellian fortresses there. An even more detailed record is found in one of the most extraordinary travel diaries in the history of central Europe, the eye-witness account written in 970 by the Jewish merchant Ibrahim ibn Ja'quab. Ibrahim was born in Muslim Spain and travelled north as an envoy for the caliph of Córdoba. Like so many masterpieces of the ancient world the diary was saved by an Arab scholar, in this case the eleventh-century Abu Obaid Abdallah al Bekri, who found it so impressive that he reproduced it in his *Book of Ways and Lands*. Ibrahim ibn Ja'quab's journey took him along the established trade routes through Prague and probably to Cracow, and then towards Mecklenburg, where it is thought he described the settlement at Schwerin.[26] He was struck by the large, secure Slavic fortresses with their high wooden walls strengthened by mounds of packed earth and protected by rivers so that one could only reach them on 'a wooden bridge over the water'. Evidence shows that even the smaller fortresses at Potsdam, Treptow and Blankenburg were built on islands and were not merely defensive but housed carpenters, weavers, tanners, furriers and other tradesmen. Ibrahim ibn Ja'quab noted that the Slavs 'are especially energetic in agriculture'. The fortresses also provided a safe haven for the priestly hierarchy who kept the shrines for Dazbag, the god of the sun, Jarovit, the god of spring, and the fertility gods Rod and Rozanicy in their midst. Ibrahim also recognized that the Slavs were skilled merchants and that 'their trade on land reaches to the Ruthenians and to Constantinople'. The fortresses of Spandau-Burgwall and Köpenick had grown powerful from their position on an important medieval east–west trade route which extended from the Rhine and Flanders through Magdeburg, on to Brennabor, over the Berlin area to Leubus and Posen and on to Kiev. Muslims and Jews were the most influential traders, regularly travelling from China to Africa and up the Caspian Sea and the Volga to the Baltic; trade with the Latin west was maintained primarily by Jewish merchants who, according to the early ninth-century geographer Ibn Khurradadhbeh, were highly sophisticated and could 'speak Arabic, Persian, Greek, Frankish, Spanish and Slavonic. They travel from west to east and from east to west, by land and sea.'[27] The Jews were not the only merchants to visit the fortresses, however, and although the Slavs themselves used cloth as currency around 1,000 foreign coins of Arabian, German, English, Scandinavian, Polish, Bohemian and Hungarian origin have been found there. Even at this early date Spandau and Köpenick were filled with international dealers: Scandinavian traders had moved in by the ninth century and Arabian and Jewish traders predominated by the year 1000.[28] Dozens of products changed hands – from skins, honey, potash, wax, textiles, slate and weapons to jewellery from Kiev and salt from the Rhineland. Slaves were bought and sold; indeed the word 'Slav' was first given to the hapless victims captured in the east and then dragged across Europe to be sold in the markets around the Mediterranean. By AD 1000 the Slavs had created prosperous, stable communities on the banks of the Havel and the Spree. Like the Semnonen before them they might well have become the founders of modern Berlin. But Europe was about to undergo another herculean change. This time people would move in from the west. These warriors and settlers would be Christian.

The spread of Christianity was one of the definitive movements in the creation of modern Europe. The advance began within the bounds of the Roman Empire during the first centuries AD; the first bishoprics were established in northern Europe by the fourth century – the bishop of Rheims, for example, was first mentioned in 314 – a process accelerated by the conversion of the legendary Frankish king Clovis.[29] For those outside the empire conversion was often brought about by force, and one of the most successful of these Christian warriors, the man who essentially created the Holy Roman Empire, was called Charles the Great or Charlemagne.[30]

Charlemagne was born in 742 and became king of the Frankish realm in 768. He was determined not only to resurrect the glory of Rome but to expand its boundaries, to spread Christianity as far as possible and to convert or eradicate the Saxon heathens. After establishing himself in his mighty castle at Aachen he spearheaded a campaign which would take him far into Germany. For eighteen years he waged a bloody war against the Saxons, putting down resistance and massacring those who opposed change. After the battle at Verden in the 782 war he had 4,500 Saxon hostages beheaded in cold blood.[31] Not surprisingly, Saxon resistance was crushed by 804 and Charlemagne's became the first imperial army to reach the river Elbe since Augustus. In 800 he was confident enough to proclaim himself *imperator et augustus*, the ancient title of the victorious empire, and he was crowned in St Peter's Basilica by the pope in a dramatic ceremony on Christmas Day.

Despite his ferocity on the battlefield Charlemagne proved himself an admirable administrator, sponsoring the arts and education and dividing the conquered territory into administrative regions called *Marken* (marches), which were governed by loyal counts or dukes known as *Markgrafen* or margraves. Charlemagne also favoured the establishment of bishoprics in the conquered lands and made Hamburg the first diocesan seat east of the Elbe. In the end Charlemagne created a new boundary down the centre of Europe called the *Limes Sorabicus* or Sorbian Wall, which effectively separated Christians from the heathen. It ran from Regensburg through Erfurt, and along the Elbe to Kiel. Berlin still lay a hundred miles beyond the border but Christianity was drawing ever closer. The nearest outpost was a settlement founded on the Elbe. It was called Magdeburg.

The first thing one sees when journeying towards Magdeburg is the great cathedral which rises up from the centre of the small city, its great spires dwarfing everything else around. The building is a mere hint of the city's role as a beacon on the edge of the Christian world, a stronghold which once lay between 'Europe' and the wilderness. Like Trier under the Romans and like West Berlin during the Cold War Magdeburg became a splendid showcase meant both to dazzle and intimidate the poor pagans to the east. The cathedral itself, which started as a small Romanesque church, was regarded as so important that it was endowed by the English king Alfred the Great's grand-daughter with eighteen casks of gold. Even in its earliest incarnation, it served as a base for missionaries determined to convert the unenlightened Slavs to the east.

Magdeburg continued to be a frontier post under Charlemagne's successors but it was not until the reign of Henry the Fowler, who ruled from 919 to 936, that a fresh attempt was made to push the borders of Christianity eastward. Like his son Otto I, Henry believed that Magdeburg should be a metropolitan see 'for all the people of the Slavs beyond the Elbe and the Saale, lately converted and to be converted to God', and from his palace in the Harz mountains he ordered the creation of bishoprics at Havelberg and the foundation of Quedlinburg and Merseburg.[32] The desire to create new strongholds was not simply the result of religious zeal; Henry and his contemporaries felt – quite legitimately – that Christian Europe was under constant threat and that such outposts were essential to its defence. In 845 the Norsemen had decimated the newly founded town of Hamburg and in 875 wiped out a great Saxon and Thuringian army on the Lüneburg Heath while the Magyars from Hungary, the 'scourge of Europe', attacked regularly and fought their way as far north as Bremen.[25] The new church settlements were built not only as religious centres but also as fortresses to protect the duchy of Saxony against the Hungarians. When Henry died in 936 his son Otto I, who reigned until 973, was determined to continue in his father's footsteps and expand eastward. This was evident in the ceremony of his investiture as duke of Saxony: 'I bring before you Otto, chosen by God, designated by Henry, formerly lord of the kingdom, and now made king by all the princes,' boomed the archbishop of Mainz. 'Accept this sword with which you are to eject all the enemies of Christ, barbarians and bad Christians. For all power over the whole empire of the Franks has been given to you by divine authority, so as to assure the peace of all Christians.'[33]

Until now the Slavic Hevellians had been spared the Christian onslaught but the peace ended suddenly in 948. In that year Otto I crossed the Elbe and attacked their capital Brennobar. The heathen settlement was overrun, Slavic protestors were killed, the celebrated pagan shrine was levelled and a bishopric was put in its place. The town was given a new name: Brandenburg.

Brandenburg was turned into a centre of evangelizing activity. Christians quickly moved in, rounded up the local Slavs and forced them to convert at swordpoint. Otto was so successful in his drive eastward that by the end of his reign he had reached the river Oder, dividing the new lands into Marks.[34] The area which would become the Nordmark or North Mark and which encompassed the territory of the Hevellians and the Sprewan Slavs extended from the Elbe to the Oder and from Lausitz to the Elbe–Peene line. Furthermore Otto finally defeated the troublesome Magyars at the Battle of Lechfeld in 955, a victory which brought him such fame that he was henceforth referred to as Otto the Great. Rather than protect his conquests in the north, however, Otto set out on three separate campaigns in Italy and in 962 marched to Rome, where the Pope placed the magnificent gold and gem-encrusted crown of the Holy Roman Emperor on his head. But his victory did not bring the desired peace. Otto I died in 973 and, rather than return to the north, his successor Otto II remained in a bid to drive the Greeks and Saracens from Italy. In 982 he faced a humiliating defeat at the hands of the Muslims of Sicily. It left him gravely weakened, and the newly won lands and new bishoprics at Havelberg and Brandenburg were left undefended. And it was then that the Slavs struck back.

The Slavs of the North Mark had been resentful at the coming of the Christians and of the strange new religion which forbade the worship of their fertility goddesses and the shrines to the spirits of nature. Worse still, the new masters had forced them to pay tributes to the Germanic religious fortresses, payments which were extracted by sheer force if necessary. When the Slavs heard the news of Otto II's disastrous defeat in Italy they were encouraged to take up arms. The response was the Great Slav Uprising of 983.

The revolt was led by the Hevellians, who were determined to retake their holy capital of Brennabor. In a well-orchestrated attack they set upon the city, sacking the new Ottonian church and massacring the Christian inhabitants there. On 29 June 983 the bishopric of Havelberg was destroyed, and the small church at the Spandauer Burg was decimated three weeks later. The Slavs then swept through the Mark, killing monks and settlers. By July most German outposts had been razed to the ground, and although a handful of bishops dared to remain they were forced into hiding and lived without cathedrals or diocese.[35] The rest of the population reverted to their pagan practices. The Germanic Christian drive eastward had been halted and Magdeburg once again became the true boundary of the German Christian world. Otto was devastated and died in 983 in the knowledge that he had failed at his most important task – the defence of Christendom against the heathen. The unhappy emperor was buried at St Peter's in Rome. Unfortunately for the Slavs in the North Mark, Otto's death was not the end of the threat to their way of life. The leader of a completely different area had also recently undergone conversion to Christianity and was now eager to expand his territory in the name of the Church. This place lay not in German lands, but far to the east of the Spree and Havel in a place which would soon be known as Poland. The Slavs of the Berlin area were now sandwiched between two powerful Christian blocs. The race was on to see which side could conquer it first.

The coming of Christianity to Poland was of immense importance not only to the Slavs of the Berlin area but to the unfolding history of the entire region. The presence of a vast Catholic kingdom to the east of Germany would shape the history of central Europe and of Berlin for centuries to come, not least because of the rivalry which even now emerged between the German Christians and their Polish counterparts.

The Germans had hoped to Christianize all of northern Europe by pushing eastward from Magdeburg and on to Kiev Rus, knowing that under the Ottonian system the establishment of religious centres was inextricably linked to political conquest. The sudden emergence of Poland foiled their plans. The early history of the Piast dynasty remains obscure but by the third quarter of the tenth century the Polish ruler was rising to prominence as quickly as the Saxon rulers had in the west. The first Polish prince, Mieszko I, was keen to extend his power throughout the region.[36] This posed a problem for the Germans, and in particular for Otto I.

When Otto made Magdeburg an archbishopric in 961 he had seen it as the base from which all territory from Saxony to Russia would be Christianized, a move which would in turn have brought all of east central Europe under German control. Mieszko objected. Not only did he want to prevent German meddling in his affairs; he also wanted to increase his own territory. The first Polish ruler was still relatively weak compared to his powerful Saxon rival and had to tread carefully; indeed at one point he only managed to forestall an invasion by agreeing to accept German Christian missions on his land.[37] To Otto's fury, however, in 966 he did the unthinkable. Instead of accepting Christianity from Germany Mieszko turned instead to Bohemia. By adopting Christianity from the south he had in one momentous act prevented the religious, administrative and political domination of Poland by the Holy Roman Emperor. Henceforth – to the annoyance of the Germans – Poland would grow to become an entirely separate and independent entity which would never succumb to the German vision of the *Drang nach Osten* – the idea that they had a civilizing mission in the east.

For a time it looked as if the religious compromise between Poland and the Germans would hold. The new Holy Roman Emperor Otto III, who was half Greek and had been brought up in Italy, regarded his own people as somewhat primitive and was not obsessed by German domination of the east. On the contrary, he had been deeply shaken by the Slav uprising and by the

14

Borderlands between Germany and Poland, 10th–11th Century

BALTIC SEA

KINGDOM OF DENMARK

NORTH SEA

POMERANIA

MARCH OF THE BILLINGS

Stettin

Hamburg

NORTH MARCH

Posen

Bremen

WESTPHALIA

Spandau

Köpenick

SAXONY

POLAND

Osnabrück

Magdeburg

MARCH OF LAUSITZ

Oder

Münster

Leubus

Breslau

GERMANY

Liegnitz

Elbe

THURINGIA

MARCH OF MEISSEN

Rhine

FRANCONIA

Prague

Mainz

Main

Bamberg

BOHEMIA

MORAVIA

Worms

Neckar

Danube

Strasbourg

Augsburg

BAVARIA

MARCH OF AUSTRIA

ALSACE

SWABIA

Salzburg

KINGDOM OF HUNGARY

Chur

Brixen

CARINTHIA

KINGDOM OF BURGUNDY

VERONA

MARCH OF STYRIA

KINGDOM OF ITALY

CROATIA

— ·—·— Boundary of the German Kingdom

– – – The Polish Kingdom

ADRIATIC SEA

disastrous campaigns of the 990s and was willing to leave the conversion of the troublesome pagan Slavs in the east to the Poles as long as they joined the confederation of Christian princes under his ultimate control. Unlike his predecessors he had a vision of Europe organized as a hierarchy of kings; indeed a diptych painted at the end of the tenth century shows him receiving the homage of four crowned women: Germany, Gaul, Rome and Slavonia – the Slavic lands.[38] He was sympathetic to the idea of Polish independence and, to the fury of leading German ecclesiastics, planned to set up a number of churches there which would be free from all German control.

Such German generosity to Poland is rare in history, but it had in part to do with the Polish response to a particular event which had deeply affected Otto III. This pious emperor had been a friend of Adalbertus, the former bishop of Prague. In 996 Pope Sylvester I had sent Adalbertus on a mission to convert the fierce East Prussians, and on his journey north that year the new Polish leader Boleslaw the Brave, Mieszko I's son, generously received him with full honours. The action was duly noted in Rome. Adalbertus continued on to East Prussia where the local tribesmen, who were not keen on conversion, simply murdered him. Rather than ignore his death the Poles purchased his body for a vast sum – its weight in gold – and created a shrine for him at Gniezno. Pope Sylvester I was so impressed by this show of piety that he took the unusual step of canonizing Adalbertus, elevating Gniezno to an archbishopric and creating bishoprics at Wrocław (Breslau), Kołobrzeg (Kolberg) and Kraków (Cracow). It was the creation of a new archbishopric which finally severed the Polish Church from control of the German archbishopric at Magdeburg. The Poles now had an independent administration and took to Christianizing the west Slavic tribes with as much gusto as the Germans had done – the great bronze doors of Gniezno Cathedral depict King Boleslaw distributing blessings and assisting at baptisms, while his sword bearer stands beside him ready to strike down those who refuse to convert.[39] The Poles were emerging as a powerful Christian country in their own right.

Adalbertus continued to play a role in Polish–German affairs from beyond the grave. In the year 1000 Otto III made a pilgrimage to his tomb, not only to pay homage to his murdered friend but also to determine what place Poland should have within the Holy Roman Empire. He was so impressed by Boleslaw's extraordinary welcome and the wealth of the Polish court that, according to the chronicler monk Gallus, 'Seeing his glory, his power and his riches the Roman Emperor cried out in admiration: "By the crown of my Empire! What I see far exceeds what I have heard!"' He took his own diadem and placed it on Boleslaw's head as a sign of union and friendship, gave him 'a nail from the Holy Cross and the lance of Saint Maurice, in return for which Boleslaw gave him the arm of Saint Adalbertus. And they felt such love on that day that the Emperor named him brother and associate in the Empire.'[40] To the horror of the German prelates Otto III decided that Poland should not be a mere tributary duchy of the Holy Roman Empire but should be treated as a kingdom alongside Germany; an (almost) equal partner in a federation of Christian kingdoms. During his stay Otto not only spoke of friendship and co-operation between Germany and Poland but even of marriage between Boleslaw's son Mieszko and his own niece Judith.

Had the relationship between the two leaders endured, the long troubled saga that is Polish–German history might have been quite different, but it was not to be. Otto III died in 1002 at the age of twenty-two and was succeeded by Henry II, a man bitterly opposed to the creation of a strong Polish state. In order to strengthen his bargaining position with Germany Boleslaw took advantage of the confusion following Otto's death and seized Meissen and Lausitz. Henry was prepared to accept this but Boleslaw did not stop there and took Bohemia as well. Henry demanded homage, Boleslaw refused, and Henry attacked the Poles. The ensuing war lasted until 1018.[41] Poland's strength was further undermined by a great Slav revolt in 1035–7, which resulted in the move of the Polish capital to Cracow.[42] The Polish–German rivalry now manifested itself in the often bitter fighting along the border from Lusitia to Pomerania, where disputed land changed hands constantly and was often referred to as 'Polish' by the ruler of Poland and 'German' by the emperor and his subjects. This confusion is still reflected in various nineteenth- and twentieth-century Polish and German school atlases which 'claim' the territory as their own. In reality, however, much of the area, including the land around Berlin, was still in the hands of the heathen Slavs and belonged to neither.[43]

By the eleventh century the Slavs were still clinging defiantly to the strip of land around Berlin despite being under constant threat from the Germans, who controlled the Elbe to the west of Spandau and Köpenick, and by the Poles, who now controlled the Oder to the east. It was a fascinating time. Traders continued to travel from German Christian Magdeburg, then east to the heathen fortresses of Köpenick and Spandau, and then on to Christian Poland. This extraordinary situation lasted for over a century, making the Berlin region one of the last parts of central Europe to become Christianized. But the Slavs were living on borrowed time. The Christians could not tolerate this isolated island of heathenism in their midst; nor could the rulers of Polish and German lands leave such valuable territory unclaimed. The centuries-old domination of the area by the Hevellians and the Sprewans was about to be broken for ever.

In the end the territory fell to the Germans. The drive to take it was spearheaded by Lothair III, the Holy Roman Emperor, who began a campaign against both the Danes and the Slavs in the early twelfth century. One of

Lothair's strategies was to send knights to conquer and settle land in his name, and in 1134, in one of the turning points of Berlin's history, he gave the North Mark to a young count of the House of Ascania whose name was Albert the Bear.[44] It was he who would finally wrest the Mark from the pagan Slavs and transform it into part of the German Christian world.

Albert the Bear was typical of the young nobles and knights who set out to make their fortunes in the heathen lands at the edges of Europe. His father, Count Otto of Ballenstedt, already held large properties in the Harz mountains and northern Thuringia and it was normal that the son should go out to earn his fortune in this way; by the time he reached his twenties Albert had already fought in a number of border skirmishes with the Slavs and the ambitious young man was determined to extend his holdings as far as possible, whether by diplomacy or conquest. In order to do this he had to recruit knights.

Knights were integral to the expansion of Europe in the Middle Ages. Many were driven by the desire for land which all knew would translate into dynastic power; if they were successful and survived the gruelling life they could expect property and fiefs, wealth and status. This international brotherhood had first appeared in France but had quickly spread from Cyprus to Hungary, from Italy to East Anglia – indeed anywhere along the fringes of Europe where there were heathen to fight and glory to be won. Their code of chivalry encompassed everything from the fierce defence of the Church of Christ to strict rules of honour towards women; it was the era of Tannhäuser and Parsifal, of troubadours and minnesingers, and it would later become the stuff of Romantic legend. The stories which grew up around these men tended to emphasize their bravery, their mercy and their dedication to God, and many were indeed fired by a genuine determination to save souls – although it is clear that others were more tempted by the spoils of conquest. Nevertheless they all shared a common ideology so aptly summarized in the medieval *Song of Roland*: 'Christians are right, pagans are wrong.'[45] The knights were truly international; according to the thirteenth-century account *The Chronicle of Morea*, Frankish knights settled in Greece, those who fought in Ireland and Wales were granted titles by the king of England, and even in the area around Berlin the Slavic princes, including the duke of Barnim and the Wedel lords of Uchtenhagen, recruited German knights to increase their own dynastic power.[46] Albert the Bear was merely one of many young noblemen trying to attract such men, and he was highly successful.

Albert organized an extraordinary mission against the Slavs which combined a strong force with clever alliances with the Church, particularly with Bishop Anselm of Havelberg and the powerful Archbishop Wichmann of Magdeburg, both of whom gave him the credibility and financial backing he needed to recruit men.[47] A typical appeal of 1108 read: 'to the leading men of Westphalia, Lotharingia and Flanders to help conquer the territory of the Wends. These pagans are the worst of men but their land is the best, with meat, honey and flour ... So – Oh Saxons, Franconians, Lotharingians and Flemings, here you will be able both to save your souls and, if you will, to acquire very good land to settle.'[48] Albert soon had Polish, Danish, German, French and Flemish men under his command and in 1147, under the motto *Tod oder Taufe* (death or conversion), began to push his way into Brandenburg and south into the lands which officially came under the auspices of the archbishopric of Magdeburg. After years of bitter fighting he eventually reached the Oder and went beyond into Pomerania. But one of his greatest triumphs was the retaking of Brennabor – Brandenburg – which had been held by the Slavic Hevellians since 983.

Brandenburg had become something of a symbol for the conquering Christian knights. They conveniently forgot that it had started as a Slavic village and were intent on revenge for that black day when the heathen had swept upon the town, murdering the Christians, smashing the Ottonian cathedral of Marienburg, setting up a shrine to the great three-headed monster Trigilaw and forcing the bishop to hide in the nearby monastery of Lietzkau. In 1150 Albert retook the town and imprisoned the Slavic prince Heinrich Pribislaw, forcing him to convert and making him promise that on his death bed he, Albert the Bear, should succeed him. Pribislaw died that year and was buried in the castle chapel and Albert seized the town. It was not a straightforward victory, however. The Slavic leader Jaxa von Köpenick, who had already converted to Christianity under pressure from the Polish bishopric at Leubus, felt that as Pribislaw's nephew he and not Albert should have Brandenburg. Jaxa was a shrewd politician. He holds the distinction of being the first man to appear on a coin (a silver brakteat of 1150) minted in the Berlin area, which depicts him sitting in his fortress at Köpenick clutching a gigantic sword and wearing a helmet.[49] Jaxa gathered his own army, made up largely of Polish troops, and in 1154 retook Brandenburg. It took three more years of bloody fighting before Albert managed to wrest the city back from the Polish-backed Slavic prince in 1157. It was this final victory which Germans came to regard as the 'Birthday of the Mark of Brandenburg'. Henry of Antwerp witnessed the celebration of 11 June and wrote in his *Tractatus de captione urbis Brandenburg*: 'So, in the year of the incarnation of the Lord 1157 the Margrave, by God's mercy, took possession as victor of the city of Brandenburg and, entering it joyfully with a great retinue, raised his triumphal standard on high and gave due praises to God, who had given him victory over his enemies.'[50] Albert the Bear took the title Markgraf (margrave) and the city became the first capital of the Mark Brandenburg, the *caput marchionatus Brandenburgensis*.[51] It was soon elevated to the status of residence city (where the ruler's palace was located). For Albert, twenty-three years of fighting and diplomacy had been amply rewarded and he had transformed himself from a mere knight into a powerful German leader.

The taking of Brandenburg broke the power of the Hevellian Slavic princes and it had a profound effect on the future of the Berlin area. Spandau became Albert's property; the first Christian graves there date from 1150 and the first Ascanian governor, Albert's son Margrave Otto II, was appointed in 1197. In 1241 Margrave Johann I took Köpenick from the Wettiner Markgraf von Meissen along with all the properties belonging to the Sprewans and built a new fortress which became a powerful administrative centre. Johann was a fierce fighter and extended his power far to the east, even seizing Gdańsk from the Poles between 1266 and 1271, the first of many Polish–German conflicts over that city. By 1319 Albert's Ascanian successors had extended their authority over territory stretching nearly 200 miles east of the Elbe. The land around Berlin had become an integral part of Germany.

The high Middle Ages was a time of extraordinary transformation and resettlement across Europe, a period when untold numbers of people made their way to new regions often thousands of miles from their birthplaces.[52] Settlers moved into the Celtic lands, along the Mediterranean and to the Oder; they moved from England to Ireland, from Saxony to Livonia, from Old Castile to Andalusia, and they transformed the Iberian peninsula from Muslim into Christian land. But of all the migrations of the twelfth and thirteenth centuries it was the *Ostsiedlung*, the Germanization of lands east of the Elbe, which was the most overwhelming; indeed it was so complete that by the end of the thirteenth century much of central and eastern Europe from Estonia to the Carpathians was inhabited by German farmers, merchants, miners, traders, churchmen and aristocrats, culminating in the conquest of Livonia by the Knights of the Sword of Livonia and of East Prussia by the Teutonic Knights. The newcomers transformed the east as comprehensively as the Normans did England after the invasion of 1066, and after generations many came to believe that the land which they now inhabited had 'always' been German.

The first people to colonize an area were often representatives of the Church. The pagans were not always willing converts and pockets of heathenism remained for centuries. The missionary Boso, bishop of Merseburg, translated the *Kyrie eleison* into Slavonic so that it could be understood by them, but the Slavs 'being sacrilegious, derisively changed it to *ukrivolsa* which was bad, since [in their language] it means "There is an alder-tree in the

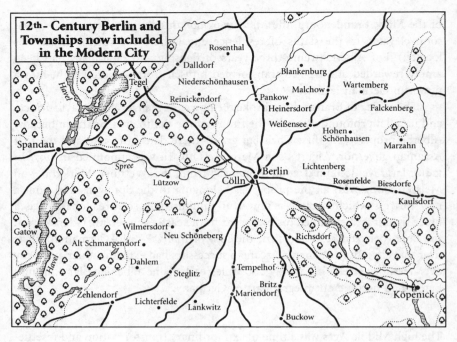

12th-Century Berlin and Townships now included in the Modern City

copse"'.[53] But changing the words of the *Kyrie* would not save the pagans, who faced a cultural revolution of epic proportions.

The churches were far mightier than the pagans could have realized and were granted enormous expanses of land and immunity from royal interference so long as they collected taxes and remained loyal to the emperor. The Christianization of the territory was marked by the spread of churches, and many cities can trace their origins back to the foundation of a monastery or bishopric. Their influence was incalculable. It was they who brought a Roman-inspired model of civilization to the area; it was they who transformed the region from an oral to a written culture; it was they who brought western arts and letters to the east and who taught grammar and rhetoric, arithmetic and geometry, music and astronomy and even practical subjects like the fortification of cities and the creation of markets. The transformation of the Mark Brandenburg into a part of the modern Europe began above all with the coming of the great religious orders.

The first to appear were members of the Premonstratensian Order sent by St Norbert of Magdeburg. Named after their mother house Prémontré near Laon, the monks of the order saw it as their duty to go amongst the heathen and convert them by preaching, hearing confession and administering the sacraments. They were often the first Christians to come into contact with the remote Slavic peoples in the Mark Brandenburg but were joined in the thirteenth century by the Cistercians, an order named in 1098 after the abbey of Cîteaux in French Burgundy. The Cistercians were enormously successful precisely because they looked upon the conversion of the heathen Slavs as an extension of the Crusades – as a true Holy War. Some have argued that the most powerful man in the second half of the twelfth century was neither the pope nor the Holy Roman Emperor but the famous Cistercian Bernard, abbot of Clairvaux, who had persuaded the pope to reward those Christians who fought in the north with the same indulgences and dispensations as were granted to the Crusaders in the south.[54]

The Cistercians might have chosen lonely wooded spots for their monasteries but they were part of a highly sophisticated organization which controlled much of Europe. Each was part of an interdependent network of houses which stretched from Ireland to Norway to Poland and which promulgated everything from religious instruction to reading and writing. The Cistercians created this network by moving on to grants of territory, often in the region of 6,000 *hufe* – around 180,000 acres – where they would build a monastery and drain the land. After this they would plan out a village, complete with houses arranged symmetrically along a straight road and with fields divided into rectangular blocks. Many towns around Berlin owe their origins to the order, including Heiligengrabe, Chorin – which in 1273 built the first brick monastery of the Mark Brandenburg – and Lehnin, whose beautiful Ottonian church became the house monastery and burial site of the Ascanians and which was, for a time, the wealthiest town in the Mark.[55]

The Cistercians were not the only order to become powerful in the Mark Brandenburg: the Franciscans and the Dominicans were active, and the town of Angermünde grew around Franciscan monasteries which were in turn protected by the margraves of Brandenburg. Religious orders created a number of districts which still exist; in 1344, for example, the grand master of the Order of St John asked Johannes Reiche to create a settlement called Marienfelde in what is now part of Berlin; Reiche was given the estate in perpetuity on the understanding that he would govern in the name of the Church. It is a common misconception that the knights and the religious orders were intent on erasing the heathen from the land or, as one commentator put it, that they completed 'the region's first Holocaust'.[56] There is no doubt that the first wave of conversions was often brutal but the notion that the knights 'waged something akin to a twentieth-century war of extermination' is inaccurate: after the regions were conquered the rulers were prepared to grant the local people generous terms to live and work on their land – it made economic sense to do so.[57] This was particularly true of the Mark Brandenburg, where the Slavs were encouraged to stay and prosper as long as they converted to Christianity. Most

Wends were permitted to retain their own language; indeed even Otto I had command of both the German and Slav languages. It was not uncommon for Slav and German nobles to intermarry, and families like the barons von Plotho from Kyritz can trace their ancestry back to Slavic Wendish princes while half the wives of the first sixteen marriages of Albert the Bear's family were of Wendish descent.[58] Groups of Wends also moved into separate villages or *Kietze*, some of which, like Spreewald, survived into the twentieth century with their culture intact.[59] For Albert the main problem was not that his population was Slavic, but that it was too small. If the area was to prosper it needed settlers.

Like other nobles and religious leaders Albert the Bear sent representatives called *locatores* to attract people to his lands. These settlers were not all Germans; indeed many thousands came from other more crowded parts of western Europe attracted by the freedom from the restrictions of feudalism already in place there. Albert's men went 'to Utrecht and the places near the Rhine, especially to those who live near the ocean and suffer the force of the sea, namely the men of Holland, Zeeland and Flanders, and brought a large number of these people whom he settled in the fortesses and towns of the Slavs'.[60] In his work *Chronicle of the Slavs*, written in the 1170s, Helmold of Bosau recorded how rulers took part in similar recruitment drives: Count Adolf II, who had conquered eastern Holstein in the 1140s, sent messengers to all the regions, 'namely Flanders, Holland, Utrecht, Westphalia and Frisia, saying that whoever was oppressed by shortage of land to farm should come with their families and occupy this good and spacious land, which is fruitful, full of fish and meat, food for pasture'.[61] The Flemish, Dutch and Franks were prized for their ability to drain the marshland, and many towns in the Mark Brandenburg owe their origins to them. The Flemish left their stamp in names like 'Fläming' and in village names like 'Flemmingen', named after the thirteenth-century bishop of Ermland, Henry Fleming of Flanders; the Danes gave their name to Dannenwalde, the Dutch named Neuholland, people from the lower Rhine settled Rheinsberg. Like those who colonized North America many centuries later the settlers were tough and hard working. They moved into woodland or swamps, cut down the forests, drained and cultivated the land, introduced the three-field system and the new heavy plough, and raised everything from fruit trees to vines to domestic animals. In the *Cronical principum Saxonie* Albert's family was praised for its work in the area; having

> obtained the lands of Barnim, Teltow and many others from the Lord Barnim (of Pomerania) and purchased the Ukermark up to the River Weise . . . They built Berlin, Strausberg, Frankfurt, New Angermünde, Stolpe, Liebenwalde, Stargard, New Brandenburg and many other

places, and thus, turning the wilderness into cultivated land, they had an abundance of goods of every kind.[62]

It has been estimated that the Ascanians brought over 200,000 people to the Mark between 1134 and 1320 alone. It was at this time that the trade routes which had passed over the sheltered fortresses of Köpenick and Spandau shifted slightly to cross the Spree at Berlin. With this, the city was born.

The city of Berlin was founded sometime in the late twelfth century although there is no single reliable date. The question of 'foundation' is itself ambiguous as the city now contains the much older settlements of Spandau, Köpenick, Lützow (Charlottenburg) and Teltow. Neither did Berlin start as a single settlement but consisted of two separate entities called Berlin and Cölln, located on opposite banks of a narrow point on the river Spree.[63] Years later the East Germans would use this to try to justify the division of the city by the Wall, claiming that Berlin had 'always' been split in two. In reality it was not unusual to have two settlements co-existing and many towns of the Mark, including Potsdam and Brandenburg, started in this way, as did many other great European cities – Paris was originally divided into three parts, with the left bank starting as a Roman settlement; Prague began as two settlements, joined in the twelfth century by the Judith Bridge (replaced in the fourteenth century by Charles IV's magnificent bridge); and Buda and Pest were only united a century ago.[64] In historical terms the two settlements at Berlin actually joined quite early.[65] But the most important factor in the prosperity of the twin town was its control of a vital crossing point on the Spree before it emptied into the river Havel, at a place where the flat and traversable Barnim and Teltow plateaux lay only five kilometres from one another.[66] The Slavs would have found the position too exposed and vulnerable but by the twelfth century the region was more secure and the very lakes and marshes which had once protected the Slavic fortresses were now seen as a hindrance to the movement of goods. From its earliest years Berlin grew strong on trade.

Much has been written over the centuries to portray Berlin as a city which was somehow predestined to play a vital role first in Prussian and then in German politics. This was not the case. For centuries Berlin and Cölln remained small trading towns of minimal importance compared with dazzling contemporaries like Augsburg or Nuremberg. Berlin lay too far north to be on the great east–west route which ran along the Harz foreland and through Thuringia, and acted only as an optional stop for merchants travelling from Magdeburg and Brandenburg on their way to Frankfurt-an-der-Oder, Leubus and Kiev. The first significant change in Berlin's fortunes came only with the increase of trade in the Baltic.[67]

The Germans had been trading in the Baltic before the year 1000 but it was their eastward expansion in the twelfth century which led to a dramatic increase in activity in the entire region. In 1241 an alliance was formed between Lübeck and Hamburg to protect the overland route from the Baltic to the North Sea, an agreement which formed the nucleus of the great Hanseatic League.[68] By 1370 seventy-seven cities, including all significant centres in northern Europe, were members, including Cologne and Brandenburg, Riga and Braunschweig, and trade extended all the way from London to Russia. Berlin joined much later and it was first mentioned only as a nominal member in 1359. Goods were moved in wooden ships known as 'cogs', which often measured over sixty feet in length; by 1368 around 700 such ships were sailing out of Lübeck harbour each year. The growth of the Baltic markets also promoted north–south trade and new routes now threaded their way over the Alps to Nuremberg and from there to Berlin over Barnim and Teltow and on to the north. Berlin's most important link was with Hamburg, with which it traded over the Spree–Havel–Elbe connection, becoming part of the route to the Oder and to the Ostsee. Important Berlin traders like Thilo von Hameln dealt in the high-quality 'Berlin rye' and local oak, which was shipped to Hamburg in cargo boats, while herring and dried cod moved back to Berlin from the Ostsee; iron was brought in from Thuringia; fine cloth came in from Flanders; saffron, pepper, cinnamon, ginger, figs, oil and other spices came in from the Mediterranean and the Orient; wine arrived from northern Italy, Spain, Greece and the Rhine and Mosel areas; and long-distance trade flourished in everything from rice to weapons. Local products were also important. Berlin beer became famous in Hamburg and Lübeck, and trade in honey, wax, feathers, leather, skins, wool, pitch, pewter and brass continued to grow.

By the mid thirteenth century special trade agreements criss-crossed Europe and in March 1252 King William of Holland opened up a favourable trading partnership between the Netherlands and Berlin so that many local merchants went to Ghent, Utrecht and Flemish cities, as well as to Hamburg, Lübeck, Lüneburg and Stettin. In that year Berlin citizens were granted the *Landesherrlichen Zollstätten*, the freedom to control tolls, while the Stendal guild gave exemption to the residents of Berlin, Brandenburg and Prenzlau from duty normally paid for most goods, including precious Flemish cloth. The new Brandenburg laws defended the rights of citizens to hold a market and ensured their personal freedom. By the end of the thirteenth century Berlin had joined the ranks of that extraordinary institution of medieval Europe – the independent town.

*   *   *

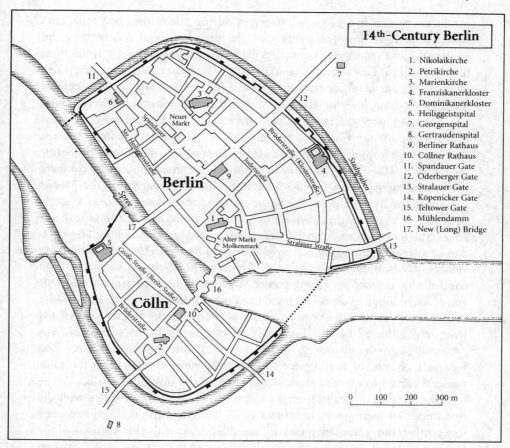

14th-Century Berlin

1. Nikolaikirche
2. Petrikirche
3. Marienkirche
4. Franziskanerkloster
5. Dominikanerkloster
6. Heiliggeistspital
7. Georgenspital
8. Gertraudenspital
9. Berliner Rathaus
10. Cöllner Rathaus
11. Spandauer Gate
12. Oderberger Gate
13. Stralauer Gate
14. Köpenicker Gate
15. Teltower Gate
16. Mühlendamm
17. New (Long) Bridge

'*Stadt Luft macht frei*', went the old German expression: 'city air makes one free'. By the thirteenth century small self-governing walled communities were flourishing throughout Europe, separated from the oppressive world of feudalism which dominated life outside. When you entered the gates of the town you passed from the immediate jurisdiction of the prince or king or bishop who controlled the territory into an independent community; you might be a serf or a knight but if you resided in the town for a year and a day you automatically became a free citizen. Townspeople had their own markets and councils, and in the centre one found not a palace but a market square and a town hall. The powerful medieval guilds controlled everything from prices to the quality of goods, from the number of employees in a given business to the accepted working hours, and inspectors regularly combed towns like Berlin ensuring that craftsmen did not advertise their products or undercut fellow producers or deal in foreign goods except during one of the great trade fairs which were held throughout Europe. The proud seals of shoemakers and goldsmiths and tailors also concealed harsh regulations and petty restrictions like the Beeskow Law which dictated that only Germans could be members of a guild, and there were fines for disobeying guild restrictions, fines for wearing incorrect clothing, fines for selling goods on the incorrect day and fines for usury.

The rules were tolerated because they were made and enforced by the townspeople themselves; kings and bishops allowed these freedoms because they benefited from the wealth generated by the towns.[69] With prosperity came the creation of their own dynasties and although Berlin had nothing to compare with the great patrician families of Europe like the Fuggers or the Medici some, like the Blankenfeldes, the Rathenows and the Rykes (Reiches), became extremely powerful in their own right.[70] Many founded new districts for themselves: the Reiche family created Rosenfelde (now Friedrichsfelde), Steglitz is named after the knight who first lived there, and many streets and surrounding villages still bear the names of their founding families. Increased patrician control was summed up in a document written on 10 April 1288 by Nikolaus von Lietzen, Johann von Blankenfelde and other leaders, in which Berlin cloth cutters were granted the right to create a guild as long as they obeyed the strict laws enforced by the dignitaries of the town – Berlin offered citizens protection and the chance to make money in return for obedience.[71] The fortunate citizens of Berlin were indeed 'free' when compared to the poor peasants forced to eke out an existence on the land outside its walls.

The increase in wealth brought a flurry of building to the town, with the first important permanent structures being churches. The ruins of two early thirteenth-century Romanesque basilicas still lie under the foundations of the St Nikolai and St Petri churches along with more than ninety early Christian graves, but the earliest church to survive was St Nikolai. Started in 1230, with walls of simple round grey fieldstones, it was rebuilt as a late-Gothic hall church. The church of St Petri was founded around 1250; the Marienkirche and the nearby Neuen Markt were started around 1270 and rebuilt after the great fire of 1380. The religious orders were central to the creation of the city: the Franciscan monks were established in the city in 1250, the Dominican monastery was founded in 1297 on the site now occupied by the grandiose Dom, while the Knights Templars set up their cloister south of Cölln, giving their name to Tempelhof. The religious orders brought the first hospitals to Berlin: the Heliggeistspital at the Spandau Gate was built in 1250 and the Georgenspital Leper House was placed outside the Oderberg Gate, now at the edge of present-day Alexanderplatz. The first Berlin wall of fieldstones piled two metres thick was started in 1247 and it was cut through by the Stralau, Oderberg, Spandau, Teltow and Köpenick gates.

In 1256 Berlin and Cölln were linked by a mill dam which could control the flow of water, making it a more convenient river crossing and providing power for a public mill; in 1307 the two towns merged in a formal union and a new Rathaus was built on the Lange Brücke – or long bridge – so that the representatives were actually suspended between the two settlements as they sat in council. The margrave of Brandenburg did not move to Berlin, preferring to stay in the much more luxurious Spandau Castle, but he was represented there by a governor known as the Schultheiss, first appointed in 1247.[72] (The name Schultheiss was given to one of Berlin's famous brands of beer.) The towns were given their own seals; the earliest dates from 14 July 1253 and was produced under the joint authority of the Brandenburg margraves Johann I and Otto III. It depicts the Cölln eagle framed by a great city gate complete with three towers. The *Sekretsiegel*, the second Berlin seal to depict a bear, dates from 1338 and shows a rather ferocious beast, all claws out, striding across the landscape and dragging behind him a small Cölln eagle attached to his neck by a leash. In 1369 Berlin Margrave Otto granted Berlin the right to mint coins which were to be honoured by the people of 'Berlin, Cölln, Frankfurt, Spandau, Bernau, Eberswalde' and others, in effect making Berlin the financial centre of the Mark Brandenburg.[73]

Despite such successes Berlin was far from becoming a great city; indeed in comparison to the rest of Europe all the towns of the Mark were backward and primitive.[74] The few churches in Berlin were small and unimaginative. There was no great representative architecture of the age and certainly nothing remotely like the magnificent Notre Dame, Westminster Abbey, St Stephen's in Vienna, the Charles Bridge in Prague, or Magdeburg Cathedral; nor were there beautifully constructed city walls or ornate public buildings. Fourteenth-century Berlin-Cölln covered a modest seventy hectares and contained around 1,000 houses at a time when Paris, Venice, Florence and Genoa contained around 80,000 people and London already had 35,000, making it the largest city in England.[75] Berlin could not compete with the great textile cities of Arras and Ghent or with ports like Bruges or Genoa and it lagged far behind in everything from financial acumen to the development of art and culture. Then, on 14 August 1319 the Margrave Woldemar died, bringing the end of the Ascanian dynasty which had governed the Mark Brandenburg from the time of Albert the Bear. Berlin had lost its powerful patrons.

There was no natural heir or successor to the titles held by the family of Albert the Bear, and the vast property passed into the hands of margraves from the houses of Wittelsbach and Luxembourg. Unlike the Ascanians these families had no interest in supporting the strange territory; on the contrary, they were eager to extract wealth to finance their estates elsewhere and increased taxes and fines accordingly. With no protection the Mark was soon targeted by marauding armies and bandits. Polish and Lithuanian troops raided in the 1330s, and in 1349 the Danish king Woldemar – the 'False Woldemar' – returned from the Crusades claiming to be Albert the Bear's long-lost ancestor. When he was denied his 'inheritance' he attacked the Mark, burning dozens of villages in the ensuing struggle.

This was not the only disaster to befall the fledgling city. In 1348 the Black Death made its fearsome way through Europe and reached the Mark the following year. Suddenly people began to develop black sores on the palms of their hands or under their armpits, only to die in agony a few days later. One tenth of the population of Berlin succumbed to the bubonic plague and more fell to influenza, smallpox and typhus. Tragically, the Black Death brought the first pogroms to Berlin. The Jews had long played an important part in the region; not only had they traded there throughout the Slavic period but the first Jewish grave dates from 1244 and the Berlin Jewish community was officially founded in 1295, after which Jews and Italians largely controlled the functions of banking and money-lending. This long history did not prevent persecution and after the outbreak of plague Berliners began to blame the Jews for poisoning the wells. There were wild outpourings of hatred, Jews were viciously attacked on the streets and in their homes, and many moved for a time to a protected alley near the present Klosterstrasse which was closed off at night by a huge iron gate. Jews were put on trial and publicly executed for their 'crimes'. Such violence was by no means unique to Berlin; over 300 Jewish communities were destroyed in western Europe and many fled east, particularly to more tolerant Poland, where they formed the largest community in Europe until the Second World War.[76] This first wave of Berlin anti-Semitism ended only on 6 July 1354, when the margrave re-established the right of Jews to reside in the city and founded a Jewish school and a synagogue.

The misery of the century was not yet over. In 1376 Berlin was ravaged by another of those demons of medieval Europe – fire. It struck again in 1380 in the 'Great Fire', which destroyed most of the city. All the churches were levelled and the Rathaus was reduced to ashes along with all early documents and records of the city's history, one of the reasons we know so little about Berlin's earliest years. A contemporary chronicler reported that only six buildings were left standing, and when it was all over an unfortunate and probably blameless knight, Erich von Falke, was accused of arson and tortured to death; his head was stuck high on the Oderberg Gate.

The era was for many Berliners a miserable time of superstition and punishment. The city enforced strict penalties for the most petty crimes and, according to the *Berliner Stadtbuch*, women caught stealing from the Church were buried alive while those caught committing adultery were killed by the sword. Crimes like alleged poisoning, witchcraft and the use of black magic were considered serious offences and between the years 1391 and 1448, in a population of no more than 8,000 people, 121 'criminals' were imprisoned, forty-six were hanged, twenty were burned at the stake, twenty-two were beheaded, eleven were broken on the wheel, seventeen were buried alive (of which nine were women), and thirteen died through other forms of torture.[77] Being broken on the wheel meant just that: the victim was tied on the ground and large wooden blocks placed under him. He was then battered until his arms, legs and spine were cracked so that his broken body could be threaded on to the spokes of a specially made wheel, which was then raised on a high post and the man left to die (the wheel was not used to punish women, who were typically drowned or boiled, burned or buried alive). The corpses of the executed were hoisted up and displayed on the Lange Brücke, their bodies left to decay and their bones put out to rattle in the wind as a warning to others.[78] Many other punishments are recorded on the bloody pages of the *Berliner Stadtbuch* – Christians who 'mixed poison' were burned, liars were boiled alive in a gigantic iron cauldron, and lesser charges could result in anything from having the eyes pushed out, the ears sliced through, the right hand chopped off, the tongue removed with pliers, or molten iron pushed between the teeth.[79] These 'minor' sentences were carried out twice a week, on Mondays and Saturdays, although the public executions took place only once every two weeks – on every second Wednesday – in front of the Oderberg Gate. Such tortures were common throughout Europe but Berlin was already proving itself to be rather a violent place.

Things were to get worse. The fire which had resulted in the execution of Erich von Falke had been so destructive that Margrave Sigismund had allowed Berlin to forgo paying taxes for a year, but even so it was dangerously weak, and from the 1390s the infamous *Raub Ritter* – the Robber Barons from Mecklenburg and Pomerania – began to ravage the area. The very mention of their names – Quitzow, Putlitz, Bredow, Kracht – was enough to send fear through the population. These destructive, barbaric men brought catastrophe in their wake and made the decade from 1401–10 the most turbulent in the history of medieval Berlin.

The robber barons were adventurers who terrorized the area, burning and looting and raping at will. An extraordinary letter sent to the people of Lichtenberg still survives in which Dietrich von Quitzow explains that 'if they do not send their wagons to Bötzow and bring me wood and ten Schock [a group of sixty] of good Bohemian Groschen for delivery which your Councillors of Berlin-Köpenick have captured from me, I will take everything that you possess. Thereupon I await your answer.' Towns like Berlin, Rathenow, Spandau, Bernau, Frankfurt, Beelitz and Potsdam desperately joined together in an attempt to defend themselves, but without money or arms there was little they could do. A contemporary woodcut entitled *The Storming of a Fortress by the Robber Barons* shows their technique for taking heavily fortified towns: in this case some hide behind baskets filled with stones, some run forward with ladders while some stand poised to skewer the defenders of the city gate with their long pikes.[80] Some documents hint at the decimation caused by the bands: in 1402 the leaders of Berlin-Cölln complained to Margrave Jobst that the Count von Lindow and the Quitzows had 'burned and destroyed 22 villages in a week' and that they were still plundering and burning 'day and night' in Barnim. In the nineteenth century the robber barons were turned into Romantic figures, and the 1888 four-act play *Die Quitzows* by Ernst von Wildenbruch became one of the greatest ever triumphs at the Berlin Opera House. In reality, however, the fierce bandits brought nothing but misery to the beleaguered residents of Berlin.

The fight over the succession of the Mark Brandenburg led to years of chaos during which Berlin fell into serious decline. The Four Horsemen of the Apocalypse – famine, war, plague and omnipresent death – became the dominant symbol of the age and the once prosperous countryside, which had been dotted with little towns and villages, declined to almost nothing. The people of the region now believed that St John's visionary prophecies were coming true and that the world was doomed, and the horrific paintings and woodcuts of the period, like the terrifying Dance of Death frieze in the Berlin Marienkirche, reveal the obsession with violence and decay.[81] It was in part because of this unending chaos that on 8 July 1411 the Holy Roman Emperor Sigismund decided to give the troublesome land to a new leader, the descendant of the wealthy burgrave of Nuremberg. It was he who would set Berlin on the road from backward medieval trading town to one of the most important cities in Europe. His name was Frederick von Hohenzollern, and his family would rule over Berlin for over 500 years.

The first task of the Hohenzollern princes was to fight the robber barons and restore law and order to the Mark. In 1411 Burgrave Frederick VI attacked the Quitzows using the new invention of gunpowder-fired cannon and, after a series of spectacular victories, defeated the robber barons and arrived in Berlin in triumph. On 18 October 1415 the entire city, including noble and patrician families, all guild members and all residents, gathered to watch as the new leader was formally sworn in as the margrave of Brandenburg. In the beginning the Hohenzollerns were not particularly interested in Berlin, and the old patrician families managed to retain their control of the city councils, trade levies and taxes. The population grew increasingly impatient with them but could do nothing without the support of the ruler. It was about to change. In 1440 the Hohenzollern Margrave Frederick II, known as 'Irontooth', became *Kurfürst* or elector, and guild members and craftsmen invited him to take over the reins of government, even offering him the keys to the city. 'Irontooth' was happy to seize power, but the townpeople's hopes of freedom were soon dashed. During his investiture he refused to confirm the privileges of the people (in fact he made the promise but refused to give the traditional vow to the saints, making it null and void in his eyes), and in 1441 he began to disband all governing bodies, including the courts and the town council. As promised he broke the control of the patrician families but, to the horror of ordinary Berliners, he also created an independent administrative network under his own personal control which effectively ended traditional citizens' rights. The new power was to be symbolized by a new palace, the Schloss Zwingburg, for which he personally laid the foundation stone in 1443. Berliners were enraged and in 1447 they fought back, attacking Irontooth's appointees, re-opening the old town hall and even flooding part of the city in an attempt to destroy the foundations of his new palace. Irontooth responded by rounding up 500 knights, crushing the revolt and throwing the statue of Roland – a traditional symbol of town rights – into the Spree. He then subjected the city to total control, appointing aldermen, seizing private property and levying his own taxes. It spelled the end of Berliners' political independence. Berlin became the official residence of the Hohenzollern of Brandenburg-Prussia in 1486.[82]

The fight against Irontooth has, perhaps predictably, become part of Berlin mythology. Chroniclers began to refer to it as *Berliner Unwille* or defiance, 'proof' of Berliners' innate suspicion of leaders ranging from Irontooth to Hitler. The myth became popular in the nineteenth century, when a plethora of patriotic stories and novels (*vaterländische Romane*) appeared, the most famous of which was the 1840 *Der Roland von Berlin* by the local writer Willibald Alexis. In this tale the honourable Bürgermeister Johannes Rathenow is shown fighting valiantly against the elector, defending the rights of the people against the oppressive ruler determined to take power for himself. The analogy fired local Berlin patriotism but it was flawed from the beginning. Berlin towns-people were not unique in their struggle against rulers trying to take away their privileges; indeed burghers throughout Germany and beyond constantly struggled to keep their hard-won rights against increasing pressure from local princes. The fight against Irontooth was representative of the extraordinary vul-nerability of many of the little towns of Europe whose citizens' freedom ulti-mately existed by the grace of kings and princes. The rulers who had granted rights could also take them away, and the towns were always at risk; those which managed to retain their status as 'free cities' – like Bremen and Hamburg – still remain fiercely proud of their independence.

Berlin was only one of many towns to fight back in vain; in 1428 the people of Stettin had risen up against Duke Casimir of Pomerania, who had retaliated by killing the ringleaders, crushing their bones and raising his castle over their remains. In 1525 the burghers of Würzburg rose up unsuccessfully against the bishop who was trying to control the town; in the aftermath the ex-mayor and great sculptor Tilman Riemenschneider, who had created some of the most beautiful carvings in all Germany, including the Altar of the Holy Blood in Rothenburg, was captured and tortured. Legend has it that the bishop ordered his hands to be broken. Berlin was not even alone in its fight against the Hohenzollerns; Nuremberg, too, had led a group of Franconian towns in an unsuccessful revolt against them in the fifteenth century. Even Machiavelli wrote of the conflicts between powerful cities and the ruling princes, although unlike later Berlin commentators he believed that the competition between the townspeople and the representatives of the pope or the emperor had fostered the vitality which had in turn led to the great success of the Italian city states at the end of the fifteenth century.

Despite such evidence the notion of *Berliner Unwille* as something unique entered into the popular history of the city and has even been used to portray the people as independent-minded and suspicious of authority, an image fostered with particular vigour after the Second World War. In reality it is difficult to imagine a city which has been more politically docile throughout its long and turbulent history. Its citizens might have grumbled about their leaders but they rarely acted against them. Berliners were not Parisians – to this day they have never initiated a successful revolution – not against Iron-tooth, not in 1848, not against the Kaiser and certainly not against Hitler. Even the mass demonstrations of 1989 which brought down the Communist regime in the GDR started in Leipzig and Dresden, not in Berlin.

The myth of *Berliner Unwille* has one final irony. It was intended to show Berliners as independent critics of the Hohenzollern princes who ruled them for so long, but the fact is that without this extraordinary family Berlin would probably be less important today than Frankfurt-an-der-Oder or Magdeburg. By the end of the fifteenth century Berlin was in a perilous state. Its trade had been eclipsed by Frankfurt-an-der-Oder, with its huge annual trade fair, and by Leipzig, which was strategically positioned on the main east–west route across Germany. English and Dutch merchants were now drawing trade towards Antwerp and Lisbon and to America and the east, and it was Amster-dam – not Berlin – which represented the future of northern Europe. Berlin did not seem 'destined' for greatness; on the contrary, it was saved from obscurity by the ambitious, aggressive Hohenzollern family, who transformed it from a small trading town into a powerful administrative centre backed by an oversized army. As Golo Mann put it, Berlin was little more than 'the creation of a few kings possessed by the fury of *raison d'état* and of servants whom they commanded'.[83]

It was the artificial nature of Berlin's success which led to the nineteenth-century desire to give the city a fresh identity; one which glossed over the 'un-German' aspects of her past while stressing those elements which could help to unite the German nation around the unpopular capital. There are many legends about Berlin, but none revealed its insecurity more clearly than the nineteenth-century story which was created to explain its origins.

Thomas Carlyle calls history a mere distillation of rumour, and nowhere is this more apparent than in the legends which explain the genesis of cities. Fables have been told over millennia to explain these exalted places; it was the goddess Ningal who was said to have built the Sumerian city of Ur; it was Zeus who controlled the destiny of Troy; and it was God who 'doth build up Jerusalem'.[84] By the nineteenth century younger European cities were beginning to rediscover their real or imagined origins and, while towns along the Rhine and into Scandinavia looked back to the *Edda* and the fabulous Nordic sagas with tales of giants and river gods, smaller cities from Trier to Bath cherished their Roman ancestry. Others looked to great founding fathers like Constantine or Alexander, to 'Good King Wenceslas', the shadowy ninth-century Slavic chieftain said to have founded Prague, or to Peter the Great, who created beautiful St Petersburg out of the dreary swamps at the mouth of the Neva. The one thing which tied these cities together was a sense of exuberance and pride in the past and a feeling that, as Tennyson said in *Guinevere*, 'the city is built to music, therefore never built at all, and therefore built for ever'. And yet there was one exception. Of all the great cities of nineteenth-century Europe only one seemed to have no great legend to explain her early history, no great tale to justify her origins, no river gods or magic gold or mighty kings to look back on with pride. That city was Berlin. It struck visitors as strange that the arrogant German capital, which was otherwise intent on creating a positive image for itself, should go to such lengths to divert interest from its distant past, almost as if it had something to hide. They were not far from the truth.

During the eighteenth century few Germans had been interested in the history of Berlin, but with its elevation to the capital of Bismarck's Reich it came under increased scrutiny and pressure to project itself as the focal point of a united German nation. One way to achieve this end was through the writing of history. The use of the past in the creation of a sense of identity was not new. As far back as the fifteenth century Germans longing to re-create the glory of the Holy Roman Empire had glorified Charlemagne and had even used Tacitus, first rediscovered in 1497, to try to prove the existence of inviolable German traits. Nevertheless, modern German historiography evolved in the late eighteenth and early nineteenth centuries primarily as a reaction against the cultural domination of France. Born in 1744, a student of Kant and friend of J. G. Hamann, Johann Gottfried Herder was one of the first to become interested in those elements which make a nation. He concentrated on the importance of language and in his *Essays on the Origins of Language*, published in Berlin in 1772, tried to show that communication was not God-given but had evolved as men had lived together in communities; each nation was unique and bound together by a common tongue. In *Von deutscher Art und Kunst* he claimed that education and culture were the distinguishing marks of national existence and that in order to discover one's true identity one had to look not to France, but back to hitherto ignored art forms like ancient folk tales and architecture.[85]

Herder was not alone in his search for the meaning of national identity, and one of the most influential converts was Johann Wolfgang von Goethe. Like his contemporaries Goethe had long ridiculed medieval culture and the Gothic style, but during a 1773 visit to Strasbourg Cathedral he changed his mind. Suddenly he decided (incorrectly) that the Gothic was a German invention:

> Since I found this building constructed on an old German site and built in the real German age, to be so highly evolved; and since the Master's name on his modest tombstone was also fatherlandish by sound and origin, the merit of the work emboldened me to change the hitherto ill-famed designation of 'Gothic' ... and to justify it as the 'German Architecture' of our own nation.[86]

It was this love of the 'true' German past which would come to dominate Berlin Romanticism of the nineteenth century.

Despite its extraordinary diversity one of the most striking features of German Romanticism was the obsession with history and the longing to find a modern German identity buried back in the Middle Ages. Many Romantics, including Clemens Brentano and Achim von Arnim, rediscovered German folk art and fostered the collection of old songs, ballads, folklore and fairy tales. In 1800 Friedrich Schlegel wrote *To the Germans*, in which he encouraged people to fulfil their cultural mission.[87] Romantic notions of the German nation appeared in the work of poets like Novalis; fairytales by the brothers Grimm and Moritz von Schwind contained lavish illustrations of German knights and castles, while paintings like Ferdinand Olivier's *The Fairytale King's Homecoming* and Henry Fuseli's *Thor Battering the Midgard Serpent* personified not only the fascination with the occult but also the desire to dig through centuries of 'foreign influence' to find that 'pure' German culture that was said to have existed in the mists of time. This was linked to the obsession with the *Volk*, the new love for 'Fatherland' and, above all, with the yearning to create a new nation-state which would reflect the glory of the German Empire of the high Middle Ages. As the nineteenth century progressed these national pursuits became more patriotic, and it was George Bernard Shaw who warned of the craving for German greatness hidden in Wagner's revival of the themes of the lust for flesh, power and gold.[88]

The rediscovery of 'true German' medieval art and culture was soon put to political use. In his 1808 *Addresses to the German Nation* given in a Berlin occupied by Napoleonic troops Fichte explained to the German people that they were a race morally superior to all others and that they had a duty to learn about their past through the study of art and architecture, poetry and language. The cry for nationhood intensified after the defeat of France: by the 1830s young people were gathering at events like the Hambach Festival of 1832 to recall the glories of the past and to call for the unification of Germany; medieval societies restored old buildings and held mock historical services and praised the lost glory of the Holy Roman Empire. Attempts to create a national identity took a new form: the writing of national history.

By the mid nineteenth century historians at the new university in Berlin had started to create a state-centred political history to justify Germany's new powerful role in the world. In the years between the failed attempt at revolution in 1848 and the unification of Germany in 1871 historians from Ranke to Droysen, from Sybel to Treitschke worked to create a nationalist version of the past, outlining the importance – and indeed the superiority – of the traditions and the language shared by all Germans. Ranke had attempted to write a history free of personal bias but his very choice of subject, the rise of the nation-state or *Machtstaat*, was thinly veiled praise of the extraordinary rise of Prussia within Germany. Treitschke replaced Ranke's conception of a balance of powers with the idea that individual states were constantly battling with one another for a position of dominance. Related to this was the glorification of war as a German destiny which would allow the nation to fulfil its cultural mission. For Droysen the concept of the *Volk* was inseparable from the desire to create a German state led by Prussia, while Friedrich Naumann defined nationalism as the urge of the Germans to spread their influence throughout the world. But it was in the years leading up to the creation of Bismarck's Reich in 1871 that historians began to legitimate Germany's new aggressive colonial and military policies, the political exploitation of cultural achievements in science, technology and the arts, the isolation of those in society who were considered not at one with the *Volk*, and above all the promulgation of German *Kultur* abroad.[89] The historian Sybel wrote in 1867 that Germans had to learn about the history of the ancient *Volk* because without this the nation would be like a tree without roots, and that they must look back to the ancient tribes described in *Germania*, for 'the Germans of Tacitus were the Germans in their youth'.[90] Tacitus was also used by xeno- phobes like Houston Stewart Chamberlain to 'prove' German racial purity and ancient Germanic national traits from loyalty to honour in battle. History was used to give the new Germans a sense of pride in their nation. The story of Berlin was no exception.

The most important author in the creation of the popular legend of Berlin was the historian Adolph Streckfuss, who coined the expression *From Fishing Village to World City*, the title of his 1864 history of the city. As a young man Streckfuss had been a democrat and a supporter of the 1848 Revolution, and it was he who popularized notions of the *Berliner Unwille*.[91] Nevertheless the myth that Berlin had been founded in a barren wasteland in the twelfth century soon became orthodoxy and by 1910 it had become a staple of the Baedeker guide. But why was history rewritten? Why was this dry story taken up with such enthusiasm – a story which ignored so much of the region's complex and fascinating history? The reason was less than pleasant. Not only had the Berlin area been one of the last areas to be Christianized; unlike 'truly German' cities like Cologne or Nuremberg, it had been populated for six centuries not by Tacitus' Germans, but by the hated Slavs.[92] Rather than acknowledge their contribution, the Wendish past was at best marginalized and at worst simply written out of history.[93]

The Berlin legend was created in an age when concepts like ethnic purity and the superiority of one race over another were taken for granted by many Germans. It was devised at a time when Germans were being taught that their own national characteristics had evolved through contact with certain geographical areas or with the *Heimat* (homeland) or even with the 'soil'; at a time when Germans genuinely believed that they were direct descendants of the pure northern race of Germans described by Tacitus. In our multi-ethnic, relativist world it is difficult to understand the importance placed in the nineteenth and early twentieth centuries on concepts like ethnic, racial or cultural 'purity'; indeed the notion of a racially 'pure' area was ludicrous in a continent in which every corner has been touched by wars, migration, intermarriage, conquest and commerce, and where even the isolated British were a mixture of Celtic, Roman, Norman, Viking and other peoples. This was particularly true of Germany, which for most of its history had been a patchwork of squabbling territories with no clearly defined borders and no real sense of unity. It was perhaps the very lack of a distinct national identity which made Germans so keen to create a coherent history after 1871 and to turn Berlin into a unifying symbol for the entire nation. But to do so meant that history had to be altered to fit contemporary demands. And the first victim was Berlin's Slavic past.

In keeping with racial Darwinism and other such theories many Germans now believed that civilization in Europe had moved from the 'superior' west to the 'inferior' east. Of course such ideas were not unique to Germany; in Britain they were reflected in the colonial policies of the Victorian age, and many nations throughout the nineteenth century created equally chauvinistic accounts of their own superiority. But while internal prejudice was being increasingly channelled into rising anti-Semitism, the external foe was seen to lie in the Slavic lands to the east. Negative views of 'the Slavs' were widespread in nineteenth-century Prussia. Friedrich Engels was voicing a popular view when he wrote that 'all these [Slavic] peoples are at the most diverse stages of civilization, ranging from the fairly highly developed (thanks to the *Germans*) modern industry and culture of Bohemia down to the almost nomadic barbarism of the Croats and Bulgarians'.[94] All Slavs were 'inferior', but for Berliners the most contemptible group were their neighbours – the Poles.

The vast borderlands between Germany and Poland have long been one of the most controversial regions of Europe. The lines between them have constantly shifted, leaving mixed populations on one or other side and, despite claims and counter-claims by both nations, there is not and never has been anything like a simple clear-cut historical border to divide the two. The mutual contempt was not merely the result of a long and troubled history but had to do with contemporary questions of political power. The Prussians, with Austria and Russia, had erased Poland from the map in 1795. Germans were taught that the re-creation of a Polish state would result in unacceptable losses to the Prussian–German eastern frontier, and instead of responding to legitimate demands for Polish independence they had tried to Germanize the Prussian-Polish lands through the *Kulturkampf* and through special bodies created to oversee German colonization; these measures included the prohibition of the use of the Polish language in schools and the purchase of Polish estates for German settlers.[95] And yet, to Bismarck's chagrin, Polish cultural and economic bodies were so well organized that despite his concerted efforts there was little decline in use of the Polish language or in the ownership of land. Worse still, his measures seemed to have intensified a sense of Polish national consciousness.

Berlin's history was rewritten at a time when Germans felt threatened by this increasing tide of Polish nationalism and when words like 'Wend', 'Slav' and 'Pole' were increasingly – and incorrectly – used interchangeably. Late nineteenth-century Germans were bombarded with images of Slavs as a chaotic people whose towns and villages were primitive and dirty compared with their pristine German counterparts. Poles were commonly portrayed as devious and untrustworthy and incapable of governing themselves. Why, it was asked, should Germany allow the creation of a Polish state which would merely collapse into anarchy? Furthermore, Engels's view that all civilization, culture, progress and advancement in the Polish lands had ultimately been introduced by Germans was widely believed. One of the most pervasive themes in popular history was the notion of the *Drang nach Osten*: the ancient German 'mission in the east' was viewed as one of the crowning achievements of European history. Wilhelm Jordan was typical when he asked: 'Are not the Germans more important and more difficult to replace from the perspective of the progressive development of the human race than the Poles?'[96] Furthermore it was argued that this was not a modern phenomenon; archaeology and ancient history could 'prove' that the Slavs had 'always' been comparatively primitive. Ancient Germanic villages could be identified because they were neat and technologically advanced, whereas Slavic ones were crude and disorganized. The archaeologist Wilhelm Unversagt, who carried out excavations between the Oder and the Elbe, said of one Slav fortress:

> The domestic and defensive buildings were constructed in the most primitive block-technique ... when one recalls that such houses appear in the residences of Slav princes, and at a time when the imposing Romanesque churches were built on the Rhine and in central Germany, which even today arouse our highest admiration, one can understand what the culturally superior Germanic West had to give to the primitive Slavic East.[97]

These 'scientific' and 'scholarly' views provided fertile ground for the National Socialists in 1933.

The process of rewriting Berlin history was intensified in the 1930s, when it became a tool of Nazi state policy through the work of bodies such as Walter Frank's Reichsinstitut für die Geschichte des neuen Deutschlands (the Institute for the History of New Germany) and the work of eminent men like Erich Marcks, Fritz Hartung and Heinrich von Srbik. And it was then that a concerted attempt was made to thoroughly 'Germanize' Berlin's history. Positive references to Jews, Slavs and other 'undesirable groups' were simply erased. In the 1936 article 'What All Berliners Must Know About Their History' Dr Hermann Rügler, the head of the Institute for the History of Berlin, wrote that 'Berlin was from the very beginning to the present day a German city'. He acknowledged that although there had been a period of Slavic settlement this had been 'insignificant', as Germans had quickly resettled the *altes deutsche Stammes-gebiet* – the old German ancestral area. He claimed that there was plenty of archaeological evidence of early Germanic settlements in the region but that the 'few Wendish finds' revealed that the Slavs had merely 'existed – nothing more'. The 1937 Nazi publications for Berlin's official birthday boasted that the city was indeed 'founded on good Germanic soil', and the mention of the city's Slavic past disappeared from the 1937 *Baedeker*.[98] In short, Berliners were taught that although there had been a brief period of 'illegitimate' Slavic settlement in a Germanic area, these people had contributed nothing to the history of the city. The message was as powerful as it was sinister. If the medieval Germans had been right to retake the 'true German' areas around Berlin and if the Slavs were not worthy of inhabiting 'German soil', why should this end in the Mark Brandenburg?[99] The same arguments were quickly extended to whip up support for the retaking of 'true German' cities like Danzig. As early as 1936 the Nazi version of the history of Berlin had become a handmaiden to the war effort.

The denial of the Slavic heritage became the first great myth of Berlin historiography. It was pathetic – rather as if the British had tried to deny the Norman Conquest – but the extraordinary notion that one could use ancient history to legitimate contemporary politics was taken with deadly seriousness. The abuse of early history continued even after the war and not only by the Germans; the ludicrous assumption that the ancient Wends were in fact Polish was used by some Polish extremists in 1945 to claim that because Slavs had at one time lived in the Berlin area the city should become part of Poland.[100] Nevertheless the most blatant abuses in the early history of the Mark Brandenburg were corrected after the war, and the Wends were finally given their rightful place as one of the many groups who had lived in and contributed to the long and complex history of the city of Berlin.

Such considerations were of course irrelevant to the Berliners of the fifteenth century. The city was still small and insignificant and paled in comparison to Paris or London, Amsterdam or even Rome, where Cardinal Odoardo Farnese could hear twenty-seven languages spoken in the refectory of the Jesuit college in the Piazza Altieri. Berlin still had nothing to compare with the marvels of the rest of Europe, whether in the Vladislav Hall in Prague or the Palazzo Vecchio in Florence or the magnificent guild hall of Ypres. But Berlin was now firmly in the grip of the Hohenzollern family and was about to be pushed on to the world stage. In the coming years it would undergo a transformation so profound that it would become one of the most important and powerful cities in Europe. It would be a traumatic birth.

II

The Capital of Absolutism

The chance is offered; take it while you can.
(*Faust*, Part II, Act 1)

WHEN EMINENT FIFTEENTH-CENTURY EUROPEANS like Copernicus and Albrecht Dürer set out on their travels through Europe they did not contemplate visiting Berlin; why should they when Florence, Venice, Padua, Paris and Rome beckoned with 'the most glorious sights for state and magnificence that any city can show a traveller' or when the Low Countries were reaching ever greater heights of art and culture?[1] Why should they go to the small German town when so many other cities, from Buda to Prague to Moscow, were being transformed by Italian Renaissance architects and artists, when Nuremberg and Augsburg and Munich were producing fabulous works of art, or when Copernicus' own university of Cracow was being transformed by the spirit of religious tolerance and Humanism of the 'Golden Age of Poland' reflected in the works of that great poet Jan Kochanowski.[2] The Dutch art historian Karel van Mander travelled not to Berlin but to Vienna, and recommended those travelling south to go to Prague, which, under Rudolf II, had become the Parnassus of the arts.[3] Compared to the great princely houses of Europe the Hohenzollern margraves were poor and their city was rough, unsophisticated and shabby.[4] Even so, Berlin was now a residence city and its culture was improving.

The sixteenth century had started well for Berlin. The Reformation, which had swept through Germany after 1517 when Luther nailed his ninety-five theses to the castle church of Wittenberg, had come to Brandenburg peacefully. The Hohenzollern Elector Joachim II had adopted Lutheranism on 13 February 1539 – the first service was held in Berlin by Luther's friend Johann Agricola in 1540 – and the people had followed him. Within a few years the great families of Berlin were commissioning paintings and monuments for themselves in the new style: the Blankenfeldes had a massive memorial carved showing the family at prayer, while the Reiches ordered a painting of the entire family mourning at the crucifixion. Most of the great painters of sixteenth-century

Germany – Albrecht Dürer, Lucas Cranach, Hans Baldung (Grien) and Hans Holbein – worked in the service of the Reformation, helping to spread its ideas and to glorify the new leaders on canvas. Luther's friend Lucas Cranach the Elder painted a magnificent portrait of Joachim I, who ruled in Berlin until 1535. In 1551 Cranach the younger painted his heir, Joachim II.

This 1551 portrait captures the self-confident air of a man not yet troubled by conflict. He stands stocky and proud, with a hint of cruelty hovering around his eyes in a manner reminiscent of Holbein's 1536 portrait of Henry VIII.[5] Joachim's red tunic is shot through with gold, his bearskin hat is decorated with pearls and his heavy fur cloak is weighted down by two enormous jewel-encrusted gold chains. There is nothing in the portrait to suggest any doubt about the future. The painting was commissioned at an optimistic moment in northern Europe's history, when Amsterdam was outpacing Antwerp as the greatest city of the Low Countries and when east–west trade was sustaining towns from Danzig to Nuremberg. The culture of northern Germany was becoming more sophisticated: great castles were built from Dresden to Stettin; princes and merchants patronized the arts and employed craftsmen, furniture makers, metal workers, sculptors and painters in the creation of their magnificent courts.[6]

The elector had started to improve Berlin. He invited the Torgau master-builder Konrad Krebs to build the electoral residence, which in the 1540s became a monumental Renaissance palace; he invited in Dutch-trained builders and hired artists and architects like Kaspar Theyss, Hans Schenk and Kunz Buntschuh to bring a glimmer of the Renaissance to the city. Under him Berlin sustained a population of 10,000 people. But the self-confidence of this generation would be short-lived. Despite the Religious Peace of Augsburg of 1555, during which all imperial rulers from the electors to the knights had promised to tolerate Lutherans and Catholics within the empire according to the principle *cuius regio, eius religio*, the divisions brought about by the Reformation were about to resurface.[7] Berlin was on the verge of another of those traumatic upheavals which mark its history, known as the Thirty Years War. This time the war would wipe out virtually all vestiges of Berlin's medieval past.

One can sometimes catch glimpses of the violence and despair of so many people's lives in the paintings of the time. There are flashes of ugliness and cruelty in the works of Holbein and Cranach; there is a sense of gloom, an undercurrent of despair in the works of Brueghel and of Bosch with their cold peasant villages, destitute vagabonds and terrifying visions of carnage. Brueghel's beggars have sunken battered faces, they wear rags, they are blind and struggle down cart tracks on crutches; Bosch's downcast pedlar wears only one shoe as he creeps slowly away from an isolated inn, its broken windows and hanging shutters just visible in the bleak light of mid-winter. Grünewald's depiction of the ugly enraged villagers in *The Mocking of Christ* shows the people dragging an accused man through the streets on a rope, beating him as he passes and leaving blood streaming down his face – common treatment of condemned men and women in the villages of northern Europe. In *Three Ages of Woman and Death* Grien shows a ghastly rotting corpse holding an hourglass over the head of a young maiden; his woodcuts with titles like *Young Witch and Dragon*, or Albrecht Altdorfer's *Departure for the Sabbath*, hint at the common fear of the occult. Even Holbein, better known for his revealing portraits of monarchs and princes, depicts horrific scenes in his series of drawings, *Der Totentanz* (Dance of Death) and *Das Todesalphabet* (Death Alphabet) of 1524; indeed it was the turbulence following the Reformation which drove him to England and the court of Henry VIII. An acceptance of violence shows in the thousands of contemporary woodcuts with their gory portrayals of battle scenes, torture and dismemberment. The images were not fantasy but reflected the harsh spirit of an age consumed by the religious and dynastic conflicts which erupted in Europe and Berlin, and they capture the despair of populations forced to endure decades of violence during that most grisly of religious conflicts.[8]

The Thirty Years War began in 1618 and raged until 1648. It left deep scars on the German psyche and it was a turning point for Berlin, destroying the old city and paving the way for the benevolent despots of the seventeenth and eighteenth centuries.[9] Even before the outbreak of hostilities it was clear that Europe was on the verge of a disaster. There had been a sense of impending doom since the 1550s, which had seen waves of unrest, peasant uprisings and a general mood of crisis. Berlin had also experienced increased poverty and social unrest; once again Jews were targeted. In July 1510 100 people were tried for allegedly stealing and selling sacred items from a Berlin church: thirty-eight Jews were burned in the Neue Markt and the rest were banished from the Mark Brandenburg. But above all there was a sense that the fragile truce between Protestants and Catholics hammered out at the Peace of Augsburg was about to fail. Governments throughout the German lands had started building up their defences, and even in Prussia, where the estates refused to pay for a militia, the elector raised taxes to pay for fortifications for Memel and Pillau and built two warships to patrol the Baltic.[10] The premonition was correct: in 1608 the imperial Diet collapsed. By 1618 four important political conflicts had emerged in Europe. The first was between Protestant princes and the Catholic Habsburgs in the Holy Roman Empire; the second was the continued hostility between Poland and the Swedes; the third, the conflict between France and the Habsburgs, and the fourth, that between the Spanish and the Dutch. These were woven into a net of related quarrels, dynastic ambitions and petty rivalries so that even before the war began treachery, broken alliances and deceit amongst rulers had become common on all sides.[11] No single religion, ruler or state was powerful enough to impose any decisive settlement on the others. War was a foregone conclusion.

In the event the Thirty Years War began in Prague. Hostilities broke out during the Bohemian revolt of 1618 when a Protestant king, the twenty-three-year-old Frederick II of the Palatinate, was chosen by the estates to rule Bohemia instead of the Catholic Habsburg successor. The Habsburgs, then in league with a number of other German states, attempted to oust the new king; they were victorious under General Tilly, who triumphed at the Battle of the White Mountain in 1620. The Habsburg emperor's success fuelled his hope that he might wipe Protestantism from the face of Europe altogether, and he decided to push northward and retake converted lands, a scheme later codified in the Edict of Restitution. With the help of his brilliant general, Albrecht von Wallenstein, it seemed that he might succeed. Wallenstein conquered great swathes of Germany, finally approaching the Mark Brandenburg in 1626. In the tenth year of fighting, the war reached Berlin.

Until then Berliners had been spared the worst of the conflict. A few troops had passed by the city in 1620, including 3,000 English mercenaries on their way to Prague under Ernst von Mansfeld, but although a fire had swept through the town that year it had had nothing to do with the troops. Now, however, the armies were drawing near. Berlin was ruled by a weak and ineffectual leader, the Elector George William, whose ideas about war were limited to the notion that if attacked one should surrender and change sides. It would prove a disastrous policy for Berlin.

With Wallenstein's men approaching fast the elector was finally forced to do something. He tried to gather a defence force but could muster fewer than 1,000 troops; when they entered Berlin in order to organize themselves the confused citizens pelted them with stones, believing them to be on a secret mission to convert them from Lutheranism to Calvinism.[12] The troops were of little use. By the summer of 1626 Wallenstein had overrun most of Germany and had based himself at Crossen on the Oder. His troops threatened to ransack the towns of the Mark if they were not paid compensation. Brandenburg's 'obligation' was assessed at 60,000 gulden, and to encourage payment Wallenstein rounded up hundreds of people and held them hostage. The money was finally paid, but it made little difference. His troops entered Berlin for the first time on 15 November 1627 and ransacked the city, looting and raping. They returned a year later, bringing another wave of terror. Forty thousand troops arrived in February 1630, and this time they remained for over a year, leaving a legacy of destruction, hunger and disease in their wake. Each occupation meant more brutality for the people, who prayed: 'Is there no God in heaven that will take our part? Are we then such utterly forsaken sheep?

Must we look on while our houses and dwellings are burnt before our eyes?'[13] This is one reason why there is only one late Renaissance building still standing in central Berlin.[14]

After four years of occupation by the Catholic forces Berlin's fortunes appeared to be changing. The apparent salvation came in the form of one of the great heroes of the Protestant cause, the king of Sweden, Gustavus Adolphus, who had landed at Usedom in Pomerania in July 1630 and had begun to march south. The imperial commander, Tilly, had already taken the outer fortifications of Magdeburg by April, but as the Swedes approached he feared that he might be caught between the city and the Swedish forces. He gave the order to attack, but tragically could not control his own insubordinate, bloodthirsty troops, and on 20 May 1631, in one of the most outrageous acts of the war, 30,000 of the people of Magdeburg were hacked or burned to death in a matter of hours. The news of the massacre infuriated the Swedish king, who was spurred on by the desire to avenge the disaster. By the end of May 1631 his men, wearing the telltale yellow and blue ribbon around their hats, had driven the imperial troops south and had reached the gates of Berlin. Gustavus Adolphus now demanded that the dithering Elector George William sign a Treaty of Alliance with Sweden. The elector's attempts to try to evade his obligation so infuriated the Swedish king that on 21 June he brought his army to the gates of Berlin and aimed his cannon directly at the electoral palace. George William cowered inside, sending his wife and mother-in-law out to pacify the king, but on 23 June the treaty was finalized, putting Berlin firmly under Swedish rule. Brandenburg and the fortresses of Spandau and Küstrin were placed at the disposal of the Swedish king, Berlin was occupied, and Gustavus Adophus himself took up residence there for a time, demanding 30,000 thalers a year for the upkeep of his troops.

Any hopes Berliners might have had for an improvement in their lives were quickly dashed. The new occupation force, which remained until 1634, behaved as badly as Wallenstein's men had done. The situation would worsen again. In 1635 the emperor's forces began to move north once more; armies swept into the Mark Brandenburg from the south and Berlin became part of the central battlefield of the war. That year marked the beginning of the last and most horrible phase of the conflict in the Mark Brandenburg; fighting between Sweden and the emperor was constant and the city changed hands and was plundered and occupied on numerous occasions. In 1638 George William fled to Königsberg, leaving Berlin under the control of the imperial Catholic general Adam Graf zu Schwarzenberg and stripping it of its *Residenz* status. Schwarzenberg was detested by Berliners. Not only did he treat the city as his own, but he took to burning down part of Berlin every time an enemy army approached to try to dissuade them from attacking; much of the city was destroyed in this manner – particularly in a raging fire of 1640. In January 1641 word spread that the Swedes were moving towards Berlin once again, and this time Schwarzenberg gave the order to burn Cölln. As the buildings blazed it was discovered that the Swedish 'army' consisted of only 1,000 poorly equipped men, 360 of whom were easily captured. To Berliners' delight Schwarzenberg died suddenly in March 1641, releasing them from his grim hold, but by now Berlin had only 845 houses left, 200 of which were empty. Cölln had been almost completely destroyed.

The devastation of the city and the surrounding area was beyond comparison with anything which had gone before, and although some parts of Germany, including much of Saxony and Holstein, were untouched there was a huge swathe of desolate land which stretched from Swabia and the Palatinate through Thuringia and Brandenburg to Mecklenburg and Pomerania. The destruction was not just the result of the battles. There have been countless wars in European history; territories have changed hands, provinces have been won and lost and cities like Berlin have been occupied many times, but few pre-twentieth-century conflicts have created so much damage as the Thirty Years War. The loss of life was proportionally even greater than that sustained in the Second World War.[15] The reason lay in part with the nature of the armies themselves. In the seventeenth century no European state had a national force; there was little in the way of conscription, proper training or effective control of troops' behaviour. Emperors, princes and others in need of a fighting force held recruitment drives in some areas, but few could afford to support an army for long – not least because the war was a death sentence for thousands of young men: in the small village of Bygdea in northern Sweden, 215 of the 230 men who fought were killed in battle, and five of the survivors returned home crippled.[16] Instead, most hired professional generals to recruit mercenaries. Many armies were made up of outcasts, criminals, vagabonds, homeless men, professional soldiers and psychopaths; some longed for adventure while others felt that it would be safer to be a soldier than a civilian. National and religious loyalties were irrelevant for most mercenaries. Poles fought for Germans, Swiss for Austrians, Dutch for the Swedes, Scots for the Danes, and former enemies often met to discuss the relative merits of an employer – contemporary reports held that the German emperor did not provide adequate shelter while the Polish king scrimped on food for the troops.[17] Such men fought only for a banner; if it was captured they simply changed sides. Autumn desertion was common but generals tended to waive the mandatory death sentence, knowing that many of the men would return for fresh booty in the spring. Armies were expensive; they were kept relatively small, the strategy of attrition dominated and campaigns were dependent on finances. Generals assumed that occupied territory was the property of the army and gave troops free rein to loot, rape and plunder at will; indeed, those soldiers lucky enough to survive often returned home wealthy men – the Swedish general Königsmark, who had started out as a common soldier, returned with assets of almost 2 million thalers (4.8 thalers were worth around £1 sterling), while the once impoverished imperial commander Henrik Holck returned home to Denmark and paid 50,000 thalers in cash for an estate in Funen.[18] The war became a relentless quest for fresh plunder – a self-perpetuating nightmare of destruction. The unruly troops rarely showed mercy to civilians; even when Berlin was occupied by her own allies she was laid waste.

Nikolaas van Eyck's *Occupation of a Village*, which hangs in the Kunsthistorisches Museum in Vienna, offers a glimpse of an everyday occurrence during the war. Van Eyck shows a hamlet surrounded by troops set on plunder, and while some soldiers push their way into houses others loll around on the cannon on the main dirt track waiting their turn to search for food, women and treasure. Helpless villagers wander aimlessly past the incoming wagons; one man comforts his wife and child while another sits beneath a tree, crying. The plundering of villages and towns was the norm. Nothing was spared. Church spires were melted down for lead, farms were stripped and set on fire, villages were burnt for amusement. Peasants were considered fair game for sport: it was common for them to be captured, rounded up like animals and tortured; some had cords tied around their heads so that their eyes were forced out, others had their thumbs pushed deep into gun barrels. Innocent people were bound and tossed into the rivers, thrown out of windows, roasted on spits or boiled in their own cauldrons. Prisoners were sometimes tied in rows and bets placed on how many bodies a bullet would penetrate. Some armies became known for particular forms of abuse: when Wallenstein took hostages in the Mark Brandenburg burghers were repeatedly tortured so that they would reveal the location of 'treasure' which had long since been plundered; priests were tied under wagons and made to crawl on all fours like dogs until they died; others were dragged 'for miles along the rough roads bound to the tails of horses'.[19]

Despite official attempts to curb the violence to civilians the Swedish occupation was equally horrific. By 1632 there were no young women left in Berlin as all had been taken by the troops; children were reportedly killed in front of their parents in order to elicit the whereabouts of the family valuables. The soldiers, keen to amuse themselves, murdered unknown numbers of Berliners by sprinkling gunpowder on their victims and setting them alight; they also poured raw sewage down the throats of prisoners, a practice so widespread that the foul mixture came to be known as the 'Swedish drink'. The hatred between the people and the occupying armies was extreme – particularly in the unprotected areas outside the city walls; civilians sometimes attacked soldiers' encampments and then endured savage reprisals, while a popular expression amongst the troops went: 'Every soldier needs three peasants: one to give up his lodgings, one to provide his wife, and one to take his place in Hell.' Colonel Monro complained of the behaviour of Bavarian peasants towards the Swedes in 1632: they 'cruelly used our souldiers (that went aside to plunder) in cutting off their noeses and eares, hands and feete, pulling out their eyes, with sundry other cruelties which they used; being justly repayed by the souldiers, in burning of many Dorpes [villages] on the march, leaving also the boores dead, where they were found'.[20] Both troops and civilians had become brutalized.

The armies consisted not only of soldiers but of whole communities, including army whores, bedraggled children and vagrants who dragged behind the wagons along with their often diseased livestock, horses and cows. All of them had to be supported and the results were ruinous for occupied territories. Berlin was badly affected by famine. Four failed harvests on the Havel between 1625 and 1628 had already weakened the population and entire encampments of wretched refugees were wiped out by starvation in the successive winters. In 1627 the crops had grown well but they were destroyed by the retreating Danes and the victorious imperial army. The land was constantly being stripped bare, crops were trampled or ripped out before they reached maturity, and starvation was widespread.[21] In 1629 the Englishman Sir Thomas Roe travelled through the area and wrote: 'I hear nothing but lamentations nor see variety but of dead bodies ... in eighty English miles not a house to sleep safe in; no inhabitants save a few poor women and children *vertend stercorarium* to find a corn of wheat.'[22] In Berlin the starvation in 1631–2 was so extreme that people were reduced to stealing dead animals from the knackers' yards. The much used gallows were regularly plundered and even graves were found emptied. In one case fresh human bones were discovered in a pit with their marrow sucked dry.

Starvation weakened the population and left them vulnerable to sickness and diseases like smallpox, syphilis, scurvy and typhus. Worse still was the return of the dreaded plague. The first outbreak reached Berlin in 1620 but it continued throughout the war. In 1630–31 2,000 Berliners died of plague; in 1637 over 500 died. Bodies lay out in the streets as there was nobody left willing to push the plague carts or dig the mass graves. Those still alive created strange concoctions of lavender, rosemary, juniper berries, garlic, white onions, vinegar, walnuts, endive, hot poultices, cold compresses, scented masks and bags of herbs in a desperate attempt to halt the disease. People were obsessed with death: drawings of skulls and skeletons appeared on plague sheets and themes of decay and mutability abounded. When the English ambassador travelled to the electoral meeting at Regensburg he reported on a country where a few bedraggled villagers who saw them coming fled in terror, fearing that his party was yet another group of invading soldiers; roads were so unsafe that several of his group were murdered near Nuremberg, and he recounts how he found bodies newly scraped out of graves, 'fair cities pillaged and burnt', and people 'found dead with grass in their mouths'.[23] In May 1631 a pastor in Brandenburg wrote in his diary: 'Catherine, my old servant, shot.'[24] There was no other comment. Such things had become commonplace.

The importance of the conflict is reflected in the mass of literature – and the myths – which it has inspired. The Thirty Years War became a subject of particular importance in the nineteenth and early twentieth centuries when German historians attempted to use it to 'prove' how much the 'all destructive fury of the Thirty Years War' had damaged German interests and to show that both the conflict and the post-war settlement was 'a monstrous iniquity perpetrated on Germany by foreign powers, especially France'; some even drew parallels between the Peace of Westphalia and the Treaty of Versailles.[25] But notwithstanding a tendency to exaggerate the results, the impact of the gruesome conflict cannot be underestimated, and many works have tried to come to terms with its effects. These range from Adalbert Stifter's 1842 novelle *Der Hochwald* and Conrad Ferdinand Meyer's 1882 *Gustav Adolf's Page* to Heinrich Laube's nine-volume novel *Der deutsche Krieg* (The German War), completed in 1866. Schiller wrote a *History of the Thirty Years War* in 1789 and his tragedy *Wallenstein* (1799) was one of his greatest works. Ricarda Huch's *Der grosse Krieg in Deutschland* (published in 1914) and *Wallenstein* (published in 1915) were praised by Thomas Mann, and modern German perceptions of the war were greatly influenced by Gustav Freytag's *Bilder aus der deutschen Vergangenheit* (Pictures from German History), published in 1859. But the impact of the war is brought to life most vividly in the works of those who experienced it at first hand; indeed, along with the music of composers like Michael Praetorius and Heinrich Schütz, Johann Jakob Froberger and Johannes Crüger in Berlin, literature was one of the few art forms to flourish in Germany during those ghastly decades.

The eyewitness accounts make grim reading. Johann Michael Moscerosch, who fought with the Swedish army and very nearly died of starvation during the war, wrote of the effect of war in his 1643 *Adventurers of Philander of Sittewald*. Two of the most celebrated poets of the day, Martin Opitz (who died of the plague in 1639) and Paul Fleming, wrote of the longing for peace. Like the other two Andreas Gryphius, born in Glogau in 1616, was forced to flee to Holland for much of the war, but his *Tränen des Vaterlands anno 1636* remains one of the most moving descriptions of the devastation caused by the conflict: in it he describes the misery of the people with their towns in flames, the strong maimed, the virgins raped, the streets running with blood and everywhere 'Fire, plague and death oppress the heart and soul'. His heart-wrenching *Epitaph on Mariana Gryphius* describes how his infant was killed: 'Born during the flight, surrounded with swords and conflagration, almost stifled in the smoke . . . I pressed forward to the light when the furious fire had consumed my country; I looked upon this world and soon said farewell to it, for in one day all the dread of the world came upon me.'[26] Soldier poets like Caspar Stieler and Georg Greflinger brought the coarse scenes of battle to life; Greflinger wrote the sombre *Der deutschen dreissigjähriger Krieg* (The German Thirty Years War) in 1657 while Stieler wrote priapic pornographic works glorifying male power under the pseudonym Filidor der Dorfferer, pieces which were clearly influenced by his experiences as a soldier. In *Leave the Dead in Peace* he warns the soldier Filidor that his lover will 'crack jokes over your coffin and sing, whoop and caper on your grave . . . she will even batter your rotting bones herself'. But he promises to torment her, to frighten her with 'thumping and bumping' so that if bruises are found on her in the morning, 'say that I have done it as my revenge.'[27] During the war itself thousands of tasteless, smutty and gruesome illustrated pamphlets were produced by the respective armies to frighten the inhabitants of local towns and to justify their own crude behaviour, and some of these survive.[28]

Above all the war resulted in the single most important German work of the seventeenth century, *Der abenteuerliche Simplicissimus Teutsch*, translated as *Simplicius Simplicissimus*, by Hans (or Johann) Grimmelshausen. He was born in Gelnhausen, Hesse, in 1622 but in 1635 Hessian and Croat soldiers ransacked his village. They kidnapped him and he was forced to spend the next fourteen years first as a boy soldier then as a musketeer; he eventually served in a number of regiments, only turning to writing in the last decade of his life. *Simplicius Simplicissimus*, first published in 1669, is a semi-autobiographical account of the war and is the most important of his works. The main character recounts how his family's farm is destroyed, how the inhabitants of his village are tortured or raped, how he is carried off by Croat soldiers, falls into Swedish captivity and ends the war serving under the Protestant forces. Its impact influenced many later German writers; nearly three centuries later Bertolt Brecht based his play *Mother Courage* on Grimmelshausen's character Landstörzerin Courasche, a woman who spent her life trailing behind Protestant troops on their campaigns through Sweden, Poland and Germany, and whose very existence had become entirely dependent on the continuation of the war.[29]

Within a decade of the beginning of the conflict the small mercantile town of Berlin had been reduced to a shadow of its former self. Much of it had been destroyed by fire; the city was stripped of anything of value, the once proud citizens scratched out a meagre existence in the ruins, the roads were in terrible shape, the Spree was so clogged up it was unfit for trading vessels, agriculture was in a dire state and the Schloss was so badly damaged that it had to be propped up with wooden slats. Much had been destroyed; the artist-historian Joachim von Sandrart, who had survived the war, wrote that 'Queen Germania saw her palaces and churches decorated with magnificent pictures go up in flames time and again, whilst her eyes were so blinded by smoke and tears that she no longer had the power or will to attend to art.'[30] The population of Berlin had plummeted from over 14,000 to a mere 6,000. It seemed for a time that the elector of Brandenburg would lose his title; as early as 1630 he had sent a plaintive letter to Vienna declaring, 'No one knows how long I shall remain Elector and master in my own land.' Berlin seemed destined to become little more than a ghost town. Then, suddenly, the Elector George William died. His successor would prove to be one of the most remarkable leaders in Berlin history; a man determined to ensure that war would never again rule his destiny. It was he who dragged Berlin from the wreckage and set it on its way to becoming the capital of Prussia. His name was Frederick William, and he came to be known as the 'Great Elector'.

Frederick William was a product of the Thirty Years War. Born in 1620, four years after the outbreak of war, Frederick William had spent many years in the safety of The Hague as a young man, where his Calvinism was reaffirmed along with its austerity and devotion to duty. Clever, dignified and utterly practical, he was well prepared to take power when his weak father died in December 1640. His greatest wish was to see the creation of a strong, independent state which would never again be at the mercy of marauding armies or dependent on the patronage of other rulers. It was he who would first brand Berlin with the mark of austerity, militarism, religious tolerance, devotion to duty and an undue respect for authority for which it became famous; it was he who ushered in the beginning of the rise of Prussia.

Frederick William had much to do. The war still raged around him, his territory was wrecked, his people desperate. The Mark was occupied by Swedish troops, Berlin was a ruin, his own slovenly army lived by moving from town to town and was as hated as the foreign troops. The elector was forced to remain in Königsberg as the Berlin Schloss was uninhabitable. If Frederick William was to bring peace to his territory his first move must be to secure an agreement between Brandenburg and the Swedes and he sent ambassadors to Stockholm to ask for a suspension of hostilities. By May 1641 they had agreed on terms; by October Brandenburg and Sweden had divided Pomerania while Stettin went to Sweden in return for a favourable settlement for Prussia of the Cleves-Jülich lands. With the Swedish flank secured Frederick William formed an alliance with the House of Orange in order to gain Dutch support. In 1643 he felt confident enough to move back to Berlin.

The desire for peace spread through Europe: Queen Christina of Sweden encouraged the French to negotiate and other powers followed suit – often out of sheer exhaustion and in the realization that the military capacity for total victory was beyond the grasp of any one country.[31] Talks continued between the delegates of 109 states from 1643 to 1648, although fighting continued throughout – as the Catholic Prior Adami of Murrhart put it, 'In winter we negotiate, in summer we fight.' The people of Europe were desperate for peace; a Swabian family put in their diary of 1647, 'They say that the terrible war is now over. But there is still no sign of a peace. Everywhere there is envy, hatred and greed: that's what the war has taught us . . . We live like animals, eating bark and grass. No one could have imagined that anything like this would happen to us. Many say that there is no God.'[32] Nevertheless progress was made and after much haggling an agreement was reached. Rumours of a settlement spread until on 24 October 1648, after thirty years of misery and months of negotiation, the European powers signed the Peace of Westphalia to an outpouring of rejoicing in the Mark Brandenburg. The music composed for the peace included some of the most powerful Lutheran hymns ever written, including Justus Schotel's extraordinary *Friedens Sieg*.

The peace was an uneasy one. War had exacerbated the rivalry between France and Spain, between Richelieu and the Habsburgs, between the king of Sweden and the Dutch, between the Russian tsar and the Poles, and between the dozens of German princes and electors. But the peace had also resulted in compromises between Protestants and Catholics, and between the Holy Roman Emperor and individual German princes. It was the latter which would prove so advantageous to the young elector of Brandenburg. The war had weakened the Holy Roman Empire and strengthened regional leaders, including the electors of Bohemia, Saxony, Hanover and the young Frederick William of Brandenburg, who was determined to take advantage of the power vacuum in Europe. Ironically it was France which opened the way for the ambitious German elector. By shattering Austrian might France had laid the foundations for the creation of a new power in Germany – a 'third power' to curb both Austria and Sweden. Frederick William was happy to fill the gap. To his relief many rival German princes chose this moment of peace to withdraw from politics and to put their energies and their money into prestigious projects like palaces and art collections and parties. Their courts expanded exponentially and were paid for by their subjects; the minister in Berlin, Count Manteuffel, said of these petty princes that despite their often dubious birth 'one would think they were put on earth to ride roughshod over their fellow men'.[33] They also created some of the most beautiful court-cities in Europe.

Frederick William was different. While his rivals amused themselves the hard-headed elector of Brandenburg set about consolidating his territory. In 1657 he signed the Peace of Wehlau and in 1660 the Peace of Oliva, which marked the end of the Swedish–Polish war.[34] Those in the eastern provinces who refused to obey him were punished: Colonel von Kalckstein, who, like many Junkers, preferred to ally himself with the more easy-going Polish nobility, was executed; the rest were forced to bow to Berlin. The elector of Brandenburg now ruled over a new entity which would eventually be referred to by a single name: Prussia.

In the nineteenth century historians of the Prussian school, including Sybel and Treitschke, were determined to show that the rise of their state was 'inevitable'; that it had been 'destined' to become the force which would eventually unite Germany, that it was a state so graced with natural virtues that it was superior to all others. But there was very little to suggest that seventeenth-century Prussia or its capital Berlin would ever be much more than a poor outpost on the fringes of the German-speaking lands. Prussia had little on which to build. It had no glorious history, it did not consist of a single ethnic group nor did its peoples speak a single language; its disparate bits of land were scattered from the Rhine to the Niemen, making it seem ill defined and incoherent. The land itself was impoverished and underpopulated, the soil was generally poor and its showpiece, Berlin, was more like a dirty provincial village than a capital city. Prussia and Berlin became powerful not because of 'natural forces' but through the ambition, hard work, determination, luck and obsession with military and economic might of a series of extraordinary rulers who were determined to increase the power and prestige of their upstart state.

The Hohenzollerns were the luckiest of the ruling families of seventeenth- and eighteenth-century Europe. Of all the great houses theirs was the only one to produce a succession of four healthy male heirs, none of whom was inept or deranged. Three were truly outstanding monarchs. This enviable continuity began with Frederick William in 1640, extended to the first king in Prussia, Frederick I, to his son Frederick William II, the 'Soldier King', and finally to Frederick the Great, who died in 1786. Three dedicated themselves entirely to building a strong state through the improvement of the economy and the creation of a sound administration and bureaucracy and, above all, of an army. The pattern began with Frederick William. Immediately after securing his place in Europe he turned his attention to making

Prussia stable and prosperous, and his reforms would become legendary.

He faced an enormous task. Berlin was bankrupt and the last Swedish troops evacuated the Mark Brandenburg only in 1650, leaving farms, hamlets and villages in ruin. Two-thirds of homes in the Mark were destroyed, as were nine-tenths of the cattle and livestock; the population of Neubrandenburg was reduced by half; Altmark towns like Salzwedel and Gardelegen had lost a third of their populations, Stendal and Seehausen lost over half, Werben and Osterburg two-thirds.[35] General Montaigne said, 'I would not have believed a land could have been so despoiled had I not seen it with my own eyes.' In terms of everything from culture to commerce Berlin lagged well behind a Paris now rising to greatness under the Sun King, Louis XIV.[36]

Any notion of reconstruction was made more difficult by the fact that pre-war commerce had been so badly damaged; the commercial middle classes had been decimated and trade had virtually ceased. In 1621 200 ships had sailed across the sound at East Friesland; by the last decade of the war it had dropped to ten ships per year.[37] Germany was now landlocked as foreign powers controlled the mouths of its rivers. The Hanseatic League, which had done so much to bolster the Berlin economy, was disintegrating and Berliners had to deal with the loss of traditional markets in Italy and east Central Europe as the English and Dutch increased their trade in the west. Powerful medieval towns and old commercial centres like Lübeck and Nuremberg, which had traded with Berlin, were now overshadowed by princely residences like Mannheim and Karlsruhe.

In the end, however, Berlin was one of the few towns to succeed in making the shift from a medieval commercial centre to a residence city. The remaining rights of the townspeople were systematically crushed but this time they did not resist. The war had brought death and misery and by the time it was over Berliners were willing to submit to any authority strong enough to prevent a similar conflict. Frederick William consciously played on their fears by using the threat of renewed war to increase his control over the estates. In this sense his rule marks the final collapse of Berliners' independent civic power and the beginning of their often excessive devotion to authority. The Hohenzollern rulers brought peace and prosperity to their lands but it was this very success which helped to convince the people that their interests were better served by benevolent paternalism from above than by the fight for political rights; later, when the French or the English or the Americans agitated for real political power and representation Berliners would be content to live as they had for centuries – under the all-powerful, all-knowing hand of a 'great leader'. In their eyes it was the Hohenzollerns who had turned their small, dusty, uninspiring state into a world leader and who had transformed their city from a

desolate backwater into a capital to be reckoned with; surely it would be
ungrateful not to follow their princes without question. This passivity was
relatively harmless under the eighteenth-century benevolent despots, but it
ultimately inhibited political change and established a precedent of obedience
and unquestioning loyalty which lasted well into the twentieth century – with
disastrous consequences. Berlin would grow powerful in the eighteenth century
but its people would remain politically unsophisticated for centuries to come.

Frederick William's solutions for the internal reforms of his lands were
bold, and it is not difficult to understand why he became a heroic figure in
the minds of his subjects. Using his own money he built a canal with eleven
locks to link the Oder and Elbe rivers, a vast project completed in 1669. He
ripped down the old medieval city wall in Berlin, regulated the flow of the
Spree and created docking facilities and a crane, attracting east–west inland
trade between Hamburg and the Low Countries through to Bohemia, Silesia,
Saxony and Poland. He built a sea-going fleet and a sugar refinery in Berlin,
hoping to turn the city into the distribution centre of colonial products to
Brandenburg, Prussia and eastern Europe, although it ultimately failed to
compete with England, France and the Netherlands. The recovery of his lands
was impeded by a severe labour shortage so, rather like his predecessor Albert
the Bear, he invited people to settle there. Many had fled religious persecution
from other parts of Europe, and Berlin became a city of refuge.

Frederick William was selective about whom he invited to Prussia, consciously choosing settlers who would bring money, expertise and skills, including Danes, Swedes, Jews, French and Scotsmen, Germans and Bohemians; by
1725 one-fifth of the population in Brandenburg had been born abroad. Berlin
was transformed by the energy and skills of the immigrants. Artisans from
Liège introduced the manufacture of weapons and armaments to the backward
town; the Walloons cultivated the new plant called tobacco; Dutchmen drained
marshland and their compatriot Benjamin Raule created a college of commerce
in Berlin; the great painter Michael Willmann travelled to Berlin in 1660; and
the influence of Rubens, Rembrandt, Ruisdael and Van Dyck reached Berlin
around the same time. A limited number of protected Jews were allowed into
the city shortly after the completion of the canal in 1669 and brought commercial contracts and business skill to the trade in luxury goods from silk and
horses to furniture, chocolate, coffee, tea, snuff and tobacco. Calvinists came
from Silesia, Scotland, Denmark and Sweden, attracted by promises of partial
self-government, a separate judicial system and by economic privileges including tax relief. But by far the largest group of refugees were the Huguenots,
the Calvinists who fled in the face of a new wave of religious persecution in
France.

In 1598 the French had passed the Edict of Nantes allowing the French

Protestants, the Huguenots, freedom of conscience, limited freedom of worship and civil status. After 1661, however, the truce began to break down. Protestants were gradually excluded from the professions and the law courts and synods were curtailed. Finally, in 1685, Louis XIV banned all forms of public worship, ordered the destruction of Protestant churches and had the ministers expelled. A seventeenth-century engraving in the Bibliothèque Nationale in Paris depicts *Louis the Great in Triumph over the Heretics*: the king stands in a wig and toga, his right foot on the head of a Huguenot, his left stamping on the pages of the New Testament from between whose pages a serpent emerges. The woodcut glorified the revocation of the Edict of Nantes, which forced over 400,000 French Huguenots from their homes. Many fled to England or to Switzerland, and it was at this point that Frederick William, the Great Elector, issued the 1685 Edict of Potsdam inviting any of the refugees to Prussia. Over 20,000 came to the state and over 6,000 settled in Berlin.

By 1687 20 per cent of the population were Huguenots, making Berlin seem more like a French than a German town. They brought over 3,000 thalers per person to the province and contributed to Brandenburg's average capital inflow of around 6 million thalers, but even more important was their contribution to Berlin industry; without them Berlin might well have remained poor and backward like many of its erstwhile rivals. It was they who made the woollen industry the most important of Brandenburg's native products by the end of the century, and it was they who improved cotton weaving with new inventions and with the importation of raw materials from as far as the Balkans and the West Indies. The French contribution was widely recognized at the time, prompting the Great Elector's grandson Frederick William to comment:

> the French are very industrious people who have made the towns in our country capable of producing manufactured goods, for fifty years ago no fine cloths, stockings, crepe, velvet or woollen goods were manufactured here, and we had to import these from England, France, the Netherlands, now our lands export considerable quantities all over Germany.[38]

The invitation to the refugees was one of the high points of Berlin history and has ever since been used to demonstrate Berlin's credentials as a city of tolerance and freedom. Nevertheless this tolerance was not without ulterior motives. The Great Elector was genuinely concerned to protect Protestants in Europe, but the Edict of Potsdam was also motivated by both international and local politics. In 1670 Prussia had cemented an alliance with France; fifteen years later it was souring, not least because the elector was furious that Louis XIV had meddled in his Baltic policy against Sweden and feared that the French were planning an alliance with the new English Catholic king James

II.[39] The French attack on the Huguenots and his subsequent invitation to the refugees gave him an excuse to signal his displeasure to the French king. The edict also had important repercussions closer to home.

The Great Elector had long been troubled by the entrenched Lutheranism in Berlin and elsewhere and longed to convert the population to Calvinism. It was not an easy task. The conflict between Calvinists and Lutherans, which was based on doctrinal disagreements on the Lord's supper and predestination, had wreaked havoc in many parts of Germany after the Reformation, when rulers from Saxony, Brandenburg, the Palatinate and elsewhere had lurched from Lutheranism to Calvinism. The two groups of clergy detested one another even more than they loathed the Catholics. The Lutheran Matthias Hoë von Hoënegg reflected this view in his 1601 pamphlet entitled *A solid, just and orthodox detestation of Papists and Calvinists*, which was followed in 1620 by *A weighty (and in these dangerous times very necessary) discussion of whether and why it is better to have conformity with the Catholics . . . than with the Calvinists*.[40] Fights over religious succession were often bitter; a regent in the Palatinate was so desperate to ensure the province remained Calvinist that he locked the young Lutheran successor away in a lonely convent and tried to convert him; in Baden the regent stole his nephew from his dead brother's wife and forced him to adopt his own religion. Berlin was at the centre of a similar conflict. The first of the Calvinist electors was Johann Sigismund, who had converted in 1613, and his successors remained faithful, swearing, 'I am a Calvinist and with God's help I shall die one.' Berliners, however, remained devout Lutherans and were violently opposed to change. When the Great Elector took power the only Calvinist institutions in Berlin were the court and the cathedral, and when the first Calvinist preacher entered the city a Lutheran mob broke into his house, beat him up and stole everything but his green underwear – in which he was forced to preach the following Sunday. Thereafter the few Calvinists in Berlin were regularly attacked in the streets.[41] If the elector could not convert Berliners peacefully he could do so by force of numbers, which could be bolstered by the refugees. As a result, when war broke out in Europe in 1672 and Catholic governments began to attack the entire Protestant community he invited them to Berlin, not only from France but also from the Palatinate, the upper Rhine and from Habsburg lands. They changed the religious balance in Berlin, and did so without bloodshed.

The townspeople were suspicious and even hostile to the large number of Calvinist refugees who suddenly appeared in their midst. The French spoke a strange language, wore strange clothing and followed a different religion; worse still, they were given tax breaks and financial assistance funded by the local population through forced collections like that of 20 January 1686, when 'each and every citizen' had to contribute to a fund of 14,000 thalers for the refugees.[42] Despite later claims of 'tolerance' these Berliners did not welcome the newcomers with open arms; Muret decried the '*Gehässigkeit*', the hateful behaviour of Berlin Lutherans towards the French, and it took generations for them to be accepted.[43] In the end, however, the Huguenots became an integral part of the city. By 1690 the institutional autonomy of the Lutheran Church had crumbled and Calvinism had become the official religion in Berlin.

By the eighteenth century 'tolerance' had come to mean the freedom to practise religion without the kind of persecution seen in many parts of Europe at the time. This extended to many groups, including the Jews. Like other cities of the *ancien régime* Berlin was far from allowing complete emancipation of Jews but it was more liberal than many in Europe; it did not have a ghetto and had ceased to persecute and expel Jews.[44] The Great Elector had invited a small number of 'protected Jews' into Brandenburg in 1650 and on 21 May 1671 issued an edict on the 'Admission of Fifty Families of Protected Jews', who were permitted to 'keep open stalls and booths, to sell cloths and similar wares . . . to deal in new and old clothes, and further, to slaughter in their houses and to sell what is above their needs or forbidden to them by their religion, and finally to seek their subsistence in any place where they live'. The Jews were not permitted to have synagogues but could meet in one of their own houses as long as they conducted ceremonies 'without giving offence to Christians'.[45] The electoral edict of 1671 attracted many more families to Prussia from Poland and the Habsburg lands; wealthy Jewish families who had been expelled from Vienna in 1670 came to the city and formed the foundation of what was to become Berlin's sophisticated German-Jewish sub-culture.[46] Frederick the Great would improve their situation further in 1750 through the 'Revised General Privilege and Regulation for the Jews in the Kingdom of Prussia', under which they were given complete control of their own schools, synagogues and cemeteries and were to be tried in accordance with the tenets of Jewish law. Berlin was not tolerant in the twentieth-century sense but it became the most permissive of all Prussian towns and was, for a time, one of the most open-minded in Europe.[47] Even so, some religions were excluded until the reign of Frederick the Great: in the Brandenburg Recess of 1653 Frederick William announced he would 'not permit the practice of their religion, in public or private, to Papists, Arrians, Photinians, Weigalians, Anabaptists, and Minists'. He emphasized that his successors 'must not tolerate Jesuits in your lands. They are devils who are capable of much evil and intrigue against you and the whole community'.[48] Catholics continued to suffer under intolerant laws until well into the eighteenth century and even 'protected Jews' were subject to myriad regulations, special taxes and discrimination.

Irrespective of their shortcomings the Great Elector's innovative policies were highly successful in creating a prosperous state out of the devastation of the Thirty Years War. The influx of skilled and talented refugees fired the Berlin economy and the city began to flourish. Increased trade and industry meant more revenue for the state, and to assist in administration and tax collection Frederick William created the General Kriegskommissariat (War Commission), a powerful new agency based on the French and Dutch models which formed the basis of a unified central state apparatus. It was the tentative beginning of Berlin's role as the administrative centre of Prussia. In 1667 he introduced a detailed excise tax on virtually every product: home distilled brandy cost 6 groschen per quart, Rhenish and Polish brandy cost 9 groschen per quart, a fattened hog cost 3 groschen, a ton of salt 4. The revenue generated was ploughed back into the most distinctive feature of the new state, the army.

It had been clear from the beginning of his reign that Frederick William had intended to create a strong army but few had realized the extent of his plan. His army was not to be a mere fighting force; it was set to become the very foundation, the very essence of the Prussian state. The army would change Berlin for ever, influencing everything from its layout and architecture to its culture, its economy and its spirit. In the short term it helped to protect Prussia and made it an important power in European affairs. In the long term, the obsession with the military would prove disastrous.

In his *Political Testament* Frederick William wrote: 'A ruler is of no consideration if he does not have adequate means and forces of his own; that alone has made me – thank God for it – a force to be reckoned with.'[49] The experience of the Thirty Years War had taught him that although alliances were useful they could not be relied upon and it was this which determined his military policy. Unlike other German princes Frederick William had not disbanded his troops after the Peace of Westphalia but had quickly added to his forces. The growth of the military was spectacular: at the end of the Thirty Years War Frederick William had an army of a mere 2,000 poorly trained, undisciplined men, but he was determined to change this. Berlin became a garrison city in 1657 and that year Prussia defeated the Swedes at Fehrbellin, making Brandenburg the strongest German state after Austria. The elector spent 70,000 thalers on the fortification of Berlin alone, building an eight-metre-high wall complete with thirteen bastions around the city. Parade grounds and guard houses began to appear everywhere and Berlin took on the arid militaristic atmosphere which would soon give it the reputation of the 'Sparta of the North'. The recruitment and generous financing brought results: when the Great Elector died the army consisted of 30,000 men. Suddenly, Berlin ruled over one of the largest forces in Europe.[50]

Frederick William died in 1688. He had not achieved the power or prestige of contemporaries like Cromwell or Richelieu but his accomplishments were extraordinary. He had raised his lands above the dismal legacy of the Thirty

Years War and created the foundations of a strong, successful Prussian state. His acceptance of religious refugees and his innovative approach to industry had made Berlin prosper, while his determination to create a strong army had made it an important European power.

After the death of the Great Elector his son Frederick III, the least impressive of the four rulers, took the throne. He had an immediate impact on the city. The new elector was tired of the obsession with fiscal policy and the army and reacted against everything his father had stood for. He was more concerned with questions of status and spent money on useless wars which he had not started and could not influence while splashing out on a grandiose life of luxury. He gave Berlin a short-lived air of decadence. Politically, Frederick's reign was unremarkable. His only real accomplishment was to use his father's army to blackmail the Holy Roman Emperor into giving him a royal title; the emperor was in desperate need of Brandenburg's military support in the War of the Spanish Succession and as a reward for a consignment of Prussian troops he elevated the elector of Brandenburg to 'King in Prussia'.[51] He would henceforth be known as King Frederick I.

Frederick was delighted with his promotion and was determined to make his coronation a European spectacle. Hundreds of carriages wound their way to Königsberg, and jewels and medals glinted in the sun as he was proclaimed king; this was followed by lavish celebrations in Berlin which were a mere foretaste of what was to come later in his reign. The new king continued to raise revenue by hiring out his army: the English and Dutch paid sizeable subsidies of around 1.5 million thalers to maintain 31,000 of his troops at war in Italy and in the Low Countries, and in all he managed to net around 14 million thalers in this way. Unlike his father, however, he did not use the money to increase his military or economic strength but poured it into the creation of a fabulous baroque court in Berlin. His personal expenditure was staggering. In the years 1705–10 he spent around 5.3 million thalers a year, with over 600,000 on personal expenses; in 1688, the year of his father's death, more than half of all state expenditure went on luxuries at the Berlin court. An indication of the massive increase in spending is recorded in the excise taxes paid by Berlin Jews, who were the primary traders of luxury goods. In 1696 they paid 8,614 thalers in tax; by 1705 it had reached a massive 117,437 thalers.[52] The large amount of money in circulation in Berlin gave it the reputation of a fortune-seeker's paradise, attracting adventurers and opportunists from throughout Europe, and the population raced from a low of 4,000 in the war years to 55,000 by 1710.[53] For the first time the city shook off its aura of gloom and began to emerge from years of cultural isolation.

The Great Elector had done relatively little to revive the culture of the city. His obsession with strict Calvinism had brought improvements to some aspects of life: there was, for example, a rise in literacy as all members of the Church were expected to be able to read before confirmation and hence before marriage; he had founded a library and a number of schools in the city. But his concentration on the military and the economy combined with strict religious beliefs had kept Berlin culturally backward. The popular recreation of dancing had been banned as it was said to lead to debauchery; street singing of 'smutty songs' had not been permitted; theatres and taverns had been closed as they led to 'indecency'; and no recreational activities had been permitted on Sunday. The comparison between Berlin and the rest of Europe was startling and the city had nothing to compare at a time when Italy had already produced Michelangelo, Bernini and Corelli, when Holland had Rembrandt and Vermeer, and Flanders Rubens and Van Dyck, when Spain had El Greco and Velázquez, England Purcell, Milton and Christopher Wren, and when the France of Racine and Poussin revolved around Versailles. It had remained distant from the artistic and philosophical debates of the age and isolated from those intellectuals from Poland to Scotland who had already begun to debate the works of Descartes, Hobbes, Galileo and Kepler; the jurist Samuel von Pufendorf had been enticed to Berlin only in 1688, the year of the elector's death. The new king was embarrassed by the cultural shortcomings of his capital and, with his consort the Hanoverian princess Sophie Charlotte, bankrupted Berlin in an attempt to make it comparable to other European cities.

One of his first important projects was the creation in 1696 of the Academy of Arts in Berlin, followed by the Academy of Sciences in 1700. The latter, which brought Leibniz to Berlin, was one of the city's first intellectual coups. Leibniz, along with the court chaplain, Jablonski, had long been interested in founding a learned society in Germany for men interested in the study of rational science, but many provincial princes had been suspicious of these ideas. It was the consort Sophie Charlotte who gave Leibniz the chance to create a society which would allow men to 'strive towards the development, improvement, complete understanding and correct application of beneficial studies, the sciences and the arts, useful information, and anything else that is relevant'.[54] Like the Academy of Arts it was based on the French model and became the third Academy of Sciences in Europe. There were eighty members, including the astronomer Gottfried Kirch, the mathematician Jean Bernoulli, and the architect Andreas Schlüter. A small observatory was constructed and in 1710 the first Berlin scientific journal, the *Miscellanea Berolinensia*, was published.

Sophie Charlotte contributed to the cultural life of the city in other ways, dedicating her court at the splendid new palace of Charlottenburg to artistic and intellectual life. The princess was influenced by those elements in Pietism which emphasized religious tolerance, personal rebirth and intellectual curiosity; she invited not only Leibniz but a host of European thinkers to the palace, including the English free-thinker John Toland, author of *Christianity Not Mysterious*. For his part, Toland praised Berlin as a city of peaceful tolerance between communities and a place of 'happy prosperity'. The queen brought Italian music and opera to the court with performances of Alessandro Scarlatti, Corelli, Giovanni Buononcini and even the young Telemann.[55] Frederick also encouraged advances in health care: the College of Medicine was founded in 1685 and the Charité-Hospital, initially started for plague victims in 1710, became a centre of medical excellence. In 1713 a vast circular operating theatre was built with rows of benches and a wooden table recessed in the centre, complete with a collection of instruments, jars of preserved organs and various human skeletons propped up on stands.

Frederick I was now king in Prussia and he was determined to make his residence look like a royal capital. He had much to do. His predecessor had made some minor changes to Berlin, creating Dorotheenstadt and Friedrichstadt for Huguenot settlers, hiring Nering to make small alterations to the old palace, rebuilding the wooden Lange Brücke in stone in 1695, planting the first small avenue of trees which eventually became Unter den Linden, and laying out the Tiergarten as a hunting ground. Nevertheless it was Frederick I who gave Berlin its first grand buildings. When he came to power Europe was steeped in the exuberance of the high baroque inspired by the fabulous Italian palaces and churches and fountains designed by Bernini and Borromini, and by the more correctly classical French style reflected in Salomon de Brosse's Luxembourg Palace in Paris, Le Vau's Institut de France and by the Palace of Versailles. Baroque had originated in the Counter-Reformation as an attempt by the Roman Catholic Church to attract people back through the joy and pageantry of its buildings, and the results were delightful. The movement in the architecture was breathtaking, and the curvaceous spires and graceful windows and ornate pastel-coloured facades the product of sheer exuberance; the drama of the chiaroscuro, the gilt and friezes and barrel-vaulted ceilings dripping with cherubs and stylized tendrils and branches came to grace some of the most glorious buildings of Europe. The style was brought to Catholic Germany by the Jesuits, but although villages and hillsides in Catholic Bavaria and Swabia are dotted with dozens of churches in this style sober Protestant northern Germany was less receptive; Berlin got a whiff of the baroque during the reign of Frederick I through the work of a handful of architects and artists invited to the city. The most important were Jean de Bodt, Johann Friedrich Eosander, Arnold Nering and, above all, the architect and sculptor Andreas Schlüter.

Schlüter was born in Danzig but soon moved to Warsaw, where he worked on a number of important commissions, including the Krasiński and Wilanow palaces. In 1694 he moved to Berlin and the following year began work on the Royal Palace, which was completed in 1707. It was ripped down by the East Germans in 1950 and replaced by the asbestos-ridden modernist disaster, the Palast der Republik.[56] Sadly, little else of Schlüter's work survived the war, although a hint of his mastery can be seen in the grand equestrian statue of the Elector Frederick William I, which now stands before the Charlottenburg Palace. The work is based on the Roman model of Marcus Aurelius in the Capitol in Rome and, although derivative, projects vigour and power in its own right. His other surviving Berlin masterpiece is the Arsenal on Unter den Linden, a long elegant building best known for the twenty-two dramatic sculptures of heads of dying warriors with their beautifully carved and emotive faces: one throws his bearded head back and cries out in agony, another bites his lower lip and grimaces in terrible pain, another lies dying with his proud, noble face tilted to one side in so realistic a pose that one feels compelled to reach out to touch the furrowed brow.

The king also commissioned other important Berlin landmarks; he had Nering build Charlottenburg Palace; he built Monbijou Palace and commissioned homes for the military as well as a number of churches.[57] Little survives; the only baroque church still standing in Berlin was commissioned for Spandau in 1712 by Sophie Luise, and its pretty butter-yellow walls and elegant dome still bring a touch of Bavaria to the northern capital.[58] The king continued to invest in Berlin, draining land on the outskirts of the city and building new suburbs. He added to the new development north of the Lindenallee in Dorotheenstadt, and in 1709 joined the districts of Berlin, Cölln, Friedrichswerder, Dorotheenstadt and Friedrichstadt under a single municipal government, forming the nucleus of the city which would become modern Berlin.

Frederick brought something of the culture of Europe to the city, but the cost was very high for a small state and did little to benefit the lives of ordinary people in Prussia. The new buildings were beautiful but they still stood amidst rubble left over from the Thirty Years War and there was an extreme contrast between the exuberant life at court, with its ballets, fashionable clothes and masked balls, and the poverty to be found in the streets. Visitors were appalled at the number of prostitutes and beggars in Berlin; Lady Mary Wortley Montagu described the kind of poverty to be found amongst the glamour of the residence city as 'a sort of shabby finery' with 'a number of dirty people ... narrow nasty streets out of repair, wretchedly thin of inhabitants, and over half of the common sort asking for alms ... How different from England!'[59] Most of the streets of Berlin remained unpaved and filthy and housing was pitiful. Even its economic wealth was illusory; most of the luxury goods were imported and did more to support craftsmen in France, Saxony and the Dutch republic than in Berlin. For most residents life was squalid and dangerous. Once again, however, Berlin was about to be transformed.

The city's political history has always been one of extremes, and the eighteenth century was no exception. The brief flowering of the baroque and the dazzling life of the Berlin court ended abruptly in 1713 with the death of Frederick I. No sooner had the fun-loving and creative king died than Berlin reverted to its tough militaristic life. The change was brought about by the new king's determination to reverse his father's excesses and to create a centre of military power. The city had entered the harsh era of Frederick William I, the Soldier King.[60]

Frederick William saw nothing but waste and vanity in his father's palaces and art collections. The new king took his austere reformed Pietism very seriously, living by its code of hard work, puritanical restraint, devotion to duty, self-sacrifice and austerity. He gave his father a luxurious funeral but then set about dismantling the court and erasing his memory. Everything went – the silk bedclothes and velvet curtains were replaced by rough cloth; furniture, jewels and carriages were sold; the orders for twenty-course dinners, wigs, silk stockings, fans, pearls, delicate gloves and pretty shoes were cancelled, and decadence was banished in favour of efficiency, cleanliness and hard work. The dismantling did not end with the court. The paintings and operas of western Europe baffled the new king and architecture bored him. The construction of the capricious baroque buildings was halted; a court jester was appointed to succeed Leibniz as president of the Berlin Academy as science was now considered 'empty formal garbage'; university lecturers were 'not even good for sentry duty' and intellectuals were referred to as 'wastrels' or 'dog food' and were banned from court.[61] Instead of lavish feasts the new king preferred simple food served on a rough wooden table. He wrote little in his own language but detested French and spoke no other foreign languages. At a time when Pöppelmann and Permoser were putting the finishing touches to the Zwinger Palace in Dresden and at a time when St Petersburg was rising out of the muck at the mouth of the Neva, construction in Berlin ceased and the city fell back into cultural darkness. It was whispered that the people there had become the most enslaved of Europe, 'worse, even, than Russia'. Frederick William had other priorities. Culture was unimportant; instead he wanted to make Prussia into one of the most powerful economic and military states in the world.

When Frederick William took power Berlin was bankrupt, and the king's first step was to begin a concerted drive to impose central control over administration, finances and industry. Local power was to be crushed and all towns, including Berlin, were to be administered by royal appointees and their budgets treated as part of the royal domain. New and detested tax commissars took control of the city's administration. In 1723 the king merged the old General War Commissariat and the General Finance Directory to create a new General Directory, which became a clearly defined administrative body whose fundamental aim was to account for every penny spent in Prussia both at the provincial and central level.[52] Frederick William took personal control over the new civil service, running it like a giant military machine. His ministers sent him detailed reports covering every aspect of their work; those who displeased him were fired. The omnipresent corruption, bribery and embezzlement which had characterized his father's government were stamped out and his employees began to develop the selfless devotion to duty which would come to characterize the Prussian civil service.

Frederick William was a fanatic when it came to controlling the lives of Berliners. State employees were told what to wear, what time to appear for work, when and what they should eat; if someone contradicted his orders he treated them to a crack across the face with his cane. He believed it was his duty to ensure that Berliners did not succumb to the sins of gluttony or sloth and insisted that they spend all their waking hours at work. He regularly sent spies to patrol the streets and, disguising himself as a commoner, walked through the city attacking those who were 'idle', breaking teeth and noses in the process. Market women and shopkeepers were expected to knit or sew when there were no customers around; street cleaners and stable boys were punished if they were found loafing; washerwomen and nurses were not to waste time gossiping.

His efforts to 'clean up the streets' were also motivated by his devotion to work. The beggars, vagabonds and prostitutes who had lived in Berlin under his father were rounded up by the Berlin police and, in keeping with the Pietist belief that nobody should receive charity for nothing, were put in workhouses where they were expected to spin wool; even children in orphanages were forced to work after a long morning of religious education. Ironically Frederick William managed to reduce the number of homeless in the city: they preferred to go elsewhere rather than face the strict regime in his Pietist workhouses. The work ethic affected everyone; when Berlin held its last witch trial in 1727 the 'guilty' Dorothea Steffin was not burned at the stake as was the custom, but was imprisoned in Spandau fortress to spend the rest of her life weaving and spinning.[63] The obsession with work made Berlin a sober, disciplined and unpleasant place. Berliners detested the new rules and regulations which governed their lives and organized watchmen to warn them if the king or one of his spies was approaching so that they could hide. Nevertheless the reforms did bring prosperity and Berlin became the prime beneficiary of the protectionist measures introduced by the king.

The king was also determined to foster domestic industries, in particular those which he deemed essential to the military, but he realized that the local manufacturers could not compete with foreign imports. His response was to demand punitive duties on imported goods and in some cases he banned them altogether. In 1724 he halted the import of all foreign weapons, but six years later armaments manufacturers in Spandau and Potsdam were exporting their goods to Denmark, Poland, Russia and the Habsburg Empire. The most blatant form of control came in the textile industry, which was so important for the supply of military uniforms. Frederick William personally controlled the prices of textile goods; in 1719 he banned the import of all foreign cloth and two years later ordered all military personnel to buy expensive new uniforms every year; if they could not afford it they were expected to supplement their incomes by spinning wool for cash. Spinners and weavers at the state-managed textile enterprises, such as the Berlin Lagerhaus, were paid 25 per cent above the going rate and the king insisted on high quality and prompt delivery, which in turn promoted the development of efficient production methods.[64] This artificial market attracted skilled workers from all over Europe; 20,000 people came to Prussia in 1732 and over a quarter moved to the Berlin area. Wool for manufacture increased from 43,969 stones in 1720 to 81,955 in 1737.[65] Increased production and revenue allowed the king to pursue his greatest ambition: the creation of a powerful army.

When Frederick William took power the army was in terrible shape.[66] The state had not been able to pay the soldiers, they had no education, lived in degrading housing and were often short of food; widows and orphans and wounded men were considered outcasts and resorted to begging on the streets of Berlin. The Pietist Jakob Spener had tried to alleviate the problem by creating a wing at the Grosse Friedrichs Hospital, where they were given food and shelter in return for regular church attendance, but when war broke out in 1701 the numbers of the destitute rose again and riots often flared when the Berlin police tried to clear them off the streets. Frederick William's solution was to put the injured in workhouses while the able bodied were expected to join the army. By now Prussia had a population of 2.25 million, of which an extraordinary 90,000 were soldiers, and the numbers were swollen by peasants expected to divide their time between army service and work on the land. Frederick William's obsession went beyond the desire to assemble a strong fighting force; one of his most notorious hobbies was the creation of a bizarre battalion of giant grenadiers: the countryside was scoured for men over six feet tall, who were then forced to serve. These men were personally trained by him, and when he was ill or depressed he would have them march through his private rooms.[67] But, above all, the king saw the army as a model way of life for all men and he issued a stream of 'articles' dictating every aspect of their behaviour. Common soldiers had to keep scrupulously clean and show unquestioning obedience to officers, who in turn were to carry batons with them at all times; visitors to Berlin were often shocked to see officers beating soldiers who had not saluted quickly enough or were sloppily dressed. Minor offences were severely punished; stocks and floggings were common, as was hard labour on construction of fortresses or barracks. The most infamous punishment was running the gauntlet, in which the unfortunate victim would be made to race past a line of around 200 soldiers who hit him with the flats of their swords. Drunkenness was punished with ten runs, insubordination with thirty runs; theft and a second attempt to desert were punished by death. The army was also meant to be part of religious life. The first military church in Berlin was located at the garrison and was directed by Lampertus Gedicke; it became renowned for its tough moral stance and bleak services. The king made officers march their soldiers to church every Sunday and guards were posted at the doors so that nobody could sneak out; one disgusted visitor noted that the men were marched in 'in the same Order, and with the same Silence, as if they were going to Battle'.[68] The king often delivered the cheerless sermons himself.

By the end of his reign life in Berlin had become inextricably linked with the army. All frivolity had vanished and the city had regained its reputation as a gloomy place devoted to the barrack square and the parade ground. Eighty per cent of all revenue went into the army; only 2 per cent was spent on the court. When it had first become a garrison city in 1657 Berlin had contained 1,500 soldiers and 579 dependants; under Frederick William one quarter of the population of 57,000 were in or dependent on the military. Soldiers were everywhere, parading around in their uniforms in bright yellow, blue, red or white, barking orders, marching in rows or filing into their barracks. The landscape of Berlin was dominated by new installations: a parade ground was set up at the Lustgarten, another in the Tiergarten, another near present-day Alexanderplatz; there was a parade ground in front of the Brandenburg Gate, another by the Potsdam Gate, another by the Halleschen Gate; there were soldiers, guard houses and exercise grounds everywhere. It was Mirabeau who quipped that '*La guerre est l'industrie nationale de la Prusse*' and by the time of the Soldier King's death Prussia had the fourth largest army in Europe despite being only thirteenth in population and tenth in area.[69] In his *Political Testament* the king warned his successor to be godly, not to take mistresses or follow 'scandalous pleasures', to beware of 'flatterers and toadies'. Above all he was to manage his finances and the army 'personally and alone'. The

Soldier King had put the imprint of the military firmly on Berlin's character. It would be left to his son Frederick II, known as Frederick the Great, to transform Berlin into one of the most important cities in Germany.

Frederick the Great was the last and the most important in the line of benevolent despots who ruled Berlin in the seventeenth and eighteenth centuries. His reign lasted from 1740 until his death in 1786, and under him Berlin was a complex and often contradictory place. It became the centre of a new kind of administration, a haven of French fashion, a centre of learning and industry, a cultural centre. But it was also despised as a city of aggressive militarism, an upstart, a sand-pit of soldiers and cannon and officers which could threaten not only Russia and Sweden, but France and England and Austria as well. These contradictions were very much a reflection of the king himself, the last of the absolutist monarchs who shaped the city in his own complicated image.

Frederick II became king in Prussia on 31 May 1740. The coronation was nothing like the spectacle enjoyed by his grandfather, and after a short traditional ceremony the king went to the balcony of the Schloss and looked out over the crowd in the Lustgarten.[70] Berliners cheered with delight. They had heard about Frederick's love of art and of music, his hatred of violence, his suspicion of the military, his passion for learning and for Enlightenment ideas, and all were hopeful that the oppressive policies of the Soldier King had come to an end. To their surprise, instead of dismantling the military he immediately started a war. Berlin, which had enjoyed peace for decades, was plunged into the middle of a bloody European conflict for which they were blamed. Once again, its future hung in the balance.

Frederick had been in power only a few months when news reached Berlin that the Emperor Charles VI of Austria had died and that the throne had passed to the young Maria Theresa. Frederick was keen to take advantage of her weakness. Without even declaring war he mobilized his army and led it into Silesia, sending word to the young empress that he would 'protect' her if only she would hand over the province without a fight. She refused and in 1741 an Austrian force was sent to attack the Prussian troops. Frederick held on to the territory in the First Silesian War, but it was difficult to protect and after years of continued conflict the Austrians made a decisive bid to win it back. The Seven Years War lasted from 1756 to 1763 and extended far beyond Silesia until all European powers were involved in some way; the British backed Prussia not because they agreed with their expansion into Silesia but because they needed them as an ally elsewhere, particularly in North America, and at one point it was money from the British government which saved Frederick from ruin because, as Pitt put it, Canada and India were to be won for the

British on the battlefields of Silesia. Macaulay said of Frederick: 'In order that he might rob a neighbour whom he had promised to defend, black men fought on the coast of Coromanel, and red men scalped each other by the Great Lakes of North America.'[71] The rest of Europe frowned on Frederick's greed and from that time Berlin was identified by many with dangerous Prussian militarism and opportunism.

The war was devastating for the city, at least in the short term. Once again Berlin found itself in the middle of a long-drawn-out conflict and a series of battles which it could not afford to finance. It suffered occupation twice. The first occurred on 16 and 17 October 1757, when 3,400 Austrian hussars took control of the city and demanded 200,000 thalers before they would leave. A more serious occupation took place in October 1760. In that year Russian troops had swept through East Prussia and had met up with the Austrians near Berlin; 44,000 Austrian and Russian troops engaged 16,000 Prussians at the gates of the city and after a five-day battle the armies took Berlin. They demanded a payment of 2 million thalers but this time money did not save the city. Palaces and houses were looted and many of Berlin's newly acquired treasures disappeared. Frederick was so angry about the sacking of the palace of Charlottenburg by Saxon troops that he wrote to Augustus III, king of Saxony, to complain; when he received no reply he retaliated by occupying his rival's hunting lodge at Hubertusburg, selling the contents and using the money for his field hospitals. When the marauding armies finally abandoned Berlin at the end of October it was left demoralized and bankrupt. Ernst von Lehnsdorf wrote in his diary in 1761 that only war profiteers had enough to eat; most of the population were hungry and the city was in a terrible state of decay. Prussia emerged victorious in 1763 but the country was exhausted, the land uncultivated and the people starving. Berlin was a shell of its former self, with the population having dropped from a pre-war high of 126,000 to a low of 98,000. Frederick returned to the city six weeks after signing the Treaty of Hubertusburg: he was welcomed with a triumphal coach, flags and flowers, but he was saddened by its decline and noted that he found nothing but 'empty walls and the memory of those he had loved' upon his return.

The rest of the world did not see it that way; Berlin was now cast as the capital of a new self-confident, aggressive power, a reputation which would be further enhanced in one of the most controversial moves of Frederick's reign. In 1772 he orchestrated the First Partition of Poland in order to – as he put it – eat the Polish provinces 'like an artichoke, leaf by leaf'.[72] On 5 August he, along with Catherine the Great and the Empress Maria Theresa, sliced off pieces of the defenceless country. Prussia took 36,000 square kilometres, Austria took 83,000 and Russia 92,000 square kilometres. The land was particularly

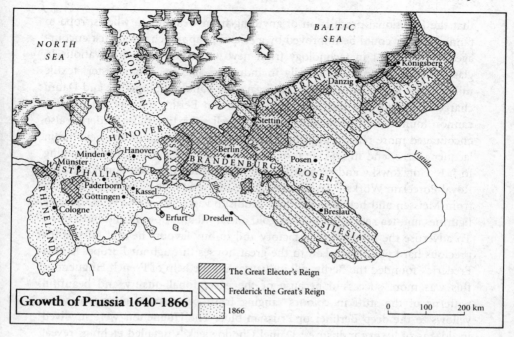

NORTH SEA

BALTIC SEA

S. HOLSTEIN

Königsberg

Danzig

POMMERANIA

EAST PRUSSIA

Stettin

HANOVER

Weser

SAXON

Berlin

BRANDENBURG

POSEN

Posen

Vistula

Minden • Hanover

Münster •

WESTPHALIA

Paderborn •

Göttingen •

Kassel •

Cologne

RHINELAND

Rhine

Erfurt

Dresden •

Elbe

Breslau •

SILESIA

Growth of Prussia 1640-1866

The Great Elector's Reign

Frederick the Great's Reign

1866

0   100   200 km

valuable to Frederick as it linked East Prussia with the west and gave her control over the river Vistula. In 1793 and 1795 the three powers would administer the *coup de grâce*, dismembering Poland completely in the final partition. It was a disgraceful act, but Berliners cared little. Through war and the opportunistic seizure of territory Frederick had made Prussia a great power, posing a direct threat to Austria and relegating the Holy Roman Empire to political obscurity. The people were proud of their king and became more so when Frederick turned his attention to rebuilding the state after the destruction of the Seven Years War and to making a capital city worthy of a new great power.

Frederickan Berlin conjures up images of a growing, vibrant city, a place feeling its self-esteem and confidence, developing its own unique identity and finally becoming something of a unifying force in Prussia. The king was responsible for many of these changes, promoting everything from the rejuvenation of industry to the creation of a sophisticated new legal code. Farmers ruined by the war were supplied with government money to rebuild their homes, purchase seed and cattle and grow strange new crops like the potato. Frederick was determined to foster trade, improving harbours on the Baltic, linking the Elbe, Oder and Vistula rivers by a system of canals and improving docking facilities in Berlin. He was also inspired by the French *Philosophes* who advocated the application of Newtonian ideas to industry and believed that the traditional production of anything from weapons to wheels, rope to tanned leather could be improved by a scientific approach. Frederick encouraged development in technology from new water pumps to innovations in glass making; he invested heavily in industries like the 'Manchester' textile mill and the Berlin clock factory, and gave the bankers Splitgerber and Daum charge of gunpowder and arms manufacture in Berlin; the city got its own cannon foundry and gunpowder works as well as textile mills. Frederick also encouraged more refined industries like furniture making and the new Berlin lacquer works, and in 1761 he purchased a small porcelain factory belonging to J. E. Gotzkowsky and renamed it the Königliche Porzellanmanufaktur, the Royal Porcelain Works.[73] To the annoyance of the Saxons he poached workers from Meissen and began to produce exquisite vases, dinner services, delicate figurines and tea sets smothered in gold and dotted in flowers and butterflies. To advertise the money-losing factory and to buy favours he sent gifts of his precious hard paste porcelain to the great houses throughout Europe. In 1755 Frederick founded the Berlin silk industry with the help of French Huguenots; this was more successful because of the exceptional quality and beautiful patterns of the stuff in colours ranging from peppermint greens or vivid yellows to the deep Berliner or Prussian blue. The Huguenots were involved in dozens of luxury industries: Daniel Chodowiecki's detailed etchings reveal the world of French merchants in Berlin as they bring new bolts of silk to potential customers or show off their elaborate dresses heavy with embroidery and ribbons and feathers; Pierre Mercier founded the Berlin Tapestry Company, which employed 283 handworkers; Pierre Froméry made guns of exquisite quality; Jean Barès created intricate pieces in gold and silver, while other Frenchmen produced everything from delicate enamelled snuff boxes to imposing carriages.

For all his attempts to promote Prussian goods Frederick had to rely on protectionism to nurture the infant industries. He was aware of the problems inherent in this but, as he explained to the French financial expert de la Haye de Launay, he could not afford to change:

I prohibit imports as much as I can so that my subjects shall be encouraged to produce those things which I forbid them to get from elsewhere. Admittedly their early efforts are crude, but time and practice will bring perfection and we must show patience with first attempts ... I have poor soil; therefore I must give the trees time to take root and grow strong before I can expect them to produce fruit.[74]

The protectionist measures were not popular; when Frederick decided that coffee was too expensive Johann Sebastian Bach was prompted to write the

Coffee Cantata, which poked fun at the king's incessant praise of the official alternative – beer.

The attempt to control all aspects of life in Prussia led to another crucial development. Although Berlin was already a military and administrative centre Frederick built on his father's legacy and transformed it into the centre of a modern civil service populated by bureaucrats who owed their allegiance to the state. He reformed the legal system, creating the foundation of the Allgemeines Landrecht.[75] Berlin became a city of offices, bureaucrats, secretaries and clerks. By the 1780s it contained not only the General Directory, but also the Administration Secret State Council, the Department of External Affairs, the Chief Audit Office, the General Supply Office, the Department of Justice, the Supreme Court, the Ecclesiastical Department – with separate sections for Lutherans, Calvinists and Huguenots – the Post, the Regie for Customs Administration, the Medical Board, the Mint, the Offices of the Fiscal, the Offices for the Administration of the Army, including the Secret War Chancery and the Commissariat, and the Colleges of the Estates. The administration of the city of Berlin came under central control and from the 1720s Berlin's Magistrat was composed of civil servants led by a president appointed by the king; Berlin's administration thereafter rested on what the great Berlin publisher Friedrich Nicolai called the 'repression of traditional corporate municipal self-government'.

Berlin's own administrative bodies included the Court Post Office, the Royal Firewood Administration Office, the Commission for Royal Buildings in Berlin, offices for the Saltworks, the Fire Society and the Porcelain Industry. Berlin social welfare administration included the Invalidenhaus for disabled soldiers, the Institute for Poor Widows and the Public Alms Houses.[76] The city also contained offices to oversee the Academy libraries, the art collections, the Royal Library and the Schloss collection of paintings; Frederick built 150 *Bürgerhäuser* or apartment blocks for the new bureaucrats. Even the buildings reflected the importance attached to these new offices; Gerlach's impressive Collegienhaus in Kreuzberg was the first specially commissioned administrative building in Berlin and still projects its importance through its balanced baroque facade and through the large allegorical figures of Justice and Mercy which recline high on the pediment over the grand entrance. The city was not yet the all-powerful administrative centre which it would become after 1871, and Prussian cities and districts still had a high degree of autonomy not least because poor communications between regions made efficient central government impossible. Nevertheless its influence was growing. So was its population. At the end of the war Berlin had a population of 98,000 people but by 1786 it had already reached 150,000. Thirty thousand people worked in industry and trade alone and there were already 3,500 administrative officials. Twenty per cent of the population was in the military and the Berlin garrison now numbered 25,000 men.[77] Berlin was increasing in size and importance. Now Frederick set about transforming its cultural life as well.

In the eighteenth century all Germany looked to France as the model of civilization. German princes spent fortunes on mock palaces of Versailles; they tried to learn French, copied French manners and imported French courtiers to populate their new palaces – indeed, in 1775 Karl Wilhelm Ferdinand of Brunswick would allow only Frenchmen at his court.[78] Frederick the Great was amused at the pretensions of these petty princes: 'there is no prince down to the younger member with an apanage who does not imagine himself to be a Louis XIV. He builds his Versailles, has his mistresses and maintains an army.'[79] Ironically, however, Frederick set about precisely the same thing and his capital became a quasi-French city. French became the language of the educated elite and of the court at Potsdam on the outskirts of Berlin; in 1750 Voltaire commented that German was reserved only 'for soldiers and horses'; Frederick had his poetry corrected by Voltaire and even his German history books were in French. An anonymous writer recorded that 'French language, French clothes, French food, French furniture, French dances, French music, the French pox ... hardly have the children emerged from their mothers' wombs than people think of giving them a French teacher ...' Young men destined for life at court took a 'Knight's Tour' to Paris, where they studied the art of conversation, wit and fashion in an attempt to lose les airs allemands. Saint-Simon referred to these ponderous youths as 'gross, ignorant creatures, very easy to dupe, whom one cannot help mocking'.[80] Educated Berliners, on the other hand, referred to Paris as the 'New Athens'.

There were other settlers in Frederickan Berlin: over 300,000 colonists were welcomed to Prussia, and by the end of his reign one-sixth of his subjects had been born abroad. Frederick claimed to be tired of looking into blue eyes and encouraged not only French, German and Polish immigrants but Greeks and other Mediterraneans to come; he had an immigration office set up in Venice and considered building a mosque in Berlin to attract Turks.[81] But the overriding influence was French, and his cultural ambitions were set by the court at Versailles.

Frederick the benevolent despot was determined to make Berlin a great city, on a social, economic, intellectual and cultural par with France. He took the ideas of the French Enlightenment seriously, encouraging a free press and banning censorship even if books or pamphlets were critical of him. At a time when people throughout Europe were being banished for stealing a loaf of bread, and long before Molière complained that in Paris 'they hang a

man first, and try him afterwards', Frederick abolished the torture of civilians
and permitted the death sentence only for those convicted of murder. He was
not religious but was tolerant of others' beliefs, even allowing a Catholic
cathedral in the city centre. He was obsessed with education, setting up training schools for teachers and making primary education mandatory. He
founded the Realschule in Berlin, which taught not only reading, writing,
mathematics and Latin but also physics, engineering, architecture, geography,
botany, book keeping and other practical skills, and he set up the Ritter-
akademie to train civil servants and created a school for diplomats. Although
Berlin would not have its own university until 1809 he rejuvenated the Academy
of Sciences, installing the mathematician and physicist Pierre Louis Moreau
de Maupertuis as its president and turning it into a centre of learning; it
was there, for example, that Johann Heinrich Pott analysed over 30,000
mineral and soil samples and discovered the secret of making Chinese
porcelain.

After decades of neglect Berlin began to develop as a centre of culture.
The king had little faith in the ability of Berliners to produce great art; he
told his sister Sophia Wilhelmina in 1746 that 'We are emerging from barbarism
and are still in our cradles. But the French have already gone a long way and
are a century in advance of us in every kind of success.' He also told Voltaire:
'You are right to say that our good Germans are still at the dawn of their
knowledge. In the fine arts Germany is still at the period of Francis I. We love
them, we cultivate them, foreigners transplant them here, but the soil is not
yet propitious enough to produce them itself.'[82] Instead he went abroad for
his treasures. He purchased classical statues, including the Polignac marbles
admired by Voltaire; he had Berlin-based French art dealers like Girard and
Michelet supply him with paintings by his favourite artists Watteau and
Lancret; he commissioned many works, including numerous portraits by the
French artist Pesne; he had copies of French furniture made by manufacturers
like J. A. Nahl. An avid flautist, he welcomed Johann Sebastian Bach to his
beloved palace of Sanssouci in Potsdam in 1747; Bach's *Musikalisches Opfer*
were written for Frederick based on a phrase composed by the king; Bach's
son Carl Philipp Emanuel became Kapellmeister to Frederick and introduced
a new musical style to the court.[83] The king also presided over the architectural
transformation in Berlin, a feat accomplished with the help of his old friend
the architect Georg Wenzeslaus von Knobelsdorff.[84]

Frederick set out to redesign the city, building monumental structures
which combined elements of baroque, rococo and neo-classical styles which
still grace central Berlin. Unter den Linden was given thirty small houses and
twenty larger palaces along with the new Academy buildings and the Royal
Library. Frederick helped to design the Gendarmenmarkt, modelled on the

Piazza del Popolo in Rome, flanked by the French and German cathedrals with their graceful baroque towers and impressive sculptures. Unlike his father he did not see opera houses as places of the Devil and commissioned Knobelsdorff to build what he called his 'Temple of Apollo'. The Opera House was unique for the age in that it was not located in the wing of a palace but was an entirely separate structure. The building remains impressive. The pedimented portico with its sweeping stairs running up the sides was inspired by English architecture; there was room outside for 1,000 carriages, and the interior was complete with moveable stages, water pumps for artificial lakes and waterfalls and myriad other innovations. Architects and musicians travelled to see it even when still under construction, and the spectacular opening on 7 December 1742 was followed by a performance of Graun's *Cleopatra e Cesare*. The Opera Platz was finished along with St Hedwig's Cathedral, a vast domed Catholic church designed in part by Frederick himself after the Pantheon in Rome. The Tiergarten, Berlin's large central park, was redesigned in the baroque style complete with mazes, avenues of trees, benches and tents, where people could enjoy tea, coffee, chocolate, lemonade or Danzig liqueur; its paths met at the Grosser Stern, near the pretty new Bellevue Palace, built in 1786 for Frederick's brother Prince Ferdinand, its debt to classical architecture most visible in its clean outline, its flat facade and its simple windows. Many private houses built under Frederick have been destroyed, although one of the most exquisite, the Ephraim House with its delicate curved sandstone facade, was rebuilt in 1985. The Nicolaihaus on Brüderstrasse, which had been given a new facade by the publisher Friedrich Nicolai in 1787, is the only baroque town house to survive, although the lighter rococo buildings along the Märkisches Ufer built in the 1760s still stand. Frederick's most ambitious project was the design of the Forum Fridericianum, a vast area flanked by the Altre Bibliothek with its great curved baroque facade, nicknamed the 'Commode', acting as a counterweight to the neo-classical Opera House, and Prince Henry's Palace, which is now the Humboldt University. The Schloss had already been transformed by Schlüter from an Italianate cloister into a French complex and for the moment remained one of the largest palaces in Europe, bigger than Versailles itself.[85] The famous equestrian statue of Frederick the Great by Christian Daniel Rauch, unveiled in 1851, is positioned so that the king sits high above Unter den Linden, poised as if ready to ride into the majestic Forum which he himself had created for Berlin.

With the erection of dozens of magnificent buildings the city began to take on the appearance of an important capital and even James Boswell was moved to write in 1764 that Berlin was 'the most beautiful city I have seen'.[86] Other visitors were less impressed. When Madame de Staël visited in 1804 she was surprised by its newness: 'one sees no traces of earlier times . . . an entirely modern city, beautiful as it is, makes no impressions; it reveals no marks of the history of the country, or the character of its inhabitants.'[87] The English minister Sir Charles Hanbury Williams wrote, 'Berlin is a very fine and large town but thinly inhabited. It is big enough to contain 300,000 souls and yet without the garrison there is not about 80,000 inhabitants, and among these there is not one at whose house you can dine or sup without a formal invitation; and that is a thing that very seldom happens.'[88] Frederickan Berlin was impressive, but it was cold. The turn to neo-classicism placed an emphasis on order and correctness and the new buildings in Berlin were characterized by their straight lines, pure tones and lack of colour. They were dignified rather than captivating, elegant rather than ebullient, detached rather than high-spirited, and they reflected the character of Berlin, with its preoccupation with military precision, order and strength.

The accomplishments of the seventeenth- and eighteenth-century Hohenzollerns were extraordinary. Berlin had been improved beyond recognition, built from nothing in the midst of a sandy wasteland by a succession of visionary leaders culminating in Frederick the Great. His accomplishments account for the cult status he has been accorded by successive regimes in Berlin. The first state meeting to be held by Frederick's tomb at nearby Potsdam was between the tsar and Frederick William III in the tumultuous month of October 1805, when the two swore eternal friendship in the face of the Napoleonic threat; William I held his first presentation of colours to new regiments beside his tomb; Hitler held the infamous 'Day of National Awakening' there in 1933, while the latest evidence of the cult was the reburial of Frederick's bones at Potsdam in 1990.[89]

But while much local history has portrayed the king as unique he was in fact only one of a number of benevolent despots who refashioned eighteenth-century Europe. The most extraordinary example of a city created from nothing was not Berlin but Peter the Great's St Petersburg to the east which, as Alexander Pushkin put it, rose in all its grandeur and its pride from the 'dank of forests' and the 'damp of bogs' at the mouth of the Neva.[90] Neither were Frederick's social and political reforms unique; after the Seven Years War the Austrians had also modernized their administrative system, while Joseph II abolished serfdom, introduced religious tolerance and made Vienna into a world centre of the arts – Haydn, Mozart and Beethoven would go there, after all, and not to Berlin. Many institutions rivalled the Berlin Academy of Sciences; the great mathematician Leonhard Euler would leave Frederick's Berlin for St Petersburg, and even the Royal Swedish Academy of Sciences of Stockholm and the university at Uppsala were centres of excellence which attracted men like Carolus Linnaeus and Celsius, who invented his thermometer there in 1741.

Furthermore Frederick's extraordinary accomplishments touched only a tiny minority of Berliners. The city was still relatively poor and with the exception of the elite and the rising middle class the majority of people still lived in poverty or squalor. In 1768 30,000 people in the city had the *Armutszeugnis*, an official recognition of poverty, and there was little support for the disabled soldiers, ex-prisoners, the failed students or beggars who wandered Berlin's foul back streets. Life remained difficult for ordinary people, who huddled in cold, damp, poorly lit houses with little furniture. Clothing for most was coarse and uncomfortable, few people bathed and food was unpleasant. The roads were terrible: it took Casanova three days to make the eighty-five mile journey between Magdeburg and Berlin.[91] Above all, the military still dominated Berlin life: the barracks, parade grounds and uniforms prompted Goethe to write to Frau von Stein of his visit to Berlin in 1778 that he could not enjoy the splendour of the royal city as it was obscured by 'men, horses, wagons, guns, ammunition; the streets are full of them. If only I could describe adequately the monstrous piece of clock-work spread out here before one's eyes.'[92]

In reality, Frederick represented the end of an era: he was an absolutist monarch who insisted on personal control of all aspects of life. He would remain one of the most important figures in the history of Berlin, but he did not understand the new force beginning to take hold even at the height of his reign. The Enlightenment ideas upon which he modelled his rule were also fuelling the rise of an independent, educated middle class which was no longer content to follow unquestioningly the dictates of the monarch. These men and women admired Frederick's reforms, but they were increasingly tired of the constraints placed upon them by absolutism. These Berliners were preparing the way for the future. And the future was being made in France.

The French Revolution of 1789 sent shock waves throughout Europe and, for a time, the champions of the Enlightenment believed that they were witnessing the triumph of reason over the 'allies of darkness' and the 'enemies of man'. For thousands of men like Karl von Mastiaux, who stood before a little German reading group in 1789, the Enlightenment had improved and ennobled the spirit and the heart: 'Its progress is long and arduous, but following a lengthy process of ripening, it bears those most noble of fruits, the true virtues, the fruit of enlightened reason and benevolent sensibilities.'[93] Mastiaux's sentiments had been repeated throughout Europe in an age when words like 'improvement', the 'brotherhood of man', and the 'light of reason' were to 'ignite the flame of teaching and banish the darkness which blighted the Christian peoples'. As one Masonic song had it: 'The noble goal of our scared quest; Light, virtue and justice blessed . . . This shall be our battle-cry.'[94] These ideas had been accepted in Frederickan Berlin.

The Enlightenment swept through Europe at the end of the seventeenth century, shaking the very foundations of human understanding and knowledge. It found its first echoes in the detached systematic philosophy of Descartes but it began in earnest in England, with the work of Sir Isaac Newton. In 1687 Newton published one of the most significant works of intellectual history, his *Philosophiae Naturalis Principia Mathematica*, in which he proposed radical new ideas about the workings of the physical universe. The discovery of natural laws by Descartes and Newton and in the work of Boyle, Hooke and Bacon had led to a new attitude to the world, one in which everything could be explained through the application of science and technology and reason.

The work had an immediate effect on European intellectual life. Newton's work on prisms and the diffraction of light was applied to everything from hydraulics and the development of water pumps to medicine. Inoculation was introduced at the end of the 1720s and was championed by Voltaire's *Philosophes*. New operations were devised to cut out cataracts and set broken bones, trepanation was developed to evacuate blood from the skull after a fracture, lithotomy was used to remove bladder stones – both Samuel Pepys and Benjamin Franklin underwent this operation. La Mettrie, later brought to Berlin by Frederick the Great, was fascinated by experiments on muscular reaction and concluded that just as the legs have muscles for walking, 'the brain has its muscles for thinking'. The world was no more than a gigantic 'system' governed by natural laws. All man had to do was use his reason to figure out how they worked, and then apply them to his own society.

The new materialism and utilitarianism was applied to all aspects of life. Old belief systems like religion, superstition and magic became irrelevant in a world in which everything could be explained. In the middle of the century a group of French writers, the Physiocrats, claimed to have identified a 'natural order' by which man could understand the natural laws of economics and thereby achieve a better standard of living – their ideas inspired Adam Smith, who developed them in his *Inquiry into the Nature and Causes of the Wealth of Nations*, published in 1776. In his 1690 *Essay Concerning Human Understanding* John Locke had tried to show how man is a *tabula rasa*, a creature which, given the correct environment, laws and education, could become a model citizen irrespective of class or nationality; of course, if man could be improved, society could be improved also. The idea was revolutionary and challenged the very assumptions upon which the existing order rested.

The Enlightenment had its roots in England, but it found its spiritual home in France, where it was led by the *philosophes* who contributed to Denis Diderot's *Great Encyclopaedia*, itself an attempt to catalogue and summarize all human knowledge. In his *De l'Esprit des lois* Montesquieu equated enlightened self-interest with the common good; Voltaire's irreverent wit cut deep into religious and social mores of the day, with *Candide* becoming one of the most famous books of the age; in 1770 Baron d'Holbach published his *Système de la nature*, in which he outlined a mechanical scheme of the cosmos and of man; Turgot attacked the current distribution of wealth, in his *Code de la nature*, Morellet launched a scathing attack on religion, concluding that 'Any moral system which bases its doctrine on this conception of the Divinity [as a beneficent god] is absolutely vicious.' Even the Marquis de Sade echoed these ideas when the philosopher-king Zamé in *Aline et Valcour* says of God: 'What you wish is that man should be just; what pleases you is that he should be humane.'[95] Condillac took Locke's ideas still further, claiming that man could never comprehend anything beyond his own experience so that abstract notions like religion were a waste of time. These works spread through France and then to the rest of Europe: Buffon's *L'Histoire naturelle* and Montesquieu's *De l'Esprit des lois* were bestsellers, the latter going to 35,000 copies. *Candide* went through eight editions in 1759 alone, while 4,000 people subscribed to the expensive *Encyclopédie*.[96] The Enlightenment in France became a revolutionary force which challenged Absolutism and which prepared the way for the French Revolution, the American Declaration of Independence and the 1791 Polish Constitution. In Germany, however, it took quite a different form.

Germany was slow to take up the ideas of the Enlightenment – the *Aufklärung* – and by the time they reached Berlin they had lost their radical edge. The progenitors of the *Aufklärung* included Christian Thomasius, who passionately opposed the witch-burnings and religious show trials of the day and wrote to this effect in a number of the new German periodicals. Leibniz, too, had been important in laying the foundations of the German Enlightenment, writing as early as 1700 that only through the use of reason could man 'strive towards the development, improvement, complete understanding and correct application of ideas'. Christian Wolff was the first influential Enlightenment thinker in Prussia, although he was forced to move to Leipzig after arguing that the Chinese were capable of philosophical virtue. Nevertheless, while the French Philosophes tended to speak up against their king and were often harassed by the monarch, many of their German counterparts became fixtures at court. Christian Wolff's *Politik* was like a handbook for kings and justified the all-powerful state with an absolutist monarch at its head. For many Germans, autocracy was rational, and therefore good. Unlike the French many defended religion, resting the *Aufklärung* firmly on Pietiest foundations and teaching

German Enlightenment thinkers that religion could be reconciled with reason. The Germans did not appreciate French attacks on the Church or on morality; rakish works like Diderot's *Bijoux indiscrets* and Montesquieu's *Lettres persanes* were firmly rejected and Berliners failed to grasp that sexual freedom was considered a mark of breeding in the France of Louis XVI. They were baffled when Parisians sneered at Rousseau's mistress Madame de Warens because she 'conceals her bust like a *bourgeois*'; they were shocked when the Parisian lawyer Barbier called Christian marriage a 'despised popular superstition', and shook their heads when he proudly recounted that 'of every twenty lords at Court, fifteen are separated from their wives and keep mistresses'.[97] Both Christian Thomasius and Christian Wolff rejected empiricism and utilitarianism in favour of religion, a stance which so disgusted Chateaubriand that he wrote in 1797: 'When all other nations have given up respect for religion it will find a haven among the Germans.' Voltaire disliked Wolff and called him a 'system builder'; he later tried to convince Frederick the Great that he was 'a mere German pedant'.[98] Ironically it would soon be Voltaire who would be ridiculed in Berlin.

Berlin was by no means the only centre of the *Aufklärung* in Germany. Christian Thomasius was a professor in Leipzig and Halle; Johann Christoph Gottsched, who at one time had been forced to flee Prussia to avoid being drafted into the Soldier King's special band of tall troops, worked in Leipzig; Kant spent his entire life in Königsberg; Christian Wolff worked in Jena and Leipzig. Enlightenment ideas first came to the city 'from above' via Frederick the Great and were first manifested at court. Only later did they begin to affect the new middle class of Berlin.

As the administrative centre of Prussia Berlin had gradually become the centre for the new groups of independent, salaried professionals, people who neither worked at the court nor laboured in a trade, who had free time for the pursuit of culture and wanted to improve both themselves and society. They were determined to distance themselves from the world of trade and commerce and were in turn excluded from court life as Frederick still preferred 'a worthless noble to a cultured bourgeois'.[99] Most genuinely admired Frederick's reforms and believed that he represented their best interests, but such deference was in part due to the fact that he still controlled all appointments in the civil service, including those in academia. But whereas in France and England natural rights were invoked to guarantee the freedom of the individual against oppression by the state, in Berlin it was assumed that the state itself was the guarantor of rights. The people looked to their benevolent despot in a way which was unthinkable in Paris or London, and Berlin's Enlightenment was anything but revolutionary; it was more cultural than political, more to do with *Bildung* (education) than with economics or power.[100] It would be a

charming and civilized episode in its history, it would allow members of the
new middle class to 'improve themselves' through education and the creation
of new institutions, it would revel in public-spirited ideals, in the pursuit of
reason, religious tolerance, education and humanitarian principles.[101] It would
also leave the city ill prepared for the political upheavals to come.

The rise of the new educated middle class changed the face of Berlin.
Elegant gentlemen carrying canes and newspapers could now be seen attending
the opera or promenading in the Tiergarten or meeting their friends to discuss
the latest articles in the new 'moral weeklies' or the 'civil journals'. By the end
of the century Berlin contained a plethora of open and secret clubs, reading
societies, debating associations, scientific groups and learned and literary circles
whose members included everyone from civil servants to professionals to the
clergy, from professors to bankers to physicians. Many had their own buildings
which contained reading rooms and conversation rooms; each society had a
complex set of statutes which usually included the banning of alcohol, smoking
and gambling, and the prohibition of conversation about personal problems
or religious or political beliefs.[102] Conversation tended to focus on sensible
reforms, on scientific innovation and on practical matters from new agricultural methods to improvements in education. There were dozens of closed or
secret societies: the Society of Friends of the *Aufklärung*, the German Society,
the Reading Cabinet, the Monday Club; but the most famous of the exclusive
secret Berlin clubs was the Wednesday Society, started in 1783, which not only
championed Enlightenment ideas but which would after Frederick the Great's
death be one of the few to advocate reforms of Prussian absolutism.[103] Its
membership included the society secretary Johann Biester, who published the
respected *Berlin Monthly Journal*, Friedrich Nicolai, Christian Wilhelm von
Dohm, best known for his 1781 essay *On the Civic Improvement of the Jews*,
which marked the beginning of the era of Jewish emancipation in Germany,
and Prussian state officials like Karl Zuarez and Ernst Klein, who were later
involved in the reform of the Prussian legal system.[104] The strict code of secrecy
allowed even government officials to speak freely at meetings without fear of
reprisal. The Freemasons were also very active in the city and were keen to
promote the 'development of men within laws of enlightened reason'. Berlin
contained dozens of lodges. The early ones like Aus trois globes (1740), Fidélité
and L'Harmonie (1758) were modelled on their French counterparts, while
those founded after 1760 were decidedly more German, with names like Hoch-
capital von Jerusalem (1760), Zu den drei goldenen Schlüsseln (1769), Zum
Pegasus (1771), and Friedrich zu den drei Seraphim (1774). Berlin's growing
importance was reflected in its being given the Mother Lodge *Zum Widder
Grosses regierendes Ordens Capital der grossen Landesloge der Freimaurer von
Deutschland in Berlin* in 1776. Lessing and Fichte were both members and

Lessing would later write, 'Freemasonry and middle-class society are of the same age. Both originated side by side.'[105]

The innovative new culture quickly spread beyond the reading rooms of the city centre. In 1749 a famous music club was opened in the Brüderstrasse in the house of the Berlin organist Sack, dedicated to the music of Telemann, Haydn, Glück and to Bach's sons; other enthusiasts championed Mozart and performed his great Enlightenment opera *The Magic Flute*. For the first time theatres were built for new middle-class patrons away from the court; in 1760 Andreas Bergé opened the privately funded 1,000-seat Pantomime in Spandau. The Danzig-born artist Daniel Chodowiecki moved away from painting court scenes in oils and executed over 2,000 drawings and etchings which depicted the merchants and beggars and fashionable ladies of Berlin; he also illustrated works by Lessing, Goethe, Bürger, Schiller and Claudius, who was himself often called the 'father of modern German popular journalism'. Chodowiecki was the quintessential Enlightenment artist and it was his allegorical work of the sun's rays piercing the gloom at daybreak which came to symbolize the 'coming of light' of the *Aufklärung*.

Berlin also became the German centre of the salons modelled on those in Paris and brought to Germany by Germaine de Staël-Holstein. These were held in the private homes of the well-to-do, allowing everyone from intellectuals to impoverished nobles, from bureaucrats to artists to form friendships across the estates.[106] The salons were unique in Berlin history for giving a remarkable group of educated Jewish women, including Henriette Herz and Rahel Levin (later Varnhagen von Ense), real influence over intellectual life in the city; the latent anti-Semitism in Berlin would re-emerge with a vengeance in 1806, but for four decades the Jewish salons were the most prestigious in the city. The beautiful and intelligent Henriette Herz wrote that she attracted 'as if by magic, all the outstanding young men who were either living in Berlin or else visiting the city'.[107] The Prussian Academy of Sciences, the gymnasia, the academies and the public lectures were now of a high standard. One of the most influential in this circle was the writer and publisher Friedrich Nicolai.

Nicolai was one of the most important figures of the Berlin Enlightenment. His father, a bookseller, left the business to his twenty-five-year-old son in 1759 and Nicolai turned it into a focal point of Berlin life. In the mid eighteenth century books were still an expensive luxury; there were no public libraries and people were obliged to share copies amongst friends. Nicolai advocated the increased production of books and pamphlets and pushed for the publication of ever more reviews, journals and 'moral weeklies' based on English journals like the *Tatler* and the *Spectator*. He promoted better education and literacy in the drive to create enlightened citizens. On 4 January 1759 he, advised by his friends Lessing and Moses Mendelssohn, began to publish some letters – *Briefe, die neueste literatur betreffend*, the most important paper of the German Enlightenment, which came out every Thursday. In 1765 he founded the *Allgemeine deutsche Bibliothek*, which was published for nearly forty years and which contained reviews of some 80,000 German titles between 1765 and 1805 alone, including memoirs, literary histories, biographical dictionaries and novels. His bookstore, the largest in Berlin, became a haven where intellectuals could meet for a glass of wine and discuss the latest publications. Nicolai also promoted the modern newspapers which combined entertainment and edification; in 1721 the *Königlich privilegierte Berlinische Zeitung* (later the *Vossische Zeitung*) began its career, and many of the 300 contributors to the *Berlinische Monatsschrift* were high-ranking civil servants who were published alongside ten army officers and five women.[108] The voracity for books meant that the number printed doubled every ten years; there were 3,000 authors in 1760 but 10,000 by 1800. Nicolai's own works were successful and his *Sebaldus Nothanker* was a great bestseller of the day. To Goethe's annoyance it sold 12,000 copies, far more than his own work.[109]

By the turn of the century Berlin had the highest concentration of 'intellectuals' of any German city.[110] Many were civil servants or bankers who dabbled in literature, but there were others of profound importance, in particular the friends Gotthold Ephraim Lessing and Moses Mendelssohn. It was they who, by moving to Berlin, pulled the city out from under the shadow of rivals like Jena, Leipzig, Göttingen, Königsberg and Weimar. In autumn of 1748 the nineteen-year-old Lessing, a Saxon by birth, came to Berlin to escape debts which he had run up while at university in Leipzig. After finding lodging in the Spandauer Strasse he set out to transform Berlin. Lessing was a true son of the Enlightenment. He fervently believed that reason was the key to progress, that humanism and human freedom were paramount, and he stood against the evils of prejudice in all its forms. In November 1748 he and his cousin Christlob Mylius, who edited the *Berlinische Privilegierte Zeitung*, met the publisher Christian Friedrich Voss and Richier de Louvain, who later became Voltaire's private secretary. Together they founded the Montagsclub (the Monday Club), which attracted luminaries like the critic Karl Ramler, the composer Johann Quantz, Friedrich Nicolai and Moses Mendelssohn, immediately making it a centre of Berlin intellectual life. Lessing became the most eloquent of German Enlightenment writers, with his works reflecting his deep longing for equality and justice: *Minna von Barnhelm* is a plea for reconciliation between the old enemies Prussia and Saxony and an attack on the outmoded notion of 'honour'; his famous critique of Johann Winckelmann's aesthetic theory in his essay *Laokoon* foreshadowed the classical revival in Germany; the tragedy *Emilia Galotti* exposed the corruption of the minor German courts.[111] Lessing was convinced that morality was more important than the dogma of conventional religion and he detested the religious intolerance which he witnessed in Berlin, the most obvious example being continuing prejudice against the Jews. His two plays, *Die Juden* of 1749 and the magnificent *Nathan der Weise*, written in Wolfenbüttel in 1779, which stands as one of the greatest works of the *Aufklärung*, challenged the stereotypical image of the Jew. Through his work Lessing demanded of his audience that they not ask if a person was a Christian or a Jew. Instead, they should ask if he is a man, a human being. The kind and noble character of Nathan was modelled on Moses Mendelssohn, of whom Lessing said: 'How free from prejudice his lofty soul, His heart to every virtue how unlocked, with every tender feeling how familiar.' It was an apt description.

Moses Mendelssohn was the third great figure of Enlightenment Berlin. Born in Dessau in 1729, he moved to the city when he was twenty-five. He began as a tutor to a wealthy Jewish family and later supported himself by running a silk factory. At the same time he wrote extensively in journals and newspapers and produced a number of philosophical works, including *Phädon oder Über die Unsterblichkeit der Seele*, which revealed his humane rationalism. Mendelssohn was a tireless campaigner for Jewish emancipation. He founded the first Jewish school in Berlin for eighty children, financed by court banker Daniel Itzig and the businessman David Friedländer, while his work *Jerusalem oder Über religiöse Macht und Judentum* was a plea for acceptance of his people; it formed the basis of the Haskalah and later for Reformed Judaism. For those Jewish families granted permission to live in the city Berlin offered many advantages: the city had no ghetto, there were few housing restrictions, and during Mendelssohn's time it was home to around 3,500 Jews – around 2 per cent of the population. Their growing prosperity was reflected in palatial houses on Unter den Linden and Spandauer Strasse and in the great salons of the day.[112] Nevertheless Jews still faced a plethora of petty restrictions and discrimination; when he came to Berlin Moses Mendelssohn could not enter the city as other men did but was forced to remain in a hostel outside the gate otherwise used for livestock. There he was questioned at length and had to pay a transfer tax similar to that applied to cattle before being permitted to enter.[113] Another of the levies forced him to purchase overpriced figures from Frederick the Great's struggling porcelain firm; as a result twenty monkeys sat in a row on a shelf in his house in Berlin.[114] Mendelssohn was a leading intellectual of his day but he faced official discrimination throughout his life: in 1763 Frederick the Great rejected his application to the Academy of Sciences because he was a Jew, a decision meekly accepted by its members even though they had unanimously supported his application. When he died Mendelssohn had still received no official recognition from the Prussian state. Lessing snorted that Frederick's renowned religious tolerance clearly did not extend to allowing a Jew into the upper reaches of a learned society.

The passive acceptance of such discrimination which went so clearly against their principles was one of the problems with the Berlin *Aufklärer*. They were innovative in their social and artistic and cultural lives, but they were politically impotent. The only serious criticism of Frederick came in the form of growing resentment against the very people who had brought the Enlightenment to Berlin in the first place: the French.

Anti-French sentiments and the rise of German nationalism are typically identified with the Napoleonic Wars, but resentment against France was simmering away in Berlin long before 1806. It was the product of increased self-confidence in Prussia: as early as 1700 Leibniz had said: 'We have set France up as a paragon of all virtues and our young self . . . [and the Prussians] have in consequence misunderstood their own country while, on the other hand, admiring everything which comes from France.' Collini, Voltaire's Italian secretary, noted that the victories of the Seven Years War had already made Prussians feel superior not only to Austria but also to France, which was sometimes referred to as 'a futile frivolous, vain deflated nation'. The rising tide against the French was found in the work of Francke and Spener; it emerged in Klopstock's epic poem *The Messiah* and later in the works of Hamann and Herder. In Berlin it took the form of a reaction against the French tax collectors, bureaucrats and courtiers with whom Frederick had flooded the city. Frederick II was a cultural Germanophobe and had consistently appointed French academics and officials to important posts; he called Shakespeare, then championed by German writers, 'abominable' and 'worthy only of the savages in Canada', and when he read Goethe's *Götz von Berlichingen* he labelled it a parody of the very worst efforts of Shakespeare.[115] By the second half of the eighteenth century the pent-up feeling in Berlin led to open denunciations of the utilitarian ideas of the French *Philosophes*, an anti-French movement which Madame de Staël would later describe in *De l'Allemagne*. But above all, the move away from French cultural hegemony was championed by Lessing.

Lessing became increasingly angry with Frederick's inability to recognize the emergence of a German national literature. He fell out with Voltaire and was furious with the king for installing Maupertuis and la Mettrie at court while excluding both himself and Mendelssohn from the Potsdam Academy. Unlike Frederick, Lessing revered Shakespeare, seeing him as a model for a theatre free of French influences and even calling him the 'father of German literature'. His anger and impatience were extended to Berliners, whom he saw as docile and submissive.

Lessing is often held up as the most important Enlightenment figure of

Berlin; his name is everywhere, his statue stands in the Tiergarten near the Brandenburg Gate and he, like Mendelssohn and Nicolai, are mainstays of a self-congratulatory myth of Berlin as a 'city of tolerance'. But Lessing had an uneasy relationship with Berlin and he was ultimately as critical of the city as it was of him. His work bristles with anger at the stifling rules and controls imposed upon him there. In his play *Minna von Barnhelm* the main character goes to Berlin to find her lover, but instead of being welcomed is immediately interrogated by the 'very exact' police, who demand to know precisely where she is from and what she is doing in the city; at the same time the maid Franziska complains: 'Where can one sleep in this devilish big city?' – where one is annoyed 'by the coaches, the nightwatchmen, the drums, the cats, the corporals who never stop clanking, shouting, sounding rolls, meowing, cursing'. The play was banned in Berlin and this, compounded with the fact that his application for a job as librarian was turned down, caused a disgusted Lessing to leave the city for good. He remained in Hamburg from 1767 to 1768 and then became librarian to the duke of Braunschweig at Wolfenbüttel, writing in 1769:

> How can one feel well in Berlin? Everything there makes one's gorge rise. Don't talk to me of your freedom of thought and publication in Berlin. It consists only of the freedom to publish as many idiotic attacks on religion as one wants – a freedom of which any honest man would be ashamed to avail himself. But just let anyone try to write about other things in Berlin ... let him attempt to speak the truth to the distinguished rabble at court, to stand up for the rights of the subject, to raise his voice against despotism as now happens in France and Denmark, and you will realize which country, up to the present day, is the most enslaved in Europe.[116]

He never bothered to visit the city again and died in Braunschweig in 1781. Lessing was not the only one to feel stifled by a place which, as Voltaire put it, had 'astoundingly many bayonets and very few books'. Voltaire left Prussia for the last time in 1753. Goethe visited Berlin only once in his life, in May 1778. He met Chodowiecki, the art collector Johann Christoph Frisch and the music director Johann André, but he had no contact with Nicolai or Mendelssohn and left thoroughly unimpressed. In 1767 Carl Philipp Emanuel Bach grew tired of the residence city and followed Telemann to Hamburg.

For all its advancements Berlin was still overwhelmed by the Hohenzollerns and by the military. Things could not have been more different in France. In the 1770s an apocryphal conversation between the dauphin and the court physician François de Quesnay made the rounds of the cafés and salons of Europe. In it the dauphin asked the doctor what he would do if he were king.

'Nothing,' de Quesnay replied. 'Then who would govern?' the dauphin asked in alarm. De Quesnay replied, 'The Law.' The story delighted the French, but it baffled Berliners. While French thinkers from Rousseau to d'Alembert now insisted that Enlightenment and despotism were mutually exclusive, Berliners continued to defend Absolutism; even the great Immanuel Kant called eighteenth-century Prussia 'the age of the Enlightenment or the century of Frederick'.[117] The unquestioning respect for Frederick and for duty and obedience struck many visitors as odd; even Nicolai was astounded in 1759 to find that the official Censor for Philosophical Works had nothing to do as nobody ever wrote anything critical of the king. Berlin still 'smelled of gunpowder'. The famous Italian playwright Vittorio Alfieri visited in 1770 and found Prussia 'like a horrific never ending guard room' and Berlin 'like a gigantic loathsome barracks'. In 1779 George Forster, best known for his accounts of his voyage with Captain Cook, spent five weeks in Berlin and commented that although it was outwardly beautiful it was 'inwardly much blacker than I had envisaged', with the new buildings and streets impressive but the people coarse, arrogant and badly educated.[118]

With such meagre defence of its ideas, it was no wonder that the Enlightenment would soon fade. The death knell was sounded when Frederick the Great was succeeded by Frederick William II in 1786, a man who opposed the Enlightenment and soon became terrified by the implications of the French Revolution. After 1789 many Berliners turned against their own Enlightenment thinkers and some societies and clubs voluntarily closed themselves down rather than be associated with the spread of Jacobinism. Those who held on to their Enlightenment beliefs were labelled 'Nicolai-iten' and treated with disdain. The self-censorship extended to all levels of society. Immanuel Kant dutifully stopped writing about religion when, in 1794, his works were declared derogatory to Christianity, noting in his papers: 'To withdraw or deny one's convictions is base, but silence in such a case as this is the subject's duty.'[119] The Berlin salons of Dorothea Veit and Henriette Herz and Rahel Levin (later Varnhagen von Ense) enjoyed a brief flurry of activity between the time of Frederick's death and 1806, attracting men from Fichte to the Humboldt brothers to Varnhagen and Schlegel, but this ended with the Napoleonic Wars, when 'friendships between commoners and nobles and the open display of Jewish wealth and culture all became deeply controversial'.[120] Rahel Varnhagen would soon lament: 'where are our days, when we were all together! They went under in the year '06. Went under like a ship: containing the loveliest goods of life, the loveliest pleasures.'[121]

Perhaps the most poignant symbol of the sad decline of the Enlightenment was the defection from the circle around the once-revered Friedrich Nicolai. Nicolai hung on to his ideals until the end. He was deeply resentful of the coming of Romanticism and was so appalled by Goethe's *The Sufferings of Young Werther* that in 1775 he wrote a lame satire called *The Friends of Young Werther*; he disliked Kant and mocked Herder's cult of folk songs and interest in German national identity. But his time had passed. Goethe and Schiller attacked him in *Xenien* and Goethe used him as the model for the ludicrous character Proktophantasmist in the first part of *Faust*. By the time of his death in 1811 he had become a figure of ridicule amongst the new intellectual elite in Berlin. The Enlightenment, the 'coming of the light', had brought a brief period of tolerance to the city, but its most fundamental principles had already been pushed aside by the time of the French Revolution. The Enlightenment would leave a legacy, but not the one envisaged by Mendelssohn and Lessing and Nicolai. By shattering the belief in traditional religion and loosening the bonds to an old way of life it had left an immense vacuum in people's lives. The Enlightenment thinkers had hoped the void would be filled by notions of tolerance, reason and universal brotherhood, but this was not to be. Instead, people turned to nationalism – not merely the cultural nationalism of Lessing and Klopstock and Herder, but the political nationalism which would be sparked off by one of the most formative events in Berlin history: the arrival of Napoleon.

III

The Emerging Giant

Bring in the wine! A toast! To liberty!
(*Faust*, Part I)

'FROM HERE AND TODAY,' Goethe said to friends shortly after the French Revolution, 'a new epoch in world history is dawning, and you will be able to say that you were there'.[1] During his eighty-two years the genius poet witnessed the dramatic changes which rocked Europe and Berlin, from the Napoleonic Wars and the coming of the Industrial Revolution to the birth of that essentially urban movement which he did so much to bring about – Romanticism. It was a time of great uncertainty, of turmoil and, for many in Germany, of humiliation. At the end of his life Goethe said sadly: 'I thank God that I am not young in so thoroughly finished a world.'

For an era of such extraordinary importance it started calmly enough. In the last years of his life Frederick the Great had become a recluse, languishing at Sanssouci with only his dogs for company. He had grown weary of life and when he died in 1786 Berliners seemed almost relieved. The Enlightenment was already faltering and the *Sturm und Drang* (storm and stress) writers were ushering in a new, wilder culture. Then, in 1789, the news of an extraordinary upheaval exploded across Europe.

The French Revolution shook every aspect of European life, from politics to the economy, from literature to philosophy. It propelled Europe headlong into the modern era. When the news from Paris first reached Germany the revolution was heralded as the precursor to a new, better age. Kant praised it, Hölderlin called it a 'beloved wonder', the young Hegel called it a 'glorious sunrise' and was so moved that he and his friend Schelling planted a Liberty Tree in the Tübingen market place, Klopstock and Schiller became honorary French citizens, Herder and Fichte and Beethoven wrote of a new age of liberty and brotherly love. Wordsworth captured the dream in his immortal lines: 'Bliss was it in that dawn to be alive, But to be young was very heaven!'[2]

The dream was short lived. Within months news of the September massacres had turned erstwhile supporters against the revolution. Iffland and

Gneisenau were now scathing about the Terror, von Gentz published Burke's critique of the revolution, Kotzebue wrote a burlesque mocking Paris, Klopstock mourned that 'our Golden Dream is shattered'. On 8 February 1793, after the execution of Louis XVI, Schiller wrote, 'I feel so sickened by these abominable butchers', and six months later fumed that the revolution had 'plunged not only that unhappy people itself, but a considerable part of Europe and a whole century, back into barbarism and slavery'.[3] The longing for *Freiheit, Gleichheit, Brüderlichkeit* had ended in the bloody crash of the guillotine.

In Germany the profound disappointment turned to fear when it became obvious that the violence would not be contained in France. War threatened on the Rhine. The Gironde party, hoping for a diversion abroad to prevent the Jacobins and Royalists from gaining power, began to churn out pamphlets and posters proclaiming that 'France owned the Rhine' and that it was France's 'mission' to bring the ideas of the revolution to enslaved peoples 'yearning to be free'. The problem for Germans was that this 'freedom' would come through the force of arms.

In April 1792 France declared war on Austria and, by implication, on her ally Prussia. It was the start of the Revolutionary Wars. The disorganized Germans were no match for the zealous French army and by September France had won the great victory at Valmy. By 1794 all German territory west of the Rhine was held by the occupying forces. Austria now fought alone in Italy against the new commander-in-chief of the Army of the Interior, a young Corsican named Napoleon Bonaparte who had already astonished the world with his military genius. On 9 November 1799 he returned to Paris and was made first consul. In 1804 Napoleon Bonaparte declared himself emperor. He was thirty-five years old.

Napoleon was determined to make German states virtual colonies of France. In 1805 he resumed the campaign in the east and by 1806 had dissolved the Holy Roman Empire, forcing the emperor, Francis II, to abdicate. Germany had ceased to exist as a unified political body. Napoleon reorganized the German Reich into a new entity: the Confederation of the Rhine.

Until now Prussia had remained neutral in the European war. In his *Annalen* Goethe wrote: 'Europe had changed shape, cities and navies were being destroyed on land and sea, but central and northern Germany profited from a certain feverish peace which enabled us to enjoy a doubtful safety.' The 'feverish peace' which had so encouraged the cultural flowering in Weimar and in Berlin itself was almost at an end. Tension was growing between Paris and Berlin. In 1805 Napoleon had tried to use Prussian-occupied Hanover as bait in his peace negotiations with Britain. Tension was exacerbated when in 1806 he had the Nuremberg bookseller Johann Palm executed for publishing an anonymous pamphlet attacking France: the trial caused a sensation and roused popular anger throughout German lands. In the end it was his violation of the Treaty of Schönbrunn which provoked Frederick William III of Prussia to make his disastrous declaration of war on 1 October 1806. Prussia was now fighting alone against the mighty French army. It was doomed to fail.

It was not surprising that Prussia lost to France in 1806. When Frederick the Great died he left Prussia in the hands of his nephew Frederick William II, who was neither intelligent nor dedicated enough to keep the worn-out system alive. He had ignored the army and the bureaucracy while creating a glittering life at court – it was he who invited Mozart to Berlin to conduct *The Marriage of Figaro*. It was renowned for its courtesans, its corruption and its domination by the strange cult called the Rosicrucian Order. The members of the sect had transformed life at court with their palace seances in which people communed with spirits of the dead or with the elements, and with their truly depraved rituals which were said to prolong human life.[4] When the system began to fall apart the king had merely increased controls and religious censorship. Instead of modernizing, Berlin had taken on the appearance of a frenzied and decadent eighteenth-century court. Frederick William II died in 1797 but his successor Frederick William III brought little change. He was less ostentatious and debauched than his predecessor but he lacked character, finding it impossible to make decisions and dithering and procrastinating at a time when Prussia needed a firm hand. It is telling that it was not he but his consort, the beautiful young Queen Luise, who would become the heroine of Berlin for taking a stand against the French and against Napoleon. By the time Napoleon invaded Prussia Berlin had languished under thirty years of incompetent rule.[5]

Napoleon needed only one week, from 10 to 17 October, to smash this once formidable opponent. Prussian divisions were knocked down one by one while the fortresses from Erfurt to Halle, Spandau to Stettin to Magdeburg surrendered in turn – only Kolberg at the Prussian Pomeranian coast held out until 1807. The final battles were fought on 14 October 1806, at Auerstedt and to the south at Jena. The latter was an unmitigated disaster. Last-minute changes in the Prussian battle plan resulted in confusion and a tangle of troops with no supply lines and no communication. At that moment the French attacked and within hours the Prussians were retreating in panic. One young man who heard the noise of battle from his room in Jena was Friedrich Hegel, who hastily scribbled the last words of his *Phenomenology of Spirit* so that he could hide it from the occupying forces. The Prussian army, which had risen to such prominence under Frederick the Great, had collapsed.

News of the catastrophe at Jena reached Berlin the following day and it became obvious that the city could no longer be defended. Panicky officials began to load wagons with everything from weapons from the arsenal to state papers; the king and queen were spirited off to Königsberg and those with means fled east. As the governor of the city, General von der Schulenburg-Kehnert, prepared to leave he posted the infamous declaration explaining how Berliners were expected to behave now that they had been defeated. 'The King has lost a battle,' it read. 'The first duty of the citizen is now to be quiet. This duty I charge the inhabitants of Berlin to perform. The King and his brothers live.' With that, Berliners were left to face French occupation alone. Henriette Herz, who calmly decided to remain in her Berlin apartments, wrote of the announcement: 'How laconic! And yet part of it is superfluous. For who in Berlin thought of disturbing his quiet? The announcement was read, but few countenances showed any expression of fear, most no expression at all; at the utmost one or two people went away shaking their heads with an air that seemed to say, really, it has come a little too quick!'[6]

Napoleon entered Berlin on 27 October 1806 and as his triumphal procession made its way under the newly completed Brandenburg Gate and down Unter den Linden curious Berliners lined the streets to watch him pass. The sculptor Gottfried Schadow, who had designed the new Quadriga atop the Brandenburg Gate, sketched the stubble-faced victor glowering at the people from under his hat. That evening French troops celebrated by breaking into churches, plundering wine cellars and raiding food stores.[7] Napoleon dismissed the acting governor Prince Hatzfeld and ordered the councillors to gather 2,000 eminent Berliners together; sixty were elected to a new city council, with seven forming the executive. He appeased Berliners by promising political reforms, the institution of the Code Napoléon and a modern constitution, but soon after the signatures were dry on the Treaty of Tilsit of July 1807 it became clear that he saw Berlin as little more than a subjugated capital from which to squeeze reparations.

Tilsit was Prussia's final humiliation. Despite the occupation of Berlin Prussia had remained formally allied to Russia and at war with France, but on 14 June 1807 Napoleon defeated the tsar at Friedland and Russia sued for peace. On 9 July Tsar Alexander and Napoleon met on a luxurious raft on the river Niemen; Frederick William was forced to wait on the riverbank while the two leaders signed the treaty which dismembered Prussia and removed her territory west of the Elbe along with most Prussian-held territory in Poland, which became the grand duchy of Warsaw under the duke of Saxony. Prussia, which had had a population of 6 million at the death of Frederick the Great, now had only 4,938,000 people. Only four provinces were left, all of which were occupied by Napoleon. The land was impoverished and weakened by war and the Prussian army was reduced to 42,000 men, 16,000 of whom were to be at Napoleon's disposal. Furthermore, Prussia was forced to pay an indemnity of over 100 million francs and also to cover the costs of the occupation of a huge foreign army of over 150,000 men, a burden which would cost 216 million francs.[8] Napoleon knew that Prussia would be unable to raise the money quickly and used this tardiness as an excuse to continue his occupation. At the same time, the French stripped Berlin of its wealth and its few treasures; the official list of plunder included 116 paintings, 96 busts and statues, 183 bronzes, 538 gems, 7,262 medals and coins, manuscripts, amber and the Quadriga, which had only just been placed atop the Brandenburg Gate. This was a meagre haul compared to the 4,000 cartloads of booty taken from Rome, which became the foundation of the Musée Napoléon (the Louvre), but the loss of their few treasures irked the population. There was also a good deal of unofficial looting and Berliners were forced to watch as officers piled goods on to boats and sent them off to Paris.[9] Berliners also resented the rowdy troops quartered in their homes and the creation of huge French barracks like the Camp Napoléonburg in Charlottenburg, which housed 25,000 men. Manufacturers and merchants suffered from a drop in trade brought about by Napoleon's 'continental system', but even when Napoleon replaced the blockade with an import ban of between 40 and 50 per cent, scarcity and price rises caused hardship. Berliners could not believe that their mighty capital had fallen so quickly and so far.

Napoleon was astounded by the ease of his victory over Prussia. When he visited the tomb of Frederick the Great he told his officers: 'Hats off, gentlemen! If he were still alive, we would not be here.'[10] Napoleon's words were echoed by Queen Luise, who lamented that Prussia had 'gone to sleep on the laurels of Frederick the Great'. The problem lay in part with Frederick's own success. His obsessive control over the army and administration had kept enlightened absolutism alive long past its natural life. His successors had ignored his advice, but for an artificial state made strong primarily by its oversized army the decision to allow it to decay had been a form of suicide.

Napoleon's occupation of Berlin did have one surprising benefit: it ushered in a period of reform which led to profound changes in the army, education and administration of Prussia. The reason was clear. Under the old system of absolutism the monarchy had seen no need to change. Napoleon's lightning strike had exposed the rot in the system. Even the reactionary king understood that if he did not introduce reforms Prussia would never again attain great power status in Europe. He did not want reforms because he felt they were right; he introduced them because he had no choice. Prussia could no longer survive as an absolutist state. It was a question of reform or perish.

Berlin was now under French military control and although the king was in Königsberg the government in Berlin did appear to be pro-French, not least because open defiance of Napoleon would have led to immediate reprisals. In return for his loyalty the king was allowed some autonomy in the running of his government and managed to appoint a number of ministers who were given unheard of authority despite being clandestine opponents of France. Frederick William advised that the Prussian state should 'replace by spiritual strength those material things which have been lost'. The reformers wanted to modernize the army, improve the educational system, and above all create a constitutional government. Under normal circumstances the king would have seen these ideas as radical and dangerous. As it was, they were his only hope if he was to preserve his own power.

The city of Berlin remains something of a shrine to the reformers who struggled to modernize Prussia under the watchful eye of the French. Statues, plaques, busts, streets and squares still bear the names of men hailed as everything from German nationalists to the 'fathers of German democracy'. Humboldt University – so named by the Soviets in 1945 – is graced by statues of the brothers Alexander and Wilhelm; statues of Freiherr vom and zum Stein and August von Gneisenau stand on Unter den Linden; Hardenbergstrasse, Hardenberg Platz, Gneisenaustrasse and Niebuhrstrasse criss-cross the west end. Ironically these 'great Berliners' had come from elsewhere: Scharnhorst and Hardenberg were Hanoverians, Niebuhr was educated in Holstein, Stein was Franconian and educated in Hanover, Blücher and Queen Luise were from Mecklenburg, and only the Humboldt brothers, Schleiermacher and von Schön were born in Prussia. Many had originally come to Berlin to work in the civil service and were shocked to find their adopted city subjugated by a foreign power. The reformers were universally anti-French. Stein had initially adopted a tolerant line but when Napoleon continued to demand larger sums from destitute Prussia he realized that the only course open to them was to wage war on France and provoke a popular uprising.[11] Gneisenau said, 'As a patriot I sigh. In the time of peace we have neglected much, occupied ourselves with trivialities, flattered the people's love of show, and neglected war which is a very serious matter.'[12] Heinrich von Bülow wrote in 1806 that leaders who let even large armies 'lie idle in garrison service, where it rusts and bastardizes and sinks into a spiritless militia of the sort that German students call Philistine . . . The fact is certain, Prussia has lost her independence since she forgot how to make use of 200,000 men.'[13] And Hardenberg had warned the king: 'a radical treatment of the defects of our administration is absolutely and urgently necessary.'[14] The most influential of the reformers was Stein, who was appointed after Tilsit in July 1807. He would be in power only one year, but his impact on the government and administration of Berlin would be remarkable.

Baron vom und zum Stein came from an old Thuringian family but had moved to Berlin to take up a post in the Prussian General Directory in July 1804. He was highly independent, had a fiery temperament and a determination which had already set him apart from his colleagues. After Jena Stein and his friend Hardenberg persuaded the king to dismiss the Kabinett, the powerful but irresponsible group of courtiers which had helped lead Prussia to ruin and included men like Lombard, Beyme and von Köckeritz and the ineffectual and stupid minister of foreign affairs Haugwitz; Lombard had in fact been a traitor, feeding information to Napoleon while pretending to advise the king. In 1807 Stein was presented to the king as the 'only man' who could save Prussia and in his memoirs Stein recalled looking out at the defeated capital, a sight which fuelled his desire to create a 'rousing, moral, religious, patriotic spirit in the nation, of inspiring it anew with courage, self-confidence, readiness for every sacrifice in the cause of independence of the foreigners and of national honour, and of seizing the first favourable opportunity to begin the bloody and hazardous struggle for both'.[15]

Stein began by taking over the Civil Organization Commission, which included men like von Schön, Niebuhr and Stägemann. Like Stein they had been deeply influenced by Adam Smith, had worked to rid Prussia of backward class divisions and hoped to set up representative institutions in their place.[16] Stein's first accomplishment was the Emancipation Edict of 9 October 1807, which freed the estates from ancient restrictions and allowed all men to engage in the occupation or business of their choice irrespective of birth; it abolished serfdom and allowed noblemen to engage in trade while curbing the restrictive guilds. Stein's government reforms were equally radical. The Edict for Local Institutions abolished all existing administrative bodies, reorganized local government districts and centralized the administration of the state to allow for coherent centralized government and for the efficient distribution of resources. The new Council of State was to be presided over by a president, ministers of the crown, royal princes, and appointed privy councillors; a smaller body, the Council of Ministers, was to deal with ordinary government business. For this five ministries were created: Foreign Affairs, War, Finance, Justice and Internal Affairs, with the first meeting held in the Berlin Rathaus on 6 July 1809. The council survived until 1918 and its creation marked the beginning of Berlin's domination of Prussian, then German, national government affairs. For the first time ministers were freed from the direct interference of the king and the court. At the municipal level Berlin was given special status, with its own elected city council and with a magistrate and an elected Bürgermeister and Oberbürgermeister. The mayors were still subject to official approval by the king, and police and justice came under state jurisdiction, but Berliners gained control over many other functions from road building to housing. These would prove crucial in regulating development in the coming era of rapid industrialization and would later make Berlin's municipal administration the envy of Europe.

While Stein reformed the civil service Wilhelm von Humboldt tackled education reform. Born in 1767, the sparkling, generous Humboldt had long been a popular figure in the Berlin salons of Henriette Herz, Dorothea Veit and Carl Laroche. He had championed classical education and the concept of *Bildung* from an early age. For him education was not merely the chance to learn a trade or set of skills but rather gave the individual the chance to develop his *Humanität*, his human spirit. He was a meritocrat and believed in education for all irrespective of birth – his reforms would do much to further the rise of the bourgeoisie in nineteenth-century Berlin. In 1808 he was appointed the king's chief of educational and ecclesiastical affairs in the new Ministry of the Interior and set about reshaping the Prussian education system. He abolished class-based schools like the Ritter or Knight's Academies, made education compulsory for all, improved elementary schooling and introduced a classical curriculum into a new kind of secondary school which he called the Gymnasium. His proudest achievement was the creation of a new university.

Berlin University came about as a direct result of the Napoleonic Wars. The Peace of Tilsit had forced Prussia to hand over the universities of Duisberg, Erlangen and, the most important, Halle; neither of the two remaining universities, Königsberg or Frankfurt-an-der-Oder, were regarded as suitable as the central Prussian seat of learning. In September 1807 the king agreed to the creation of a new university in Berlin and on 16 August 1809 he pledged an annual sum of 150,000 thalers and donated the beautiful Prince Henry's Palace on Unter den Linden to the new university. The Humboldt brothers now travelled throughout Germany recruiting for the faculty, and the list of luminaries they attracted was impressive – the first rector was the famous professor of jurisprudence, Schmalz, while the first *elected* rector was the philosopher Fichte. The university could soon boast Schleiermacher and De Wette in theology, Friedländer, Hufeland, Reil and Holrausch in medicine, Wolf, Buttman, Rühs and Niebuhr in history, Tralles in mathematics (Gauss turned down the offer), Savigny in law, Oltmanns in astronomy and a host of other prominent intellectuals of the day.[17] The university opened on 15 October 1810 and the first work published was Niebuhr's *Roman History*. It quickly became a central feature of Berlin life and a magnet for leading German intellectuals, many of whom, from the Humboldts to Fichte, from the Grimm brothers to Schelling, from Hegel to Ranke, would leave an indelible mark on German intellectual life.[18]

It was here that the concept of *Bildung* and of *Wissenschaft* (knowledge) evolved into a movement which would sweep nineteenth-century Germany and Europe. The student was not to focus on a specific subject or learn a practical profession through repeating a restricted programme, but was to learn how to be curious, how to explore new subjects and to pursue knowledge for its own sake. Berlin University became something of a temple to knowledge, and its professors were treated with reverence not because of their birth, but because they embodied the classical ideal of the educated man. The magnanimous Humboldt was perfectly serious when he said that it was 'no less useless for the carpenter to have learned Greek than it is for the scholar to make tables'. Berlin came closer to achieving his ideal of a free classical education for all in the first half of the nineteenth century than at any time since.[19]

The other institution to undergo reform was the military. For centuries the Prussian army had been a state within a state, living in a world of its own with its own police, its own codes of conduct, its own church, and with virtually no links to civil society. Prussians had been amazed to see French soldiers march into their country, fired up with patriotism and nationalistic pride. The introduction of conscription in 1792 had not only created an endless supply of recruits, it had also unified the nation and the army. The French soldier was not a *sujet* harangued and beaten like his Prussian counterpart; he was a *citoyen*. The French military, it was said, was the French people in uniform. The reformers in Prussia hoped that if they could harness the will of the people in a similar way they could provoke a national uprising and rid Prussia of the French occupiers.

The main reformers, including Gneisenau, Boyen and Count Götzen, were brought together in Hardenberg's Military Organization Commission, but the most influential of all was General Scharnhorst, whose story mirrors the revolutionary nature of his times. In any previous era this boy of peasant stock would have been barred from a military career but he lived in a revolutionary age. As a young man he entered military school in Hanover and his brilliant strategic mind soon brought him to the attention of his superiors. He moved to Prussia where he entered the service and, although he was constantly put down by men – including General Yorck – for being a commoner, his lectures were recognized for their brilliance. Scharnhorst was eventually ennobled. His influence cannot be underestimated; Arndt called him the 'greatest of the reformers' while Clausewitz called him the 'father of my mind'.[20]

The military reforms were radical and reflected Scharnhorst's meritocratic views. In 1807 he dismissed 208 woolly-minded officers and replaced them with professionals; he opened the army to commoners; he dissolved the old cadet schools; he set up new institutes, including the Berlin Academy, and abolished the infamous and degrading punishments so characteristic of the Prussian military. More revolutionary still was Scharnhorst's idea of the creation of a new force, a militia called the Landwehr. Napoleon had limited the Prussian army to 43,000 troops but Scharnhorst quietly sent soldiers on leave every month and replaced them with new recruits, building up a secret reserve which would ultimately enable Prussia to raise 280,000 men. On 17 March 1808 Napoleon permitted the creation of the Landwehr for all men between seventeen and forty not in the regular army, and in April allowed the Landsturm for all those capable of auxiliary work. Napoleon had assumed that they would be cannon fodder for his own armies; in fact they would eventually fight against France in the Wars of Liberation.

Napoleon became increasingly suspicious of the reformers and flooded Berlin with his spies to watch over them. Stein realized the danger – he advised the king to remain in far-off Königsberg so as not to come in Berlin 'into immediate contact with all the machinery of domestic and foreign intrigue which is now set in such violent motion'.[21] The French period of repression began on 15 August 1808 when a letter discussing a future War of Liberation from Stein to Prince Wittgenstein was intercepted. Napoleon had it printed in *Moniter* and in the *Berliner Telegraf* and Stein was forced to flee to Bohemia pursued by assassins; he only saved himself by going on to Russia, where he worked against the French in the service of the tsar. After Stein's escape the French started a reign of terror in Berlin and anyone suspected of anti-Napoleonic sentiments was in danger. Von Troschke, who co-owned property with Stein, was arrested and was for a time condemned to death. Prince Wittgenstein was arrested and accused of planning to poison Napoleon at Bayonne. The eighty-year-old Countess Voss was detained for plotting to kill Napoleon, this apparently confirmed by the fact that she had taught her parrot to screech obscenities about the Corsican.[22] Fichte was put under observation and Hardenberg and Schleiermacher were followed and harassed. Theodor Schmalz was arrested. Scharnhorst was removed from office in 1810. Prussia fell behind in her reparation payments and Napoleon used this as an excuse to increase his control over the city. Depression, fear, frustration and anger no longer had an outlet in politics. Instead it spilled out in a new culture – Romanticism. Berlin, once the centre of the Prussian Enlightenment, was now transformed into a cultural centre of the fight against French tyranny.

Berlin is rarely thought of as a centre of Romanticism; rather, the label is usually applied to regions like Bavaria with its Ludwig II fairy-tale architecture, or to the Rhine with its great ruins towering above the water and its legends of river gods or magic rings. The image is wrong. Despite Berlin's post-war attempts to distance itself from a movement now associated with everything from nationalism to Nazism it was in fact the most important centre of German Romanticism in the Napoleonic period.[23] It was Berlin which became the focal point of the diverse artistic, literary and intellectual output of that troubled age, and it was in Berlin that the sentimentality and *Schwärmerei* was channelled into a fledgling political movement. It was there that the resentment against France and against political impotence began to be mixed with its notions of the German *Volk* and *Vaterland*, with calls for German unity and, more ominously, with increasing claims to German cultural superiority and, later, racial purity as well. Berlin became important in an age in which middle-class Germans, barred from political life, began to be passionate about their own culture and their own past. They were permitted to pursue their cultural revolution under the noses of the French only because Napoleon refused to believe that such scribblers and artists threatened his rule. He was only half right.

The sheer number of artists and writers attracted to Berlin was staggering. When Kleist returned from Paris to carry on the struggle against Napoleon he chose Berlin as his base; in 1815 the world traveller Adelbert von Chamisso called it the 'Father City'.[24] A number of Romantics, from Hitzig and Tieck to Eichendorff and Varnhagen, were Berliners but many more were drawn to the city to meet and to argue and to hear the latest works at the salons of Bettina von Arnim, Henriette Herz, Rahel Varnhagen, Karoline Schlegel and Henriette Sontag. Achim von Arnim settled in Berlin in 1809, where he married Bettina Brentano; the great Berlin critic Wilhelm Wackenroder, who stressed the importance of feelings over analysis, remained there for most of his life; Karl Philipp Moritz taught at the Academy of Arts and published the *Magazin für Erfahrungsseelenkunde* between 1783 and 1793, the first ever periodical of psychology produced in Germany. Friedrich de la Motte Fouqué, the grandson of Frederick the Great's famous general, married Karoline von Briest there and retired to her home near Berlin, where he wrote myriad Romantic tales, plays and novels, including *Der Held des Nordens* and his masterpiece *Undine*. E. T. A. Hoffmann moved to Berlin in 1798, where he wrote his evocative and fantastic stories and drank with friends like Ludwig Devrient at 'Lutter und Wegner'; he died in Berlin in 1822, aged forty-six. Clemens Brentano, a friend of Arndt with whom he had written *Des Knaben Wunderhorn* (The Boy's Magic Horn), moved to Berlin from Heidelberg in 1810; here he met Müller and Eichendorff and the Schlegel brothers. Zacharias Werner, the most important dramatist of the Romantic movement, wrote poetry and songs while working in the Prussian civil service during the Napoleonic occupation; Adelbert von Chamisso, whose family had fled the revolution in France when he was a boy of nine, wrote many of his poems and stories in Berlin, including *Der Soldat* about a man ordered to execute his closest friend. Heinrich Heine studied in Berlin for two years and spent much of his time at Rahel Varnhagen von Ense's salon. Kleist, who had spent most of his extraordinary life travelling, returned to Berlin in 1807, was arrested and spent time in a French prison but returned in 1810 to continue the fight against Napoleon and to complete his most famous work *Prinz Friedrich von Homburg*. He killed himself at Wannsee in Berlin on 21 November 1811 after shooting a terminally ill friend. Friedrich Schleiermacher helped to found Berlin University and emphasized the religious dimension of Romanticism; his lectures and sermons as a professor of theology filled young Berliners with patriotic fervour.

Romanticism in Berlin was born out of the indignity, the shame, the degradation felt by those living in the humiliated and occupied capital. German Romanticism was a reaction against France – against French manners, French ideas, the French *Philosophes* and finally against French aggression. Young Germans now saw Enlightenment rationality, classicism and utilitarianism as the culture of the enemy, a culture which lacked something fundamental, something spiritual, and above all something German. Romanticism started as a literary movement and can be traced to the short-lived whirlwind aptly named *Sturm und Drang*.

Sturm und Drang ran its feverish course between the years 1765 and 1785. Frederickan Berlin was still very much an Enlightenment city, and it was left to Weimar to lead the headlong charge into the new age. Wieland arrived in 1772. Three years later Karl August became duke and invited Goethe to stay. He would remain for the rest of his life. Herder moved to Weimar in 1776 and Schiller thirteen years later. The concentration of talent in the small town would later give rise to the inane notion that Germany was somehow divided into two mutually exclusive groups, the *Dichter und Denker* (poets and thinkers) represented by Weimar, and the arrogant Prussian militarists of Berlin; in fact the two strands in German life have always been linked. Nevertheless in the late eighteenth century Weimar was experiencing its golden age and was receptive to the ideas introduced to Germany by that *Citoyen de Genève*: Jean-Jacques Rousseau.

Rousseau was the 'wild man' of Europe, the uncouth genius with a deep love of nature who travelled on foot preaching a new 'natural religion' and leaving a string of mistresses and abandoned children behind him. For him the Enlightenment man was a fallacy for underneath all the trappings of civilized life lurked an earthy, spiritual, natural human being. Being free meant breaking the restrictive chains imposed by society and allowing the natural man to shine. 'I would rather be dead than be taken for an ordinary man,' he exclaimed. The longing to break with the refined views of the Enlightenment was one of the key undercurrents of *Sturm und Drang*.

The name itself was derived from the title of a play written in 1777 by Friedrich Klinger.[25] In contrast to the characters in the typical bedroom farces of the day Klinger's characters seethed with unbridled emotion; the hatred between the two families on stage raged so intensely that it could only be countered by passionate love. The very style, the tone, the wild abandon of the characters marked this out as quintessential *Sturm und Drang*. The new movement challenged conventional morality; the rule of law was scorned while anything which allowed man to follow his true nature was praised. Jakob Lenz actually lived the new carefree life, which included well-publicized attempts to bed married women; many of his works from *Die Engländer* to *Der Waldbruder* revolve around the idea of unrequited love. In Wilhelm Heinse's 1780 novel *Ardinghello* the hero, a Florentine painter, commits two murders in the name of love but this was acceptable because the artist had thrown away stifling convention and had abandoned himself to his emotions. Schiller, too, fore-shadowed the Romantics with his belief in the primacy of art and in the idea that beauty could restore to man all that he had lost through the Enlighten-ment. His heroes were to be respected not because of their deeds but because of their inner responses to life. In *The Robbers* of 1781 the wrenching conflicts suffered by his main character, Karl, glorify the anarchic liberty of the indi-vidual; Karl becomes a tragic hero despite the crimes he has committed as the head of a robber band.[26] These ideas were echoed by Hamann, the 'Magus of the North', in his anti-rationalism and his belief in instinct and in the primacy of poetry and imagination. But above all, *Sturm und Drang* found its leading spirit in Goethe. Later in his life this many-faceted character would mock his youthful outbursts, but in the late eighteenth century he was the undisputed master of the new movement.

Goethe enjoyed the kind of adulation in his youth now typically reserved for pop stars, and his works, especially his *Bildungsroman* or novel of experi-ence, caused a hitherto unheard of sensation. The young Goethe appealed to his generation precisely because he rejected conventional rules and codes; for him a genius did not follow a path laid down by others: instead such talent revealed itself by rejecting convention, by 'overstepping existing law, breaking established rules and declaring itself above all restraint'. The early novels always featured such characters: *Wilhelm Meisters Lehrjahre* (William Meister's Apprenticeship) is the story of a young man who leaves his comfortable middle-class life to journey into the unknown; he experiences love and illness, he sees lost children and joins a wandering acting troupe, he is moved by a production of *Hamlet*, he is robbed and beaten and is rescued by a beautiful Amazon, and in the end he is taken in by a secret society in a great tower, populated by men who appreciate what he has been through and who declare him a *Meister* – a master. So too with the hero of *Götz von Berlichingen*, the young man who cries to God that he feels free under the sky, 'how free!' even as he dies. Goethe foreshadows the Romantics, too, in his accounts of Italian journeys and in his beautiful poems, *Prometheus* and *Willkommen und Abschied* and *Neue Liebe*. But it was the success of *Die Leiden des jungen Werthers* (The Sorrows of Young Werther) of 1774, a bestseller in its day, which went farthest in creating the image of the tortured Romantic soul. This is the story of a young man who longs for the freedom to fulfil himself but who cannot find happiness in the world as it is. He falls passionately in love with a girl, Lotte, who rejects him; he leaves her to find work but is misunderstood by the society in which he lives, returns to see his beloved and is finally driven to suicide. The book mourns for the misunderstood youth, the man who is too fine, too sensitive for the harsh world in which he finds himself. Such a person will always be misunderstood, just as all exceptional people 'who have created something great, something that seemed impossible, have to be decried as drunkards or madmen'.[27] It was the birth of the German cult of genius, and it was taken with deadly seriousness. Hundreds of young people identified themselves with Werther and dressed in the blue coat and yellow trousers of their champion; many left their homes to write poetry or to make pilgrimages to Weimar. There were dozens of copycat 'Werther' suicides; one Christel von Lassberg even drowned herself, Ophelia-like, in the stream near Goethe's house with a copy of the book wrapped in her clothing. The new ideas were exhilarating, inflammatory, alarming and intoxicating, and with the dawn of the nineteenth century, the coming of the French Revolution and the menacing period of uncertainty and war, *Sturm und Drang* moved seamlessly into the Romantic movement. Goethe soon turned his back on it but it was too late. The ideas had taken on a life of their own.

It was Lord Bacon who said 'there is no excellent beauty that hath not some strangeness in the proportion'. It was this need for 'strangeness', the worship of nature, the thirst for the bizarre and the erotic, the glorification of the uncontrollable, the belief in the great man, the desire to free oneself from urban restraint and to run through desolate, untamed woods or along black, craggy shores with the sinister spirits and dark forces unlocking the mysteries of the German soul, which characterized the Romantics. The term 'Romantic' was first used to describe medieval tales and songs written in Latin languages and by the seventeenth century already evoked something that was mythical, distant or fantastic. It was Madame de Staël who in 1813 first used the term to describe the poetry of the heirs of *Sturm und Drang* as the works concentrated not on events, but on the emotions of the main characters. The diverse artists, writers, poets, painters and philosophers who called themselves 'Romantics' were brought together by a common world view or *Weltanschauung*, and although there were expressions of Romanticism throughout Europe from England to Italy the movement reached its most intemperate heights in Germany. The private world of melancholy, darkness, fatalism, death, despair and cultural pessimism seemed to touch something in young Germans, and their new hero – the lonely misunderstood genius – was one they instinctively understood.

The new artistic hero was the antithesis of the hated French savant who had reduced the individual to a mere cog in the machine. For the Romantics there was no law higher than art; only the artist was sensitive to the laws of nature, only he could free himself from the restrictions of society and dedicate himself to the pursuit of truth. The Romantics revered men like Beethoven who had so spectacularly broken with convention. They repeated stories of his bravado and independence – how wonderful it was that in 1806 he had turned to his erstwhile protector and friend Prince Lichnowsky and said: 'Prince, what you are you are by the accident of birth; what I am, I am of myself. There are and there will be thousands of princes. There is only one Beethoven!'[28] There was, of course, a price to be paid. The genius would almost certainly be misunderstood by the masses; he would probably suffer, struggle, be cast out by family and friends; he would be laughed at, he would be cold and hungry and lonely, and he would probably die young. But it would be worth it, for the suffering he bore would heighten his awareness and make him greater still. This belief in the benefits of pain became a self-fulfilling prophecy; Charlotte Stieglitz was so convinced of its power that she stabbed herself in her Berlin house so that her husband could write better poetry; sadly it did not work.[29] Countless young men and, to a lesser extent, women struggled in garrets and lonely rooms trying to paint or write or compose *Lieder* and, as Sheehan has put it, 'often poor, almost always insecure and unsettled, the Romantics paid dearly for the artistic autonomy they celebrated in their work'.[30] Many died young – Hardenberg (Novalis) at twenty-nine, Wackenroder at twenty-five; Kleist committed suicide in Berlin aged thirty-four.

The notion of the individual against the world was echoed in all Romantic literature. Shakespeare's tragedies were held up as the first role model because of the human conflicts they revealed; Hamlet was seen as the quintessential Romantic youth tormented by ghosts and drowning lovers and his own fears – 'that dread of something after death' – which made him incapable of action. King Lear was a tragic figure staggering towards his death blind and betrayed; the play *Macbeth* was filled with Romantic symbolism from hideous witches on the bleak moor to the bloodstained hands that could not be cleaned, and the eternal punishment for 'unnatural deeds' committed by 'infected minds'. The German Romantics wanted nothing to do with society novels and had no time for Jane Austen or pretty French farces; their works were about suffering and pain and fate. In *Ahnung und Gegenwart* Eichendorff describes the traumatic experiences of a young man during the Napoleonic occupation; in *Undine* a mermaid is visited by her husband on the forbidden day and is forced to return to the sea for ever; Friedrich Schlegel's *Lucinde*, subtitled 'An Apology for Nature and Innocence', describes a heroine who is so carried away by her own passions and natural urges that she flouts all norms of conventional morality. It is a tale of such eroticism, raw emotion and sexuality that it caused a scandal when it was published in 1789, but Schlegel defended his creation, announcing that Lucinde was innocent because she had merely been following her true nature.

The new mood was echoed in the Romantic music which combined the cult of genius with deep human passion. Beethoven, Weber, Schubert and Schumann were venerated and E. T. A. Hoffmann called music 'the most Romantic of all the art forms'; he was so enamoured of Mozart that he added 'Amadeus' to his name. Liszt said that music is 'the embodied and intelligible essence of feeling; capable of being apprehended by our senses, it penetrates them like a dart, like a ray, like a dew, like a spirit, and fills our soul.'[31] Music itself featured in Romantic works: Wilhelm Wackenroder's *Joseph Berglinger* is about a composer torn between the inspiration of his music and the mundane life he is forced to lead. *Lieder* and programme music often evoked Romantic themes. Schubert's *Die schöne Müllerin* and *Winterreise*, which echoed around the Berlin salons of the 1820s, captured a world in which sensibility was all; Carl Maria von Weber included themes of wonder and magic in *Der Freischütz* of 1821 in which a forester goes into the woods in search of a magic spell which will restore his marksmanship but instead meets the sinister Black Ranger.[32]

The forester's journey into the wood was another of the great Romantic themes linked to the love of nature and the fascination with the dark forces of life. Rousseau had said 'no flat country, however beautiful it may be, ever appeared so to me. I need torrents, rocks, firs, dark woods, mountains, rough tracks to climb up and down, precipices by my side.'[33] The German Romantics echoed this fascination with nature and landscape; they wanted nothing to do with fussy manicured lawns or carefully laid out paths; they wanted eerie forests, deep streams, strange grottoes and lonely seascapes far away from town and people. Nature, real or imagined, was the antithesis of and an escape from the city, where so many of these prophets lived; from the increasingly troubled world of the Industrial Revolution, and from the oppression of occupied Berlin. Even the 'English garden', the rage at the time, was planted to look as if it had grown naturally. Poetry and stories were filled with references to nature: Hölderlin lovingly describes the forest in the evening: 'Now there is a breath which moves the tree-tops in the wood, and look, now the shadow image of our earth, the moon, is on her way in secret too; night the dream-laden is coming.'[34] Goltz wrote: 'Of all nature's scenes it is the wood in which all of her secrets and all of her favours are found together ... What the evil over-clever, insipid, bright cold world encumbers and complicates, the wood – green mysterious, enchanted, dark, culture-renouncing but true to the law of nature – must free and make good again.'[35]

The love of landscape was reflected in the painting of the day. In the landscapes of the old world, from the Dutch masters to Poussin, nature had been portrayed as a mere backdrop to the relationship between God and man and had been executed in a highly stylized, symbolic manner which evoked a sense of harmony and a divine order. Romantic painters changed this view. The old ideas of balance and construction and man's control over nature were swept aside in favour of unfettered, uncontrollable nature which reduced man to a mere speck in an unfamiliar, frightening, painful and menacing world.

The greatest and most moving of these paintings came to Berlin in 1810, in an exhibition at the Academy of works by Caspar David Friedrich. The artist caused a sensation in the city with his chilling portrayals of destiny and the helplessness of man against the elements. His *A Monk on the Seashore* reveals a lonely windswept figure standing out against the threatening, turbulent water, an image of infinity with its terrible dark emptiness, the figure with no hope of redemption or eternal life. *Wanderer above the Sea of Fog* has the lone figure again, this time a man dressed in black standing on craggy rocks watching the crashing sea below. In *Two Men Contemplating the Moon* cloaked figures look out from the edge of the forest at the misty moonlight shining through the gnarled fingers of an ancient tree, and are overpowered by the spectacle before them.[36] Like so many of his generation Caspar David Friedrich had been influenced by the *Naturphilosophie* – the pantheism of men like Friedrich Wilhelm Schelling, who taught that the spirit of the world manifested itself in nature. The forest paths which led down rocky cliffs and past shadowy caves were both a source of revelation and a source of fear. The traveller seeking fundamental truths had to make his way through the German forest alone.

This endless journey, the search for meaning and truth, was another essential element of Romantic literature. The artist suffered the Romantic agony because he could never be content with the world as it was. He was driven on by the deep longing, *Sehnsucht*, to find something which, tragically, could never be achieved in his life. In his *Evening Fantasy* Hölderlin exclaims: 'But where am I to go? Mortals live by wages and work; in alternate toil and rest everyone finds satisfaction: why is it always in my breast that the goad is never still?'[37] In his poem *Sehnsucht* Eichendorff describes how a lonely man suddenly hears the sound of a post horn echoing over the distant hills, a call which awakens his lost memories and desire: 'My heart caught fire within me, and I thought secretly to myself: O, how wonderful to go along too in the glowing summer night.'[38] The most famous symbol of *Sehnsucht*, and indeed of German Romanticism itself, was Novalis's 'blue flower'. This remarkable image first appeared in his unfinished novel *Heinrich von Ofterdingen*, which was published posthumously in 1802. In it the young poet Heinrich meets a stranger who tells him of treasures in far-off lands and that night he dreams of the mysterious, magical light-blue flower. Heinrich becomes obsessed by this thing of perfection and beauty; the flower has awakened an 'indescribable longing in me ... I cannot get it out of my mind'. He is driven to search for this perfect object, but the blue flower can never be found in this world.

Heinrich's dream was not unique. If the *Philosophes* had championed the coming of the light the Romantics preferred the murky world of apparitions and darkness. Hundreds of works were written on the themes of sunset and nightfall. Beethoven's *Moonlight Sonata* was the first of many pieces ranging from Robert Schumann's *Nachtstücke* (Night Pieces) of 1839 to Brahms's *Der Tod, das ist die kühle Nacht* (Death, that is the Cold Night). Poetry, too, ranged from Hölderlin's *Sunset* to Brentano's *Evening Serenade*, in which he describes the flute wafting over the dark hills: 'How sweetly it speaks to the heart! Through the night which holds me embraced.' Nightfall brought with it the terrible, wonderful world of dreams which gave the human being access to the secret world beyond reason. In *Die Symbolik des Traumes* (The Symbolism of Dreams) Gotthilf Schubert asserted that dreams gave human beings access to the subconscious, to the soul and to God.[39] E. T. A. Hoffmann's dream sequences are the most disturbing in Romantic literature and range from fairy-tales like *The Mouse King* to sinister stories like *Ignaze Denner* and novels like *Elixiere des Teufels*, which delve into the horror of insanity and which would later inspire the genre of crime fiction. The world of dreams tied into the bizarre and the occult, into a world filled with strange apparitions, ghosts, rotting corpses, and spirits. Mesmer, who gave his name to his own particular brand of hypnotism, created a sensation in Berlin when he preached that all living creatures are linked by a mysterious substance called animal magnetism. He charged substantial sums of money to hypnotize members of the audience and to perform 'miracles' and 'magic cures' for them. Terrible dreams recurred in Romantic painting, as in the pictures of a goblin lying on a sleeping maiden in Fuseli's *The Nightmare* or in Alfred Rethel's *Death as Assassin*, complete with its hideous dancing skeleton.

The Romantics were obsessed by themes of fate and death. Popular *Schicksalstragödien* (tragedies of fate), which were often modelled on Greek plays, had individuals or even whole families fated to die because of a crime committed in the past. In his sensational success *Die Schuld* (The Guilt) Adam Müller portrays a count who murdered a man in his youth and then married his widow. As the play unfolds he, and the audience, slowly come to realize that the dead man was his own brother. The obsession with death was everywhere. In *Hyperion's Song of Fate* Hölderlin described how 'suffering human beings dwindle and fall headlong from one hour to the next hurled like water from precipice to precipice down through the years into uncertainty'. In *Hymns to the Night* Novalis cries, 'Oh draw me, Beloved, powerfully on, so that I can fall into slumber and can love. I feel the rejuvenating stream of death ... Eternal life has been revealed in death; you are death and it is only by you that we are made whole.'[40] This love of death came through in Achim von Arnim's phrase 'We live to die, we die to live.'[41] Even in Wilhelm Müller's cycle of poems *Die schöne Müllerin*, so beautifully set to music by Schubert, the young miller drowns himself when he learns that the woman he loves desires another. Gradually the fascination with mortality took on a new theme – the idealization of violence and violent death and the creation of apocalyptic visions of warfare and honour in battle. In *Fragmente* Schlegel writes about giving one's life for the nation: 'the noblest and most beautiful must be chosen, above all, the human being, the flower of the earth ... only in the midst of death is the lightning of eternal life ignited.'[42] Tieck wrote, 'The desire for death is the warrior-spirit.'[43] Joseph von Eichendorff's *Ahnung und Gegenwart* ends with: 'We were born in struggle and in struggle we will go down conquered or in triumph. For out of the magic incense of our making a ghost of war will materialize, armoured, with the blanched face of death and bloody hair.'[44] It was not surprising that this was written in 1815, in the wake of the Wars of Liberation. The idealization of violence and war began to touch for the first time on the world of politics. This new, much more dangerous strain of Romanticism, found a natural home in Berlin.

Berlin's role was central in the transformation of Romantic ideas into political ideology. Whereas in other parts of Germany it was possible to remain aloof from political life, even the most unworldly philosophers and poets could not shield themselves from the national problems of unity and independence so visible in the occupied city. Suddenly their themes began to take on a new patriotic meaning; characters could still walk through the woods but now they had to be German woods; they could admire buildings, but they had to be 'German' Gothic buildings; they could talk of history but it had to be 'German' history. Images of national regeneration, of rebirth and greatness, of a lost world of the German *Volk*, of medieval pageantry and honour, found their way into the works of Novalis and Arndt and Körner and Schenkendorf. Novalis wanted to bring back the glory of the lost Germany and said that 'the magic of the imagination can unite all ages and all worlds'. Now Hölderlin referred to the German nation as the only one which was pure and called Germans 'incomparably diverse, wonderfully deep', while Schlegel wrote that the spirit of Europe 'now lived in Germany'.[45] Folk tales and legends were now treated as a lifeline back to a 'true German' past, and Arnim and Brentano's folk songs, *Des Knaben Wunderhorn*, or Wackenroder and Tieck's *Der getreue Eckart und der Tannenhäuser* and *Tod des kleinen Rotkäppchens* were read with intense interest; even tales like *Die schöne Melusine*, which had originated in France, were presented as quintessentially German. The Grimms' fairy tales, published between 1812 and 1814, were decidedly nationalistic; glorious German epics like the *Nieblungenlied* were resurrected along with ancient German heroes. The figure of the huntsman, for example, now stood for the magical Teutonic character Siegfried.

History, too, became part of the idea of national rebirth. It was important to discover the 'true' German past because, as Friedrich von Schlegel put it, only people with 'great national memories' have survived in history, 'history is the self-consciousness of a nation'. The real Germany was said to have existed far back in the Middle Ages, a perfect age when Germans had pursued pure and noble goals. The Berliner Ludwig Tieck had explored the monasteries and villages of the Mark Brandenburg with his friend Wackenroder in search of a medieval past; like so many of his generation he became enamoured of Dürer – his 1798 story *Frank Sternbald's Wanderungen* was a fictitious tale about one of the master's pupils. The reverence for the medieval past had religious undertones and was connected not only to the new reverence for Luther as the 'father of the German language' but to German Pietism, which held that religion was above all a deeply personal, emotional experience rather than one dictated by empty formal institutions admired by the previous generation. Adam Müller, a member of the Berlin salons and the Christlich-Deutsche Gesellschaft, believed that Germany was essentially Christian; in order to survive it had to rediscover the community of the faithful, united once again by an emotional sense of belonging to the nation, the feeling which had once produced a 'beautiful brilliant' Christian age. Such vague Romantic ideas had not initially been part of a single political message but were soon channelled into a specific national political programme by those united against Napoleon. One of the most important was the revolutionary nationalist prophet and propagandist, the philosopher Johann Gottlieb Fichte. It was he who articulated the link between Romantic notions of history and culture with a new concept of German nationalism. He used the lecture halls of Berlin as his pulpit.

Fichte was born in Rammeau in 1762 and first studied theology before becoming a student of Kant's. In 1794 he was appointed to a chair of philosophy at Jena, where he met Goethe, Schiller, the Schlegel brothers and the Humboldts, but he was dismissed for being an atheist. Instead he moved to that 'Godless city' Berlin, where he became the first elected rector at the new university. It was there that he turned against the Enlightenment and against Kant, and moved towards a Romantic view of German history and the German nation. For him Germans – the *Urvolk* – were morally superior to other races, not least because they had remained uncorrupted by other cultures, especially

those of the Latin and Roman worlds. It was this vision which prompted
Fichte to write his *Speeches to the German Nation*, delivered in Berlin during
French occupation in 1806–7.[46]

The speeches came at an important time. The Spanish had revolted against
the French and some, including vom Stein, hoped that Berliners might also
rise up against Napoleon. In his addresses Fichte asked, 'What is to be done
with Germany?' and in fourteen lectures proceeded to outline a new vision of
German nationalism. He asked what made a German 'German'; why, despite
the fact that Rome had been a superior civilization, had the ancient Germans
resisted it for so long? His answer was that freedom meant rejecting foreign
cultures and 'just remaining Germans'. There, in the heart of occupied Berlin
and with French officers in the audience, he asserted that 'only the German
has character' and went on to stress that individuals must be taught to feel
part of this national group. The key to this was education, which would teach
young Germans that fulfilment in life would only come about if they were at
one with the German nation. The message was clear: Berliners might not be
as sophisticated as the French but to be true to themselves they had to rid
themselves of the occupiers and re-create a glorious past through the resurrection of folk tales and medieval history. It was a provincial idea born of humiliation and loss of prestige, an idea which would later be twisted into the service
of racists and chauvinists whom Fichte would have hated. And yet with his
help Germanic fairy tales, the Gothic cathedrals, the poetry of 'longing', the
patriotic songs, the slanted versions of history and the many other trappings
of German Romanticism became mixed up with the new political movement
– nationalism.

By 1808 other patriotic Germans had joined Fichte in the effort to rouse
Berliners against the French. Schleiermacher, who had been exiled from Berlin
by Napoleon, returned and spent his time whipping up popular support for
war against France, for 'one could not abandon the nation to the foreigner'
but had to create 'one true German Empire, powerfully representing the entire
German *Volk*'. Kleist said of the French in 1808:

> Bleach every space, field and town,
> White with their bones;
> Spurned by crow and fox,
> Deliver them unto the fishes;
> Dam the Rhine with their bodies;
> Let her, swollen with their limbs
> Flood the Pfalz with foaming waves,
> May she then be our frontier.[47]

Ernst Moritz Arndt cried, 'let the unanimity of your hearts be your church, let hatred of the French be your religion, let freedom and Fatherland be your saints, to whom you pray!'; and in his 1813 speech 'What is the German's Fatherland?' he spoke of the need to unite Germans in a great nation. For him, Germans did not appreciate their own country: 'We live in a beautiful large rich land, a land of glorious memories, undying deeds, unforgettable service to the world in remote and recent times.'[48] It had been lost, now it must be recovered. Publications, too, began to reflect the new mood. As early as 1807 Wilhelm Gubitz, a teacher at the Academy of Arts, had attempted to publish a nationalist newspaper Der Vaterland, although the first edition was seized and he was imprisoned. In 1808 Kotzebue published a number of anti-Napoleonic articles in Der Freymüthige; the paper was banned after K. M. Müller submitted an inflammatory article called 'Über die Nemesis', but the papers continued to circulate underground.

Anti-French feelings began to take more practical forms after news of the Spanish Uprising and the Austrian Wars of Liberation in 1809, the return of the king from Königsberg at the end of that year and the death of Frederick III's consort Queen Luise in July 1810 – a woman who was revered for her stance against Napoleon and whose death brought people together in mourning. A plethora of illegal and secret organizations sprang up: Reimer's bookshop on the Kochstrasse became a centre of clandestine activity for anti-French groups; men from Chamisso to Savigny, from Varnhagen to Arndt continued to meet at the Herz salon to discuss possible moves against France. One of the most powerful organizations was the Tugendbund, started in April 1808 in Königsberg, with a chapter in Berlin. It called itself the 'Moral and Scientific Union' for 'the revival of morality, religion, serious taste and public spirit' but was in fact a secret society directed against the French. Friedrich von der Marwitz said that they got 'intelligence from all quarters, to create irritation against the French . . . and then to make report how discontented the people are here'.[49] Schleiermacher was the leader of the Berlin Committee, which included military men amongst its members and which met secretly even when 'the enemy was still in the land'. The groups communicated between Königsberg and Berlin using codes to deceive the French; in one the king and queen were referred to as 'Quednow and his wife', vom Stein was called 'Christ', and Gneisenau was referred to as 'the Call'.[50] In 1812 the Hauptverein or Berlin Central Club was founded to further the nationalist cause and in November 1810 the Deutsches Bund or German Confederation was formed by the student Friedrich Friesen and the teacher Friedrich Ludwig Jahn to ensure 'the survival of the German people in its originality and self-sufficiency, the revival of German-ness, of all slumbering forces, the preservation of our nationhood . . . aiming at the eventual unity of our scattered, divided and separated *Volk*.[51] Jahn was obsessed by the idea of strengthening the German *Volk* by ridding it of the foreign presence; in 1811 he put these ideas into practice by forming the *Turnerschaft* in Berlin's Hasenheide. Two hundred gymnasts gathered not only to exercise together but to stage medieval tournaments, complete with crossbow competitions and mock sword fights. Young people were to be ready for war and all these activities – from poetry readings to night marches – were meant to instil a communal spirit. By 1812 the Deutsches Bund had spawned other groups, including the Charlottenburger Bund which included Gneisenau, Schleiermacher and Reimer amongst its members. The wave of anti-French activity increased dramatically when Napoleon began preparations for a new campaign in 1812. In the end, however, it was neither the reformers nor Romantic ideas nor the patriotism of men like Fichte or Görres which drove Napoleon from Berlin. It was the result of Napoleon's one great mistake – the invasion of Russia.

By the end of 1811 relations between France and Russia had started to break down and both sides began to plan for war. The French preparations were staggering. Napoleon assembled an army of 1,100,000 men in Europe. Five hundred thousand, including Dutch, German, Polish and Swiss troops, were moved to the east. To the annoyance of the local population thousands were stationed in Berlin. Worse still, Napoleon forced the Prussian king not only to maintain the troops on his soil but to provide 20,000 troops for the army. From March 1812 Berlin once again endured the economic hardships of the occupation of a vast army. Many of the reformers were so disgusted by the king's support of France that they left the country: around 500 officers resigned their commissions – Boyen and Clausewitz went to Russia, Gneisenau went to England, and the head of the Prussian police went to Prague. Civil servants, journalists, writers, philosophers and others who yearned for a war of liberation continued to organize underground. Some Berliners were visibly hostile to the French troops in their midst; when the foreign soldiers celebrated Napoleon's birthday on 15 August a handful of people pelted them with stones and had to be driven back with bayonets. The Deutsches Bund and other groups began to sabotage French supply lines and attack guard posts. This did not amount to a popular uprising against the French – far from it – but some Berliners used the opportunity to demonstrate their hatred of France for the first time.

The war began on 24 June 1812. A vast army of 422,000 men struggled across the river Niemen and entered Russia. Napoleon had high hopes of victory. He believed that the Russian serfs would rise up and join him in their demands for the principles of liberty, equality and brotherhood. But the Russian serfs knew little of the principles of 1798. Napoleon hoped he might be reconciled with the tsar before Christmas and decided not to burden his troops with heavy fur coats, boots or ice shoes for the horses. But the tsar did not negotiate. Compared to the mighty French force bearing down on it the Russian army was weak and Napoleon thought it would be easy to crush. But instead of fighting it continued to retreat into the vast landscape, burning villages and fields on the way thereby depriving the French army of food. By the end of that fiery August the invaders had already lost 150,000 men to illness and desertion and so many horses were dying in the heat that the basic provision of food and supplies simply ceased.[52] Just before Moscow, at Borodino, Marshal Kutuzov finally turned and fought the French, but although it was a Russian bloodbath their army remained intact. The French continued on to Moscow with 100,000 troops but found the city deserted and emptied of supplies. It was a hollow victory. By the time Napoleon arrived there winter was closing in. As he paced the Kremlin wall and looked over his latest conquest he realized that he had been trapped.

The winter of 1812 was particularly bitter. Napoleon ordered his army to retreat down the Smolensk road pursued by Kutuzov. Many were killed by Cossacks and partisans but more simply froze to death on the way home as temperatures reached −21°C at Smolensk, −24°C at Minsk, −30°C at Molodeze. The suffering was immense. On 5 January the pro-Russian activists vom Stein and Arndt left a liberated St Petersburg to the sound of church bells and followed the retreating French army down the road from Pskov. The carnage was terrible to behold. Their sledge passed over the dead bodies of horses and men which were strewn on either side of the road; all the villages they passed had been ransacked or burned. On 11 January they reached Wilna and found a pyramid of corpses in the courtyard of the monastery 'as high as a third storey window and all frozen together'. Stein wrote to his wife: 'We see nothing but wagons full of corpses which are found in the high road partly eaten by wolves or are carried out of the hospitals (in Wilna alone there are 15,000 in hospitals) or gangs of prisoners in rags, hollow-eyed, with blue-grey skin, awaiting death in sullen silence.'[53] Over 20,000 men were lost crossing the river Berezina alone, and when the remnants of the Grande Armée finally struggled over the Niemen into Poland only 18,000 troops remained. Napoleon had lost 380,000 men, making this one of the most costly campaigns in history.[54]

The majority of Berliners had remained passive throughout the French occupation, unmoved even by Fichte's speeches and the activities of the *Bund*, but rumours of Napoleon's defeat in Russia brought anti-French sentiments to life. French army soldiers quartered in people's homes were turfed out on to the street. By the end of 1812 the remnants of the Grande Armée had started to struggle back into Berlin; Ludwig Rellstab saw the wagons filled with wounded men roll slowly into the city and noted that 'the appearance of the unfortunates was terrible'.[55] As the Grande Armée struggled west General Hans Yorck, then in command of a Prussian auxiliary corps of 14,000 troops, had deliberately disobeyed the king – unthinkable behaviour for a Prussian officer in an army whose motto was 'Obedience' – and had changed sides. The Convention of Tauroggen, signed in December 1812, opened the border to the tsar's army and the two had pursued the French into Prussia together. Gustav Parthey noted that above all it was 'the young generation which greeted [Yorck's action] with joy'.[56]

On 6 February 1813 Berliners had their first contact with the victorious Russian army when an advance party of 300 Cossacks entered the city and demanded the surrender of Napoleon's 10,000 troops there. The French barricaded the city but Russian reinforcements arrived and on 4 March Berlin was liberated. Many who had remained loyal to France fled the city in disgrace and on 17 March General Yorck made his triumphal entry into Berlin. At the same time Stein had travelled to Breslau to try to persuade the king to change sides and enter the war against France. On 23 February Frederick William, who had finally broken his ties with Napoleon, read the proclamation *An Mein Volk* (*To My People*), appealing to his subjects to rise up and volunteer for service. On 3 March he introduced a new medal for bravery in battle to be awarded irrespective of rank. It was designed by Schinkel, and was called the Iron Cross.

Friedrich William III's change of heart heralded the true start of the Wars of Liberation. The Prussian army openly called for men and the clandestine organizations were transformed into recruitment centres: members of Jahn's organization rushed to join the Landwehr under Adolf von Lützow, who adopted the uniform of black frock coat, red lapels and gold oak branches – the first manifestation of the black-red-gold which would later become the colours of the German nationalist movement. Theodor Körner wrote poetry glorifying the national fight; he was later killed in action and became a hero – there are still two streets named after him in Berlin. Thirteen thousand Prussians from all walks of life joined up – 6,500 from Berlin, including Schadow, Fichte and Iffland, who came in outlandish medieval outfits. Berlin businessmen raised 1.2 million thalers to pay for the volunteer army and many women gave their gold jewellery in return for ornate filigree iron bracelets and necklaces which were worn with patriotic pride. On 24 March Frederick William finally returned to his capital confident that the city was now safe. The final battle near Berlin took place at Grossbeeren on 23 August 1813, when a French force of 70,000 men met an army of Swedish, Russian and Prussian troops under Bernadotte. The French defeat there foreshadowed the most important battle of the Wars of Liberation, the 'Battle of the Nations' at Leipzig.

This battle was the largest so far in history. It was fought by the coalition of Austria, Prussia and Russia; Austria alone contributed 127,000 men, Prussia 228,000 infantry and 31,000 cavalry, while Napoleon had a force of 442,000. The battle began on 16 October 1813. The mammoth armies clashed for three days and when smoke finally cleared the rolling fields, now hills of mud, could be seen littered with dead and wounded men, mutilated horses, discarded weapons and twisted wreckage. The French lost a staggering 38,000 men while 30,000 were taken prisoner.[57] The battle was a disaster for Napoleon and it broke him. War continued for months, but his hopes for the mastery of Europe ended in 1815, at Waterloo.

When news of the rout at Leipzig reached Berlin the city erupted in a wave of jubilation. The sense of pride and optimism carried on into the summer, when the Prussians reached Paris and cartloads of property stolen from Prussia were brought back to Berlin. On 17 and 18 January 1816 a great victory celebration was held under the restored Quadriga on the Brandenburg Gate. The anti-French activists had now become heroes and Baron vom Stein was made a Knight of the Order of the Black Eagle – the highest decoration in the land. The victory had freed Berlin and Prussia from foreign domination.

Reformers and fledgling nationalist groups now demanded social and political reforms. Liberal nationalists like Jahn and Ernst Moritz Arndt wanted to see the creation of a unified German nation and in 1814 Arndt wrote in *Germanien und Europa* that Germany should be a single monarchical state with its own army, its own laws and its own representative institutions. To this end he started to organize the creation of monuments and festivals, including one at the site of the Battle of Leipzig. But the hopes of the reformers were soon dashed. The king was safe, Napoleon was gone and things could go back to the way they were. The political class found to their disappointment that not only was there little real desire for change amongst the ruling elite; there was little interest amongst the people either. The drive for national unity remained strong amongst liberals and reformers but they were a tiny minority. Democratic reforms were halted before representative government could be put into place in part because the mass of Berliners remained suspicious of it, even referring to democratic constitutionalism as 'un-German'. Nineteenth-century attempts to portray the time as one of mass movement for national unity were mere fantasy; after all, even the Landwehr had consisted of only 20,000 volunteers, and the war had been won not by them but by the mammoth regular armies. Only later would men like Arndt and Fichte or the reformers like Stein and Scharnhorst become national heroes; at the time they were treated with suspicion both by the populace and by the aristocrats keen to retain power. With Napoleon gone liberal nationalism was increasingly seen as a threat. As Madame de Staël had said of Prussia, 'the two classes of society – the scholars and the courtiers – are completely divorced from each other. The thinkers are soaring in the Empyrean and on the earth you encounter only grenadiers.' The 'grenadiers' had fought the war for the restoration of stability and to retain Prussia's status as a great power. They wanted to return to their own privileges. Society as a whole was unwilling or unable to stop them, and that is precisely what they did.

Men like Stein were bitterly disappointed by the general apathy of the population at large and by the fact that there was no real stomach for reform amongst the majority of Berliners. Peace had come at last and most wanted to settle down and rebuild their lives. Stein had already complained about Berliners' pathetic response to Napoleon compared to the fervour of the masses during the Spanish revolt or of the Muscovites, in whom he had witnessed 'heart-elevating inspiring scenes'. After the war he was even more scathing about Berliners' lack of interest in reform. 'It is a misfortune for the Prussian State that the capital is situated in the Electoral Mark,' he said. 'What impression can those dry flatlands make on the mind of their inhabitants? What power can they have to rouse or exalt or cheer it?' He continued, 'What can you expect from the inhabitants of those sandy steppes, those smart, heartless, wooden, half-educated people, cut out for nothing but corporals and calculators ... fellows that think only of places, privileges, increased salaries.'[58] Niebuhr told Wilhelm von Humboldt: 'It is an utterly mistaken view to think that the mass of the German population has a democratic tendency; that appears in our savants, our pamphleteers, our beardless youths, but nowhere in the people, the nobles, citizens or peasants.'[59]

This view was soon codified in the post-war settlement of Europe. The bizarre Congress of Vienna in 1814–15, best known for the many amorous liaisons which took place behind the scenes, settled Europe's borders after the defeat of Napoleon but did not end German fragmentation and absolutist rule. Stein had hoped for the creation of something akin to the old German empire and Hardenberg had wanted a close German federation and representative government, but such developments were impossible at a time when neither Prussia nor Austria would concede power to the other, when smaller states like Württemberg insisted on sovereignty, and when the people of Germany remained passive. The result was a loose confederation of states with a weak parliament in Frankfurt-am-Main made up of non-elected representatives. There was no constitutional reform in Austria or Prussia and the new German Confederation was little more than a collection of princes determined to retain power and prevent change. Ironically, the most important change had nothing to do with reform, but took place because the tsar wanted large chunks of Polish territory which was then in Prussian hands; Prussia was compensated with Saxon territory and with extensive areas in the Rhineland and Westphalia, giving it control over a swathe of territory from East Prussia to the new industrial areas in the west. Although the significance of this was little understood at the time it marked a crucial turning point in German history. For the first time ever Prussia's focus had shifted to the west; for the first time ever Berlin was responsible not only for the defence of the east, but also for the border with France. The attempts to join these divided Prussian regions would now in effect shape the drive for German unity. But this lay in the future. Berlin was not yet the focal point of Prussia; neither Rhinelanders nor Saxons felt any loyalty to their new state capital. Goethe noted that whereas other countries had great cities which served as the capitals of a united nation Berlin remained a mere provincial city: 'Paris is France,' he wrote. 'All the main interests of that great country are concentrated in the capital ... It is quite different here in Germany ... We have no city, we have not even a region of which one could say: "Here is Germany!" '60

Some tried to maintain the nationalist momentum after the Wars of Revolution. *Turnvater* Jahn hoped to expand his patriotic gymnastic groups and in Jena the student movement or *Burschenschaft* was founded and quickly spread throughout Germany. These young people still longed for the creation of a united Germany; they dressed in what they believed to be old German national costumes, carried the black, red and gold colours of the old imperial order used by the Lützow volunteers, and they began to act out Romantic stories of medieval knights and folk tales in secret rituals and gatherings. In October 1817 they gathered at the symbolic Wartburg castle perched high on a rocky crag in Thuringia to merge all the local groups into a national body. Nearly 500 torch-bearing students dressed in costumes trudged up the hill to the site where Luther had translated the Bible, to the very room whose wall was still marked with the ink he had thrown at a vision of the Devil. There they held a ceremony commemorating both the victory at Leipzig and the anniversary of the Reformation which had brought 'freedom from Rome'.61 In memory of Luther's burning of the Papal Bull they gathered works of conservative and anti-nationalist writers together and burned them in a huge bonfire.

The idea of a group of nationalists agitating in the German universities made the leaders of the newly restored absolutist regimes nervous. The chance to silence them came when the student and *Burschenschaft* member Karl Sand assassinated the reactionary playwright Kotzebue on 23 March 1819 – the student was later decapitated in public.

All liberal democratic and nationalist groups were to be punished under a new set of laws: the infamous Carlsbad decrees. These were masterminded by the wily Austrian statesman Wenzel von Metternich, who was bitterly opposed to any participation of the people in government. All democratic clubs, liberal organizations and anyone suspected of involvement in 'revolutionary agitation' were now to be suppressed and police state techniques used to hunt down all those opposed to the restoration of absolutism. The press was censored along with all printed matter of less than twenty pages; universities became bastions of conservatism as professors who criticized the system were sacked and rebellious students sent down. Beethoven's *Fidelio* was banned, as were Fichte's *Speeches to the German Nation*; Friedrich Jahn was arrested and his gymnasia closed down and Frederick William III dismissed the last of the reformers, including Wilhelm von Humboldt; on 20 March 1820 Humboldt revealed the extent of the censorship when he began a letter to Stein with: 'I have refrained from saying to you through the post anything about public affairs ... All our letters are opened.'[62] Berliners did not defend them; most longed for peace and agreed with Niebuhr when he said that there was no need to fight for political change when liberty was 'based more on administration than on constitution'. The disillusioned poets and writers and artists were not powerful enough to rouse the city from its complacency; how could they when even Goethe taught that he would 'rather cause an injustice than tolerate disorder'. The 'quiet years' of the Biedermeier period had begun.[63]

Biedermeier represented a great retreat from politics and from the national questions left unsolved after the Wars of Liberation. It was also a reaction against Romanticism, which by now was sinking under the weight of its own obsession with tuberculosis and opium and death. There was a sense of insecurity and helplessness amongst the bourgeoisie, captured by the anguished term *Weltschmerz*, the pain of being in the world. People were too tired or too disappointed to face the issues churning beneath the placid surface of life and drifted into a period of restoration, of security and of conservatism. They turned inward to the small things in life, to local politics, to the *Heimat* and to the family.

The name Biedermeier was invented in the 1850s, long after the period had ended, and was a gentle dig at the dull, sentimental bourgeois culture which flourished after the defeat of Napoleon. The Biedermeier world was one of *Bildung*, of classical education, of innocence and naïveté. Its air of respectability and quiet dignity hid a degree of prudishness and hypocrisy. Contemporary paintings capture its spirit, filled as they are with their images of pretty but not grand interiors, of young men in their libraries or young ladies practising the piano or having tea or singing Christmas carols. The rooms were cosy and homely, with wooden floors and striped silk wallpaper, filled with dainty furniture of lavender and cherrywood. The centre of this world was the family.

The new morality made the family into the highest achievement of bourgeois life; children were seen not merely as future providers but as a way for a middle-class couple to ensure immortality: they represented hopes for advancement and success in the next generation.[64] Marriage was no longer strictly controlled by the community or regarded as a financial transaction or dynastic contract between two families. Love matches were suddenly fashionable. The new morality influenced sexual mores. In the eighteenth century love and sexuality had been seen as two distinct things and open libertinism and erotic adventures had been a source of amusement, particularly amongst the aristocracy. In the early part of the nineteenth century Wilhelm von Humboldt was famous for his visits to Berlin's better brothels, and yet his marriage had been held up as a paragon of virtue. Thomas Jefferson had told Humboldt in 1807 that 'When a man assumes a public trust he should consider himself as public property', but neither man would have thought this included scrutiny of his private life. Now Humboldt's personal life was criticized; Hardenberg was castigated for keeping a mistress and both Wieland, who had had a splendidly decadent sex life, and Kotzebue, who had at least seventeen children and perhaps more, were labelled lascivious and immoral. Men still frequented brothels and had mistresses on the side but it was no longer polite to talk about it openly. This prudishness extended to all aspects of life, including the world of politics. Bourgeois Berliners knew they had no political power but they rejected the inflammatory work of Heinrich Heine who, writing from Paris, railed against the repression in Berlin. Rather than heed his warnings of the dangers lurking in Prussian life Berliners called him 'radical' and 'dangerous'.[65] In reality, the educated elite remained firmly under the control of the Hohenzollerns and the military. Personal and political doubts were pushed underground in a world of censorship and conformity and repression. Even Humboldt, who had done so much for the city's academic life, called Berlin an 'intellectual wasteland, small, unliterary, and therefore overly malicious'.[66]

Given the pervading climate it is not surprising that Biedermeier Berlin produced little art of note. Sadly many of the great artists who had been drawn to the city during the heady days of the Romantic period now found their careers blocked. Felix Mendelssohn, who in 1820 had re-introduced Bach's *St Matthew Passion* to Berlin and who should have succeeded to the directorship of the Singakademie, was passed over for the dull Karl Friedrich Rungenhagen. Carl Maria von Weber, who had inaugurated Romantic opera with the première of *Der Freischütz* in 1821, was rejected by the court composer

Gaspare Spontini and moved to Dresden: the Berliner Giacomo Meyerbeer was forced to leave for lack of work and was only offered the position of director of the Opera in 1842 under Frederick William IV; Hector Berlioz and Richard Wagner both spent time in Berlin but were disappointed by its repressive atmosphere and moved elsewhere. Even the great sculptor and artist Johann Gottfried Schadow, who had created the Quadriga and who had been so scathing about the French occupation of Berlin, received no more commissions in his own city. He was superseded by the more solid Christian Daniel Rauch, who completed the great equestrian statue of Frederick the Great and had statues of the successful generals of the Napoleonic Wars – Blücher, Yorck, Gneisenau, Scharnhorst and Bülow – lined up along Unter den Linden. But Berlin still failed to impress. When Pastor Karl Philipp Moritz first saw London he exclaimed: 'How great had seemed Berlin to me when I saw it from the tower of St Mary's and looked down on it from the hill at Tempelhof . . . how insignificant it now seemed when I set it in my imagination against London!'[67] The only field in which Biedermeier excelled and served to change the spartan view of Berlin was in architecture. This was largely thanks to the gift of one man, Karl Friedrich Schinkel.[68]

In 1826 the Viennese writer and friend of Beethoven's, Franz Grillparzer, journeyed to Berlin in one of the new post coaches: 'Finally the towers of Berlin,' he wrote. 'Through the gates. Beautiful. The collection of buildings more beautiful than I have seen together. The streets wide. Kingly.'[69] Such praise was rare before the arrival of Schinkel, the greatest German architect of the nineteenth century. It was he who, over the space of a long and dynamic career, transformed central Berlin, giving the city centre a unified feel with his elegant neo-classical buildings in the 'Prussian style'. Schinkel gave form to Unter den Linden, the Platz der Akademie, the Lustgarten and, with Lenné, the Tiergarten. If, as it is said, the first Roman emperor 'found a city of brick and left it marble', Schinkel found a city of wood and left it brick. But much of Schinkel's brick was covered with plaster, swathed in marble and surrounded by columns of Saxon sandstone, sculptures and elaborate wrought iron. His gifts ranged from interior and set design – he created fabulous iron furniture, was one of the first to do lithographs, and designed the magnificent star-studded set for the Queen of the Night in Mozart's *The Magic Flute* – to draughtsmanship and painting. But Schinkel's career also reflected the triumph of reaction in Berlin. He had started out as an ardent Prussian reformer but, like so many of his generation, had retreated from political life after the disappointment following the Wars of Liberation. Instead he became a pillar of the establishment in the apolitical and naive world of Biedermeier Berlin.

Schinkel's life spanned the era from the end of absolutism to the end of the Biedermeier years. He was born in 1781 in the little garrison town of Neurippen to the north of Berlin. It was a time of extraordinary change. By the time the family moved to Berlin in 1794 Kant had published *The Critique of Pure Reason*, Frederick the Great had died, and the ideas of the French Revolution were reverberating across Europe. The young Karl was sent to school at the famous Graue Kloster but in 1797 decided to become an architect after seeing Friedrich Gilly's plans for a vast monument to Frederick the Great. He studied with Gilly and was given his first commission – a garden pavilion – in 1806. The revolution and ensuing turmoil had a powerful influence both on his personal and professional life. Schinkel watched from his rooms on the Alexanderplatz as French troops marched into Berlin in 1806 and like many of his contemporaries he was roused into a patriotic fervour by Fichte's 1807 *Addresses to the German Nation*. He joined the Berlin Romantic literary circle and was befriended by Achim and Bettina von Arnim, Clemens von Brentano, Karl von Savigny and others; like many of them he volunteered to serve in the Prussian Landsturm after the declaration of war on France. Schinkel's ardent patriotism was reflected in his work. By 1805 he had already designed a monument to Martin Luther; he would soon create sets for *Undine* and *Faust* and planned to illustrate Brentano's fairy tales. His paintings, like the melancholy *Bohemian Mountain Range at Sunset*, were executed in the high Romantic style and were clearly influenced by Caspar David Friedrich's lonely landscapes which he saw exhibited in Berlin in 1810. During the occupation he painted large dioramas of historic scenes to bolster public morale and in 1812 exhibited the vast *Burning of Moscow* to emphasize Russian fighting spirit against the Grande Armée: it showed thick brown clouds of smoke billowing over Moscow and the people stoically walking away as the French moved up towards the high towers of the Kremlin.

Schinkel's patriotic service continued after the defeat of Napoleon. He designed the decorations which streamed from the Brandenburg Gate for the victory parade in 1814 and he helped to organize the great exhibition of war booty returned to Berlin from Paris. He produced a medal for Blücher showing the great general as Hercules in a lionskin on one side and St Michael defeating Satan – a reference to Napoleon – on the other. He designed the Iron Cross – and created the *Pickelhaube* or pointed helmet, which would later become the very symbol of Prussian militarism. Above all, his patriotism was reflected in his architecture, and in his use of the 'national style' – Gothic. Schinkel believed that Gothic architecture represented Romanticism, eternal Christianity, the lost Germany of the Middle Ages, even the 'German soul'. The Gothic style provided a model for the development of Prussia and embodied the call for liberty and freedom, for reform and for the creation of a unified German state. Most of his early plans were in this style. When Queen Luise died in

1810 Schinkel submitted to the king drawings for a memorial chapel complete
with guardian angels, high arches and tracery windows meant to evoke the
very entrance to paradise. After the war he designed a vast Liberation Fountain,
which had the Germanic chieftain Hermann rearing up on his horse and
holding a spear to the belly of the fallen Roman Quintilius Varus who, weighed
down by his imperial armour, bore a striking likeness to Napoleon. He designed
a great Gothic cathedral to commemorate the Wars of Liberation and submitted plans for the rebuilding of the Petrikirche. But none of these huge projects
was ever built. The reasons were political.

During the Napoleonic period Frederick William III had appeared to
support the reformers, the German nationalists, the volunteers for the Landsturm, and the liberals who wanted political change, but with the defeat of
France he quickly reverted to his old ways. Calls for political reform, for a
unified Germany, for a constitution and for a representative government were
now considered subversive and dangerous and the Gothic style was intrinsically
linked to them. As such, it fell out of favour. Instead, the king now preferred
buildings which gave an air of stability and safety, above all those designed in
the neo-classical style.

Schinkel's work was greatly affected by this change in royal preference.
Frederick William III chose a Doric mausoleum over a Gothic tomb for his
wife and halted plans for the great Gothic cathedral in Berlin because of a
lack of funds. Schinkel had to make do with the cast iron Gothic monument
in Kreuzberg created under the direction of Major von Reiche, the nephew
of the eminent general ennobled after Waterloo, and although the crown
prince commissioned a number of small Gothic monuments they did not
amount to much. By 1820 Schinkel had been forced to abandon the Gothic
in favour of classicism. Some saw this as tantamount to a betrayal of the fight
for German unity, but despite his love for medieval architecture Schinkel
wanted above all to build. For over a decade his most important work would
reflect the needs of the reactionary Prussian state.

To be fair Schinkel did not see the two styles as mutually exclusive. Other
artists, from Beethoven to Hölderlin to Möricke – and even Goethe in *Faust*
– had mixed elements of Romanticism and neo-classicism and Schinkel convinced himself that educating people about the values of ancient Greece was
the next best thing to evoking the spirit of medieval Germany. For him Greek
architecture had been the product of a harmonious, integrated and free society
which could be seen as a model for Prussia – 'the most felicitous state of
freedom within the law'. And art and culture were the key: beautiful buildings
could, in Schinkel's words, 'ennoble all human relations'. But the view epitomized the problem of the Biedermeier world. It was naive to think that the
creation of buildings and paintings and sculpture could somehow educate

the people in democratic principles. Schinkel had convinced himself that his buildings were somehow 'liberating' Berlin. On the contrary he was legitimating the rule of one of the most reactionary regimes in Europe.

Schinkel's career as an architect began in earnest in 1818, four years after the Congress of Vienna, with the completion of his first great commission – the Neue Wache or New Guard House. It was a small monument to Prussia's victorious army. Built in the shape of a Roman castrum with a Doric portico of six simple columns it remains the most striking monument on Unter den Linden. The king liked it and it led to new commissions. Within the next two decades Schinkel touched virtually every corner of the city centre, converting the baroque cathedral across from the Schloss, planning the Lustgarten, creating the Schlossbrücke, building the Schauspielhaus or theatre, which opened in 1824, and a number of private houses and palaces, including a residence for Prince William on Unter den Linden and the Palais Redern on Pariser Platz, and drawing up plans for everything from a new library to gatehouses for the Potsdamer Platz. In a letter to Sulpice Boissière in 1822 he said he hoped his work would create 'beauty in itself and for the city'.[70]

His crowning work in the neo-classical style, and the building which he considered his greatest work, was the Altes Museum, which was completed in 1830. It remains a great Berlin landmark. From the outside it looms like a vast Greek stoa with its grand row of eighteen Ionic columns marching in perfect symmetry across the northern end of the Lustgarten. The vast rotunda, modelled on the Pantheon in Rome, is hidden from view from the outside and comes as a marvellous surprise to the visitor. Schinkel intended the rotunda to be a temple to art and culture; a sanctuary where 'the sight of a beautiful and sublime room must make the visitor receptive and create the proper mood for the enjoyment and acknowledgement of what the building contains'.[71] After studying the exhibits the visitor could leave via the Treppenhaus, which connected the museum-temple to the busy secular world of Berlin. The position was vital. The museum was placed across from the Royal Palace, flanked by the arsenal and the cathedral, and next to the Stock Exchange and the Neue Packhof or New Customs House, which was completed in 1832. By placing it here Schinkel was trying to prove that art could fit into the civil order and to demonstrate that culture was indeed equal to the pillars of Prussian society represented by the military, the monarchy, the Church and the new emerging power of industry. It was an absurd delusion. Art was not as powerful as the rival institutions and never would be. When Robert Smirke designed the British Museum in 1824 it was placed miles from Whitehall and St Paul's and the City, and the English would have thought it absurd that culture could be seen as a rival to parliament or the military or industry in the running of their country. Schinkel's notion that culture was a substitute for political action was typical of Biedermeier Berlin. However beautiful his symmetrical, clear, austere neo-classical buildings, he had come to mirror that fatal tendency in the Berlin educated middle class: the belief that they could influence politics through culture.

What Schinkel did not seem to recognize was that far from being a political activist he had in fact become a pillar of the Prussian establishment. He was a trusted public servant and in 1838 was considered reliable enough to be elevated to the highest office of public works in Prussia. The sheer number of commissions and projects which came to him through the royal family made him the most famous architect in Prussia, but he was a court architect in all but name. His claims to be leading Prussians to a better, more democratic world through his architecture and his art rang increasingly hollow.

In many ways the Altes Museum heralded the end of pedagogic architecture in Berlin and by the time it was finished the Biedermeier world was beginning to crumble. Even Schinkel foreshadowed the change and in the last decade of his life began to explore other forms of architecture by developing an ahistorical functional style inspired in part by British industrial architecture.[72] His new designs included plans for a shopping bazaar on Unter den Linden and the surprisingly modern purple brick Bauakademie, so wantonly destroyed by the East Germans after the Second World War. His late works hinted at a new age to come, when the edifying public buildings of the past would make way for hotels, factories, department stores and train stations, built not to educate or to ennoble the public, but to facilitate trade and commerce.[73]

By the time Schinkel died in 1840 many of those excluded from the Prussian elite were growing increasingly angry at the censorship and repression which still characterized Berlin. If Schinkel had renounced the fervent nationalism and politics of his youth there were many in Berlin who had not, and the work of those in exile was finding its way back to the city. Groups of reform-minded individuals were forming political groups disguised as poetry clubs, literary circles and music societies to defy the ban on the fledgling political parties; works written during the Napoleonic occupation were rediscovered; the longing for national unity was growing stronger. However civilized and sedate the Biedermeier years had been, however gracious Schinkel's neo-classical masterpieces had appeared, they had represented the artificial calm of a middle class shielded from the political realities of the day. Heinrich Heine was suspicious of the new elegant city with its 'long stretches of uniform houses, the long wide streets ... but with no care given to the opinion of the masses.'[74] In his famous lines he foreshadowed things to come:

'Berlin, Berlin, great city of misery! In you, there is nothing to find but anguish and martyrdom . . . They respect rights as if they were candles.'[75] Biedermeier, and all it stood for, was set to come to a sudden and violent end in the revolutionary year of 1848.

IV

From Revolution to *Realpolitik*

Needs must, when the Devil drives!
Business and duty rule our lives.

(*Faust*, Part I)

BY THE LATE 1820s the absolutist systems bolstered by the Congress of Vienna were starting to break down. Europe was changing. Its population was growing, industrialization was bringing social and economic change and people were becoming increasingly impatient with the outmoded system which blocked any chance of reform. In Germany young men who had been exhilarated by their experiences in the Wars of Liberation resented retreating to a dull, stifling world. Artists and writers and ex-soldiers fuelled the Young Germany movement led by Karl Gutzkow and Heinrich Laube, who in turn introduced themes of rebellion and emancipation in their *Zeitromanen* (novels of the times). New oppositional poets and songwriters, including Hoffmann von Fallersleben (who wrote the German national anthem but lost his job because of his political views), Georg Herwegh and Ferdinand Freiligrath (both of whom were sent into exile), and the continuing influence of Heinrich Heine, began to challenge the status quo.[1] The students in the *Burschenschaften* dressed themselves in medieval clothes, grew long hair and beards, and gathered secretly in old ruins to reaffirm their calls for a unified German fatherland. Then, in the 1830s, revolutions began to erupt all over Europe. News of the fall of the Bourbons in France in 1830 raised hopes that the period of reaction might soon be at an end. The Belgians began to fight for independence from the Dutch, while Poland rose up and fought for independence against Russia. The Polish insurrection was particularly important in Berlin. It lasted nearly a year and despite the fact that the Prussian king backed the tsar's brutal repression, there was much sympathy for the victims in the city itself. Thousands of Poles found sanctuary in Berlin and were championed by the population; Harro Harring wrote *Freedom's Salvation* in their honour and Richard Wagner, then in Leipzig, wrote: 'The victories achieved by the Poles during a short period in May of 1831 aroused my ecstatic admiration: it seemed to me as if the world had been created anew by some miracle.'[2] Two years later while staying in Berlin he wrote the overture *Polonia* and Berlin salons were now filled with music by Chopin and the rousing poetry of Mickiewicz.[3]

Then in May 1832 German students organized the Hambach Festival: 20,000 liberal supporters gathered with black, red and gold banners to honour the new political spirit of the age. In Berlin despite constant repression intellectuals again began to call openly for German unity; Dahlmann wrote that the civil service should be open to all, and others called for a representative government. When William Jacob visited Berlin in 1819 he had noted that liberals there seemed uncertain of their goals, but by the mid-1830s a coherent set of calls for political reform found expression.[4] Some merely wanted to lift the most repressive censorship laws; others wanted to challenge the power of the aristocracy and the military, but for most the underlying hope was that Germany could unify as a nation state based on the rule of law – a state which would represent the common will. Liberals demanded basic rights: freedom of expression, of association, of right to property and education; they wanted to retain the monarchy but have participation of the nation in government. For them the people – the *Volk* – did not mean the masses but rather an educated elite; universal suffrage was still considered a dangerous idea best left to the radical democrats. But nationalism was a powerful force; the idea of the *Kulturnation* and the liberal idea of the *Staatsnation* had begun to fuse, and when the French demanded the Rhine as a frontier in 1840 Germans reacted in a wave of patriotism.[5] Nikolaus Becker's *Rheinlied* became a hit with the lines 'They shall not have it, the free German Rhine'. *Die Wacht am Rhein* (Watch on the Rhine) was heard everywhere, as was Hoffmann von Fallersleben's *Deutschlandlied*, now the German national anthem, whose sentiments, like Verdi's *Nabucco* in Italy, mirrored the longing for unity. Far from being an aggressive song of conquest it called for people to forget their petty differences and put a united 'Germany, Germany above all'.

The political changes were reflected in many aspects of culture. Berliners now wanted to discuss politics, to be active, to have news from other nationalist groups in the rest of Germany. This thirst for information contributed to the sharp rise in the number of newspapers. The first liberal newspapers to break through the censorship of the Metternich era had to be smuggled into the city from other German states. Oppositional publications founded by Young Hegelians and Young Germany – including Görres's *Rheinischer Merkur* and the *Rheinische Zeitung* edited by Karl Marx – were under constant threat; Görres was forced into exile in 1827 and Marx's paper was banned in 1843. In 1846 the liberal *Deutsche Zeitung* was founded in Heidelberg to cover not a single region, but the whole of Germany. Berlin also produced publications of its own, including the *Vossische Zeitung* whose circulation doubled to 20,000 between 1840 and 1848; it was also home to conservative papers like the 1831 *Politische Wochenblatt*, and the *Neue Preussische Zeitung*, known as the 'Cross Newspaper' because of the Iron Cross on its front page.[6] The cutting, satirical magazine *Kladderadatsch* was started in 1848 and had reached a circulation of 39,000 by 1860. By 1862 Berlin would publish fifty-eight weekly papers and thirty-two dailies.

Newspapers were not the only means of spreading information in the era of repression. The university was still a centre of independent thought; Hegel, the champion of the state, held a chair of philosophy at the university from 1817 and his influence was already widespread. Literary societies and educational groups, choral and gymnastic festivals, shooting matches and poetry groups were increasingly used as covers for political meetings, and liberalism flourished in the German coffee houses and *Konditereien* of Berlin like Josty, Spargnapani and Stehely. Literary societies like the 1824 Mittwochsgesellschaft (Wednesday Society) or its rival Der Tunnel über der Spree, founded by Moritz Saphir in 1827, and newspaper reading rooms like that started by Gustav Julius, provided places where people could meet in relative safety to discuss the works of Hegel, Heine, Ludwig Börne and later Karl Marx and Friedrich Engels.[7] Despite police controls increasing numbers of periodicals, pamphlets and cartoons appeared which were critical of the government. Finally, there was a flurry of excitement in liberal circles in 1840 when the repressive king died and was succeeded by his son Frederick William IV. This, they hoped, was the chance for reform they had been waiting for.

King Frederick William IV came to the throne on a wave of optimism in the city. He was a humane man and seemed to espouse liberal ideas; indeed one of his first acts was to free political prisoners and to appoint the liberal heroes, the brothers J. and W. Grimm, Savigny, Schelling and Tieck, who had been turfed out of Göttingen by the king of Hanover, to professorships at Berlin University.[8] Unlike his father he loved the grandiose neo-Gothic architecture then coming into vogue and hoped to build an enormous national cathedral on the banks of the Spree. He loved ceremony and colour and show and used Berlin as a personal parade ground, holding mock manoeuvres and even mistakenly blasting out windows with his cannon. Despite his liberal tendencies, he was first and foremost the king of Prussia. He liked the appearance of freedom and he genuinely wanted to be liked, but he refused to accept any diminution of his power. Frederick William IV was an impulsive man who could be kind and charming one minute and violent and brutal the next; this neurosis ultimately ended in mental collapse. As one observer put it, his people were like an animal on a long string; he liked them to enjoy 'freedom' and was distressed if they hurt themselves by pulling on it, but he still would not cut the string. After a short period of grace he once again began to oppress those intent on reform.

There was widespread disappointment in Berlin when it became clear there would be nothing but cosmetic change. Once again people began to be prosecuted for minor infringements: Johann Jacoby, a regular at the liberal Siegel's *Konditorei*, was arrested in February 1841 for publishing a pamphlet called *Vier Fragen* (Four Questions), which was mildly critical of the government. But Berlin was heating up. The Industrial Revolution was finally reaching the city, its population was growing and social problems like destitution, homelessness, rising disease and crime rates were putting pressure on the old system. The problem was made worse by a simmering economic crisis in the east which resulted in the 1844 revolt of the Silesian weavers and the famine in Silesia and East Prussia of 1847. When the new king refused all demands for fundamental reform the frustration amongst the intellectual elite and the political classes increased. They could never have started a revolution on their own – Berlin was no Paris or Warsaw or Vienna. But revolution was coming. Once again, the spark was ignited in France.

The turbulent year of European revolution started in Paris on 22 February 1848. The bourgeois king Louis-Philippe had infuriated the populace by prohibiting a banquet which had been planned in order to raise money for reforms. Within hours students, workers and the national guard were raging through the streets of Paris demanding an end to political repression. The king was forced to flee and France was declared a republic. News of the triumph spread rapidly through Europe: the patriotic movement had begun in Italy and the writer Massimo d'Azeglio proclaimed the 'principle of open conspiracy'; Garibaldi was forced out of the country. The wave of violence spread east. The first uprisings in Baden and Saxony saw demonstrators demanding freedom of assembly and of the press, trial by jury and the creation of a people's militia. Unrest spread rapidly through the rest of Germany and people used petitions, strikes, demonstrations and the fear of revolution to extract political reforms from the terrified rulers.[9] By March Berlin was a tinderbox ready to explode. Berliners now gathered daily at the Zelten in the Tiergarten to hear speeches, read pamphlets and sign petitions for change.[10] Then, on 13 March, the news broke that the revolution had reached Vienna and that the architect of the hated Carlsbad decrees, Metternich, had been forced to flee to England hidden in a laundry basket; Frederick William IV was convinced he had to act quickly to avoid the same fate. On the evening of 17 March he drafted a series of political reforms in order to appease his people. He also appointed the hard-line General von Prittwitz as military commander of Berlin.[11]

Sunday 18 March 1848 dawned peacefully in the city. A large crowd, including radicals, students, craftsmen and apprentices, gathered at the palace to hear the king speak; most were unarmed, although workers from the Borsig factory had brought axes with them. The municipal authorities had agreed to admit a deputation demanding a modern constitution, freedom of speech and of the press, the right of citizens to bear arms and the withdrawal of troops from Berlin. The group of representatives was received by the king that morning but was surprised to learn that he had already passed a law which granted freedom of the press, abolished censorship, called for a united Diet and the reorganiz-ation of the German federal constitution, and that he had drafted a modest constitution for Prussia itself. However, he had said nothing about withdrawal of the troops.[12]

Berlin was still very much a military city but the oppressive presence of a disproportionate number of soldiers had long been a source of friction between Berliners and the government. The people were tired of barracks and parade grounds and abusive officers in their midst; after the Napoleonic Wars they had demanded a military which represented the people – a people's militia. They had a point. On that March day there were more than 20,000 troops on the streets, many of whom stood and jeered at the civilians in front of the palace. None of the citizens had guns nor any intention of fighting the Berlin garrison; they cheered the king when he appeared to announce the reforms. But when the speech ended, and still nothing had been said about the military, people began to chant: 'Withdraw the troops! Withdraw the troops!' The king was horrified.

Frederick William was willing to introduce some reforms but the call to banish the military challenged the very legitimacy of the Prussian monarch. In his eyes it amounted to a call for the king to renounce the very power on which his authority had rested since the Thirty Years War.[13] He did not respond; indeed, in an attempt to appease the army he told the cavalry to 'clean up' the palace square. The order was misunderstood. Rather than simply clearing the area the troops began to ride towards the crowd brandishing their swords and pushing the people back into the side streets; Major von Falkenstein chased one group to the Breitestrasse while a second was pushed towards the Lange Brücke. Suddenly two rifle shots rang out. These were probably acciden-tal but the crowd thought that the troops had opened fire. Cries of 'Assassins!' rang through the air and the people began to fight back. The army opened fire in earnest amidst screams from the public. The revolution in Berlin had begun.

Within minutes barricades were being put up throughout the city centre. The first, made out of two hackney coaches, an overturned carriage, the sentry box from the front of a bank and some old barrels, was constructed at the corner of Oberwallstrasse and Jägerstrasse. The barricade in Friedrichstrasse was made out of Mother Schmiddecke's fruit stall; and the biggest of all, at the corner of Königstrasse on the Alexanderplatz, was put together out of blocks of granite. Republicans and socialists manned the barricades with students, craftsmen, workers, liberal intellectuals and destitute migrants from the east. Some had firearms but most were armed with makeshift weapons like pitchforks and bricks; a small brass cannon had also been found and loaded with marbles. The king refused to speak to the people, further increasing suspicions that he had been behind the order to shoot. Fighting intensified throughout the afternoon. Fierce battles were raging by nightfall.[14] The violence was made worse by rumours that the military were tying prisoners in cellars and beating them with rifle butts. Berlin was ablaze; the artillery sheds at the Oranienburg Gate and the iron foundry went up in flames and all the customs houses were burning. Citizen Hesse took the reservist arsenal in Lindenstrasse and distributed weapons while women and children pelted the troops from windows and rooftops with paving stones and tiles. Over 230 people were killed in the fighting on the night of 18 March. The king feared a civil war. On 19 March, to the fury of the military, he ordered the troops to stop firing. In a dramatic gesture he rode up to the barricades and through the city draped in a flag bearing the black, red and gold colours of the revolution, and followed this with the famous speech 'To my dear Berliners', in which he called for the cessation of violence and the removal of the barricades in the 'true old Berlin spirit' of reconciliation. Negotiations began at the palace. This time, when the citizens demanded the withdrawal of troops from Berlin, the king obliged. He also promised a national assembly to debate the draft for a constitution and promised to find a solution to the national question.[15]

Berliners celebrated their successful revolution, and a huge funeral for the 'March Heroes' who had died in the fighting was planned. On 22 March a grand procession moved through Berlin, under trees and past buildings which had been draped with thousands of black banners paid for by the people of the city. Factory workers walked the route with professors, the mayor stood beside Alexander von Humboldt and Theodor Fontane, Poles and Italians marched together, each carrying their national flags, and Berlin societies and clubs sent representatives with ceremonial banners and wreaths. In all 20,000 people marched that day, and when they passed the palace the king and ministers stood on the balcony and bared their heads. The bodies were laid to rest with much ceremony at the Friedrichshain cemetery, and the graves would become a site of pilgrimage for liberals, social democrats and communists from that day on.[16] The people basked in feelings of goodwill and loyalty to their king.

Despite its great promise the 'Springtime of the Nations' would turn out to be one of the great false dawns of Berlin history. King Frederick William IV's order to send the army out of the city and his perilous ride through the streets of Berlin dressed in the flag had seemed genuine. The street fighters really believed that he had undergone a miraculous transformation – there would be no need to storm the palace or to see noble heads roll; the bloodshed and terror which had so shaken Europe during the French Revolution would not be necessary in Berlin; theirs had been a 'civilized revolution' and cries of 'We have won!' rang out in the streets. August Borsig, who was soon to become Berlin's first great industrialist, was one of many who believed in the king's promises of elections and a new constitutional monarchy. In his impassioned speech by the graves of the fallen street fighters he had announced: 'the ground which has closed above our beloved heroes has for ever buried all hatreds and fraternal strife. We demand that a brotherly hand of forgiveness be extended to our army. Honour those soldiers who fell in obedience to their oath.' A 'new era of co-operation' between the army, the king and the people would now begin; an era which would be marked by 'men of goodwill'.[17] He had not seen that the monarch's romantic gesture was the promise of a man already tottering on the brink of madness, nor had he understood that the military had withdrawn under duress like 'a great dog which has been slapped on the nose'. The humiliation of the army had only increased the generals' thirst for revenge against the troublesome citizens. The people had not realized that the reforms were temporary and that a king who could grant them so easily could also take them away. The revolution had stopped before any real change had taken place in the power structure of Prussia. By not taking advantage of the temporary split between the king and the army, they lost their chance for ever.

Given its power it was perhaps inevitable that the Prussian army would get its way in the end. The officers put pressure on the king to allow the military back into the city, and on 20 September 1848 General Wrangel led 40,000 soldiers, twice the number of the original Berlin garrison, back to their barracks. Berliners did nothing. Instead, they continued to squabble amongst themselves at the new Berlin National Assembly, which had been formed in March.

The Assembly had been fraught with problems from the beginning. Unlike its counterpart in the Paulskirche in Frankfurt, which was made up of professionals and professors, the Berlin body was one-third peasants and craftsmen and one-quarter low-ranking civil servants. The most important group gathered around Benedikt Waldeck, a jurist who represented the moderate left, and on 26 July the Assembly passed the Waldeck Charter proposing a strong parliamentary system for Prussia. But there were many splits and disagreements, particularly between the liberals and the radical left. On 16 October river-boat workers began to protest at the loss of jobs due to the installation of steam pumps on the Spree; they destroyed one pump and the liberals sent in the moderate people's militia. Eleven men were killed in the fighting; the radicals in parliament accused the liberals of following in the footsteps of the Prussian army, the fights became more bitter and divisive, and radical demands grew increasingly strident. By the end of August new motions had been introduced calling first for the abolition of hereditary titles and much-prized feudal hunting rights, and finally of the nobility itself. The conservatives grew increasingly nervous. But the real conflict was caused by proposed army reform. The National Assembly wanted to create a state army, a people's army removed from the king's command and made up not of Junkers but of the citizens. The king saw this as a direct threat to his power. His sympathy for the reformers began to wane and the military were only waiting to nudge him back into the counter-revolutionary fold.[18]

The moment of truth came on 28 October. The king, now influenced by his conservative council, rejected the liberal candidates proposed by parliament and appointed the conservative Graf von Brandenburg as Prime Minister and Otto von Manteuffel as Minister of the Interior. The parliament did nothing and the young Bismarck concluded that the babbling body had 'no stomach for a fight'. Meanwhile the arch-conservative General Wrangel, the new commander-in-chief of the Brandenburg region, prepared to use his troops to disband the troublesome parliament for good. Berlin's democratic experiment was about to come to an abrupt end.

On 10 November Wrangel's men marched into Berlin and surrounded the theatre where the National Assembly was in session. It was the beginning of the end. Wrangel ordered a chair to be set up in the middle of the street. A nervous officer of the militia emerged from the playhouse and proclaimed that he was there to 'defend the freedom of the people and the safety of the National Assembly', and would surrender 'only to a superior force'. Wrangel merely nodded to his troops and said in broad Berlinerisch, 'Tell your militia, force is ready for 'em!' He added that the members of parliament and the militia had fifteen minutes to leave the building or suffer the consequences. The officer retreated. Within minutes the dignitaries came to the door and meekly left the building in neat rows, never to return. There were no barricades, no fights, no protests, nothing. The Assembly was formally dissolved on 5 December and the king imposed his own constitution. The revolution was over.

Endless works have been written on the failure of the 1848 revolution in Germany. It has been seen as the point at which Germany took the *Sonderweg* (the 'other' path) and 'failed to turn' towards a Western liberal democracy. Its failure has been blamed on liberals or radicals for splitting the opposition; it has been seen as the moment when the unification of Germany under Prussia became inevitable; it has been linked to the First World War, even to Hitler. All this, however, is ahistorical. It is unlikely that the revolution could have succeeded even if the radicals and the liberals had not split; even if they had not been beset with the problem of national unity, or the problem of reconciling freedom and unity in all Germany. Not only were the 'forces of reaction' keen to maintain power in Berlin but the monarchy, the aristocracy and the military were stronger than they had first appeared. Furthermore, as Nipperdey has pointed out, the 'monarchic sense and a sense of legality were still widespread among the people'. If the people were not willing to fight their king and their army in the name of the revolution it was doomed to fail.[19] The revolution could not be won by people who refused to touch the king's palace because somebody had posted a notice on it declaring it to be the 'property of the people'. Alexis de Tocqueville remarked bitterly that 'There are no revolutions in Germany, because the police would not allow it.'[20] Unless the Prussian elite were physically removed from power, which in 1848 would have meant civil war, the old power structures were bound to remain. The feudal aristocracy and the military understood that to accede to the people's demands would have meant the erosion of their own dynastic and feudal privileges – something which they were not prepared to tolerate. Liberals had been terrified of a second revolution akin to the Jacobin uprising in France, and instead of siding with the radicals they moved to the right; but for their part the radicals were as yet too weak to bring about a complete overthrow of the system. When General Wrangel moved to disband the National Assembly in Berlin he did not encounter any resistance from supposedly 'revolutionary' Berliners. The would-be activists who had rallied so proudly at the graves of the fallen in March had quietly packed up and gone home.

The authorities now moved quickly to prevent any unrest. A three-class voting system was imposed, reflecting the new compromise between right-of-centre liberals and the monarchy – the Junker Herrenhaus evolved from this body in the 1850s. The rights of the crown were retained and the king still controlled virtually every aspect of state power. The military was now exempt from the constitution and pushed for the enforcement of a state of emergency.[21] Once again, Berlin became a centre of repression.

Known activists and street fighters were rounded up and arrested, a curfew of eleven o'clock was imposed and citizens were forced to carry identification with them at all times. Strict controls were introduced at the city gates and all visitors had to register with the police. House searches became the norm, with 20,000 'suspected weapons' being confiscated in 1848–9 alone. Contemporary drawings show the police bursting into liberal clubs and coffee houses, breaking up political gatherings, arresting agitators and gathering incriminating literature which included liberal newspapers such as *Reform* and the satirical *Kladderadatsch*, and the more radical *Volksblätter*, *Republik* and *Berliner Krakehler*. Papers were strictly censored; General Wrangel decreed that articles which were 'insolent, cheeky, irreverent or disrespectful', which 'questioned the implementation of law and order by the state', which expressed 'unhappiness or dissatisfaction with the government' or which 'criticized the sovereign' were forbidden. As most liberal and radical articles came under this broad brush editors were constantly harassed and their papers threatened with closure.[22] The worst days of the Carlsbad decrees had returned with a vengeance. Berliners could only dream of the time a few months before when Metternich and their 'cartridge prince', later to become Kaiser William I, had fled to London in fear of their lives. Now the crown prince was back in Berlin, and the hunter had become the quarry.

The repression was to get worse. The officials used whatever means were necessary to consolidate their hold on the capital, and the abuses of power became part of Berlin folklore which fuelled the innate distrust of the ruling elite. An infamous example occurred after the attempt on the king's life on 22 May 1850. A young junior officer had run up to the monarch crying, 'Freedom lives!' and fired a small pistol. Although he had barely touched the king the incident was used as a pretext to launch fresh attacks against the revolutionaries. Varnhagen said sarcastically that it was 'particularly irritating' that the assassin had been a military man as 'it would have been so *nice* if he had turned out to be a member of democratic societies and a reader of democratic newspapers!' By the end of 1850 the only social reform left was the Berliners' right to smoke in the street.[23]

The form of subjugation had a further sting in its tail. During the revolution Berliners had fought hard to increase local police powers. The force had been enlarged, but instead of protecting the new laws and freedoms it was now reorganized along paramilitary lines and became a highly effective instrument of control. Intimate knowledge of the local landscape and a huge network of informers made the force adept at tracking down political suspects. Police presidents became powerful figures and were given jurisdiction over many other aspects of city life, such as the fire department and street cleaning, the construction of public baths and sewer and water systems and the granting of building permits, all of which made control of 'enemies of the state' even easier. Contemporary manuals described the 'Prussian policeman's foolproof arm-lock for troublesome detainees' and outlined where new recruits should look in people's homes for hidden magazines and newspapers. A journal called *In the Police School* showed the 'old Prussian Police grip', with an officer bringing in a well-dressed but clearly very uncomfortable 'liberal' by the scruff of his neck and the back of his trousers.[24] The first police president to be appointed after 1848 was Carl Ludwig von Hinckeldey, who had already made himself unpopular through his unrelenting harassment of the 'Red Democrats' and his determination to erase all traces of revolution from the city. Even the famous Berlin 'Litfass columns' were put up as a means of social control. On a visit to Berlin in 1891 Mark Twain described them as 'pretty round pillars . . . 18 foot high and about as thick as a boar's head', and even recommended that they be brought to the United States. The columns had in fact been invented by Ernst Litfass, Frederick William's court printer, who put one up in front of his house to protest against the new ban on public notices. To his chagrin the columns were used by the very people against whom he had protested. Hinckeldey had seen their potential and had columns put up all over the city and Berliners were now forbidden to put posters elsewhere but had to apply for permission to use the columns; those requesting space for politically dubious material were noted on police files.

The repression went further. The new police system saw trials against communists and democrats; the press was controlled through taxation and a new system of licences, all those in the civil service with liberal tendencies were dismissed, school teachers were carefully monitored, factory inspectors were sent round to check political unrest, even the courtiers and the king were spied on. It was at this point that the Berlin civil service became the true organ of the conservative government; advancement now depended not merely on a neutral political attitude but on positive proof of commitment to its policies; Prussia might have had a constitution and respected the rule of law, but in practice the bureaucracy and the military were controlled by the conservative forces of reaction. Ironically the new system was accepted by many Berliners as being 'for the best' or good for their 'own protection' against the increasing tide of radicalism. This shift was visible in the change of attitude to Hinckeldey, whose rule ended in a duel which turned him from a hated figure into a hero of the city.[25]

Hinckeldey's transformation began in 1856, when the police chief organized a raid at the exclusive gambling club in the Hotel du Nord. While there he got into a heated exchange with the arrogant young Count von Rochow-Plessen, who objected to the intrusion. The argument ended when Rochow-Plessen threw down the gauntlet. Duels were not uncommon in Berlin at the time but were fought between 'men of honour' or men of equal social rank; Carl Gottlieb Svarez, the author of the Prussian General Legal Code, wrote in 1794 that only 'officers and noblemen' should be permitted to duel; 'when persons who belong neither to the nobility nor to the officer corps issue or accept a challenge to a duel, such action shall be deemed to be attempted murder and be punishable as such'. By the nineteenth century duels between members of the middle class had become more common but these were also governed by a strict code of honour. When two Berlin waiters fought a pistol duel in 1870 they were not allowed into 'honourable detention' in a castle but were sent to a 'dishonourable' prison because, as the Prussian Minister of Justice Eulenberg had put it, 'the condemned belong to a class of society in which it is not customary to settle one's affairs in a duel'.[26]

Given the social difference between the nobleman and the police chief the challenge was seen by many as somewhat unfair. Furthermore, duels to the death with pistols were usually reserved for grave offences such as cuckoldry, with less lethal swords being preferred for insults such as this. Nevertheless on a cold March morning in 1856 the two men and their seconds met at the Berlin Jungfernheide; the pistols were chosen, the men walked, turned, and fired. The police chief missed, but von Rochow-Plessen, a crack shot, hit his target squarely in the chest. Hinckeldey didn't utter a word, but 'quietly made a half turn, fell to the earth, and died'. Suddenly the hateful image changed. Now the police chief was hailed by Berliners as a 'great protector of freedom', a 'fair Prussian bureaucrat', who had, after all, done a great deal to modernize the city. Had he not introduced a new water system to curb disease, and brought in a 'new fangled sewer system' which despite making the city reek to high heaven had modernized waste management? Had he not also introduced new laws governing factory health and safety, and brought in strict fire regulations? Had he not defended the rights of poor Berliners against the Junkers and 'paid for it with his life'? Ten thousand tearful Berliners attended his funeral.[27]

Bitterness and disappointment prevailed in the aftermath of the revolution. The makeshift Berlin parliament had been dispersed and the all-German Frankfurt parliament had effectively collapsed before the Prussian king rejected their 'crown from the gutter'. A quarter of a million people left Germany every year throughout the 1850s and many of her most energetic, forward-looking and innovative citizens forsook their depressing country and went to North America in search of the freedoms denied them at home.

Most of the liberals who remained in Berlin now abandoned their futile struggle for political reform. They felt powerless against the mighty state and convinced themselves that the restrictive three-class voting system and constitution were preferable to a bloody revolution or to the harsh system still in place in Austria. The *Bildungsbürgertum*, the educated middle classes, reverted to their comfortable pre-revolutionary lives, enjoying the prestige associated with posts in academia and in the bureaucracy, while some found an outlet for their liberal ideas in the quieter world of administrative reform. Theatres reopened and families enjoyed outings to their favourite parks and lakes. Schopenhauer and Wagner were fashionable.[28] Even General Wrangel became popular; he was renamed 'Papa Wrangel' and his uses of the Berlin wit and dialect were fondly quoted. A contemporary joke told of a little boy who bumped into the general while walking down Unter den Linden. He was whistling but immediately fell silent when he saw the general. Touched by this show of respect Wrangel asked him to carry on, whereupon the boy said, 'When I see you I have to laugh, and when I laugh, I cannot whistle!' A cartoon in *Kladderadatsch* showed a hilarious series of drawings of Wrangel being transformed from a priggish young Junker into a kindly old man. But in the end these jokes were a sign of powerlessness; Wrangel might have become a likeable figurehead but it was he, and not the liberals, who controlled Berlin. The failure of 1848 had meant that even rapid industrialization and the rise of the economic bourgeoisie would not result in fundamental change in the social or political structure of Prussia. The number of aristocrats in the officer corps continued to rise so that they controlled all top positions and 65 per cent of the officer corps, police power was strengthened, the old estates remained in place.[29] It seemed as if the Junkers would keep the city a sleepy capital on the edge of Europe, governed by the tenets of enlightened absolutism.

The liberals might have abandoned politics but they had not given up on their hope to unify Germany. If they could not do it by political means, perhaps they could through economics and industry. The Industrial Revolution which had swept England was moving east and many Berliners were eager to forget their political impotence and to join in the tangible world of business. A harsh realism soon replaced the Romantic nationalism of the revolutionary period. The age of accepting political constraints, of recognizing limitations, of *Realpolitik* had arrived. Berlin would experience its 'first industrial revolution' and grow powerful on iron, coal, steam, metal working, textiles, machine construction and the railways. The second would follow quickly, with its concentration on electricity and chemicals and pharmaceuticals.

Ludwig August Rochau coined the term *Realpolitik* in 1853. It captured the spirit of his time.[30] His message was simple. The liberal nationalists had been crushed in 1848 because they had lacked any understanding of savage political realities. The Berlin and the Frankfurt parliaments, with no real power, no access to an army and no grasp of international relations, had been destined to fail. Germans had to learn to be tough and unsentimental. They had to understand geopolitics, military power and, above all, economic might, for these things alone could forge a united Germany from its disparate and feuding states. In 1869 Rochau wrote that freedom was not to be achieved through political change but through the 'acquisition of property'. For him the achievement of German unity was to be like some extraordinary business meeting which joined the different divisions of an enterprise together. This 'new realism' swept through Berlin. Philosophers, poets and literary men fell out of fashion; historians and economists – or 'national economists', as they preferred to call themselves – became the new demi-gods. Like Marx the new thinkers believed that natural economic laws determined history and that to understand them was to hold the key to the future. Economics was a central part of post-1848 political liberalism and the very term became synonymous with the new nationalist movement. Liberals began to concentrate on aspects of trade, money, power, productivity, public opinion and economic policy unheard of before. Its most fervent disciples were in Berlin.

The new Berlin economists envisaged Prussia, and not Austria, as the future economic heart of Germany. The vehicle for this was to be the German Customs Union, the Zollverein.[31] Before the creation of the Zollverein in 1834 the thirty-eight German states had been separated by hundreds of obsolete medieval trade barriers; Berlin itself was surrounded by a customs wall until well into the nineteenth century. The tolls had posed one of the most annoying obstacles to German unity and liberals had long wanted them abolished; indeed in 1830 revolutionaries had attacked and demolished customs posts throughout Germany, chopping up the little houses and gates and throwing the toll keepers out on to the roads, and the 1848 revolutionaries had burned all the customs houses in Berlin. The importance of the Zollverein cannot be underestimated; amongst other things it marked the beginning of a German national economy, of a national state and of Prussian dominance over Austria. It came about because of Prussia, and because of Bismarck.[32]

After the Congress of Vienna Prussia had been divided into unconnected territories stretching over 7,500 kilometres from east to west. In 1818 the state had introduced a new customs bill to create a free trade zone between its provinces, but it also forced smaller states to join. Some, like the Anhalt principalities, were opposed to any policy which excluded Austria, and Metternich rejected it, calling it a 'state within a state'. Nevertheless as early as 1834 a number of states had joined with Prussia, including Saxony, Frankfurt and Baden.

Throughout the 1840s and 50s Berlin used the Zollverein to further Prussian interests in Germany. The Minister of Finance Christian von Motz openly referred to it as an 'independent policy for German unification', insisting that the 'political unity' was a 'necessary consequence of commercial unity'. In 1844 a Braunschweig liberal commented that 'the Zollverein has become in fact the nourishing ground of the idea of unity'. Bismarck, who became Chancellor in September 1862, was desperate to make Prussia the key state in Germany and to keep his great rival Austria out of the Zollverein. His chance came that year when he signed a commercial treaty with France. When Austria demanded entry in 1865 Bismarck blackmailed the small- and medium-sized German states by threatening to disband the Zollverein altogether if its members supported Austrian entry. Berlin now controlled 90 per cent of the mining and metal industries, two-thirds of heavy industry and almost the entire textile industry of Germany; the smaller states supported Bismarck, and Austria was excluded.[33] In July 1862 Berlin formally recognized the creation of the kingdom of Italy against Austria's wishes, further widening the gap between Vienna and Berlin. Prussia had assumed the leading economic role in Germany; now it was putting this to its political advantage. Prussian victory in the race to unify Germany was now merely a matter of time.

Control of the Customs Union had become increasingly important to Berlin's burgeoning power in Germany. The 1850s and 60s had been a period of extraordinary growth; the economy was booming and Germany was experiencing an industrial revolution which Prussia was keen to harness. Individual liberal bureaucrats promoted economic reforms in Berlin through bodies such as the Prussian Ministry of Commerce. One of the most important was the 'schoolmaster of Prussian industry' Peter Christian Beuth, who worked tirelessly to make Berlin into an industrial powerhouse. Beuth was the Minister of Trade, Industry and Construction who in 1821 had founded the Association for the Encouragement of Industry in Prussia and the Gewerbe-Institut (Institute of Trade). He also formed the Association of the Promotion of Industrial Knowledge and established a number of technical schools in Berlin, including the Berlin College of Trade and Industry in 1824, the Society of Architects and Engineers, and the School of Artillery and Engineering in 1822. He planned the new Customs House for the Kupfergraben, worked with Schinkel on the handbook for workers – the *Vorbilder für Fabrikanten und Handwerker* – and oversaw the 1828 creation of the Customs Association of Central and South Germany and Prussia-Hesse. Beuth was deeply influenced by his journeys to Industrial Revolution Britain. He saw the new cities as role models for Berlin and spent many months travelling through England, Scotland and Wales, visiting factories and interviewing industrial magnates – he even went with Schinkel in 1826 to examine the potential of new industrial architecture. He stole a number of designs from British manufacturers and introduced modern centralized factories in the city, doing away with the old 'piece work' system of production wherever possible. He also masterminded the first Prussian Trade and Industry Exhibition in Berlin held at Treptow Park, now the site of the vast Soviet war memorial where 5,000 Red Army soldiers lie buried. It was a huge success and, although it could not rival the Great Exhibition in London, was still impressive with its 176 exhibitors and 998 displays; 750,000 people attended.[34]

Beuth and his contemporaries researched, financed and promoted mechanization in every way. He was friendly with all rising young industrialists: 'Hummel, Egells, Freund, Borsig, Hoppe, Tappert, Wöhlert, Arnheim, Ade, Hamann, Siemens, Schwartzkopff, the Müller brothers, the Kunheims and Kahlbaums, all were his friends and most were his personal students.'[35] Beuth encouraged innovation and the use of technology from abroad – for example, bringing a British company to Berlin to install gas lighting in 1827. The ministry oversaw the granting of new business subsidies and donations, including funds for the 1822 Egells iron works and for the Borsig iron foundry and machine factory founded in 1837.[36] They supported vocational education and even gave prizes for the best new products or designs created in Berlin. The Prussian government was deeply involved in business, a development which set Berlin apart from the English industrial giants – and indeed from other German industrial cities like Leipzig, which was still controlled from far-away Dresden. By now wealth had become more important to the one-time revolutionaries than the struggle for political rights, but despite the innovations Berlin still lagged far behind the great industrial cities of Britain. Something had to be done.

By the mid nineteenth century Berlin was in danger of being left behind in the race for industrial power. Granted, this was in part due to her reliance on the textile industry. This had made Berlin the single largest industrial city in Germany in the late eighteenth century – indeed uniforms from Berlin had clothed not only the Prussian army but the American and Russian armies as well. But after the 1848 revolution it had slumped and Berlin's location worked against recovery. Furthermore the city had no raw materials of its own and it was too far away from the rich coal, lignite, iron and steel of Prussia's western provinces to compete in the production of raw materials. It needed to turn itself into a manufacturing centre which took raw materials from elsewhere and turned them into finished goods. This would only be made possible by that most spectacular innovation of the Industrial Revolution – the railroad.[37]

On the eastern edge of the Askanischer Platz stands the jagged brick ruin of the Anhalter Bahnhof, all that remains of one of the largest and most imposing train stations in Europe. Only the entrance portico survived the 1950s demolition of the war-damaged structure, but remnants of the intricate and beautiful terracotta work can still be seen on its dingy facade. Flowers, wreaths and vines curl around the lonely figures of Day and Night, which sit high above the entrance. These statues once held the great clock which welcomed people from Frankfurt-am-Main, Basel, Leipzig, Munich and Dresden; now they prop up an incongruous brick circle framing nothing but a piece of Berlin sky. On the other side of the entrance lies a desolate expanse of Brandenburg sand where the hall – 30 metres high, 60 metres wide and 87 metres long – once stood. Despite its sorry state this 'cathedral of industry' remains a powerful symbol of the wealth and power of industrial Berlin. It was built to project success, and Berliners were proud of it.[38]

Interest in rail travel had already gripped the city in the pre-revolutionary period; even Goethe had complained in 1826 that 'railways, express mail, steamboats and all possible means of communication are what the educated world seeks'. The first German rail line was opened between Nuremberg and Fürth in 1835, and the first Prussian line was opened in September 1838.[39] At high noon a small engine puffed and ground its way out of Berlin and was greeted forty minutes later in Zehlendorf by an ecstatic crowd throwing flowers and tossing their hats in the air. The crown prince openly supported the new and daring form of travel and grandly announced that 'these carriages which now travel throughout the world can be stopped by no man'. For his part the unpopular king snubbed Berliners with his remark that getting to Potsdam a couple of hours sooner really did not constitute 'a major contribution to human happiness'. The king's disapproval did nothing to quell popular enthusiasm; train travel had arrived with a vengeance.[40]

The first train between Berlin and Potsdam was a roaring success and the astounding financial returns led to a flurry of speculation and an increase in private investment in new lines. Hundreds of miles of shiny track were soon snaking their way across Prussia: over Dessau to Köthen in 1842, to Stettin in 1843, to Frankfurt-an-der-Oder in 1842, to Breslau and to Hamburg in 1846; the original Berlin–Potsdam line was extended to Magdeburg in 1846. By 1848 there were 5,000 kilometres of track in Germany; by 1870 this had risen to 18,810 kilometres. Berlin placed itself at the centre of eleven radiating main lines, making it the prime rail node in Europe. Major international crossings ran through it: if one wanted to travel to Moscow via Warsaw from Paris, or from Milan and Vienna to Scandinavia, one was forced to stop in Berlin. On contemporary rail maps the city looks like a contented fat black spider perched in the centre of a dense web extending the length and breadth of Europe.

Once in Berlin the traveller was faced with a confusing array of stations dotted around the city. Berlin never had a Hauptbahnhof or central station because of the old Customs Wall which still encircled the city, but the peripheral stations became district landmarks and were built in an ever more fanciful and elaborate manner as the century wore on. Many became the catalyst for new urban development of plazas, squares and hotel and restaurant complexes to serve the travellers. In the mid nineteenth century the Hamburger Bahnhof was replaced by the grand Lehrter Bahnhof for trains to Hanover and

Hamburg, while the Stettin, Potsdam and famous Anhalt stations were remod-
elled in the ostentatious neo-Gothic or mock Renaissance styles.[41] The influx
of traffic soon began to change the face of the city. The horse omnibus which
had run ten kilometres along the Customs Wall was replaced in the 1860s by
an S-Bahn (city train), which cut through its heart and eased the problems
of interconnection between stations. The old city walls and gates were pulled
down and the track was extended so that Berlin became the first continental
city with an S-Bahn network. Other forms of travel were improved simultaneously: the already extensive canal system was enlarged and made more
efficient.[42] The 'great age of Prussian road building' between 1845 and 1870
coincided with the building of the railroad: the total length of main roads
more than doubled between 1840 and 1860 and the streets of Berlin were
widened and paved. Some Berliners protested at the dramatic changes wrought
by the new networks; August Orth complained in 1871 that the traffic had
destroyed the intimacy of the city and that old streets had 'completely lost
their meaning', but the young industrialists began to feel confident that they
could rely on steady supplies of coal, iron and other essential items. This
confidence in turn encouraged investment in industry.

Trains were also instrumental in making the city a political powerhouse.
Prussian lines were initially financed privately but military planners were quick
to see their enormous strategic potential.[43] A complex military masterplan was
devised and any new lines which did not fit into it were refused planning
permission by the Prussian state.[44] This fascination with the new form of
transport was in stark contrast to the obdurate Austrian General Staff, who
rejected the 'ridiculous notion' that railways might one day be of some strategic
importance; indeed they made the inane decision to allow Italy's northern
railways to be sold to a French company at precisely the moment when they
were preparing for war with France. By refusing to accept the new technology
they set themselves up for their humiliating defeat at Königsgrätz in 1866,
when the Prussians used their new trains to devastating effect.[45]

The rest of Europe has not forgotten the importance of these Prussian
trains; in 1991 the *Spectator*, warning against the creation of a new Europe in
Germany's federal image, cited the German reference to themselves as the
'locomotive' of European unity. The author claimed that there was something
'archetypally German about a train ... trains occupy an important place in
German national mythology ... the German train is punctual and powerful,
a symbol of the strength of industry and the power of the state'. The train
did for Germany 'what geography did for Britain'. In the 1890s the train was
synonymous with German assertiveness and with the single-minded pursuit
of a selfish national interest, but few in nineteenth-century Berlin would have
disagreed. The German novelist Wilhelm Raabe once said, 'the German Empire

was founded when the first railway system was built'. Berliners watched as the railroad forged the weak and shapeless Prussia into a state so powerful that it could subjugate all Germany. But the train also put Berlin at the heart of Europe, and for that reason it remains one of the city's most cherished symbols.[46]

The military men in Berlin were not only interested in the promotion of railroads; they began to support industrial expansion, with greedy eyes fixed on the prospect of more guns, artillery, ammunition, uniforms and pharmaceuticals. In their minds, industry meant power. But the new weapons, locomotives and machinery did not bear the names of the Junkers; instead they were stamped with the signatures of as yet unknowns like Egells, Pflug, Wöhlert and Schwartzkopff. The Zollverein, economic reforms and the railroads had brought iron, steel and coal within reach of Berlin; between 1848 and 1857 pig iron production in the Zollverein increased by 250 per cent, coal production by 138 per cent and iron ore and coal mining by over a third.[47] Furthermore, freight traffic on the Prussian railways increased seven times over between 1850 and 1860. This had paved the way to success for a new breed: the Berlin entrepreneur.

One of the first great self-made men of Berlin was the committed liberal who had spoken over the graves of the revolutionaries in 1848, August Borsig. He had started as a carpenter, moved to a vocational school in 1823 and joined a small iron foundry in 1825, beginning his own business in the courtyard of a Berlin *Hinterhof* or tenement block a few years later. His first contract was the installation of pump machinery in the fountains of Frederick the Great's palace Sanssouci. In 1836 he scraped together enough money to buy a small piece of land at the corner of Thorstrasse and Chausseestrasse in the Moabit district, and by July 1837 he was producing his first pieces of iron. He managed to get a contract to supply 117,000 spikes for the new Berlin–Potsdam line and with that money immediately installed a twelve-horsepower steam engine, paying soldiers from a nearby barracks to work the bellows. He then turned his attention to locomotives.

Borsig's locomotives dominated the German market between the 1850s and the 1870s. He started by copying English designs but soon modified them and in 1841 became a local hero when his new engine 'destroyed the myth of English speed' by streaking from Berlin to Jüterbog ten minutes faster than its great English rival, the Stephenson Model.[48] By the late 1840s his main factory hall was so enormous that it could accommodate twenty-five locomotives at a time. The flamboyant coal merchant Emanuel Friedländer described it as the giant of Berlin: 'on approach one sees about 15 chimneys belching smoke and hears at the same time the 3 colossal steam machines which set the whole works in motion. The great main hall, surrounded by dozens of buildings and chimneys, looks like a small city.' By 1850 Borsig employed over 1,200 workers and his had become the largest private enterprise in Berlin. When the Berlin–Potsdam line was built virtually all parts had been purchased abroad. Borsig changed that. By the 1850s Berlin was supplying the world with entire railway lines complete with everything from track, cable and signalling equipment to the locomotives themselves. Borsig had proved it was possible to create a mighty industrial centre even if one had to import raw materials, and he had paved the way for the future of Berlin industry. It was said that he had gone '*Vom Handwerksburschen zum Millionär*' – from journeyman to millionaire – but it was said with pride.

Borsig was still deeply committed to the ideas of 1848 and saw his factory as a step in the advancement of civilization. He dreamt of the day when capital, the workers, and the natural sciences would 'all be as one under the guiding hand of great industrial enterprise'. His famous villa, with its gardens, birds and tropical plants, was built near the factory to 'bring beauty and harmony' into the emerging industrial society. His ideology came through in all he did, and never more clearly than in the festivals held to mark factory anniversaries. The first great jubilee was held on 20 September 1846 to mark the completion of the 100th locomotive. The flower-bedecked engine was described as the darling of Berlin; little children looked at it in awe, beautiful ladies in enormous hats gossiped about it, and even the king and queen were shown admiring it. Such spectacles were repeated often, but the most extravagant was held on 21 August 1858 after the completion of the 1,000th engine.

The festival was a tribute to August Borsig and the events were clearly meant to emphasize the importance of his historical and cultural mission as well as to commemorate the 'peaceful revolution' which the factories had brought to Prussia.[49] The local Moabit newspaper announced that the Borsigs planned to celebrate 'in the grand style of a Renaissance prince', and that is very much what they did; all Moabit was invited to the villa and 30,000 people ate, drank and danced at the factory. In the evening Albert, August's son, staged an extraordinary play in the Viktoria Theatre written by the editor of *Kladderadatsch*. With hindsight it is difficult to imagine anyone wanting to sit through this bombastic extravaganza, but the employees of the day loved it. It took the form of a quasi-Greek drama which recounted the adventures of the busybody, Hans Dampf, amongst the gods. The terrible rivalry which had raged between the deities since time immemorial was vividly described: Vulcan, Mercury, Minerva and Venus ran around the stage in their Olympian finery brandishing weapons and fighting amongst themselves. The young man approached them and declared that, as he could harness steam, he was more powerful than they; he represented 'the highpoint of industrial civilization' and heralded 'the dawning of a new Golden Age'. Only the great new force, steam, could bring the warring gods and the opposing elements into a new and happy co-existence. At the end of his demonstration Venus turned to Vulcan crying, 'Yes! Yes! Steam now rules the world/And you and I are his loyal servants!'

The play had a clear political agenda. Albert Borsig, like his father, wished to see the creation of a strong united Germany. In one of the final scenes Minerva, 'the Goddess of machinery and the art of war', appeared with all the elements needed for a 'strong Germany': water, wind, coal, iron, fire, Father Rhine, the four winds, along with gnomes, dwarves and a cyclops carrying various Borsig products from cables to cannon. 'Great industry', they sang in chorus, could 'make Germany into one true nation using tools of both war and peace'. At the end an image of the 1,000th locomotive, *Borussia*, was brought in. 'This great *Borussia*' possessed 'revolutionary properties', it 'welded Germany together' and brought 'work, a sense of purpose, and happiness to the German nation' by 'giving people a future and distributing material and spiritual wealth'. Borsig's trains were driving Germany towards unification.[50]

Some did not see these developments in such rosy terms: one contemporary wrote of the 'debasement of man' brought by Borsig's new heavy industry while another called his factory a 'terrible torture chamber ... filthy, noisy and inhuman'. Some saw steam as the '*Demon Dampf*', a great enemy which was ruining the traditional way of life and which should be stopped at all costs. But these voices were few and far between and for many liberal Berliners industry was the way of the future. August Borsig's factory became the largest in the district of Moabit – '*la terre Moab*', as he called it – and he turned the area around the Chausseestrasse and the Oranienburg Gate into the first great modern industrial centre of Berlin.

Borsig's success was shared by others: in 1800 there had been 130 small firms in the area; by 1849 there were 2,000. Egells iron was joined by Schwartz-kopff torpedoes, Pflug founded his train carriage factory in 1838, Wöhlert his machine works in 1843 and his iron foundry in 1844. The new industries needed workers and the district grew twenty-five times in less than fifty years, with the population rising from 6,534 residents in 1858 to 159,791 by 1900. Locals were fascinated by the new industrial landscape, which they called 'The Fireland', and 'Herculean Berlin'; a essayist wrote that Chausseestrasse was a 'wonder of the world' with 'every chimney spewing out great showers of sparks and thick billows of smoke, as if it were the fire city of Vulcan'.

A list of firms founded in Berlin during this period reads like a contemporary *Who's Who* of German industry. Schering, Borsig, A EG, Siemens, Osram, A GFA, and dozens of others took advantage of the boom and expanded to proportions hitherto unknown in Germany. The Schering concern started in 1852 as a local pharmacy called the 'Green Apothecary', but soon began to produce the new wonder drugs chloroform and.cocaine. Schering later made a fortune by pioneering the use of synthetic drugs to avoid importing raw materials.[51] Berlin also became a huge centre for another kind of drug – alcohol – and the brewing and distilling industries flourished. The Aktiengesellschaft für Anilinfabrikation or AGFA started with aniline production but soon became a German leader in photographic materials, optical instruments and precision tools. Following AGFA's lead the city became a centre for precision instruments such as microscopes, nautical equipment and medical supplies. Loewe turned his small machine tool factory into an enormous concern for arms and ammunition which competed with Krupps in the Ruhr region.

At the same time Berlin became the capital of the German clothing industry. The *Konfektion* or 'putting together' had been started in the eighteenth century by Huguenots, who had produced uniforms for the Prussian army, but in the nineteenth century clothiers took modern technology from England and set up factories; entrepreneurs like Valentin Manheimer from Magdeburg and David Levin made the Hausvogteiplatz the centre of the 'rag trade'. Berlin was heralded as the 'German fashion capital' although it was ridiculed throughout Europe for slavishly copying Parisian designs.

New industries produced a plethora of goods, from rubber bicycle tyres to decorative brassware. Berliners showed great inventiveness: one hit on the idea of using puréed peas instead of meat to make long-lasting 'sausages' for the Prussian army; another invented margarine, 'workers' butter', from pressed palm oil; a third developed the insulated Thermos flask. The city grew at an amazing rate with hundreds of new firms being set up every year. Berliners became renowned for their technical prowess: one joke described two Bavarians sitting in a bar, one madly shaking and banging at a salt cellar. A Prussian sitting nearby brashly reached over and poked the holes of the container with a fork. 'Damned Prussians,' the Bavarian swore to his friend, 'but you just can't beat them!' The two greatest firms founded by Berlin's most famous entrepreneurs exhibited all the know-how of their Prussian contemporaries. Their names were Werner Siemens and Emil Rathenau.

Berliners became better informed through the inexorable growth in the newspaper industry. The titles which had been founded in the 1840s now reached mass circulation and Berlin was widely referred to as the *Zeitungstadt*, the 'newspaper city'. There was a rise, too, of professional journalists and full-time editors, many of whom had broader political ambitions – the conservatives Hermann Wagener and Joseph Jörg, the liberal Eduard Lasker and the socialist Ferdinand Lassalle, among others.[52] There was criticism of the new popular medium: Burckhardt and Nietzsche were disgusted by the prefabricated relationship to the world created by newspapers and by the pretension of the readership that they were informed, when in fact they were living on superficiality and half-truths; as Theodor Fontane put it, 'Ninety-nine among a hundred people simply parrot what they read in the paper and nothing else.' But there was no stopping newspapers and they in turn encouraged the growth of printing and publishing – so much so that Berlin soon challenged the traditional centre of printing, Leipzig.[53] Communications of a different kind were also being developed in the city. Long before the telegraph was invented Berliners had transmitted messages over distances by waving flags from tops of local church steeples. Werner Siemens transformed communications in the city and in the process became one of Berlin's most remarkable industrialists.[54]

He was born in Hanover in 1816. He joined the Prussian army as a cadet and attended the United Engineering and Artillery School in Berlin, after which he was appointed a second lieutenant in the artillery. He was always fascinated with new gadgets and inventions and began to experiment in his own time with the new force, electricity. Siemens first caught the public eye when he defied his critics and patented a galvanic process for gilding and plating in 1842; his brother sold the patent to a firm in Birmingham for a staggering £1,500. It was Siemens who realized the potential of the electric telegraph, inventing a process to insulate overhead wires so that they could be used along railways; the first of these was installed in 1847 along the famous Berlin–Potsdam line. In that year he teamed up with a mechanical engineer Johann Georg Halske and set up a small workshop with a handful of employees in the Schöneberger Strasse; by 1914 the huge firm employed more than 60,000 people. Siemens-Halske specialized in laying telegraph and submarine cables; one of the most extraordinary was the overland telegraph line which stretched from Britain to India by way of Prussia, Russia and Persia, and was completed by three Siemens firms under their London-based Indo-European Telegraph Company in 1867.

Siemens was a brilliant inventor and came up with a number of electrical instruments, the most important being the electric dynamo demonstrated at the Paris International Exhibition in 1867. The first ever elevator, built in a New York department store, had been steam powered; but in 1881 Siemens installed the first ever electric elevator, which astounded everyone with its smooth and quiet ride. He was fascinated by transportation and built an ingenious miniature electric railway which later served as a model for a full-scale service, as well as an electric trolleybus. Siemens and Halske electric trams first glided through Lichterfelde in 1881 and soon linked the city together.

The new Bell telephones had been invented in America, and despite official disapproval Siemens was determined to install them in Berlin. The first 200 subscribers were hooked up in 1880. Electric street lighting illuminated Berlin in the same year. Until the 1820s Berliners had lived in almost complete nocturnal darkness, and during what they called the 'dark season' between November and March one in three homes had to have a petroleum lamp outside the door. When gas street lamps were finally introduced they were said to have a 'bad influence on people's morality, undermining fear of the Lord and terror of the dark'. The introduction of Siemens's electric light half a century later was greeted with more enthusiasm. The first lamp was put up in 1880, outside the Bauer Restaurant on Friedrichstrasse, and the first street to be fully electrified was the Leipziger Strasse. Berliners crowded around waiting for the 'magic lights' to be switched on, and the result was impressive. Never had the shadows been so sharp or the vision so clear. Despite the great expense – 1 kilowatt of electricity cost 40 pfennigs, more than twice the cost of gas – Berliners saw it as a matter of pride to put electric lights up throughout the city as soon as possible. The first coloured electric sign for Manoli cigarettes was hailed as a landmark, but before long all the clubs on the Friedrichstrasse were dazzling visitors with their blue and green and red lights.

Siemens's great rival was a charming man by the name of Emil Rathenau, whose son Walther was later assassinated under the Weimar Republic. Born in Berlin in 1838 Emil studied engineering at technical college and worked as a draughtsman at Borsig's firm in Moabit. He travelled extensively in England and on his return to Berlin purchased a small engineering plant in a converted dance hall in the famous Chausseestrasse. His forty employees started by building steam engines, equipment for gas works and props for the State Opera House; indeed one of his first contracts was to build a ship for Meyerbeer's *Die Afrikanerin*. Rathenau's life changed in 1881 when he saw Edison's incandescent electric bulb at the Paris exhibition. At his funeral his son said:

> when Emil Rathenau saw that little bulb alight for the first time, he had a vision of the whole world covered with a network of copper wire. He saw electric current flowing from one country to another, distributing not only light but also power – energy that would become the life blood of the economy and would stimulate its movement and growth . . . he vowed that he would devote his life to electricity.[55]

In 1883 Rathenau founded the German-Edison Company in order to produce Edison's inventions in Berlin, and it was over the production of the humble light bulb that he first clashed with Siemens. Neither could outproduce the other and after a long and expensive struggle the two giants agreed that Siemens should have the sole right to manufacture white carbon filament bulbs while the German-Edison Company had the right to produce yellow incandescent bulbs. Berliners supported the two companies almost as if they were rival teams. Rathenau challenged Siemens again by designing and building power stations: the first in the city was put up by his Municipal Electricity Works, and really made his fortune. AEG was created from a number of his smaller companies and rose to fame in 1891 when it laid the first long-distance electric power cable of 175 kilometres between Lauffen and Frankfurt-am-Main. Thanks to Siemens and Rathenau steam was superseded by electricity, and Berlin remained the centre of the industry until the outbreak of the First World War.[56] The new force had once again captured the Berliners' imagination, and their endless catalogue of insults was expanded to include references to 'crossed wires', 'weak currents', and the need for a 'new bulb'. With characteristic arrogance Berlin began to call itself 'the light of the world' and the 'city of light', labels which played an important part in the image of modernity and the metropolis which swept Berlin in the early twentieth century.[57]

The railroads and new industries gobbled up resources and their voracious appetite called for 'money, money, and more money'. Behrenstrasse, the new financial district, was created to fill the need. In the age of absolutism banking had been strongest in German residence cities where, given the Church ban on usury, Jewish bankers (*Hoffaktoren* and *Hofagenten*) had managed the finances at court.[58] The Rothschilds, for example, were descendants of a financial agent of the richest German prince, the elector of Hesse-Kassel, while others like the Kaullas in Stuttgart, the Kaskels in Dresden and the Oppenheims in Cologne had dominated their respective princely courts. Conversely, in free cities such as Hamburg and Bremen where there were no ruling princes, banking was almost non-existent. Berlin was the exception: although bankers like Ephraim and Isaak were employed by the Hohenzollerns they had been constricted by the unique and highly developed Prussian bureaucracy.[59] Berlin's lack of a banking tradition therefore left the way open to newcomers who pioneered modern financial practices in the nineteenth century. By the time of unification it was the new financial capital of Germany.

Berlin owed its new status to the ingenuity of a new group of Jewish families, the most important being the Mendelssohns and Mendelssohn-Bartholdys, Bleichröder-Schwabacks, Magnuses, Warschauers and Plauts. These were bankers for the new age, and quickly overtook the old private banks, which did not have the means to meet the increased demands for capital. The vast demand for money from government and railway consortia[60] led to involvement in the formation of joint stock banks like the Berliner Handels-Gesellschaft. The first modern German credit bank, the Darmstadter, was founded in 1853. There was a great deal of initial resistance to it, both from the established small family banks and from the conservative Prussian elite, who wanted to see the creation of a larger state bank over which they could exert direct control. Frederick William IV saw the new bank as a 'disgusting example of French speculative fever and corruption' and demanded it be closed. Bismarck leapt to its defence, albeit for typically devious reasons. The new bank posed a direct threat to the Rothschilds, who were aligned with the Austrians; damaging them would also hurt his enemies in Vienna. Whatever Bismarck's motives, the victory of the Darmstadter Bank over the conservative forces was of great significance, and the bank paved the way for many others of its kind.

By the 1860s even the most conservative elements in Prussia had come to see that industrial expansion had outgrown the smaller banks and would best be served by joint stock companies. These would also be based in Berlin. In 1856 David Hansemann founded the Diskonto Bank, which was soon followed by the Berliner Handels-Gesellschaft and the Berliner Bankverein.[61] Soon even banks such as the Darmstadter and Dresdner moved to Berlin. By 1870 the 'D-Banks' – the Disconto Gesellschaft, Deutsche Bank, Dresdner Bank and the Darmstädter – were playing a vital role in rapid industrialization by raising capital for new enterprises, capital which in Britain had been supplied by the City of London. Here, however, the banks combined commercial banking with long-term industrial financing and provided the investment capital for a number of the new heavy industries in Germany which in turn gave them immense control over important sectors of the economy.[62] The Reichsbank was founded in Berlin in 1857 to keep a watchful eye on the dealings of the new financial institutions.

Berlin's economic importance increased dramatically: in 1850 the circulation of notes in Prussia was around 18 million thalers; by 1875 it was 290 million. The Berlin banking quarter came to reflect this increasing prosperity and security: all along the Behrenstrasse, which ran parallel to the south of Unter den Linden, enormous marble palaces were erected which projected Berliners' unshakeable faith in the new system. (After the war the ruins of the old banks were torn down and the blocks of stone used to construct the new East German zoo.) Bankers themselves became well-known figures: Carl Fürstenburg was adored by Berliners for his biting wit; in describing a dinner given by the Prussian Minister of Finance he said, 'Madame Minister appeared in a low but unsuccessful décolleté, a bit like her husband who also sports an uncovered deficit.' When asked if he knew who had died that day he retorted, 'Today, anyone will do!' Hermann Sudermann hinted at Bleichröder's new status in his notorious play *Sodoms Ende* when the character Weisse explains: 'We cannot all scale the luminous heights of humanity where Goethe, Bismarck and Bleichröder stand . . . although if you open a newspaper in the provinces you will find my name.'[63]

The new Stock Exchange was closely linked to the industrial transformation and between 1851 and 1857 119 joint stock companies were founded in Prussia. In its second year the Berlin Stock Exchange reported a 'very considerable and lively turnover in stocks and shares in internal and foreign accounts and for investment and speculation purposes'.[64] Berlin trading was heaviest in commodities such as grain, coal and iron, but money was soon needed for growth in industries from metalwork to textiles. The resources of the propertied classes were restricted and financing with one's own credit and capital was risky, so even in the 1850s entrepreneurs were going to the public to collect capital assets and use them to finance their new projects. The share quickly became a fashionable object in Berlin, a status symbol and topic of polite conversation amongst the very new members of the middle class. The money generated by industry helped to fuel investment, and Berlin found itself in a seemingly endless upward spiral of growth and prosperity. The immensely optimistic newly rich middle class began to change the social face of the city, and the late nineteenth century was to become the golden age of the *Besitzbürgertum*.

These propertied middle classes initially consisted of self-made men, often the sons of craftsmen or skilled labourers like Borsig or professionals like Siemens who had, through skill and sheer hard work, made fortunes for themselves in the new industries. These men could not aspire to ennoblement and instead worked towards non-hereditary titles and conferments which became highly coveted until well into the 1890s. Receiving the title of *Kommerzienrat* or Privy Councillor meant that a businessman had 'arrived'; a title could greatly enhance the standing of the recipient's business and substantially improve its credit rating. The titles were granted by the king on the recommendation of the Minister of Commerce and holders were nominated by public figures, noblemen, municipal corporations or dignitaries; sons sometimes recommended their fathers in connection with some business jubilee. At least until 1886 a candidate had to pass through a rigorous selection procedure. He had to own or be part owner of a successful enterprise and be active in its management; he might have developed a new branch of industry or enhanced Prussia's business reputation abroad; he should have done charitable or Church or municipal government work; he had to have good labour relations in his factories, and he had to be considered a 'notable' and play a prominent public role. In Berlin a candidate required a minimum personal fortune of 1 million marks, although candidates from the provinces needed half that much. The political restrictions were made very clear: the candidate had to be 'politically reliable' – support for the liberals was a tremendous handicap which had to be compensated for by other qualifications; opposition to government made it very difficult for one to get a title and liberal activists and active supporters of the Fortschrittspartei (Progress party) were barred without question.[65]

The preferments were something of a meritocracy in the otherwise class- and code-ridden city, and one measure of this was the large number of titles granted to Jewish businessmen. The later tragedy of the Holocaust was particularly difficult to accept in a city which rose to prominence largely because of its entrepreneurial Jewish population; indeed without the input of these Jews the city would never have reached the economic and financial heights of the nineteenth century. Unlike areas such as the Ruhr, where most title holders were Gentiles, over 40 per cent of those in Berlin were Jewish and it was estimated that about half the economic activity in the city was generated by Jewish businessmen.[66] Their success attracted more Jews to the city so that by the 1870s 80 per cent of Prussian Jews had moved to Berlin. The Jews were important in industries and services centred there; whereas Gentile millionaires tended to be in the coal, iron, steel, metallurgy and machine-building industries, Jews were particularly successful in banking, manufacturing and trade, all of which were highly represented in the Prussian capital. Berlin industrial history was shaped by important Jewish families not only in banking and finance but, like the Reichenbeims and Goldschmidts, also in clothing; the silk manufacturers the Meyers had royal patronage; the Liebermanns were an old trading family which made a fortune in calico and pioneered the use of mechanical manufacturing. Jews were also prominent in brewing and distilling and all the service industries. Thanks to the capital generated there economic decision-making came to be concentrated in Berlin, at the expense of Frankfurt-am-Main, Cologne, Hamburg and other older centres. Berlin was never free of anti-Semitism but Jews were given more freedom and were increasingly seen as important and respected members of mid nineteenth-century Berlin society. One measure of this acceptance was the increase in official recognition of their contribution in the form of orders which gave them a seal of respectability in the Gentile world. The fact that a candidate for honours like the *Geheimer Kommerzienrat* was Jewish was mentioned in the confidential reports as a minor flaw but not insurmountable as long as he showed Christian or patriotic 'virtues' – to be a liberal or even a Catholic was often seen as a more serious hurdle to advancement. One report stated that 'the candidate, although Jewish, employed in his office mainly Christian clerks' or 'although a Jew, he has always acted in a Christian spirit'; of another, 'it is precisely because he is a Jew and a traditional liberal, but in times of need a generous patriot, that his appointment would be generally welcomed'.[67] It was only in the final quarter of the century, when racial anti-Semitism was on the rise, that such recommendations became rare. Ironically one of the triggers would be jealousy of increasing Jewish wealth and success which Berliners themselves had championed in the mid nineteenth century.

The economic rise of Berlin throughout the nineteenth century is one of the most remarkable success stories in history, made all the more dramatic given the depths to which it had fallen under Napoleon. In the early part of the century Berlin had been an economic backwater languishing on the edge of western Europe; when Napoleon marched in it had only one steam engine in the Royal Porcelain Works, and even that did not work. Compared with the new English industrial cities like Birmingham and Manchester Berlin was little more than a village and, locked as it was in the midst of a sandy wasteland, seemed an unnatural place for an economic giant. And yet, within decades, it had become the mightiest industrial capital on the continent. No European city rose from obscurity so quickly, and none would be so drunk on its success. By the end of the century Berlin had mushroomed at a breathtaking pace and had outstripped its formidable rivals, Paris and London, in industrial output. The population growth was staggering: in 1800 it stood at 915,000; by 1890 it had shot up to 2 million, and by 1914 it would be nearly 4 million, making it the largest city in Europe. Berlin's transformation was due to an explosive combination of factors which included the importance derived from its role as the Prussian capital, the coming of the railway, Otto von Bismarck's early support of the Zollverein, and the new breed of Berlin entrepreneur determined to put his city on the map.

But despite its success it was not a city at ease with itself. Political reforms were non-existent, social reforms were grudgingly introduced, and all this at a time when hundreds of thousands of people were moving to the city to fill the new factories and the tenement blocks. They would become part of a force so powerful that by the end of the century Berlin would act both as the conservative capital of Germany, and the centre of the German working-class movement – the 'other' part of the city known as 'Red Berlin'.

V

The Rise of Red Berlin

God help the poor.
(*Faust*, Part I)

ON A DAMP AFTERNOON in October 1836 a black and yellow postal coach pulled into Berlin and a young student stepped out on to the pavement. He had just written a short verse to his beloved in Bonn: 'The two skies. On the journey to Berlin in a carriage. The mountains pass, the forests recede. Gone from sight they leave no trace behind.'¹ It was not a promising start. After finding rooms in Lessing's old house in the Mittelstrasse (with 'cultured people') the gaunt man, his face adorned by a rather unsuccessful moustache and wispy beard, set off to register at the university. Had he remained in the Rhineland the world might have been spared a great deal of turmoil and bloodshed, but his experiences in Berlin would redirect his career and change him from a drunken, duelling provincial student into the creator of scientific socialism and the driving force behind the international Communist movement. Berliners can be forgiven for ignoring the arrival of Karl Heinrich Marx, forced to Berlin by a father tired of his loutish behaviour in Bonn, but they would hear of him soon enough.² And Marx was only one of the litany of Communist saints who would be drawn to this burgeoning industrial city; Friedrich Engels, Ferdinand Lassalle, August Bebel, Karl Liebknecht, Karl Radek, Rosa Luxemburg and even Lenin, who visited twelve times and who later slid through Germany on his way to lead the Russian Revolution, would be drawn to the new centre of the European working-class movement. Between Marx's arrival and the end of the First World War the sprawling industrial city became known as 'Red Berlin', a powerful symbol lionized by the left and feared, even loathed, by just about everybody else.

When Marx first arrived in Berlin he found a city charged with pre-revolutionary tension. He threw himself into the radical circles at the university, joined the Doktorklub, a group of earnest young men who met over coffee and the eighty newspapers of the reading room of the Café Stehely, and was inspired by the latest works by the Young Germans like Heinrich Heine,

153

Ludwig Börne, Karl Gutzkow and Theodor Mondt.[3] But above all it was in Berlin that the young Marx came into contact with the works of Berlin's most prominent philosopher: Georg Wilhelm Friedrich Hegel.[4]

'Only one man understands me,' Hegel muttered towards the end of his life, 'and even he does not.'[5] The complaint was widespread; Hegel's cryptic style, coupled with the fact that many of his works were published from lecture notes, added to the difficulty in deciphering his already obscure and abstract writing. Schopenhauer would call Hegel's work 'pure nonsense' created by 'stringing together senseless and extravagant mazes of words, such as had previously been known only in madhouses', which had resulted in the 'most bare faced general mystification that has ever taken place . . . and will remain as a monument to German stupidity'.[6] It did not help that Hegel had attempted nothing less than the placement of all human knowledge into a coherent philosophy of history. Despite the savage criticism his work was, in Engels's words, a 'triumphal procession which lasted for decades' and was later used to legitimate two of the most influential – and mutually exclusive – developments in history: the rise of chauvinistic Prussian nationalism, and the creation of scientific socialism. Hegel would be given the dubious honour of being invoked both by William II and by Marx.

Hegel was born in Stuttgart in 1770 and struggled for many years as a poor and unknown lecturer, confiding in his friend Schlegel that he had often gone hungry. His house at Jena was stormed by Napoleon's soldiers and he barely managed to survive while in Nuremberg and Heidelberg, but by the time he reached Berlin in 1818 he had become the well-known author of *Logic* and the *Encyclopaedia of the Philosophical Sciences* and his birthday was jointly celebrated with that of the other icon of the fledgling German nation – Goethe.

Hegel was above all a product of his age. Golo Mann has said of him: 'What Napoleon was to the political history of the period Hegel was to its intellectual history.'[7] One sees in his work the desperate search for answers to the political turmoil which had ripped apart the Europe of his youth. For Hegel, the most important aspect of existence was the notion that everything – every idea and every situation – must always change, be torn down, and give rise to its opposite. If there is peace there will be war and, although this will result in violence and pain and bloodshed, eventually the warring parties will come to some reconciliation which will form a 'higher stage', a greater whole. The new status quo would not last either – it too would spawn its opposite, and the same process would be repeated again and again. This was the dialectic which swung through history like a giant pendulum, affecting everything from art to philosophy, from fashion to politics. For Hegel the great dualisms of history – the divisions between public and private or between the individual and society – would one day be reconciled through this relentless process. Only then would man achieve complete knowledge and fulfil the world spirit – Geist.[8]

Hegel died in 1831, and his followers immediately split into two antagonistic groups known as the Old Hegelians and the Young Hegelians. The first were ultra-conservative and would eventually use his defence of the all-powerful state – the Machtstaat – to legitimate Bismarck's unification of Germany in 1871 and to justify chauvinistic nationalism and militarism well into the twentieth century. Because of this Hegel has been called everything from the father of nationalism to the harbinger of totalitarianism, but although he defended the Machtstaat, it is ahistorical to suggest that he either foresaw or would have approved of the policies later carried out in his name. He would have been appalled to see his face staring out gloomily from the pages of Nazi propaganda.[9]

Hegel's other disciples, the Young Hegelians, saw his work as proof of precisely the opposite view. For them Hegel's dialectic proved that what is 'rational' today is 'irrational' tomorrow, and that everything from religion to culture to politics must be destroyed to make way for something new, something better. Using Hegel as their guide they began to denounce their own society.[10]

Hegel had been a religious man all his life but his followers set about proving him wrong. Using his own methodology they tried to show that religion was a human construct whose time had passed. In 1835, four years after Hegel's death, David Friedrich Strauss wrote his Life of Jesus, in which he used the dialectic to 'prove' that the New Testament was a myth. In his Kritik der evangelischen Geschichte der Synoptiker Bruno Bauer denied that Jesus was the son of God, and in The Essence of Christianity Ludwig Feuerbach tried to show that it was not God who had created man, but rather man who had created God, and that the deity was nothing more than a projection of human needs and desires. It was Feuerbach who coined the now famous expression 'You are what you eat' – by which he meant that man is not fashioned in the image of God but is nothing more than biological matter.[11] Arnold Ruge became the leading Young Hegelian of the 1848 era and, using Hegel's 'terror of reason', attacked everything from politics to the Romantics. He called for an end to ephemeral liberal theorizing and proclaimed that democracy would not simply 'happen' but must be fought for using principles of science and reason. He also chided Germans for being as passive about politics as they were 'about the weather'. In 1838 Arnold Ruge and Theodor Ernst Echtermeyer founded the Hallesche Jahrbücher für deutsche Wissenschaft und Kunst, which became a rallying point for radical intellectuals; it was banned by the Prussian government in 1841 and Ruge was forced to flee to Paris, but not before he and others – above all Bruno Bauer – had influenced the young Marx.[12]

Marx was captivated by the new ideas sweeping 1830s Berlin and wrote to his father that he was attaching himself 'ever more closely to the current philosophy'. His father sneered that he had merely replaced 'degeneration in a learned dressing-gown and uncombed hair with degeneration with a beer glass', but Marx was serious and had already started to struggle with Hegel's troubled legacy.[13] Marx agreed with Hegel that society was moving towards a Utopia but for him human beings had to make their own history, albeit under conditions which they had not chosen. To do this they had to act politically. Marx turned Hegel on his head, transforming Hegel's passive view into a call for action. The epitaph on his gravestone in Highgate cemetery reads: 'Philosophers have only *explained* the world in different ways, what matters is that it should be *changed*.'

In Berlin Marx drank in the theories of the Young Hegelians: religion became the 'opium of the masses'; political action was necessary to create the perfect society; and it was possible to achieve an ideal world if one followed rational scientific principles. Nevertheless at this point in his development the young student showed more interest in the coffee houses, the theatres and the salons of Berlin than in the working-class districts to the north and it was only later, in Paris, that he first noticed the 'nobility' in the 'toil-worn bodies' of the workers and discovered his own 'agent of history' – the proletariat. Only then would the Hegelian ideas absorbed in Berlin fit into a vast system which explained how society was dominated by a class struggle between capitalists and workers and how, when the workers were made aware of their class consciousness, they would inaugurate a revolution and bring about a Communist society in which there would be plenty for all, classes would disappear, ideology would vanish, the state would wither away, and all human beings would live together in peace and self-fulfilment. It was a seductive idea and, although Marx left Berlin in 1841 as a virtually unknown academic, all of 'Red Berlin' would have his name on their lips by the time of his death in 1883. The city was growing, the Industrial Revolution was bringing inexorable change, and the urban working class was becoming a force in its own right. The new industrial areas north of the Oranienburg Gate would soon be fertile ground for the revolutionary ideas spread by Marx and his disciples.

The radicals, the neo-Hegelians, and indeed Marx himself came to maturity during a particularly grim phase in nineteenth-century industrialization. Berlin was no exception. Long hours, terrible working conditions, exploitation and brutality were the rule in the early factories and even before Marx's arrival many were beginning to understand that however prosperous industrial Berlin appeared to be to the casual visitor it was a savage and terrible place for many of its inhabitants. Contemporary posters show the city haunted by a hideous black devil hovering above the buildings, waiting to devour those foolish enough to venture through the gates.[14] Mothers in the villages of the Mark Brandenburg warned their children of the evil and depravity of the 'Demon Berlin', and conservatives grumbled about the hazards of having such a hotbed of radicalism in their midst. But the vast majority of the new working class who made up the overgrown industrial slums had not wanted to live in Berlin at all; they were immigrants who flooded into the city after their traditional way of life had collapsed in the east.

Berliners have created a great many myths about themselves, and one of the most enduring is the image of the 'typical Berliner'. Every tour guide, local historian and *Kneipe* (bar) philosopher will expound at length about the collective wit, disrespect for authority, suspicion of leaders and tradition of tolerance which epitomizes a true Berliner. He will invariably point to medieval examples of *Berliner Unwille* or to Goethe's musings about the audacious local temperament, or recall Queen Victoria's daughter's description of Berliners as 'bristly, thorny ... with their sharp tongues, their cutting sarcasms about everybody and everything' as proof of this heritage. But like so many modern myths, it is largely a nineteenth-century creation. It is true that Berlin has always been a magnet for immigrants, and everyone from the Wends and the French Huguenots to the Jewish merchants and Dutch and Bohemian craftsmen left their mark on the city, but nothing could compare with the wave of people which swept into Berlin from Saxony and the east Elbian lands throughout the late nineteenth and early twentieth centuries. By 1900 more than 60 per cent of Berliners were either immigrants or the children of immigrants and this percentage skyrocketed in the years between 1900 and 1914, when the population doubled again.[15] Visitors commented that Berlin looked more like a New York or a Chicago than any equivalent European city, and it developed a culture to match. A quick look through a modern telephone directory still reveals a plethora of common Bohemian, Moravian and Polish names, but these destitute strangers were brought together not by a common language or religion, but by poverty and fear, by the factory floor and the rental barrack. It was from these reluctant migrants, and not their earlier counterparts, that the caricature of the coarse, tough, witty, irreverent Berliner was born.

The reasons for the mass migration to the city were complex but ultimately lay in the fact that the land in the east could not sustain a large rural population. If one journeys overland from Berlin through the Mark Brandenburg into Poland and what were then the provinces of Mecklenburg, Pomerania and West and East Prussia one passes a seemingly endless patchwork of sandy fields broken by a few straggly pine forests and small villages. It was here that the Junkers, descendants of the settlers who had accompanied the old Teutonic conquerors to the area, lived on their estates, and fiercely defended their feudal privileges. Some were as poor as the French *hobereaux* who had to stay in bed while their only pair of trousers was being mended, but the larger landowners had become wealthier throughout the nineteenth century as rational methods of production, Liebig's mineral fertilizers, and modern equipment triumphed over the sandy soil.[16] They would suffer later when cheap imports of Russian and American grain undercut their products, but they prospered for much of the nineteenth century and were particularly important to the recovery of Prussia after the Napoleonic Wars. The 'agrarian revolution' which took place after the victory was bolstered by the reforms introduced between 1807 and 1821, but although they improved production and strengthened the Junkers' power they had unforeseen consequences. Serfs were able to 'buy' their freedom from the lord by returning half the land they had once worked, but they were then left with tiny plots of poor soil from which it was impossible to make a living. Few could afford to buy seeds, farming equipment or supplies, and as the lord's woodlands, grazing areas and common fields were now out of bounds few could survive for long. A desperately poor rural substratum emerged, with ex-serfs drifting around the countryside collecting wood, poaching, begging or stealing.[17] The new, large-scale agriculture was achieved at the expense of peasant ownership, and between 1811 and 1890 the number of large estates increased by two-thirds in the east Elbian region. For their part the estate owners became increasingly powerful and continued to exert an extraordinary influence on the Prussian (and later the German) government. At the same time improved efficiency saw a vast increase in the population – Prussia's grew by 26 per cent between 1840 and 1860 alone – but as fewer people were needed to work the land unemployment rose. Many were drawn to the new industrial cities.[18] By the end of the century thousands of immigrants had moved in from West and East Prussia, Brandenburg, Pomerania and Mecklenburg.

To make matters worse, the crisis in agricultural labour coincided with the introduction of free trade in the North German Confederation and with the corresponding breakdown of the medieval guild system. Before 1810 only a privileged few had been entitled to become master-craftsmen, but the free trade laws did away with the strict code which required all silversmiths, jewellers, furniture makers, stone masons and a host of others to join one of the exclusive guilds. In 1820 there had been thirty masters and journeymen per 1,000 Prussians, but this had already doubled by 1850. Independent artisans were forced to work from home or to hire themselves out for menial repair work on battered furniture or church silver, and a newcomer could only hold his own against new mass-produced items by constantly increasing the length of his working day. Many simply gave up and went to the city.[19]

The Industrial Revolution hit the traditional cottage industries just as hard. There were half a million small linen and wool looms and tens of thousands of spinners in Prussia alone in the early nineteenth century, but as the shining new factories began to spring up in Europe's cities life for traditional workers became a struggle for survival. Hollow-eyed children were sent to work at the age of four; *Huhn* (chicken) on a menu could mean *Hund* (dog); and even the cannibalistic jokes running through Kayssler's social commentary, akin to Swiftian satire about Irish children, were not considered far fetched by those who visited the region. Linguet's observation that 'you can be sure that [the city] where the most human beings are at the point of dying of hunger is the one where the most hands are employed in working the shuttle' was an apt description for much of the east.[20] It was clear that the cottage weavers were fighting a losing battle.

The spark which ignited the powder keg was started by famine. From 1843 Prussia experienced successive failures in both the grain and potato harvests, and food riots became increasingly common in Berlin after 1845. By this time around 70 per cent of a labourer's income was spent on food – a dire situation when, according to the great liberal scientist Rudolf Virchow, workers' real wages dropped by 45 per cent between 1844 and 1847.[21] The latter was the year of the 'Potato Revolution', which saw violence on the streets of Berlin provoked by endless food shortages and an outbreak of typhus, a disease brought on by malnutrition.[22] It was put down by the military. But the situation was worse in Silesia. There linen weavers could no longer compete with new mechanical production techniques employed in Britain and they were penniless and starving. Eighty thousand people contracted typhus and around 16,000 people died that winter. Thousands rose up in desperation against the local merchants and middlemen in a pitiful attempt to get food and to somehow reverse the course of the Industrial Revolution. The weavers blamed the wealthy middlemen, who were detested for flaunting their coaches and clothes and estates as the people went hungry. Three hundred weavers attacked their factories and homes in 1847, smashing property and burning the records of their debts. Not amused by the cartloads of 'German Luddites' bearing down on them with sticks and pitchforks, the merchants asked the Prussian military to intervene and the latter, nervous about the persistent whispers of revolution floating around Europe, crushed the revolt with brute force.[23]

In more settled times an incident like this would soon have been forgotten, but the story of the revolt became one of the first great rallying myths of the emerging working class; indeed it fuelled the Marxist belief that industrial capitalism must inevitably lead to the degradation and impoverishment – to the pauperization – of workers. Heinrich Heine wrote about it in his early poem of social protest *The Silesian Weavers*; it was taken up by Gerhart

Hauptmann in his eerie, disturbing – and banned – play *Die Weber* (The Weavers) and by Käthe Kollwitz in her black lithographs of the same name; it cropped up in Franz Mehring's essay *Hauptmanns Weavers*, in Friedrich Kayssler's *The Weavers' Social Drama*, and was later alluded to by many a left-wing Berlin writer of the nineteenth century. The frightened and starving cottage weavers would never know of their place in history, but they packed up their belongings and left for Berlin, adding to the mass of new arrivals there. Evidence of this exodus has long since disappeared under the weight of the more terrible things which have since happened in eastern Germany and Poland. Perhaps the closest equivalent one can find today are the chillingly quiet villages near Chernobyl in Ukraine which resemble the abandoned settlements that once littered the territory east of the Elbe. There the evidence of rapid departure is everywhere: small brightly painted wooden houses line the dusty roads, old bottles stand on kitchen window sills, benches where neighbours once chatted in the sun lie at the edges of overgrown gardens, and rusting wire still clings to empty chicken coops. In the 1980s the fear of radiation forced people to move; in the mid nineteenth century it was starvation, but the end result was the same: a destitute population compelled to emigrate in search of a better life.

In 1847 400,000 peasants, merchants and artisans left the eastern provinces; by 1870 it was over 800,000 per year and over 2 million Germans emigrated in the years between 1850 and 1870. Of the 133,700 who officially registered in Berlin in 1870 (many did not) over half were young men of working age. The city population surged to 1 million following demobilization after the war of 1871; twenty years later it doubled again, and it had reached 4 million by 1914. Most continued to come from the east; in 1911 alone 1,046,162 people came to Berlin from German lands along with 97,683 from Russia; this was in contrast to the mere 7,611 who came from western countries like Holland or 3,682 from Italy.[24] Huge tent cities sprang up on the fringes of a Berlin bloated with desperate people hoping to get work – older men with families to feed and a few qualifications, or rural untrained youths with no idea about life in the city. Many had hoped to make enough money in Berlin to buy a passage to America but had been trapped by their poverty.

The mass migration caught officials by surprise, but the indifferent city councils pretended that nothing was happening and refused to make provision in the hope that the troublesome people at their gates would simply go away.[25] In the end the Prussian government had to order the Berlin police to prepare plans for new housing developments, but it was not until 1858 that the young architect and civil engineer James Hobrecht was appointed to draw up plans for huge districts to house the newcomers. It took Hobrecht four years to produce the Generalbebauungsplan (general development plan), a quintessentially Prussian piece of work which was brilliant, meticulous, all-encompassing, and fundamentally flawed. The police president, who ran the city in much the same way as the *préfet* de la Seine ruled Paris, could have rejected the plans outright, but the combination of the relentless wave of people coupled with the demands of burgeoning industry for cheaply housed labourers encouraged him to make disastrous decisions which turned the 'Athens on the Spree' into the biggest working-class slum on the continent.[26] As the peasants huddled in their tent cities, huge barracks were built within the city walls which would soon house them like virtual prisoners.

Nobody else in Europe noticed when Hobrecht was appointed in Berlin as all eyes were on Paris, and the architect Baron Haussmann. When Louis-Napoleon lived in exile in London between 1838 and 1840 he had been much impressed by the new developments around Regent Street which he passed when visiting his mistress in St John's Wood.[27] Back in Paris he appointed Haussmann to copy the London style and, guided by the motto 'air, open prospects, perspective', Haussmann created a city of such beauty and spaciousness that it has never been equalled.[28] The Rue de Rivoli, the Champs-Élysées, the Place Vendôme, and the Place de la Concorde became the envy of Europe and were copied around the world just as Versailles had been before. The burgomaster Anspach attempted to Haussmannize the lower part of Brussels; in Mexico City in 1860 Emperor Maximilian opened the most bizarre imitation of the Champs-Élysées called the Paseo de la Reforme, which was designed to join the Aztec city to the palace of Chapultepec. Most Italian cities were given Haussmannesque main roads to connect the centres with the new railway stations, including the Via Nazionale in Rome and the Via Independenza in Bologna. The 1864 reconstruction of Florence was a slavish copy of Haussmann's style; even the Vienna Ring was influenced by him.[29]

Not all of Haussmann's contemporaries appreciated his work. Delvau spat that Paris 'is no longer Athens but Babylon! No longer a city but a station!' For him the city of Balzac had been destroyed; Paris was now little more than a 'tasteless circus'. Sadly, Hobrecht was another of Haussmann's critics, but for different reasons. For him Haussmann's Paris was not well organized or efficient, and it could not possibly house enough people. There would be little room for glorious boulevards and spacious avenues in his grand plan.

For centuries architects from Alberti to Le Corbusier have tried to create ideal communities for human beings, and for just as long the disorderly and difficult creatures have refused to conform to their ideas. Frederick the Great was the first to make this mistake in Berlin when, as early as 1747, he passed a Housing Law which allowed property speculators to build 'ideal' three-storey apartments around Leipziger Platz. As Werner Hegemann fumed in his 1930 work *Das steinerne Berlin* (Berlin in Stone), these cramped buildings became the most despised houses in Berlin: 'Frederick the so-called Great was too busy composing French poems with Voltaire to realize that with haughty indifference he determined the well-being and suffering of hundreds of thousands of people.'[30] For his part Hobrecht wanted to create a vast number of high density residential districts between the old Customs Wall and the S-Bahn ring railway. He despised London, claiming that the wealthy lived in elegant districts while the poor lived in areas entered 'only by the policeman and the writer seeking sensation'.[31] Hobrecht's Berlin was to be 'integrated', with expensive flats at the front of the houses, and small, dark, cheap ones at the back. After drawing a gigantic ring around the city (the 1862 plan was never completed) he divided land into large 400-square-metre blocks separated by a grid of connecting roads. Then he let the developers loose, assuming that they would add small airy side streets, parks, footpaths and gardens to break up the blocks. The developers ignored all pleas for lawns and lanes and proceeded to build on every available inch of land by constructing enormous rectangular seven-storey brick barracks divided around successive paved courtyards. They could not have been less Haussmannesque, but these miserable buildings became the dark, infested, despised *Hinterhöfe* – the tenement blocks – of Berlin.

Within a decade acres of these red and ochre brick buildings had spread like cancer over the city. The rooms within were tiny and badly lit, the air was poor, the facilities abysmal and made worse by the relentless flow of newcomers who filled every available space. Like many experts of his day Hobrecht had assumed Berlin would not reach a population of 4 million for at least a century; in fact it passed this mark in a few decades. The feverish growth and physical pressure for housing fuelled ever more crass speculation; in 1871–2 forty building societies were set up with capital of 194 million marks; in 1860 9,878 sites had been developed; in 1870 this had reached 14,618. Rental barracks sprang up so quickly on the farms of Wedding, Kreuzberg and Prenzlauer Berg that local peasants became millionaires overnight. The change was so startling that even the calm sociologist Rudolf Eberstadt said that the disorientation would prove immensely damaging to the health, and Georg Simmel warned of the damage caused by the *Steigerung des Nervenlebens*, an increasingly stressful life.[32]

Hobrecht's rental barracks are still grim. As a research student in East Berlin I lived in a typical *Hinterhof* which, as it had not yet been 'sanitized' (a euphemism for renovation), had changed very little from pre-war days. The only door from the street led to a short dark corridor which in turn opened on to the first of four dingy courtyards of 28 square metres, the space once required for horse-drawn fire engines to turn. Rubbish was piled near the entrance, the wooden windows and doors were rotting in their frames and the grey-green stucco, a colour peculiar to Communist Europe, fell from the damp walls. Its oppressive nineteenth-century character was made all the more unpleasant by the sense of decay and fear which was omnipresent in the back streets of Honecker's Berlin, and by the occupants of the ground floor, the Stasi 'caretakers' (they usually got the nicest flats), who would peer out from behind their filthy net curtains to check on the comings and goings of all the occupants. The flat was on the top floor and consisted of two grimy rectangular rooms and a small kitchen which was covered in turquoise plastic and fitted out with a few old appliances. One of its most pleasant features was the ceramic tile oven, which devoured bricks of the acrid brown coal that I was obliged to haul up from the cellar once a week in the winter. The back court was completely isolated from the streets outside; at night one could lean out of a window and smell the mixture of rubbish, coal smoke and sausages which rose through the gloom, or listen to muffled quarrels interrupted only by the echo of footsteps in the courtyard below. But whatever the drawbacks of life in late twentieth-century East Berlin my existence was luxurious compared with that endured by the original inhabitants.[33]

When my flat was built in 1870 Berlin had the highest urban density of any city in Europe. Each small block contained an average of fifty-three people compared with a mere eight in ghastly Dickensian London; by the turn of the century there were a staggering 1,000 people per hectare. Each room contained an average of five people but according to Berlin records, which were by their very nature incomplete, 27,000 had seven, 18,400 had eight, 10,700 nine, and many had more than twenty per room. A tiny flat like mine might well have housed fifteen people. Over 60,000 people 'officially' inhabited coal cellars; I shudder to think of people living in my dank, airless underground room with its walls glistening with slime and the numerous rats scurrying past in the dark.[34]

Some areas were notorious for overcrowding even then. The barracks between Luisenstadt and the Landwehrkanal housed more than 250 families and these numbers do not take into account the thousands of *Schlafburschen* or *Schlafmädchen* who rented a bed for a few hours a day, or the *Trockenwohner* who occupied rooms in building sites while the fresh plaster dried. The 1905 census showed that over 63,425 homes took in such part-time tenants, some of whom had young children.[35] The most infamous development was the 'Meyers Hof' in Wedding, built in a tough street which was later made famous – or infamous – through Georg Grosz's graphic etching *Sex Murder in the Ackerstrasse*. Six *Hinterhöfe* were squeezed on to a site 150 metres long but only 40 metres wide, giving the effect of a long dark tunnel from which there was no escape. According to the magazine *Architekten Verein* the 300 flats housed well over 2,000 people a matter of days after completion, but the numbers were bound to rise, making it a breeding ground for illness and disease; indeed infant mortality in Wedding as late as 1905 was an extraordinary 42 per cent.[36] The complex was smashed by bombs in 1944, with the last remaining section pulled down a decade later to make way for the Ernst-Reuter development. Today the only thing that survives is the deceptively pretty mock Renaissance facade which was fastened to the front of another building nearby.[37]

Sanitary conditions in the slum rental barracks were totally inadequate; only a few outhouses were built for each back block and at the end of the century only 8 per cent of Berlin dwellings had a WC; even the residents of well-to-do areas would be woken at night by the sound of women clattering down the street in rickety carts, collecting sewage in large tanks and dumping it into the river. Again the officials disregarded calls for change. When residents in the Prenzlauer Berg complained that there was only one toilet for every ten flats the official Prussian response was typical: because most men were away for most of the day 'when most stools are passed', they were told, the toilets had only to accommodate ten or eleven women, and as 'one sitting takes an average of 3–4 minutes or five including time to adjust one's clothing even though this is not necessary for women ... even allowing 10 minutes per sitting there should still be time in 12 daytime hours for 72 people to use the closet ...'[38] Raw sewage ran in the streets for decades. Naturally, outbreaks of typhus and other illnesses were common. Cholera was another killer: in 1831 an outbreak killed around two-thirds of those infected, including Hegel, and it was the terrible epidemic of 1868 which prompted the liberal scientist Rudolf Virchow to promote the development of sanitary systems like the Rieselfelder sewage works.[39] The smallpox epidemic of 1871 struck so many that the Berlin garrison allowed health workers to set up hospital tents on their parade ground at the Tempelhof field, on the very site where the Wright brothers would soon test their planes: 6,478 people died, which was not surprising given that the only prescription for the 'poor person's illness' was turnip soup. Every day, wrote Rosa Luxemburg, homeless people die in Berlin, broken by hunger and cold: 'nobody notices them, particularly not the police reports'.[40] Venereal disease was rampant and Virchow estimated that around 3.8 per cent of men in the Prussian army and 5 per cent of the population of Berlin were infected. But the great national disease of the century was tuberculosis. For some reason this became a romantic disease, said to create 'radiant beauty' as it killed, and could only be 'cured' with opium. For the poor who were stricken, the strange potions, the blood letting, the laxatives and the poultices administered by quack healers did little good. According to Virchow, around

15 per cent of all fatalities in Prussia in 1860 could be attributed to tuberculosis, and many thousands coughed and sweated to death in conditions which bore little resemblance to the glorious sets of *La Traviata*.

As the century wore on the numbers of migrants steadily increased, and even the over-filled rental barracks failed to meet the escalating housing needs. Thousands of people slept in courtyards, at train stations or under makeshift shelters; some were forced into the infamous workhouses such as the eighteenth-century Ochsenkopf on Alexanderplatz or the Rummelsburg. Homelessness surged on collection days, 1 April and 1 October, when the thousands who could not pay the high rents were forced on to the street. Eyewitnesses described families sitting dejectedly amongst their possessions or pushing them along in small hand or dog carts; streets in Luisenstadt, at the Halle Gate or by the Lustizer Platz were piled so high with furniture and belongings that it was impossible for pedestrians to get by. During the particularly bad Easter move of 1872 there were so many people on the street that the city officials were forced to build a temporary shelter in Moabit; between 1900 and 1905 the shelter on Fröbelstrasse took in 2,000 people every night. But for most the only option was to move under a bridge or into a deserted building site, a stable, an empty train carriage or a warehouse. A group of families at the Stralau Gate hauled an old river barge on to land and lived under it, a novelty which soon became a local landmark.

The authorities had little sympathy for the destitute families and were often remarkably brutal when breaking up their settlements. After the Easter move of 1871 dozens of people had settled around the Blumenstrasse and the Kottbus Gate, and as the fire brigade had not managed to shift them by July the police were sent in to move them on. In one street battle alone 159 people lay bleeding on the roads, having been cut down by sabres.[41] The following year during another insurrection the police ripped down the white flag with the red Brandenburg eagle which a carpenter had nailed to a flagpole as a rallying mark. The carpenter took out his red handkerchief, and nailed it in its place. It became the first red flag raised in Berlin since 1848. The public prosecutor was so disturbed by this that he forced the socialists, who had not been directly involved in the fighting, to pay the revenue lost to the landlords.[42]

The police tended to overreact to anything reminiscent of 1848, when Berliners had torn up paving stones to slow down cavalry and infantry, carried projectiles to upper floors and thrown them at passing troops, and tried to strangle soldiers who entered their homes. But for the new working class these street battles became part of the local culture which bound the poor together against the Berlin police, and which marked the beginning of a radical split between the Berlin 'underclass' and the city authorities. As Ringelnatz put it: '*Die Dichter und die Maler, Und auch die Kriminaler, Die kennen ihr Berlin*' (the poets and the painters, and also the criminals, they all know their Berlin).[43]

In his efforts to create the perfectly planned city James Hobrecht had unwittingly created a maze of slums, back corridors, hidden rooms and hiding places which made the new districts difficult to control. As the population soared the crime rate rose with it and a huge underclass of thieves, criminals, prostitutes, blackmailers and confidence men began to flourish in the dark areas stretching out behind Alexanderplatz to the north, the north-east, and on the outskirts of southern Berlin. Homelessness and begging were made illegal in 1843, and the Poor Law or 'Eberfeld System' forced people who were caught committing petty crimes to work on civic projects, but these measures had little effect on illegal activity. The slums of Berlin began to resemble Chicago in the 1920s or even Moscow in the 1990s, with extortion, black marketeering and dubious business deals becoming the norm. The city began to acquire the reputation as a 'fount of perversion, criminality and evil'. Döblin called Berlin a 'peculiar debauched city of sin, joined by trains, swarming with agitated worker-animals . . . whose lungs filled with the poisonous vapours from the factories emit the death rattle . . . It was rotten here from the beginning.'[44]

The Berlin authorities were slow to tackle the root cause of the problem, which was poverty and overcrowding, but they remained obsessed with political control and with reversing the decline of moral standards in the city. The Lex Heinze of 1900 was one attempt to improve morality in Berlin. It listed items to be banned, including 'obscene literature, pictures or representations' and 'objects suited for obscene use' which they found offensive.[45] Berlin's chief of police, Horst Windheim, set up the much-derided Sittenpolizei or 'Morality Police' unit, which took to following suspicious characters on the streets or swooping down on rubber-goods suppliers, barber shops and pharmacies to confiscate any obscene photographs or objects which could be used for contraception or other 'degenerate purposes'.[46]

One of their most obvious targets was rampant female, male and child prostitution which was fast becoming a feature of the industrial city. Unlike Hamburg, Paris and Vienna, brothels had been outlawed in Berlin by the mid nineteenth century so that contact between prostitute and client was made in cafés, pubs, dance halls and along the main shopping streets. A woman could register with the police and if she promised to keep away from cultural and government centres, train stations, museums, palaces and army barracks and any other 'sensitive areas' she might be permitted to work without being arrested, but of an estimated 50,000 prostitutes only 4,000 signed up.[47] In his book on prostitution, in which he reports that, as one woman told him, 'only the stupid ones register!' Abraham Flexner described the unique style of Berlin prostitution: the slow glance, the deliberate walk, the striking clothing, the longing stare into a café window. He described ridiculous scenes where innocent bourgeois women were hauled off to the station by the police for apparently looking at someone in an 'alluring manner', although according to Hans Ostwald it was easy to make mistakes:

> In the streets between the Zoo Railway and Wittenbergplatz and along the Kurfürstendamm there is a crowd of strollers at all times of day in which women predominate ... here one doesn't know; perhaps she is the daughter or wife of the man who walks beside her – for here the glittering colour of the demimonde is also the style of dress. And that plain woman over there is perhaps soliciting.[48]

As the inevitable consequence of rampant prostitution there was a spate of unwanted pregnancies. The numbers of illegitimate children rose in the mid nineteenth century. In 1750 around 4 per cent of births in Berlin were illegitimate; by 1816–20 the number had climbed to 18.3 per cent. It dropped to 14.5 per cent by 1866–70 but this was still extremely high compared to the Prussian average of 7 per cent.[49] Added to this was a so-called 'abortion epidemic' in the late nineteenth century.[50] Max Hirsch, the famous Berlin gynaecologist and proponent of the holistic study of women's health, tried to reduce the pressure on women who had abortions by arguing that modern life, and in particular factory employment, with its foul air, dim lighting and loud noise, noxious fumes and glass or metal particles in the air, contributed to the high incidence of miscarriage. He also pointed out that given hard physical labour, poor living conditions and a high incidence of smallpox, influenza, cholera, typhoid fever, tuberculosis, syphilis – all hazards of the Berlin slums – women stood a high risk of not being able to carry to full term.[51] But the police argued that the incidence of abortion was too high to be accounted for by Hirsch's findings, and new health insurance records showed that 10 per cent of female recipients suffered from the side effects of illegally induced abortions. Some women broke limbs throwing themselves from trams while others had to be treated for shock or hypothermia after being fished out of the Landwehr Canal, but the vast majority were found out because they had to be treated for the after effects of quack remedies peddled by the charlatans and frauds who fed on the desperation of others. One of many dangerous common remedies for those who could not afford a good surgeon was to eat hundreds of phosphorous match heads, a practice which only stopped when the substance was banned in 1907.[52] To add to this, many women died because of air bubbles in syringes, unsterilized instruments or internal injuries inflicted during backroom abortions; the mortality rate after complications was over 25 per cent and the Prussian Statistical Office estimated that over 2 per cent of *Berlinerins* died this way.[53] Women of all different ages and classes had abortions, but those most often caught were the factory workers, prostitutes, seamstresses and servants, for whom there was no protection even if they had been made pregnant by an employer and could not afford 'reliable' care. The crisis eventually became a political issue; in July 1871 even the conservative *Kreuzzeitung* expressed concern about the increasing number of 'unknown graves' being found throughout the city.

The terrible conditions for many women from factory workers to domestic servants fuelled the fledgling women's movement in Berlin. The concept of female emancipation first reached Berlin from France, where well-to-do women like Aurore Dupin, better known as George Sand, had called for women's rights as early as 1830. The climate in Berlin was hostile. When in 1835 the Berliner Karl Ferdinand Gutzkow published his novel *Wally die Zwei-flerin* about an emancipated woman, it was banned and he was imprisoned for a month under federal law for bringing the Christian religion 'into disrepute'. Young Hegelians also began to champion equal rights in the 1840s but they offered little practical help. The first active groups were founded in Berlin by liberal women who hoped to educate girls in domestic sciences and give them skills to cope in the city. In 1848 Luise Otto-Peters, already known for feminist articles and novels such as *Die Freunde* and poetry such as *Lieder eines deutschen Mädchens*, founded the Allgemeine deutsche Frauenverein (All German Women's Society) in 1865.[54] The group also published a journal, *Neue Bahnen*, which demanded education and equal work opportunities for women. In 1865 the more conservative Society for the Advancement of Employment for the Female Sex was founded to help young women to find placements in 'respectable households' and to train them in the new 'women's professions' such as teaching. Writers such as Helene Lange and Gertrud Bäumer motivated women through their 1901 journal *Handbuch der Frauenbewegung* and Bäumer wrote a number of other feminist works, including a biography of the historian and novelist Ricarda Huch, who in 1891 became the first German woman to get a D.Phil. This described how Huch had been forced to go to Switzerland for her degree as German universities did not accept women.[55] Social Democratic groups were greatly influenced by August Bebel's famous work *Die Frau und der Sozialismus*, which called for women's rights, improved health care and a list of other improvements for women, and before long hundreds of small self-help clubs, groups and charity organizations had been set up to try to bring about change.[56] By the First World War the Berlin Social Democratic women's movement had become the largest in the world with over 170,000 members.

Despite such innovations the industrial workers, both men and women, endured filthy manual labour, low wages, minimal security, overcrowded housing, miserable food and dangerous, cramped and disease-ridden working conditions. As early as 1828 General von Horn had complained that the children from the industrial districts were so 'stunted in physical and mental develop-ment' that they would be unable to fill the ranks of the army, concerns which led to the first piece of protective labour legislation, which stated that children should work no more than ten hours a day. But abuses still took place, and many a child spent his early life with no education and no freedom, surrounded by the filth and noise of machinery.[57] The adult working day increased from twelve or fourteen hours a day in the 1840s to as much as seventeen hours a day in the 1870s and if the breadwinner became ill the dependants could quickly plunge below subsistence level.[58] The clothing industry was particularly repugnant. Women were forced to work in sweat shops for starvation wages in utterly degrading conditions; one presser, Ottilie Baader, described her life as endless grey drudgery in which years passed without her noticing that she had 'once been young'.[59] Cheap labour kept German textiles competitive and there were nearly 500 wholesale garment dealers in Berlin in 1895 which exported goods all over the world, but the price was high. The women sewing and pressing in the Berlin sweat shops lived to an average age of twenty-six.[60]

Industrial workers made up between 55 and 60 per cent of Berlin's popu-lation by 1900, as compared with 43 per cent in London or 38 per cent in Paris.[61] And yet, few affluent Berliners knew or cared what was happening at the edge of their city. The closest most came to the slums was a glimpse from the new Ringbahn, where for a few pennies the well-to-do could look down on the dangerous but mysterious districts without having to go out on to the streets.[62] The *Bärenführer* or 'bear guide' for Berlin recommended trips above the 'other' Berlin on the Nordringbahn so that the adventurous visitor could catch a glimpse of the 'pulse' of the 'north', which stretched out behind the Weidendamm Bridge where the *Menschenmasse* – the masses – lived. One could explore the 'dark areas', and as long as one was 'tactful' even a stranger could 'study and experience the night life without undue fear'. Nevertheless the guide advised that it 'would be better to leave the ladies in the hotel', and carry valid papers 'in case of a police *Razzia*' (raid).[63] For most middle-class Berliners the poor were a nuisance; as Franz Held put it:

> Sick beggars with hunger in their eyes
> Stretch out an arm for a penny piece
> The satisfied public push past:
> 'And the police tolerate this!'[64]

As Georg Hermann put it, the different areas of Berlin were 'worlds apart'.

But a few were looking at the vast brick barracks and the teeming mass of people below and seeing the force of the future. After a visit to the slums

Engels wrote that the city, 'the breeding places of disease . . . the infamous holes and cellars in which the capitalist mode of production confines our workers night after night', would not disappear until the conditions which produced it disappeared also. 'As long as the capitalist mode of production continues to exist', he continued, 'it is folly to hope for an isolated solution of the housing question, or any other social question affecting the fate of the workers.' The Communists believed that this teeming mass would soon realize its tremendous power, and would act.

Before the Wall collapsed central East Berlin was a dreary shrine to a falsified version of the history of the working-class movement in Germany. On May Day plastic cutouts of proletarian leaders were paraded down Unter den Linden in front of a forcibly gathered crowd to illustrate their place in the rise of the working class. Marx and Engels, Luxemburg and Liebknecht, and finally Erich Honecker himself were put high on the list of Communist heroes, and Berlin was duly portrayed as the focal point of the smooth transition from one leader to another; from effete Social Democrats to vigorous Communists; from corrupt capitalism to the workers' state, from one stage of history to the next. Erich Honecker's reedy voice would float down to the bored Young Pioneers who were forced to stand around holding flowers and placards and singing the *Internationale*, which by the 1980s had lost any of its original meaning.

The actual history of the working-class movement in Germany was much more complex and less harmonious than the glib version peddled by Honecker and his government. East Germans could have been arrested for saying so, but it was by no means inevitable that Marx and Engels were destined to become the spiritual leaders of the Berlin working-class movement. Berlin was best known first as a liberal city; the Social Democratic Party had adopted Marxism almost by accident. Marx had been largely ignored in Berlin until after his death; his *Communist Manifesto* only became popular after it was re-imported by his followers, and even *Das Kapital* was better known abroad than at home. The political development of workers began not with the proletariat or factory workers, who were excluded from political life, nor did it start with radical intellectuals such as the Young Hegelians. The earliest champions of the workers were not Marxists at all, but well-to-do liberals who lived in the elegant centre of town, the very people who had first helped and encouraged Marx and whom he later grew to despise.

The liberals were naive, but well meaning. Bettina, the wife of the Romantic poet Achim von Arnim and author of *Goethe's Exchange of Letters with a Child*, was so shocked by the hopeless misery of the workers during the cholera epidemic of 1831 that she wrote *This Book Belongs to the King*, one of the first works of social criticism written about Berlin.[65] But the work was ignored by Frederick William, and it was not until the 1850s that charitable associations began to care for the destitute; a handful of fortunate Berliners received alms from the city but the 3 thalers and 2 silvergroschen per month was barely enough for food. Private citizens sometimes organized charity kitchens: Lina Morgenstern's People's Kitchen served out 2.2 million portions in 1871 alone and there were dozens like her, while liberal *Bildungsvereine* or cultural associations were set up to foster the 'improvement of the moral and economic condition of the working class'.[66] The irony of these groups was that the object of their concern, the 'uncouth workers', were themselves kept at arm's length by high fees and membership requirements.[67]

The problem of the liberal approach to workers was characterized by the kind-hearted and well-meaning Hermann Schulze-Delitzsch. He was not interested in philosophy or in revolution – on the contrary he believed in providing practical help to the workers of the city. He sought a free market economy, freedom of movement and freedom of occupation, and the destruction of old guild restrictions. Politically he supported the view that the middle class should unite with the workers to prevent the kind of failure which happened after 1848.[68] But his plans were fundamentally flawed. Schulze-Delitzsch and his associates believed that workers should not participate directly in politics until they had become educated, had been rid of ignorance and prejudice, and had earned their 'passport to civil society'. When he talked about 'workers' he was referring to the ambitious man who wanted to pull himself into the middle class, not to the inarticulate slum dweller. Schulze-Delitzsch tried to bring these changes about by founding workers' and consumer and production co-operatives to enable workers to become self-employed and financially independent. He also helped to set up the Central Association for the Welfare of the Working Class to provide support funds for company pensions. Nevertheless, most of these 'workers'' organizations had few working-class members and some, like the Nationalverein or German National Society, imposed such high membership fees that workers were excluded altogether. Schulze-Delitzsch might have referred to workers as 'honourable members' but in practice they had no power and no say in 'their' organizations. The leaders of the Fortschrittspartei or Progressive Party might have called the workers the 'pillars of the emerging German nation', but they insisted that workers must learn the ways of the bourgeoisie before they could have a political voice. All such groups rejected the idea of universal male suffrage. It was inevitable that, as industrialization spread, workers would become better organized, more independent, and increasingly resentful of liberal paternalism. The first groups formed by and for workers appeared in Berlin in the 1860s.

Like their liberal predecessors the first true working-class activists were moderate and, like Schulze-Delitzsch, wanted to introduce simple, workable measures to ease life in the factories and in the slums, and to give people a chance to work their way out of poverty.[69] Two of the most prominent were Friedrich Held, who was deeply concerned about conditions for factory workers and became popular among machinists through his publication *Lokomotive*, and Stephan Born, who published *Das Volk*, the most sophisticated of the labour papers. Both had read Marx and Engels but rejected the call for a revolution, saying that it would 'only bring anarchy'. They were the forerunners of those trade unionists who advocated careful organization, political pressure and steady improvement rather than a violent overthrow of the system. By the 1860s over sixty workers' associations had been formed in Berlin, including education societies and bourgeois foundations for workers. It was tragic that these moderate voices were ignored by the rulers of Prussia. The reformers were practical and decent men who simply wanted to give the new underclass some kind of place in society. The 'fourth class' was not yet agitating for revolution and most of its members still wanted to be part of the existing system. But the elite, from the newly declared Kaiser to the army to the new industrialists, were terrified of any threat to their power and rejected change out of hand, opting for a course of ever greater repression, banning workers' groups and arresting leaders. In the end the lack of acceptance at this early stage helped to radicalize the working-class movement. It would not be Schulze-Delitzsch or Friedrich Held who would lead them into politics; it would be the heirs of the radical tradition who as early as 1848 had hoped that the Frankfurt parliament would collapse in a second revolution. They were led by a young man who detested the liberals and who hated Schulze-Delitzsch above all – Ferdinand Lassalle.

Lassalle was an extraordinary figure in Berlin history. He was a mass of contradictions: a working-class leader posing as an aristocrat; an activist longing for academic life, and a friend of two of the most powerful enemies of the nineteenth century, Marx and Bismarck. And it was Lassalle who defied the liberal agenda and who explained to workers that they should demand more than honorary membership of the bourgeoisie. It was he who put 'Red Berlin' on the political map of Europe.[70]

Even as a schoolboy in Breslau, Lassalle was convinced that he was destined for great things and confided to his diary: 'Had I been born a prince I would be an aristocrat body and soul. But as I am merely middle class I shall be a democrat.' At twenty-one he met Heinrich Heine, who was impressed by his wit and perception; in the same year he met the wealthy Countess Hatzfeldt, who was losing in a spectacular divorce suit against her loutish husband. Lassalle, moved perhaps less by her plight than by the social opportunities afforded by association with her, helped her to win one of the most sensational divorce cases of the century. In return the grateful countess presented Lassalle with a pension for life which allowed him to pursue his political career. He threw himself into the radical movement and set off to the Rhineland to join his hero, Karl Marx.

Lassalle became a devoted member of Marx's sycophantic entourage, and the Düsseldorf police soon noticed that his 'energy and powers of persuasion', his 'wildly leftist ideas' and his 'not inconsiderable financial resources' made him a most dangerous enemy in his own right. But in 1857 a bitter quarrel erupted between the two men, and Lassalle moved to Berlin by himself. While Marx was working alone in the British Library, Lassalle was dashing around Berlin, agitating for change and inciting the workers to act. Marx referred to the 'would be labour dictator' as 'that ridiculous person'. He once complained that 'not only did Lassalle consider himself the greatest scholar, the most profound thinker, the most gifted investigator, etc., but in addition he was also Don Juan and the revolutionary Cardinal Richelieu'.[71] The men clashed on three fundamental issues: Marx believed that the revolution was inevitable, while Lassalle did not; in his view one had to create a state in which the working class could have real political power. Second, Marx believed the state would wither away, whereas Lassalle saw the state as the future guarantor of workers' rights. Finally Marx believed in the International, while Lassalle was concerned with change only within the state itself. By the 1850s it was clear to all who knew them that the two men detested one another.

To Marx's chagrin Lassalle took Berlin by storm, setting himself up in beautiful apartments at 13 Bellevuestrasse which he crammed with expensive works of art and priceless books. Monday evenings would find him at Fanny Lewald's for dinner; later in the week he would visit the Varnhagens or Lina Dunker's salon, and everyone from Ernst Dohm to Fürst von Puckler-Muskau were guests in his house. He must have been an extraordinary sight, fulminating about the future of the working class from behind the red velvet curtains and marble pillars, or expounding about factory conditions over the customary champagne and hashish, but in his spare time he did work hard for his cause, writing pamphlets and rushing off to factories in his beautiful clothes and top hat and white gloves to tell the spellbound audience how to fight their capitalist oppressors.

The decisive moment came in 1862. That year the liberal German National Society sent a delegation of workers to the World Exhibition in London. The visitors were so impressed that upon their return they decided to call for the formation of their own General German Workers' Congress. A mass meeting was held in Berlin that year to choose delegates for the conference to be held in Leipzig. The liberals, who had initially supported the idea, were horrified to find that the delegates chosen were not their own members but were radical democrats who called for universal suffrage and even for the creation of a separate workers' party, a move which the liberals knew would effectively wipe out their mass support. Schulze-Delitzsch began a massive campaign against the Congress. The delegates were forced to turn to the one man in Berlin who could help them: Ferdinand Lassalle.

On 1 March 1863 Lassalle responded to their demands in his *Open Reply*; he made it clear that the liberals were the arch enemy. The 'iron law of wages' meant that capitalists would always keep workers poor unless the cycle was destroyed, but the only way to do this was to split from the liberals and organize their own political party.[72] The Berlin workers were divided between support of Schulze-Delitzsch and of Lassalle, but in 1863 the dream of a working-class political party became reality with the foundation of the General Working Men's Association. It was a turning point in the history of Germany.[73]

Ironically it was also the mutual hatred of the liberals which brought Lassalle and Bismarck together in Berlin to form one of the most unlikely friendships of the century. A bundle of letters found in 1928 revealed that the two shared a great many things, not least a lust for political power; Lassalle wrote to his mistress, 'Do I look as if I would be satisfied with any secondary place in the kingdom? . . . No! I will act and fight, but I will also enjoy the fruits of the combat.' The words could have been Bismarck's. Their friendship was a calculated political gamble: Lassalle wanted Bismarck to help smash the Prussian constitution if in return he would curb the economic absolutism of the capitalists and give the workers social security; but Bismarck, by far the more crafty of the two, wanted to use Lassalle and the threat of universal suffrage to frighten the liberals into political obedience.[74] Bismarck used Lassalle to help him to crush the centre, and then he threw him away. Lassalle did not live long enough to retaliate, and one can only imagine the sigh of relief breathed on opposite sides of Europe by both Bismarck and by Marx when they heard the news that Lassalle had been killed in a duel fighting over his lover on 28 August 1864. Although only thirty-nine years old he had already become a pivotal figure in Berlin working-class history. Karl Kautsky would later write that 'In so far as the origins of German Social Democracy may be viewed as the work of a single individual, it was the creation of Ferdinand Lassalle.' But without his leadership the Berlin working class was destined to follow the powerful Marxists who were putting pressure on them from the south.

After his death Lassalle's General Working Men's Association continued to gather support, but a rival, the Eisenach Party, was created in June 1869 under August Bebel and Wilhelm Liebknecht and it soon began to dominate workers' politics in southern Germany. This bizarre and disorganized group recruited under the slogan 'Down with sectarianism, down with the leadership cult, down with the Jesuits who recognize our principle in words but betray it in deed.' In a desperate move to gain socialist credibility, Liebknecht and Bebel linked up with the Marxist First International.[75] This gave the Marxists a foothold in Germany, making the ideology much more fundamental to the working-class movement than might well have been the case.

In reality the deep rift which marred early relations between the Eisenach group and the Lassalleans had less to do with differences about Marx than with conflicting views on German statehood. Lassalleans supported Prussian unification of Germany while Liebknecht and Bebel were both Saxons who hated Prussia and hated Berlin. The party's early speeches were filled with appeals to 'all democrats and Prussian-haters' to join them, and it was only because German unification brought such dogged persecution of both groups that the two were forced to either work together or perish. They reluctantly came together to form the Socialist Labour Party at the May 1875 Gotha Congress, but without Lassalle's towering presence it was overwhelmed by the Marxists, who stood for everything Lassalle had come to detest. Ironically Marx refused to attend because of the very presence of the Lassalleans and instead put his energies into writing a Critique of the Gotha Programme; the commemorative scroll for the Congress shows Marx and Lassalle standing shoulder to shoulder, but looking in opposite directions.[76]

Despite its shaky beginnings the new party became the largest and best organized in Europe and began to exert an extraordinary political, economic, social and cultural hold on the working class of the city. One reason was the essential rootlessness of the workers in Berlin. Most were immigrants who were not integrated culturally or socially into the community or the Church, which left them more open to socialist ideas. Its members founded new organizations which took the form of political clubs, cycling and rambling societies and singing groups (by 1880 there were 200 of these), and all manner of cultural and social gatherings which combined entertainment with political indoctrination. Earnest women met to discuss their rights at sewing parties; youth groups commemorated the victims of 1848 and went to salute their graves even though the police confiscated the wreaths which they brought to the Friedrichshain cemetery. The party organizations were cheap copies of their bourgeois counterparts, but Marxist jargon, revolutionary rhetoric and naive optimism made up for the shabbiness, and their popularity increased rapidly. Most important of all, the Social Democrats began to mobilize the hundreds of thousands of immigrants and workers to vote. The establishment was shocked by their phenomenal success.

The SPD first participated in Berlin municipal elections in 1883 and secured five seats, but it had already entered the national scene in 1871, gaining 124,000 votes and sending two deputies to the Reichstag. In the elections of 1874 they increased their share to 352,000 votes and nine deputies, and in 1877 the vote went up by 40 per cent to twelve deputies. In the following election the SPD would get more votes than any other German party. This new political force horrified Bismarck, and he began to search for an excuse to crush the menace which might one day threaten his powerful empire. His chance came in 1878.

On 11 May the old Kaiser was being driven in a carriage down Unter den Linden, enjoying the sights and sounds of his city, when a man who had been hiding behind a cab leapt up and fired at him. He missed, and after capture the demented mechanic announced that he was only trying to draw attention to the plight of the working classes. On the basis of this confession Bismarck immediately tried to introduce anti-socialist laws, but he failed when it was revealed that the man had actually been barred from the party because of his extremist views. Fortunately for Bismarck, a second, more damaging attempt was made a few days later. On 2 June 1878 the Kaiser was once again being driven along Unter den Linden when Karl Nobiling fired from a nearby apartment window, hit him with about thirty pellets of swan shot in the face, arms and back, turned the gun on himself and attempted suicide. The Kaiser was rushed to the palace streaming with blood, and this time it took months for him to recover.

Bismarck wasted no time on the state of the king's health; indeed it would be over a week before he visited his monarch. Instead he shouted gleefully, 'Now we'll dissolve the Reichstag!', rushed to parliament and began to ram through his anti-socialist laws. The growing conservative middle class and the old aristocracy backed Bismarck in his campaign, and the Reichstag passed the Bill by 221 to 149. As a result of the vote the SPD, the left-wing Progress Party and the Catholic Centre Party were denounced as enemies of the state, and the first clause of the new law read that 'Associations which aim by social democratic, socialist or communist means to overthrow the existing state or social order, are banned.'

The workers, who had never heard of Nobiling and who rather liked the old Kaiser, were shocked to see the police bearing down on their districts in retribution for his crime. The industrial areas were soon in a state of siege; hundreds of people were arrested and sixty-seven leading socialists were rounded up and deported from the city without a court hearing and with no provision for their families. Police shut down the earnest new working-class clubs and associations. The socialist press was silenced; in 1878 forty-five out of forty-seven leading newspapers were banned, including *Vorwärts*, *Die neue Rundschau*, *Die Zukunft* and *Berliner freie Presse*; over 150 periodicals and 1,200 non-regular publications were suppressed and all 'social-democratic, socialist, or communist associations, assemblies and publications' were forbidden.

Bismarck justified his actions to the general public by announcing that Nobiling's evil deed had been inspired by 'Socialist agitators', and the popular response in Berlin was unpleasant and extreme. Scores of people were reported to the police for harmless remarks 'against the Kaiser', with the courts viewing all charges with utter seriousness. A woman who had quipped, 'At least the Emperor is not poor; he can have himself cared for,' was given eighteen months in prison. On a single day in June 1878 the Berlin court sentenced seven people to twenty-two years and six months for 'insulting the Emperor'. Employers were called upon to dismiss all workers with socialist inclinations and most obliged. Bismarck had so exaggerated the threat of the 'Red Menace' that people genuinely believed the social and political order to be in imminent danger of collapse if all left-wing activity was not stopped immediately; indeed Otto Vossler once remarked that Bismarck's attacks against the socialists were of such a fanatic severity that they were not used against the country's most dangerous external enemies even at war. In what was supposed to be a modern constitutional state the treatment of the socialists was absurd. It was also counter-productive.

Far from stamping out the party, Bismarck's policy served not only to strengthen it, but to radicalize it. The 'heroic years', as they were later called, became the foundation upon which dozens of working-class myths were based. Some of the tales were based on fact; activists did sneak out at night and hang red banners on bridges, on public buildings, even on the statue of Frederick the Great. The new party newspaper *Sozialdemocrat*, founded in Zurich in September 1879 and edited by Georg Vollmar and later by Eduard Bernstein, was printed and smuggled into Berlin along with dozens of other papers. The party postal service delivered the more than 3,600 different pamphlets printed before 1879, and although there were 1,500 members in prison and the socialists were forced to hold their congresses abroad Berliners continued to organize secret meetings throughout the city. The clandestine world of protest would become the stuff of left-wing legend. One typical 1920s socialist film showed an illegal *Hinterhof* meeting suddenly interrupted by the police, but although they turned the flat upside down they found nothing. On their way out they stopped, puffed out .their silver-buttoned chests and saluted an enormous smiling bust of the Kaiser perched on a shelf by the door. Once they had gone the socialists picked up the statue and, laughing at the police and their 'Kaiser cult', pulled out the wads of paper hidden inside. Despite their clear propaganda value such films had a point: the police could not stop the meetings, the funerals, birthday celebrations, picnics or other gatherings where information was passed or mass demonstrations organized; they could not force workers to be antagonistic to those who had been taken prisoner; they could not stop people from treating men like Ignaz Auer and Heinrich Rackow with kindness as they made their way into exile, or lining up along the platform to salute the elderly August Bebel as he was led to prison accompanied by his pet canary and a cartload of books.[77] This callous treatment of innocent men persuaded many to join the party of the downtrodden, the poor, the factory worker and the slum dweller.[78] (Later, when the Nazis carried out a much more brutal 'cleansing' of the Berlin working-class districts, the Social Democrats and the Communists deluded themselves into thinking that they could once again fight the police and win, and the tales of the 'heroic years' obscured the fact that their new enemy was not merely an extension of the Bismarckian repression, but was far more deadly.) When it finally became clear to Bismarck that his policy of repression had failed he tried another tack that Hitler would never have accepted for the despised radical left: appeasement.

Bismarck was not accustomed to losing a battle, and if the troublesome workers could not be intimidated, perhaps they could be bought. His change of heart was inspired by a number of factors, including a new-found faith in the Prussian tradition of state paternalism embodied by Frederick the Great, who had at one time referred to himself as the 'King of the Beggars', and by Napoleon III, whom he believed had at one time 'secured the loyalty and allegiance of the peasantry by means of his social legislation'. Above all Bismarck was influenced by his friend Disraeli, whom he had met during the Berlin Congress of 1878. In his novel *Sybil* Disraeli had described the two groups 'between whom there is no intercourse and no sympathy . . . The Rich and the Poor', and he, like Bismarck, had been shocked to think that there were people in Berlin or London who were living 'lower than the Portuguese or the Poles, the serfs of Russia or the Lazzaroni of Naples'. Bismarck was so taken by the British Prime Minister that he put his portrait beside the only others on his desk – 'My monarch, my wife, and my friend' – and when his policy of repression failed it was Disraeli who inspired him to push through his social reforms.

The first state insurance measure was announced by the Kaiser in 1881. Health insurance was introduced in 1883 and over 14 million were covered by 1913; accident insurance was introduced in 1884, accompanied by the most sophisticated and thorough code of factory legislation in Europe. At the same time a number of projects were completed in Berlin: hospitals were set up in the densely populated areas of Friedrichshain, Wedding and Kreuzberg, a new sewer system was built, a central slaughter house and market were completed in 1881 and hundreds of schools were put up. But although the changes were far-reaching it was too little, and far too late. The workers were happy to take advantage of the new measures but they were certainly not going to forget the recent repression, or the dreams of fundamental political change which had been nurtured by it.

It says something of the immense ignorance of Berlin's ruling class that they vehemently opposed Bismarck's modest proposals. The nationalist historian Heinrich von Treitschke proclaimed that the workers were 'poor and should remain so'; the highest values of culture and politics were never intended for the masses because 'the millions must plough and hammer and plane in order that the several thousand may carry on scientific research, paint and govern'. For him 'the masses must for ever remain the masses', and the 'poor man should know that his lament: why am I not rich? is no more reasonable even by a hair's breadth than the lament, why am I not the German crown-prince?'[79] There were thousands like him in imperial Berlin, and they made compromise with the moderate left virtually impossible.

Faced with this intransigence the Social Democrats became ever more radical. Their growing hatred of the government, their unorthodox views on the family, their attacks against religion, their internationalism and their ever more vehement opposition to German patriotism brought them into further disrepute with the respectable elements of society. It did not help that venerable leaders like Bebel declared that he wanted to 'remain the deadly enemy of this bourgeois society and this political order in order to undermine it in its conditions of existence and, if I can, to eliminate it entirely'.[80] Each side began to fear and loathe the other, a division which was summed up by the chief of police in 1889:

> The antagonism between the classes has sharpened and a gulf separates the workers from the rest of society. The expectation of victory among the socialists has grown. The German socialist party holds first rank in Europe because of its superior organization. It has outstanding leaders, especially Bebel and Liebknecht, and it is united. Clandestine papers continue to appear in spite of all confiscatory measures. The trade-union movement increases steadily, and the party can look forward to considerable gains in the next elections to the Reichstag.[81]

But the 'heroic years' also allowed the Social Democratic Party to develop a private world which was so self-sufficient that it began to lose touch with the normal aims and function of the state – an isolation which prevented them from making the politically crucial transition from a labour movement to a broad-based democratic party. Had the political elite been aware of and receptive to the problems of the workers they might have acted on their behalf; had they later offered the SPD full participation in the government the pseudo-Marxism of the party programme might soon have been dispensed with and the radicals might well have been integrated into society. But the nation lacked an effective parliamentary system and the workers were made to feel that they had no place in the new Germany. Those who had tried to work within the framework of the state had found that their state rejected and despised them. Even the American ambassador James Gerard was moved to say that the Berlin workers 'probably work longer and get less out of life than any working men in the world'. But the arrogant William II continued the backward-looking policies of his predecessors, proclaiming whenever he got the chance that he regarded 'every Social Democrat as an enemy of the Empire and Fatherland ... such a gang of traitors are a breed of men who do not deserve the name of Germans ... and their party must be rooted out to the very last stump'.

In the end neither Bismarck nor the Kaiser nor anyone else could have stifled the rise of the working class or the increasing power of the left for long. By 1890 'Red Berlin' was already a fact of life. The SPD was Germany's largest party, netting over 1.5 million votes. Its nerve centre was the most powerful working-class city on the continent, and its importance began to affect all other aspects of life in the city.

For decades Berlin had remained a cultural backwater, falling well behind other German court cities – let alone the centres of Paris or London. When Balzac visited Berlin in 1843 he was disgusted by its provincialism: 'Imagine Geneva, lost in a desert,' he wrote, 'and you have an idea of Berlin. It will one day be the capital of Germany, but it will always remain the capital of boredom.' Things became worse under William II, who actively tried to stop artistic impulses from decadent centres like Paris from reaching his city. But despite his control of bodies such as the Academy of Fine Arts even he could not completely stifle influences from abroad. Brave Berlin authors like Julius Meier-Graefe, patrons like the 'Red Count' Harry Count Kessler, museum directors like Hugo von Tschudi, art dealers like Paul Cassirer and the editors of journals such as *Pan* or *Kunst und Kunstler* defied him and promoted contemporary artists from Manet and Degas to Strindberg and Ibsen. This in turn encouraged a new generation of artists in Berlin, artists who rejected the stale official art of the court and who wanted to address the issues of their day. As the playwright Samuel Lublinski put it: 'The future is the truth. Our puffing locomotives, our restless hammering machines, our technical prowess and our science – it is there we find the truth, the only subject that should concern a modern poet.'[82]

Given the spirit of the times many aspiring young authors took great risks with their careers. Conservative critics openly shunned most of the greatest writers of the nineteenth century and rejected those Berliners who identified with them. Balzac, who had the added stigma of being Karl Marx's favourite author, was viciously attacked, and works like *La Comédie humaine* were criticized for their 'dangerous classifications' of human society. But the critics could not stop his work, or that of the brothers Goncourt or Emile Zola in France, Tolstoy in Russia, or Ibsen in Norway, from reaching Berlin altogether. By the 1880s a number of young writers from Johannes Schlaf and Hermann Conradi to Karl Henckell and Gerhard Hauptmann had moved to the city, had formed literary clubs like Durch on the Spittelmarkt, and had started to write in the new style. The first 'Berlin Naturalists', the Hart brothers, produced their 1884 *Kritische Waffengange* after reading Zola's *Les Rougon-Macquart*. In the *Kritischen Jahrbuch*, written five years later, they wrote: 'Until 1880 there was no youth, no literary youth. Now it is here, and with them as in nature, movement, foment, storm.'[83] Karl Bleibtreu followed with his *Revolution der Literatur*, followed by Arno Holz, who in *Das Buch der Zeit* was the first to write about the lives of the Berlin masses. The Webercolonie am Müggelsee (part of the small outlying district of Berlin beside the pretty lake Müggelsee) in Friedrichshagen became a meeting point of the new Friedrichshagener Kreis, where Heinrich and Julius Hart, Wilhelm Bölsche and Bruno Wille met with and discussed the works of Gerhart Hauptmann, Frank Wedekind, August Strindberg and dozens of others. The Naturalists and their sympathizers came to shun classicism and instead looked, as Eugen Wolff put it, at 'the alcoholism or the prostitution, beggars and suicides, degeneration and bestiality, marriage breakdown and child labour, illnesses of poverty and slavery to machines'.[84] Erwin Bauer claimed that the 'Berlin Modern' reflected the passions of the French Revolution – freedom, equality and brotherhood.[85] These ideas helped to create a new theatre which burst on the Berlin scene in 1887.

When the electrifying Théâtre Libre visited Berlin that year a group of artists were so moved that they decided to defy the Kaiser's censors and start their own company. In April 1889 the Hart brothers met with Maximilian Harden and the editor Theodor Wolff behind the steamy windows of the Kempinski on the Leipziger Strasse; after hours of discussion they held up their glasses and toasted the foundation of the Verein Freie Bühne. As it was to be an 'association' the police could have little control over its programme. The new director Otto Brahm said of the project, 'we are creating a free stage for modern life. Art shall stand at the centre of our endeavours; the new art which shows reality and the future.'[86] It came as no surprise that the first posters at the Lessing Theatre were soon advertising the Berlin première of Ibsen's *Ghosts*. This extraordinary play, which revolved around the taboo theme of inherited syphilis, shocked the prudish Berlin audience, but the theatre was allowed to remain open. The opening night of the second production, Gerhart Hauptmann's *succès de scandale*, *Sonnenaufgang* (Sunrise), turned out to be one of the most memorable evenings in the history of the Berlin theatre.

Even before the curtain went up the audience was restless, and by the time the play had started the jeering made it virtually impossible for the players to get through the first act. The tension continued to mount and finally, during the graphic birth scene, the theatre erupted into a fist-fighting free-for-all; people leapt over seats towards the stage trying to punch the actors, and an enraged doctor threw a pair of forceps at the main character. This time, the play was banned, and William II permanently cancelled his subscription to the 'Kaiser's Loge' in the Deutsches Theater.[87]

Gerhart Hauptmann continued his battle against the Berlin censors, producing play after play criticizing the existing system and exposing the misery and desperation of the Berlin underclass. *Hanneles Himmelfahrt* is a grim story of the fragility of existence in the slums in which Hannele's mother dies and she is viciously beaten by her alcoholic father. The girl is taken to a poor house, where she has a series of visions before dying of her injuries. *Die Ratten* (The Rats) showed the hopelessness of life in a Berlin rental barrack. A young couple, the Johns, are herded together with human beings who are so degraded that they have 'become' rats, picking over refuse, nibbling, sniffing and scraping at everything. They drive one man to murder and the heroine to suicide but in the end the loathsome creatures are seen as victims of a society which denies them any self-respect. Hauptmann's most famous work, *Die Weber*, played with a similar theme of mass psychology, this time showing people mesmerized and controlled by the eerie monotonous sound of the spindles which dominate the stage. This fierce attack on existing social order was banned on the grounds that 'it was an open appeal to rioting', but the liberal press defended it; Fritz Stahl praised it in the *Deutsche Warte* as 'the greatest work of German Naturalism to date', while Julius Hart wrote that it was 'certainly not the revolutionary speech of a party politician, but was simply the voice of humanity reflecting tremendous suffering, love and hate'. The theatre company was taken to court and won only because the court decided that the high ticket prices 'precluded the attendance of an appreciable number of workers at the performances'. Even so, Hauptmann was rejected by polite society; Prince Chlodwig zu Hohenlohe-Schillingfürst called his *Hanneles Himmelfahrt* 'A monstrous wretched piece of work . . . social-democratic-realistic, at the same time full of sickly, sentimental mysticism, nerve-racking, in general abominable. Afterwards we went to Borchard's, to get ourselves back into a human frame of mind with champagne and caviar.'[88] Hatred of Hauptmann extended to Berlin University; as late as November 1922 a party organized for his sixtieth birthday was boycotted by the Berlin Student Society because he was not considered to be 'a German of strong character'.

It was ironic that the Social Democrats did not come to the aid of these struggling artists, but they were already exhibiting the confusion and muddle-headedness which would plague them in later years. Unfortunately for them Marx had never clarified whether or not the dictatorship of the proletariat should produce a wholly new kind of art, or if bourgeois art could still be appreciated after the revolution. He gave no hint as to whether the proletariat should reject or affirm the culture of the past, nor whether critical art produced under the capitalist system was acceptable. Engels had attempted to deal with these questions after Marx's death but had failed, and the local Berlin leaders like Bebel and Liebknecht considered the task of getting into power far more important than wasting time on painting and theatre. In the end it was agreed that 'new art' should be positive, optimistic, inspiring and uplifting. It should fill the worker with love for his fellow revolutionaries and point the way to the glorious future, an attitude which would be taken to its logical conclusion in Stalin's Soviet Union. In the meantime there was no place for depressing, realistic portrayals of life in the slums. The Social Democrats refused to support Hauptmann because, as Eduard Bernstein put it, the works 'portrayed human suffering without advancing any remedies for it'. Marxism was supposed to have a magic formula to cure all social ills, and one 'couldn't have workers leaving the theatre in despair'.[89]

Attempts to create alternative 'inspiring' Social Democratic works were a disaster. In June 1890 Bruno Wille founded a workers' theatre, the Freie Volksbühne at the Böhmischen Bräuhaus (Bohemian Brewery) in Fried-richschain, and in order to make it affordable to the masses kept admission down to 50 pence and sold tickets by lottery amongst 2,000 trade union and Social Democratic members. The venture was a spectacular failure, not least because the plays, with their carefully worded Marxist solutions to social problems, were mind-numbingly dull. Social Democratic leaders promoted all manner of escapist kitsch which was surprisingly close to the official culture of imperial Berlin, reinforcing the very 'Philistine petty bourgeois art' which they professed to hate while finding nothing of value in the Naturalists or the modern theatre. Wilhelm Liebknecht was typical: 'I have no time to go to the theatre, and did not visit the Freie Bühne productions,' he said, but having read their plays he found them a 'disappointment'. 'I will not name names,' he sniped, 'but the breath of Socialism or, in my opinion, the Socialist move-ment, is not to be found on the stage of the *jüngsten Deutschland*'.[90] Frau Piscator had a different view: 'The proletarians did not care for the proletarian theatre,' she wrote. 'It died without mourning in April of 1921.' The only genuine working-class culture which was acceptable both to the avant-garde and to the party was vaudeville, and it was here that the image of the working-class slum dweller was developed, refined and projected on to the whole of the city. The 'true Berliner' as we know him today was largely created and introduced through the cabaret of the nineteenth century.

The first Berlin cabaret acts were born in local *Kneipen*, of which there were thousands in working-class Berlin; in the 1880s there was one for every 135 Berliners.[91] These small smoke-filled rooms, with their wooden planks for a stage – the *Brettl* – surrounded by tables and chairs, would serve beer and schnapps along with bread and sausage or thick soup, and local entertainers would get up at the front to tell their jokes and rustic stories drawn from Berlin life. The first purpose-built cabaret, the Überbrettl or Buntes Theatre, was opened in January 1901 by Ernst von Wolzogen, who hoped to copy the tradition of the Montmartre and bring political satire and music to a small audience. It was a sensation and by the autumn no less than forty-three such Überbrettl had opened, including the legendary Schall und Rauch. Middle-class theatre owners had also seen the potential of the local *Kneipe* performers and had put on revues of their own: the Tonhallen Theatre, founded in 1870, the Bellevue in 1872, the Neues American Reichs Theatre in 1877, and the Reichs-hallen Theatre in 1877, had all switched from conventional programmes to vaudeville within a few years, scouting for local talent in the *Kneipen* and teaching the amateurs how to perform on stage. Even the Wintergarten, with its 2,300-square-metre glass-covered hall, converted to vaudeville in 1887 and became the most prestigious stage of its kind in Europe. A cabaret journal of 1902 noted that 'Julius Baron, the former director of the Wintergarten, was probably the first person to build a large and wide bridge between vaudeville artistry and bourgeois society', taking the coarse language from the street and gentrifying it for the middle classes.

The most cutting satires were often censored through the Lex Heinze, but the best cabaret acts disguised their critiques under layers of *double-entendre* understood only by local audiences. A range of 'Berlin characters' emerged, from lower-class cab drivers, hawkers and apprentice shoemakers to the *Ecken-steher*, or men who stood on street corners and hired themselves out as labourers. Whereas the old Berliner had been funny but rather slow and phlegmatic, the image of the new Berliner was of a cunning, street-wise character who could keep up with the hectic tempo of the big city. He or she was poorly educated but witty, self-assured, irreverent, crass, vulgar and spoke *Berlinerisch* in a more aggressive fashion than his or her predecessor. The new Berliner was subversive of authority, directly critical of the court and indirectly critical of the Kaiser, ridiculing official Berlin culture, the cult of subservience to the Prussian army and anything that smacked of bourgeois or upper-class life. He joked about attempts by Wilhelmine state officials to encourage loyalty, patriotism and morality through the Church and he was sympathetic to other oppressed groups, from prostitutes and prisoners to those under the colonial yoke and Poles and Catholics targeted in Bismarck's *Kulturkampf*. He was resilient, amoral and permissive; in short he was all the things that were anathema to the official culture. The *Meyers Konversations-Lexikon* of 1874 reported that 'The Berliner is always quick at repartee, always able to find a sharp, suggestive, witty formulation for every event and occurrence', and newcomers learned to ape these characteristics or for ever be treated as outsiders. By the twentieth century, this image of the Berliner had been accepted as historical fact by both locals and foreigners alike. A nineteenth-century myth had become reality.

Despite the encroachment of popular cabaret into middle-class society, Prussian officials continued to exert strict controls over the 'higher forms' of art, and suspicion of revolutionary art extended beyond Naturalist theatre to the new forms of painting and sculpture. Those who refused to follow the official guidelines were rejected by the Academy, and Franz Servaes warned that young artists who came to Berlin must expect to be called 'talentless', must become 'as hard as steel – or go under', and must 'learn to mix his colours with his lifeblood'.[92] In 1892 the Association of Berlin Artists dared to invite Edvard Munch to exhibit in the city but the conservative reaction was swift and decisive. Munch was labelled 'vulgar and disgusting', his work 'lacked form', he was 'talentless', he was 'brutal and fiendish', even 'ruthless'. The exhibition doors were locked after two days. The insults continued. For the 1889 Academy exhibition Walter Leistikow submitted a very beautiful painting, *Grunewaldsee*, which owed a clear debt to the French Impressionists. The work showed the placid lake in evening light, the surrounding trees silhouetted against a darkening sky, and a small path snaking along the shore. He had high hopes for the painting but it was refused by the Academy. Richard Israel thought it of such high quality that he purchased it and donated it to the National Gallery, where it came to the attention of the Kaiser. Shortly after the Academy refusal the gallery director Hugo von Tschudi tried to persuade the Kaiser to invest in some French Impressionist paintings, and he hoped that by showing him a great work in the same style by the 'Painter of the Mark Brandenburg' he would approve the expenditure. The opposite happened. Instead of admiring Leistikow's work William announced that the picture was terrible, and did not look like nature at all. He was certain of this not only because he personally 'knew the Grunewald' but because 'apart from anything else he was a huntsman'.[93] Tschudi was forced to resign, and it became clear that the Academy would remain closed to Leistikow. In 1898 he and eleven other artists, including

Lovis Corinth and Max Slevogt, broke away in protest and founded the Berlin Sezession. Max Liebermann became its first president.

The first Berliner Sezession exhibition was held in a small building in the garden of the Theater des Westens in the Kantstrasse; the freshly prepared walls were so damp that the paintings had to be taken down every evening and rehung the next day to prevent damage. Most officially approved artists refused to have anything to do with the gallery; Menzel 'spat with contempt' when asked if he would exhibit there.[94] Nevertheless, the gallery became an underground success and moved to larger premises. A 1905 guidebook informed tourists that the Sezession had moved to Kurfürstendamm 208: 'Regular summer exhibitions from May to September. Small but powerful . . . Officers go in civilian clothes!' (the Kaiser had threatened to punish officers seen entering the gallery).[95] Despite official condemnation the gallery exposed Berliners to some of the greatest works of the late nineteenth century. The young art dealer Paul Cassirer was instrumental in bringing paintings by Monet, Manet, Renoir, Lautrec, Rodin, Whistler, Israëls, Beardsley and Maillol to Berlin, and it was he who introduced the as yet unknown Cézanne to Germany. During a trip to Copenhagen Leistikow had seen works by Van Gogh and brought them to the gallery. According to Corinth the paintings 'baffled Berliners . . . there was much ironic laughter and shrugging of shoulders' but the Sezession continued to exhibit Van Gogh's works long before they were generally appreciated as masterpieces.[96] The gallery also showed an increasing number of German artists and soon works by Beckmann, Grossmann, Purrmann and Walser were shown along with those by Hans Baluschek, Lovis Corinth, Käthe Kollwitz, Heinrich Zille and Frank Skarbina.

Industrial Berlin itself was becoming an acceptable 'subject' for the first time, and paintings began to show the desolation and misery of life in the working-class city. Lesser Ury exhibited his first 'street paintings' in 1889. Skarbina's *Railway in the North of Berlin* depicts a proletarian couple trudging through the dirty snow on a Ringbahn bridge high above a railyard, framed by dreary smokestacks and rusty ironwork and bathed in icy artificial light. Poor tattered women huddle under a cold yellow sky waiting for their husbands in Hans Baluschek's *Midday at Borsig*, while in his *Berlin Landscape* a lonely female figure hurries furtively past a Berlin municipal railway and row of tenements, concealing a small red wreath meant for a socialist demonstration. Baluschek captured the new Berlin which 'like a lucky speculator, lacked the breeding and culture to play the new role with decorum, without meanness'.

Heinrich Zille's lithographs were inspired in part by the revelations of a Dr Ebelin who, after talking to Berlin slum children, discovered that '70 per cent have no idea of what a sunrise looks like, 76 per cent don't know what dew is, 82 per cent have never seen a lark, half have never heard a frog'. Zille showed people crammed together in their high rental barracks accessed by tiny staircases or living in wretched wet cellars and over stinking stalls without air and sun. 'There, one could kill a man', he commented wryly, 'just as easily as if one used an axe.'[97] His drawings for popular magazines were tragic, witty and ironic at the same time; one showed a boy yelling to his mother to throw down the flower pot because his dying consumptive sister wanted to sit 'in the garden'. But of all the works shown the most passionate and moving were by Käthe Kollwitz. Her shocking portrayals of starvation, disease and filth, of death in the slums, of human tragedy behind the brick walls of the rental barracks were wrenching and terrible. The Kaiser refused to allow the Association of Berlin Artists to grant her their gold medal: 'Please, gentlemen, a medal for a woman,' he exclaimed, 'that would really be going too far.' It hadn't helped that she had incited 'revolutionary tendencies' by producing engravings for Gerhart Hauptmann's banned play, *The Weavers*.[98]

Although these artists would reach dizzying heights of fame during the Weimar Republic they were lonely pioneers in imperial Berlin. The official critic Broder Christiansen once sneered that the Naturalists were interested only in 'the crass, the shrill, the caustic, the repulsive and the common ... the miserable people of Berlin in Heinrich Zille's paintings do not want to move,' he said, 'they are not there as a social indictment, but rather as a means of producing intense nervous stimulation. Their putrescence gives a stimulant to art, and in Zille's paintings the latrine is seldom missing.' Herwath Walden published a marvellous article simply listing the words used by Berlin critics against the new artists, expressions which might well have appeared in Hitler's *Degenerative Art* catalogue, including 'sensation seekers', 'motley coloured louts', 'Niggers in frock coats', 'Hottentots in dress shirts', 'rabid simpletons', 'shitty and laughable clods', 'bluffers', and 'a horde of colour spraying howling apes'.[99]

In those days of pettiness, repression, misunderstanding and hatred it was difficult for the industrial poor to see that the glittering Wilhelmine system was drifting towards collapse, and that it would be struck a mortal blow in the mindless butchery of the First World War. But between 1871 and 1914 the squalid life in the factories and the rental barracks carried on as before, and the artists who tried to address these issues were kept well away from the official culture, and the ever increasing wealth and prosperity of the swaggering imperial city.

VI

Imperial Berlin

Fame surrounds her, blazing, glorious,
shines to dazzle all men's eyes:
and her chosen name, Victorious,
Goddess of Man's enterprise.

(*Faust*, Part II, Act 1)

IMPERIAL BERLIN, THE BRASH, *parvenu* capital of the German Reich, exploded on to the world stage in 1871. In its brief forty-seven years the imperial city would change from a small provincial town into a garish giant, and for most Berliners its sheer size and wealth was enough to prove that their city had finally arrived. Berlin was no longer a mere *Residenz*; it was the Reich capital, complete with parliament and bureaucrats, banks and enterprises and burgeoning industries. The opportunities seemed limitless and the optimism was intoxicating as the city became the showcase of the new energetic German state. The capital might have been chauvinistic, militaristic and undemocratic but few well-to-do Berliners noticed, and for many the late nineteenth century would be remembered as Berlin's golden age. As one of Gerhart Hauptmann's characters put it: 'Berlin is splendid! . . . Berlin is the most wonderful city in the world . . . Berlin is life.'[1]

On 16 June 1871 Berliners woke to find their city in festive mood. Acres of bunting and flags smothered the grey buildings up and down Unter den Linden, and the Brandenburg Gate was heavy with greenery. Academy artists from Gustav Richter to Carl Becker, Otto Heyden, Georg Bleibtreu and Adolph von Menzel had worked since May to decorate the route between the Halle Gate and the Lustgarten to be used by the Prussian troops for their triumphal march. Great painted awnings hung across the road for five whole streets, and the facade of the Academy itself was hung with portraits of the victorious commanders-in-chief of the army.[2] By mid morning tens of thousands of people had flocked to the city centre, pushing for a vantage point and jostling the little groups of schoolchildren already rehearsing their poems and patriotic songs like Freiligrath's *Hurrah! Hurrah! Germania!* along the well-marked parade route.

The sense of expectation was palpable, for today marked Berlin's coming of age; the Prussian town was to be officially recognized as an imperial city. Prussia had defeated France, Germany was unified, and Berliners were to rule over it all.

Suddenly a group of figures appeared in the distance, and the crowd began to cheer. The first in line was not Kaiser William I but their real hero of the day, Prince Otto von Bismarck. He was followed by Field Marshal Count Helmuth von Moltke and General Albrecht von Roon, the representatives of Prussian military might. Only then did the old Kaiser come into view, progressing slowly down the road followed by his sons. Behind them were the non-commissioned officers holding aloft the eighty-one captured French flags and eagles, which were laid at the feet of the new monument to Frederick William III, the man who had been so humiliated by Napoleon Bonaparte half a century earlier. Then came 42,000 men in full battle dress, some crowned with laurel wreaths, looking for all the world as if they were at a procession in ancient Rome. The parade lasted a full five hours, and for Berlin it marked the dawning of a new age, a time of peace and prosperity, of flamboyance and energy, of greatness and power, industrial growth and modernity.

Berlin was in the process of re-inventing itself yet again, this time transforming itself into a powerful world capital. Even the liberal-minded Fontane, the greatest and most critical of Berlin's nineteenth-century writers, was overwhelmed by a sense of pride and patriotism. The mood was lighthearted and later, as the Landwehr battalions returned home, the writer Sebastian Hensel watched as the men walked up Unter den Linden arm-in-arm with their wives and children.[3]

But such relaxed displays of civilian life would soon disappear under the worst aspects of Prussian military culture. The last Kaiser would give Prussian officers virtually unlimited powers to behave as they wished in 'his' city; indeed the Kaiser saw himself rather like a warrior chief who alone stood above the General Staff, the Ministry of War and the Military Cabinet. Wilhelm von Hanke, chief of the Military Cabinet between 1888 and 1901, maintained that the army 'should remain a separate body, into which no critical eyes should be permitted to gaze'.[4] The officers under their control would become ever more abusive, bolstering the foreign stereotype that the city was the very heart of narrow-minded Prusso-German nationalism. The writer Jankowski spoke for the world when he said that Berlin 'fed itself by war and became fat through war', and Churchill would later refer to this Prussia as the embodiment of German evil. The military success which made the 1871 triumph possible was brought about by one of Berlin's most influential and controversial sons, the man who had led the parade, Otto von Bismarck.[5]

*   *   *

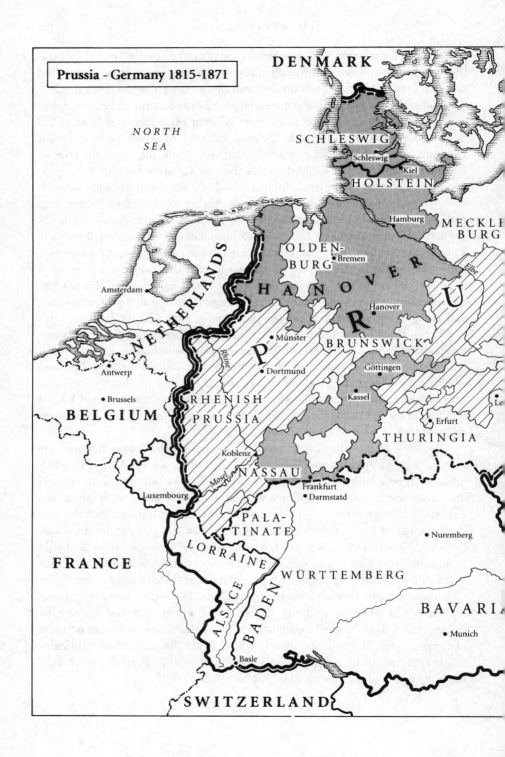

Prussia - Germany 1815-1871

DENMARK

NORTH
SEA

SCHLESWIG
Schleswig
Kiel
HOLSTEIN
Hamburg

MECKLE
BURG

OLDEN-
BURG
Bremen

HANOVER
Hanover

Elbe

P R U

Amsterdam

NETHERLANDS

Münster
Dortmund

BRUNSWICK

Göttingen

Kassel

Le

Antwerp

Brussels

BELGIUM

RHENISH
PRUSSIA

Rhine

Koblenz

Mosel

NASSAU

Erfurt

THURINGIA

Luxembourg

Frankfurt
Darmstatd

PALA-
TINATE

LORRAINE

Nuremberg

FRANCE

ALSACE

BADEN

WÜRTTEMBERG

BAVARIA

Munich

Basle

SWITZERLAND

SWEDEN

BALTIC SEA

Tilsit

Königsberg

EAST
PRUSSIA

POMERANIA

Danzig

WEST
PRUSSIA

Stettin

S   I   A

Warthe

POSEN

Vistula

Posen

in

RANDEN-
BURG

RUSSIA

POLAND

resden

Breslau

Oder

SILESIA

Prague

OHEMIA

Danube

Vienna

AUSTRIA

	Prussia in 1815
	Acquired by Prussia 1815-66
————	Boundary of German Confederation of 1815
– – – –	Boundary of North German Confederation 1866
▬▬▬▬	Boundary of German Empire 1871

Shakespeare said of Julius Caesar,

> he doth bestride the narrow world
> Like a Colossus; and we petty men
> Walk under his huge legs, and peep about
> To find ourselves dishonourable graves.
> Men at some time are masters of their fates.

It was a fitting description of Bismarck. Germany might never have been unified and Berlin might never have become Germany's capital without this crafty political genius at Prussia's helm, guiding it to power through his own particular brand of *Realpolitik*. Bismarck was able to create and maintain a system riddled with contradictions and preserve a semi-feudal style of government within an otherwise modern state. When he left his careful system of checks and balances unravelled and paved the way for the rampant aggressive nationalism of William II. But Bismarck was not a warmonger, as is often thought, and he did not engage in conflict for its own sake. He was a masterful technician of power, and used it first to create a nation state and then to protect it. And at the heart of his system was the capital, Berlin.

Bismarck was born outside Berlin on his father's estate in Schönhausen on 1 April 1815. He cultivated his Junker image and harboured a deep suspicion of Berlin, but it was his mother, the daughter of a well-known Prussian bureaucrat and one-time adviser to Frederick the Great, who adored the city and who introduced him to urban life. It was she who had him educated at the great Berlin school the Graue Kloster, and who taught him that there was more to life than tending his father's run-down estates and drinking at the officers' club. Although Bismarck would later deny his middle-class roots it was his mother who first opened his eyes to the fascinating world of politics.[6]

Bismarck's early career contained few clues to his future success. His first port of call was Göttingen University, where he was stirred not by the words of his liberal colleagues, but by literature, particularly the fiery work of Sir Walter Scott. After Göttingen he studied in Berlin, sat the rigorous Prussian civil service exams, spent a year in the military and then suddenly took eight years off to help manage his father's crumbling estate. Despite the much professed love of his Junker heritage the years at Schönhausen dragged slowly by and according to his brother he spent hours dreaming of great battles and future glory to come. When the 1848 revolution broke out he decided that it was time to act. He rounded up the peasants on his estate and prepared to march them to Berlin to save his beleaguered king. Although his mission ended in failure he decided from that moment on to become actively involved in affairs of state. He rejoined the civil service and managed to get himself appointed as ambassador to the Frankfurt Diet, where he nurtured a budding contempt for parliamentarians. His next posting in St Petersburg taught him the advantages of the tsar's autocratic regime, which he admired, while his stint in Paris made him despise the effete French. But wherever he went his love for all things Prussian continued to shine through; he wrote to a friend in Berlin that 'as soon as it was proved to me that something was in the interest of a healthy and well-considered Prussian policy, I would see our troops fire on French, Russians, English or Austrians with equal satisfaction'. His tough patriotism endeared him to his fellow Junkers – already threatened by the rise of the industrialists and the urban working class – and when a fight began to brew between the liberal parliamentarians and the king Bismarck was eager and ready to act on their behalf.[7]

The conflict which propelled Bismarck to power, and which ultimately crippled the might of the Prussian bourgeoisie, centred around the question of army reform. This confrontation emerged in 1860 when a new law was put before the Diet to implement reforms introduced by von Roon which included the provision for a three-year term of compulsory military service, for an annual intake of 63,000 recruits, and the weakening of the popular Landwehr, which had been created by the Scharnhorst-Boysen reforms during the Napoleonic Wars. The old liberal parliamentarians were against the reforms but both sides held firm until the king tried to break the deadlock by dissolving the Assembly and holding new elections. He actually did this twice, but to his chagrin the new Deutsche Fortschrittspartei, which included a number of liberal civil servants, became the largest political grouping.[8] William was deeply troubled – what was the point of being king if he could not determine basic military policy? Finally he could stand it no longer, and when the second election result was announced he stormed to the palace and drafted a letter of abdication. The struggle between the Berliners and the Hohenzollerns appeared to be turning in the civilians' favour when a conservative ultra-royalist candidate was proposed for the office of Prussian Prime Minister. His name was Otto von Bismarck, and this time the parliament had met its match.

The news of the possible abdication had terrified the Junkers, who knew that if William left he would be succeeded by his liberal-minded son Frederick William, who could not be relied upon to protect their feudal privileges. In a last-ditch effort to save William, the Minister of War, Albrecht von Roon, sent an urgent message to Bismarck. He was to return from Paris at once; 'Delay is dangerous,' he wrote. 'Hurry!' Bismarck arrived in the city on 20 September, and two days later, during a walk in the gardens at Babelsberg, persuaded the king to rip up his letter of abdication and promised to govern as Prime Minister without a majority and without parliamentary approval of the budget – in other words, illegally. The king grumbled that the Berliners would 'cut off your head and later on mine on the Opernplatz beneath my windows. You'll end up like Strafford and I like Charles I.' But Bismarck knew Berliners better than that. He remembered the failed revolution of 1848, the lack of action, the fear of real revolution. Berliners were 'all talk and no action', and the parliamentarians were worst of all. They were mere 'chatter-boxes who cannot really rule Prussia ... they know as little about politics as we knew in our student days'. The conservative *Kreuzzeitung* newspaper predicted that he would 'overcome domestic difficulties by a bold foreign policy'. They were right. When Bismarck stood before the budget committee a short time later he rammed home his triumphant message in his high-pitched voice: 'Germany does not look to Prussia's liberalism but to her strength ... The great questions of the day will not be decided by speeches and the resolutions of majorities – that was the mistake of 1848 – but by blood and iron!'[9] The fateful pact at Babelsberg between Bismarck and the king marked the beginning of twenty-eight years of the Iron Chancellor's rule, and true to his word he set about unifying Germany by force.[10]

Bismarck's genius shone through in his ability to transform liberal nationalism from an oppositional ideology into an integral one and to make the principle of nationhood the unifying factor for Berlin and for Germany. Before Bismarck the Junkers and conservatives had been overwhelmingly opposed to German unification as they feared it would inevitably diminish their power. It had been left to the liberals, radicals and progressives to try to unify Germany. They had hoped to bring this about under a democratic Prussia, which they assumed would ensure parliamentary democracy, freedom of speech and a host of other rights and privileges – as Arnold Ruge put it, 'Prussia, with all its repugnant police barbarism, is the only salvation for Germany.'[11] Bismarck essentially gave both groups what they wanted: he preserved the traditional power of the Junkers, but he gave the liberals their united Germany, achieving in five months what the people had failed to do in five decades. The fact that he succeeded not by the workings of liberal democracy but through 'blood and iron' distressed many, but his success was enough to drown most dissenting voices and turn erstwhile liberals into ardent supporters of the new Reich. He, von Moltke and the Prussian Junkers were destined to become the heroes of the new Germany.

The first of Bismarck's three strategic wars was waged against Denmark in 1864. A speedy victory resulted in his ally, Austria, being given the territory of Holstein while he took Schleswig as his own, quickly establishing a German naval presence at the port of Kiel. This war created new enemies and a new fear of Prussia; the Frenchman Émile Ollivier said bitterly that 'England failed France and France failed England and both failed Europe'.[12] Bernhard von Bülow once commented that for Bertie, the Prince of Wales, the word German became synonymous with 'the narrow-minded moral preaching, drilling and brute force', and when his Danish wife Alexandra found out that her second son had been made an honorary colonel in a Prussian regiment she snapped, 'So, my Georgie boy has become a real life, filthy, blue-coated, Picklehaube German soldier! Well, I never thought to have lived to see that!'

Denmark had been easily beaten and Bismarck turned his sights on Austria. Many in Berlin were against war with Austria, seeing it akin to *Brüderkrieg* – a civil war. Bismarck managed to provoke the conflict by denying the Austro-Prussian agreement and claiming that Prussia had as much right to Schleswig as to Holstein. Austria felt it necessary to defend her new territory, and the two states were soon at loggerheads. The historian Wilhelm Oncken was in no doubt that Bismarck had both wanted and provoked war with Austria, calling the disagreement over Schleswig-Holstein tantamount to 'a declaration of war against Austria and its allies'.[13]

When the Seven Week War started Prussia was by far the smaller of the two combatants. The Habsburg empire had a population of 35 million subjects, bolstered by a further 14 million from some of the smaller German states. Prussia had a mere 19 million. But papers in Berlin were confident. For them Prussia had 'the most modern army' headed by the 'brilliant strategist' Field Marshal Helmuth von Moltke, and their technology, transportation networks, troops and armaments were 'second to none'. The decisive battle took place at Königgrätz (Sadowa), where 500,000 men and 3,000 guns faced one another in the first modern battle in history. Within a few hours the Austrian side had collapsed. In a single battle Prussia had destroyed Austria's bid to lead Germany to unification and the *Grossdeutch* solution was forgotten.[14] Berlin's dominance over her arch rival Vienna was won on the bloodstained battlefield of Sadowa. A liberal leader, Mevissen, wrote of the Prussian troops' return to Berlin: 'I cannot shake off the impression of the hour. I am no devotee of Mars ... but the trophies of war exercise a magic charm even upon the child of peace. One's view is involuntarily chained and one's spirit goes along with the boundless rows of men who acclaim the god of the moment – success.'[15]

The Prussian victory shocked the world, but it shocked the French most of all. A sorrowful Adolphe Thiers concluded that 'it is France which has been beaten at Sadowa', and his countrymen were now even more terrified of Prussian might than they had been after the Danish war. Their only hope of maintaining a dominant position in Europe was to keep the German states divided, but they knew that Bismarck wanted to unify Germany under Prussia and rule from Berlin. They also knew that to do this he had to win a decisive victory against France. Neither William of Prussia nor Napoleon III wanted war and it is testimony to Bismarck's ingenuity, his cunning and his ruthlessness that, despite their own wishes, the two men would face one another on the battlefield in less than four years. Berlin's new status was just within her grasp.

'War', said the General Helmuth von Moltke, 'is a necessary part of God's arrangement of the world.'[16] Men could also arrange war, and that is precisely what Bismarck set out to do. In the days before all-consuming nationalism it was common for countries to invite foreign princes to take over their empty thrones, and when Walachia and Moldavia united to form Romania the kingdom was offered to a Swabian Hohenzollern, a distant cousin of the Prussian ruling family. Prince Carol I of Romania was crowned in 1866. At the same time the Spanish deposed their bumbling debauched Bourbon and were also in search of a new king. The crown was offered to another Hohenzollern prince and the French were furious. The loss of the first throne had been bad enough, but the Spanish offer was too much for a nation terrified that they would be boxed in by Prussia or her allies to the south and east without having fired a single shot. Napoleon III's Foreign Minister, the duc de Gramont, declared that 'The honour and interests of France are in peril', and threatened that if the Hohenzollern accepted the Spanish throne France would go to war.[17] William of Prussia was a peaceable man and encouraged his cousin to back down, but when Bismarck heard that war had been averted he went white with anger. War with France was essential to his plan, not least because he knew that only this would persuade the south German states to join the new Reich. Somehow he had to provoke conflict with France.[18]

William was confident that the crisis was over, and decided to recover at the elegant Ems Spa. But the duc de Gramont, who had apparently just achieved one of the great coups in diplomatic history, was not satisfied and was determined to get Prussia to promise to keep out of Spain for ever. A few days later he sent the ambassador Benedetti to Ems where, during a pleasant garden stroll, he contrived to bump into the king. On Gramont's orders Benedetti demanded that Prussia not only renounce all present family claims to the Spanish throne, but that it should do so in perpetuity. The king politely refused and had his aide Abeken send a telegram to Bismarck outlining the conversation. Thinking no more of it, he went off to bed.

As it happened, Bismarck was dining at home in Berlin with Moltke and Roon that evening. The three men had spent their time complaining that war with France seemed further off than ever; Bismarck and Roon shared Moltke's sentiment that God could 'take my old bones' if only he could only live long enough to go to war against France. Bismarck was contemplating resignation.[19] Suddenly the telegram was delivered. Bismarck picked it up, read it, and gave a cry of joy. He began scribbling on the paper and, by cutting out some of William's text, he made the bland wordy message look like a terse declaration of war.

ABOVE The Thirty Years' War – 1618–1648 – saw Berlin's population reduced by over half, to 6000 people. The torture and execution of civilians was common; Jacques Callot's etching, *The Tree as Man's Gallows* is from the series 'The Miseries and Ills of War'.

RIGHT The 1685 Edict of Potsdam attracted over 20,000 persecuted French Huguenots to Prussia – the newcomers transformed the cultural, economic and religious face of Berlin, creating something of a French city in the Mark Brandenburg. David Chodowiecki's 1775 engraving is entitled *Pilgrimage to French-Buchholz* – referring to the Huguenot settlement of Buchholz-Pankow.

Frederick III, later King Frederick I in Prussia, took the throne in 1688 determined to transform Berlin into a great centre of the arts. He is shown seated in the studio of the sculptor Andreas Schlüter studying the equestrian statue of his father, the Great Elector. (Engraving after a painting by Zöpke, 1875.)

Fortune smiled on the Hohenzollerns in the 17th and 18th centuries. They produced a succession of male heirs, three of whom, Frederick William I (the Great Elector), Frederick William II (the Soldier King) and Frederick II (the Great) were extraordinary leaders by any standard. Here the young crown prince, Frederick (the Great), and Prince Heinrich pay their respects to their grim father, the Soldier King. The painting is by Dismar Daegen, 1736.

Frederick the Great transformed the centre of Berlin; the Königliche Bibliothek (nicknamed the 'Commode') was only one of the new buildings on the Unter den Linden. The military spirit was retained, however, and the area in front was used as a parade ground.

Napoleon enters Berlin through the Brandenburg Gate on 27 October 1806. The French occupation heralded an era of Prussian reforms, but it also provoked the rise of German nationalism and turned Berlin into a centre of that essentially urban movement – Romanticism.

INSET The reforms of 1848 were quickly revoked when it became clear to the king and the army that the people were not going to fight to keep them. Here the 'German Michel once again gives everything of himself' – freedom of assembly, the right to bear arms, freedom of the press, freedom of the people. By 1850 the only social reform left was Berliners' right to smoke in the street.

BELOW Berliners on the barricades. Over 230 people were killed on the night of 18 March 1848, and the cemetery at Friedrichshain became a shrine to the memory of the failed liberal revolution.

ABOVE In 1836 the young August Borsig purchased a small plot of land in Moabit and started an iron foundry. By 1860 he dominated the German locomotives market and the little factory had become one of the largest in Europe. Borsig was typical of the farsighted entrepreneurs who turned Berlin into the German centre of the industrial revolution.

INSET The image of the 'true Berliner' – quick-witted, coarse, amoral, resilient – evolved in the 19th-century industrial city. Far from representing 'eternal' traits, he was based on the cab drivers, hawkers and *Eckenstcher* (men who stood on the street and hired themselves out as labourers), who became ever more prominent as Berlin grew into a modern giant.

The mass migration from the land to the city swelled Berlin's population, which rose from one million in 1871 to nearly four million in 1914. Here, young farm labourers from Silesia arrive in Berlin. The photograph was taken in 1900.

ABOVE Industrial workers made up between 55 and 60 per cent of Berlin's population by 1900 but few of the affluent residents had any contact with them. A 1912 guide book recommended that the 'adventurous' take a tour on the Ringbahn or Hochbahn for a glimpse of the 'other Berlin', to see where the *Menschenmasse* lived. This picture commemorates the opening of the Hochbahn in 1902.

LEFT 'Who calls for a butcher?' Gill's 1871 caricature highlighting Bismarck's role in engineering the war against France.

A somewhat retouched photograph of the Prussian Garde at attention during the proclamation of the German Empire in Versailles in 1871. Berlin became the capital of a united Germany for the first time in history.

The Year of the Three Kaisers. Frederick William, married to Queen Victoria's eldest daughter, was terminally ill when the old Kaiser died in 1888. He was succeded after only 99 days by Kaiser William II. This picture shows the dying man being taken through the Schlosspark at Charlottenburg.

Kaiser William II created the 700-metre long Siegesallee or
Victory Boulevard in the Tiergarten lined by 32 marble statues of
his ancestors. The project was meant to instil pride in Berlin –
indeed, he compared the work favourably to that of Michelangelo
– but even Baedeker refused to grant him a single star for his
monuments.

The boulevard was dismantled after 1945 and some of the
statues thrown into the Landwehr Canal. Here, William I,
Johann II and Otto II of Brandenburg as they appeared in 1950.

espite official disapproval,
erlin became a centre of
odernism even before the
rst World War. In 1898
alter Leistikow submitted
e beautiful painting
runewaldsee for the
cademy exhibition. It was
fused, and he and eleven
her artists broke away to
und the Berlin Secession
hich brought artists ranging
om Edvard Munch to
odin, Max Liebermann to
äthe Kollwitz to public
tention.

This photograph captures the moment on 29 March 1890 when the ageing Bismarck, rashly dismissed by Kaiser William II, left Berlin from the Lehrter Bahnhof for an unhappy retirement. Bismarck would later turn coins over so he would not have to see William's 'false face'. When he died in 1897, William did not give Bismarck a state funeral, prompting the French ambassador to exclaim: 'Whatever the Germans say or do, they will never be a great people.'

Kaiser William II competed with the English in virtually all he did; when he decided that Berlin needed a new library, the architect Ernst von Ihne had one brief: to make the reading room bigger than that of the British Library. It opened in 1914. This photograph dates from 1925.

The original telegram consisted of two long paragraphs filled with diplomatic protocol and inoffensive niceties. One phrase explained that the French ambassador had 'presented to His Majesty the King at Ems the demand to authorize him to telegraph to Paris that His Majesty the King would obligate himself for all the future never again to give his consent should the Hohenzollerns revive their candidacy'. But it had continued in a gentler vein, in which the king had explained: 'I refused to agree to this, the last time somewhat earnestly, telling him that such obligations dare not and cannot be assumed *à tout jamais*. Naturally I told him that I had not received any news as yet and since he had been informed earlier than I via Madrid and Paris he could see that my government was once again out of the affair.' But Bismarck deleted the second part of the paragraph leaving a terse, provocative statement.

The original had included a long explanation of how the king was expecting a communication from the prince, and for this reason would not receive Count Benedetti again. Bismarck cut that out as well, and ended the telegram with the clipped phrase: 'His Majesty the King thereupon refused to receive the French ambassador again and sent word to the latter through his Adjutant that His Majesty has nothing further to tell the ambassador.' As a result Bismarck made the overall message much harsher and more abrupt than the king had ever intended while completely changing its meaning.[20] Moltke gloated that the innocent note now ended like 'a flourish in answer to a challenge'. Bismarck said, 'If I not only publish this text . . . at once in the newspapers . . . but also transmit it by telegram to all our embassies, it will be known in Paris before midnight, and not only because of its contents but because of its mode of publication, it will have the effect of a red cloth upon the Gallic bull.'

Bismarck sent the telegram without consulting the king and, as he predicted, the story was printed in the *Norddeutsche Zeitung* in Berlin and picked up on both sides of the Rhine that night. Napoleon III was informed of the Prussian duplicity and was left with no honourable choice but to talk of war. When he saw the text, Count Waldersee, who was then in Paris, said that it was so '*grob*' (rude) that 'I could hardly believe it was possible'. The morning editions in Paris were filled with anti-Prussian venom and had TO THE RHINE and À BERLIN! printed across their front pages.[21]

When poor befuddled William awoke the next day he was shocked to hear the news. 'This is war!' he said sadly and left immediately for Berlin, determined to stop the terrible events from unfolding. But Bismarck was always a few steps ahead of his king. The Chancellor intercepted him at the train station and convinced him that total mobilization was the only sensible option for Prussia. He was a persuasive man. On 19 July France declared war on an expectant Prussia.

Berliners knew nothing of Bismarck's manipulation of the Ems telegram, and rose up in a frenzy of patriotism and anti-French indignation. Thousands rushed to the palace singing, 'I'm Proud to be a Prussian', declaring their loyalty to the king and yelling insults at the French for forcing their innocent army into war. Baroness Spitzemberg reflected the popular mood when she wrote that 'In Berlin they are in great excitement . . . The French could not have arranged things more unintelligently . . . instead of dividing us they have contrived to complete Germany's unification.' Sybel wrote: 'the excited masses swayed to and fro; men embraced one another amid tears of joy and thunderous cheers for King William rent the air.'

Once again Europe watched as small Prussia took on a European giant; France had after all been the greatest power on the continent for 200 years and few believed Prussia could win a sustained war against her. They were wrong. Once again they had not counted on the deadly combination of Bismarck and Moltke, backed by an efficient, powerful and well-informed army. The Franco-Prussian war was a vicious and bloody affair; Theodor Fontane went to the front shortly after Napoleon's surrender and was shocked by the horror and the bloodshed he found there; indeed he was almost shot as a spy while trying to find Joan of Arc's village. Adolph Menzel, too, was appalled by the scenes on the battlefield and said that he now knew 'from where Schlüter had got his masks of the Arsenal'.[22] Napoleon III surrendered after the Battle of Sedan and the anniversary became a German national holiday. The French Republic, which was declared at the infamous Hôtel de Ville, faced the siege of Paris with inadequate supplies and a demoralized army.

Initially most Europeans had believed France to be the aggressor and had sympathized with Prussia, but opinion turned against the Germans during the four-month bombardment of Paris and it solidified further after the forced annexation of Alsace and Lorraine. The liberal Crown Prince Frederick warned that if Prussia was too belligerent it would 'no longer be looked upon as an innocent victim of French aggression but rather as an arrogant victor. The nation of thinkers and philosophers, poets and artists, idealists and enthusiasts' would be portrayed 'as a nation of conquerors and destroyers'.[23]

The Prussian generals were unimpressed by such sentimental nonsense.[24] They were winning a vital war, carving out an empire by crushing their greatest historical enemy; Paris had not even surrendered when Bismarck decided to make his move and announce the unification of Germany. His timing was perfect. With the Prussians winning on all sides nobody, least of all the other German princes, was in a position to refuse him. The German army headquarters, the king, Bismarck, the Prussian court, the government of Prussia and the representatives from the North German Confederation were all crowded together in Versailles, along with the courts of twenty German princes. On 18

January 1871 the representatives were called in to Louis XIV's magnificent Hall of Mirrors and forced to watch as King William was declared German emperor. At the stroke of a pen Berlin had been elevated to the capital of a united Germany.

Not all Germans were pleased by these developments. The south German states had conformed but many resented Prussian dominance and the exclusion of Austria – and Vienna – from the new Germany. Some complained that the state could not be considered 'unified' despite the foundation of the Reich as one-third of the German speakers of Europe remained outside its borders. Furthermore Germany remained a land of regions: there were still kingdoms within the Reich, including Saxony and Bavaria, grand duchies (including Hessen), and free cities like Hamburg and Bremen – each proud of its identity. Berlin was not a popular choice for capital in much of the rest of Germany and there were many in Nuremberg, Frankfurt and beyond who felt that their cities would have made better, worthier and, best of all, anti-Prussian centres; Munich above all saw itself as a rival to Berlin, particularly as a centre of the arts, and Prince Otto of Bavaria was not atypical when he said, 'I cannot even describe . . . how infinitely sad and hurt I felt during the ceremony . . . Everything was so cold, so proud, so glittering, so showy and swaggering and heartless and empty.'[25]

But despair was not confined to other Germans. Many conservative Prussians were dismayed at the loss of their little kingdom and even King William of Prussia wept, overcome by what he saw as the destruction of his ancestral Prussian crown. He had never wanted to be emperor of Germany, but with Bismarck dictating policy he had little choice. He pointedly refused to shake Bismarck's hand during the ceremony and would soon be heard to mutter that 'it was not easy being King under such a Chancellor'. But none of these things bothered Bismarck.[26] He had fulfilled his dream to become leader of the Second Reich. He had ended two centuries of Austrian involvement in Germany and the particularist tradition of the Old Reich. He had stifled German dualism and German confederation, and he had destroyed Old Prussia. Bismarck was now eager to assume power in Berlin. He sought to be made Chancellor and Foreign Minister of Germany as well as Minister President of Prussia, and set out to rule a country in which the Reichstag had no real power and the people had no popular representation and no Bill of Rights. Erstwhile liberals became increasingly conservative and Germany developed an ever more aggressive chauvinistic nationalism.

These developments fuelled the ahistorical post-1945 thesis that the nation had followed a *Sonderweg* by not developing 'correctly' into a Western liberal representative democracy like England or the United States. The thesis was absurd; Germany was not unique – Russia also refused to follow the so-called 'correct path' – and the notion that history follows such 'courses' is simplistic. Even so, Bismarck stymied the creation of a stable parliamentary system and retained some of the most oppressive aspects of Prussian rule. It was this inflexibility which would ultimately lead to its complete collapse.[28]

After 1871 Berlin's political power increased dramatically. It now housed the federal government, including its executive – the Kaiser and the Chancellor, who personally controlled all aspects of German foreign and military policy as Article XI of the constitution declared that 'presidency of the union belongs to the King of Prussia who shall, in this capacity, be termed German Emperor'. Berlin was the main benefactor of the German Constitution of 1871, which turned it into the centre of the federal union of twenty-five allied states. Although each had a representative assembly of its own, they also now sent delegates to the Bundesrat or Federal Council and to the Reichstag or National Parliament, made up of representatives elected by male suffrage and secret ballot. The Bundesrat and the Reichstag controlled most aspects of German commerce, transportation, communication, patents, tolls and matters relating to the economy. The individual states were left to govern their own police forces, education and health, but any important measures had to pass through the Berlin Bundesrat which was dominated by the Prussian state government. This was a backward, undemocratic parliamentary system which represented the landowners, aristocrats and Junkers through an electoral system which based status on the amount of taxes paid by the candidate.[29] And yet as the largest state, with seventeen out of fifty-eight votes in the Bundesrat, Prussia could control most important decisions in the federal government. Berlin's own political structure reflected this conservatism; the mayor-elect of Berlin had to be confirmed by the Kaiser and despite its large urban proletariat the three-tier voting system ensured a politically 'reliable' mayor, as reflected in the continuing electoral success of Adolph Wermuth, *bürgerlich* mayor of Berlin until 1920.[30] Politically, there was no question that Bismarck's Berlin was the powerhouse of the Reich. Berliners were impressed by their status and many put aside their reservations to bask in the glow of the power and authority of the post-unification city. Above all, they began to make money.

Within months of the grand victory parade the city had become wildly prosperous, its fortunes boosted by the 5 billion francs indemnity pouring in from France. Felix Philippi wrote, 'Everyone, everyone flew into the flame . . . the market had bullish orgies; millions, coined right out of the ground, were won; national prosperity rose to apparently unimagined heights. A shower of gold rained down on the drunken city.'[31] Industry boomed, the population skyrocketed, and a frenzy of luxury and materialism marked the glorious age of the *Gründerzeit* or 'time of foundations', a term which alluded not only to the Empire, but also to the sheer number of new companies created at the time.

The years following the creation of the empire were undisturbed by war. Bismarck had achieved all he wanted through the military; now he tried to avoid conflict through a carefully balanced foreign policy dictated by *Realpolitik*. He survived the stock market crash of 1873, which saw the destruction of economic liberalism, and he enhanced his comprehensive system of social security reforms. But a shadow was soon to pass over the prosperous new capital. Years before, the revolutionary citizens had hated the 'Cartridge Prince' who had tried to crush the 1848 revolution, but by the 1880s their old Kaiser William I had become a revered and beloved figure. Revolutionary talk had moved to the slums and the back streets, and the well-to-do had become enthusiastic supporters of the new order which had brought them such wealth.

In 1887 rumours began to fly through the cafés and offices that the Kaiser was ill; loyal subjects gathered beneath the palace windows waiting for news, and bulletins were put up every few hours. After a short illness the Kaiser died at the age of ninety-one, sixteen years after the birth of the empire.

For decades, the crown prince Frederick William had waited in the wings for a chance to rule, nurturing his liberal values and holding an alternative court on Unter den Linden with his wife Vicky. Young Etonians had cheerfully pushed the royal carriage from the train station to Windsor the day the prince married Queen Victoria's eldest daughter, and the young man was popular in England. The gentleman prince had been the great moderate hope of the future; his preference for British liberalism and hatred of Bismarck made him the only man who might successfully have challenged the all-encompassing power of the Junkers, and many hoped that he would introduce a constitutional monarchy modelled on the English system. But fate intervened. The pair had waited thirty years for the throne, but when Frederick finally succeeded he was a dying man. The throat cancer which now ravaged his body had made him speechless and he could only breathe through a little silver tube pushed into his windpipe. His illness had become a great source of tension between England and Germany; German doctors had pronounced his tumour malignant early on and would probably have saved him had they operated immediately, but Vicky had relied on the incorrect diagnosis of her Scottish doctor, sentencing her husband to an early grave and fostering anti-English sentiments in Berlin.[32] This tragic and largely forgotten figure ruled from the palace in Berlin for a mere ninety-nine days, and his premature death paved the way

for the accession of his thirty-year-old son, Kaiser William II. That year –
1888 – was later known as the 'year of the three Kaisers'.[33] It was also the
beginning of the end for imperial Berlin.

It was a tragedy for Germany that William came to power, and although there
is no doubt that he was bright and quick witted, he was also vain, arrogant
and rash.[34] Some of this might have been due to his difficult youth; his mother
nearly died in childbirth and by the time anyone attended to the infant his
wrenched and twisted arm was beyond repair. As he grew the poor boy was
forced to endure painful shock treatments, take disgusting quack medicines
and have frequent baths in the blood of freshly slaughtered animals to try to
bring the withered arm back to life. The prince forced himself to ride despite
constantly falling off his horse because of his lack of balance, and he learned
how to hide his arm under ever more grandiose uniforms or by resting it on
the hilt of his sword.[35] The need to overcome his physical weakness combined
with the belief that he had been chosen to rule by God made him arrogant
and something of a bully. His friend Eulenburg noted his sheer blood lust
during his hunts in the Romintern Forest and his delight in watching 'the
panting desperate brutes as they hurl themselves perpetually against the farthest
hedges'. It was not uncommon for William to kill 1,000 animals in a week,
and when he was forty-three he put up a monument to commemorate the
bagging of his 50,000th beast.[36] He was rude to important guests at court
whom he often teased in an offensive, even sadistic manner; he sometimes
forced visitors to do gymnastics on the deck of his yacht, the 'perpetual floating
casino', and would push them when they were bending over or kneeling down.
He became known as the 'showman of Europe', the 'crowned megalomaniac',
the man who 'wanted every day to be his birthday'. Max Weber called him
the 'Imperial Clown'; Bismarck complained that he was like a balloon pushed
around by sudden gusts of wind, and even the once indulgent Queen Victoria
called him a 'hot-headed, conceited, and wrong-headed young man, devoid
of all feeling'.[37]

When his father died the young prince moved fast to wipe out all traces
of his memory and take control of his city. Robert von Dohme remembered
how, on the very day of Frederick's death, William cordoned off the palace
and imprisoned his mother in her rooms for allegedly sending vital documents
to England. He rifled through state papers, erasing the memory of his hated
parents and destroying anything which might threaten his authority. Then he
filled the palace with his sycophantic friends. His lust to increase Germany's
imperial might and to compete above all with England meant that the military
was given a free hand in the city, and civilians had to get used to being jostled

by arrogant officers in the streets. William had always disliked Berlin and he was happy to fill it with his own kind. Berliners found themselves increasingly identified in the rest of the world with the most arrogant, militaristic, expansionist tendencies of the Prussian army. Liberals were silenced, and the 'Red Radicals' were forced underground.

The pervasive presence of the military was the product of the foundation of the empire itself. The new state had been created not by the German people but by the army, by the Junkers, by Bismarck and by 'blood and iron'. Instead of turning into a liberal democratic state Berlin had become the centre of an ever larger military machine. By the time the foolish young Kaiser had pushed his people to the brink of world war it was too late for them to regain control of their own destiny. On the surface the imperial period was stable and prosperous, but the seeds of its own destruction had been sown during the militaristic ceremony which marked its birth in the Hall of Mirrors in 1871.

'In Berlin', it was said, 'the air stinks of powder.' Whereas the sight of uniformed officers in Piccadilly or on the Champs-Élysées usually meant that some state occasion was underway, it was the norm in Berlin. The army had always shaped the life of the city, but despite the old parade-ground atmosphere the military had remained decidedly separate from civilian life under the Soldier King and Frederick the Great and William I. The officers had formed a tight-knit group of pious, frugal and unostentatious men devoted to the Protestant Church and to their monarch – they had not played polo, for example, because it had made the distinction between rich and poor too obvious. They had led quiet, even reflective lives; the old Count Helmuth von Moltke, whose family had been poor, had translated Gibbon's *Decline and Fall* to meet the expenses of his appointment to the General Staff. Most had been forced to wait until their forties or even their fifties before they could afford to marry. Exclusive regiments like the Guards or the Cavalry lived by Frederick II's dictum that 'only nobles are noble enough to command', and no amount of money, power, prestige, social or political influence could overcome the barrier of birth; indeed the old Kaiser had known all 3,000 of his aristocratic officers personally. This old way of life was transformed under William II.[38]

Within a few years of taking the throne William expanded the officer corps to 20,000 men; indeed the strength in officers and men increased by almost 100 per cent between 1880 and 1913.[39] There would have been a great deal to be said for widening the social base of recruits if it had led to a more moderate, meritocratic system, but it had the opposite effect. The power of the aristocrats was never really broken; in 62 per cent of the Prussian regiments more than 58 per cent of officers were nobles, while sixteen regiments had an exclusively aristocratic officer corps. Although middle-class recruits could now hold junior positions up to the rank of colonel, noble Prussian officers held most General Staff posts, numbering 625 officers by 1914; the Minister of War, von Heeringen, criticized plans to expand the Prussian army because it would lead to the inclusion of social groups which were 'not really suitable for supplementing the officer corps', exposing it to 'democratic influences'. Jews were treated with barely concealed contempt; there was not a single Jewish regular officer in the entire Prussian army between 1878 and 1910.[40] Bourgeois officers fortunate enough to obtain a commission renounced their backgrounds and slavishly copied the manners, ideas and activities of their aristocratic fellows. The army encouraged this by developing a policy of indoctrination and coercion which taught them how to think and behave. National pride was the order of the day and, as the Polish writer Józef Kraszewski put it, the army 'is a school which teaches without fail'.[41] New recruits were told that the army was 'the only fixed point in the whirlpool, the rock in the sea of revolution that threatens us on all sides, the talisman of loyalty, and the palladium of the prince'. Albrecht von Roon told his men: 'The army is now our fatherland, for it is the only place which has not yet been infiltrated by impure and restless elements.' Recruits were expected to swear an unswerving oath of loyalty, which by the early twentieth century had led to an abdication of personal responsibility far beyond anything in equivalent armies in western Europe. This would reach absurd heights during the Nazi period, when officers still refused to act against Hitler even though they knew he was leading the nation to ruin because they had sworn an oath. They had forgotten the lesson of Tauroggen.[42]

The new Wilhelmine officers were insufferable. The great historian Eckhard Kehr wrote that 'the Prussian lieutenant, who up to this time had been on the average relatively modest', had turned into 'the unbearable prig of the Wilhelmine era'. The writer Wesenhof declared, 'everyone knows that Berlin is an eastern city, which means it lacks taste . . . but the fact that the French, English or Italians are full of themselves is not nearly so irritating to the foreigner as the arrogant stance of a Prussian officer or bank director'. Most nineteenth-century visitors were amazed by the sheer number of rude uniformed men who pushed people around on the streets. The American ambassador James Gerard wrote that

> on one occasion I went to the races at Berlin with my brother-in-law and bought a box. While we were out looking at the horses between the races a Prussian officer and his wife seated themselves in our box. I called the attention of one of the ushers to this, but [he] said he did not dare ask a Prussian officer to leave, and it was only after

sending for the head usher and showing him my Jockey Club badge and my pass as an Ambassador that I was able to secure possession of my own box.

Even after minor disputes on the street he noted how officers would 'instantly cut the civilian down'.[43] When the Kaiser went to the opera or the theatre his entourage of officers would not only take up most of the seats but would delight in disrupting the proceedings. Soldiers could send enormous packages through the post simply by writing '*Militaria*' on the front. Officers still settled their disputes through duels, and failure to follow this code of honour meant dismissal from the army. Parades and manoeuvres were a daily occurrence throughout Berlin; Fritz von Unruh had his sleep interrupted 'every morning by the trumpet in the infantry barracks across from me', and recalled his irritation when endless parades forced traffic to grind to a halt.

But however much they complained, Berliners were deeply affected by the military ethic. Everybody seemed to wear a uniform. State and municipal officials wore dark sober jackets; cab drivers wore red braided coats and top hats; even Friedrich Engels once wrote to his sister from Berlin: 'here you see me in my uniform, my coat very romantic and artistic.' Sybil Bedford compared Berlin unfavourably with London, complaining that 'uniforms, no longer the livery of duty, were worn like feathers, to strut the owner and attract the eligible', and as Schlettow in Carl Zuckmayer's play put it, wearing mere civilian clothes in Berlin was like being 'half a portion, with the mustard left out'.

Berliners' obedience to uniforms went to absurd lengths. In October 1906 a company of twenty soldiers commanded by a 'captain' arrived at Köpenick Station, marched to the town hall and occupied the building. The 'captain' was in fact Wilhelm Voigt, an unemployed shoemaker and petty criminal who had purchased a musty old uniform in a second-hand shop, ordered a company of soldiers in the street to follow him – which they had done without question – and cheekily commanded the mayor to hand over the town funds 'by the Order of His Imperial Highness'. The mayor may have had his doubts about this strange little man but the power of the uniform was too much. He handed over 4,000 marks – an enormous sum at the time. The 'captain' took it, marched his company out, and promptly disappeared. He was caught a few days later but when they heard about his prank Berliners laughed uproariously and even the Kaiser was amused enough to release him from prison after only two years. The soldiers who had been duped had all charges against them dropped because they had 'unquestioningly obeyed the command of an officer'. The 'Captain of Köpenick' became a Berlin celebrity: *Die Welt am Montag*

published a long interview with him; he entertained audiences in an arcade
on Unter den Linden and sold his story on the new wax sound discs, some
of which were found in a junk store in 1966 and given to the Köpenick
Museum.[44] Carl Zuckmayer wrote a play about him which was later made
into a popular film. But however entertaining it was, the 'Captain of Köpenick'
story exposed Berliners' pathetic and widespread deference to authority on a
scale unthinkable in any other European capital. By laughing at him Berliners
were laughing at their own impotence.

The spotlessly clean city was well managed and highly efficient; Christian
Otto once commented that 'in no other German city is the attention to the
law greater than here'. But if the city was clean it was also oppressive, and
most visitors found it cold and antiseptic. People were 'arrogant' or 'haughty'.
Penderewski found the bars and cafés crowded and noisy, but heartless and
without 'genuine laughter', and in a letter to his wife the Polish writer Boleslaw
Prus exclaimed that 'Berlin is beautiful – too beautiful . . . and as cold as ice.'
Jules Laforgue, the French writer, invited to the court to converse with the
Empress Augusta, was scathing about the oppressive atmosphere in Berlin
which he captured in his book *Berlin, la cour et la ville*.[45] He recalled how in
his native France one immediately got a whiff of absinth and freedom from
the train attendants and heard them call to one another, 'Will I see you later
this evening?'; but in Germany 'the personnel are military, they don't say a
word but busy themselves with running the train, performing the same task
yesterday as today'. He was amazed to see how when an officer walked past
a group of soldiers the latter stood to attention, stamping their feet on the
spot until he had passed, a scene repeated 'every day all around Berlin'.[46] Carl
Ludwig Schleich and his friends the writers Strindberg and Hartleben were
nearly arrested for simply trying to measure the curvature of the earth at the
corner of Unter den Linden and Friedrichstrasse, while Kraszewski commented
that even with civilians one could see that 'either he was, or he will be a
soldier': they adopted the manner of their military brethren, and treated visitors
'as if you are meant to fetch their shoes'. He found the city 'severe, ordered,
serious, obedient and disciplined . . . as if in a permanent state of siege'. Not
only did the soldiers move along the street with rigid measured steps like
machines, but they were 'copied by the street-seller, the coachman, the porter,
even the beggar'. Rosa Luxemburg was even more critical. 'Berlin made a
ghastly impression on me,' she wrote; 'it is a cold, tasteless, massive barrack
filled with those *darling* arrogant Prussians, every one looking as if he has
swallowed the stick with which he had just been beaten.' The new militarism
was detested by many; after a brief visit in 1898 Wesenhof complained that
there was 'nothing left of the elevated idealism which led philosophy, poetry
and even sometimes politics in Germany . . . Where is the old cradle of art,

the co-parent of Gothic, the Fatherland of Dürer, Goethe and Heine? It is no longer in Berlin.'

In the meantime Berlin's propertied middle class was becoming rich beyond its wildest dreams. Members of the old liberal *Bildungsbürgertum* (or educated middle class) were marginalized and although they continued to live in the quiet elegant Tiergarten, read their pleasant journals and attend their lectures at the university, they could not win against Berlin's new brassy culture.[47] Berlin was a city which epitomized the nineteenth-century literary paradigm of 'new' and 'old' money, but the new money was winning. By the turn of the century there were dozens of millionaires in the city, with forty-five families each possessing fortunes exceeding a staggering 3 million marks. Names like Siemens and Borsig, Ullstein, Gerson, Mosse and Wertheim became synonymous with the new wealth and in many ways it was these families who created the thriving heart of the new Berlin.[48] Even so they remained shut out of the political, military and social life of Berlin and Potsdam, which was still controlled by the 7,000 aristocrats in the city – less than 1 per cent of the population. In England a public school education, appointment to high political office or a life peerage could propel a nineteenth-century industrial family into the upper reaches of the establishment, but this was impossible in Berlin, where a distinct line existed between the aristocrats and everyone else. Instead of trying to create their own independent culture the new rich copied the upper classes, competing with one another for imperial recognition and attempting to get their sons into the officer corps and marry off their daughters to the younger sons of minor nobility. Many of the new rich laid claim to 'family crests' and bought up old and unprofitable Junker estates in the hope that the prestige of the ex-inhabitants would rub off on them. They took up riding and hunting, art collecting and charity work, and they fought for membership in the Union Club or the Kaiser's Automobile Club. This 'neo-feudalism' was parodied in endless cartoons and articles but it was a fact of life in imperial Berlin.

Identification with the existing system extended to the quest for orders, medals and distinctions, which reached a ridiculous level amongst the bourgeoisie at the height of the empire. They were not eligible for noble orders such as the Black Eagle or the Red Eagle of the Crown, but there was no shortage of lesser honours which could be handed out to them. Invitations to the Kaiser's annual *Ordenfest* (Order Festival) were fought over by businessmen and professionals: there, an old palace servant might be seated near an officer who had obtained *Pour le Mérite* for distinction in battle, while an artist might be next to an arms manufacturer. Berliners were obsessed with questions of rank: when Madame Essipoff gave a concert at the palace she insisted upon being referred to as the 'Palace Musician', a title which was utterly meaningless but which she used until her death.[49] When the great nineteenth-century historian Ranke was ill the papers solemnly reported that 'Dr Wirkliche Geheime Rat Professor Doktor von Ranke has had a restless night'. Wives expected to be addressed as 'professor' or 'doctor' like their husbands, and even people who had been friends for decades would use these cumbersome prefixes. Theodor Storm once commented that 'even in educated circles in Berlin an individual is not judged by his personality but by his rank, orders and title'. But as Gerard pointed out, the silly emphasis on empty labels tended to 'induce the plain people to be satisfied with a piece of ribbon instead of the right to vote, and to make them upholders of a system by which they are deprived of any opportunity to make a real advance in life'.[50]

Whatever their political restrictions the new rich Berliners had wonderful lives and their optimism and wealth quickly changed the appearance of the city. Sybil Bedford commented on the 'big money, big enterprise, big buildings, big ideas' which made Berlin a city of 'Wagnerian flourishes'. A nineteenth-century Polish visitor who compared Vienna with Berlin said: 'Vienna is a Grand Lord, ruined but proud, and in a noble lordly fashion disinterested in the future. Berlin is a *nouveau riche*, a boorish peasant who is determined to see that what he has acquired he will retain.' Berlin began to be called the *parvenu* capital of Europe; loud, pushy and ostentatious. And nowhere was this more obvious than in the buildings which were erected after 1871.

One of Adolph Menzel's most cutting paintings, *Beati Possidents* (Happy Owners), looks at first like a Dutch bourgeois genre painting of the early seventeenth century. Upon inspection one sees that it was painted in 1888 and depicts a smug, self-satisfied bourgeois couple before the balcony of their new villa, surrounded by gardeners, artists and others busy transforming it into a 'historic' house. Menzel saw these vast megalomaniac villas as little more than 'freshly painted forgeries' as false as the painting itself.[51] Everything in imperial Berlin was built for show. Huge new apartment houses and pseudo-palaces went up in areas like Charlottenburg and in the new 'villa colonies'. The enormous structures looked impressive, but they were nothing but cheap brick smothered in plaster and stucco. Isherwood described these houses as 'shabby monumental safes crammed with tarnished valuables', and although the writer Prus was initially impressed by what he found he soon wrote: 'I long to see something small and simple ... Berlin houses are simply overloaded with ornaments – and behind the palaces you can see breweries and behind turrets there are factory chimneys. Even the churches in Berlin are swamped by these private houses.' Maximilian Harden said they were built so that the new Berliners could 'show off for the people across the road'. They had 'monumental facades designed to look impressive even if the inhabitants actually live in tiny bedrooms at the top of the house'.[52] George Hermann described a typical villa with its NUR FÜR HERRSCHAFTEN (social elite only) and PLEASE WIPE YOUR FEET signs at the edge of the decorative garden complete with yellowing miniature fir trees and new busts of Dante, Luther and the Belvedere Apollo.[53] Christian Friedrich Hebbel said that at first glance Berlin reminded one of Paris and Rome but that one must not look too closely as the squares were shoddy and the buildings 'unsolid'.

There was no consistency in the architecture and there was no new 'Berlin style' to replace the Prussian style of the eighteenth century.[54] The Berlin villa colonies were more like a Beverly Hills or Reno, Nevada, than a Knightsbridge, with a pastiche of styles copied from other cultures and periods. Rathenau described these areas as full of all manner of cheap and expensive ugliness which made one feel caught in a feverish dream: 'Here is an Assyrian temple beside a patrician mansion from Nuremberg, a bit further on is a glimpse of Versailles, then memories of Broadway, of Italy, of Egypt – terrible abortions of a polytechnical beer – imagination.'[55] Christian Morgenstern wrote a sketch on this theme for Schall und Rauch in which the millionaire Kalkschmidt tells a horrified old professor that he wishes to build his restaurant not so much in the 'Old Bavarian' style as the 'Venetian church' style, complete with 'great pictures and all gilded with painted ceiling and real Carrara and old wood carvings and columns and stained glass windows'; when the professor objects Kalkschmidt chides: 'You do not know the modern Berlin, Herr Professor.'[56] Adolf Behne complained that one could no longer see anything of the walls as they were covered in 'Caryatides, columns, cartouches, busts'.[57] Some projects were even more ostentatious: in 1894 a family from Pankow Wollank had their oriental palace built in the shape of an Indian mosque which floated on a raft in a nearby lake. It vanished in flames a few years later. And naturally William II had to outdo his subjects. Cecilienhof, the site of the 1945 Potsdam Conference, was an extraordinary copy of an Elizabethan manor house and contained a room built in the shape of a ship's cabin suspended on leather straps so that he could be rocked to sleep as if at sea. He ordered that it should be completed in a mad frenzy when Germany was already well on its way to losing the First World War. No matter what the cost, appearance was everything. For Spender even the most sordid tenements never lost 'some claim to represent the Prussian spirit, by virtue of their display of eagles, helmets, shields and prodigious buttocks of armoured babies'.[58]

Charles Dickens's *Our Mutual Friend* is a novel about the new money coursing through nineteenth-century Europe. The Veneerings were typical of the new rich:

All their furniture was new, all their friends were new, all their servants
were new, their plate was new, their carriage was new, their harness
was new, their horses were new, their pictures were new, they themselves were new ... from the hall-chairs with the new coat of arms
to the grand pianoforte with the new action ... all things were in a
state of high varnish and polish. And what was observable in the
furniture, was observable in the Veneerings – the surface smelt a little
too much of the workshop and was a trifle sticky.[59]

The Veneerings might well have lived in imperial Berlin. The interiors of the
new villas were even more outlandish than their facades and were crammed
with pillars, statues and staircases. Ceilings dripped with plaster cherubs and
fruit-laden vines, grand bourgeois rooms groaned under the weight of dark,
heavy stuffed furniture, ornate mirrors, thick carpets, full-length curtains and
palm trees; fountains spurted champagne and ornamental gardens and conser-
vatories were replanted every few months. Billions of marks circulated in Berlin
and the beneficiaries spent it on luxury; as Siegfried Kracauer, Berlin review
editor of the *Frankfurter Zeitung*, put it, everything in Berlin 'was glittering
and absolutely new'. Even for those somewhat less well off life was getting
better. Over two-thirds of Berliners rented apartments rather than owning
their own homes, which allowed for easy mobility. Rooms in flats no longer
ran into one another; they were now divided so that nurseries and bedrooms
were separated from the public spaces, making life more private both for
residents and servants. Urban life had become easier for all; kerosene and then
gas lamps replaced candles; linoleum floors were easier to keep clean and solid
fuel briquettes and safety matches made homes easier to heat. A service sector
quickly developed to cater to the whims and desires of the well-to-do.[60]

Since unification Berliners had become keenly aware of their status in comparison to other European capitals. They had defeated France and Austria on the
battlefield and now they were determined to outdo Paris and Vienna as centres
of pomp and luxury. The new department stores which were built at the end
of the century quickly became symbols of great local, if not national pride.
Tietz, Ka De We and Wertheim's became synonymous with the new urban
Berlin, providing customers with thousands of new and wonderful goods from
around the globe.[61]

Hermann Tietz was typical of the new optimistic, energetic and daring
Berliner. In order to build his store he had to rip down a house which was
featured in Lessing's *Minna von Barnhelm*, and although the destruction of a
place immortalized by a great national writer would have been unthinkable a

decade before there was little room for sentimentality in the new Berlin. Tietz delighted in introducing products to the city; the humble tomato was first sold on his food floor, although it took a while before suspicious Berliners took to the fleshy, watery 'fruit'. Rice, once a luxury item, became commonplace. But Tietz was not alone; the first major development in the New West was the Kaufhaus des Westens or Ka De We, which would later become a famous anti-Communist landmark in West Berlin. The unusually restrained and refined building was innovative in that it combined the sale of goods with a central ticket office for all travel and entertainment, a beauty salon, a café and other services previously found only in separate outlets.[62]

In 1909 the beautiful Sarotti shop on the prestigious Leipziger Strasse opened its doors after costly refurbishment. A year later it was gone. The building was demolished to make room for the most sumptuous of all Berlin stores, Wertheim's, which was built at a staggering cost of 12 million marks.[63] All the new stores were large versions of the bourgeois villas, resplendent with grand entrance halls, huge chandeliers, staircases, mosaics and mirrors, but Messel's extraordinarily modern design for Wertheim was the most sumptuous of all. A hundred thousand lights illuminated the staircases, the fountains, the palm trees, and the soft rose-coloured tiles which had been supplied by a factory owned by the Kaiser. Glass replaced solid walls, giving the building a light, airy feel, and people came just to see the new atrium which was lit from above. Berliners loved this new place, called the 'greatest department store in the world', and they flocked to buy, to see and to be seen.

But the new department stores alone could not make a *Weltstadt* (world city). Harden noted that 'one finds nothing elsewhere to compare with the department store of A. Wertheim ... those who first come to Berlin must believe that they have stepped onto the earth of the richest city in Europe. Only those who remain longer ... see that the rich facade has merely dazzled and the spectacle begins to appear shoddy and shallow.'[64] Imperial Berlin glittered, but it lacked substance and depth, a fact reflected in everything from architecture to fashion.

In the past, few Berliners had been exposed to western fashion trends, but they were determined to make up for lost time. Men who had avoided beards in the 1840s because of their 'liberal' connotations began to sport 'emperor's sideboards', made popular by Franz Joseph and Kaiser William. Wives and daughters wanted to be well dressed for their dinners and balls and promenades on Unter den Linden, and new styles were not merely copied, but embellished by Berlin manufacturers so that they would be 'better than in Paris'. Gone were the demure empire-line dresses and ringlets of the Bieder-meier era, which had made women look more 'mother than mistress'; now opulence was everything. Hats had to be wider, skirts fuller, shoes higher and fabric more colourful than elsewhere, and gowns became ever more expensive and outlandish. Even the fashion magazine *Die Mode* lamented that 'the tendency of fashion at the moment is to go to extremes'. Hats began to reach extraordinary dimensions, extending far beyond each shoulder; theatres had long since requested that ladies leave them in lockers but they became so enormous that according to the *Berliner Tageblatt* tram passengers would take bets to see if fashionable ladies could get through the doors.

For foreigners these desperate attempts to outshine the fashion capitals of Europe were pathetic; when Jules Laforgue left France for the Berlin court he 'hoped to dispel the image of the terrible taste of the Germans', but his visit had the opposite effect. For all their money, he said, Berlin women simply did not have a sense of style: 'one piece goes so badly with others that it is often grotesque to see'. The overall impression was frightful, as 'the Berlinerin never has her hair done properly, never wears proper shoes, her walk is without grace, the movements too natural and voice loud and monotone.'[65] For the writer Przervwa-Tetmajer even the words 'ugly, shitty and horrific' were too mild to describe the women he encountered in Berlin.

By now, of course, comments made about Berliners by Frenchmen, Russians, Austrians, Englishmen and Italians were tainted with a mixture of surprise, jealousy and fear of this upstart capital in their midst. When Berlin was a small provincial city nobody had cared how its women dressed, but all of a sudden it was important. Europeans began to be curious about this strange place in the Mark Brandenburg and for the first time the city became a stop on the nineteenth-century version of the grand tour for the non-military who were interested in learning about the art of war.[66] By 1900 a million visitors a year were arriving via the new water and rail networks which encircled the city, and the small dank inns of old gave way to the newest additions to the Berlin skyline, the grand hotels.

In the late nineteenth century the size and style of hotels were considered a measure of the city's greatness, and Berliners were eager to compete with their rivals. They had started very late – the first hotel large enough to call itself 'grand', the elegant Kaiserhof, was only completed in 1875. When the Kaiser saw it he said he had seen 'nothing like it' and Bismarck admired the elegant sandstone building so much he insisted that it be used as the venue for the Berlin Conference of 1878, at which the European powers attempted to halt Russian expansionism in the Balkans.[67] Other hoteliers tried to imitate its success, and soon the Grand Hotel de Rome, the King of Portugal, the Central Hotel, the Hotel d'Angleterre and the elegant Bristol were vying for business in the area around Friedrichstrasse and Unter den Linden. By 1914 Berlin had twelve grand hotels with a capacity of 3,355 rooms, and they soon became important settings of novels and later films; Vicki Baum, who wrote

People in the Hotel, would work as a maid at the Excelsior, and Greta Garbo would murmur 'I want to be alone' into one of its great pillars.[68] But all paled in comparison with the 'best address in Berlin', the famous Adlon at Number 1 Under den Linden.

The Adlon has now been rebuilt, but for those who stayed there before the war the mere mention of the name still evokes wistful sighs. Debutantes and foreign dignitaries danced the night away in its ballrooms while heads of state and grand industrialists stayed in its lavish apartments. The hotel came into existence through the bad luck of Count Redern, who lost his pretty Schinkel palace while gambling one night with the king of England. The property went up for sale and Lorenz Adlon bought it, ripped down the palace (the equivalent of demolishing a Wren building in London) and, with the Kaiser's blessing, built the hotel. Like Wertheim's the hotel epitomized the new city: it was huge, opulent, and filled from top to bottom with frescoes, carpets, elaborate glassware and silver gilt; lights replaced service bells and its 140 bathrooms were awash with onyx and marble. The 'Wonder of Great Berlin' became another proud landmark and the Berlin design periodical *Innendekoration* was not being ironical when in January 1908 it called the Adlon a symbolic building which 'outshone all others not only in Berlin or in Germany', but even in 'New York, Paris and London'. The Adlon was 'great and important', it stated, 'because it loudly proclaimed to the world that Germany is rich!'[69]

Berliners had endured long periods of starvation and deprivation in their chequered past, which might explain why prosperity and success were so closely associated with food. The proprietors of the grand hotels joined in the race to build great restaurants and dining halls, cashing in on the fact that the bourgeoisie still equated gluttony with success. The images of the Berlin businessman bursting out of his waistcoat while cramming in yet another sausage, so brutally portrayed by Georg Grosz and Otto Dix, were not far from the truth. An American visitor quipped that Berlin ladies could not get through an entire performance of *Hamlet* without having a *Schinkenbrot* – a smoked ham sandwich – between acts, and it was considered quite normal in well-to-do families to have at least one seven-course meal a day.[70]

The hallmark, however, was quantity, rather than quality. Dishes were based on the rustic peasant food of their forefathers – Conrad Alberti described the heavy smell of frying, alcohol and sauerkraut mixed with tobacco smoke which hovered in the thick air of the local *Kneipe* where, 'as it was Thursday', the main dish was *Eisbein*.[71] A French visitor once complained that in a 'delicatessen' one could only get coarse sausage and in a 'bakery' one could only get black bread. Preserved foods from pickled cucumbers to sauerkraut remained Berlin staples long after Frederick the Great had ceased to force his subjects to buy huge quantities of salt; local fish included carp, canal trout, eel and pickled herring, while other specialities included *Bouletten* or small hamburgers, pork cutlets and, above all, beer. Meals were a serious ritual; Arno Holz joked in *Phantasus* that his family remembered the day he was born because they could recall 'the roast with plums they had for lunch, and I had arrived by coffee time'. The restaurants were as outlandish as the hotels; the Rheingold at the Adlon greeted its 4,000 customers with a facade which looked more like the nave of a medieval cathedral than a place in which to eat, while Borchardt, Dessel, Kranzler and Kempinski on the Leipziger Strasse (known as the Café Egomania because of the posturing of its customers) became city landmarks.

Berlin had done well, but it was still desperately trying to catch up with its rivals in Europe. With their new money and their new look Berliners could not understand why outsiders remained so critical or why they were so slow to acknowledge Berlin's greatness. The Kaiser was keenly aware of his city's subservient position in Europe. In 1896 he wrote that 'Berlin is a great city, a world city (perhaps?)'. It was no Paris, for

> Paris is the whorehouse of the world; therein lies its attraction ...
> There is nothing in Berlin that can captivate the foreigner, except a
> few museums, castles and soldiers. After six days, the red book in
> hand, he has seen everything, and he departs relieved with the sense
> that he has done his duty. The Berliner does not see these things
> clearly, and he would be very upset, were he told about them.[72]

But despite his harsh words William was desperate for the city to reflect the power of his Germany. He wanted visitors to marvel at the ingenuity and wealth of his people, at the 'powerful, surprising and almost incomprehensibly rapid progress ... the result of the reunion of the German races in one common Fatherland'. But his insecurity and defensiveness shone through in his words: 'The more we are able to wrest for ourselves a prominent position in all parts of the world the more should our nation in every class and industry remember that the working of Divine Providence is here manifested. If our Lord God had not entrusted to us great tasks He would not have conferred upon us great capacities.' With this in mind William set about making Berlin the symbolic focus of the nation. A romantic version of Berlin's importance in history was reinforced through everything from museums of local history to the creation of gigantic war memorials, Winged Victory statues and images of Berlin's goddess Berolina, all smothered in ancient symbols such as eagles, oak leaves and laurel wreaths.[73] Museums, schools, public buildings and patriotic paintings were commissioned to enhance this national iconography.

The sense of rivalry with Vienna and Paris never waned in Berlin.[74] Bismarck had been particularly keen to emulate Napoleonic Paris – itself modelled on imperial Rome – which he saw as the ideal imperial capital. Bismarck was impressed by Napoleon's monuments of war, and the column made of melted down cannon from Austerlitz in the Place Vendôme, which chronicled his exploits, found an echo in Berlin's own victory column.[75] The presence of Pope Pius VI at the ceremony at which Napoleon crowned himself emperor and the attempt to install the pope in Notre Dame found an echo in the desire to create a 'Vatican of the North' in Berlin. Bismarck admired Napoleon's creation of wide streets like the Rue de Rivoli and was so impressed by the Champs-Élysées that he created the Kurfürstendamm in its image to connect the city centre with the elegant suburb of Grunewald.[76] Napoleon had wanted to make Paris into the centre of European culture and had not only plundered the great art treasures of Europe for the Musée Napoléon but had also stolen entire archives from occupied countries in order to create a single great European reference archive; if Berlin could not achieve this it could at least build schools and museums and libraries. Paris was the unrivalled administrative and political centre of France and whereas Louis XIV had moved the French capital to Versailles Napoleon had moved it back, shunning, as Bismarck had done, the particularist interests of petty princes. Bismarck introduced many elements of imperial Paris to the new German capital. But if Paris was Bismarck's ideal, the young William II looked increasingly to another rival – London.

The Kaiser became increasingly obsessed with the desire to outdo the new industrial and military giant of Europe, a country in which he had spent some of the happiest days of his youth.[77] England had colonies, great wealth, grand buildings, a powerful navy, and much more besides, and William entertained the childlike belief that anything which England could do, Germany could do better. If London had grand hotels then Berlin needed them. If London had museums and department stores Berlin could have twice as many. The Kaiser Wilhelm Gesellschaft, founded in 1909, was to be an 'Oxford in Dahlem'. The Lichterfelde Botanical Gardens, with its arboretum, pools and collections of native and foreign vegetation, was to rival Kew Gardens, as was the Great Tropical House, built in 1906, with its iron and glass cantilever construction. When William decided that Prussia needed a new Royal Library the architect Ernst von Ihne had one brief: it had to be bigger and better than the reading room of the British Library. Only the shell remained after the war, the huge battered clock frozen at 6.30 when it was bombed, but when standing it was the largest reading room in the world. It had cost Berliners 25 million marks. Having been built for show it was quite impractical; not only did the enormous dome magnify the slightest whisper but it was so difficult to heat that scholars had to dress in winter coats in order to work; the historian Droysen could always be seen with an enormous green and black blanket wrapped around his feet. But the Kaiser was delighted with the result.

The competition between London and Berlin went further. London had Houses of Parliament and a magnificent new Foreign Office so Berlin would have to have a Reichstag, something 'huge, heavy and Imperial'. It was not that William wanted to do anything for politicians, whom he hated so much that after leaving a German Colonial exhibition he declared that he would like to have all parliamentarian heads shrunken and put on sticks like the ones he had just seen. He called the parliament buildings the *Reichsaffenhaus* or 'empire ape house', and he even objected to the 'revolutionary' slogan 'To the German People' which was to be emblazoned across the front.[78] This was only added in the dark days of 1916. Nevertheless 183 architects competed for the Reichstag contract and in 1882 it was awarded to the heavy-handed Paul Wallot. The mock Renaissance building with its arches and its oversized dome would later play a key role in Berlin history, burning as the Nazis seized power, acting as a backdrop to the vicious hand-to-hand combat between Germans and Russians in May 1945, standing beside the Wall as an important symbol of West Berlin, and finally crowned the centre of the reunified capital by a glass dome designed by the English architect Sir Norman Foster. But when it was new it was simply another hollow showpiece for the upstart imperial city.

The gesture to political life was also to be extended to the religious life of the nation. Berlin had its hotels and political and industrial palaces and now William wanted a grand cathedral for his capital city. He was not modest; this was to be nothing less than the focal point of the 'greatest Protestant dynasty in Europe'. Above all, the church was to encourage unquestioning loyalty to the Hohenzollern dynasty.

By the time William II came to power the Protestant Church had an established history of supporting secular authority, a tradition which had started with Martin Luther himself. Despite his sublime plea for intellectual liberty Luther had been politically conservative, teaching that an individual must pray to God but must obey his prince. The links between Church and ruler increased in Protestant areas well into the seventeenth century; in Berlin the Hohenzollerns appointed faithful Calvinist preachers as civil servants and educators, who consistently managed to combine their devotion to God with service to the state.[79] In the wake of the Napoleonic Wars theologians, including the Berlin professor Schleiermacher, author of *Über die Religion*, pushed for the creation of a Church which would formally merge all Lutheran and Calvinist (Reformed) elements of Prussia and northern Germany and in 1817, on the tercentenary of the Reformation, Frederick William IV created a 'national Church'. It would become a pillar of Prussian state power.

By the late nineteenth century conservatives were increasingly frightened by the spectre of revolution; as Ranke put it, 'the whole order of things ... is threatened by anarchic powers'. One way to counter the dangerous ideas disseminated by Social Democrats and revolutionaries was to 'Christianize' Prussia and to entice people back to a Church which conformed to state policy. In order to achieve this Bismarck actually began to interfere in Church appointments, barring Young Hegelians and others suspected of holding radical political views from the clergy. His political views also affected the state's relationship with German Catholics. Bismarck was not anti-Catholic per se but wanted to curb the power of the Catholic Centre Party and admitted that religion was a convenient excuse by which to accomplish this: 'it is not a matter of a struggle between faith and unbelief. What we have here is the age-old struggle for power, as old as the human race itself . . .'[80]

The struggle had started in 1864 when Pope Pius IX had published the encyclical *Quanta Cura* claiming Church supremacy over all civil authority. Bismarck had seen this as a challenge to his own political authority and had unleashed the *Kulturkampf* against them. Catholics were labelled a 'fifth column' who dared to put Rome above Berlin; as a result they suffered discrimination, priests were no longer permitted to work in the state service, the Prussian government imposed official requirements for the ordination of Catholic priests and Catholic schools were harassed.[81] The *Kulturkampf* proved counterproductive, serving only to unite Catholics against Bismarck and eliciting much sympathy from non-Catholics throughout Germany. It was abandoned in 1875. Nevertheless the idea that no religion should act against the interest of the state but should rather inspire patriotism and loyalty persisted under William II.

The young Kaiser believed that he was God's instrument on earth and that to criticize his policies was to go against God's will. He expected complete loyalty from the Protestant Church but was in return willing to make Berlin the 'Vatican of the North'. He believed it a 'disgrace' that London had St Paul's, Paris Notre Dame and Rome the Vatican while Berlin had nothing but a handful of small medieval and eighteenth-century churches. Germany was unified; four-fifths of the population was Protestant, and now it needed a powerful symbol at its centre. In 1884 William commissioned the Berlin cathedral. The old church, once redesigned by Schinkel, was ripped down and a massive baroque-style building erected in its place to tower above the palace, the Reichstag and the Armoury.[82]

The Dom was opened in 1905 in a wave of nationalistic celebration, and sermons delivered from its pulpit gave William II complete support in his dangerous foreign and domestic policy. In 1914 the sermons rang in the ears of young Berliners off to war, and twenty years later it served as the focus of

Hitler's Nazi state Church and as the site of Nazi ceremonies, including Göring's outlandish wedding. After being bombed and gutted during the war it was partially restored by Erich Honecker both to reward those East German Protestants who supported his corrupt regime and to project the 'pride and legitimacy' of the DDR. It remains one of Berlin's most controversial buildings.

In May 1993 a ceremony took place in the centre of reunified Berlin to mark the end of fifty years of dereliction, but the day was not a happy one. Although some in the congregation were clearly moved by the ceremony many Berliners complained that the project had been too expensive and that the money should have gone to more pressing projects such as countering right-wing radicalism or helping refugees from Bosnia. The event could not have been more different from the proud, arrogant spectacle staged there in 1905 which so aptly demonstrated the links between the Protestant Church and Wilhelmine Germany.

The Dom was not the only church built at the time. The empress shared William's passion for heavy neo-Gothic architecture, which she combined with an obsession for building churches: forty-two went up in a mere ten years. Dozens of these brick or sandstone edifices still stand in the old working-class districts, where they were intended to inspire the secular proletariat. Before William churches in Berlin had usually been named after saints or other biblical figures, but in the new Berlin the houses of God were named after the Hohenzollerns themselves. One of Berlin's most famous landmarks was the church at the northern end of the Kurfürstendamm, the Kaiser Wilhelm-Gedächtniskirche (Memorial Church), built to honour William's esteemed grandfather. The architect Schwechten created an outlandish mock late-Gothic Rhenish church, which the well-to-do of Berlin paid for out of their own pockets, and the design became ever more colourful as William insisted on more plaques, more carvings and more colourful gold, blue and pink mosaics. The church was consecrated on Sedan Day in 1895 in a wave of rampant nationalism and civic pride, and it was only after the war that the surviving ruin became the striking and impressive symbol of West Berlin. Gerhard Masur called it 'one of the few buildings to have been improved by the fall of bombs and the ravages of fire'.[83]

Dozens of other ostentatious buildings went up under William II. Berlin was not yet a unified city (this would happen in 1920) and the autonomous districts built town halls to reflect their fierce local pride.[84] Charlottenburg, which claimed to be the most prosperous town in the empire, built a huge sandstone town hall to project its importance; not to be outdone the central Berliners built the 'Red Rathaus' in 1879. With its clinker-brick construction, ninety-seven-metre mock Renaissance tower and thirty-six red terracotta panels depicting Berlin's history it remains a landmark in the city.[85] Commercial buildings also became ever larger and more ornate; banks and offices were mock Renaissance or neo-Gothic palaces; the Viktoria-Insurance on Lindenstrasse had a monumental facade 130 metres long, while the Imperial Naval Headquarters, with its 800 offices, was an expression of William's new military ambitions; Hitler was so impressed by it that he turned it into his Wehrmacht headquarters. William had little interest in preserving old buildings which got in his way; Rathenau recounted how the Gendarmenmarkt was to be elongated, cutting into the Leipziger Strasse and on to the site of the old Academy of Arts to create a 'new and colossal Via Triumphalis', while left and right on Unter den Linden *Kaisermonumente* were to be erected which would end in the facade of a huge new opera house, and the front of the Josty Eck was to become a monumental cascade in the form of the Trevi Fountain.[86] The pretty Opera House on Unter den Linden was to be replaced by a huge neo-Gothic affair and William ignored the public outcry which found expression in the popular street song, *There Was Once an Opera House*. Only the outbreak of the First World War halted the demolition. The historicist imperial style which had been inaugurated by Hitzig's huge mock Renaissance Berlin Bourse of 1863 had been copied in museums, galleries, theatres, universities, bank buildings and private villas, in Hitzig's central bank building on the Jägerstrasse and in the mock Renaissance Technical University. At the high point of this historicizing style, Renaissance, Gothic, baroque and classical features were all muddled together so that by the end of the Wilhelmine period heavy gaudy buildings dominated the Berlin skyline, and large sections of the medieval or Frederickan city had vanished for ever.

William had great hopes for his capital but, in his attempts to create a great cultural centre in the heart of Europe, he often stifled the very artists and trends which might really have put his city on the map. He called everything from Impressionism to Naturalism 'art from the gutter', and while Schiele, Freud and Klimt were busy exposing the internal decay of Vienna the backward-looking military values imposed from above drove many great German writers and artists away: Schopenhauer hated Berlin, calling it a 'psychologically and morally cursed nest' and he moved to Frankfurt; Wagner stayed in Bavaria; Jakob Burckhardt refused a professorship there: he considered 1846 Berlin to be 'repulsive, ugly, vile, mean to the point of malevolence, and with all this fortunately ridiculous'; Nietzsche despised the crass bourgeois aspect of the city; Brahms left after a short stay.[87] In the end only one great writer stayed in imperial Berlin to become its most perceptive critic. It was Theodor Fontane who looked past the glittering surface and exposed the conflicts and the turmoil which haunted the shadows of the new imperial city.

Fontane was born near Berlin and spent his youth travelling throughout the Mark Brandenburg with his debt-ridden father, an experience which later inspired his famous 1862–82 *Wanderungen durch die Mark Brandenburg* (Travels in the Mark Brandenburg) and the 1889 *Fünf Schlösse* (Five Castles). His family was too poor to pay for a formal education and he was sent to a trade school in Berlin to learn pharmacy. Nevertheless he was able to journey to London and eventually returned to Berlin to write poetry. He joined the literary club Tunnel über der Spree whose programme, written by Arno Holz, began 'Zola, Ibsen, Leo Tolstoy, A world lies in their words' and ended with the cry: 'Our world is not Romantic, Our world is only modern!' The journalists, artists and writers there encouraged the young Fontane; each member was given a nickname (Theodor Storm was 'Tannhäuser' and Emanuel Geibel was 'Bertrand de Born'); Fontane was accepted, and nicknamed 'Lafontaine'. After a short stint on a newspaper in London Fontane joined the conservative *Kreuzzeitung* and began to write about Berlin in earnest.[88] His articles, letters, and above all his social novels bring the imperial city to life. To read him is to begin to understand the pretensions of the new rich, the decline of the educated middle class, the struggles of the workers, the arrogance amongst the officers, the separateness of the aristocracy, and the universal problems of family pride, honour, passion, marriage and adultery, life and death in the brash imperial city. Above all he deals with the social pressures which in the strict hierarchy of the new Berlin conspire to destroy true love. The Berlin novels were written as a series and were meant to cut through and expose all strata of life, but they were written with such humour, gentle irony and compassion that they rose above being mere criticism. The novels share similar themes: *Irrungen, Wirrungen* (Error and Confusion) describes the impossibility of marriage between a working-class girl and an officer, while *Stine* focuses on a forbidden love between a nobleman and a middle-class girl which ends in death. *Die Poggenpuhls* is about the widow of a Prussian Junker and her impoverished children who are saved in part by the paintings of one daughter which are bought by a wealthy Jewish banker; *Frau Jenny Treibel* is a scathing criticism of a new rich family's snobbery. *Effi Briest*, the German *Anna Karenina*, is the story of a young woman trapped in a loveless marriage, who is banished and dies alone after a handful of old love letters are discovered by her husband. Fontane was naturally sympathetic to the old bureaucrats and university professors, judges and lawyers, doctors and journalists who were now part of a fragmented group with no organized political voice and who were slowly being pushed aside by the materialistic and militaristic values of Berlin. These feelings come through in his last novel, *Der Stechlin*, in which he describes an endearing nobleman Dubslav von Stechlin and his encounters with virtually all layers of Berlin society. Dubslav and Count Barby are portrayed as honourable anachronisms of a vanishing world, and Fontane praises Dubslav's modesty and integrity while heaping contempt on the insufferable upstart Herr Gundermann, who has recently been granted a 'von' by the Kaiser. Fontane's works remain a unique and invaluable exposé of life and of the rapid changes in imperial Berlin, but for all his perceptive wit, his insight and his criticism he was largely ignored during his lifetime. He in turn saw Berliners in a jaded light, commenting in a letter to Georg Friedländer in 1884 that 'The Berliner remains a selfish, narrow-minded provincial' and that although the town continues to grow it is 'ruled by imitation, the lowest common denominator, respectable mediocrity'.[89]

The Wilhelmine period produced a number of extraordinary artists and writers and architects, from Fontane to Messel, and saw the birth of everything from Expressionism to modern industrial architecture in Berlin. Indeed while many visitors were disappointed by its ostentatious yet uncertain style they were impressed by its great department stores, train stations, hotels and industrial buildings. It was not the Reichstag or the Dom, but rather the Borsig works and the extraordinary 1909 turbine factory built by Behrens for AEG which made Berlin seem so energetic, so modern, so like Chicago. Berlin succeeded in impressing not because of, but despite its Wilhelmine pretensions. New cabaret and revues were intent on projecting Berlin as a *Weltstadt*. Performers like Claire Waldoff sang of Berlin's 'big city' character in songs like the *Lindenlied*, which compared Berlin's main street with the great boulevards of Paris and Vienna; revues at the Metropol included glitzy productions extolling the virtues of Berlin, including hits like Paul Lincke's 1908 *Donnerwetter – tadellos!*, his 1909 *Halloh! Die grosse Revue!* and Rudolf Nelson's 1912 *Chauffeur – in's Metropol!!* and the cheekily titled *Das muss man seh'n!* (You Gotta See It!). The new reviews extolled the virtues of the big city, glorying in its consumerism and cosmopolitan nature and advertising new forms of entertainment which would later be associated exclusively with the Weimar period, from the six-day bicycle race to boxing and from the new facilities at Wannsee beach to the creation of the Luna Park. One song from the Metropol's 1910 production of *Hurra! Wir leben noch!* dared to place Berlin ahead of other European capitals: 'As soon as day has turned to night,' it complained, 'London has shut up tight.'[90] If some complained that Berlin was crass or *parvenu* the revues argued that this was because the city was so new – a *Metropolinchen*. As a song in *Das muss man seh'n!* put it, Berlin was still trying to find its feet: 'I have the foibles of my youth, I'm still a young metropolis.'

References to Berlin's modernity made little impact on the 'official culture' controlled by William II. He continued to control the cabaret through rigorous censorship which banned political criticism and 'obscenity'. In one example the Kaiser forbade officers to attend performances of *Donnerwetter – tadellos!* because the expression, translated as 'Goddamn – perfect', was one of his own favourites and was mercilessly ridiculed in the performance. His views on art in general were clearly demonstrated during a speech in 1901, when he decried all things modern: 'Art should help to educate the people; if art does nothing more than paint misery more ugly than it is, it sins against the German people.' Art in his city was meant to 'proffer a hand to uplift, rather than to debase'. The art and architecture he commissioned should present Berlin's greatness, not its weaknesses, and there was constant tension there between 'acceptable' art and the great trends sweeping the rest of Europe.[91]

Music remained a mainstay of Berlin cultural life and retained a high standard – in part because it was less prone to censorship than the theatre. Concerts had become popular among the bourgeoisie in the early nineteenth century and Berlin attracted the first musical celebrities, including Paganini and Liszt, nurtured choirs like the Singakademie and the Philharmonischer, where Bach and Handel had played. Berlin was a musical city which boasted schools like the Musikhochschule and the Sternsche Konservatory; orchestras included the Royal Orchestra for the Opera House and the Philharmonic Society, founded in 1826. The Academy of Music, founded in 1869, attracted Schumann, Wagner, Brahms and Dvořák, and the Berlin Philharmonic, founded in 1882, was conducted by Richard Strauss, Tchaikovsky, Mahler and Edvard Grieg. Berliners idolized musicians, and little porcelain busts and photographs of Wagner, Brahms and Saint-Saëns, the likes of which can still be found in the homes of central European music teachers, were sold at Berlin newsstands next to those of the violinists Eugène Ysäye, Sarasate, Wilhelmj, and the pianists d'Albert, Rubinstein, Liszt, Frau Schumann, Graf Zicy (who played only with his left hand), and the magnificent Hans von Bülow, who told his orchestra while rehearsing the overture *Oberon* that 'it sounds as if he is calling a regiment of heavy cavalry when they are supposed to be elves!' But however high the standard of performance, few composers could bear to live in the stifling militaristic city, and even Rubinstein admitted that 'Berlin offended my spirit'. Paderewski was shocked at the conservative tastes, and although he called it one of the great musical centres of the world he muttered that 'the traditions of Handel, Bach, Mozart and Beethoven are kept with such severe seriousness and with such reverence that these composers have almost become false idols'. Felix Mendelssohn complained of Berlin's contradictions, which in turn influenced musical life: 'the huge pretensions, the tiny achievements; the exact criticisms, the miserable performers; the liberal ideas, the royal servants crowding the streets'.[92] Bülow gave a farewell concert in Berlin in 1892 shortly after William's speech damning everything from socialism to modern art: after long applause Bülow turned to the young Kaiser and said sarcastically: 'Your Majesty has in the last days been gracious enough to inform us that the best way for grumblers to improve the miserable and woeful state of the Fatherland is to shake the German dust from his slippers and to leave as quickly as possible. I do this forthwith and take my leave of you.' With these words he took his handkerchief from his sleeve, dusted the lacquered stand, and deserted the podium. He left Berlin for good, returning only once for a concert shortly before his death in February 1894.[93] Few other respected figures dared challenge the Kaiser's views so openly.

The same conservatism was evident in opera. Like concerts, opera had moved from being the preserve of the aristocracy and was now an essential part of the nineteenth-century bourgeois world. The new audiences called for romantic and patriotic subject matter and the houses obliged. Berlin had dozens of opera houses, including the Theater des Westens, which opened in 1896, the Komisches Oper of 1905, the Kroll Theater in the Tiergarten, the Charlottenburg Opera of 1912, which was replaced by West Berlin's gloomy Deutsche Oper after the division of the city, and the old Royal Opera House. Caruso sang in Berlin every year between 1906 and 1913, and because Berliners had the curious custom of allowing stars to sing in their own language one might hear Erwin Booth in English, Rossi in Italian and the chorus in Russian all at the same time. But in Wilhelmine Berlin there was no doubt who was the master of opera – Richard Wagner.

Wagner took the inspirations of middle-class Berliners and transformed them into music. Political works such as the patriotic *Kaiser March*, written for the 1871 victory celebrations in Berlin, were rare; for the most part Wagner was an apolitical critic of his age despite the fact that the themes he chose would fit comfortably into the world view of increasingly chauvinistic nationalists. Wagner did not want to write 'mere music' but *Gesamtkunstwerk* – a complete work of art which over the course of the evening would transform the fragmented, alienated bourgeois audience into a collective whole. His work, with its crescendos and chromatic passages, was designed to bring the listener to ever greater levels of ecstasy so that by the end he would be submerged in a world of honour and glory and history which would make the materialistic society around him seem crass and vulgar by comparison.[94] Wagner was immensely popular. When he came to Berlin for a performance of *Tristan und Isolde* at the Royal Opera House in 1876 he was mobbed by the crowds; at a performance of *The Ring* in the Viktoria Theatre five years later thousands of wild fans gathered in the streets to cheer him on, while well-to-do Berlin ladies competed with one another to entertain him and see to his every whim.

For his part William disliked all new tendencies in opera. When the Wagner memorial was unveiled in Berlin he asked, 'Why do people really make such a fuss of this Wagner? The fellow was after all only a simple conductor, nothing more than a conductor – a quite common conductor.' And, as the programme at the Royal Opera House had to be approved by him, it remained backward and stale. His aversion to modern pieces and his wife's hatred of the late nineteenth-century themes of sensuality, decadence and corruption ensured that the most innovative works of the period were not performed in Berlin. The great Richard Strauss gave over 1,000 performances at the Royal Opera in nearly twenty years of direction but was forced to première his own operas in Dresden because they were considered too risqué for Berlin; the most insulting incident occurred when his great work *Salome* was banned because the empress could not tolerate its eerie music, sexual overtones and wild erotic dancing. She was not alone; the Count von Hülsen-Häseler thought Baron Ochs auf Lerchenau in Strauss's *Der Rosenkavalier* was 'too lusty and vulgar', an amusing observation from the man who was later to die of a heart attack while dancing in a ballet tutu in front of the Kaiser. Hypocrisy was never a problem for William's courtiers.[95]

The Kaiser's negative influence was even greater in the theatre. He had an intense dislike for the avant-garde and venues such as the Freie Bühne, which were dedicated entirely to the great works of Ibsen, Strindberg, Hauptmann and Wedekind, were officially ignored. Instead, Berliners were given an insipid diet of nationalistic drama. Ernst von Wildenbruch's historic plays such as *Die Quitzows*, which distorted the exploits of the pre-Hohenzollern Berlin robber barons, were common fare. The Theater des Westens in Charlottenburg was notoriously dull; Bernhard Sehring's pseudo-Renaissance building 'For the Care of Art' was later described as one of the great sins of the imperial period. But the most dreary of all was the Kaiser's own Royal Theatre, where the director Hülsen-Häseler commissioned nothing of which the 'All Highest Master' might not approve. A critic who saw a 1905 production of *Prinz Friedrich von Homburg* said that all was 'inadequate and superficial' and that the actors were 'beneath contempt'. It was said that even productions in the New Theatre, the Lessing Theatre and the Little Theatre were better despite the fact that money, pensions, orders, decorations and official praise were showered down on the Kaiser's favourites. Artists like Max Reinhardt struggled on, producing works by Wedekind and Shaw and Chekhov at the Deutsches Theater and the Kammerspiele and even opening his famous Grosse Schauspielhaus before the collapse of the empire. But despite their increasing appeal the works would only become 'acceptable' after the First World War.[96]

William was as disgusted by contemporary art as he was by the new theatre. Like many of his contemporaries he had been influenced by the eighteenth-century interpretation of Greek culture which assumed that there was such a thing as an absolute artistic ideal.[97] All forms of modern art were rejected and he continued to ban the French Impressionists and to attack the local Berlin Secessionists who were, in his words, 'vulgar', 'crass' and 'revolutionary'.[98] Despite the fact that they were attracting the attention of artists and critics throughout the world Max Liebermann, Lovis Corinth, Käthe Kollwitz, Max Slevogt, Ernst Barlach and Max Beckmann were treated with such contempt that Franz Servaes was moved to call Berlin 'the scullery maid of Europe'.[99] In return for conformity the Kaiser gave his appointees a free hand to control the Berlin art world. Anton von Werner, the conservative President of the Academy of Fine Arts, had soon become to painting what Hülsen-Häseler was to opera.

Werner echoed the tastes of his master. For him, historical painting was the rightful subject of the modern artist and themes of national history were the most important of all. Art and nationalism coincided as paintings were meant to portray the greatness of the German past as well at to instruct the viewer about decisive world historical moments. On the other hand Werner commonly referred to any form of modern art as 'dreadful' or 'worthless trash', and even insulted Berlin's liberal press by complaining that 'art was better when the critics were better'. For a man who claimed to have 'no sympathy, no understanding and no apology for historical lack of genius' his inability to see the great gifts of contemporaries from Manet to Munch was astounding. Artists of whom he approved included the now forgotten Franz Krüger, Eduard Gaertner, Michael Aschenbach, and Ernst Hildebrandt, and the top floor of the National Gallery in Berlin still bears witness to his limited taste; after a visit in 1913 the American critic James Huneker wrote, 'The sight of so much misspent labour, of the acres of canvas deluged with dirty, bad paint raises my bile.'[100] Hans Rosenhagen complained that he ranked Bonnat with Rembrandt, Anton Graff with Holbein and Gustav Richter with Reynolds, and concluded that 'When one knows that Herr von Werner is one of the artists who advises the Kaiser ... one cannot be surprised that so much meaningless art finds its way to the throne, while none of the painters who are creating the art of our time are found anywhere near the palace.'[101]

The artist who captures the era was the Kaiser's friend Adolph Menzel. Menzel was one of the few outstanding Berlin painters of the period to be accepted at court. He had started on the road to fame with lithographs illustrating the works of Frederick the Great which were recognized for their brilliance. His early paintings, particularly landscapes like *Houses in the Snow*, were similar to those of Corot or Constable (whose work he knew), and he was open to new ideas – as can be seen in his paintings of construction and industry such as the *Iron Rolling Mill* of 1875. This momentous work depicts the interior of a huge rail factory with its cavernous interior lit by the glow of molten iron in which around forty workers hurry to lift a bar on to a set of rollers while in the foreground a young girl brings them a basket of bread. The work is reminiscent of Courbet's *The Stone Breakers*. Menzel broke new ground with works like *Travelling through the Countryside* (1892), one of the first pictures to depict rail travel. Such works bring to mind Theodor Fontane's comment that Menzel was possible only in Berlin – 'indeed Berlin was for him a necessity'.[102]

Sadly the more famous Menzel became the more he was seen as the chronicler of the showy Wilhelmine court. This began with his paintings of Frederick the Great, including *The Flute Concert* in which he created an image of life at Sanssoucci which has impressed leaders ever since – from William II to Hitler – and continued with depictions of *Hofbälle* and galas and processions for which he was increasingly criticized by his fellow artists. Even his friend and admirer Fontane once referred to him as a 'grandiose little bauble', and when he was awarded Prussia's highest decoration Gerhart Hauptmann called him a traitor to art: 'Imagine him receiving the Order of the Black Eagle: what horrible blasphemy!'[103] Although they were friends Liebermann said of him that for all his pretensions he was backward and provincial 'like all Brandenburgers'.[104] Liebermann admired Menzel but saw him as an artist of the past who dismissed Impressionism with its 'fuzzy lines' as the 'art of laziness'. The art critic Julius Meier-Graefe saw two distinct 'Menzels', both the 'Impressionist' and the 'painter of Frederick the Great'.[105]

Despite the opprobrium since heaped upon him it must be said that Menzel's attempts to create realistic portraits of the great men and events of the past were executed with a skill unmatched by any Berlin painter of his generation. As a result of William's admiration for his historical works he became a fixture at court and when he died in 1905 the city staged a grand procession with so many flags and officers in uniform that Oskar Loerke remarked that 'it looked more like a carnival than a funeral'. The Kaiser himself walked behind the coffin; the only other European artist to have been so honoured by his monarch was the incomparable Velázquez, who had died in 1660. But it was clear which aspect of Menzel William admired, saying he was 'the most distinguished of German artists . . . not of course the Menzel who anticipated in his street scenes, landscapes and interiors what the younger generation strove for, no, the posthumous Chronicler of old Fritz'.[106]

Historically Berlin art collections had never compared with those in the old German court cities like Munich or Dresden, and it certainly had nothing to match the Louvre or the Hermitage. Thankfully William had nothing against the Old Masters and was determined to bring Berlin galleries up to the standard of his rivals. Thanks to men like Carl Osthaus, Hugo von Tschudi, Ernst Wichert and, above all, Wilhelm von Bode he came closer to his goal than might have been expected.

Berlin owes a great debt to Bode.[107] An extraordinary art historian in his own right, he had a marvellous eye for lost masterpieces or forgeries; legend has it that he spotted a Frans Hals in a flea market from a street car, which he then bought for a mere 50 marks. He began his spectacular career by collecting Renaissance bronzes but he soon attracted a tremendous group of specialists and art historians who between them turned Berlin into a centre of the European art market and art journalism. He also developed a network of 'informers', such as his friend Hainhauer, who would tell him if there was anything of interest for sale in Paris or Rome. He was a most charming man and managed to beguile most of the famous private collectors of the day from the coal magnate Eduard Arnold to the newspaper baron Rudolf Mosse. He befriended the mine owner Oscar Hulschinsky, whose collection included a Frans Hals, a Botticelli and a Rembrandt, along with other important and generous friends – among them Jacoby, who collected Japanese art, and Eugen Gutmann, the founder of the Dresdner Bank who had works by Van Dyck, Ruisdael, Rubens, Tintoretto and Rembrandt. Bode worked closely with the Kaiser to persuade collectors to give to the Berlin museums; if a potential donor was spotted Bode would ask William to 'have coffee' with them, and the Kaiser would then casually promise the collector honours or titles if he would consider donating his treasure to the state. Bode's Berlin acquisitions were spectacular by any standard before or since, and included works by Filippo Lippi, Dürer, Botticelli and Bellini, Rembrandt, Raphael, Correggio, Veronese, Titian, and dozens of others. Felix Braun once wrote from Vienna that he was amazed by the works he had seen in Berlin, the likes of which were 'missing from our Hofmuseum', while Jacob Burckhardt said in 1882 that 'nowhere else offers the chance to become familiar with the best of so many periods of art'. The Kaiser-Friedrich Museum, which juts out into the Spree and is crowned by a great dome, was filled with Bode's treasures and was later renamed the Bode Museum in his honour.[108]

But the acquisition of Old Masters was not enough for the Kaiser; it had not escaped his attention that the other great European cities were building up collections of archaeological and ethnographical treasures to rival their art galleries, that while the British Museum and the Louvre were being filled with Greek statues and Egyptian mummies, Berlin was lagging far behind.

As ever, William's motives were linked to his desire to increase the importance of the German state. In the nineteenth century new museums and institutes dedicated to archaeology and ethnography went hand-in-hand with the rush for colonies which became yet another symbol of national pride. Germany had come late to the race for colonies; indeed Bismarck had been against the idea of rushing around the globe for land for fear it would upset his carefully balanced equilibrium in Europe. But in the summer of 1884, urged on by German nationalists as well as by merchants, bankers and entrepreneurs who sought markets and raw material overseas, and with the help of the English (who appreciated his support in Egypt), he changed course and within a few years he had acquired South-West Africa (Namibia), German East Africa (Tanzania), Togo and the Cameroons in West Africa, the Bismarck Archipelago (Solomon Islands) and much of New Guinea. The colonies were not particularly successful: most holdings in South-West Africa were 'only good for diamond mines' and German East Africa was uninhabitable; indeed by the outbreak of the First World War only 25,000 Germans had settled there. But they remained a source of great pride. The Berlin department stores and speciality shops sold racks of tropical clothes and outlandish gear and the city was host to organizations from the German Colonial Society and the Colonial Lottery to the Colonial Troops and the Colonial Congress. Germans felt themselves to be as much of a 'civilizing force' as other Europeans and no one batted an eyelid when, for example, the learned Professor Doktor Emil Steudel debated whether or not one should best use 'a rope or a hippopotamus whip to keep plantation workers in line'.[109] It was during this period that the museums of Ethnology, Arts and Crafts, the Colonial Museum and the Natural History Museum grew most rapidly, and even the Maritime Museum, built in 1906, was little more than an excuse to present more nationalistic propaganda about the need for a large German navy to defend the new colonies or trade routes.

Berlin's archaeologists first flexed their muscles in North Africa. The fearsome leader Mohammed Ali had kept all Europeans out of his ancient territory for years, but the Berlin Egyptologist Carl Lepsius managed to get an audience with him and exchanged a few pieces of Prussian porcelain for permission to remove all the treasures he could find. It was a great coup. He returned to Berlin in 1850 with crates and boxes bursting with artefacts, leaving the French and the British green with envy. German archaeologists never looked back, increasing their theoretical and practical knowledge while actively participating in German foreign policy. Like their British and French counterparts they took to working alongside the military as spies, gathering intelligence and keeping their government informed of the local political situation while unearthing the treasures of ancient Egypt, Babylon, Assyria, Mesopotamia and Greece. Interest in the cultures of the Nile delta reached new heights during the Suez Canal project, which led to the creation of the Egyptian Museum, a fantastic collection which still houses the breathtaking bust of Nefertiti discovered by Ludwig Borchardt at Tell al-Amarna in 1912. The Islamic Museum was founded during the construction of the railroad line to Mecca. The eighth-century palace of Mshatta which had stood in the way was summarily torn down, but in 1903 the sultan of the crumbling Ottoman empire, keen to ingratiate himself with the Kaiser, presented Berlin with the lavish 45-metre rock facade. The Pergamon Museum was named after the extraordinary Pergamon Altar. The city had once rivalled Athens in the ancient world, but it had been forgotten by westerners for over 300 years until the German archaeologist Carl Humann rediscovered it in 1878. He spent thirty years excavating and reconstructing the massive line of stone columns which includes a huge frieze depicting Zeus fighting the giants for Mount Olympus. The Market Gate of Miletus, built by the wealthy citizens of the city in AD 120 under Hadrian, soon joined the Pergamon Altar with its giant two-tiered Corinthian marble columns. This fabulous gate had once greeted traders from all civilization, but the structure had collapsed in an earthquake around the year 1000 and was only excavated and transported to Berlin in 1905.[110] The Middle East Department was built to contain the fantastic Ishtar Gate of Babylon, which was built at the height of Nebuchadnezzar's influence in 580 BC, and it still dazzles visitors with its brilliant blue-glazed tiles and mosaics of glorious mythical animals.

Berlin produced other pioneers as well: in 1873 Heinrich Schliemann discovered the ancient city of Troy. He dug through precious layers looking for the city of King Priamos, and discovered a fabulous cache of exquisite gold jewellery, later modelled by his wife Sophie in one of the most famous photographs of the century. The find changed fashion trends all over Europe, much as did Carter's later discovery of Tutankhamun's tomb in the Valley of the Kings, and there was no well-dressed Berlin lady in the *Gründerjahre* (the years following the foundation of the empire) who did not have at least one piece of gold jewellery inspired by Priamos' treasure. The Trojan hoard was thought to have melted in the fires of the Second World War; in fact it had been stored in the Zoo bunker in 1945 and was stolen by Soviet troops. It has recently turned up in Russia along with dozens of other treasures and was shown in a magnificent exhibition at the Pushkin Museum in Moscow.

The sight of all the colonial artefacts in the heart of the Mark Brandenburg helped to reinforce the idea that Berlin was now a great and powerful capital, and the Kaiser encouraged these sentiments by building outlandish monuments of his own. Since 1871 Berliners had been swept along by the tide of nationalism and militarism which was reflected in the *Kaiserkult* or 'Cult of the Kaiser'. Busts and statues of Bismarck and William, von Roon and von Moltke, including the three enormous works which still stand forlornly on the Grosser Stern, had sprung up like mushrooms; over fifty statues of Bismarck had been raised by 1890 alone, and new versions were reproduced in glass or bronze for household use. Everything from schnapps to pickled herring was named after the Iron Chancellor, while grown men swooned at the thought of living in

Bismarck's city; Hermann Bahr wrote in 1884: 'even today my heart beat quickens when I remember how I stepped off at the Anhalter Bahnhof: to be in the same city as Bismarck, to breathe the same air . . . here [where he] wanders amongst the people!' Children were taught about the greatness of the Kaiser; when the sun was shining Berliners called it 'Kaiser weather', and bourgeois children were dressed up in military outfits and Hussars' hats. When William II began to build up his navy little boys were squeezed into dark-blue sailor suits complete with gold buttons and caps with *SMS Rügen* or *SMS Helgoland* emblazoned across their brims. During his 1897 visit Rubinstein was amazed to see that over half the men of Berlin had copied the Kaiser and 'enthusiastically adopted the fashion of wearing the enormous W-shaped moustache'. That grown men should so slavishly sport such a strange style seemed ludicrous to him.

William II dreamed of filling every street in his city with grand statues and monuments to rival those of the ancient world. For him these were an important way of projecting historical legitimacy, of demonstrating the power and the might of the German capital and its new place in the world. He did not understand that since the early nineteenth century great and profound works of art had no longer been asked to fit within a given tradition, but were increasingly judged by their ability to break from it. Thanks largely to Romantic notions of the creative spirit, artists were now supposed to be original, to be emancipated, to be 'free'. William disregarded this trend; for him art was to reflect the historical greatness of the Prussian state, and of the new capital city of Berlin.[111] The huge nationalistic monuments he sponsored were meant to remind troublesome Berliners of the glorious victories of the past, and would become the focus for parades and ceremonies of all kinds.

When the angels in Wim Wenders's classic Berlin film *Himmel über Berlin* (*Wings of Desire*) met to look over the lonely city they chose one of its most impressive vantage points, the top of the Siegessäule (Victory Column) which towers high above the Brandenburg Gate. The massive structure was built to commemorate Bismarck's victorious campaigns against Denmark, Austria and France, and symbolized the pomp and splendour of the imperial capital. The red Swedish granite structure was decorated with captured cannon barrels and enhanced by mosaics depicting a glorified version of the victories of the Prussian army throughout the ages, and it was topped by a rather beefy golden Goddess of Victory. It was meant to commemorate the unification of Germany but, in the spirit of true Prussian chauvinism, failed to depict the contribution of any other state. But this was only one of dozens of huge monuments put up by the Kaiser.

William could not tolerate boring single figures in the 'old style', and the works he commissioned were always of heroes (usually Prussian) standing amongst cannons, draping flags, angels, fearsome animals and anything else that could be squeezed in. His favourite sculptor was Reinhold Begas, who designed everything from the Schiller Memorial to the Bismarck Monument on the Kaiserplatz and, the most overblown of all, the national monument for Kaiser William I. In this 'William the Victorious' peeked out from a plethora of angels, horses and enormous lions, earning it the name 'William in the Lion's Den'. The Kaiser generously awarded his favourites with honours and medals of all kinds; in 1905 he even awarded Count Gortz, the designer of the ghastly Coligny Memorial in front of the Schloss the Order of the Black Eagle. The Kaiser was not particularly tactful and his commission of a new 'Roland' was one of his less sensitive projects. In medieval Hanseatic cities a Roland statue had been a symbol not only of free trade but also of the political independence of citizens. The free city of Bremen still has a Roland statue in the town square, complete with the spikes on its knees which were once used to measure standardized lengths of cloth. But soon after the Hohenzollerns took over Berlin in 1440 they destroyed all symbols of local autonomy and threw the Roland into the river. The original has never been found but as a goodwill gesture William commissioned an 11-metre-high red granite structure to take its place. History was now a device for the instilling of national pride. The history it represented bore little resemblance to actual events but had become meaningless kitsch. This exaggerated form of historicization was personified in the most outlandish monument of the era, the Siegesallee or 'Victory Avenue'.

William was convinced that Berlin had risen to greatness because of his own ancestors, and the monument was designed to commemorate their influence throughout the ages. The lane was 700 metres long and stretched through the Tiergarten from the Königsplatz to Kemperplatz, along the axis of the Siegessäule and the site of the new Roland fountain. It was flanked by thirty-two busy Carrara marble statues of Hohenzollern figures, from the twelfth-century Albert the Bear to Kaiser William I. Berliners soon named it the 'Puppenallee' or Doll's Lane, and laughed to discover that the statue of the fourteenth-century Margrave Heinrich dem Kinde looked exactly like the satirical caricaturist Heinrich Zille. Oskar Bie, who published the *Neue deutsche Rundschau*, said in 1902 that 'there are only five or six [of the figures] that could affect a modern person', while Rathenau criticized the 'feudalism' of the project. The marble statues of the Siegesallee were dismantled by the Allies in 1947 and some have recently been discovered buried like corpses in the mud of the pumping station at the Landwehr Canal.

When he opened the lane William made a speech in the Schloss to promote 'International Respect for German Sculpture'. He began by proclaiming his Berlin art to be 'of a quality rarely seen even during the Renaissance', and compared Michelangelo unfavourably with his own Begas. He warned 'his' artists against going down the wrong path of 'new art', and finally declared that 'art which transgresses the laws and barriers outlined by Me, ceases to be an art'.[112] William had wanted to make Berlin the greatest city in the world. He believed he had succeeded. He claimed to have 'watched with sharp eyes' all developments in art and stated that although he had seen many great cities Berlin had now become the 'most beautiful'.[113] Instead, he made it at best a laughing stock and at worst a hated symbol of pomp, arrogance and Prussian militarism.

Bie was critical of the political control of art; while in the Florence of the Medicis the nobles and patrons had remained separate from the artists and craftsmen, he said, in the Kaiser's Berlin the Siegesallee was a last vestige of the long-dead Louis XIV – *Kultur* and the Meyerheim Exhibition was little more than 'dog and ape theatre-art'. For Bie the official art was fighting against the Secession movement, through which freedom 'opens its small door'.[114] Przervwa-Tetmajer said that the 'appalling and crass Victory Boulevard with its padded officers on parade and its grim brutal seriousness is an excellent image of Prussia'. He continued: 'This is the most ghastly city known to me and every time I am there I get the same impression.' Even Princess Blücher said, 'Berlin seems so ostentatiously clean and parvenu, and its absolute lack of style verges on vulgarity.' For his part Jules Laforgue complained that all he could see from the Princess Palace where he was living were 'pillars and statues everywhere ... I have five windows, and all I see are monuments surrounded by officers with monocles'. Kraszewski deplored the fashion for military statues: 'it is impossible to have a civilian hero here,' he wrote; 'even the monuments and statues wear uniforms' – and even Berolina, the armour-clad Goddess of Berlin, was 'decidedly masculine, strong and obese with a serious expression'. Karl Baedeker refused to award even a single star to any of the Kaiser's monuments, stating that Berlin could 'not compete in antiquity or historical interest with other great European capitals'.[115] His only positive comment was to say Berlin was a 'model of cleanliness' – faint praise indeed. Berlin was pompous not grand, theatrical not regal, showy not elegant, and bombastic not magnificent; its real treasures lay in its new industrial architecture and in the attempts to bring modern art to the city, not in the Kaiser's grandiose attempts to outdo the Renaissance. It was a city which was trying too hard to impress and by so doing made itself an object of ridicule; as Fontane put it in 1898, 'as far as Berlin is concerned, all chicness and elegance is gone'.

The insults cut deep. Baedeker's snub deeply offended William and made him even more determined to prove Berlin's worth on the international scene. If he could not do it through culture, he could do it by force. His mood changed from friendly competitiveness to aggressive nationalism and many Berliners who felt isolated and resentful began to find comfort in this increasingly belligerent chauvinism. The Kaiser and his representatives had trained them well. In a questionnaire to mark the turn of the century, Berliners were asked who was the most important German of the century; most named Bismarck and then Kaiser William I. The greatest thinker was said to be Helmuth von Moltke, who beat Darwin and Schopenhauer. The greatest artist was Adolph von Menzel, the greatest sculptor Reinhold Begas. The most important event in world history had been the creation of the German Reich, thus the most important event for Berlin was being named capital of a united Germany.[116] The answers were indicative of the tragic combination of provincialism and fervent nationalism which would sweep the city in the next decade and would push Berliners on to fight in the First World War. In a few short decades Berlin had grown from a backwater into the most powerful capital on the continent, but this brilliant flame was about to be extinguished in the bloody trenches of France and Flanders.

VII

The Road to the First World War

The wise man worries when the soldiers come.

(*Faust*, Part II, Act 4)

WHEN BERLIN WAS DECLARED the capital of a united Germany it seemed nothing could stop her meteoric rise to power. Max Weber was struck by the wealth and speed of the new metropolis with its 'tramways, underground railways, its electric . . . lamps, display windows, concert halls and restaurants, cafés, smokestacks, masses of stone, and the wild dance of impressions of sound and colour'. Berliners had longed for unification but found the expectations heaped upon the new capital a heavy burden and the tensions which resulted from it were, if anything, greater than they had been before 1871. Weber's 'wild dance' papered over deep divisions which quickly resurfaced when the boom began to turn sour.

By the mid nineteenth century Berlin had become a battleground for the dominant ideas of the age. In the period leading to unification it had been seen as living proof of progress and the triumph of capitalism, the epitome of modernity and a society which admired industry and success. Nevertheless even in the boom years Berlin contained dissenting voices: some were frightened of change, suspicious of all new trends, contemptuous of men who made money and prospered at the expense of traditional values. The unity of 1871 masked the beginnings of an epic struggle between opposing ideologies: between those who advocated modernity and those who felt that progress was destroying everything for which Germany should stand, between cosmopolitans and agrarians, between new money and old, between progressives and conservatives, between the 'asphalt' and the 'soil'. These divisions in the Reich capital were exposed by a single, now largely forgotten event – the stock market crash of 1873.[1]

With hindsight it is clear that a financial catastrophe was inevitable after the orgy of spending and speculation which had swept Berlin after 1871. Defeated France had quickly paid 5 billion francs in reparations, the Stock Exchange had gone mad, thrift and modesty had been thrown aside and easy money had attracted ever more entrepreneurs. Those who lived through that time wrote of the fever, the reckless drunken mania which seemed to overcome even the most steady and sensible of men. This ostentatious behaviour may have appalled Nietzsche and horrified Jacob Burckhardt, but it electrified Berlin. The years 1871 to 1874 had seen a 15 per cent annual increase in productivity: an amazing 857 companies were formed with a share capital of over 1.4 million thalers. The tremendous property boom had resulted in the creation of new developments from Wilmersdorf to Grunewald and from Schöneberg to the Kurfürstendamm; in some areas prices had risen 600 per cent above the 1871 purchase price. A new breed of Berliners had emerged, the *Gründer* or promoters who had encouraged ordinary people to buy shares in all kinds of ventures no matter how shaky. Berliners had poured money into property, the stock market, new banks, chemical plants, factories and railways – nearly twice as many companies were created in 1872 alone than in the entire century preceding unification. And for a few years these investments had paid extravagantly, encouraging people to take ever greater risks. The essentially conservative, non-entrepreneurial middle classes had been lured by the promise of instant risk-free wealth and thrown themselves headlong into the dizzying spiral of upward mobility.[2] Those who had not invested had watched sullenly as their friends paraded around in smart new clothes or moved to houses in the affluent suburbs.

Of all the investors and entrepreneurs in Berlin one man had become the very symbol of the age, the Jewish investor Henry Bethel Strousberg.[3] At the height of his career he had owned dozens of factories, mines and railroads, had bought himself a beautiful villa by the Brandenburg Gate which later became the British embassy, and had become one of the richest men in Germany. There is no doubt that Strousberg's business practices were less than sound; although born in Prussia he had spent twenty years in London, where, as editor of two trade journals, he had come into contact with British businessmen. His first venture in Germany was as the agent for the English financiers who had secured the 1862 concession to build the Tilsit to Insterburg line in East Prussia. He had quickly gained control of it himself and went on to build a handful of other railway lines. Strousberg was controversial not because he was a wealthy and successful businessman – of which there were now hundreds in Berlin – but because of the way he raised his money. He tended to avoid the banks, preferring to sell shares to small savers. He attracted interest by advertising in local newspapers and could often be found bribing editors with cash or shares to print articles predicting that the proposed railway would make a huge profit in a short time; he also invariably persuaded a few noblemen or senior civil servants to sit on the board of directors and give the latest venture credibility. Strousberg then set up nominally independent subsidiary finance and construction companies which were in fact controlled by the railway company. The contractors were paid in shares but as they usually needed money quickly they tended to sell as soon as the line was running, lowering the stock price and ruining the other investors. Strousberg left a string of bankruptcies in his wake and quickly became a hate figure in Germany and the target of increasing anti-Semitism; even Engels said of him in 1869, 'Strousberg is without doubt the greatest man in Germany. He will soon be made Emperor! . . . His guiding principle is to swindle investors, while acting fairly toward his suppliers and other industrialists.'[4] Nevertheless, as the massive cash injection from war reparations began to dry up Strousberg's empire faced collapse along with the rest of the German economy. A warning was sounded in May 1873 when the Viennese banks crashed. Werner Siemens wrote to his brother: 'The storm over Vienna is more threatening than ever and here too the lightning will strike.' Berliners ignored the ominous signs from the south.

On 28 October 1873 the Prussian bubble burst. The Quistorp Bank collapsed, followed by twenty-seven others, and the Berlin Exchange followed suit. By now it had become clear that the Berlin crash was part of a world-wide economic crisis which, as Engels put it, was 'one of those earthquakes that cause bourgeois society to shake at its foundations'. Fights erupted at the doors of the Bourse as people rushed to sell their worthless pieces of paper; anger mounted when savings, homes and businesses were lost. Hans Blum wrote:

> Railway companies, bank construction companies, large factories, joint-stock companies as well as companies with unlimited liability were ruined . . . At the same time countless unfortunate private individuals were horrified to discover that they had lost their capital or savings, or that – as shareholders in companies with unlimited liability – they faced the prospect of losing everything that they possessed to satisfy the companies' creditors.[5]

Newspapers were filled with reports of gruesome suicides and Berliners faced a long winter of bankruptcies and funerals.

In retrospect the true economic effects of the 'Great Depression of the Bismarck Era' were exaggerated. Many small investors lost everything and prices dropped dramatically for a time but industrialization carried on virtually uninhibited; indeed nearly 900 new companies were founded in 1874 alone, and wages remained stable.[6] But it was the psychological impact of the crash which changed Berlin's history. The *Mittelstand* (or middle classes) forgot that they had voluntarily risked everything on the stock market for the promise of easy money, and instead of accepting their losses as part of the risk of investment they wallowed in self-pity, calling the crash the 'modern catastrophe', the 'blackest day in history'. They nursed their wounds on rumours of the corruption and fraud of the *Gründer*, and on stories about the evils of capitalism. For those who had been stung Berlin became a symbol of everything that had gone wrong with the new Germany. Their disappointment was channelled into protectionism, virulent nationalism, anti-Semitism and a sharp reaction against 'foreign influences'.

In political terms the first of the many victims of the crash was economic liberalism.[7] Before unification Bismarck had promoted free market capitalism but the crash had exposed the vulnerability of German markets to cheap grain imports from Russia and America, iron from England and textiles from Lorraine. The Junkers and industrialists began to demand massive protective tariffs to defend their enterprises. Bismarck obliged by cementing the 'marriage of iron and rye'.[8]

For the small investors now wary of the free market this state intervention seemed inherently 'right'. Bismarck followed Frederick's lead, turning his back on *laissez-faire* policies and introducing a heady cocktail of protective tariffs and social legislation in the so-called 'Second Founding of the Reich'.[9] Berlin became a centre of protectionism. The National Liberal Party slowly became part of the pro-government establishment, although liberalism was labelled the 'Grey International', as dangerous as its 'Red' counterpart. Words like 'overproduction' and 'speculation' became terms of abuse. The crash had shattered the appearance of unity in Berlin, class divisions became more pronounced, and opportunities to gain wealth and power seemed once again to lie in the hands of the very few.[10]

The winners in this wholehearted rejection of liberal policies were members of the powerful coalition of agrarian and industrial interests. The Junkers' staying power had been extraordinary. They were anachronisms in a modern industrial state, with no counterparts in the United States, France or Britain, and yet they had set themselves up, along with the army and the Kaiser, as the protectors of German national pride. They argued that their expensive feudal estates were vital to the German economy even when critics like Max Weber exposed this as a fallacy. Above all they continued to provide the military elite and this in turn led to the spread of military values and codes of conduct throughout society.[11] Even at a time of rapid industrialization civilians were made to feel inferior to officers; as Wehler has put it, 'Social militarism could be seen at every turn; in the precedence at Court of the most junior of nobles in lieutenant's uniform, in the way one stepped aside to let an officer pass in the street, in the employment of ex-NCOs as postal officials, in the drills which formed part of physical education in the grammar-schools.' At the same time many of Berlin's most powerful industrialists gave up on the liberal ideas they had once held dear and became increasingly conservative, aping the aristocracy, vying for positions in the military and marrying their daughters to minor nobility. The old Borsigs and Siemenses who had lived and worked at their own factories gave way to successive generations who managed the firms from large suburban villas or newly acquired pseudo-aristocratic country estates. Bismarck succeeded in forging the powerful Junkers and the conservatives and the industrialists into an anti-liberal coalition and, as Fritz Stern has put it, 'precisely at the moment of Germany's modernization the anachronistic and economically declining elements of a modern society were once more exalted.'[12]

The crash had another more sinister side. With the fear of change and the rejection of modernity came the rise in *völkisch* beliefs adopted by those thousands who felt trapped and frightened by the changes which had engulfed them. They included the small shopkeepers, clerks, minor civil servants, teachers, artisans, craftsmen, farmers, and the small traders of the *Mittelstand* whose old privileges had been eroded. As Fontane put it in a letter of 1894, 'The civil servant sinks ever lower through no fault of his . . . he is surpassed tenfold in point of money and consequently in all other aspects.'[13] These men and women were desperate not to slip into the dark world of the working poor, and they blamed materialism and other 'foreign' ideas for the destruction of their old way of life. Richard Wagner spoke for many when he complained that a united Germany had been created at the cost of the 'German Spirit'. For his part Nietzsche said: 'One pays heavily for coming to power. Power *makes stupid*. The Germans, once called the nation of thinkers – do they still think at all today? . . . *Deutschland, Deutschland über Alles*, I fear that was the end of German philosophy.'[14] But the fear, the envy, the panic led to a deep suspicion of the liberalism, cosmopolitanism and modernity epitomized by the 'effete' democracies of the west.

The mistrust was not new. Berliners have periodically struggled to catch up with their counterparts in London or Paris or Rome but whenever it became clear that they could not outdo their western rivals they often rejected them altogether. Berlin's competition with the west began even before the Thirty Years War when the city was isolated from many of the great civilizing influences of western Europe. It had seen little of the Renaissance and its citizens had produced little to compare with the intellectual, artistic and cultural achievements of Italy or France or indeed other German cities like Nuremberg or Augsburg. As if in self-defence Luther and the Reformation had made poverty almost desirable and had fostered an idealism steeped in anti-rationalism, disdain of all earthly pleasure and a deep suspicion of the decadent west.[15] It was not surprising that Lutheranism was taken up with such zeal in Berlin.

Attempts by various rulers to counter this inward-looking nature had always failed.[16] When Frederick the Great sought to reverse the stagnation in his capital he had looked to France, dutifully building his copy of Versailles, speaking French, following French fashion and filling his capital with Parisian courtiers. The French, with their intellectual arrogance, cosmopolitanism and individualism, had alienated their dowdier Berlin counterparts – who comforted themselves by insisting that a deeply moral inner spirituality was of far greater worth than the shallow existence of the powdered and plucked gadflies at court.[17] Frederick's championing of French culture was rejected after his death, when German thinkers began to emphasize the importance of their own historical identity, language, customs, fashion, ideas and expressions. Immanuel Kant was not a petty nationalist and he firmly supported the ideals of the French Revolution, but his attempt to link reason and belief later influenced the speculative idealism of Romantics from Fichte to Schelling. After the Napoleonic Wars the ideas of the French Revolution were identified not with universal emancipation but with the enemy; Beethoven captured this mood when he scratched out the dedication on the 'Eroica' to the self-styled Emperor Napoleon and scribbled 'To the Memory of a Great Man' in its place.[18] New ideas of German nationalism began to emerge, which stressed the importance of the 'national community'. According to Gottfried Herder's concepts of *Volksgeist* and *Nationalgeist* identity lay not in Enlightenment reason or universalism but in local history, language and customs. For Hamann, Berlin was little more than a poor version of Paris, crawling with pseudo-Frenchmen living by the creed of the *raisonneurs* and destroying the true natural spirit of the German soul, while Friedrich Schiller emphasized the need for man to resort to the inner will in order to defy the constrictions of society. In his Berlin lectures Hegel taught that specific nations were the carriers of *Geist*, an idea echoed by the Körners, the Jahns, the Arndts and Fichtes who began to preach the superiority of German culture and the heroic qualities of the German *Volk*. Many of these ideas, benign in themselves, were now taken up and twisted by the German neo-Romantics and by the rabid nationalists of the late nineteenth century.

When Bismarck founded the German Reich in 1871 it had been seen as the fulfilment of the aspirations of the ordinary person, the true German who had fought so long against French tyranny. Berlin, as the new capital, was the focus of all these hopes: 'Rome, Paris, London were yesterday's cities,' went the saying, 'Berlin is the World City of the future.' The 1873 crash dashed expectations that economic and political unity or capitalism, materialism and liberalism would lead to endless wealth.[19] Now the Germans looked to some other force to prove their worth, and to provide an identity for the new state. It was at this moment that virulent nationalism began to turn into a mass movement. The result was to prove disastrous, both for Berlin and for the rest of Europe.

The anger of those who had suffered in the crash led them to turn against the modern cosmopolitan city into which they had poured their dreams. The journalist Glagau, who had lost all his money, wrote, 'how quickly the glory, so recently won, paled and waned!' There was a widespread feeling that Berlin had become the 'vile cess pit' which would ultimately destroy German culture and debase the German people. Irrational voices rose to denounce the 'mechanized and artificial life' of the big city, and small-minded, resentful people – both in Berlin and in other parts of Germany – began to point an accusing finger at the 'foreigners and Jews who run Berlin' and search instead for an identity to which they, 'the dispossesed Germans', could belong. Real Germans did not need smokestack industries or stock markets – all they needed was the *Volk*. When the harsh realities of the modern world seemed to conspire against them they looked back to a mystic past, a figment of their collective imagination. At the height of Berlin's headlong rush into modern capitalism they rejected the modern and began to immerse themselves in everything from nature movements to rural Romanticism, from vegetarian pacifism to 'blood and soil' mystique.[20]

Modern Berlin, the 'Whore Babylon', became a particular target for the new ideologues. Conservatives like Oswald Spengler associated the city with the decline of traditional cultural and moral values and with the end of Germandom, calling the 'Red Berlin workers' the 'rootless denizens of the big city'.[21] Berlin's growth had paralleled the growth of American giants like New York and Chicago, but Americanism was now seen as a curse. The sociologist Werner Sombart complained that while Vienna was a European bulwark against Americanism Berlin was 'a victim of it'. Karl Scheffler was distressed by the blatant Americanism which he found there as well as by the diverse un-German population, the robust materialism, the lack of culture, the pioneer spirit which reminded him of 'American or Australian cities that arose deep in the bush'. For him Berlin streets had 'no essence, no pattern of character peculiar to them. The squares are empty spaces without dimension or form; the houses do not blend with the streets, are loud, conspicuous and yet without effect.' In his famous book *Berlin, Ein Stadtschicksal* he commented that 'not a trace of the born gentleman does one find in the modern Berliner', for here was a 'dull and dreary' colonial population which had 'streamed into the city from the eastern plains, lured by the promise of Americanism' – it was a 'utilitarian city on the Spree'.[22] Anderson Nexo wrote 'after a number of months in Berlin I saw that over there two men had lifted their hats to one another. That was an experience; in this Babel two men who knew one another.' He complained of the alienation which led 'most people to marry through advertisements in the newspaper'. Berlin terrified people because it was so pitiless, so inhuman, so technologically advanced, so new. A contemporary *Baedeker* guide commented that 'three-quarters of its buildings are quite modern'; Princess Blücher called it 'ostentatiously clean and *parvenu*'; and Karl Scheffler called Berlin the 'Capital of All Modern Ugliness'.[23]

The alienation of the individual became a common theme of the time. The big city was demonized both by the left, who abhorred the alienation of workers, and by anti-urban conservatives and cultural pessimists of all kinds, who mourned the loss of the traditional German community. For different reasons all saw in Berlin varying degrees of brutality and unhumanity.[24] The poet Alfred Lichtenstein wrote that when one saw Berlin 'the world collapses; the eyes cave in', while Glagau described the times as ones in which

> the most serious and unnatural crimes are the order of the day, murder and robbery, burglary and theft . . . fraud and embezzlement spread like the plague, suicide has assumed epidemic proportions. Beggars and vagabonds roam about in droves, the prisons and penitentiaries are full, the number of civil and criminal trials, of bankruptcies, seizures and enforced sales is legion.

Rathenau noted that doctors were now treating patients so used to the built-up areas of the city that they suffered from *Platzangst*, a fear of open, windswept areas. The Berlin sociologist Georg Simmel claimed that the city dweller was confronted by unnatural stimulae every day, that 'economic, work and social life' created a way of life which contrasted sharply with the 'slow, familiar, even flowing rhythm' of existence in the country or in the village. The big city dweller must therefore create 'a protective organ for himself against the profound disruption with which the fluctuations and discontinuities of the external milieu threaten it'.[25]

The crisis of modernity gave rise to a host of conservative cultural critics, from Wilhelm Heinrich Riehl and Oswald Spengler to Justus Moser, who despised the new Berlin and were only too happy to tap into the resentment and disappointment felt by the *Mittelstand*.[26] Houston Stewart Chamberlain, German by choice, attacked democracy, liberalism and Jews; in 1881 Paul de Lagarde denounced the Reich as un-German and advocated settlement in a large part of Russia to be called 'Germanien'.[27] In *Rembrandt as Educator*, a book which was highly popular until the end of the Nazi period, Julius Langbehn described Rembrandt as a German artist and used him to illustrate that Germanic culture was superior to all others. He was anti-urban and anti-intellectual, claiming that 'in the end it may happen that the farmer will kill the professor; that what is innate in the nature of the German will predominate over what is artificial and conquer it'.[28] Some of these theorists began to agitate for real change in society. Wilhelm Forster founded his pseudo-Christian Ethical Society in 1892, while Moritz von Egidy gathered a small circle of members of his new pacifistic religion in his Berlin apartment in order to explore the spiritual utopian mystical forces of nature.[29] All these figures shared common beliefs about the horrors of modernity and the need to recreate a truly German way of life.[30]

The dominant theme in this maelstrom of *völkisch* ideas was the belief in the need for a new national revolution which would lead to a spiritual regeneration of the German people, the recreation of a mythical Germany of peasants and small-town craftsmen who shared a love of Teutonic myths and glorification of battle. The new Germans called for the elimination of the artificial divisions of class, party and religion so visible in Berlin. They looked instead to the universe, to a cosmos filled with mysterious life forces, to a world which could be experienced only if the individual immersed himself in the landscape of Germany, the homeland of the *Volk*. Young Berliners could not travel to the mountains, the rivers and the dark forests of Germany, so they created a romantic version of German *Kultur* at home based on a shared history, culture and language, and on ideas of pre-Christians who had lived on their hallowed soil for thousands of years and who had spilt their blood in order to protect it. Rural village life with its hard-working family values was contrasted with the decadent materialism of the city's feckless inhabitants – how could one touch the great German soil when it was covered with asphalt? The idea of a *Volksgemeinschaft* or mystic community of the *Volk* came to have quasi-religious significance, and was directed against all 'un-German' traitors, including socialists, Catholics, Jews, freemasons, Slavs, western Europeans, large-scale capitalists, cosmopolitans, all other foreigners and just about everyone else who inhabited the 'diseased capital at the heart of Germany'. New societies and clubs sprang up dedicated to the preservation of German culture; there was even a Bund für deutsche Schrift (Society for German Script) which rejected Antigua or Latin letters in favour of the 'true German' Gothic-style *Fraktur* derived from medieval script.[31]

Racism was part and parcel of the *völkisch* movement and it was at this time, long before the emergence of Nazism, that the disciplines of ethnology and anthropology were used to justify the superiority of the Germanic race. The selective reading of Darwin's theory of evolution, combined with the rediscovery of Mendel's work on genetics in 1900, led many scientists to believe that all human traits, including intelligence, were the result of biological evolution. These notions soon took on the trappings of 'pure science'. Germans, it was said, had evolved as a 'superior race' over thousands of years, and as such they must be protected from 'infection' by 'inferior races'. In 1904 the Archive of Race Theory and Social Biology was founded, with its rows of wax heads of racial 'types', eye colour charts and cranial calibration equipment – later used to distinguish Aryans from non-Aryans.[32] The *völkisch* nationalists had also been encouraged by the racist aspect of Bismarck's *Kulturkampf*, which had started as an attack against Catholics but had ended up in a campaign against minority groups, especially Slavs, who at the time made up over 10 per cent of the Reich.[33] New racial laws were introduced from the turn of the century; in 1908, for example, mixed marriages were forbidden and earlier marriages annulled in the German colony of South-west Africa. In 1913 Dr Fischer published his book about the children of Boer men and Hottentot women, the *Bastards of Rehoboth*, and recommended that they be given 'the minimum amount of protection . . . for survival as a race inferior to ourselves'. But by far the most insidious form of racism in Berlin was the new form of anti-Jewish prejudice which arose after the 1873 crash – racial anti-Semitism.

As in most European centres religious prejudice against Jews had long been a feature of Berlin life, nevertheless the people had always been relatively tolerant and there had been no Jewish ghetto or even a Jewish quarter in the city. The Enlightenment and the French Revolution had tempered some of the medieval prejudices and in the nineteenth century legal emancipation had coincided with new economic possibilities heralded by the Industrial Revolution. As a result many Jews had built up highly successful careers in professions from publishing to medicine, from manufacturing to banking, and the population of Jews in Berlin rose steadily from just under 50,000 in a population of 826,000 in 1871 to 170,000 in a population of over 2 million by 1910. The great success of Berlin's nineteenth-century Jewish community can still be seen in the magnificent reconstructed synagogue in the Oranienburg Strasse, which served as the centre of the Jewish community from the 1860s onwards, and in the Weissensee cemetery which remains one of the great landmarks of Berlin.[34] Weissensee was opened in 1880 when the older Jewish cemetery had been filled to capacity, and amongst the 100,000 headstones are names of great families from Rathenau to Tietz, from Mosse to Ascherode.[35] But all was not well and the Jews of Berlin were 'immeasurably useful and they were immeasurably resented'.[36]

It is particularly sad to chart the rise of anti-Semitism in a city whose wealth, prosperity and power owed so much to its Jewish citizens, and it was often resentment of their success which made Berlin Jews the target of the new ideologists.[37] The Englishman Shepard Thomas Taylor wrote of 1870s Berlin that the Jews 'inhabit the best houses in the best quarters of the town, drive about the parts in the most elegant *équipages*, figure constantly in the dress circle at the opera and theatres, and in this and other ways excite a good deal of envy in the minds of their less fortunate Christian fellow-citizens.'[38] But despite their wealth Berlin Jews had continued to suffer varying degrees of prejudice – they were still barred from the army, from diplomacy, from the other traditional bastions of the aristocracy, and were subject to much petty abuse.[39] Bismarck's banker, Bleichröder, the first Jew to be ennobled without having converted to Christianity, was shunned by much of polite society and although he spent millions of marks emulating the aristocracy and throwing extravagant parties in Berlin many 'upstanding families' declined his invitations. At one *Hofball* men refused to dance with his wife until a young officer was ordered to do so; he obliged coldly but returned to his friends to apologize for having broken the regimental code by dancing with a Jew.[40] Princess Catherine Radziwill was surprised by the level of anti-Semitism:

> Berlin is not Paris. In the capital of the new German Empire, as in Russia, prejudices still exist that have long since disappeared in France. Among these prejudices, one must include a certain repugnance to shake the hand of a Jew in front of a witness or to go to his house or to receive him at one's own . . . There is no city in the entire world where the children of Israel are more repulsed by society or where that society makes greater use of them.[41]

When the crash came many turned against the Jews, whom they blamed for their losses. The most visible target was Strousberg, who was thrown into debtors' prison in Moscow after his empire had collapsed and who would die a lonely and despised pauper in Berlin in 1884. But hatred was extended to all Jewish promoters and bankers and even Bleichröder received letters asking: 'how could you have allowed this to happen to me?'[42] Within weeks of the crash all things Jewish were being targeted; the liberal press, which was largely Jewish owned, was accused of having conspired to dupe investors, Jews were accused of deliberately exploiting Germans, while the rumour was circulated that established Jewish banking and industrial families had not suffered in the crash. Many angry Berliners believed Glagau when he claimed, incorrectly, that '90% of *Gründer* and speculators who had caused the crash were Jews'.[43]

With the depression of the 1870s Berlin became a target for anti-Semites. Wilhelm Riehl labelled the city 'the domain of the Jews' and in 1879 Constantin Frantz declared Berlin to be 'more like the capital of a Jewish Reich than a Germanic one'.[44] Some began to see Jews at the 'heart of an international conspiracy that was corroding the German character and the European order', and words like 'modern' and 'Jewish' were used interchangeably in attacks on Berlin. A new contempt for the city became inextricably linked to anti-

Semitism; modern art, particularly Expressionism, was associated with 'Jewishness', and the most important critics of the day, including Alfred Kerr and Siegfried Jacobsohn, were accused of being biased because they were Jewish.[45] Nietzsche was struck by the rising prejudice and wrote in 1885, 'I have not met one German who is well-disposed towards the Jews.' In *Human, All Too Human* he tried to explain this phenomenon, stating that 'the whole problem of the Jews exists only in nation states, for here their energy and higher intelligence, their accumulated capital of spirit and will, gathered from generation to generation through a long schooling in suffering, must become so preponderant as to arouse mass envy and hatred'. He went on to say that there was a growing tendency to 'lead Jews to the sacrificial slaughter as scapegoats for every possible or private misfortune'.[46] Nietzsche might have regarded the 'young stock exchange Jew' as 'perhaps the most disgusting invention of mankind' but unlike many of his contemporaries he insisted that German culture owed much to Jews, who had given human beings 'the noblest man (Christ), the purest sage (Spinoza), the most powerful book, and the most effective moral law of the world'. Furthermore, Nietzsche insisted that the Jews had helped to save German culture: 'in the darkest times of the Middle Ages . . . Jewish free-thinkers, scholars and physicians . . . clung to the banner of enlightenment and spiritual independence . . . We owe it to their exertions, not least of all . . . that the bond of culture which now links us with the enlightenment of Greco-Roman antiquity remained unbroken.'[47] Nietzsche referred to anti-Semites as those who cannot forgive Jews that they have *Geist* and money: 'Anti-Semites – Just another name for the *Schlechtweggekommenen*' (underprivileged).[48] Despite such criticism, however, anti-Semitism continued to rise. Now it was levelled not against 'outsiders' but precisely against those assimilated Jews who were an integral part of Berlin culture. The most dangerous development was that anti-Semitism would now be based not on religion, but on race.

In 1879 Wilhelm Marr published his highly influential book *The Victory of Judaism over Germandom*, in which he explained why racial anti-Semitism now had to replace medieval religious anti-Jewishness in the struggle against the 'foreigners'. Even if 'these people' had lived in Germany for generations, spoke German, had contributed to German culture and had died for Germany in war they were not and could never be 'German' because they were of a different racial type. The Berlin economics lecturer Eugen Dühring took up this idea in his 1881 book *Die Judenfrage als Rassen- Sitten- und Kulturfrage*, teaching his students that Jews were born inherently inferior and corrupt and could never be compared to the honest, forthright, upstanding German. It was now accepted as scientific fact that racial characteristics were literally determined by the group's native 'soil'. Germans were richly mysterious

Lichtmenschen who had emerged from the ancient dark forests of the north, while the Jews were desert people and therefore shallow, arid, uncreative and parasitic. The 'Jew' became an invention backed by pseudo-scientific facts and as the social stereotype was multi-faceted it could be made to fit any category: Jews could be scapegoats for all Germany's ills.[49] The evils of capitalism, modernity, materialism, corruption, socialism and moral decay could all be heaped conveniently on their shoulders. Furthermore as they were of a 'different race' they could never really become German: the Jew would for ever live 'under the inescapable influence of his blood'.[50]

Before 1878 anti-Semitism in Berlin had been politically unfocused. That year Alfred Stöcker, who equated Jews with socialism and blamed them for rousing the industrial proletariat, founded his Christian Social Party – the first in Berlin history to campaign on a specifically anti-Semitic ticket.[51] By the 1880s the conservatives had recognized the political possibilities of this phenomenon and began to associate themselves with groups such as the Agrarian Association of Landowners, who amongst other things believed that Jews were genetically incapable of farming. The more tolerant attitudes of the early part of the century gave way to increasing tension between Jew and Gentile, with the former coming up against new unofficial barriers in society; as one jurist put it, it was 'the reversal of the Constitution by the administration'.[52] Examples of overt anti-Semitism became more common: the 'Horse-tramway affair' of 1880 flared up when two teachers sitting on a Berlin tram made loud anti-Semitic remarks.[53] After listening to their conversation for a time an outraged Jewish passenger went up to them and asked them to stop. Instead of obliging they insulted him further and the three men began to fight until they were stopped by the police. When the scandal hit the press the public sided with the teachers, whom they saw as perfectly entitled to make such remarks in a public place. One teacher was publicly cheered when he claimed that the fight had been 'part of the historic struggle between the German people and the Jews'.[54]

The fact that the men on the tram were teachers was significant, for all *völkisch* ideas began to find resonance amongst young people through youth movements and in the schools.[55] The first true German youth movement had evolved during the Wars of Liberation against Napoleon, when Jahn had founded the fraternity movement of *Burschenschaften* with the aim of promoting Germanic culture and teaching German youth the importance of their own heritage, but by the end of the century these fraternities had developed a maze of highly codified pseudo-Teutonic rituals of loutish drinking and duelling as proof of loyalty to the Germanic tradition. The emphasis on 'Germanness' meant that foreigners and Jews were excluded from the rituals; no Jews were permitted into fraternities after 1906, nor could they duel with

German nationalists in search of the prized facial scar as they were said to be 'unworthy of a weapon'. The Verein deutscher Studenten or Federation of German Students was modelled on the *Burschenschaften* and promoted nationalistic Pan-German anti-Semitic ideas well into the twentieth century.[56]

The gentler Wandervögel originated in a Gymnasium in the Berlin suburb of Steglitz under the motto 'youth amongst itself'. The modern city was rejected in favour of the virtues of old folk songs, the beauty of nature and the joys of the German landscape. Little bands of young Berliners could now be seen heading out for rambles in the countryside and trips to important German landmarks to 'escape from the brick of Berlin'.[57] Other groups followed suit – from the urban allotment movement and the nudist Naturmenschen to those dedicated to German folklore, whose members scoured the countryside in the search for closed cultural regions untouched by railways, pavements or crowds.[58] A new anti-modern movement, Heimatkunde or 'lore of the homeland', emerged in 1890: its members set out to find their ancient roots on the outskirts of the city under the slogan '*Los von Berlin*' (away from Berlin). But the most important group was that founded by Karl Fischer in the Berlin suburb of Steglitz; he treated the members of the 'Wild Horde' as equals and would hold long discussions in his distinctly urban 'den', but he was revered by his young charges, who greeted him by stretching out their right arms in unison and crying the word '*Heil*' – Fischer would later be seen as the founder-leader of the entire Wandervögel movement. Most of these groups became willing vehicles of the new *völkisch* nationalism, and students and young people who did not comply were targeted by the fanatical members of the Kyffhäuser Verband der Verein deutscher Studenten or VDS, a hypernationalist and monarchist movement determined to rid Germany of all alien influences. Disillusioned with the 'sterility of urban life' these young people felt a deep yearning for some vague 'revolution of the spirit', and a deep desire to 're-Germanize' their country.

These ideas were soon taught in the schools. Teachers had been deeply affected by the crisis of modernity and had lost prestige and influence to the new moneyed middle class. They were only too happy to adopt the views of the new *völkisch* nationalists. Friedrich Diesterweg produced a scheme intended to combat the excessive cosmopolitanism of Berlin in the classroom, claiming that the purpose of education was to 'create German national conviction . . . and the inner feeling of affection for all who speak German, live on German soil', which was to be united with 'the hatred of all things foreign'. In 1881 the General German School Union was formed, an alliance of teachers and academics who wished to promote German language and culture. Eight years later a Prussian royal edict declared that all school texts should be controlled, and rewritten if necessary, to ensure that their content was in keeping with 'the interests of the state'. Children were exposed to the new nationalism from their first years at school to the most advanced classes at university.

The University of Berlin was one of the city's great nineteenth-century triumphs. From meagre beginnings in 1908 it became one of the great European centres of learning and was home to some of the most distinguished scientists, physicians, jurists, sociologists and historians of the age. In 1877 2,000 students matriculated; this number had nearly tripled by the turn of the century.[59] German scholarship, both in Berlin and the other great universities from Heidelberg to Göttingen, went through an explosive period of growth during this time; science departments attracted figures like Hermann von Helmholtz, Rudolf Virchow, Adolf von Harnack, Robert Koch (who in 1905 won the Nobel Prize for his work on tuberculosis and cholera and who ran the Institute of Hygiene of the University of Berlin set up in 1885 and the Royal Institute of Infectious Diseases set up in 1890), Kirchhoff (who developed the spectroscope), Hertz (who discovered radio waves), Röntgen (who discovered X-rays), Ehrlich (who discovered a treatment for syphilis), the psychologist Wilhelm Wundt and the chemist Justus von Liebig. By 1890 there were twice as many academic scientists in Germany as in Britain. The universities were also a great centre for the social sciences, and philosophers like Karl von Hartmann, Wilhelm Dilthey, Ernst Cassirer and Edmund Husserl, sociologists like the founder of the discipline Max Weber, as well as Ferdinand Tönnies and Georg Simmel, historians like Theodor Mommsen, Heinrich von Treitschke, Leopold von Ranke, the biblical scholar Wellhausen, Delitzsch (who deciphered Assyrian and Sumerian and trained most great Assyriologists of the day), economic historians like Schmoller and Brentano and the German linguist Wilhelm Scherer, either worked in Berlin or influenced academic life there.[60] Nevertheless, Berlin University had never resolved its greatest conflict: between *Geist* and *Macht* (spirit and brute force), and sadly the prestige of the university gave academics near godlike status and the licence for some to teach nonsense without being challenged.[61]

It is very difficult for those in Anglo-Saxon cultures to understand the glorification of the German professor which persists to this day. In Berlin it can be traced to the end of the last century, when the image of the professor changed from the grubby tattered figure described by the writer Kurt Tucholsky as the vacant man 'in slouch hat and wrinkled coat' to the figure of great eminence. Humboldt had argued that education, not birth, was to be the 'true qualification of the true nobility' and by the late nineteenth century professors were treated with extraordinary deference. This elite despised anything which hinted of 'vocational study' or the nasty business of making money – which in turn made them enemies of the new rich bourgeoisie of Berlin. It was at this time that novels began to appear in which students would describe the near religious experience of listening to the lecture of a senior professor; the 'pure German man' removed from the dirty world of politics or money, pursuing the higher goal of knowledge. By the end of the century Berlin University had become an avid supporter of German nationalism and *völkisch* ideology and the professors were its chief orators.

The acceptance of these ideas had something to do with the structure of the university and its relationship with the government. The universities were state institutions and professors were state servants who needed government money in order to survive. Some early Ministers of Education actively controlled university appointments to ensure that professors taught the official line; Friedrich Althoff, Prussian Minister of Education from 1897 to 1907, told professors that he would punish them if their views did not coincide with those of the imperial government. In 1899 when Hans Delbrück, professor of history at the University of Berlin, criticized the government's policy of Germanization in Schleswig-Holstein he was put before a disciplinary court and only avoided dismissal because of support from his colleagues and because he delivered a speech to a large audience in support of the government's naval policy.[62] A Social Democrat had little hope of a successful academic career. The law passed in 1898 by the Prussian government declared that 'the deliberate promotion of Social Democratic purposes [was] inconsistent with a teaching post in a royal university'. In fact the law had been specifically designed to deprive Leo Arons, the young physics lecturer at the University of Berlin, of his post because of his active involvement in socialist politics.[63]

Academic appointments were usually political, and men with 'incorrect' views were often denied chairs. Admission to universities was generally restricted to the sons of the conventional *Bildungsbürgertum*, and the procedure for recruiting future *Ordinarien* or holders of chairs meant that the scholar was dependent upon the established professor for whom he wrote his *Habilitation* or second dissertation. This could be blocked by secret vote of the chairholders, thus preventing the candidate from admission into the profession. This led to the exclusion of most people with 'radical' views and of Jews. Anti-Semitism was rampant in Berlin University by the end of the century, and although in 1909 almost 12 per cent of all instructors in the city were Jewish there were far fewer professors, and in that year not a single faculty included a full Jewish professor. When professors began to teach *völkisch* ideas to their students their judgement was rarely questioned and universities became dedicated to preserving the existing power structure.[64] Nowhere was this more clear than in the teaching of history.

After the unification of Germany historians had been expected to help create a new national identity. Conservative historians dominated chairs in Berlin and they were happy to give their new state a coherent version of its past. One of the most influential was Leopold von Ranke, who had demanded that history should be written 'Wie es eigentlich gewesen' or 'as it actually occurred'. For him the proper subject for historical study was the maintenance and growth of the power of the state, particularly the German state, which was for him 'a living, individual, unique self'.[65] Through his work Ranke had unwittingly laid the foundation for the nationalistic Prussian School which emerged at the end of the nineteenth century. Early in their careers younger historians such as Droysen, Sybel and Treitschke had identified themselves with German liberalism and had criticized Ranke's political conservatism, but after unification they switched sides, referring to the primacy of the German state, the importance of the German nation, the superiority of German culture above all others, and even the need for the powerful capital city of Berlin. In his book *Germans and Their Entrance into History* Heinrich von Sybel described how the Germanic religion had come from a deep instinctive understanding of nature, which allowed the *Volk* to shape human history and culture. Aggressive colonial and military policies were defended through carefully selected historical texts; Friedrich Naumann defined nationalism as the urge of the German people to spread their influence over the globe.[66] Others concentrated on Germany's innate superiority and its 'sacred mission to preserve and disseminate German *Kultur*'. Historians like Troeltsch and Hintze extolled the virtues of *Kultur* and claimed that it was proper for Germans to teach the rest of the world about the glories of superior German painting, sculpture, literature and philosophy. The backlash against France was now complete. Berlin no longer had to compete with Paris; she was simply better. For the Teutomaniacs who became the self-appointed guardians of *Kultur* German virgins were more virginal, German loyalty was more selfless and German culture was deeper and richer than that found in Paris or, for that matter, anywhere else.[67]

Heinrich von Treitschke became the most influential of the historians after replacing Ranke as professor of history in Berlin. He was a highly popular figure in the city. Students would queue for hours to get into his lectures, he was greeted with reverential devotion on the street, and his words were copied out and distributed to those who were unlucky enough not to have seen him in person. He was also a German chauvinist and his five-volume *History of Germany in the Nineteenth Century* was filled with calls for Germans to throw off the yoke of the past and immerse themselves in the *Volk*: for him the task of the individual was to 'forget himself and feel part of the whole, he must realize how insignificant his life is compared with the whole'. In 1879 and 1880 he published an influential series of articles in the *Preussische Jahrbücher* in which he advocated the destruction of the socialists, defended permanent poverty of the working class, and warned his students of the scourge of foreigners in Germany. It was here that he wrote those fateful words which would reverberate around Germany in years to come: 'The Jews are our national misfortune.'[68]

Treitschke was also a tireless campaigner for the need to increase Germany's power on the world stage. For over twenty years the historian fuelled nationalistic fervour in Berlin, glorifying war as a German destiny which would allow the nation to purge itself of its 'sins of materialism' and to fulfil its destiny as the dominant power in Europe. He taught future leaders, including Alfred von Tirpitz, the man behind German naval expansion, and Heinrich Class, the founder of the Pan-German League.[69] Cheers erupted in his lecture when he bellowed: 'The State is not an Academy of Art! It is Power!'

The professors and teachers taught their students to admire the military men and the industrialists who ultimately directed the policy of nationalism and chauvinism from their offices a few blocks away from the university. By the turn of the century the dominant culture in Berlin stood for colonial expansion, naval supremacy, suppression of Polish separatism, a 'place in the sun', national unity in the face of the Social Democratic menace; German *Kultur* should be passed on to other nations and Berlin should be purged of 'foreigners and Jews'. Politically these people sought a coalition of all 'state conserving forces', which included everyone from the National Liberals to the extreme right, and they were allied with the Commercial Employees Union, the Pan-German League, the Army League, the Colonial Society, the Navy League, and many other groups whose members shared the love of the *Volkstum* and racial purity, and a deep opposition to parliamentary politics and liberal values. The highly militaristic Pan-German League under Class's presidency had corporate membership of over a hundred other groups and was itself full of politicians, top bureaucrats, university lecturers and the heads of student societies.[70] Even more extreme was the Deutschbund, founded in 1894 by Friedrich Lange, the editor of the *Deutsche Zeitung*, who was consumed by *völkisch* ideology and by racism. Its journal *Rünen* was decorated with the swastika. The aggressive, radical chauvinism finally came to a head in 1914, when, laughing and cheering, Berliners sent their young men off to war, convinced that victory would make their nation the most powerful in the world.

All Europe saw outbursts of nationalism before 1914 but the bluster which emanated from Berlin made the others look positively restrained. Most of its inhabitants supported the national mission and believed that the city would emerge from the coming conflict as the most important and powerful capital on the continent. The widespread acceptance of aggressive foreign policy and militarism boosted the prestige of the leaders in their midst. From the students to the professors, the Junkers and the shopkeepers, the newspaper editors and the politicians Berliners rallied around the Kaiser and his generals and urged them on. Although the rise of virulent nationalism can be traced to the stock market crash of 1873, the military and diplomatic structures which led to war were part of the legacy of Otto von Bismarck.

It would of course be ludicrous to suggest that Bismarck caused the First World War, any more than he was responsible for the rise of Hitler. Unlike his successors he despised the Pan-Germanism and the unpleasant chauvinism which swept the country at the end of the century. He had masterminded three wars but he never believed in Germany's inherent right to dominate her enemies; after the defeat of Austria he had to restrain William I from seizing territory and staging a victory parade in Vienna, and he fell out with Moltke in 1870 for interfering in the latter's plans to subjugate Paris. In a world of five great powers – Germany, France, Austria, Russia and Great Britain – his strategy had been 'always be part of an alliance of three'. Rather, Bismarck made a world war possible because he managed to maintain a retrogressive political structure in an otherwise modern German state. When he was pushed from power there was nobody capable of maintaining his complicated system.

History is littered with great leaders who believe themselves to be indispensable and the Iron Chancellor was one of them. Bismarck had been the elder statesman of Europe for a quarter of a century and when the thirty-year-old William II took the throne he was convinced he would retain his place in the Wilhelmstrasse. He had prepared young William for his role as emperor, teaching the boy that Germany was merely posing as a constitutional state, that as emperor he would be all-powerful, and that the Hohenzollern mystique had given him 'special genius' and 'divine right' to rule, but Bismarck had always assumed that the emperor would continue to rely on him and leave him in charge of political affairs. By supporting William's megalomania he had unwittingly sown the seeds of his own destruction, and it was not long before William grew impatient with the old man of seventy-three whom he referred to as a 'mere servant of the state'. Stöcker once claimed that William had said: 'I will let the old man snuffle about for six months and then I will rule myself,' and Count Waldersee whispered to him, 'If Frederick the Great had such a Chancellor, he would not have been "the Great".'[71]

The first disagreement between the two flared up over differences in social policy; William wanted to introduce legislation to help the poorest worker in the filthiest slum in Berlin by introducing restrictions on child and female labour. Bismarck was utterly opposed to this, calling it 'humanitarian humbug' and claiming that it would merely play into the hands of the socialists, and he succeeded in barring the motion.[72] In retaliation William began to ignore him, and when Bismarck tried to reintroduce an old decree of 1852 which stated that Prussian ministers could not talk to the Kaiser without him present William demanded that it be withdrawn at once. Tension mounted and, keen to put the young pup in his place, Bismarck purposely let him see papers in which the tsar had called the emperor 'a badly-brought-up man of bad faith'.[73] William left defeated, but three days later he challenged Bismarck's authority in foreign policy. Bismarck threatened to resign as he had done so many times before under the old Kaiser. This time William called his bluff, and on 18 March 1890 accepted his resignation. The moment was captured in a *Punch* political cartoon, one of the greatest ever sketched, entitled *Dropping the Pilot*. It showed the feckless young Kaiser leaning nonchalantly against the railing of a great ship, smoke curling from a cigar, watching the old Bismarck, dressed in a naval outfit, descending the gangplank.[74]

Bismarck was devastated by this turn of events and bitter at those colleagues who had let him down. He left Berlin as quickly as possible, stopping only to remove hundreds of packing cases of documents and a few thousand bottles of wine from the Chancellery cellar; on 28 March he laid a bunch of roses on William I's grave, 'saying goodbye to my old master'. On 29 March he left Berlin. Baffled crowds lined the streets of the city and a guard of honour saw him off, but the young Kaiser did not turn up. From his lonely exile Bismarck continued to spout smouldering insults at the Kaiser; he would even turn coins over so he would not have to see William's 'false face'. But his days in power were over.[75]

From that moment William sabotaged Bismarck's reputation whenever possible. He managed to keep him out of Berlin for the most part but was horrified when Bismarck accepted Kuno von Moltke's invitation to come to the capital to celebrate his birthday. Berliners knew little of the rift between William and the Iron Chancellor and on 21 January 1894 Bismarck made a triumphant return through the Brandenburg Gate and along Unter den Linden to the steps of the palace. To keep up appearances William went out amid the cheering of the crowd, who broke into loud renditions of *Deutschland, Deutschland über Alles*, but once inside the palace he ignored the old man, banishing him to his estate at Friedrichsruh. Bismarck's home became a place of pilgrimage for fanatical youth groups and nationalistic organizations, whose members he would toast from his balcony with a glass of champagne, but that was the sole extent of his involvement in the Germany which he had done so much to create. Fontane later said that the power of the Hohenzollern monarchy had been stronger than both Bismarck's 'genius and his falsehoods'. When he died in December 1897 he was not given a state funeral but was buried quietly at Friedrichsruh. William was forced to attend for publicity's sake but he was sullen and rude and refused to speak to the family. When the great monument to Bismarck was unveiled in Berlin on 16 June William was reluctant to appear. The Kaiser's treatment of Bismarck led the French ambassador to exclaim angrily that 'Whatever the Germans say or do they will never be a great people.'

With Bismarck finally buried there was nothing to keep William in check; there was no imperial Cabinet, the Chancellor and the Foreign Secretary could merely advise him, and he had complete control over the army. Only the tsar of Russia and the sultan of the Ottoman empire possessed such power; it was a ridiculous state of affairs in a modern industrial state. Dazzled by his own omnipotence, surrounded by sycophants who did not dare to criticize him, and convinced of his personal link to God, William II set out on the road to war to become, as his uncle Edward VII would say, 'the most brilliant failure in history'.

It was Mirabeau who said, 'war is the national industry of Prussia', but if the army had been powerful before William II it became ever more arrogant in the final years of the empire. Officers justified their behaviour by reminding critics that Germany would not have been unified and Berlin would still be a provincial capital had it not been for them. The 1871 victory of the Prussian army was called a 'moral triumph', a glorious *Sieg* which had been predetermined by history as a reward for German excellence. Gustav Rümelin called it 'one of the guiding lights of humanity . . . history hardly provides us with a more impressive event than this change of scene in the world theatre, as the hitherto dominant people steps behind the curtain and another long kept standing in the wings steps to the centre of the stage'. According to Gustav Freytag, never before had any army had 'such warmth, such inspiration and such a deep poetic sense of the fact that the dreadful work of the battlefield served a higher ethical purpose'. The victory was 'predetermined', 'logical', 'righteous' and 'just'. The new industrialists, ever keen to expand their armaments industries, joined forces with the Junkers, and when that mercurial genius Nietzsche warned that this frenzy would end in disaster or defeat, 'the defeat, even the death, of German culture' for the benefit of the German empire his warning fell on deaf ears.

Between 1900 and 1914 Germany's defence and foreign policy decisions under the Kaiser became ever more inept and inflammatory. Berlin had become the largest and wealthiest capital of the most powerful nation on the European continent, but for all the self-congratulatory talk few understood the responsibilities that such a position brought with it. Instead of respecting the fears of their neighbours Germans became ever more keen to wave their flags, sing their national songs and extol the virtues of the German race. Berliners from all walks of life soaked up propaganda outlining the importance of the Teutons' historical struggle against the Gauls or the Slavs. Although none of the great powers really wanted to discuss arms limitation at The Hague in 1899 or 1907, it was the delegation from Berlin which claimed that it would be 'unfair' on Germany.[76] A terrible lack of trust grew between the giants but criticism of Berlin's foreign policy fell on deaf ears; in his last speech in the Reichstag Bebel said:

> There will be a catastrophe ... sixteen to eighteen million men, the flower of different nations, will march against each other, equipped with lethal weapons. But I am convinced that this great march will be followed by the great collapse (*at this moment many in the chamber began to laugh*) – all right, you have laughed about it before; but it will come ... What will be the result? After this war we shall have mass bankruptcy, mass misery, mass unemployment and great famine. Are you denying this?[77]

He was drowned out by laughter in the chamber. Finally from a right-wing bench came the self-assured reply. 'Herr Bebel, things always get better after every war.' With this attitude prevailing in the corridors of power in Berlin, it is easy to understand how the stream of foreign policy blunders led to war.

The first of these mistakes can be dated to 1890, when it became clear that Bismarck's carefully crafted foreign policy was going to be allowed to unravel.[78] The Kaiser's main adviser was the shady and mysterious Baron von Holstein, who had been Bismarck's friend until he realized the Iron Chancellor was about to fall, when he shifted allegiance to the Kaiser's friends Count Philipp Friedrich, Prince zu Eulenburg and Bernhard von Bülow. Through them he increased his influence at the Foreign Office, dictating policy to the new Chancellor Caprivi from his dark office at 76 Wilhelmstrasse. Holstein rarely went out, avoided publicity and official functions, met the Kaiser only twice despite numerous invitations to the palace, and was commonly referred to as the 'Monster of the Labyrinth'.[79] But in 1890 it was he who allowed the three-year Reinsurance Treaty with Russia to lapse, pushing Russia straight into the arms of France.[80]

The Reinsurance Treaty had a complex history but in essence it stated that if either Russia or Germany was attacked, the other would at least remain neutral. With the treaty no longer in force, the Russian bear became an active threat on Germany's eastern flank. France rushed to take advantage of the mistake and by July 1890 the French commander Admiral Gervais was holding up his glass in Moscow, announcing grandly: 'I drink to Holy Moscow, the great Russian nation and its noble Tsar.'[81] France and Russia now hemmed Germany in on both fronts. It is some measure of William's lack of judgement that he did nothing to reverse this disastrous error. Worse still, he chose this moment to begin to alienate Germany's most natural ally, Britain.

When my Hanoverian ancestors enthused about a foreign nation it would invariably be Britain. They served its kings and fought its wars as allies; my great-great-great-great-great-great-grandfather, Bernhard von Moltke, lost two of his sons at Waterloo. Many Hanoverians emulated the British way of life, travelled in Britain, were educated there and married there, but this easy friendship was also true of the great merchant families in the Hanseatic cities, which had long histories of trade with Britain, and even of Berlin, which had old diplomatic and military links with the country. Nineteenth-century Berliners might have been jealous of Queen Victoria and of the wealth and breadth of the British empire but they wanted to emulate it, not destroy it. For their part the British might have found their Teutonic cousins somewhat provincial but they were certainly preferable to their old revolutionary enemy, the French, and to the autocratic Russians. However, William was able to destroy the bond of centuries in only two decades.

William had always vacillated between a sentimental love for his mother's country and intense jealousy of it. He was both fascinated and infuriated by his relatives but he became increasingly frustrated by the effortless power of the British empire and reacted by showing off. At a 1903 dinner for former Prussian and Hanoverian officers he bellowed: 'We must never forget that the German legions and the German troops of Blücher on the day of Waterloo saved the British Army and the Duke of Wellington from annihilation' – an outburst which was neither tactful nor historically accurate. In many ways William's problems with Britain stemmed directly from a rivalry with his uncle Bertie (who became King Edward VII) which first became apparent during yacht racing at Cowes.

During the early 1890s William visited Cowes almost every year, but his behaviour was consistently rude and erratic. He insisted that official functions be carried out by rank so that he, not the Prince of Wales, would be treated as the most important guest. When he lost a race in 1895 he did the unthinkable and lodged a complaint about the club rules. When Bertie vowed never to race with him again William decided to start his own regatta at Kiel. His experiment was a flop. With his brass bands and heel-clicking officers William could never hope to emulate the easy, relaxed atmosphere of the British event, and his invitations were only accepted by minor nobility and wealthy Americans impressed by a royal invitation. The failure only encouraged William to search for a way to impress the British. He began sending messages to the British navy, in which he held honorary rank, explaining how they could improve their ships; upon receiving one of these papers Lord Salisbury commented to Lord George Hamilton that it rather looked as if the Kaiser was not 'all there'. He later asked Queen Victoria to recommend that William adopt 'calmness, both in his policy and in the speeches which he too often makes'.

In the age of imperialism, with its emphasis on overseas trade and colonial expansion, it was assumed, first by theorists like MacMahon and then by virtually everybody else, that the nation with the greatest navy would also be the greatest power. Admiral von Tirpitz, who had been Treitschke's student at the university, persuaded William that the only way Germany would ever compete with Britain was to have a powerful fleet of battleships.[82] In the past Prussia had shown little interest in the sea, its power having been backed by the army. The Prussian Admiralty was created in 1853, but at that time it had no ships, no officers, no seamen and no serious naval base until Bismarck captured Kiel in 1863. But William II was encouraged to change this state of affairs. The First Navy Law was passed in 1898 and called for the construction of nineteen ships. On 12 June 1900 – despite opposition from socialists in the Reichstag including August Bebel and Karl Liebknecht, who opposed the rise in taxes needed to pay for the ships – the second was passed by 201 votes to 103. Over the next five years a battleship would be launched every four months, and William told officers of the Berlin garrison: 'As my grandfather did for the army, so will I for my navy.'[83]

The nationalism which had developed in Berlin since the economic crash led to support for the Kaiser's expansionist naval policy. Pan-German groups wanted to acquire more colonies, trading posts and the other trappings of greatness. 'To say that Germany should cease its *Weltpolitik*', William said, 'is like a father telling his son: If only you would not grow, you troublesome youth, then I would not need to buy you longer trousers.' Sitting in his headquarters in Berlin Admiral Tirpitz declared that German overseas expansion was 'as irresistible as a law of nature'. Ernst Hasse, the founder of the Pan-German League, echoed the dominant view when he said, 'we want territory even if it belongs to foreigners, so that we may shape the future according to our needs'. The situation demanded 'more battleships'. The Boer War gave Tirpitz the excuse he needed to double the order.

Berliners first heard of the impending war through news of the Kaiser's infamous 'Kruger telegram'. When Jameson raided the settlers Berlin papers heaped abuse on the British, charging them with trying to crush the 'plucky little Boers' and exclaiming that Germany would never allow them to 'stamp out the Transvaal'.[84] The Kaiser had wanted to send an expeditionary force to Africa but was persuaded only to send a much publicized telegram to Kruger which read: 'I express my sincere congratulations that . . . you have succeeded by your own energetic action against armed bands [the British] which invaded your country.' Berlin papers happily endorsed the Transvaal's bid for independence against the British and congratulated themselves for finally taking part in international relations in a way which befitted a *Weltmacht*. The British were furious and Londoners vented their anger by smashing German shop windows. The popular image of Germany began to change for the worse.

Relations between Britain and Germany deteriorated further during the Boxer Rebellion in China. This erupted suddenly in 1900 when Chinese activists, resentful of foreign domination, forced Europeans to take shelter in the diplomatic quarter of Peking. William had wanted to crush it and to avenge the death of the German minister Baron von Ketteler, and sent a German expeditionary force with the words: 'Take no prisoners! Kill him when he falls into your hands ... even as, a thousand years ago, the Huns under Attila made such a name for themselves as still resounds in legend and story, so may the name of German resound through Chinese history for a thousand years.'[85] The Germans arrived too late to be of any use and annoyed the British force by goose-stepping around Peking in large straw hats which Waldersee described as 'some Berlin tailor's idea of appropriate headdress ... for a campaign in the East'.[86] The only thing William accomplished was to burden the German army with the term 'Hun' for decades to come. But Germany's fear of annoying Russia led to the decision not to back British policy in China in 1901, a decision which did little to endear Germany to the British.[87]

By the turn of the century the British had shifted their alliance in Europe away from Germany and in 1904 signed a convention with France and in 1907 an *entente* with the Russians. When the King met Tsar Nicholas II in Estonia in 1908 they got along so well that he spontaneously made him an admiral of the fleet. William complained bitterly about the 'evil encirclement' of his country, but even now he seemed oblivious to the fact that the new alliances which threatened Germany were at least in part the direct result of his own actions.

The following year Berlin papers were filled with the bizarre story of the 'Endangered German' of Morocco, an event which marked the next stage of German isolation. Tension had been mounting for years between France and Germany over the control of Morocco. In 1880 a convention signed by France, Spain, Germany, Italy, Britain and the United States had supported the idea of Moroccan independence but in 1911 the French had claimed that her citizens were in danger in Fez and required the protection of a French expeditionary force. If France could take the north, what was preventing Germany from taking the south which, it was rumoured, contained untapped mineral resources?

The problem was that there were no Germans living there. Bethmann-Hollweg set out to convince the rest of Europe that there were and persuaded William to send the battleship *Panther* to Agadir while he ordered a poor

German by the name of Herr Wilburg to walk the seventy-five gruelling miles from Mogador to Agadir. When the half-starved wretch finally arrived at the beach he was picked up 'under the protection of the German Navy'. German newspapers cheered the bravery of their men and printed detailed stories of the 'Endangered German' and the mythical settlers supposedly under attack by local tribesmen. Nationalists took to the streets yelling, 'Western Morocco to be German! When do we march?' But by mid August it had become clear that no other European power was ready to risk war for the German claim and on 4 November 1911 Germany backed down. The Kaiser was given a 'useless slice of the Congo'. Berlin erupted in furious protest, and even liberal newspapers printed stories describing how the French had besmirched German honour and made her a laughing stock. Sir Edward Grey, the British Foreign Minister, commented, 'out of this mountain of a German-made crisis came a mouse of colonial territory in Africa', but when Bethmann-Hollweg went to the Reichstag to explain the situation he was shouted down from all sides of the chamber. The Agadir crisis increased tension between Britain and Germany; as Winston Churchill said, 'Germany's action at Agadir has put her in the wrong and forced us to consider her claims in the light of her policy and methods.'[88] Germany had made another powerful enemy.

Many Berliners now believed propaganda which claimed that the other European powers were merely trying to keep Germany weak, and many became more shrill in their demands for increased global power. It was at this time that Max Weber commented on the changes in his countrymen, noting 'the striking lack of grace and dignity in the overt bearing of the German'. Newspapers were filled with conspiracy theories about the treachery of their neighbours.[89] Bertie, the 'Great Encircler', had died in 1910, and the British had made an attempt to come to an understanding with Germany by sending British War Minister Richard Haldane to Berlin in February 1912 to talk to Bethmann-Hollweg, Tirpitz and the Kaiser. The talks had faltered because the Germans had demanded a pledge of British neutrality in the event of any future Franco-German war.[90] It was not yet clear whether Britain would intervene in a future conflict but war between Germany, Austria, Russia and France seemed a foregone conclusion. In December 1912, as war raged between Montenegran, Serbian, Bulgarian and Greek forces aligned against Turkey, the British sent a warning to Germany not to interfere on the side of Austria should the latter attack Serbia. The Kaiser was furious and held a 'war council' on 8 December with Tirpitz, Moltke, Heeringen of the Naval Staff and Müller, chief of the Naval Cabinet, during which he condemned the British attitude and accepted the principle of a preventative war against Russia; Moltke approved with the words 'the sooner the better'. It was Bethmann-Hollweg who tried to regain British confidence by searching for a diplomatic solution to the Balkan crisis.[91]

Nevertheless, the military build-up, the international rivalries, the tensions in the Balkans, the increasing German fear of Russia and talk of preventative war led to a feeling by the long hot summer of 1914 that a war in Europe was now inevitable.[92] Elegant ladies dining at Borchardt's would talk of the coming war as if it were merely a social engagement and young men yearned for the chance to get into uniform and march in the name of Germany. It was now a matter of time.

The international fiascos which dogged the Kaiser in the years leading to the First World War were paralleled by a number of domestic incidents played out in Berlin. The rapid expansion in Berlin's population had not been matched by an increase in food production, and the state's support of rural producers in order to win their support for a naval build-up raised the cost of basic foods in the city. This in turn led to unrest in Berlin, particularly in 1903 and in 1912, which in turn fuelled the rapid expansion of support for the Social Democrats. It was not surprising that in 1912, the year of the second crisis, the socialists won the majority of the vote in the city and more seats – 110 out of 397 – than any other party in Germany. In Berlin districts socialist candidates were now regularly obtaining between 55 and 90 per cent of the vote although they were blocked from exercising a predominant role in local politics and had only one Social Democratic deputy that year.[93] Power still lay very much in the hands of the Kaiser, the Junkers and the industrialists, who were increasingly concerned about the menace from the left, but the constitutional crisis which had brought about Bismarck's downfall had not been solved, and neither the Kaiser nor Bismarck's successors – whether Caprivi or Hohenlohe or von Bülow – were able to overcome the growing divisions between the Chancellor, the Reichstag, the Kaiser and his court, the Prussian ministries and the state governments, powerful industrialists and landowners and smaller interest groups. Most worrying for Berlin's elite and its middle class was that it could no longer rival the left in terms of the sheer number of voters. Rather than compromise William continuously attacked the left, calling their supporters untrustworthy and disloyal, which only served to alienate them still further; he was aided by his sycophantic Chancellor von Bülow, for whom the greatest task of the nation was 'combatting Social Democracy and making it obsolete'.[94] At the same time William tried to whip up patriotic support by holding grand celebrations such as the commemoration of the bicentenary of Frederick the Great's birth, while the conservative press increased coverage of the armaments race, naval expansion and colonial aggrandizement. William was becoming increasingly rash; when he returned from pleasure trips such as his journey to Palestine he ordered Berlin to be hung with flags as to greet a victorious war hero and in 1906 Zedlitz wrote that 'The Emperor is more autocratic than ever'. Although he was still popular with the general public the Kaiser's credibility was being increasingly challenged. One of the most damaging in a series of incidents was the Eulenburg affair of 1906, during which an unscrupulous editor tried to expose the rot at the palace.[95]

In the years before the war one of the great pleasures of the middle class was to read boulevard newspapers filled with endless stories about the royals. Magazines such as the *Berliner illustrirte Zeitung* were packed with pictures of 'The Kaiser hunting at Sandringham' or 'Princess Auguste Victoria of Schleswig-Holstein-Sonderburg-Augustenburg attending the *Hofball*', with polite court gossip and in-depth discussions of the latest in royal fashion. There was satire too; *Kladderadatsch* always contained a sprinkling of cartoons poking fun at the Kaiser's bizarre pronouncements and his penchant for dressing up in ridiculous uniforms, but details of his personal life and those of his family and friends were taboo. All that changed when Maximilian Harden appeared on the scene.

Harden was the son of a Berlin silk manufacturer who became interested in politics at a young age. He had an obsessive hatred of the Kaiser, and in 1892 founded the newspaper *Die Zukunft* (The Future) in order to launch an attack on the Hohenzollerns and the servile bourgeoisie. Ironically his hatred was fuelled by a resentful Bismarck, who was quite happy to feed Harden with gossip after being dropped by the young Kaiser. Harden published dozens of critical articles but his circulation remained too small to have much effect on public opinion. If he was going to do serious damage he needed a German 'diamond necklace affair', a juicy scandal which would cause maximum embarrassment to the royal family. His chance came in 1906.

In that year the Kaiser fired Baron von Holstein, who was brought into contact with the editor by their mutual hatred of the Kaiser and his entourage. It was too dangerous to attack William II directly so they targeted his friends – in particular Prince Philipp Eulenburg.

Eulenburg was a member of one of the oldest and most respected of Prussian noble families. He was tall, handsome and elegant, witty and fun, and he kept the Kaiser entertained, encouraging him to dress up in ever more outlandish costumes or helping him to design new belts, chin-straps and other features on the uniforms of the armed forces. Although he had held a couple of important diplomatic posts his chief talent, according to one friend, was his 'unequalled gift for anecdote by which he could entertain the Emperor from morning until night' and his 'endless fund of stories and jokes of every nuance'. His friendship with the self-proclaimed '*Allerhöchsteselber*' – the All-Highest – made him an easy target.

Holstein was convinced that Eulenburg exerted a harmful influence on the Kaiser and that the group of prominent men, the Liebenburg Round Table, which met regularly at Eulenburg's palace, cultivated 'treasonous contacts' with the French and British governments. Above all, he erroneously believed that Eulenburg had been the architect of his downfall. The editor Harden saw in Holstein's information the makings of a sexual scandal which would rock the throne. In June 1907 he published an article in which he accused Prince Philipp Eulenburg and Count Kuno von Moltke, aide-de-camp to the emperor, of homosexual tendencies, referring to Moltke's *Süsslichkeit* or 'sweetness'. By so doing he broke one of the most sacred taboos in imperial Germany.

At the time there was considerable hypocrisy surrounding homosexuality in Germany; on the one hand it was so common amongst the upper classes, particularly in the elite Prussian officer corps, that it was known abroad as 'the German vice.'[96] However, the boulevard newspapers studiously avoided compromising the elite. In retrospect, newspaper restraint had been extraordinary, particularly when scandal threatened to touch the Kaiser. Fritz Krupp, a good friend of William's and the heir to the family fortune, was well known for his homosexuality.[97] When not playing in his erotic grotto on the isle of Capri he travelled around the Mediterranean searching for young men, whom he then sent with letters of introduction to the elegant Hotel Bristol in Berlin. The boys would be hired without question on the understanding that when Krupp came to stay they would be temporarily released from their duties to take part in his orgies. Krupp's penchant for young men only became public after the Social Democratic paper *Vorwärts* published an article describing exactly why he had been banished from Capri, and Krupp committed suicide rather than face trial.[98] Despite the considerable evidence against him most newspapers fastidiously defended him: *Der Tag* wrote that the Social Democrats were guilty of 'barbarism' and had 'savagely made Fritz a hunted animal'. The Kaiser accused them of having 'murdered a gallant member of the Reich'.[99] Without media coverage the sordid affair was soon forgotten.

Such incidents were not unique. When William was visiting the estate of his friend Prince Maximilian Egon zu Fürstenberg, the chief of the Reich Military Cabinet, General Count Dietrich von Hülsen-Häseler, appeared at the fête dressed in a pink ballet tutu adorned with a wreath of roses. He whirled gracefully around the room, stopped in front of the Kaiser for his farewell bow, and suddenly dropped dead of a heart attack. Rigor mortis had set in before the guests had the presence of mind to dress the general in his uniform; even so Hülsen-Häseler was given a sombre funeral with full military honours.[100] The reluctance to report on people's private lives extended to heads of state. At the time it was known that the king of Württemberg was in love with a mechanic, the king of Bavaria with a coachman, Franz Joseph's brother

Archduke Ludwig Viktor – 'Luzi-Wuzi' – with a masseur, and that William's own son Prince Eitel Fritz was homosexual. Hundreds of eminent citizens were under investigation by the German Criminal Commissioner for breaching Article 175 of the Criminal Code but there was never a hint that the findings would be made public. The disclosures about Eulenburg and Moltke certainly did not surprise anyone 'in the know', but for a city fed on a diet of bourgeois morality the revelations were shocking. *Die Welt am Montag* now wrote about '*die perverse Kamarilla*' accused of bringing down the liberal Chancellor Caprivi and in *Die Zukunft* of 17 November 1907 Harden wrote that Eulenburg was 'an unhealthy late romantic visionary' who encouraged the Kaiser in the dangerous belief that he was infallible and 'incomparably blessed'. The Kaiser realized the potential danger and quickly cut himself off from his friends, publicly stripping them of their rank and threatening to banish them from their estates. The whole thing would probably have been forgotten had Kuno von Moltke not exhibited considerable lack of judgement by calling for a civil action against Harden. It became one of the most sensational trials in Berlin history.

Harden had been gathering information on the Kaiser's entourage for over a decade, using servants, highly placed courtiers and other informants who were dotted strategically around Berlin. His extensive sources enabled him to keep detailed dossiers on anyone of potential interest and he used his information to maximum effect. During the trial he astounded the public by claiming that the entire imperial court was poisoned by a 'heady romantic atmosphere' and implied that nobody, least of all the Kaiser, had a grasp on political reality. Most sensational of all were his colourful 'eye witness' accounts of Moltke and Eulenburg, including a description of the two men meeting in the forest. Harden managed to provoke four lengthy court cases using allegations of sexual misconduct to attack the political elite; this included the introduction of over sixty witnesses – among them a fisherman who at the age of seventeen had taken Prussian noblemen out on the lake, where they had done 'dirty things'.[101] Harden's real aim was not to reveal homosexuality at court, but rather to expose the influence that this group of noblemen had over the Kaiser. Some continued to defend William's circle. Count Robert Zedlitz-Trutzschler wrote: 'it appears that neither in the case of Prince Eulenburg nor that of Count Moltke is there any evidence ... this whole thing is simply the result of moral fanaticism which only breeds hypocrisy'. A friend of Eulenburg's later said that it was a shame he had not 'horsewhipped or shot' Harden immediately, because 'the good people assume the truth of all the accusations which this clever, but none too scrupulous a writer has brought against him'. But the evidence against the accused had been overwhelming and the trials had exposed a world of homosexuality, blackmail and deceit which had hitherto been kept from the general public. The notion that the Kaiser was surrounded by dangerous men of dubious character persisted.

The Kaiser's reputation was further damaged by the 'Daily Telegraph affair' of 1908, in which foreign and domestic policy overlapped. The text of informal conversations between the Kaiser and Major General Stuart-Wortley during William's visit to England, during which the Kaiser had tried to patch up Anglo-German relations, were written up by the latter, sent to and apparently sanctioned for publication by the Foreign Office. The text of the 'interview' was given to the English Daily Telegraph, and it caused a sensation.[102] Far from improving relations between the two countries the Kaiser's remarks annoyed everyone. He upset the Russians and the French by claiming that they had proposed a coalition against the British during the Boer War; he worried the Japanese by suggesting that his large navy was essential to 'guard against eventualities in the east'; he infuriated the British by claiming that they had consistently undermined his sincere attempts to improve relations between the two countries, and angered Germans by implying that he had no faith in parliament and had supported the British in the Boer War (an unpopular cause in Germany). The British Foreign Secretary Grey wrote: 'The German Emperor . . . is like a battleship with the steam up and screws going, but with no rudder, and he will run into something some day and cause a catastrophe.'[103]

The Eulenburg and Telegraph affairs caused many of his subjects to doubt William's ability to lead. His position was not helped by the fact that rather than go to Hamm, where 300 men had been killed in a mining accident shortly after the Telegraph affair, he remained on a hunting trip. This apparent callousness annoyed many and the Austrian ambassador was surprised to find that Berliners had temporarily turned against their Kaiser: 'Never before in Prussian history have all circles been captured by such deep resentment against their sovereign.' The socialists immediately demanded more restrictions on the monarchy and even conservatives criticized him openly. The Berliner Tageblatt wrote: 'the events of the last few days have made it clear that the German people will not continue to allow their vital interests to depend on the mood of a single individual whose impulsiveness they have once again had the opportunity to witness.' The Kaiser was astounded by these attacks but rather than change he blamed von Bülow for the recent disasters and fired him.

The Bismarckian system was now breaking down. William II was also becoming concerned about the relative weakness of his army and when on 2 December 1911 Helmuth von Moltke 'the younger' advised him that in a future war 'the decisive events will be on land and will be brought about by the army' he introduced an Army Law to fund his military machine: 'I intend to put through this Army Bill, cost what it may . . . I'll see that drivelling Reichstag be damned if it opposes me!' When the 'Zabern affair' broke out in 1913, in which officers in part of Alsace were accused of bullying the local population, Berliners began to grumble about the excessive power of the military.[104] This coincided with an economic recession which saw rising unemployment and price increases. Many, including the new Chancellor Bethmann-Hollweg, were terrified that the left might seek to win the support of the disillusioned middle classes and the General Staff recommended countering Germany's domestic problems by preparing for war, arguing that nothing would rally the population behind the Kaiser more quickly than a victory over France or Russia. Reports of foreign 'encirclement' and 'treachery' became more frequent in the Berlin press, and there was much talk of Russia's decision to build fortresses along their western frontier, of France's introduction of three years of military service and of the instability of the crumbling Austro-Hungarian empire. The American artist Marsden Hartley, who came to the city in 1913, captured something of this cult of the warrior in works such as *Officer in Berlin*, filled with badges and regalia and uniforms then so prevalent in the city, which he painted for his lover, the young officer Kurt von Freyburg.[105] For such men war was nothing less than the ultimate glorious adventure, and they thirsted for battle. Finally, the long hoped for event arrived in the form of the Balkan crisis of 1914.

It was Bismarck who said that it would be 'some damned fool thing in the Balkans' which would ignite the next war. His prophecy was fulfilled when, on 28 June 1914, Archduke Franz Ferdinand of Austria was assassinated by the Bosnian Serb Gavrilo Princip, setting in motion a flurry of diplomatic activity which led to war. On 28 July Austria declared war on Serbia, bombarding Belgrade and goading Russia into the conflict. On 1 August Germany declared war on Russia, and two days later on France. The 'War to End All Wars' became the most bloody, wasteful conflict the world had yet known, but each of these powers entered with bravado and confidence. France had waited forty-three years for revenge against the German 'criminals of 1871', Russia was eager to stop the rot after defeat in the far east in 1905 and humiliation in the Balkans in 1908, and the Austro-Hungarians were willing to fight to keep their crumbling empire together.

Berliners, who had only months before shown some doubt about their Kaiser, were thrilled by the prospect of war and rallied behind him; indeed it brought all Berliners together under one banner for the first time in history. Each group wanted something different from the conflict. The Junkers and military saw the inevitable victory as a chance to increase prestige and maintain their hold on power. The government hoped it would divert attention from domestic problems. Berlin industrialists wanted the chance to produce weapons, rolling stock, electrical goods, chemicals and textiles and increase their markets abroad. Youth groups welcomed war as an escape from the boredom of a comfortable but stifling bourgeois world. Socialists and workers viewed war as a chance to speed the creation of a democratic Germany and finish off despotic Russia and the mighty British empire. Whatever their motives, the vast majority of the people and all parties from the Centre Party to the Social Democrats were caught up in the patriotic fervour – even the left-wing anti-war campaigners melted away. Walther Rathenau would later ask: 'Who were those who cheered jubilantly on 1 August, 1914? It was almost everybody . . . There were many good Socialists among them.'

Berliners supported the war effort with gusto. When on 31 July Germany issued an ultimatum to Russia to demobilize within forty-eight hours or face war the mood was one of excited expectation. From early on the morning of 1 August Berliners gathered on Unter den Linden and milled around outside the Kaiser's palace, their nervous but excited expressions captured for ever in Max Beckmann's terse drypoint *Declaration of War 1914*. They waited by newspaper kiosks for the latest edition, and even factory workers came out of the back streets, their socialist rhetoric fading with the prospect of war with the 'Slavic hordes' of Russia. At five o'clock a policeman appeared at the palace gate. The Russians had not responded to the ultimatum. Mobilization was announced.

Suddenly the mood changed. The crowd struck up the national anthem. People began to cheer hysterically, hugging one another and waving banners and flags, hooting horns and whistles and waving handkerchiefs.[106] Mobs went to the Russian embassy and hit the ambassador and his party in the face with sticks. 'Russian spies' were beaten to death in the centre of the city. Rumours abounded that the Russians had poisoned the water at the Müggelsee or that they were running around the city disguised as women. Spy fever would later extend to the other Allied powers; in some cases innocent people were simply seized on the street and summarily shot.[107]

Mobilization transformed the face of Berlin. The army came under federal jurisdiction and Berlin was at the centre of the III Corps district of Brandenburg; most young recruits joined the Fifth and Sixth Divisions (III Brandenburg Corps) and the Fifth and Sixth Reserve (III Reserve Corps) as well as the Prussian Guard.[108] Men hurried to their designated depots and were issued with uniforms and arms. They formed companies which became battalions, joined by cavalry, cyclists, artillery, medical units, cook wagons and blacksmith wagons, all of which were sent to points along the frontier. Berlin was the nerve centre of a vast operation involving thousands of trains and millions of men, and when troops marched through the streets on their way to the train stations with their rifles and spiked helmets and rucksacks Berliners lined the streets, cheered and threw flowers. On the eve of war the actress Tilla Durieux wrote

> Every face looks happy: We've got war! Bands in the cafés and res-
> taurants play *Heil dir im Siegerkranz* and *Die Wacht am Rhein* without
> stopping, and everybody has to listen to them standing up. One's
> food gets cold, one's beer gets warm: No matter – we've got war!
> People line up to offer their motorcars for service ... Soldiers at the
> railway stations are offered mountains of buttered sandwiches, saus-
> ages and chocolate. There's a super-abundance of everything: of
> people, of food, and of enthusiasm![109]

Berliners began chalking slogans on everything: EVERY SHOT WILL HIT A
RUSSIAN, or EVERY STAB WILL DOWN A FRENCHMAN were popular.
Berlin's cosmopolitan era was over. All foreign place names were changed: the
Café Piccadilly became the Fatherland Café, the Hotel Bristol on Unter den
Linden vanished; the Hotel Westminster became the Lindenhof, the Cumberland Hotel could keep its name because the Duke of Cumberland was related
by marriage to the Kaiser, but the *Confiserie* sign had to go. The word *Chauffeur*
was banned and replaced first by 'Power Wagon Driver' but later by the term
Schauffoer; the word *bonbon* was targeted until a Breslau confectioner said he
would only stop using the term if the officer who gave the order stopped
calling himself by the French word 'general' – so the word *bonbon* remained.

The frenzied outpouring of emotion in Berlin made reactions in Petersburg
or Vienna look bland by comparison. Berliners chose to believe that their
country was fighting a 'legitimate war', a 'defensive war', but above all they
wanted to prove that their nation had to be taken seriously on the world stage.
It may have been this belief in their own righteousness, in the blamelessness
of the German army, that prompted Berliners to support the single event
which would damn Berlin in the minds of other Europeans – the invasion of
neutral Belgium.

It was clear from the outset that war would not be confined to Russia.
The interlocking system of European alliances made it inevitable that Germany
would fight a war on two fronts, against both Russia and France. Based on
the principle of concentration of forces, Count Alfred von Schlieffen, who had
been chief of the General Staff from 1891 to 1906, had decreed that in a
two-front war Germany must first destroy France and then turn to the powerful
but poorly organized Russian army. The French campaign would, he had said,
take six weeks. To use his favourite expression, it would inflict a 'modern
Cannae' – the total annihilation of the enemy – in the west. Nevertheless, it
would mean going through Belgium.[110]

The Germans offered Belgium a choice. If she did not resist the German army she would be offered independence after the war and perhaps territory carved from France as a reward. If she blocked their path she would be treated as an enemy. Belgium chose the second option. At six o'clock on the morning of 4 August 1914 Herr von Bülow delivered a note to the Foreign Office saying that in view of the rejection of his government's 'well intentioned proposals' Germany would be obliged to invade.

The Reichstag gathered in Berlin. After a rousing service in the new cathedral the deputies marched across the road to the Great White Room in the palace. The Kaiser stood up. 'The war', he declared, 'has been provoked by Serbia with the support of Russia.' 'Shame!' they all yelled. After decrying the encirclement of Germany he continued: 'From this day on I recognize no parties but only Germans!' and he called upon party leaders to step forward and shake his hand. Amid 'wild excitement' all did.[111] Then, at two minutes past eight that morning, the first wave of field grey broke over the Belgian frontier at Gemmerich, thirty miles from Liège. Belgian gendarmes in their sentry boxes opened fire. The war in the west had begun.[112]

'You will be home before the leaves have fallen from the trees,' the Kaiser told departing Berlin troops in that first week of August. With Bismarck's decisive wars still in their minds most people believed him. Count Oppersdorf said he expected to eat at the Café de la Paix in Paris on Sedan Day and families gave their departing sons lists of the clothes and perfume they would like from Paris fashion houses for the winter season. Bethmann-Hollweg wrote of the 'gigantic national uplifting' and 'complete enthusiasm of all parts of the population' and Tirpitz praised the 'immense moral exaltation with which our whole nation took up the perfidious brutal gauntlet'. Hertling saw 'a marvellous patriotic wave passing over the Empire'. Princess Blücher said of Berlin, 'The excitement and enthusiasm all over the city are enormous. The Kaiser is the most adored man of the moment.' She watched as soldiers covered in garlands of flowers and singing *Die Wacht am Rhein* marched past her: 'I think I shall hear these words ringing in my ears to my dying day. The whole life in the Germany of today seems to move to the rhythm of this tune.'[113] But few understood the implications of the invasion of Belgium.

When war was first announced Berliners believed that Britain would refuse to come in against them and indeed the British had been reluctant to get involved in this continental skirmish: when news of the Austrian bombardment of Sarajevo reached London Trafalgar Square was filled with anti-war demonstrators chanting that Britain would not go to war for the Russian 'Criminals of Crimea', or indeed for France, and many – including Lord Chancellor Loreburn – believed war in this 'purely French quarrel' was unnecessary.[114] Britain could have chosen to remain neutral, but the argument put forward most forcefully by Sir Edward Grey and Winston Churchill to interfere eventually won the day – following news of the imminent invasion of Belgium crowds pushed into Whitehall to urge the government to defend the tiny neutral country. On the day of the invasion the British sent Germany an ultimatum telling them to withdraw by midnight, or face war.

Berlin was stunned by the news. How could the British be so treacherous? Bethmann-Hollweg told the British ambassador that his country was doing an 'unthinkable' thing, that 'it was like striking a man from behind while he was fighting for his life against two assailants', and that it would be Britain which would be judged responsible for all the dreadful events that might follow. They would do this, he said, 'all for just a word – "neutrality" – just for a scrap of paper'. The phrase echoed around the world, bringing disgrace to Germany and her capital. The Kaiser became the 'Beast of Berlin', the city was the 'Home of the Hun'. On 4 August crowds engulfed Whitehall singing 'God Save the King', German shops were smashed and dachshunds were stoned in Hyde Park. Germans living in England were forced to leave; Prince Blücher's English wife Evelyn, who had followed her husband into exile, described the mood as one of 'sadness and bitterness ... they all blamed the officials in Berlin who, they said, had grossly mismanaged the negotiations'.[115] That night Lord Grey is said to have looked down from the Foreign Office window at St James's Park and muttered: 'The lamps are going out all over Europe.'

Each of Europe's great capitals was on edge, and Berlin most of all. Rumours of alliances and betrayals rippled through the crowds until suddenly, just after eight o'clock, thousands of posters and leaflets began to appear on the streets. They read: 'England declares war on Germany. The British Ambassador has asked for his passport.' Berliners rushed into Unter den Linden and into the Wilhelmstrasse. Sir Horace Rumbold, who was in the British embassy at the time, wrote: 'Almost immediately after we had seen the poster we could hear the howls of the mob outside the Embassy, although we were separated by two very large rooms from the street. The howling was continuous, and almost reminded me of a typhoon in Japan.' The British party moved to a front room and turned on a light, at which point stones began to smash through the windows.

> I looked out on to the street for a moment. It was crammed from kerb to kerb with a crowd consisting of quite well-dressed individuals, including a number of women. Two or three mounted policemen were vainly trying to prevent the demonstrators from climbing up on to the window-sills. The crowd seemed mad with rage and was howling 'Down with England! Death to the English pedlar nation! Race treachery! Murderers!'

A man climbed on to a window sill and smashed a pane of glass. His umbrella fell into the room, and was later presented to *The Times*. Another witness wrote:

> Certainly no civilized community on earth ever surrendered so completely to all-obsessing brutality as the war mob which thirsted for British blood in Berlin on the night of August 4, 1914. It gave vent to all the animal passions and breathed the murder instinct said to be inherent in the average human when unreasoning rage temporarily supplants sanity. If it had caught sight of or could have laid hands on Sir Edward Goschen, or anyone else identifiable as an 'Engländer' it would undoubtedly have torn him limb from limb.

Blücher could not understand 'the absolute revulsion [of England], when I think of the almost exaggerated expressions of admiration and affection which were so widely spread formerly'.[116] People with connections to England were advised to wear an American badge and it was forbidden to speak English on the telephone or in any public place in Berlin. When a rumour spread through the crowd that the Japanese had declared war on Britain hundreds ran to the embassy shouting, 'Long live Japan! Long live Japan!' until the ambassador came out and told them to go home. Secretary of State Gottlieb von Jagow told the British ambassador that he was 'ashamed' at the behaviour of his countrymen, and that they had left 'an indelible stain on the reputation of Berlin', but his was a lonely voice. The old ties, the common bonds between Europeans were coming apart, and before long all manner of propaganda and deceit and brutality would become acceptable. Behind the walls of the palace that night was the pathetic sight of the men who had led Berlin to this, the Kaiser and his entourage, temporarily unnerved by the events unfolding before them. Bethmann shook his head and asked, 'How on earth do you think this could have happened?'

The support for the war was fuelled by the virulent nationalism and the *völkisch* ideology which had evolved in the city after the crash of 1873, and which had risen to fever pitch and new levels of fanaticism by September 1914. Old differences were forgotten in the jubilation of imminent victory. The young men who marched down Unter den Linden with flowers in their gun barrels, Nietzsche in their back pockets and patriotic songs on their lips had put their differences behind them to revel not simply in the pride of being German, but in the belief that they were fighting for *Volk* and *Vaterland*. Berlin had played a pivotal role in the creation of this new movement, and now with this final victory their city would be the most powerful in Europe. Russia would no longer threaten them in the east, and France and England would be forced to listen to the demands of the Wilhelmstrasse.[117]

The belief that the war would end in six weeks, the 'short war fallacy', had led to extraordinary developments in Berlin. The Social Democrats had voted with the government for war credits; to do otherwise would have been 'unpatriotic'. The Reichstag had renounced its power and recessed until December, when the 'war would be won'. War hid the divisions between left and right, rich and poor, and even Bethmann-Hollweg told the Democrat Conrad Haussmann that the war had created German 'unity' and thus 'a nation', had diminished class distinctions and would cause a 'new time' after the war when 'barriers would fall'. People from all walks of life gloated over soon-to-be-won German spoils. Pan-Germans were the most extreme, but even National Liberal supporters like Gustav Stresemann favoured seizing land in Russia and Catholic Centre Party members like Matthias Erzberger advocated German domination of Europe and opposed an early peace. Even moderate socialists pushed for the annexation of territory. Industrialists like August Thyssen, Emil Kirdorf and Karl Rochling wanted to extract a promise from the government that the French mines in Briey-Longwy would soon be annexed, the War Committee of German Industry urged Bethmann-Hollweg to prolong the war rather than conclude peace, which might cause Germany to give back Belgium, and there were many more who wanted to see the annexation of French and Belgian territory. Four hundred and fifty German professors signed a document endorsing Germany's expansionist aims in 1915 and the majority of Berlin professors, who had done so much to legitimate nationalism in the first place, agreed; some even suggested Germany use Napoleon's empire as the model for the future Germany, incorporating Russia and France. The complete annexation of Belgium was a common goal. Even the historian Friedrich Meinecke, who had hoped for peace in September 1914, asserted 'we now want to win for ourselves room to breathe and security for a century'.[118] The moderate Hans Delbrück said that Germans now wished to be secure for ever, 'which could happen only if we conquer'. Winckler urged incorporation of what he called the 'old German lands', namely Belgium and Luxembourg, whereas the Baltic professor Theodor Schiemann demanded German annexations in the east. Solf, the Minister for Colonies, said: 'the wish for as much land as possible from our enemies is expressed with complete confidence not only by Pan-Germans but by wide circles throughout Germany.' The support for German expansionism was popularized in Friedrich Naumann's pamphlet *Mitteleuropa*, which envisaged Germany taking enormous chunks of Europe. As French or Belgian towns and cities fell to the advancing German army Berlin church bells rang out, houses were decorated and cannon were fired throughout the city. The philosopher Max Scheler wrote of the German bombardment of Rheims Cathedral: 'If the cathedral had been capable of thinking and feeling it would have realized that the force firing the cannons was part of the same force that had once created this heaven-storming Gothic masterpiece.'[119]

For all their early advances, the Germans were soon to learn that wars never go as planned. They had hoped to win against France quickly before turning to defeat Russia, but stopping Russia was easier than expected. It was the fighting in the east, culminating in the Battle of Tannenberg, which brought home to Berliners that they were really at war. Hundreds of thousands of soldiers took part in the campaign and before long the troop trains which had headed east filled with fresh young recruits began to arrive back with their tragic cargo of maimed and injured men. Stories began to filter back to the city of the pincer movement which had forced the Russians into two huge lakes to drown. One witness said that he would never forget

> the shrieks and cries of the dying men and horses ... so fearful was the sight of these thousands of men, with their guns, horses and ammunition, struggling in the water that, to shorten their agony, we turned the machine-guns on them ... And the mowing down of the cavalry brigade at the same time, 500 mounted men on white horses, all killed and packed so closely that they remained standing.[120]

The Russian army was in disarray, and the Germans won a decisive victory; Hindenburg and Ludendorff supplanted William as the great heroes of the day.

On the western front, however, things were quite different. The initial German thrust through Belgium and into France was weakened by von Moltke's last-minute decision to transfer two army corps to East Prussia. The French had counter-attacked and halted the German advance, and by November 1914 the front was frozen. It would stay virtually unchanged for four long, bloody years. Overwhelming popular support for the war had been based on the 'short war fallacy' and it was only after the terrible and bloody defeat at the first battle of Ypres that it became clear to the generals that a quick victory had eluded the German army. Thousands of men were dying each day as the French and British met the German army head on, diverting them from Paris and leaving the 'infallible' Schlieffen Plan in ruins.

The government had been so confident that their carefully thought out strategy would deliver victory by Christmas that they had made no contingency plans for the continuation of war. New units were hurriedly created in October 1914 and Berliners were now called to serve in the 201 to 206 Infantry; volunteer regiments made up of young men below the age of twenty-two were formed in the autumn of 1914, which helps to explain why 20 per cent of all present and former pupils of the Kaiser Wilhelm Gymnasium were killed in the war. The Berlin metal-working and other industries were in chaos not least because

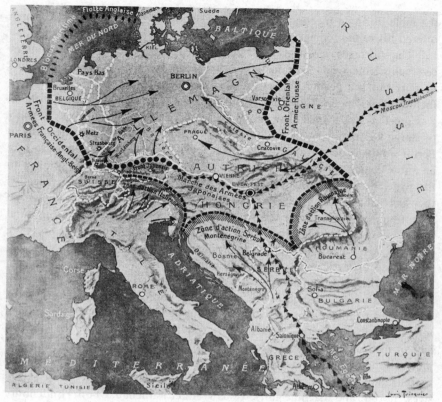

Purported 'Encirclement' of Germany, 1915

of a sudden labour shortage and an increase in wages as industries sought to attract workers; a new policy, the *Zurückstellung* process, was introduced which allowed skilled workers to return to Berlin from the front; 700 were called back in 1914 alone.[121] By October 1914 ammunition supplies had run out. While the Allies could buy weapons on the open market the Kriegsrohstoffabteilung (War Materials Procurement Department) and the Munition Service could not because of the international blockade against Germany, forcing German officers, businessmen and shady characters of all kinds out to scour Europe for illegal arms. One Captain von Rintelen, a young naval officer, was given the task of procuring machine guns in a hurry, 'even if they come from the moon'. He managed to find sheds in Copenhagen filled with guns which had recently been bought by the Russians and, posing as an Englishman, he set up an elaborate ploy to purchase them. This was foiled by his assistant, a Prussian lance corporal, who, forgetting that he was in disguise, went up to the table during a meeting, clicked his heels together and in perfect German offered his captain a cigar.

The shortages were aggravated by the German decision to carry out intensive submarine warfare against the Allies. The German navy was confined to port but the deadly U-boats stalked the seas, targeting all enemy ships, including passenger ships from North America. The sinking of the *Lusitania* was greeted by Berliners as a moral victory 'against those who wish illegally to starve Germans', but it was universally condemned abroad. Americans in Berlin stopped socializing with Germans and their newspapers began to take an anti-German turn. Worst of all, American munitions began to pour in to the western allied nations. Their shells were considered particularly deadly; they were not made of cast iron like European ones but of steel, a 'diabolical invention', ribbed and grooved so that when they exploded the casing burst into thousands of small pieces with terrific force. At the beginning of 1915 the Supreme Army Command wired in from the front: 'We are at our wits' end to defend ourselves against American ammunition.'

The crisis and the massive losses sustained at Verdun led to a revision of armaments policy in August 1916; control over munitions manufacturing was transferred from the Ministry of War to the Kriegsamt (War Office) and in 1916 Hindenburg decided that the only way to compensate for the German lack of troops was to fight with technology and to vastly increase armaments production; the result was the Hindenburg Programme, which called for the mobilization of all available resources for the manufacture of ever more explosives, mortars and machine guns. It was Walther Rathenau, whom Hindenburg put in charge of the War Materials Procurement Department, who allowed Germany to carry on for as long as it did, not least because of his policy of appointing industrialists rather than *Beamten* to powerful positions.[122] Before long Berlin was being stripped of raw materials for the armaments factories; at first only scrap materials and railings were used; later church bells and organ pipes were melted down and in 1915 Berlin lost her copper roofs. The district of Spandau became the centre of new armaments industries, employing 120,000 people; Moabit became the centre of mustard gas production, and carts filled with basket-covered glass bottles rolled out of the factory and on to the trains heading west.

But despite all attempts to produce armaments for men at the front Berlin industry was faced with severe shortages, both of manpower and resources, which became more acute as the war continued. The workforce was expanded, hours were increased and over 2,000 Berlin firms received more workers, but the high death toll on the front continued to drain the labour market and in July 1917 alone there was a shortage of nearly 6,000 people in the factories; the demand for workers continued to exceed the numbers available until the end of the war.[123] A 1916 report from the Verband Märkischer Arbeitnachweise stated, 'the shortage of workers is reaching such proportions that it exceeds the capacity of the placement system to satisfy industrial needs.'[124]

Berlin was a huge city and was highly dependent on imported food. As a result it was particularly vulnerable to the Allied blockade. Rationing began to bite even in the first winter, when Rosa Luxemburg wrote, 'Gone is the ecstasy, and gone are the patriotic street demonstrations . . . No more do trains filled with reservists pull out amid joyous cries from enthusiastic maidens. No longer do we see laughing faces smiling from train windows.' At first only alcohol production was limited and beloved Berlin *Kneipen* began to close. The sausages and chocolate and beer which had been consumed so readily in 1914 soon gave way to watery soup and turnips. In February 1915 Berlin was given the distinction of being the first German city to be given bread ration cards. Meat and flour supplies were placed under official control, potatoes, lard, eggs and milk were rationed and it became a criminal offence to bake a cake in Charlottenburg. The winter of 1915–16 was called the 'turnip winter'; in May 1916 butchers' shops were closed for three weeks, and people forced to move from one line to another were said to be dancing the 'butter polonaise'. Women would often get up in the middle of the night to be first on the scene, bringing their knitting or sewing with them; some even brought sewing machines to the queues. *Ersatz* became a common word in the Berlin dialect; coffee, jam, soap and bread made of potato flour became the norm and unscrupulous dealers made easy money by selling black ash as 'pepper' or starch mixed with bicarbonate of soda as 'butter'. By 1916 the situation was so chaotic that the government formed the Kriegsernährungsamt or K E A (War Food Office) but they were unable to regulate the fair distribution of food. Berliners were now permitted two eggs a month, small amounts of meat and a handful of vegetables, all controlled by tiny cardboard ration cards, but whereas farmers in the villages or those with connections could fall back on the traditional barter system and the rich could obtain goods *hintenerum* – by the back way – most Berliners were utterly dependent on the goodwill of hoarders and speculators. Inflation meant that average wages no longer covered the cost of basic household goods and in contrast to Paris and London the Berlin black market flourished.[125] In the winter of 1917 the potato crop failed, causing widespread starvation; rats were used as food and there were riots at the weekly market in eastern Berlin that summer. By 1918 the consumption of meat had dropped to a mere 12 per cent of its pre-war level, the consumption of eggs to 13 per cent and of fish to 5 per cent.[126] According to the war-time mayor of Berlin, Adolf Warmuth, hunger began to 'reap its reward in the hospitals of the city'. Berliners faced a bitterly cold winter with temperatures remaining below freezing throughout January and plunging to an average daily low of −18.5 degrees Celsius in February 1917. Transportation bottlenecks meant that 1,200 of the 2,000 wagons which came to Berlin every day could not be unloaded, which led to a severe shortage of coal, and *Vorwärts* complained on 11 December 1917:

> [The bureaucrats] sketch out a distribution plan, ration the individual districts, distribute ration cards to the individual consumers, and then think that they have done their duty. Whether, when, where, and how much coal will be delivered, however, doesn't concern them at all . . . Whoever has connections enough to discover where the coal is arriving, and then queues up for it, or has someone else queue up for it, may actually obtain something. Others come up empty handed, and these are naturally the sick, the old, or those who work throughout the day.[127]

Thousands of Berliners died each month from illness and disease associated with malnutrition and cold.

Other pleasures were soon curtailed as well. Theatres, museums and street markets closed soon after the outbreak of war, there were cuts in public transport and electricity and street lights were put out at 1 a.m. Some clubs were permitted to stay open but the productions became increasingly dry, with entertainers making excuses for the high death toll and the increasing shortages at home. One song backing the government's attempts to make women buy dresses made out of cellulose fibre ended with the lines: 'Miss Fashion accommodates herself to the seriousness of the times, and the gentlemen say, "That paper dress, oh no, how modern it is!"' Songs about 'great men' from Zeppelin and Tirpitz to Hindenburg and Frederick the Great shared the bill with nationalistic ditties like Ernst Lissauer's *Song of Hate Against England* and Claire Waldoff's *Soldier's Song*. Life became increasingly restrictive. Colonel von Kessell began to carry out house searches and arrests in the name of 'order' in 1915 and Christmas that year was grey and dismal. Princess Blücher remembered the 'white-faced black-robed women who glide so sadly through the streets, some bearing their sorrow proudly as a crown to their lives, others bent and broken under a burden too heavy to be borne'. The midnight mass at the Convent Hospital was crowded with 'wounded soldiers, nurses, nuns, and pale-faced heart-broken women'. By late 1916 wool and cotton were in desperately short supply, clothes were rationed, and the once thriving Berlin textile industry churned out nothing but uniforms. Shoes and boots were made of poor quality leather and grey cloth which fell apart. Anti-Semitism rose as Jews were accused of hoarding and speculation. A report by a Landrat from the area of the Twenty-first Army Corps was typical: 'the population clearly expresses its displeasure at the fact that Jews are given preferential treatment, especially in the institutions of the war economy, and the war is frequently described as a *Geldkrieg* [money war]. Comments such as: "The Jews have not yet earned enough, that is why the War has not yet ended" are not uncommon.'[128]

As men were moved off to the front women began to run the city. At first they were assigned to nursing, caring for prisoners of war, working for the Red Cross, driving horse-drawn buses and post wagons, and setting up soup kitchens. Women of independent means set up small nursing homes; Frau von Ihne, for example, set up a home for blinded soldiers in the Bellevue-strasse. The National Women's Service had 7,000 women working at their base in Berlin, distributing state relief for the wives and children of fallen soldiers. They also instructed women how to cook without milk, eggs or fat and helped widows and destitute women to find work sewing or wrapping packages for the front. By March 1915 women had been given jobs in the once male domains of banking and insurance companies, in military and government offices, and in heavy armaments factories and on the railroads. Women now worked in the production of everything from chemicals, electrical equipment, metalwork and machine tools to precision instruments and leather goods; they dug out and built large sections of the Berlin underground. Berlin women had a particularly difficult time compared to their counterparts in Britain or France; the pressure to work was much higher and by December 1917 the proportion of women in chemicals, metalworking and machine tools was over 50 per cent, over twice that in Paris or London. Health regulations were relaxed: young mothers in Paris were prevented from working; in Berlin they were not, and although there were rules against night work these were often ignored. Sixty-hour weeks were not uncommon. Severe food shortages added to their problems and, as a Gewerbe-Aufsicht report put it, 'exhaustion at work was common because these women, some of whom had recently been delivered or had very young children, suffered from malnutrition'.[129] Many women suffered from tuberculosis; indeed the death rate for young adults between the ages of twenty and twenty-nine rose to 32 per 10,000 in 1917; many of the victims were women who probably had latent tuberculosis from childhood and who succumbed to the disease as a result of the exhaustion, poor nutrition, cold and poor ventilation of the factories. This sudden change of roles was to fuel the later drive for equal rights, but at the time women were given opportunities because of the desperate shortage of men.

The face of Berlin changed in other ways: old horses, donkeys and even the elephants from Hagenbeck's circus were used to pull coal carts from the train stations. Prisoners of war worked in crews around the city building roads around Lichterfelde, while British soldiers were kept at the Ruhleben racecourse. The latter received packages from home and later in the war they were often better fed than Berliners themselves. One escapee was recaptured only because he had made himself white bread sandwiches and when he began to eat them at a train station he was besieged by Berliners demanding to know where he had found this amazing product.

Life in Berlin became increasingly depressing. Black crosses and the names of those who had died a 'hero's death' filled the newspapers and the lists of casualties which appeared daily at the War Ministry in the Dorotheenstrasse grew longer and longer. Queues of anxious women hurried there every day to search for references to brothers, fathers and husbands. Another clue to the carnage was provided by the Nachlass Bureau, where small articles picked up on the battlefield were kept for identification; crushed and bloodstained cigarette cases containing photographs or scraps of paper were piling up in their hundreds, along with monographed handkerchiefs, torn letters, jewellery, and all manner of small items which awaited identification in vain. News filtered back through wounded troops that entire regiments were being replaced every few months; the First Garde Regiment was not unusual in that it had been replaced five times between the Battle of the Marne and 1916. On a Berlin train one day people began to laugh at a woman who kept pulling at her fingers, but the man sitting next to her said, 'Do not laugh at my wife, ladies and gentlemen . . . she has lost her five sons.'

The gaudy veneer of imperial Berlin had soon worn off, and the city revealed itself as an ugly and brutal place. Georg Grosz wrote of 1916:

> The Berlin to which I returned was a cold and grey city, the busy cafés and wine-cellars merely accentuating the gloom of the dark unheated residential districts. The self-same soldiers who frequented the former, singing, dancing and clinging to the arms of prostitutes in a drunken stupor, could later be seen weary and with the dirt of the trenches still on them, dragging their feet and their packs from one station to another . . . I drew men drunk, men vomiting, men with clenched fists cursing the moon, men playing cards on the coffins of the women they had murdered . . . I drew scenes of army life based on sketches I had made during military service . . . I drew soldiers without noses; war cripples with crab-like limbs of steel; two medical orderlies tying a violent infantryman up in a horse blanket; a one-armed soldier using his good hand to salute a heavily bemedalled lady who had just passed him a biscuit; a colonel, his fly wide open, embracing a nurse; a hospital orderly emptying a bucket full of pieces of human flesh down a pit. I drew a skeleton dressed up as a recruit taking his medical.[130]

Terrible stories filtered into the city through nurses, who heard about conditions in the trenches: how men were forced to watch their friends die a few yards away from them in No Man's Land, unable to move amid the torrents of machine-gun fire; how people were pushed 'over the top' again and again because 'if you did not go forward you would be shot', how at Christmas the guns fell silent and men from opposing sides would sing carols or play football in No Man's Land before blowing each other up again the next day. The young soldier Willy Kurtz hated the trenches: 'There were times when my feet were never dry for weeks at a time . . . My whole body was wet most of the time. We just sat in misery day after day, hating the life we were living, yet fearing the dreaded order to charge.'[131] When the over-protected emperor went to see how things were going at Verdun, a battle of immeasurable suffering where in 1916 1,000 soldiers died per square metre, he saw a whole company of men blown up by a French mine and became ill for days afterwards. The 'cripple brigades' were manned by people who had been disfigured but were still capable of work; they used to bury the dead and could well 'do' 4,000 corpses a day in a place like the Somme or Ypres or Vimy Ridge. Towards the end of the war these pathetic, exhausted, injured, half-starved German soldiers were sent headlong into the lines of fresh American troops. Wounded men began to refuse consent to operations which might heal an injured limb for fear of being sent back to the front and a soldier's greatest hope was to be hit in the ankle or the foot so that he could go to a field hospital and get away from the shelling, the mud, the rats, the gas attacks, the endless noise, the death. Carl Zuckmayer, then a young artillery officer, had returned to the front after only a week in an army hospital where he had been sent because of a terrible head wound. He could barely stand up when he was told by a captain of the medical corps that he must go back to the front as he was fit enough to get himself killed: 'that's what we need young officers for now.' Others were treated equally badly. Kokoschka, Barlach and Klinger all served at the front and would later depict graphic accounts of the misery they saw there; Ernst Kirchner's depressing *Self Portrait as a Soldier*, painted in 1915, captured his pathological fear of being recalled to the army: 'New draft calls of the reserves stay close at my heels and who knows when they will stick me in again.' Beckmann's pre-war self-portrait with its handsome, elegant face was replaced by the grim, war-wearied, frightened image of the soldier; Otto Dix, who spent the entire war at the front, later used his experiences in his brutal and shocking *War Portfolio*; many more of the city's talented poets and artists were killed. Grosz wrote of them: 'My friends, hacked up, scattered, duped, bewitched into battle-grey comrades of slaughter!! . . . cadaver upon cadaver, already green rotting corpses grow among the rank and file – If only it would end soon!!'[132]

When I was working in West Berlin in the 1980s I once came across a bizarre collection of artificial limbs made of wood, metal, rubber and fibre which had been made for the crippled soldiers of the First World War. There were hundreds of these gruesome objects, and the sheer extent of the damage done by the shrapnel and the bullets was brought home by the crudely shaped foot pieces, the plates for bits of the skull which had been blown away, the glass eyes, the nose pieces, the pathetic, clumsy re-creations of knees and elbows. Germany sustained over 4 million wounded in the war, and Berlin was an important medical centre even though it was far from the front.[133] The Rudolf Virchow hospital alone treated over 200,000 men and the military hospital at Busch treated 30,000; the Charité had 1,175 beds and there were specialist hospitals run by religious denominations – Berlin hospitals accommodated 253,000 men during the war and these figures did not include patients in clinics, convalescent centres and homes for long-term care.[134] When Georg Grosz was recalled to the army in 1917 he tried to drown himself in a latrine and was sent to hospital to recover. He wrote: 'We in the hospital were fed on dried vegetables, turnip coffee and synthetic honey which corroded the lining of our stomachs.' One day he woke up next to a Berlin coachman who had had half his stomach blown away, and who told Grosz he couldn't find his legs. 'He tried to point to his lumpy middle, but his hand and finger let him down once more. He gave a semi-conscious groan and sank into a coma. That night he died . . . a shapeless bundle of flesh.' The man next to him had been shot in the groin.

> 'No more fun with the girls for him,' the orderly said. The sergeant was of a different opinion. 'Don't believe it, my boy,' he said. 'They'll bloody well give him a brand new custom-built cock made of bloody wood. We've seen the lot here. And artificial legs are as good, partially, as the real thing, even better for some things, if you ask me, like bloody hurdling, or high-jumping.'[135]

Another man nearby seemed to be swelling up and growing bigger and bigger, and Grosz's neighbours told him of another case where a friend gassed in the trenches had bloated so much that he looked 'like a bloody balloon'. Another of Grosz's companions in the hospital had been driven mad by his experiences at the front and he babbled: 'we had just been ordered up front . . . we had no steel helmets, but everything else was just fine . . . Then we went down that bloody log road, you know, that's where we spotted them bastards . . . My God, when I came to, my head felt just like a bloody sandbag.' He kept tearing at his injury until they tied him up in a horse blanket and moved him to Berlin, where he kept shouting, 'I just want to get the bloody sand out, can't you see the bloody sand?'

*   *   *

The armies on the western front were slowly bleeding to death in a terrible war of attrition and each side became more desperate to break through the defences of the other. They tried stacking barbed wire in different directions in order to herd infantrymen into killing zones; they built checkerboards of camouflaged concrete machine-gun bunkers to kill more men as they ran into the open; they tried spacing their second trenches beyond the range of artillery fire; they built complex underground networks like the Allied labyrinth at Arras, which accommodated 30,000 men; they tried using gas, and they tried building armoured vehicles and tanks that would somehow get through the thick mud. Conditions at the front were appalling for both sides and by the end Germany had lost 1.2 million young men – half her youth – in the trenches. My great-grandfather, General Henry Thoresby Hughes, had served in France and Flanders during the war, and in 1918 headed the Commonwealth War Graves Commission which erected memorials to those who had died.[136] Although the fighting had stopped the parties had to negotiate the twisting muddy roads and trenches, dugouts and barbed wire – places so pounded by bombs and shells and machine guns that it was difficult to identify exactly where battles had taken place. The debris left after the fighting was terrible: spent shells, bully cans, shovels, bayonets, lumps of twisted metal and masses of barbed wire, ghostly wooden posts, and everywhere pieces of human beings – hands, pieces of jawbone, legs, all protruding from the mud of the trenches, lying at the bottom of flooded bomb craters or covered by scraps of rotting uniform in No Man's Land. These were the unknown soldiers, the thousands of young men on both sides who would never be accounted for, and who still lie in unmarked graves.

Perhaps the most spectacular new weapon designed to outmanoeuvre the other side was the bomb which was to have been dropped on Berlin. By 1918 the capital had become a universal Allied symbol of German evil, and the Allies were keen to pay Berliners back for the raids on their cities. London and Paris had been bombed by Zeppelins since the beginning of the war and although Count Talleyrand had said, 'a bomb from a Zeppelin could not hit a Dreadnought,' they did cause fear in the cities. By 1918 both sides had developed bombers and the Germans struck Paris seventeen times, killing 303 Parisians and wounding 539; my English grandmother remembered watching in horror as a German plane was shot down near her house in Surrey. 'Big Berthas' – 8.26- and 9.13-inch guns – also blasted at Paris and were specifically designed to weaken French morale. The Royal Air Force was founded in April 1918 in order to increase British strength in the air, and British multi-engined aircraft could already carry 2,000-pound bombs, which were being dropped on border cities, including Trier, Cologne and Mainz. In October 1918 Lloyd George decided that the British people were 'entitled to a bit of revenge' and that they should try to bomb Berlin. The RAF devised a strategy whereby they would fly from Norfolk, drop their load over Berlin and land in Prague. The plan had enormous propaganda value but did nothing to give the Allies a decisive strategic advantage. That would come from politics abroad.

When the first Russian Revolution broke out in February 1917 there was widespread hope in Berlin of a separate peace in eastern Europe, and the Bolshevik *coup d'état* and Russian withdrawal from the war which culminated in the Treaty of Brest-Litovsk gave the Germans renewed hope of victory. But the expected military benefits did not come. Negotiations were long and hard and German troops had to remain in the east to keep order; grain from Ukraine did not materialize as quickly as had been hoped. In the end it was not the Russian collapse but the 1917 American entry which would end the war, making it just a matter of time before Germany was defeated.

Nationalists in Berlin refused to accept the evidence of inevitable defeat and were determined to resist. In his diary entry for 10 July 1917 Walther Rathenau said: 'The occupation of Paris alone would probably not be enough to satisfy the desires of our annexationists; the occupation of London would probably have to be added as well.'[137] In 1917 the extreme right-wing Fatherland Party was formed, headed by Admiral Tirpitz and Wolfgang Kapp, and encouraged the government to erect an enormous and hideous wooden statue of Hindenburg in uniform near the Reichstag. Berliners could pay money for a 'victory nail' which they could then drive into the statue. The money was to fund a final great offensive which most believed would deliver victory, a belief which was fuelled by the increasingly shrill and belligerent propaganda which engulfed the city.

It was Hiram Johnson who in 1917 said to the American Senate: 'The first casualty when war comes is the truth.' Since 1916 the High Command had taken complete control of both the war and civilian affairs, including information and propaganda, and from the beginning the government had decided not to tell its people the truth about the reversals on the western front; Admiral Hintze refused to allow news of the defeat at the Marne to be disseminated because it was essential to 'deny defeat' and 'nurse the patriotic feelings of the German people'. This wall of propaganda, lies and deceit fooled most Berliners into believing that glorious victory was imminent and that the German army was successfully fulfilling its heroic mission to dominate Europe. When Paul von Hindenburg and Erich von Ludendorff announced the great German offensive on the western front on 21 March 1918 – the so-called Emperor's Battle – Berliners eagerly prepared for victory and headlines cheerfully announced NOW WE HAVE THEM! They were wrong. Three quarters of a million men and 6,000 heavy guns were set against the Allies, but the Germans were repulsed. They tried again at the Marne in July and again they were beaten back. The campaign was such an enormous failure that Hindenburg forbade anyone to speak of the position unless they said something positive. Germany suffered 800,000 casualties in those battles alone, and morale at the front began to crumble. By the autumn of 1918 it was close to total collapse but on 28 September Ludendorff still had the audacity to report to Berlin that 'complete victory was within his grasp'. Berliners entered the final month of war still dreaming of victory but they had been lied to. They were not facing a great victory at all.

VIII

The Bitter Aftermath of War

Their epic struggles tire me: soon as one
is finished, then another has begun.
They say they are fighting to preserve Democracy,
but it's just slave against slave, as far as I can see.

(*Faust*, Part II, Act 2)

THE STREETS AND SQUARES of Berlin are haunted by the ghosts of war. They are there in the old Prussian parade grounds and the massive barracks, with their mock Tudor towers and tiny windows constructed to isolate troops from the citizens. The ghosts are there in Schinkel's neo-Gothic Kreuzberg monument, built to commemorate the defeat of Napoleon; they sit at the Siegessäule constructed out of brick and cannon in honour of Bismarck's wars, and they stare from the gigantic bronze-green faces of Roon and Moltke who stand alone amidst the traffic on the Grosser Stern. War is there in Hitler's architecture: in the cold walls of the Olympic stadium and in the impregnable burnt facade of the Air Ministry which, because of its immense strength, survived the bombing of the Wilhelmstrasse. War lingers in the enormous Stalinist memorial to the Russian soldiers who were killed taking Berlin street by street in 1945. It wafts around the few remaining shards of the Cold War Wall and the burned and jagged tooth of the Kaiser Wilhelm Gedächtniskirche, the symbol of post-war West Berlin and memorial to the Second World War. All these events have left their mark on the city and have been commemorated in some way; all, that is, except the Great War of 1914–18.[1]

One can walk in vain for hours through the streets of Berlin in search of a great monument to that terrible conflict. The mass graves and the *Totenburgen* remain deep in the territory of France and Belgium and Poland but the 'War to End All Wars' has no grand memorial, no equivalent of London's Cenotaph or the catafalque created beneath the Arc de Triomphe at the Étoile in Paris.[2] During the war the people of Hackney and Ealing and Camberwell had spontaneously built memorials for those who had died in battle and the street-shrine movement of London reached a climax in 1918 with the completion of an enormous shrine in Hyde Park, a site which was quickly smothered by 10,000 wreaths of flowers.[3] Even during the war Berliners had refrained from such unmilitary forms of mourning, limiting themselves to private ceremonies or to the hammering of a nail into the official Hindenburg statue in order to raise money for the war effort. Schinkel's monument to the victory of 1871 was temporarily adapted in the 1920s to mark the Great War and a new memorial was planned but it was never built. It was only in late 1931 that the eighteenth-century neo-classical Guard House on Unter den Linden, the Neue Wache, was inaugurated as the Tomb of the Unknown Soldier. It was a failure. Few Berliners went there; other Germans regarded it as 'too Prussian' and 'too Berlinisch' to represent the dead of Bavaria or of the Rhineland at a time when the capital was losing its power to unify the nation. The combination of the loss of hundreds of thousands of young men, coupled with the realities of defeat, was too much to bear. Only the Nazis were keen to use images of fallen heroic soldiers in their own propaganda, replacing the simple rites of remembrance with pompous ceremonies which made little distinction between soldiers and their own 'martyrs' like Horst Wessel. Even so, most of their commemorations tended to be held at a local level, far from the decadent capital now blamed for the German defeat.[4] In 1946 the interior of the bomb-damaged Neue Wache was treated like any other Nazi monument and destroyed. It was resurrected by the East Germans in 1960 to 'Honour the Victims of Fascism and Militarism' and goose-stepping guards returned to Unter den Linden in a sickening Communist parody of Hitler's 1933 ceremony. Berlin had lost her only important central First World War memorial for good. Few people even noticed.

This momentous act of forgetting is startling in a city whose future was so deeply affected by the war. Although not touched by the front-line fighting the four long years of battle had reduced the proud capital to a shadow of its former self. Between 1918 and 1924 Berlin would be pounded by a relentless stream of traumatic events, from the collapse of the monarchy to the November Revolution and the Spartacus Uprising, from the rise of the Freikorps and the list of bloody political assassinations to the Kapp *Putsch* which foreshadowed Hitler's coup, and from the Treaty of Versailles and the resulting hyper-inflation to the demise of all traditional values which had once held the imperial city together. The war brutalized and impoverished Berlin and it would never truly recover. The first in this wave of crises was the shocking news of defeat on the western front. It hit the unsuspecting city like a thunderbolt.

The Berliners who had gone off to war in 1914 had been convinced that they could not lose. War had been a great adventure which would bring prosperity, huge territorial gains, glory, power and respect to their new empire.

Victory had failed to materialize at Christmas 1914, but the Germans had fought on. The front lines had frozen and the casualty lists had spilled over into the hundreds of thousands, and life on the home front began to deteriorate, but still they fought on, convinced that the sacrifice and loss would be amply rewarded in the end. The very nature of the war made it difficult for Berliners to foresee its outcome. Whereas in 1945 they would watch in helpless terror as the Red Army swept towards them through East Prussia and Poland, in the First World War the front lines remained virtually stationary in far-off France and Flanders. Even by 1918 not one inch of German territory had been occupied by the Allied armies, a fact which was taken as further proof of inevitable victory.

This powerful illusion was sustained by the High Command, whose shrill promises became ever more preposterous as war dragged on: Germany would keep Belgium, would reign over large chunks of France, would keep all gains in the east and would demand ruinous reparations from the British and the French.[5] The German generals clearly believed their own publicity; as a young officer Walter Gropius recalled overhearing General Ludendorff laugh in disdain when he was informed that the United States had joined the Allies. 'Americans?' he snorted. 'Bah!'[6] Even in the final days of September 1918 Berlin was awash with extreme nationalist propaganda. Plays like *Der Hias*, which glorified the noble sacrifice of war, drew record crowds while patriotic films like *Fifi – the Daughter of the Regiment* were daily fare in the West End. Oskar Messter's newsreels, the *Messter Woche*, showed heroic soldiers eagerly blowing up bridges and taking Allied soldiers prisoner; newspapers reported the Kaiser's comment of March 1918 that 'if an English delegation came to sue for peace it must kneel before the German standard'; the B U F A (official film company) films dared to glorify Ludendorff's offensive even as Allied soldiers were pouring in from the west and when, between March and July, Germany was in the process of losing 1 million men. The self-delusion was extraordinary: on 27 September 1918 Berlin dailies announced that the war was won.[7]

In reality the German army had been losing strength rapidly throughout 1918. At the height of summer Marshal Foch had opened a massive counter-offensive against Ludendorff's troops and on 3 August Sir Douglas Haig suggested an attack with tanks from Amiens which resulted in the complete crushing of six divisions of the German second army. On 8 August 1918 tanks pushed the Germans back to the Hindenburg Line. On 25 September the final assault began on the western front. The Americans pounded the Meuse, firing more artillery shells in three hours than had been fired in their entire Civil War. It was followed two days later by a powerful French offensive at the Argonne. On 27 September the British army pushed forward, followed on the 28th by the Belgians. On 15 September the French had attacked in Greece and, with the help of the reconstituted Serbian army, fought against Germany's ally Bulgaria; on 29 September the latter sued for peace, leaving a huge gap in Germany's southern flank and exposing Constantinople to attack. The Turkish army, long since decimated, concluded an armistice with the British. The Austro-Hungarian army had been attacked while retreating from Italy and the royal and imperial army fell apart with 1 million men killed and 800,000 taken prisoner. A few days before, a German Foreign Office official who had dared mention the possibility of a German defeat had been haughtily dismissed for his insolence.[8] Now even Hindenburg and Ludendorff had to admit that they had failed.[9] On 29 September they went before the Kaiser and Foreign Secretary von Hintze, and revealed that the war was lost.[10]

The next day the leaders of all political parties were summoned to the Reichstag, many convinced that they were finally to hear news of the promised victory. When the truth was announced there was a deafening silence. Ebert went 'as white as death' and the conservative leader clenched his fists, muttering, 'We have been deceived and cheated, deceived and cheated!' The news quickly spread. How could this be? Had the High Command actually lied to them? Had an entire generation of young men been sacrificed for nothing? In the cold grey gloom of 1918 imperial Berlin began to disintegrate before their very eyes. Some were unable to face reality and hung on to the extraordinary belief that if Germany could just keep fighting for another few weeks she would be victorious, but when men began to return home from the front on furlough with first-hand accounts of the crushing losses Berliners' patience suddenly snapped. They turned with breathtaking speed against the monarchy and those they deemed responsible for the war, and they reacted bitterly to the endless stream of lies. Suddenly, as if out of nowhere, the government faced the worst threat of all – a repeat of the Russian Revolution.

The small, quiet district in Wilmersdorf near the Nollendorfplatz is today a calm suburb dotted with small apartment buildings, second-hand bookshops and markets. In 1918 it looked completely different.[11] The streets teemed with strange-looking people and the place was filled with restaurants, shops, cafés, laundries, hairdressers' and anything else that could be squeezed in. All the signs were written in Cyrillic. When the omnibus drivers reached the Bülowstrasse they would yell out, '*Russland!*' for this was the centre of the Russian emigration, the place where those fleeing from the Bolshevik Revolution would stay – at least until they could move on to Paris, London or America.[12] By 1918 there were 50,000 Russians in Berlin, by 1922 there were 100,000, two years later there were 300,000, and they included everyone: poets, artists, aristocrats, soldiers, musicians and writers from Nabokov to Pasternak and from

Mayakovsky to Gorky.[13] Ehrenburg was amazed by the mixture of humanity thrown together by fate: 'some had flown out of terror, others because of hunger, others because they had simply shot their neighbour. Who emigrated and who remained was often a matter of chance ... chance decided the fate of millions of people.'[14] Alfred Döblin recalled that the first wave of émigrés was not poor and did not fit well in Berlin's working-class districts; instead they were 'well dressed bourgeois who prefer to spend their time in the west end and go to balls. Finally they have their own Russian cabaret in the Blaue Vogel.'[15] But as it became clear the Bolsheviks were not a temporary intrusion their lives became harder. Precious jewels were pawned, elegant clothes became shabbier, and cruel cartoons began to appear showing the decline of the Russian émigré from socialite to taxi driver.[16] But the one thing which tied the émigrés together was first-hand knowledge of the staggering power of the Bolsheviks, and of the speed with which revolution can strike.

Of all European capitals Berlin had been the most keenly affected by news from Russia. For the bourgeoisie, the factory and property owners and the moderate Social Democrats, whispers of Bolsheviks shooting landlords, lynching officers and seizing property were terrifying. For the radical workers of 'Red Berlin', however, the revolution was seen as a great achievement and as a blueprint for what they could achieve in their own country. Whatever their views, all had seen how a small and obscure group could take over one of the world's great powers in a matter of days, and none of them doubted that it could happen again, in Berlin.[17] It was for this reason that the announcement of the defeat on the western front at the end of September and the spiralling unrest sent such electric currents through the city. Lenin, too, was watching keenly from Moscow, for he was determined to see that the German capital become the focal point for the new 'World Revolution'. Lenin's interest predated the 1914 war, but his active involvement in the coming upheaval can be traced back to early 1917.[18]

It is one of the great ironies in Berlin's history that Lenin was helped into power not by Berlin's working-class radicals, but by conservative German generals. They believed they had good reason to support him. In 1917 their army was locked in a deadly war on two fronts, a war which the High Command knew it could not sustain. It was imperative that they get Russia out at any cost but their only option was to stir up trouble from within. The American ambassador Gerard reported to Washington as early as 1915 that the Germans were combing prisoner-of-war camps, supplying radicals with money and false papers and sending them back to fight the tsar.[19] In 1917 unusually cold weather in Petrograd (St Petersburg) led to food and energy cuts which led in turn to widespread strikes. As these became more violent the rag-tag Petersburg Garrison rose in revolt. The tsar refused to act, believing as Louis XVI had in 1789 that he was facing a minor skirmish and not a revolution and when his men lost control of the streets on 27 February it was too late to act. Nicholas was deposed and the provisional government took power. To the chagrin of the Germans, however, Kerensky refused to pull Russia out of the war. The High Command decided to try again.

The legion of 'Russian experts' in Berlin now informed the government that their greatest chance lay with a ruthless political exile named Vladimir Ilich Lenin, then languishing in political exile in Switzerland.[20] Parvus called him more 'raving mad' than Kerensky, and Count Brockdorff-Rantzau agreed, but in a chilling top-secret message transmitted to the Ministry of Foreign Affairs stated: 'We must now definitely try to create the utmost chaos in Russia ... we must secretly do all we can to aggravate the contradictions between the moderate and the extreme parties, since we are extremely interested in the victory of the latter, for another upheaval will then be inevitable, and will take forms which will shake the Russian state to its foundations.'[21] Bethmann-Hollweg gave instructions that Lenin be taken from Switzerland to Russia immediately.

German attempts to overthrow enemy governments from within were not new; the traitor Joseph Caillaux, later imprisoned by the French, and Sir Roger Casement, later shot in Britain, were both financed by the Germans, but unlike his counterparts Lenin proved worthy of the investment. He understood exactly why the Germans needed him and squeezed concessions from them, even dictating terms of transport through a country at war with his own.[22]

On 31 March the Assistant Secretary of State von Stumm had ciphered a message to Ambassador Romberg in Berlin: 'Urgent! the journey of the Russian émigrés through Germany should take place very quickly, since the *Entente* has already started counter-measures in Switzerland.'[23] Contrary to legend the train procured by Ludendorff was not sealed but was treated as an 'extraterritorial entity'; Krupskaya later confirmed that there had been no baggage or passport checks. The identity of all thirty-two passengers still remains a mystery, although it is known that Lenin, Krupskaya, Zinoviev and Radek were amongst the nineteen Bolsheviks on board. At midday on 11 April 1917 the train glided into Berlin and came to a halt at Potsdamer Platz. Lenin waited there for twenty hours before being taken under full police escort to another train waiting at the Stettiner Station. From there he departed for the Baltic port of Sassnitz. The Germans had ensured that he was well fed, clothed and rested when he arrived in Petrograd.

Lenin stepped out at the Finland Station to cheering crowds singing *La Marseillaise* but he was not quite the triumphant hero later depicted in Communist propaganda. Many of his erstwhile supporters now rejected his radical ideas; Stalin initially called his *April Thesis* 'short on facts' and the Bolshevik paper *Pravda* refused to publish them, claiming that their printing presses had broken down. Only after much persuasion was Lenin able to push through his now infamous programme calling for revolution. This was to result in the transfer of all power to the Soviets, the creation of a popular militia, the nationalization of land, the creation of a single Soviet National Bank, Soviet control of all agriculture and industry and the creation of a new Socialist International. Lenin also promised that if he was successful he would end the war.

Russian radicals might have had reservations about Lenin, but the Germans were delighted by their new charge; as early as 4 April their agent in Stockholm reported 'Lenin's entry into Russia is successful. He is working exactly as we wish.' As a reward the military government continued to deposit large sums of money into a Bolshevik account in the Diskontogesellschaft in Berlin, sent money to Petrograd sewn into the coats of reliable agents, and even printed counterfeit banknotes for use in Russia. Eduard Bernstein estimated that by the October Revolution the Germans had given the Bolsheviks more than 50 million Deutschmarks – more than nine tons – in gold.[24]

Lenin set about wearing down the provisional government. Despite his long-winded rhetoric he thought purely in terms of military strategy, believing as Napoleon had done that a battle is won or lost in the minds of men long before it actually begins. He created the illusion, even in the minds of his victims, that the defeat of the provisional government was inevitable. When it finally came the October Revolution was a simple *coup d'état*, a brutal, calculated bid for power that worked not because Lenin had a vast popular following, which he did not, but because he was cunning, ruthless and very lucky. The small group of radicals who walked gingerly into the Winter Palace bore little resemblance to Eisenstein's epic hordes but it did not matter. After the coup Marx's advice given after the fall of the Paris Commune was put into practice: one must not work with existing political, social or economic institutions, one must coldly crush them as one would crush an insect. After the October Revolution Lenin ruled by decree, liquidating all those who stood in his way – beginning on 5 January with the Constituent Assembly; indeed it was Lenin who provided the model for the treatment of real and imagined enemies for both Stalin and Hitler. Like his successors Lenin felt no remorse for his victims; the ends justified the most barbarous of means.

At the time, Berliners knew little about Lenin's plans. The Terror had not begun in earnest and conservatives who would soon live in fear as the red flags were raised in their own city celebrated the news of Lenin's victory, blissfully ignorant of the monster they had helped to create. All that mattered was that Lenin had promised imminent Russian withdrawal from the war.

Peace did not come quickly enough for the Germans and when Lenin tried to delay signing a treaty they invaded Russia. By 2 March they had gone so far that they bombed Petrograd, an act which forced Lenin to hurriedly move the capital to Moscow, where it has remained ever since. The Germans had helped him to power; now they forced him to sign the draconian Treaty of Brest-Litovsk, a treaty which put Berlin quite literally at the centre of Europe for the first time in her history.[25]

On the surface Brest-Litovsk was a fabulous coup for Berlin, making her the focal point of a vast eastern empire which fulfilled Naumann's 1915 dream of annexations stretching from the Baltic to Ukraine to the Caucasus. The people of Lithuania, Courland, Ukraine and Poland were to be made into part of a *cordon sanitaire* and Russia was to be pushed completely from continental Europe. The immense resources of the area would be used to fuel the German war effort and to bolster the prestige of the German empire. The Kaiser decided to make himself the duke of Courland and spent hours designing a new coat of arms resplendent with aurochs which he thought roamed there. An Austrian archduke asked to be made the king of Ukraine while the Kaiser's brother-in-law demanded the kingdom of Finland. Russia was deprived of territory as large as Austria-Hungary and Turkey combined; she lost 56 million people, one-third of her railway mileage, 79 per cent of her iron, 89 per cent of her coal and 28 per cent of her industry.[26] The acquisitions only fanned the flames of German greed. Berlin's generals dreamt of commanding the Adriatic and the Aegean, controlling Turkey, the Persian Gulf and Suez, and the Baltic; taking precious iron ore from Sweden and heavy industry from Lorraine, the Saar and Bohemia, breaking the British naval blockade and conquering Egypt and North Africa. Berliners became ever more proud of their new status, but it was a pyrrhic victory. The hoped-for food and supplies did not materialize and a million troops were needed to control the new territories, troops which were desperately needed in France.[27] As the Kaiser busily scribbled his new coat of arms the western front headed for collapse. At the same time, Lenin began to target Berlin, telling Trotsky that 'we will go under without a German revolution'.[28]

Lenin knew Berlin well. He had visited often, even living there in 1895, when German doctors had saved his life after a bout of pneumonia, and again in 1912, when he told his sister he 'almost felt at home' there. He was impressed by her industrial might and was convinced that her workers could carry the revolution forward if given the correct guidance: 'The German revolution is vastly more important than ours,' he wrote. The ink was not yet dry on Brest-Litovsk when he began to pour money, supplies and agents into Berlin, transforming the ex-tsarist embassy on Unter den Linden into a powerful

Bolshevik nerve centre.[29] Lenin continued to pump the German High Command for money and in an extraordinary document written on 14 August 1918 he refers explicitly to German financing of Communist activity. In a letter to Y. A. Berzin he states: 'I am using an opportunity to dash off a few words of greeting. I thank you from the bottom of my heart for the publications: do not spare *money* and effort on publications in three (or four) languages and distribution. The Berliners will send some more money: if the scum delay, complain to me *formally*. Yours, Lenin.'[30]

On a pleasant April morning in 1918 Berliners on their way to work were confronted by a most peculiar sight. There, in the most conservative section of the old city, a gigantic hammer and sickle could be seen rising slowly above the grand Russian embassy on Unter den Linden. It was soon followed by an enormous banner which proclaimed: WORKERS OF ALL COUNTRIES – UNITE! The new ambassador, Adolph Joffe, had arrived in Berlin. Over the next two weeks hundreds of cases, boxes and files filled with Soviet documents were sent to the building along with 300 diplomatically immune 'staff', who were in fact all skilled agitators fresh from the Bolshevik Revolution. It was clear from the beginning that Joffe had no intention of playing the role of a conventional ambassador. He categorically refused to meet the Kaiser or attend the round of drinks parties and receptions expected of him and insulted the government by inviting 'dangerous radicals and enemies of the state' to his embassy gatherings.

Thanks to Lenin, Joffe was rich. Twelve million marks had been deposited in the Mendelssohn & Co. Bank alone, and he used the money to finance Bolshevik newspapers, letters, meetings and offices. Trainloads of diplomatic bags continued to arrive from Russia stuffed with revolutionary propaganda but the Germans could do nothing to stop them. Joffe also played a masterful game of deception, cementing relationships with the Berlin capitalists and industrialists which, in one form or another, would continue well into the Nazi period. He was able to convince Berlin businessmen and bankers that he was not really interested in revolution but was merely using its rhetoric for cynical political reasons. They were blinded by self-interest and were already sending prestigious trade delegations to Moscow by the summer. Joffe boasted to Lenin, 'the director of the Deutsche Bank frequently visits us, Mendelssohn has long sought a meeting with me, and Solomonssohn has already come three times under various pretexts.' For Lenin equally interesting contacts lay on the radical left.

The moderate German Social Democratic Party, with its vast headquarters in Berlin and its 1 million members, was the largest political party in the world and was internationally recognized as the leader of the Marxist labour movement. Lenin despised it. He hated its leaders because they fought for gradual social change within a democratic framework instead of for revolution. He hated them because they had supported the Kaiser's war effort, because they openly disagreed with his one-party dictatorship and his use of terror. He hated them because they threatened his authority with the workers in a way the 'doomed' upper and middle classes did not.[31] The Social Democrats returned his hatred. The vast gulf which separated them was described in 1918 by the SPD figure Karl Kautsky, who in *The Dictatorship of the Proletariat* and later *Terrorism and Communism* vehemently attacked Lenin and his methods. With no support amongst Social Democrats Lenin was forced to rely on a small splinter group which had abandoned the Social Democratic Party in 1916. Named after the leader of the Roman slave rebellion, Spartacus, it was led by two of the most remarkable characters in the history of the period, Rosa Luxemburg and Karl Liebknecht.

'Red Rosa', the slight figure seen at Berlin rallies usually sporting a distinctly bourgeois parasol and large hat, was of Polish-Jewish origin and had worked for years in the Polish Socialist Group before moving to Russia. She had come to Berlin illegally via Bromberg to escape the tsarist police and had entered into an arranged marriage to avoid deportation. Luxemburg was an idealist with a passion for revolutionary theory, and although she spent much of the war in prison serving time for sedition and treason she continued to guide the radical left through work smuggled out by her friend Clara Zetkin. She would later found the Communist daily the *Rote Fahne* (Red Flag), about which Silvia Rodgers would later write: '[it was filled with] calls for strikes, for the release of political prisoners, for equal pay and rights for women, the role of Britain as the exploiter of black and brown people, and the *Klassenkampf* ... Above all and whenever possible, the paper vilifies the German Social Democratic Party, the SPD, whose politics were moderate.'[32] Karl Liebknecht was a lawyer and son of a moderate Social Democrat, but unlike his father he nursed a passionate hatred of the army and the imperial system. Nervous and energetic, with small glasses sitting uneasily on his pinched face, he was a tireless agitator and was first arrested in 1907 for writing anti-militarist pamphlets. After months of burying war dead on the Russian front he returned to Berlin in disgust and began to mobilize support against the war. Lenin had high hopes for him. Even in his speech at the Finland Station in 1917 Lenin had declared his support for Liebknecht and for the German revolution.

The Berlin workers had been remarkably docile in the early years of the war but by 1917 they were becoming increasingly difficult to control. Deprivation and war weariness had begun to take its toll.[33] There was a deep contempt for those who profited from the war and spent money in the grand hotels or for the officers who, as Princess Blücher put it, enjoyed pheasant and champagne while others starved. She remembered 'a man looking in at the "Esplanade" the other night, his face pressed against the glass of the door, [who] showed an expression of hatred and disgust at the elegant public within at their supper, in which there were few signs of the frugality expected in times such as these'. The anger was not confined to poverty-stricken civilians. One young officer, forced to watch helplessly as his men were mown down by machine-gun fire, was disgusted that evening to see the highest staff authorities sitting at a grand banquet and discussing the war in a flippant way: 'I could have killed them all,' he said. 'We . . . are half cripples; they think it better to send us back as "cannon fodder"; we can get killed off and no loss to the state.' Resentment grew and treasonous street demonstrations became more common and more violent. Berlin became the centre of political agitation between veterans and nationalists; in May 1917 a Berlin lawyer, Erich Kuttner, who had been wounded at Verdun, organized disabled veterans to fight for provisions and help, and to call for an end to war; the result was the Bund der Kriegsbeschädigten und Kriegsteilnehmer. The organization became increasingly radical, and on 7 January 1918, when disabled veterans disrupted a Fatherland Party rally at Alexanderplatz which was calling for the prolongation of war, they were attacked and many posted their decorations to Admiral Tirpitz in protest. There was little help for them in impoverished Berlin, and many were reduced to begging in the streets.[34] Princess Blücher passed the Esplanade Hotel on 1 May 1916 only to find it surrounded by a police cordon after a mob had stolen all the bread from the kitchens. Anyone who wore fur or jewellery was suspected of being a *Kriegs Gewinner* (war profiteer) and was liable to be beaten up and robbed. People already spoke of revolts and riots and disturbances. By 1917 their patience was beginning to run out. On 16 April that year an astounding 300,000 people marched to protest at the halving of the bread ration. Liebknecht was arrested on the same day for organizing an anti-war rally at Potsdamer Platz and 50,000 machine workers turned up to support him at the trial. Then, at the end of January 1918, Berlin was shaken by the most serious strike it had ever seen. Nearly half a million metal and munitions workers put down their tools and demanded not only food but also 'the speedy bringing about of peace . . . in accordance with the principles formulated by the Russian Peoples Commissioners in Brest-Litovsk'.[35] Angry mobs overturned trams and buses, revolutionary shop stewards combed the city recruiting workers and military personnel to join their cause and dozens of red flags went up in the main streets. Hindenburg wrote to General Wilhelm von Groener that the Berlin workers should be punished or, as he put it, 'further enlightened'. A state of siege was proclaimed and all labour press was forbidden. Seven of the great Berlin industrial firms were placed under military guard, fifty policemen were stationed permanently at the Brandenburg Gate and the men were ordered to resume work under martial law. Thousands of workers known to be involved in the protests were sent to the trenches. The strikes were eventually crushed by the Berlin Garrison but the sheer scale of support had frightened the government. Indeed it was the ferocity of the Berlin strikes which finally prompted Ludendorff to launch his disastrous offensive in March.[36]

The unravelling of discipline in Berlin was augmented by demoralization of troops on the front line. The Bolsheviks had been targeting German soldiers in the east since Brest-Litovsk, where fraternization was encouraged and thousands of German troops and prisoners of war were systematically exposed to Bolshevik propaganda; indeed the army was so well infiltrated that in October 1918 General Max Hoffmann, Chief of Staff Ober Ost, refused to use troops from Ukraine, claiming that 'Our victorious army on the Eastern Front had become rotten with Bolshevism. We got to the point where we did not dare transfer certain of our eastern divisions to the West.'[37] Some of the men were sent back to their depots in Berlin, bringing with them Lenin's cry of 'peace and bread'.

The 'rot' in the front line continued throughout the spring of 1918. The endless butchery meant that older men, including left-wing factory workers, were now being sent out as troops but they brought with them the rhetoric of the factories. They were soon joined by the ringleaders of the January strikes who had been sent out as punishment; this had the unwanted effect of sending revolutionaries straight into the divisions of already demoralized troops. The front was also awash with the 'Spartacus letters', which openly denounced the war and the Kaiser and which reached the front hidden in empty sandbags or boxes of equipment; Liebknecht even sent thousands through the post.[38] The propaganda had a powerful effect on the tired and hungry troops and as reserve divisions marched to take their positions they were jeered at by departing front-line soldiers, who told them to 'go back! go back!' Gropius wrote that 'the mood of the front against the government is becoming dangerous, thank God!' At the end he wrote, 'For four years I have given my all for this insane war and have lost, lost, lost, while a lot of those at home fatten themselves on our backs . . . What a gloomy fate to have to sacrifice everything that makes life worthwhile for an ever more doubtful patriotic ideal! We have had no bread for two weeks . . . I rack my brain over what is to become of us.'[39] Troops in training on Sedan Day did the unthinkable, and sang *The Marseillaise* in the very heart of the German capital.

The drastic decline in morale might have been reversed had Ludendorff's final offensive been successful. But his defeat marked the beginning of the end for imperial Berlin. By 1918 the city had lost all pre-war affluence. Food rations had been cut again, coal was non-existent and the influenza epidemic or *Blitzkatarrh* was sweeping through the city and claiming 300 people – mostly young women – a day.[40] The centre looked shabby and desolate; broken windows remained smashed, people fainted on the pavement while dead horses were ripped apart and slabs of meat carried off to frozen homes. Consumption of fats was 12 per cent of the pre-war level and crime began to soar in the frenzied struggle for food. Local authorities noted a marked increase in theft by armed gangs: 'One abuse which the shortage of food has created is to be found in the daily plundering expeditions by train to the country, where food has been carted off in great quantities either through persuasion or through force.'[41] Max Weber described the devastating effect of 'more than four years of camphor and morphine injections to keep up emotions – no nation has endured anything like it'. In his poem *War* Georg Heym wrote of the demon which calls men to fight, of the rivers 'already full of blood' and the numberless bodies laid out in the reeds covered with birds of death. At the end, he describes the great city which sank into a cloud of yellow smoke, a city which has 'hurled itself without a sound into the belly of the abyss'. Philipp Scheidemann said it was now hopeless to attempt to shore up civilian morale: 'It is a question of potatoes. We no longer have any meat . . . misery is so great that one poses a riddle when one asks oneself "What does North Berlin live on and how does East Berlin exist?" '[42]

When the front finally collapsed, Ludendorff and Hindenburg scrambled to avert a revolution. They quickly relinquished power to a constitutional government under Max von Baden which was to be answerable not to the Kaiser but to the Reichstag. Berliners had waited for hundreds of years for such a system but it was no longer enough. All wanted an immediate end to the war, but the choice now lay between merely deposing the Kaiser or getting rid of the entire system. The city teetered on the brink of revolution.

Liebknecht's release under the new government's general amnesty brought the second choice one step closer. Thousands of workers paraded him around Berlin in a flower-covered carriage. Scheidemann was amazed: 'Liebknecht has been carried shoulder high by soldiers who have been decorated with the Iron Cross! Who could have dreamt of such a thing happening three weeks ago?' It was also some measure of his importance to Lenin that when the report reached Russia a national holiday was declared, streetcars stopped running, factories closed and Lenin, Stalin and Sverdlov (the man who murdered the tsar) sent him a telegram conveying 'immediately . . . our very warm greetings'. Lenin called the demonstrations a 'visible sign' in the new epoch of 'triumphant socialism'. For his part Liebknecht immediately began to mobilize the workers, persuading them that peace would come only if the Kaiser was forced to abdicate. The situation in the capital was unbearably tense. The spark which finally ignited the November Revolution was the mutiny in Kiel, the port city north of Berlin.

The Kaiser's obsession with the German navy had been one of the primary causes of the First World War. As with so many follies of history the battleships had never been used, having been 'embalmed' in port while the war at sea was carried out by U-boat. When notification of Ludendorff's defeat reached Admiral Scheer he decided at least to save the honour of the navy by mounting a last stand, a 'death ride' straight into the heart of the British fleet.[43] In his ignorance he believed that this would improve the German bargaining position at the peace talks.

The sailors in Kiel had a different view. The mothballed 'iron prisons' had become hotbeds of radicalism and by 1918 had turned Bolshevik; Seaman Richard Stumpf recalled that by the end of the war 'mass refusals to obey orders had become routine'. The war was clearly lost and the men were not keen to risk their lives in an insane mission that would get them all killed, and they refused to provision the ships or put out to sea. The mutiny soon spread to the dock workers of Kiel, and by 4 November 1918 angry sailors were swarming through the city demanding the 'destruction of militarism, the termination of social injustice and the overthrow of the ruling class'. Above all, they wanted a quick end to the war.[44]

News of the mutiny spread rapidly and soviets sprang up all over Germany. On 9 November the revolution reached Berlin and hundreds of thousands of people rampaged through the streets, demolishing everything that had to do with the old order which had cost the lives of 1.2 million men. Soldiers' councils were formed on the Bolshevik model and factory workers threatened a general strike if the Kaiser did not go. Conservatives were terrified; it was just like Russia all over again. When rumours reached Max von Baden that thousands of mutinous sailors were descending on Berlin he had the tracks of the Berlin–Hamburg line ripped up.

There was a widespread feeling around the world that Berlin was going to fall. When the first reports of the mutiny reached Washington, Breckinridge Long, Assistant Secretary of State, said, 'This is the worst news of many months. If true, it means the advent of Bolshevism in force in Germany.' William Bullitt told President Wilson that the Kaiser was doomed and the power struggle was now between moderate socialists like Victor Adler and Scheidemann and the Spartacists such as Liebknecht and Mehring. He wrote, 'The conclusion is inescapable that social democracy throughout the continent of Europe is inevitable and that the question still before the world is only whether the evolution to social democracy shall be orderly and peaceful under the leadership of the moderate leaders of the working classes, or shall be disorderly and bloody under the dominance of the Bolsheviki.' It was clear who the Americans preferred; Lansing called the Bolsheviks 'a crew of murderers ... appealing to the criminal and the mentally unfit'. When Lenin offered the people of Berlin wheat in exchange for their loyalty to the Spartacist cause Lansing told Washington that ideology was irrelevant and it was food that mattered in Berlin. It could be simply put: 'Empty stomachs mean Bolsheviks. Full stomachs mean no Bolsheviks.' This view was echoed by the young British Flight Lieutenant Campbell, who noted: 'They are hungry, very hungry . . . the one question in Berlin is: When are the Americans or the English troops coming, and will they give us food? . . . They fear that food will not be given to them until all fear of a Bolshevik Revolution is past.' As crowds gathered in the streets Philipp Scheidemann said wearily: 'we have done all we can to keep the masses on the halter.'

By midday on 9 November tens of thousands of armed workers, wearing red armbands and carrying their rifles upside down to signify they had mutinied, took to the streets on foot or in lorries festooned with red banners made from bolts of cloth stolen from Berlin department stores; onlookers were amazed at the sheer amount of red material they had been able to find despite the grave textile shortages. Well-to-do Berliners hid as the mob paraded under their windows singing the *Internationale*; some bribed policemen to protect them but within hours even the police had vanished. The army refused to fire on the workers, and soldiers began to turn on their officers; the militant crowds spat on them, beat them up, ripped off their insignia and their medals or threw them into the Spree. High-ranking officers disappeared from sight as bands went from house to house; General von Beseler was given an anonymous note which alerted him to the fact that his house was on a 'hit list', so that when the mob arrived at his door they were told he was still in Warsaw. Many were not so lucky. When the dishevelled German delegation left Berlin to sign the armistice the city was in turmoil; by 9 November it was in the grip of revolution. Unless the Kaiser abdicated and the government was reformed it was feared that Berlin would fall to the Bolsheviks. Max von Baden now realized that the Kaiser would have to go and quietly handed power to the Social Democrats at 11.30 on the morning of 9 November. He then issued a statement through the Wolff Press Agency which read: 'The emperor and the king has decided to renounce the throne.' In fact the dithering William was informed of his own 'abdication' some hours later.[45]

In 1915 the Kaiser and his family had celebrated 500 years of Hohenzollern presence in the Mark Brandenburg, during which he had boasted that the dynasty would rule for ever. By the end of the war it was an empty memory and the Kaiser a pale shadow of his former self. A German Foreign Office official in Geneva described him as 'having practically ceased to exist. He is not even formally consulted in Berlin . . . he is treated as an annoying child who gets under foot or in the way.'[46] His popularity amongst the troops had been in question for over a year; when he inspected soldiers in 1917 the men were ordered to unload their weapons and hand in their bayonets. His son, the Crown Prince William, was despised by troops not least because he would wave them off to be massacred in the trenches dressed in his tennis flannels. Jokes about the Kaiser had become more bitter with each passing month: 'Which family do you guess will get through the war with its six sons alive?'[47] In the cold grey gloom of 9 November 1918, amidst the turmoil of a burgeoning revolution, the Kaiser's abdication was announced in Berlin. The first democratic German republic was declared, and the armistice followed a few days later. Ludendorff knew that the war was over for Germany; he also knew that the Allies were unwilling to negotiate with a military dictatorship. For this reason he bestowed parliamentary democracy on Berlin and recommended she appeal to the Allies for a peace settlement on the basis of President Wilson's Fourteen Points. The Kaiser waited for news which would reverse Germany's fortunes on the battlefield, but he waited in vain. General Groener suggested that he might retain his throne if he went to the front line and allowed himself to be wounded but William refused. His only course of action was to abdicate.[48]

The announcement of the abdication was greeted with enthusiasm by the revolutionaries but it shocked the nationalists, the conservatives and the *Mittelstand* to their very core. The Kaiser had stood for all they believed in; he was the symbol of all the dreams and ambitions they had nurtured since unification and he had provided German society with a sense of security and common purpose. With him gone the whole edifice collapsed. Suddenly their lives were in ruins and the angry mob was in the street. Young officers committed suicide rather than face life without the monarch, but there was also a deep sense of betrayal, a feeling that the Kaiser should have gone to the front and died a hero's death, or at least 'become wounded', as General Groener had suggested, thereby saving the throne for his sons.[49] It has left one of the great questions of German history unanswered: namely, if the monarchy had survived in some form would Germans have poured their dreams and ambitions into Hitler only a decade later? As it was, vast groups of silent Berliners dazed by the enormity of events watched in horror from the safety of their apartments and their villas, buried their valuables and prayed for a quick end to the tempest which was now engulfing them.

Friedrich Ebert was now appointed Chancellor. As hundreds of thousands of workers and soldiers marched together through the city Philipp Scheidemann rushed to the Reichstag to tell his colleagues of the appointment. The building had become a giant military base. 'Soldiers came and went. Many were armed . . . The great entry hall presented a dramatic picture. Rifles were stacked in pyramids. From the courtyard, one could hear the stamping and neighing of horses. In the hall itself, thousands of milling people seemed to be talking or screaming simultaneously.'[50] After telling his colleagues of Ebert's appointment, he decided to have a bite to eat in the Reichstag restaurant. Berlin politics were about to descend into farce.

Scheidemann's meal was interrupted by the news that Liebknecht was on his way to the palace to call for a republic modelled on Soviet Russia. If Scheidemann was to avoid a Spartacist coup he must speak to the crowds at once; as he put it, 'Whoever could bring the masses into motion, whether "Bolshevistically" from the Palace or "Social Democratically" from the Reichstag, would have won. I saw the Russian madness before me, the replacement of the Czarist terror by the Bolshevist one. "No! Not in Germany."' He left his meal, and at two o'clock flung open the French windows of the Reichstag library. 'Thousands of arms extended, waving hats and caps. The cries of the crowd echoed loudly. Then everything became still.' Scheidemann gave a short speech in which he described the horror of the war and the misery of defeat. Almost as an afterthought he shouted down to the crowd, 'The rotten old monarchy has collapsed. Long live the new! Long live the German Republic!' The onlookers cheered as he went quietly back to his meal.[51]

Like many other moderate Social Democrats, Ebert had wanted to see the establishment of a constitutional monarchy, but Scheidemann's hasty declaration could not now be reversed. This hurried, half-hearted speech marked the official beginning of a republic that nobody really wanted, a system of government which for most of its troubled life would merely be tolerated until something better could be found to replace it. Even on the day of its inception it was in mortal danger. Having heard Scheidemann's speech the excited crowds set off down the street towards the palace. A huge red servant's blanket fluttered on the roof. A mere two hours after Scheidemann's declaration from the Chancellery, Liebknecht walked to the balcony from which the Kaiser had declared the mobilization in 1914 and yelled: 'I proclaim the free Socialist Republic of Germany, which shall comprise all Germans ... We extend our hands to them and call on them to complete the World Revolution. Those amongst you who want the World Revolution raise your hands to an oath.'[52] The crowd raised their hands in unison and cheered.

The Social Democrats hoped simply to ignore Liebknecht. They now formed the legitimate government of Germany and they congratulated themselves on the success of their 'revolution'. Their supporters eulogized the speech from the Reichstag as beginning a proud new age in German politics: the *Frankfurter Zeitung* wrote that a 'glorious feeling of liberty and brotherliness has taken hold of the entire nation', while Theodor Wolff wrote in the *Berliner Tageblatt* that 'the greatest of all revolutions has, like a suddenly onrushing storm, overturned the Imperial regime ... yesterday morning, at least in Berlin, everything was still there; yesterday afternoon nothing of all that existed any longer.' Ernst Troeltsch was more realistic; in his 'Spectator Letters' of 10 November he wrote of Berlin: 'Everything is somewhat subdued, like people whose destiny is being decided somewhere far off in the distance . . .'[53]

For all the self-acclaim, the Social Democratic 'November Revolution' had been a revolution in name only. The Kaiser had been deposed and the war ended but power had been given to them from above, not least because the Allies had refused to negotiate with a German military government. It had been more like a simple transfer of power than a revolution, more like the French collapse of 1871 than the revolution of 1789. For his part Liebknecht refused to accept the new status quo and with the cheers of the palace crowds still ringing in his ears he vowed to fight on. In a final attempt to integrate the Spartacus members into the new regime Ebert called for a mass meeting of representatives of all the German soviets in the great round hall of the Circus Busch, in which most of the 3,000 delegates voted to support Ebert's Social Democrats. The SPD and Independent Socialist executive council again invited Liebknecht to join them but he refused. Instead, he opted for civil war.

For the next three months nobody seemed to know exactly what to do. The Social Democrats were in power but they had no idea of how to govern, and they had lost control of the streets. Few believed the republic would survive into the new year. Berlin had been badly affected by the armistice; the Allies had seized vehicles and trains, putting severe pressure on Berlin's transportation system which was still carrying a million passengers a day; the amount of coal for household use fell by 27 per cent between April 1918 and March 1919 and for gas works and electric works by 86 and 79 per cent respectively. Industries were closing down rapidly, starvation was widespread, the flu epidemic continued to kill and there was mounting anger against the seemingly ineffectual government. Crowds of young men rode around in lorries terrorizing people and demanding that they 'join the revolution', but as they all wore bright red few could tell if they were Social Democrats, Spartacus members or something else entirely. One adjutant reported to his commanding officer: 'Disorder, lack of discipline, looting, wild commandeering and house searching . . . The troops go their own way, the barracks are like a madhouse. Sentry posts don't exist. There are soldiers' Soviets in every corner and alley . . . The true masters of Berlin are indiscipline, vice and chaos . . . Day and night senseless shooting out of exhilaration and fear.'[54] Princess Blücher said, 'Berlin, the cleanest and most orderly of European towns is now the most disorderly and a perfect bedlam . . . everyone is convulsed with rage, despair, hunger and cold.' The situation was not helped by the massive unemployment, which reached a high of 276,420 in Berlin in February 1919.[55] Some industries like the manufacture of clothing and paper began to expand but armaments industries laid off increasing numbers of workers, particularly women; the Deutsche Maschinenbau AG had let all of its women employees go by February 1919, as had the Runge-Werke rubber factory in Spandau, and shifts for men were cut drastically.[56] Berlin had suffered a net population loss of 16 per cent during the war. It now attracted returning soldiers and thousands of refugees, who flooded in from Posen, East Prussia and Russia, leading to a sudden population increase of over 230,000 people between 1 November 1918 and 31 January 1919. Many were homeless, unemployed and vulnerable to those who promised radical change. There were plenty of 'revolutionaries' of every hue but Liebknecht's 'Council of Deserters, Stragglers and Furloughed Soldiers' slowly began to dominate. His 60,000 'shock troops' raced around Berlin drinking and looting, generously signalling their intention to ransack a house by suspending a grenade on the victim's front door handle. Liebknecht began to occupy important buildings, beginning with the officers of the conservative newspaper the *Lokal Anzeiger*. Guided by Rosa Luxemburg, Spartacus workers began to print their paper, the *Rote Fahne*.[57]

Increasing turmoil in Berlin gave Lenin and Liebknecht cause to be optimistic. They saw the November Revolution as only the first step towards their own seizure of power, just as Kerensky's February Revolution which toppled the tsar had heralded Lenin's own success.[58] Now the second phase could begin in earnest. In January 1919 Lenin sent his agent Karl Radek back to the city to direct events in accordance with his revolution of October 1917. Radek was to ensure that the soldiers, workers and unemployed would overthrow Ebert's interim government and disrupt the January elections to the National Assembly, elections which he knew Spartacus could not win. As in Russia two years before, the resulting chaos was meant to give them a chance to seize power.

As the new year passed Berliners could sense that something was about to happen. The streets were suddenly more dangerous; the atmosphere more strained. Otto Schmalhausen, a soldier just back from the western front, remembered being suddenly confronted in the Hohenzollerndamm by a bourgeois man who offered him free board and a meal of veal cutlets if he would stay the night and protect his family. When he refused he was given a bottle of Château-Lafite for 'future security'. Georg Grosz also walked through Berlin on the eve of the Spartacus uprising and found the streets empty, not only because of the curfew but because of a pervading sense of fear. It was strangely dark as the power stations were either shut down by strikes or occupied by the Spartacists. 'The smell of civil war was in the air . . . the stucco had fallen away from the houses, windows were broken, and many businesses had lowered their iron blinds, although through them and the dingy plate glass behind them you could just make out dummies that had not been dusted for years.' Even so, he 'ducked in and out of the tall doorways keeping close to the small porters' lodges – many people, unable to bear their frightened and cooped-up existence, had made for the rooftops and would take pot-shots at anything they saw, whether birds or people'.[59] Ordinary people were armed with everything from Mausers to machine guns.

The bloody Spartacus Uprising began in earnest on 5 January 1919, sparked off by Ebert's decision to fire the self-appointed 'police chief' Eichorn. Spartacus appealed to the Berlin proletariat to defend him: 'March out in a mass! Your freedom depends on it, your future depends on it! The future of the Revolution depends on it!' The demonstrations started at the police headquarters at Alexanderplatz and soon extended for many blocks east and west along the Königsstrasse. Revolutionary leaders spoke from the balcony of the Regierungsbank and the Spartacus leadership voted overwhelmingly to overthrow the Ebert government. Count Kessler remembered seeing two processions, one made up of Social Democrats and the other of Spartacists. They looked alike with 'the same sort of clothes, waving the same red flags, and moving in the same sort of shambling step. But they carry slogans, jeer at each other as they pass, and perhaps will be shooting one another down before the day is out.' Within hours his prediction had come true.

By afternoon the demonstrations had become violent and by nightfall Spartacus had seized all important government buildings in the city centre. On 6 January 200,000 workers joined the general strike and the mob raged in the streets, attacking the Wolff Telegraph Agency and the newspaper offices of Ullstein, Mosse and Scherl.[60] The Vorwärts newspaper offices at the Belle-Allianz-Platz were again taken over and an entire issue was seized and dumped into the Spree. Riflemen controlled the top of the Brandenburg Gate and Unter den Linden, the Charlottenburger Chaussee and north along the Königsstrasse. The government printing office was seized, all the Berlin railway stations were taken, the enormous Botzow Brewery was occupied and the Reichstag was attacked. Liebknecht was driven triumphantly through the city surrounded by a ring of trucks with machine guns mounted on top and hailed as Berlin's 'Lenin', poised to emulate the Bolshevik success at the Smolny Institute. Spartacus confidently prepared a document announcing: 'The Ebert-Scheidemann Government Has Been Deposed'. But there were differences between Berlin and Petersburg. Unbeknownst to Spartacus the Social Democrats had made a secret pact with the army, and even then its leaders were planning their attack.[61]

When a militaristic state collapses there are always those who resent its demise. The Kaiser had gone but the basic socio-economic structure of Germany remained virtually intact. Ebert had not introduced any serious reforms and while his Council of People's Representatives had called for a constitution to be drafted by a National Assembly, the bureaucracy, judiciary, education, religious establishments and, above all, the army remained in place.[62] Faced with the Spartacus threat the moderate socialist government decided that their only chance of survival was to co-operate with their erstwhile oppressors. Their decision would affect the entire future of the Weimar Republic, and indeed the very fate of Germany.

The first step towards this fateful alliance had already taken place on 9 November, the day that Scheidemann and Liebknecht had declared republics from their respective balconies. Late that night Ebert had returned to his new private office in the Wilhelmstrasse. Suddenly a telephone rang. When he picked it up he was speaking to the chief of staff, General Groener, at the army headquarters in Spa. Groener informed him that the Kaiser had just fled to Holland and that Germany needed a new government which would support the officer corps and oversee the massive demobilization from France. He offered to put the army at Ebert's disposal 'to fight against Bolshevism', but on one condition: he must never meddle in army affairs.[63] The first Chancellor, and future President of Germany's first republic, secretly agreed to their demands, in effect promising to preserve Prussia's backward military tradition even in a democratic republic. Now, surrounded by the Spartacus mob, he called on the military for help. He had every reason to think they would succeed, for he had just caught a glimpse of their new secret force. It was called the Freikorps.

Only two days before the Spartacus Uprising Ebert had been taken on a surprising journey to the little town of Zossen on the edge of Berlin by his Defence Minister, the 'bloodhound' Gustav Noske.[64] When he had stepped from the car he could not believe his eyes. There, on a small snow-covered parade ground, were 4,000 well-turned-out troops who looked as if they had just stepped out of an imperial postcard. It was the first time in Prussian history that a military review had been staged for a civilian and it was a welcome sight for a desperate man. Ebert could not have known that some of these very troops would soon threaten his own government and form the basis for Hitler's Stormtroopers; for him they represented a chance to restore order to his shattered city.

The Freikorps was an almost inevitable consequence of the collapse of the army in 1918. When the nine Berlin infantry divisions had straggled home after the armistice the men faced a bleak future. The parade held in their honour was a sad affair: a few strands of greenery had been hung on the Brandenburg Gate, some of the helmets had been decorated with oak leaves, and a few brown flags symbolizing the new republic had fluttered amongst the imperial colours. Despite these preparations the mood was tinged with melancholy. Well over a million young men were dead, over 4 million had been wounded, and one out of every eleven Germans was a casualty of the conflict. Of 350,000 young men who had been enlisted from the central districts of Berlin 54,000 had died and it has been estimated that in all over 350,000 young men from greater Berlin were killed in the war.[65] And despite this sacrifice, the German army had lost the war. The troops trudged by in the cold, the misery and suffering of the trenches still etched on their faces. Chaplain Raymund Dreeling described them as weary beings dazed by defeat and stunned by the new situation: 'The unshaved faces beneath the helmets are haggard, wasted with hunger and long peril, pinched and dwindled to the lines drawn by terror and courage and death.' There is no doubt that if the army had been victorious Berliners would have turned out in their hundreds of thousands to cheer them with flowers and songs, as they had so many times before, and to take them back into society, but this time the dejected troops quickly disappeared and became easy prey for anyone who could offer them food, shelter and a future. Those not attracted by the left were ideal recruits for the Freikorps.

The Freikorps started small. The first groups were based on the legendary elite battalions which had led the suicidal attacks over No Man's Land to the enemy trenches; the officers had always been under twenty-five, were expected to be 'physically perfect' and had been hailed as 'New Men'. They were also ruthless; Hermann Göring would later refer to them reverentially as the men who could not be 'debrutalized' after the war. But the Freikorps also attracted ordinary soldiers – those with nowhere to go, those too young to have seen the front and who wanted to 'do something' for their country, and those who, horrified by the threat of Bolshevism, believed that joining was the patriotic thing to do. In the beginning the Freikorps was used to repress Communist revolts throughout Germany and to provide some security for the young republic, but it also did much to sustain the militarism and aggression which fuelled the right-wing paramilitary groups of the 1920s.[66]

Noske was impressed by the calibre of the new groups and officially sanctioned them in January 1919. With Ebert's approval he set up headquarters in an empty girls' school in Dahlem, equipping it with everything from a map room to radio transmitters. When Spartacus began to take Berlin he prepared for battle and on 9 January he gave the order to march. That night 1,200 Freikorps troops of the Potsdam Regiment began to move towards the Belle-Allianz-Platz. Anyone who came within ten steps of them was shot.

The first target was the *Vorwärts* building in the newspaper quarter, where over 350 Spartacus members sat in waiting. The famous photographs of radicals firing over huge rolls of newsprint, later used in every East German history textbook, belied the fact that within hours most had been captured or killed. Poorly organized Spartacus fighters had no chance against the howitzers and tanks of the Potsdam Freikorps; even after the white flag was raised the bombardment continued and when they surrendered seven people were beaten to death or shot on the spot. Following this success Noske gave the order to liquidate all other Spartacus strongholds in Berlin. Bourgeois Berliners who had been hiding from the Bolshevik menace came out on their balconies to cheer them on. Artur Iger, a Freikorps supporter, described it as an

> unforgettable procession . . . Man after man, faces as if cast in bronze, shoulder to shoulder, these magnificent figures, the liberators of Berlin . . . and behind them a column of the prisoners – disgraces to their uniforms, the three hundred Spartacists, some of them women, seem ready for the rope . . . A single thought enlivens the crowd, a single feeling envelops the throng of happy women and men and seizes the youths who have survived the terror: The criminals have not won their criminal game, the beautiful metropolis on the Spree has not become the spoil of this human dross.[67]

The night of 11 January saw a vicious and bloody battle to recapture the red-brick police station on Alexanderplatz and the next day troops based in the beautiful Charlottenburg Palace attacked from the south, while troops based at the Eden Hotel went for targets on Unter den Linden.[68] On the 13th Maercker's Volunteer Rifles (with headquarters in the Crown Prince's Palace), Roeder's group, based in the Viktoria School, Wissel's troop near Treptow Park, and General von Held's Seventeenth Division Volunteers, based in the Neukölln town hall, attacked Berlin simultaneously. They moved in one block at a time, rounding up suspected radicals and flushing out Spartacus supporters who had taken to shooting from the roofs of occupied buildings. Bloody street fighting broke out all over Berlin but this time the Freikorps gained control. They set up machine guns on the main squares in the city centre and recaptured the Brandenburg Gate, pushing Spartacus into tiny pockets of resistance which were then brutally crushed.[69] On 13 January the revolutionary shop stewards called an end to the general strike, but when the workers would not disperse after a peaceful demonstration at the Reichstag troops under the command of General Lüttwitz opened fire with machine guns. Within seconds forty-two lay dead and 105 wounded. Noske claimed that the demonstration had been 'an insurrection' and ordered a state of siege throughout northern Germany, clamping down on all subversive organizations and killing dozens of suspected radicals; it was reminiscent of the June Days in Paris, with the role of Cavaignac filled by Gustav Noske. The Spartacus Uprising was over.

Its failure was ultimately due to the superior strength of the army, but it was also due to the ineptitude of its own leaders. Despite its brave face Spartacus was hopelessly divided.[70] Rosa Luxemburg, the idealist of the group, had protested against the January uprising on the grounds that the proletariat were not yet 'ready' to fulfil their historic task. Karl Radek told her that the proletariat would never be 'ready' but that they always had to be led, and when she attacked him for supporting Lenin's tactics he retorted that she was a naive idealist, that even the Bolsheviks had been weak and isolated and that ruthlessness had been essential to their survival. 'How can you deny the need for terror in such circumstances ... particularly against classes whom history has sentenced to death?' to which Luxemburg replied that he belonged in 'the whore category'. None of this was conducive to revolutionary harmony.[71]

Luxemburg's 'weakness' had caused Radek to doubt the ruthlessness of the Berlin Spartacists and he too withdrew his support for the uprising, hoping to later replace the impotent German leaders with people more in keeping with the Russian Bolshevik line.[72] The decision to proceed was taken by Karl Liebknecht, but the man hailed by Lenin as the next leader of Germany turned out to be vain, self-serving and utterly disorganized. He was an inept tactician and he lacked a grand plan. When his troops took over buildings or train stations they received no orders on how to proceed and even Luxemburg admitted that the demonstration on 9 January had been the largest, 'but most useless', in Berlin history. There was no equivalent of the Petrograd Military Revolutionary Committee to direct proceedings in Berlin. Liebknecht was no Lenin.[73]

With the quashing of Spartacus the Freikorps leaders set out to capture the ringleaders. Ebert offered 10,000 marks for Radek's arrest, and he was quickly rounded up, along with Georg Ledebour and Ernst Meyer, Leo Jogisches and Hugo Eberlein. But Karl Liebknecht and Rosa Luxemburg evaded capture. It seems that Luxemburg was unaware of the great danger she was in and continued to write editorials for the Rote Fahne, one of which was bitterly entitled 'Order Rules in Berlin'. Liebknecht hid in the working-class district of Neukölln but on the night of 14 January he moved to the more affluent 53 Mannheimer Strasse in Wilmersdorf. Luxemburg and Wilhelm Pieck joined him there. Suddenly, at 9 p.m., a patrol from the Horse Guards Division surrounded the building, having been tipped off by a 'trusted neighbour'. They seized the Spartacus leaders, and took them to the Eden Hotel for interrogation.

Luxemburg and Liebknecht were questioned separately, and were released without charge. Liebknecht left the rooms first. As he emerged from the plush interior a burly Freikorps soldier named Runge brought the butt of his rifle down hard on Liebknecht's head. Dazed and bleeding he was pushed into a waiting car which was driven to the Tiergarten. The driver pretended that the car had broken down and Liebknecht was shoved out towards the dark trees. He staggered for a moment and began to walk. After a few steps, he was shot in the back.

Luxemburg had followed Liebknecht through the door. Runge smashed his rifle butt down again, this time crushing part of her skull. She was bundled into another car and after a few minutes a pistol was put to her head and her brains were blown out in the back of the moving vehicle. Her body was pulled from the seat and dumped from the Leichtenstein Bridge into the dark Landwehr Canal. She crashed through the thin sheet of ice and was trapped there; the bloated, rotting corpse was discovered the following May. Rosa Luxemburg and Karl Liebknecht became martyrs and essential elements of Communist Party iconography, but a great proportion of Berliners heaved a sigh of relief, glad to be rid of the Bolshevik menace. Few yet realized how high the cost had been.[73]

The violence did not end with the defeat of Spartacus; indeed the two brutal murders marked the start of a new kind of savagery, the deadly combat between Communists and the radical right which would continue well into the Nazi period. By 19 January the First Freikorps had occupied the entire city, tracking down 'radicals' and ensuring they were 'shot while trying to escape' or 'shot resisting arrest'. Many people simply disappeared after being taken into custody; dozens of unknown corpses joined Luxemburg's in the canals of the city.[74] Noske began to use force to suppress unrest in other parts of Germany – in Bremen, in the Ruhr, in Halle. The tactics learned in Berlin were becoming universally useful and before long they would be directed against the government itself. On 15 January 1919 the *Manchester Guardian* reported: 'The formidable military machine, which seemed to be crushed for ever, has risen again with astounding rapidity. Prussian officers are stalking the streets of Berlin, soldiers marching, shouting and shooting at their command. Indeed Ebert and Scheidemann very likely got more than they bargained for.' Haase wrote that 'the officer caste has never made such a great show of themselves as now ... the military spirit has never been revealed in so unpleasant a fashion as at present'.

In the second week of March Independents and Communists called for a general strike in Berlin following the election victory of the bourgeois Volkspartei and the forced disbanding of the soldiers' soviets, and began attacking police stations throughout the city.[75] Noske spread the rumour that Spartacus members had murdered sixty police officers in cold blood and sent 42,000 Freikorps troops, the 'White Terror', under the command of Colonel Wilhelm

Reinhard and Captain Pabst of the Guard Cavalry Rifle Division. 'Any proletarian seen carrying arms' was to be 'instantly executed'. The brutality in the March battles was extreme: people were shot in the back after giving themselves up; machine guns were turned on a group of soviet sailors who had surrendered and twenty-eight were killed in cold blood; Communists and Freikorps members were ambushed in the back streets and tortured before being stabbed or shot. Mortars and heavy artillery were used liberally by both sides. Over seventy of Noske's men and 1,200 Communist supporters were killed in the street fighting. On surveying the scene around him Count Kessler concluded that 'every horror of the most pitiless civil war is perpetrated by each side. The hatred and bitterness which are being sown now will bear fruit. The innocent will pay for this cruelty.'[76] Continued Social Democratic support for the Freikorps disillusioned many who had supported them during the November Revolution. Rilke now saw the whole enterprise as a failure; for him the government was the same as before 'in which the old want of character persists'. Paul Cassirer now called the revolution 'nothing but a great swindle', the only difference being that 'a few cousins' had been shoved into positions of power, and Count Kessler noted during the 1919 May Day celebrations that people were in 'national mourning for a revolution that misfired'.

The state of siege was lifted on 6 December, but military brutality and 'overkill', cold-blooded murder and summary justice continued. The general acceptance of violence was part of the legacy of the war, but it shocked those visitors who had seen the prim imperial capital before 1914. Berlin was awash with violent reminders of the trenches: the war wounded and their con-artist imitators hung around all major street corners and the weapons trade continued to flourish. Some, like Erich Maria Remarque and Hermann Hesse, actively spoke out against violence but few listened. Georg Grosz wrote that

> the times were certainly out of joint. All moral restraint seemed to have melted away. A flood of vice, pornography and prostitution swept the entire country ... The city was dark, cold and full of rumours. The streets were wild ravines haunted by murderers and cocaine pedlars, their emblem a metal bar or a murderous broken-off chair leg. People denied all knowledge, but whispered about secret manoeuvres by the Black Reichswehr or a newly-formed Red Army.[77]

The obsession with death increased as the ghastly influenza pandemic made its fearsome way through the population; 4,732 Berliners died in December 1918 alone.[78] The city was full of the thousands of war veterans 'who had not been able to find their way back from the trenches to the factory floor. In any case there was no regular work even for those who sought it.'

Berlin began to attract extremists who delighted in translating war-time language into political discourse. For members of the radical left or radical right politics was no longer a question of compromise but was an all-out war – a battle which was to end in the enemy's utter destruction. The Freikorps came to symbolize the continuation of wartime camaraderie, with young men working to 'crush the revolution, crush the Bolsheviks, crush the Poles in Upper Silesia' and beat the 'blood red women', the 'Bolshevik whores' to death. They took sadistic pleasure in their work. Political murders became commonplace, and the street fighters talked about the matchless pleasure of killing, of the 'power of the sword'. Ernst von Salomon remembered his time in the Freikorps as one laced with excitement and death: 'We were a band of fighters drunk with all the passion of the world; full of lust, exultant in action.' The popular writer Hermann Lons described man as an essentially primitive being, who was destroyed by the 'un-German' urban centres like Berlin. Although Ernst Jünger was a complex figure and far from the Nazi sympathizer he was made out to be, his work exalting German nobility in battle and his 'new race' built for war fanned the militaristic flames. In his *Der Kampf als inneres Erlebnis* he described combat as a time 'when the blood courses through the brain and arteries as before a long-desired night of love, but much more hotly, more madly'. He wrote of war as the 'father of all things' and warned that 'Under the skin of all cultural and technical progress we remain naked and raw like the men of the forest and of the steppe . . . That is the new man, the pioneer of the storm, the choice product of central Europe.'[79] Brutal 'primitive' posters with sadistic and pornographic undertones were pasted on every street corner in the city. Death and violence were mundane.

The popular novels and trashy serials which began to appear were often horrific combinations of savagery and sex, with titles like *Jack the Mysterious Maiden Killer*. Viktor von Falk's *The Executioner of Berlin* contained 3,000 pages of graphic murder, beatings, agonizing tortures and sexual perversion, and it sold well over a million copies. Plays were also violent; in 1918 Max Reinhardt produced Frank Wedekind's *Pandora's Box*, in which the main character, the sweet Lulu, is graphically butchered by Jack the Ripper. New cabaret was macabre and the satire savage; the sketches were no longer expressions of the self-confidence of the imperial capital but reflected its defeat: 'Berlin, Berlin, you just aren't what you were – The Friedrichstadt now looks like Myslowitz [a dingy provincial area].' The period abounds with violent sketches and songs; Klabund wrote lyrics like 'Come on, give me some cash, dear . . . I want to booze and to carouse, I want to buy a lovely house – Or perhaps a shroud.[80]' The new characters enjoyed murder for the fun of it: in his *Cheerful Murderess* Klabund recounts the story of a lesbian who put acid in her husband's food and gleefully watched him die. Franz Hessel's songs were full of grisly tales of dire poverty; in the *Tenement Lullaby* a night watchman hangs himself in desperation, while 'A small boy laughs till he is sick; And other children jeer and mock; While dancing round the tenement block.' Walther Mehring's *Fortune Teller* gives 'Elli the slut' a filthy abortion in her 'dingy stinking cellar', and is later murdered for the money she has made. Erich Kästner captured the sense of helplessness in post-war Berlin: 'All together in the same train, we're driving through the night. We feel our journey was in vain; All together in the same train . . . It seems we've lost the fight.'[81]

The psychiatrist Otto Binswanger was appalled at this moral decay and tried to explain it in terms of the defeat. For him patriotism had been distorted into 'cruel hate' and he warned that the wish to utterly annihilate the war-time enemy was being applied directly to civilian life. Without the normal restraints of pre-war society the troops were carrying on as before, attacking 'enemies' as if they were still on the front. Criminologists noted that brutal acts were now commonly committed by men with no previous records and attributed this to war-time experiences combined with the perilous social and economic situation in the capital. In Arnold Zweig's novel *Pont und Anna* a former officer and member of the Freikorps commits a brutal murder during a rape, an act which is applauded by his colleagues. Berliners now seemed immune to violence; one eyewitness described how men who had just been outside fighting would 'without the slightest hesitation wipe their bloodstained hands and come in from the street battles to the cabarets to dance and drink and dine with women'. There were even a number of infamous cases of serial killers who skinned and processed their victims and sold them as bottled goat's meat or preserved pork, making a fortune on the black market. The perversity in popular literature was merely a reflection of a society gone mad.

The frenzied art which began to appear immediately after the war also reflected this moral decay. One manifestation of it was Dada, an attack on traditional values which paraded under the slogan 'Art is Shit'. Originally founded in the Cabaret Voltaire in Zürich it was brought to Berlin by Richard Hülsenbeck in 1919. The Dadaists were appalled by the slaughter of the First World War but, although associated with the radical left, their agenda was simply to expose the madness of a world at war by turning it on its head.[82] They attended meetings in the Romanisches Café and Sunday morning 'matinées' in a cheap little theatre in the West End, letting loose a frenzy of anarchism and nihilism. Walther Mehring would yell poetry accompanied by the tapping of a typewriter, John Heartfield and 'Dada-Oz' Schmallhausen (in his bowler hat and yellow gloves) would come on stage drunk and hurl abuse at the 'pillars of society' and at the audience. The 'Propagandada' Georg Grosz would read earnestly from Baader's *Dadacon*, a collection of random newspaper clippings pasted together, or would urinate on pictures by establishment artists; Schwitters would build 'statues' from pieces of rubbish, giving them names like 'Germany's Greatness and Decline in Three Stages', Hülsenbeck and Raoul Hausmann held a race between a sewing machine and a typewriter; when the latter 'lost' Hülsenbeck smashed it on stage. The largely unrehearsed performances were always guarded by the police, who were incapable of controlling the inevitable raucous fights. The imperial madness which had driven Germany to war was ridiculed at every turn: at the first Dadaist exhibition Rudolf Schlichter set up a giant mannequin dressed as a German general with a pig's head, and labelled it 'Hung by the Revolution', while Dix's huge, twisted 'war cripples' hobbled along on the wall beneath it. After hearing one of Mehring's poems Stefan Zweig wrote, 'All values were changed . . . no tradition, no moral code was respected.' The more the bourgeois critics were taken in, the more the Dadaists despised them.[83] The movement began to fade as the artists grew ever more cynical about the November Revolution and the failure of Spartacus, but much of the seething discontent remained in their later work.

The Berlin Expressionists and the 'Neue Wilden' also reflected the aftermath of war and the emotional hope that the revolution would sweep all memory of it away. In 1914 the young German Expressionists had gone to the *guerra festa* with wildly idealistic beliefs that it would bring about fundamental change. George Heym had captured the prevailing mood: 'if only there was war I would be healthy again,' he said; 'everything is so boring.' The mass slaughter soon put a stop to these notions; Gropius wrote from the front in 1918 that he was 'livid with rage sitting in chains through this mad war which kills any meaning of life . . . The war will ruin people.'

The Novembergruppe of 1919 was the Berlin Expressionists' answer to the war and to the Russian Revolution. Artists like Max Pechstein and the sculptor Rudolf Belling were determined to 'link art to the revolution', and were joined by a list of eminent artists – including the painter Emil Nolde, the architects Walter Gropius and Erich Mendelsohn (who built the famous observatory or Einstein Tower at Potsdam), the playwright Bertolt Brecht, the composers Kurt Weill and Paul Hindemith and the art dealer Alfred Flechtheim. Their first manifesto read: 'The future of art and the seriousness of this hour forces us revolutionaries of the spirit (Expressionists, Cubists, Futurists) towards unity and close co-operation.' The movement was to achieve a 'new unity of art and life' and there were endless pronouncements on the 'sacred solidarity' of painters and poets. The eruptive intensity and bitterness was meant to give expression to the 'wildest raging era of human history'.

For all their ambitions the Expressionists and those already dabbling with Verism reflected more of the uncertainty of the times than any kind of utopian future. Heady canvasses were filled with tortuous images of death. They showed visions inspired by the morphine, cocaine and heroin then in vogue with the avant-garde; they showed the Berlin gangs and the seedy cafés, and they explored the erotic rituals and bizarre cults which had sprung up in those hopeless days. War was reflected in plays like Ernst Toller's drama *The Transformation*, which had the actors dressed as skeletons trapped in a mock trench. Film also reflected the macabre life in the city: Robison's *Warning Shadows* was filled with evil, death and dreams, mediums and magicians, hidden chambers of lust, and walls which were alive. In Lang's later work *Dr Mabuse* Count Told asks the doctor why he thinks Expressionism is merely a game: 'but why not? Today everything is a game.' Robert Wiene's 1919 *The Cabinet of Dr Caligari* was the most famous Expressionist film, made as it was of strange twisted sets of dark rooftops and alleys and with its evil protagonist creeping through the blackened city. Rudolph Kurtz's review of it captured the pervading mood in Berlin: a city of the

> distraught souls caught in the web of fate . . . the delirium and hallucination, stemming from a much wilder time, darkened streets, the shouted commands of republican troops, from somewhere the harsh screeching of street-corner rhetoricians – a city clothed in the deepest darkness occupied by radical revolutionaries, with the rattle of machine guns, chains, rooftop snipers and hand grenades.

Some artists who had made their names in Berlin before 1914 portrayed ever more terrible images of the post-war city: Heinrich Zille continued to chronicle the deprivation of the urban proletariat, Käthe Kollwitz depicted tragic views of suffering in the violent slums beside the 'saintly head' of the murdered Karl Liebknecht; Meidner depicted the terror of urban life, Kirchner painted grotesque, garish, distorted prostitutes preying on the city.[84] Georg Grosz and Otto Dix outdid each other in their visions of black marketeers, Freikorps assassins, crippled veterans and sex murderers, which reversed the values of the imperial era. Dix's drawing of an ex-soldier who had lost most of his mouth and lips was taken from one of Ernst Friedrich's series of photographs *War Against War*, pictures which were so horrific that they encouraged the popular myth that secret hospitals existed for men so hideously wounded that they were not to be permitted out.[85] Wieland's journal *Neue Jugend* became a vehicle for the new aggressive style; Franz Jung ripped at contemporary life through poetry while John Heartfield produced his collages plastered with coffins and death masks and strange symbols which frightened the uninitiated. His work, as Grosz put it, 'reflected the spirit of the age, of a world in the process of being dismembered'. Even the great burst of creativity offered by the Russian émigrés was tinged with bloodshed; Nabokov's father was murdered during a skirmish in a Berlin theatre. Stefan Zweig, who hated Berlin, referred to the city as a centre of madness, while Georg Grosz called it 'a seething cauldron'. It was hardly the sort of place to inspire political loyalty in the rest of Germany or confidence in the rest of the world.

Nothing represented Berlin's sudden fall from grace more dramatically than the decision to convene the first meeting of the National Assembly far from the capital, in the small town of Weimar. From the middle of the sixteenth to the end of the nineteenth century Weimar had attracted revered figures in German history, including Lucas Cranach, Johann Sebastian Bach, Friedrich Schiller, Franz Liszt and, above all, Johann Wolfgang von Goethe. Ebert consciously played on Allied war propaganda which distinguished between the Prussian militarism of Berlin-Potsdam and the humanistic tradition of Weimar, but in reality he feared that Berlin was too dangerous and too unstable to act as a focal point for the republic. While the streets of Berlin were in chaos Weimar was peaceful, quiet, provincial and safe, and where Berlin espoused a strange, decadent morality Weimar represented Pan-German values. But the decision was naive. The problems in Berlin were representative of those faced by the entire nation; they were simply closer to the surface in the sprawling urban centre.

In 1848 the German liberals had genuinely believed that the mere introduction of their Frankfurt constitution would give birth to a liberal Germany; likewise the architects of Weimar hoped that their constitution would produce a population of convinced democrats and quickly heal the rifts of war. They refused to see that Germany had never been a democracy and its people did not yet understand the individual responsibility which such a system demanded. To the new groups of young Communist and right-wing thugs already longing for radical solutions to the shame of 1918 the 'effete' Weimar democracy became a symbol of political weakness. Peter Suhrkamp noticed that even in its early days people preferred the idea of hero-worship to slow constitutional change: 'Without heroes they feel nothing. They resign, they take off. They have never grasped the difficulties, the dangers, and the harsh laws of reality.' Weimar represented a dream world, and when the National Constituent Assembly opened on 6 February 1919 it was bound to disappoint the expectant nation.

For a population which could still remember the pomp of glittering imperial state occasions the first gathering of the National Assembly was a terrible anti-climax. There were no banners, uniforms, horses or grand speeches, no Kaiser or royal family or military parades, just a few grey men in civilian clothes shuffling into a makeshift chamber. The first meeting convened in the New Theatre. A 'Gothic room' had been constructed out of tatty *Lohengrin* sets intended to evoke the Houses of Parliament at Westminster, but the illusion failed. Other symbolic gestures also fell flat. The new government decided to use the black/red/gold flag of 1848 but it was highly unpopular as most Germans preferred the traditional colours of black, white and red, constantly referring to the yellow as 'mustard' or 'chicken shit' or 'pus'. It was no accident that Hitler resurrected the imperial colours on the Nazi swastika. The controversy over the flag merely reflected the lack of legitimacy of the republic as a whole, and its situation was not helped by the continuing state of crisis. Only five months after its birth Weimar was dealt another devastating blow: the Treaty of Versailles.

Throughout the war Berliners had exhibited an uncanny ability to misunderstand the effect of their actions on others. For all their wit and intelligence they lacked the self-criticism which might have prepared them for defeat and its aftermath. This blindness took many forms. Although Berlin was delighted to act as the strong German capital after 1871 its inhabitants were offended when the Allies identified the city with the very Prussian militarism which had won them that status. Although they openly demonstrated in support of the invasion of neutral Belgium and the sinking of the *Lusitania*, they could not understand the hostile Allied propaganda directed against them both during and after the war. Although Berliners had avidly supported chauvinistic, aggressive German war aims in 1914 they refused to accept responsibility for its consequences, claiming until the end that they had been 'forced' into the conflict by Russian 'brutality' and Allied 'encirclement'. It was in this atmosphere of self-delusion that Berliners waited to hear the terms of peace. Although they had not been invited to send a representative to the talks in Paris, they assumed that they would be treated fairly, as one nation amongst equals; they expected to simply put the brutal war behind them and resume their role on the world stage as if nothing had happened between 1914 and 1918. They were to be bitterly disappointed.

The treaty reached Berlin on 8 May, and it hit the capital hard. It was worse than even the most pessimistic among them had dreamed possible. France demanded Alsace-Lorraine, and was to occupy Germany west of the Rhine for fifteen years as well as the coalfields of the Saar. Poland was to be given the important industrial area of Upper Silesia, and West Prussia was to be turned into a Polish corridor, giving Poland vital access to the sea but cutting East Prussia off from Germany. The predominantly German Danzig was to become a 'free city'. Germany was to be stripped of her colonies; the army was to be reduced to 100,000 men and the General Staff disbanded, military equipment, including aeroplanes, fighting vehicles (such as tanks) and large ships were to be banned. Germany was to lose 13 per cent of her territory,

German Territorial Gains –
Treaty of Brest - Litovsk
March 1918

Territory effectively controlled by
the Central Powers after the treaty
of Brest-Litovsk

Territory ceded by Russia under
the treaty of Brest-Litovsk

Petrograd

ESTONIA

(LIVONIA)
• Riga
(COURLAND)
LATGALE

Moscow

Baltic Sea

LITHUANIA

Hamburg

Danzig

• Berlin
GERMANY

Warsaw •
Brest-Litovsk •
POLAND
Cracow •   • Chelm

• Kiev   • Kharkov

Nuremburg
• Prague

Lvov •
UKRAINE

Munich

AUSTRIA-HUNGARY
• Vienna

• Budapest

• Odessa

• Zagreb

ROMANIA
Bucharest •

Black sea

ITALY

• Belgrade
SERBIA
BULGARIA
• Sofia

0   200   400 km

10 per cent of her population, 15 per cent of arable land, 75 per cent of
iron ore, 16 per cent of rye, 13 per cent of wheat, 6 million people and
70,000 square kilometres. One of the most damaging sections of the treaty
was Article 231, the so-called 'War Guilt' clause, a humiliating addition which
saddled Germany with sole responsibility for starting the war. This had little
real value for the Allies but had the effect of utterly discrediting the treaty
in the eyes of most Germans.[86] The reaction ranged from stupefaction on
the left to bitter nationalist resentment on the centre and right. Even the
Independents and pacifists were appalled: in their eyes they had laid down
their arms expecting mercy and understanding; now they were defenceless.
Berlin was not to be a thriving confident capital but the symbol of a vanquished
nation, and its people gathered outside the American military mission in
droves, yelling, 'Where are our Fourteen Points? Where is your "peace of
justice".'[87] Allied nationals were told to disguise themselves in civilian clothes
to avoid attack on the streets. The Chancellor accused the *entente* powers

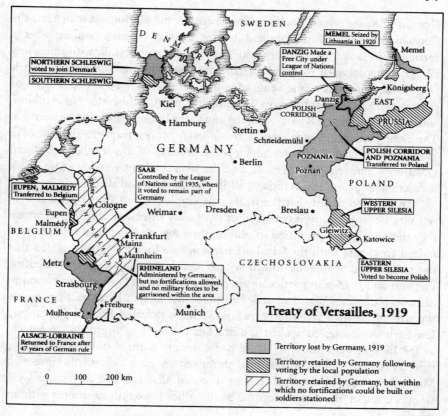

Treaty of Versailles, 1919

Territory lost by Germany, 1919

Territory retained by Germany following voting by the local population

Territory retained by Germany, but within which no fortifications could be built or soldiers stationed

of seeking to make the Germans 'slaves and helots ... doing forced labour behind barbed wire and prison bars'. The Democrat Haussmann cried, 'If our Army and our workmen had known on the fifth and the ninth of November that the peace would look like this, the Army would not have laid down its arms.'

There were tense scenes in Berlin as the deadline loomed. Germany had been given fifteen days, until 19:00 hours on 23 June, to sign. If she did not, she would be invaded. The war was still technically underway and some argued that Germany should fight on, but by now most knew this was hopeless. On 19 June Scheidemann resigned as Chancellor, unable to sign the document that would make any hand 'wither'. The Social Democratic government did not want to sign, but they had no choice. Versailles was ratified one hour before the deadline by the new Foreign Minister Hermann Müller on Saturday 28 June in the Hall of Mirrors. Right-wing newspapers in Berlin appeared with a thick black band of mourning around the front page. The Pan-German

Deutsche Zeitung wrote: 'In the place where, in the glorious year of 1871, the German empire in all its glory had its origin, today German honour is being carried to its grave. Do not forget it! The German people will, with unceasing labour, press forward to reconquer the place among the nations to which it is entitled. Then will come vengeance for the shame of 1919.' Versailles was portrayed on all sides as the most vengeful document in the history of mankind, with Berlin the innocent party, isolated and alone in a sea of vindictive enemies. The right naturally ranted against it but even moderates were shaken. Max Weber said that 'A new order which is the product of this terrible defeat and violation is unlikely to take root', and the liberal Count Kessler wrote of his indescribable dejection 'as though all life in the soul had died'.

There is no doubt that the treaty was vindictive, but in the great tide of self-pity Berliners conveniently forgot the heady threats of retribution which they themselves had promised to visit on their enemies had they won the war; indeed from 1914 until the failed offensive in 1918 they had openly stated that the vanquished would be forced to pay dearly for any German suffering. England and France in particular were to be 'ruined'. There was no reason to disbelieve them; in 1871 Bismarck had made Berlin rich by extracting double the cost of German war-time expenditure from defeated France, and in 1917 few Berliners protested against the draconian Treaty of Brest-Litovsk which, as the Independent Socialist Haase had correctly pointed out, was far worse than Versailles. Berliners remained unmoved by such arguments. Friedrich Meinecke spoke for many when he wrote that all states and all nations were sinners but that 'the sins committed by the Allies since 1918 are almost without parallel'.

The treaty was ultimately counterproductive for the Allies. It caused Germany to suffer not only humiliation and territorial loss (which it might have borne), but also social and economic collapse, which destabilized the nation and united the forces of reaction which would later turn against all of Europe. It was the new Social Democratic government and not the old imperial order which was saddled with the epithet 'November Criminals', giving the far right a powerful propaganda weapon with which to attack the fledgling democratic republic. Millions harboured a secret lust for vengeance and eagerly listened to the demagogues who promised to smash it. Out of Versailles came the *Dolchstoss* or 'Stab-in-the-back' legend which blamed the defeat not on military loss but on the 'saboteurs, the gangsters, the war profiteers, the Socialists and Jews who populated Berlin'. The powerful legend took hold early; on 9 November 1918 General Schulenburg cried: 'our men will claim ... that they were stabbed in the back by their comrades-at-arms, the navy, together with Jewish war profiteers and shirkers.' Three days later General von Scheuch declared: 'if ever anybody should affirm that the German army was beaten in this war,

history will call it a lie. Let the consciousness of having returned home unde-
feated never be taken from you!' One of the greatest advocates of the lie was
Adolf Hitler, who made it the central theme of *Mein Kampf*. Early in his career
he delivered the same speech again and again, describing how he had received
news of the revolution and defeat while recovering from a poison gas attack:
'Had they died for this, the soldiers of August and September 1914?' It was
the shameful Treaty of Versailles, he would say, which encouraged him to
enter politics.

The Deutschnational Volkspartei, the People's Party, officers' groups, the
newly established Reichswehr, urban academic circles and professors and
students at the university took up the cry. The November Revolution and the
republic became symbols of the destruction of traditional German values.
Völkisch and anti-Semitic associations began to operate openly and legally in
the heart of Berlin, while secret terrorist groups in the tradition of the Freikorps
carried out violent acts of immense brutality. Political assassination, the Feme
murders, became their speciality and the dozens of victims included the republican Matthias Erzberger, who was assassinated in 1921 for the 'crime of signing
the armistice agreement in 1918', and the great statesman Walther Rathenau,
who was murdered in 1922 for being a Jew, an intellectual, and an influential
and respected member of the government.[88] The protests against his murder
and the solemnity of his state funeral in Berlin were drowned out by the
shrill rhetoric of the right. Their assassins and accomplices were protected by
sympathizers in the Reichswehr and in the police and judiciary. Of the twenty-
two murders committed by the left, seventeen of the perpetrators were severely
punished, ten with the death sentence; but of the 354 murders committed by
the right between 1918 and 1922, only one was punished.[89] Vigilante groups
made up of unemployed ex-officers and criminals continued to occupy the
capital, murdering at will, clubbing and beating people accused of 'unpatriotic'
activities. The Freikorps and the related civilian organizations were increasingly
disloyal to the government, marching under the swastika which had been their
symbol long before Hitler adopted it, waiting for the day the hated republic
would fall. Theorists from Spengler and Moeller van den Bruck to Alfred
Rosenberg and Anton Drexler laid the intellectual groundwork for the anti-
liberalism, anti-Semitism and anti-Marxism which would intensify a decade
later. Grosz described Berliners as lost in an unstable world 'like boats in a
storm' heading for disaster. It was only a matter of time before the right would
try to take over by force. They waited less than a year.

The first attempt to take the capital came in the form of the infamous
'March on Berlin', the Kapp Putsch. In February 1920 Noske had, in keeping
with the terms of Versailles, ordered the dissolution of one of the toughest
Freikorps groups in Berlin, the Ehrhardt Brigade. General Lüttwitz refused,

called for the demise of the new National Assembly and ordered Ehrhardt and his associate Wolfgang Kapp to seize the capital. When the beleaguered government heard of the plans at three in the morning of 13 March they fled Berlin more like a group of poor fugitives than elected leaders, taking a train to Dresden and then travelling on to Stuttgart with nothing but a suitcase each. At seven in the morning Freikorps soldiers marched cockily through the Brandenburg Gate and occupied the government quarter. 'We need two things, order and work,' declared Lüttwitz. 'Agitators will be exterminated without compassion.' The only important member of the government who had remained behind was the Privy Councillor Arnold Brecht, who called for a general strike. Berliners had been unimpressed by Lüttwitz's threats and were tired of months of Freikorps violence. They turned against Kapp and his troop. The result was the only effective general strike ever held in the capital.

Although Kapp now occupied the entire government quarter the city had shut down. All utilities, including gas and water, were cut. No trams ran, offices and factories remained closed, people pulled down their blinds, bolted their doors, and stayed at home. The army sensed the mood in Berlin and finally withdrew all support for the putschists.[90] Kapp fled to Sweden in disgrace and the sullen troops of the Ehrhardt Brigade marched out of the city, leaving a trail of murdered civilians in their wake for whom Gropius later built his famous memorial.[91] The departure of Kapp gave the republic a brief respite, but the truce would not last. The debacle served as a model for Hitler, who decided to stage his own Beer Hall *Putsch* and march on Berlin in 1923.

There are thousands of images which capture the senseless violence and the crazed moral decay of the immediate post-war period in Berlin. Some of the most disturbing have little to do with murder and bloodshed, but depict the devastation faced by ordinary people trying to survive the next of the grave crises to hit Berlin. Pictures show workers struggling to carry home wages in laundry baskets, women buying a single potato with a wheelbarrow full of paper notes, or children playing on blocks of worthless billion-mark notes, for the Kapp *Putsch* was barely over when Berlin was racked by hyper-inflation.

Inflation had started during the war and was in part the fault of imperial fiscal policy. The government had financed the war through loans and bonds rather than through taxes, and the war economy had only hidden the decline in the real value of the mark. The leaders had taken the risk, convinced that the money would soon be paid back by the defeated Allies. The gamble failed. Hyper-inflation was triggered off by the Allied reparations which were finally fixed at the Paris Conference in January 1921.[92]

The initial figure demanded of Germany was a staggering 269,000 million gold marks, and although this was reduced to 132,000 million gold marks at the London Conference a few months later the amount remained almost too great to comprehend. The Berlin press angrily reported that they would be paying 2.5 billion marks annually until 1966 and 1.5 billion annually until 1988, and protested that their children would languish in 'debt slavery'.[93] Inflation was also fuelled by Wirth's 1921 'Policy of Fulfilment', in which the currency was allowed to founder in the vain hope that the Allies would take pity on the despairing nation.[94]

The final push into rampant hyper-inflation came in 1922, when the French marched into the Ruhr under the pretext that the Germans had not delivered a shipment of telegraph poles on time. It was clear that France hoped to split the Rhineland and the Ruhr from the rest of Germany. Berliners were outraged and led the call for strikes and for passive resistance in the occupied areas. The policy was a disaster.

The strike meant that the government was suddenly faced with a huge bill for wages and salaries; 100,000 Berlin metalworkers alone had to be supported.[95] The cost devastated the already fragile German economy and could only be covered by printing money. Inflation spiralled out of control and the currency collapsed completely.[96] In 1921 the value of the mark had dropped from the pre-war level of 4 to 75 marks per dollar. In February 1923 it was already 48,000 marks. On 4 October 1923 a dollar was worth 440,000,000 marks and by 20 November it was 4,200,000,000,000. At the height of hyper-inflation paper money was worthless; it was packed into boxes and sold as waste paper for less than old bones and rags. A pensioner who might have invested the substantial sum of 100,000 marks before the war would have found his account worth less than a few cents in 1923. Berlin again became the suicide capital of Europe; reports abounded of desperate people withdrawing their entire savings for one last tram ride across town or for a single stamp on a letter to be posted before they committed suicide. People carried wages home in huge crates; by the time they could spend it even their trillion-mark bills were virtually worthless.[97] Over 300 paper mills and 2,000 printing presses worked on twenty-four-hour shifts to supply the Reichsbank with notes; old bills were stamped over to increase their value and even newspaper presses were used to print money. At the same time the food supplies failed and malnutrition spread, barely checked by the soup kitchens which sprang up around the city. Peasants in the surrounding villages were made rich by demanding valuables in exchange for a few eggs or potatoes although there were numerous often deadly fights over crops in nearby fields. Even so the 'hamster trains' which took people to the outskirts of town were packed and for years afterwards visitors were astounded to find seedy local farmhouses filled with Meissen porcelain, paintings, pianos and beautiful furniture, the spoils of inflation. Confidence in the republic was dashed in waves of fear, panic, strikes and misery so poignantly expressed in Döblin's shattering trilogy, *November 1918*. The collapse ripped at the fabric of the city and destroyed the faith of the middle class in the democratic system. It wiped out old strict values of thrift, the tradition of painstaking saving and the tough work ethic which had made Berlin so prosperous in the past.

The situation was made worse by traders known as *Schieber* or *Raffkes* who had access to hard currency and could buy goods in Germany, sell them in foreign markets and return with food and other essential items which were sold at hugely inflated prices and sometimes in doctored form. They, along with banks and heavy industry who had access to borrowing facilities, purchased every physical asset available: factories, mines, stocks of raw materials, shops, farms, whatever had a good chance of retaining its real value. The most spectacular *Raffke* was Hugo Stinnes, the Strousberg of the 1920s, who built a vast paper empire which included interests in iron and steel, shipping, transportation and lumber. Cartoons show him as a sinister figure gloating over Berlin and he was universally hated by those facing ruin. Worse still, the new rich were seen squandering their money on ostentatious entertainment and luxury, gulping down champagne and caviar while chanting the slogan: 'one lives for such a short time and is dead for so long.'[98] As the cabaret song put it, 'Sweet corpse, let's dance round your coffin and holler, three-seven-oh marks is the rate for one dollar . . . here's to grandma's lovely little cottage – and to mortgage number one and number two.'[99]

Berlin also began to attract foreign visitors drawn by the cheap freedom of the city. Although the life of the average Berliner was, as Grosz put it, 'wholly negative' the city was

> all frothy on the top, and many took that froth for the true face . . . Foreigners, in particular, were taken in by the gay whirl, by the abandoned night-life, by the so-called freedom of expression and the flowering of the arts. But close beneath all the glittering frivolity lay a swamp of fratricidal hatred and internal dissension, and the troops were even then lining up for the final battle.[100]

Many Berliners resented these adventurers, who would have been down-and-out at home but who were wildly rich in Berlin. While locals fought over discarded cigarette butts and starved on a diet of rats and birds the newcomers were waited on hand and foot at Berlin's grandest hotels. One could buy a row of elegant houses, or hire the Berlin Philharmonic for the night for a mere $100.

Hard work now seemed to mean nothing; one could only get ahead through crime, black marketeering or prostitution. Berliners experienced an inversion of values and a new moral relativism far more acute than that seen after the 1873 crash, and by the mid 1920s many of the social ties which had bound the Berlin upper and middle class together had completely broken down. Retired generals or diplomats on fixed pensions could be seen rummaging in the streets for scraps of food. Arnold Bauer remembered 'the tragedy of old people, despairing people, people on small fixed pensions ... who simply couldn't grasp what was going on'. Public monuments had to be removed from the city centre as they were plundered by scavengers, while door handles, mailboxes, garden rails, roof tiles and anything else that could be taken disappeared. Girls of twelve or fourteen prostituted themselves after school with their parents' approval. Illegitimate births had already increased to 22 per cent of all births by 1917 (as compared to 5.4 per cent in London at the same time) and illegitimate infant mortality soared to an extraordinary 300 per thousand by 1920.[101] Every kind of sexual perversion was catered to and hotels like the Excelsior and the Adlon hired 'in house' male and female prostitutes to entertain the guests. As things grew increasingly dire Berlin threw itself into an orgy of dancing, drinking, pornography and prostitution with *je m'en fous* being the order of the day. The higher prices rose the greater the abandon, the madder the nightclubs, the faster the dance steps, the louder the jazz bands, the more plentiful the cocaine. But this was not yet the joyful dancing of the so-called 'Golden Twenties'; it was an insane dance of forgetting, a dance of despair.

The inflation became a lasting image in Berlin culture, the figures of broken people recurring in the vivid paintings of Baluschek, Skarbina, Zille and Grosz. In his 1922 scene of the Mühlendamm Bridge, Karl Hubbuch drew unemployed boatsmen standing around drunk and unshaven, indifferent to the fact that one of their number was about to kill himself. Stresemann said that 'The intellectual and productive middle class, which was the traditional backbone of the country, has been paid for the utter sacrifice of itself to the state during the war by being deprived of all its property and by being proletarianized.' In Remarque's novel about the inflation, *The Black Obelisk*, a widow explains how her husband committed suicide because the bank would not allow them to withdraw their life savings from a term deposit. Stefan Zweig's *Invisible Collection* tells of the wife of a near blind collector who secretly sells his precious objects for scraps of food.[102] The old man proudly shows his treasures to a dealer unaware that they are now nothing but worthless paper. For outsiders the city was a thrilling whirlwind of sensual pleasure but for most Berliners it was a living hell. It was only after the introduction of the Rentenmark in 1923, when the currency went from a trillion marks to one, that Berliners again began to experience a sense of stability.

The First World War had marked a terrible turning point for Berlin. The imperial dream was swamped in a wave of violence, revolution and decay, and the missed opportunities and terrible mistakes of those years sowed the seeds which radicalized the city and ultimately made Hitler's rise to power possible. Yet even in the atmosphere of impending doom Berliners began to slowly build a new identity for their city. For a few brief years it would become the scene of one of the greatest cultural flowerings the west has ever seen, acting like a magnet to the most talented artists, composers, actors, theatre directors, film makers and architects of the age. 'Weimar Culture' would provide a glimmer of hope in the years of anguish which had preceded it, and in those which were soon to follow.

IX

The Golden Twenties

Dear God, how short is Life, how long is Art!

(*Faust*, Part I)

THERE ARE TIMES IN HISTORY when a city transcends its earthly role and becomes the very stuff of legend. Ninth-century Europeans from Genoa to Valencia to Flanders listened in awe to tales about the shimmering city of Constantinople rising majestically above the Bosphorus, resplendent with jewel-encrusted rooms, gold-plated palaces and mechanical statues from which wine and honey flowed on feast days. Even after being sacked by crusaders in 1204 it continued to exert a magical influence on the European imagination, becoming a legend which has endured for centuries. Although none has equalled the impact of Constantinople, at their height a handful of other cities have also become symbols able to conjure up powerful images in the modern mind. Assumptions about ancient Athens still influence every aspect of western culture from architecture to philosophy; Brunelleschi's dome epitomizes the exquisite beauty of the Florentine Renaissance, while the graceful figures in Renoir's *Moulin de la Galette* still capture the sweet essence of *belle époque* Paris.

Throughout her history Berlin had always been considered a cultural backwater by the rest of the world, and it had never reached the exalted status of a Paris or a Constantinople. There was no indication that this would change in the desperate years following the First World War. Yet it was in this atmosphere that Berlin surprised both itself and the rest of the world by becoming the centre of a cultural explosion which dramatically changed its dismal image. Suddenly the city threw off the Prussian imperial mantle, becoming the capital of modernism and the undisputed centre of the 'Golden Twenties'.

Like all legends, that of Weimar Berlin is a heady mixture of fact and fiction, much of it concocted long after (and partially because of) its pitiable end at the hands of the Nazis. It was only after 1945 that Weimar began to be seen as a glittering time sandwiched between the arrogant pomp of the imperial age and the indescribable blackness of Hitler's Germany. Artists who had been forced into exile after 1933 began to portray it as the only period when Berlin had embraced its 'un-German' modernity and revelled in its speed, its light, its Americanism, its moral freedom, and its passion for experimentation. There was another aspect of the legend which concentrated on the new decadence: the smoky jazz clubs and naked dancers, the Haus Vaterland and the Wintergarten, which in the popular imagination took on a certain seedy glamour and romance of their own. Although the post-war image bordered on sentimentality and *kitsch* and ignored how much Weimar culture owed to the late nineteenth century and how much lingered well into the Nazi period, there is no doubt that something quite extraordinary happened in Berlin between the wars. For a few brief sparkling years the city attracted a sheer concentration of talent which has not yet been equalled in Europe. Berlin heralded a new vision of modernity, and introduced it to Germany. When Germans rejected it her exiles brought it to the rest of the world.[1]

The list of achievements is overwhelming and includes novels from *Berlin Alexanderplatz* to *All Quiet on the Western Front*, films by Fritz Lang and Josef von Sternberg and Billy Wilder; the satire of Georg Grosz, the icy paintings of Christian Schad, the collaboration of Brecht and Weill in *The Threepenny Opera*, the architecture and artistry of the Bauhaus, of Max Beckmann, Otto Dix, Mies van der Rohe, Walter Gropius, Moholy-Nagy and Wassily Kandinsky, the seductive talents of Josephine Baker, Greta Garbo and Marlene Dietrich, the music of Wilhelm Furtwängler, Otto Klemperer, Arnold Schoenberg and the work of publishers like Sam Fischer, who from his office on Mehrenstrasse issued books by Thomas Mann, Hermann Hesse, Gerhart Hauptmann, Stefan Zweig, Carl Zuckmayer, Hugo von Hofmannsthal, Alfred Döblin and dozens of other giants of the age.[2] The cultural rebirth was unexpected after the havoc of the First World War and is often attributed solely to the genius of Weimar artists themselves. In fact the conditions which made it possible had little to do with them but came about through a combination of sheer hard work on the part of the unloved Weimar politicians like Walther Rathenau and Gustav Stresemann, and Germany's changing role in the international community.

In the first year after the war, Berlin had struggled to find a place in a world which had so forcefully rejected her at Versailles.[3] Berliners staunchly refused to question the role of their own aggressive military leaders, their cultural chauvinism or the importance of the insane messages which had been issued from the Wilhelmstrasse in the years before the war. Instead, they blamed their 'encirclement' and 'isolation' on the anti-German bias of the other great powers and, later, on the Kaiser's decision to allow the Reinsurance Treaty with Russia to lapse. Seething resentment against Versailles had caused many to turn their backs on the west; why should they follow a democratic European policy based on Franco-German understanding or try, as Mierendorff put it, 'to transcend Versailles by Europe' when they had been treated so poorly by France and Britain?[4] Those who believed this version of history wanted the new government to restore their tattered prestige by re-establishing Germany on the international scene. Their overtures were directed not at the west, but at Russia.

Shortly after the disastrous Spartacus Uprising, Lenin's agent Karl Radek had been captured and thrown into solitary confinement in Berlin. When the Treaty of Versailles was published he was suddenly moved to luxurious quarters, was permitted to communicate with Lenin, and was encouraged to receive visitors. His rooms were turned into what he called his 'prison salon', where he entertained guests ranging from prominent Bolsheviks to the highest ranking members of the German ex-imperial order.[5] The latter had engineered the change in the hope that Radek would help design a treaty with Russia which would counter the Treaty of Versailles. What instantly united the two countries was the desire to eradicate the new Poland, the so-called 'Bastard of Versailles'.

At least since the days of the Polish partitions in the late eighteenth century, both Russians and Germans regarded their Polish neighbours as troublesome because they refused to accept foreign domination. General von Seeckt said that the existence of the new Poland was 'unbearable' and 'irreconcilable with the living needs of Germany'.[6] 'Poland', he wrote, 'must disappear and will disappear through its own internal weakness and through Russia – with our help.'[7] The German desire to erase Poland went so deep that they were even prepared to tolerate the Red Army on their own frontier, failing to see that for all his conciliatory words Lenin was still intent on fomenting revolution in Berlin.[8] When the Poles repulsed the Red Army in the 'Miracle on the Vistula' in 1920 the Germans were furious with them, still oblivious to Lenin's plan to march into their own country after he had crushed Poland. The battle at Warsaw is rightly remembered as one of the most decisive in history as it halted the westward spread of Bolshevism, forcing Lenin to rethink his policy of aggressive expansionism and ushering in his policy of 'Communism in One Country'.[9] Unaware of the significance of the battle the German right merely redoubled its efforts to co-operate with their compliant Bolshevik allies, secretly hoping that through such contact they would be able to nudge Russia back into the capitalist fold. This was the origin of the bizarre slogan which was issued from the German Foreign Office: 'The Bolsheviks will save us from Bolshevism.'[10]

Reports exposing the Russian double-dealing were ignored by the Germans and on 16 April 1922 the western powers were forced to look on helplessly as the two political outcasts signed one of the most controversial documents of the period, the Treaty of Rapallo.[11] This cancelled all war indemnities between them, established diplomatic and economic relations, and included a secret protocol which broke the terms of Versailles by allowing Germany to build weapons and train troops on Russian soil. Trotsky hailed it as a prodigious achievement and at the Fourth Congress of the Comintern in 1922 Radek spoke glowingly of the 'mutual necessity' of the German–Russian bond. Berliners also saw it as a serious step forward; the *Tägliche Rundschau* referred to it as 'of world historical importance' and supported the new links with the soulful land of Tolstoy and Dostoevsky. Only a few, like Walther Rathenau, cared less about improving relations with Russia than forcing the west to rethink the terms of Versailles.

Since 1871 Berliners had seen themselves as a 'bridge between east and west', as close to Russia as to the democracies of France or England. As they could never quite decide if they were really western Europeans or were best allied with Russia, they preferred the dangerous game of playing one off against the other. The Weimar period was no exception. Berlin continued to woo Russia throughout the 1920s, but after the conclusion of Rapallo decided to look west again. This two-pronged strategy was made possible by the reversal of American and British attitudes towards the vanquished German nation after 1919.

When the Germans were handed the Treaty of Versailles they knew nothing of the serious wrangling which had hindered the proceedings, nor were they told that the terms were little more than a hasty compromise between those who were intent on revenge, and those who wanted a fair-minded peace.[12] Clemenceau had advocated the most vindictive line, pushing for ever greater concessions to France and to Poland, while many American representatives – from John Foster Dulles to Norman Davis, who served on the Reparations Committee – had balked at their demands.[13] On the night before the treaty was handed over President Wilson had muttered, 'If I were a German, I would never sign it.'[14] General Smuts wrote to Lloyd George and President Wilson that the French policy of trying to weaken Germany 'for all time' would fail because she was ultimately too powerful to be suppressed. By 1920 the general attitude towards Germany had started to change. Many began to see the war as little more than a 'terrible accident', a war which Europe had 'stumbled into' because of the 'international arms race'. They began to talk of renewing ties with a Germany that had 'been punished enough'. John Maynard Keynes argued in his *Economic Consequences of Peace* that Germany had been too harshly treated, and statesmen began to argue that German economic recovery was essential if there was to be lasting stability in central Europe. They also hoped that by accepting Germany into the western fold she would renounce her marriage of convenience with Russia and act as a defence against the westward spread of Russian Bolshevism. By 1922 these views were having an effect on the terms of peace themselves, with a number of articles being modified or remaining unenforced. The demand that 900 Germans, including the Kaiser, be tried as 'war criminals' was dropped because it would put a terrible strain on the already weak republican government; only six Germans were actually tried.[15]

At the same time the Allies began to realize how little could be squeezed from the German economy in the way of reparations. Germany could of course be made to pay but she would have to rely on increased exports, a solution which was simply not possible in war-torn Europe. Germany could also have exchanged finished goods in lieu of cash, but the Allied governments did not want to ruin their own manufacturing sectors by taking on her products. The British were among the first to accept this and to the fury of the French began to lose interest in the reparations issue, abandoning Lloyd George's pledge to squeeze the German lemon 'until the pips squeak' and adopting a more forgiving policy. The British ambassador in Berlin was also conscious of increased American sympathy, commenting that even their businessmen were 'pro-German'.[16] This change of heart coincided with Stresemann's introduction of the Rentenmark and the end of passive resistance against the French in the Ruhr. The Treaty of Rapallo temporarily halted this sense of Allied goodwill, but in 1924 the Allies and the Germans accepted the American-inspired Dawes Plan, which set a lower scale of annual reparation payments.[17] Inflation was halted, the German financial system was reorganized, and it was agreed that Germany could receive Allied loans. The scale of borrowing soon reached fantastic proportions: between 1924 and 1931 Germany received 33 billion marks in (mostly American) short-term loans, and it was for this reason that 1920s Berlin was characterized by a surge of apparent prosperity, growth, easy money and optimism.[18] Few in Berlin ever acknowledged the extent to which they were living on credit, but the short-term benefits had a dramatic effect on the city.

In 1918 Max Weber had compared Germany to the shattered mess left after the Thirty Years War and had predicted a long hard struggle back to pre-war life. He was wrong. Within months of the Dawes Plan Berlin had resumed her role as one of the foremost industrial cities of Europe. Inflation had cleared industry's debts, loans were pouring in and production was soon up to pre-war levels. German exports doubled in the five years after 1924 and by 1929 was 12 per cent higher per capita than in 1914. Germany was now second only to the United States in world exports, and indeed exported more finished products than any country in the world.[19] James W. Angell called it 'one of the most spectacular recoveries in the world's entire economic history'.

The economic boom was enhanced by new foreign policy successes; Gustav Stresemann, who became Foreign Minister from 1923 until his death in the momentous year of 1929, saw France leave the Ruhr in July 1925, and the signing of the Locarno Treaty which guaranteed that neither Germany, France nor Belgium would alter their borders by force, making the 'Spirit of Locarno' an expression of optimism in mid-twenties Berlin.[20] In September 1926 Germany became a member of the League of Nations, and in January 1927 the Inter-Allied Military Commission overseeing Germany's disarmament was withdrawn. Economic rapprochement between France and Germany continued while German diplomats mediated between the USA and France for the 1928 Kellogg–Briand Pact. In the Young Plan of August 1929 reparations payments were lowered again, foreign controls were removed and in 1930 military occupation forces left the Rhine.[21] In *The Collapse of German Idealism* Paul Ernst had called for the dawning of a 'new age . . . that will be different'. This was now taken to mean the promise of stability, prosperity and a decent life.

The economic and political healing of the 1920s affected Berlin more profoundly than any other German city. Suddenly the giant had a future, not as the stuffy bastion of the tired imperial order but as a leading light of modernity. When the composer George Antheil returned to Berlin in the mid twenties he found it transformed: 'The electric lights were back in their sockets. The red carpets, new ones, were down on the floors of the expensive hotels. People had their brass doorknobs out again – whereas in 1923 you couldn't find a brass doorknob in all Berlin: people would just steal it in the night.' Heinrich Mann was suddenly calling Berlin 'a city of excitement and hope'. The future, he said, was being 'anticipated by Berlin' and anyone who wanted to see the shape of Germany to come should look there. 'Yes,' he said, 'Berlin will be the beloved capital little though it imagined it would be.'[22]

One of the most significant changes was the final unification of the city under the Oberbürgermeister Gustav Böss.[23] Throughout history Berlin had consisted of a collection of loosely linked urban civil parishes, including Charlottenburg, Köpenick, Lichtenberg, Neukölln, Schöneberg, Spandau and Wilmersdorf, aligned with fifty-nine rural civil parishes and twenty-seven rural estates, which had been informally known as Berlin but whose regional differences had often stymied growth and development. It was the war which prompted centralization and in 1920 the districts were legally combined to create a city which ballooned from an area of 6,572 to 87,810 hectares. The city continued in its role as the unquestioned centre of Germany. Foreign policy was still determined from the Wilhelmstrasse; it remained dominant in banking and finance and continued to attract leading industrial firms from Siemens and Schering to Sarotti and AEG. The city exploded outwards as people moved to the huge new suburbs and as the larger industrial firms made use of rail lines and waterways to move away from the urban core. By 1928

Siemens had completed the electrification of all the central and suburban railway lines and in November that year the Berlin Transport Company or BVG was formed, making it the largest community transport system in the world. The population increased exponentially, racing from 1.9 million to 3.8 million in just over a decade; by 1933 the city had a staggering 4.2 million inhabitants and was the third largest city after London and New York. Berliners became increasingly proud of their size and strength and reverted to their pre-war habit of proving their status as a *Weltstadt* in headlines which proclaimed WE HAVE 1.5 MILLION MORE PEOPLE THAN PARIS; WITH 500,000 LINES THE CITY HAS THE HIGHEST RATIO OF PEOPLE TO TELEPHONES; and WE HAVE THE FASTEST UNDERGROUND RAIL SYSTEM IN THE WORLD. Klaus Mann said that the city was bursting with pride and that Berliners were now 'prepared for anything'.

The republican government fuelled this optimistic spirit by borrowing money and spending it like water.[24] Berlin got new roads and trains, new canals and housing projects, new employment and welfare schemes, new factories and new hospitals.[25] The city looked like a large building site, and 14 million marks were spent on the reconstruction of the Berlin Opera alone. For artists, poets, writers and architects Berlin was the place to be. It had money, it was pulsating with life and ideas, and it was able to draw on the museums, the theatres, the operas and the concert halls, the newspapers and publishing empires, the political cabarets, the film studios, indeed the entire infrastructure which had been established under the Kaiser but which was now freed of all Wilhelmine constraints. Censorship laws were the least repressive in Europe; *The Blue Angel* was banned in Paris but considered tame in Berlin; in the smart new journal *Weltbühne* sexual freedom and pacifism were exalted and middle-class values savaged; and Kurt Tucholsky could produce films with titles like *Scenes from a Man's Girlhood* with no fear of recrimination. The war and hyper-inflation had destroyed the old system of values, and modern attitudes were becoming institutionalized. Leading museums began to buy new paintings and sculptures, opera houses staged atonal works, Otto Dix was made a professor and art theorists like Carl Einstein and Max Dvorak put abstraction and Expressionism within the tradition of mainstream European art. Herwath Walden's gallery had led Europe by exhibiting Léger, Chagall, Klee, Mondrian, Hans Arp, Kurt Schwitters, Moholy-Nagy and Robert Delaunay and continued to show new works long before they were seen on the Left Bank. It was this official acceptance of the modern which suddenly made the avant-garde, treated so shabbily under the Kaiser, into a new cultural elite.

Within a few years Berlin had brushed away the cobwebs of the imperial world and overcome the misery of the post-war years. Carl Zuckmayer said that Berlin gobbled up talents and human energies 'with tornado-like powers'.

It was like a 'hugely desirable woman, whose coldness and coquettishness are widely known', and although she was called arrogant, snobbish, *parvenu*, uncultivated and common, she was the centre of everyone's fantasies and the goal of everyone's desires. 'Everyone wanted her, she enticed everyone ... The man who had Berlin owned the world.'[26] Other cities had also achieved new status in the new decentralized Germany; Bauhaus started its life in Dessau, Schwitters worked from Hanover, Otto Dix in Dresden; but in the end most of the notable German artists and writers were drawn to the capital.[27] Natives joked that 'famous Berliners' were more likely to have been born in Hanover or Düsseldorf, Prague or London. Willy Haas said that 'the fewest Berliners I knew were real Berliners' but 'to become a Berliner – that came quickly'. He loved the 'toughness of the place', the 'indescribable dynamic, the love for work, the readiness to take hard blows – and to go on living'.[28] Berlin was a city of immigrants and of 'outsiders' suddenly promoted to the highest levels of the new society. Herwath Walden proclaimed that the Berliners had their own dialect that, aside from them, only Russians understood. 'It is only spoken by real Berliners throughout the world, but one cannot find it in Berlin.' Even the hookers used the pick-up line, 'I am a stranger here myself.' Alfred Kerr called the twenties a 'new Periclean age' and Brecht wrote: 'I am at home in the asphalt city.' Peter Gay described the old Berlin as impressive, the new Berlin 'irresistible'. To go to Berlin was the aspiration of 'the composer, the journalist, the actor; with its superb orchestras, its hundred and twenty newspapers, its forty theatres, Berlin was the place for the ambitious, the energetic, the talented. Wherever they started, it was in Berlin that they became, and Berlin that made them famous.'[29]

Berlin also had another, less romantic side which reflected the drastic changes brought by war and hyper-inflation. In 1923 the writer Georg Kaiser was sentenced to a year in prison for stealing to feed his family. Inflation had destroyed the old way of life. The essayist Siegfried Kracauer lamented its passing, commenting that

> among the members of the independent professional classes – doctors, authors, journalists, actors – having two jobs is now virtually the rule ... the leisure which used to nourish intellectual activity and permit the cultivation of ideas is no more; the sense of security in old age, that cushion for those who live on their wits and nerves, has vanished.[30]

Writers and painters turned more to modern mediums like journalism or photography; indeed the figure of the harassed journalist living at the mercy of the proprietor or at the whim of the market replaced that of the elegant pipe-smoking writer as the symbol of the 1920s intellectual. Some were bitter that the old life of the mind had been pushed out by the new life of the cultural producer, but most Berliners accepted the change. At its worst the new approach legitimized cheap reportage and glorified uninspiring art simply because it was modern. At its best, it challenged the heavy Germanic stereotype of the self-possessed Romantic artist and opened the door to the very best of twentieth-century culture.

The change in mood was reflected in all forms of art. The terrifying Expressionist madness of *Caligari*, the horror of Meidner's Berlin, the gruesome visions by Grosz and Dix, the searing criticism in Kästner's production of *William Tell*, the images of twisted war cripples and the harsh political cabaret had managed to capture the spirit of the frightening, unstable post-war years. Now it looked increasingly tired and passé; a product of war and revolution looking backward instead of to the glowing future. Max Weber had come to criticize Expressionism and pleaded for a more sober form of art; the editor of the *Neue Rundschau* Rudolph Kayser said that the tendency towards a new reality and objectivity was becoming palpable in all areas of life.[31] The leading Expressionist Paul Kornfeld turned his back on his own movement, writing in the comedy *Palme oder der Gekränkte*, 'Let us hear no more about war, revolution and the salvation of the world! Let us be modest and turn our attention . . . to smaller things.' The art historian Gustav Friedrich Hartlaub cast around for a term which would capture the new sober mood, and in 1923 coined *Neue Sachlichkeit* or 'New Reality'. It would stand for the objectivity, the new matter-of-factness and rationalization which would characterize Berlin in the 1920s. It did not matter that the war had ripped the country to pieces or that the revolution had misfired; Berlin had been given a fresh start, and it was time for artists to move forward.[32]

The new realism was imbued with a longing for something whole and with an enthusiasm for things as they are rather than as they should be. It was as if Germans had finally given up the search for an identity informed by *völkisch* tales of ancient dark forests or misty mountains and had decided to place themselves in the real world, with all its industry, its toughness and its urban ugliness. Berlin led Europe in the transition from the art of the bourgeois milieu to the caustic world of popular culture. By the mid twenties *Neue Sachlichkeit* was being applied to everything from film to theatre, from cabaret to painting; the title song from the famous revue *Es liegt in der Luft* began: 'A new reality is in the air . . .' Berlin itself was said to embody progress and success: Henry Nelson captured this spirit in his 1926 revue *Es geht schon besser* (It's getting better). The Berlin artists were also influenced by the Russian avant-garde, who had been flooding into the city after the signing of the Treaty of Brest-Litovsk.

*   *   *

The attempt by Lenin to create a brave new world of Soviet Communism now lies shattered and discredited. That the experiment would fail was not apparent to everybody in the 1920s, and least of all to the left-wing intellectuals in Berlin. In the post-revolutionary years many still believed in the seductive theories of Marx's economic determinism and in the grandiose claims of Bolshevism. With Lenin preaching the need for 'industrialization' and 'electrification', his country seemed to some like the very embodiment of progress. The early years of Soviet Russia, before Stalin crushed the avant-garde, saw a frenzy of experimentation, and the list of those who visited Berlin in the 1920s was impressive. In 1919 Arbeitsrat für Kunst (Working Council for the Arts) was held in Berlin by the architects Walter Gropius and Bruno Taut. Many artists from eastern Europe attended, including Alexander Archipenko, Ivan Puni, El Lissitzky, Wassily Kandinsky, Marc Chagall, Naum Gabo and Kasimir Malevich. Many stayed on to make Berlin their centre of activity; by 1922 it is estimated that over 200,000 Russians lived in Berlin and had six newspapers, twenty bookshops, and their own cabarets and cafés and theatres.[33] The legendary First Russian Art Exhibition opened at the Galerie van Dieman in 1922 under the auspices of the Russian Commissariat for Popular Education and Art and held 'for the benefit of the starving Russian population' and drew artists from El Lissitzky and Wassily Kandinsky to Kasimir Malevich. The following year Vladimir Mayakovsky gloated in his essay Berlin Today that the Russians on the Kurfürstendamm (nicknamed the 'Nöpski Prospekt') were no longer refugees from the revolution but were 'the true representatives of Russia', intent on sealing the friendship between the two peoples.[34] Russian and Hungarian Constructivists like László Moholy-Nagy had developed a new style based on 'labour, technology, organization'; artists were told to abandon the 'bourgeois studio' for the factory, and even Dadaists like Grosz and Heartfield adopted the new style. 'Art is dead,' they announced, 'long live the new machine art of Tatlin.' The Russians started a host of galleries and journals, including the tri-lingual Veshch (Object), which introduced Berlin to the work of Prokofiev and the Petrograd novelists Pilnyak and Zamyatin. They claimed that they wanted to break the hold of traditional institutions on the world of art or, as Ladovsky put it, to show that 'the future belongs to those who are extraordinarily untalented for art'. They also wanted to break down the traditional walls which separated art from everyday life. In this they influenced, and were influenced by, one of the most important products of Weimar Germany: the Bauhaus.[35]

The Bauhaus School was started by Walter Gropius shortly after his return from the western front in 1919. Located first in Dessau, it finally moved via Weimar to Berlin, where it remained until it was disbanded by Hitler. Gropius was passionate about breaking down barriers between art and craft, and hoped to bring people together rather like the medieval master builders, who had used stone masons, woodcarvers, glass makers, painters and jewellers to complete their celebrated cathedrals. 'Let all, forgetting snobbish distinctions, collaborate in the new building of the future,' he said. The new building was to be 'everything together, architecture and sculpture and painting in a single shape, rising to heaven from the hands of millions of craftsmen as a crystal symbol of a new emerging faith'. As the 1920s progressed the Bauhaus members, like their Russian counterparts, became obsessed with technology. Machines were no longer to be treated as dehumanizing but were to become an integral part of 'the whole'. Buildings were to be 'machines for living' and to stand, as Schlemmer put it, for 'the American spirit, progress, the marvels of technology and invention, the urban environment'. They were to become a celebration of urban life.[36]

The group of artists and architects assembled by Gropius is testament to the dynamic and ever-changing style of the school. Berliners were soon living in buildings designed by Erich Mendelsohn, Hans Poelzig, Hans Scharoun, Josef Albers and the brothers Bruno and Max Taut, they used Lissitzky's new graphics, listened to the music of Hindemith and Bartók, read typeface by Herbert Bayer and followed Kurt Schwitters's recommendation that Germans abandon frilly Gothic script. They watched Stravinsky's 1928 *Oedipus Rex* with sets designed by Moholy-Nagy, bought the paintings of Paul Klee and Wassily Kandinsky, used steel-tubed chairs designed by Marcel Breuer, and worked in offices designed by Mies van der Rohe. The expression 'less is more' was to be applied to every aspect of design from a simple teapot to a huge housing estate. Nothing was too small for their attention; when my uncle was a child in Holland his cousin Paul Citroën, a member of the Bauhaus School, had Gropius design a country house for the family. Every detail, from door handles to window frames, from lamps to furniture to wallpaper, was specifically made for the building. Those Berliners fortunate enough to live in one of the new housing estates built by Bauhaus enjoyed the same attention to detail. The style was quickly accepted; only two years after Mayor Böss had complained about the design for the furriers Herpich on Leipziger Strasse, it had been given protected status.

When one flies over Berlin one can still see a large horseshoe shape which dominates the landscape along the Fritz-Reuter-Allee. This startling find is the Hufeisen of the Britz estate by Bruno Taut, one of the many residential estates commissioned by the Weimar government in an attempt to stem the housing shortage which had struck Berlin after the war. Thousands of newcomers had once again been forced to live in cellars and tiny attic rooms or share on a rotational basis. The government, ever keen to prove its socialist credentials and bolster its popularity, decided to introduce a housing tax on the Austrian model with which to fund the estates. A group of architects, from Martin Wagner and Hans Scharoun to Walter Gropius and Bruno Taut, were commissioned and they created some of the renowned landmarks of Berlin, including the Britz, the Grosssiedlung at Siemensstadt with its 1,685 homes, Onkel-Toms-Hutte, named after an old local inn), the Karl Legien estate on Prenzlauer Berg, and the Friedrich Ebert flats in Reinickendorf.[37] There were many others, all of which provided comfortable rooms and lavish gardens, light, open space, centralized heating, hot water systems, community centres, even piped-in radio.[38]

These estates were built in the heady days of modernist fantasy, when architects sincerely believed that they could create a new type of person simply by shaping their living conditions. The Berlin designs worked because they were built on a relatively small, human scale. Sadly when the architects were forced out of Germany their inflexible modernism was taken up because they were fleeing from Hitler's tyranny and because some, like Gropius and Mies van der Rohe, proved to be adept self-publicists in the west. Virtually everything they recommended was taken seriously and they spawned monstrous projects which came to blight many a city with their well-intentioned walkways and tunnels acting more as havens for drug dealers and muggers than as ideal homes for 'model humans'. These later disasters helped to bring all modern architecture into disrepute, but to go back and look at the few remaining originals in Berlin is to be reminded of the freshness, creativity, craftsmanship and vision for which the architects originally stood. Nobody who looks at the gentle curves of Emil Fahrenkamp's 1930 Shell House on the Reichpietschufer with its wavy facade and delicate windows reflecting the water of the canal could compare it with the brutal concrete blocks which went up all over the world after 1945. The extraordinary power plant at Rummelsburg with its dramatic chimneys was a marvel of new industrial architecture, and Bruno Taut's comprehensive school in Neukölln, badly copied in Britain after the war, was a practical yet attractive alternative to the stuffy schools of the Wilhelmine era.

The new building schemes reflected the belief that modern technology had almost limitless power to create a new world, and for a short time the utopianism of the mid twenties seemed to be coming true.[39] City planning was 'rationalized'. Sewage systems and water supplies were integrated with health and hygiene improvements, which in turn led to an almost complete disappearance of smallpox, cholera and tuberculosis. It was argued that if rationalization could provide such obvious benefits in health care, surely it could cure all the ills of modern society. As a result the mid twenties saw a drive for better housing, social security, public health insurance and other well-intentioned reforms. In his autobiography Henry Ford claimed that a society could escape poverty by means of modernization and improved efficiency, and both the government and the trade unions urged the acceptance of 'Fordism' in the belief that it legitimated claims for higher wages, shorter working hours and safer conditions in factories. The ideas were revolutionary for the time, but the reformers failed to take into account the fragility of their own weak economy. Germany could not yet afford such vastly expensive projects. Even so, cautious warnings about spending borrowed money on such reforms fell on deaf ears.

To those in its midst, the progress of the mid twenties seemed unstoppable, and this encouraged many intellectuals to impart a deeper meaning to modernity than might otherwise have been the case. Suddenly they began to claim that modern Berlin contained within it a new 'energy' or dramatic power which could help to create a 'new man'. It was almost as if they believed that modernity alone could heal the rifts in Germany and make up for the political and economic instability simmering angrily under the surface. The call for radical change was now over; Ehrenburg left Berlin for Moscow in late 1923, disgusted because there had been no revolution: 'I had spent two years in Berlin,' he wrote in his memoirs, 'with the constant feeling of a gathering storm, and suddenly I realized that the wind had died down. To tell the truth, I was dismayed.'[40] The rest threw themselves into the new trend. Descriptions of Berlin by otherwise sober observers were laced with pronouncements of the faith. The doctor Willy Hellpach called the Berliners *homines novi*, Adolph Behne earnestly stated that the streets create 'a new type of person', Marcel Breuer called the movement of traffic and people the 'Drama of the Big City', and Julius Meier-Graefe swooned that Berlin was so resilient it 'could be completed today and be ripped apart again tomorrow'. Even the usually steady Stresemann called it a 'Metropolis of Brain Power'.

As the years went on intellectuals seemed to lose all sense of proportion about their new modern playground. Otherwise critical men were captivated by the idea of *Berliner Luft* (Berlin air), which supposedly did everything from encouraging original thought to curing hangovers. They echoed Conrad Alberti, who in the 1870s described 'the nervous, endlessly quivering Berlin air ... which works upon people like alcohol, morphine, cocaine, exciting, inspiring, relaxing, deadly; the air of the world city'. There seemed to be a universal desire to glamorize things which were in fact quite normal in all big cities: traffic, noise, speed, technology, machines, transportation links and department stores. In his extraordinary work *The Philosophy of Money* Georg Simmel described the need to surprise blasé Berlin residents with increasingly 'enticing' displays so that even window shopping became a form of entertainment in the nervous, agitated city.[41] Walther Mehring's poem is still quoted by Berliners as proof of their erstwhile cosmopolitanism: 'Giddy-up! Along the Linden! Gallop! Gallop! On foot, on horse, in pairs! With watch in my hand and the hat on my head. No time! No time! No time!'[42] Otto Elsner was so impressed by 1920s traffic that he published his own reverential pamphlet about Berlin which raved about the 'racing tempo' in the heart of the Reich with its 4 million people 'in quick step!' Werner Sombart called it 'the fastest city in the world'. In his *Um die Schönheit der grossen Stadt* (On the Beauty of the Big City) August Endell guided the reader through the varied districts of Berlin, asserting that the big city was the new *Heimat*, with an environment as beautiful, complicated and interesting as any place in nature: 'Despite all the ugly buildings, despite the noise, despite every fault that one can find in it, the big city is, for him who has eyes, a miracle of beauty and poetry.'[43]

Technical developments were praised: Berliners thought of film as their own civic invention because the first public screening had been at the Berlin Wintergarten.[44] Trains and new transportation links were eulogized; Döblin's Biberkopf got his bearings in *Berlin Alexanderplatz* by reading the names of train and S-Bahn stations upon his release from prison, and even the caustic Siegfried Kracauer seemed genuinely moved by the 'heavy express trains rushing toward famous cities such as Warsaw and Paris'. Trains were still used to promote Berlin's central position in Europe, and Heiner Müller did not flinch when he wrote that Berlin was like a 'magnetic field' between a 'west and an east pole'. The Anhalter Bahnhof marked the point, he said, where 'the Holy Roman Empire of the German nation ends', and the Schlesische Bahnhof marked 'the west gate of the Balkans'. He even tried to demonstrate Berlin's relation to American cities by way of an imaginary railway line which went from the United States to China via Berlin. For him, as for everyone else in Berlin, comparisons to the United States had become a source of pride.

When Rathenau wrote, 'Athens on the Spree is dead and Chicago on the Spree is emerging,' he had meant it as an insult. But the Berliners of the 1920s took it as a compliment. The United States had emerged after the disastrous world war as the success story of the twentieth century, and as the historian Arthur Rosenberg put it, America was 'a good idea'. Berliners looked longingly across the Atlantic and tried to become like a piece of America in Europe. Julius Meier-Graefe suddenly announced that Berliners had the strength of the American colonists, while the normally taciturn Herwuth Walden called Berlin the 'capital of the United States of Europe' and 'America in microcosm'. Even left-wing radicals took up the call after Stalin announced in 1924 that the Russians must adopt a 'combination of American matter-of-factness and Russian revolutionary spirit' in order to get industry moving. Berliners wanted

American-style products and German factories obliged by producing motorcycles, radios, lighters, elevators, escalators, hairdriers, Siemens electric irons, AEG toasters, Protos vacuum cleaners, Mercedes electric typewriters, 'Prograph' dictaphones, Jupiter pencil sharpeners and BUG calculators.[45] 'American kitchen buffets' became essential status symbols in the modern home. People took their Americanism seriously, and typing pools, telephone exchanges, post offices, shining new 'rational factories' full of dials and switches and recessed ceiling lights 'proved' – as Ilya Ehrenburg put it in 1927 – that Berlin had become 'the apostle of Americanism'.[46] American fashions copied from Hollywood films were available in the 'palaces of consumerism', the department stores which Edwin Redslob called the 'academy of modern living culture'. Richard Ziegler painted *Vor den Schaufenstern* (Before the Window Display), showing overdressed ladies staring longingly at goods; Karl Hubbuch painted the *Dream of the Tietz Girls* in which glassy-eyed women were sitting in the store fantasizing about their purchases. One of Weimar's most successful revues, *Es liegt in der Luft*, written by Marcellus Schiffer and Mischa Spoliansky, was set in a department store and sent up characters from clerks to customers.[47] The new Karstadt department store on the Hermannplatz was a monumental building, praised not least for the 15-metre column of light which could now help to guide planes to the sparkling new Tempelhof Airport. The *Börsen Courier* wrote that it was a tower 'to the World City Berlin', and the *Berliner Tageblatt* paid the ultimate compliment, assuring its readers that it had stirred interest in America. Werner Hegemann wrote about Karstadt in a manner usually reserved for Romantics musing on the beauty of nature: when darkness fell on the 'living being of the department store', he said, one could see 'the high column of light, its silver shaft pushing into the dark sky, [and] the utopian world of technology comes alive like the fabulous novels of Jules Verne or Wells'.[48]

The fascination with the modern was pushed to extremes. Some took Sergei Tretyakov seriously when he called for 'factographies of things' in the form of biographies of forests, bread, coal, iron, flax, cotton, paper, locomotives and factories. 'We need them,' he announced earnestly. Some argued that as wood and stone were old and bourgeois all new structures must be made of 'modern' iron, glass and concrete. Others who could not afford a new building simply knocked down the old nineteenth-century cherubs and plaster balustrades and attached 'modern' cement cladding to the facades; the neo-baroque Excelsior Hotel at the Anhalter Bahnhof was one of many buildings defaced in this way. The translation of the Russian novel *Cement* was popular and the American artist Charles Sheeler's works, such as the 1922 *Skyscraper* or his photographs of Henry Ford's factories, were praised as they glorified a world in which love of the organic and the natural was replaced by worship of the machine. One of the most peculiar events was the 'Berlin in Light' exhibition of October 1928. A huge rectangular column was erected with a sign proclaiming that the city was now a 'world city' of light, and pamphlets and newspapers were filled with praise of the artificial glow which dominated the Berlin night. Light was 'modern' and was therefore 'good'. Christian Morgenstern wrote of Berlin, 'I love you in fog and by night, when your lines swim into each other – above all at night when your windows glimmer and people bring your stones to life.'[49] Kirchner wrote that 'the modern light of cities, in combination with the movement of the streets, continually gives me new stimuli. It spreads a new beauty out across the world.' Léger was caught up by the mood when he wrote, 'Berlin is modern, modern through its light . . . its war against the night . . . Light at six, at midnight, at four, unceasing light. Paris is like a city of varying shades of grey. Berlin is a single block of light.' Isherwood commented that Berliners loved their modern traffic lights and bright street lamps, while August Endell claimed that the beauty of the metropolis could only be enjoyed when the ugly facades of Berlin were 'enveloped by light'. The old *völkisch* idea of the German as the natural *Lichtmenschen* was translated into the new obsession, and even the normally sceptical Kurt Weill wrote a *Berlin im Licht* song for the exhibition. Entire revues were based on the glorification of light, including Nelson's 1927 *The Lights of Berlin* and Paul Linckes's popular hit which urged the glowworm to 'shimmer, shimmer'.[50] Berliners' characteristic arrogance again began to show through: London was not a 'true metropolis' because it closed up at midnight. Berlin was the new model of the world city because its citizens played under the artificial canopy well into the early hours of the morning.

There was a chilling naïveté in the belief that one could measure 'modernity' by displays in a department store or by the number of lights in the streets. Sefton Delmer was right when he said Berliners 'like to think of themselves as a world city; it was rather a Middle Western idea, the American idea of a successful city. It was really very provincial and has been overglamorized and misrepresented by nostalgia.'[51] Erich Kästner's wit turned against Berliners' need to promote the city by numbers: 'Let's look at Berlin in statistical terms. You can find all you want within this city's bounds, like 190 life insurance firms and 916 hectares of burial ground.'[52] Even so, in the heyday of the 1920s most Berlin artists and intellectuals took the new trend with deadly seriousness, and it was clearly reflected in the shift from Expressionism to the new obsession with all urban themes.

By 1924 virtually all Expressionists had abandoned the movement in favour of the *Neue Sachlichkeit*. Carl Zuckmayer, whose first play *Am Kreuzberg* had been the epitome of Expressionism, now called the style artificial, even hysterical, and greeted the detached Bertolt Brecht as the writer of the future. Hans Richter went from being an Expressionist painter to a Constructivist film-maker; Hans Fallada, who had written the revolutionary *Young Goedeschal*, now produced *Little Man, What Now?*; Georg Kaiser, made famous by his disturbing *Hell Road Earth*, wrote the lighter *Side by Side* with Cubist sets designed by Georg Grosz.[53] There was an increasing tendency for artists to move between new technical mediums – with varying degrees of success; novels like *Berlin Alexanderplatz* or *The Threepenny Opera* were made into films; Moholy-Nagy experimented with photography; Hindemith developed new mechanical instruments; Brecht wrote *The Song of Machines* and praised the writing of poetry on a typewriter. Schlemmer wrote, 'If today's arts love the machine, technology and organization, if they aspire to precision and reject anything vague and dreamy, this implies an instinctive repudiation of chaos and a longing to find the form appropriate to our times.'

There were few scenes of rural bliss in the work of the *Neue Sachlichkeit* artists, a development which would be vividly contrasted by the Nazi 'blood and soil' paintings soon to take over. Berlin itself had attracted the artists; now 'big city themes' became the primary focus of their work. Kurt Wolff's 1925 woodcuts called *Die Stadt* were typical, as were Carl Reissner's *Bilder der Grossstadt*. Kurt Jooss created a ballet called *The Big City*, while Robert Seitz and Heinz Zucker published the anthology *Um uns die Stadt*, for which Lion Feuchtwanger, Walther Mehring and Kurt Tucholsky wrote their 'big city poetry'. Above all it was the new urban Berliner who captured their imagination. Georg Grosz created harsh revealing portraits like that of the poet Max Herrmann Neisse collapsed in a chair in his flat; Otto Dix painted hideous images of exhausted prostitutes and nightclub players, captured the 'new Berlin woman' in his painting of the journalist Sylvia von Harden, and questioned the twisted efficiency of the scarred doctor Hans Koch shown holding a syringe and a rubber hose and standing menacingly in front of a steel stirrup chair. The large cold eyes of Christian Schad's subjects capture the very essence of the Berlin *Neue Sachlichkeit*. Severe blank faces stare from the canvas even when the subject is, like Graf St Genois d'Anneaucourt, surrounded by transvestites, lounging prostitutes or society beauties. In the hands of another artist the *Zwei Freundinnen* masturbating for the viewer would verge on pornography, but for Schad they were bored, unfeeling automatons; when Schad himself poses in a poisonous green diaphanous shirt beside a lover lying indifferently on a chaise-longue, a narcissus flower pushes itself into the centre of the picture. Even the men in Rudolf Schlichter's *Treffen der Fetischisten* or 'Meeting of the Fetishists' seem weary of the women splayed on chairs or bending over red velvet steps, naked except for their high black leather boots. Sex had been reduced to auto-eroticism and people to the mere machines of the city.[54]

The new clinical spirit transformed even the sacrosanct realm of music. Berliners had long enjoyed one of the most impressive musical cultures in Europe with the city's excellent imperial orchestras and schools. Erich Kleiber was not asking the unthinkable when he insisted on 130 rehearsals for a new opera, and with the Philharmonic under Wilhelm Furtwängler, Artur Schnabel teaching at the Academy of Music, Otto Klemperer conducting the Berlin State Opera and Erich Kleiber at the Municipal Opera, Berliners were accustomed to the best. Even so, by the mid 1920s musicians and composers were scrambling to adapt to the new 'rational' atonal music and the influence of jazz, as well as trying to bridge the growing gap between the old elite and the new mass audience being created by gramophone and radio.[55] The composer Ferruccio Busoni, described by his student Kurt Weill as the supreme pianist of his generation, had introduced Debussy, Delius and Sibelius to Berlin; when he died his progressive legacy was continued at the Berlin Hochschule by his successor Arnold Schoenberg. The atonal champion turned the Berlin musical world on its head with works from *Von Heute auf Morgen* to *Erwartung*. Hanns Eisler described his new mechanistic style as 'the manifestation of nervousness, hysteria, panic, confusion, the lost, the terror ... the base character of Schönberg's music', he said, 'is Angst.' Schoenberg attracted colleagues from the Vienna Circle to Berlin, including Webern and Alban Berg.[56] *Wozzeck* had its première at the State Opera in 1925, the perfect twelve-tone musical structure unfolding as the tragic main character, the hapless ignorant soldier, struggled under huge soft trees waving like giant sea-anemones to mock his humiliation, his crime, and his suicide. The effect was electrifying. Conservatives hated it: the critic in *Germania* called it 'Ingenious pretence, sensational pretence, but, in any case, pretence!' but *Vorwärts* reflected that the composer had raised 'the brutality of a single fate to the spirituality of an unreal, dreamlike, unworldly experience'.

Berlin attracted other sensational musicians, from the Russian singer Feodor Chaliapin, the young prodigy Yehudi Menuhin to the great Louis Armstrong; the 1929 Berlin Music Festival featured Richard Strauss and Bruno Walter, Furtwängler and Klemperer, Toscanini, Casals and Thibaud. Hanns Eisler wrote in the 1928 *Berliner Skizzenheft* that dailies invariably carried three pages dedicated to discussion of orchestra concerts, piano and song; in Berlin on every evening of the 'season' one found eight to ten concerts. 'What is going on?' he asked. 'Is ... the hunger for art [*Kunsthunger*] of the bourgeois fed through such a collection of events, through such a list of talent?' Viscount d'Abernon spoke of Berlin as a shimmering city of culture, 'as if all the eminent artistic forces were shining forth once more, imparting to the last festive symposium of the minds a many-hued brilliance before the night of barbarism closed in.' When Sergei Diaghilev came to Berlin with the *Ballets Russes* he said that it was like no other city: 'Faced by Berlin I'm like a schoolboy in love with a grande dame, and I cannot find the key to her heart.' With everything from an ultra-modern production of *The Flying Dutchman* to the première of Hindemith's *Neues vom Tage*, Weimar Berlin managed to surpass even its own formidable pre-war reputation, constantly extending the boundaries of 'acceptable' art and embracing works not yet tolerated by the rest of the world.

The passion for experiment extended to the theatre, making 1920s Berlin the unquestioned centre of Europe.[57] Bruno Walter said that the accomplishments of the thirty-five serious Berlin theatres could 'hardly be surpassed in talent, vitality, loftiness of intention, and variety'. Visitors marvelled at the sheer choice at the Deutsches Theater and the Kammerspiele – where one could see 'Shakespeare, Hauptmann and Werfel, from Molière to Shaw and Galsworthy, from Schiller to Unruh and Hofmannsthal' – the Tribune and the State Theatre, where Leopold Jessner raised 'dramatic interpretive art to new levels'. The most notable development was the attempt to create 'mass' or 'epic' theatre of urban industrial tales far removed from the official pre-war fare. The first of the celebrated directors, Max Reinhardt, had started his career at the Deutsches Theater and then moved to Otto Brahm's Freie Bühne, renowned in the imperial period for producing Gerhart Hauptmann's controversial Naturalist works. He had become increasingly impatient with Brahm's style and in 1900 founded the cabaret Schall und Rauch, which poked fun at Naturalist drama, and created the famous 'Serenissimus' character who sat in one of the boxes alongside the audience and commented loudly on the performances. Reinhardt championed the works of Wedekind and Hofmannsthal in his Neues Theater on Schiffbauerdamm and in the Deutsches Theater, which he took over in 1905. During the war he managed the Berlin Volksbühne and became one of the founding members of the Salzburg Festival, and in the Weimar period he took over the Schumann Circus on the Schiffbauerdamm, where his innovative talent was given full expression. Reinhardt began by commissioning the architect Hans Poelzig to turn the tired space into a new theatre in the round. The result was breathtaking, with Poelzig creating a vast arena complete with enormous white wooden icicles hanging in rows from the dome, giving audiences the impression that they were sitting in a cave of stalactites. Reinhardt's legendary attention to detail enabled him to turn otherwise dour productions like *The Dawn of Humanity* and *Upsurge*, both inspired by Russian revolutionary works, into a new kind of people's theatre which the public actually wanted to see.[58] But by 1923 his fiefdom was already being challenged by the two newcomers on the Berlin theatre scene, Leopold Jessner and Erwin Piscator.

Leopold Jessner dominated the Theater am Gendarmenmarkt and was the first in Berlin to make theatre abstract. It was there that he invented the 'Jessner stairs', a huge prop which ran up the centre of the stage and had the effect of freeing the theatre from conventional or representational scenery. Erwin Piscator also challenged Reinhardt with his Epic Proletarian Theatre, funded largely by the Communist Party.[59] Following Eisenstein's lead he used rolling steps, huge pieces of scaffolding and enormous flags to create a vast noisy colossus on the stage. His production of Hašek's *The Good Soldier Schweik* had treadmills weighing a ton each, and the round steel sets for *Rasputin* and for Mehring's *The Merchant of Berlin* were designed by Moholy-Nagy with music for the latter by Hanns Eisler. The prominent actors of the day – Heinrich George, Albert Bassermann and Elisabeth Bergner – appeared regularly in their respective theatres.

This vigorous life attracted the best writers and playwrights in Germany. In 1924 another man joined the artistic migration to Berlin, his carefully presented proletarian image completed by a dark leather jacket, permanently dirty white shirt and well-chewed black cigar.[60] It was Bertolt Brecht, the archetypal Weimar genius, who had finally succumbed to the lure of the city which would become the subject of his greatest works, and which would make him famous.

Brecht had already made something of a name for himself as an Expressionist playwright with the ominous *Drums in the Night* but he had turned against the movement, mocking it mercilessly in *Baal*. Once in Berlin he met the composer Kurt Weill, with whom he wrote the opera *The Rise and Fall of the City of Mahagonny*, the imaginary city which lay 'somewhere between Florida and Alaska' acting as a thin disguise for modern Berlin. The two also joined forces to produce one of Weimar's most famous pieces and a triumph of the age, *Die Dreigroschen Oper* (*The Threepenny Opera*). Here was Berlin again, this time dressed up as nineteenth-century London, presented on stage with all its crime, its seedy prostitution, its cynicism, its inherent violence. Harold Paulsen created the immortal Mack the Knife, strutting around menacingly in his suit and his bowler hat, attacking the values of the middle class: 'First comes feed, then the morals,' he sneered. The right-wing press attacked it viciously, the *Kreuzzeitung* calling it literary necrophilia, and Alfred Kerr, critic for the *Berliner Tageblatt*, dismissed it as 'Rubbish. Junk.' Even so it was an enormous success; Ihring called it 'the breakthrough not of a worldly or a society-oriented theatre ... because morality is neither attacked nor negated, but simply suspended'.[61]

Ihring's phrase was prophetic. The artists and playwrights of Weimar Berlin were prodigious, but for all their claims to be changing the world through art most remained out of touch with the desperate political problems of their time. Like Brecht, they lived in a world of suspended morality, revolving in a glittering, glamorous, intellectual limbo which had little to do with the real world.

Many of the left-wing intellectuals in Berlin insisted that they were creating art 'for the masses' and that they represented the working classes. In reality, few had any idea what that meant. Most avoided the north of Berlin, few dirtied their hands in the factories or forfeited a late night on the town in order to get up with the 6 a.m. shift; as Robert Walser put it, these were the people, the dreamers who had adventures 'through the night and half the morning', the 'lazy dogs' who 'wake up for the twentieth time, yawn and go back to snoring', the artists who say: '*a was, quatsch, früh aufstehen*' (oh what, rubbish, getting up early).[62]

For their part, the workers remained distinctly unmoved by the artistic innovations carried out in their names. The lives of some had been improved in the mid twenties by the introduction of the forty-hour working week, the new housing projects and the health and education reforms, but most of 'Red Berlin' remained old and shabby, and life was hard. A handful of artists ventured to depict it as it was: Gustav Wunderwald's paintings, such as the 1927 *Underground Station*, showed how little north Berlin had in common with the slick modern thoroughfares of the West End. Another who actually knew the area personally was the doctor and author of *Berlin Alexanderplatz*, Alfred Döblin, who lived and worked in the seedy Frankfurter Allee. It was his experiences in the slums which inspired his portrayal of Franz Biberkopf, the tragic figure who struggles to remain honest after his release from prison, but ends up corrupted and broken by Berlin, the 'Sodom on the eve of its destruction'. Döblin was critical of the hypocritical socialists and Communists who spent their days asleep and their nights on the town; he mocked the 'Communist' Erwin Piscator, who had an extravagant villa built for himself in the Grunewald, and who arrived at plays for the commemoration of the Russian Revolution in a chauffeur-driven new Rolls-Royce.[63] Even an article in Ullstein's *Dame* asked, 'This is a Communist?' Few were as honest as Döblin; they preferred the easy life in the West End.

The self-imposed isolation of the Berlin avant-garde was epitomized by their new café society. There were dozens of cafés in Berlin but only a handful, like the Café des Westens, really mattered in the new social hierarchy. The grandest of them all was the vast neo-Gothic expanse by the Kaiser Wilhelm Gedächtniskirche, the Romanisches Café. Max Krell wrote that it was the place 'where ideas and plans were exchanged, a spiritual exchange', and Elias Canetti remembered the Romanisches Café as playing a pivotal social role in the artistic life of the city, acting like a cement for an essentially rootless society. The most celebrated figures in Berlin met daily at the Romanisches: the Dadaists in a large room called the 'swimming pool' at the back, the Secessionists and Expressionists on the terrace, and writers and directors, painters and art dealers all in their separate sections. The hierarchy was clearly defined; minor figures were treated with barely concealed disdain and seated near the entrance and the porter Herr Mietz acted like the doorman of a London gentlemen's club, turning away 'non-members' – including the champion heavyweight boxer Max Schmeling. For those in the charmed circle, however, life was fabulous.[64] Hans Tasiemka said that though 'the coffee was bad, the cake old, the eggs in a glass expensive', everybody who could get in went as often as possible. The sheer number of works depicting artists and their friends drinking, talking, smoking, sitting or standing in the cafés gives some measure of the incestuous nature of their world: Christian Schad met and painted his quintessential Weimar model Sonja at the Romanisches Café; Otto Dix painted the poet Iwar von Lucken there, Willy Jaeckel painted Lesser Ury, Oskar Kokoschka painted Tilla Durieux, Höxter painted Frank Wedekind, whom he called the 'Star of the Cafés'. Titles revealed this self-obsession: Kirchner, Karl Hubbuch, Jeanne Mammen and Eduard Braun painted works entitled *Berliner Café*; Meidner painted his *Berliner Caféhaus* at the Romanisches; Walther Mehring did his *Selbstbildnis im Café* there; Paul Citroën broke ranks by painting the *Café des Westens*; Karl Arnold, Frigl and Emil Orlik each painted works entitled *Im Romanischen Café*, and the list went on.[65] Here were the left-wing intellectuals at play, men and women who continued to see the new-found artistic freedom as an inevitable privilege of modern society even when it was nearing its end. And the end was approaching fast.

The list of refugees eventually forced to flee Weimar Berlin is one of the most impressive testaments to its history. Hundreds of leading twentieth-century writers, poets, film makers, theatre directors and painters who had lived or worked in Berlin would see their works burned or ridiculed, and many, from Walter Gropius to Alfred Döblin, from Fritz Lang to Bertolt Brecht to Max Reinhardt, would be forced into lonely exile in London or New York or California, left in alien worlds to dream about the unique time of freedom and creativity which was their Berlin. It was then, from outside, that the legend of the Golden Twenties began to take hold in the west. But the image was flawed, for although they described the freedom with a passion most failed to mention that they had done little to defend it while they had the chance. There were many amongst them who had epitomized the *Vernunftrepublikaner*, the Rational Republicans, complaining bitterly about the failings of the republic but doing little to help change it, reflecting a deep traditional Germanic disdain for politics. How could they be inspired when Stresemann, the very symbol of the republic, maintained that Weimar was an affair of reason, not of the heart. The young Thomas Mann had captured this attitude in his 1918 *Reflections of a Nonpolitical Man*: 'I hate politics and the belief in politics, because it makes men arrogant, doctrinaire, obstinate, and inhuman.'[66] Mann later changed his views and openly, courageously defended the republic, but his was a lonely voice in a sea of arrogance and denial.[67] Ultimately even Mann's politics were little more than an intellectual exercise, the examination of an interesting concept to be dissected and put back together as he did in the quintessential Weimar novel, *The Magic Mountain*.[68]

At least Mann tried. Most of the great writers of the day preferred to remain in the world of the spirit rather than enter the nasty business of politics. Of the serious writers of the age from Gerhart Hauptmann, Jakob Wassermann, Rene Schickele, Arno Holz, Georg Kaiser, Ricarda Huth, Arthur Schnitzler and Hans Werfel, few actively worked to support the republic. Franz Neumann later said that the German intellectuals' state of mind was one of 'scepticism and despair, bordering on cynicism'. While most artists and writers refused to raise their voices in defence of the republic some, from Brecht to Piscator to Heartfield, viciously attacked it from the radical left. Kurt Tucholsky, normally a strong defender of republican values, lashed out that the real danger in Germany was the intra-party Stresemann type: 'German democracy [is] a facade and a lie.'[69] Johannes Baader regularly interrupted both church services and the Weimar National Assembly as a protest against the new status quo, while Raoul Hausmann, who had been one of the founders of Berlin Dada, said in 1919: 'I am not only against the spirit of Potsdam – I am above all against Weimar.'[70] Communist writers on the Bund proletarisch-revolutionärer Schriftsteller (Federation of Proletarian-Revolutionary Writers) attacked Alfred Döblin, Heinrich Mann and Ernst Toller because they were 'social fascists' (Social Democrats); as early as 1924 Johannes R. Becher, a lyricist who would later become a minister in the German Democratic Republic, attacked intellectuals who defended the republic as 'a parasite exuding pink-red mimicry'.[71]

The apolitical nature of Weimar is reflected even in the great 'political' cabaret, which tended to attack all aspects of Weimar with equal vehemence, as in the classic sketch by Robitschek for the Kadeko, which satirized the political nature of Berlin's newspapers. The stage is set by the *conférencier*, who explains that the audience is about to hear how each of the Berlin newspapers would report the minor incident of a collision between a bicycle and a dog. The sketch begins:

The optimistically liberal *Berliner Tageblatt* claimed that 'dog and bicyclist race along the Kurfürstendamm, they hurry – despite a little scratch here and there – towards the brilliant future of the German republic'. The pessimistically liberal *Vossische Zeitung* complained that the appearance of *red* blood on a *black* dog with *white* spots turned the incident into an expression of reactionary politics; it called for more laws to defend the republic. The nationalist *Lokal-Anzeiger* claimed that 'a foreign bicyclist ran over the dog of a retired general. Fifteen years ago the German people would have stood up as one body and would have swept the bicyclist away with ringing manly fury, but today our faithful dogs lie limply on the ground, shattered by the Treaty of Versailles'. The Communist *Rote Fahne* reported: 'On the Kurfürstendamm, that pompous boulevard of satiated capitalism on which the proletarian revolution will march against the imperialists in the very near future, a dog attacked a simple proletarian bicyclist!!!!! That's how it starts! First one dog attacks a single bicyclist, then all dogs unite against the Soviet Union!' Finally, the Nazi *Völkischer Beobachter* asserted: 'Once more one of our party comrades has been attacked from behind in the dark of night by a bow-legged, flat-footed dachshund. Bow-legged – that betrays the true race of these eastern Jewish pets, with their sagging ears and curls, who suck the marrow of our countrymen and steal the bones from under the noses of our German shepherds. Tomorrow our Führer Adolf Hitler will speak in the sports palace about this national affair. Party comrades should appear in simple battle dress, with hand grenades and flamethrowers.'[72]

Such satires kept the audience laughing but punchier jokes were unpopular with the general public. Robitschek considered jokes by Tucholsky, Mehring and Erich Weinert 'too political' and said in 1929: 'how many people would show understanding for such an ideal cabaret? Twenty journalists and three hundred schnorrers of free tickets. The Cabaret of Comedians has 950 chairs, they seat people of all political persuasions, all social classes, all *Weltanschauungen*. Try to cook up a sauce that all of them will find tasty!' For him, 'politics did not belong in the cabaret'.[73]

However naive or unaware they might have been about the threat of Nazism the intellectuals alone could have done little to stem the rise of *völkisch* nationalism seeping into German life. Walter Laqueur was right to point out that it was 'Hitler, not Tucholsky, who buried the Weimar Republic'; that 'even if the left-wing intellectuals had been more positive about their new political system, even if they had been less embittered about the fact that their noble dream had not been realized in Weimar, even if their perspective had not been dictated by utopian visions and moral absolutes, even if they had all rallied to the defence of the Republic, the outcome would most probably have been the same'.[74] Ernst Wichert said of the Weimar writers that they had a 'cool sharp intellect, a cold eye, the capacity for analysis, the incisive knife, the sure hand'; that they saw life in its naked pitiless reality and tore down all the old conventions and objects of piety; that 'there was little that they shunned in the means they used'. But for all their willingness to attack and rip apart, they offered precious few solutions to the terrible problems of the age. Their lack of support did nothing to help save the system. Even in the relatively stable years, or perhaps because they were stable, the artists and intellectuals seemed oblivious to the fact that the real danger lay not with the admittedly flawed republic, but with the forces slowly gathering strength on the right. The artists' complete inability to understand the realities of German society and political life was illustrated by Friedrich Holländer, who in his revues at the Tingel-Tangel portrayed Hitler as a harmless fool who would never succeed in politics, or in the proposal by the men at the *Weltbühne* to have Heinrich Mann run as a serious contender against Adolf Hitler in the 1932 presidential elections.[75]

If the intellectuals were out of touch with political reality, they were also out of touch with the needs of the 'average Berliner'. While the workers struggled to make ends meet the new white-collar middle class grew from 8 to 18 per cent. Traditionally the *Mittelstand* had consisted primarily of shopkeepers and craftsmen, but they had been joined by a new breed of skilled workers who were employed, not self-employed, and who worked in the new offices, department stores and government ministries. They became managers in the new factories, acted as administrators in the new government offices or hospitals, and included doctors, engineers, lawyers, accountants and financial advisers who worked in the new service sector. They had money and leisure time and saw themselves as quite separate from the industrial workers.

The emergence of the new group had a profound effect on the role of the middle class, and particularly on women, who had traditionally taken care of the children or worked in agriculture or in small family businesses.[76] The war had changed all that. With the men at the front line women had been expected to take on jobs traditionally held by men, and when the fighting had stopped they refused to settle back into the old way of life. They were finally granted the right to vote in 1918 and many continued to work, not least because the mass slaughter had resulted in a shortage of eligible men.[77] By the 1920s nearly a quarter of the Berlin labour force was made up of women, with the largest increase being in the white-collar sector. The less skilled worked in factories or found jobs in the new shops and department stores while others became typists, telephone operators and secretaries. Many were encouraged to study and, although they were paid less than men and tended to be given less responsible jobs, they found work in industry, commerce, government and in the private sector; they also took degrees and worked in the new disciplines of psychology, sociology and education. For the first time in Berlin history, women became independent and important in their own right. Role models included not only singers and actresses like the great Elisabeth Bergner, Tilla Durieux, Fritzi Massary and Trude Hesterberg; there were also 111 women serving in the Weimar Reichstag. Vicki Baum captured the 'new woman' in novels such as *Stud. Chem. Helene Willfüer*, which told the story of a young professional woman who led a thoroughly independent life, even having a child out of wedlock. She was able to defy the old professor who was determined to stifle her career, and finally became a leading research scientist.

The new liberation took many forms; the corset was gone, skirts were shortened to the knee, women bound their breasts to fit into the new boyish fashions and 'bob' haircuts like the *Bubikopf* and *Herrenschnitt* gave women new freedom, as satirized in Friedrich Holländer's hit song *Die letzte Haarnadel* (The Last Hairpin). Suddenly modern girls were *sachlich* and could drive cars, smoke cigarettes, drink alcohol, take drugs and have sex before marriage. There were many impudent flappers and nude dancers on the Berlin stages, but the liberation also gave more women greater freedom. They worked for a salary and spent their money 'on the town', and although few could expect to live up to the glossy image of the vamp portrayed in the new women's magazines they had a changed role in society. They too fed on the new consumerism sweeping Berlin. For some this was an ominous symbol of the rationalistic, empty world of industrial modernity. For others, it was the way of the future.

In his extraordinary series of essays about Berliners 'Amongst Themselves' for the *Frankfurter Zeitung* Siegfried Kracauer described Berlin as a city inhabited by white-collar workers who wanted nothing but mass culture. The 'new women' Berliners were so proud of worked in stores and offices; 'young girls come mostly from a poorer milieu and are attracted by the glamour'. They worked in the typing pool, visited department stores with 'their cheerful rooms flooded with light' and 'need hit songs and films to keep them going'. Popular entertainment, shopping excursions and sporting events provided the distractions. 'The exact counterpoise to the machine world of the office . . . is the world of bright lights. Not the world as it actually is, but the world as it is portrayed in hit songs. A world which has been gone over by a vacuum cleaner, so that not a single speck of the dust of everyday life remains.'[78] He was writing about Haus Vaterland, but he might as well have been describing the new members of the Berlin middle class.

Nothing illustrates the differences between the needs of the new intellectual elite and the white-collar workers more clearly than film – the quintessential medium of Weimar Berlin. For many intellectuals forced to leave Berlin, and for many in the west, Weimar Berlin is still epitomized by *Caligari* or *Nosferatu*; by Fritz Lang's *Metropolis* or Marlene Dietrich in *The Blue Angel*.[79] In reality, these cultural icons have come down to us through the film schools and screens of New York and Hollywood. *The Cabinet of Dr Caligari* might have transformed cinema history with its synthetic world of bizarre sets filmed in a studio without lighting, but it only had a run of four weeks in Berlin. Instead, the themes of the *Doppelgänger*, the portrayal of the evil world of death and dreams were served up in melodramatic soap operas filled with black-robed magicians, evil spirits and mad apparitions chasing scantily clad young ladies around graveyards and dark, bat-filled caves. These long-forgotten films had titles like *The Tophar Mummy*, *The Hunt for Death* and *The Sign of Malay*. It was not edifying stuff.[80]

The same fate awaited the best films from Russia. These extraordinary works did affect the artists; after seeing *Battleship Potemkin* Max Reinhardt is said to have muttered, 'I am willing to admit that the stage will have to give way to the cinema.'[81] Piscator's sets were a deliberate attempt to rival film, so much so that in his 1926 production of *Trotz Alledem!* he projected a film of naval battles and crowd scenes on the huge screen behind the actors. Nevertheless few Berliners bothered to go to Willi Münzenberg's showing of Eisenstein's films. The new German–Soviet co-productions like *Superfluous People* and *The Cigarette Girl from Mosselprom* quickly faded, and Münzenberg's attempts to found Communist cinema for the working class outlined in his 1925 book *Conquer the Film* – later turned into the first Marxist film for the masses, *Kühle Wampe* – was a failure and drove him to bankruptcy.[82] Melodramatic social dramas like *Mutter Krausens Fahrt ins Glück*, the story of a poor working-class Mother Courage and her struggle to keep her family together, fared little better. To the chagrin of the idealists intent on shaping society in the Soviet image, the workers seemed to prefer light films and American-style musicals to the dreary fare churned out by Münzenberg and his supporters.

Despite the presence of the great directors from Billy Wilder, Max Ophuls, Alexander Korda and Josef von Sternberg, Berliners preferred the endless diet of light entertainment created by UFA (the great German private film company) at Tempelhof and Babelsberg and the cheaper productions from smaller studios at Friedrichstrasse, at Weissensee and the old Zeppelin hanger near Spandau. Many of the films were popular simply because they glorified the new 'Metropolis Berlin', helping to create identity and pride in the *Grossstadt*. 'Street films' included *Symphony of a Grossstadt*, which was a collage of Berlin 'big city scenes', Joe May's *Asphalt*, which had a Berlin traffic policeman as its hero, *The Night Belongs to Us*, filled with cars speeding through the streets, *The Adventures of a Ten Mark Note*, showing a 'cross section' of Berlin society, Greta Garbo's first film outside Sweden, *Joyless Street*, and *Nie Wieder Liebe*, which was filmed at the Luna Park swimming pool. Silly romantic comedies starring the 'screen couple' Willy Fritsch and Lilian Harvey also featured Berlin, but with names like *The Empress and I*, *Hungarian Rhapsody*, and the first hugely successful operatic musical, *The Congress Dances*, set behind the scenes at the 1815 Congress of Vienna, they were also forgettable.[83] Added to these were the dozens of cheap romantic Berlin dramas, some of which bordered on pornography and which liked to emphasize the immoral and dangerous side of the metropolis: they included *The Prostitute's Daughter*, *Woman: Love for a Night*, *The Girl from Counter 12*, *The Secrets of the Big City*, *The Girl from the Revue*, *Big City Butterfly* and *Woman in the Moon*.

Another of the ground-breaking films which Berliners failed to support in large enough numbers was Fritz Lang's *Metropolis* which, despite its enormous futuristic sets and its elaborate crowd scenes, told a rather disappointing story of the futility of the fight against authority. The film had an important political consequence; it nearly bankrupted UFA, and in 1927 the company fell under the control of the right-wing magnate, the nationalist Alfred Hugenberg, who was one of the first to court Hitler. The new owner preferred another kind of film, an 'educational' product meant to instil good German values in the audience, in part by condemning every aspect of the struggling republic. His favourites were nationalistic dramas based on the 'true to life' stories of historic leaders like Frederick the Great, the so-called *Fredericus* films.[84] This highly popular genre would continue well into the Nazi era.

The 'Golden Twenties' legend rests in part on the nostalgia for the cabaret, a popular image created by Dietrich and Isherwood and the film *Cabaret*, starring Liza Minnelli. In the years following the war political cabaret had indeed been exciting and provocative, with its mockery of the generals and the nationalists who had started and lost the war and the consequences of hyper-inflation and the Treaty of Versailles. It regained some of its sparkle in the short tragic years between 1929 and 1933, when the great Kabarett der Komiker or Kadeko, founded by Kurt Robitschek and Paul Morgan, satirized events like Hitler's Beer Hall *Putsch*. The famous *conférenciers* or masters of ceremonies reigned supreme and included men like Paul Nikolaus at the Kadeko, Ernst Busch, Jushny at the Russian cabaret Blue Bird, the incomparable Werner Finck, who would ask Nazis in the audience if he should speak more slowly so their poor small brains could understand the jokes, and Karl Schnog – who later set up a 'cabaret' in Dachau. The very best Weimar cabarets included Max Reinhardt's Schall und Rauch, Leon Hirsch's flying cabaret Die Wespen (Wasps), which moved from place to place in the working-class districts in the north and east of Berlin, Trude Hesterberg's Wilde Bühne (Wild Stage), which she opened in the basement of the Theater des Westens in 1921, and Werner Finck's Katakombe, founded in October 1929. Noteworthy composers included Friedrich Hollaender, Kurt Tucholsky, Rudolf Nelson, Hanns Eisler, Erich Kästner (now best known for *Emil and the Detectives*) and Walther Mehring.[85] Their works were performed by singers like Rosa Valetti (who had her own Club Megalomania), the razor-thin Margot Lion, the great Kurt Gerron, who performed the 'Rat Catcher' which lambasted black marketeers and inept politicians, Karl Wilcynski, the Communist performer Ernst Busch, Josephine Baker – who often appeared in Berlin in the 1920s – Wilhelm Bendow, who appeared as 'Lydia Smith the Tattooed Lady', and Trude Hesterberg, who performed on her own stage in the Wilde Bühne where Anita Berber, already burnt out on heroin and cocaine, also danced her elaborate striptease.[86] The city itself became the subject of the stage as epitomized by the darling of Berlin, Claire Waldoff.

Waldoff was touted as the epitome of the true *Berlinerin*; short with red hair and with a rasping voice and vulgar sense of humour, she had the *Schnauze*, the Berlin coarse wit and repartee which endless commentators claim marks the 'true Berliner' from all others. The Berliner *Schnauze* was itself a whimsical invention, rather like the Scottish paraphernalia devised by Walter Scott in the nineteenth century, but by the 1920s it had become a self-fulfilling Berlin character trait. Claire Waldoff's persona was also an invention, and she had all Berlin fooled. The young aspiring actress had actually arrived penniless from her school in Hanover and decided to go on the stage, but quickly realized that if she wanted to survive in a city filled with talented and conventionally beautiful performers she would have to change her image. She studied the Berlin dialect and turned herself into the epitome of what the well-to-do believed the *Echt*, genuine working-class Berlin woman was like. She delighted middle-class cabaret audiences, most of whom had never been to the slums, with lyrics about the poverty of the *Hinterhof* or the back-breaking work in the factory, acts which always ended with a cheerful piece of advice, such as one should not 'dwell on hardship' but should 'get out and take Berlin'. She was already well known before the war but her career took off after 1918 and the success of this *ersatz* character was a comment on the age.[87] Whatever the attractions of these cabaret divas, the most popular forms of mass entertainment had nothing whatever to do with real cabaret, let alone political satire.

The image of the hard-hitting political stage has been greatly exaggerated since 1933 and even during the heyday of Weimar cabaret its most perceptive writers lamented that Berliners were not really interested in satire at all. As Peter Jelavich has pointed out, much cabaret applauded the aggressive nationalism which marked the era while 'writers and performers who espoused liberal and democratic values had great difficulty finding a proper voice and an appreciative public'.[88] Kurt Tucholsky, who in 1919 had set out to write ferocious satire, found the audience unresponsive: 'the middle class, the bourgeois, is indignant and feels his most sacred values attacked if ever some-one on stage should dare to express an opinion different from his own – he will not stand for radicalism in a variety show and will never forgive a singer for it.'[89] He complained to a friend three months after the relaunch of Schall und Rauch that 'Everything is so sad: even here pandering to the consumer, that is the audience, which is mostly loathsome. A truly literary cabaret would not work. It is very, very sad.'[90] Restrictive nineteenth-century censorship laws had been directed not so much against political satire but against obscenity, but with the lifting of these restrictions after the war everything from nudity to sexually explicit lyrics were suddenly permitted. Far from supporting the new political freedoms the majority of Berliners flocked to vaudevilles and revues and naked dancing evenings, many of which continued seamlessly into the Nazi period. If Weimar revues had a common theme it was not political satire, it was Girlkultur.[91]

The one thing which tied shows at the Metropol, the Apollo, the Haller Revues at the Theater am Admiralspalast, the Klein Revues at the Komische Oper and the Charell Revues at the Grosses Schauspielhaus together was the presence of naked women. Any women would do, whether single nudes, chorus lines or pairs of erotic dancers, and there were literally hundreds of revues in the style of Klein's Berlin Without a Blouse, in which the girls were implored to strip to songs like Tucholsky's Take It Off, Petronella. Girl reviews became ever more elaborate and risqué. It was not unusual for 'Black and White Girls', the 'Admiral Girls' or the 'Paris Mannequins' to appear in 'dramas' with titles like Dancing Girls, Over and Under, On and On, On and Out, When and Where, baring ever more as they went along.[92] Typically, some Berliners attempted to justify it in terms of modernity. Giese wrote a learned study in 1925 entitled Girlculture. Comparison between American and European Rhythms and Feelings of Life, in which he said that the Tiller Girls were the epitome of the technical age because their 'dancing bodies drilled and trained' like 'mobile machines'.[93] Paul Simmel drew a cartoon in 1926 showing Tiller Girls being created on a Ford factory production line. Polgar noted that there was more than 'just' erotic magic to them, but that they represented the 'submersion of the individual into the group, the concentration of bodies into a single collective body'.[94]

There was some criticism of the trend; Walter Benjamin, always ready with a serious cultural critique, said that the revue was at the point of exhausting its store of inspiration: 'Ever since it undressed the female body to the point of total nudity, its only available mode of variation was quantity, and soon there will be more girls than spectators.'[95] Another critic wrote that if one wanted to sum up the shows one could simply 'multiply a naked woman by fifty, and you have the main idea'. But the revues revealed the acceptance of nudity and prostitution and the fact that for most jaded Berliners of the late 1920s sex was just another commodity. People were satiated after the crazed post-war climate of sexual experimentation, and even the innovative clubs had been replaced by seedy playboy-style bars where the indifferent nude waitresses could be fondled by the customers. In his novel *Iron Gustav* Hans Fallada described a post-war scene in which a young girl brought home by the maid began to dance for the master of the house, and when his wife walked in she was so overcome that she stripped off and joined her. This was a typical theme in the *Ballet Celly de Rheidt*, whose performances Celly's husband Alfred Seweloh promoted as 'beauty evenings' but which were nothing but nude dancing, starring his wife with beautiful girls as young as twelve. Numbers had titles like *The Vampyr, Salome, Opium Intoxication* and *Dance of the Gladiators*; one featured a nun who in a fit of ecstasy threw off her clothes, ran around the stage and finally leapt towards an altar and embraced a crucifix.[96] A court case against Celly's 'ballet' led to a ruling that although women who stood still on stage could be naked those who danced had to cover their private parts in some way. The police dutifully went to each revue to ensure that the small pieces of opaque fabric stayed in place during the dances. The reports are often obscene in themselves; one written about a 1926 performance by the infamous Anita Berber ended with the phrase: 'The sexual parts, around which the pubic hairs seem to have been shaved off, are clearly visible and are so imperfectly covered by the band between the thighs, that the labia bulge out to the left and the right of the band. The posterior is uncovered.' Another policeman noted the extensive use of binoculars and opera glasses in the Berlin dance halls, employed 'from a distance of 5 to 10 metres, whereby they could see only individual parts of the body, or could scrutinize at most a single person'.[97] As the decade wore on, however, even the infamous *Nackttanz* evenings were seen as 'boring' and 'predictable'. According to Landauer the blasé attitude towards sex in the night life of Berlin 'destroyed for many of us younger men all the illusions about sex that some people retain throughout their whole lives'.

Berlin had become famous for its tolerance of homosexuality immediately after the war, but by the mid twenties it was not merely part of a subculture but a necessity of avant-garde fashion to arrive at parties or go to the opera with a member of the same sex: it proved that one was 'modern' and that one had broken with the 'tired bourgeois morals' of the pre-war era.[98] Margot Lion and Marlene Dietrich's hit song *Wenn die beste Freundin* (When My Best Girlfriend) became the unofficial lesbian anthem in the late 1920s.[99] Nightclubs like the Silhouette or the Grotto for women or the El Dorado for men eventually became little more than stops on the tourist round; Felix Gilbert wrote that foreigners visiting the city usually wished to see something of the amorality of Berlin life about which they had heard so much. Consequently, Berliners – and I was no exception – often guided visitors to a restaurant and large dance hall frequented exclusively by homosexuals. The foreigners usually went away happily content that they now could talk on the basis of personal experience about the licentiousness of the city.[100]

Eugen Szatmari wrote, 'the real clubs are known only to the initiated . . . the magnets of the Berlin night', but he was still keen to make fun of the Germans from the provinces shocked by the goings-on in Berlin, snickering at 'the nice gentleman from Saxony who dances with the blond singer [but] doesn't have the slightest idea that his blond lady is a man'. But the overriding mood in the late 1920s was a sense of boredom and listlessness.

The demand for mass entertainment and escapism fuelled the need for ever more variety. The Scala, with its Grock the Clown and other shows, became a Berlin landmark; the Wintergarten was constantly packed with audiences keen on seeing the latest varieties, and the Luna Park drew Berliners with its enormous swimming pool complete with 'Atlantic wave maker' at which 'naked days' were particularly popular with families. The 'Panoptikum' at the Luna Park offered entertainment in the form of revues and freak shows: Berliners went in their thousands to see the Siamese twins Rosa and Josefa Blazed, the 'Huge Machnow – the largest man that ever lived', 'Princess Elisabeth the living puppet', 'Madame Dimanche – the horned lady from Paris', the famous transvestite Anton Krotoschin or the shrunken heads from 'deepest Africa'.[101] The ever-popular Haus Vaterland, with its enormous fake marble columns and its 'palm room', was filled with a collection of 'thematic restaurants' like the Rhine Terrace or Bavarian Beer Hall or Wild West Bar and was fondly remembered long after the war.[102] It was *ersatz* cosmopolitanism, *ersatz* authenticity, and *ersatz* worldliness, and much of the worst of popular entertainment carried on into the Nazi era with no break at all.

Mass spectator sports were another new twentieth-century phenomenon taken up with a passion in Berlin. Horse racing, association football, champion eights on the Havel and tennis tournaments became part of life. World records were set on the Avus racing track with its famous 44-degree north curve; Manfred von Brauschitsch in his Mercedes, Hans Stuck racing for Auto-Union and the stars Veers and Charon in their Bugatti became household names, and when in 1928 Fritz von Opel won with the first rocket-powered car (which went from 0 to 100 in 8 seconds) he became a hero overnight. Cars became highly fashionable; when Lilian Harvey bought herself a 'snow white 7.7 litre Mercedes' it became a star in its own right. Special shops sold clothing and gadgets for motorists and slick new petrol stations with their lights and dials went up around the city. The hit film *Die Drei von der Tankstelle* (Three from the Petrol Station) was shot in one of them, while Wilhelm Speyer had his character Charlotte tear around Berlin in a little red sportscar. There were over 300,000 privately owned cars in the city by 1929 and, like so many other technical innovations, motorways were being built long before Hitler introduced them to the easily impressed provinces and took to driving around the country in his super-charged Mercedes.

Fascination with 'modern' transportation extended to everything from U-Bahns to Zeppelins. Ullstein had the journalist Arthur Koestler accompany the LZ127 *Graf Zeppelin* to the North Pole; when he arrived back he reported on the spectacle of crowds of people waiting at Tempelhof and breaking into spontaneous singing of *Deutschland, Deutschland über Alles* as the Zeppelin docked; 'Berlin', he wrote, 'has Zeppelin fever.' The theme was taken up throughout Berlin; even the newly modernized main Dresdner Bank building had enormous wall paintings covered with Cubist planes and Zeppelins whizzing towards the centre of Berlin. The planes were also a source of pride – as was the highly advanced Tempelhof Airport, which was opened in 1923 for civilian traffic. In 1926 Luft-Hansa was formed and soon provided a service to fifteen European destinations. Berliners celebrated every new record with gusto; when three pilots started off from Berlin and became the first to cross the Atlantic from east to west every movement was followed with intense interest. When the pilots landed in America on 28 April 1928 enormous paintings of their heads were stuck on to the front of the Tietz department store and Berlin was decorated as if for an imperial parade.

The Berlin Sportpalast also came into its own during the Weimar period as the venue for everything from skating championships to boxing matches. Boxing reached new heights of popularity when Max Schmeling became world heavyweight champion; Georg Grosz painted him, Rudolf Belling sculpted him in bronze and Bertolt Brecht wrote a boxing poem called *Hook to the Chin*.[103] The most famous event at the Sportpalast was the six-day bicycle race which became an important function in the social calendar. When Curt Morek saw it he noticed that everybody in Berlin seemed to be there, from office workers to the greatest stars of the day. The people in the gallery would 'stamp their feet for their favourites. The riders race around at high speed. The music plays endlessly. In the shimmer of light in the loggia one sees the beautiful shoulders of elegant women next to black "Smokings".'

By the mid 1920s Berlin seemed the epitome of a glittering capital enjoying its new-found prosperity. It was all breathless, thrilling frothiness, but it was an illusion which would soon prove to lack resilience and depth. The elite which had replaced the Kaiser and the court now consisted of film starlets and sports heroes, theatre directors and business moguls, artists and writers. It was flamboyant and it was fun, but it was also essentially rootless. There was no equivalent of the social register, the Paris *gratin* or London society to filter out charlatans and confidence tricksters, and social life revolved around parties at the Adlon or at the embassies and gatherings at the six-day bicycle race. The highlight of the year came in the form of subscription balls such as the Alpine or the Colonial, the most prestigious of all being the Ullstein Press Ball, which continued until 1933. The new aristocrats were constantly on the lookout for thrills and mixed everything from mysticism to Taoism to astrology, fervently worshipping, as Franz Werfel put it, both 'God and the Foxtrot'. As they enjoyed their narcissistic pleasures they showed a wanton disregard of political reality. It proved to be suicidal.

The legend of Weimar which persists to this day reflects the unique modern culture which swept through Berlin between the wars, but it is an uncritical view. Amongst other things it ignores the fact that with the exception of the artists themselves few Berliners realized they were living through a cultural Renaissance. The myth severs Weimar Berlin from the imperial era and ignores the fact that many of the cultural and intellectual developments of Weimar Berlin, from cabaret to Expressionism, originated in the period before the First World War. It also assumes that no aspects of Weimar were carried on into the Nazi period and that 1933 represents a radical break with all aspects of the past, whereas in reality many elements of the 1920s found their way into Nazi Germany, albeit in altered forms. Those Berliners who were able to glide comfortably from the Weimar period into the new regime still have difficulty separating the 1920s from their own memories of what was for many the 'Golden Thirties'. The uncomfortable fact was that while the avant-garde was destroyed after 1933 much of the popular culture and the seedy glamour of the nightclubs and films and revues and restaurants carried on well into the Nazi period with little obvious change; one still meets Berliners who warmly reminisce about the delights of the Wintergarten or the Haus Vaterland or the Funkturm or the cabaret which were as much a part of 1930s Nazi Berlin as they had been of Weimar Berlin. As such the myth ignores the uncomfortable fact that even when avant-garde culture was at its height the majority of Berliners were ignorant of it, even frightened by it. The image of the Golden Twenties which has come down to us is a grotesque distortion of one of the most complex and tragic periods of Berlin history. The Nazis were able to destroy the avant-garde precisely because it was a minority affair despised by many and treated with suspicion by most, while the real Weimar culture – the popular culture – already laced with *völkisch* imagery and themes of nationalism and anti-Semitism, would continue to flourish.[104] The social, political, economic and cultural constellations which allowed Nazism to take hold were falling into place long before the weary Weimar supporters finally lost the will to carry on with their lonely, thankless task of trying to keep the country together. When the end came most Berliners were relieved to see the capital 'cleansed' of the 'un-German' artists in their midst.

The novelist Georg Hermann once remarked that Berliners have an ambivalent relationship to their city, as 'they cannot do without it, but neither can they come to terms with it. And least of all can they comprehend [it].' His comment can be applied to many aspects of the period but none more so than to Josef von Sternberg's The Blue Angel, the film that made Marlene Dietrich famous.

The Blue Angel, made in 1929 as Germany's first talking film, lies at the heart of the myth. Set in the seedy world of a cabaret, it attacked the bourgeois values of pre-war Germany by depicting the painful humiliation of an old schoolmaster at the hands of a femme fatale cabaret singer, Lola Lola. The Weimar image of the leggy blonde perched on the edge of a barrel, top hat tilted back and singing Ich bin vom Kopf bis Fuss, a song about falling nonchalantly in and out of love irrespective of the pain it causes others, is perhaps the best-known in the rest of the world. But myth is not reality, and however important the film was to the post-war Berlin tourist trade it was clearly not enough to overcome many Berliners' deep resentment towards Marlene Dietrich and the world for which she stood.

Dietrich left Berlin shortly before the Nazi seizure of power not for political reasons but because von Sternberg promised her a career in Hollywood.[105] Americans had not seen The Blue Angel and what is commonly thought of as the 'Dietrich Legend' was created not in Berlin but in the United States. It was there that von Sternberg perfected it after 1930 in films like Morocco and The Devil is a Woman whose plots invariably revolved around the male characters' erotic obsession with the femme fatale.[106] Berliners were indifferent to her Hollywood career but many were highly critical of her subsequent support of the Americans during the war, even though she was actively speaking out against Nazism and for the resurrection of what she thought of as 'her Berlin'. When she returned for a concert in 1960 she was stunned by the behaviour of the crowd, who chanted, 'Marlene Go Home!' She never set foot in Germany again. During the following decade Berliners' anger seemed to cool. Many in 1970s West Berlin were eager to resurrect her in an attempt to link their half of the city with the culture of the 1920s and to try to recapture the sense of glamour and excitement of an era said to be untainted either by the imperial period or by the evils of Nazism. It was particularly important in a city which had lost its political and economic role in a divided Germany and which was forced to rely on its importance as a cultural centre. That this failed to impress many Berliners was made painfully clear in May 1992.

When news of Marlene Dietrich's death reached Berlin the city was peculiarly ungrateful. In a place which prides itself on its 'resistance movements' and its 'anti-Nazi stance' the reaction to the news was startling. Many people I talked to seemed openly pleased that she had died; one man was glad that 'that bitch' had gone; others referred to her as a 'whore' and a 'traitor' or as a woman who had come back to Berlin in 'enemy uniform'. These same Berliners were furious to hear that she was to be buried in the city; local papers were filled with letters asking why 'that foreigner' should be allowed back to the city which 'she had rejected'. Shortly before the coffin was moved on an open Cadillac towards the cemetery some people actually spat in the freshly dug grave. I had observed a disdain for Weimar figures in West Berlin before; hatred for Bertolt Brecht was understandable – not least because he had foolishly thrown his lot in with the East Germans; but I remember a conversation in which Walter Gropius was derided for his 'Communist buildings' and another in which Thomas Mann was called a pervert because he had openly written about homosexuality in *Death in Venice*. Marlene Dietrich's funeral illustrated the dangers of taking the myth at face value, for it is the reflection of an idealized world which exonerates those thousands of Berliners who stood and applauded as works by Brecht and Mann and Hauptmann and Döblin were heaped upon the flames, along with those who spat on Dietrich's grave in 1992.

In 1927 another funeral was held in Berlin, this time for the cabaret star Anita Berber. Unlike Dietrich, Berber had achieved cult status in Berlin in her own day and was one of the most famous people in the city. She had been a gifted ballet dancer but in Berlin she had opted for the cabaret circuit, making a name for herself dancing with famous stars and performing complicated erotic striptease numbers at clubs like the White Mouse. She lived in a world steeped in sexual scandals involving lovers of both sexes, parading at the six-day bicycle races and the grand hotels surrounded by bodyguards and admirers. She drank with wild abandon, took morphine, heroin and cocaine, and helped to finance her habits by casual prostitution. By the age of twenty-eight she had contracted consumption, but it did not stop her from going on a tour of Greek, Egyptian and Beirut nightclubs. One night she collapsed in Baghdad, and her Berlin colleagues took up a collection to get her back home. It was said that 'her beauty had damned her', and she died within the year. The world which she once loved gathered at her coffin; as one witness put it, 'Prominent film directors marched beside the whores of Friedrichstrasse, young male hookers with hermaphrodites from the "Eldorado", famous artists next to barmen, men in top hats beside the most famous transvestites of Berlin.'[107]

The cortège reflects all the ambiguities in the legend of Weimar, its burst of creativity, its seedy glamour, its short dazzling life. Berber herself represented both its energy and its superficiality. Weimar culture had become enamoured of itself; the new artists and intelligentsia had turned their backs on politics and on the prudish sensibilities of the majority of Germans. They had made powerful enemies.

As the coffin wound its way through the streets of Berlin the storm clouds which had long been gathering began to encroach upon the city itself. Berber's funeral was almost in time to mark the end of Weimar Berlin. Within three years the devastating financial crash would sink it back into chaos. In six years Adolf Hitler would be in power, and the men and women who had attended Berber's funeral would themselves be in exile, in prison, or living in fear of their lives. 'Weimar Berlin' would be given its place in the list of exalted cities only after its death. Like the memory of Berber herself, it would be remembered as a shimmering dream whose life was brutally cut short.

X

The Betrayal of Weimar

These people simply fail to recognize
the Devil, standing before their very eyes.

(*Faust*, Part I)

ON THE MORNING OF 30 January 1933 the forty-three-year-old corporal
Adolf Hitler met the ageing Hindenburg at the Presidential Palace in Berlin.
Shortly before noon he emerged flushed with excitement and rushed to his
headquarters at the Kaiserhof Hotel. As he burst into the room Joseph Goebbels
noticed that his eyes were filled with tears. 'Now we are on our way!' he
gasped. Adolf Hitler had just been made Chancellor of the German Reich.

When the news reached the street cheers went up from the crowd of
Berliners gathered on Unter den Linden. They continued to cheer when at
seven o'clock that evening thousands of brown-shirted storm troopers, the
SA, along with their elite, the black-outfitted SS, marched through the Tiergarten to the Brandenburg Gate, down the Wilhelmstrasse, past the British
embassy and the Ministry of Justice to the Reich Chancellery, carrying row
upon row of torches which lit up the dark drizzling sky. The atmosphere was
electric. As the marchers came closer to the Chancellery they could just make
out the figure of Hindenburg standing in Bismarck's old room and moving
his hand in time to the military marches. Fifty feet away stood Hitler in
evening dress at an open window. He was saluting his troops. Many who lined
the streets remembered it as a night of relief and expectation similar to the
nationalistic frenzy of August 1914. Theodor Düsterberg, a Stahlhelm member,
said, 'I had never believed it possible that our steady, disciplined nation could
become so aroused. Anyone who experienced the torchlight procession will
remember hundreds of thousands of people with torches, singing and whoop-
ing in an indescribable state of ecstasy.'[1] An SA man recalled the Wilhelmstrasse as 'a seething, red, clear burning sea of torches'. According to Douglas
Reed, 'Berlin was buzzing like a beehive from morning till night, the nerves
of four million people were quivering like harp strings.' Joseph Goebbels wrote
in his diary, 'It is simply moving for me to see how in this city, where we

began six years ago with a handful of people, the entire people is now rising up, marching by below me, workers and middle class and peasants and soldiers – a great community of the *Volk*!'[2]

Not everyone shared this view: a number of apprehensive Communists had gathered to monitor events and were identified as they refused to give the Hitler salute. That night they were left alone, for the last time. The painter Max Liebermann, watching from his studio near the Brandenburg Gate, made the wry comment that it would be impossible to 'eat as much as one wanted to vomit'.[3] But he was in the minority. Goebbels had already been quick to see that Berlin was not only a bastion of 'Red radicalism' but was awash with *völkisch* and nationalistic ideas long before his arrival. Post-war attempts to portray Berlin as an 'anti-Nazi' city are ahistorical, for deep within the universities, the civil service, the schools, the military, the small businesses, the slums and the middle-class suburbs there were groups of people who had been licking their wounds and nurturing deep resentment against the German defeat, the Treaty of Versailles, the loss of imperial prestige, the inept government, the strange artists and writers in their midst – and against the increasing power of the radical left.[4] Hitler did not need to 'crush Berlin' into submission; he found a ready audience eager to listen and to give him their votes. The overriding mood on the streets the night Hitler took power was one not of fear, but of relief and celebration.

By the mid 1920s some of the more astute members of the Berlin avant-garde had recognized that their world was coming to an end. In 1926 the brilliant writer Carl von Ossietzky, who would soon die as the result of wounds sustained in a concentration camp, surveyed the situation in Berlin and was terrified by what he saw. Where a few years before there had been tolerance and experimentation he now saw a battle raging between two cultures, between two mutually exclusive world views. In an article in the left-wing journal *Die Weltbühne* he pointed to the increased use of the disquieting term 'Cultural Bolshevism', now used to attack anything which offended the provincial sensibilities of the right. The term was used even

> when Klemperer takes tempi different from Furtwängler, when a painter uses a colour for a sunset not seen in Lower Pomerania, when one favours birth control, when you build a house with a flat roof, when you admire Charlie Chaplin and Albert Einstein, when you follow the democracy of the brothers Mann and when you enjoy the music of Hindemith and Kurt Weill – all that is 'Cultural Bolshevism.'[5]

Most dangerous of all was the appeal of Nazism to the young.

In many ways the story of Hitler's success is the story of the ability to capture the imagination of youth. Germany had undergone profound demographic change at the turn of the century, when the increased prosperity and optimism of the imperial age had resulted in a sharp rise in the birth rate. The First World War shattered these young families, leaving millions of young men dead or wounded, 533,000 German war widows and 1,192,000 orphans. The children had been born into the imperial bombast of pre-war Germany and most had just missed war-time service, but they came to adult-hood in a shattered and hopeless world and were forced to watch as their friends and families lost everything in the political and economic turmoil which followed defeat. Structural unemployment and low wages left hundreds of thousands disillusioned and the politicians of Weimar seemed unable to offer them a future. Anti-republican sentiments flourished, and even the inept Kapp *Putsch* had the support of over 50,000 students. The young men and women of the 'lost generation' were ideal recruits for extremists of all kinds, including the *völkisch* nationalists and, later, the Nazis. They were a powerful force. By 1920 over one-third of Berliners were under thirty years of age.[6]

The new generation began to develop a culture quite different from that which harked back to the failures of the older generation. As they gained in confidence they began openly to attack the republic and the politicians who had come to power after signing Versailles, the 'shame of the nation'. The front-line soldiers who had sacrificed their lives only to be 'stabbed-in-the-back' became their new heroes in a general romanticization of the First World War. The young Berliner Annemarie Wittemberg was typical: 'At the end of the school year during which we had studied the Versailles Treaty, we commemorated it with a mourning procession in the schoolyard. At the end of it, we solemnly tore up a copy of the treaty, threw it in a prepared garbage pail and set fire to it.'[7] They began organizing battlefield tours and asked that mass-produced crosses be forbidden in war cemeteries because they rep-resented 'soulless modernity' and denied the 'proper reverence' for the indi-vidual dead. In the journal *Volksbund* the new manager of the German Association of Landscape Architects went so far as to condemn English mem-orials as frivolous because poppies were permitted to grow on the graves: 'The Germans do not disguise the tragic and heroic death of the fallen by planting colourful flowers. They confront it instead, for to affirm the tragic is a sign of culture, while mere civilization seeks to ignore it.' Young Berliners joined students from all over Germany to plant 'serious' oak trees near their war memorials.[8]

The problem with this 'lost generation' is that most never really accepted that they had lost the First World War. The majority believed that Germany was a nation wronged by history and they simply wanted to redress the injustice. There was never any proper analysis of the reasons for the German defeat, nor was there an admission that had they won they would have treated the vanquished with as little regard as they themselves were treated. By heaping the blame for their post-war woes on Versailles they could criticize the Allies for keeping Germany down. It was therefore logical that if they reversed their policies the nation would simply return to pre-war splendour. Few understood that they were in fact much poorer than they had been in 1913 and that Germany had become impoverished not because she had lost the war, but because she had fought it in the first place. But the blindness continued, and the young generation began to yearn for a new purpose in the ruined and crisis-ridden world in which they lived. They hungered for a new culture which would express their frustrations and which would push the decadent world of Weimar Berlin aside, and they revelled in the 'stab-in-the-back' legend which explained everything so neatly. New books which played on the nationalism, militarism, anti-Semitism and neo-Romanticism of the 'emerging Germany' were eagerly devoured. Wilhelm Stapel, editor of the nationalist paper *Deutsches Volkstum*, captured the mood when he proclaimed that he wanted to see the 'growth of a national myth, a myth that is not sweated out of the nerves, but one that blossoms forth from the blood'.[9] Werner Beumelburg, later to become a prominent Nazi writer, Josef Magnus Wehner, who also continued to write his war novels under the Nazis, Hans Zöberlein and Walter Bloem and his son, who became a member of the Waffen-SS and went missing in Berlin in 1945, began to portray German nationalism as the most noble of ideas. In his *Ruf der Jungen* (Call of the Young) Max Boehm attacked the revolution of 1918 as a travesty which had betrayed the fighting men at the front and asserted that only a 'truly high minded racialist feeling' could overcome the 'decomposing influence of the Jewish spirit' and 'save' Germany from the terrible stigma of defeat. Like many of the new writers Boehm wanted to wipe away the trappings of modern life and retreat to pre-modern life free from the strains of technology or modernity.

Other such writers focused on the intense joy and satisfaction found in the camaraderie amongst fighting men. Franz Schauwecker, who would later become one of the Nazis' favourite writers, romanticized these feelings: 'We saw our blood drench the living earth in which we had buried two million brethren. We came back and had experienced the nation. Only where there is destruction can there be such a mighty revelation.' The mysticism of Jacob Boehme and the motto 'Stirb und Werde' (Die and Become), which portrayed death as part of the supreme transformation of man, became a recurring theme. The respect for the fighting man was carried on in Ernst Jünger's works; for him battle was a trial of endurance and national pride and in his *Stahlgewitter* (Thunder of Steel) he called the soldiers who had joined the storm troopers the 'aristocracy of the nation'. He was captivated by the idea of the *Männerbund* – male bonding between warriors who had faced death together – and challenged the youth of Germany to cast aside ideas of tolerance and spineless compromise in favour of 'the sword', preaching that wars were not fought for reasons of international politics but were ends in themselves, waged for the sheer thrill of battle, for glory, honour and the lust for blood.[10] All these works shared a number of fundamental themes: Germany had lost her honour after 1918, a loss which could only be regained through war. Germans must abandon the notion of subservience to the western Allies and prepare for a new conflict which would result in a great victory over Germany's external and internal enemies. In *The Junk Heap* Mariaux described the 'great drunkenness of madness' in which the old world would be destroyed and from which would rise the phoenix of a new Germany. War was to be declared on all those who had contributed to the 'diseasing of Germany' – a huge group said to include everyone from the 'Jewish speculators' and 'Bolshevik agents' of Berlin, to the teeming Slav millions encroaching on and 'infecting' German territory in the east.[11] These frenzied, irrational, intoxicating ideas began to take hold in Berlin. Some, like Bertolt Brecht and Thomas Mann, were appalled at the change, but there was little they could do. These spokesmen for the modern were now being labelled as 'outmoded has-beens' by the aggressive new cultural leaders, and productions of *Mahagonny* and Toller's *Hinckemann* were now marred by noisy demonstrations.

To the annoyance of the celebrated Weimar writers, the young refused to read books like *The Magic Mountain* or *Berlin Alexanderplatz*, preferring the works of now long-forgotten *völkisch* authors. Reprints of Gustav Frenssen's *Jörn Uhl* shot to the top of the bestseller list. Hans Grimm's *Volk ohne Raum* (People Without Living Space), which popularized the German need to expand its territory and which asserted that 'the German tradition has gone to the Devil', sold 315,000 copies following publication in 1926 and became a standard matriculation text in German schools.[12] In it he asserted that the most decent, most honest, most efficient and most industrious 'white nation on earth lives within too narrow frontiers'. It ended with the words: 'It is also true, German children will laugh even less as war and Versailles Locarno weigh heavier on us, we who are without *deutschen Raum*.'[13] Frau Ellen Frey's response as a young woman was typical: 'We read it and said, "Man, there are so many people in Germany and we're in such a narrow space, they can give something up for us, no?"[14] It was Walther Darré, soon to head the Race and Settlement Office of the SS, who coined the term *Blut und Boden* or 'blood and soil' literature to characterize these books, and many took them to be serious works of art far superior to the *Dreck*, the 'garbage' of the Manns and the Döblins.[15] Some were of a scientific nature, like *Verbrechen als Schicksal* (Crime as Destiny), which demonstrated how some individuals of inferior breeding were genetically programmed to become criminals.[16] The new authors laced their books with a muddle of *völkisch* themes, racism, hero worship, anti-Semitism and *Heimatkunst* – the sentimental portrayal of the 'homeland'. The urban Berliner, alienated by modern mechanized and industrialized society, was told that he still formed part of the great German community based on the soil. For the middle classes and the white-collar workers trapped in a fast downward cycle these books provided much-needed escapism. It was tempting to see the catastrophes of war, inflation, unemployment and the threat to livelihood in terms of 'disease' caused by Jewish speculators, Bolshevist agitators, the Slavs and other 'enemies' of the *Volk*.[17]

The ideas put forward in the novels of the mid 1920s were slowly given a veneer of respectability by a new breed of intellectual 'theorists' who began to find favour in academic institutions in the city. Exquisite gold-embossed editions of Novalis and Schlegel began to appear once again in Berlin bookshops, as did simplistic nationalistic analyses of Herder, Fichte and Hegel. The new theorists began to develop ideas which within the decade would become the basis of the German state. In *Revolution von Rechts* Hans Freyer put forward the startling idea that perhaps political revolution could be sparked not only by the left, but by the radical right. In his early articles with titles like 'Immorality in the Talmud' (1920) or 'The Crimes of Freemasonry' (1921) the future Nazi ideologist Alfred Rosenberg began to weave his web of alleged conspiracy against the German people. His *Der Mythus des 20. Jahrhunderts* (The Myth of the Twentieth Century), later hailed as 'the most important book of National Socialism next to Adolf Hitler's *Mein Kampf*', he explained that the history of the world was a question of the history of race. 'The history of the religion of the blood . . . is the great world story of the rise and downfall of people, their heroes and thinkers, their inventors and artists.' It had sold hundreds of thousands of copies by the time Hitler came to power. Moeller van den Bruck's *The Third Reich* was a plea for a new way of governing Germany which would have nothing to do with either capitalism or Marxism but would rely on a quasi-mystical 'spiritual revolution'. He also stressed the need to protect the German minorities in Poland, and predicted the rise of a strong leader, a Führer who would lead Germany to victory.

These writers exerted a great influence on the men soon to control Germany. Dietrich Eckart befriended Adolf Hitler in 1919 and introduced him to *völkisch* ideas through his seething anti-Semitic smear sheet *Auf gut Deutsch* (In Plain German). In 1919 Eckart outlined his idea of the future saviour of Germany, insisting, amongst other things, that he 'must be a bachelor'. Hitler's disgusting chapter on syphilis in *Mein Kampf*, in which he displayed an almost pathological hatred of women, was inspired by this unpleasant character. Hitler ended *Mein Kampf* with a dedication to him and later named part of the massive Olympic complex in Berlin after him.[18] Perhaps the most influential of all these writers was Oswald Spengler, whose sweeping history of the world, entitled *Decline of the West*, captivated a number of would-be leaders, including Hitler and Joseph Goebbels. Spengler saw man as a mere 'zoological expression', a creature locked in a neo-Darwinist biological struggle of life and death. Humans could expect nothing but death, whether of individuals, nations or cultures. Some, however, could still rise to greatness, and in this Germany had a special place reserved by history. This 'young nation' had been 'kept back' by its vindictive neighbours, but she was about to make use of her vast potential and would soon rule Europe. Albert Speer would later claim that Spengler's book was the one work which drew him towards National Socialism. As he said in his memoirs, 'Spengler's *Decline of the West* had convinced me that we were living in a period of decay strongly similar to the late Roman Empire: inflation, decline of morals, importance of the German Reich.'[19] In the midst of their traumatic lives bourgeois Berliners who read these muddled works once again began to believe in a future. All they had to do was to draw on their ancient heritage, on pre-Christian customs and on their inherently powerful and pure race, and they would find victory.

By 1927 these *Blut und Boden* writers were openly challenging the position of the avant-garde in Berlin, including the eminent figures at the Prussian Academy of Art. In that year Hans Blüher, Friedrich Blunck and Paul Ernst began to attack Heinrich and Thomas Mann, Alfred Döblin and others at the Academy for being so-called Asphalt writers – 'rootless internationalists' and 'traitors to art out of touch with the real needs of the German people'. In 1929 Alfred Rosenberg established the Kampfbund für deutsche Kultur (Fighting League for German Culture), in which he categorized art as either 'beautiful' (which reflected the nature of the racially pure German) or as 'degenerate' (which did not). According to him, works such as Dürer's *Hare* and Mozart's *Eine kleine Nachtmusik* expressed the 'same cultural capacity of the Germans' – a capacity for realism and German themes which was missing from the Asphalt Weimar artists. Professor Ewald Geissler, who hated the abstract modernism of the avant-garde, declared that only art that was easy to remember could prove its 'Germanness'.[20]

The resurgence of these ideas was not limited to painting or to literature, but became important in the transformation of Berlin's universities and colleges. In the early years of the Weimar Republic Berlin had been at the centre of an explosion in German intellectual life: Einstein had lived there and made relativity a household word; the Institute of Psychoanalysis had actively promoted the work of Freud and it had accepted Jews, Social Democrats, even women into its hallowed halls. But the appearance was deceptive, and it soon became clear that for every scholar willing to support the republic there were many more who longed for a return to the ways of the past. The rector of

Berlin University, Reinhold Seeberg, a staunch critic of Versailles, had long called his students 'the defeated who shall emerge victorious'.[21] Count Kessler warned of this growing trend in Berlin when he attended a celebration in 1922 in honour of the playwright Gerhart Hauptmann. 'The most remarkable thing about the festivities was the grotesquely narrow-minded conduct of students and professors,' he noted. 'The Berlin fraternity council solemnly resolved – I believe with a majority of two to one – not to participate in the Hauptmann celebration because Gerhart Hauptmann is no longer to be considered a reliable German, after professing himself a Republican!'[22] The trend was clear. Supporters of the republic were not to be trusted, and the drive to expel them was underway.

Opponents of the republic soon became more confident and more visible. They included the men around Eugene Diederich's journal *Die Tat*, Heinrich von Gleichen's *Gewissen*, in Moeller van den Bruck's Juni-Club and the sophisticated gentlemen at the Ring Kreis, who were opposed to modern rationalism, and the members of the exclusive and radical Herren Klub, from which von Papen and his cronies would later plot to bring Hitler to power.[23] The economist Werner Sombart began to introduce mystical alternatives to all scientific procedures and rejoiced in the idea of the 'Führer principle'. When Hitler came to power he would cry, 'I, for my part, say Thank God that this is so!' The brilliant jurist Carl Schmitt launched a series of devastating critiques against the flawed republic, furnishing those intent on destroying the 'system' with powerful ammunition. Not all these intellectual giants were to be found in Berlin but the city was greatly influenced by their ideas. Far away in Heidelberg, Martin Heidegger attacked the republic as 'that pathetic creature of Reason', and was cheered by the students in the capital.

Berlin had retained its position as a centre of historiography throughout the Weimar period, but even here the mood was changing. Troublesome young historians interested in subjects other than the greatness of the Prussian military tradition found their careers discreetly blocked. The brilliant young Eckart Kehr was chastised for his provocative articles in the socialist periodical *Die Gesellschaft*, and for his deeply critical doctoral thesis which attacked the domestic impetus behind the naval build-up at the turn of the century. As his friend Felix Gilbert later recalled, Kehr realized that 'he might encounter difficulties in the pursuit of an academic career'; as a result he went to the United States, where he would die in exile. Gilbert remembered that 'for people who were antagonistic to the rise of nationalism and authoritarianism – even for those lacking Kehr's missionary spirit – the pursuit of an academic career was becoming very difficult. One could not overlook the fact that there were many aspirant historians who were better fitted to the spirit of the times.'[24] This was not just Gilbert's imagination. Like the artistic community, the institutions of higher learning were divided between those for and those against the republic. Albert Speer, a student of the architect Tessenow in Berlin, said that the famous Institute of Technology had 'become a centre of National Socialist endeavours. The small group of Communist architecture students gravitated to Professor Poelzig's seminar, while the National Socialists gathered around Tessenow.'[25] Although not a National Socialist, the latter 'decried the metropolis and extolled the peasant virtues' in his classes. The student population in Berlin was almost wholly supportive of the new right. Speer first heard Hitler speak in Berlin because his students had implored him to attend; after the gathering he joined the Nazi Party. 'It seemed as if nearly all the students in Berlin wanted to see and hear this man whom his adherents so much admired and his opponents so much detested. A large number of professors sat in favoured places in the middle of a bare platform. Their presence gave the meeting an importance and a social acceptability that it would not otherwise have had.'[26]

The professors' support did not waver. Shortly after Hitler took power, on 3 March 1933, 300 university teachers declared in an election appeal that they supported him. The response from the universities and from other educational bodies would prove so overwhelming that Hitler actually frowned upon the sudden 'mass conversion', warning in September 1933 against those 'March violets' who had 'suddenly changed their flag' in order 'to have the main say in the realms of art and cultural policy; for this is our state and not theirs'.

Other areas of Berlin academic life were aligning themselves with the Nazis not only in fields such as pre-history, folklore and linguistics, but also in the fields of genetics, anthropology and eugenics. By this time it was widely believed, not only in Berlin but in many parts of Europe, that all aspects of sexual behaviour and all hereditary disease could be predicted and conquered by genetic engineering and that a better society could be created using selective breeding. Even in the early 1920s it was quite common not merely to counsel parents-to-be about the dangers of inherited illness, but to discuss genetics in terms of improving the national genetic stock. These ideas became ever more extreme. In his book *Rassenverbesserung* (The Improvement of Race) Dr Rutgers explained in scientific terms how 'fewer children but strong humans is the solution for the rebuilding' (*die Lösung für den Wiederaufbau*).[27] Scientists began to talk in terms of mass sterilization in order to rid society of hereditary diseases which were now said to include everything from schizophrenia and alcoholism to short-sightedness. In Berlin a genuine concern for public health fostered by the republican government shifted to an obsession with racial biology, and when this was combined with the notion that some races were of inherently higher value than others it became a potent cocktail of hatred and prejudice. Perfectly normal people would soon be talking about 'selection', and then 'eradication', of groups of people who were deemed harmful to the German gene pool and the German race.

Another cornerstone of Nazi ideology was already in place by the late 1920s, as the new science was increasingly used by historians and anthropologists keen to promote the idea that the 'Nordic stock' or the 'Aryan race' or the 'Germanic race' was inherently superior to all others. In his 1932 book *Die nordische Seele* (The Nordic Soul) Ludwig Ferdinand Clauss, a lecturer and racial scientist at Berlin University, tried to prove that an individual's appearance was the manifestation of the soul, and that the soul was determined by the landscape in which it had evolved. The book, which taught Germans that they were genetically honest, forthright, hard working, physically attractive and natural leaders, raced through eight editions. In 1929 Eugen Fischer, the director of the Kaiser Wilhelm Institute for the Study of Anthropology, Human Heredity and Eugenics in Berlin-Dahlem, tried to show that a racial type always showed a uniformity of characteristics. If the child of two apparently racially pure parents had features not in keeping with their race, then one of the parents was not 'pure'.[28] The laws of racial purity were now considered a proven scientific fact and the history of the world was reinterpreted as the history of the struggle between one race and another. Hans Günther asserted that the Nordic race had proved itself to be superior to all others throughout history: 'the relatively great number of Nordic people among the famous and outstanding men and women of all Western countries is striking,' he said, 'as is also the relatively low number of famous men and women without noticeable Nordic strain.'[29] Jakob Graf received high acclaim when he asserted that 'ethnological historical research has proved that the Nordic race has produced a great many more highly talented people than any other race.' Max Brewer not only believed that all great men of history were ultimately 'Nordic', but even 'proved' not only that Christ had not been Jewish but that he had in fact been the product of 'good Westphalian stock'. Schoolchildren were asked to collect propaganda posters and caricatures 'for your race book and arrange them according to racial schemes'.

This strange pseudo-science was used by a number of professional bodies – even in court, to determine the 'character' of the witness. Ironically, after the failed Beer Hall *Putsch* of 1923, Hitler himself was examined by a leading racial hygienist, Dr Gruber, who was called as an expert witness before the People's Court in Munich. Gruber testified that Hitler's face and head were of a 'bad racial type', which showed that he was 'crossbred'. he had a 'low receding forehead, ugly nose, wide cheekbones, small eyes, dark hair'. From this he deduced that Hitler had both an absence of 'objective brainpower' and an 'exceedingly subjective character'. Gruber also characterized Hitler as typically 'un-Nordic East Slav'. The subjectivity of this 'science' was revealed some years later when Hitler's own racial scientists fell over themselves to reverse Gruber's analysis and prove the Nordic characteristics of the Nazi leadership. One scientist would later declare Hitler 'a pure Aryan-Germanic type' and Alfred Richter, a Nazi specialist in racial characteristics, described Hitler's facial expression as 'that of a genius, a creative spiritual leader, powerful, tenacious, filled with great love, unspeakable pain and renunciation'. He even went so far as to say, 'Hitler is blond, has pink skin and blue eyes, and is therefore of a pure Aryan-Germanic character, and all contrary statements concerning his appearance and personality have been sown in the people's soul by the Black and Red press, which I hope herewith to have corrected.'[30] From there Hitler could be compared to all great Germans of the past, from Frederick the Great to Bismarck: the historian Ritter von Srbik compared him to the great Freiherr vom Stein.

If the Nordic race was said to be the pure force of 'good' in the world, the advocates of racial history identified 'evil' with that other 'pure race', the Jews. As before, the Jews were blamed for all ills that had befallen Germany, but as the crisis of Weimar became worse, the indignities heaped upon them increased. Jews became universal scapegoats: they were the 'November criminals' responsible for Germany's shameful surrender and oppression at the hands of the Allies; Jewish 'hoarders and speculators' had been responsible for the post-war misery and inflation, 'Jewish Bolsheviks' had caused both the Russian Revolution and the Spartacus Uprising, 'Jewish capitalists' had fattened themselves up at Germany's expense, the *Ostjuden* flooding in from the *Shtetl* in the east were responsible for everything from increased crime to a rise in the Berlin rat population. Some maintained that as Jews did not have souls they were not really human. In the popular *völkisch* novels sweeping the market, Jewish characters were invariably portrayed as greedy, pushy and unpleasant types who met 'well deserved' ends. The words 'Jewish' and Bolshevik' and 'capitalist' were regularly used as interchangeable prefixes for anything said to go against the 'true Germany'. Some, annoyed by the Jews' visible success in Berlin, became obsessed with the notion of Jewish conspiracies; it was 'obvious', they said, that Jews controlled the press, academia, cultural life, foreign capital, industry and international relations. The most infamous case centred around the publication of *The Protocols of the Elders of Zion*, a work concocted for the Russian political police but taken in 1920s Berlin as proof of a genuine Jewish conspiracy.[31] One of the most disgraceful manifestations of this shift in attitudes was the enquiry into Jewish activity during the First World War. Thousands of German Jews had been killed in the trenches in the 1914–18 war, but this did not stop the persistent rumours that they had shirked front-line service. The army had held the so-called 'Jew count', but the results – which Franz Oppenheimer called 'the greatest statistical monstrosity that a public authority had yet been guilty of' – showing that 10,000 Jews had been killed, were never published.[32] Jewish veterans were excluded from the Stahlhelm, making it the first national veterans' organization to ban former comrades at arms.[33] Jews were soon forbidden to join student fraternities and other nationalist organizations and in 1929 the German National Party, a member of many Weimar coalition governments, officially forbade Jewish membership. Shortly after Hitler came to power the Nazis again claimed that Jews had been shirkers and had contributed to the defeat. The names of Jewish soldiers who had fallen in battle were banned from German war monuments and Hitler was particularly adamant that their names should not appear on the enormous memorial arch he and Albert Speer planned for Berlin. It is still eerie to walk through the German First World War cemeteries in Flanders and France and to see the headstones of young German Jews killed in the trenches, which were ripped out in the 1940s and were only replaced after 1945.

Anti-Semitism manifested itself in other ways. Some academic subjects were now classified as 'Jewish', and were attacked accordingly long before Hitler came to power. The International Psychoanalytical Association in Berlin was one such target. The institute was a huge facility which drew students from Karen Horney to Wilhelm Reich, and Freud made his last visit in 1922, when he outlined the now famous theory of the id, the ego and the superego. Nevertheless those involved in psychoanalysis were castigated for trying to 'undermine the German character'. As Freud was being vilified for his 'Jewish' analysis of the mind, the Nobel laureates Johannes Stark and Philipp Lenard led the attack against Einstein's 'Jewish physics', an approach to science which, they said, sought to undermine the absolute laws of nature. For them, 'German science' was factual and objective while 'Jewish science' was mere opinion. Ultimately their attack on Einstein's Theory of Relativity impeded attempts by Nazi scientists to develop a nuclear bomb; according to Albert Speer Hitler's knowledge of atomic science 'was limited to anything that appeared even remotely associated with Einstein, for whom he had conceived an irrational hatred'. It did not help that Heisenberg and Max Planck were called 'white Jews' because they agreed with Einstein. Although research in atomic physics did continue throughout the Nazi period, anti-Semitism might have been the crucial factor which prevented Hitler getting the bomb before the United States.[34]

Racial anti-Semitism was not the only ideology which had become deeply entrenched in German society long before Hitler took power; many other ideas and organizations later adopted by the Nazis were already in place before

1933. This did not mean that the Nazi seizure of power was inevitable, but the widespread acceptance of many of their basic tenets certainly made their task easier. The obsession with race, with mystical blood ties and ancient links to Nordic gods, led to waves of Nordic spiritualism and occultism in the 1920s, and Berlin was awash with charlatans, seers and pseudo-druids throughout the decade preceding Hitler's seizure of power.[35] Guido von List, author of *The Secret of the Runes* which explored the mystic Germanic past, was convinced that the strange little man who called himself Tarnhari was the reincarnation of the leader of a Germanic tribe known as the Völsungen. The hypnotist Erich Jan Hanussen became the Berlin chief of police's astrologer although he was found murdered in a Berlin forest when it was revealed that he was not a foreign mystic but a German Jew. The ancient art of sun worship was rediscovered and thousands of Berliners from all walks of life and political persuasions took part in the elaborate ceremonies on the eve of the summer solstice.[36]

Ideas of racial purity began to manifest themselves in new images of 'ideal' blond blue-eyed youth, popularized by painters like Karl Höppner, who painted 'temple art' inspired by frescoes and mosaics from the ancient world. Young Germans were portrayed in sandals and togas perched high on cliffs framed by huge glowing images of the sun. The new look was popularized in photographs and in films such as Dr Adolf Fanck's 'mountain films' in which Leni Riefenstahl, soon to become Hitler's master film-maker, got her start as an actress. One right-wing critic praised the films, calling mountains 'pure' and 'eternal like the German *Volk*'. Riefenstahl claimed to love the mountains because they were ruled by a different system of values, with 'no telephone, radio, post, railway or motorcar'. She claimed to detest modern Berlin but then proceeded to work there and used the most advanced medium of film, making her living using 'modern' equipment and techniques, and depending on the urban audiences for her livelihood. Like so many people later to make it in the Nazi world Riefenstahl proved herself to be something of a hypocrite.[37]

The desire to attain the Greek ideal of physical beauty led to the development of hundreds of sport and gymnastic clubs which catered to all political and social groups in Berlin throughout the Weimar period. The socialist Fritz Wilding said, 'the progress of history indicates that in every class-oriented society sport served a political function . . . sport becomes the means for the social struggle . . . turning people from being lonely, persecuted, tortured, and destroyed back to their rightful human dignity.' Carl Diem opened a college for gymnastics in Berlin in 1920, and it was he and not Goebbels who first created startling spectacles of lines of young tanned maidens in identical costumes, performing synchronized routines with hoops and medicine balls. One could be forgiven for thinking that photographs of the vigorous athletes

of the Teutonic Sports Club running in perfect formation under the Brandenburg Gate were taken in Hitler's Berlin; in fact, they date from 1925.

Nudist clubs were also taken with great seriousness in Weimar Berlin.
These were said to have nothing whatever to do with sex and everything to
do with the creation of a 'healthy Germany'. The clubs were often divided
along political lines; the nationalists went to a huge camp at Motzensee run
by a Dr Fuchs while the most important socialist club was run by Adolf Koch,
who had been banned from teaching when parents complained that their
children had been forced to do school gymnastics in the nude. Those who
attended the clubs adhered to a strict set of rules which they believed anchored
them to a nineteenth-century puritanical morality.[38] The hundreds of photographs of young people leaping about in fields or picnicking together in the
nude were harmless enough but there were more disturbing aspects to this
body cult. Although the cover of the 1925 edition of *Die Schönheit* showed a
naked adult couple jumping over a flaming Olympic-sized torch, the issue
itself was filled with semi-pornographic photographs of children and with
advertisements for books on 'race improvement'.[39] Sports and gymnastic clubs
were also used to disguise the true nature of various political groups. The
armed squads which Hitler was gathering around him in the summer of 1921,
soon to become the 'Storm Detachments' or S A, started life as the 'Gymnastic
and Sports Section' of his fledgling National Socialist Party.

The ideal of physical beauty which would become such a mainstay of Nazi
culture was already accepted in the 1920s. To be 'beautiful' now meant to be
young, fair, 'Aryan' and healthy. In a personal column in the mid-1920s
'Renewal of Life' issue of *Schönheit* hopefuls invariably described themselves
as 'light blond' or 'dark blond with blue eyes'; as 'Wandervögel', as 'followers
of the *Körperkultur*', as 'gardeners' or as 'German maidens'. A typical ad read:
'Educated young woman, Protestant, healthy, North German, 30 years old,
daughter of businessman, musical (piano-organ), interested in art, nature and
sports, fiancé fell in the war ... write to number 4265 at the *Schönheit* Publishers.'[40] During his first visit to Germany in the summer of 1929 Stephen
Spender found young people intoxicated by the sun: 'I went to the bathing
places, and I went to parties which ended at dawn with the young people
lying in one another's arms. This life appeared to me innocuous, being led
by people who seemed naked in body and soul, in the desert of white bones
which was post-war Germany.' But, he continued, there was a certain heart-
lessness at the centre of it, a product of 'the saga of all this German youth
which had been born into war, starved in the blockade, stripped in the inflation
– and which now, with no money and no beliefs and an extraordinary anonymous beauty, sprang like a breed of dragon's teeth waiting for its leader, into
the centre of Europe'.[41]

The ideas might have remained of marginal importance to Berlin history had they not been taken up with such fervour by German youth. Young people gathered together in a multitude of associations and clubs, separating themselves completely from the older generation and pursuing these ideas with a passion. By the end of the 1920s over 80 per cent of young Berliners belonged to a youth group. Most developed complicated rituals and drew on elaborate symbolism complete with flags, uniforms and 'ancient' German customs. Swastikas, first used before the First World War, became so common that the Prussian Ministry of Education had to restrict their use in schools. Many nationalistic groups continued to use 'Heil' as a greeting. The groups ranged from Communist to conservative, from pantheistic to Utopian, from the Wandervögel, with their emphasis on healthy living, sports and folk songs, to those dedicated to the preservation of ethnic Germans in 'occupied lands'.[42] Most eschewed drugs, alcohol and cigarettes in favour of healthy diets, vegetarianism, cycle rides, trips to battlefield sites or Teutonic castles, and all were dedicated to the search for a 'better' Germany which often included calls for the removal of the hated Weimar 'system'. Above all they detested modernity and reason and longed for a world of passion and irrationality. Their spiritual leaders were the poets of Germany.[43]

Since the Second World War many have asked what happened to the *Dichter und Denker*, the 'good Germans' under the Nazis. In fact the *Dichter und Denker* also formed part of the 1920s youth culture, albeit in bastardized form. The problem with turning to the German poets in this period of uncertainty was that they were profoundly unpolitical. Schiller, Hölderlin and Goethe were men of genius but their work contained nothing which could guide young people through the pitfalls of a failing democracy – how could they when professors like Petersen, dean of German studies at Berlin, were set to identify Schiller and Goethe as 'archetypal National Socialists'.[44] Stefan George, with his band of elitist disciples, and Rainer Maria Rilke, with his lyrical poetry, became the spiritual voices for an entire generation but they led them headlong into irrationality. When Goebbels visited Weimar for the first time he walked around in awe, muttering, 'Weimar *is* Goethe.'

Some despised this trend. On the centenary of Goethe's death in 1932 Carl von Ossietzky said, 'Official Germany celebrates Goethe, not as poet and prophet, but above all as opium.' When the magazine *Die literarische Welt* held a poetry competition in 1927 and asked Bertolt Brecht to judge the 400 entries the playwright was so disgusted by cheap imitations of George and Werfel and Rilke that he gave the prize to a piece he found in a bicycling magazine. 'Here they are again,' he snarled, 'these quiet, refined, starry-eyed people, the sentimental element of a worn out bourgeoisie with which I refuse to have anything to do! ... These people should first join the army.' As for the poets themselves, he said, 'I would draw your attention to the fact that Rilke's form of expression, in dealing with God, is wholly homosexual.' As for George, his poetry was 'empty', the views it expressed were 'trivial and haphazard'. 'He has absorbed a mass of books with nice bindings and associated with people who live on their incomes,' Brecht continued. 'The result is that he makes the impression of being an idler instead of an observer.'[45] Brecht had every reason to be vitriolic; as a member of the 'literary opposition' he had hoped to lead the young generation himself but found he could not compete with the appeal of the poet-kings. But his criticism was more apt than he knew.

The poets were not alone in the crusade to create a better Germany. Many teachers and lecturers sympathized with the anti-Weimar sentiments of German youth and did not object when students openly attacked the Weimar Republic. Walter Gehl, a Berlin teacher, was typical when he spoke out against the increased industrialization of the city, and advocated the use of textbooks such as Hermann Pionn's *History*, which attacked the transformation of Germany from a pastoral to modern mechanized society, or the work of the Berlin economic professor Max Sering, who preached that Germans should resettle in the east to stem the tide of Polish immigration into 'German lands'. Students flocked to racial science and genetics courses and, in Berlin, Jewish students and teachers lived in fear following waves of new anti-Semitic propaganda. Some intellectuals, including Thomas Mann and Friedrich Meinecke, appealed against this but to the young they now seemed outdated and tired and had lost their ability to influence the new generation. On the other hand there were dozens of university professors, teachers and intellectuals who gave the rising National Socialists a veneer of respectability with their acclamation of the 'rebirth of creative life forces', their anti-Enlightenment views of Luther's 'whore reason', and their search for the 'primitive' and the 'sacred darkness of ancient times'. 'The young' now included men like Horst Wessel who, after registering at Berlin's Friedrich Wilhelm University in 1927 and joining the right-wing Bismarck and Viking youth groups, had thrown himself into the SA after hearing Joseph Goebbels speak in Berlin. They included Julius Streicher, who would soon say to a gathering of Berlin university professors: 'You old men with beards and gold-rimmed glasses and scientific faces are really worth next to nothing. Your hearts are not right, and you can't understand the people as we can. We are not separated from them by so-called higher education.'[46] They also included Heinrich Himmler, who had joined the Artaman group, which sent young Germans to work on the large estates in East Prussia so that the land would not be 'polluted' by Polish workers. The ideas honed in the 1920s resurfaced a decade later when he had archaeological excavations carried out in search of the original pure Aryan race, funded anthropological work in Japan and Tibet to confirm, as Speer put it, 'the Germanic origin of these admirable Asian nations', and studies made of the skulls of 'Jewish-Bolshevik commissars' in order to arrive at a typological definition of the 'sub-human'.[47] He would later take his fanaticism to extremes when, as Reichsführer of the SS, he introduced a bizarre series of rituals based on racial and blood ties. Building on the ideas of his youth he was determined to follow 'Mendel's Law' and make his country 'authentically German' within the magical time span of 120 years. To this end he created a privileged SS caste which would be encouraged to reproduce at will, even in special brothels, and he planned to create a network of Germanic villages, a 'paradise of the Germanic race' in the conquered lands of the east. On 4 October 1943 he would say to the SS Group Leaders, 'we must be honest, decent, loyal, and comradely to members of our own blood and to no one else. What happens to the Russians, what happens to the Czechs, is a matter of utter indifference to me ... Whether or not 10,000 Russian women collapse from exhaustion while digging a tank ditch interests me only in so far as the tank ditch is completed for Germany.' He continued,

> I shall speak to you here with all frankness of a very serious subject
> ... I mean the evacuation of the Jews, the extermination of the Jewish
> people. It is one of those things which it is easy to say. 'The Jewish
> people is to be exterminated,' says every party member. 'That's clear,
> it's part of our programme, elimination of the Jews, extermination,
> right, we'll do it.' And then they all come along, the eighty million
> good Germans, and each one has his decent Jew. Of course the others
> are swine, but this one is a first-class Jew. Of all those who talk
> like this, not one has watched, not one has stood up to it. Most of
> you know what it means to see a hundred corpses lying together,
> five hundred, or a thousand. To have gone through this and yet –
> apart from a few exceptions, examples of human weakness – to
> have remained decent, this has made us hard. This is a glorious
> page in our history that has never been written and never shall be
> written.[48]

In all these obscene and murderous ideas one can find traces of his days on the racially pure farms of East Prussia, and of his development in the Germany of the 1920s.

One of the final and most dangerous aspects of this swing to the right was the deep, passionate, obsessive longing for a heroic leader, a 'saviour' who, it was believed, would soon sweep down and save the German nation. As Kurt Hesse put it in his 1922 work *Feldherr Psychologos*:

Where he comes from, no one can say . . . But everyone knows; he is the Führer, everyone cheers him and thus he will one day announce himself, he for whom all of us are waiting, full of longing, who feel Germany's present distress deep in our hearts, so that thousands and hundreds of thousands of Germans picture him, millions of voices call for him, one single German soul seeks him.

Völkisch nationalists developed a notion of ideal leadership, the idea of a man of the people invested with the will of the nation. He would be radical, ruthless, strong; he would wipe away class differences and he would bring about a new beginning, uniting people in a racially pure 'national community'. For every attack on the weak, dithering Weimar politicians there would be an equally strong call for a true Führer, and as the crises of the republic deepened and all faith in the politicians faded this hope intensified. The idea was given impetus by the success of the *Duce* Mussolini, who staged his successful March on Rome in 1922.[49] Ernst Werner Techow, one of Walther Rathenau's assassins, captured the expectant mood when he said that 'the younger generation was striving for something new . . . They gathered in themselves an energy charged with the myth of the Prussian-German past, the pressure of the present, and the expectation of an unknown future.' And the future was approaching fast. Far off in Bavaria Adolf Hitler had joined an obscure group known as the German Workers' Party and was fashioning it into his own image. As early as April 1923, Hermann Göring said that 'many hundred thousands' were already convinced 'that Adolf Hitler is the only man who could raise Germany up again'. Meanwhile, the man who would lead Berlin to Nazism in Hitler's name was being transformed from a mild-mannered Catholic youth into a rabid nationalist. Within a decade he would become the most powerful man in Berlin. It was he who would transform the Nazis, a local Munich group, into a national movement, a step achieved by the move to the capital. His name was Joseph Goebbels.

The story of Goebbels's rise to power is inseparable from the history of Berlin in the dying years of the Weimar Republic. His life mirrors the terrible struggle which took place for the hearts and minds of young Germans in the 1920s, a struggle which he brought with him in his mission to take Berlin and deliver the city to Hitler. Goebbels shows how the Machiavellian struggle for power turned the city into the centre of the civil war, which was waged until all opposition was crushed in 1933. Without him, Hitler might well have failed in his bid for power, but his success in the 'Red capital' was one of the decisive factors in the Nazi takeover. Goebbels was Berlin's undoing.

Joseph Goebbels was typical of the 'lost generation' of the post-war era. Like so many of the Nazi leaders, he is proof of the ideological war raging in Germany after 1918, and of the power of the challenge to the avant-garde.[50] Born in 1897 to a lower-middle-class Catholic family in Rheydt, near Düsseldorf, his childhood was marked by poverty and unhappiness. A clubfoot caused by infantile paralysis led to a sense of self-loathing and isolation which encouraged him to spend time alone and to find solace in books. The student, with a passion for the bombastic history classes typical of the Kaiser's Germany, was desperate to prove his worth to the nation. Like so many of his generation his life was changed by the First World War. When mobilization was announced on 4 August 1914 he joined his town, lining the streets and cheering his friends on to certain victory, and he wrote in his diary that his one wish was to join his brother at the front. The euphoric parades and speeches made it easier for Goebbels to fit in: for the first time in his life it seemed to him that people ignored his poverty and his deformity and treated him as an equal member of the community, as part of the *Volk*. It was a lesson he would never forget. Later, in the massive propaganda spectacles he staged for the Nazis, he would always try to give even the most timid individual in the audience the sense that he was 'at one' with the nation.[51]

To Goebbels's amazement Germany lost the war. The teenager who had so fervently believed the stories of victory right up until 1918 was devastated by the news. The resulting collapse of national unity, the abdication of the Kaiser, the revolution and the 'shameful Diktat' of Versailles all seemed unreal to him. He fell into a deep depression, and began to see the fate of the nation as his own.

From school Goebbels went on to university in Würzburg, spending some time in Munich, where he first encountered radical right-wing student groups. Although life was a constant struggle against poverty and loneliness he spent much of his time dreaming about a national rebirth and imagining the role that he might one day play in it. He was searching for a mission and as he read the new *völkisch* and nationalistic literature flooding Germany he began to dream of a new German revolution. He was one of the tens of thousands of university students who supported the Kapp Putsch in far-off Berlin.

Despite the obstacles thrown in his way Goebbels was determined to write a doctorate. He was enamoured by the German poets, and Stefan George in particular, and went to study with one of the George Circle, the Jewish literary historian and biographer of Goethe, Friedrich Gundolf. Goebbels referred to him as 'a charming and agreeable man' and although he was not taking on new students he continued to help Goebbels and recommended him to Max von Waldberg, who assigned him the topic of a little-known Romantic dramatist, Wilhelm Schütz.[52] The doctoral thesis, an unbridled mixture of *völkisch* passion and nationalistic jargon, was laced with incongruous references to 'love of the *Vaterland*' and notions of 'spiritual greatness'. It had more to do with his vision of Germany than with an obscure Romantic writer, and was a sentimental, shallow piece devoid of content and filled with flourishes designed to impress. Even so the proud scholar received his doctorate on 18 November 1921. He would later be referred to as 'the Doctor' by Nazis: as there were so few doctors of philosophy amongst the Nazi leadership everybody knew who this meant; for those who did not he insisted on signing even the most trivial Nazi memos 'Dr G.'.[53] But as Albert Speer has pointed out, Goebbels was perhaps the most clever of the Nazis in the group around Hitler: 'He was, I think, a genius in propaganda, and I think one can say that he made Hitler as much as Hitler made him. His was a very complex personality – totally cold.'[54]

Like so many of his generation Goebbels was deeply impressed by the irrational outpourings of the new German theorists and he thought of himself as one of the future writers of the new Germany. His own novel, *Michael Voormann: A Man's Fate in Leaves from a Diary*, was a semi-autobiographical work which he dedicated to 'the spirit of resurrection, the rejection of material-ism ... towards passionate surrender'. Here was Goebbels the fraud, already claiming that his leg had been smashed in the war (a charade he would keep up until he was found out in 1927), pontificating on his destiny and littering the pages with pompous and irrelevant references to the Bible, to Nietzsche, to Dostoevsky, to Spengler and to the other German writers currently in vogue. Hidden amongst it all was the call for the one thing which could save Germany: a strong leader. He first heard of a little-known orator named Adolf Hitler in 1922. Three years later Goebbels would finally meet the man whom he would bring to power in Berlin.

In any other time or place Hitler would probably have been instantly forgettable. As a young man he was unattractive, sullen, lazy, irrational and decidedly unpleasant. Born in 1889 in Braunau on the Austro-German border, he tried and failed in his attempts to study architecture at the Academy of Fine Arts in Vienna. He stayed on in the city, eking out a living by painting watercolours for tourists, spending much of his time lonely, miserable, and jealous of those who had the good fortune to be well off.[55] He might well have remained drifting in Vienna had it not been for the First World War, about which he would write: 'I sank down upon my knees and thanked heaven from the fullness of my heart for the favour of having been permitted to live at such a time.'

Hitler volunteered to fight in the German army, and threw himself into the war effort with the ferocity of a man who has nothing to lose. His experiences in battle were terrible. He sat thirty feet underground in the mud-filled trenches at the Somme waiting as the British bombarded the German forward line for days at a time and then emerged only to find himself wounded amongst the thousands of men slaughtered in the first hour of the battle. Later he became a runner, a job in which life expectancy was measured in weeks. There is no doubt he had courage; by the end of the war he had been made a corporal and had won the Military Merit Cross and the coveted Iron Cross First Class. In the last weeks of the war Hitler was caught in a gas attack, and it was during his convalescence that he heard about the defeat and the revolution in Berlin. Huddled in a military hospital, his 'aching head buried between the blankets and pillow', he cried 'with bitterness and shame'. He emerged from the ward to find his world shattered. He would later claim that it was the news of the shameful surrender that drove him into politics.[56]

There is no telling how much the experiences of gore and death on the front affected him in later years, but they transformed him from a lazy would-be architect into a cunning, hardened, brutal political animal.[57] Hitler would later pretend to be shocked by the brutality of the SA or the SS, and he preferred not to get personally involved in violent 'actions' or to see evidence of them afterwards, but he knew perfectly well what was being done in his name, and he was not squeamish. The Nazi supporter Rudolf Diels remembered sitting with Hitler in his headquarters at the Kaiserhof in 1931 when a woman rushed in holding a small package. Her name was Frau Stennes, the wife of an SA man recently murdered at Hitler's command. She ripped open the package and threw a shirt down on the table in front of him. It was covered in the blood of her dead husband. Diels recoiled in horror but when he glanced at Hitler he found him staring at the woman with terrifying coldness. Human life meant nothing to him.[58]

When Hitler returned to Munich the army sent him to a political indoctrination course, where he began to lecture and where he discovered a talent for public speaking. His fervour drew him to the attention of Captain Mayer, the head of the Bavarian Press and Propaganda section of the army, who sent him to report on the various political groups then springing up around the city. One of these was the German Workers' Party, the DAP, which had been founded by the railway mechanic Anton Drexler and the sports journalist Karl Harrer. Their ideas attracted Hitler and, with few other prospects, he joined in 1920. Hitler began to speak on subjects ranging from anti-Semitism to hatred of the new government. The strange little man with greasy black hair and a nervous manner seemed even then to have an almost mesmerizing hold on his audiences. He began to attract a following.[59]

By 1921 the DAP had changed its name to the National Socialist German Workers' Party and Hitler had been made party leader. Membership had increased to 3,300. Hitler's original black ski-outfit design for his troop was forsaken after an abandoned cache of khaki uniforms once destined for the German army in East Africa was found, giving rise to the 'brown shirts'. By 8 November 1923 Hitler had attracted 55,000 members, including the men who would form his Munich power base: Hermann Göring, Rudolf Hess and Alfred Rosenberg. With membership came interest from others, including the Reichswehr, the Freikorps, and from Field Marshal Ludendorff himself, all of whom were keen to harness this growing party for their own political purposes. After the failed Beer Hall *Putsch* and 'March on Red Berlin' in 1923 Hitler was arrested, but even then he used his trial as a political soapbox, making ardent speeches about the patriotism of his actions. The sympathetic court gave him the minimum sentence of five years, with an understanding that he would be let out early. He had just enough time to finish *Mein Kampf.*[60] The failed *Putsch* taught Hitler a great deal about the limits of armed rebellion in a modern state like Germany, and set him on the road to a 'legal' seizure of power. The trial also made Hitler into a national hero for many young Germans. One of these was Joseph Goebbels, who was so impressed that he scraped together some money and headed for a National Socialist rally in Weimar. 'It was a god', Goebbels wrote, who had given Hitler the 'strength to voice our suffering'. The journey to Weimar would change his life.

Ironically, the rally which brought Goebbels into the National Socialist camp was held in the National Theatre, the very place in which the republic had been proclaimed less than a decade before. Now, the shaky opera sets were gone and the theatre was bathed in the late summer sunshine, and filled with swastika flags. There Goebbels stood during the closing ceremonies, watching his hero General Ludendorff surrounded by men from all parts of the Reich standing at attention and yelling '*Heil!*' at the top of their lungs whenever Hitler's name was mentioned. The old feelings of pre-war euphoria washed over him. This was the 'new Germany', the 'elite of the honest and true'. For the first time in years he was treated like part of the 'brotherhood', and it made him feel as if he was in 'a big house with many children ... It is so heart warming and provides a great sense of security and satisfaction'.[61] Goebbels immediately decided to join the movement under the auspices of the left-leaning Strasser wing of the party. He raced home to found a Gladbach chapter, and began to campaign for Hitler.

On 12 July 1925 he met his new leader face to face. After his second meeting he wrote: 'This man has everything it takes to be a king' and began to think of himself as Hitler's instrument of 'divine will'. For his part, Hitler recognized Goebbels as the brains behind the Strasser wing and rewarded him for his idolatry by advancing his career.[62] Up until now the Nazis' sphere of influence had been limited to Bavaria, but Hitler was on the road to power and he knew it. He was unwilling to risk going to Berlin too early but he needed a trusted and devoted man to establish a power base in the powerful 'Red' capital. Goebbels was the perfect choice. Not only was he intelligent and dedicated, but Hitler felt sure that his socialist leanings would enable him to find the key to winning over at least part of the working-class population. The appointment was of the utmost urgency, for Hitler recognized that 'whoever has Berlin has Prussia', and whoever has Prussia 'has the Reich'. On 28 October 1926 Hitler appointed Joseph Goebbels Gauführer of Berlin. It was probably the single most important appointment Hitler ever made. Goebbels would soon be known by his admirers as the 'Marat of Berlin'; by his detractors as the 'ratcatcher', or the *nachgedunkelte Schrumpfgermane* (dark shrivelled Teuton), or the 'Goblin' who 'circles around the great city like a vulture'. He would retain his post until his suicide in the Führer bunker on 1 May 1945.

On 7 November 1926 the twenty-nine-year-old Goebbels stepped from the train at the Anhalter Bahnhof. Small, frail, insecure, he looked anything but a conquering hero. Goebbels made his way to the Nazi head office, which proved to be nothing more than a dingy little room in a cellar in the Potsdamer Strasse. The Nazi Party was virtually unknown in the city. It had been banned after the failed 'March on Red Berlin', and the first troubled branch was only founded in February 1925 under the inept direction of Ernst Schlange. The Berlin division of the SA, called the 'Sports Club of Greater Berlin', was established only a short time before Goebbels's arrival on 22 March 1926. The organization had fewer than 200 members.

It is often said that Goebbels despised Berlin, and those keen to promote Berlin's anti-Nazi credentials point out that when he first heard of his possible appointment he sneered, 'Thanks for the desert of stones,' and that on his first day there he spat: 'Berlin by night [is] a sink of iniquity. And I'm supposed to plunge into this?' What they fail to mention is that he quickly changed his mind.

Goebbels's initial scepticism had very little to do with Berlin and a great deal to do with his desire to stay near Hitler. The Nazi leadership was never monolithic but was already made up of antagonistic rivals from Göring to Himmler, who competed for the fickle favours of their leader. Goebbels already knew that the only hope of success in the Nazi Party was to keep in Hitler's intimate circle and that, he believed, meant staying in Munich. His attitude changed dramatically, however, when Hitler's chauffeur told him that the capture of Berlin was one of the Führer's highest priorities.[63] Suddenly Berlin was 'magnificent' and 'electric', and when he was shown around the city on his second day by a 'charming lady' he wrote in his diary that his visit to Frederick the Great's tomb in Potsdam had been one of the 'great moments' of his life. He began to refer to Berlin as a 'metropolis', a city of excitement and challenges, a city in which one could feel the 'breath of history'. Although he would constantly attack the republicans, the Jews and the avant-garde or, as he put it, the 'madhouse of Bolshevists and Jews', he had also seen with his own eyes how many people in Berlin shared the nationalistic and *völkisch* ideas which underpinned the Nazi movement; indeed some districts like Spandau had, in his eyes, shown '*völkisch* potential' as early as 1921 when they had made the German Socialist Union with its swastika emblem the fourth largest party in the district. He quickly saw through the glamorous facade of the Kurfürstendamm to the vast, increasingly alienated middle classes longing for a change and he even believed, correctly, that he might one day win support from the vast army of workers in the poor industrial areas of the city. He began to sense the potential for 'action' on the streets of the giant city: 'Berlin needs sensation as a fish needs water', he wrote in his extraordinarily frank *Kampf um Berlin* (Struggle for Berlin). 'Any political propaganda that fails to recognize that will miss its target.'[64] In the 'age of the masses' one needs to 'conquer the street' for 'history is made in the street'.[65]

Goebbels's first task was to try to boost party membership, and in order to do this he had to gain publicity. After a failed demonstration in which his supporters were beaten up by Communists he began to organize talks throughout the city, targeting student fraternities, youth clubs and beer halls, and opening the doors of the new Nazi headquarters in the Lützowstrasse. He quickly developed a loyal following of young people devoted to 'their Goebbels'. Horst Wessel was typical of the students attracted to the fledgling Nazi Party: 'The oratorical gifts and organizational talent this man displayed were unique,' he wrote. 'There was nothing he couldn't handle. The party comrades clung to him with great devotion. The SA would have let itself be cut to pieces for him.'[66] Within months Goebbels had increased the membership to 2,000 but despite this obvious success he had not yet been mentioned in the Berlin press. He began to prepare for the battle which would get him the attention he needed. His first task was to reorganize the Sturmabteilung, the SA, into a tough fighting unit modelled on the powerful Communist 'Red Front Combatant's League'. He complained that he was hard-pressed to make 'political soldiers' out of these unemployed thugs who would fight anyone and anything, including one another, at the slightest provocation, and one can see in the early photographs of the Berlin SA the sullen bullying faces leering at the camera as if threatening the photographer. But Goebbels knew that they would be useful for the coming battle and he would soon put them to work in the beer house brawls, the surprise attacks, the beatings, shootings and cold-blooded murders which would soon rage between the Communists and the SA. In *Kampf um Berlin* he would call this phase the 'Bloody Rise'. His motives were not ideological. He had read Le Bon's *Psychology of the Masses* and was convinced that publicity was an end in itself: 'That propaganda is good which leads to success and that is bad which fails to achieve the desired result ... no one can say your propaganda is too rough, too mean; these are not criteria by which it may be characterized.'

In the post-war legend of Berlin the Communists and the Nazis are invariably shown to be intractable enemies on opposite sides of the political spectrum. Goebbels, at least in his early years, did not think this way. Throughout his youth he had been a great admirer of Russia and an avid reader of Dostoevsky and Tolstoy; he had been sympathetic to the Russian Revolution and as a student had even supported the Communist struggle against the hated Weimar Republic. He wrote in his diary that anything seemed better than the endless empty debates, the fatuous politicians and the immoral world of capitalism, which 'has learned nothing from recent events ... because it places its own interests ahead of those of the other millions'. 'It is better to go on with Bolshevism than live in eternal capitalist servitude,' he wrote. After reading van den Bruck's *The Third Reich* he proclaimed that the Germans and the Russians had much in common and that the Germans would soon experience a 'rebirth' similar to that which took place in Russia under Lenin.[67] Goebbels saw that the Communists and Nazis shared anti-democratic and anti-republican aims, and when making his early speeches he would even insist on being called 'Comrade Dr Goebbels'. He realized that the Communists were his main rivals in the working-class areas but his overriding aim was not to destroy the KPD (German Communist Party), but to topple the republic. His increasingly shrill rants against the 'Red murder squads', the 'Bolshevik menace' and the 'Red Terror' all had, like his ever more fervent attacks against the Jews, a hysterical, insincere ring to them. None the less, Goebbels faced a daunting task when doing battle with the Communists in the working-class districts of 'Red Berlin'.

After Moscow, Berlin was the largest Communist stronghold in the world and it was an old and established force in the giant industrial city. When Goebbels arrived in Berlin it was headquarters to a party of 250,000 members, with twenty-five newspapers, eighty-seven affiliated groups and 4,000 active political cells.[68] It had a highly developed courier service, a vast network of informers and sophisticated surveillance systems. It was home to the Communist Party headquarters, the Communist Delegation, which sat in the Reichstag, and the infamous Soviet Trade Delegation. The Soviets poured money into Berlin, teaching local party members 'Passology' (the art of forging documents and signatures and making fake Brazilian passports), how to build covert networks, how to infiltrate enemy groups, and how to produce effective propaganda. Goebbels, with his pathetic handful of supporters, envied this powerful rival. It is a measure of his genius as a propagandist and political activist, and testament to the stupidity of the Communist leadership, that within seven years the situation would be completely reversed.

Goebbels's first attack against the Communists took place on 11 February 1927, with a carefully staged rally 'in the lion's den', the Pharus Hall in the heart of 'Red Wedding'. He had advertised the event throughout Berlin, replacing the small NSDAP announcement with enormous posters done in a bright blood red specifically to provoke the Communists. Goebbels had barely climbed on to the platform when a group of Communists moved in on the assembled SA men and began to attack. This was not mere brawling but tough hand-to-hand combat with both sides armed with heavy chains, brass knuckles, sticks and iron rods. The fighting continued outside, where people from both camps had their jaws and noses broken and were knocked unconscious. According to an SA report the KPD had eighty-five wounded whereas the SA had three badly wounded and 'about 10–12 slightly'.[69] Goebbels was delighted. The superior SA forces made the Communists withdraw, and for the first time the Nazis were given broad coverage in the Berlin press. Goebbels called the 'Battle of Pharus Hall' a 'good beginning' and made much of the 'terror' experienced by the 'innocent' Nazis, who had merely wanted to hold a peaceful meeting. The report concluded: 'When the police appeared the fight was already over. Marxist terrorism had been bloodily suppressed.'[70]

Goebbels did not let the momentum slip. On 20 March 1927, the so-called 'Mark Brandenburg Day' which marked the anniversary of the founding of the Berlin SA, Goebbels gathered his men a short distance from the city. After whipping them into a frenzy he directed them to march into Berlin. Over 400 men in uniform set out, beating up any Communists they found in their way. Later that day Goebbels instructed them to attack Jews, or anyone 'of Jewish appearance', and by nightfall many had been taunted and injured by SA men singing the SA *Song of the Storm Columns*, which had the words 'Only when Jews are bleeding/Only then shall we be free' as its refrain. Many Berliners came to watch these events. Some were disgusted and some showed their disapproval but nothing was done to stop the SA during this first overt Nazi anti-Jewish 'action' in Berlin. The beatings were still going on when Goebbels spoke at the closing ceremony at the Wittenbergplatz. Here, in the middle-class West End, he refined his speech to conform to his new audience. 'We came publicly for the first time into Berlin, with peaceful intentions,' he lied. 'The Red Front Combatants League has compelled us to spill our blood. We won't let ourselves be treated like second-class citizens any longer.' The group of well-heeled listeners cheered. Goebbels would later boast that he had played on the psyche of the middle class as if he had played 'on a piano'. By 2 September 1928, at the annual general meeting of the party, the Nazis could proudly announce:

The disintegration spreads slowly but surely; there is hardly any serious resistance. But anti-semitism grows as an idea. What was hardly
there ten years ago is there today: the Jewish question has been brought
to people's notice, it will not disappear any more and we shall make
sure that it becomes an international world question; we shall not let
it rest until the question has been solved. We think we shall live to
see that day (*enthusiastic applause*) . . .'[71]

In the following months Goebbels stepped up the violence in the working-
class districts, always being careful to avoid the well-to-do sections of the city.
A particularly violent phase led to a ban on the SA, but the organization
simply turned itself into 'hiking' or 'swimming' clubs and the uniform became
a white shirt with a brown rubber bottle top wrapped around one button. A
new 'marching band' was formed, its real purpose clearly to be seen in the
photographs of scarred and coarse thugs posing with musical instruments they
clearly did not know how to play. Goebbels also used this time to found his
own propaganda paper to complement Hitler's *Völkischer Beobachter*. He called
it *Der Angriff* (The Attack) and, following Hitler's dictum that the masses
should never be turned against more than one enemy at a time, he hit out at
the Jews, a target which he now deemed particularly appropriate for Berlin.
Here were the early Nazi cartoons by Hans Schweitzer and vulgar stereotypes
of hideous and 'lecherous' Jewish capitalists, 'destructive' Jewish Bolsheviks,
'parasitic' Jewish businessmen, 'immoral' Jewish professionals, 'intellectual'
Jewish Berliners – said to be doing their utmost to undermine the honest,
hard-working Germans in their own capital. There were no depths to which
Der Angriff would not sink.[72]

As with his attacks on the Communists, Goebbels did not take the
racial theories or anti-Semitism of the party seriously; indeed he had once
ridiculed the coarse anti-Semitism of the Nazis. His motives were purely
self-serving. He wanted attention, and he wanted to give the people something to hate. Goebbels had not been brought up in an anti-Semitic
environment, and it was only after reading Houston Stewart Chamberlain's
Foundations of the Nineteenth Century that he first began to refer to the
'historical struggle' between the two 'pure races', Aryans and Jews. When
he was refused a job at the Ullstein Press after completing his doctorate he
blamed it on Jewish control of the media and in some of his subsequent
articles for the *Westdeutsche Landeszeitung* he identified 'Jewish materialism'
as the root of 'all political, intellectual and moral confusion of our times'. But
he had never been a radical anti-Semite like, say, Himmler, and it was only
in Berlin that he transformed himself into Hitler's prime Jew-baiter. He
would say: 'God gives you aims, it doesn't matter which!' although the phrase

FLOTTEN-
Schauspiele
Kurfürstendamm 153/156

Täglich **2** Vorstellungen 4 u. 8 Uhr,
Sonntags **3** „ „ 3, 5½ u. 8 Uhr.

Stadt- & elektr. Bahnverbindung.
Näheres durch die Tageszeitungen.

ABOVE In the age of Imperialism, with its emphasis on overseas trade and colonial expansion, it was assumed that the key to great-power status was a mighty navy. By 1904 Berliners could visit this Kurfürstendamm attraction – a gigantic pool in which model battle ships engaged in mock manoeuvres.

RIGHT On the eve of war in August 1914 the actress Tilla Durieux wrote: 'Every face looks happy. We've got war! Bands in the cafes and restaurants play *Heil dir im Siegerkranz* and *Die Wacht am Rhein* without stopping, and everyone has to listen to them standing up. One's food gets cold, one's beer gets warm. No matter – we've got war!' Here, a young woman puts flowers in the buttonhole of a young recruit.

At first the war seemed to be going well. Here, a concert is held in the tower of the Berlin Rathaus, in celebration of the fall of Antwerp – 11 October 1914.

The optimistic mood did not last. Berlin's first casualty list is posted at the War Ministry in the Wilhelmstrasse. In the end, 350,000 young Berliners would die as a result of the conflict.

RIGHT Although far from the front line, Berlin was utterly changed by war. The gaudy Imperial veneer soon wore off and Berlin revealed itself to be an ugly and impoverished city. Even the elephants of Hagenbeck's circus were used to haul coal.

BELOW Berlin was an important medical centre and its hospitals accommodated 253,000 men during the war. Georg Grosz recalled: 'in hospital we were fed on dried vegetables, turnips, coffee and synthetic honey which corroded the linings of our stomachs.' Here, war-wounded in the Moabit hospital celebrate Christmas 1918.

3 March 1918. The Russian delegation on its way to sign the draconian Treaty of Brest-Litovsk. The central figure is Adolph Joffe, soon to be Soviet ambassador in Berlin who would spearhead Lenin's attempt to foment revolution in the German capital.

10 December 1918. When the frontline troops returned to Berlin they faced a grim future. Chaplain Raymund Dreeling described the scene: 'The unshaven faces beneath the helmets are haggard, wasted with hunger and long peril, pinched and dwindled to the lines drawn by terror and courage and death.' They were ideal recruits for the radicals on both left and right.

Revolutionary troops before the Brandenburg Gate, November 1918. The Spartacus Uprising was finally crushed in January 1919.

In January 1919 Lenin had sent his crack agent Karl Radek back to Berlin to direct the coming 'revolution'; he was to ensure that unemployed soldiers and workers overthrew the Ebert government and disrupted the January elections to the National Assembly. He quickly quarrelled with Rosa Luxemburg, who disagreed with his support of Lenin's violent tactics.

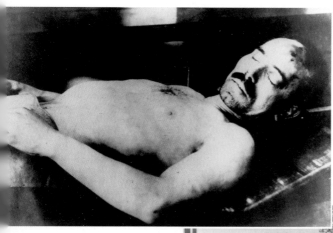

The leaders of the Spartacus Uprising, Rosa Luxemburg and Karl Liebknecht (shown here), were murdered in Berlin in January 1919. Luxemburg's body was left to rot in the Landwehr Canal; Liebknecht was shot in the back in the Tiergarten.

ABOVE For a few brief sparkling years
Berlin attracted a concentration of artistic
talent which has not since been equalled.
It heralded a new vision of modernity and
introduced it to Germany. When Germans
rejected it, its exiles brought it to the rest of
the world. Here Herwarth Walden holds an
artistic festival in his gallery Der Sturm in
1923. Paintings by Sonia Delaunay-Terk hang
in the background.

RIGHT Scene from the classic Expressionist
film *Das Kabinett des Dr Caligari*, 1919.
One can just catch a glimpse of the eerie
Expressionist sets.

Few Berliners actually saw the great
films of the era; *Dr Caligari* had a run of
only four weeks in Berlin. Instead people
went to melodramas filled with black-
robed magicians, evil spirits and mad
apparitions chasing scantily clad young
ladies around graveyards and dark,
bat-filled caves. They had titles like
Tophar Mummy and *The Hunt for Death*.
Der Teufel und die Circe was typical.

ABOVE The legend of the Golden Twenties is a heady mixture of fact and fiction. While the avant-garde wiled away the hours at the Romanisches Cafe, the majority of Berliners flocked to the revues, which were distinguished only by the ever-increasing numbers of naked women. Here, the 'girls' of the Haller Revue pose as the Quadriga statue atop the Brandenburg Gate.

Anita Berber, a famous cabaret star of her day, was the epitome of Weimar. She died in 1928 after collapsing in a Baghdad nightclub. She represented both Weimar Berlin's energy and its superficiality.

Department stores were symbols of modernity in Weimar Berlin – a view of the KaDeWe in 1932.

Adolf Hitler as an infantryman in France in the First World War.

INSET Weimar Berlin was a centre of innovative architecture, as seen in the Shellhaus on the Reichpietschufer, built by Emil Fahrenkamp between 1930 and 1932. Berlin was also the last home of the Bauhaus before it was disbanded by the Nazis.

BELOW The Hufeisen (horseshoe) designed by Bruno Taut and Martin Wagner (1925–7) was one of the best known of the innovative residential estates built during the Weimar Republic.

would have been more apt had he replaced the word 'God' with 'Hitler'.

There has been much speculation about this change in Goebbels's behaviour towards the Jews. Some have questioned whether he was merely trying to please Hitler, or whether there was a deeper need to rid himself of his own insecurity, to drum from his memory the taunts at school when the shy, bookish child was called 'Rabbi' and bullied by his classmates. Perhaps he was trying to protect himself from the inner party circle which never quite forgave him for having been one of Friedrich Gundolf's students, or maybe he felt he had to atone for the fact that his wife Magda Quandt had been brought up in a Jewish household after her mother re-married; his obvious inability to comply with the blonde, physically perfect Nazi ideal may have made him ever more desperate to prove his *völkisch* and racial qualifications to a critical party.[73] This was not unusual; Reinhard Heydrich, who was to become one of the most brutal anti-Semites of the Third Reich, was almost certainly of Jewish ancestry although this may never be conclusively proved as he diligently destroyed all of his family headstones and removed incriminating documents from church and registry offices in Leipzig and Dresden. Whatever the reasons, Goebbels stepped up his attacks on the 'un-German' presence in Berlin, slavishly currying favour with Hitler in the process. One of his most vindictive personal vendettas was against the Berlin police president Bernhard Weiss, who had been responsible for the ban on the SA. Goebbels code-named him 'Isador', a name which he took from Communist propaganda and which he mistakenly believed to be Jewish.[74] When a friend criticized him after a particularly disgusting article he responded that he did not care at all about Weiss himself; all he cared about was whether the propaganda was 'effective'. 'Propaganda', he said, 'has nothing to do with the truth.'

Despite his hard work, Goebbels's advancement in Berlin seemed painfully slow. In the elections of 20 May 1928 the Nazis did poorly, scraping only 1.5 per cent of the vote in Berlin compared to the Social Democrats' 28.4 per cent, and the Communists' 24.6 per cent. They fared little better in the nation as a whole, netting only 2.6 per cent of the vote and twelve seats in the Reichstag. The apparent prosperity had kept people away from the Nazis with their prophecies of doom and, at the time, it looked as if the Weimar Republic might actually survive. Things had settled down in Berlin, the Communist and Nazi clashes had not yet moved from the slums into the city centre, and for visitors and residents alike the city had a heady, carefree attitude. It was all about to change. The illusion of success was shattered by the devastating world economic crisis which reached Germany at the end of 1929, a crisis which destroyed the last vestiges of support for the republic and which pushed the moderate left towards the Communists and the frightened middle classes into the waiting arms of the Nazis. The terrible images of Weimar Berlin in its death throes, with its extremism, its lines of starving unemployed workers, its increasingly brutal street violence and the scenes of Jews and other 'enemies' of the community being harassed and beaten up foreshadowed that which was to come.

From the devastation of the city in the Thirty Years War to Bismarck's *Gründerzeit* crash to the hyper-inflation after the First World War Berlin has faced a number of economic crises in its history, but none was as devastating as that which began in the autumn of 1929. 'Black Friday' on Wall Street heralded the beginning of the Great Depression in the United States, and the consequences for Berlin were dire.[75]

Hitler's success was based on the misery and fear caused by the slump. Election results from the 1920s indicate that when the economy was doing well support for the Bavarian rabble-rousers remained low. The bizarre *völkisch* beliefs, the 'socialism' and the aggressive nationalism they espoused would always have been popular amongst certain segments of society, but there is little reason to believe that Hitler would have been able to put his schemes into practice had the country remained stable. There were many other factors which contributed to Hitler's victory, but without the international financial crisis his ruthless bid for power would almost certainly have failed.

Black Friday marked the turning point in Hitler's career. The crash froze the vital flow of foreign capital into Berlin as American financiers recalled the numerous short-term loans which had given Weimar its veneer of opulence. Bankruptcies followed, export markets disappeared, businesses were forced to close, the demand for housing was severely reduced and industrial wages dropped to 10 per cent below those of 1914. In December 1929 the Secretary of State Hermann Pünder surveyed the increasing misery in the city and could only compare it to the 'terrible years of 1918–19'. Berlin itself was in serious financial trouble, over 400 million marks in debt and facing bankruptcy. Tariffs were levied on everything from water to electricity to transportation and all building projects were halted, including work on the U-Bahn. At the same time a scandal broke out involving the mayor of Berlin, the Sklarek brothers, and a missing 20 million marks which further undermined middle-class faith in the system.[76] The Communists ruthlessly exploited the scandal, crying that 'the lost millions of the three Sklarek brothers is proof of the spreading evil of the bourgeois social fascist corruptionists', and the Nazis followed suit, pointing to the 'general corruption' in all those associated with the Weimar Republic. Most damaging of all was the quick, relentless, seemingly unstoppable rise of unemployment, a feature of the depression which hit industrial Berlin particularly hard.

The unemployment figures were staggering. In 1929 31,800 Berliners had been out of work. By the end of September 1931 it was 323,000. By the beginning of April the following year 603,000 were registered unemployed, and the actual figure was estimated at over 700,000. Berlin now contained more than 10 per cent of the total unemployed population of Germany. The persistent poverty wore people down. It was the second time in a decade that the Weimar system had failed them, and their anger was palpable.

The carefree 1920s were over. The innovative films and theatre productions were replaced by escapism or a brand of caustic black humour born of extreme misery. For a few years the cabarets resurfaced as organs of scathing political satire, reflecting the fact that for the vast quiet majority of its citizens Berlin had again become a place of poverty and despair.[78] The crisis quickly spread beyond the industrial slums. Many white-collar workers and public employees who had once enjoyed the new department stores and their 'rationalized' offices were fired or forced to take swingeing salary cuts. Small businesses closed and thousands lost their financial security. Large new city apartments stood empty as the humiliated lower middle classes were forced back into the *Mietskasernen*. Spender felt that an 'all-pervading smell of hopeless decay ... came out of the interiors of these grandiose houses now converted into pretentious slums'. This coincided with the failure of the much-publicized republican welfare system, which became tangled in a web of red tape and could not begin to meet payments to the mass of new applicants. Production fell so rapidly that many thought the capitalist system would fail completely. Some described Berlin as a city of aching hopelessness. Horse meat restaurants opened again, and lines of unemployed men with no place to sleep waited around the meagre soup kitchens in their frayed, dirty clothes and cloth caps, or went to live in the desolate tent camps such as Kühle Wampe on the outskirts of the city.[79] One observer noted that these camps consisted of orderly rows of tents with men sitting outside day after day, staring into space. This was the 'clean, adult and neat misery' of the Berlin unemployed, Berlin's experience of the Great Depression, with hundreds of thousands of people living from day to day, without work and without hope for the future.[80] As a child Karma Rauhut remembered seeing people on streetcar platforms collapsing from hunger. There were 'people everywhere on the streets offering themselves for *any* work. Experienced salesmen stood on the Kurfürstendamm or Unter den Linden, carrying cardboard signs saying who they were and that they desperately needed work.' A family friend took her to eastern Berlin, where for a meagre sum women rented out a bed for a few hours to men who could not afford a room; while they slept the children lay in their parents' bed or on the floor: 'we were so shaken,' she recalled.[81] The crisis seemed to have no end, and poor, desperate people found themselves watching their youth ebb away and their dreams for a future crumble before their eyes. Fragile, unstable, damaged Berlin was too weak to survive such a crisis unscathed, and people began to search for radical solutions.

Even so, it is still startling in retrospect to see how quickly the republic collapsed; how quickly Berliners gave themselves up to the radical ideas of the new right and to those who promised a utopian Germany free of the people who had 'caused' the problems. All the post-war arguments resurfaced: the defeat had been unjust, Germany had been stabbed in the back, the 'November Criminals' had set Germany on the road to ruin; the Jews had caused the collapse. The works of the *völkisch* writers which had appeared in the mid 1920s were suddenly sold out. The notions of race, national mission, the need for living space, anti-Semitism, the hatred of the 'system', the belief in the coming of a great leader – all began to be taken as serious doctrine. Spender felt a 'sensation of doom' on the Berlin streets:

> For years the newspapers contained little news but of growing unemployment and increased taxation necessary to pay reparations and doles. The Nazis at the one extreme, and the Communists at the other, with their meetings, their declamatory newspapers, their uniformed armies of youths, their violence against the Republic and against one another, did all in their power to exacerbate the situation.[82]

It was a tragedy that, in the midst of this misery, a man was waiting to exploit the gullible population, to give them the sense of hope and belonging they were looking for, and to tap their sense of nationalism and self-sacrifice. For Hitler, the crisis was an extraordinary stroke of luck, and he used it to the full.

In his pamphlet *Die zweite Revolution* of 1926 Goebbels had predicted: 'We shall achieve everything if we set hunger, despair and sacrifice on the march for our goals.' He was right. Three years later he moved to take advantage of the suffering of Berliners. His chance came in the Berlin City Council elections of 17 November 1929. Goebbels pulled out all the stops for the campaign, setting Hitler up as the saviour of Germany and blaming the economic situation on the evil workings of 'International Jewry', but he also made use of everything from unemployment to the Sklarek scandal to the general ineptitude of the government in his vitriolic attacks. The propaganda struck a chord and the Nazis came from nothing to win 132,097 votes in the city – 5.8 per cent of the total. The Communists were still much stronger, with 40.6 per cent, but Goebbels had tasted success and rapidly stepped up his propaganda war.

The attacks on the Communists continued, with the SA pushing ever deeper into working-class districts. Goebbels now began to create martyrs to the cause. The 'Unknown Soldier' of the First World War now became the 'Unknown SA Man', and Goebbels held ceremonies and commemorative speeches honouring those 'untold heroes' who had already died for the Nazi cause. They were soon replaced by real 'sacrificial victims'. Goebbels could not have cared less for the lives of those who fought for his cause; for him the death of his own men was seen as the best way of making the headlines. The first of these 'martyrs' was Hans-Georg Kütemayer, an SA man who had actually committed suicide by throwing himself into the Landwehr Canal in 1928. Goebbels turned his death into a Communist crime: his grisly article described how the innocent man's pale face had been 'crushed' by iron rods wielded by 'Red hoodlums'.[83] When the SA member Walter Fischer was killed in a fight with Communists Goebbels organized a huge rally on the Fehrbelliner Platz during which he, Hermann Göring and Horst Wessel called for revenge against the 'Red murder squads'.

A few weeks later a young SA man named Werner Wessel, Horst Wessel's brother, died of exposure while on a ski trip. The details of his death were falsified at the extravagant funeral, which saw 500 Berlin SA men march past the Communist Party headquarters brandishing torches and yelling abuse at those inside. The greatest propaganda coup came a few weeks later, when Horst Wessel himself was murdered by Communists. Wessel, a Sturmführer in the SA and a pimp, was shot in a fight over a woman in the spring of 1930. He was rushed to hospital with a bullet lodged in his brain. Fortunately for Goebbels he took weeks to die so that each stage of his decline could be reported in agonizing detail in the Nazi and eventually in the national press. When he died on 23 February Wessel was instantly transformed into an icon and all Nazis were instructed to wear mourning for three weeks. The funeral was another triumph, with 20,000 Nazis gathered in Berlin to hear Goebbels proclaim, 'when the SA assembles for the great roll call ... the Führer will also call your name, Comrade Wessel!' The Communists had daubed the cemetery with 'To Wessel the Pimp – a Last *Heil* Hitler!' and to Goebbels's relief they launched a huge attack after the funeral, providing him with yet another opportunity to portray the KPD as thugs with no respect for the honoured dead. Wessel's most lasting contribution was a song he had scribbled in March 1929, which Goebbels predicted would be sung throughout Germany 'in a decade'. In fact it would take only three years for the 'Horst Wessel Song' to become the *de facto* German national anthem.[84] Despite the hypocrisy the ceremony surrounding the deaths of these 'patriotic' Germans appealed to a large segment of the Berlin middle class, who were taken in by Goebbels's anti-Communist rhetoric. It also impressed the German right. Goebbels knew that this popularity was growing but he and the Nazis needed an election. Once again, fate played into their hands.

Chancellor Brüning had come under increasing pressure as a result of the economic crisis. This was in part to do with his own economic policies, which reflected his desire to prove to the Allies that Germany could not afford to pay reparations. This might have evoked some sympathy in Washington or London but offered little hope to the individual in Germany. Brüning was now governing by decree and the brawls between twenty-nine different political parties were broadcast over the radio, producing the impression of a cabinet which, as Spender put it, was like 'a little boat manned by a hopeless crew, trying to navigate an unending storm'. For him the feeling of unrest in Berlin

> went deeper than any crisis. It was a permanent unrest, the result of nothing being fixed and settled. The Brüning regime was neither democracy nor dictatorship, socialism or conservatism, it represented no group nor class, only a common fear of the overwhelming disorder, which formed a kind of rallying place of frightened people . . . Berlin was the tension, the poverty, the anger, the prostitution, the hope and despair thrown out on to the streets. It was the blatant rich at the smart restaurants, the prostitutes in army top boots at corners, the grim, submerged-looking Communists in processions, and the violent youths who suddenly emerged from nowhere into the Wittenbergplatz and shouted: 'Deutschland Erwache!'[85]

In the midst of all this, late in 1930, the 'Hunger Chancellor' was forced to dissolve the Reichstag and call new elections for 14 September of that year. These elections mark Hitler's breakthrough into national politics.

On 26 April 1930 Goebbels had been made Nazi Director of Propaganda and had set out finally to convince the German people that Hitler was their 'saviour'. He adored Hitler and knew that his own success depended on Hitler's rise to power. 'The greater and more towering I make God, the greater and more towering I am myself,' he wrote in his diary. Hitler was increasingly impressed by him, once saying, 'I have heard them all but the only speaker I can listen to without going to sleep is Goebbels. He really can put it over.'[86] Goebbels worked obsessively, co-ordinating the national campaign, creating new slogans, writing for Der Angriff and using press campaigns, films and posters to attack the republic and develop the image of Hitler as the Führer. He targeted all levels of society, using the faintly Leninist slogan 'Freedom and Bread' for the working class while attacking the 'Reds' in middle-class areas. No detail was too trivial for his attention. His instructions for one of the signs read:

> Hitler Poster. The Hitler poster depicts a fascinating Hitler head on a completely black background. Subtitle: white on black – 'Hitler'. In accordance with the Führer's wishes this poster is to be put up only during the final days [of the campaign]. As experience shows that

during the final days there is a variety of coloured posters, this poster with its completely black background will contrast with all the others and will produce a tremendous effect on the masses.

Goebbels also had a fanatical belief in his own success. Hitler had sent him to Berlin to establish a Nazi political presence there but Goebbels had done much more than that, capturing middle-class support and even making inroads into the working-class population. He now wished to present a willing and pliant capital to his Führer. Ultimately he wanted to persuade Hitler to move from Munich to Berlin, and thereby make himself indispensable to his leader.

Until now, Hitler's power base had been firmly centred in the 'Brown House' in Munich. Goebbels had often fallen foul of the 'fascist oriented Munich tycoons', whom he blamed for 'keeping Hitler from Berlin'; for example, he held Rudolf Hess and Göring personally responsible for preventing Hitler from attending the triumphant Horst Wessel funeral.[87] There had been dozens of examples of in-fighting between Nazi leaders and Hitler had deliberately encouraged this in his successful efforts to remain the ultimate authority in the Nazi Party.[88] Goebbels's elevation to 'Director of Propaganda' had been Hitler's compensation to him for helping to bring down the Strasser brothers in Berlin.[89] Goebbels also fell out with those who advocated abandoning the revolutionary socialism of the party in favour of co-operation with the industrialists and bankers, whom Goebbels loathed; this lay behind his rivalry with Hermann Göring: he hated his fellow Nazi for his patrician ways and for his connections with the German establishment. As a result, Goebbels knew that his only chance of continued success in the Nazi Party was to encourage Hitler to look to Berlin as the future Nazi headquarters. He outdid himself.

On 10 September 1930 Hitler prepared for his first official speech in Berlin. It was to be held in the gigantic Sportpalast. According to Goebbels 100,000 Berliners had requested advance tickets and when the hour arrived the hall was packed to capacity. The spectacle was carefully planned and rehearsed in a format that would be repeated countless times throughout Germany in the coming years: the hall was bedecked with banners and swastika flags, the lighting and the sound system had been carefully designed, the audience had been allowed in early and had waited for hours to intensify the feeling of suspense. Suddenly they could hear the cries from the crowd outside as Hitler approached the building. As he stepped out on to the platform he was greeted with a standing ovation, wild applause and shouts of '*Heil* Hitler!' During his hour-long speech Hitler exhibited his consummate skill as a public speaker, starting slowly and quietly and gradually building up into a frenzy of slogans and gestures which kept his audience spellbound. 'Fellow Germans!' he yelled. 'Join forces with the brown front marching at the head of an awakening

Germany!' The Sportpalast erupted in thunderous applause. For the people who heard him – the student with no future, the poverty-stricken shopkeeper, the middle-class family man with his back to the wall – Hitler suddenly *was* the future. As Albert Speer put it,

> Both Goebbels and Hitler had understood how to unleash mass instincts at their meetings, how to play on the passions that underlay the veneer of ordinary respectable life. Practised demagogues, they succeeded in fusing the assembled workers, petits bourgeois, and students into a homogeneous mob whose opinions they could mould as they pleased ... for a few short hours the personal unhappiness caused by the breakdown of the economy was replaced by a frenzy that demanded victims. And Hitler and Goebbels threw them the victims. By lashing out at their opponents and vilifying the Jews they gave expression and direction to fierce, primal passions.[90]

Hitler was delighted with the reaction in Berlin but he was even more pleased with the election results, which exceeded all his expectations. The NSDAP won 6.5 million votes and with 107 seats became the second largest party in the country. They won 395,000 votes in Berlin, ten times more than only two years before. The Nazis polled 14.7 per cent of the vote in 'Red Berlin', as compared to 27.3 per cent for the Communists and 27.2 for the Social Democrats. Increasingly, Berliners were turning away from the democratic and centre parties towards the anti-republican radicals. Count Kessler called it a 'black day' for Germany but Hitler's star continued to rise. To Goebbels's relief he began to spend more time in the capital, using the top floor of the Kaiserhof Hotel as his temporary base – this was adequate although Goebbels was convinced that the kitchen staff had been infiltrated by Communists, who were poisoning their food, and invited him home virtually every evening. Hitler was now preparing for the 'inevitable' day when he would take power and for a time believed he would be asked to form a government. He even promised Goebbels a cabinet post, and when Hanfstaengl played a new song called *Deutscher Föhn* Hitler proclaimed: 'This is what we will have the band play when we march into Berlin.'[91] Hitler's hopes were only stymied by the Social Democrats' tactical decision to co-operate with the centrist Brüning government, which kept him out of power. It was but a temporary setback.

The economic crisis intensified in the summer of 1931, finally destroying any hope of recovery for the Weimar system. The Austrian Creditanstalt had collapsed in May 1931; the German Danat Bank followed in July, the American economy was in deep trouble and the Bank of England was only saved by its abandonment of the gold standard. People in Berlin rushed to withdraw their savings and the government responded by closing all banks. Christopher

Isherwood described the long lines of people standing around outside a bank with its iron lattices pulled down: 'Most of the people were staring intently and rather stupidly at the locked door. In the middle of the door was fixed a small notice, beautifully printed in Gothic type, like a page from a classic author. The notice said that the Reichspresident had guaranteed the deposits. Everything was quite all right. Only the bank wasn't going to open.' The banks did not reopen until 5 August, and the Stock Exchange remained closed until 3 September. By now one in three Berliners of working age was out of work, and barely two-thirds of these received help from the state. The others turned to begging or crime, or to the Communist and Nazi armies that offered food and shelter.

Goebbels quickly took advantage of the worsening situation, stepping up his appeal to the devastated middle classes. New Nazi organizations were set up in Berlin to attract doctors, lawyers, teachers, civil servants, war veterans and, above all, the young. Goebbels was quick to capture the student movement, but this was not difficult in a city where, in 1931, a third faced unemployment after graduating from university. The Hitler Youth alone, founded in 1922, had over 100,000 members a decade later. Goebbels used the romantic radicalism and emotional appeal of the movement to give young people an identity they could believe in. With the Nazis they felt they were working towards something; they could march, they could agitate, they could advance rapidly in the party; it offered them 'a future of work and prosperity . . . and even gave them present opportunities to strut about in uniforms and feel important'.[92] In 1931 almost 40 per cent of Nazi members were under thirty years of age, and hundreds and then thousands of baffled middle-class parents had to face their children as they appeared in their Berlin apartments or suburban homes and strutted around in the uniform of the Hitler Youth or the SA, parroting the slogans of the radical right. Even the leadership were attractively young: Goebbels was twenty-nine when he went to Berlin; Hitler forty-four when he took power.

It was to these young people that Goebbels appealed in his 'actions' in the centre of Berlin. By now anything associated with Weimar was considered a legitimate target, including its 'un-German' art and culture. One of his most successful protests was the sabotage of the American-made film of Erich Maria Remarque's *All Quiet On the Western Front*, a moving testimony to the futility and waste of war. The film embodied all that Goebbels hated about Weimar culture. It was 'unpatriotic' as it showed death on the front as meaningless, and it was pacifist and therefore undermined the 'spirit' of the German nation. Furthermore it was supported by the Berlin avant-garde, for which reason alone it was a target.

Goebbels began his attack on the night of its second showing in December, when he joined the 150 SA men who had bought tickets and positioned themselves throughout the Mozartsaal cinema in the West End. As the film started they began to shout abuse and attack other members of the audience. One let a group of white mice loose at the front, others let off stink bombs, and innocent people were pushed and beaten.[93]

Goebbels had chosen his target well. Many Berliners now claimed to be 'outraged' by the unpatriotic tone of the film, and when Goebbels called on Berliners to fill the streets in protest over 6,000 supporters showed up on the first day alone. For the next two days the area was the scene of 'legitimate protests' and rallies, which attracted ever greater crowds. Hitler came to review the procession of protesters as if they were soldiers going to war.

At the same time Karma Rauhut remembered a man approaching her father for help. The man's daughter worked as a chambermaid in one of Berlin's hotels and the Nazis believed she had helped Erich Maria Remarque flee the country: 'They took the poor man into the SS barracks, there was a big Gestapo headquarters, and then they interrogated the man and smashed his glasses, smashed out all his teeth, and [beat him] blue.' Herr Rauhut, a director of a private bank, gave him money.[94] Few heard of such intimidation behind the scenes, and Goebbels's provocation had its desired effect. The Film Board withdrew the work, calling it 'a threat to German honour', and for the first time Goebbels boasted that he had 'made government policy'. For many in the Weimar artistic community this event marked the beginning of the end. Carl von Ossietzky noted the marked increase in hostility to the avant-garde. The 'club-footed psychopath', he said, had scored another victory.[95]

Two months later Goebbels struck again, this time attacking Jews who lived in the West End. On 12 September 1931 Jewish worshippers emerging from Rosh Hashanah services at the synagogues in Fasanenstrasse and Lehniner Platz were attacked by over 1,500 Nazis who yelled, 'Kill the Jews'. The Café Reimann was destroyed, and cabarets like the Kadeko suffered a sharp drop in attendance.[96] A few days later at the Tingel-Tangel Friedrich Holländer produced a satire about Berlin anti-Semitism set to the habanera from Bizet's *Carmen*. It went:

> If it's raining or it's hailing,
> If there's lightning, if it's wet,
> If it's dark or if there's thunder,
> If you freeze or if you sweat,
> If it's warm or if it's cloudy,
> If it thaws, if there's a breeze,
> If it drizzles, if it sizzles,
> If you cough or if you sneeze;

It's all the fault of all those Jews!
The Jews are all at fault for that![97]

And in December Werner Finck performed the following joke in the Kata-
combe: 'In the first weeks of the Third Reich, parades will be staged. Should
the parades be hindered by rain, hail, or snow, all Jews in the vicinity will be
shot.' Tragically the audiences still thought these performances so outlandish
as to be funny. They would not think so for long.[98]

Hitler's spectacular electoral success had attracted the attention of the
bankers and industrialists on the centre-right of the political spectrum.
Although they looked down on the Bohemian corporal they could not deny
his appeal to the masses and hoped to use his sudden popularity for their
own ends. At a massive right-wing rally in Bad Harzburg in October 1931
Göring arranged for Hitler to meet leading industrialists, including Hugenberg
and von Thyssen, and representatives of the Stahlhelm and the military. One
of the speakers was Hjalmar Schacht, the former director of the Reichsbank.
This powerful group joined forces, ostensibly to create a 'front' to fight Bolshevism. The collaboration was essential for Hitler, bringing much-needed funds
and, above all, respectability. The British ambassador, Sir Horace Rumbold,
reported from Berlin that there was 'nothing in Herr Hitler's speech to suggest
that he has sacrificed any part of the Socialist section of his programme in
order to fall into line with Herr Hugenberg and the big industrialists'. Rumbold
was right to say that Hitler had no intention of compromising his own programme, but the businessmen had not noticed. They simply saw a man who
not only had a mass following, but also opposed the Marxist left and sought
to rebuild German greatness. General Schleicher called the Nazis a 'healthy
reaction on the part of the *Volk*' and said that if they had not existed 'one
would have to invent them'. As Goebbels continued to encourage the street
fighting in Berlin, Hitler began publicly to distance himself, blaming it on
unruly elements in the SA. With Göring's help, the 'presentable' officer who
held Pour le Mérite – Germany's highest military award of the First World
War – continued to polish his image and ingratiate himself with the German
establishment. The deception would soon bear fruit.

In 1932 Hindenburg's seven-year term of office expired. He was eighty-four
years old and senile, but he was willing to run for another term of office. It
was ironic that Hindenburg had been a staunch enemy of the republic from
its inception, but as President he had attempted to uphold its constitution as
best he could. By 1932 he seemed to represent the only hope for Weimar, and
the Social Democrats did not even put up their own candidate, knowing that
only the 'Old Gentleman' could keep the constitution in place and check
Hitler's rise to power.

When Goebbels announced Hitler's candidacy at the Sportpalast on 22 February he was overwhelmed by the 'storm of enthusiasm' which greeted him. 'Wild demonstrations for the Führer. The people stand up and cheer and shout. The roof threatens to cave in.'[99] Hitler warned Hindenburg: 'You are too venerable for us to let those whom we intend to annihilate hide behind you. You must stand aside.' To keep a firm grasp on the campaign Goebbels moved the Reich propaganda directorate from Munich to Berlin, and launched a concerted drive in the Führer's name. He had propaganda films made of Hitler to be shown in the squares of local districts and towns to 'bring the Führer nearer to the people'. He made 50,000 small gramophone records of Hitler's speeches; he himself made endless speeches playing on the misery and suffering experienced by the average German and he sent half a million posters throughout Germany, setting up round-the-clock SA guards on the huge displays in Berlin to prevent Communist vandalism. He had Hitler fly through-out Germany, swooping down from the sky to talk to expectant audiences, who greeted him with shouts of '*Heil* Hitler', often with tears streaming down their faces.[100] Hitler did not win, but his gains were extraordinary. In the run-off election between the two Hindenburg won 53 per cent of the vote compared with Hitler's 47 per cent. 'By the time I am 85, Herr von Hindenburg will have been long gone,' Hitler announced smugly. 'Our time will come.'

Events moved very rapidly after 1932. Poor muddled, tired Hindenburg swayed from one policy to another, first banning the SS and the SA, then dismissing the Defence Minister who had implemented the ban. Soon after the election he dismissed Brüning and his government and replaced him with the oily smooth, insincere and selfish Franz von Papen and his 'cabinet of barons'. One of von Papen's most foolish acts was to fabricate evidence against the legitimate Social Democratic government of Prussia, forcing Hindenburg to dismiss it. The Prussian leaders slunk off to Switzerland without a fight, leaving von Papen free to name himself the National Commissioner for Prussia and purge the bureaucracy and police of Social Democratic supporters. Von Papen had hoped to start a conservative revolution which ultimately sought to restore the monarchy, but the government was a failure, and in June 1932 Hindenburg dissolved the Reichstag and called for new elections. He also lifted the ban on the SA and the SS.

The July election campaign was the most savage in Weimar history. The Berlin SA had become very powerful; aside from possessing an arsenal of rubber hoses, brass knuckles and iron rods, various gangs began to compete to blow up buildings, burn offices and use firearms. Each gang had a well-defined territory; one gang in Wedding was called the *Raübersturm* (Robber band), and local leaders had names like '*Revolverschnauze*' (Revolvernose). Hitler and

Goebbels managed to control the SA by promising them greater riches to come once the Nazis came to power, a promise which would end in the bloody Night of the Long Knives. The constant battles whipped up by Goebbels and Röhm were carefully designed to show Germany that only the Nazis had the power to save them from a Communist revolution. As the SA wagons rumbled over the streets of Berlin, politically motivated murder became a daily occurrence. In July 1932 there were 400 battles on the streets and 200 people were killed in Prussia alone. On election day, 31 July, nine people were murdered. The fighting was not only between the Communists and Nazis but had spread to all political groups as a result of the general brutalization of the streets. Anarchy and violence ruled Berlin. As the journalist Edgar Mowrer put it in his courageous book *Germany Puts the Clock Back*,

> Brown shirts were everywhere in evidence again and now four private armies, equipped at the very least with jack knives and revolvers, daggers and brass knuckles, were shooting in the squares and rampaging through the towns. Processions and meetings, demonstrations and protests, festivals and funerals, all wore the same face but a different uniform – except that the SS and SA of the Nazis, and the Red Front of the Communists marched more obstreperously, the Sozi-Reichsbanner more fatly, the Stahlhelmers more sedately. The Reichswehr, the one legal force, was least in evidence, even though it was, in a sense, the private political tool of Hindenburg.[101]

The mood was violent, the atmosphere tense. Berlin had become completely radicalized.

The mood fuelled Nazi success. They became the strongest party in Germany, with 37.3 per cent of the vote and 230 seats. In Berlin Goebbels netted 28.6 per cent of the vote; the next largest party, the Communists, won 24.4 per cent. To Hitler's chagrin Hindenburg refused to make him Chancellor and named von Papen instead, but Hitler was determined to bring down his government even if it meant collaborating with the other mass party, the Communists. There was little need to panic. Von Papen dissolved the Reichstag immediately after his opening speech, prompted by the knowledge that the Nazis and Communists were poised to table a joint motion of no confidence. New elections were called for November, the fourth that year. Shortly afterwards, Goebbels made a speech which captured the political mood in Berlin: 'Things cannot go on as they are,' he said. 'There must be a change. We have the choice: from here on into Bolshevist anarchy or from here on into National Socialist order and discipline.'

* * *

The role of the Communists was crucial at this stage of Hitler's rise to power. Contrary to the legend of Red Berlin, the working-class was far from united. By the end of 1932 one-third of Berlin's labour force was out of work, 60 per cent of metal workers and 90 per cent of those in the building trade were unemployed. Far from uniting them, the Depression set workers against one another, each fighting to save his job or his factory. The shrinking labour market had a particularly devastating effect on the older Social Democratic membership, comprising skilled and white-collar workers, many of whom would be drawn to the Nazis; indeed in the 1930 elections 25.6 per cent of the Berlin Nazi Party were white-collar workers. The other beneficiary of the turmoil was the KPD, the Communist Party.

The Communists of Berlin are often portrayed as the group that resisted the Nazis and 'saved the honour' of Berlin. In reality, they were a destructive force which helped to pave the way for Hitler's rise to power.[102] Much of the blame for this must rest with Stalin.

In 1928 tensions in Berlin between the Nazis and the Communists were mounting fast, but Stalin chose this moment to launch a vicious attack, not against the Nazis, but against the Social Democrats. He sent a message to the Communist Party headquarters warning that the German party was 'lagging behind revolutionary developments'. He reminded the KPD's leaders that although the road to Communism was inevitable the one thing that might divert the masses from their revolutionary destiny was the centre-left Brüning government, and it was important to recognize that the real class enemies were the Social Democrats. The Berlin KPD leadership was to do anything it could to topple the government, even if it meant collaboration with the Nazis. That is precisely what the Communists did.

The timing for this decision was extraordinary. Stalin might have been influenced by the fact that in 1927 the Chinese Communist Party, which on Stalin's instructions had collaborated with the Kuomintang, had just been wiped out by its former ally, making him somewhat reticent about 'common front' tactics. At the same time Russian domestic policy was becoming increasingly extreme, with preparations for the first show trial well underway.[103] The Comintern was equally radical on the international scene and preached to its members that the collapse of capitalism was 'imminent'. Stalin genuinely believed that the Nazis were merely a staging post on the road to Communism which explains why, even after their victory in 1933, he urged the establishment of friendly relations with the Nazis, accepted the persecution of the German Communists, bolstered the links between the Reichswehr and the Red Army, and renewed the German–Russian trade agreement. Stalin's blindness meant that real Communist resistance to the Nazis in Berlin started far too late and was utterly ineffectual.

Obedient as ever the Berlin Communists relentlessly attacked the Weimar government. Silvia Rodgers, whose mother was a Berlin Communist, remembered that she 'put all the blame on the Social Democrats . . . Rosa Luxemburg was right to despise the Social Democrats and regard Ebert, the Social Democratic Chancellor, as the enemy'.[104] In June 1929 Erich Weinert wrote that 'Social Democrats have now become fascists!'[105] Communist agitprop groups such as Die Ketzer (The Heretics) performed skits showing how the SPD had ordered the murder of Rosa Luxemburg and Karl Lieb-knecht; the Red Rockets performed a scene in which the SPD danced to the music of the Krupp concern; and, in November 1930, the Red Torches pre-sented a spectacle in which the audience was asked to decide a punishment for those on stage said to represent capitalism, the Church, the police, the judiciary and the SPD. According to the police report, the audience made 'the most nauseating suggestions about how to punish them'. The police, for example, were to be thrown into the room in which revolutionary sailors had been shot in 1919 and a grenade thrown in after them.[106] On 11 February 1930 Stalin's German representative Ernst Thälmann actually declared that, as the head of government was a Social Democrat, he believed that 'fascism' was 'already in power'. He would later die in Buchenwald at the hands of the Nazis who, needless to say, behaved somewhat differently from the government he had done so much to destroy. As late as September 1932, at a secret conference of KPD functionaries, a speaker called the Socialist Trade Unions and the SPD 'the greatest brakes on our revolutionary policies. If we do not succeed in smashing them, we will never attain the revolution.'[107]

Much has been made of the street fighting between the Nazis and the KPD and there is no doubt that much of it was brutal; even so the brawls were often undertaken by both sides for cynical publicity purposes. Christopher Isherwood noted that there was something false and ritualistic about many of the attacks; the short, violent conflicts would last 'fifteen seconds, and then it was all over and dispersed'. Both sides enjoyed the violence, both wanted to prove that anarchy reigned in Berlin and that the republic had lost control of the streets. In short, the Nazis and the Communists were playing the same game.

In the end the Communists were not so much frightened by the Nazis as increasingly jealous of their success. They were resentful that thousands of their members were defecting to the Nazis. Silvia Rodgers said of her parents: 'My mother and her comrades had to be very cautious about each one of their members. There was danger from infiltrators, but also from their own deserters who could easily turn into informers and betray their former comrades. Too many joined the Nazi bandwagon.' Her parents were stunned when one day a good Communist factory worker turned up at their flat in Nazi uniform.

> My mother and father were stunned. This man, their comrade, stood there in those brown boots, that coarse-textured diarrhoea-coloured uniform, with the aggressive armband of the black bent cross in its white circle on red. He stood there among our furniture ... and he praised Hitler. The Führer, he insisted, was good for Germany and good for the German people. My parents were disgusted and afraid.[108]

The KPD were also jealous of the cult of leadership around Hitler and they tried to turn the dull Ernst Thälmann into a similar figure, selling him as the 'Leader of the German Proletariat'. When this failed they tried to put Hitler's attraction down to support from hysterical females who knew nothing about the realities of politics. In 1932 the left-wing journal *Das freie Wort* carried an article entitled 'The Woman Hitler – Psychology Around a Leader', which dismissed his success as little more than 'feminine quasi-erotic appeal'. The Communists completely underestimated the dynamics of Nazism or the extraordinary power of Hitler as a leader.

The most damning aspect of Communist activity during this period was their deliberate collaboration with the Nazis, which finally helped Hitler to power. There were a number of examples of this. The two parties worked together in the Berlin Transport Strike of November 1932, which had been sparked off by a small reduction in wages. The sight of Joseph Goebbels and Walter Ulbricht (who later became Party Secretary of the East German SED) demonstrating together is one of the most chilling in Berlin history; one witness recalled seeing Nazis and Communists standing arm-in-arm near his house, one shouting 'Red Front' and the other waiting to shout '*Heil* Hitler!' Many in Berlin saw the Nazis and Communists as two sides of the same coin, attested to by the rows of alternating swastika and hammer-and-sickle flags flying side by side from the windows of the *Mietskasernen*.[109] Ernst Thälmann and Hermann Göring often joined forces in the Reichstag to turn parliamentary procedure into farce, and together they pushed through the referendum which forcibly removed the legal Social Democratic government in July 1930. They also collaborated to draft the vote of no confidence which forced von Papen to dissolve the Reichstag and hold the elections that would eventually result in Hitler's victory. Far from 'saving' Berlin, the Communists greatly contributed to its downfall. Both the Nazis and the Communists offered appalling choices for the future. For all those who point to the relatively low vote for the Nazis in the final years of Berlin as somehow saving the reputation of the city, another statistic proves far more revealing. In the final election of 1932

720,000 Berliners voted for Hitler but over 70 per cent voted either for the Communists or the Nazis, the two totalitarian parties which sought the complete destruction of the Weimar Republic.[110]

The final blow to Weimar came after these elections of 6 November. The Nazis remained the largest party in Germany, followed by the Communists. The Nazis had lost support in the rest of Germany but not in Berlin, and the Communists had for the first time overtaken the Social Democrats. Between them the two radical parties held an absolute majority in the Reichstag. To Hitler's disappointment Hindenburg again refused to make him Chancellor, giving the post to General von Schleicher instead. Hitler's bid for power was rescued by the bitter von Papen, who also resented Schleicher's appointment. He decided to use Hitler as a 'stalking horse' to regain his throne. That summer saw a flurry of hurried secret meetings between Hitler, von Papen, the financier Schacht, who, along with von Papen, Oskar von Hindenburg and Otto von Meissner, now lobbied Hindenburg on Hitler's behalf. The demand was simple. Hitler wanted to be Chancellor, and his only other demand was that he be given two further cabinet posts. Von Papen would be made Vice-Chancellor. Surely, it was argued, the conservatives, with their eight ministers, could box Hitler in and prevent him from being anything more than a figurehead. They would simply use him to 'sell' their ideas to the adoring masses. When von Papen was asked about the wisdom of this strategy he proclaimed that he was not in the least bit worried about having Hitler as Chancellor. 'We've hired him,' he said.

Nobody knows what finally weakened Hindenburg's resolve against Hitler but on 30 January 1933 the Austrian demagogue was made Chancellor. Göring became acting Prussian Minister of the Interior, which meant that he controlled the police in three-fifths of the Reich, and Wilhelm Frick became Minister of the Interior. Goebbels, who had brought Hitler his success in Berlin, was passed over for a cabinet post because he was not deemed to be respectable enough. This did not improve relations between Goebbels and the victorious Göring, but within a few weeks the decision was forgotten. A spectacular cabinet room was later built in Hitler's new Reich Chancellery with the names of the ministers embossed in gold on heavy blue ink blotters, but it would never be used. Parliamentary democracy was dead, and for all practical purposes Hitler now controlled the German Reich. Mowrer referred to Hitler's victory as 'the rejection by Germany of 1,000 years of civilisation'.

By 30 January 1933, under the flicker of the torches filing up Unter den Linden, many who had at least nominally supported the Weimar Republic knew that they had finally lost to the advocates of blood and soil and the *Volk*, of racial purity and anti-Semitism, who had been slowly gathering strength in Berlin since the mid 1920s. The dream was over. Many fled or committed suicide; others would soon end up imprisoned, tortured or murdered. Almost immediately the order went out that works of art with 'cosmopolitan and Bolshevist symptoms' were to be burnt, and that 'the names of all those artists who have been swept along by the flood of Marxism and Bolshevism must never be mentioned again in public'. The new Reich Centre for the Advancement of German Literature quickly banned hundreds of 'un-German' books, while the National Socialist Cultural Community began to dictate its pathetic and banal artistic and cultural vision, enforcing the ban on the hated Weimar artists it had despised for so long. In 1933, a few weeks after Hitler came to power, the Hugenberg Press Trust writer Friedrich Hussong wrote in his book *Kurfürstendamm* of his contempt for the Weimar avant-garde, saying of Erwin Piscator's production of *The Good Soldier Schweik*: 'Women wearing *décolletage* down to their navels and diamonds on their shoes screeched their delight at the worst obscenities.' But now:

> A miracle has taken place. They are no longer here. They claimed they were the German *Geist*, German culture, the German present and future. They represented Germany to the world, they spoke in its name ... What they did not permit did not exist ... Whoever served them was sure to succeed. He appeared on their stages, wrote in their journals, was advertised all over the world; his commodity was recommended whether it was cheese or relativity, powder or theatre, patent medicine or human rights, democracy or Bolshevism, propaganda for abortion or against the legal system, rotten Negro music or dancing in the nude. In brief, there was never a more shameless dictatorship than that of the democratic intelligentsia and the *Zivilisationsliteraten*.[111]

Tragically, many of those who lined up on that grey night to cheer Hitler's accession to power were also cheering this vision of a 'cleansed' Berlin. After over a decade of drinking in theories about the *Volk*, the race and the Führer, and after years of social, economic and political turmoil, many Berliners allowed themselves to sink into a collective madness. Despite the brutality, the violence, the purges and the murder soon to stain the streets of Berlin, Hitler's popularity would continue to rise. Over 50,000 Berliners joined the Nazi Party in the month following his accession to power. The blackest period in the history of the city had begun.

XI

Nazi Berlin – Life Before the Storm

> dear son beware
> do not go there
> or you will die
>
> (*Faust*, Part I)

WITH THE NAZI SEIZURE OF POWER Berlin was set to become one of the most important symbols of the 'Thousand Year Reich'. As he surveyed the old industrial streets in 1933 Hitler boasted: 'In ten years nobody will recognize the city.' He was right. The creation of a new capital – to be called 'Germania' – was fundamental to Hitler's vision of the future.[1] 'As the Reich capital of a nation of sixty-five millions ... Berlin must be raised to such a high level of urban planning and culture that it may compete with all the other capital cities of the world.' The renewal of Berlin would be 'the very epitome of what can be accomplished with present-day means'. Hitler promised that the Reich capital would be more beautiful than Paris, more splendid than Vienna, more powerful than ancient Rome; 'Berlin was to be rebuilt and expanded to serve a potential estimated population of eight million people', a task which 'exceeded anything one could imagine'.[2] Far from hating Berlin, Hitler wanted to make it more powerful than it had ever been.

A few months before Hitler took power Siegfried Kracauer wrote: 'Whoever stays for any length of time in Berlin hardly knows in the end where he really came from.' He might well have been speaking about Adolf Hitler. Hitler was no longer the small-town boy from Linz but had already convinced himself of his omnipotence, and the change in his attitudes towards 'modern' Berlin drove the point home. During the 'years of struggle' the city had been criticized as the centre of decadence and modernism; after the seizure of power references to the 'downgrading' of the capital and to the glorification of *völkisch* rural life were gradually abandoned, speeches against technology and progress were toned down and the exploitation of the deep crisis of modernity which had simmered since the nineteenth century was thrust aside. From 1933 it became clear that Berlin was not to be 'peasantized' but would go through the Nazi period with its modern industrial culture intact.[3] To the chagrin of doctrinaire followers the city was no longer to be treated as 'inherently decadent' but was merely to be 'cleansed' of its 'Jewish-Bolshevik' elements; others would be permitted to stay as long as they accepted the new order. Hitler may not have liked Berlin as it had been, but he was determined to create a capital city worthy of being at the centre of his Thousand Year Reich.[4]

The co-ordination of all ministries and government offices in Berlin con-tradicted the early Nazi-*völkisch* ideal, but was consistent with the creation of a system which could sustain the future war effort. When fanatics like Himmler and Rosenberg complained that Hitler had turned against their *Blut und Boden* ideas by concentrating all power in the city they were told to conform. Resentment towards Berlin was particularly strong in the rest of the country after Hitler cancelled the independence of the eighteen German states and Hansa towns and transferred all sovereign power to the Reich capital, and many local authorities complained that this went against his promise to devolve power rather than extend Bismarck's 1871 policy of centralization.[5] Hitler did not care. By the end of the 1930s he had made Berlin the mightiest city in Europe, and as Bavarians and Rhinelanders fumed its industrial, political and military power overshadowed them all.

Senior Nazis moved to the capital with remarkable speed and competed with one another for offices close to the Reich Chancellery and their venerated Führer. The new cluster ranged from Goebbels's Ministry of Propaganda and Enlightenment, to Göring's Air Ministry; from the Foreign Office, where the ridiculous 'von' Ribbentrop would later play the elder statesman, to the head office of the Reichsbahn, where the transports of human beings would be so meticulously planned; from the Interior Ministry to the headquarters of Himmler's SS, which would become the most feared address in the world. The lives of millions would be manipulated from the offices which bristled down the Wilhelmstrasse, the Bellevuestrasse, Prinz-Albrecht-Strasse and Unter den Linden, and when orders 'came directly from Berlin' they would be obeyed without question. For the next twelve years Berlin was the very seat of Nazi authority and its name would provoke envy, terror, wrath or pride – but rarely indifference – in all who heard it. The infamous expression, 'Hitler is Germany and Germany is Hitler,' was soon extended by locals to read: 'Berlin is the Reich, and the Reich is Berlin.'[6]

The torches which sizzled and smoked down Unter den Linden on 30 January signalled the beginning of Hitler's so-called 'bloodless revolution'. The SA fighting had stopped, the streets were safe for the first time in years and many Berliners believed that Hitler had brought lasting peace. Hitler had not turned against violence; he was merely waiting until he could strike with impunity. In those first weeks he was still relatively weak: he depended on Hindenburg's signature to pass his emergency decrees, he had to avoid antagonizing the army and he was forced to restrain his attacks on the Communists for fear of shattering the brittle veneer of legality which he needed for the final elections in the spring. His only controversial action was to pass the 5 February 'Law for the Protection of the German People', which empowered the police to raid the Communist headquarters at Karl Liebknecht house, an act which Hitler hoped would provoke a Communist backlash. When nothing happened he paced up and down in his office in frustration, hurling violent abuse against his fellow cabinet members who were preventing him from taking action.[7] It is difficult to know how long this 'legalistic' phase would have lasted had it not been for another of those extraordinary events in Berlin history: the Reichstag fire.

At 9.10 p.m. on the cool evening of 27 February 1933 a young printer named Werner Thaler was walking home from work. As he approached the Reichstag he heard the sound of breaking glass. Fearing it was being burgled he told a nearby policeman, who saw flames licking up inside the old tinder-box and called for the fire brigade. Shortly afterwards a half-witted Dutch plasterer, Marinus van der Lubbe, was dragged from the blazing building. He readily admitted to having set the fire 'so the workers could have power', but he also insisted that he had acted alone. Thus began an unsolved mystery which gave Hitler the excuse he needed to crush his opponents, and which changed the course of German history.[8]

Nobody is certain who masterminded the fire – did the strange Dutchman act alone, or was the fire instigated by the Nazis in order to speed their consolidation of power? The obvious advantages accruing from it have led many to believe that Hitler must have been involved, but others see it as one in a series of providential accidents which he then ruthlessly exploited. No evidence has as yet emerged which directly links Hitler to van der Lubbe.

On the evening of the fire Hitler had gone to a small party at Goebbels's house to discuss the plans for the upcoming elections and for the celebration of the Day of National Awakening. Ernst (Putzi) Hanfstängl, then head of the Foreign Press department, had been invited by Magda Goebbels but had decided to remain at Göring's residence, where he was staying to nurse a severe cold. His sleep was interrupted late in the evening by a flickering light. At that moment the maid burst in and told him that the Reichstag was on fire. Hanfstängl immediately telephoned Goebbels and shouted the news but Goebbels, convinced that it was a practical joke, hung up. Hitler told Goebbels to phone back. A few minutes later he told Hanfstängl that Hitler wanted to know what was going on but that he wanted 'no more of your jokes, now'. Hanfstängl repeated that the Reichstag was burning, and that if they did not believe him they should come down and see for themselves. He then slammed down the phone.[9]

Hanfstängl disliked Goebbels intensely, referring to him as a 'consummate liar'. Even so, he later said that both Goebbels and Hitler had sounded genuinely surprised by the news. The two men rushed to the Reichstag, which by now had been cordoned off by the police. A vast crowd watched as every fire engine in the city sped to the area while fire boats on the Spree poured a huge fountain of water over the blazing landmark. There was a gasp as the Kaiser's great cupola collapsed in a crash of glass and copper. One of the first foreign journalists on the scene was Sefton Delmer, who learned that the police had captured one of the arsonists and was told that given the size of the blaze 'there must be more inside', but nobody else was found. Hermann Göring was also at the scene and Delmer heard him say he was convinced that this was the signal for the start of a Communist uprising and that he had given the order that all other public buildings be guarded. Later that evening Göring greatly exaggerated the amount of fuel found at the scene in order to implicate the Communists. It was rumoured amongst foreign journalists, including William Shirer, that Karl Ernst, head of the Berlin SA, might possibly have used the tunnel between Göring's office and the Reichstag, but although the passage existed there was no evidence that anyone had been through it. Delmer recalled that when they met von Papen Hitler had ranted, 'God grant that this is the work of the Communists ... you are witnessing the beginning of a great new epoch in German history. This fire is the beginning ... you see this building? You see how it is aflame? If the Communists got hold of Europe and had control of it for but two months the whole continent would be aflame like this building.'[10]

Whoever was ultimately responsible for the blaze, it was the excuse Hitler needed. All through the night Hitler, Goebbels and Göring drafted anti-Communist policies and spread their net to capture other 'enemies of the state'. They were joined by the 'Communist specialist' Rudolf Diels of the Gestapo (then under Göring's control), who had just interrogated van der Lubbe. He reported that he believed the Dutchman had acted alone but he nevertheless provided Göring with a list of prominent Communists who could easily be rounded up 'on suspicion' of complicity in the 'plot'. The reign of terror began on that night, exactly one month after Hitler had taken power.

The shell of the Reichstag was still smouldering when the SA were let loose in the city. Four thousand functionaries of the KPD and other prominent left-wing activists heard the dreaded pounding at the door in the early hours of the morning and well-known Berliners – from Carl von Ossietzky to Egon

Kisch – were dragged from their beds. Social Democrats were also rounded up, their party offices occupied and all their newspapers banned; the SPD would officially cease to exist on 22 June. Social Democrats and Communists were astounded at the accusations levelled against their respective parties and many showed up at police stations protesting their innocence. The most famous of these was Ernst Togler, the head of the Communist Party Reichstag Delegation, who went to assure the police that his party had not started the fire and were in no way plotting to overthrow the government. The delighted SA men simply threw him into prison. Meanwhile, Hitler and Goebbels read out the proclamations justifying the incarcerations as necessary for the crushing of a 'planned Communist revolution', and in an article written for *Der Angriff* early that morning Goebbels asserted that the Communists were to be annihilated so that not even the name remained to sully German history.

Hitler moved extraordinarily quickly. The next day, 28 February 1933, he passed the Reichstag Fire Decrees and began the process known as the *Gleichschaltung*, the 'bringing into line' or 'co-ordination' of power, which not only made him the master of Germany but also made Berlin the undisputed centre of the Reich. 'Co-ordination' spelled the official end to autonomous provincial governments and agencies, and shifted ultimate authority over virtually every aspect of life to Berlin.[11]

The new laws had far-reaching consequences. Hindenburg, who believed the fatuous claims of a Communist conspiracy, signed an emergency decree which suspended all constitutionally guaranteed rights and which extended the death penalty. The decree 'For the Protection of the People and the State' was enhanced by a decree 'Against Treason against the German People and Seditious Actions'. Civil liberties ceased to exist.[12] People could be arrested without charge, the Prussian state police was turned over to the head of the Berlin SS and the Berlin police was put into the hands of Göring's men. Entire housing estates in Berlin's working-class districts were sealed off and meticulously combed by the SA, SS, police, fire brigade and Technical Emergency Service for any evidence of resistance. All weapons and illegal literature were seized and even footballs or musical instruments which might hold suspect material were taken away. The thoroughness of these raids made it virtually impossible for opponents of the regime to organize any serious protest.[13] At the same time, Berlin prisons, cellars and deserted factories began to fill with 'enemies of the state'.

The most brutal members of the SA, those who had proved themselves in the years of street fighting, were given the task of dealing with the prisoners. The round-ups continued throughout March 1933, with SA men searching out their Communist counterparts and settling accounts from the street-fighting days. The thugs broke into flats and houses, threatening people at gunpoint and tormenting their frightened victims. Passports were routinely confiscated so that even if prisoners were released from custody they could not escape abroad. Famous Berliners from Social Democrats like Julius Leber to trade union officials like Wilhelm Leuschner, from the heads of radio stations and newspaper columnists to the anarchist Erich Mühsam, simply disappeared. Silvia Rodgers recalled that when a cell of eight men was infiltrated by the Brownshirts they did not arrest them but 'simply locked the place up so the cellar could not be opened from the inside. No food, no water, no air. The eight men died within two weeks.'[14] 'Ali' Höhler, the Communist hooligan who had murdered Horst Wessel, was dragged from a cell in Berlin to a forest on the outskirts of town and hacked to pieces, the murderers cutting into the tattoos which criss-crossed his body.

The SA now took over the Berlin prisons. The vast Berlin police head-quarters on Alexanderplatz, once the office of Goebbels's nemesis 'Isador' Weiss, became the central collecting post.[15] The labyrinthine corridors were replenished every night with the bewildered victims of the latest round-up. The 600 spaces were soon filled as ever more people were crammed together in the tiny cells. Newcomers were made to kneel on carbines and were hit in the face until they confessed to whatever crime it was they were supposed to have committed, and it was standard practice for new arrivals to have their noses or jaws broken. Those lucky enough to get out at this stage were often unrecognizable to their families and friends. One eye witness wrote that his cell in Alexanderplatz was filled 'with sixty-two other prisoners. These men, mostly working men and Jewish passers-by, had been beaten half to death. I saw men whose eyes had been gouged out. The teeth of most of them had been knocked out with rifle butts. Their hands had been burned. All the Jews had been thrown on the floor and the Nazi storm troopers had jumped on them until they fainted.'[16]

The influx of prisoners was so great that even the vast Alexanderplatz and the huge Tegel Prison, which had held Döblin's Franz Biberkopf, could not accommodate more people. A 'practical remedy' had to be found. The solution was one of the blackest inventions of Berlin history, for it was then that the first random or 'wild' concentration camps were created – camps which would evolve into larger and more deadly places. The first 'wild' camps were known simply as 'beating stations', and there were more than fifty of them in Berlin in 1933–4 alone.[17] There was another reason for the creation of these camps; the SA, the Gestapo and the SS were still in the throes of a power struggle and Diels's Gestapo would often snatch victims from the clutches of the SA and bring them to his headquarters in the Prinz-Albrecht-Strasse for his own purposes. The SA resented this interference and knew that if prisoners 'dis-appeared' into the dark recesses of one of the camps they would be difficult to find. Many of the camps were located in cellars or back courtyards of buildings in central and popular streets like the Friedrichstrasse, Rosinestrasse, or the Kastanienallee. SA strongholds included the Gladenecksche Villa in Köpenick, and the Universum Exhibition Centre in the middle of the Tiergarten. Several still stand unmarked, including the Kaserne in the General-Pape-Strasse and the disused water tower on the Knaackstrasse in Prenzlauer Berg. The SA devised appalling tortures for their victims. In the SA Feldpolizei on General-Pape-Strasse an ex-prisoner reported how he had been brought to the dark red-brick building.

I was 18 years old . . . I was called into a first-aid room. The SA called out. 'The young one there, pants down, penis out!' They injected something into my urinary tract although I tried to hinder its progress by constricting my muscles . . . Then I had to move up a passage on my knees. Two SA-men escorted me and kicked me in my groin and then in my buttocks so that I fell forward. I was handed over to other SA-men . . . six of us were forced to lie on our stomachs with our hands flat on the floor. The men then stepped on our feet, our legs, our hands . . . a pair of them had some flat-nose pliers with which they pulled out fingernails and hair . . . On the next day when I relieved myself I noticed that the acid had done its work and it burned painfully.[18]

The SA were particularly bloodthirsty; in the infamous June 'Köpenick Blood Week' over 500 people were rounded up in a few days and were systematically tortured. Ninety-one were murdered. The Gestapo were also brutal; Ernst Thälmann was imprisoned in the Prinz-Albrecht-Strasse between 9 and 23 January 1934 and was repeatedly interrogated. Four of his teeth were knocked out and then 'a uniformed Gestapo officer with a whip of hippopotamus hide in his hand beat my buttocks with measured strokes. Driven wild with pain I repeatedly screamed at the top of my voice. Then they held my mouth shut for a while and hit me in the face, and with a whip across the chest and back. I then collapsed.'[19]

The SS also had its own centres, including the infamous Columbia Haus which was located on the Potsdamer Platz. A SOPADE secret report recorded the experiences of dozens of people who managed to live through the tortures meted out there.[20] One was a Social Democratic functionary who was brought to the centre, stripped naked and repeatedly beaten. 'I was dragged outside, was sprayed with a water hose, and pissed on. I was thrown in a cell without a bed or window and although it was November there was no heating. I was forced to lie on the floor . . . in eight days of this I lost forty pounds.' Another typical case was that of Hans Litten, a Stahlhelm member and a lawyer, whose 'great crime' had been to question whether the Nazi Party was 'law abiding' in 1931.[21] Litten was rounded up one night and taken to the camp at Sonnenburg. By the time he got to Spandau his jaw had been broken, his cheeks were in rags, his teeth had been bashed in and his hearing and vision were impaired. He was removed by a Gestapo detective who wanted to reverse the verdict of one of his last trials. Under severe torture he agreed to sign anything, but later scrawled a letter to the Gestapo declaring his confession false. He then tried to commit suicide. Next he was moved to Columbia Haus, where he was beaten with whips which left his flesh lacerated. When he was finally moved to the Brandenburg camp he was so misshapen and his injuries so terrible that none of the other inmates would share his cell. Even so, the SS, already exhibiting signs of their inhuman perversity, found former clients who were forced to beat him directly in the face. Litten was then thrown into a pit of filth and prison urine, where he eventually died.

The SA and the SS were already developing a peculiar brand of sadism. They devised situations in which fellow prisoners were forced to beat one another, and they entertained themselves by meticulously recording how long it took before the man or woman would pick up the whip or how many times they would have to be threatened before they acted. They particularly enjoyed forcing friends to beat one another, revelling in the debasement and the dehumanization of their victims. Karl Billinger, prisoner number 880 in Columbia Haus, reported how one Jewish prisoner was forced to attack another:

> The SS began to rain blows thick and fast over their heads and necks and backs, while like a maniac the officer kept yelling, 'Forward! Forward!' Hesitantly, appalled by what he was doing, then more rapidly to escape the onslaught of the guards, the older Jew struck the younger a blow – and another – until at length he was laying about him in a frenzy, his face racked with agony, his eyes glaring with madness. The younger man never so much as lifted his arms to ward off the blows about his head ... Erect and silent, he stood till he collapsed.[22]

Another victim, the *Weltbühne* journalist Kurt Hiller, was taken to Columbia Haus, had his nose and teeth smashed in and was beaten nearly senseless. He was then put on a wooden table in the basement, where some twenty SS men stood and laughed as he was given fifty searing lashes. With his back and buttocks a bloody mass he was doused with freezing water and forced to stand upright in an empty cell. Whenever he flagged he was hauled out for the 'bear dance', a humiliating ritual in which prisoners were forced to skip around the courtyard in oversized boots with no laces while singing children's songs. Hiller's kidneys, which had been badly damaged by the beatings, began to fail.

As his legs swelled he was put in tight shackles to increase the pain. A doctor was brought in and recommended bed rest and salt tablets, but when he left the guard yelled that the visit had been a hoax. Hiller was again made to dance around the prison yard until he dropped, was picked up and forced on again, his enormous legs in excruciating pain. He was fortunate to survive his ordeal.[23]

The memories of these people still linger in Berlin. When I lived in West Berlin I discovered that an innocuous café near the U-Bahn station across from my house was a place from which the SA had sometimes seized their victims. Late in the evening in November 1933 the handsome young actor Hans Otto, a leader of the German Workers' Theatre League, was having a quiet meal in the back when the SA arrived. He had been betrayed, probably by someone in the café. The thugs brought him to the SA centre called the Café Komet, which was another little SA joke. As the band played, the victim was beaten, kicked and hit in the face in time to the music. After four days Otto was moved to Köpenick and chained along with other men and women, some of whom had been there for weeks. From there he was brought to the Möllendorfstrasse, and then to the Gestapo headquarters in Prinz-Albrecht-Strasse, where he was starved of food and water and regularly beaten. Shortly afterwards he was moved to the Vossstrasse, where his friend Gerhard Hinze saw him. 'It must have been around midnight,' Hinze wrote. 'He could no longer speak, but only mumbled. His mouth and his eyes were thickly swollen ... a few hours later I saw him for the last time. He was half naked, and I could no longer recognize his face. His body was a bloody mass. He was unconscious.' The next day Hans Otto died.[24]

The sufferings of many of these prisoners must have been aggravated by their proximity to normal life. Merrymakers on their way past the SA building near the Friedrichstrasse nightclubs could have heard the screams of the tortured victims floating up from the cells; the SA Feldpolizei building in the General-Pape-Strasse was next to pretty residential homes and gardens; Hiller died within sight of Tempelhof Airport, through which foreign dignitaries and movie stars passed every day; and other victims at Columbia Haus noticed that loud music was played during torture sessions in order to cover the noise. Even so, the plight of the thousands of prisoners was generally ignored by a people who believed in the propaganda about 're-education' areas and in the urgent need for order. Hundreds of people rotted in the basements and stinking deserted factories of Berlin and many 'committed suicide' or were 'shot trying to escape'. When the torturers were challenged, even by fellow Nazis, they yelled that they were sick of being told what to do by party members who had been sitting in safety while they were 'having their heads bashed in by these red bastards you want to help now'.[25]

The situation was to deteriorate further with the opening in March 1933 of the first permanent concentration camp in an old brewery in Berlin – Concentration Camp of District 208, or Oranienburg. This place became a model for future camps throughout the Reich. The Nazis forced the prisoners, none of whom had been convicted of any crime, to build rows of sheds filled with cramped bunk-beds. The prisoners were made to rise at 5.30 in the morning, were given some bread and *ersatz* coffee and were marched out to work as labourers in full view of free Berliners. Many humiliating tortures were devised in the camp, the most notorious being the cells or 'coffins' made of stone, which were so small that a human being could barely be squeezed in. Prisoners singled out for punishment were forced to stand in these terrible boxes for days on end. One victim described them as a horrendous medieval torture in which prisoners underwent inexpressible torment, slowly feeling 'their limbs becoming numbed from below and beginning to ache, the knees beginning to sag and graze the walls, eternally wondering where to put one's arms and how to go on standing ... it is simply a hell, and the man who devised it is not a human being but a beast'.[26]

Nobody knows how many Communists, Social Democrats, Jews or pacifists were arrested, tortured, beaten or killed in the first months of Hitler's rule. Hitler himself claimed that there had 'only' been 300 killed and 40,000 wounded in the first three months – which enabled him to continue to boast of a 'bloodless revolution' – but he was pleased by the 'actions'. In 1933 Göring was heard reporting to Hitler: 'I have just had to sign twenty-two death sentences for your approval.' They were 'very satisfied with themselves, rubbing their hands ... It had obviously become a matter of routine, and no clemency was exercised'.[27] Rudolf Diels estimated that between 5,000 and 6,000 KDP and SPD members had been imprisoned in Berlin alone in the two months since Hitler came to power and that a 'substantial number' of these people had been killed. By the end of July 1933 there were more than 10,000 Germans languishing in 'protective custody' in the camps around Berlin, including Oranienburg, while others were now sent to concentration camps like Dachau and Esterwegen. The initial attacks on the Communists and Social Democrats would soon spread to the Jews, to members of the Roman Catholic and Protestant Churches, and then to anyone who dared to voice dissent against the regime. Hitler distanced himself from the violence and pretended to be shocked by the excesses although he was well aware of what was going on.[28] The vast majority of Berliners chose to ignore the rumours or the testimony of those who had managed to get out of this system alive, and it was in this atmosphere of furtive violence and mass self-deception that the final contested democratic elections were held in Nazi Germany. This would have been the last realistic opportunity for a mass protest against the Nazis and their increasingly bloody repression, but many people quietly approved of Hitler's policies. For them he was simply 'cleaning up the streets'. The election date was set for 5 March 1933.

Forced to proceed 'legally' Hitler was determined that these would be the 'last elections', whatever the outcome. Goebbels's propaganda machine went into high gear, with its speeches, parades, and full use of the radio. One of his most cynical creations was 'Potsdam Day', symbolizing the national awakening and the reconciliation of the 'old' and 'new' Germanys. All the sentimental kitsch of the mythical Prussian past was there: Frederick the Great's tomb, the black and white banners of Old Prussia, the pretty Potsdam setting. There, in front of banners and bunting and flags, Hitler joined the mass of First World War generals and Prussian aristocrats, Hohenzollern princes, industrial magnates and heel-clicking sycophants, all of whom pledged their allegiance to the 'new Germany'. With tears in his eyes, Hindenburg, in the uniform of imperial field marshal, shook hands with a deferential Hitler, who bowed before him dressed in sombre top hat and tails. This image became a powerful symbol of the new era, while the sight of polished boots and uniforms and medals glinting in the sun gave Hitler the appearance of legitimacy and stability; a great theatrical parody of Prusso-German reconciliation posing as a legitimate political act.[29] Postcards began to appear with the heads of Frederick the Great, Bismarck, Hindenburg and Hitler arranged in a long logical line, an image which made conservatives feel more at ease with the Austrian corporal.[30]

The elections were not the overwhelming triumph Goebbels had hoped for. The Nazis captured 43.9 per cent of the vote and so remained nominally dependent on the compliant nationalist DNVP, with their 8 per cent. In Berlin Hitler received 34.6 per cent of the vote, and Goebbels quickly turned the results into a 'victory and a glorious triumph'. Two days later the Reichstag convened in the Kroll Opera House, its entrances patrolled by the black-uniformed SS and their ferocious dogs to prevent unwanted delegates from entering to vote against Hitler's 'Enabling Act'. The Nazis had little to fear. The Communist deputies were in prison, as were twenty-one Social Democratic representatives. All parties, with the exception of the few remaining Social Democrats, voted of their own free will to hand over dictatorial power to Hitler. To his great credit Otto Wels, the SPD leader, delivered one of the most courageous speeches ever made in Berlin, risking his life to condemn the Nazis openly. It was the last oppositional speech made in the Third Reich, but it fell on deaf ears. The Act was passed. Anyone who stood in his way could now be legally removed, and the outlawed Communist Party was quickly followed by the right-wing Nationalists and then by the People's Party.

Notwithstanding the terror thousands of Berliners now flocked to join the Nazis.[31] Goebbels was particularly impressed by the number of former Red

Front fighters who came over to the SA and, as further inducement to the working classes, he announced that the first of May was to be a German national holiday inaugurated by a huge event on the Tempelhof field. The master plan still exists, giving some insight into Goebbels's meticulous skill. Each section of the vast field was blocked out and allotted to a particular group; the parade routes were outlined and the 'spontaneous demonstrations of joy' carefully rehearsed.[32] As a result, the impact of the event was staggering; aerial photographs show a swarm of people over the area and Goebbels wrote in his diary that Berliners,

> who only a few years earlier had been shooting each other with machine guns, had all turned out for the event – with wives and children – workers and middle class, high and low . . . A wild intoxication of enthusiasm has seized hold of everyone. Full of strength and conviction, the 'Horst Wessel Song' soars toward the eternal night sky. The airwaves carry the voices . . . across all Germany . . . we have become a united people of brothers.[33]

Goebbels was exaggerating, of course, but encouraged by such vast staged events workers turned their backs on their parties and unions, and on 2 May SS and SA units moved in and occupied union headquarters and workers' credit unions and seized all remaining Social Democratic property and financial holdings. There was no resistance.[34] A new law of July 1933 banned all remaining parties, including the Social Democrats, and all rival organizations, including the once venerated Stahlhelm. There was now only one thorn in Hitler's side. This time it came from his own party, in the form of the troublesome SA.

The militant revolutionary members of the SA had for years been the most important fighting force in Berlin. In their own eyes they had 'taken' the city for Goebbels and had been instrumental in agitating against the Communists, frightening the middle classes and bringing Hitler to power. Now, the 2.5 million members wanted their just reward. They were growing impatient with what they saw as Hitlers' deference to the forces of reaction. They detested his kow-towing to Hindenburg and the army and the industrialists. 'Adolf has gone soft,' they muttered as they talked of a 'second revolution' which would create a true SA soldiers' state made by and for the fighting man. The most anxious to fulfil this dream was Ernst Röhm, the head of the SA, who wanted to see the 'grey rock' of the Wehrmacht swallowed up in the 'brown flood' of the SA. He repeatedly told Hitler that he wanted the SA to form the basis of the new Germany army, and that he wanted to be its commander-in-chief. Röhm was becoming increasingly belligerent and attacked Hess, Goebbels,

Göring, Himmler and Hitler, whom he scathingly referred to as 'the artist'. He was a dangerous and unruly force, but he had made powerful enemies and his days were numbered.

Hitler had long mistrusted Röhm and as early as January 1933 had begun to gather evidence against him, concentrating primarily on his bi-sexuality and his lecherous private life. Ironically it was the corpulent 20-stone Hermann Göring who took on the task of cataloguing Röhm's moral indiscretions – this from a man who, when not washing his cocaine down with Dom Pérignon, would dress in jewels and bearskin coats and ridiculous uniforms which would have made even Kaiser William II blush. By June 1934 Göring, Himmler and Heydrich had convinced Hitler that Röhm was indeed plotting a coup against him, and Hitler decided to act. He telephoned Röhm, asking him to gather the top SA men together on 30 June for a meeting in a small *pension* near Munich. Röhm was delighted to comply, convinced that at last Hitler was about to offer him a new army. Like so many others, he had badly underestimated the Führer.

The round-up began almost immediately. Hitler flew to Munich and drove to the hotel at Bad Weissee, where Röhm and his men were still sleeping. The SA had been celebrating their 'victory' the night before and when Hitler got there many had passed out while others, like Edmund Heines, were in bed with young men. Hitler, Goebbels and their aides rushed through the corridors kicking in doors and herding the baffled and joking SA men into waiting cars. When Hitler reached Röhm's room he was alone, although the rumour would later be planted that he had been in bed with a young SA recruit. Röhm just managed a garbled '*Heil* Hitler' before he too was bundled into a waiting car. The SA men were taken to Munich's Stadelheim Prison, assembled in the central courtyard, and shot. Hitler already knew about Röhm's homosexuality in 1932, when letters from the lover he had taken while a mercenary in Bolivia had fallen into his hands; nevertheless he feigned horror at the discovery of Röhm's 'perversion' during the Night of the Long Knives. As Hanfstängl put it, this was 'pure invention' and a convenient excuse for his death.[35] Röhm, one of Hitler's oldest friends and one of the few people he addressed with the informal '*du*', was placed in a cell and shot after the Führer had left for Berlin.

Berliners out on the streets on the afternoon of 30 June could sense that something was about to happen. The American ambassador, Dodd, described the atmosphere as 'tense and edgy', like 'Paris on the eve of the Great Terror'. Albert Speer, who was unaware of the impending bloodbath, felt that there was definitely 'something cooking' when he saw groups of the SS milling around the Reichstag. It was Göring who had been left in charge of the Berlin operation and when Hitler relayed the code-name *Kolibri* (Hummingbird) to him the local operation was launched. The Night of the Long Knives in Berlin was particularly bloody. Dozens of SA men were rounded up by SS firing squads and shot in the courtyard of the Lichterfelde cadet school and at Prinz-Albrecht-Strasse. Hitler also used the opportunity to rid himself of 'difficult' figures who had nothing to do with the SA but who might at some point challenge his authority. Gregor Strasser, who had long opposed Hitler's 'conservatism', was taken by ten men to Gestapo headquarters, where he was murdered. General Kurt von Schleicher was shot in the study of his beautiful Berlin villa along with his wife, who had tried to protect him. Another Reichswehr general, Kurt von Bredow, was shot in the head after answering his doorbell. The Catholic Action leader Erich Klausener was also murdered. Von Papen was spared only because Hitler thought he might still be of some use, although his private secretary Edgar Jung was shot. When the dust settled Berliners learned that over 200 people had been killed that night. Astoundingly, most Berliners celebrated, convinced that it spelled the demise of the SA and the street violence which had racked Berlin for over a decade. Hitler was praised for his 'courage', and when Goebbels ordered flags to be hung for 2 July Berliners celebrated the victory over the 'criminal revolt'.[36]

These events marked a fundamental change in the face of Nazi Berlin. Röhm's enormous SA organization had been made up of men who enjoyed street fighting and brawling for its own sake, and their methods were obvious and crass. These would be replaced by an altogether different kind of violence, masterminded by Heinrich Himmler.[37]

The Night of the Long Knives was the most important moment in Heinrich Himmler's career. When Hitler required a tough force to murder fellow Nazis he called not on the police or the Gestapo or on any other body; he called on Himmler and his elite SS. In early 1929 the SS had consisted of only 300 men, but by 1933 Himmler had increased the Munich-based force to 50,000. He and his assistant Reinhard Heydrich had patiently worked their way up in Hitler's favour, finally moving to Berlin in 1934 and wresting control of the Gestapo from the resentful Göring. The secret police, which had been created under Rudolf Diels in April 1933, already had the power to shadow, arrest, wiretap, interrogate and intern without reference to any other state authority. Himmler quickly rid himself of the comparatively mild Diels and turned the Gestapo into an arm of his terrifying security system, augmenting it with Heydrich's SD (Sicherheitsdienst), which had carried out all the intelligence work for the Night of the Long Knives. With every drop of blood shed that night, Himmler climbed higher in Hitler's favour.[38]

The changes wrought after 1934 brought Himmler immense power. He was given responsibility for the fifteen SA detention camps, including Oranien-burg, and soon co-ordinated all of them under a special arm of the SS, the Totenkopfverbände (Order of the Death's Head), which would carry out unspeakable crimes even before it was put in charge of the creation of more camps and then organizing mass exterminations in special camps like Treblinka and Auschwitz-Birkenau. By the end of 1938 the Verfügungstruppen and Death's Head units already numbered 20,000 men. Himmler moved fast to consolidate his power in other areas. His dream was to create a new 'elite' Germany, a 'state within a state', and in many ways he succeeded.[39] On 17 June 1936 he was appointed head of the now unified police forces of the Reich and Reichsführer of the SS, and from this position of strength he created hundreds of SS organizations throughout Germany, from SS mobile troops to SS economic and administrative offices. Himmler would head the Office for Race and Settlement and, to the fury of the Wehrmacht, would create the rival Waffen-SS, which grew to an unbelievable forty divisions. The thousands of people attached to the SS were not governed by the state but operated under a law of their own, responsible to Himmler, who in turn answered only to Hitler.

It was Himmler above all who changed the face of Nazi terror. Unlike Röhm, Himmler disliked obvious violence and he quickly replaced the SA thuggery with a well-organized but largely covert system of control. The coarse brown shirts were replaced by the black-uniformed SS, who carried out the 'cleansing' and murder of human beings in a quiet, dispassionate, clinical, systematic way. Ideally, there would be no photographs, and all rumours could easily be refuted in propaganda. Himmler's methods influenced every level of Berlin society. The legal system became a travesty of justice. People were arrested on a whim; they had no rights, and sentences were often ignored once an individual was in a prison camp. Freisler's 'People's Court' punished the nature of the offender rather than the crime; if a tall 'Germanic' youth committed a minor offence he would merely be reprimanded, whereas if a Jew or a homosexual committed the same offence he would probably die in a camp. Himmler vigorously enforced punishment of the bizarre new 'race crimes' to prevent sexual relations between Aryans and 'non-Aryans'. For sexual relations between Jews and Aryans the normal ten-year sentence was often increased to death if coitus could be proved to have occurred. Later, when Berlin was flooded with foreign slave labourers identified by large letters (Poles, for example, were forced to wear a large letter 'P'), relations between German women and foreign labourers was a grave offence — the German woman often had her head shaved and was paraded through the streets while the man was either imprisoned or hanged.[40]

It is still shocking to look through SS, SD and Gestapo files and to see how many people both accepted and aided the Nazis in their quest for total conformity. Not including figures for the SS or the SD, in 1943 alone there were over 45,000 Gestapo men in Germany who employed over 60,000 agents and had over 100,000 official informers; this does not include the millions of people who in one way or another spied, reported and informed of their own volition or worked as part-time agents. Some informers were motivated by self-interest – they sought promotion by showing loyalty to the state, or immunity by diverting attention from their own indiscretions. Some concocted evidence in order to settle old personal vendettas; others were genuinely motivated by Nazi ideology. Whatever the reasons, those few who harboured Jews, those who gave food to forced labourers, those who made rude jokes or questioned Nazi foreign policy always had to fear a knock at the door in the early hours of the morning, a hurried lonely trip to the Prinz-Albrecht-Strasse, interrogation, beating, and possibly death by execution or in a camp.[41]

Nazi informers were everywhere: the system could not have functioned as it did without the participation of thousands of people – men, women and even children – who made it very dangerous for those trying to help someone evade the system. Berlin cafés and *Hinterhöfe* and offices were filled with people willing to betray others, perhaps by letting a bit of gossip slip to a local party boss, or by having a quiet word with the Gestapo, or by writing to the police. This occurred at every level of Berlin society; people reported everything from treasonous behaviour, which carried the death penalty, to the most pathetic and petty indiscretions.[42] When Hess made the announcement in 1933 that 'Every Party and fellow comrade impelled by honest concern for the movement and the nation shall have access to the Führer or me without the risk of being taken to task', he and Hitler received such a flood of letters from people with something or somebody to 'report' that he had to make another speech reversing the plea. The government was later given the task of dealing with the many informers on 'anti-state' activity but by the mid 1930s the response was again so great that Minister Lammers, the head of the Reich Chancellery, appealed to Goebbels to somehow curb this enthusiasm. New signs posted on the public transportation system reading A FARE-DODGER'S PROFIT IS THE BERLINER'S LOSS led to thousands of non-paying passengers being reported to the police; Goebbels's request for information on those who dared to utter 'unpatriotic' thoughts was soon answered by friends, relatives and neighbours eager to give evidence. When Karma Rauhut defiantly brought a copy of *The Threepenny Opera* to her school in Berlin a friend contemplated denouncing her. After the war Karma discovered that she had refrained because 'I talked about it with my parents and [they] said not to do it. You don't know what her parents are and what kinds of connections they have . . . *That* was the reason.'[43] To Rauhut it seemed as if the organizations 'were *everywhere* and the human beings reported each other and one watched the other'. Her father was reported for going to see a film with an English newsreel while on a business trip in Switzerland; once back in Berlin he was hauled in for questioning and asked to explain his behaviour.

There was little sympathy for the victims of denunciation, while those known to have informed were rarely ostracized by their neighbours. One *Berlinerin* I talked to remembered being taken in for questioning about her son in full view of the other residents in her apartment block. Although she was quickly released even her 'friends' stopped talking to her upon her return, some out of fear and others out of obvious disdain. An element of *Schaden-freude*, a delight in the misery of others, crept through the city under the Nazis, and the files hold a miserable catalogue of treachery amongst ordinary people, with children denouncing their parents for telling jokes about the Führer, or wives arranging for the secret police to overhear the treasonous talk of their unwanted husbands, or spies in the *Hinterhöfe* reporting everything from prostitution to listening to foreign radio. People who helped the Jews were at particular risk and by 1937 it was dangerous to even be seen speaking to a Jew. This was taken to extremes: a Berlin woman went to visit some Jewish friends only to find that they had disappeared; rather than explain the situation the porter's wife told her not to ask questions and to 'go quickly, otherwise someone hearing us talk will tell the Gestapo'.[44]

As Himmler increased his power over everyday aspects of Berliners' lives, Hitler strengthened his hold on the state. Shortly after the Night of the Long Knives President Hindenburg became mortally ill. He died on 1 August 1934. This removed the final obstacle to Hitler's complete control of Germany. He immediately declared himself President as well as Chancellor, and later named himself Supreme Commander of the Armed Forces. The army did not object. Reichswehr Minister Blomberg made the German Wehrmacht swear a personal oath of loyalty to the Führer, leaving many young men with the wrongheaded but fervent belief that they were honour bound to 'do their duty' and to defend their leader no matter how absurd or brutal or evil that duty became. Soon afterwards Hitler declared himself 'Führer', a title which made no distinc-tion between his position as head of the party and head of state. All these changes were ratified by a plebiscite in which 39 million people voted; 90 per cent voted in favour of Hitler's new powers, and he could now proceed with his ultimate aims of destruction and war without fear of serious opposition. His first aim was to give vent to his seething, irrational, obsessive hatred of the Jews.

* * *

Jewish families had lived and worked in Berlin here for centuries, forming an intrinsic part of the fabric of the city. Now Berlin's 160,000 Jews would find themselves gradually excluded from normal life. Years of anti-Semitic propaganda had encouraged Berliners to resent the cultural, intellectual and economic contributions made by generations of Berlin Jews and by the time the Nazis came to power many were willing to admit that, even if they did not agree with the excesses of the SA or the SS, they could 'see something in the Nazi view'. A few brave people stood up to the harassment of their fellow citizens. Hanns Peter Herz, labelled a 'half Jew' by the Nazis, remembered being harassed by a boy named Lippert, the youngest son of the mayor of Berlin. 'I came into the classroom and found a Star of David scribbled on my desk bench. And in the few minutes that I sat at my desk with my back turned, he wrote "JEW" on the back of my jacket.' When the teacher saw what had happened he said, 'Lippert! Get the sponge, wet it, wipe off the bench, clean off his jacket, and then bring me the sponge.' When Lippert gave him the sponge, the teacher squeezed it out and slapped Lippert right and left across the face. He said, 'I don't want this happening in my classroom again.'[45]

However, the vast majority of Berliners did nothing. As William Shirer put it, 'A few Germans . . . were disgusted or even revolted by the persecution of the Jews, but though they helped to alleviate hardship in a number of cases, they did nothing to help stem the tide. What could they do? They would often put the question to you, and it was not an easy one to answer.'[46] Many Berliners were embarrassed by the behaviour of the Nazis in their midst but there is a yawning chasm between embarrassment and action. Few people were willing to put their reputations, let alone their lives, at risk for people they now considered to be 'aliens'. As a result, few intervened as Jewish doctors who had faithfully served their patients were chased out of their surgeries or when Jewish businessmen were spat on or forced to walk in the street carrying placards reading I AM A FILTHY JEW. Few complained when bankers were stripped of their shoes or their trousers and made to stand silently in a square and listen to abuse, or when old men were told to pick up rubbish deliberately thrown down on the street or were made to scrub the pavement with brushes.[47] There were endless petty, hurtful humiliations meted out by 'decent' Berliners; Jews were subject to strict rationing and neighbours who smelled coffee would denounce them for imbibing 'forbidden substances'; people ignored them in shops and avoided them on the streets, and Hans Albers remembered a neighbour yelling to her own dog as it ran up to his dachshunds, Plisch and Plum, 'Don't play with those non-Aryan dogs.'

The first serious SA attacks against Jews had occurred before Hitler came to power but by February 1933 they had become commonplace. Jews were treated particularly badly in the 'wild' concentration camps: one Communist named Bernstein, arrested on the night of the Reichstag fire, was given fifty lashes because he was a Communist, and another fifty 'because he was a Jew'. On 18 March Siegbert Kindermann, a member of the Bar Kochba Jewish Sports Society, was beaten to death by the SA in retaliation for a court case brought by him during the Weimar Republic. His body was thrown out of a window into a Berlin street with a swastika gouged into his chest.[48]

Hitler and Goebbels fully intended to increase pressure on the Jews in the hope that they would be forced to emigrate, and together they hit upon the idea of a boycott on Jewish businesses. Goebbels introduced it to Berliners by calling it an 'atrocity campaign' – by which he meant atrocities perpetrated by Jews against the German people. The boycott was to be sold as a 'defensive' measure against 'subversive Jewry' who were, amongst other things, 'strangling' Berlin. On 28 March 1933 the party headquarters ordered a national boycott of all Jewish businesses and professions to take place on 1 April. It was a great test of Berliners' fortitude, strength of character and independence from the Nazis.[49]

The tension on the street was palpable as the appointed hour – ten o'clock on Saturday morning – approached. SA men set up cordons and blockades in front of shops and held up placards announcing JEWS OUT or GERMANS DO NOT BUY FROM JEWS. According to Lady Rumbold, wife of the British ambassador, every Jewish-owned shop in Berlin was plastered with notices 'warning people not to buy in Jewish shops. In many cases special notices were put up saying that sweated labour was employed in that particular shop, and often you saw caricatures of Jewish noses.' Eyewitnesses recalled the division amongst the crowds – between those who forced their way into shops despite the abuse hurled at them; those who hurried by with an embarrassed glance in the direction of the store or building; and those, like the mass of people in front of the Ka De We, who stood around the entrance spontaneously giving the Hitler salute and chanting anti-Semitic slogans. Goebbels organized a mass rally in the Berlin Lustgarten and made a speech which was broadcast throughout the Reich, although it was difficult to hear him as he was constantly interrupted by Berliners shouting, 'Hang them! Hang them!' Most of the shops along the Kurfürstendamm were daubed with the word JUDE in white paint; others simply had their windows smeared or covered with large Stars of David. Jewish surgeries and legal offices had ACHTUNG JUDEN! BESUCH VER-BOTEN (Attention Jews! Visits forbidden) posted outside, and even when established organizations were attacked nothing was done. One hour after the Berliner Zeiting rolled off the presses at lunchtime on Saturday the SA invaded the huge Ullstein building and marched up and down the corridors yelling, 'To Hell with the Jews!' and demanding the dismissal of all Jewish workers. Bella Fromm, a Jewish journalist soon to lose her job, remembered having her car parked by the Ullstein doorman in his grey uniform with a large 'U' on the breastpocket. A few hours later he was dressed in his SA uniform and had joined the marching columns in the halls, although he averted his eyes when he saw her. When she left the building to go home he was once again in his Ullstein uniform, and graciously fetched her car as if nothing had happened.[50] Some brave Berliners showed their displeasure at the boycott and carried on with their Saturday shopping despite the abusive crowds and SA men, who recorded their names for 'future reference'. When one woman drove up to the huge Tietz department store and marched in the crowd almost lynched her. An SA man who had run after her returned to the crowd and calmed them down by explaining that 'It's all right, she's from an embassy.'

Berliners have often claimed that they resisted the boycott, and that it was their stand which persuaded Hitler to call a halt. But Goebbels and Hitler were told that, although the event had not been popular, people had not offered large-scale resistance to their measures. Hitler decided to shorten the boycott to fourteen hours only because it was receiving terrible coverage in the international press.[51] The stock market had already started to fall on Friday and New Yorkers had gathered in Madison Square Gardens to demand a counter-boycott of all German-made goods if Hitler's measures were not abandoned. The overt action on the streets was stopped, but discrimination continued.

Slowly, steadily, Jews lost their rights. On 7 April 1933 the first anti-Semitic law was passed in the infamous 'Aryan Clause' of the Law of the Restoration of the Professional Civil Service, which divided the population into 'Aryan' and 'non-Aryan' categories. It meant that officials of non-Aryan descent were to be forcibly 'retired'. Goebbels justified the law thus:

> From graves in Flanders and Poland two million German soldiers rise up to charge that in Germany the Jew Toller was allowed to write that 'the heroic ideal is the most stupid of ideas'. Two million rise up to charge that the Jewish *Weltbühne* was allowed to write 'Soldiers are always murderers', the Jewish professor Lessing was allowed to write, 'German soldiers fell for something not worth a damn.'

This new law led to the dismissal of all civil servants 'not of Aryan descent'. A week later notices were posted outside the university which read STUDENTS AGAINST THE UN-GERMAN SPIRIT and OUR MOST DANGEROUS OPPONENT IS THE JEW. Jewish professors were dismissed, leaving the way open for those willing to conform to the regime; these included eminent academics like C. G. Jung, who took over the editorship of the *Zentralblatt für Psychotherapie* in December 1933. A few days after this the German government passed an 'Act against the excessive number of students of foreign race in

German schools and universities'. Jews were now to be considered a foreign race even if their families had lived in Berlin for hundreds of years.[52]

By early May no Jewish painter, sculptor or engineer was permitted to contribute to the annual Academy Exhibition. By 1 August no Jewish law student could sit exams in Berlin, and the Berlin mayor, Julius Lippert, ordered all Jewish doctors in the city hospitals to give notice at their next appointment. By 7 October there were none left in Berlin's hospitals. Party members were now legally forbidden to shop in Jewish stores and products were stamped with labels showing that they were 'Rein deutsches Erzeugnis' (pure German goods), while Berlin newspapers, even Jewish-owned papers, practised self-censorship and refused to take Jewish advertising or personal notices, including announcements of births or deaths. In Lichtenberg foreign Jews were forbidden to put up stalls in the market and no Jews could display their wares in the huge Hauptmarkthalle vom Handel, cutting many off from an important source of income. On 20 July 1935 the Berlin police chief ordered Jewish businesses on the Kurfürstendamm to close, a move accompanied by vehement attacks against the Jews in the press. Four years later Rita Kuhn remembered sitting with her father in their flat and listening with increasing fear to the sound of heavy boots coming up the staircase. It was a policeman coming to take away their radio which, along with cameras and a list of other items, were now forbidden to Jews. The following year the Kuhns were forced to move from their home.[53] Indignities and crimes mounted; thirty-two deaf Jews were suddenly expelled from their local relief organization, including one old lady who had been a fully paid-up member since 1876.

The anti-Jewish measures began to affect many aspects of Berlin culture, including the newspapers. Berlin had long prided itself on being the *Zeitungstadt*, Germany's 'newspaper city', and with over 2,000 dailies during the 1920s it had published more newspapers than all of France and Britain together. The great Jewish publishers Mosse and Ullstein were responsible for the most important dailies, with the latter publishing the influential *Berliner Tageblatt* and the popular *Berliner Morgenpost*, which had a circulation of over half a million. Ullstein's empire had long been a source of pride for Berliners. The enormous building on the Kochstrasse covered a city block and employed over 10,000; indeed a joke about an escaped leopard which entered the offices and attacked the editors ended with the punchline that 'nobody had noticed', as there were over 200 of them. In 1913 the Ullstein brothers had purchased the venerable 'Auntie Voss', the *Vossische Zeitung*, which had been published in Berlin since 1703, and spent tens of thousands of marks supporting this cultural institution. In addition to these highly respected papers, Ullstein published the *Berliner illustrirte*, the *Grüne Post*, the *Tempo*, an evening paper, *Die Dame* for the height of fashion, *Uhu* for literature, and *Querschnitt* for intellectuals who wished to read Shakespeare or Proust in the original. For Berliners who had lived through the Weimar Republic, it was unthinkable that the Ullstein empire could be destroyed, but it was.

The various Nazi controls on newspaper publishing led to the slow, painful death of many great papers. By the end of 1933 the Nazi publisher Max Amann controlled the membership of the Reich Press Chamber.[54] Jewish or 'undesirable' publishers could simply be shut down and by 1936 Amann had personally eliminated four-fifths of the German press. The *Reichsschriftstellergesetz* of October 1933 made writers and editors personally responsible for the content of their articles and banned Jewish journalists from working. Goebbels himself dictated what was 'acceptable news' down to minute instructions on acceptable jokes and foreign events. In March 1933 Theodor Wolff, the chief editor of the *Berliner Tageblatt*, was forced to leave. By the end of 1933 the Mosse concern had been sold and all its famous titles had disappeared by 1938. The Ullstein empire was damaged by violent anti-Semitic attacks, which increased after the Jewish boycott. Berliners stopped buying these 'Jewish' products and businessmen refused to buy advertising space. The street paper *Tempo* was forced out of business in August 1933 through lack of sales; the *Vossische Zeitung* became Nazi property in March 1934 for the same reason; Goebbels forced Ullstein to sell the weekly *Grüne Post* and the *Berliner illustrirte Zeitung* in the same year so they could be 'Aryanized', and although the latter had a circulation of 1 million it was sold for the paltry sum of RM 6.5 million. By 1940 there were only ten newspapers left in Berlin.

Berliners would not have been able to halt Goebbels's drive to take over the press after 1933, but their abandonment of papers such as the *Vossische Zeitung* after the boycott damages their claims to have been 'anti-Nazi'. Ullstein had been one of the most important figures of the Weimar Republic. His annual Press Ball, the last of which was given the night before Hitler became Chancellor, had been the highlight of the Weimar social season, but it soon became clear that many of the starlets and journalists and generals who had enjoyed his hospitality had felt little true sense of loyalty. Very few turned down invitations to attend the Nazi Press Ball, which replaced Ullstein's in the following years.

The economic boycott was a powerful weapon in Nazi hands. The Mosse concern was the first large Jewish-owned business to collapse but many others soon followed. The 'Aryanization' or 'transfer of Jewish businesses into Aryan hands' was a despicable process whereby Jews were forced to sell their enterprises for drastically reduced prices. Many were impoverished, making them more vulnerable to repression. Of the 1,200 Jewish firms sold in Berlin in the early 1930s, 700 were 'Aryanized' while the others were simply closed down. The change of hands sometimes led to confusion: Israel's department store had all its windows smashed because the SA were not aware that it had already been 'Aryanized'. These expropriations have continued to cast a shadow over many firms, particularly those which celebrated their fiftieth anniversaries in the mid 1980s. In a special anniversary publication in 1986 a large department store group, Horten, doctored a facsimile of a 1936 advertisement to hide the fact that it was founded through the 'Aryanization' of Alsberg, a Jewish company. Many other companies have taken similar steps to conceal their past: Tietz, a famous Berlin department store, became 'Hertie'. Few Germans realize that this is an acronym for the Jewish founder Hermann Tietz, who built up the group in the 1930s into the largest family-owned retailing concern in Europe. Tietz and his family were forced to flee, only reaching the United States in 1941.

The banks, with their vast offices in Berlin, were also affected by the anti-Jewish measures. The Dresdner Bank, the largest in 1930s Germany, absorbed the Berlin houses Bleichröder and Hardy, while the Deutsche Bank took over the Mendelssohn Bank. Of the 1,350 private banks which existed before Hitler came to power, only 520 were still there in 1939.[55]

In the early years of his rule Hitler hoped to drive the Jews from Germany by excluding them from economic life. On 26 April 1936 he issued a decree which required all Jews to register holdings of over 5,000 marks. After studying the lists Goebbels concluded that there were 'many rich people and quite a few millionaires among them', and that compassion towards them would be 'totally out of place'. The registration and decrees of 14 June 1938, which required all Jewish businesses to be visually identified and registered, provided a basis for further confiscations. In August 1938 Jews were forced to make themselves more recognizable. All had to adopt the name 'Sarah' or 'Israel', which was registered on their passports. Goebbels had already replaced Berlin's mild police chief von Levetzow with Count Wolf-Heinrich von Helldorf, a rabid anti-Semite. 'Bravo!' Goebbels cried. 'We'll clean up Berlin. With united forces.'[56] The purge against the Jews was stepped up to make the capital *Judenfrei*.

At the party rally in Nuremberg in September 1935 a special Reichstag session was held to pass the Reich Citizenship Law and the Law for the Protection of German Blood and German Honour. These defined Reich citizenship in terms of race.[57] Under the first law, citizenship could only be given to a national of 'German or kindred blood'; under the second, all Jews were defined as 'not of German blood'. Ironically, the definition of Jewishness was ultimately based on the religion, and not the race, of one's grandparents and parents, but this obvious contradiction did not bother the Nazis. Marriages between Jews and German 'nationals' were forbidden, as were sexual relations between the two outside marriage. Jews were to be allowed no further part in

German life: they were without citizenship, without rights, and without recourse to the law. Racial anti-Semitism was given legal expression and Goebbels patted himself on the back. 'This is a hard blow against the Jews,' he wrote in his diary.

Mass arrests of Berlin Jews continued in the following years. Goebbels told police officers, 'legality is not the watchword, but harassment,' and in May 1937 alone over 200 Jews were picked up in highly visible places such as cafés and cinemas, humiliated on the streets, and sent to camps. On 5 December 1938 the Berlin police chief pushed through the *Ghettodekret*, which forced Jews to move away from government buildings and from the affluent western section of the city. They were now forbidden to rent accommodation from Germans. One by one districts were declared *Judenfrei*. Jewish banking and business families were forced to leave the beautiful villas built by their grandfathers in the West End. According to Frank Foley, the British passport control officer in Berlin, 'the methods of persecution have been particularly harsh in Berlin'; it was 'no exaggeration to say that Jews have been hunted like rats in their homes, and for fear of arrest many of them sleep at a different address overnight'.

The *Kristallnacht* of 9–10 November 1938 was one of the most vicious attacks against the Jews, but it was very much in keeping with earlier measures. The pogrom was supposed to look like a 'spontaneous' reprisal for the murder in Paris of a German diplomat by a Jewish youth but had in fact been planned to the last detail by Goebbels and local officials.[58] Police president Count von Helldorf ensured that Jewish buildings were isolated and that gas and electricity supplies had been cut off. The fire brigade was on full alert to prevent damage to adjoining 'Aryan' property.

At two in the morning the hundreds of Nazis who had been loitering in the streets began to smash shop windows and set fire to Jewish property. Nine out of the twelve large Berlin synagogues were plundered and destroyed that night, including the magnificent synagogue on Oranienburger Strasse, which was consumed as Berlin firefighters stood by and watched. As day broke swarms of Berliners ran through the streets, beating Jews and looting their property. Over 20,000 Jews were loaded on to trucks like cattle and hauled off to Oranienburg, Buchenwald or Dachau. The correspondents for the *New York Times* and the *Daily Telegraph* noted that some members of the public had shouted, 'Down with the Jews!' and that mobs of looters had gone to work after the SA had finished. Hugh Carleton Greene of the *Daily Telegraph* had seen many examples of racial hatred in Berlin, 'but never anything as nauseating as this. Racial hatred and hysteria seemed to have taken complete hold of otherwise decent people.' However, other reporters noted that the majority of people had been 'deeply disturbed' by the events, not least because they resented the re-emergence of lawlessness, vandalism and destruction of private property. The British *chargé d'affaires* reported that he had not met 'a single German from any walk of life who does not disapprove to some degree of what has occurred'. David Buffam, the American consul, wrote at the time that the event 'draws attention to the powerlessness of the public'. A SOPADE report of November 1938 noted that there was 'great indignation' amongst the population. In one case SA men smashing a shop after dark were pelted with stones from an orchard opposite; furthermore 'many people are looking after the Jewish women and children and have put them up in their homes. Housewives are shopping for the Jewish women, because it is now forbidden to sell food to them ... protests by the people of Berlin against the robberies and arson and the evil deeds done to Jewish men, women and children of all ages were plain. They ranged from looks of contempt and gestures of disgust to overt words of revulsion and harsh abuse.'[59]

The Nazis had no patience for such 'weakness'; as Goebbels put it on 24 November 1938, 'there still existed a class of whining Philistines' who spoke of the 'poor Jews' and took their part at every turn. It was not acceptable that 'only the state and the party be anti-Semitic'. Nevertheless there was no overt protest after *Kristallnacht* and Hitler even issued bogus warnings against individuals who attacked Jews on their own initiative. Many chose to believe that the events had been yet another example of the unruly elements of the SA taking matters into their own hands, and fervently argued that Hitler 'could not have known' about the excesses of his underlings. And if, as the SOPADE reports indicate, *Kristallnacht* caused indignation amongst many Berliners, the imposition of the yellow star and the deportations seem to have had little effect on public opinion.[60] This was selective blindness on a mass scale, which continued long after Berlin's once proud Jewish citizens had been reduced to helpless, furtive, dispossessed people who lived in fear for their lives.

By the mid 1930s Berlin had become a living nightmare for thousands of Jews, Catholics, Social Democrats, homosexuals, Church activists and others deemed 'unacceptable' to the 'new Germany', and the record of Nazi crimes reveals terrible savagery long before the outbreak of war. The question remains: Why was so little done to help these victims? Many Berliners may have been disgusted or frightened by Nazi violence, but once again very few acted. For every person who risked his life to save somebody else there were thousands of street fighters, SS men, Nazi bureaucrats, party members or ordinary Berliners willing to condone the Nazi atrocities. According to Gestapo and Social Democratic SOPADE reports many Berliners salved their consciences by telling themselves that those being punished must somehow have deserved it. One young SA recruit told the journalist Louis P. Lochner that he enjoyed beating a prisoner because it was 'safe to assume that he is guilty of something or other, else he would not have been arrested and brought here'.[61] Berliners were not inherently evil, as immediate post-war histories liked to make out, but many were naive, cowardly, greedy or indifferent in an age when such weakness could mean the difference between life and death. In the early years Hitler's most effective method of control had little to do with the persecution of the Jews or even with the terror instilled by Heydrich's leather-coated Gestapo men; for a people racked by years of deprivation and misery it was enough to deliver economic recovery and national pride. There is nothing like success to silence dissent, and by the mid 1930s it seemed to many that Hitler had worked a miracle.

When Hitler stood before the German people in 1933 and shouted, 'Give me four years' time,' the country was in the throes of the Depression. Berlin had the highest unemployment rate in Europe, the weekly wage had fallen by over a third, and to hundreds of thousands the future looked hopeless. It was Hitler's good fortune to come to power when the economy had already moved into an upward cycle. Unemployment had bottomed out in 1932 and in his first year the standard of living rose to a few points above subsistence level. By 1936 employment was back to the level of the best years of Weimar. The birth rate, a reliable measure of confidence, rose by 22 per cent within a year of Hitler's coming to power and continued to grow throughout the 1930s.[62] Contrary to the popular view there was continuity between the Weimar system and the new regime which provided much-needed stability. The machinery of the state was kept running smoothly by obliging ex-Weimar bureaucrats, while labour affairs were dealt with by ex-union officials who now slid into Nazi positions. As Speer put it, 'the directors who helped to achieve the extraordinary increase in armaments production ... were ones who had already made names for themselves before 1933 ... great successes resulted from combining these old proven organizations and carefully selected officials from them with Hitler's new system'.

The 'new system' which Speer referred to was a make-work programme which Hitler called 'a great programme of road building and improvement of railways and communal facilities'. The Reinhardt Plan, named after the Secretary of State of the Finance Ministry, was intended to kick-start the German economy by investing in roads, buildings, housing and industry.[63] Hitler's pet project was the creation of gigantic concrete Autobahns, which soon employed 200,000 people and gave work to 20,000 building firms from cement manufacturers to haulage companies. The fact that they also made use of forced labour was conveniently ignored by most of the population.[64] After all, the Autobahns provided jobs for workers, architects, engineers, those in the automotive industry and in a host of related areas, and Hitler's gleaming super-charged Mercedes became a popular symbol of the era.[65] Hitler designed a number of new projects specifically for Berlin in his 'reshaping of the Reich capital'. Six different Autobahns were to shoot into the city through the giant Berliner Ring, mimicking the pattern of rail lines which had made Berlin the focus of European travel in the nineteenth century. Hitler ordered that the roads must be tied in to other projects, such as the area around the Funkturm, the famous Berlin radio tower. In 1933 alone 10,000 Berliners were given jobs on the Autobahn projects and the demand for labour rocketed. They were also a highly popular symbol of the 'new Germany'; Albert Speer wrote in *Segments of Life* that

> when the abolition of the multi-party mess removed the obscenity of unemployment, and the first 1,000 kilometres of *Autobahnen* opened up a new era of mobility, I too saw the light: this was the time when Churchill said he hoped Great Britain would have a man like Hitler in times of peril, and when high church dignitaries and distinguished academics paid the Führer homage.[66]

The drive to reduce unemployment was stepped up with the 1934 plan designed to 'dry out the red unemployed sewer of Berlin'. The mayor, Julius Lippert, initiated a make-work programme which exiled 20,000 Berliners to the provinces; these left-wing 'Göring workers' were treated with disdain in their new communities but the exodus did wonders for Berlin's employment statistics. At the same time Hitler introduced an obligatory six-month Labour Service for young people, and it became a common sight to see rows of teenagers armed with shovels and pickaxes marching off to dig ditches and gardens throughout the city.

One of the enduring myths about Berlin is that the period after Hitler came to power was one of deprivation and misery. True, there were some food shortages, but these were primarily due to a series of disastrous agricultural reforms undertaken by the fanatic *Blut und Boden* theorist Walther Darré. His Reich Food Office implemented strange schemes to 're-Germanize' farms, and his inept management was responsible for cutting wheat and barley production by 15 per cent between 1933 and 1935. The food shortages were aggravated by a dearth of foreign capital.[67] Hitler had always been adamant that foreigners would never again dictate the course of the German economy and he strove to make Germany as self-sufficient as possible. At the same time protectionism was rife amongst its trading partners and the lack of trade was reflected in the barren foreign exchange centre at the Berlin Ritterstrasse. The most obvious shortages were in agricultural products, ranging from Danish bacon to foreign wheat, but Berliners were far from starving. The 1933

'10-Pfennig meal' of boiled buckwheat mixed with animal fat was soon replaced by better food. The consumption of staples like bread, butter, fat, cheese and potatoes rose dramatically, and even sales of expensive luxuries like coffee rose by a fifth between 1933 and 1937. Beer consumption shot up and cigarette consumption increased by 50 per cent. Some *ersatz* products were introduced early on, but serious food shortages did not bite until well into the war. Ironically, some workers turned down new canteen meals in favour of their old menu of bread soaked in beet juice or sandwiches of thick brown bread and sausage, but this was purely a matter of taste. When there were shortages the Nazis called for self-sacrifice, and during the 'fat emergency' of 1936 Hess wrote in the *Völkischer Beobachter*: 'We are prepared – in the future too – if need be, to consume a little less fat now and then, a little less pork, fewer eggs, because we know that this small sacrifice signifies a sacrifice on the altar of the freedom of our *Volk*.' This would help in the rearming of Germany: 'Because a world under arms has forced us to rearm we are rearming fully: each new piece of artillery, each new tank, each new aeroplane means increased security for the German mother that her children will not be murdered in an unholy war – or be tortured by Bolshevik hordes.'[68] In general life was immeasurably better than it had been in the years before 1933. The Berlin beer gardens, cafés and restaurants flourished, and while some places still allowed Berliners to boil their own water for coffee, most customers could now afford the full service. For the average person, life was improving rapidly.

Hitler had been very lucky to pull this economic rabbit out of the hat. He had known nothing about economics and despised professional economists, but his commonsense approach had led him to invent a new fiscal policy: deficit spending.[69] To the horror of his critics Hitler had simply printed money to pay for the huge building projects, and with the help of Schacht, the president of the Reichsbank, he was able to borrow vast sums on the promise of future tax payments. Fortunately for him the recovery quickly overtook the debt, increasing government revenues and actually reducing the budget deficit to a level far below that which had existed during the Weimar Republic. But there was more to his success than the printing of money. Hitler created a mood of such optimism and hope that people were willing to invest in the future. Industrialists no longer worried about troublesome trade unions; savers now felt confident enough to entrust their money to the banks rather than storing cash in the sugar bowl or under the mattress, and people spent money in the belief that they would soon be earning more.[70] The university, which had stopped issuing doctorates as a 'passport to unemployment' in 1932, granted them again after 1934, the bureaucracy expanded by 800,000, and industry demanded ever more workers. As Otto Dietrich put it in 1935, the leader was now seen as 'the symbol of the indestructible life-force of the

German nation, which has taken living shape in Adolf Hitler'. Even the crusty Hindenburg was moved to write in early 1934 that 'Much has happened in the past year with regard to the removal of economic distress and the reconstitution of the Fatherland, and great progress has been made.'

Hitler had managed to rejuvenate the economy with his building projects, but this masked a more sinister purpose. His real aim was conquest, and he longed to lay the foundations for war. To this end he initiated a rearmament policy which transformed the German economy. Hitler had made no secret of his intentions. The first practical step was his withdrawal from the League of Nations in October 1933. In 1935 90 per cent of the population of the Saar voted for integration into the Reich and on 7 March 1936 German troops marched into the de-militarized part of the Rhineland. On 11 March 1937 Hitler announced unexpectedly but to great acclaim that he was introducing universal military service despite the fact that it breached the provisions of Versailles. Berliners lined up to cheer the birth of the new German Wehrmacht and the leaders of all three armed services attended a spectacular ceremony at the Berlin Opera. It was no accident that Hitler chose the typically sombre German Memorial Day to announce the change, and Berliners shouted with joy as the steel-helmeted troops goose-stepped down the Wilhelmstrasse. The restoration of military strength, the right to rearm, and independence from Versailles became the main themes of foreign policy. In 1936, using language borrowed from Stalin, Hitler and Hermann Göring introduced the Four Year Plan, in which Hitler openly declared that 'the German Armed Forces mut be ready for combat within four years', and that the 'German economy must be mobilized for war within four years'. Foreign dignitaries ignored it at their peril, for Hitler meant every word.

The Four Year Plan had an immediate effect on Berlin, making it the industrial powerhouse of the Third Reich and bringing it enormous prestige. Dozens of gleaming new factories rose on the edge of the city, including the huge Daimler-Benz plant, the Henschel Works and the new Arado and IG Farben plants, the Focke-Wulf aircraft factories, the Argus aero engine plant, the Rheinmetall Borsig and the new Deutsche Industrie Werke. Many of them benefited from Hitler's drive to create synthetic products such as rubber, fats and cheap metals; IG Farben received money for the production of synthetic fuels and it combined with Wintershall to create Brauhag, which led the way in the production of gasoline from lignite. Thousands of Berliners were employed in the new industries and during labour shortages few complained about the increased use of slave labour. Sachsenhausen would soon supply labour for AEG, Argus, Borsig, Demag, Registrierkassengesellschaft-Krupp, Siemens and Sehlendorfer-Spinnstoffwerke. Henschel would soon be the first of many companies to use women labourers from Ravensbrück, but this too would be accepted.

By the end of the 1930s Berlin was the largest and most powerful industrial centre in Europe and the biggest single armaments producer on the continent. More than 2.3 million Berliners produced 14 per cent of the output of the entire German economy. Thirty per cent of all workers and 90 per cent of those in the metal industry worked in the production of weapons, war materials and other armaments. Soon Berlin would be producing every second aircraft engine, every second gun, and every fourth panzer in Germany. Most of the electrics for planes, panzers and U-boats were manufactured in the city. The Four Year Plan introduced a strange kind of 'socialism' in which private property and enterprises were left intact but were strictly regulated through the allocation of raw materials and foreign capital, and finally through administered scarcity. Everything from the supply of labour to wages, the place of employment and other vital considerations were centrally governed from Berlin.

By 1938–9 Hitler was spending RM 17 billion a year on weapons, bringing prosperity to the city. Few seemed to care about the ultimate goal of the rearmament drive; the streets buzzed, clubs stayed open all night and Hitler enjoyed wave upon wave of adulation, particularly after his march into the Rhineland. In the plebiscite to test the popularity of the move the Nazis polled 98.9 per cent throughout Germany, and although the results were rigged (the Gauleiter of Cologne managed to get 103 per cent as he had given his men too many duplicate ballot papers) it was clear from secret police and SOPADE reports that the overwhelming majority of Berliners supported Hitler's new economic and foreign policies.[71] Hitler was mobbed everywhere he went: people waited for hours around the Chancellery just to catch a glimpse of him. Charlotte Müller, daughter of a Berlin Social Democrat, recalled passing the Wilhelmsplatz on her way to visit her mother: 'In front of the palace, there's a view of the Wilhelmsplatz and it was *full* of ladies who were screaming, "We want to see our Führer. We want to see our Führer" ... They were completely in love with him. It's a mentality like with soccer, the whole stadium goes crazy ... That was the mentality back then.'[72] Albert Speer recalled that the people regarded Hitler as 'the leader who had made a reality of their deeply rooted longings for a powerful, proud, united Germany. Very few were mistrustful at this time. And those who occasionally felt doubts rising reassured themselves with thoughts of the regime's accomplishments and the esteem it enjoyed even in critical foreign countries.'[73] Hitler was overcome by his success and made the fatal mistake of believing in his own omnipotence. He increasingly saw himself as one of the 'great men' of history: 'Heretofore only one German has been hailed like this,' he told Speer. 'Martin Luther.'

*   *   *

Shortly before Hitler's seizure of power Communist and Social Democratic functionaries had comforted themselves with the notion that he would never win over the workers of Berlin. But control of the troublesome workers in big industrial centres was of paramount importance to a leader who was determined that the dangerous revolutionary mood of 1918 should never return to Germany. Hitler converted many to his cause but, even more important, was able to control dissenters with a dual strategy of terror and bribery. The former was achieved after the Reichstag fire with the crushing of all forms of worker representation through political parties or trade unions, the prohibition of any form of strike or organized protest, and the persistent use of persecution and terror. By 1935 SOPADE had to concede that 'the National Socialists have destroyed the workers' self-confidence; they have crushed the forces of solidarity and crippled their will to resist.'[74] The second half of the strategy, the 'bribery', was achieved by convincing the workers of the benefits of Hitler's Germany. For many, Hitler had brought about an 'economic miracle' which had raised the gross national product from RM 58,000 million in 1932 to RM 93,000 million in 1937; armaments production rose from 1 per cent in 1932 to 13 per cent in 1937, and unemployment was down from just over 6 million in 1933 to 1,051,500 in 1938. It was this – particularly falling unemployment – which made such a difference early on; as the SOPADE report of 1935 put it, 'the fear of the renewed misery of unemployment is worse than the misery itself,' and it had caused workers to 'become apprehensive' about resistance of any kind. Those who had experienced unemployment were 'anxious not to make themselves conspicuous'. Hitler also played up to the workers, feigning concern for them and pretending to defend their interests over those of the 'bosses'. 'I only acknowledge one nobility – that of labour,' he declared, and during a speech before the Reichstag in 1939 he claimed, 'During the last five years, I too have been a worker.' When a group of labourers were killed while working at a site on the Berlin Underground Hitler attended their state funeral and the contractors became defendants in a carefully staged public show trial.[75]

With no serious organized resistance Hitler was able to introduce labour policies aimed strictly at appeasement and control of the working class.[76] One of his main allies was the party hack Robert Ley, who set up the DAF or German Workers' Front in 1933; modelled on the now banned trade unions, it was intended to streamline and control Germany's workforce under Nazi control. Ley built up a personal empire, an enormous fiefdom which became the biggest of its kind in history and through which he controlled every aspect of workers' lives.[77] He masterminded a scheme whereby every worker was issued with a card which carried his identity and his work history; without the card he could not get a job. In order to sustain an appearance of worker independence he set up factory councils – the National Socialist Works Cells

Organization – but in practice these represented Nazi views; according to a SOPADE report of April–May 1934, some workers were becoming 'increasingly disenchanted [with the NSBO] because they have to pay more than they did when they were in unions and, instead of "red" bosses, they have got "brown" ones'.[78] At the same time Ley organized state benefits for workers and carried out systematic campaigns to improve working conditions. These exercises were called *Schönheit der Arbeit* (Beauty of Labour) and *Kraft durch Freude* (Strength through Joy).

The 'Beauty of Labour' and 'Strength through Joy' campaigns were blatant attempts at Nazi social engineering, in which Ley sought to win over the workers by giving them a wealth of cosmetic benefits without conceding real power.[79] The Beauty of Labour scheme forced factory bosses to modernize their offices, installing new safety equipment, lighting, furniture and the latest technology. At the same time 'volunteers' planted trees around the factories and created little parks for their own use. Berlin was awash with Strength through Joy posters, which played on the earlier, and distinctly un-Nazi, infatuation with the metropolis. Now, the city was proudly portrayed as BERLIN – WORK FEVERED METROPOLIS, or BERLIN – SOURCE OF STRENGTH OF THE REICH, or BERLIN – TIRELESS CITY OF WORK.[80]

Strength through Joy may not have converted sceptics to the Nazi cause but it was effective in pressuring workers to conform and to become integrated into National Socialist culture. Factories now offered evening classes, amateur cultural events, exhibitions, concerts, sports facilities, and although these activities had a political agenda a number of working-class Berliners I have talked to who claim to have disliked the Nazi regime still refer to their clubs, bands, sports associations and theatres with nostalgia. The most popular aspect of the project was cheap organized travel. The Nazis built huge holiday resorts in the Harz mountains and on the Baltic and sent worker there at heavily subsidized prices. Better still, they offered cruises to 'exotic' locations like Madeira or Norway on which everyone from managers to blue-collar workers were allocated cabins by the drawing of lots. Fewer people were able to travel than was implied by Nazi propaganda but in the end around 10 million German workers participated in the KdF trips; one in three vacationed in Germany and one in every 200 Berlin workers took a cruise abroad. Another of the popular KdF innovations was the promise of the Volkswagen or 'people's car', designed by Ferdinand Porsche. The production of this affordable means of transportation was halted by the outbreak of war, although over 300,000 Germans had already paid for their own vehicle by 1940. Many were impressed by these gains in material wealth. After surveying Ley's work Sir Nevile Henderson wrote in his 1940 book *Failure of a Mission* that 'There are, in fact, many things in the Nazi organization and social institutions, as distinct from its rabid nationalism and ideology, which we might study and adapt to our own use with great profit both to the health and happiness of our own nation and old democracy.'[81]

One reason for Hitler's success at winning even sceptical Berliners to his cause was the move away from *völkisch* Nazism towards the pursuit of a modern, fast-paced industrialized society. Far from insisting on a return to medieval German *völkisch* life Hitler actually encouraged Berlin to continue much as it had in the Weimar era and his fascination with modern technology often contradicted many of his *völkisch* pronouncements. Before 1933 the Nazis had portrayed 'asphalt' Berlin as the epitome of the evil of Weimar – a 'corrupt' cesspit to be 'Germanised' at all costs. After 1933 Hitler openly praised selected aspects of the modern city and promoted everything from technological innovation to industrial might. Far from decrying modernity he began to claim that 'without motor-cars, sound films and wireless' National Socialism would not have achieved its great victory.[82] He was the first to use aeroplanes as an electioneering tool and took a great interest in new airports, including the extension to Tempelhof; he championed inventors like Porsche and in the early years increased the production of modern consumer goods from hair-driers to washing machines. One of the most obvious volte faces was in Hitler' treatment of the great Berlin department stores. In the years leading up to 1933 these had been vilified as symbols of 'Jewish materialism' and the opening of new branches of Woolworths or Bata had always attracted an SA demonstration. Department stores were centres of 'interest slavery' because they enticed people to buy goods they could not afford, they undermined true German craftsmen and local shopkeepers, they promoted 'cosmopolitan' products like cosmetics and cigarettes, and Berliners were reminded that the Jewish stores should be avoided at Christmas. A 1932 drawing in *Der Stürmer* had shown a department store as a concrete shell with a monstrous black octopus oozing out to strangle the small stores in the vicinity. It seemed inevitable that once Hitler came to power Tietz, the Ka De We and Wertheim's would be closed down. Instead, they were 'Aryanized' and kept open, acting as city landmarks until closed, usually by war-time bombing.

Under Hitler's guidance Berlin tried to reclaim its place as the most modern city in Europe and *völkisch* rhetoric was retained only when it did not interfere with industrial output – workers in their gleaming chrome and glass factories were summoned by a peal of bells rather than clocking in and foremen were told to refer to themselves by the medieval guild term *Meister*, but none of this affected production. Nazi ideology had never been particularly coherent but now it became a muddle of contradictions – a cross between *völkisch* romanticism and a hard, practical modernism.[83] In the 1934 exhibition 'German People, German Labour', held in the new ultra-modern Deutschlandhalle, Hitler was praised both for having brought industrial greatness back to Germany *and* for having come from 'four generations of farmers'. Berlin's image was also transformed: no longer was it the 'un-German' capital but the 'true German' capital. In the film *Der Weg ins Freie* nineteenth-century Berlin was deemed to be a fitting precursor to the Nazi city because whereas Polish migrant labour was able to carry the 'revolutionary virus' into 'mongrelized Vienna', 'racially undiluted Berlin' had proved resistant to 'infection'.[84]

Hitler justified his change of attitude by blaming the Jews. His theory went as follows: the old class system was the fault of Jews, who had 'forced' industrialization on traditional German society in the nineteenth century. As the clock could not be turned back the only way out of the class-ridden, divided Germany which they had 'created' and which he had 'inherited' was to industrialize further and thereby eliminate class barriers through increased wealth and strength. The root cause of the problem – the Jews – would be eliminated at the same time. With this neat twist Hitler made modernity acceptable so long as it was of the '*völkisch*' and not the 'Jewish' variety. Berlin could remain the 'progressive work fevered Metropolis' as long as this benefited German national causes such as rearmament. This peculiar notion explains how Hitler could undertake enormous modern projects while stressing their *völkisch* elements. The Autobahn was one such example. By 1936 2,000 kilometres of slick new road were under construction or already finished. According to the 1939 propaganda film *Roads Bring Happiness* the Autobahn was not only great because it was an engineering marvel or because it created jobs; it also brought 'joy' through technological progress as Germans 'could now ride on the most modern, the safest and the most beautiful roads in the world'. Hitler declared that the project was 'truly German' because it brought the *Volk* from all over the Reich together: advertisements and films showed good German families picnicking together beside the long cement ribbons running through idyllic countryside. Propaganda also focused on the bridges which, although of modern construction, were clad in hand-hewn stone and topped by enormous sculptures to make them look like ancient monuments. Fritz Todt boasted that his roads were 'works of art' not least because they followed the 'craftsman's principles of building and implantation in the earth'.[85] The most advanced technology in the world had been used to create both a modern marvel and a symbol of the union of the German *Volk*.

The strange mix of modern and *völkisch* themes crept into many other aspects of society. People would gather round their new mass-produced radios to hear Hitler extol the virtues of the simple life on the land (over 80 per cent of Berlin families had a radio by 1939 and Hitler made fifty broadcasts in his first year in office); he used the latest in mass transportation and crowd control to bring tens of thousands to his spiritual rallies; and new scientific techniques were used to determine whether someone was of pure ancient Germanic stock. The paradoxes became ever more sickening. The brutally efficient Buchenwald concentration camp was built in a truly beautiful historic landscape overshadowed by Goethe's favourite oak tree, while the prisoners sent to Auschwitz were greeted by a hand-made iron sign which, like something from a needlepoint decoration in a country kitchen, read ARBEIT MACHT FREI. Modernism was acceptable as long as it could in one way or another be sold to the general public as *völkisch*; as long as it was available, at least in theory, to all Germans irrespective of birth or position in society it was considered symbolic of the German community.

The confusion over what was acceptable in Berlin increased as the economic and political situation changed. Nowhere was this more clear than in the role women were expected to play.[86] When Hitler first came to power women were forced back into the home in the drive to reduce unemployment. In 1933 one-fifth of Berlin university students were women but admission was drastically restricted so that in 1934 only 1.5 per cent of those who qualified for entry were given places. Married women, including doctors and civil servants, lost their jobs immediately and were given financial incentives and motherhood medals to stay at home and produce babies for the Reich.[87] Hitler closed birth control clinics and stopped the advertising of contraceptives, while abortions were called 'acts of sabotage against Germany's racial future' and Berlin doctors were jailed for sixteen years for the crime. But, like so many others, these measures were quickly reversed when they became inconvenient. Restricting women's access to jobs was fine when unemployment was high, but by 1936 labour shortages were starting to make themselves felt and employers re-hired skilled female labour, which was also much cheaper. In 1937 the Nazis rescinded the decree that granted marriage loans only if women promised to stay out of the labour market. Women were once more employed as tram conductors and postal workers, and by 1938 10 per cent of civil servants were female. Hitler also decided that women should take the place of all waiters, although this had more to do with his belief that it was not 'manly' to serve food.

The attitude to women changed most rapidly in Berlin. Local magazines and newspapers were soon praising working women; in 1936 the *Berliner illustrirte Zeiting* ran articles about the well-dressed modern women working in 'the shop', in 'the lab' or in 'the office', and proudly advertised the fact that out of 207,000 Berlin employees in health care 136,000 were women; of all workers in shops and businesses the ratio was two to one, and of the 6,300 writers and artists in the city 1,500 were women.[88] The 'peasant' image also changed: Berlin women ignored the bans on make-up and followed the lead of Magda Goebbels, who became patron of the German Institute of Fashion in Berlin. Even her husband publicly championed beautiful women, defending the right of Gauleiters to trade in their old wives for younger and more desirable women, thereby making an 'essential contribution to the public good'. When the ideologists tried to ban trousers he said, 'whether women wear slacks is of no concern to the public . . . The bigotry bug should be wiped out. Long live the Metropole and the Scala [dance halls]!' Despite the risk of being called 'whores' or 'Jewish *cocottes*' by passers-by on the street daring *Berlinerins* dyed their hair (usually blond), wore make-up, and even sported nail polish.[89]

Berlin became an island of modernity in a world of Nazi provincialism. Contrary to popular belief the Americanization of the Weimar period was not erased but continued at a fast pace, with American skyscrapers and technology remaining the symbol of 'progress'. Two new Coca-Cola plants opened in the 1930s and the city was awash with Hollywood films. Although jazz was officially banned throughout the Reich dozens of Berlin clubs played a form of jazz and swing music without fear of punishment; at the Press Ball in 1936 both Göring and Goebbels could be seen gyrating across the floor to the tune of 'Dinah'.[90] The city quickly became the playground of prominent Nazis who, in the safety of the Reich capital, could flagrantly break laws which were rigorously enforced in the provinces, and life was terrific for those free to enjoy the delights of rich, powerful Berlin.

Hitler knew about the abuses of power in Berlin, but he did nothing. He himself cultivated an image of purity; he was the 'new broom' waiting to sweep away the scandal of the Weimar period and stop crime and corruption. Many people were impressed by his anti-criminality drive and a number of Berliners have commented to me that 'at least under Adolf it was safe' and that 'even old ladies could walk the streets at night'. Hitler also cultivated the image of a law-abiding, decent man. He did not drink or smoke, he was a vegetarian, and he pretended to put the welfare of the nation above his personal happiness. Much of the image was a lie. He claimed he never needed sleep and worked tirelessly for Germany, but in reality he was inherently lazy and quickly became bored and distracted by the humdrum realities of running the state. He pretended to lead an 'asexual life' and to put his 'energies' into the state even when Eva Braun was sneaking up the back stairs of the Chancellery. But the myth spread and when local party bosses became corrupted people would say: 'If only Hitler knew about this.' A Berlin Gestapo report of 1936 read:

It is said that the Führer cannot fail to see the effect of the human failings of a whole array of his subordinates, how now this one and now that one is having a huge villa built, how several of his colleagues are living a luxurious existence which has a directly provocative impact on the mass of the people. Such conversations usually end with the questions: 'Why does the Führer put up with that?' ... In broad sections of the people the opinion has spread that the Führer is surrounded by an invisible wall no longer penetrable by reports reflecting the truth.[91]

But by the standards of the Nazi leadership Hitler was one of the least corrupt. Nazi greed and hypocrisy were embodied in the corpulent bulk of Hermann Göring.[92]

Göring's appetite for ostentatious self-gratification seemed insatiable. Amongst many other things he skimmed off huge sums of money from his self-appointed 'public offices', which included being National Hunt Master, and from a host of directorships, shares in newspapers, aircraft manufacturers and other firms. His wedding was the pinnacle of the 1935 Nazi social calendar, and although many Berliners were reminded of the pomp of 'the days of the Kaiser' as the bridal pair thudded down the steps of the Dom with Hitler beaming in the background, few realized how much the circus had cost them. In order to pay for the wedding Göring's ministerial employees had been forced to give 'voluntary' contributions from their salaries, and other groups were pushed to make lavish 'donations'. The National Industrial Group was faced with the choice of giving either a painting, an estate, or a porcelain dinner service – they decided on the latter as it was the cheapest at 30,000 marks. As Prime Minister of Prussia Göring could legitimately seize beautiful estates for himself and hand them out at will; he gave ex-imperial figures like Hindenburg houses and bought the favour of younger generals and high bureaucrats by giving them land, castles and expensive gifts. Göring himself took a number of properties, not least the Kaiser's old hunting lodge which he had demolished to make way for the sumptuous Karin Hall; his state huntsman and foresters were all paid out of the state purse. He strutted around Berlin in ridiculous uniforms with epaulettes 'the size of a fruit-tart', and he collected medals and decorations and blackmailed old princely families to give him the grand cross of their ancestral order – Prince Windischgrätz told Hanfstängl that the 'little pleasure had cost him £150'.[93] Later, during the war, his greed would become uncontrollable and his private army of contact men who specialized in collecting bribe money and other 'gifts' would start to compete with Hitler's men in the rush to seize the most beautiful and priceless art treasures of Europe. Before the war was out he had amassed one of the finest private art collections ever known.

Göring was merely the most blatant of the venal Nazi elite. Goebbels, the 'he-goat of Babelsberg', never made as much money as his counterparts although he was not averse to profiting from forced sales of Jewish-owned property. But for all his *völkisch* morality he was a notorious womanizer and kept a string of UFA starlets at his disposal. Others were worse. Julius Streicher was involved in racketeering and corruption on a grand scale. This editor of the Nazi smear sheet *Der Stürmer* publicly admitted the great sexual excitement he felt when whipping prisoners in the camps, although he also had his own string of young women whom he blackmailed for more conventional pleasures.[94] The Hitler Youth leader Baldur von Schirach shot himself after it was discovered that he had embezzled RM2 million. Robert Ley, a slob and an infamous alcoholic who headed the 1939 abstinence drive, regularly stole money from the DAF, which was exempt from public audits. When, by 1939, it was clear that the Volkswagens ordered and paid for by hopeful Germans would never be built he simply pocketed the 100 million marks for himself; he was neither caught nor punished. Gauleiters like the brutal mass murderer Erich Koch took to aping the aristocracy; Koch had Polish slave labourers build him a palace which he staffed with white-gloved SS functionaries who would carefully pass tea to the 'Frau Gauleiter' in a parody of aristocratic life; Gauleiter Hildebrand, an ex-poacher, also craved identification with the old military elite – when he informed Countess von Schulenburg of her husband's arrest by the Gestapo in connection with the July 1944 plot against Hitler she noticed that he had a bust of the great commander General von Schulenburg on his desk.[95]

The elite were quick to seize Jewish property supposedly earmarked for the state; when the Foreign Minister Konstantin von Neurath wanted a new house he drove through the streets of Berlin, stopped by the most beautiful Jewish-owned villa he could find, and simply took it over. His successor, von Ribbentrop, had the young von Remnitz imprisoned on trumped-up charges and murdered in Dachau so that he could take his splendid estate. Count Helldorf, the Berlin chief of police, was also utterly corrupt. It was he who supervised the 'Aryanization' of Berlin, and he made vast amounts of money in the process. He would send his cronies to the houses of targeted Jews, seize their passports, and demand a 250,000 mark 'contribution' for their return. This was, of course, no guarantee that the victims would be able to get out of Berlin. The property of Jews forced to leave their homes was supposed to be sealed off and treated in the 'proper manner'; mere looting was fiercely prosecuted. But official Nazi appropriation was rampant. The local bosses would divide up property between themselves and would regularly take their wives into the vacated flats or houses to choose jewellery and fur coats. Truckloads of furniture and paintings could often be seen trundling up to the front doors of party functionaries while private markets allowed Nazi officials to exchange 'their' diamonds, jewellery and antiques. They were not shy about their new wealth; Göring would bring out bulging purses of gems after dinner at Karin Hall. Hundreds of officials were involved in this corruption, not least the deputy Gauleiter of Berlin under Goebbels, Karl Holz, who made a small fortune from the illegal transfer of property after *Kristallnacht*.[96] Hitler also ensured that Eva Braun was given a large collection of precious gems, although she rarely wore them as they would not have suited her childlike image. This sanitized looting and abuse of power flourished at all levels of the party hierarchy. At the same time, average citizens were bullied and coerced into giving ever greater donations to the state through bodies like the Winterhilfe, which ostensibly gave money to the unemployed in Germany but in fact went to line the pockets of various functionaries.

The Winterhilfe was called a 'voluntary charity' but by the mid 1930s had become a method of social control.[97] The Winterhilfe ground into gear each year with the *Eintopf*, or one-pot meal: families were asked to forgo their normal fare once a month and donate money to the cause. Thousands of official collectors ran up and down the back streets and *Hinterhöfe* of Berlin demanding money and reporting those who did not comply. The Gestapo was inundated with reports about people who had not contributed enough, and there are hundreds of documented cases of people who were punished and ostracized because they only gave clothes or a small amount of money. Some Berliners I have spoken to resented the Winterhilfe but seemed equally indignant about those who had not contributed to it; one lady had to be protected by the police when her neighbours discovered she had given only an old pair of boots to the 'charity', while a block warden would coerce those in his *Hinterhof* to give more so that the house would not get a 'bad name'. The resentment against this ritual intensified in the late 1930s, and even as people made donations they would glance at one another when party bosses drove by in their new cars and new clothes and say, 'There goes the Winterhilfe.'

The rot at the top began to work its way through the entire system of government. Any remaining ethic of thrift and honesty vanished in wave upon wave of greed. The Prusso-German bureaucracy, hitherto famous for its incorruptibility, was inundated with new employees who had no respect for its previous good name; corruption was particularly common in the new bodies like Goebbels's Ministry of Propaganda, whose employees found over 200 jobs for relatives in its first year.

The vast expansion of Nazi bureaucracy also caused something of a social revolution in Berlin, for the new placements often had no qualifications and would never have been hired under the old system. Anyone could now be promoted into a powerful position, whether in the party, in Ribbentrop's new foreign policy department, in the civil service, in Robert Ley's empire or in the SS. Hundreds of thousands of Berliners took up their new positions with pride, gaining prestige and stable incomes never dreamt of by their forefathers. With their new salaries the fledgling functionaries could afford middle-class luxuries like radios and big flats, they could wear uniforms with shiny boots and buttons and click their heels like the Prussian officers in their favourite UFA films, and they could lord it over others. The new aristocrats of Berlin included men who had joined the party before 1933 and who had proved their loyalty on the street; indeed, in 1935 Hitler decreed that 10 per cent of all vacancies in all but the highest posts of the civil service were to go to the 'old fighters' and not only to the 'March violets'. By the mid 1930s 80 per cent of civil service jobs had been given to party members. These crass, uncouth men willingly enforced the most ridiculous of Nazi policies, directly affecting all aspects of life in the capital. They owed their position to the Nazis, and they followed orders to the letter. Many who lived through the period have described the intense frustration of looking into the blank eyes of such people while they dictated the party line, seemingly incapable of understanding the implications of their own words. The bureaucrats were particularly intransigent when enforcing the new doctrines on art and culture, unaware of the value of the people and the objects which they so callously banned and destroyed.

Hitler saw himself as an artist and took particular interest in the shaping of German culture. The 'de-Jewification' of Berlin and the 'cleansing of culture' took a terrible toll on the city, reducing it from the centre of European art to a dull provincialism from which it has never recovered. Nevertheless, although Goebbels detested the 'Jewish intelligentsia' who had no place in the true Berlin, he did not dismiss all Weimar culture out of hand. In his 1928 article 'Around the Memorial Church' he wrote: 'That is Berlin W! The heart of the city turned to stone. Here the spiritual leaders of the asphalt democracy sit together in the nooks and crannies of cafés, in cabarets and bars, in the Soviet theatres and fancy apartments ... One would like to think that it is the elite of the people ... [but] it is only the Israelites.'[98] Goebbels entertained the ludicrous notion that Berlin could still nurture a dynamic and innovative culture even after it was 'cleansed' of Jews and others critical of the regime. The result of his attempt to retain Berlin as a world-famous cultural centre was that the 'cleansing' of German art was far from consistent and many Weimar traditions survived, albeit in radically altered form.

The cultural *Gleichschaltung* began in earnest in September 1933 with the creation of the Reichskulturkammer, a body which was divided into separate sections regulating every aspect of culture from painting to the press. The first target was the Prussian Academy of Arts, which was already thriving under

Frederick the Great. When a number of writers decided to band together to fight against Hitler in the March 1933 elections, Goebbels and Rosenberg demanded a purge. In May 1933 many of the finest works of German literature were targeted for destruction.

On 7 May groups of Berlin students entered libraries throughout the city and began to pull books off the shelves, in accordance with a list compiled by Dr Wolfgang Hermann, the man in charge of 'Reorganizing the Berlin City and People's Libraries'. The works of 160 authors were removed and tons of books brought to the student fraternity headquarters on Oranienburger Strasse. Many were sold for pulp to pay for the torches and banners needed in days to come but on 10 May the students of Berlin, in their green and purple fraternity caps, loaded the remaining books on to trucks and marched through the city to the Brandenburg Gate and up Unter den Linden, ending up at the Opernplatz. It was midnight by the time they arrived in the dark, rain-soaked square. The books were piled on to a ceremonial log pyre (favoured by the Nazis for its *völkisch* overtones), soaked with gasoline and, after some difficulty, the whole thing was set alight. Louis P. Lochner, the head of the Associated Press, wrote that 'every few minutes another howling mob arrived, adding more books to the impressive pyre. Then, as night fell, students from the university, mobilized by the little doctor, performed veritable Indian dances and incantations as the flames began to soar skywards.' E. M. Remarque was burned as the students chanted, 'Against literary betrayal of the soldiers of the World War. For the education of the nation in the spirit of military prepared-ness.' Tucholsky and Ossietzky were burned 'Against arrogance and presump-tion. For veneration and respect for the immortal German national spirit.' Freud was burned 'Against the overvaluation of instinctual urges that destroy the soul.' Lochner recalled that when the orgy was at its height, a cavalcade of cars drove into sight. 'It was the Propaganda Minister himself . . . "Fellow students, German men and women," he cried as he stepped before the micro-phone for all Germany to hear him. "The age of extreme Jewish intellectualism has now ended."' He praised the students for their hard work in 'clearing up the debris of the past'. For him, the 'healthy instincts of the *Volk*' would now determine the future of literature and art in Germany. Over 20,000 works were consumed by the flames that night.[99]

Attacks against writers continued and while Goebbels and Rosenberg squabbled over the relative merits of works the police continued to seize anything which 'endangered public order'. The confusion was not resolved until 1939, when a national index of books and 576 authors was finally compiled. It banned 261 émigrés or 'traitors', along with 178 Marxist and Soviet authors, fifty-six 'pornographers', and eighty-one 'others'. Despite the fuss surrounding 'degenerate' art, Nazi policy was far from consistent; on a recent trip to Norway my brother and I found a cache of Nazi literature in an isolated German bunker, and scattered amongst the novels, which were stamped *Sonderdruck für Wehrmacht* (special army issue), was pornography hidden behind plain covers with titles like *Art of the People*. Less privileged Germans had to make do with works by uninspiring writers like Erwin Guido Kolbenheyer and Werner Beumelberg and Hans Friedrich Blunck. In justification of the ban on some of Germany's greatest writers in 1933 the novelist Börries von Munchhausen said, 'What matters if, in sweeping away the chaff, a handful of golden grains are lost?'[100]

Painting in the city was also devastated by the Nazi ideologues, but again the censors were inconsistent. The more sophisticated Goebbels fought a constant battle with the dogmatic Rosenberg over what was to be allowed, and for a time he even defended the idea of allowing famous artists to stay on even if they were of Jewish descent. When he renovated the Propaganda Ministry he 'borrowed' a number of Nolde watercolours from the Berlin National Gallery and hung them in the main hall. The paintings would certainly have remained had Hitler not expressed his violent disapproval, after which Goebbels told Speer, 'The pictures have to go at once; they're simply impossible!' Ironically Nolde himself was desperate to be accepted by the Nazis, as were Kirchner and Pechstein, but they were never rehabilitated. Shortly after the 'Nolde incident' Hans Weidemann, who was head of the art section in the Propaganda Ministry, put together a collection of paintings of what Speer called the 'Nolde-Munch' school and recommended them to Goebbels. So recently stung by Hitler's attack, he forbade their display and when Weidemann tried to salvage them he was immediately demoted.

The 1937 'cleansing' of the art galleries and museums went some way to ending the confusion; Expressionism was officially banned, although the *Neue Sachlichkeit* and Verism of the late 1920s was still permitted in certain forms, and elements of these styles resurfaced in some Nazi paintings by men like Adolf Wissel and Paul Roloff. In general, however, modernism was doomed. Hitler personally led the attack, lashing out at artists who painted what he saw as

> misformed cripples and cretins, women who inspire only disgust, men who are more like wild beasts, children who, were they alive, must be regarded as under God's curse . . . it is clear that the eye of some men portrays things otherwise than as they are, that there are really men who on principle feel meadows to be blue, the heaven green, clouds sulphur-yellow . . . in the name of the German people I have only to prevent these miserable unfortunates, who clearly suffer from defects of vision . . . from presenting them as 'art'.[101]

The modern section of the Nationalgalerie in Berlin was closed and 16,000 of Germany's finest paintings, drawings and sculptures by Dix, Grosz, Kirchner, Nolde, Schlemmer, Kandinsky, von Barlach, Klee and others were removed, as were works by Van Gogh, Picasso, Matisse and many more.[102] Following the purge in Berlin, galleries throughout Germany were emptied and many of the works were piled up in a vast exhibition called *Entartete Kunst* (Degenerate Art). This was intended to show the depths to which 'the art of the period of decadence' had sunk and to reveal to Germans the 'diseased spiritual condition' of the artists' minds. The exhibition first opened in Munich in July 1937 and moved to Berlin later that year. Six hundred works by 110 artists were hung in a chaotic and ridiculous manner, often without frames and with insulting captions. A Klee drawing was hung beside that of a schizophrenic to demonstrate their similarity. Further on, two sculptured heads were placed side by side: the first, created by 'an unhealthy, crazy man' in the Heidelberg psychiatric clinic, had the caption: 'That deranged people who are not artists should produce such work is understandable.' Next to it stood a Hofmann masterpiece, under which it said: 'The title of this monstrosity is "Girl with Blue Hair".' It was 'a measure of Hofmann's diseased mind that the girl's hair has been painted purest sky blue'. Another section showed three sketches with the caption, 'Which of these three was drawn by an inmate of an asylum?' Two out of three, the exhibitors sneered, were done by 'the master' Kokoschka.[103]

The reaction to the Degenerate Art exhibition was startling. Over 2 million people attended and in Berlin it attracted 20,000 visitors a day. Some might have come to see works for the last time, but judging by the reaction of visitors the majority came to heap scorn on the 'Jewish-Bolsheviks' who had 'controlled' their culture for so long. One visitor suggested that each artist be tied up next to his work so that 'every German can spit in his face'. When it was over hundreds of artists found themselves barred from teaching, exhibiting and even painting, and they were subject to frequent visits by the SS, who would break into their homes to see if they had purchased paint, if any canvases had recently been stretched or even if their paint brushes were wet; some, like Oskar Schlemmer, were permitted only to apply camouflage paint to gasometers. In 1939 yet another fire swept through a courtyard in Berlin, this time at the headquarters of the city fire brigade. In an act reminiscent of Savonarola's in Florence over 4,000 of the finest works of German modernism were burned. Some have survived, but only because Goebbels decided to sell them abroad for hard currency.[104]

There was very little protest from the thousands of lesser artists who remained in Germany, for if one was 'accepted' by the 'art-loving regime' state support was generous and opportunities for prestigious exhibitions increased. Not surprisingly most of the Nazi art was uninspiring and concentrated on banal rural peasant scenes and rosy-cheeked maidens enjoying their rustic evening meals of brown bread and beer. There are few redeeming features in the work of Fritz Mackensen or Franz Stahl. Urban themes, so popular in Weimar Berlin, were frowned upon, although Oskar Graf's bridge or Christian Hacker's images of Nazi buildings were acceptable because they had a *völkisch* theme. Artists like Heinrich Knirr, with his portrait of the Führer, Herman Otto Hoyer, through his picture of Hitler addressing an early meeting in Munich captioned '*Am Anfang war das Wort*' (In the beginning was the word), Richard Schwarzkopf's *Deutsche Passion VI* and, the most ridiculous of all, Hubert Lanzinger's *Bannerträger* (Flag Bearer) or *Führerbildnis* (Führer Portrait), which showed Hitler perched on a horse and wearing shining medieval armour, did their utmost to bolster the myth. The Führer favoured Hellenic classicism, boasting in a manner reminiscent of Kaiser William II that 'never was humanity in its eternal appearance and frame of mind nearer to the ancient world that it is today'.[105] His promotion of Hellenism resulted in the production of hundreds of nudes in blatantly pornographic poses, which were deemed to be 'high culture'. Paintings of female nudes were everywhere: Ivo Saliger's cold *Das Urteil des Paris* (The Judgement of Paris) and Johann Schult's *Erwartung* (Waiting) were sexually explicit, as was Adolf Ziegler's dubious *Die vier Elemente* (The Four Elements), which hung above Hitler's mantelpiece in his Munich residence and about which he would lecture his spellbound visitors. Perhaps the most apt summation of the values of Nazi art was given by Count Baudisson, who toured Germany ordering the removal of 'degenerate' paintings from galleries and museums: 'The most perfect shape, the sublimest image that has recently been created in Germany has not come out of any artist's studio,' he said proudly; 'it is the steel helmet.'

Sculpture, too, suffered. Modernist sculpture was banned and dozens of fine works by artists like Wilhelm Lehmbruck, Christoph Voll and Otto Freundlich were pilloried in the Degenerate Art exhibition; indeed Freundlich's famous stone sculpture of a primitive head was plastered on the cover of the catalogue before being destroyed. The banned sculptures were replaced primarily by gigantic, sexually explicit muscular nudes by artists like Adolf Ziegler, whose detailed work in this area earned him the nickname 'Reich Master of Pubic Hair'. Sculpture such as Bernhard Bleeker's figure of a youth were sentimental *kitsch*, while others like Max Brumme's *Berufung* or Anton Grauel's *Abend*, which depicted in explicit detail a young woman writhing in the throes of sexual passion, were simply pornographic. One of the most important sculptors of the Nazi period was Josef Thorak, who produced gargantuan figures of heroic men, busty Amazons and snorting horses fighting it out as if on an enormous Wagnerian set. The other was Arno Breker, whose enormous studio in Berlin was frequently visited by an admiring Hitler and his entourage.

He too specialized in gigantic nudes, many of which were commissioned for the most important buildings in the Reich capital. Breker's aim was to create the ideal Germanic type in stone and at the same time to demonstrate the all-encompassing power of the state; his works, like all Nazi art, were meant to educate and intimidate at the same time.[106] The two enormous bronze statues which flanked the entrance in the inner courtyard of the Reich Chancellery were typical. Entitled *The Party* and *The Wehrmacht*, each stood 3.7 metres tall. *The Party* was a bulging muscular man holding a torch aloft as if to lead the masses to victory. According to Breker the body was to be 'natural, classless, evoke sexuality, historicization, and eternity'. The head was to be of 'Nordic appearance' and the phallus was to evoke 'sexuality, reproductive power, manliness, strength and energy'.[107] A number of these sculptures still exist, including Fritz Klimsch's figures for Goebbels's Propaganda Ministry and works by Breker for the Round Room of Hitler's Chancellery. It is strange to stand beside these cold figures which survive in the shadows of Berlin, some still hidden from public view.[108]

The *Entartete Kunst* exhibition finally set guidelines for 'acceptable' painting and sculpture, but the dictates governing film, music, theatre and other areas remained much more contentious and were often contradictory.[109] As in all other areas, the 'de-Jewification' devastated Berlin musical life. Otto Klemperer, conductor of the Berlin State Opera, was awarded the Goethe Prize in 1933 and was then promptly dismissed 'for racial reasons'. Dozens of the most eminent composers and musicians emigrated, including Schoenberg, Artur Schnabel, Lotte Lehmann and Elisabeth Schumann, along with three of Berlin's great conductors, Walter, Klemperer and Kleiber. Severus Ziegler, who set himself up as a judge of 'degenerate music', banned Mahler, Milhaud, Stravinsky and Weill. Goebbels refused to allow Hindemith to remain in Germany despite Furtwängler's pleas. Eventually the bans were extended: Ravel, Debussy, Chopin, Bizet and Tchaikovsky were no longer played after the outbreak of war. Nothing was above reproach; Mozart's *The Magic Flute* was criticized by party hacks for its masonic theme until Hitler publicly declared it to be acceptable, while Handel's *Judas Maccabaeus* was renamed *Wilhelm von Nazzau* and given a suitably *völkisch* libretto. Wagner remained the epitome of Nazi musical taste and the Bayreuth Festival was personally supported by Hitler. Even so, *Parsifal* was dropped during the war because its Christian theme offended the ideological extremists around Rosenberg.[110]

Despite the purges, however, most Berliners continued to enjoy their musical life as if nothing had happened. A number of prominent musicians remained in the capital, preserving the veneer of continuity between Weimar and the 'new age'. Furtwängler chose to stay despite misgivings about the dismissal of Jews from his orchestra, and Richard Strauss became the first president of the Reich Chamber of Music. By the time he left in 1935, after official protest over his friendship with the Jewish writer Stefan Zweig, who had written the libretto for *Die schweigsame Frau*, he had added enormously to the prestige of the regime. The Nazis were typically contradictory in their approach to music and allowed some 'modern' composers to remain: Werner Egk found success when Hitler unexpectedly applauded his *Peer Gynt*, and Carl Orff, who became one of the most successful young Nazi composers, was fêted because Hitler liked *Carmina Burana*.[111] Thanks to those who stayed behind, the Nazis were able to maintain a facade of musical excellence through-out the 1930s; the theatres and opera houses carried on even during the bombing and Missie Vassiltchikov remembers watching Herbert von Karajan's career flourish after the departure of his rivals; she once bumped into him rushing for the air-raid shelter at the Adlon Hotel. Although the regime commissioned vast amounts of terrible new music, from the *Horst Wessel Commemoration Cantata*, which aimed to 'evoke the genius of Bach', to dozens of pieces for Nazi festivals and celebrations, more conventional fare continued throughout the period. In the 1941–2 season alone over eighty separate operas, operettas and ballets were produced in the capital.[112]

The same veneer of normality existed in the once-famous Berlin theatre. Many great actors and film directors were forced to leave after 1933, and attempts to create a 'people's culture' were not particularly successful; the open-air 'Thing-Theatres', built to resemble ancient amphitheatres, were a flop, as were the endless heavy-handed *Blubo* (*Blut und Boden*) party pro-ductions, and no great Nazi playwrights emerged. Nevertheless, for many naive Berliners things even seemed to improve under the Nazis. Twenty-three of the city's forty-five theatres had closed during the Depression, and the Nazis reopened many of them; 'theatre for the masses' was promoted and workers were given subsidized tickets through the 'Strength through Joy' organization. Only a handful of theatres were overtly politicized and some good productions were mounted with actors like Käthe Dorsch, Hermine Körner and Eugen Klöpfer playing in heroic costume dramas and historical plays, which soothed the consciences of educated Berliners.[113] The Nazi censors were particularly accommodating when it came to works of past masters, and Hebbel, Kleist, Goethe and Shakespeare were performed with regularity. There were countless lighter dramas, from *Uproar in a Tenement* to *Petermann Sails to Madeira*, although one of the hits of the 1935 season at the Lessing Theatre was a ballet in which two farmers fought over a live pig. Even at the height of the offensive in the east, over a hundred plays were produced annually in the city.

The same was true of film production, which seemed to many to continue almost seamlessly from the Weimar into the Nazi period. Again, Jewish actors and film directors were forced to emigrate and films in which Jews had starred were banned, but many actors and directors happily moved in to fill the gaps left by their erstwhile colleagues. Much damage had already been done in the late Weimar years through Hugenberg's control of UFA, and few noticed when Goebbels forced him out and took control of the company, with its 5,000 employees and 120 cinemas. Under Goebbels Berlin retained, even enhanced, its role as the largest and most powerful centre of film production in Europe. It is ironic that this ultra-modern medium, which is now such a staple of the legend of Weimar, should become a particular favourite of the Nazis.

Goebbels was the first to appreciate the power of light entertainment to enliven propaganda and he allowed film companies to go on much as before, protecting them against the worst of the party hacks and ideologues. As a result, film attendance rocketed, quadrupling between 1933 and 1940 and overtaking all other forms of entertainment. Goebbels's genius for propaganda led him to steer clear of 'official' films; indeed of the 1,097 films made under him only ninety-six were initiated by the Ministry of Propaganda, the most famous of which included Leni Riefenstahl's documentaries of the Berlin Olympics and the Nuremberg rallies. Other films were openly propagandistic but were so well made that they achieved high attendance ratings. These included the anti-Semitic *Jud Süss*, Wolfgang Liebeneiner's *Ich klage an*, which was a dramatic appeal for euthanasia, and Gustav Ucicky's *Heimkehr*, which 'documented' Polish atrocities against the German minorities.[114] The *Fredericus* films, already popular in the 1920s, continued to glorify Frederick the Great through Johannes Meyer's *Fredericus* of 1936 and Harlan's *Der grosse König* of 1942. These were extended to include the Bismarck films in the 1940s.

The medium of film naturally posed problems for the Nazis, particularly when it came to dealing with representations of Berlin. Images of peasant life might have sufficed for paintings or sculptures consigned to quiet galleries but Goebbels realized that barnyard scenes and peasant humour would not appeal to the average film audience. Furthermore, he realized that the city of Berlin had been one of the most exciting and provocative 'characters' in Weimar film, and he set about devising ways through which the 'decadent' city could be rehabilitated. The changing image of the city in Nazi film mirrors the ideological change in Nazism itself. Where early films reflected the decadence and foreignness of Berlin, later films positively delighted in the big city where Nazi bosses like Goebbels now felt at home.

The early anti-Berlin films clearly reflected the anti-Weimar prejudices prevalent during the years of Nazi rule. They often revolved around the plight of a 'good German' visiting Berlin and being shocked by the appalling 'Jewish-Bolshevik' influences there. In Putzi Hanfstängl's pathetic film based on the Horst Wessel story, *Hans Westmar – One Among Many*, the young Westmar is shown struggling to make sense of the seething city streets. When an old

Berliner, long emigrated to the United States, comes to visit him he too is shocked by the changes wrought in Berlin by the decadent Weimar politicians; he shakes his head and mutters that this 'foreign' place could not possibly be the German capital. As if to reinforce the point the neon signs which flash across the screen are in foreign languages, particularly English and French. The people in cafés and restaurants cannot understand German; revues have 'un-German' titles which reflect Berlin's 'Jewishness' (*A Jew Goes Through the World*) and its shameless licentiousness (*Berlin Without a Blouse*). When Westmar follows the old man to his pub they find it is no longer a Berlin *Kneipe* but is now called Chez Ninette, and when he asks for a beer in German the waiter mistakenly sends him to the cloakroom. The other clients are nothing but fat lecherous drunkards who ogle the women and puff on their enormous cigars, looking for all the world like something out of a sketch by Georg Grosz. 'Germany is now somewhere utterly different,' Westmar mutters in dismay.

The battle between the good Germans and the evil of Berlin continued in films like Hans Steinhoff's *Hitlerjunge Quex*, which was set in a working-class district of the city. The story revolves around a new Nazi recruit who is first drawn to the Hitler Youth when he stumbles across one of their ceremonies held around a campfire:

> He ran up the hill . . . Reaching the top, he found himself staring in terror at a dazzling flame. He was blinded by the sudden light . . . At least a thousand youths were standing around a burning pile of wood . . . *Deutschland, Deutschland über alles* swept over him, from a thousand voices, like a scalding wave. I too am a German, he thought; and he was filled with profound knowledge, stronger and more unexpected than anything he had felt in his life before . . . This was German soil, German forest, these were German youths; and he saw that he stood apart, alone, with no one to help him; and he did not know what to make of this great and sudden feeling.[115]

The boy finally admits to his handsome, clean-cut Hitler Youth leader that his father is a Communist. The old man is initially portrayed as an evil drunkard, but as the film proceeds the wise Hitler Youth leader learns about the conditions in Weimar Berlin which made the poor man desperate enough to turn to the radical left. He looks beyond his Communism and sees the true German below, and explains how the Nazis will make life better for him and for his son. The film was also an attack on local working-class district loyalties. According to the Hitler Youth leader Berliners were to forget their local identity and throw themselves into the great community of the city and of the German

Volk, which was already united by blood and not class. It is no accident that the young Communist's name is 'Völker'.

Other early films carried the attack on Weimar decadence further. Scenes were filmed in a deliberately provocative manner; Jews and capitalists were always made to look as ugly as possible and loose women appeared diseased and filthy under their layers of crusty make-up. The hated figure of the *femme fatale* was always treacherous and identifiable because she smoked and wore make-up, while the heroine was invariably blond and well scrubbed. In the film *Togger* the hero of the story is made ill by the sight of a black man dancing with a German woman, while in *Pour le Merite* the honest captain who tries to earn a living after returning from war is constantly crushed by the 'un-German' elements in Weimar Berlin. As Westmar says, 'Three million had to die. And they – they are dancing . . . boozing . . . howling!'

The anti-Weimar films continued throughout 1934, but it soon became clear to Goebbels that they were now dated. Berliners wanted to see their city projected in a positive manner. They rather liked their big buildings and their racy cars, and Goebbels was forced to dictate a new formula. The 'new city' was now to be shown as a place 'cleansed' of 'Jewish-Bolshevism'; it was therefore free to celebrate its greatness, its economic strength, its technology. Now that the enemy within had been dealt with it was time to concentrate on the common enemy across the German border. This change conveniently meshed with Hitler's armaments drive and his increasingly aggressive foreign policy. Berlin was being groomed as the capital of war.

The change in film was noticeable after 1935. Old genres were still produced, but the emphasis had shifted. In First World War films Berlin was no longer shown as the treacherous capital responsible for the 'stab-in-the-back'; suddenly it too was the home of honourable fighting men. In *Urlaub auf Ehrenwort*, made in 1937, a First World War regiment stops briefly in Berlin on its way to the western front. All the young soldiers come from various parts of the city, and the young captain grants them a few hours' free time, knowing he will be court martialled if even one does not return. The camera follows the soldiers through the city as they visit family and friends from working-class slums to the villas and apartments of the West End. '*Heimat*' Berlin is now part of the war effort and the embodiment of good German family values. Naturally, all the young soldiers, including the working-class youths, appear on time, and the honour of Berlin is saved.

Berlin was once again a positive 'central character'. Lovers in sentimental Nazi musicals could now meet on the U-Bahn or in the Funkturm or in one of the huge modern offices in the city centre; they could now spend an evening together in a club or have dinner in one of the grand hotels. The city was used more frequently as a national symbol of unity as Germany moved closer to war. The plot of the 1940 film *Wunschkonzert* (Wish Concert) revolved around a radio request programme uniting soldiers with their loved ones over the airwaves. The film was almost like a Nazi version of the Weimar *Berlin – Die Symphonie der Grossstadt*, filled with a moving photomontage of Berlin life. It began with spectacular shots of the Olympic Games, where the two main characters meet and fall in love. The scenes of Berlin's 1936 triumph were clearly meant to boost morale and remind Berliners what they were fighting for. When the hero is sent to the front the two lovers are brought together by the radio request concerts; as the music plays the director showed patriotic scenes of Berliners listening to the request of a loved one while doing their bit to support the war effort: mothers write to their sons while knitting items for the winter, and happy new babies who have yet to see their young fathers gurgle at the camera.[116]

The new films reflected the new tendency to mix *völkisch* themes with images of Berlin as a modern centre of technological and military strength. In *Der Herrscher* (The Ruler) of 1937 the city was portrayed as an industrial powerhouse run by good Germanic males, while in the 1941 *Heimkehr* (Going Home) and *Amerika – Ein mann will nach Deutschland* (America – A Man Wants to Go to Germany) it was also a beacon drawing Germans home.

The most successful of Goebbels's films were love stories and musicals in which the propaganda message was hidden in a flood of sentimentality mixed with toe-tapping fun. The most famous was *Die grosse Liebe* (The Great Love) of 1942, in which once-decadent Berlin nightlife was used as a backdrop. By now the women who worked in the dance halls and revues were portrayed not as harlots but as honourable members of society, although in this case the heroine, Zarah Leander, a dancing girl, wears a military uniform rather than suspender belt and sequins. Leander has a passionate affair with a Luftwaffe officer and belts out some of the most famous of the German war songs: *That Won't Be the End of the World* and *I Know Someday a Miracle Will Happen*, but in the end this moral 'artiste' recognizes the importance of her country, and nobly bears the pain of self-sacrifice. As the war dragged on directors became less coy about depicting its effects, and a number of films, such as *Der verzauberte Tag* (The Magic Day), depicted love stories between nurses and soldiers on leave or, later, wounded men. The war began to creep into even the most banal fare: at the end of the 1942 musical *Wir machen Musik* the hero turns to the audience, pulls down his ultra-modern skylight blind, and reminds them to black out their windows when they go home.

Berlin society of the 1930s benefited from the large film studios as many of the 'great stars' of the Weimar period stayed on to add prestige to Nazi Berlin. The multi-talented Emil Jannings, who had played opposite Marlene Dietrich in *The Blue Angel*, took to the new masters with gusto; after the filming of the anti-English Boer War film *Ohm Krüger* he was heard boasting about the number of extras who had been killed during the filming. Otto Gebühr added immensely to the prestige of Nazi film by agreeing to continue playing Frederick the Great in the seemingly endless productions about the life of the Prussian monarch. Frederick cropped up in dozens of other films as well: *Ein Schritt vom Wege* was a comic love story about a young couple who get lost on the tour of Sanssouci, and walk reverentially around touching Frederick's library books and furniture until they see a vision of the great man himself. Goebbels adored the film stars and courted all, from the directors Veit Harlan and Leni Riefenstahl to the 'great stars' Jenny Jugo, Karl Ludwig Diehl, Willi Birgel, Lilian Harvey and, until Hitler insisted upon her removal, his infamous Czech mistress Lida Baarova. The man responsible for the elimination of 'decadent' culture would sit in the Berlin Club of Comradeship of German Artists, surrounded by scantily clad starlets, drinking and toasting and dancing to the jazz and Broadway numbers forbidden to other Germans. Goebbels was not the only hypocrite where film was concerned. Hitler's favourite, *The Blue Angel*, was publicly banned but even after Heinz Hilpert had failed to woo Dietrich back to Berlin Hitler would secretly watch the film in the comfort of the Chancellery. Hollywood films were a regular feature there – Hitler liked *King Kong* and Goebbels gave him thirteen Mickey Mouse films as a Christmas present.[117]

It was not unusual for clubs and variety halls to carry on from Weimar into the Nazi period without a break; indeed, many of Weimar's famous clubs and *Lokale* remained open, including the Haus Vaterland, with its collection of *kitsch* restaurants, the Admiralspalast, with revues like *Heut bin ich verliebt* (Today I am in Love) which featured the Admiral girls until the early 1940s, and the Schiffbauerdammtheater, which continued to produce musicals like *Mädel ahoi!* (Maidens Ahoy!) until well into the war. In the early years even Hitler sometimes went over to the Wintergarten or Scala to watch the kicklines of Tiller Girls or Hiller Girls, whom he claimed to admire because their training pushed them 'to the breaking point of the human body'. Others went to the Plaza to see insipid shows by Willi Kollo, Hans Brennecke and Paul Lincke, or to the Scala to watch the musicals and revues which, despite open attacks on the work of James Klein and Herman Haller, still featured their rows of scantily clad girls – the Scala girls – dancing away to 'Aryan' jazz numbers. A Propaganda Ministry official noted that the Scala was now engaged in the 'utilization of naked women on a very large scale . . . It is outright embarrassing to see a rebirth of the long-dead genre of "living sculptures", in the form of living reproductions of the paintings of classical masters.' One young party member was shocked by a risqué 'Adam and Eve' revue at the Scala: 'Is it not disgraceful for us Aryans, when we allow the appearance of dancers whose "costumes" lay bare with every movement the charms of woman – a woman who as a German mother should be holy to us, as we have intoned again and again?'[118] Shortly afterwards an angry storm trooper wrote to the Reich Culture Chamber decrying the 'Semitic-oriental-erotic veil-games' played by loincloth-clad 'beauty dancers' at the Stella-Palast: 'One feel that one has been sent back to the worst times of the Weimar era.'[119] But the Nazis realized that the revues were highly popular, and justified displays of nudity by reminding Germans that the healthy Aryan body should be celebrated; even the SS newspaper *Das schwarze Korps* tried to point out the difference between the 'chaste' pictures of nude German women and the 'lascivious' pictures of the women of the stage.[120]

The Nazi policy on cabaret was equally confused. Most of Weimar's brilliant and mercurial cabaret artists had been forced to flee Berlin in 1933 and a number of them, including the great writer Kurt Tucholsky, the satirical cartoonist for the *Berliner illustrirte Zeitung* Paul Simmel, and the *conférencier* at the Kadeko, Paul Nikolaus, committed suicide in despair.[121] Even so, a few notable performers were permitted to remain in the city. Some quickly conformed to the demands of the new regime. Paul Schneider-Duncker, who had founded one of Berlin's first cabarets with Rudolf Nelson, became a staunch supporter of the Nazis and an overt anti-Semite; Paul Lincke continued to write and direct for the Nazi cabaret; Wilhelm Millowitsch (or rather his wife) wrote letters to the Nazis denouncing Jews in a vain attempt to allow him to keep his job, and Trude Hesterberg proved herself an opportunist by joining the Nazi Party and the Fighting League for German Culture, even denying her earlier friendship with Heinrich Mann, all of which meant that she was given official permission to open her own cabaret called the Musen-schaukel in 1933. When this folded a year later she became a successful freelance performer and spent the rest of the Nazi period as a guest of cabarets like the Kadeko. Although not an overt Nazi sympathizer Claire Waldoff was beloved by the party and remained in Berlin throughout the Nazi period, grinding out the same 'Berlin' songs and giving many the false impression that little had changed in the world of Berlin cabaret. A number of Jews stayed on in Berlin and tried to continue in the cabaret. Max Ehrlich was allowed to give performances, but only for Jewish audiences sponsored by the Kulturbund deutscher Juden; he even managed to bring Rosa Valetti back from Austria for a number of guest appearances in 1934. Erwin Lowinsky, or 'Elow', was actually permitted to start a new cabaret called Elow's Kunstlerspiele Uhlandeck on the Kurfürstendamm, which he ran until it was 'Aryanized' in 1934.[122]

Some famous 'Aryan' performers braved the threat of the camps to poke fun at the Nazis themselves. Werner Finck stayed on in Berlin and opened a smaller version of the Katakombe, where his carefully coded attacks on Nazism ruffled important feathers: he performed a skit which implied it was better to sit in a café with a prostitute than with a woman collecting for the Nazi Winterhilfe. The Tingel-Tangel remained open until performers were accused of 'defaming' the state by, for example, giving the Nazi salute and then tapping their heads as if to say it was lunacy. The Katakombe and the Tingel-Tangel were closed down in May 1935 and a number of performers, including Werner Finck, Heinrich Giesen, Walter Trautschold, Walter Lieck, Walter Gross and Eckehard Arendt, were sent to Columbia Haus and then for brief periods to concentration camps. The Kadeko remained the most important venue in Nazi Berlin and although it usually pandered to official taste there were brief moments of real satire, as when Helmut Buth, Manfred Dlugi and Wilhelm Meissner, otherwise known as 'die drei Rulands', who now worked with the reinstated Finck, dressed themselves in architects' smocks and made acerbic comments on the plans to rebuild Berlin: the city had always been considered ugly, they quipped, until Hitler's hideous construction sites made whatever was left look truly beautiful. As a result of these jokes Finck, the conférencier and die drei Rulands were dismissed from the Reich Culture Chamber in February 1939, although Finck was permitted to write a weekly arts review for a newspaper. There was a great deal of street humour about the Nazis, particularly about the lower ranking Bonzen (big-wigs), and even Hitler was not exempt. Jokes were often of a crude sexual nature and took the form of innocent questions about the consequences of Göring's weight problem on his love life, or why the Führer held his cap tightly against his groin while reviewing parades. Recently such jokes have been cited as an indication of resistance to the regime, but they were nothing of the kind, and even the Gestapo distinguished between those who made crude jokes but were otherwise model Nazis and those whose comments betrayed dubious political loyalties.[123]

For those who did not ask too many questions about the true nature of the regime, life improved dramatically throughout the 1930s. It seemed to many that the Nazis had preserved the very best of Weimar Berlin: films were everywhere, restaurants opened by the dozen, and much of Weimar social life which had revolved around the grand hotels and the embassy parties continued almost as before, the difference being that the starlets now hung on the arms of prominent Nazis. Even institutions like the Berlin Press Ball continued, as did the Opera Ball, upon which the new impresario Göring lavished literally millions of marks. With the moralizing of the early 1930s over, Berliners enjoyed a relatively relaxed atmosphere. Swing and jazz began to emerge from the Nazi clubs for the enjoyment of the general public. Nazi radio, magazines and advertising began to entice Berliners with the promise of goods, food and drink which they had not enjoyed since before the Depression. Many Weimar nightclubs remained open, like the Femina, with its table telephones and pneumatic tubes. The famous Kurfürstendamm clubs like the Atlantic Bar, the Kakadu Cabaret, which served hot meals until 3 a.m., the Königin Café, which featured Felicitas Henrich's late-night dance music, stayed open; the Russian vodka and caviar clubs like the Don and the Troika on the Wittenbergplatz flourished well into the late 1930s. The best bands played at the Delphi and the St Pauli; the new Berolina Roofgarden Club at Alexanderplatz became a popular spot, while the Resi still featured indoor watersports. Restaurants were somewhat less exotic; traditional German food was the norm – along, of course, with German-Italian cuisine, which became popular as Germany strengthened her ties with Mussolini. Even so, from the Kroll Garten to the Linden Restaurant to the Prälaten am Zoo the food was plentiful, and for those who could afford Hörcher's or the Adlon or the Kaiserhof champagne and caviar were never in short supply. Foreigners noticed that the quality of food was not up to the standard of Paris or New York but Berliners rarely travelled now and for them it seemed like paradise after the post-war deprivation. This provincialism affected other luxury goods available in the Berlin shops; perfumes had unpleasant names like Schöne Frauen Sympathie, Rosa Centifolia, or the particularly dire IA-33, which promised to be 'temperamental and racy until the last drop' but which apparently smelled like a combination of axle grease and dead plants, and compared to the output of the Paris fashion houses Magda Goebbels's fake silk gowns were hideous. All this might have seemed grim to visiting Parisians and New Yorkers but in the eyes of most other Germans Berlin was decidedly sophisticated and modern. Some provincial Nazi leaders were shocked by the goings-on there, and would leave shaking their heads and wondering if Hitler was aware of the state of his capital.

One of the problems was that Berlin still looked modern; indeed contradictions between the new Nazi modernity and the *völkisch* aesthetic were rife. The Bauhaus, which by 1933 had moved to Berlin, had been closed down when Hitler came to power but many of the items produced under the Nazis clearly owed more to Gropius than they did to anything else and it is sometimes difficult to accept that the shiny chrome surfaces, the steel-tubed chairs, the rounded cutlery, the plate glass, the recessed lighting built for Ley's new factories, and the sparse wallpapers which were popular in Nazi circles, were produced after 1933. When Goebbels moved into the nineteenth-century Schinkel building on the Wilhelmsplatz he wrote of his contempt for the nineteenth-century style: 'Workmen will . . . have to get rid of all this stucco, and throw away the musty plush curtains: I can't function in these dark rooms; I need sunlight, clean, clear lines . . .'[124] Two days later he added that the old bureaucrats who opposed the changes 'haven't caught on that our revolution will not be stopped either by old men, old files, or old stucco'. Even Hitler, who had been greatly influenced by Troost, had a penchant for enormous plate-glass windows and harsh rectangular rooms which were decidedly 'modern'; in fact Speer noted that many top Nazis favoured what he referred to as the 'cruise liner' style, with its chrome and art deco elements, as opposed to the pointed-roof village style touted in official propaganda. After 1936 many Nazis began to openly praise modern Berlin architecture even if it had been built before 1933; the Rummelsburg power plant was described as a 'marvel' and even the Shell building, today seen as the quintessential symbol of the Weimar era, was described in a Nazi brochure as a masterpiece, with its hundreds of windows and beautiful wavy facade mirrored in the Landwehr Canal. New structures were also praised for their 'modernity'; the wind tunnels and accelerator in Dahlem or the enormous eight-storey refrigeration house at the Berlin Osthafen were shown to have put Berlin ahead of other cities, as had 'the modern city buildings at Fehrbelliner Platz with their gigantic curved facade' or Hitler's Deutschlandhalle, which was one of the 'largest halls in the world'.[125] The bizarre love of traffic was resurrected for the 1930s city and Potsdamer Platz was once again proudly referred to as the 'busiest intersection in the world'. In a thinly veiled copy of Walther Mehring's poem, the Nazi columnist Max Ehlert wrote in 1937: 'Is there another picture that so personifies modern Berlin as the Potsdamer Platz today? This haste and movement of cars and people and yet the highest order reigns . . . an unforgettable image.' Modern technology was now as popular as it had been at the height of the 1920s and people were encouraged to buy new gadgets such as cameras, which were actively promoted through events like the Berlin photography exhibition of 1937.

The new image for Berlin seemed to contradict all that the Nazis had stood for before 1933, but as Hitler moved Germany closer to war he wanted a strong, contemporary, industrial capital at the helm. Berlin was now the symbol of the German Reich, and he and Goebbels devised a number of spectacular events which would ram this message home. The most famous was the Olympics of 1936, which was widely seen as the moment at which Germany reasserted herself on the world stage.[126]

Although initially sceptical Hitler became convinced of the propaganda opportunities afforded by the Olympic Games in 1933 and he threw his weight behind the project. Berlin was to be turned into the greatest host city since the Games left Greece, and he ordered the construction not only of an enormous stadium to seat 100,000 people, but a grand Olympic bell and a complex which was to include a vast open-air parade ground, a swimming stadium, a hockey rink and the huge Deutschlandhalle. New underground stations were built linking the buildings to the city centre, roads were widened, and the chief architect

Otto March was instructed to build his structures from natural stone: 'When a nation has four million unemployed,' Hitler said, 'it must seek ways and means of creating work for them.' The construction programme did indeed put Berliners back to work; the labour force on the main stadium, built of limestone, basalt and marble blocks, consisted of no fewer than 2,600 men. A monthly propaganda magazine called the *Olympic Games* was published to inform Berliners of progress on the site, an exhibition called 'Sport in Hellenic Times' was mounted in the Berlin Museum, and an Olympic caravan toured the country bringing news of forthcoming events in the Reich capital.[127] Berliners got their first glimpse of the new stadium in April 1936 and the reaction was overwhelmingly positive. The building was greater than anything yet built in the city, and the assembly area outside could hold 250,000 people.

If Berliners wanted proof that Hitler was a consummate liar they would have needed to look no further than his cynical moves to ensure that the Games stayed in Berlin. Amidst the cheers for the new buildings the international community became increasingly worried by reports of abuse, terror, concentration camps and the harassment of the Jews.[128] Concern grew when Hitler decreed in July 1934 that no Jews would be permitted in the German team or when the magazine *Der Dietwart* wrote, 'We cannot afford to keep any Jews as members because (a) we see ourselves being viciously attacked from within, and (b) they are organized as an international movement and put their racial interests above national ones. It is for this reason that we keep the Jews at a distance from our own organizations.' International observers were also worried about the fact that many young Germans were being forced into competitive sport under the motto: 'Your body belongs to your country, as it is to your country that you owe your existence.' The concern increased further after Jim Wango, a thirty-eight-year-old black wrestler under contract to a German trainer, appeared in an international contest in Nuremberg in March 1935. After he had defeated a number of white wrestlers Julius Streicher appeared in the ring and forbade Wango to continue, claiming he was appalled that the organizers had 'put a negro on view and let him compete with white people'. When Wango fell ill soon after the fight he was refused treatment in Nuremberg and by the time he reached a hospital in Berlin he had died of a kidney ailment. It was Wango's death, above all, which nearly lost Hitler his Games. The British ambassador strongly warned against participating in Berlin, while the French ambassador sent a message to Paris raising questions about 'how, in general terms, the German Government intends to treat coloured people . . . and in particular, at the time of the Olympic Games'. The Americans were furious, not least because they did not want to see some of their best athletes maltreated because of their race, and by the summer of 1935 many thought that the United States should boycott the Games. Anxieties mounted after 15 September, when the Nuremberg laws were passed legalizing racial discrimination in Germany. In the end the Olympics were saved by Hitler's clever manoeuvring.

By the time the controversy broke Hitler had already invested heavily in the Games and to have them cancelled would have been a personal blow to his authority. Suddenly he announced that German Jews could participate after all and rejected accusations that Germany was racist. Famous German-Jewish athletes in exile were invited to return, including the high-jumper Gretel Bergmann, who had fled to England, and the fencing champion Helen Meyer. The international community was not fooled, but it had been pacified.[129] Some saw through Hitler's ploy: E. L. Woodward, professor of history at All Souls, wrote,

> Facing the situation means realizing that you cannot trust any promise these people make. Of course they are trying to beguile us — why not? ... I should be quite open and say that we cannot trust the present regime, and will come to no agreement with them. If agreements are worthless, why make them? ... We know that about 300 people a month are still being done in by the Nazi police, but we shall hurrah all right at the Olympic Games.[130]

And they did.

With the Games now certain to take place, Hitler was even more determined to show Berlin's best face to the world. Orders flew from the Chancellery to 'clean up Berlin'. The veritable forest of signs all around Berlin reading, JEWS NOT WELCOME, JEWS THE ROAD TO PALESTINE DOES NOT GO THROUGH HERE! or NO JEWS OR ANIMALS were removed and stored in the basements of the local town halls. No anti-Jewish comments were to be made in public between 30 June and 1 September. Der Stürmer was removed from public view. People were given detailed instructions as to how to treat 'foreign-looking' visitors, and Walther Darré explained that even if Jewish tourists arrived Berliners must treat them 'just as politely as Aryan guests'. The city became like a fantastic stage set. The entire East–West Axis was beautifully decorated; the government buildings on Unter den Linden were hung with 45-foot-long swastika banners and flags of all the German towns; the Brandenburg Gate was festooned with gigantic flags and oak garlands, and Berliners replaced the vegetables in their window boxes with specially designed flower displays. All houses on the main thoroughfares were repaired and painted and then smothered in swastikas, and the entire six-mile route from the Brandenburg Gate to the Reich Sports Field was decorated with ribbons and banners looping from tree to tree. The Games were to go ahead. In the process they would give Hitler one of his greatest propaganda victories and would further blind the world to his ultimate goals. It would have been a bloodless move to boycott the Games, but by ignoring the plight of the thousands of Germans already languishing in Hitler's prisons and camps the international community had unwittingly set out on the slippery slope of appeasement.

As it was, the Games were a great success. On the eve of the opening the city was buzzing with excitement. Thousands of people braved the rain to camp overnight by the Brandenburg Gate and in the morning they were rewarded for their patience with parades and spectacles. At eleven o'clock that morning an emotional ceremony was held at the War Memorial, after which 100,000 boys and girls gathered at the Lustgarten for a Festival of Youth. A few hours later over half a million people lined the street to watch the procession of the Olympic flame through the city. A hundred thousand spectators had already gathered in the stadium to watch the airship *Hindenburg*, which floated overhead. At exactly three o'clock Hitler's black Mercedes pulled out of the Chancellery into Unter den Linden. The crowds were so large that it took him an hour to reach the stadium. A roar went up as he walked between the athletes and took his place to the sound of the national anthem. The stadium erupted in loud cheers for each team, particularly for the French, with whom many now hoped to bury their differences – to Hitler's visible annoyance. To an enormous wave of applause Hitler declared the Games open, the torch was lit, 20,000 pigeons were set loose, music played, people cheered; the atmosphere was overwhelming. The adulation of Hitler was frightening for non-Germans; people yelled themselves hoarse crying '*Heil* Hitler' and stared at his box to catch his every movement. There were famous incidents which gave a glimpse of the Nazi ideology – including Hitler's anger at the performance of the great American athlete Jesse Owens. According to Baldur von Schirach, Hitler responded to a request for him to congratulate the hero with: 'The Americans should be ashamed of themselves, letting negroes win their medals for them. I shall not shake hands with this negro.' But few Berliners noticed the snub and cheered Owens on. The city was basking in positive international attention for the first time since before the war, and nothing could spoil their fun. Clubs and dance-halls opened up and real jazz was permitted; Jack Hylton played in the Mocca Efty bar and prostitutes were allowed back.

Over 1.2 million visitors came to Berlin that summer and became convinced that the horror stories they had heard about Hitler's Germany were simply untrue. The novelist Thomas Wolfe wrote about the golden spell which the Olympics cast over Berlin in *You Can't Go Home Again*, poking fun at the 3,000 foreign journalists who refused to see beyond the glamour and the dancing and the parties. The visitors were fêted with rounds of lunches, dinners, dances, embassy gatherings, government engagements and cocktail parties which recalled the *Kaiserzeit*. Göring was the most ostentatious of the hosts; at a lunch held at the Air Ministry he decorated the lawns with lights and filled with pool with floating lilies and as the *corps de ballet* from the Berlin Opera danced on the lawn giant screens were pulled away to reveal a Viennese fun fair. Göring also acted as host at the government dinner at the State Opera House: all seats were removed, the stage was made level and guests ate from round gold tables which were soon cleared away to make room for opera singers and a night of dancing. Hitler's dinner for 200 was held in the new Chancellery, which was being shown off publicly for the first time. By far the most dramatic event was staged by Goebbels, who was determined not to be outdone by his detested rival. He had the Wehrmacht construct special pontoon bridges for access to the Peacock Island for the 2,500 guests, while the path was lined with girls from various Berlin nightclubs dressed up as eighteenth-century pages. The island was decorated with fairy lights and torches, champagne flowed and at the end of the evening guests were entertained with a spectacular fireworks display.

When the Games were finally over Berliners surveyed their city with satisfaction. According to the *Völkischer Beobachter* Berlin had been a magnificent host city and Germany had 'shown the world its true face'. Only a few saw through the pretence. The United States consul general in Berlin, George Messersmith, said, 'To the Party and to the youth of Germany, the holding of the Olympic Games in Berlin in 1936 has become the symbol of the conquest of the world by National Socialist doctrine.' But few listened. Many visitors returned home with the impression that Hitler was a peace-loving man whose only ambition was to return Germany to her rightful place among nations. Most Berliners had been swept along by the Olympics and, like the rest of the world, believed that they heralded the dawn of a new era of self-confidence free of the humiliation of the past.[131]

The momentum of the Olympics did not let up. On 30 October, while the anti-Semitic signs were quietly replaced and the more obvious prostitutes cleared from the streets, Hitler staged a huge party to mark the tenth anniversary of Goebbels's posting as Gauleiter of the city. An exhibition was mounted in the City Hall on Alexanderplatz, and *Der Angriff* reported that Berliners had generously donated a house to Goebbels on the shores of one of Berlin's loveliest lakes where, 'after the strain of his daily work serving the people and the Reich, he can find peace, relaxation and a place to collect his thoughts'. In fact he would use the house for his numerous affairs. That evening there was a rally at the Sportpalast where Hitler spoke in praise of his faithful servant, who had begun an almost hopeless struggle in the outpost of Berlin a decade before and had

marched on ahead of this Berlin, this awakening Berlin, a fanatic filled
with faith . . . Therefore I thank you, my dear doctor, thank you today
especially for taking the flag from my hand ten years ago, which you
then planted in the capital of the Reich as the banner of the nation.
And your name stands inscribed over this ten-year struggle of the
National Socialist movement in Berlin! It is forever linked with this
battle, and will never be obliterated from German history.

The propaganda spectacles continued during the following months. The
Olympics were quickly followed by the '700th' anniversary celebrations in
Berlin. It was Hitler who decided to create a date for the founding of the city
– a date which had less to do with history than with the need for a grand
occasion. During the Weimar era the historian Ernst Kaeber, then the director
of the City Archives, had suggested a number of possible dates which could
be used to commemorate the development of Berlin-Cölln. The year 1237 was
significant only because of the existence of a document which proved the
existence of Berlin's sister city, Cölln, but it certainly did not mark the founding
date of Berlin. Kaeber had been forced out of his job when the Nazis came
to power as he was married to a 'non-Aryan'; he was forced to watch as
his idea for a minor celebration was transformed into a National Socialist
extravaganza. Dr Hermann Rügler was made the head of the Nazi Association
for the History of Berlin, and it was he who verified for Hitler that Berlin
'could be said to have been founded in 1237'.

The 700th Anniversary was carefully calculated to send a political message
both to Berliners and to other Germans. A huge exhibition was set up at the
Funkturm and special histories of the city were created to teach Berliners
about the past. The prehistory was shown to have been exclusively Germanic,
despite evidence of the Slavic settlements in the area, and Hitler was directly
linked to the glorious Prussian military past embodied by his hero Frederick
the Great. Figures as diverse as von Arnim, Hegel, Kleist, Fichte, Menzel,
Theodor Mommsen and Heinrich von Treitschke were hailed as 'great Berliners', although Horst Wessel was said to have been more important to the
city's literary history than E. T. A. Hoffmann or Wilhelm Raabe. The history
of the nineteenth and twentieth centuries was encapsulated into a neat Nazi
version in which all the 'good' in Berlin history could be linked to Adolf
Hitler. The display of photographs of the *Reichshauptstadt Heimat Berlin*
showed stirring pictures of the brave Berlin soldiers marching to war in 1914
positioned next to photographs of 'shameful Spartacus rabble rousers' attacking them in 1919. To ensure that there was no misunderstanding, one photograph was captioned: 'Soldiers of the unbeaten German army of the World
War risk their lives in the fight against the *Untermenschentum* [the sub-

humanity] which had flooded Germany'. These were followed by photographs of Hitler on the balcony of the Reich Chancellery: 'Out of the blood of the World War, out of the blood of the fallen victims, out of the fourteen year hero's war, emerged the Third German Reich. Your *Führer* fulfils the dreams of the city, and the dreams of the *völkisch* unity of Germany.' The commemorative *Berliner illustrirte Zeitung* demonstrated how historic areas of Berlin were linked to the Nazis; the Wilhelmplatz 8/9, built '200 years ago for the Master of the Order of St John', was now the centre for the Propaganda Ministry where the 'Berlin citizen' Joseph Goebbels had his office. Königsplatz 6 was shown with enormous photographs of the field marshal General von Moltke at work beside a picture of 'the new master at Königsplatz 6, the Minister of the Interior Wilhelm Frick'. Berlin was described as the 'movie star capital', the city 'with happy youth on its streets' (complete with pictures of pretty blond children), and the 'great centre of science' (shown beside atomic experiments being carried out at the Kaiser Wilhelm Institute for Physics). Berlin was the European city 'with the greatest theatre culture', it was a 'fashion capital', a 'sports capital', a 'music capital'. The military was never far away: a shining Tempelhof airfield was shown beside rows of fighter planes while Hitler Youth boys were pictured at 'weekend weapons training'.[132]

The 700th celebrations reached a climax on 16 August 1937 with a huge parade in the city centre. Again, Berlin was in a festive mood. One and a half thousand young men and women dressed in period costumes paraded along a six-mile route, while elaborate floats showed a stylized portrayal of Berlin history from the foundation of the ancient 'Germanic' settlements, through the Middle Ages and into the reign of the Hohenzollerns and the great victories of the Prussian military. In the events which followed at the Olympic Stadium armed forces personnel dressed up in costumes recreating battles and historical milestones under Speer's spotlights surrounded by hundreds of flags and banners. One witness recalled the 'special moment' when Frederick the Great's army arrived in the stadium, 'the picture of military discipline and splendour ... One hundred thousand people roared out in unison!' They roared again when the Nazi victory was recreated, and although Hitler himself did not attend (fuelling the post-war myth that Hitler hated the city) Berliners cheered loudly at the very mention of his name. Berlin was referred to as the 'centre of the Reich', the 'new focal point for Germany', the 'much loved capital', the 'most powerful city in the world'. One essay in the *Berliner illustrirte Zeitung* dealt frankly with the problems of Berlin's identity, but it also hinted at a new important role in Nazi Germany. Weimar Berlin had been 'sick', the author said, but this period of illness had clearly come to an end. Now, under the guiding hand of the National Socialists, Berlin could be as 'fresh and healthy' as the 'smallest village', for National Socialism would not leave any part of

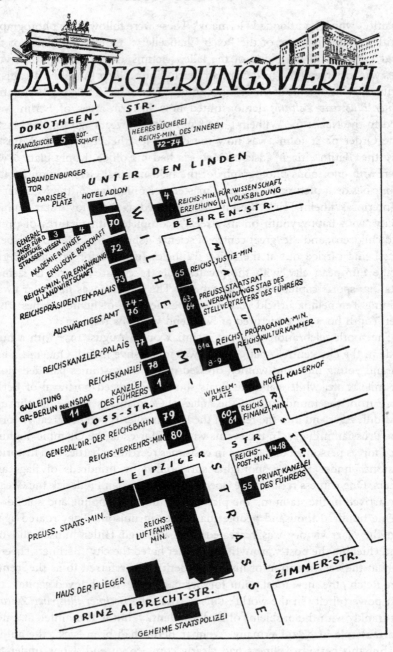

DAS REGIERUNGSVIERTEL

The Government Quarter

Germany isolated. The message was finally one of great joy: Berlin might be the antithesis of the *völkisch* German community, but it too had its place in the Reich. 'Berlin has been transformed,' the article crowed, 'and can and will maintain its new life as long as "Berlin is the Reich, and the Reich is Berlin".'

Hitler had missed the Berlin spectacle as he had spent the previous weeks in Bavaria, but he rushed back from Bayreuth for the greatest propaganda event of the year, the state visit of Mussolini, to be held on 27 September 1937. If there had been any doubt about Hitler's interest in promoting Berlin it was silenced during the following days. The celebrations were of gargantuan proportions and were clearly meant to impress the Italian leader with the loyalty and dedication of Berliners. The Führer and the Duce both delivered speeches at the Olympic Stadium which were relayed around the world and which again thrust Berlin to the forefront of Hitler's Germany. Goebbels claimed that 3 million people had lined the streets and that a third of those had stood on or around the Maifeld to hear the speeches. Hitler, betraying his increasing megalomania, said to the assembled crowd, 'We have just witnessed a historic event, the significance of which has no parallel. More than a million people have gathered here, participating in a demonstration which is being closely followed by the national communities of two countries, numbering one hundred and fifteen millions, besides hundreds of millions more in other parts of the world . . .' Mussolini was somewhat less impressed by Berlin, finding it grey and uncivilized; he caught a cold after standing in the rain for hours and when he went to have a bath in the Reichspresident's Palace he found that there was no hot water and had to go to the Adlon instead. An embarrassed Hitler had the people responsible arrested to find out if the incident had been a deliberate act of sabotage, but it proved to be caused by little more than old age. Hitler fumed to Speer that Berlin had let him down. The city was run-down and ugly. Something had to be done.

Hitler's greatest problem with the 'old' Berlin was that it had not been built in a grand style. His predecessors, he said, had no idea how to build to impress; everything in the capital seemed shoddy and second rate. With the exception of the restrained buildings in the eighteenth-century Prussian style and a few of the Kaiser's monstrosities Hitler dismissed Berlin as little more than ugly industrial sprawl. He attacked virtually every building, from the 'old shack' of the Reichstag to the Berlin Rathaus: 'Here Vienna is worthily represented,' he said. 'By contrast, consider the Berlin Rathaus. We will give Berlin a more beautiful one than Vienna's, no doubt about it!' As for the city as a whole, he complained that it lacked distinction. 'Berlin is a big city, but not a real metropolis,' he complained. 'Look at Paris, the most beautiful city in the world. Or even Vienna. Those are cities with grand style. Berlin is nothing but an unregulated accumulation of buildings. We must surpass Paris and Vienna.' To that end, he and his sycophantic architect Albert Speer worked to create plans for a new city called Germania which was to house 8 million people. It was a project which commanded Hitler's undivided attention.

As a young man Hitler had ambitions as an architect and both Speer and the Germania project occupied much of his time, becoming something of an obsession even in the darkest years of the war. All new projects from the Autobahn to the Deutschlandhalle to the Olympic complex were to be incorporated into the new plans. Hitler had initially relied upon local Berlin officials for assistance but had found them obsessed with costs and 'incapable' of comprehending his grand vision. He treated them with his usual disdain: 'Let them think we're considering building our new capital on the Muitzsee in Mecklenburg,' he said. 'You'll see how the Berliners come to life at the threat that the federal government may move out.' And he was right. When he suggested he would build a 'Washington-style' political capital elsewhere the locals became more than co-operative, although he was still frustrated by their provincialism.[133] When Mayor Julius Lippert disagreed with the Führer's proposal to chop down Berlin's famous trees in order to widen Unter den Linden Hitler told Speer, 'Lippert is incapable of governing a metropolis and incapable of understanding the historical importance I intend to give to it.' Goebbels was ordered to find a replacement mayor.

In January 1937 Albert Speer was officially named 'Inspector General of Buildings for the Renovation of the Federal Capital', and was given complete control of the Berlin project. After this Berliners heard only vague rumours about the plans for their city. The scale models were top secret and were kept locked in Speer's office at the Academy of Arts on Pariser Platz. Speer's secretary Annemarie remembered that

> The model Speer had built downstairs took up almost a whole huge room. It was so beautiful, so complete, you know, with all the streets and trees and flowers and fountains, and all the buildings finished and lit to perfection ... There was a special entrance to this room from the Chancellery gardens, and that is how Hitler would come ... Sometimes very late at night, sometimes after lunch. But whenever he came – and this went on long into the war too – he would stay for a long time, and however tense he seemed when he arrived, he would visibly change as he looked at this vision of the future.[134]

Speer was not as dismissive of old Berlin as his master and tried to protect Berlin landmarks, maintaining that 'our aim in general was to appease the feelings of the public in carrying out our plans'. Speer and Hess also designed new residential housing while Willie Schelkes tried to preserve the green areas around the city.[135]

Speer's appointment and the new plans reflected Hitler's mounting ambitions. In 1933 the Führer had been ready to move into Bismarck's old residence but after his success in the mid 1930s he decided that this was too restrained. With much banging of fists he declared:

> I am too proud to move into former palaces. That I refuse to do. The new Reich will create new spaces for itself and its own buildings. I will not move into the old palaces. In the other nations – in Moscow they're squatting in the Kremlin, in Warsaw they're squatting in the Belvedere, in Budapest in the Königsburg, in Prague in the Hradschin. Everywhere they're squatting in some old building. My simple ambition is to present the new German Reich with buildings it need not be ashamed of . . . But above all, this new German Republic is neither a boarder nor a lodger in the royal chambers of bygone days![136]

His 'simple ambition' was to build a fitting palace for himself which would be not twice, not ten times, but 150 times the size of Bismarck's residence; together with its gardens it would occupy 22 million square feet in the very centre of Berlin. The reception rooms were to lead through several long marbled halls and salons into a dining room, which could accommodate thousands, and then into a 400-seat theatre/cinema. When Goebbels pointed out that this did not quite square with the simple 'man of the people' image he and Hitler had worked so hard to create the Führer retorted, 'I myself would find a simple little house in Berlin quite sufficient. I have enough power and prestige; I don't need such luxury to sustain me. But believe me, those who come after me will find such ostentation an urgent necessity . . . my spirit will have conferred tradition upon the building. If I live in it only for a few years, that will be good enough.'[137] Anyway, he said, he would still sleep on his small iron bed, which presumably could be photographed to reassure the German people that he had not lost touch with them.

Not only the palace, but the entire city was to be rebuilt in Hitler's oppressive Nazi 'neo-classical' style. His motivating idea was that everything had to be longer, bigger, wider, taller and more massive than the buildings in any other capital. The plans, most of which survived the war, are memorable not for their beauty but for their cold and forbidding giantism. The plan included the creation of a 'cross of four main thoroughfares of unprecedented generosity [each of them wider and greener than Hitler's favourite avenue, the Champs-Élysées in Paris] and, with money no object, an entire new railway system'.[138] The main Anhalt and Potsdam railway stations were to be shifted to release enormous strips of land in the city centre for an imposing three-mile north–south avenue. Visitors arriving by rail would alight in a building bigger than New York's Grand Central Station, and step out on to a 3,300-foot-long marble plaza which would end in a huge Arch of Triumph engraved with the names of the 1,800,000 Germans who died in the war. From there one would see the great domed Volkshalle – so massive that St Peter's in Rome would fit into it several times over – which would in turn be faced by a huge ornamental water basin 350 metres wide and 1,000 in length.[139] The avenue would have a new cinema for 2,000 people, a new opera house, three theatres, a new concert hall, a congress hall, hotels, restaurants, an indoor swimming pool in the Roman style, luxury shops and plenty of courtyards and colonnades, all built of solid stone so that in future centuries they would become ruins like those of the ancient world.[140] 'Berlin must change its face,' Hitler said, 'in order to adapt to its great new mission.'[141]

Berliners were finally given an indication of the scale of the plans when the construction of the East–West Axis got under way. The new stretch of road still cuts through the Tiergarten and was unveiled on 20 April 1938 – Hitler's fiftieth birthday. Hundreds of thousands of Berliners cheered as the 60,000 troops marched past his podium with their guns, trucks, tanks and other weapons of war. The parade lasted for four hours. The axis itself was lined with enormous eagle and swastika pillars which stood between Speer's characteristic double-headed bronze lamps and ran past the Siegessäule, to which another layer of cannon had been added, by then moved to its present spot at the Grosser Stern. The only surviving relic of the second phase, the North–South Axis, is nothing more than a lump of concrete. Hidden behind greenery and fencing near the railway bridge at the Dudenstrassse is a large spherical mass which locals erroneously refer to as an air-raid shelter. The lump of cement is in fact the first trial foundation for Hitler's triumphal arch, and even this small segment dwarfs those who stand beside it and gives a hint of the oppressive scale of the plans.

Such scattered remnants of Hitler's dream are a stark reminder that he intended Berlin to be the centre of a huge and powerful empire which was to rule not only Germany, but Europe and Russia as well. Looking at the architectural model in 1937, he turned to Speer and pointed to the eagle perched atop the gleaming Volkshalle. The swastika in its talons, he said, must be changed to a globe, for Germania was to rule not only Germany, 'but the world'. Two years later he would say, 'Berlin must be the true centre of Europe, a capital that for everybody shall be *the* capital.'[142]

Hitler's fanaticism and his madness were gradually revealed in part through his obsession with the Berlin-Germania plans. When he learned that Stalin was erecting a socialist-realist monstrosity to himself in Moscow he was, according to Speer, visibly shaken. On the day he invaded Russia, one of the most significant days in German history, he actually turned to his architect and said, 'Now, this will be the end of their building for good and all.' This idiocy continued well into the war. The London Blitz was unleashed not after serious military deliberation but was the result of a childish tantrum when Hitler heard that a few scattered British bombs had hit Berlin in late 1940. In a fit of rage he ordered the Luftwaffe to top bombing British airfields and attack London instead, a move which spared precious British planes and which ultimately led to his defeat in the Battle of Britain.[143] The obsession with Germania continued until the end. Even as the fronts crumbled and the enemy moved on the city Hitler would bring out the plans and ramble on about his vision of the city. When Goebbels's Propaganda Ministry received a direct hit only weeks before the end of the war, Hitler told him in all sincerity that he would soon build him another. Surrounded by death and smouldering ruins, he could still say that the bombing of Berlin was a blessing in disguise because it would save on costly demolition work later on.

By the late 1930s the idea of the Thousand Year Reich and Germania had become inextricably linked in Hitler's mind. To create a true imperial capital, however, he must have an empire. Hitler's huge scale models, his gigantic buildings and his triumphal cannon-lined avenues advertised his intention to wage a war of conquest, and made it clear that Germania was not meant to dominate Germany alone.[144] Even when they were finally shown the plan, however, most Berliners chose not to question its true meaning.

The first years of Hitler's Reich had seen thousands of Berliners imprisoned, tortured and murdered, but for the majority he had brought unprecedented prosperity, and they adored him. The attention lavished on the capital had raised the standard of living and increased the quality of life beyond their wildest dreams. As they enjoyed the fruits of Hitler's 'Golden Thirties' with the glitzy revues and the new fast cars, the glamorous grand hotels, the thriving cinema, the safe streets and the impressive goose-stepping parades, few stopped to think about where it was all leading. The ease of life mixed with a new sense of pride blinded many to Hitler's crimes against his own people, and against his ultimate aims of conquest.

The attitude of Berliners to the Nazis remains difficult to understand. Frau Margerete Fischer, wife of the historian Fritz Fischer, explained: 'Many who nowadays always say, "Yes, we were a hundred per cent against it" – all of that one can say very easily afterward ... there were certainly eighty per cent who lived productively and positively throughout the time ... We also had good years. We had *wonderful* years.'[145] The problem has been compounded by post-war notions of 'collective guilt', which led ordinary Germans after 1945 to deny and to avoid and to forget the early years of adulation in favour of memories of their shock after Stalingrad or their anger at the bombing raids or their fear of the approaching Red Army. True, the prosperity of the 1930s and the 'Hitler myth' faded and was replaced by increased cynicism and terror by 1945, but Hitler would not have been able to start a war in the first place had he not secured the support of the vast majority of the population in the 1930s.

There was very little scepticism in the early years precisely because Hitler seemed to have accomplished everything most Germans wanted. At the same time the Nazis preyed on a host of human frailties, ranging from gullibility and cowardice to pride and cruelty. Hitler's genius lay in his ability to create a dual system which used both terror and material success simultaneously: terror against those who did not fit into the new 'racially pure' Reich, and increased prosperity for those who were fortunate enough to belong to the new Germanic community. Nineteen-thirties Berlin was a schizophrenic mixture of both extremes, with the victims gradually becoming dehumanized and isolated and the 'members' of the new Germany turning away from disturbing scenes on their streets, stopping their ears to rumours of torture in the prisons and in the new camps, quietly accepting that increasingly unpleasant measures needed to be taken against Jews and other 'enemies of the state' and exhibiting a stupefying naïveté as regards Hitler's ultimate aims.

They ignored them at their peril. A loathsome spectre was already hovering over the city, and for those with eyes to see the vision was terrifying. By the late 1930s Berlin was already well down the road to a war which would cost millions upon millions of innocent lives. Berlin, and the world, would pay a terrible price for the attempt to turn the capital city into the imperial Germania.

XII

The Second World War

Their violence is allowed to rage, unchecked:
already half the world is ruined, wrecked.

(*Faust*, Part II, Act 1)

WHEN THE SECOND WORLD WAR BEGAN Berlin was at its most arrogant, its most pompous, and its most dangerous. When it ended, 45 million human beings lay dead, Europe was in turmoil, and the once prosperous capital was a ruin. The German nation had been comprehensively shattered in a nightmare of gruesome violence.

Studying the period one is faced with a web of conflicting interpretations and memories. Berliners tend to see their city primarily as a victim of war, crushed by endless bombing raids, its heroic dissidents murdered by the Nazis and its suburbs overrun by the brutal soldiers of the Red Army. This image contains elements of truth, but it is highly selective. Berlin had another more sinister side. It was the pinnacle of a ruthlessly centralized Nazi state and housed the hundreds of ministries, departments, offices and institutes filled with tens of thousands of willing employees who directed the most criminal aspects of the war. Other towns had their dutiful party bosses but it was Berlin which became the oppressive administrator of Nazi terror.[1] The history of the city at war is contentious precisely because its citizens played a complex role; Berliners were both perpetrators and victims of this terrible chapter of history.

Long before war broke out Berlin was being transformed into a military powerhouse and it had become obvious that Hitler was preparing a staging post for future conflict. By the mid 1930s it was the headquarters of three armed services swollen by conscription, contained nearly a hundred military barracks and other installations, and was awash with steel-helmeted troops.[2] The sight cheered some Berliners, but it sickened the rest of the world. Terrified by the thought of another war and bewitched by Goebbels's masterful propaganda newsreels, Europeans convinced themselves that accommodation with the mighty new Germany was the safest policy.

The road to war was hidden behind a latticework of lies and hypocrisy

475

which culminated in Hitler's charm offensive in the late 1930s. He had come to power openly declaring what he intended to do. References to retribution for Versailles and the desire for *Lebensraum* (living space) littered *Mein Kampf* and were rammed home in virtually every one of his speeches from 1933 until 1939. Germany was to become a racially pure Reich with Berlin – to be renamed Germania – at its heart; the new empire was to reach from Jutland to the Brenner and 'from the Riga Dom to the Strasburger Kirche'. The question was not if, but when. And yet Hitler's impersonation of a peace-loving states-man, backed by a thinly veiled threat of military might, was one of the most successful deceptions in history. On 7 March 1936 Hitler re-militarized the Rhineland. The French did nothing. In July 1936 Hitler and Mussolini joined forces with the Fascists in Spain, leaving the other side open to Stalin's own brand of treachery. The world stood by. In October 1936 the Germans and Italians declared that they had formed an 'axis' around which Europe was soon to revolve. After Mussolini's visit to Berlin in November 1937 the Italians, Germans and Japanese concluded an Anti-Comintern Pact. Hitler openly stated that he intended to go to war, but the French and the British did not respond. The delay would prove disastrous.[3]

On the cool afternoon of 5 November 1937, as Berliners basked in the fond memories of their 700th Anniversary celebrations, Adolf Hitler assembled his political and military minions in the Reich Chancellery to discuss his plans for the expansion of Germany which, in the event of his death, was to act as his 'testament'. All the top military men were there, from the commander-in-chief of the air force, Göring, to the commander-in-chief of the army, Colonel-General Baron von Fritsch; from the Minister for War Field Marshal von Blomberg to Baron von Neurath, the Minister for Foreign Affairs; the minutes were taken by Hossbach. Hitler began to outline his plans. Germany's arma-ments were, he said, superior to those in any other European state at that moment, but this situation might not last. Even now Germany's potential enemies might be planning to overtake her. Furthermore, Germany needed to grow; it needed more space, and that space lay in the east. It was clear 'that Germany has nothing to gain from a long period of peace'. The question was where one could gain the most 'agriculturally useful space' at the lowest cost. The first phase should be to 'consolidate the Reich', which meant reclaiming territory, the flesh ripped from Germany in the hateful *Diktat*. The second was to be expansion into central Europe. With *Mitteleuropa* under her command Germany could get food supplies, raw materials and cheap labour which would fuel even greater campaigns into the tantalizing wealth of Ukraine and beyond.[4] Citing Frederick the Great's struggle in Silesia and Bismarck's wars against Austria and France, Hitler declared that Germany had no choice but to use force.

The room became silent. The generals did not want war; neither did the people. With much hand-wringing Blomberg warned Hitler of the strong Czech fortifications while von Fritsch said France would certainly attack in the west and this would lead to a feared war on two fronts. Even Göring expressed doubts, saying that at least Germany should retrieve her troops from Spain before moving ahead. Hitler rejoined that they were all cowards, they had no vision, they did not understand German destiny. Before long most of the men in the room would be removed from office, and Göring was advised to take a long holiday in San Remo.[5] The first of the four great crises which would eventually lead to war was just around the corner – the German annexation of Austria.

Austria had floundered badly after the loss of the Habsburg empire in 1918, and by the late 1930s it was a sea of discontent. Whatever the claims of post-war Austrians the painful truth was that the majority of its people wanted to join the German Reich.[6] On 12 February 1938 Hitler bullied the Austrian Chancellor Kurt von Schuschnigg into signing an agreement under which all Austrian Nazis were to be released from prison; some were to be appointed to the cabinet. He then flew to Berlin, where he made a sabre-rattling speech promising to 'protect' the 10 million Germans outside the Reich. When Schuschnigg hesitated Hitler simply marched into the welcoming country; when he visited Vienna on 14 March 1938 a mass of people surged towards him calling, 'Heil Hitler!' and paraded up and down singing Deutschland, Deutschland über Alles – a sight which did little to substantiate Austria's later claims to be Hitler's 'first victim'.[7] An orgy of anti-Semitic violence followed, during which hundreds of Viennese Jews were beaten and humiliated, their shops smashed, their belongings stolen, their lives wrecked in a few brief, devastating hours. Hitler gave a triumphalist speech on the Heldenplatz in the heart of the city surrounded by thousands of cheering Austrians. Those who did not raise their hands in the Nazi salute had their shins soundly kicked by their neighbours. Berlin was not alone in this particular method of social control.

Berliners greeted the news with self-satisfaction: 'Austria! And not a shot fired!' they said. Centuries of rivalry between the Habsburg and the Prussian capitals had seemingly come to an end, and Berlin had won the decisive victory. Gentle Vienna with its yellow baroque buildings and its air of grace had been transformed into the willing vassal of the tough, coarse capital of the north. Hitler was dazzled by his own success and immediately set out for greater conquest. The next target was the Sudetenland, a German-speaking area which had been granted to the new Czechoslovak state in 1918. It would lead to the second great crisis on the road to war.

For years Hitler had been complaining about the plight of German nationals who had been torn from their own states by the Treaty of Versailles.

One such population lived in the Sudetenland. The Depression and its accompanying misery had been shared by the Sudeten Germans, who had also endured short-sighted discrimination at the hands of the new Czech government. A combination of factors had encouraged many to turn to Hitler, who by now was offering them everything from guaranteed jobs to outright bribes, and the German propaganda war waged in the Sudetenland in 1938 was so overwhelming that the Czech government finally demanded the return of all radios to the post office. Göring summed up the German view in a speech in Berlin on 10 September: 'A petty segment of Europe is harassing human beings ... This miserable pygmy race [the Czechs] without culture – no one knows where it came from – is oppressing a cultured people and behind it is Moscow and the eternal mask of the Jew devil.' On 28 September Hitler made a vitriolic speech at the Berlin Sportpalast, during which he hurled insults at the Czech president and demanded the return of the ethnic Germans. If the Czechs did not comply, there would be war.

Once again, Hitler faced opposition from his own generals. During his interrogation by the Allied Military Intelligence officers at Nuremberg in 1945 General Franz Halder, chief of the General Staff, recalled that a group of officers headed by himself, Generals von Witzleben, Beck, Stülpnagel, the commander of the Potsdam garrison Brockdorff, and the police president of Berlin, Count von Helldorf, had planned to depose Hitler in 1939 in order to prevent war. All these men would later be implicated in the July 1944 plot. Berlin's civilians were also nervous. They were not opposed to Hitler's aims as such but their memories of the First World War were fresh and they were frightened. William Shirer remembered seeing a motorized division driving through the centre of Berlin at dusk on 27 September on its way to Czechoslovakia. There was no fanfare, no parade and no cheering mob. Two hundred people milled around Hitler's balcony as he half-heartedly reviewed his troops, clearly disappointed by the meagre showing. Hitler had expected wild cheers and Hewel, von Ribbentrop's man at the Chancellery, reported that Hitler declared, 'I cannot yet fight a war with this people.'[8] If the world had stood up to him then he might have been stopped, but Hitler was fortunate to have struck his second blow during the era of appeasement. Opposition was deflected by the announcement of the Munich Conference.

Hitler's saviour came in the nervous owl-like form of the British Prime Minister Neville Chamberlain, who, aware of British military weakness and secretly sympathetic to German territorial claims, simply gave in to all Hitler's demands.[9] The French Prime Minister Daladier and Chamberlain decided to permit the Germans to take the Sudetenland by 28 September 1938 if Herr Hitler sincerely promised that this would be his last such claim in Europe. When von Ribbentrop, who had been eager for war, criticized the agreement

Hitler responded, 'Ach, you don't need to take it so seriously. *Dieses Papier hat doch weiter keinerlei Bedeutung* – This paper is really of no great importance.'[10] When Chamberlain alighted from his plane and walked to the microphone in the chilly wind at the Croydon aerodrome, he clutched a little piece of paper with Hitler's signature on it, an agreement which guaranteed 'the peace of Europe' – peace in our time. From No 10 Downing Street he talked of his horror that a war might have been started 'because of a quarrel in a far-away country between people of whom we know nothing'. For a brief moment he was a national hero but some had already seen the awful truth: Duff-Cooper resigned his government post in disgust over the treachery to Czechoslovakia. Churchill spoke against the climb-down:

> It is the most grievous consequence . . . of what we have left undone
> in the last five years – five years of futile good intention, five years
> of eager search for the line of least resistance, five years of uninterrup-
> ted retreat of British power, five years of neglect of our air defences
> . . . We are in the presence of a disaster of the first magnitude which
> has befallen Great Britain and France. Do not let us blind ourselves
> to that.[11]

In fact Hitler was mildly annoyed by the interference of Chamberlain, whom he privately referred to as 'the arsehole': 'That fellow has spoiled my entry into Prague,' he sneered to Schacht. As the worthless piece of paper was fêted in Britain, Hitler began to mobilize his troops for an invasion of the remainder of Czechoslovakia. It was the start of the third crisis on the road to war.

The propaganda assault began first. From 12 March onwards the Berlin press began to print tales of violent Czech attacks against peaceful Germans in Bohemia. By 14 March Keitel had placed fourteen divisions, some 200,000 men, on the frontier of Bohemia and Moravia and Göring had been called back from his 'holiday' in San Remo. All was in readiness. During the afternoon of 14 March Hitler summoned President Hácha to Berlin. In an act of unbelievable cynicism the ailing old man was received with the full honours accorded to a head of state and driven through the snow to the Adlon Hotel. Hitler gave his daughter a box of chocolates. The next morning, 15 March, he was called to a meeting with Hitler, Göring, Ribbentrop and State Secretaries Weizsäcker, Meissner and Keitel at the new Reich Chancellery. On the table lay a piece of paper – an agreement to make Bohemia and Moravia a protectorate of the Reich; Slovakia was to be a republic. Hitler told Hácha that the German army was moving and could not be halted and that he should instruct his Minister of War not to resist if he wanted to avoid a bloodbath. Then he stormed out, leaving Ribbentrop and Göring pushing a pen into the old man's hand and yelling, 'Sign or half of Prague will lie in ruins within two hours! Sign it! Sign it!' Hácha collapsed, and was revived with injections.[12]

At 3.55 in the morning the deed was done; Bohemia and Moravia 'legally' became part of the German Reich and the Nazis marched into Prague. The newsreels documenting this moment of triumph showed the Wehrmacht stomping past groups of shocked civilians with their heads in their hands, crying and mourning the loss of their country. As the news was relayed to Berlin, however, the mood changed from fear to relief. Once again the Führer had won a stunning victory; few spared a thought for the Czechs now suffering the arrests and round-ups soon to become characteristic of Nazi rule. Berliners cheered as Hitler made his way through the teeming city. In their eyes, he now seemed invincible. Sir Nevile Henderson, who watched the policy of appeasement unravel around him, wrote bitterly that 'The Germans are a strange people. They seem utterly incapable of seeing any side of a question except their own or to understand the meaning of civilized decency and moderation.'[13]

Hitler's infamous fiftieth birthday on 20 April was a thinly disguised victory parade to celebrate the conquest of Czechoslovakia. The newsreels had made this quite obvious:

> Preparations for the Führer's fiftieth birthday . . . The entire nation expresses its gratitude and offers its wishes of happiness to the founder of the Greater German Reich . . . Gifts from all the Gaue of the Reich are continuously brought to the Reich Chancellery . . . Guests from all over the world arrive in Berlin . . . On the eve of the birthday, the Inspector General for the Construction of the Capital of the Reich, Albert Speer, presents to the Führer the completed East–West Axis . . . The great star of the newly erected victory column shines.[14]

Hitler beamed for four and a half hours as the 50,000 troops and columns of military hardware rolled by in the 'greatest military spectacle' ever. At the front of the box, well away from the Nazis in their uniforms and their tin-pot medals, stood a lonely figure dressed in a solemn black coat and top hat. It was Dr Hácha, 'President of the Protectorate of Bohemia and Moravia', forced to stand there as Hitler reviewed the troops that had taken his country. Such ritual humiliation was typical; indeed Hitler had specifically asked Ribbentrop to invite 'as many cowardly civilians and democrats as possible' in order to intimidate them. Ironically, it had the opposite effect. The treatment of Czechoslovakia finally brought the rest of Europe to its senses. On 16 March *The Times*, the *Daily Telegraph* and the *Daily Express* criticized Hitler with one voice and warned of his territorial ambitions in Poland. But just when they were poised to tear the mask of respectability from the face of their enemy the west received a harsh blow: on 23 August 1939 Goebbels announced that Hitler and Stalin had signed a non-aggression treaty. The west was stunned.[15]

The Germans have always been ambivalent about Russia, on the one hand fearful of her barbaric might and on the other mesmerized by their notions of the 'Russian soul' and impressed by her vastness and the endurance of her people. By the time Hitler came to power opinion in Berlin was firmly divided between two conflicting schools. The 'Pan-German' school, which included many in the General Staff, believed that only Germans were fit to rule the territories of the east. All eastern peoples, including the Russians, were uncouth peasants and anything resembling *Kultur* there could inevitably be traced back to German influence. These men had been behind the rapacious Treaty of Brest-Litovsk and now called for a new eastern German empire stretching from Berlin to the Urals so that their capital could rule Warsaw and Kiev, Leningrad and Moscow.

The other group, the 'eastern school', contained the remnants of Bismarck's followers who saw friendship with Russia as essential to German survival. According to them the Germans needed to co-operate with their formidable eastern neighbour in order to divide and control the troublesome nations which lay between them. They also needed Russian backing to prevent any possibility of having to fight a two-front war. This school had recommended the Treaty of Rapallo, in which central Europe had been carved up between Russia and Germany. Its master theorists were men like von Seeckt, von Maltzan and von Brockdorff-Rantzau, and it included men like Keitel and Ribbentrop. In their eyes Berlin was destined to share the spoils of eastern Europe with Moscow, for mutual benefit and mutual protection. No group advocated self-determination for the peoples of central Europe.

Ever since his emergence on the political stage Hitler had always seemed to embody the aims of the first school.[16] For him the Slavs were the second most detestable racial type on earth after the Jews and he was well aware of Stalin's 'Asiatic' brutality – he even spoke with disgust about the crimes of Beria and Vyshinski. But Russia and central Europe was also *Lebensraum* territory, and mention of the rich black soil of Ukraine or the vast mineral deposits lying in the Urals made him greedy.[17] Hitler's sudden treaty with Russia was not prompted by a new love for the Slavs but was motivated by the desire to safeguard Poland's eastern flank in preparation for his invasion, and to discourage the western Allies from risking a war with Germany. He had initially hoped to forge an agreement with Poland for the return of Danzig and for the right to transect Poland with the Berlin-Königsberg Autobahn, but these plans had been rejected by the Polish ambassador and on 28 March 1939 Hitler finally abandoned the non-aggression pact with Poland. Instead, he turned to his fellow tyrant Stalin and called on the remaining members of the 'eastern school' to secure a treaty with the Soviet dictator. One member of the team was the German ambassador in Moscow, Count Werner von der Schulenburg, who was fascinated by Russia and delighted by Hitler's change of heart. He wanted to see a solid, indefinite bond of friendship between the two nations and the permanent end to Poland. It was Hitler's eventual invasion of Russia which would shock Schulenburg and the men of the 'eastern school' into joining the anti-Nazi resistance.

In May 1939 Ambassador von der Schulenburg received instructions to approach Molotov, the new Commissar for Foreign Affairs, who was keen to open links with Berlin. Stalin had been negotiating with the west with a view to signing an anti-Nazi pact but the chance to join Hitler in the dismemberment of Poland and central Europe proved far too tempting. He abandoned the west and in a friendly ceremony in the Kremlin signed a treaty with his arch-enemy, toasting Hitler's health with Russian champagne while the assembled party sang a little ditty in Ribbentrop's honour: '*Spassibo Jesche Ribbentropu, Shto on otkryl okno w Jewropu!*' (Thank you, dear Joachim Ribbentrop, for opening the window to Europe.)[18] The Ribbentrop–Molotov Pact was officially a non-aggression treaty but contained a secret protocol. Its first point held that in the event of a 'territorial and political rearrangement' in the areas belonging to the Baltic States (Finland, Estonia, Latvia, Lithuania), the northern boundary of Lithuania 'will form the boundary of the spheres of influence of Germany and the USSR'; the second held that 'in the event of a territorial and political rearrangement of the areas belonging to the Polish state, the spheres of influence of Germany and the USSR shall be bounded approximately by the line of the rivers Vistula, Narew, and San'; the third essentially gave Russia a free hand to do as it wished in south-eastern Europe, and the fourth point stated that 'this protocol shall be treated by both parties as strictly secret'.[19] The 'transformation' alluded to was already well underway when the protocol was signed; indeed the first stage had already been ordered by Hitler on 3 April in a top-secret directive informing his senior commanders that he intended to attack Poland. With Stalin preparing for simultaneous invasion from the east, Hitler prepared to strike.

The news of the Hitler–Stalin pact took Berliners by surprise. Goebbels suddenly halted all anti-Soviet propaganda, disbanded the infamous Anti-Comintern Propaganda Unit and began to churn out articles stressing the historical links between Germany and Russia. The *Frankfurter Zeitung* described the atmosphere after news of the treaty as 'relaxed and placated'. Berliners seemed oblivious to the fact that the treaty had impelled them headlong towards the final crisis which would lead to the outbreak of the Second World War.

Long before the ink was dry on the treaty Goebbels had been bombarding Berlin with anti-Polish propaganda, subtly preparing the city for war. The people were told that the Corridor and Danzig belonged to them, that the Poles were mistreating Germans there and that the territory should be returned immediately. Minor incidents perpetrated by Poles against the German minority after Versailles were blown out of all proportion and fed to the German people as appalling abuses which 'called for revenge'. There is no doubt that Poland *had* adopted a discriminatory policy towards its Germans, giving Goebbels ample fuel for his propaganda machine, but now even the most insignificant incidents were portrayed as terrible crimes. The propaganda worked. When Goebbels stood on the balcony of the Berlin Staatstheater on 17 June and yelled for the return of Danzig Berliners chanted, 'Home into the Reich! Home into the Reich!' The headline of the *Berliner Zeiting* of 10 August read: POLAND? LOOK OUT! By the end of August Goebbels was producing photographs, articles, pamphlets and books documenting 'Polish atrocities' and portraying Poles as mere savages who would rip Germans apart limb from limb if given the chance. One woman, who still believed in the propaganda, remembered hearing that in peacetime the Poles had killed 'sixty thousand Germans' in the Polish Corridor. 'Then Hitler said on the radio one day, I heard it, "We cannot allow that any more." We wanted to avoid war at all costs. But the Poles were so hateful to all the Germans there and those who lived along the border.'[20] Another remembered reading leaflets allegedly dropped by the Poles over East Prussia (actually printed by Goebbels), which read: 'Tomorrow you belong to us' – tomorrow East Prussia will be Polish.[21] The propaganda was to be particularly brutal, Goebbels admitted privately, 'lest this last phase of the war of nerves be lost'.

Much of the anti-Polish propaganda was accepted at face value in Berlin that summer. When people woke up to the first food and clothing rations on 28 August they did not blame their own government but pointed the finger at the Poles for 'disturbing the peace of Europe and threatening Germany with armed invasion'. Shirer could not accept that Berliners were so gullible as to believe these lies. 'Then you talk to them,' he said. 'So many do.'[22]

Meanwhile Hitler was preparing a pretext for the attack. This did not have to be too convincing because, as he put it, nobody would care about how the war had started when he returned victorious. This was to be a war of conquest, a war to capture *Lebensraum*, a war to rid 'ancient German land' of the hated Poles. It was to be brutal. He told his generals in August: 'I have assembled my Death's Head Formations . . . with the command to send man, woman and child of Polish origin and language to death, ruthlessly and

Hitler's Planned Autobahn Extension
Straddling the Polish Corridor, 1939

mercilessly. This is the only way we can win the living space we need ...
Poland will be depopulated and settled with Germans.' At 12.40 p.m. on 31
August 1939 Hitler issued the Directive OKW/WFA No. 170/39 g.k. to the
commanders-in-chief of the army, navy, air force and general headquarters.
The document contained orders to invade Poland and stated that the attack
'will be called Operation White and will take place on September 1'.

On the same afternoon Heydrich ordered SS-Sturmbannführer Alfred
Naujocks to take an SS commando unit to the German town of Gleiwitz. The
SS men were dressed as Polish troops and staged a false attack on the radio
station, complete with the sound of gun-fire in the background and a 'Polish'
appeal to rise up against the Germans. At the same time Polish-speaking SS
troops, also dressed as Poles, took over the German customs station at Hoch-
linden in a staged skirmish; six corpses of Sachsenhausen concentration camp

prisoners dressed in Polish uniforms were left there as proof of the battle. The German police reported the incidents, saying that Polish attackers had been killed by German frontier guards.[23] When Goebbels 'heard' about the attacks on the 'innocent Germans' he pretended to be furious. How dare Poles attack Germans in their own country? 'German *Volk* will not take another attack lying down,' he raved; until now 'terrorist acts' had only been directed against Germans living on Polish soil but 'now they also occur on German soil!' The headlines in the *Völkischer Beobachter* read POLISH PARTISANS CROSS GERMAN BORDER. This 'provocation' was too much. Hitler immediately ordered the German army to attack Poland. Berliners, furious at the Polish 'insolence', entered the Second World War with their eyes firmly shut. When asked in 1990 if Germany should have invaded Poland Irene Burchert, a German woman who had lived through the period, replied: '*Ja*. Poland provoked.'[24]

In the grey light of the early Baltic dawn on 1 September 1939 the first shots of the war rang out. They were fired by Germans and were aimed at the Polish fortification on Westerplatte. Shirer wrote, 'It's a flagrant, inexcusable, unprovoked act of aggression. But Hitler and the High Command call it a "counter attack".' Five hours after the first shots were fired on Danzig Hitler went to the Reichstag to give his speech.

> This night for the first time Polish regular soldiers fired on our own territory. Since 5.45 a.m. we have been returning the fire, and from now on bombs will be met with bombs. Whoever fights with poison gas will be fought with poison gas. Whoever departs from the rules of humane warfare can only expect that we shall do the same. I will continue this struggle, no matter against whom, until the safety of the Reich and its rights are secured.

Berliners were frightened of war but they believed that Germany was innocent. There were rumours that the treacherous Poles meant to fight with terrible new weapons and with deadly bacteria. Goebbels continued to depict the Poles as monsters, making much of the few examples of Polish brutality against ethnic Germans, such as the incident at Bromberg when retreating Poles had cruelly killed German civilians in retaliation for being fired upon. He failed to mention that the German corpses had been 'doctored' for propaganda photographs, their noses and arms cut off as if by savage Poles; or that SS units had then moved into the town and liquidated the Polish youth organiz- ation and about 300 other civilians; or that Roland Freisler had a further 100 Poles executed. All Polish crimes were used to justify the much more widespread and serious German murders.[25] Goebbels was not taking any chances with his propaganda drive; on the night of the invasion he drafted the law prohibiting the population from listening to foreign broadcasts; failure to comply could in 'particularly grave cases' result in death.

While Berliners backed Hitler's latest act of aggression the rest of the world looked on in horror at what he had done. London demanded a ceasefire and the German withdrawal: otherwise Germany faced war. Hitler was stunned. He had expected the British to cave in as they had over Prague. The chief interpreter at the Foreign Office, Paul Schmidt, remembered the moment Hitler received the news: 'Hitler sat there as if turned to stone and gazed straight ahead . . . "What now?" he asked his foreign minister with a furious look in his eyes.'[26] One hour later France had also delivered an ultimatum. Göring turned to Schmidt and said, 'If we lose this war, may heaven have mercy on us.'[27]

As the news was piped out to Berliners on loudspeakers over the Wilhelmsplatz their trepidation turned to cold anger. How could the British object to Germans defending themselves against Polish aggression? How could they deny them the right to reclaim their own territory? How could they declare war on an innocent nation? Their naïveté was astounding. There was nothing of the euphoria of 1914: Nevile Henderson, a long-time appeaser, later wrote that 'the mass of the German people, that other Germany, were horror-struck at the whole idea of the war which was being thus thrust upon them . . . the whole general atmosphere in Berlin itself was one of utter gloom and depression.'[28] Albert Speer remembered scurrying to a public shelter during a false air-raid. 'The atmosphere was noticeably depressed,' he said, 'people were full of fear about the future.' On the evening of the English declaration of war Hitler had his bags packed and quietly left for his headquarters in Pomerania. There were no crowds to see him off; he crept out of Berlin under the cover of darkness, leaving a confused, frightened, angry city behind. But the sombre mood did not last long. As news of victory flowed back to Berlin, the city became ecstatic.

The Poles fought bravely but they were no match for the Germans and their new form of warfare, the *Blitzkrieg*. Stuka dive-bombers hurtled down from the sky, Messerschmitt fighter planes and Heinkel bombers targeted areas and were then followed by massive tank attacks which smashed through the Polish defences and which were in turn followed by motorized infantry. By 5 September the Poles had withdrawn behind the Vistula. By 6 September the Germans were in Cracow; on the eighth they were at the outskirts of Warsaw, while the Tenth Army had Kielce and the Fourteenth took the town of Sandomierz, the point at which the Vistula meets the San. Excited Berliners were stunned by the success of their army and lined up outside the store windows to stare at the large maps with little red pins showing the progress of the troops. As the good news poured in the cafés, restaurants and clubs filled with cheering people who periodically stood up to sing the national anthem and to toast their troops. As Polish civilians were being rounded up and shot in Warsaw Berliners crammed into *Tannhäuser* and *Madame Butterfly*, while the Metropole announced a new revue. Shirer said: 'I have still to find a German, even amongst those who don't like the regime, who sees anything wrong in the German destruction of Poland. All the moral attitudes of the outside world regarding the aggression against Poland find little echo among the people here ... As long as the Germans are successful and do not have to pull in their belts too much, this will not be an unpopular war.'[29] On 27 September, after a valiant fight, Warsaw capitulated. On 5 October Hitler reviewed the German troops in the battered city. The campaign had lasted only five weeks, the destruction of Poland being completed by the Soviet invasion from the east on 17 September. The Germans lost only 10,000 troops but Polish casualties were severe; 700,000 prisoners were captured by the Germans, 200,000 by the Soviets.

The war against Poland was a milestone – not only in military strategy but for a new kind of brutality which would come to characterize the war in the east. For those Poles who had last encountered German troops during the First World War the transformation was extraordinary. Honourable codes of behaviour had been replaced by gratuitous violence on a scale as yet unheard of in modern Europe. Hitler was determined to punish the Poles for not yielding to his territorial demands but he was also motivated by a deep racial hatred and announced he would be 'forced' to use every means at his disposal to show the Polish civilians the 'pointlessness of their resistance'.[30] In short, the Polish nation was to be destroyed or enslaved, an aim largely shared by Stalin in the east. During the celebration to mark the reoccupation of Marienburg Hans Frank said, 'the Poland of Versailles no longer exists and will never re-arise again. Marienburg is German today, Cracow is German and both will remain German.' Professors in Berlin explained that Poland had always been an 'unviable state': eighteenth-century Warsaw had been ruled by 'drunken, chattering nobles' and priests who 'preached the most laughable stupidities to the people', whereas Berlin had been filled with 'well-trained soldiers' who exemplified 'unity, readiness to make sacrifices and love of country'.

This attitude was translated into deadly policy. When Hitler returned from his victory parade in Warsaw he told Goebbels that the people of Poland were 'more animal than human' and he wanted no filthy assimilation with them.[31] Instead, the newly created 'Generalgouvernement' under Hans Frank was to purge the population of its elite and use the rest as slave labour. Security police and security service units of the SS were sent from Berlin to target specific groups of Poles. Like the Soviets in their zone, the Germans carried out systematic arrests, deportations and murders of intellectuals, professionals, landowners, the clergy, officers, civil servants, ex-army settlers, policemen and all those connected in any way with the running of the Polish state. The most infamous Nazi camp, Auschwitz, was actually opened for the Polish intelligentsia in June 1940 and was only enlarged to include the extermination camp – Birkenau – in 1943; my father-in-law, Wladyslaw Bartoszewski, was taken on the second transport of 22 September 1940 and imprisoned there for no other reason than that he lived in a particular district of Warsaw – he was eighteen years old at the time and was one of the few people freed by the Red Cross, for whom he worked, on 8 April 1941.[32] Reports on the treatment of Poles were dutifully sent back to headquarters in Berlin: in his memo of 21 September 1939 to the chief of the SS commandos Heydrich wrote of his intention to round up the Jews and force them into ghettos, and he was careful to send a copy to a handful of top bureaucrats in Berlin, including des Heeres, the head of the Oberkommando or OKH (Army High Command), Neumann, the director of the Four Year Plan, Stuckart, the Minister of the Interior, and to all those responsible for the civilian populations in the occupied territories. The deportations of Poles out of 'ancient German' areas was also recorded; one memo of 15 November accounted for the 'evacuation' of 303 special transports of Poles, including '234,620 Poles from Wartheland' and '30,758' from West Prussia, into the Generalgouvernement 'to make the Reich ready for German re-settlement' – the memo confirmed that since 14 May 1940 the Poles had used 1,401,774 kilos of food, for which they would now be expected to pay. The bill was duly processed through Eichmann's office in the Kurfürstenstrasse. Professor Voss of the Anatomical Institute in Posen watched as the Gestapo disposed of the bodies of over 4,000 Poles in the ovens in the basement of the institute. On 24 May 1941 he wrote in his diary: 'The Poles shot by [the Gestapo] are delivered by night and burned. If only one could reduce the whole of Polish society to ash!' On 15 June he visited the 'corpse cellar' again. Almost daily, he noted,

> a grey van arrives with men in grey uniforms, i.e. SS men from the Gestapo, bringing material for the oven. Since it was not in action yesterday, we could look inside. The remains of four Poles were in there. How little remains of a person when all organic matter has been burned! A glimpse inside the ovens is very thought-provoking ... At the moment the Poles are very uppity, and consequently our oven has a lot to do. How nice it would be if one could chase the whole society into such ovens. Then there would finally be peace in the East for the German people.[33]

Voss was not alone in his belief that Poland should be 'cleansed'; ultimately 3 million Polish Gentiles and 3 million Polish Jews would die under German rule.

As the news of victory sank in Berliners became increasingly arrogant. A young German officer accompanied the American journalist Howard Smith on a walk down Unter den Linden a few months after the fall of Poland. 'Look around you,' he said. 'Not the slightest difference from two years ago. Is that not the best argument for our strength? We shall never be beaten.'[34] When the new film *Feuertaufe* (Baptism by Fire) was released, a film which included numerous brutal scenes of the bombing of Warsaw, it was greeted with hoots of joy in the cinemas up and down the Kurfürstendamm. Christmas that year was wonderful: rations were relaxed and people enjoyed huge dinners surrounded by trees and lights, toys and presents. The Nazis celebrated the New Year in Berlin in style. All the clubs, the restaurants, the grand hotels and the shops were open, and although there were fewer luxury goods most people could wheedle something from contacts and friends. Berlin had defeated a hated enemy; now they longed for peace. It was not to be.

Hitler was convinced that the decadent British had declared war only for the sake of public opinion and that, faced with the fall of Poland, they would now make peace. But the British saw things differently: they had given Hitler every possible chance to avoid war but he had refused. They had declared war not 'for Danzig' but because they were convinced that Hitler ultimately threatened their own way of life. Hitler decided to teach them a lesson. On 9 October he ordered his horrified generals to plan an invasion of western Europe.

Hitler moved remarkably quickly. His first targets were Norway and Denmark, which would give German forces access to the Atlantic and protect the shipments of iron ore from Sweden. The invasion of Scandinavia was rapid. The Germans handed notes to the Foreign Ministers of the two countries at 5.20 a.m. on 9 April explaining that their countries were now under the protection of the German Reich. Any resistance to the occupation would be crushed. The Danish crumbled quickly, and despite resistance and an attempt by British, Polish and French troops to fight at Narvik, Norway was occupied by 9 June. Berliners greeted the invasion with nervous indifference. Smith remembered overhearing a conversation at the Berlin Zoo between a ticket collector and an old man out walking his dog: '"See we invaded Norway this morning?" one said. "Ja," said the ticket collector, removing the cigar from his mouth, "and Denmark too." "Ja," said the ticket-taker, handing back the punched ticket. "Auf Wiedersehen." "Wiedersehen," and the old man and his dachshund went in to observe the strange manners of the animals.'[35] By now,

the occupation of Norway and Denmark was merely a 'side issue', for Hitler
had suddenly turned on Germany's great western rival: France.

France had been bled white by the First World War and ended 1918 victorious
in name only. Since then it had concentrated on building an immense ribbon
of fortifications along the German border – the Maginot Line – a great concrete
dinosaur suited only to First World War conditions. The French hid behind
the line but had lost the will to fight; when they declared war over Poland
the army merely tiptoed over the Maginot Line and then tiptoed back again,
thankful not to have met any Germans despite promises that they would
mount a sustained attack. During the endless *drôle de guerre*, the 'phoney war',
the troops had lived an uneasy truce, peering out from their concrete bunkers
and hoping that the Germans would leave them alone. The French High
Command had refused to go to Poland's aid at the very point when this might
have crippled Hitler. By the time the Germans turned to France it was in
disarray.

Hitler had learned a great deal from his experiences of the First World
War and, knowing the Maginot Line was virtually impassable, simply went
round it. On 10 May 1940 he began the invasion of Holland and Belgium
with a small but highly trained force. Berliners were again subdued but
they need not have worried. The airborne assault and seizure of the Eben
Emael fortress, 'the strongest fortress in the world', on the first day permitted
a rapid crossing of the Alber Canal. The Germans sped through the area,
sending policemen ahead with white gloves and *Michelin* guides to direct
the troops. At the same time the Luftwaffe struck at the Allied planes, which
were lined up in neat rows on the ground; fifty airfields were attacked on
the first day alone. The Dutch and Belgian armies were unable to delay
the German advance; Berlin celebrated as the Dutch surrendered on 15
May, followed by the Belgians on 28 May. The west, believing that Hitler
was re-enacting the Schlieffen Plan (in which Germany was to encircle
Paris), rushed their troops to the north to meet his army. But they had
been duped.

The second, most ingenious part of the attack took place in the Ardennes.
French fortifications there were dismal, with the vital crossings over the river
Meuse held by only a few divisions. Hitler ordered his troops down the narrow
mountain roads in the dead of night, camouflaged and unnoticed. By 12 May
the Wehrmacht were poised to attack. They charged south of Sedan, crossed
the river and raced into France. The Luftwaffe attacked over Sedan the next
day. For fuel and supplies the Germans simply plundered the now abandoned
depots, while amazed French troops dropped their weapons and ran. One

soldier, Ferdinand Krones, remembered receiving a radio message from his company commander shortly before he reached Sedan:

> We are now at the spot where in 1870 Napoleon III surrendered his sword to Bismarck and said, 'Since I did not have the pleasure of dying at the head of my troops, I present your excellency with my sword.' And Bismarck graciously asked him to keep his sword 'as a symbol of respect for the bravery of the French soldiers'. This time we took everyone by surprise ... They were captured without a shot being fired.[36]

In one instance a column of 10,000 men tossed aside their guns and walked towards the German lines with their hands up. France was doomed.

As the rout continued the Allies in the north, including the British Expeditionary Force, were driven back on to the beaches of Dunkirk. The famous evacuation, in which ships of all shapes and sizes raced to France to haul troops off the beaches, continued until 3 June, with the rescue of 350,000 men. As the *Blitzkrieg* swept through the country the French leaders fumbled. The eighty-four-year-old Marshal Pétain was recalled to boost French morale, but he merely blamed France's predicament on '30 years of Marxism'. His generals drew 'halt lines' on their maps but by the time the orders reached the troops the Germans had long since passed them. On 11 June Paris was declared an open city. The Allied resistance had been demolished; the Germans had lost only 25,000 men. Two days after the fall of Paris the French government under Marshal Pétain started peace negotiations with Hitler.

At the beginning of the western offensive many Berliners had been fearful. Old soldiers had warned of the miseries of the trenches, the horror of Verdun, the likelihood of defeat at the hands of the strong French army. But this was a different kind of war and as news of victory reached them the mood changed rapidly. The German army had rolled effortlessly over battlefields which the old soldiers had failed to capture in four long and bloody years of fighting. As the Somme and Vimy Ridge and Passchendaele fell the veterans clasped one another and gave thanks; when Dunkirk fell the churchbells of Berlin rang continuously for three days and the victory was described as the 'greatest ever in German history'; when Paris was taken Berliners were convulsed with sheer joy and sang marching songs and danced in the streets. On 17 June, the day of the ceasefire, they gathered spontaneously at Goebbels's Ministry on the Wilhelmsplatz, singing the *Deutschlandlied* and crying out for him to appear. The signing of the armistice was trumpeted in minute detail via telephone reports from Compiègne. When one young soldier got his pilot to land on the Champs-Élysées it was reported with giddy delight in the press. The young pilot, Werner Bartels, and Captain Galland were the first Germans to walk down the Champs-Élysées after the French capitulation: 'We made plans to be the first ones to walk down Bond Street in London as well.'[37] Hitler's critics were silenced by waves of euphoria and pride – not even the doubting generals dared challenge him now. It had taken him ten weeks to conquer virtually all of western Europe. Berlin – and Germany – adored him.

Hitler now humiliated the French by forcing them to sign the armistice in the old railway carriage in which Germany had been forced to sign the armistice in 1918. The carriage was then brought to Berlin as a trophy. France was disarmed, the Vichy government was set up to rule southern France, while the north came under direct German rule. Hitler's tour of Paris was strangely quiet: three days after the armistice he landed at Le Bourget airfield at 5.30 in the morning, accompanied by Speer and Breker. They sped to Berlin's rival city and looked at the famous landmarks from the Opera House to the Champs-Élysées and Napoleon's tomb. After three hours it was over. Hitler told Speer that he felt 'honoured' to see Paris, and would refrain from destroying it if the new plans for Berlin could go ahead quickly: 'Berlin is to be given the style commensurate with the grandeur of our victory,' he said.[38] Meanwhile, the German capital prepared to welcome its leader home.

On 6 July Goebbels inspected the final preparations for the return of the Führer. As he passed the huge crowds which had gathered he congratulated himself on his handiwork. The entire city 'was decorated with thousands upon thousands of Swastikas, a band and cameras waiting, the tension extraordinary'. Hitler's train pulled in at three o'clock. Goebbels could barely contain himself. 'Mad enthusiasm fills the station,' he wrote. 'The Führer is very moved. Tears come to his eyes.' To the roar of a city cheering and yelling the motorcade made its way from the Anhalter Bahnhof to the Chancellery, pushing its way through crowds of people waving flags and raising their arms in the crush while the churchbells rang out. Millions of Berliners surged towards Hitler's balcony; film footage shows the pride on Hitler and Göring's faces as they leaned over and realized that the crowd stretched far out of sight in all directions. To the people standing in the vast street below Hitler seemed to have achieved the impossible and they celebrated as if they were reliving Bismarck's glorious return in 1871. The shame of the First World War had been expunged, and Berlin was once again destined to be the greatest city on the continent.

William Shirer watched the proceedings and was astounded by the ignorance and pomposity of the people during those hot summer days. 'Nothing pleases the Berliners – a naive and simple people on the whole – more than a good military parade,' he noted, and on 18 July the city staged the first victory march since 1871.[39] A holiday was declared and thousands upon thousands packed the streets to cheer the beaming troops of the 218th Infantry Division as they walked back under the banners festooned over the Brandenburg Gate. Goebbels stepped up to the magnificent platform on the Pariser Platz and addressed the crowd. After a rousing welcome he reminded Berliners that the troops of 1918 had also deserved such a welcome but had faced only gangsters and strikers. 'Not this time!' he bellowed. The soldiers returned to find the swastika still in place, just as it was when they left. As they marched beneath the gigantic banners they were greeted by children holding bunches of flowers, by clouds of confetti and by loud military bands. Women tried to break through to kiss them. The crowds on the East–West Axis were twenty rows deep and people hung from lamp-posts, scaled trees and statues and perched on balustrades for a better view. Everyone was happy. 'Looking at them,' Shirer mused, 'I wondered if any of them understood what was going on in Europe, if they had an inkling that their joy, that this victorious parade of the goose-steppers, was based on a great tragedy for millions of others whom these troops and the leaders of these people had enslaved. Not one in a thousand, I wager, gave the matter a thought.'[40]

Shirer was right. Berliners knew little and cared less about the fate of those in Poland or in France. Their feelings were not simply expressed by their presence on the streets; the SD secret service reports spoke of their 'deep joy'. Most were delighted that the First World War had finally been put behind them but they also foolishly believed that the war was over. Hitler and Goebbels fostered this notion while trying to persuade the British to make peace – even the victory parade had been staged as a threatening display of might. If they did not co-operate Hitler had already resolved to invade. Indeed, enormous reviewing stands were erected along the Wilhelmsplatz, Pariser Platz and Unter den Linden to welcome the entire army home after the defeat of Britain. Hardly anyone believed that the war would go on for more than a few weeks.

The illusion of prosperity and peace in Berlin was fuelled by the spoils of war. As Bismarck had done in 1871, Hitler charged the French enormous sums to cover the cost of the occupation, setting up an artificial rate of exchange between the franc and the Reichsmark which was greatly to Berlin's advantage, and sanctioned the plundering of the occupied territories. The soldiers in Bohemia sent home crates of beautiful crystal and coloured glass, those in Norway shipped fur coats and whalebone trinkets back to their girlfriends, the troops in Poland sent foodstuffs and vodka and fine linen, there was an abundance of Dutch tobacco and coffee, and soldiers pilfered everything they could carry from the Paris shops. By the summer Berlin was awash with beautiful clothes, food, perfumes and luxuries of all kinds. Enormous crates arrived filled with furniture and porcelain, shoes and boots and fine woollens, silk stockings and underwear, paintings and *objets d'art*; the little provincial

German shops which had specialized in schnapps now sold French champagne and the coarse Berlin *Kneipen* offered Armagnac and Courvoisier. Fine restaurants served up the spoils taken from the cellars of Maxim's and any self-respecting Berlin civil servant had amassed a well-stocked cellar by the end of the summer. Hitler and Göring sent their agents to steal art treasures for their own collections. The mood in the city was reminiscent of the best days of the Golden Twenties and few stopped to think that they were still at war.

At the same time, Berlin was starting to feel the economic benefits of the Hitler–Stalin pact, which relieved pressure on the domestic economy. Soviet support for the Third Reich was considerable. In the twelve months following the signing of the trade agreement of 10 February 1940 the Soviets shipped 900,000 tonnes of petroleum, 500,000 tonnes of phosphates and iron ore and 300,000 tonnes of raw steel to Germany. For their part the Germans supplied Stalin with precision instruments, radios, telegraph and telephone equipment, and plans for tanks and ships, including those for the 40,000-tonne battleship *Bismarck*.[41] The eagerness of the Soviets to fulfil their side of the bargain was extraordinary and caused turmoil within the underground Berlin Communist Party. Stalin was so keen to please Hitler that he began to denounce German Communists to the Gestapo, and many who had fled to the Soviet Union were returned to the Nazis; in March 1940, 150 German Communists were handed over by the NKVD at Brzesc-on-Bug and promptly executed, while Nazis and Communists held a secret conference in Cracow to discuss ways of jointly controlling Polish resistance.[42] The importance of the pact was brought home to Berliners on 12 November 1940, when Viacheslav Molotov, Premier and Foreign Commissar of Soviet Russia, made his first official visit to the city. He arrived at a lavishly decorated Anhalter Bahnhof and was met by dignitaries, including Ribbentrop and Ley, Field Marshal Keitel, the press chief Otto Dietrich, Heinrich Himmler and Franz von Papen. Berliners were still confused about the pact with the Soviet Union but they were content to have co-operated with them in the annihilation of Poland and the division of central Europe. Behind the scenes, however, the visit was a disaster for German– Soviet relations, primarily because Molotov wanted Hitler to step up promised shipments of goods to the Soviet Union and because he refused to abandon Soviet aspirations in Finland. To make matters worse he was obsessed with being poisoned by bacteria and insisted that all his glasses and plates must be boiled.[43] Relations were strained but the friendly facade was maintained – for the moment.

With the eastern border now secure and the battle for France over Berliners were longing for peace. To their annoyance, the British still refused to surrender. Hitler turned all his most vitriolic propaganda against them, castigating Churchill as a warmonger and blaming him for the imminent destruction of his own nation. Speer remembered sitting with Hitler as he watched the final scene of a film about the bombing of Warsaw:

> We were sitting with him and Goebbels in his Berlin salon watching the film. Clouds of smoke darkened the sky; dive bombers tilted and hurtled toward their goal; we could watch the flight of the released bombs, the pull-out of the planes and the cloud from the explosions expanding gigantically. The effect was enhanced by running the film in slow motion. Hitler was fascinated. The film ended with a montage showing a plane diving toward the outlines of the British Isles. A burst of flame followed, and the island flew into the air in tatters. Hitler's enthusiasm was unbounded. 'That is what will happen to them!' he cried out, carried away. 'That is how we will annihilate them!'[44]

On 13 July 1940 Hitler called for an air war against England, and Göring's *Adler Tag* (Eagle Day) was launched on 15 August. Hitler ordered his troops to be ready to launch Operation Sealion – the plan to attack Britain across the Channel – in ten days. Detailed lists were drawn up of English men and women who were to be arrested after the invasion, and an enormous fleet of barges was assembled in preparation for the landings.[45] But Hitler made a fatal mistake. He switched his attention from the British airfields to the cities. Thousands of civilians were killed in the Blitz, but the British maintained air superiority which meant invasion was impossible. Hitler had lost the Battle of Britain,[46] and he was forced to postpone Operation Sealion until October and then until the following spring. Even the most obtuse Berliners began to realize that the war was not yet over. The long-term consequences of this miscalculation were profound, for the western Allies retained a secure base from which to prepare for an invasion of the continent.[47]

In the meantime Berliners were having a 'good war', and the troublesome skirmish with England was only brought home by the occasional RAF bombing raid on the city. Göring had boasted that if an enemy plane ever reached Germany his name was not Göring but 'Meier', and as the first bombers broke through people were reduced to telling crude jokes about 'Herr Meier' in the shelters.[48] These first bombs to hit Berlin were in fact dropped by a solitary French plane, the *Jules Verne*, on 7 June 1940, but the RAF began its attack on 25 August 1940 after a German pilot accidentally dropped bombs on London which had been intended for the oil tanks at Thameshaven. Churchill, thinking it had been deliberate, demanded retaliation against the German capital. Bombing continued until September, but during this early phase it did more to boost morale in England than to damage Berlin.

Berliners slowly adapted to the new routine of sleeping in cellars and bomb shelters. Hitler had planned to build 2,000 open rooms with more than 400,000 places, although only 15 per cent had been completed by 1940. Some of these still exist beneath Berlin, complete with their steel doors and phosphorescent signs which still point the way to areas like the *Gasssleusse* (the gas-proof shelter). People also created solid air-raid facilities in their own basements, digging out cellar floors, knocking holes between adjoining houses and equipping them with everything from fire-fighting equipment to food.

The external face of Berlin also changed as a result of the bombing raids. Hitler's new five-mile East–West Axis looked like an arrow pointing bombers straight to the heart of the government quarter and Berliners erected two miles of steel poles covered with netting in order to disguise it. The entire Lützensee was covered with scaffolding while open spaces like the Adolf-Hitler-Platz were filled with false buildings. There were attempts to build 'false cities' outside Berlin to disorient pilots and the sparkling golden Goddess of Victory on the Siegessäule was stripped and painted a dull bronze colour. Gauleiter Hoffman, who was in charge of Berlin fortifications, positioned huge anti-aircraft guns on prominent buildings, including the Reichstag; forty-five heavy- and twenty-four medium-flak gun batteries and eighteen searchlight batteries were placed in and around Berlin, while three hideous 130-foot-high cement flak towers were built in the parks around the government quarter. These were so massive that it was virtually impossible to destroy them after the war.

Despite these preparations Berliners never developed the spirit which characterized London during the Blitz, not least because of the increasing presence of the Gestapo and the bossy air-raid wardens, who bullied people with endless lists of new regulations. There were posters everywhere about tackling incendiaries and taking precautions against excessive temperatures. Blackouts were rigorously enforced; one Berlin poster had a gruesome skeleton of Death riding a plane and tossing a bomb on a building with a light showing. *Der Angriff* started an anti-rat campaign by encouraging people to put food away before a raid: 'imagine coming into your dining-room and seeing two rats on the table eating your piece of bread.' Berliners were told that there would be no insurance damages 'for death or injury unless the victim had taken refuge in a shelter'. The Gestapo announced that anyone caught committing a crime during a blackout would be beheaded; two Berliners were duly executed in the first month of the raids, one for snatching a woman's purse and another for stealing coal. When the raid was over the Gestapo would round up political prisoners and make them defuse any unexploded bombs; those fortunate enough to survive were given a reprieve.

Despite the inconvenience of shelter life the early raids caused little damage, destroying only a handful of buildings and causing 200 fatalities. Bombing was still rather exciting and people would gather to look at damage done to landmarks like the Opera House. When the Tauentzienstrasse, a main shopping street, was hit just before Christmas a crew of forced labourers was sent to repair the water, gas, subway and storefronts so that shoppers would not have their holiday spoilt. Life in Berlin carried on much as before and the city continued to prosper. By now there were shortages of luxuries like chocolate and coffee and shops were no longer permitted to sell cigarettes to women but the optimistic mood had not been dampened. People in the provinces were appalled when they visited war-time Berlin; one irate critic wrote to Goebbels that while the country was at war 'what is going on in the Reich capital Berlin?' There followed a list of transgressions, including the appearance of naked women at the Metropol, the Admiralspalast, the Scala and the Kadeko.[49] In fact, contrary to the popular belief that Berlin was a dour and repressed city at war, such performances continued – indeed increased in number – as the war progressed precisely because they were considered an appropriate diversion for soldiers on leave. Restaurants at the Adlon, Bristol, Esplanade, Kaiserhof and Eden as well as the Propaganda Ministry Club on Leipziger Strasse and the Foreign Office Club had no problems finding roast beef and fine wines, while the Carlton Club, Jockey Bar and Hörcher's restaurant still produced lobster and *foie gras* for its privileged Nazi customers. Few people invested their money in the government's 'Iron Saving scheme', preferring to spend their spare cash on black market goods or on gambling or entertainment; one Berlin wine waiter was able to buy a country estate with the tips he made from giving Nazi customers preferential treatment.[50] Ordinary Berliners also ate well; the diet consisted of staples like potatoes, cabbage, along with a pound of meat, a quarter of a pound of butter and three pounds of bread a week. Some things, like oysters, were not rationed, and there were still ample supplies of sausages, pork chops and *ersatz* coffee made from chicory. Dancing carried on after the French campaign, with bands playing the supposedly banned jazz or swing; Magda Goebbels held her society fashion shows and her husband supervised the screenings of *Snow White* and *Gone with the Wind*. An SD report claimed that the mood of the population was positive: 'Under the impact of the great political events, and enthralled by the military successes, the entire German people now has an inner unanimity as never before . . . Everyone is looking with gratitude and confidence to the Führer and to his armed forces as they speed from victory to victory.'[51] The Führer had the fullest confidence of the people. He would need it. He was about to begin the greatest gamble of his life – an attack on the Soviet Union.

After the failure of Göring's Battle of Britain Hitler lost interest in England. The country was far away, isolated, and increasingly weakened by the Battle of the Atlantic. He assumed it would no longer pose a serious threat to the Reich.[52] On 15 June Hitler told a delighted Goebbels that he intended to turn on Russia. 'The Führer is very moved when I take leave of him . . . This is a very great moment for me. Driving through the grounds, out the gate, and then into the city where people are walking innocuously in the rain. Happy people who know nothing of all our care . . . It's for all of them that we work and struggle and take every risk. So our people may live!'[53]

The preparations for the attack remained top secret and this time Berliners were not 'softened up' by Goebbels's propaganda.[54] Astute observers might have wondered why all positive references to Russia were suddenly cut from newspapers and broadcasts. Howard Smith noticed that Hitler's half-brother Alois Hitler had removed the only Russian book, a small collection of short stories by Michael Soistshenko, from his bookshop on the Wittenbergplatz and replaced it with works like *The TRUTH About the Soviet Paradise* or *My Life in the Russian Hell*.[55] When rumours about troop movements in the east reached Berlin Goebbels generated the rumour that it was merely a diversion to mask an imminent attack on England.

Hitler had hoped to invade Russia in the late spring but Mussolini's disastrous invasion of Greece had led him into Yugoslavia on 6 April 1941 and then into Greece itself, where he attacked the British in Crete on 20 May. He did not turn to Russia until late June, delayed by a fatal five weeks.[56] Undeterred, Hitler pushed ahead with plans for 'Barbarossa', named after the red-bearded emperor who had defeated the Slavs centuries before. Over 3 million German soldiers divided into three gargantuan armies were quietly amassed on the Soviet border. Hitler was about to order the biggest land offensive in history: 'Our task in Russia has to be to destroy the Red Army and to dissolve the Soviet state,' he said. 'We are going into a battle of annihilation. If we don't accept it as such, we may, being militarily stronger, gain a temporary victory now, but the enemy will be able to re-emerge . . . In the East, gentlemen, severity now is an act of kindness for the future.'[57]

At two in the morning on 22 June Valentin Bereshkov, the first secretary at the Soviet embassy, was working quietly at his desk. Suddenly, he received a telephone call. An official from the German Foreign Ministry barked out that he was to accompany Ambassador Dekanozov to the Foreign Office; a car would be sent in half an hour. When they arrived Ribbentrop stepped up to the bewildered men and curtly informed them that Germany was declaring war on the Soviet Union. They were to return to Russia at once.[58]

German troops were already swarming over the border. Karl Rupp, serving in a German armoured division, remembered that they had been 'given three days to get ready to go to Russia'.[59] This time, nobody bothered to pretend that the enemy had attacked radio stations or threatened the German people.

Goebbels called dignitaries and newspaper men to the Propaganda Ministry and told them that he would soon be making an important announcement. Rumours flew through the crowded room. At 5.30 a.m. the Liszt fanfare sounded and Goebbels began to read Hitler's speech. 'People of Germany! National Socialists! The hour has now come. Oppressed by grave cares, doomed to months of silence, I can at last speak frankly.' The Führer had decided 'to place the fate and future of the German Reich and our people in the hands of our soldiers'. Barbarossa, the invasion of Russia and home of the Jewish-Bolshevik beast, had begun.

Berlin was abuzz with excitement. Many people openly said that they had never supported the Hitler–Stalin pact and had 'always considered Russia as the great enemy'. Now, with Ukraine, the Urals, Crimea and the Black Sea within their grasp, Germany would be invincible and Berlin would rule over the greatest land empire in the world. Some were worried about the possibility of a two-front war but Hitler assured the people that he would crush Russia before Christmas, and his sheer nerve coupled with memories of his previous sweeping successes silenced most doubters.[60]

For their part the Soviets were shocked by the invasion. Stalin had refused to believe Allied warnings of Hitler's intentions, he had rejected the advice of his own spies, he had discounted rumours of the troop movements on the eastern front as British propaganda, and he had even had a German deserter shot when he came over the border to tell the Soviets that they were about to be invaded.[61] His willingness to appease Hitler was extraordinary; trainloads of goods were still rolling into Germany even after the invasion had begun. When Stalin finally grasped what was happening he went into hiding and did not emerge for five days. The poorly organized Soviet front-line troops waited like sitting ducks on the 'Stalin Line' and were slow to respond. This was largely due to another of Stalin's policies: the purges. Between 1937 and 1938 Stalin had murdered 90 per cent of his own generals and half of his corps commanders. Every single division commander had been killed and replaced by inept party hacks who knew nothing of modern warfare. Furthermore, Stalin had halted the production of the very good T-34 tanks, while innovators like the great aircraft-designer Tupolev had been sent to labour camps or killed. The Russians had amassed a fairly large arsenal before the purge years, with 12,000 aircraft and 10,000 tanks compared with Germany's 3,350 aircraft and 3,550 tanks, and there is no doubt that Stalin was preparing for war, but without proper leadership the force was not yet a match for the Wehrmacht.[62]

Hitler was convinced that the Red Army would fall in a matter of weeks: 'all we have to do is kick in the door, and the whole rotten structure will collapse,' he said. He had good reason to think so: after the signing of the

Hitler–Stalin pact German officers had met Soviet troops on the new border and had reported to Hitler that their equipment seemed woefully out of date and run-down. According to Speer, Hitler often cited this report 'as evidence that the Russians were weak and poorly organized. Soon afterward, the failure of the Soviet offensive against Finland confirmed him in this view.'[63] Stalin's barbaric treatment of the non-Russian nationalities such as the Ukrainians now worked in Hitler's favour as many saw the Germans as liberators and were, at least at first, willing to fight for them.[64] Hitler had surprise, well-trained troops and modern equipment on his side, and his advances into Russia were sudden and deep.

As the tanks rolled across the border the Luftwaffe targeted the Soviet air force, destroying 2,000 aircraft in the first two days alone. One soldier remembered watching Soviet aircraft at the river Bug being destroyed in a matter of seconds. As the world's largest air force was being flattened the Wehrmacht tackled the Russian divisions. Frontier armies simply faded away – when the Wehrmacht reached Bialystok they were amazed to see three divisions shoot their commissars and surrender. Guderian's tanks on the southern wing of the German pincer movement and Hoth's on the north raced together, and within five days the claws closed at Slonim. Fifteen Russian divisions were caught in the Minsk area and 300,000 prisoners were taken in a few days. Six thousand Russian tanks were lost at Minsk and Smolensk alone. By early July Army Group North were at Riga and bearing down on Leningrad. Meanwhile the southern force raced into southern Poland and the centre advanced into central Russia. Between 16 and 20 September Timoshenko's huge force was caught in a pocket at Kiev. Army Group South went on into Ukraine; Odessa fell on 16 October, Kharkov on 24 October, and the Donbass, the centre of Russian coal mining and hydro-electricity, was taken in November. By the time von Rundstedt reached Rostov-on-the-Don he had captured enough mineral wealth to sustain the German war effort well into the next year. In a week the Wehrmacht was halfway to Moscow; in a month they had taken a chunk of territory twice the size of the German Reich. Half a million Russians became casualties in the first two weeks alone.[65]

In Berlin the news of the great advances was again greeted with delight. On the first day of the offensive the extra editions were sold out in minutes, with the *Völkischer Beobachter* headlines reading: WAR FRONT FROM NORTH CAP TO BLACK SEA IN BRINGING TO RECKONING OF THE MOSCOW TRAITORS! TWO-FACED JEWISH BOLSHEVIST RULERS IN THE KREMLIN LENGTHEN THE WAR FOR THE BENEFIT OF ENGLAND. There was a sense of exhilaration in the city: as Harry Flannery put it, 'I listened to their conversations around the newsstands and on the subways. I talked with a number of them. For the first time they were excited about the war. "Now," they said, "we are fighting our real enemy."[66] Loudspeakers were erected throughout the city centre and regular programmes were interrupted to warn of an important announcement. Stirring music sounded and a voice would boom, 'From the headquarters of the Führer', followed by the news that Minsk or Kiev had just fallen. Everyone would stand in silence during the broadcasts; waiters would stop serving, conversation would die down and all would strain to hear. After the announcement they would stand to attention up and down the main streets as a tinny rendition of *Deutschland, Deutschland über Alles* crackled out from the loudspeakers. Then they would turn to one another and say, 'Fantastic! Unbelievable! Wonderful!'

The mood in Berlin was at its height that autumn. Berliners thronged to the Ruhleben racetrack, to the Olympic Stadium for German championship football, to the lakes at Grünau for an international regatta. By October the headlines were screaming of imminent victory: THE GREAT HOUR HAS STRUCK! they read, or, LAST GREAT DECISIVE BATTLE. Rumours that Stalin had sued for peace were greeted with sheer joy. People hung wreaths of late summer roses on German tanks rolling through the city. Bookshops now stocked Russian grammar books and street maps of Moscow; ambitious young Germans said that the 'future lies in the east' and prepared to move and build factories and farms. Dr Walther Funk, the Economics Minister, wrote a much-publicized speech about the ancient German colonial mission in Russia, and schoolchildren learned the difference between a Ukrainian and an 'Asiatic'.

Hitler, too, had begun to rave about his visions of vast slick new Autobahns cutting through Russia, and of German settlers overseeing the Slavic workforce and ruling the 'sub-humans' there with an iron fist. In September he ordered eighty divisions to begin their move on Moscow in the final push for glorious victory. On 3 October he made a rousing speech at the Sportpalast, declaring that the enemy was already broken and would never rise again. Victory seemed imminent. But it was not to be. It was at that moment, as the troops neared Moscow, that the offensive began to grind to a halt. The first snow came and the following thaw turned the dirt roads to deep mud. 'The entire country has turned into a thick, dark gravy, frozen at the surface,' one soldier wrote. 'Above the black-brown mud hangs a heavy, low sky; everything is grey on grey ... The road is deeply rutted. German army vehicles are bogged down bumper to bumper.'[67] The winter had arrived.

As the first flakes of snow fluttered from the sky the generals asked Hitler to stop the advance. He would not hear of it, urging the Wehrmacht on relentlessly although supply lines were stretched to breaking point and the troops had only summer boots and clothes. Karl Rupp remembered that we were twenty miles from Moscow at that point. There was a streetcar stop nearby, and at night we could see the Moscow flak shooting at our planes ... Our *Landser* were a pitiful sight ... light coats, rags wrapped around feet or shoes. I myself had managed to get some Russian felt boots; I'd taken them off a dead Russian. You had to do this right away, because rigor mortis set in very quickly in that cold.[68]

Willi Nolden, an anti-tank gunner, recalled having only

regular winter clothes, a thin coat and nothing else. We got some civilian stuff, mufflers and a few gloves. But the worst thing was that we didn't have any felt boots. When we unloaded our equipment, everything was frozen solid, covered with ice. Every battery was dead. So we put all of our trucks and half-tracks in an open field and built fires around them ... We had heavy casualties from frostbite – fingers, toes, sometimes whole arms and legs.[69]

The tide had turned against Germany and despite their bad start the Red Army was beginning to fight back. A crop of new young leaders, some of whom had been released from the Gulag, were moving into positions of command and Soviet troops began to show a tenacity and courage that the Germans had not yet encountered in Europe. Wehrmacht soldiers began to tell nervous tales about how much pain the Russian soldier could endure, how he would play dead and then ambush groups of Germans, how he never cried out even when mortally wounded.[70] Hugo Volkheimer remembered that 'the Red Army fought like men possessed. They used mine dogs that were trained to crawl under tanks. The dogs wore a bomb harness with a primer that stuck up vertically and would detonate the explosive as they crawled under the tank. This made short work of our tanks.'[71] By November the temperature had dropped to −40 degrees. German equipment began to seize up, and the mighty Wehrmacht had to commandeer peasant horses to pull their guns towards Moscow. The newsreel footage which was never shown to the German people showed the first grim pictures of soldiers huddled over in the wind, their faces racked with pain, their noses bleeding, their hands blackened as they froze to death under a dusting of snow. Berliners received urgent calls to donate gloves, fur and warm clothing to the Winterhilfe, but their contributions reached the front far too late. 'When furs did finally arrive at the front they turned out to be ladies' fur coats,' one soldier scoffed.[72] Of the 3,250,000 Germans who died in the Russian campaign over 100,000 literally froze to death in the snow; as one soldier put it, one night without shelter meant amputation or death.[73] Hitler seized upon the weather as an excuse for his failure – 'I have always detested snow, Bormann, you know. I've always hated it. Now I know why.

It was a presentiment.'[74] But failure was ultimately due to his profound under-estimation of the Soviet army and the vastness of the terrain in which he fought: 'The German people were being told that only the cold winter was to blame for the disaster, and not the Russian army. Well, it was just as cold on the other side. The Russians were better and more thoroughly prepared to deal with the severe conditions. They knew what was at stake: their homeland . . . We felt like we'd already been written off.'[75]

It is still an eerie experience to journey to Moscow over land and to stand at the memorial on the edge of the city which marks the point where, in November 1941, the exhausted Wehrmacht troops were forced to a grinding halt. It is chillingly close to the city centre. Hitler was so convinced of his imminent victory that he ordered huge blocks of red granite to be transported to the outskirts of Moscow for the construction of a monument to the Third Reich.[76] But Moscow held fast. Stalin did much to boost morale in those tense weeks before Christmas, reopening the churches, easing the grip of the NKVD and appearing at Red Square to calm the people. Memories of Borodino and Napoleon stirred a religious feeling of sacrifice in the people of the front-line city, and they worked by the thousand to build tank traps and fortifications.[77] The Germans never reached them. At the very moment when Moscow seemed in greatest danger Stalin heard from his spy Sorge in Tokyo that the Japanese were planning an attack not against Mongolia, but against Indo-China.[78] He immediately transferred his forty crack Siberian divisions, including 1,700 tanks and 1,500 aircraft, to Moscow. The men were specially trained and equipped to fight in the snow. They had fur coats, fur-lined boots and hats and gloves; some had skis and white uniforms and their T-34 tanks did not seize up in the bitter −40-degree weather. They reached Zhukov on the Moscow front at the beginning of November and were unleashed on the miserable Wehrmacht soldiers. The Germans did not know what had hit them.

Having experienced victory after victory the Wehrmacht were now deeply shocked to find themselves being pushed back. The Soviets moved so quickly that the Germans were forced to use the carcasses of frozen horses to mark their panicked retreat. The Russians took few prisoners and the German soldier Peter Pechel, injured and in imminent danger of capture, said he contemplated suicide after seeing the tortured and mutilated dead of another German com-pany.[79] For the first time Berliners heard whisper of defeat. Speer remembered talking to Fritz Todt, head of Organization Todt, which oversaw construction for the Third Reich's Four Year Plan, on 27 December 1941:

He was just back from a long inspection trip to Russia and he told me how horrified he was by the condition of our soldiers. Later I would remember his words and the utter sadness in his face when he said that he didn't think we could possibly win the war there. The Russian soldiers were perhaps primitive, he said, but they were both physically and psychologically much hardier than we were. I remember trying to encourage him.

He answered, 'You are young. You still have illusions.'[80] Then, on 7 December 1941, the Japanese attacked the American fleet at Pearl Harbor, opening the war in the Pacific.[81] On 11 December Hitler declared war on the United States. Berlin was now at the centre of a world war, a conflict which she herself had started.

As hope for a quick victory in the east waned life in Berlin became more difficult. Rations were cut, casualty lists began to grow and people began to question the wisdom of attacking Russia. But it was too late. The German offensive had not been a simple military matter but had turned into a two-pronged war, with the SS overseeing a brutal racial extermination conducted throughout the occupied territories of the east. By the time the Germans reached Moscow they had already committed crimes which made an easy peace out of the question. The invasion of the Soviet Union had marked a decisive turning point in German history, and the atrocities already committed during the invasion of Poland increased to a terrifying scale. The crimes were widespread and included the barbaric treatment of civilians, the murder of Soviet prisoners of war, the 'scorched earth' policy of the retreating army, the extermination of the gypsies, the euthanasia programme, and the beginning of the extermination of the European Jews which has since come to be known as the Holocaust. These crimes were meticulously planned, directed, sanctioned and recorded by the thousands of bureaucrats and officials who sat in their offices in the centre of Berlin.[82]

In May 1985 a group of young historians armed with shovels and pickaxes walked to the deserted site of the Prinz-Albrecht-Gelände, which lay in the shadow of the Wall in West Berlin. The SS and Gestapo headquarters, which had once taken up the entire city block, had been dynamited on 27 and 28 April 1949 and demolished in 1953. The area remained an empty weed-covered lot. After a few weeks of digging they discovered a maze of ruins beneath the sandy soil which turned out to be part of the basement and kitchen area of the Gestapo headquarters; they decided to create a small exhibition on the site outlining the role of the SS and the Gestapo in time for the 750th Anniversary celebrations in West Berlin. It was to prove a controversial proposal.

The first stage was to erect a number of signs outlining the location and function of particular buildings under the Nazis. I remember walking over the area a few days after they had been put up, only to find that most had been knocked down or vandalized. Persistent attempts to destroy the site itself led to the cellars being fenced in. There were loud protests against the 'dredging up of the past' and many Berliners complained that such a display was inappropriate; one man later told me that it had probably been funded by the Communists.

The exhibition, which finally opened in June 1987, was a small, balanced and poignant display of documents, photographs and films showing the role of the Berlin-based SS and Gestapo, from their imprisonment of the July 1944 plotters to the abuse of Russian prisoners of war; from the importation of slave labour into the Reich to the extermination of the gypsies and the European Jews. In a series of interviews with a cross-section of Berliners I found that although there were many positive voices a number of people disliked the display and in particular its emphasis on crimes committed in the east. Some did not understand the 'obsession with the Holocaust' and complained that 'that is all one hears about'. One student told me that 'Stalin had murdered many millions more than the Germans, so why constantly talk about the Jews?' Others compared the killing of the Jews with the genocide perpetrated against Armenians and Cambodians; another told me that he was tired of seeing the same film footage of Bergen-Belsen and that the camps 'did not look so bad'. Another asked if Germany only had 300,000 Jews before the war, 'how could six million Jews have been killed?' One woman said that although she had lived through the war in Berlin neither she nor any of her friends had known about the 'goings on' in the east and thought that much of it was propaganda invented to besmirch the name of Germany. An old woman said it was all very well to talk about German crimes, 'but what about crimes committed by Russians to the Germans – nobody ever talks about that!' But the most frequent reaction to the exhibition was to ask, 'What have the crimes to do with the history of Berlin?' One man yelled that Berliners had been victims of Hitler just as surely as the Poles or the Russians or the Jews. Another said that what the SS did in the east was 'a terrible business', but it was irrelevant to Berlin. In all the discussions, interviews and conversations I had with Berliners it became clear that despite the vast amount of information available about the Nazi period few understood the enormity of the role played by their own city in the unfolding terror of the Second World War.[83]

Thousands of Berliners were deeply involved in these events. Berlin was unique – it was no Frankfurt, Braunschweig, Hamburg or Cologne – for it was the centre from which the crimes and the mass murder in the east were directed. Although relatively few of the victims were German and the killing took place far away it was Berliners, or those drawn to the capital to enhance their careers, who drew up plans, made decisions, gave orders, correlated mountains of data and ensured that the vast machine functioned smoothly. The blackest crimes committed in the name of all Germans are inextricably bound up in the history of Berlin.[84]

Hitler had made it quite clear that he intended the war in the east to be very different from any other Europe had yet seen – a war of conquest combined with a racial war of extermination. On 22 August 1939, just before the invasion of Poland, Hitler had hinted at things to come:

> Our strength is our speed and our brutality [he said]. Genghis Khan drove many women and children to death, deliberately and joyously. History sees him as a great founder of a state. What weak western European civilization says about me doesn't matter. I have given the order – and I will have anyone shot who expresses even one word of criticism – that the aim of the war is not to reach definite lines but rather the physical destruction of the enemy.[85]

Literally million of people were to be killed in cold blood. The treatment of Polish civilians had been brutal; the violence against the Soviets would be worse still.

The first sign of the savagery was revealed in the abuse of Soviet prisoners of war captured in the first days of the fighting. The treatment of these men remains one of the most appalling and unexplored chapters in German history. The Soviet soldiers were not protected by the Geneva Convention and many were simply murdered. One Waffen-SS Untersturmführer on leave told his friend Peter Petersen that

> he had been at the front and had taken prisoners. He asked the battalion staff what he should do with them. The Waffen-SS general in command of the sector said, 'Shoot them.' My friend then protested that the prisoners were not partisans, but regular soldiers, and that he could not legitimately shoot them. He was ordered back to the battalion, where he received a terrible bawling out. He was told that he would learn that this was no kindergarten war. He would be sent to take command of a firing squad where he would be shooting partisans, German deserters, and who knows what else. He told me that he had not had the courage to refuse to obey this order, since he would have been shot.[86]

When Kiev was taken in mid September 1941 the Germans captured three-quarters of a million Russian prisoners. Only three out of every 100 men returned alive. Of the total of 5.7 million Soviet prisoners captured by the Germans 3.3 million had died or been killed by 1945.[87] Those who survived the first weeks were sent to the vast network of forced labour camps and armaments factories which stretched the length and breadth of the German-occupied territories; I remember coming across a Russian prisoner-of-war camp in northern Norway, its barrack blocks still visible in a field set between the freezing sea and once heavily mined hills. In the grass lay an enormous concrete roller with an iron handle much like those usually hitched to oxen. Erik Svendson, one of the local residents, recounted how the Russians had been forced to build the enormous bunkers there – seven storeys deep – or to drag the roller over the roads which they had hacked out of the rock. One German Hitler Youth member, Lothar Loewe, who was captured by the Russians in 1945, was amazed to find that 'the average Russian sympathized with young boys like us' – the Russians gave them food and one soldier lent him his mess kit and spoon. Loewe was shocked:

> I had seen many Soviet POWs during the war. And I had also seen how they were treated ... The Soviets were always beaten, really, and they never got anything to eat. They were made to look like the subhumans we imagined them to be. The idea that a German soldier would give a Russian prisoner his mess kit and spoon to eat from was simply unimaginable to me. And the fact that this Soviet gave me his, voluntarily, happily, because he felt sorry for me, shook the foundations of my image of them.[88]

Of the 300,000 slave labourers sent to the armaments factories in Berlin over half perished through hunger, disease, or in the bombing raids. Russian prisoners in particular were treated little better than animals.[89]

It is a sobering experience to travel slowly through eastern Europe and Russia and to remind oneself of the events which took place there over fifty years ago. The German invasion of the Soviet Union was the most brutal yet seen in history, and it was partly for this reason that the Red Army retaliated with such ferocity against Germany in 1944–5. From the very beginning Hitler intended the war against the USSR to be, as he put it on 30 March 1941, 'a war of extermination'.[90] His soldiers were instructed to 'close your hearts to pity' and to 'act brutally' as they advanced: 'Every war costs blood, and the smell of blood arouses in man all the instincts which have lain within us since the beginning of the world: deeds of violence, the intoxication of murder, and many other things.'[91] Those labelled *a priori* as criminals or 'subhumans' were to be killed outright; on 12 May 1941, for example, General Warlimont drafted an order stating that 'Political officials and leaders are to be liquidated.'[92] But the most grim orders concerned the treatment of ordinary civilians, people whose lives meant nothing to the conquerors. On 6 May 1941 the OKH issued an order sanctioning the 'shooting in action or while fleeing' of all local residents 'who participate or want to participate in hostile acts, who by an act of theirs resisted the German Armed Forces'. At the same time German soldiers committing 'punishable acts' on occupied soil 'out of bitterness against atrocities or subversive work of carriers of the Jewish-Bolshevik system' were not to be prosecuted.[93] The order was approved by Hitler along with the note that troops should 'defend themselves without pity against any threat from the hostile civilian population'. Some generals were appalled by this and quietly refused to pass the order on to their troops; Generals Oster and Beck, who would join the anti-Hitler conspiracy in 1944, agreed with General von Hassell's view that 'it makes one's hair stand on end to learn and receive proof of the systematic transformation of the military law concerning the conquered population into uncontrolled despotism . . . the Army must now bear the onus for the murders and burning which up to now have been confined to the SS'.[94] But the die was cast, and the Einsatzgruppen and even Wehrmacht soldiers were permitted – indeed encouraged – to commit horrific acts of violence against civilians without fear of censure. There were countless acts of brutality in the east, many recorded in the neatly typed reports sent back to Berlin; each day these listed the numbers of people rounded up and shot or herded into buildings which were then set alight. The German ambassador Ulrich von Hassel remembered terrible scenes of violence: a young officer was ordered to shoot 350 'partisans' (including women and children) who had been forced into a nearby barn. He had hesitated, only to be told that if he did not carry out the order he would be shot. To his obvious shame he finally complied, using a machine gun to mow them down.[95] The commander Otto Ohlendorf admitted at Nuremberg that in the first year of the campaign his group had liquidated about 90,000 men, women and children, but that the activities had not been dictated by 'military necessity but purely by ideological considerations'.[96] On 16 September 1941 the OKW issued an order explaining that as 'atonement for the life of a German soldier, a death sentence for between fifty and 100 Communists must be generally deemed commensurate'. It added chillingly that 'The means of execution must increase the deterrent still further.'[97]

Hitler's army pushed relentlessly on throughout the autumn of 1941; by 12 November Chudovo, Vitebsk, Smolensk, Kaluga, Mtsensk, Orel and Kharkov had been taken; by the end of the year Army Group Centre was thirty-five miles from Moscow, Army Group South was at the Donets, and Army Group North had reached the outskirts of Leningrad. Villages and towns had been overrun and ransacked; in October 1941 the commander of the Sixth Army, Field Marshal von Reichenau, stated that the burning of structures was acceptable as 'the disappearance of symbols of past Bolshevik rule, including buildings, falls within the framework of the struggle for annihilation. Neither historical nor artistic considerations play a role in the East in this context . . .'[98]

Even that most beautiful of Russian cities, Leningrad, was to be 'sealed off hermetically', the population was to be 'weakened by terror and growing starvation'; in the spring of 1942, after the survivors had been 'dealt with', the city was 'to be occupied', razed to the ground 'with high explosives' and its destruction blamed on the Soviets. Hitler argued, 'I suppose that some people are clutching their heads with both hands to find an answer to the question, "How can the Führer destroy a city like St Petersburg?" Plainly I belong by nature to quite another species.'[99] In the event Leningrad was besieged, hundreds of thousands of people died of starvation and cold – but the city did not fall. And, even in the midst of this carnage, the most systematic butchery was reserved for the Jews.[100]

In 1939 Hitler had announced that any war would result in 'the destruction of the Jewish race in Europe'. During the first months of the invasion of Poland he ordered that all Jews in the newly occupied territories be herded into ghettos: 'fence them in somewhere, where they can perish as they deserve'.[101] After October 1940 the ghettos were sealed, and thousands died of disease and starvation. But it was the invasion of the Soviet Union which marked the start of mass murder on an unprecedented scale. The groundwork was carefully laid in Berlin before the actual invasion took place. On 23 March 1941 Himmler presented Hitler with a memorandum listing 'Some thoughts about the treatment of foreign peoples in the eastern territories ... I hope to see the very concept of Jewry completely obliterated'.[102] At a conference on 26 March 1941 Dr Gross, the head of the Race Policy Bureau of the Nazi Party, said, 'the definitive solution must comprise the removal of the Jews from Europe', and eugenicist and rector of Berlin University Dr Fischer said that 'the morals and actions of the Bolshevist Jews bear witness to such a monstrous mentality that we can only speak of inferiority and beings of another species'.[103] The process of extermination began with the deployment of Einsatzgruppen, who started their grisly task on 22 June 1941.

The Einsatzgruppen were killing squads composed of commandos of up to 1,000 men – hardened SS men, members of the SD, the Gestapo, the police and local volunteers. Heydrich and Himmler had carefully worked out where each group would be sent and an order issued from the SS Office IV in Berlin on 17 July 1941 confirmed that they were to target Communist functionaries, members of Soviet intelligence, and 'all Jews'.[104]

The methods were exceedingly brutal. The commando would enter a village and kill any Communists, the infirm and suspected partisans, and they would invade the Jewish quarter, burn the houses and shoot everyone, including all women and children. In larger settlements the Jewish population would be rounded up and marched to a clearing, where they would be forced to dig their own graves; pitiable photographs still exist showing rows of shivering men, women and children standing beside deep trenches, waiting to be shot. One officer, Christoph von Gersdorff, remembered a friend coming into his room 'chalk-pale'. He had just flown out of Borisov, 'over a dreadful execution scene. Thousands of people, probably Jews, had dug deep ditches and were then shot with machine guns and pistols. The next shift had to step on top of the fallen, dead or alive, and they were shot in their turn. Also babies and naked women, begging for their children.'[105] Karma Rauhut remembered when a family friend 'came to our house and told us he had seen, in Poland, an entire airplane hangar full of corpses ... Such information just does not "fit in your head". Can you picture a whole airplane hangar full of corpses if you haven't seen them? It surpasses one's power of imagination. This inhuman criminality surpassed every power of imagination.'[106]

Precise records of each killing were sent back to Berlin in a continuous stream of notes and memos: one document sent from Einsatzkommando 3 from the Kovno, Schaulen and Wilno regions on 1 December 1941 carefully listed the murder of 99,804 civilians, most of whom were Jews; the entry for Kovno on 29 November alone listed the deaths of '9,012 Jews, Jewesses and Jewish children' and '573 active Communists'.[107] Another internal memo of 1 June 1943 from the Generalkommissar of the Politics Division in Minsk described his 'action' in Witoniż, in which he had herded the villagers into a barn, ordered his men to mow them down and had set the whole thing on fire. He admitted disappointment at finding that a number had lived and had managed to free themselves from under rows of charred corpses.

This bloody mass murder began to take its toll on the men ordered to carry out the executions. Most knew that the terms used by the Nazis to categorize their victims – words like 'agent', 'bandit', 'spy', 'partisan' or 'saboteur' – were simply pathetic attempts to mask a policy of brutal mass extermination of innocent men, women and children; many became alcoholics or went mad and had to be dragged back to Berlin for treatment.[108] In the winter of 1941 Helmuth-James von Moltke ran into a nurse from a Berlin SS hospital who was walking around blind drunk because she had to work with the men 'who cannot shut out what they have done and seen, cry out all the time, "I can't do it any more! I can't do it any more!" If you have to listen to that all day, you reach for the bottle at night.'[109] Himmler called the breakdown of his men a 'sign of weakness', but as the cases mounted it became clear that the efficient SS leadership had to find a new method for murder on such a scale. The solution would be the creation of 'factories' of death, places where human beings could be quietly transported and then killed cleanly, efficiently and secretly; forced labour would carry out the most filthy jobs.

On 20 January 1942 fifteen top Nazi ministers and officials met at a villa in the peaceful Berlin suburb of Wannsee.[110] It was to be one of the most infamous meetings in history, for it was there, at No. 56/58 Am Grossen Wannsee, that the 'Final Solution' became official Nazi policy. The Einsatz-gruppen were to be replaced by efficient death camps which would no longer rely on hundreds of executioners; they would be so well planned and co-ordinated that they would require only a handful of people to do the actual killing. The ever efficient Berlin bureaucracy would ensure that it ran smoothly: it was no accident that the participants at the conference included important ministers of the Reich, from Dr Stuckart, the Minister of the Interior, to Staatssekretär Neumann; from the Justice Minister, Dr Freisler, to the Reich Chancellery Ministerialdirektor Kritzinger. They were joined by top SS men – the head of the Race and Settlement Office, SS-Gruppenführer Hoffmann, SS-Obersturmbannführer Eichmann, SS-Gruppenführer Müller and SS-Obergruppenführer Heydrich. It was clear that the project was to involve thousands of Berliners at every level of society.

The minutes of the meeting, taken by Eichmann, head of the Gestapo's Jewish Emigration Office, have an almost surreal quality to them. The powerful men sat chatting and drinking cognac together before calmly turning to the question of the extermination of the European Jews. Precise lists were shown outlining the remaining populations, including the 330,000 Jews in Britain, and it was agreed that despite the efforts of the Einsatzgruppen over 11 million still remained to be dealt with. Plans were to be drawn up for mass deportations from all over Europe to camps in Poland and Russia. The able-bodied could be worked to death (the phrase later used was 'scrapped through labour') while the others were to be exterminated. At the end there was much toasting and mutual self-congratulation, and Heydrich got drunk on Cognac. At his trial in Israel in December 1961 Eichmann was read an extract from the minutes in which Heydrich had said: 'Those [Jews] who might possibly still remain, and they undoubtedly will be the toughest amongst them, will have to be treated accordingly.' When asked what the term meant Eichmann answered: 'Killed, killed, certainly.'[111] The fate of Europe's Jews had been sealed: they were to be liquidated using poison gas.

The use of gas was not new in Nazi Germany. Gas vans into which people were locked and poisoned by carbon monoxide from the exhaust fumes had been developed under the auspices of the Berlin Technical Referat of the Inspector of Security Police in the late 1930s; the first mass murder carried out by this method occurred in 1941, when Himmler gave Gauleiter Artur Greiser of the Wartheland permission to kill 100,000 Jews in his district at Kulmhof (Chelmno). Carbon monoxide had also been used to kill Germans in the infamous euthanasia programme, which had been devised largely by eminent eugenicists and anthropologists in Berlin.[112]

This programme was intimately connected with the evolution of the 'Final

Solution'. Literally hundreds of professors, scientists and technicians obsessed with the question of 'race-hygiene' sought to determine which human beings exhibited 'inferior' racial, genetic or physical characteristics. Dozens of Berlin institutions were involved in the detailed classification of undesirable human beings, including the Race Policy Bureau of the NSDAP, which dealt with theoretical questions of race; the SS Head Office for Race and Settlement, which determined who was to be Germanized or murdered in the occupied territories; the Reich Commission for the Scientific Registration of Hereditary and Constitutional Severe Disorders, which determined whether non-Aryan or handicapped infants and children were to be classed as 'negative human material' and killed; the Reich Department of Public Health and Hygiene, which singled out those in concentration camps who lived *Ballastexistenzen* (valueless lives) and should therefore be killed (decisions were made by a board of Berlin physicians); the Kaiser Wilhelm Society for the Advancement of Science, including a vast anthropology section which dissected the brains of handicapped children or the eyes of murdered gypsies to determine racial and hereditary properties; the SS Foundation for the Heritage of our Fore-fathers; and the Reich Kinship Bureau, which was responsible for judging the difference between Jews and Aryans. The respected neurologist Robert Ritter headed the Establishment for Research in Hereditary Science in Berlin, which evolved into the Institute for Criminal Biology and was merged during the war into Himmler's Head Office for Reich Security; Ritter used his complicated scientific method to divide human beings into three types: 'good' or not genetically disposed to criminality; those individuals who despite mixed herit-age could be educated to conform to society; and the 'bad types' of inferior or mixed genetic stock, including 'half caste gypsies', who were 'ineducable' or 'biologically depraved' and therefore to be removed from society.[113] Highly respected Nazi 'professionals' from Werner Blankenburg to Werner Heyde and Hermann Paul Nitsche developed the technology which led to the creation of the extermination camps.

The euthanasia programme was directed from part of the Berlin Chancel-lery complex code-named T-4 after the address 'Tiergartenstrasse 4'. The T-4 scientists collaborated with Himmler and Reichsamtsleiter Dr Brack to perfect the use of bottled carbon monoxide; over 70,000 mentally ill and handicapped Germans were gassed between 1939 and 1941. It was the success of the murders at Kulmhof as well as the efficiency of the euthanasia programme which convinced the men at Wannsee that mass extermination of the Jews was possible using a combination of gas and secluded camps.

The first camps were set up almost immediately after the Wannsee confer-ence, when Dr Brack agreed to go to the east and set up his gassing apparatus in the three new sites being prepared for the purpose, which were both secluded and close to railway lines. They were called Belzec, Sobibór and Treblinka. Dozens of German specialists went east to help set up the machinery of mass murder: Dr Mennecke, a psychiatrist, wrote to his wife from Berlin:

> My dear little wifey ... I have just had an explanation from Dr H. [Hefelmann] of these brand new arrangements, which Miss Schwab had previously hinted at over the telephone. The day before yesterday, a large contingent from our euthanasia programme moved under the leadership of Brack to the Eastern battle-zone. It consists of doctors, office personnel, and male and female nurses ... This is all top secret. Only those who, for the most pressing of reasons, cannot be spared from our euthanasia programme are not coming along.[114]

The doctors and other medical personnel who had honed their murderous skills in the asylums of Germany went to supervise the mass murder in the new extermination camps.

Unlike concentration camps such as Oranienburg or Dachau these new camps had no room for prisoners, and the majority of victims were dead within two hours. Trains were shunted down special tracks to stations which – in Treblinka, for instance – were sometimes disguised to look like innocuous village stations. Before they knew what was happening the disoriented prisoners would be pushed from the train into a dark narrow passage, 'sorted', undressed, and herded into the gas chambers. Very few people were retained as workers. The victims were murdered and their bodies burned as quickly as possible so that the camp would be ready for the next transport. Auschwitz-Birkenau, with its four gas chambers and huge crematoria, was the last of the extermination camps to be completed in early 1943, but it was here that use of the gas Zyklon B began.[115]

The first attempt to use Zyklon B took place at Auschwitz under the direction of SS Captain Karl Fritzsche in August 1941.[116] Höss, who had been the Kommandant of Oranienburg at Berlin, was moved to Auschwitz and wrote in his 1946 testimony *Commandant in Auschwitz* that Fritzsche had come up with the idea of using this cyanide-based insecticide on human beings. Höss was excited by the find, and wrote:

> During this first experience of gassing people I did not fully realize what was happening, perhaps because I was too impressed by the whole procedure. I have a clearer recollection of the gassing of nine hundred Russians ... the doors were sealed and the gas shaken down through the holes in the roof. I do not know how long this killing took. For a little while a humming sound could be heard (the prisoners had been told they were to be deloused). When the powder was

thrown in, there were cries of 'Gas!' then a great bellowing and the trapped prisoners hurled themselves against both the doors. But the doors held ... I must even admit that this gassing calmed me, for the mass extermination of the Jews had to start soon.[117]

The procurement of Zyklon B again reveals the importance of Berlin as an administrative centre of the mass murder in eastern Europe. The SS factories did not produce Zyklon B themselves and the gas had a shelf life of only four months, which necessitated a continuous supply. It was produced by two German factories and its distribution was controlled by Speer's ministry in Berlin. A special committee, which included such esteemed men as Dr Rose of the Robert Koch Institute, Dr Christiaensen of the Interior Ministry, Dr Schreiber of the Obercommando der Wehrmacht or OKW (Armed Forces High Command) and others, decided how much Zyklon would be needed by the SS, the Wehrmacht and the other organizations which used it for fumigation (the navy, for example, used it to rid its ships of rats), and it was they who sent the SS 'quota' to the Armed Forces Main Sanitation Depot.[118] There, another lot of bureaucrats decided upon the amount which should go to the Wehrmacht and to the SS. The Waffen-SS Central Sanitation Depot then allocated gas to SS offices which carefully judged how much was needed for the projected numbers of transports. Hundreds of people were involved in the allocation of the gas, and many would have known what it was used for. The use of gas chambers combined with crematoria which could burn over 4,000 corpses a day made Auschwitz particularly efficient, and by 1943 transports were arriving from all over Europe. Only when the process was well underway did these men turn against the Jews in their own city.

The man directly responsible for making Berlin 'Judenfrei' was none other than Joseph Goebbels. Goebbels had expressed his longing to rid Berlin of Jews after his first visit to Poland in 1939; after seeing the Jewish ghetto in Lodz he wrote, 'These aren't human beings any more; they're animals ... one must operate here, and radically.'[119] Upon his return to Berlin he stepped up his anti-Semitic propaganda campaign. The films *Jud Süss*, *Die Rothschilds* and the vile film *Der ewige Jude* (The Eternal Jew) were all released in 1940. The latter was meant to unmask the 'real ghetto Jew' of Poland which lurked behind even the most assimilated Jew in 'civilized Berlin'; it depicted a graphic scene of Kosher butchering from the Warsaw ghetto and compared the migration of the Jews to the spread of the plague. In late 1940 and early 1941 the film was shown in over sixty cinemas in Berlin simultaneously, and according to secret service reports received a positive reception.[120]

On 20 March 1941 Goebbels's deputy Leopold Gutterer reported that there were still 60,000 to 70,000 Jews in Berlin. Goebbels was furious and said that

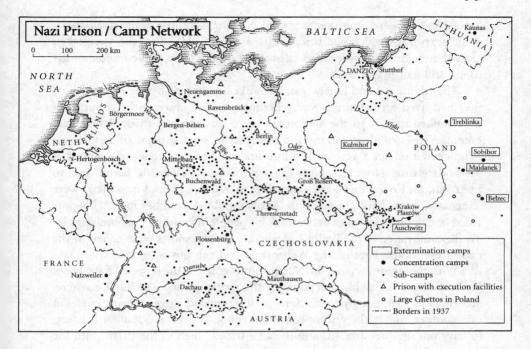

it simply was not right 'that the capital of the National Socialist Reich' should still 'harbour such a large number of Jews'. Adolf Eichmann was personally asked to 'work out a proposal for Gauleiter Dr Goebbels for the evacuation of the Jews from Berlin'. As this was being drafted the impatient Goebbels sought further measures to restrict the lives of Jews in the city. According to him only 26,000 of Berlin's 77,000 Jews were 'in employment', but on 18 August 1941 more were pushed into factories and forced to do twelve to fifteen hours of manual labour daily regardless of age or sex. The curfew was extended, rations were cut and food cards were stamped with little purple 'J's entitling shop keepers to serve them last. Jews could buy yarn twice a year, but no clothing. On 19 September Goebbels introduced the measure forcing Jews to wear the Star of David.[121] Then, in October 1941, while all attention was focused on the Russian front, the Gestapo prepared for deportations of Berlin Jews to ghettos in Poland.

Late on the night of 16 October groups of Gestapo agents spread out over Berlin and began to knock at the doors of Jewish homes yelling out the ridiculous charge that they were 'hoarding goods'. The prisoners were permitted to pack one small bag before being marched through the city past the ruin of the synagogue on Fasanenstrasse, which had burned on *Kristallnacht*. The doors of their homes were sealed with Gestapo stamps (an eagle gripping a swastika). Howard Smith remembered catching a glimpse of the small apartment next to his which had belonged to a pair of old ladies who were taken away that night. Two little china cups stood on the table in the middle of the room, still half full of tea.[122]

The frightened and lonely people had been betrayed by the city in which they had lived for centuries. Many Berliners turned away as the columns of Jews walked quietly to the stations or were loaded onto trucks late in the evening. The first deportations left from Berlin on the night of 16 October 1941, when 4,187 Jews were packed into unheated railway cars and dropped at the Łódz ghetto. Nine transports quickly followed, dispersing Berlin Jews to Łódz, Minsk, Kovno and Riga. According to Wolters around 4,500 Jews were 'evacuated' from Berlin between 18 October and 2 November 1941; 'This provided one thousand further habitations for people affected by the bombings.'[123] To the annoyance of the Berlin bureaucrats the transports were halted at the end of the month because the Wehrmacht had run out of trains.

With the residents gone the Nazis would return to the deserted flats, break the seals and hold public auctions for the sparse goods. The auctions were, according to Smith, 'ugly spectacles with ill-tempered citizens crying curses at one another and at the auctioneer, threatening with all the standard threats to have one another arrested and to call a friend "high in the Party" into the squabbles'. Many Berliners participated, although some were disgusted at the treatment of the Jews. One woman was arrested for saying, 'Thank God, this mess is over. They've sucked the last measly penny out of the Jews now; they can do nothing more.'[124]

Goebbels was angry at the delay and looked for any excuse to step up the 'cleansing' of Berlin. On 18 May 1942 his new anti-Soviet exhibition at the Lustgarten was attacked by a small resistance group and he used this as an excuse to target the remaining Berlin Jews:

> My campaign against the Jews in Berlin will be waged along similar lines [he wrote]. I am currently having a Jewish hostage list put together. Sweeping arrests will follow. I have no intention of possibly letting a 22-year-old East European Jew – characters of this type were found amongst the assassins at the anti-Soviet exhibition – fire a bullet into my belly. Ten Jews either in a concentration camp or six feet under are preferable to one roaming at large. There is no room for sentimentalism here.[125]

Five hundred Jews were arrested; 250 were shot in the Lichterfelde Cadet College and the remainder were sent to Sachsenhausen. On 29 May Heydrich was ambushed and killed in Prague, which gave Goebbels a pretext for seeking Hitler's permission to kill the remaining Berlin Jews. He now referred to them as 'unconditionally exterminable'; shortly afterwards he met Himmler to plan the deportation of Berlin Jews to Auschwitz.

These deadly transports began on 19 October, with Jews being herded to the three railway stations of Grunewald, Putlitzstrasse, and the main Anhalter Bahnhof. A hundred and seventeen 'old-age' transports took 14,979 Jews to Theresienstadt. A number who had been married to Aryans were also deported, including Sigrid Görtz's mother whose Aryan husband had been killed in the First World War fighting for Germany. When the daughter tried to save her mother, a functionary at the SD headquarters looked at her and said, 'It's a pity your father – who was not Jewish – is no longer alive, for in that case this would not be necessary. Your tough luck!'

Many Jews who heard that they had been targeted for the transports committed suicide. Of the 3,580 Jews seized for deportation on 3 April 1942 fifty-seven killed themselves; when over 900 were seized for a transport destined for Estonia 208 committed suicide; in all around 6,000 Berlin Jews died by their own hand. Some of these deaths were 'uncomfortable' for the regime: the great actor Joachim Gottschalk was something of a Cary Grant figure to many Berliners, and although he was Aryan his wife was Jewish. When the Gestapo arrived at the door to take his wife and child they found all three dead. Many Berliners were shocked by the news, but the transports continued.

On the night of 27 February 1943 Goebbels raided the Berlin munitions factories, forcing Jewish workers into trucks that took them directly to trains and the camps. 'I won't rest', he yelled that night, 'until at least the capital has become completely Jew-free.' The IG Farben plant in Auschwitz had been promised skilled workers and eagerly awaited the arrival of the Berlin Jews but two days later Obersturmführer Schwartz complained that most of the transport had been made up of women and children, and had therefore been subjected to 'special treatment'. 'If the transports from Berlin continue to have so many women and children as well as old Jews,' he wrote, 'I don't promise myself much in the matter of labour allocation.'[126] In the following four transports from Berlin only 1,689 qualified as factory labourers; the 2,398 women and children who had so recently walked through the streets of Berlin were gassed.

By 11 March 1943, in a total of sixty-three transports, 35,738 of the 66,000 Jews still living in Berlin had been deported to Auschwitz and most had been murdered. Three months later the Gestapo finally closed the office of the Jüdische Gemeinde in Berlin and transported all those still waiting for permission to emigrate to Auschwitz. On 19 May 1943 Goebbels proudly declared Berlin 'Judenfrei', a feat which he termed his 'greatest political accomplishment'.

*   *   *

The anti-Jewish measures were not popular amongst Berliners although only a few brave individuals did anything to help. Some managed to sneak food to Jews, helped them to hide from the SS and sheltered them during bombing raids: Hildegard Dannenbaum survived in the basement of the shell of a house but after some months of this a well-known physician and his girlfriend hid her in their home in the Lichterfelde area of Berlin; 'after we were bombed out there he and his girlfriend moved into a one-room summer bungalow. I slept on a folded rug under their roof.' The couple had saved her life.[127] Rita Kuhn, who had a Jewish father and an Aryan mother, remembered being ordered out of an air-raid shelter by a Gestapo woman but then being taken to a small room nearby and comforted by a lady doctor who openly defied the Gestapo order. In a strange twist of fate the Gestapo woman, named Frau Müller, actually befriended them shortly after this incident. After the war Rita Kuhn discovered that the family files had been deliberately stamped to indicate that they had died – an act which meant they would no longer be searched for. Rita believes that the Gestapo woman might have done this to save their lives.[128] Others assisted organizations such as the Herbert Baum Group; on 18 May 1942 most of its Jewish members were shot for putting up anti-Nazi posters. Some supported the Chug Chaluzi Pionierkreis, which helped Jews to escape from Germany with foreign passports. Other groups, including the Bekennende Kirche, the Hilfswerk beim bischöflichen Ordinariat, the Berlin Quakers and the Gruppe Emil, tried to shelter Jews. A handful of brave individuals like Maria, Countess von Maltzan, hid people in their flats and helped them to escape to Sweden, while the Catholic priest Bernhard Lichtenberg drew attention to their plight in his sermons. The Nazis sometimes caved in to mass protest: when 4,700 Jewish factory workers were seized for deportation their Aryan wives went as one to the makeshift prison on Rosenstrasse chanting, 'We want our husbands!' Before long other Berliners had joined them, making this a protest unique in the history of Nazi Germany. The women remained defiant even when the SS trained machine guns on them. The extraordinary demonstration lasted for several days; the SS, clearly unwilling to shoot thousands of women on the street, let the men return home, where they remained in limbo until the end of the war.[129]

Overall, however, the Berliners' record was unimpressive. There were no public acts of solidarity for the Jews; no boycotting of films like *Jud Süss* such as occurred in occupied countries and would have cost nothing; no local protests like that against the bookseller in Sweden who was attacked after he put up a JEWS NOT PERMITTED sign in his shop window; no moves to knock down the anti-Jewish signs in the parks or at the edges of leafy suburbs. Of the entire population of Berlin Jews only about 6,100 survived the war and most of those slipped through the net as partners in 'privileged mixed marriages'. Out of a population of 4 million Berliners only a few hundred people helped to shelter the 1,400 unprotected Jews known as 'U-boats' and, as Raul Hilberg has pointed out, most of those saved were either related to their protectors, were part German, or had converted to Christianity.[130]

On the other hand, Berlin contained thousands of people who actively participated in the Holocaust, albeit from a distance. The city's supreme role in the crime was undeniable – it contained the twelve vast SS headquarters, including the SS Main Office under Berger, the Reich Security Main Office under Heydrich, the Hauptampt Ordnungspolizei under Daluege, the Economic-Administrative Main Office under Pohl, the SS Personnel under Schmitt, the Main Office of the Reichskommissar for Strengthening of Germandom under Greifelt, and the Race and Resettlement Main Office under Hofman. The offices employed hundreds of people who were directly involved in the mass murder of the Jews and related atrocities in the east. The city also contained the most important Reich administrative bodies, including Ministries of the Interior, of Justice, of Food, of Finance, of the Economy and of Foreign Affairs, of the Eastern Territories, of the Post, of Armaments, of the Reichsbank and of Propaganda. These, too, were intimately connected with the crimes. These thousands in their Berlin offices may not have pulled a trigger or closed an oven door, but they made a vast logistical undertaking like the Holocaust possible: they had the power to 'destroy a whole people by sitting at their desks'.[131]

The complicity in the crime took place on many levels, reaching all the way from the top of the SS hierarchy down to minor officials in the Reichsbahn. Berlin bureaucrats directed virtually every aspect of the Holocaust, from the planning, building and maintenance of the concentration and death camps to the provision of SS brothels and gas and equipment for medical experiments. There are literally thousands of small examples of their involvement: the minions in the Food and Agriculture Ministry allocated a certain number of calories to each camp, taking into account the deaths through disease or in the gas chambers. The WVHA Amt B-V under Standartenführer Scheide at the SS Führungshauptamt carefully assigned weapons to the camp guards and decided how much ammunition would be needed for each guard tower in case of escapes. Himmler conferred with his officials in May 1943 before charging the Finance Ministry RM 150,000,000 for the razing of the Warsaw ghetto. Berlin bureaucrats dealt with unforeseen problems such as the payment of outstanding gas and electricity bills left by Jews forced to leave at a moment's notice – these were sent to the German offices responsible for public utilities and finance. The SS statistician Dr Korherr spent hours trawling through the meticulous SS documents in Berlin so that he could send a report to Himmler on 1 January 1943 proudly showing that 2.4 million Jews had already 'received special treatment' in the east. There were endless conferences and meetings to discuss everything from disease control to the number of doctors permitted at a given camp. The infamous medical experiments had to be specially ordered and processed through the 'proper channels' in Berlin: when the chief of the Air Force Medical Service became curious about the chances of pilots surviving a crash into the Atlantic he put in a request for a series of grim experiments to test the possibility of resuscitation after drowning. When Stabsarzt Dohmen of the Army Medical Service wanted to do experiments on jaundice he had to ask the SS Reichsarzt in Berlin for permission to inject prisoners with diseased serum. Himmler was particularly interested in medical experiments on humans and supported everything from mass sterilization to Mengele's experiments on twins, but he insisted that doctors follow correct procedure and make their official requests to the SS offices first. Berlin was also the centre of the rail network, and the Ministry of Transport and the German Reichsbahn were involved in the smooth functioning of the camps, for it was they who worked out the complicated logistics of moving Jews from all over Europe while still providing trains for the war effort. The minions at the Reich Railway office in Berlin carefully wrote out thousands of bills for the one-way transport to the camps, knowing perfectly well why the Jews were never coming back: adults were charged 4 pfennigs a head per rail kilometre for their own transport to their deaths: children went at half price. The Reichsbahn also organized the return of goods collected from the Jews to the Reich capital, another complicated procedure which involved hundreds of people.[132]

When Jews left for the death camps some still believed that they were about to start a new life in the east. Many dressed in their best clothes and carried their most precious possessions with them. When they arrived they were quickly forced to part with their suitcases and were herded into waiting rooms to undress. Women's hair was cut or shaved before they were directed into the gas chambers. As the victims died the camp workers began to sort their goods. Clothing and jewellery, watches and money were taken, and when the corpses were dragged from the chambers the gold teeth were pulled from their mouths. All items were meticulously inventoried before being put on the return trains to Berlin. Money, foreign currency, precious metal and coins were delivered directly to the Reichsbank storage room, where dozens of people worked to sort items: coins were sent to the precious metals divisions, stocks and bonds went to Securities, jewellery went to the Berlin Pawnshop (although there was much grumbling about items damaged 'in transit'), and the piles of gold teeth were sent to the Prussian State Mint to be melted down. Those involved in such gruesome work knew precisely where the items had come from.[133]

Other less valuable items, such as watches, fountain pens and fur coats, were sent to the SS Economic-Administrative Main Office to be repaired and put on sale for the troops. Some of the best watches were given to SS men as gifts from the Reich. Every item was accounted for and distributed to the 'competent' agency: men's underwear and clothing was sent to the Volks-deutsche Mittelstelle for distribution to ethnic Germans, and precious silk items such as women's underwear and stockings were sent directly to Funk's Economy Ministry. Piles of spectacles and dentures were sent to the Medical Referat D-III to be redistributed to German patients. After 6 August 1942 the collection of human hair became mandatory and bags of it were sent back to Berlin to be turned into felt footwear for U-boat personnel and Reichsbahn employees. Occasionally plasma was collected from young women, who were literally bled to death in the camp hospitals, although the use of corpses in the manufacture of soap has never been conclusively proven.[134] The horror of the Nazi mentality was revealed to the fourteen-year-old Martin Bormann (Bormann's eldest son) during a visit to Himmler's 'special lair' with Himmler's mistress Hedwig Potthast and their two children:

> When she opened the door and we flocked in, we didn't understand what the objects in that room were . . . It was tables and chairs made of parts of human bodies. There was a chair . . . the seat was a human pelvis, the legs human legs – on human feet. And then she picked up a copy of *Mein Kampf* from a pile of them . . . She showed us the cover – made of human skin, she said – and explained that the Dachau prisoners who produced it used the *Rückenhaut*, the skin of the back, to make it.[135]

Despite the nature of their work the thousands of Berliners who carried out these myriad tasks seem to have remained detached from what they were doing: the most horrific requests were treated as mere jobs to be done quickly and efficiently. Most of these bureaucrats were not particularly interested in the extermination of the Jews per se; indeed many officials saw the 'Jewish question' as a nuisance and an added burden which interfered with more urgent tasks related to the war effort.[136] Nevertheless, the memos were written, the telephone calls made, the files kept and the blueprints drawn up so that the system continued to function smoothly until the final days of the Third Reich. Many of these men (there were very few women involved at this level) seemed oblivious to the fact that they were tiny cogs in the vast apparatus of murder; after the war it was easy for them to distance their remote functions from the horrific crimes now coming to the attention of the world. Even important figures resorted to denial: Schacht claimed that he had tried to help Jews to emigrate; Hess reminded the Nuremberg tribunal that the Nazis were not the first to have established concentration camps; Streicher claimed that he was a Zionist; a food official said that he had been overworked and that an eye disease had prevented him from reading all the papers he had signed; Professor Abel, department head of the Kaiser Wilhelm Institute in Berlin, which was connected with the extermination of gypsies and Jews, said that anthropology and human genetics had 'no significance' for Nazi policies.[137] This vast army of Berliners wrote no memoirs, left no testimonies, and faded into the background of the post-war world as if they had never existed, leaving the histories to be written by the handful of dissenters and victims.

For those Berliners not involved in the workings of the ministries and SS offices in their city, the fate of Jews and gypsies were subjects of little interest. Few believed the rumours about the murders in the east and anyway, they argued, there was little they could have done. What they really cared about was the progress of the war, and by 1942 things were beginning to take a turn for the worse.

Berliners had cheered the invasion of the Soviet Union, convinced that the fight would last no more than five weeks. By 1942 they had already given up hope of a quick victory and settled in for a long war. There was as yet no talk of defeat; during the Memorial Day speech in 1942 Hitler said: 'we can already be certain of one thing today: the Bolshevist hordes which failed to conquer the German soldiers and their allies this winter will be beaten by us next summer and will be destroyed!' The SD report revealed that 'the Führer's words have enormously strengthened the hopes entertained by the greater part of the people that Bolshevism will be destroyed this year'.[138] People longed for victory so that they could return to 'normal' life. They did not understand that by now their lives could never return to the pre-war status quo.

The 1942 summer offensive had started on a positive note for the Wehrmacht: there was good news as Rommel, the legendary 'Desert Fox', swept through North Africa and after a long siege took the fortress of Tobruk, forcing the British to retreat to El Alamein. Meanwhile on the eastern front the Führer Directive of 3 April had concentrated German resources into a vast force set to secure the Caucasus oil fields and drive into Russia from the south. The revitalized force pressed forward towards the Donets; the Soviet army retreated, and by the beginning of August the Wehrmacht had chased them to the foothills of the Caucasus, while the Sixth Army crossed the Don and approached the Volga. On 23 August Stukas began bombarding the Soviet city of Stalingrad.

Hitler had wavered over the tactical importance of Stalingrad but on 30 July had declared it to be the key objective of the campaign, no doubt swayed by its importance to Stalin, who had held the city – then called Tsaritsyn – against the White Russians in 1918. The battle would cost around 1 million lives. It also marked the turning point of the war.[139]

On 13 September the German Sixth Army under General von Paulus launched an offensive against the city, expecting to capture it within days. As the German infantry broke through its southern defences the Nazis predicted the city's demise. Many Berliners assumed that the reversals of the previous winter had been temporary and that Hitler would, after all, prove victorious. But despite their numbers, which amounted to only a few hundred men, the Russians hung on. As the battle raged Stalin appointed his most brilliant general, Georgi Zhukov, to the post of deputy supreme commander and on 19 November he launched a major counter-offensive, attacking the German lines around the city. By 23 November the 250,000 beleaguered Germans of the Sixth Army had been surrounded, but rather than allow the trapped men to retreat Hitler ordered them to hold their ground. General von Paulus found himself locked in a street-by-street struggle through burnt-out factories and derelict buildings. The German troops were soon caught in a trap.

As time elapsed all chance of breaking free vanished. Supply lines were cut and the men received no aid except occasional food drops organized by Göring; among these were useless boxes of iron crosses which were left to freeze in the bitter cold. Christmas was terrible; Count Friedrich von Solms remembered: 'We ate cats and dogs, we had only a little bread. Even the horsemeat had run out. Our morale was bad ... The soldiers didn't want to fight any more.'[140] A division commander, General von Hartmann, climbed up on to a railway track embankment and just stood there 'until a bullet hit him'.[141] On 24 January General Paulus asked for permission to surrender but the Führer snapped back: 'Surrender out of the question. Troops will fight to the last bullet.' In this he revealed his First World War training, which had taught that no piece of territory was to be voluntarily relinquished no matter what the cost. On 30 January the soldiers huddled around their radios waiting for a message of encouragement from Hitler, but none came. I remember talking to a young medic who was one of the last Germans to escape Stalingrad on a transport ordered by Field Marshal Milch; the sight of the desperate starving men waiting in the snow shocked him into the realization that the Nazi leaders simply did not care about the fate of the German soldier. The Catholic chaplain Josef Kayser, trapped near Stalingrad, remembered that 'instead of saying Mass, I held heads and gave shots. One time I left the operating table to get some fresh air. When I got outside I saw a dog running around with a man's arm in its mouth – a wedding band was still on the ring finger. The last two Masses were, of course, cancelled.'[142] The young soldier Heinz Pfennig remembered the terrible conditions: 'both my hands and feet froze. I got shrapnel in my right thigh, and my circulation was so bad that months later my toes had to be amputated. My fingers were so swollen that they looked like blood oranges. After two days, my fingernails and my skin came off with my gloves.'[143] On that day, 10 January, the final Russian assault began and the remaining terrified Germans were flushed out from cellars and burned-out buildings. On 31 January Paulus disobeyed Hitler's order and surrendered. Of the 260,000 Germans trapped in the city only 90,000 lived long enough to be captured and only 5,000 men ever returned from the Gulag. Soviet treatment of German prisoners of war was as brutal as that meted out by the Germans themselves; most were marched through the snowy steppes to provisional camps and those who fell on the way from illness or exhaustion were shot or left to freeze to death. 'The initial months were the worst,' said one prisoner; 'our men died like flies. But the Russians themselves in the Stalingrad sector had nothing to eat either.'[144]

Hitler tried to carry on as if nothing unusual had happened. Paulus's 'treachery' was not to be mentioned again, but behind the facade he was deeply shaken by the defeat. For Stalin, however, the battle marked the moment when he knew he would win the war. There was to be no chance of a negotiated peace; the Germans could be beaten – it was just a matter of time.[145]

By Christmas rumours about Stalingrad were spreading through Berlin. On 23 January Reich Press Chief Dietrich gave news to the press of 'the great and stirring heroic sacrifice which the troops encircled at Stalingrad are offering the German nation'. Finally, to the strains of Beethoven's Fifth Symphony – a piece which always heralded solemn news – Berliners awaited a dreaded Special Announcement.

> The struggle in Stalingrad is over [they heard]. Loyal to their oath down to the last breath, the Sixth Army, under the exemplary leadership of General Field Marshal Paulus, succumbed to the superior force of the enemy and the unfavourable conditions ... Generals, officers, non-commissioned officers, and men fought shoulder to shoulder down to the last shot. They died so that Germany might live.

People looked at one another, and then turned away. Some now feared that the war was lost. This was the greatest single shock of the war, and afterwards some people began to openly criticize the party, and even Hitler himself. Secret service reports show that many soldiers began to feel a creeping cynicism and bitterness about their 'great Führer' and the assumption that victory was near at hand was gone.[146]

Hitler retreated to his East Prussian headquarters, the 'Wolfsschanze' or Wolf's Lair, rarely coming to Berlin and gradually losing touch with his people.[147] Goebbels implored him to appear in public or at least to speak to them; when he refused Goebbels tried to propagate the myth of the lonely Great Man in the mould of Frederick the Great, who would soon deliver Germany with some secret strategy or wonder weapon. Despite his best efforts, morale plummeted. Goebbels saw that the 'Hitler myth' was losing its potency and that something had to be done. A new strategy was devised – not to boost morale, but to rouse the German sense of duty, self-sacrifice and fear of defeat. Drawing on Churchill's great war-time speeches he prepared for one of the greatest performances of his life.

On the afternoon of 18 February 1943 Goebbels stepped into the shining new bulletproof Mercedes which Hitler had given him as a Christmas present and drove through Berlin. He entered the Sportpalast, which was packed with the party faithful and top officials, and stood beneath an enormous banner which read TOTAL WAR – SHORTEST WAR. The theme of his speech was simple: the Russians were coming, and every last shred of effort would be needed to defeat them and drive them back. The Battle of Stalingrad could not be seen as a mere clash of arms; it was a symbolic battle for all Germans, who were in fact fighting a Holy War to preserve Europe against the Bolshevik Asiatic beast, 'the hordes from the Steppe'. If they looked closely, he said, they would be able to see the hateful Soviet divisions bearing down on the glorious German troops; behind them were 'Jewish liquidation commandos', and behind them lurked 'terror, the ghost of famine, and complete European anarchy'. Terror had to be met with terror or German civilization would perish. After a pause he turned to his audience and asked them in a booming voice whether they wanted 'Total War – more total and radical than we can even imagine today?' The hall erupted into a frenzied, stomping, hysterical mass. Berliners now had a clear choice: either fight with everything they had, or perish in a maelstrom so terrible that it would make Stalingrad look mild by comparison. Few understood that by following Goebbels they were simply prolonging a war which was already doomed to failure. The wily Propaganda Minister would wring every last drop out of the country before the end.[148]

From that moment Goebbels did everything in his power to whip up terror of the approaching Red Army. The treachery involved was astounding: at Nuremberg Fritzsche admitted that when the Soviets allowed German troops captured at Stalingrad to send postcards back to their families Hitler ordered them to be destroyed because they belied his claim that the Germans had held out 'until the last shot'. There was no doubt about what the Berliners were meant to think of the Russians; when the embassy on Unter den Linden was closed the Nazis hung up an enormous sign saying it was being fumigated. Goebbels's propaganda worked; from now on the faster the Red Army moved the more desperate the people became, and after the call for 'total war' everything in Berlin changed. The pleasant life enjoyed until now was replaced by a hard, cold, grim regimen marked by deprivation and terror.

Goebbels began by 'radically eliminating' frivolous vestiges of civilian life. Aided by the new Reich Minister for Armaments Albert Speer he issued an order that anyone not fighting at the front would have to work at home to manufacture weapons. Many young men who had coasted through the war as merchants or factory managers found themselves on troop transports heading for the front. Goebbels closed down all businesses not vital to the war effort and trawled through the government quarter removing those who might be of more use as soldiers – he even sent three minions from his own ministry and replaced them with women. Civil government became more corrupt than ever before: knowing someone 'who knew Goebbels' could mean the difference between life and death. Rations were reduced to 60 per cent of the 1939 level; staples like potatoes ran out, clothing ration cards became redundant and women made shoes out of straw and cork. Berliners were encouraged to grow their own produce on allotments, but although one propaganda article claimed that 700,000 Berliners were cultivating plots and had 200,000 chickens and a million apple trees the city began to run dangerously short of food. Goebbels launched an operation to close down all remaining luxury restaurants in Berlin; knowing Göring would protest at the closure of his favourite restaurant Hörcher's, he simply sent SA men over to smash all its windows. The theatres were officially closed at the end of August 1944, but many had already ceased to function; the Kadeko and the Scala were destroyed in 1943 and the Wintergarten was bombed out in 1944. The bar Rio Rita remained open but all but two other clubs were closed down and these were restricted to soldiers in transit who had nowhere to go between midnight and five o'clock in the morning; dancing was forbidden and Berlin's prostitutes were sent to the eastern front to entertain the troops.

It was the Russian campaign which finally brought the seriousness of the situation home to Berliners. Up until then the Germans had lost only 200,000 men, a minute percentage in an army of up to 6.5 million troops. The Russian campaign changed this; the death notices filled ever longer columns and the newspapers of Berlin were thick with black-rimmed pages. In 1944 the numbers were so high that those who had died a 'hero's death' were lumped together in a single black notice while thousands of letters to the front were now returned to their senders marked 'Fallen'.

Berlin filled with wounded troops. Flannery noticed them 'in every block along the principle streets – young men with their arms in slings, with an arm gone, walking with crutches and canes, or without one of their legs. Previously, too, there had been few women in mourning, but I began to see them everywhere.'[149] The sight of these broken bodies and minds began to remind people of the worst scenes of 1918. The maze of tracks around the big stations were now filled with long trains covered in red crosses, and as the hospitals were filled hundreds of untrained women started working as nurses. The hospitalized soldiers brought bad news: some described what they had seen in the east and declared that they would rather die than go through another winter; others blurted out that the war could not be won.

Goebbels countered these rumours by demonstrating what would happen if the Germans fell into the clutches of the enemy. Newsreels released at the cinema each Saturday suddenly became remarkably brutal. The films were made by Goebbels's PK units, who went into the thick of the fighting and travelled with the troops in everything from bombers and tanks to submarines. Many of the reporters were killed, but their footage was remarkable.[150] The newsreels always opened with a German eagle clutching a swastika to the sound of rousing military music but now, rather than jovial scenes of soldiers marching through Paris, there were graphic pictures of enemy dead and wounded. Flannery remembered that 'some were so horrible that many German women, picturing their own men in the same scenes, could not look at them and stopped going to the theatres ... they were some of the most revolting pictures I had ever seen'.[151] Some pictured Russian soldiers being taken prisoner, others showed the 'conditions in Bolshevik villages', making much of their uncivilized lives; others showed towns being burned and piles of dead bodies waiting to be buried. In one early film the announcer yelled that this destruction had been 'the work of the Jews', after which the SS were shown beating Jews with the butts of rifles and with clubs as 'retribution'. Some died on screen. Goebbels did not seem to care that these pictures were deeply incriminating.

With the films came the admission that the Soviet troops were much tougher than the Germans had initially thought. The *Frankfurter Zeitung* admitted, 'The enemy has proved himself harder than the one we faced in the west. In contrast with our opponents on the other front, the Russians have for years equipped themselves for offensive battle. They show a fanatical hate.' The Soviet soldiers were consistently shown as hideous brutal 'Asiatics'. Goebbels was handed a great propaganda coup by Stalin when, in April 1943, the SS-Unterscharführer to the Central Office for Reich Security (RSHA) reported on a mass grave discovered near Katyn which proved to contain the bodies of thousands of Polish officers who had been murdered by the NKVD in

1939.[152] Goebbels screamed that the same fate would await Germans who fell into the hands of this 'pestilential world enemy'.

Goebbels's second strategy for controlling Berliners was to increase the terror in the city itself. As the war turned against them the top Nazis became ever more obsessed by the fear of 'another 1918', when the home front had 'stabbed the German army in the back'. On 8 November 1941, in a speech to old party comrades, Hitler had described how he would deal with any internal opposition: 'I will keep an eye on him for a certain period,' he said. 'You know my methods. That is always the period of probation. But then there comes the moment when I strike like lightning and eliminate that kind of thing.' The Nazi organization 'reaches into every house and zealously keeps watch that there shall never be another November 1918'. On 11 December he again spoke to the Reichstag: 'At a time when thousands of our best men, the fathers and sons of our people are falling, no individual at home who blas- phemes the sacrifice of the front, can reckon with remaining alive.'

To this end, Goebbels and Himmler increased the number of agents working in Berlin. Himmler came up with the idea of creating a 'Volksmeldedienst' (People's Reporting Service) to make every German spy on his neighbours; now every secretary, janitor, office worker and charwoman was to report on all unpatriotic utterances. In the wake of the first defeat outside Moscow the Berlin Gestapo was increased by 10,000 young agents fresh from their training camp in Bavaria; the numbers would continue to rise until the end of the war. After 19 March 1942 it was legally possible to punish anyone who challenged 'publicly known principles of the National Socialist leadership of the Volk', and Goebbels began an all-out attack on 'defeatists', including housewives grumbling about food prices or people in shelters mourning the 'meaningless' deaths of their sons. At best they were made to scrub floors in police stations, but 'serious' defeatists were beheaded.[153] Everyone was frightened of talking openly, even with families and old friends, for fear one might prove to be an informer, and they developed the Berliner Blick, the quick look over both shoulders to check for spies. In the first three months of 1943 the Berlin Gericht (court of justice) passed fifty-one death sentences against Feindhörer – people who had simply listened to an enemy radio broadcast – or those who had made a bitter comment about the conduct of the war. Denunciations became more common as the Germans faced defeat; hundreds were arrested by the Gestapo in the last years of the war for being a Volkssschädling (enemy of the people) and many were condemned to death by the People's Court. In 1944 at least 5,764 people were executed for 'grave' offences and resistance to the Nazis, while 5,684 people were executed in the first months of 1945. Some were killed immediately, including seventeen post office employees who, when found to have stolen chocolate and other items from Wehrmacht parcels, were marched to a square in Vienna and shot.[154] One drunken sailor was executed after blurting out: 'If things go wrong here, the bigwigs will surely have planes ready to fly them off to their villas in Switzerland; nothing will happen to them.'[155] Those who were found looting bomb sites were often killed. Men seen to be evading service were also denounced; Christine Weihs, whose husband had a serious kidney ailment and was declared unfit for service, was nevertheless ostracized by her Berlin neighbours, who called him a 'shirker'. When she was attacked by a neighbour she retorted: 'should he just allow himself to be shot out of hand?' Frau Weihs was quickly reported, hauled before a tribunal of twelve SA and SS men, and only released because a Gestapo man knew her family and said in her defence: 'She married young, she defended her husband. She really did not do anything bad.'[156] Soldiers also denounced one another: when Emmi Heinrich's husband was asked by a trusted group of friends what he thought of the war with Russia he replied that the Soviet system was not as bad as Nazi propaganda had made out and had some positive sides. A man in the group reported him that night. 'My husband was taken in a special boat to Germany and appeared before a military judge.' He was sentenced to three years in prison for the 'disruption of the state and the people'.[157] The SS and Gestapo terror created a climate in which it was virtually impossible to organize resistance.[158] In the space of a year Berlin had been transformed from the swaggering capital celebrating imminent victory over Russia to a dingy and nervous city.

Goebbels's ability to control Berlin was greatly helped by another aspect of the war – the bombing. The first Bomber Command raids of 1941 had been mild and short lived. Berliners were not prepared for what awaited them now.

The fresh wave of raids began under the new leader of British Bomber Command, Sir Arthur 'Bomber' Harris. After a lull of fourteen months he ordered a surprise attack on the night of 16 January 1943, with 190 Lancasters and eleven Halifaxes dropping 370 tons of bombs. It marked the beginning of one of the most controversial aspects of the British war – the terror bombing.[159]

The city was caught off guard by this first surprise raid. Sirens were sounded very late and people at the 'Mensch, Tiere, Sensation' circus at the Deutschlandhalle just managed to escape before the building received a direct hit, an escape which many saw as a miracle. The raids intensified. On 1 August, a week after the firestorm in Hamburg, the RAF dropped leaflets on Berlin calling on all women and children to leave the city, and a million people were evacuated. A few weeks later 'Bomber' Harris launched the Battle of Berlin.

Berlin was seen by all the Allies as the ultimate Nazi target: it was the ambition of many airmen to fly to the 'Big B' and to 'get the Hun in his evil capital'; one recalled: 'It was the target every aircrew member wanted to see in his log book for the prestige that name gave it, but it also caused the greatest surge of fear.' Shortly after Goebbels's 'total war' speech Harris told his men, 'Tonight you go to the Big City. You have an opportunity to light a fire in the belly of the enemy and burn his Black Heart out.' Other Germans were not sad to see privileged Berlin finally facing the bombs which had pounded them for months. Workers in the Ruhr chanted the song:

> Tommy, please don't drop that bomb;
> All we are is miners, Tom.
> Berlin's where you want to drop it.
> They said 'Yes' so let them cop it.[160]

The Allies believed that if they could take Berlin they would have defeated Hitler's Germany. The assumption was correct for a land-based attack; but it was not true of bombing.

Berlin seemed the ideal target for an air attack: it was Germany's single largest industrial city – a powerhouse containing dozens of gigantic armaments factories from AEG to Siemens, Heinkel, Argus, Focke-Wulf, Rheinmetall-Borsig and dozens of others, producing everything from planes and tanks to field artillery to small arms. It also housed the gigantic government machine which administered all aspects of the war effort and the mass murders, and was the focal point of domestic terror. Nevertheless by the time Harris's planes reached Berlin it had become apparent that carpet bombing would not achieve his military objectives; there was little evidence that the dropping of 42,000 tons of bombs and the loss of 718 aircraft had significantly reduced German industrial output by 1943.[161] Indeed, it was argued that inaccurate night-time drops were ineffectual and failed to crush morale. Harris ignored the evidence and in July 1943 the almost complete destruction of Hamburg led him to hope that bombing cities would work. By that summer he had become obsessed with the desire to destroy Berlin, the soft spot in the 'German armour'. He told Churchill, who had been very impressed by the Hamburg firestorm, that he expected to repeat that kind of terror in Berlin.

Fires in Berlin were common but they never reached the same scale as the inferno in Hamburg – largely because of the capital's wider streets, sturdy brick houses, and the precautions taken after the Hamburg disaster such as clearing out attics and removing coal from storage rooms. Production was not significantly reduced and, as Speer put it, 'It may well be that the estimated loss of 9 per cent of our production capacity was amply balanced out by increased effort.' Speer was also critical of the choice of targets, claiming that if Harris had concentrated on the ball-bearing industry the production of tanks, aircraft and motor transport would have been halted. Berlin's output remained steady until the final months of the war. On 28 November Goebbels could write that, however bad it looked, the British were 'greatly overestimating the damage done to Berlin'.

Harris was genuinely convinced that the bombing of Berlin would end the war: 'It is my firm belief,' he wrote to Portal on 12 August 1943, 'that we are on the verge of a final showdown in the bombing war, and that the next few months will be vital ... I am certain that given average weather and concentration on the main job, we can push Germany over by bombing this year.'[162] Then, on 3 November, he told Churchill, 'We can wreck Berlin from end to end if the US air force will come in on it. It will cost between 400–500 aircraft. It will cost Germany the war.'[163] The decision to go for Berlin over other targets, such as those which might have reduced German fighter strength, was a grave miscalculation.

On the night of 18 November 1943 the first planes of the Battle of Berlin droned through the night sky over the North Sea, finally turned at the German coast and headed south. Berlin was at the extreme range of the Allied aircraft but the 444 planes managed to drop their loads. Four days later, on 22 November, 764 aircraft bombed the city again, killing about 2,000 people and engulfing many buildings in flames. As the winter progressed the frequency and ferocity of the attacks increased, culminating in fresh raids on 27, 28 and 30 January, 15 February and 24 March 1944. It was now common for over 1,000 Lancasters, Halifaxes and Stirlings to home in on the city with over 2,000 tons of bombs, including the high explosive devices used to destroy streets and block the fire crews, the 4,000-pound 'blockbusters' which blasted off roofs and smashed windows, and the hundreds of 4-pound incendiaries which burned everything in their path. The city had become a place of terror.

The Battle of Berlin was the longest and most intensive single bombing campaign of the Second World War. More bombs would be dropped on Berlin than on England during the entire war – a total of 33,390 tons. Between July 1943 and October 1944 concern was such that 66 per cent of children were evacuated from the West End.[164] By March 1944 1.5 million people in Berlin had been made homeless; by the end 70 per cent of the city centre would be in ruins. Entire areas were flattened during single raids; 19 April saw the carpet bombing of the working-class districts of Wedding and Pankow; 26 February saw 2,796 tons of bombs plaster Alexanderplatz; on 19 March 3,276 tons of bombs decimated the West End. Bomber Command mounted 9,111 sorties against Berlin in sixteen major attacks between 18 November 1943 and March 1944, and Americans joined in daylight raids with B17s and B24s of the US Eighth Air Force in the spring of 1944. The final momentous American raid took place on Hitler's birthday, 20 April 1945. By the end of the war Harris had ordered an amazing 14,562 sorties over the city.[165]

The suffering of those trapped in the bombed city was acute, the destruction terrible. Night after night the air-raid sirens wailed, people rushed to their shelters and waited in the cold for the distant sound of the planes. Each shelter had its own character and 'obsessions'; in some the people were afraid of fire and kept extra pails of sand in the corners; in others they would light candles for fear of leaking gas. The waiting was interminable; people would endure sleepless hours as the bombs and flak pounded above them, listening to the explosions in the street as they moved closer for the dreaded direct hit. Then a bomb would crash through the structure, blasting everything in its path and spewing shards of deadly shrapnel in all directions. Direct hits often crushed an entire building, trapping people under piles of smoking debris. If they could not crawl through into the next shelter or be dug out in time they would die there, sometimes screaming or moaning for days afterwards. Some drowned when water boilers or pipes burst below the encasing rubble. Missie Vassiltchikov remembered watching a young girl aged about sixteen standing on a pile of rubble picking up bricks, dusting them off carefully and throwing them away; the entire family had been buried under the building and the girl had gone mad. After incendiary bombs fell rivers of phosphorus would run down the streets or drip from the shards of buildings, burning everything in their path and setting people on fire; civilians were often badly burned but there was little the overstretched hospitals could do. Even seriously wounded patients would be evacuated to the cellars, where the nurses sat with candles burning night after night. When the raid was finally over and the siren called the all-clear people would creep back out on to the street from the U-Bahn stations, shelters and cellars, and search amongst the smouldering buildings for survivors in the dense smoke. Leo Welt remembered that

> the air raids kept on getting worse. Sometimes the whole city was on fire. At times, you could not differentiate between night and day. When you went outside you had to have a wet cloth over your face, because there was so much dust and dirt in the air that it was impossible to breathe ... incendiary bombs fell by the thousands every day. Sometimes we could even stand in front of our house and see the sky just glistening in the distance with incendiary bombs.[166]

Shelters were stocked with equipment from rubber gloves and disinfectant to torches and bolt cutters for removing jewellery from the dead. Dismembered corpses were reassembled whenever possible to prevent double-counting of casualties and tags were attached to the pieces. Bodies were often horribly mutilated; some survivors found only the heads of relatives, others retrieved only limbs and were forced to identify the dead by a ring or a tattered shoe. Corpses were piled on the street corners ready for collection but by the end there was no energy for niceties; Russian prisoners were forced to dig graves and the dead were put into the ground with little ceremony and covered with quicklime. Notices appeared on buildings and lampposts listing those who had died; desperate messages sought news of relatives.

Well-connected party members did not suffer; many started spending more time on 'urgent business' in the safe hills of Bavaria, while those forced to remain in Berlin had access to the enormous and comfortable bunkers in the government quarter or to their own private shelters. Many of the elite government ministries had been evacuated by 1945, leaving lower-level functionaries in Berlin – of the 10 million Nazi Party members around 9.5 million would survive the war.[167]

Of those forced to remain in Berlin the people who suffered most were the vulnerable refugees or those who fell into the category of *fremdvölkische Arbeitskräfte* – the 'alien labourers', many of whom had little protection from the pounding bombs. By 1943 there were 800,000 foreign workers in the city, brought in to take the place of German factory workers now perishing at the front; one-third of all workers in the armaments industry were foreign.[168] The western European prisoners included French, Belgian and Dutch workers, who were given German ration levels and allowed to use air-raid shelters, but most of the Slavs were forced to endure the bombing raids without proper protection. Poles made up about 200,000 of the total and were forced to wear the yellow and violet letter 'P' on their uniforms, while Ukrainians had a blue and white '*Ost*'; both groups were marched to work under armed guard; their rations were meagre, their shelter inadequate and contact with Germans was forbidden – a Gestapo report of December 1941 recorded that four people in Berlin were arrested for 'prohibited contact with Poles or POWs', and 545 workers – both German and foreign – were arrested for 'refusal to work'.[169] The most malicious treatment was saved for the hundreds of thousands of Russian prisoners of war who were brought to Berlin to be worked to death. They had almost no protection from air-raids, were kept in concentration camp conditions, received low rations and were inevitably given the most difficult, filthy and dangerous jobs. Tens of thousands of these men and women died in the enemy capital; of the 720 people killed in a typical raid on 16 December 1943 249 were slave labourers and three were prisoners of war.[170] There was little ceremony for them; they were simply dumped into unmarked graves and forgotten.[171]

When the raids began in earnest Goebbels was terrified that Berliners might rise up in protest against the regime. He drew up hasty contingency plans to crush any revolts in the streets or a possible storming of the government quarter; he increased the size of the Gestapo in Berlin, and he even created secret SA units to crush unrest in factories. But he need not have

worried. Berliners did nothing. Both Goebbels and 'Bomber' Harris had miscal-
culated their will to act against the regime and, as Speer put it, '[The British]
were as mistaken about their forecasts on German morale as we were about
the effects of the rocket attacks on London.'[172] Thanks both to swift and severe
retaliation against any grumblers and 'defeatists' and to a widespread sense of
apathy Berliners failed to rise up even when the Nazi leaders were at their
most vulnerable. Despite the grim existence in the remains of the blackened
city the routine continued much as before. Red-eyed, pale, hungry people
trudged to work in filthy factories for twelve hours a day, struggled home for
their meagre rations and then moved to the cellar for a long night of bombing.
Berliners might have been worn out by the raids and many hated the war but
they worked on in a kind of daze. Thanks largely to Goebbels's propaganda
most saw the approaching Red Army, the 'Red Ghengis Khan', as a far worse
threat even than the bombing. Most still regarded Hitler as their only hope.
Frau Ursula Meyer-Semlies was typical: 'Goebbels did say we're sitting in a
moving train and no one can get out.' By 1945 Ursula no longer wanted
victory, 'just a settlement somehow'. Nevertheless, like many Germans, she
viewed unconditional surrender as unthinkable: 'Can one answer it in one's
conscience, for one's children, for the future, simply to "throw the rifle into
the cornfield"? No, we have to keep going until the end.' She spent the final
months of the war digging anti-tank ditches in preparation for the battle
against the Red Army.[173]

Top Nazis were astounded by Berliners' compliance. Albert Speer said
that 'the air raids had shown that life could continue on an orderly basis in
the severely affected cities'.[174] People continued to pay their taxes even after
bombs had destroyed their documents in the Treasury offices – the Nazis took
the money anyway. As the bombing raids became more frequent the will to
carry on intensified: 'In the burning and devastated cities we daily experienced
the direct impact of war,' Speer reported; 'neither the bombings nor the
hardships that resulted from them weakened the morale of the populace. On
the contrary, from my visits to armament plants and my contacts with the
man in the street, I carried away the impression of growing toughness.'[175]

After 'Big Week' in February 1944 Speer and Milch marvelled at the
manner in which the aircraft workers laboured on temporary open-air
assembly-lines in freezing winter weather. Workers everywhere 'went back to
their plants even after the firestorms. They repaired damage, restored production – even made their own shattered homes somehow habitable.' Goebbels
noted a marked stiffening of national morale, matched by an increasing hatred
of the enemy; the Allies were baffled by the German will to fight on even
when it was clear that they were going to lose the war.

Goebbels must take some credit for propping up morale in Berlin. Unlike many other top party people he stayed in the city and began to claw back some respect for himself by visiting bombed-out sites after the raids. He had been called 'Conquerer of Berlin', he said, and now he wanted the title 'Defender of Berlin'. He was indignant at the destruction of the city, commenting, 'It drives one mad to think that some Canadian boor, who probably can't even find Europe on the globe, flies here from a country glutted with natural resources which his people don't know how to exploit, to bombard a continent with a crowded population.'[176] He began to direct civilian operations and emergency services from the luxurious and well-stocked bunker of the Kaiserhof Hotel. At the sound of the all-clear he would hurry through the burning city, directing fire-fighting crews and offering encouragement to the people. As the chairman of the New Interministerial Committee for the Relief of Air Raid Damage he behaved much like the royal family in London, showing himself to be 'a Berliner' who was sharing the suffering of other Berliners. His tours through the ruins did wonders for his image: people clustered around him in droves, greeting him with smiling faces and shaking his hand. Even in 'Red' districts like Wedding, which would later claim to have resisted Nazism until the end, working-class people rushed from their homes to cheer him on. He went everywhere – to fire stations, to commemorative talks, to apartment block meetings and to the hasty funerals – offering the only words of comfort Berliners would get from the moribund regime. Helmuth-James von Moltke wrote: 'All the military officers are alike. They think of making their lives more comfortable and are indifferent to everything else. On the other hand Ribbentrop and Goebbels, for whom I have no love, concern themselves with everything: they visit their wounded and homeless, inspect the damaged sections of their offices, and see to it that their office functions again.'[177] In 1944 Hitler rewarded Goebbels for his diligence by making him the president of the City of Berlin, giving him 'absolute authority for leading and directing the capital of the Reich'.[178] He would use his power to full effect in the final weeks of the Third Reich.

Even when it seemed obvious that the bombing was not working Harris continued to pound the city. It was a policy of weakness directed by a man who desperately wanted to participate in crushing Hitler but had few other options. In pursuing his goal Harris squandered the lives not only of civilians, but of many of his own men. Berlin was the most heavily defended city in Europe. By early 1944 Harris was losing 6.1 per cent of all aircraft sent there; 1,047 planes were lost over Berlin and 2,690 bomber crew members died, many of whom are buried in the Commonwealth Cemetery in Grunewald. Berlin was a huge city covering 883 square miles, and Harris's assertion to Churchill that it could be utterly destroyed was ludicrous; many of the heavy industries were on the outskirts of the city and were notoriously difficult to pinpoint,

particularly at night. When the first attempts to smash Berlin proved futile
Harris merely demanded more time, saying on 29 December 1943: 'It is naturally impossible to state with arithmetical precision the acreage of German
built-up area which must be destroyed to produce capitulation.' Harris's fanaticism continued until the very end, and even after the war he continued to
disregard the evidence against his strategy, arguing that if he had been given
the resources he wanted the war could have been ended months sooner. The
arrogance of Bomber Command was astounding: on 5 November 1943 Air
Vice-Marshal F. F. Inglis, Assistant Chief of Air Staff (Intelligence), wrote,
'We are convinced that Bomber Command's attacks are doing more towards
shortening the war than any other offensive including the Russians'.[179]

Harris's policies had more far-reaching consequences. Not least they led
to a rift between the British and Americans, as the latter believed that the
prime purpose of the air force was to knock out the Luftwaffe. Through the
'Pointblank' directive of May 1943 they had tried to encourage Harris to go
for relevant targets, such as airfields and ball-bearing factories. Harris provoked
anger by making excuses for not bombing the Pointblank targets while still
sending his planes off every night to bomb cities. Harris's obduracy meant
that the greatest achievements of the Allied strategic air offensive were accomplished by the American Eighth Air Force, which arrived in England in 1943,
for it was they who defeated the Luftwaffe with their Mustangs, and it was
they who carried out the massive raids on the oil refineries which crippled
the German war machine in 1944–5.[180] Many others could see that Harris's
policy was not working: he had long been criticized by colleagues like Air
Commodore Bufton, and in January 1944 the Japanese embassy in Berlin
reported to Tokyo: 'Internal collapse will certainly not be brought about by
means of air raids . . . the fighting spirit of the people has been intensified to
the pitch of seeing no course but to fight to the finish.' Field Marshal Milch
confirmed this view after the war: 'The British inflicted grievous and bloody
injuries upon us, but the Americans stabbed us to the heart.'

Harris was only saved from the embarrassment of being proved wrong
by the Allied invasion of France. He was sceptical about the Normandy landings
and still maintained that Germany was 'about to surrender' under the pressure
of his raids. By 1944 the Americans were openly insulting his policies, stating
that British bombing had done little to 'fatally weaken' German resistance in
preparation for Operation Overlord. It was only after the establishment of the
Allied bridgehead in Normandy that the Americans began to participate in
the more accurate daylight bombing of cities. This last phase of the bombing
was marked by the devastating American raid on Berlin on 8 February 1945
by the Eighth Air Force, which killed about 22,000 people. Harris's contribution
to this unpleasant chapter is best remembered by some of the most contro-

versial raids. The most infamous was the bombing of Dresden, one of Europe's most beautiful – and strategically unimportant – cities. It saw the deaths of between 30,000 and 100,000 people, many of them refugees, and it was this which caused Churchill to write on 28 March 1945: 'The moment has come when the question of bombing German cities simply for the sake of increasing the terror, though under other pretexts, should be revised . . . The destruction of Dresden remains a serious query against the conduct of Allied bombing.'[181] Harris did not understand why anyone should object to the destruction of the city: 'In Bomber Command we have always worked on the assumption that bombing anything in Germany is better than bombing nothing.' Later he summed up his view, saying, 'I would not regard the whole of the remaining cities of Germany as worth the bones of one British grenadier.' Harris's obsession with hailing fire and brimstone down on the Germans blinded him to the moral ambiguity of his actions; As Liddell-Hart has pointed out, morale or terror bombing was incompatible with the Allied aim of forcing unconditional surrender. It merely convinced Germans that they had no option but to fight on, trapped as they were in a ghostly landscape of ruins and twisted metal.

The controversy surrounding Harris in the Anglo-Saxon world has more to do with his strategic errors and his failure to shorten the war than with his ultimate intentions. It is understood that the damage and loss of life caused by the bombing would have been justified if it had caused Germany to surrender, just as Hiroshima is seen as a military success precisely because it forced the Japanese capitulation and saved thousands of Allied lives. It is a strategic, not an emotional criticism. The argument about the bombing is seen differently in Berlin.

When I lived in East Germany I was regularly taken to bomb sites and lectured on the destruction caused by Allied raids. It was irrelevant that bombs had been dropped to hasten the end of the war; they represented a 'war crime' and would no doubt have been seen as such even if they had ended the war. In some ways this was not surprising as the bombing was the only first-hand experience many civilians had of the war. It was easier to avoid questions of guilt about the horrors of the camps or the front when one could point to one's own suffering in the bombing raids. Nevertheless my own questions about German attacks on Warsaw, Rotterdam, London or Malta were met with a stony silence, as were reminders of horrific incidents like the siege of Leningrad, in which the city was surrounded and starved for 880 days.[182] During the war many Germans knew – and approved of – attacks on other civilian populations. Albert Speer's secretary Annemarie Kempf remembered:

'When all these things ... were going on, we thought London was destroyed, with its government and virtually its entire population in flight from our rockets; that's what they told us, no doubt to emphasize ... how wonderful Berlin was by contrast, in ruins but still functioning.'[183] After the war many Berliners preferred to forget what Germans had done to others and to blame the western Allies for their suffering rather than ask the most perplexing question of all: why, when they were faced with increasing attacks from the air and when defeat became inevitable, did so many continue, actively or tacitly, to support the regime? Where was the resistance?

When reading contemporary histories of Berlin one might be forgiven for thinking that the war-torn city was teeming with anti-Nazi activists. Berlin is called the 'city of resistance'; lists of anti-Hitler jokes (which were popular throughout Germany) are held up as proof of widespread disenchantment with the Führer, and the important resistance circles are sometimes portrayed as popular movements. This view of Berlin is a post-war phenomenon created in both East and West Berlin during the Cold War. In reality, however, resistance in Berlin was conspicuous by its absence; those who actively fought the regime can be measured in their hundreds.

The lack of a resistance movement was due to many factors – ranging from SS and Gestapo terror to the fear of another defeat like that of 1918, from dread of the Russians to genuine loyalty to the Nazi regime. Hitler's broad appeal meant that even when the war began to turn sour many clung to the belief that he was their only hope and would somehow engineer a miraculous victory. This baffling loyalty was not limited to the general public; only a few of those in the officer corps broke their personal oath to Hitler even when they realized that he was leading the country to ruin.[184] In the end the city of Berlin did become the focal point of German resistance, but this had little to do with the behaviour of Berliners themselves. The city was chosen largely because it was the 'eye of the Nazi storm' and allowed plotters to hide behind official government posts and offices and to meet semi-legally under the noses of the Gestapo. Although the individual plotters risked their lives and demonstrated enormous courage in the face of terrible odds, most attempts ended in abject failure. Years of propaganda churned out by the East German regime could not conceal the fact that the Communists of 'Red Berlin' also failed.

Until the demise of the GDR East German museums and school history texts were filled with legends about the Communist resistance. Hundreds of men and women were said to have fought Nazism every step of the way, escaping from concentration camps and clearing the path for the Red Army. Images of Erich Honecker and Ernst Thälmann, Georgi Dimitroff and Werner Peuke were everywhere, shown in Gestapo prisons or in camps. In reality, the

Communist resistance was misguided and ineffectual, and by the time the KPD realized that Nazism was more than simply the 'death rattle' of capitalism it was too late for them to regroup. They were fatally weakened by the mass arrests of 1933–4. Those small organizations formed later were heavily infiltrated and hundreds of people were executed; they were not helped by Stalin's betrayal of large numbers of German Communists after the signing of the Molotov–Ribbentrop Pact. After the outbreak of war only a few groups managed to survive for more than a year and they accomplished very little. The groups included the Herbert Baum Group, which led the attack on the 'Soviet Paradise' exhibition on 17 May 1942 after which Baum committed suicide and hundreds of Berlin Jews were murdered; the groups around Robert Uhrig, who maintained contact with the workers' underground and produced illegal newsletters until the arrest of all members in 1942; and the 'Red Orchestra' under Arvid and Mildrid Harnack and Harro Schulze-Boysen, which fed information to the Russians via secret radio transmitters. They, too, were quickly infiltrated and fifty-five members were arrested in August 1942. As the East Germans desperately searched for evidence of resistance to fuel their propaganda machine some saw the failure more clearly: as the Communist Heinrich Galm put it after the war, 'the people who now say that they engaged in resistance against the Nazis – they mainly distributed leaflets.'

Like the Communists, many Social Democrats were imprisoned and killed by the Nazis after 1933 and most resistance cells were quickly infiltrated by the Gestapo. They refused to work with the KPD, who became ever more dependent on Moscow, and leaders like Julius Leber and Carlo Mierendorff saw that Hitler could only be overthrown with the co-operation of the Wehrmacht. As a result, a number of prominent members of the SPD became involved in broader resistance networks, including that of the July 1944 plotters. In the meantime they rejected terrorism and continued to compile the invaluable secret reports in the *White Book of German Opposition to the Hitler Dictatorship*, published by SOPADE – the exiled SPD – and they kept in touch with the illegal Berlin Regional Committee under Walter Löffler and Alfred Markowitz, which published *Neuen Vorwärts* and *Sozialistisch Aktion*. These activities were highly dangerous not least because many workers supported the Nazis, and elaborate codes and signals were used when moving around the working-class suburbs of Berlin. The fundamental problem with the working-class resistance was that although there was widespread grumbling against the Nazis most workers continued to function within the system until the final days of the war, and many proved loyal informants to the Gestapo. Only when the Red Army appeared at the gates of the city did anti-Nazi graffiti begin to appear on blackened brick walls in the working-class districts, but there had never been any danger of another revolution. Hitler's propaganda had done its work even here.

'First they came for the socialists,' said Pastor Niemöller in his famous post-war speech, 'and I did not speak out – because I was not a socialist. Then they came for the trade unionists, and I did not speak out – because I was not a trade unionist. Then they came for the Jews, and I did not speak out – because I was not a Jew. Then they came for me – then there was no one left to speak for me.' The text reveals Niemöller's deep regret that so few acted to help those around them even when they faced mortal danger in the streets of Berlin. His criticism was aimed largely at the Church.

The German Churches were constrained by their history. They were deeply conservative and most had supported Hitler's anti-Weimar appeals against godless 'Jewish Bolshevism', against the collapse of solid German values, and against everything from decadence to modern art and from materialism to the Treaty of Versailles. After coming to power the Nazis quickly created the 'German Christians', which mixed *völkisch* ideas with elements of the traditional Church, complete with racial clauses and 'Brown Synods'. Although Hitler ultimately intended to do away with Christianity he was careful to hide his intentions for fear of provoking popular resistance early on. Many Church officials were fooled by his pious facade, and thousands of Berliners flocked to the new Nazi faith.[185]

For anti-Nazi Catholics the Concordat with the Holy See in the spring of 1933 was a disaster. It was this agreement which resulted in the infamous pictures of German cardinals lining up in Berlin to give the Nazi salute, and it effectively stymied Catholic opposition. Hitler had no intention of keeping his side of the Concordat and quickly started closing down Catholic schools, newspapers and youth groups, but there was surprisingly little resistance. A few Berliners protested, including Erich Klausener, leader of Berlin's Catholic Action Movement, who held mass meetings of over 60,000 people and called for an end to anti-Catholic activities. Klausener was murdered by the Nazis in 1934. Some Berlin Catholics were later inspired by examples of resistance outside the city, including the most effective by Bishop Galen, who called attention to the grisly euthanasia programme and forced Hitler to halt it temporarily and thereafter to hide it more effectively. Another notable exception was Bernhard Lichtenberg, a lowly priest at St Hedwig's Cathedral in Berlin who worked tirelessly and with little support to help all victims of Nazism regardless of origin and ended every service after *Kristallnacht* with a prayer 'for the Jews and the poor prisoners in the concentration camps and my fellow priests there'. He prayed not only for baptized Jews but for all Jewish victims and was the only Berlin churchman to speak publicly against the Holocaust. When arrested on 23 October 1941 he proclaimed that he was an enemy of National Socialism and demanded to share the fate of the Jews in the east in order to give them comfort there. This extraordinary man died on his way to Dachau. Few had heeded his message.[186]

The Protestants also largely failed in their obligation to offer moral leadership in the Nazi period; they too were constrained by their history. Berlin Protestants had a long history of obedience to authority, of opposition to the Weimar Republic and of anti-Semitism. A great number welcomed Hitler's 'national revolution'; most supported the new regime, and many joined Hitler's 'German Christians'. The most important resistance to the popular Nazi Church was the creation of the Confessing Church and the Pastor's Emergency League, a protest against Nazi intervention in Church appointments which was started by the Berlin-Dahlem pastor Martin Niemöller. Hitler was furious and told Niemöller to restrict himself to Church business as *he* would take care of the German people. Niemöller replied: 'We too, as Christians and churchmen, have a responsibility to the German people which was entrusted by God. Neither you nor anyone else in the world has the power to take it from us.' As a result of this defiance Niemöller was arrested at his house in Dahlem on 1 July 1937 and eventually sent to Dachau as Hitler's 'personal prisoner'. Dozens of other members of the Confessing Church ended up in camps, where they were forced to wear the pink triangle for homosexuality. Another important member of the Confessing Church who was later involved in the military opposition to Hitler was Pastor Dietrich Bonhoeffer. He was arrested in April 1943 and murdered in Flossenbürg in April 1945. A few Churches actively stood up to the Nazis, but on the whole they exhibited a baffling degree of accommodation and compliance with the Nazi regime. The men who resisted often did so without the support of their peers, and as such were highly vulnerable to Nazi terror.

From the beginning Hitler had made it very clear that he intended to die in office. The power base in Nazi Germany meant that deposing Hitler would require the support of the army. He had never been popular amongst a group of conservative army officers and since the late 1930s some, including Generals Beck, Goerderler and Witzleben, had been planning to oust the 'Austrian corporal' from the Chancellery. Hitler's extraordinary successes had changed the minds of many and they vacillated, hedged their bets, and waited. Most dissenters began to regroup only after it had become clear to them that Germany was going to lose the war.[187] From about 1942 onwards Berlin became the centre of their activities.

One of the most important of these groups was formed by Helmuth-James von Moltke and later named the Kreisau Circle after his Silesian estate. Moltke was associated with the anti-Hitler activist Admiral Canaris, the head of the Abwehr or Military Intelligence, and was himself a lawyer in the International

Law sector, which gave him freedom to travel and meet potential allies. Moltke regularly met a group of landed aristocrats, members of the Foreign Office, the civil service, the SPD and the Church either in Kreisau or in his flat in Berlin to discuss topics ranging from the abuse of Russian prisoners of war to the crimes of the Einsatzgruppen. These decent men risked their lives by creating the detailed blueprint of a government which could take over in the event of Hitler's death, but many rejected the idea of assassination on moral grounds. Those in favour of killing Hitler joined with the plotters gathered around Count Schenk von Stauffenberg.

Many of those involved with Stauffenberg had long hated Hitler but they had been unable or unwilling to act. As the war dragged on and the German position became weaker it became a matter of urgency to try to kill the Führer while the country could still sue for peace. In 1943 the conspirators developed a plot code-named 'Valkyrie' – the name of an existing plan drawn up for the Reserve Army in Berlin. The conspirators intended to assassinate Hitler, give the Valkyrie order and seize the city. The top Nazis and SS were to be rounded up and arrested by a number of officers, including Generals Fromm and Beck, while the centre of Berlin was to be surrounded by the Reserve Army. The same procedure was to be followed in other cities, including Paris. For months secret meetings and conferences were held in Berlin, and upon receiving news of the sudden military crises on both fronts in June 1944 the conspirators decided to act.[188]

The man who volunteered to kill Hitler was Colonel Claus Count Schenk von Stauffenberg who, because of serious injuries to his hands and eye, had decided to use a bomb as the murder weapon. Having made two previous unsuccessful attempts, he was given a final chance in July, when he was invited to Hitler's Wolfsschanze to put forward designs for a new set of uniforms for the Reserve Army. He set out from Berlin on 20 July.

The plan began to go badly wrong from the beginning. There was no car to take Stauffenberg to the compound and he was late arriving for the confer-ence. He had to set the fuses in a hurry and was interrupted in the lavatory, managing to activate only one of them before going to the meeting. The conference was held in a wooden hut and not in Hitler's bunker, which might have deflected a bomb blast inwards. The plot was set to fail.

At the start of the meeting Stauffenberg placed the suitcase under the table near Hitler. After listening to the Führer for a short time he made an excuse to leave the room to take a prearranged telephone call. From a short distance away he heard the explosion, saw bodies and debris thrown from the hut, and assumed that Hitler had been killed. He was wrong. The force of the bomb had knocked Hitler backwards and had ripped his trousers to shreds, but the Führer was not seriously hurt. Acting on the assumption that he was dead Stauffenberg phoned Berlin, told the headquarters the news, and ordered Operation Valkyrie to proceed immediately. When he arrived in Berlin some hours later he found nothing but chaos and confusion in the Bendlerstrasse headquarters. General von Hase had failed to take control of the city as planned; the Guard Battalion under the junior officer Major Ernst Remer had started to cordon off the government quarter but he had been taken to see Goebbels instead. From the Chancellery Remer learned that Hitler was alive and he actually chatted with the Führer on the telephone. The news quickly spread that Hitler was unhurt. General Fromm, who was to have led the Reserve Army, tried to save himself by turning against the plotters. He allowed General Beck to commit suicide, but shot a number of others in the light of car headlamps in the courtyard at the Bendlerstrasse. Stauffenberg cried, 'Long live Germany!' as he fell to the ground.[189]

Hitler was in a state of shock, but he was alive. At 6.30 p.m. the Deutsch-landsender (German radio) announced that there had been an attempt on Hitler's life but that it had failed. When Mussolini arrived at the Wolfsschanze that evening he sat through an extraordinary tea party during which the ashen-faced Hitler alternated between sitting in stony silence and emitting blood-curdling screams at the band of 'criminally stupid' men who had tried to kill him. They were to be 'strung up like slaughtered meat'. The next day he made a radio broadcast announcing that a conspiracy had been hatched by 'a tiny clique of ambitious, irresponsible and at the same time stupid and criminal officers ... I was spared a fate which holds no terror for me, but would have had terrible consequences for the German people. I regard this as a sign that I should continue the task imposed upon me by Providence.' Hitler genuinely believed that he had been saved from death by some 'higher purpose' and he turned on the plotters with a vengeance. The round-up of suspects and their families began immediately.

Himmler put 400 special Gestapo officers on the case. Fifty-six men were arrested within the first four days and hundreds of people were eventually rounded up on suspicion of involvement. The most prominent conspirators were forced to endure long imprisonment, hunger and medieval torture in the basements of the Prinz-Albrecht-Strasse before being hauled before Roland Freisler's People's Court for a series of nauseating show trials. The accused were brought in starved, unshaven, with no belts on their oversized trousers, and were made to stand while Freisler screamed at them at the top of his voice. After hours of this mindless ranting the men were invariably sentenced to death and executed.

The small white execution chamber at the Plötzensee prison is a chilling reminder of the heavy price paid by these brave men. The first to be killed included von Trott zu Solz, von der Schulenburg and von Moltke, who were slowly strangled by a thin cord as they hung from meathooks attached to a long iron girder. The executions were filmed, although Albert Speer doubts whether Hitler watched them as he preferred to distance himself from graphic depictions of violence (Speer claimed that this was one of the factors which prevented him from visiting bomb sites in Berlin and elsewhere).[190] The other plotters were held in Flossenburg concentration camp and were killed during the last months of the war. Canaris, Oster, Karl Sack and Bonhoeffer were amongst those murdered on 9 April 1945. Just before he died Canaris tapped a message to Hans Lunding of Danish intelligence, who was trapped in the next cell: 'I die for my country and with a clear conscience,' he said. 'I was only doing my duty to my country when I endeavoured to oppose Hitler and to hinder the senseless crimes by which he has dragged Germany down to ruin.' It is estimated that over 200 people were directly implicated in the plot and murdered between July 1944 and May 1945; they included twenty-one generals, thirty-three colonels and lieutenant-colonels, two ambassadors, seven senior diplomats and the head of the criminal police.[191]

For all their bravery and for all attempts to turn them into German national heroes after the war, the plotters remain ambiguous figures. Their plans to create a post-war Germany had become utterly unrealistic by 1944 and reflected the longing to re-create a nation that had died in 1914; indeed the men seemed unaware of their nation's true situation at the time. Many of the plotters had been hostile to the Weimar Republic and its egalitarian and democratic tendencies, which they thought 'unsuitable' for Germans, and by 1944 most wished to see the creation of a new united Germany which would not only retain the 1933 borders but would regain those of 1914, including the Polish Corridor and the German-speaking territories of the old Habsburg empire. Their social and constitutional plans were hopelessly out of date and many of their ideas were unpleasant: Schulenburg and the rest of the 'eastern school' had fully supported the destruction of Poland, and the rabidly anti-Semitic von Helldorf had helped Goebbels to 'cleanse' Berlin of the city's Jews. The plotters were angry that Churchill had ignored their peace initiative, even though by 1944 they were in no position to sue for peace; the brutality of the Nazi occupations, the cruel murder of millions of people and the appalling losses inflicted during the war would have prevented any such agreement. They failed to understand that the Allies sought an 'unconditional surrender' for fear the Russians might be tempted to make a separate peace. The plot failed because it did not have the support of important members within the government: neither Goebbels nor Göring, Ribbentrop nor even the vacillating Himmler yet had the will to act against the Führer. But most important of all, the plotters never would have had the support of the people. Even in 1944 a murdered Führer would have become a martyr.

The July 1944 plotters were indeed saviours of German honour and should be remembered with the respect and sympathy they earned with their lives. As an admittedly distant relation of Helmuth-James von Moltke I was brought up in Canada and in England to respect the Kreisau Circle and those 'good Germans' who had given so much of themselves; I naturally assumed that most Germans shared this view. It was something of a shock to visit Germany in the early 1980s and to meet those who still referred to the July 1944 plotters as 'traitors'.[192]

When the news of the assassination attempt reached Berlin in 1944, many people were not relieved, but disgusted. Secret service reports from the city reveal an overwhelming sense of relief at Hitler's escape and there was widespread outrage that the 'arrogant officer clique' had tried to kill the Führer. Some women were reported to have burst into tears of joy on the streets, saying, 'Thank God the Führer is alive.'[193] Even workers in the north of the city were reported to have been 'horrified' at the plot. Some might have been too frightened to admit their true feelings; one young soldier heard of Hitler's 'death' while waiting to be sent to the eastern front and remembered that the entire troop transport erupted in cheers of joy. The young men were quickly silenced by the arrival of a group of SS men, who threatened to shoot anyone who uttered another word. For the majority of civilians, however, Hitler remained a figure of hope and the plotters were detested. This attitude was reflected even after the war: in a poll taken in the summer of 1952 a quarter of the West German population claimed they still had a 'good opinion' of Hitler and 10 per cent believed he was the greatest statesman of the century after Bismarck. Even then one-third of West Germans still claimed they opposed the 20 July 1944 attack on Hitler's life. The 1944 plotters have become heroes of the new Germany, but their status is a post-war creation. The 'resistance' has itself become another of the myths of the history of Berlin.

The plot had failed, and Berliners were now faced with a gruesome fight to the death. The Allied armies were beginning to mass around Germany and were slowly moving in for the kill. On 6 July 1944, just two weeks before Stauffenberg's bomb, the Allies launched Operation Overlord and opened up the western front on the beaches of Normandy. On 22 June the Russians started a fresh offensive on the upper Dnieper, recapturing Minsk on 3 July and parading 350,000 humiliated German prisoners in Red Square. Berlin was about to be squeezed by armies advancing from the south, east and west and by fierce bombing pounding down from the skies. Hitler would soon move back to the bunker at the Chancellery and turn the city into a gigantic armed fortress. The Führer had chosen Berlin, his Germania, to be the focal point of the terrible *Götterdammerung* of the Third Reich. He summed up the importance of the city as a symbol in July 1942. In a discussion about how the conquered peoples of the east should be educated he concluded that 'Instruction in geography can be restricted to a single sentence: "The Capital of the Reich is Berlin." '[194]

XIII

The Fall of Berlin

*The entrance they are free
to choose, but not the exit.*

(Faust, Part I)

THE SECOND WORLD WAR IN EUROPE reached its nadir in the terrible Battle of Berlin. It was fought in the spring of 1945, but the crucial decisions which helped to determine its final form were taken much earlier in Washington, London and Moscow and at the Allied conferences at Tehran and Yalta. Allied armies had started to squeeze Europe by early 1944, with the vast Red Army moving towards Berlin from the east, and the Anglo-American forces closing in from the west. The race to defeat Germany had begun.

The western offensive began with the Normandy landings in the summer of 1944. General Eisenhower had moved to England on 16 January to take up the post of Supreme Commander of the Allied Expeditionary Force for Operation Overlord, and on 6 June 9,500 aircraft and 600 warships crossed the Channel on their way to France in the greatest amphibious operation in military history.[1] Within twenty-four hours 176,000 troops were ashore and advancing into German-held territory but Hitler refused to heed the danger. When Avranches fell to the US Eighth Army Corps on 31 July General von Kluge told him it was 'questionable if the enemy can still be stopped'; he was stripped of his rank and forced to commit suicide. On 25 August, amidst great celebration, General Jacques Leclerc led the French Second Armoured Division into Paris along with the US Fourth Armoured Division. The Canadian First and British Second Armies under Montgomery advanced into Belgium and liberated Brussels on 3 September. In the south the US First Army under General Courtney H. Hodges went into Liège; Patton's Third Army went east to the river Mosel to meet with General Patch's French-American Seventh Army, which had fought north from the Riviera. By September the western Allies were only 400 miles from Berlin. But behind the spectacular military success there was a growing rift between the two western powers. The controversy raged over the ultimate question: who should take Berlin.

Churchill saw the city as the ultimate Allied target – to be reached as quickly as possible.[2] By 1944, however, Roosevelt and Eisenhower disagreed over this issue. The situation was made more complex by changes in the chain of command. General Montgomery, 'Monty', had been forced to relinquish overall command to Eisenhower on 1 September during the Normandy campaign because the Americans were now contributing the bulk of the forces and they did not want an Englishman commanding their troops. Monty deeply resented this and treated Eisenhower with barely concealed disdain. The rift was not caused by a mere clash of personalities; it mirrored the profound shift which had taken place in world power since the American entry into the war. Britain was already being eclipsed by the young and vital great power, which in 1945 would become the first superpower, but the feud between Montgomery and Eisenhower soon began to affect the conduct of the war.[3]

Montgomery shared Churchill's view that if Berlin could be taken quickly the 'knock-out blow' would win the war. Germany would be defeated, and Stalin would be sent a clear message that he could not have central Europe. On 4 September Montgomery wrote to Eisenhower: 'I consider we have now reached a stage where one really powerful and full-blooded thrust towards Berlin is likely to get there and thus end the German war.' He wanted all available resources dedicated to the advance, and intended to leave Bradley's forces to 'do the best it can with what is left over'. A division of the forces would be fatal: 'If we attempt a compromise solution and split our maintenance resources so that neither thrust is full-blooded we will prolong the war.' His plan was to put all resources into a single-pronged drive by the Twenty-first Army Group and the US Twelfth Army Group across Holland and through northern Germany to Berlin.

Eisenhower did not appreciate interference from the British field marshal and on 5 September, influenced by General Patton's strategy of 'bulling ahead on all fronts', replied: 'While agreeing with your conception of a powerful and full-blooded thrust to Berlin I do not agree that it should be initiated at this moment to the exclusion of all other manoeuvers.' Instead, Eisenhower split the available resources between Montgomery's and Bradley's armies. Montgomery was furious, firing back on 9 September that if they had the ports of Dieppe, Boulogne, Dunkirk and Calais, and 'with 3,000 tons a day through Le Havre WE CAN HAVE BERLIN'. He persuaded Eisenhower to meet him in Brussels on 10 September to discuss his plans. Both men prepared for a showdown.

This fateful meeting revealed the depths to which the Anglo-American relationship had sunk by 1944. Montgomery pushed his way into the cramped cabin of the American aeroplane and began to lecture the Supreme Commander as if he was an 'errant staff college pupil'. Eisenhower listened for a

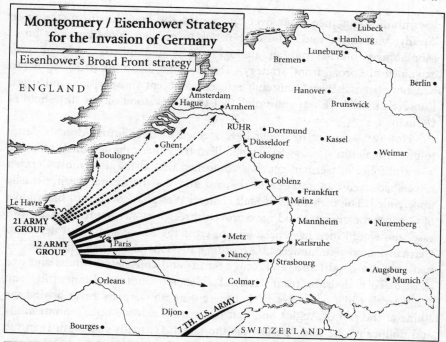

Montgomery / Eisenhower Strategy
for the Invasion of Germany

Eisenhower's Broad Front strategy

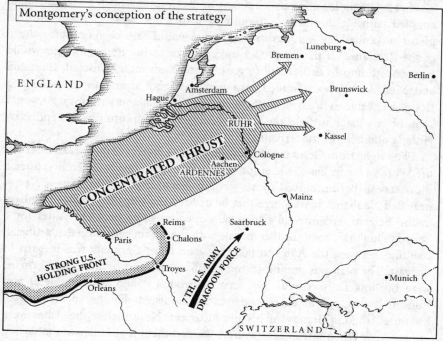

Montgomery's conception of the strategy

few minutes and then leant over and patted the Englishman on the knee: 'Steady, Monty,' he said. 'You cannot talk to me like this. I am your boss.' Montgomery blurted out an apology and waited quietly as Eisenhower explained his 'broad front' strategy.[4] The idea of a 'lightning strike' on Berlin had now been shelved. Churchill refused to accept the decision and urged Roosevelt that 'there was still time'; that the Allies stood on the 'threshold of Germany'.

However arrogant he might have seemed to Eisenhower Monty's desire to push for Berlin was less far-fetched than the Americans assumed. After the war a number of German generals confirmed that at the time most German forces had been concentrated in the east and that Berlin had been virtually undefended. The then Chief of Staff General Westphal said, 'Until the middle of October the enemy could have broken through at any point he liked, with ease, and would then have been able to cross the Rhine and thrust deep into Germany almost unhindered.' According to General Student the Germans had only 100 good tanks, and 'only recruits and convalescent units and one coast-defence division from Holland'. General Günther Blumentritt, von Rundstedt's Chief of Staff, said that there were no German forces behind the Rhine at the end of August and that the front was 'wide open'. 'Strategically and politically,' he said, 'Berlin was the target. Germany's strength is in the north. He who holds northern Germany holds Germany. Such a breakthrough, coupled with air domination, would have torn the weak German front to pieces and ended the war. Berlin and Prague would have been occupied ahead of the Russians.'[5] If the Allies had succeeded in taking Berlin the war would have ended months earlier and to great western advantage. Instead, Churchill and Montgomery were vetoed. Antwerp was ignored and 100,000 German troops were able to flee over the Schelde and into Holland – troops who would soon be sent back to fight the western Allies. The opportunity was ended by Hitler's offensive in the Ardennes.[6]

The signs from Germany were ominous. On 20 November 1944 Hitler left the Wolf's Lair in East Prussia for the last time and on 16 December, after a short stay in Berlin, moved to his western headquarters – the Eagle's Nest – near Bad Nauhaim. It was there that he devised the surprise counter-offensive in the Belgian Ardennes in which he hoped to drive back the Allies for a 'second Dunkirk', break British morale with the V2 rocket, cause the 'artificial' coalition between the Allies to fall apart and leave Germany free to turn to the east. The plan was grandiose and absurd – not least because the Germans were by now far too weak to carry it through – and when General von Rundstedt was put in charge he was so disgusted that he spent most of his time drinking brandy in his headquarters. Nevertheless the Allies were unprepared. When intelligence sources warned them that Hitler was amassing troops in the west Eisenhower's Chief of Staff Bedell-Smith said that such an attack was impossible: 'No goddamned fool would do it.'[7] But it was precisely this irrational element which gave Hitler an advantage, and the Germans advanced rapidly in what would later be called the 'Battle of the Bulge'.[8] Eisenhower became convinced that the Germans intended to assassinate him and hid in his headquarters. Monty was given overall command on 19 December and fought back, and on Christmas Day 1944 the Germans were forced to concede defeat, having lost 120,000 men. The Americans also suffered heavy losses – 80,000 were killed, wounded or taken prisoner. Worse still, the victory did little to smooth the relationship between the British and the Americans. Montgomery held an ill-judged press conference in which he took credit for the victory, which had been won primarily by American soldiers, insisting that if his original strategy had been followed in September the battle would not have happened at all. The Americans were furious, and Churchill was forced to stand in the House of Commons and make a conciliatory speech. It failed to heal the rift. After the Battle of the Bulge the Americans and British fought two virtually separate wars, and Montgomery's subsequent pleas to be allowed to advance on Berlin continued to be ignored. By the beginning of 1945 the western Alliance was in tatters and the Americans had now become convinced that Hitler's forces were much stronger than they actually were. The Battle of the Bulge proved to be the final German offensive of any consequence in the west. However, when the western Allies got a second chance to take Berlin they were over-cautious, and the opportunity was missed once again.

The new chance came as a surprise to the western forces. It was not the result of any military strategy, but of a new outlook amongst many Germans in the west. The Battle of the Bulge had been their last major attempt to push the Anglo-American forces out of Europe; when it failed many realized that the war was lost. Resistance suddenly lessened, and by the time the Allies crossed the Rhine even high-ranking German officers spoke openly of defeat; one SS colonel remarked in Hitler's presence that he would have to move to Berlin because the troops would soon be able to take a streetcar from the eastern to the western front – fortunately for him Hitler thought it a preposterous joke and merely laughed. Most civilians now reasoned that it was far better to be taken prisoner in the west than die fighting or be taken prisoner by the Red Army in the east. Furthermore, if Germany was to fall, let it fall to the western Allies and not to the barbarous Russians; some even believed that the west would soon join them in a war against the Soviet Union. Many German soldiers in the west began to surrender, throwing down their weapons, waving white flags and travelling to prisoner-of-war camps with a look of relief on their faces. Goebbels was appalled by this and complained in his diary on 27 March 1945:

General Patton is letting it be known that practically nowhere is he meeting any firm resistance and consequently can drive around in our country unimpeded. This is in fact the case ... With our anti-bolshevik atrocity campaign we succeeded in reconsolidating our front in the East and making the civil population completely ready to defend themselves. That this has not happened in the west is primarily due to the fact that large sections of the German people and also of our troops think that the Anglo-Americans will treat them more leniently. As far as day-to-day procedures are concerned this may be true.[9]

On 31 March he wrote again: 'In contrast to the Soviets the Anglo-Americans are not feared by the people – as we have long known; on the contrary large sections of the people are glad to see them come so that they may be protected from the Soviets ... they are now throwing themselves into the arms of the Anglo-Americans.' He was particularly upset when his home town of Rheydt hung a sea of white flags from all the buildings to welcome the American troops on 5 March: 'I can hardly believe it, especially not the fact that one of these white flags flew from the house where I was born ... It makes a first-class sensation for the Americans of course just as it is harmful and humiliating to me. If we ever return to Rheydt, however, I shall try to clear the matter up.'[10] In his 31 March BBC broadcast Wynford Vaughan-Thomas expressed astonishment that the Germans were allowing the Allied armies to pass without resistance: 'it's the strangest possible sensation to be driving almost at will, utterly unmolested, through the heart of your enemy's country. It just doesn't seem possible.' Richard Dimbleby saw the German civilians as 'neutrals in their own country' who did not really see the western armies as invaders. The photographer Robert Capa wrote in *Slightly Out of Focus* that 'GIs fought their way ahead, meeting less and less resistance and finding more and more cameras, Lüger pistols and fräuleins.'[11] Despite sporadic fighting the western Allies were able to move quickly through Germany; by April they encountered a surrender rate of 30,000 men per day, whereas on the eastern front the Red Army was meeting fierce resistance at every turn.[12] Once again, Churchill saw the prospect of an early conquest of Berlin, and urged his men on to the heart of the enemy capital.

Churchill had many reasons for wanting Berlin. Not only did he see it as the key to victory over Hitler; he also knew it would send an important signal to Stalin. Churchill had become increasingly concerned about the Soviet dictator's behaviour and his voracious appetite for territory. Furthermore, he was alarmed by the treatment of civilians in Russian-occupied areas, where tens of thousands of anti-Communists and others were being rounded up and were disappearing deep into the Soviet Gulag.[13] Churchill tried to persuade

Roosevelt that if Stalin was capable of backing out over agreements related to places like Poland he could do the same in Germany and in Berlin. The only solution was to get to the capital first: 'I say quite frankly that Berlin remains of high strategic importance,' he repeated. The Americans, determined not to cause a rift with Stalin, decided instead to meet the Red Army further south. They were also convinced that the Germans were creating a stronghold, the 'national redoubt', in Bavaria. Eisenhower seems to have sincerely believed in this notion. After the war a supporter of the plan, General Omar Bradley, would write sheepishly: 'The National Redoubt existed largely in the imaginations of a few fanatical Nazis. It grew into so exaggerated a scheme that I am astonished we could have believed it as innocently as we did. But while it persisted this legend ... shaped our tactical thinking.'[14] Instead of making for Berlin, Eisenhower directed his troops to the south. On 28 March 1945 he sent the now infamous cable to Stalin in which he proposed that the Americans and Soviets link up not in the capital city, but in the area around Leipzig and Dresden.

It is almost certain that had they pushed forward the Anglo-American troops would have reached Berlin before the Soviets. The Ninth Army under the command of Lieutenant General William Simpson, part of Montgomery's army group, reached the river Elbe on 11 April. The spearhead was at Zerbst – only forty-eight miles from Berlin – while patrols were reaching as far as Potsdam. Soldiers were chafing at the bit, eager to go along the 'path of glory' and enter Hitler's capital. Suddenly, they were told to stop. Simpson received a call from General Bradley just as he was about to move ahead telling him that he had been ordered to halt. Simpson could not believe this and demanded to know 'where in the hell' the order had come from, only to be told that the order had come 'from Ike', as advised by General Marshall. It had been sanctioned by Roosevelt.[15]

Churchill was beside himself and tried desperately to get Eisenhower to change his mind. Having fought doggedly since 1939, surely the British would not be forced to stop just short of Berlin. He sent a cable asking,

> why should we not cross the Elbe and advance as far eastward as possible? This has an important political bearing as the Russian armies of the South seem certain to enter Vienna and overrun Austria. If we deliberately leave Berlin to them, even if it should be in our grasp, the double event may strengthen their conviction already apparent, that they have done everything ... I do not consider myself that Berlin has yet lost its military and certainly not its political significance. The fall of Berlin would have a powerful psychological effect on German resistance in every part of the Reich ... The idea that the

capture of Dresden and junction with the Russians there would be a
superior gain does not commend itself to me . . . While Berlin remains
under the German flag, it cannot, in my opinion, fail to be the most
decisive point in Germany.

For Churchill, the fall of Berlin would be 'the supreme signal of defeat for
the German people'.[16] After haranguing Eisenhower he told Roosevelt that 'we
should march as far east into Germany as possible and that should Berlin be
within our grasp we should certainly take it'.[17] But Roosevelt was unmoved
by arguments about the effect this would have on the post-war settlement of
Europe. General Bradley would later say that, as soldiers, 'we looked naively
on this British inclination to complicate the war with political foresight and
nonmilitary objectives'. But it was Bradley who had come up with the absurdly
high estimate that taking Berlin would cost the Americans 100,000 men: 'It
would be a pretty stiff price to pay for a prestige objective.' In the coming
years Berlin would prove to be much more than that.[18]

Churchill was not the only one to be appalled by the halting of the Allied
army; many Americans, including General Simpson, were furious. In a 1972
interview he said, 'I had six or seven divisions on the Elbe . . . I had two army
corps there and was in very good shape to have gone on and made the advance
. . . we could have gone right on to Berlin and put up a darned good show.'
In his view the Germans would simply have surrendered. 'I have a feeling that
maybe the Germans might have welcomed us . . . They were in terrible shape,
you know.'[19] According to his own calculations, if he had been given the
chance, Simpson's Ninth Army would have entered Berlin two weeks before
the Soviets.

Roosevelt had given away the chance to conquer Berlin. Not only did he
not understand the strategic importance of the city with respect to post-war
settlements with the Soviets; worse still, he had actually 'given' the city to
Stalin at the Yalta Conference. Between 4 and 11 February 1945, just after the
Battle of the Bulge, the 'Big Three' had met as Stalin's guests in the great
white-granite Summer Palace built by Tsar Nicholas II in the Crimea. By now
it was clear that the Germans would be defeated but it was Stalin who was
most skilful at manipulating the post-war settlement to his own advantage.
He was keen to control as much of Europe as possible, and although his main
territorial demands had already been granted at Tehran Roosevelt gave the
final seal of approval to the plan at Yalta. This now included handing over a
large chunk of eastern Germany. Unbeknownst to Churchill it was here that
Roosevelt had promised Stalin a most tantalizing gift – the conquest of the
city itself.

This crucial offer took place at a secret meeting between Stalin and

Roosevelt, one of the many from which Churchill was now regularly excluded. Roosevelt told Stalin that 'bets had been made' aboard the American cruiser which had brought them to Yalta 'as to whether the Russians would get to Berlin before the Americans got to Manila'. The notes of the meeting recorded that 'Marshal Stalin remarked that he was certain that the Americans would get to Manila before the Russians got to Berlin since there was at present very hard fighting going on at the Oder line'. The exchange was crucial. Stalin understood that Roosevelt had, in effect, excluded Berlin from the American sphere of influence. Churchill, still unaware of this hidden agenda, continued to encourage Montgomery to reach Berlin as quickly as possible.[20] The secret understanding between Roosevelt and Stalin was only revealed when the Americans rejected the second opportunity to take the city.

The reasons for Roosevelt's extraordinary – not to say criminally stupid – behaviour are still unclear. Why would a commander-in-chief deliberately restrict the advance of his own army in such circumstances? Perhaps he believed that this important gift would convince Stalin of his good intentions, or maybe that it would make the Soviets more co-operative in the post-war world. Wolfgang Stresemann, Chancellor Gustav Stresemann's son, claimed that 'Roosevelt had little idea himself of what the programme was really about. He had not the slightest notion of foreign policy, and little knowledge of history. He concerned himself only superficially with things of this nature.'[21] We do know that Roosevelt had a bizarre relationship with Stalin and was determined to see 'friendship' where there was no such thing. But why was he so taken with the Soviet dictator? After all, he knew that Stalin had attained power through murder and deceit, had joined with Hitler in the dismemberment of Poland and the Baltic States, had already sanctioned the murder of countless millions of people through the Gulag and in the engineered famine in Ukraine. Many tried to warn the President: war-time correspondence between Churchill and Roosevelt, and the papers of ambassadors such as William Bullitt, Admiral Standley and Averell Harriman and of Russian experts from George Kennan to Charles Bohlen, were filled with information about Stalin's pursuit of expansionist aims which they realized would ultimately threaten American interests. But Roosevelt thought of himself as Stalin's 'friend' – he was the only man in the west in whom the Soviet leader would confide; in short he believed he had a special relationship with him. On 18 March 1942 Roosevelt wrote to Churchill: 'I know you will not mind my being brutally frank when I tell you that I think I can personally handle Stalin better than either your Foreign Office or my State Department. Stalin hates the guts of all your top people. He thinks he likes me better, and I hope he will continue to.'[22] By 1943 Roosevelt considered Russia to be America's most important partner; it was now referred to as 'America's natural ally' and much closer to a 'true democracy' than the 'imperialist' states of Britain or France. As for eastern Europeans, they 'belonged' in the Russian sphere of influence; as Roosevelt put it repeatedly in 1943, 'I really think those 1941 frontiers [those devised between Hitler and Stalin] are as good as any . . . and all those Baltic republics are as good as Russian.' To Churchill's horror Roosevelt began to send Stalin warm offers of friendship, weapons, money, supplies and promises of ever more territory. When, at the fateful Tehran meeting on 29 November 1943, Stalin was granted huge chunks of Polish and German territory Churchill tried to warn Roosevelt about Russia's long-term ambitions in Europe, even requesting that the western Allies pursue a Mediterranean strategy to cut them off in central Europe. His suggestions were ignored. Roosevelt seems to have decided by Yalta that the war would soon be won and that Americans would go home in two years and leave the messy business of running eastern Europe to his new ally. As a result, Roosevelt stopped his own American army from taking Berlin, leaving the prize to Stalin. The Red Army now moved in for the kill.

While the west dithered and prepared for a fight in far-off Bavaria Stalin had not wavered from his course. He did not really believe that Roosevelt could be so stupid as to let him have the city so easily and so, for him, it remained a great race – one which he was determined to win. After the spectacular victories at Stalingrad and at Kursk Stalin knew he had a chance. From then on no effort would be too great, no division too valuable, no resources too precious to be spared in the drive for victory. Stalin sent his best generals to compete for the prize, the three most important being General Zhukov, General Rokossovsky and General Koniev. Under them the Battle of Berlin would be fought not as a war of liberation, but as a ruthless war of territorial conquest.[23]

Georgi Konstantinovich Zhukov was the most important of Soviet generals. It was he who had bolstered Stalin's morale during the disastrous first months after Hitler's invasion, becoming invaluable for his tactical genius, for his ability to harness new technology and for his ferocity. Zhukov was a tyrannical commander. Like Stalin and Hitler and Napoleon – who had referred to his dead men lying at Eylau as 'small change' – Zhukov valued a soldier's life at almost nothing. He thought little of sacrificing thousands of troops in a single battle. His men feared him more than the enemy itself; all those – from soldiers to senior officers – who did not show total obedience were simply shot. During the sweep through Poland in 1944 a general of the Forty-fourth Division hesitated slightly after being given an order. He was sent to the penal battalion and made to lead one of many terrible suicide attacks on German lines. He was killed almost instantly. Zhukov had an exceptional relationship with Stalin and had led the dictator through the early years of the war. General Belov had the impression in early 1942 that it was Zhukov who was giving orders to the dictator; in his 1966 memoir *The Soldier's Debt* Rokossovsky recalled how Zhukov told the omnipotent Stalin to his face that one of his orders was impractical. When he commented on this Zhukov answered, 'That's nothing. You should see us on other occasions.' In August 1942 he was made Deputy Supreme Commander of the Red Army and his name is attached to some of the greatest Soviet victories of the war: the defence of Leningrad and Moscow, Stalingrad, Kursk and, finally, Berlin. Although Stalin became increasingly afraid of his popularity Zhukov managed to stay in favour until 1946, when he was exiled to the provinces.[24]

The second of Stalin's extraordinary leaders was Marshal Konstantin Rokossovsky, the half-Polish soldier who after the revolution had joined the Red Guard and then the Red Army. He had risen quickly through the ranks, but like so many other promising military men had been arrested in the purge of 1937 and condemned to death. He was released in 1940 but his death sentence was not commuted until much later; Stalin would helpfully remind him that if he did not perform well he would be killed. After proving himself on the central front, notably at Kursk, he was made a marshal in July 1944 and given command of the First Byelorussian Army. Stalin never forgot that he had been an 'enemy of the people' and in 1944 appointed the top agent Nikolai Bulganin to follow him around and report back on any signs of disloyalty. Despite such controls Rokossovsky became the second most successful Soviet field commander of the war and was invaluable in the long struggle for Berlin.

Marshal Koniev was the third of Stalin's generals who conquered Berlin; his career had been markedly different from those of the other two. Whereas Zhukov and Rokossovsky had risen through the army he had been made a Communist Party political commissar in 1926 and was a feared agent of the NKVD. Koniev had been deeply involved in the intelligence required for Stalin's purges, which included preparing cases against 'enemies of the people' and extracting 'confessions'. It was only in February 1939 that he moved into the army, being promoted to the post of commander in the far east. Koniev was one of the most tyrannical men in the Red Army; it was he, for example, who on 16 February 1944 won the battle at Korsun in Ukraine at which 55,000 Germans were killed.[25] Twenty thousand of these men had been trapped in a valley near the city, and Koniev watched with delight as the tanks rolled backwards and forwards grinding bodies into a bloody pulp. This massacre so impressed Stalin that he promoted Koniev to the rank of marshal. Koniev's sense of loyalty was as underdeveloped as Stalin's; it was he who helped to engineer the show trial and death of his old NKVD colleague Lavrenty Beria in 1953.

Much has been said about Stalin's exploitation of the rivalry between his generals on the road to Berlin, but although he played them off against one another there was none of the destructive dissension that lay between Montgomery and Eisenhower. Furthermore, as Speer pointed out, Stalin gave his commanders an independence in military matters unheard of in the Wehrmacht:

> Hitler and Stalin were very alike in some dreadful respects ... but there is one fundamental point on which they differed absolutely. Stalin had faith in his generals and, although meticulously informed of all major plans and moves, left them comparative freedom. Our generals, on the contrary, were robbed of all independence, all elasticity of action, even before Stalingrad. All decisions were taken by Hitler and once made were as if poured in cement, whatever changing circumstances demanded. This, more than anything else, lost Germany the war.[26]

This did not mean that Stalin was an easy task master. The dictator had become increasingly paranoid about the military, and all generals were spied on by party members appointed to his military council; at Stalingrad, for example, Yeremenko was 'chaperoned' by none other than Nikita Khrushchev. Stalin was vicious with his officers. When Churchill's military assistant General Ismay visited Moscow in October 1944 he noted that when Stalin entered the room 'every Russian froze into silence and the hunted look in the eyes of the generals showed all too plainly the constant fear in which they lived. It was nauseating to see brave men reduced to such servility.'[27] Progress was slowed by the General Staff in Moscow, who tried to fight the war along Marxist-Leninist principles; when Rokossovsky told Stalin that a single frontal attack against Germany would be highly risky the party protested that a divided front contradicted Lenin's pronouncements on war. Fortunately for the Soviets Stalin listened to the advice given by Zhukov, Rokossovsky and others. Their influence would become clear in the race through central Europe to Germany and its capital.

It was an epic race. It took the Red Army two and a half years to get from Stalingrad to Berlin, and despite Stalin's criminal disregard for his own men individual Russian soldiers fought with a tenacity and bravery rarely seen in history. Largely as a result of their superhuman efforts Stalin was set to launch the offensive against the German defences in the summer of 1944. The plan was laden with symbolism. The attack itself was code-named Bagration after the commander who had fought in the 1812 war against Napoleon; he, like Stalin, had been a Georgian. The date chosen was 22 June, the anniversary of Hitler's invasion of the Soviet Union three years earlier.

On that day heavy infantry divisions began to move across a front which stretched an amazing 800 miles. The Soviets vastly outnumbered the German forces, and on the central front alone they killed or captured 1.5 million Germans, 31,000 artillery and mortar pieces, 5,000 tanks and over 6,000 planes in a matter of days. By July the Red Army troops had driven the Germans out of Soviet territory and were moving through Poland and Romania; in July 60,000 humiliated German prisoners of war were paraded through Moscow on their way to the Gulag.

Hitler had dismissed all reports of Russian forces amassing at the Polish border, joking that Stalin must be using fifteen-year-old boys to fill a few divisions. The Russians overran Poland with a staggering 163 divisions – over 2 million tough, battle-hardened men. By the end of July they were heading towards Warsaw.

Stalin's indifference to human life had become obvious as the Red Army began to 'liberate' territory in eastern Europe. As the army moved forward the NKVD moved with them, dealing out its own brand of retribution not only against anyone suspected of sympathizing with Germans, but with large groups Stalin had designated as untrustworthy. Entire national groups – from the Crimean Tartars to villagers in the northern Caucasus – were rounded up and forcefully moved from places where their ancestors had lived for centuries. Four million Ukrainians were transported east, as were the Volga Germans, whose descendants now live in Kazakhstan. The same fate awaited many of those unfortunate enough to come under Soviet control in central Europe. The treatment of the Poles, who unlike most Europeans had fiercely resisted the Nazis from 1939 onwards, was particularly cruel. Stalin detested the Polish government in exile, the 'London Poles', who had the support of the majority of the Polish population and who were fighting for the creation of a democratic, independent state free from both Soviet and German domination. Stalin wanted to win the war against the Germans, but he also wanted to create a docile Polish 'buffer' state run by a Communist puppet government. The nationalist Poles were therefore also treated as 'the enemy'.

Throughout July 1944 Soviet radio had called on the Polish Home Army to fight for Warsaw and for months they had prepared to do so despite Stalin's taunts that they were standing with their weapons 'at ease'. The Poles in Warsaw were anxious to participate in the liberation of their own city, but they waited until the Red Army was approaching the far bank of the Vistula before ordering a general uprising, assuming that the Russians would quickly move across the river and help to free the city from German control. But when the fighting started the Russians did nothing. Stalin now declared that he had no intention of helping 'the criminals who have unleashed the Warsaw adventure' and watched with satisfaction as the Germans did his killing for him. Rokossovsky's First Byelorussian Army refused to offer any help, even denying British and American planes the right to refuel after dropping supplies. Despite the terrible conditions the citizens of Warsaw held off the Germans for sixty-three days, crawling through the sewers of the city and battling from street to street. But the fight was hopeless, and the Germans were victorious. The city was cleared, and detachments were sent in to blow up Warsaw block by block, building by building. In the end the city was utterly destroyed. Only then did Stalin proceed through Poland, imprisoning those members of the Home Army who had escaped from the Germans. Stalin's refusal to help the embattled Poles for his own political reasons should have sent a clear signal to the western Allies as to his post-war intentions for that country, but most refused to listen.

The Soviet military successes in Poland led to jubilation in Moscow. By New Year's Day 1945 the people were convinced that victory was imminent; Alexander Werth reported for the BBC that the big hotels had stayed open through the night and the 500 guests at the Hotel Metropol predicted that the war would end within the year. On the streets of Moscow the usual greeting was replaced by 'How far to Berlin?' All waited eagerly for Stalin to turn on Germany itself. The attack began in January 1945.

The incredible offensive pounded its way through the German lines by sheer brute strength. Stalin ordered Zhukov to take Warsaw and move down the Warsaw–Berlin axis towards the city while Koniev was to advance towards Breslau and Silesia. Over a million tons of supplies were brought up to Zhukov's lines alone. On 12 January, amidst bitter wind and driving snow, Koniev's offensive opened with a massive artillery barrage which shattered the Fourth Panzer Army and decimated the German lines. Zhukov's offensive began two days later. The Red Army had a five-to-one advantage over the Germans in manpower and armour, a seventeen-to-one advantage in aircraft, and there were sixty-four Russian guns and twelve tanks per kilometre along the front. Warsaw fell on 17 January, Łódz and Cracow fell on the 19th, and a day later Zhukov's advanced columns were pressing on across the Silesian border. On 31 January they reached the Oder. Only a last-ditch counter-attack by General Wenck encouraged Zhukov to clear the east bank of the Oder before attempting to cross.

The name 'Berlin' was specifically mentioned for the first time in orders issued on 27 January by Marshal Zhukov in relation to the imminent attack at the Oder. He told his commanders to establish bridgeheads on the western bank of the river before the Germans could regroup. 'If we succeed in capturing the west bank of the Oder the operation to take Berlin will be fully granted.' The effect on the generals was momentous: 'The word "Berlin" on that memorable order sounded like our next mission. One can well imagine how excited

we were when we read it . . . We were now approaching the ultimate target.'
Ilya Ehrenburg, now acting as an official Soviet spokesman, wrote proudly
that 'the Red Army is heading for Berlin' and *Pravda* reported,

> if we are determined to be in Berlin, it is because we owe our children
> a real peace and not an *ersatz* peace, which the Germans would like
> to palm off onto us. That will never happen. Our people cannot be
> expected to build new towns and new houses if they know people in
> Germany are already quietly manufacturing new weapons of war, new
> V2's or 3's or 20's, and that the executioners of Maidanek are designing
> even bigger and better concentration camps.[28]

It was then that Stalin received Eisenhower's telegram asking him to meet
the western Allies in the Dresden–Leipzig area instead of in Berlin. He was
immediately suspicious of American motives.

Stalin could not believe Eisenhower's message; as Henry Kissinger has
pointed out, he was not in the habit of receiving telegrams from mere generals.
But he pretended to play along and expressed the desire to meet up with the
Americans in the south; he even sent Eisenhower a note on 1 April which said
that 'Berlin has lost its former strategic importance'. Secretly, however, he
believed that the western Allies were trying to divert him from Berlin in order
to take the city themselves; surely they would not be naive enough to give it
up when it lay within their grasp. Stalin's suspicions were further aroused
when his spies procured a copy of Montgomery's (long-abandoned) plan to
drive for the capital. In a fit of panic he called Zhukov and Koniev to the
Kremlin on 1 April for a conference, during which he waved Eisenhower's
telegram at them and told them that the Allies were secretly planning to beat
them to the prize. They must go directly to Berlin without delay and beat the
western Allies to it. Standing in front of his generals he demanded '*Tak kto
zhe budet brat Berlin, my ili soyuzniki?*' ('Well, who is going to take Berlin,
will we, or the Allies?') Zhukov told Stalin that his First Byelorussian Army
was ready to move. Not wanting to be outdone Koniev interrupted, claiming
that he too was ready. In the end Stalin unleashed them both, calling on
General Rokossovsky to join them some days later. General Antonov of the
General Staff asked how Zhukov and Koniev's armies should be disposed and
who should have the honour of taking the city. Stalin drew a line on the map
forty miles from the city boundary and said grandly: 'Whoever breaks in first,
let him take Berlin.'

The battle which was to decide the fate of Berlin for decades to come
started on 16 April on the Oder–Neisse rivers. Both Zhukov and Koniev
ordered their armies to cross the Oder and dive into the 1 million badly
equipped and disorganized Germans. Two and a half million Red Army soldiers

fought towards the highway from Küstrin to Berlin, with the Wriezen–Berlin
road and the Frankfurt–Berlin Autobahn as secondary objectives. For the first
time in the war the Russians reintroduced the 1917 practice of carrying banners
and colours into battle to boost morale – flags which the soldiers were told
to picture fluttering over the Reichstag. Koniev raced forward in the south,
crushing German defences as he went. Zhukov faced a more difficult problem
at the Seelow Heights – a long expanse of marsh on the approach to Berlin
which ended in a long escarpment. The Germans had deliberately flooded the
Oderbrück valley bottom, turning it into a soggy swamp over which it was
virtually impossible to move tanks and troops. Zhukov spent two days pum-
melling the German lines with the greatest massing of artillery yet in history
– over 40,000 guns firing 1,200,000 shells at the enemy lines – but despite the
fact that the Soviets outnumbered the Germans ten to one Seelow itself changed
hands a number of times and the Russians lost 30,000 men. The road from
Seelow to Berlin is dotted with Red Army and Wehrmacht cemeteries; many
of the latter are filled with the remains of boys of sixteen or seventeen years
old, a testament in itself to the state of the German forces by 1945. Zhukov
finally managed to break through the tough defences and on 19 April
announced that he was closing in on Berlin. The next day he reported in from
the Hangelsberg Forest only eight miles from the city. In the meantime Marshal
Koniev sped through Cottbus on the Spree towards Zossen, which led in to
the Anhalter Bahnhof and to the heart of the city, while Rokossovsky's Second
White Russian Army moved in from the north. Marshal Zhukov issued a
proclamation to his troops:

> Comrades! The decisive hour of battle has come. In front of you lies
> Berlin, the capital of the Nazi state, and beyond Berlin, the meeting
> with the troops of our Allies and complete victory over the enemy
> ... You are faced by Berlin, Soviet warriors. You must take Berlin,
> and take it as swiftly as possible so the enemy has no time to come
> to his senses ... Forward to the assault on Berlin!

The Battle for Berlin was to be the final act in the Great Patriotic War and
the subjugation of the German capital the ultimate act of revenge against the
nation which had caused the Soviet people such suffering.

As Berliners heard of the advance they became increasingly terrified. Hitler
had sworn that the Red Army could not reach Germany – now it was moving
towards the Berlin suburbs. The panic was increased by the endless lines of
refugees trudging through the city, recounting stories of the Soviet occupation
of eastern Germany. The advance of the Red Army was one of the most

destructive in history, eclipsed only by the German invasion of Russia four years before. It has remained something of a taboo subject both in Germany and elsewhere, not least because after the war the Russians and their Communist puppet governments attempted to portray themselves as 'liberators' rather than barbaric oppressors, rewriting history to legitimate what was, in a sense, a form of 'ethnic cleansing' against Germans and others in the region.[29]

It must be remembered that none of the crimes committed against the Germans after 1944 matched the level of barbarism to which the Germans themselves had sunk in the east between 1939 and 1945. The Red Army would never have been in the western regions had the Germans themselves not swept through Soviet territory and created such a wasteland out of the region between the Bug and Moscow. By the time the Red Army had reached the outskirts of Germany they had seen the results of the German occupation: the unspeakable cruelty, the waste, the scorched earth, and the murder. Many had themselves been victims of German barbarity either on the front of in prisoner-of-war camps. For many of these men human life had become virtually meaningless and they had pity for no one. They would treat German civilians accordingly.

The Red Army was, broadly speaking, divided into two main groups. The front line of modern elite guards divisions with their tanks and artillery were well disciplined and professional, but they made up only a tiny minority of the Soviet force. The second line was made up of thousands of men – the vast majority simple peasants – who had endured years of the most extreme battle conditions without leave, had rarely been paid and had lived under the threat not only of the enemy, but also of the hated NKVD. Red Army troops were often treated as expendable and unknown numbers died as a result of stupid or irresponsible orders by their commanding officers. If they were not party members their families were rarely informed of their deaths. Neither Stalin nor his generals cared how many died in battle and sometimes the lives of thousands of men were sacrificed for no real gain. The generals thought nothing of losing a third of a battalion in a single confrontation, of sending groups of men into the open to draw the line of fire, of dropping them from low-flying planes without parachutes when silk ran out on the assumption that enough would survive to fight on, or of sending men through mine fields in order to clear a path for the troops. One Soviet veteran of the Battle of Kursk remembered being forced to carry out the often deadly task of digging up German mines, which were more reliable than their own and were sometimes re-used eight or ten times.

It was this vast second tier of troops which baffled the Germans – they did not seem to fight by the same rules as ordinary armies: they were harder and braver. General von Manteuffel was amazed by the tough, almost primitive character of the men: 'Behind the tank spearheads rolls on a vast horde, largely mounted on horses. The soldier carries a sack on his back with dry crusts of bread and raw vegetables collected on the march from the fields and villages. The horses eat the straw from the roofs – they get very little else.'[30] As the Red Army advanced its ranks were swollen by thousands of prisoners of war released from German camps. Those fit enough to march were kitted out and sent on as second-line troops. By the time these men reached the German border they longed for some release from the pressures of life on the front. They thirsted for revenge.

When the Red Army finally crossed into German lands they were told to exact a price for the years of suffering. Signs were posted at the German border reading YOU ARE NOW ENTERING BLOODY GERMANY or YOU ARE APPROACHING THE LAIR OF THE FASCIST BEAST. There were to be no rules of conduct, no restraint; instead, the men were told that Russia would never be safe until 'every German' was punished. Ilya Ehrenburg told the men to 'exact two eyes for an eye' and 'a pool of blood for every drop of blood' as there is 'nothing funnier for us than a pile of German corpses'. He encouraged Russians to rape with impunity: 'Soldiers of the Red Army, the German women are yours!' This was taken as official doctrine. The thirst for revenge finally erupted into an orgy of violence, and as the Red Army crossed through Silesia, Pomerania and East Prussia they behaved with a ferocity not usually associated with a 'liberating' force. The first Germans they encountered were inhabitants of backward rural farming communities which, until then, had been largely untouched by the war. The troops were infuriated by the tidy villages and well-maintained houses before them; Dmitri Shchegolev wrote of the farmers' kitchens, 'I'd just love to smash my fist into all those neat rows of tins and bottles.'[31] The civilians – mostly women, children and old men – were unprepared for what awaited them. Many had wanted to escape but had been forced to remain in their towns and villages by the SS, determined that the Germans should fight to the end or die. As a result they became the first to pay the price for the crimes committed in Germany's name. There was widespread looting, pillaging, raping and murder underpinned by a grotesque element of sadism. Women were systematically gang raped, tortured and muti-lated, their tendons cut so that they could not run away, their bruised and battered corpses left in the road or rammed on to fenceposts. John Erickson, no critic of the Red Army, described the 'speed, frenzy and savagery' which characterized the Soviet advance.

> Villages and small towns burned, while Soviet soldiers raped at will and wreaked an atavistic vengeance in those houses and homes decked out with any of the insignia or symbols of Nazism ... Columns of refugees, combined with groups of Allied prisoners uprooted from

their camps, and slave labor no longer enslaved in farm or factory, trudged on foot or rode in farm carts, some to be charged down or crushed in a bloody smear of humans and horses by the juggernaut Soviet tank columns racing ahead with assault infantry astride the T-34s. Raped women were nailed by their hands to the farmcarts carrying their families . . . families huddled in ditches or by the road-side, whimpering for what seemed the wrath of God to pass.[32]

In *Prussian Nights* Solzhenitsyn recalled the bloodthirsty sweep of the 'asiatic hordes' under Ghengis Khan:

> The mother's wounded, still alive.
> The little daughter's on the mattress, Dead.
> How many have been on it,
> A platoon, a company perhaps?[33]

The behaviour of his men did not concern Stalin as long as their pillaging and raping did not impede the rush to Berlin. Vengeance became the byword of the Red Army, now officially the 'Soviet' army, during those terrible winter days. Millions of Germans fled in panic, joining the long rows of refugees already snaking westward towards the safety of the American lines. They did not know it yet but their homes, some of which had been settled by Germans for centuries, had already been given to Poland and the Soviet Union. They were leaving for the last time, victims of a war which had been started and fought in their name. Even western leaders like Montgomery were appalled: 'From their behaviour it soon became clear that the Russians, though a fine fighting race, were in fact barbarous Asiatics who had never enjoyed a civiliz-ation comparable to that of the rest of Europe. Their approach to every problem was utterly different from ours and their behaviour, especially in their treatment of women, was abhorrent to us.'[34]

The influx of refugees had a profound effect on Berlin, for at last there was incontrovertible proof that the Red Army was closing in and would treat them in the manner long predicted by Goebbels. A Soviet airman flew over Berlin in early 1945 and was amazed at the sight: there was 'an uncanny stillness in the east of the city with trams standing motionless on the tracks, their roofs covered in thick white snow while none of the factory chimneys were smoking. Only in the west of the city was there the constant stream of cars, carts and pedestrians moving out as civilians, women and children poured through Berlin from east to west.' A Swedish reporter said that the newcomers were wide-eyed and 'looked out from under their caps at the ruined streets of Berlin, which they were obviously seeing for the first time'. Some tried to find refuge there but the majority continued to trudge west, desperate not to fall victim to the Russians a second time.

On 7 March 1945 Goebbels drove through the 'heap of ruins into which the Reich capital has been transformed' and met 'one refugee convoy after another, mostly Black Sea Germans. The type of people entering the Reich calling themselves German is not exactly exhilarating,' he sneered. 'I think there are more Germanic types entering the Reich from the west by force of arms than there are Germanic types coming in peacefully from the east.' Despite his bitter comments he quickly realized that the refugees brought with them a great propaganda opportunity which could be used to stiffen German resolve to fight against the Russians. Radio reports talked of forty-mile-long columns of refugees being shot at by Soviet tanks or being strafed from the air. Berlin newspapers recounted atrocities in great detail: the *Völkischer Beobachter* published a daily list of rapes under lurid headlines like SEVENTY YEAR OLD WOMAN RAVISHED or NUN VIOLATED FOUR TIMES. Stories spread quickly: all men were being rounded up and sent to Siberia, children were being forced to clear mines, and wives and mothers were being raped to death in front of their families. No story was too grim for Goebbels's *Gruelpropaganda*, which called for Germans to 'throw themselves into the last defence with the conviction of what will happen to wife, child, and family members if they fall into the hands of the Bolsheviks'.[35]

But Goebbels had another pressing reason to call for the defence of the capital: on 16 January 1945, after the failure in the Ardennes, Hitler had moved back to Berlin. He had already started to set the stage for a terrible last battle in which the city would either emerge victorious, or perish. If the 'people failed him' Berlin was to become a gigantic funeral pyre fit for the death of a 'great man'. If he succeeded, the city would be rebuilt as Germania and would rule over Europe with an iron fist. There was to be no compromise, no middle ground. Berlin was to conquer or die. It had long become clear to those in his inner circle that Hitler was suffering a serious physical and mental decline. Now, back in the city, he became quite deranged.[36]

Hitler's descent into madness was one of the most eerie aspects of the end of the Third Reich. If he had 'embodied the nation' of the 1930s, with its weapons and parades and its overweening pride, he now reflected the decrepit, crumbling nation of 1945. Like Germany itself he had shown a steady deterioration after Stalingrad and Kursk, becoming increasingly unstable. He had been deeply shaken by the July 1944 bomb, which not only caused some damage to his balance and hearing but also made him suspicious and reclusive. He retreated into a kind of self-imposed exile, shielding himself from all but his closest associates and firmly shutting out knowledge of the real world. He had chosen to direct the war not from the military headquarters at Zossen or in Bavaria, but from a deep bunker in the very heart of his Germania.

The oppressive concrete chambers in the midst of bomb craters and flaming buildings became the setting for extraordinary scenes of absurd melodrama and madness. The bunker itself was part of a vast secret underground complex which snaked its way under the old government quarter of Berlin. It was connected to the enormous shelters at the Foreign Office and the Propaganda Ministry, and contained everything from a field hospital to multi-car garages and numerous secret entrances, some of which still lead up to the pavements of busy streets. Although the first bunker was started in 1936 Hitler ordered the New Chancellery bunker to be rebuilt at the end of 1944 by the firm Hochtief, which had carried out the original work. His quarters, which lay three floors – over ten metres – below the ground, were encased in three metres of concrete, which were in turn covered by thick layers of steel mesh and enormous granite slabs. The structure was designed to deflect even the most powerful explosion. It was the single most heavily fortified place in the Reich.

The journey – and it was a journey – to reach Hitler in his headquarters required a perilous climb down a long iron spiral staircase blocked at the bottom by large gas- and waterproof steel doors. The bunker was guarded by dozens of members of the Waffen-SS Leibstandarte 'Adolf Hitler' Regiment, who meticulously searched all visitors as they entered each section of the gloomy complex. One passed first through the Vorbunker of around twenty rooms, which housed offices, a dining room, kitchen, the Reich security service and rooms for Hitler's bodyguards. Magda Goebbels would later poison her children in one of its rooms. From there one passed down another long corridor and more steps into the Führerbunker itself, which covered an area of 548 square metres. This section had its own electricity supplied by noisy diesel generators, a pump room which procured fresh water from an artesian well, a telephone switchboard, storage areas and a whining air-conditioning system which Hitler occasionally turned off during meetings, causing terrible stuffiness. The complex was divided into eighteen cramped and unpleasant rooms, including reception rooms, offices, Goebbels's bedroom, a room for Hitler's Alsatian, Blondi, and his own suite. The latter contained his carpeted study, complete with atlas and portrait of Frederick the Great, a conference room, and bedrooms for himself and Eva Braun.[37] All those who saw the bunker found it a dismal, even terrifying place. The grey walls were rough and unpainted; in some areas the concrete was not yet dry. The rooms were tiny and pools of water stood in the stairwells. There was no natural light, no

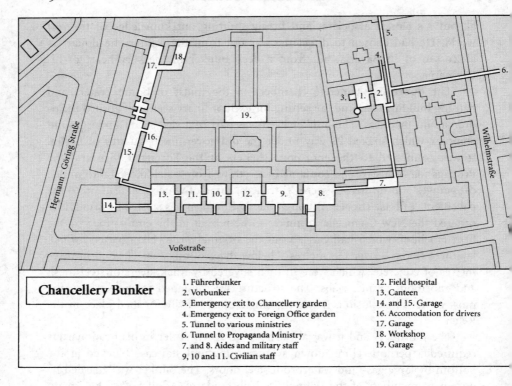

Chancellery Bunker

1. Führerbunker
2. Vorbunker
3. Emergency exit to Chancellery garden
4. Emergency exit to Foreign Office garden
5. Tunnel to various ministries
6. Tunnel to Propaganda Ministry
7. and 8. Aides and military staff
9, 10 and 11. Civilian staff

12. Field hospital
13. Canteen
14. and 15. Garage
16. Accomodation for drivers
17. Garage
18. Workshop
19. Garage

fresh air, and no sense of time – Hitler would regularly end his daily meetings at six in the morning and resume late the next afternoon. Albert Speer noted that 'This withdrawal into his future tomb had, for me, a symbolic significance as well. The isolation of this bunker world, encased on all sides by concrete and earth, put the final seal on Hitler's separation from the tragedy which was going on outside under the open sky. He no longer had any relationship to it.'[38]

The life in the bunker reveals the depths to which the Nazi leadership had fallen by 1945. Hitler had long stopped talking to the German people and no longer cared what happened to them. He ventured out of Berlin only twice after January 1945 – once to attend a secret meeting of Gauleiters on the outskirts of Berlin on 25 February, and once to visit General Busse of the Ninth Army on 3 March to discuss the by now hopeless 'defence' of the Oder. On both occasions he pulled down the blinds in his car to block out the view of the ruined capital and prevent any glimpse of its filthy, toilworn citizens. He never once visited a bomb site, preferring to remember the capital as it had been in the 1930s; perhaps this was why he could chat happily with Speer about the future of glorious Germania or reassure Goebbels almost until the end that Berlin would be rebuilt by the end of the decade. On 17 March he crawled up to the bombed-out Chancellery gardens, making his last appearance before the cameras to decorate some members of the Hitler Youth for bravery, even stopping to tweak one boy's sunken cheeks. He held a similar ceremony on his birthday on 20 April, although contrary to popular belief this was not filmed. He never went into the fresh air again, retreating into the recesses of the cement labyrinth until his death.

His reclusive behaviour resulted in much speculation both in Germany and abroad about the state of his health. The *Washington Post* guessed that Hitler might be 'seriously ill'; the *Daily Express* believed that he had been injured in the July 1944 bombing, and the *Daily Mail* quoted the psychologist William Brown as saying that 'the Führer may now be approaching the final phase of his mental sickness'. They were closer to the truth than they knew.

Goebbels worked hard to contradict damaging foreign press reports, urging Hitler to speak in public and, when he refused, speaking for him, but it did little good. The Führer was heading towards collapse. Hitler made a rare speech on New Year's Day 1945, ranting that the war would end by 1946 – not by German capitulation, which would 'never come', but by 'German victory'. His voice cracked and wheezed and his speech rambled. People who saw him in the last months of his life were astounded by the changes in his features. According to Speer, who went to see him in April 1945, he was

> shrivelling up like an old man. His limbs trembled; he walked stooped, with dragging footsteps. Even his voice became quavering and lost its old masterfulness. Its force had given way to a faltering, toneless manner of speaking. When he became excited, as he frequently did, his voice would start breaking. He still had his fits of obstinacy, but they no longer reminded one of a child's temper tantrums, but of an old man's. His complexion was sallow, his face swollen; his uniform, which in the past he had kept scrupulously neat, was often neglected in this last period of life and stained by the food he had eaten with a shaking hand.[39]

The young officer Siegfried Knappe saw him a few days before his death: 'I was shocked by his appearance. He was stooped, and his left arm was bent and shaking. Half of his face drooped, as if he'd had a stroke, and his facial muscles on that side no longer worked. Both of his hands shook, and one eye was swollen. He looked like a very old man, at least twenty years older than his fifty-six years.'[40]

One of the reasons for Hitler's extraordinary physical collapse had been the diet of drugs administered by his 'trusted personal physician', Dr Theo

Morell. Hitler received frequent injections of amphetamines, belladonna and strychnine, took large quantities of glucose and vitamins, and used eye drops made of cocaine. According to the Chief of the General Staff, Hitler 'no longer recognized limits' and had slid into a fantasy world populated by ghost armies and phantom warriors. 'Anyone who speaks to me of peace without victory will lose his head,' he ranted. And yet, even in this state, he was able to direct the war, not least because his officers continued to obey his often suicidal orders.

The bunker-dwellers began to behave like the members of a cult: they had lost touch with reality and instead put their faith in Hitler, horoscopes and mediums. In early 1945 Eva Braun's sister Ilse arrived in Berlin, having fled the advancing Russians in Silesia. Eva took her to the Adlon for lunch, where Ilse recounted her experiences, looked at her and said: 'all Germany is lost ... Your Führer is a fiend, he's dragging you into the abyss with him.' Eva refused to listen, retorting that her sister deserved to be shot for what she had just said. On 15 April Eva Braun, the epitome of Nazi womanhood, joined Hitler in the bunker. This was taken as a serious omen by his secretaries, who jealously referred to her as the 'Angel of Death', but in fact Eva Braun was typical of the courtiers around the Führer, who hung on his every word – no matter how absurd – and encouraged him to fight on. Many of the party bosses and SS men hiding beneath the ground whispered about defeat behind his back but none had the courage to defy him openly.

Of all those in Hitler's entourage Bormann remained the most powerful and the most dangerous, but it was Goebbels who did most to rouse his flagging spirits. When Hitler's optimism faded it was he who persuaded him to carry on; when news from the front was black it was he who boosted his morale, thus delaying capitulation and in effect writing the death warrant for thousands of innocent people killed in the final weeks of war. Still jealous of his rivals, particularly Göring and Himmler, he connived and plotted to regain his place as Hitler's favourite, seemingly oblivious to the fact that this was now meaningless; on his last ever social call outside the bunker Hitler visited Goebbels's villa, bringing his own cake and flask of tea. When he left Magda Goebbels crowed that 'He would not have gone to the Görings!'

Goebbels's diary is filled with equal doses of bile against his rivals and praise for Hitler's 'strength' and 'courage' in the 'dark days', but it was his belief in mystical links with history and with the occult which had the greatest effect on Hitler's morale in the final weeks. Goebbels would spend hours reading rousing passages from Carlyle's *History of Frederick the Great*, concentrating on the period in the Seven Years War when Frederick's arch-enemy the Russian tsarina Elisabeth died in the 'Miracle of the House of Brandenburg', leaving her successor to make peace and allowing the Prussians to go on to victory. Goebbels believed that if it had happened once it could happen again for the new Frederick – Hitler; instead of the tsarina, perhaps Churchill or Stalin would die and open the way to peace. The two men also relied on horoscope readings which 'confirmed' the path of recent history and spoke in glowing terms of Germany's future. The stars apparently revealed a 'difficult' period for Germany in mid April, stagnation until August 1945, then peace followed by three hard years, after which it would 'rise again' in 1949 and achieve even greater glory. It seems that the two men genuinely believed the message from the stars – Hitler was so delighted by these findings that he encouraged Goebbels to issue a proclamation forecasting imminent victory which began: 'The Führer has declared that there will be a change of fortune in this very year.'[41] This faith in the occult reached ludicrous heights when Roosevelt died on 12 April 1945. Both Goebbels and Hitler were convinced that this was the 'sign' that they had been waiting for – Hitler's own Brandenburg miracle. Later that day there were jubilant celebrations in the bunker as Hitler awaited a call from the Allies for the negotiation of a separate peace, still convinced that the west would now join the Nazis and turn against the Soviet Union. Even the news that Vienna had fallen to the Soviet army could not dampen his spirits that evening. But the mood did not last. By 20 April – Hitler's fifty-sixth birthday – the Allies had still not offered peace. Something had gone wrong.

That last birthday party was a turning point in the collapse of the Third Reich. Goebbels delivered his customary eulogy over the radio and Hitler held a conference at which he stormed: 'You will see – the Russians are about to suffer the bloodiest defeat of their history at the gates of Berlin.' That afternoon Goebbels, Himmler, Goering, Bormann, Speer, Ribbentrop, Keitel, Jodl, Krebs and others clambered up the long bunker steps to Hitler's old Chancellery study. Although it was one of the few rooms which had not yet been destroyed Albert Speer remembered it as very run down, with 'stains on the wallpaper, gaps in the furnishings, scattered newspapers, empty glasses and plates, a hat that someone had tossed on a chair'.[42] Eva Braun had managed to find a gramophone and one record – *Red Roses* – which she played over and over again while Bormann, Ribbentrop and the others danced around with the secretaries, trying to look cheerful. But behind the smiles many of Hitler's closest associates were plotting their escapes. Some tried to persuade Hitler to leave the Führerbunker and flee to Bavaria, where he might be safe. He refused, still insisting on victory. Speer was aware that the end was near and even tried to help some Berliners to escape the city. In the process he organized one of the most bizarre events of the Battle of Berlin – the final concert given by the Berlin Philharmonic. Speer had long been trying to persuade Wilhelm Furtwängler to flee to Switzerland but he had declined, saying: 'what about my orchestra?' As a result Speer promised that he would warn the musicians when the end was near by requesting Bruckner's 'Romantic' Symphony as a signal that they should pack up and go into hiding. The request came on 12 April. Speer was determined to put on a last real show and despite the electricity rations lit up the whole concert hall: 'Absurd, I know, but I thought that Berlin should see that lovely hall, miraculously still intact, just once more fully lit.' Nicolaus von Below attended the extraordinary concert and remembered: 'It was unforgettable. I sat with Speer and Admiral Dönitz and listened to Beethoven's Violin Concerto, the finale from the *Götterdämmerung* and Bruckner's symphony. Can there ever have been such a moment, such an experience? Silently the three of us walked afterwards across the totally destroyed Potsdamer Platz back to the Reich Chancellery.'[43] Annemarie Kempf, Speer's secretary, was also there. At the end she noticed that 'baskets [were] offered to spectators on the way out – cyanide capsules. Speer was just horrified. We never found out who organized it, but doubtless the party. The baskets were offered by Hitler Youths in uniform – children.'[44]

It was only when he heard of the failure of SS-Obergruppenführer Steiner to carry out an attack along the Finow Canal for the relief of Berlin that it finally dawned on Hitler that the city might be lost. Two days after his birthday he gathered his military advisers together and began to rant at them in uncontrolled paroxysms of rage, screaming insults at his men and then collapsing in a heap and sobbing. Keitel and Jodl tried to persuade him either to surrender or to try to escape before Berlin became 'a battleground of house-to-house street fighting', but Hitler accused the military of betrayal, cowardice and corruption. Finally, he announced that he was determined to stay in Berlin until the bitter end. 'I will never leave Berlin again: I will defend the capital with my dying breath. Either I direct the battle for the Reich capital . . . or I shall go down with my troops in Berlin fighting for the symbol of the Reich.' He would not be captured and 'exhibited in a Moscow Zoo'. If there was to be no peace, he would die in the city. That night Goebbels and his family moved into the bunker. Those senior Nazis who had not yet done so prepared to escape the funeral pyre of Berlin.

By now Goebbels had ordered all people capable of bearing arms to remain in the city and fight to the death. Ordinary civilians were forbidden to drive cars or use trains or public transport or to leave Berlin by any other means. The Nazi High Command and those with connections ignored the rules, and a flood of privileged men obtained special passes which would get them past the deadly guards – over 2,000 were issued on Hitler's birthday alone. Most had private cars, secret hoards of petrol and food, and money and other forms of loot with which to buy their way out. Himmler went to his castle at Ziethen, Speer went to Hamburg, Göring fled to Bavaria, Dr Brandt sent his family to

Thuringia; all the hotels in Garmisch were reserved for the ministry personnel who had long since relocated to the Harz mountains. One Berlin woman watched as the gold-braided Admiral Raeder stepped into his car and drove away: 'The rats are deserting the sinking ship,' she said bitterly. They were wise to leave when they did. On 24 April, four days after Hitler's birthday, nine Soviet armies encircled the city. Escape was now virtually impossible.

If Hitler's birthday had marked a turning point for the Nazi elite it also marked a dramatic shift in the fortunes of ordinary Berliners. Most knew nothing about the goings-on in the bunker, and although in the past Hitler's birthday had seen a celebration it would have passed virtually unnoticed in 1945 had it not been for two special announcements. The first was the news that the British and the Americans were to stop the bombing raids which had pounded the city day and night for months. The last raid was on 20 April, a 'birthday present for Hitler', but the skies fell silent after ten in the morning. Rumours spread through the capital that the Americans and the British wanted to make peace and that the Russians would not attack. The second announcement was that special rations were to be distributed in honour of Hitler's birthday. Thousands of hungry Berliners crawled from their cellars for the first time in days, finally able to walk without fear of the bombs. They searched for water and lined up outside shops for their rations of bacon or sausage, rice, sugar, tins of vegetables and other staples. According to the SD reports there was something of a holiday atmosphere in the city that sunny afternoon and people told jokes and exchanged gossip, hopeful that there would be no Russian advance; no 'Schlacht um Berlin'. The optimistic mood was suddenly interrupted by the sound of heavy guns.

By 20 April Soviet army units under Vladimir Abyzov had reached Müncheberg, halfway between the Oder and Berlin. On the afternoon of Hitler's birthday an artilleryman raced in and made the surprise announcement that the Soviet guns were within firing range. Hundreds of officers and men gathered around and Kolmogorov shouted: 'On the den of the enemy, Berlin – fire!' The Russians cheered as shell after shell roared towards the city, shells which shattered Berliners' last hopes of peace.

The American and British bombing raids had been highly destructive, reducing 6,340 acres of the city to complete rubble; 52,000 people had lost their lives. But however terrible the raids there was usually some advance warning, and they had lasted a relatively short time. The Soviet shelling was different. Artillery fire was random, there was no warning, and it was equally deadly. At 2 p.m. on that April afternoon shells suddenly began to explode in the midst of the hundreds of people queuing for their rations. Within seconds human remains littered the streets and blood was spattered on the walls of shops and houses. Shells hit every few seconds, devastating Unter den Linden, the Kurfürstendamm, the Tiergarten and elsewhere. Rita Kuhn remembered one of her neighbours leaving to get bread when 'we heard this tremendous sound, whistling . . . It was what they called the "*Stalinorgel*". It was very highly explosive and made a huge noise.' After the explosion she headed for the bakery:

> As I walked on, and I looked at the trees, and I saw pieces of clothing on the trees. Pretty soon, as I got closer to the bakery, there were pieces of human flesh. They were all over, everywhere. On the trees, on the balconies, pieces of clothing, pieces of human flesh . . . I almost fell over a woman, lying there in the street, dead, with her legs blown off. And I couldn't find the bakery. I walked on and I passed a house, and I could see a lot of people, moaning, crying. And I came to where I thought the bakery was, and there was just a big hole. Sure enough, that's where it had hit, and people hadn't had time to take cover.[45]

Even Hitler's bunker was rocked by the explosions. The Führer immediately contacted General Karl Koller by telephone and ordered him to silence the Soviet guns. The general retorted that the Soviets were not, as Hitler thought, using a captured German heavy battery but were actually within range of the city. Hitler refused to believe this and yelled down the phone that he must 'do something'. It was pointless. Dead and injured Berliners were left lying in the street as the population fled back to their cellars for a long, terrifying wait.

When Hitler recovered from the shock of the initial shelling he began to outline a hopeless strategy against the Russians. There was to be no talk of surrender and the soldiers were to fight on until they were all dead. As Siegfried Knappe put it, 'For Hitler to be so disrespectful toward the men who were sacrificing their own lives every day just to keep him alive one more day filled me with anger . . . We were perhaps only now, at the last possible moment, beginning to see clearly what kind of man we had been following.'[46] It was then that Hitler issued the 'Nero Order'. According to Albert Speer the Nero Order dictated that every useful item in Berlin was to be destroyed rather than allowed to fall into the hands of the Soviets.[47] It called specifically for the destruction of all industrial plants, electrical facilities, water and gas works, food and clothing stores, all bridges, all railway lines, all communications equipment, all waterways, all ships, all freight cars and all locomotives. This was to 'intensify to the most fanatical level' and as such it 'permits no consideration for the population to be taken'. Everything was to be destroyed; it was irrelevant if those trapped in the city starved or froze to death. If the city was to fall, then it was to perish in a spectacular inferno irrespective of the cost in innocent human lives.[48] The dreaded 'scorched earth' policy which had caused such destruction in the east was to be turned on the capital itself.

Hitler had no sympathy for the people of Berlin; in his eyes they had 'let him down', unable to appreciate his great gifts or his vision of Germany's future. They had clearly not 'deserved' to have him as a leader, nor had they deserved to be victorious:

> If the war is lost, the people will also be lost [and] it is not necessary to worry about their needs for elemental survival. On the contrary, it is best for us to destroy even these things. For the nation has proved to be weak, and the future belongs entirely to the strong people of the East. Whatever remains after this battle is in any case only the inadequates [*Minderwertigen*], because the good ones will be dead.[49]

The chief proponent of the Nero Order in Berlin was the ghastly General Helmuth Reymann, whom Hitler had appointed commandant for the Battle of Berlin and who told Speer he would follow orders 'to the letter'; both Speer and General Gotthardt Heinrici, Commander-in-Chief of Army Group Vistula, tried to limit the effects of the order wherever possible but were not able to prevent the destruction of supplies. The petty cruelty and pig-headedness of the Nazi officials intent on 'doing their duty' to the very end was unbelievable, and vast stores of food were carefully counted and then destroyed in front of starving civilians.

Goebbels was convinced that he could keep the population under control. When reports had reached him of the storming of a bakery in the district of Rahnsdorf some weeks earlier he had decided to 'make an example of them' and on 8 April had the ringleaders executed. 'I am convinced that the people of Berlin can always be persuaded to support maintenance of public law and order,' he wrote. But Goebbels forgot that in early April the Russians were still far away and there had been talk of peace. By the end of the month even Berliners realized that they were doomed. They were terrified of starving in their cellars and even fear of the SS and the shelling was not enough to keep them from looting. Rumours of the planned demolitions spread like wildfire and finally broke the discipline of the city. People rushed to break into storage facilities, trains and deserted shops. One watched as a bread truck in Köpenick was looted by passing women, children and old men: 'The driver stood there, unable to do anything about it except make parrying gestures. His truck was emptied within a few minutes.'[50] Even official buildings and military barracks were attacked by a frenzied population. A woman joined in the pillage of a Luftwaffe barracks and came away with real coffee, chocolate, meat and bottles of the finest Burgundy. A fellow looter was furious: 'They have everything in there,' she cried; 'a fine life they had, those devils!' Another came across tons of luxury foodstuffs near the Olympic Stadium. The SS quickly began to shoot civilians who approached the storage facilities: a number of people were mown down on the Warschau Bridge for trying to reach a cache of tinned meat. There was widespread fury when the giant food depots in Neukölln were detonated on 30 April.

Events in Berlin at the end of April bordered on the surreal. When the SS decided to blow up the Karstadt department store to prevent the 29 million marks of supplies from going to the Soviet army Berliners flocked to the building and demanded to be let in. The troops allowed them to take limited amounts of food but stood at the door, machine guns in hand, forcing them to drop other goods. Before long piles of linen, eiderdowns, fur coats, pullovers and other items were stacked by the exits and when the last of the food was gone the SS blew up the building and its contents, killing a number of civilians in the process. Hitler now gave the order for Berlin's 950 bridges to be destroyed, a demand which, had Speer not secretly disobeyed it (only eighty-five were actually blown up although most were charged), would have cut all electricity, food and other supplies off from the hundreds of thousands trapped in the city centre. For all the misery they caused to the civilian population these reckless measures did nothing to slow down the Soviet advance. On 25 April the telegraph office received one last message from Tokyo before closing down. It read: 'Good luck to you all.'

By the end of April all hopes of a counter-attack were fading away. The Ninth Army, on which Hitler had pinned so many of his hopes, had been surrounded in the woods of the Spreewald, and when the commanding officer, General Walter Wenck, realized that Berlin was bound to fall he allowed his men to turn away from the city and held a line open so that civilians and troops could escape; many thousands reached the Elbe, where they were captured by the Americans. Even after the Soviets had encircled the city hundreds of soldiers tried to break out rather than die in the hopeless fight for the capital. A Berlin resident, Margret Boveri, remembered returning to her street after scavenging for water and finding a German panzer sitting outside her house. The five men were a terrible sight, filthy and unshaven. She learned that they had fought in France, Africa, Russia – including Sevastopol and Stalingrad – on the Aachen front, in Stettin and had then come through Grunewald and Charlottenburg. Theirs was the last tank left from their unit. They, too, realized that the fight for Berlin was hopeless and would simply result in the loss of thousands of civilian lives, and they told her they intended to desert Berlin and make a dash for the western Allies. As Erna Dubnack put it, 'we always wished the "Amis" came to Berlin first. The Americans. We wanted the Americans here.'[51] One young Volkssturm (People's Storm) recruit remembered that it was the courage of desperation which motivated the soldiers. Berlin was defended so bitterly only because so many of the soldiers, so many of the civilians were afraid of Soviet imprisonment. They wanted to save themselves, to keep the Russians out of Berlin for as long as they could. Everything possible was done to stop them, to gain a little more time. If we were lucky, the Americans or the British would get to Berlin first. This is what any intelligent person hoped for.[52]

Churchill's words rang true – if the Anglo-Americans had insisted on taking the city, the vast majority of German troops would have surrendered without a fight.

Berlin on the eve of its annihilation was an extraordinary place. Almost 3 million people were trapped in the cellars of the vast flak towers and their homes and in underground bunkers. Zealous Nazis found themselves next to prisoners of war; hardened SS men willing to fight to the death sat with innocent civilians who simply wanted to survive. Some even tried to go on as if nothing had changed, carrying out orders and enforcing discipline as they had for over a decade. They included the bureaucrats, the SS, the Gestapo, the police and party functionaries determined to pursue the Nazi vision or at least to do their duty and maintain order until the end.

Berlin's role as the centre of the Nazi administrative machine had not ended with the Soviet advance; indeed Berlin had become increasingly important as other secondary centres of power fell to the advancing armies, and although most ministers had moved out of Berlin thousands of bureaucrats still struggled over mounds of burned-out rubble to get to their offices and continued to give orders, write memos and direct the functions of the Reich. This was one of the most terrible periods of Nazi crime, for although it was patently obvious that Germany was going to lose the war these men were obsessed by the need to complete the 'Final Solution' at any cost, and they ensured that the murders, executions and killing carried on until the very end. The final stage of the Holocaust involved dismantling the extermination and concentration camps, destroying evidence and either executing inmates or forcing them to go on long and murderous 'death marches' to camps or holding areas still in German hands. Despite the chaos in the capital this was still co-ordinated from the central offices in Berlin.

The men at SS headquarters had been kept well informed of all Soviet troop movements and of the likelihood of a particular camp being overrun. It was they who determined when a camp should be evacuated and destroyed. In acts of pitiless barbarism they refused to allow inmates simply to be liberated by the Soviets but insisted on killing them instead. The Generalgouvernement camps Treblinka, Sobibór and Belzec were given orders to evacuate in the autumn of 1943. The camps were to be destroyed, leaving no trace; Treblinka was to be turned into a farm while Belzec was to be levelled and the site planted with pine trees. By the end of 1944 only Auschwitz was still operating at full capacity, but in November Himmler decided that it was time to announce the Jewish question 'solved' and to close down the last killing installations. Inmates were set to work 'cleansing' the site at Auschwitz, which included the grisly tasks of removing human ash and bone from the ovens and scraping off eighteen-inch thick deposits of fat which had built up in the chimneys.[53] By 16 January 1945 the Soviets were approaching the camp and on 17 January the SS took the last roll-call, recording 35,118 prisoners in Monowitz and 31,894 in Auschwitz-Birkenau. The central office in Berlin had been thrown into chaos by the speed and strength of Koniev and Zhukov's offensive and this was reflected in the contradictory orders fired every few hours to the SS at Auschwitz. Finally the German staff were told to leave; on 17 January Dr Mengele personally saw to it that his bulky files documenting experiments on twins were sent to Berlin. The guards were now to escort their prisoners on foot or by train into Germany; over 7,000 of the weakest inmates who could not walk were permitted to remain in the camp on the assumption that they would soon die although hundreds of prisoners, including a group of 200 women, were shot. The corpses and living skeletons were found by the Soviets on 27 January, along with 368,820 men's suits, 836,255 women's coats and dresses, and over seven tons of women's hair. The remaining prisoners were forced to march. The order was given at Auschwitz on 18 January 1945: some walked to nearby railway junctions and were taken to camps in Germany; the others were forced to march hundreds of miles on foot. The marches were deadly. Raizl Kibel recalled:

> In a frost, half-barefoot, or entirely barefoot, with light rags upon their emaciated and exhausted bodies, tens of thousands of human creatures drag themselves along in the snow ... But woe is to them whose physical strength abandons them. They are shot on the spot. In such a way were thousands who had endured camp life up to the last minute murdered, a moment before liberation.[54]

Prisoners from thousands of other labour camps throughout north and eastern Germany were forced on to similar marches; some ended up in central camps like Buchenwald, Sachsenhausen, Dachau and Ravensbrück, others were marched with no apparent destination around Germany.[55] But it was not only the big camps which had to be dealt with; the men at Berlin headquarters were obsessed with tying up all 'loose ends', which meant murdering all remaining Jews and other prisoners who still languished in the dozens of smaller camps or prisons in the Reich. Terrible acts of cruelty were committed:

in January a forced march of over 6,000 prisoners began from East Prussian labour camps to the Baltic coast, where 3,000 Jewish women were separated out and shot on the shore or thrown into the water to drown. On 27 April three barges of remaining prisoners from the eastern labour camps were loaded with inmates and went ashore at Kiel and Neustadt near Lübeck. There, the victims were machine-gunned by SS men and naval personnel as they tried to struggle ashore. As before, the reports of 'successful' operations were sent back to the capital. It is estimated that around 250,000 people died during these marches and evacuations. Some died in the final days of war; on the day Hitler killed himself 2,775 Jews from Rehmsdorf were being marched to Theresienstadt; only 500 reached their destination alive.[56] The killing was actually carried out by the guards, but the obsessive bureaucrats showed no mercy either, and continued to give the orders for mass murder.

Despite attempts to finish the job it was clear by March that the strict central control had finally started to break down. Little documentary evidence now exists of the orders given during the final weeks of war; we know that Himmler was now secretly trying to negotiate with the Americans and ordered that Jews must no longer be killed outright, although the terrible marches were to continue.[57] Like many other camps Bergen-Belsen, its number now swollen by prisoners from the east, was forgotten by Berlin. No more food was sent there, the roll-calls ceased, rats attacked prisoners now too weak to fight them off, and there were incidences of cannibalism. The Berlin administration began to dissolve itself and top bureaucrats and functionaries who had not already left now attempted to flee and to re-invent their pasts. On 23 April the director of the Generalbetriebsleitung Ost, Präsident Ernst Emrich, who had overseen the death marches and the destruction of camp sites, called his staff together in his comfortable Berlin bunker and advised them to disappear for good. When the Soviets reached Berlin they managed to capture and identify some of these powerful men; for example, when the offices of the Generalbetriebsleitung were overrun they caught Reichsbahnoberinspektor Bruno Klemm, who had presided over many of the Berlin conferences on Jewish transports and who had failed to get out in time. Minor officials and functionaries were encouraged to stay and keep Berlin going.

Some Berliners showed an astounding ability to carry on as if nothing was happening. Erna Tietz, a young woman who worked as an anti-aircraft gunner, actually had to undergo an annual fitness assessment on 2 April 1945. The neatly typed document read: 'Mental and physical predispositions – Mentally good, capable, physically strong, athletically proportioned' – and this only a few weeks before capitulation.[58] SS-Commander Leon Degrelle noted the extraordinary mixture of order and chaos when he visited the Adlon on Hitler's birthday. The hotel was 'still operating in spite of the bombs and the shells falling right in the streets. In the brilliantly lit restaurant tuxedoed waiters and maîtres d'hôtel in tails continued solemnly and impassively to serve purple slices of kohlrabi in the huge silver platters for state occasions ... Tomorrow or the day after the building would probably go up in flames.' Degrelle praised their 'comportment, their self-mastery, and their self-discipline right down to the most minor details and until the last moment'. In his eyes the Berliners' last stand would 'be a noble memory of mankind for all those who lived the end of the Third Reich' and he was overjoyed when a group of young women, clearly impressed by his SS uniform, decked his Volkswagen out with red tulips and pansies as he prepared to leave for the front even though 'the worst humiliations lay in wait for every one of them'.[59]

Some opted for a hedonistic end, drinking, dancing, plundering stocks of fine brandies, champagne and chocolates, and making their final toasts to the Führer; others quietly spat when someone spoke his name. Jacob Kronika, who was in Berlin during those final days, likened the city to a great sinking ship struck by the *Untergangsatmosphäre* as it 'went under'. Soldiers now had an 'unquenchable' appetite for sex and by early evening the dark areas around the Zoo, the Wittenbergplatz and the Kurfürstendamm became an 'erotic wilderness'. 'The women are no different and offer men cigarettes for sexual favours,' Kronika reported. He was surprised by the promiscuity in the enormous air-raid shelters, where thousands of people were crammed together for days at a time, and noted that Berlin doctors seemed to have lost the battle against VD and under-aged pregnancy. The young defended their actions, saying: 'we want everything now – the *Knochenmann* [undertaker] might collect us tonight.'

For those removed from the privileged life of the Nazi elite, who spent their time in the grand hotels and in well-stocked private bunkers, life had become deplorable. When Berliners finally realized that they were surrounded morale plummeted. SD reports showed that the *Stimmung*, the spirit of the people, had sunk to rock bottom. One agent heard a man tell his companions at a train station at Ostkreuz that 'only crazy people believe in victory', while another agent huddling in a shelter heard: 'If our soldiers were as clever as they were in 1918, the war would already be over.' Frau Ursula Meyer-Semlies remembered that 'some people were still thinking, "The Führer won't leave us in the lurch," but she laughed secretly: Not leave us in the *lurch*? The situation is completely out of his hands.'[60] The black market flourished in those tense days; a cigarette cost 5 marks and a prostitute cost 50 marks – the same price as a loaf of bread.

The social breakdown occurred partly because people were simply shocked at the speed of the Soviet advance. Hitler and Goebbels had long promised that the Russians could never reach the Oder and that Berlin was in no danger. It was only in the final weeks of the war that Hitler decided that Berlin should be a 'fortress city', defended until the end not just by troops, but by each and every person left alive in Berlin. The notion of a 'fortress' evokes ideas of medieval Europe – of knights and armour, moats and drawbridges. To declare a modern, sprawling, industrial city a fortress was sheer madness. Hitler had already ensured the demolition of beautiful cities like Königsberg and Breslau – until then unscathed by Allied bombs – by declaring them 'fortresses'; this did little to halt the Soviet advance but caused the loss of thousands of lives and saw these places decimated by shelling and street fighting. Hitler's generals muttered that the city could never be defended and the fight would simply result in the deaths of countless innocent civilians, but even at this late stage they lacked the courage to defy orders.

Goebbels was insisting even in March that Berlin could be defended:

> Taken as a whole the situation is extraordinarily satisfactory. According to the figures submitted to me it may be assumed that with the men, weapons, food and coal available Berlin could hold out for some eight weeks if surrounded. Eight weeks is a long time during which a lot can happen. In any case we have made excellent preparations and above all it must be remembered that, if the worst should happen, an enormous number of men with their weapons would flow into the city and we should be in a position to use them to put up a powerful defence.[61]

Nazi 'experts' assured Goebbels that even if the Soviets reached Berlin the ruins and skeletons of thousands of burnt-out vehicles would be excellent material for barricades. Berlin suddenly became the subject of much rousing Nazi propaganda; Reich Labour Minister Dr Robert Ley declared that 'We shall fight before Berlin, for Berlin and behind Berlin', and Goebbels wrote in *Das Reich* that if the city fell 'the whole of Europe including Britain will be thrown into disaster'. In an extraordinary feat of self-deception both Hitler and Goebbels continued to insist almost as an act of faith that the Soviet army would be repulsed before it reached the suburbs. 'A game is not lost until the final whistle,' Hitler told Bormann. 'If Churchill were suddenly to disappear, everything could change in a flash. We can still snatch victory in the final sprint!' On 5 March Hitler had given Lieutenant-General Helmuth Reymann a half-hearted order to arrange some protection for the city, but there were no longer any legal evacuations of children or the elderly, no food supplies for the general public, and no proper defences in the form of road blocks or tank traps. When asked about the need to provide milk for the children Goebbels retorted that if necessary he would bring cows into the suburbs –

although he knew this was impossible as there would be no food, shelter or milking facilities for them. When asked about evacuations he replied that he did not intend to 'throw Berlin into a panic' when there was as yet no danger of the city falling into enemy hands. On 9 March Goebbels issued an order 'For the Defence of the Reich capital' but it was a ridiculous document full of empty phrases and grandiose visions: 'The capital will be defended to the last man and the last bullet,' he declared. In the event of an attack Berliners were to fight for 'every building, every house, every floor, every hedge, every shell crater'. Goebbels then repeated the message that it was better to die fighting for the city than to die at the hands of the Soviets. Slogans like 'Victory or Siberia!' began to appear on notice boards and walls. The city was divided into zones, with the outer ring of defence sixty miles in circumference and the second line of defence following the nineteenth-century S-Bahn ring. The third ring circling the crucial government and city centre was called Sector Z or Zitadelle. It was not until the end of March, only weeks before the final Soviet offensive, that an attempt was made to create a 'defence force' for the city and to build fortifications, but Goebbels still refused to declare Berlin a war zone. Neither he nor Hitler wished to face the fact that the city was doomed and for others to have pointed this out was still a treasonable offence.

Without troops, military equipment or resources it was impossible to 'fortify' a vast city like Berlin. Degrelle, returning there on 22 April from the eastern front, expected to find a well-defended ring bristling with fortifications;

> I was shocked when I found the prepared defence ring around Berlin. It was empty foxholes and trenches and roadblocks – *completely unmanned*! Disgustedly, I realized that it was no more than a line on a map. It had been Goebbels's responsibility, as defence commissar for Berlin, to prepare these defences, but it was painfully obvious that he had no idea how to do it . . . Incompetence seemed to be the order of the day in Berlin.[62]

Goebbels had hoped that the Wehrmacht would flock to Berlin but thousands had already been killed to the east and many others had fled to the American lines. By April there were about 150,000 men left to defend the city with only forty tanks and hardly any ammunition; as Degrelle put it, the fight against the Soviets 'should at least have been facilitated by a preparation of heavy artillery fire. But how could they fire? With what ammunition? . . . Firing was limited to one shell per day per muzzle. One shell! Only one!'[63] The haggard Wehrmacht soldiers now dragging through the city streets bore little resemblance to the proud troops who had marched off to invade Russia in 1941. One woman watched as carts rolled past through the rain; they were covered by sodden tarpaulins, under them soldiers. Filthy, grey-bearded faces, typical 'front' types, all of them old. All the carts drawn by small Polish horses, black and shiny with rain. Their loads: hay. It no longer looks like a motorized *Blitzkrieg* . . . All these creatures are so wretched, they are no longer men. One neither hopes nor expects anything from them. They already give the impression of being defeated and taken prisoner. They looked past us with expressionless faces. Evidently we – we the people, the civilians, Berliners or whatever we are – have no interest for them whatsoever.[64]

The side streets were slowly filling with guns, lorries and wagons; near them soldiers cooked, slept, cavorted with women or exchanged goods. 'Nothing is said about the war. It is clear that all of them are fed up.'[65]

When the Wehrmacht failed to materialize Goebbels called on an even more pathetic force: the Volkssturm, made up of tired old men or young teenaged boys. Goebbels and his henchmen swept through the city forcing those under sixteen and over fifty to join. The results were pitiful. The groups came under party control, which meant that they spent hours practising Hitler salutes rather than learning how to defend themselves; they had no battle experience, little equipment and no uniforms except a small armband. Most had no will to fight and die for this lost cause; the commanding officer of Forty-two Battalion reported that

> None of the men had received any training in firing a machine gun, and they were all afraid of handling the anti-tank weapons. Although my men were quite ready to help their country they refused to go into battle without uniforms and without training. What can a Volkssturm man do with a rifle without ammunition? The men went home; that was the only thing we could do.[66]

Isa Vermehren remembered watching as the Volkssturm prepared for the final battle; some men were hauled out of their houses at night and forced to join in, others were school or refugee children of fifteen or sixteen years of age who gathered at the Lustgarten and were shown how to fight. Their helmets were far too big for them and some had to wear woollen knitted hats to keep them from slipping off their heads; they had no boots but wore battered shoes repaired with straw. Fifteen-year-old Hugo Stehkämper was drafted into the Volkssturm: 'They stuck us in the old black SS uniforms which you hadn't seen any more during the war, brown Organization Todt coats, and blue air force auxiliary caps. We thought we looked like scarecrows.'[67] The tragi-comedy continued when old men arrived directly from their offices dressed in hats and coats intended for a day's work. Horst Lange was reminded of 1918 as he surveyed the ridiculous barricades and tank traps which the Volkssturm had made out of the rubble from bombed buildings. He noted that the men who had been told to defend the city were old and carried rusted weapons which 'had probably been used in the fight against Spartacus'. One man who had no gun insisted on carrying a mandolin locked in an exquisite leather case. Some of Goebbels's 'new' units existed only on paper: the 'Tank Destroyer Division' was no more than a group of old men on bicycles who were sent out one morning to confront Soviet T-34s. They were blown to pieces.

When Goebbels ran out of Volkssturm recruits he ordered his men to search military hospitals for soldiers who, although injured, were still strong enough to hold a rifle – they were then drafted into the ironically named 'stomach' and 'ear' battalions. Hitler heartily approved, declaring that these inferior men should not be permitted to shirk their duty when healthy Germans were dying at the front. As a result, sick men swooning with pain or racked with fever were sent out to certain death in the final weeks of the war. Prisoners of war and slave labourers were forced at gunpoint to work for the defence of the city: Lance-Corporal Norman Norris, a British POW, was marched through Berlin in early April and noted that 'huge tank traps were now being dug, one at Königsarterhausen by Polish Jews. They looked plaintively at us; the look in their eyes showing that they knew they would eventually be murdered was unforgettable.' The SS also went to camps housing Soviet prisoners-of-war, lined up the inmates and asked them if they would help to defend Berlin. If they refused, they were shot. Tragically those Russians forced to work for the Nazis were later branded as traitors by Stalin and thousands were executed after the war.[68]

Many Berliners were sickened by the sight of these pathetic, gaunt old men and young boys being sent to fight; some doctors wrote fake medical reports to excuse them from duty while others hid them in their homes. False papers could be purchased for 80,000 marks. Yet for all the thousands who were forced to fight against their will there were many in Berlin who remained supporters of Hitler until the end; who were determined not only to die for their Führer, but to kill all those suspected of desertion. Goebbels had scraped together the remaining men of the Waffen- and Allgemeine-SS, the labour service, the Gestapo, the fire brigade, the Plant Protection units and members of the Hitler Youth to join in the final battle. But the most shameful were his special 'Werewolf' execution squads, who combed the city looking for 'deserters' and who were made up of fanatical SS, Gestapo and Hitler Youth members who still believed in their old motto: 'We are born to die for Germany.' Hundreds of men who had tried to burn their uniforms, hide in cellars or attics or feign illness were found by the squads, dragged through the streets, and either shot or hung. The young Berliner Helmut Altner remembered being pulled from his bed by the SS and ordered to fight; he also recalled that when his platoon leader refused to go into battle he 'was strung up on the nearest tree by a few SS and an SA man – but then he was already fifteen years old'.[69] The suburbs were filled with such victims, many of whom were murdered only minutes before the Russians arrived; near the Berliner Strasse, according to one woman, 'a soldier in underpants is hanging, a sign saying "Traitor" dangling from his neck'. He was hanging so low that the young boys of the neighbourhood played by twisting him by his legs, winding the rope and spinning the dead man around. Similar signs scrawled on pieces of cardboard and hung around the wretched victims read I HAD NO FAITH IN THE FÜHRER, or ALL TRAITORS WILL DIE LIKE THIS. There were many tragic cases of boys being killed while trying to find food for their families, or of sick or old men being shot as 'shirkers' simply because they looked 'too healthy'. Margret Boveri watched in horror as a man was killed on 24 April in front of her house: 'Yesterday was the first day of the *Wehrwölfen* in our district: a professor . . . tried to throw his local Party uniform in the Lietzensee, he was captured and his throat was cut. The pool of blood was 100 metres in front of our house.' The word 'traitor' was left on the site. Lothar Rühl, then a teenager, remembered being picked up 'for desertion' by the SS.

> They told me to go along with them and said that all cowards and traitors would be shot. On the way, I saw an officer, stripped of his insignia, hanging from a streetcar underpass. A large sign hung around his neck read, 'I am hanging here because I was too much of a coward to face the enemy.' The SS man said, 'Do you see that? There's a deserter hanging already.'[70]

Leo Welt remembered that

> The SS shot a lot of German soldiers because they were not interested in fighting any more. They killed not only young boys who were crying they wanted to go home, but many soldiers because they had lost their will to fight. They were even hanged from the lampposts as traitors. And I remember quite clearly when my brother and his friends went into the basement of a house that had been bombed: there were five German soldiers sitting there, all shot.[71]

It is not known how many hundreds of Berliners were killed by these fanatics but by the end of the war the trees and lampposts of the city were festooned with the bloated corpses of those accused of desertion.

The city descended into a kind of civil war between Nazi supporters who insisted on a fight to the death, and those who tried to lay down their arms because they wanted to live. The situation was chaotic, with one side of a street or district held by fanatical Nazis and the other by the Russians.

> There were terrible scenes . . . The Russians retreated, and then I had a horrible experience. This had all happened on one of the side streets of the Kurfürstendamm. People who lived there had put out white flags of surrender. There was this one apartment house with white bed sheets waving from the windows. And the SS came – I'll never forget this – went into the house and dragged all of the men out. I don't know whether these were soldiers dressed in civilian clothing, old men, or what. Anyway, they took them into the middle of the street and shot them . . . Even when the Russians were already in sight, you could see police a hundred yards farther on, still trying to check people. Whoever didn't have the right papers or the correct pass was strung up as a deserter, and hung with a sign saying, 'I am a traitor', or 'I am a coward'.[72]

People were now terrified of helping others to hide; one young soldier remembered that 'the civilians [are] afraid to accept wounded soldiers and officers into their cellars when so many are being hanged as real or presumed deserters and the occupants of the cellars are concerned with being ruthlessly turfed out as accomplices by the members of the flying courts-martial'. He noted that most of the death squad members were 'very young SS officers with hardly a decoration between them, blind and hysterical. Hope of relief and fear of the courts-martial keeps us going.' For these 'deserters' it had been something of a relief when news reached them on 21 April 1945 that the Russians had crossed the city boundary.

The Soviet advance was met by pockets of fierce resistance which made progress painfully slow and extremely violent. By 24 April Koniev's forces were pushing rapidly in from the south, joining with Zhukov's forces in the east and Rokossovsky's in the north. Late on the night of the 24th Zhukov and Koniev's forces met up on the Schönefeld airfield, the two generals now competing for the glory of being the first to take the city. Koniev flung all his resources into a fight along the Teltow Canal, pushing through Zehlendorf, Dahlem, Lichterfelde and Steglitz to reach the S-Bahn ring defence. After heavy fighting they reached Schöneberg on 27 April and engaged in a fierce battle around the Olympic Stadium and the Kantstrasse. Chuikov, under Zhukov, advanced against the ferocious SS 'Nordland' Panzer Division into the heavily defended Tempelhof Airport and surrounded it with special tank groups to prevent any Nazis flying away at the last moment. He then fought across the Teltow Canal into Neukölln and reached the area dominated by the huge concrete hulk of the Zoo flak tower, now filled with hundreds of civilians and SS men, on 27 April. Meanwhile the Third Shock Army struggled past the Humboldthain flak tower to the Wedding S-Bahn station, only reaching the Museum Island on 30 April.

As the experience of Stalingrad and Warsaw had already shown, the taking of a besieged city is one of the most difficult tasks facing an army. Superior firepower cannot prevent enemy guerrilla tactics, cannot stop a single deadly sniper. As a result of the dogged resistance of a sizeable number of men the battle was hard – both for the invaders and for those still trapped within the city limits. Shells blasted through walls; tanks rolled over gardens and cemeteries, and fires blazed unchecked. The Soviets were forced to fight for every street using heavy artillery, tanks and lines of troops. An anonymous woman, known as the Berlin diarist, watched as 'twelve assault tanks appeared, flanked left and right by infantry, approximately one company, armed with submachine guns, and spraying the walls of the houses whilst moving from door to door at the double. They were followed by anti-aircraft guns. Behind these assault troops came carts drawn by two or four horses containing food and ammunition as well as loot.'[73] As soon as they arrived the men 'dug individual foxholes and took care of the wounded and their weapons'. Colonel-General Chuikov, now attacking from the south, described the difficulties he faced.

In street fighting, when squares and streets are empty and the enemy is defending himself in buildings, attics and cellars, the tank crews cannot see the opposing troops. Neither can they drive their tanks into buildings let alone cellars or attics. At the same time they were an excellent target for enemy tank hunters armed with incendiary bottles or, worse still, with Panzerfausts.[74]

The Soviets attempted to break resistance by shelling a street or district for hours on end before advancing. Thousands of civilians died in these massive barrages but they were effective; Colonel-General Nikolai Erastovich Berzarin later boasted that whereas the Allies had dropped 65,000 tons of bombs on Berlin 'we fired 40,000 tons of shells in two weeks!' Streets and buildings which had survived the Allied bombing raids were now reduced to rubble.

Despite the successful Soviet tactics resistance grew more fierce as the Soviet army approached the city centre. Wehrmacht and SS troops, backed by Volkssturm and pro-Nazi civilians, often fought frantically using anti-tank weapons and grenades. Some areas were teeming with snipers, who managed to hide in blasted-out buildings or in cellars and attacked the Soviets from the rear with Panzerfausts or grenades. These acts resulted in high civilian casualties: if even a single shot came from a building it would be blown to pieces irrespective of the number of civilians sheltering within. Countess Maria von Maltzan managed to avoid that fate by preventing two young SS men from setting up a machine-gun post by her flat. She pointed a pistol at them and said they could either burn their uniforms and hide in the house or she would shoot them. They chose the former, and the area was taken by the Soviets only an hour later. Other civilians were not so lucky; any person suspected of carrying a weapon was killed and there were numerous accidents and misunderstandings: a man was shot for trying to move an abandoned Soviet gun away from his front door. Civilians huddled in their cellars as the Soviet troops moved forward from house to house, one group on the main street and another covering from the backs of houses, clambering over gardens and roofs. They would smash in doors and search for soldiers or snipers; anyone suspected of carrying arms was killed on the spot. Once an area had been captured the mass of infantry would move in and secure it.

As each district was 'liberated' there was a mixed sense of fear and relief amongst the civilians. For some the terror of retribution had been too great and an estimated 6,000 Berliners committed suicide rather than fall into the hands of the Soviets – most used the plentiful 'KCB' cyanide capsules or shot themselves. Others saw their first Russians while peeping out from the cellars or from their boarded-up windows and found them a curious sight. The Russians literally set up camp in the middle of urban streets so that some areas began to resemble farmyards, complete with wagons, horses, chickens and cows. It was then, after a sense of calm had been established, that the raping and looting began.

The front-line soldiers tended to be well disciplined, but those who followed were often poorly educated young men to whom even shattered Berlin seemed luxurious. Jürgen Graf remembered that when the Russians reached his street

> all went well for 48 hours. Then the next wave of Russian troops arrived, and they settled in to stay. These Russians were really bad. Their main problem was liquor, and they were the ones who started the period of rape and destruction in Berlin ... The first troops were friendly and gave us food ... These officers explained that first they would take Berlin, and then a form of self-administration could be set up to replace Nazi rule. All of this was very encouraging. Just 48 hours later, houses were burned, women were raped, and people who had gone underground, who had worked against the fascists for years, were taken away and shot.[75]

Marshal Koniev and Marshal Zhukov's troops were known to be relatively disciplined compared with others like Marshal Malinovsky's army, which included many released prisoners.[76] Bunhilde Pomsel, who had worked in Goebbels's Propaganda Ministry, remembered being picked out from a group along with an elderly White Russian lady who could speak to them: 'The Russians didn't touch a hair on our heads ... We were lucky to have been captured by these particular soldiers, who were part of Zhukov's troops.'[77] There were from the beginning many incidents of great kindness; Russians would sometimes protect women from fellow soldiers or give the children gifts or befriend entire families; Ellen Gräfin Poninski recalled that they were either extremely kind or viciously cruel and Peter Bloch noted that they were 'unpredictable, brutal as Huns and innocent as children. One never knew where one stood. They could calmly shoot down people and rape women; give children chocolate, and stand before a stall of young rabbits and carry on laughingly and wonderingly.'[78] But the majority of Soviet troops felt no restraint. For months they had been encouraged to take what and whom they wished once in the 'lair of the fascist beast'. The Berlin diarist, who had travelled in Russia before the war, wrote:

> I try my best to imagine how the Russians must feel surrounded as they are by all this unprotected property. Every house has deserted flats completely at their mercy ... There's nothing in this city that isn't theirs for the taking ... As a result they casually grab at any shiny thing that comes to hand, lose it or give it away; many an object they simply lug off only a little while later to throw it away as too cumbersome ... As a rule they don't know how to make use of things, have no idea of quality or value. How, after all, could they have acquired such knowledge?

Watches were the most coveted possession and some soldiers walked around with both arms covered in them; they also took bicycles as long as they had tyres; Berliners quickly learned to ride on metal rims.

The single worst feature of the Soviet occupation was the rape. All women were treated as the soldiers' rightful property. Attacks were particularly vindictive in the last days of April and the first week in May, although they continued long into the occupation. Soldiers came into cellars brandishing revolvers and dragged the women into hallways or half-bombed rooms; there they were taken by individual soldiers or gang raped and sometimes murdered. Regina Frankenfeld remembered that 'as the Russians came, they just raped the women. They lined them up against the wall, they dragged my mother and my grandmother out ... they raped her, too ... just like they did me, dear God ... as they stood there with their machine guns, my mother said, "Well, now we'll probably be shot." And I said, "It's all the same to me." It *really* was all the same to me. I mean, we had nothing more to lose.'[79] Some women tried to hide but the need to scavenge for food and water made it difficult to stay indoors for long; others tried to use make-up to appear old – one friend of mine cut her hair very short and disguised herself as a boy; others 'borrowed' children as it was thought the Russians would leave mothers alone; some lived in attics as the soldiers seemed to prefer to stay on the ground floors. Hedwig Sass remembered, 'We wore old rags on purpose. But then the Russians always said, "You not old. You young." '[80] There was little attempt to distinguish between Nazis and non-Nazis; Rita Kuhn was once saved from soldiers by a German prostitute who had befriended her: 'three Russian officers came into the room ... And they looked around at everybody, and they looked at me. And they came toward me ... And she [the prostitute] saw that. Lydia was her name. She saw them come toward me, and she came to them and she says ... "Come". And she took all three of them. They all followed her.'[81] Hilde Naumann recounted how one Jewish survivor who had been living underground with her mother said, 'her mother frantically tried to forestall rape by showing their Jewish identity cards to a Red Army soldier, but to no avail, he could not read German.'[82] It was not uncommon to find dead women or girls in Berlin houses after the Russians had gone through: 'someone by the name of Inge, a couple of houses down the street, has been found with her skull bashed in after a drunken night with four unknown, so far undiscovered men,' one woman wrote. 'Drunk Russians are dangerous, see red, rage against themselves and anyone in sight the moment their anger is aroused.' Leo Welt was shocked when 'a woman friend of ours was shot in the back when she tried to run away after having been raped many times. A doctor came to treat her, and asked me to get some water ... The lady did recover physically. Mentally she never recovered.'[83] Ellen Gräfin Poninski wrote in her diary that 'Almost no evening went by, no night, in which we did not hear the pitiful cries for help from women who were attacked on the streets or in the always open houses.' Others were more fortunate; one mother and daughter hid unmolested in their second floor flat for a week and only realized why when they crept downstairs and found that the families on both the ground and first floors had committed suicide. They left the bodies hanging in the rooms for a number of weeks.

At the same time a strange role reversal took place.[84] Men, many of them hiding first from the SS and then from the Soviets, were forced to watch as the women were taken night after night. Hanna Gerlitz, the wife of a Berlin banker, remembered being raped by Russians in front of her husband. 'When they were done, they fired their guns into the air. The others thought the Russians had shot me until I yelled out, "It's over with!" Afterwards, I had to console my husband and help restore his courage. He cried like a baby.'[85] The tough Nazi soldiers, the party elite and the powerful bureaucrats who had lived by the creed of male superiority were now reduced to the role of helpless spectators while the rapes went on. Women were forced to became tougher and more self-sufficient. Frau Margarete Fischer recalled that 'during the war, we women here at home replaced all male work . . . Now, when the men came home and tried to re-establish their authoritarian presence, when it didn't lead to divorce, which in many families it often did, at the least it burdened a lot of marriages.'[86] Of the dozens of *Trummerfrauen* ('rubble ladies' – women who cleared the city of debris) I interviewed in Berlin in the 1980s many remarked bitterly that it had been virtually impossible to return to a 'normal' life after that time in Berlin, particularly when men treated women who had been violated as 'damaged goods'. Soldiers returning from the front often had no idea of the conditions under which their wives or girlfriends had lived and felt alienated from their matter-of-fact approach to sex. When the woman diarist met her fiancé, who had just returned from the front, she 'started describing some of the adventures in which we had all shared, then the real trouble began. Gerd: "You've turned into shameless bitches – every one of you in this house!" And he made a grimace. "I can't bear to listen to these stories. You've lost all your standards, the whole lot of you!" ' She gave him her diary to help him understand her ordeal but he could not read the short-hand. ' "What does that mean, for instance?" he asked, pointing at: "Rp." I had to laugh. "Rape, of course." He stared at me as though I'd gone out of my mind.' He left her shortly afterwards.[87] In the weeks following the surrender women who met one another on the street or in the food queue would begin a conversation with 'How many times . . . ?'

There were protests about the Soviet behaviour in the city. The first anti-Fascist mayor of Charlottenburg complained that 'Innumerable cases of rape occurred daily . . . It is difficult to grasp the full extent to which rape is practised.'[88] According to the Vatican representative in Berlin in October 1945, Monsignor G. B. Montini, women had hidden on the roofs for weeks in order to avoid rape but of those caught 'women from 10 to 70 and 75 years of age have been ravished'. The Soviet attitude to rape was dismissive, to say the least. The crime was not officially recognized and, if acknowledged at all, was blamed on 'bandits in Soviet uniform'. When questioned about the rapes the editor of the Soviet paper *Red Star* simply retorted: 'war is war, and what we did was nothing in comparison with what the Germans did in Russia.' When Milovan Djilas complained to Stalin about Red Army rape in Yugoslavia Stalin laughed it off, saying, 'Can't you understand it if a soldier who has crossed thousands of kilometres through blood and fire has fun with a woman or takes a trifle?'[89] When the German Communists in Moscow warned him about the profound political consequences of the rapes 'for German socialism' he retorted, 'I will not allow anyone to drag the reputation of the Red Army in the mud.'[90] But the women of Berlin would never forget their experiences in those first days of occupation – the scenes in places like Dahlem, where Russians 'stand in lines of dozens in front of lone women. In their eagerness, they don't even notice that they are dying, perhaps because they swallowed poison or from internal bleeding of the organs ... The women are herded together into rooms. Soldiers pry open their mouths and force them to drink.'[91] Erika Trackehnen wrote: 'The Russians come every night – Dear God I beg you, let me sleep and forget.'

By the end of April the Soviets had taken virtually the entire city. Siegfried Knappe recalled that by late April

we no longer had any chance of defending Berlin. The horrible, hopeless battles in the streets continued, but our divisions were little more than battalions, our morale was poor, and our ammunition was almost gone. Theoretically we had four divisions with which to defend the city, but in fact the divisions were at less than half strength, and that included many wounded. By including Hitler Youth and Volkssturm we may have had enough bodies to man four full divisions, but the Volkssturm was staffed by old men and the Hitler Youth composed of children ... Even if we'd had four fully staffed experienced, and rested divisions, we were still a corps fighting *two army groups!*[92]

As Soviet soldiers moved towards the government quarter from all directions Berlin became an unrecognizable maze of twisted metal, shattered buildings, piles of rubble and dead bodies. The Russians now used special combat teams consisting of a platoon of infantry, two tanks, sappers, flame throwers, anti-tank guns and field guns, including 203mm howitzers, to penetrate the heavily defended central areas. Heavy artillery was crammed into every available open space and directed towards the government quarter; rocket launchers were sometimes trundled to the upper floor of buildings and turned towards Unter den Linden and the Alexanderplatz. Tens of thousands of troops moved carefully through the buildings, often facing ambush. Zhukov described the valour of dozens of his men: Senior Lieutenant I. P. Ukraintsev of the 283rd Guards Regiment was commended because during the attack on a house 'hand to hand fighting broke out and he rushed at the enemy. The brave officer knifed nine Nazis to death. Following his example, Guards Sergeant Stepan Grobazai and his section killed several dozen more Nazis.'[93]

On 27 April the Russians finally encircled the city centre – the Zitadelle – which included the government quarter, the Reichstag and Defence headquarters and the Führerbunker. They faced formidable fighters from the Berlin Guard Battalion, including the Grossdeutschland Division which had crushed the July 1944 plot; a number of SS units – the Charlemagne Assault Battalion of French SS men and a detachment of the SS Walloon Division of French Belgians; the Freikorps Adolf Hitler, along with thousands of experienced SS men including 1,200 individuals from Hitler's personal bodyguard, an SS division under the command of SS-Brigade Führer Wilhelm Mohnke and more than 2,000 volunteers who had actually travelled to Berlin in order to fight the Russians. Goebbels also organized groups of Hitler Youth teenagers who genuinely believed it was their duty to die for the Führer and who would sometimes race into the path of oncoming tanks holding their Panzerfausts.

By the end of April the city had become the site of indescribable carnage. Dieter Borkowski, a sixteen-year-old Hitler Youth member now forced to fight in the Friedrichshain flak tower, wrote in his diary of 29 April:

> We could already hear the 'Hurrah's from the attacking Soviet troops in Kniprodestrasse. There were dead and wounded lying everywhere in the five stories of the Flak-tower, and an unpleasant sweet smell permeated the tower. We received the order to occupy the new front line in Höchstestrasse. The two Flak-towers now stand like islands in the sea for the Russians have long since forced their way past these fortresses . . . The provision of supplies and ammunition has become very bad.[94]

While the Soviets fought for every building and street an equally terrible battle was going on beneath the city. Thousands of people had moved into the subterranean world of tunnels and shelters under Berlin. The bunkers beneath the Chancellery had become something of an underground city, filled with government employees who no longer bothered to go home and the countless others who had taken refuge in the more exposed U-Bahn tunnels and mingled with troops taking refuge from the shelling. The Soviets followed them down into the maze of tunnels leading from the Anhalter Bahnhof, but when the SS realized what was happening they decided to flood them, indifferent to the number of civilians who might perish: the engineers were ordered to blow up the safety bulkhead control chamber on the Landwehr Canal. A young fighter from the 'Müncheberg' Panzer Division described the strange scenes before the flooding began, with people huddling on the platforms and in niches, sheltering from the fighting above: 'Shells hit the roof, cement crumbles from the ceiling. Smells of powder and smoke in the tunnels. S-Bahn hospital trains trundle slowly by.' The young soldier watched in horror as the water suddenly began to pour in:

> Shrieks, cries and curses. People are struggling around the ladders leading up the ventilation shafts to the street above. Gurgling water floods through the tunnels. The crowds are panicky, pushing through

the rising water, leaving children and wounded behind. People are being trampled underfoot, the water covering them. It rises a metre more, then slowly runs away. The panic lasts for hours. Many drowned. The whole time heavy fighting continues above ground.[95]

He was then moved to the Potsdamer Platz, where he was met by heavy Russian fire. 'Terrible sight at the station entrance, one flight of stairs down where a heavy shell has penetrated and people – soldiers, women and children are literally stuck to the walls.'[96]

The mangled dead lay everywhere and the wounded could no longer be treated. The city centre became a sea of mud and death. One witness remembered 'the howling and explosions of the Stalin Organs, the screaming of the wounded, the roaring of motors and the rattle of machine guns. Clouds of smoke, and the stench of chlorine and fire. Dead women in the street, killed while trying to get water. But also, here and there, women with Panzerfausts, Silesian girls thirsting for revenge.' Leo Welt remembered the night the Zoo was hit: 'The next morning alligators and snakes were crawling across the streets. Chimpanzees were hanging from the trees.'[97] The young diarist from the Müncheberg Panzer Division wrote of the last assaults at the Zoo aquarium:

> the streets are steaming. The smell of the dead is at times unbearable. Last night, one floor above us, some police officers and soldiers celebrated their farewell to life, in spite of the shelling. This morning, men and women were lying on the stairs in tight embrace and drunk. Through the shell holes in the streets one can look down into the subway tunnels. It looks as though the dead are lying down there several layers deep. Everyone in our command post is wounded more than once; General Mummert carries his right arm in a sling. We look like walking skeletons ... In the cellars, the shrieking of the wounded. No more anaesthetics. Every so often, women burst out of a cellar, their fists pressed over their ears because they cannot stand the screaming of the wounded.[98]

The centre of Berlin today is filled with reminders of those terrible weeks but none is so startling as the wall murals painted deep inside the Potsdamer Platz bunker which were found shortly after the wall was taken down. In June 1991 an area that once lay in East Germany's 'no man's land' was being cleared in preparation for a Pink Floyd concert when part of the bunker complex was discovered virtually intact from the last days of the war. It measured about 300 square metres and could have contained around thirty officers; when it was opened there were still boxes of ammunition, piles of weapons, including a rocket launcher, and crates of empty Bordeaux bottles lying around. The smell was unpleasant; filthy water and debris floated at knee height and the walls were covered in propaganda paintings which depicted victorious SS men protecting German farmers, women and children, rounding up surrendering British soldiers at Dover and standing proudly in shiny boots and helmets as German nuns (representing the old timid Germany) cower behind trees. Most of the murals were ringed with oak leaves and crowned with eagles – often used by the SS in their elaborate symbolism. The glorification of the Nazi ideal grimacing from these mouldering walls afforded an insight into the fanaticism of those men who, with only days to live, insisted on painting images of victory. Shortly after its discovery the bunker was sealed by large concrete slabs so that it should not become a neo-Nazi shrine.[99]

On 28 April Zhukov's troops finally broke through the German defences and into the Zitadelle, past the 'Red Rathaus' and Alexanderplatz and the Potsdamer Platz bunker in which the officers had painted their murals. Zhukov was now determined to carry out Stalin's order and raise a flag on the Reichstag by 1 May in the name of the Red Army. He knew that if he did not succeed his own life would be in danger. Ironically the Reichstag, which had remained an empty shell since the fire in 1933, had become the symbol of Soviet victory, chosen over the more significant Brandenburg Gate or even Hitler's Chancellery; the Soviets were unaware that it had stood empty during the Third Reich and had only been occupied by the SS in the final weeks of the war.

The struggle for the Reichstag was bitter. Chuikov's troops moved in from one side and fought a series of gruesome battles for surrounding German strongholds, including the nearby Moltke Bridge and the Ministry of the Interior. The German defenders were by now merciless both to their enemy and their own men. The Soviets could not turn against the Reichstag until they had cleared the Kroll Opera House, from which the Germans were covering the building. After another heavy battle it was taken on 30 April; the Russians now brought ninety heavy guns up to the front of the Reichstag to begin the final assault. The building was heavily fortified but the Soviet guns blasted large holes through the bricked-up windows and doors, allowing Red Army troops to rush in. The balconies, statues, columns and alcoves provided cover for the suicidal Germans and the fighting was fierce: according to Colonel-General Malinin 'the enemy resisted our advancing troops desperately, having turned every building, stairway, room, cellar into strong points and defensive positions. The fighting within the main building of the Reichstag repeatedly took the form of hand-to-hand combat.'[100] Soviet assault groups diverted German attention as a group of Communist Party and Komsomol members brought an enormous banner to the roof and placed it on the statue of Victory – a scene which was captured in one of the most famous photographs of the war, showing the hammer and sickle unfurled on top of the blazing building with a view of the shattered streets below.[101] The Soviets claimed that the flag was raised over the Reichstag just seventy minutes before the dawn of 1 May 1945. To the chagrin of Koniev and Rokossovsky it was Zhukov who had reached the symbolic building first and who would consequently be known as the victor of Berlin, but Zhukov's drastic push to carry out Stalin's order on time had cost many lives: 2,200 Soviet soldiers and 2,500 Germans died in the battle for the Reichstag building alone. This was one of the reasons why the Russians chose this as the site for the first Soviet war memorial in the city.

As the Soviets advanced deep into the Zitadelle the area around Hitler's bunker came under heavy fire. Siegfried Knappe made the journey between the bunker and the Zoo flak tower several times at the end of April. He described the city centre as a hell on earth:

> The acrid smell of smoke mingled with the stench of decomposing corpses. Dust from pulverized bricks and plaster rose over the city like a heavy fog. The streets, littered with rubble and pockmarked with huge craters, were deserted. I had to be careful not to get entangled in the streetcar wires dangling everywhere ... The streets were full of both debris and bodies although the bodies were hardly recognizable as such. The corpses of both soldiers and civilians who had been killed in the shelling and bombing were under debris and everything was covered with a grey-and-red powder from the destruction of the buildings. The stink of death was suffocating. We had no way to dispose of the bodies, or even to collect them, because we were under constant air and artillery bombardment and infantry fighting was now everywhere. The city smelled like a battlefield, which in fact it was, with the smell of the plaster and brick dust from disintegrating buildings, of burning wood, of burned gunpowder, of gasoline, and of decomposing corpses. Fortunately the nights were still cool, so the smell of death was still just bearable.[102]

By 28 April the Führerbunker was completely surrounded. The Russians had occupied Saarland Strasse and were almost at the Air Ministry. On the other side they were in the Tiergarten, only 150 metres away from the Führerbunker.

Hitler, by now completely mad, had continued to hold out for some miracle, ranting against his generals and blaming them for the military fiasco which now engulfed him. On the evening of 28 April news reached him which changed his mood: his 'true Heinrich' Himmler had secretly been negotiating

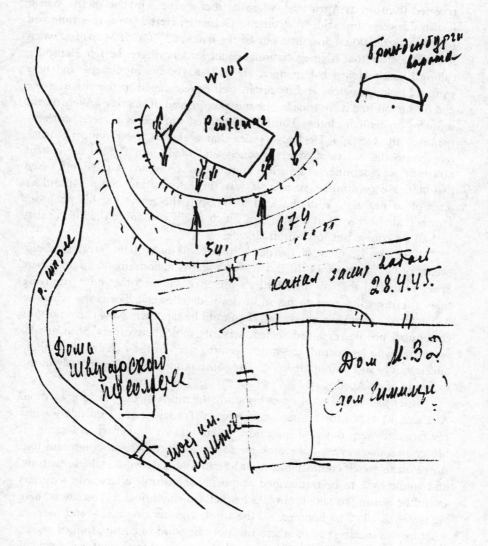

Sketched Plan for The Soviet Attack on The City Centre

with the west via Count Bernadotte of Sweden. Himmler had given up on Hitler and now secretly hoped to create a National Socialist government in Schleswig-Holstein from which he could negotiate with the Allies. He apparently believed he might even be instated by the Allies as the new German leader. His complete lack of understanding of the magnitude of his crimes revealed itself on 21 April 1945, when he met a representative of the World Jewish Congress and said: 'Welcome to Germany, Herr Masur. It is time you Jews and we National Socialists buried the hatchet.'[103] On 21 May 1945, when it became clear that his negotiations would lead nowhere, he left Flensburg calling himself Heinrich Hitzinger. He had shaved his moustache and now wore a black eye patch, and he might well have escaped in the chaos at the end of the war had he not made one mistake. Instead of wearing a Wehrmacht uniform or civilian clothes Himmler disguised himself as a mere sergeant-major of the Gestapo. He had no idea that even this lowly uniform struck terror into the hearts of other prisoners and made him eligible for instant arrest; he was identified at a British control post by Major Randell and taken prisoner. He committed suicide. It was the information about Himmler's attempt to negotiate with the west along with the news that his phantom armies had not moved in to save him which finally convinced the Führer that he had no course but to commit suicide.

Hitler clearly intended his death to become one of the great symbolic events of German history. In fact it was a seedy, melodramatic affair. Albert Speer remarked that by then Hitler's presence had become more annoying than awe-inspiring even to his most devoted followers: 'Formerly, when he had entered a room everybody had risen until he sat down. Now conversations continued, people remained seated, servants took their orders from guests, associates who had drunk too much went to sleep in their chairs, and others talked loudly and uninhibitedly.'[104] The painstaking process began early in the morning of 29 April 1945.

Hitler had been brooding in his study for much of the previous evening. At 2 a.m. he called for his personal secretary Traudl Junge. 'I quickly washed my face and went down to his study ... He was very quiet when I came in, but courteous as ever ... he took me to the large conference room and told me to make myself comfortable, what he had to dictate would take some time, and would have to be transcribed as quickly as possible afterwards. Couriers would be waiting to take it out.' As he dictated she thought: 'You know, here we were ... all of us doomed ... the whole country doomed – and here, in what he was dictating to me there was not one word of compassion or regret, only awful, awful anger.'[105] This last will and personal testament was a ridiculous document. Hitler believed that Nazism would somehow carry on after his death and he even named a cabinet with Admiral Dönitz as President and head of the armed forces, Goebbels as Chancellor and the ever faithful Bormann as head of the party; Himmler and Göring were expelled for having had treasonous contact with the enemy. He then declared that the war had been justified, that he had been the victim of foreign treachery, that his officers had been disloyal, and that above all Germans should continue to adhere to 'scrupulous observance of the laws of race and to merciless opposition to the universal poisoner of all peoples, international Jewry'. He had already sorted out his papers, having them flown out to Munich in ten separate planes (one crashed on the way, fuelling a number of myths including that of the infamous 'Hitler diaries'), but the testament was taken by four separate couriers in order to preserve it for posterity. Hitler then surprised his staff by announcing that he intended to marry Eva Braun, whom he had met in a Munich shop run by the Nazi photographer Heinrich Hoffmann fifteen years earlier. The table in his private quarters was set with a silver service and champagne glasses; Goebbels found a qualified member of the Volkssturm to conduct the ceremony and the small entourage gathered in his private rooms. Both partners swore that they were of pure Aryan descent and the nervous bride began to sign her maiden name on the certificate, crossing it out and replacing it with 'Hitler'. Goebbels and Bormann acted as witnesses. 'She will go to her death with me at her own wishes, as my wife,' Hitler wrote in his testament. 'This will compensate us for what we both lost through my work in the service of my people.' They would be married for less than thirty-one hours.

On 30 April Hitler began to prepare for his own death. As the bunker shook from the Soviet shelling he held a pathetic lunch, during which he mumbled about dog breeding, insisted that French lipstick was made from grease from the Paris sewers, and otherwise sat there 'apathetic and distractedly brooding, indifferent to everything going on around him'. Traudl Junge remembered that 'Nobody said anything. We couldn't very well toast their future.'[106] Finally Eva and Adolf Hitler went to his private quarters. According to Rochus Misch the Führerbunker had been cleared of most people, leaving 'me at my switchboard, Günsche standing guard in front of Hitler's living room, and two orderlies'. Amazingly, a raucous party was going on above them in the canteen of the ruined Chancellery; Hitler sent one of the orderlies to get Misch to tell them to be quiet: 'I rang and rang, but there was no answer; they probably couldn't even hear the phone.'[107] At one point a hysterical Magda Goebbels pushed past the guards and broke into Hitler's room; he ordered her out but she, Axmann, Linge, Kempka, Bormann, Goebbels and Burgdorf gathered near the door and waited. At 15.30 they heard a shot. Goebbels, Axmann, Linge and Günsche rushed in and found Hitler lying on his now blood-stained sofa. Heinz Linge recalled that

Hitler was sitting on the left of the sofa with his face bent slightly forward and hanging down to the right. With the 7.65mm he had shot himself in the right temple. The blood had run down on to the carpet and from this pool of blood a splash had got on to the sofa. Eva Braun was sitting on his right. She had drawn both her legs up on to the sofa and was sitting there with cramped lips so that it immediately became clear to us that she had taken cyanide.[108]

Hitler had taken poison and then shot himself, although the Soviets would later claim that he had not used the gun, presumably because poison was seen to be a less honourable form of suicide. Hitler had written in his will that he and his wife wanted 'our bodies burned immediately in the place where I have performed the greater part of my daily work during the course of my twelve years' service to my people'. Linge and the rest in the bunker carried out his wishes. 'I took Hitler by the neck. Behind me were two other officers of his bodyguard so we took Hitler's body and proceeded with it into the park.' The bodies were brought into the garden, wrapped in blankets and laid in a trench. Tins of petrol were poured over them and after some difficulty they were set alight with a flaming rag. The bodies were not completely destroyed and a second attempt to burn them was made some hours later. The charred remains were finally buried in a shallow pit close to the unfinished watch tower, where they were later discovered by the Soviets. Goebbels was now the Chancellor of Germany.

Hitler's faithful Propaganda Minister was overwhelmed by his new sense of power and genuinely believed that he could still guide the nation to victory. His plan was to make peace and to obtain Soviet recognition of the new government. He sent General Krebs, ex-military attaché in Moscow, to make the treacherous journey through the shelling to General Chuikov's command post in a house near Tempelhof Airport. Krebs reached the small suburban apartment house on 1 May. The Russian was not certain what to do with him and asked him to state his business. Krebs began with the extraordinary news that Hitler was dead. Chuikov was astounded but calmly answered: 'We know that!' Krebs tried to impress the Soviets by telling them in detail the events of the preceding few hours. They learned a great deal; they had not, for example, known about Hitler's relationship with Eva Braun, nor even that Hitler was living in a subterranean bunker. Chuikov quickly contacted Zhukov, who in turn contacted Stalin with the news, but Stalin retorted that the Soviets would accept nothing less than unconditional surrender. Krebs had no authority to grant this and struggled back through shelling and sniper fire to inform Goebbels that the Russians had refused his request. Finally, even

Goebbels realized that there was no hope. He would also have to commit suicide or face capture.

Goebbels's suicide was particularly gruesome: his wife and six young children died with him. Magda went to the children's crowded room in the Vorbunker with Dr Stumpfegger in the late afternoon and fed them hot chocolate laced with a drug to make them drowsy. When they were asleep she and the doctor opened their mouths and pushed cyanide capsules down their throats. When the Russians recovered the bodies they found bruises around the neck of the eldest daughter, Helga, implying that some force had been needed to poison her. Goebbels and Magda then walked the long flight of steps to the Chancellery garden so that nobody would have to carry the bodies up; Goebbels shot his wife as she took poison and then crunched on a glass capsule as he shot himself in the head. A tin of petrol was poured over them and their bodies set alight, but again the corpses did not burn. Graphic Soviet photographs captured the evidence of Goebbels's clearly recognizable corpse with its small head, the crow-like left hand slightly raised, the metal brace still holding his deformed leg in place. The bodies were left lying amidst the shelling and explosions raining down on the garden.

With Hitler and Goebbels dead the remaining dignitaries in the bunker busied themselves with plans for escape. All streets leading to the Chancellery were now blocked by the Soviets and some, like General Krebs and General Burgdorf, committed suicide in the face of what they considered hopeless odds. Dozens of others, including Bormann, Mohnke and Axmann, made a run for it. Despite the numerous post-war 'sightings' of Bormann in South America it is almost certain that he and Stumpfegger died in the Invalidenstrasse on the night of their escape. When one of many unmarked graves was discovered at the side of the road in 1965 a series of coincidences led to a positive check against Bormann's dental records.[109] Many others managed to escape dressed as civilians or Volkssturm members.

By 1 May all Berlin knew that Hitler was dead. Radio Hamburg announced that he had 'died for Germany in his command post in the Reich Chancellery this afternoon, fighting to his last breath against Bolshevism'. It was a lie, but it encouraged some extremists to fight on. Berlin streets remained highly dangerous; there was no chain of command, the murder squads were still carrying out summary executions and hapless civilians were being rounded up to fight. Although the Russians were celebrating May Day with much drinking and raping, Stalin called for a renewed offensive that afternoon and heavy fighting continued around the Zoo flak tower and the Chancellery. General Weidling, disgusted at the continuing loss of life, decided to take the initiative and surrender the city of Berlin to the Soviets. On the afternoon of 1 May he transmitted a radio message to Russian headquarters: 'Hello! Hello!

This is the LVI German Panzerkorps. We ask you to cease fire. At 0500 hours Berlin time we are sending envoys to parley at the Potsdamer Bridge. The recognition sign is a white square with a red light. We await your reply.'

Chuikov allowed a temporary ceasefire and met the military representative. On 2 May General Weidling crossed the Landwehr Canal via a hastily erected suspension bridge and went to Chuikov's headquarters, where he signed the surrender of Berlin. It was to take effect at 1300 hours that day, although some fanatics continued the fight into the evening. By the night of 2 May the war in Berlin was over. The German capital had fallen and, as Churchill had predicted, it would be only a matter of days before the rest of Germany followed. The inhabitants of the shattered city continued to cower in their cellars for fear of the Soviet 'celebrations' as drunken and revelling soldiers went on the rampage in the city along with freed prisoners of war and slave labourers keen to exact revenge on the population which had subjugated them for so long. Berlin became a sea of crime, violence, rape and murder which only eased a week later with the general surrender of Germany.

The cost of the Battle of Berlin had been very high: 304,000 Soviets were killed or wounded in the fighting. If one includes the hundreds of thousands of Germans who were captured defending Berlin and who never returned from the Gulag, German military losses numbered over 1 million men. An estimated 100,000 civilians were killed by shelling and by summary execution.

On 7 May Generaloberst Alfred Jodl signed an act of surrender for Germany at 1245 hours in Eisenhower's war room at Reims in front of representatives of the French, British, American and Soviet forces. Eisenhower then sent a cable to the British and American Chiefs of Staff which read: 'The mission of the Allied force was fulfilled at 0245, local time, May 7, 1945.'[110] Stalin vigorously refused to accept this surrender as genuine, arguing that it had taken place in a French town, on a document other than the one agreed between the Allies, and that the Soviet representative General Susloparov had not been authorized to sign anything – indeed the unfortunate general was recalled to Moscow, where Stalin had him killed for disgracing the Soviet Union. The next day the Allies were forced to fly their representatives to Berlin for a repeat of the ceremony, which was held at the Russian military headquarters at Karlshorst. Generalfeldmarschall Wilhelm Keitel, head of the army, Generaloberst Stumpff of the Luftwaffe and Generaladmiral von Friedeburg of the navy were flown into Tempelhof Airport under guard and were brought to the imposing brick building – one of the few in the area left unscathed by the bombing. The Germans were marched in under the gaze of

Marshal Zhukov, Eisenhower's representative Sir Arthur Tedder, General Carl Spaatz of the US Strategic Air Force in Europe, and General de Lattre de Tassigny of the First French Army. According to Marshal Zhukov the Germans were bitter:

> I asked the German delegation to come over to this table and sign the instrument of German unconditional surrender. Keitel quickly rose, shooting a malign glance at us. Then he lowered his gaze . . . and walked unsteadily to our table. His face was covered with red blotches . . . Putting his monocle in place Keitel sat down on the edge of the chair . . . His hand was shaking slightly.[111]

It was 2243 hours Berlin time. Keitel signed the paper, and the German delegation was escorted into captivity. The Second World War in Europe ended in the place from which it had started, and from which it had been directed for five murderous years. As the Allies celebrated at a lavish party that evening the people of Berlin faced an uncertain future in the ruins of their former capital. Few realized that they were about to enter into a new kind of conflict: the Cold War.

XIV

The Berlin Crisis and the Cold War

The earth endures, and so does Life.

(Faust, Part I)

THE SECOND WORLD WAR ENDED in May 1945, but for the peoples of central Europe the misery was far from over. The continent had been thrown into economic, social and political turmoil; hunger was widespread and millions of refugees stumbled hopelessly around its broken cities. In those early months of peace Berlin was seen by the world as the very symbol of Nazi terror, a pariah which had forfeited its rights as a capital city in the civilized world: it was to be occupied and administered jointly by the war-time Allies. But the world was changing fast. Berlin was not merely the former capital of Hitler's Reich; it was also emerging as a vital pawn in a tense international struggle for post-war Europe. The ruined city would soon lie at the centre of a new conflict.

It is ironic that Berlin should have been so quickly transformed from the symbol of Nazi terror into a coveted prize, but the conditions which led to this had been put into place long before the end of the war. Had the western leaders not given so much away at the war-time conferences, had they taken Berlin in early 1945, post-war history would have been quite different for those millions who became trapped under Soviet control. Stalin would still have tried to extend his power as far west as possible but he might not have been quite so successful; indeed we might even have spoken of the 'Warsaw airlift' or the 'Prague Wall'. Instead, the Red Army was permitted to enter Berlin first and Stalin quickly began to treat it as a part of the Soviet empire. Yalta and Potsdam put the international seal of approval on a carving-up of Europe and of Berlin which, given the mutually exclusive aims of the Soviet Union and the west, virtually guaranteed an eventual conflict between the two blocs.[1] The Soviets had Berlin, and their occupation marked one of the most harrowing periods in the history of the city.

As the Red Army moved through the streets in the final days of the war Hitler's brittle totalitarian structure collapsed. On 2 May 1945 General Weidling ordered the capitulation of all German troops; 70,000 were taken as prisoners of war. The Soviets took over the city.[2]

There is something profoundly shocking to the western imagination about the razing of a great city, and Berlin was set to take its place alongside Rome, Carthage and Troy in the annals of history. Compared to cities conquered by the Nazis – blockaded Stalingrad, whose inhabitants had been reduced to cannibalism during the siege, or poor battered Warsaw, which lost over 80 per cent of its buildings – Berlin had had a relatively 'good war' until the final year of bombing and street fighting. But the suffering was set to increase after capitulation.

There can be few places as haunting as a vast city on the day of its surrender. Fires burn, gasoline still pours from abandoned equipment, dead soldiers lie frozen where they fell. A number of Soviet testimonies were written about the fall of Berlin but one of the most evocative was by Konstantin Simonov, the Soviet diplomat and war correspondent who struggled through the smoking wreckage on the day after capitulation.[3] The city looked as it had in the throes of battle. Many of the U-Bahn tunnels had been split open by bombs, and far down in the gloom he could see layers of twisted and blood-soaked bodies, 'some on their backs, others with their faces to the ground'. He was amazed to find a number of SS women scattered amongst the men – although not uncommon in Russia, it was unusual in Germany to use women in combat. Simonov climbed over the Zoo wall and came across the pathetic sight of an emaciated elephant wandering around its compound. An old warden emerged and told him that although he had nursed it through the war the beast was starving; Simonov was touched that he asked for food not for himself, but for his animals. The warden took Simonov to the cages of what had been the largest chimpanzee and gorilla in Europe. Two dead SS men lay inside; a third corpse was propped against a pillar with a machine gun still resting on his knees. The warden broke down when he saw his animals lying in huge black pools of blood which had spread across the cement floor, the sight of the dead animals clearly affecting him more than that of the more commonplace dead men. A little further on Simonov found a group of Soviet soldiers standing at the edge of the monkey pit. 'The soldiers looked very tired,' he wrote. 'They smelled of smoke, were caked with dirt.' One curious Russian climbed into the pit to play with the animal and was bitten, and Simonov feared that the soldier would instinctively lash out and kill it. Instead the weary man clambered slowly out of the pit, found a spot near a group of dead Germans, curled up, and went to sleep.[4]

Next to the Zoo was the massive bunker which had held out until capitulation. The vast corridors and cement rooms were filled with men and women who had clearly committed suicide after an orgy of drinking and sex on the

last night of the war. Simonov made his way to the second floor, shining his
flashlight into the dark cubicles to reveal macabre scenes of death. At the end
he found a dead SS general lying on a bed wearing a clean shirt, open jacket
and boots and staring straight ahead with open eyes. He was about forty-five
years old, had short hair and 'a pleasant, quiet face'. His left arm rested on
the shoulders of a young woman, who lay with closed eyes between him and
the wall. Simonov noticed that she looked 'pretty in her short sleeved white
blouse and skirt'. The two had committed suicide together; the general still
held a half empty bottle of champagne between his legs.

Later that day Simonov made his way through the wrecked streets to the
Chancellery, where the search was still in progress for Hitler's body. Goebbels's
charred remains and those of his wife and children had already been taken to
Plötzensee, but Hitler's body still eluded them.[5] On 5 May the soldiers Deryabin
and Tsybochin recovered two badly burned corpses thought to be Hitler's and
Eva Braun's; they were put in two wooden crates and taken, together with the
bodies of two dogs, to the medical centre at the Shock Army headquarters in
the Berlin suburb of Buch. The building is now an anonymous clinic and few
of its patients know that it was there that the chief anatomical pathologist of
the Red Army, Professor Krayevski, performed the autopsy on Hitler on 8
May. Although Hitler's skull had caved in under the impact of his self-inflicted
bullet wound it was at this time that the Soviets decided to spread the myth
that Hitler had taken poison.[6]

As the hunt for bodies continued in the garden Simonov was able to visit
some of the most important Nazi buildings. The Chancellery had been bombed
but a number of the rooms were still recognizable, including the cavernous
main reception room and Hitler's office. The floors were strewn with debris,
papers, office equipment and books containing Hitler's *ex libris*. Simonov
gathered up a number of photographs, one of which showed a smiling Hitler
surrounded by adoring young girls and another captioned: 'Fight with Spar-
takus, Munich. 1919.' In another room he found boxes filled with thousands
of decorations, ranging from iron crosses to medals for fire-fighting. The
bodies of dead SS men and unexploded bombs still littered the garden but
the area was already becoming a favourite spot for Soviet souvenir hunters.[7]
Jim O'Donnell of *Newsweek* would later write that

the victorious Russian soldiers had ransacked the place. There was
nothing much of any intrinsic value left, no full liquor bottles, no
usable weapons, no blankets or articles of clothing, no dress-daggers,
radios or cameras. Everywhere the floors, corridors, and duckboards
were littered with glass shards, bottles, rusty picture frames, German
Army cheesecake photos, warped gramophone records, scattered sheet

music, dented air raid warden helmets, empty first-aid kits, bloodied bandages, old knapsacks, tin cans, ammunition drums, empty pistol clips, scattered playing cards, film magazines, cigar and cigarette butts, slimy condoms.

Nietzsche once said: 'He who fights with monsters might take care lest he thereby become a monster.' By 1945 the Soviet 'liberators' had sunk to depths reached only by the Nazis before them. For two months Berlin was completely surrounded, cut off from the rest of the world and at the mercy of the rapacious victors. Red Army soldiers were left alone to carry on raping, looting and murdering in an indescribable orgy of violence. When they were later asked about their behaviour they would shrug their shoulders and say, 'it was retribution'. Tragically, the retribution did not fall on the party bosses, the concentration camp guards, the SS functionaries or even the minor officials. In Berlin, it was saved primarily for the women.

The civilian population had already suffered the wrath of the Red Army as they battled through the streets, but the violence did not cease with victory. The terror unleashed by Soviet soldiers hastened a complete breakdown of the shaky framework of civilization. The nervous energy and local camaraderie which had sustained neighbours and the 'cellar tribes' during the bombing raids vanished in a vicious battle for survival. Theo Findahl watched as old friends and neighbours turned against one another: 'Everyone plunders every-one else,' he wrote. 'War is robbery.' Nothing was sacred in the scramble for food, shelter and protection.[8]

In his post-war novel *Die Stadt hinter dem Strom* Hermann Kasack describes a ghostly city of the dead which lies across a railway bridge in some far-off part of Germany and whose inhabitants move like spirits amongst the ruins. He might have been describing Berlin. One and a half years of heavy bombing and weeks of Soviet shelling had left 884 square kilometres a vast ruin. Berlin contained one-seventh of all the rubble in Germany. The city centre was almost totally destroyed – a ghostly sculpture of shards of buildings – burning wood, twisted metal and broken glass. The roads, canals and sewers were clogged with debris. Bodies lay everywhere and thousands of corpses had been left to rot under the immense piles of brick and stone. The stench was unbearable and one witness wrote: 'All Berlin stinks to high heaven. Wherever one looks there are heaps of rubbish covered with flies – flies and more flies, black, blue and fat.'[9] Raw sewage flowed in streets which now crawled with rats. Dysentery alone killed 65 per cent of Berlin's newborns in 1945, while typhoid and diphtheria raged through the filthy city. Wolfgang Leonhard, who had spent the war in exile in Moscow, was horrified when he saw Berlin for the first time in May 1945:

Slowly our train wound its way through Friedrichsfelde towards Lichtenberg. It was an infernal picture. Fire, rubble, ghostly starving people
in rags. Lost German soldiers who no longer knew what was happening. Red Army soldiers, singing, celebrating and often drunk. Long
lines of people patiently waiting in front of water pumps in order to
fill small containers. All looked terribly tired, hungry, exhausted and
decrepit.[10]

Walter Ulbricht returned on 17 May 1945 and noted that the smoke was so
thick that 'we could barely find our way through the rubble'. Willy Brandt
remembered Berlin as

Craters, caves, mountains of rubble, debris-covered fields, ruins that
hardly allowed one to imagine that they had once been houses, cables
and water pipes projecting from the ground like the mangled bowels
of antediluvian monsters, no fuel, no light, every little garden a graveyard and, above all, like an immoveable cloud, the stink of putrefac-
tion. In this no man's land lived human beings.[11]

The infrastructure of the once bustling city had been reduced to a primitive
state. There was no electricity, three out of four fire stations were out of action,
the water mains had been ruptured in over 3,000 places, which meant that
there was no safe drinking water, and there was no fuel with which to boil
the sludge from the canals. Many bridges had been destroyed, radio and postal
services had ceased, and in a city which had at one time prided itself on its
sophisticated transportation network fewer than forty buses, 100 subway cars
and a handful of trams remained, none of which worked. Most roads were
impassable although some people managed to move from one area to another
by pushing small rafts along the flooded U-Bahn tunnels. Berliners were largely
ignorant of what was happening in the rest of the world: one wrote that 'we
exist without newspapers, without any clear idea of the time, live by the sun
like flowers'.[12] Most trees in the city had been cut down for fuel and Berliners
scratched over the debris looking for bits of wood or rubbish to burn; the
anonymous woman diarist wrote: 'I am gradually acquiring a real sharp eye
for wood, hardly a twig escapes me now. Every day I find new, uncombed
spots in cellars, ruins, and deserted barracks.'[13] The Russians posted bulletins
all over the city announcing the unconditional surrender, the armistice and
the first orders governing the city but for many these events occurred in a
kind of haze: 'I lived and felt like an animal,' the diarist remembered. 'I hid
from the men, I tried to keep warm, and I searched for food – that was all.'[14]

Food, already scarce by the end of the war, became desperately short. Half
the pre-war Berlin population had been killed, imprisoned, or had fled, but

even so over 2 million Berliners, mainly women and children, lived in the wreckage; most were starving.[15] The Soviets forbade barter for food but every day hundreds of desperate people went on 'hamster trips' to the countryside armed with rucksacks, bags and suitcases filled with jewellery, household items and anything of value which they might trade for a few potatoes or some bottled preserves. These long and difficult journeys were often made in vain as the Soviets seized the goods on the return trip. Zhukov was right when he announced that Berlin was to undergo the 'severest occupation'.[16]

The Soviets had plans for the city. The war-ravaged Russians desperately needed hard currency and industrial goods with which to rebuild their shattered country, and they set out to strip Berlin before the western Allies could move into their zones. The city was booty, a conquered territory which by virtue of Soviet blood spilled there was 'Russian', and over which they now felt they had a moral right irrespective of Allied agreements at Tehran and Yalta. The Soviets changed the Berlin clocks to Russian time, put up Russian street signs and erected notices calling Berliners to SALUTE THE GLORIOUS RED ARMY, WHICH BY ITS BRAVERY AND SKILL HAS FREED EUROPE FROM THE FASCIST TERROR. There was no mention of the contribution made by the west; Berlin had become an extension of the Soviet Union.[17]

The population was seen as a source of slave labour and people were immediately put to work dismantling their own city. In the absence of radio or newspapers the Soviets sent town criers through the streets to call all people between the ages of fifteen and fifty-five to report for duty. They had no choice but to obey. Anneliese Boehnke remembered clawing around the piles of debris, moving barricades with her bare hands, and being rewarded for hours of work with a bowl of watery cabbage soup. Another Berlin woman remembered her first day as a rubble lady:

> Armed with bucket and dustpan I started out to work in the grey, drizzly early morning. While still on my way it began to pour. I could feel my knitted dress soaking up the water. It rained and rained. Nevertheless, we kept shovelling and filling bucket after bucket with rubble to prevent the chain of hands from being interrupted. The next day ... we worked hard; there were even two men shovelling with us – though they worked only when they felt the supervisor's eye on them.[18]

By 13 May the first bus route was cleared. The first U-Bahn moved on 14 May, and by 1 June there were 115 Soviet-run cars on the freshly cleared main roads. The airfields at Tempelhof, Berlin's civilian airport, Schönefeld and Dalgow were quickly repaired for use by the Sixteenth Air Army combat squadrons, which formed the Soviet Air Force of Occupation.

As the transport system improved gangs of Soviet special agents or 'Trophy Brigades' were sent to scour the city for money, gold, art, documents and anything else of value. The most obvious targets were banks and loan houses and there is no way of accounting for all the gold, currency, bonds, bullion, gems and other items seized from Berlin in 1945, not least because some of it had been stolen from others by the Nazis. The contents of the treasury, the Reichsbank and of safes, strong rooms, deposit boxes and caches all over the city were emptied into large sacks and flown to Moscow. The Trophy Brigades also searched everywhere from bunkers to bell towers in the quest for valuables. Thanks to Hitler the takings were rich indeed.

Hitler had expressly forbidden the removal of art treasures from Berlin; to suggest such a thing was 'defeatist' and tantamount to treason. It was only on 8 March 1945 – after the Soviets had reached the Oder – that he permitted a fraction of Berlin's possessions to be removed to the Kaiseroda-Merkers salt mine in Thuringia. The mines were occupied by the Americans in 1945; 202 of Germany's finest paintings were taken to Washington, although they were returned to Germany in 1948.[19] But the overwhelming majority of objects were still in Berlin when it fell to the Soviets. The stage was set for plunder on a monumental scale.

After the war it was assumed that a great many treasures which had gone missing in the last days of the war had been burned or destroyed or looted and melted down.[20] Great myths grew up around some of these, like the great room with walls of amber which had disappeared from Königsberg at the end of the war. Another of these 'lost' items was the gold of King Priam – the treasure of Troy - which had been excavated by the German archaeologist Heinrich von Schliemann in 1872. Imagine my surprise when on a visit to Moscow in the 1990s I heard that the art historians Konstantin Akinsha and Gregori Kozlov had 'discovered' the treasure in the basement of the Pushkin Museum. In 1996 I returned to see the breathtaking collection of fabulous intricate diadems with their cascades of gold, polished ceremonial axe heads carved from semi-precious stone, and magnificent solid gold vessels. At the same time another cache of paintings, including a Cranach and an El Greco, had also been 'discovered' and were exhibited under the disingenuous title 'Twice Saved'. Although the displays left one grateful that such beauty had not been destroyed they were a tantalizing hint of the treasures which were taken from the Soviet-occupied countries at the end of the war, and which still lie hidden in Russia.[21]

The order to remove Germany's art treasures came directly from Stalin. He had several motives: first he saw all German possessions as 'reparations' for everything stolen or destroyed by the Germans on their march eastwards. He also wanted to create his own 'Super Museum' in Moscow. His leading art expert M. Khrapchenko was so delighted by the quality of treasures coming out of Germany that when Raphael's *Sistine Madonna* was put in front of him he declared that the Pushkin could now become one of the world's great museums.[22] Many institutions, including the Academy of Sciences, sent out special orders for the seizure of particular works, not least for important artefacts which had themselves been stolen by the Germans; these included the priceless Scythian treasure from Kherson, which the Nazis had hidden in Schwerin, and the magnificent collection from the Novgorod Museum, which they had stored in the Prussian Secret Archives. But the Soviets did not stop at recapturing their own property. Within days the Trophy Brigades had found the cache of over 450 paintings and sculptures in the gigantic anti-aircraft bunker at Friedrichshain, works which had been stored there from two of Berlin's great museums, the Gemäldegalerie and the Nationalgalerie.[23] The Russians took the lot. The works included three Caravaggios, altarpieces by Fra Bartolommeo and Andrea del Sarto, eight works by Peter Paul Rubens, four paintings by Anthony van Dyck and many others. At the same time over 3,000 paintings from state-owned palaces and 150 works from the Märkisches Museum were either stolen or destroyed; nearly 200 paintings were stolen from the Schlösserverwaltung (Palace Administration) and are currently hidden from view in the basement of the Hermitage in St Petersburg.[24] Thousands of other paintings which the Nazis had put into storage – some in mines in southern Saxony – were also flown to the USSR. There was also a comprehensive looting of objects which had themselves been stolen by the Nazis, including works belonging to private Jewish collectors and to the museums of Nazi-occupied countries. Some of the German paintings were returned to East Germany in 1958, and some have trickled on to the international art markets over the years but the vast majority remain hidden from view.[25] Over 134,000 catalogued works and countless other pieces are still hidden in the vaults and cellars in St Petersburg and Moscow.

The Russians did not stop at works of art; they also set about removing priceless documents, manuscripts and archives from Berlin. Throughout 1945 the Education Department of the Soviet Military Administration (known as SVAG in Russian and SMAD in German) under the auspices of the Council of People's Commissars (Sovnarkom) oversaw the removal of untold numbers of boxcars filled with millions of documents, including the contents of the Prussian State Archives, the Prussian Secret Archives and hundreds of thousands of Nazi documents, ranging from SS files to myriad technical, scientific and medical papers. Nobody knows how much was taken; the information on the German rocket industry alone was removed on a train of thirty cars.[26] Books were also highly prized and officials from the Lenin Library had already moved into Berlin in June 1945 to oversee the shipment; Vladimir Semenov personally took documents and books for the library of the Ministry of Foreign Affairs. The enormous task of packing and shipping was overseen by the Education Department of SMAD but it was so overwhelming that more people had to be brought in from Moscow in December 1945. The number of volumes stolen is staggering. The contents of twenty-five libraries were seized and it is estimated that 1 million volumes were taken by the special SMAD sorting group known as the 'A-Z factory', 1 million by Rudomino from Sovnarkom, 1 million by the Academy of Sciences, 1 million by other government groups, 2 million by SMAD, and around 1 million by a variety of specialists, including representatives from medical and scientific libraries. Berlin lost around 7 million volumes in all.[27]

The official looting was carried out on a grand scale but as in the western zones there was also small-scale theft by officers and men. Many shipped furs, jewels and less valuable works of art back to Russia, and even Zhukov managed to furnish a number of large Moscow flats with furniture, carpets, paintings and other items stolen from Berlin.[28] The Soviets left some artefacts for the reconstruction of the Goethe Museum in Weimar and a collection of musical instruments which had been stored in the basement of the Reichsbank and which were used to create a Bach museum, but they left little else.[29] The end result was disastrous for Berlin; the city has never recovered from the looting of so much of its heritage.[30]

As the cultural Trophy Brigades went to work on the museums and libraries of the city others moved to capture German scientists and laboratories; still others set about dismantling German factories. The material wealth removed from Berlin during the four and a half years of Soviet occupation was immense but the appetite was particularly voracious during the first phase (from April to August 1945) after the failure to reach a firm agreement on reparations at Potsdam. Soviet ministries targeted specific factories and sent in their own dismantling teams but there were no guidelines and SMAD did little but organize transport and labour. German civilians were sent to work stripping the factories, breaking them up and putting the pieces on rail cars ready for the journey east. Of 17,024 major industrial concerns in the Soviet zone 4,339 had been dismantled and transported by the autumn of 1945, including the entire capacity of Berlin's electricity giants Siemens, Borsig, AEG and Osram. Eighty per cent of machine-tool productive capacity and 60 per cent of light and specialized industrial production was removed, along with hundreds of railway cars and tracks.[31] The seizure of property caused great resentment amongst workers: they could see that it was being dismantled in such a way that it could in all probability never be reassembled. In some instances factory workers and managers were forced to sign 'voluntary' transfer papers and were sent east with the piles of equipment, in effect exiled to lives as virtual prisoners in new Soviet industrial towns. In a great number of cases, however, the Soviets could not reassemble the factories and piles of machine parts were left to rust; they could be seen lying by railway sidings well into the 1950s.

The Soviet dismantling crews were chronically short of labour and began to round up people off the streets and put them to work; in one case Major Orlow of the Ninth Trophy Brigade surrounded a football stadium and ordered all those at the game to join a dismantling crew. The workers were often badly treated and even Soviet reports expressed concern about the whipping and maltreatment.[32] Even German Communists noted that the Russian 'liberators' seemed to take particular pleasure in humiliating Germans, often reminding them that the war had proved that Russia was the 'superior' civilization. For their part the Soviets found the Germans difficult to work with and frequently reported that they were 'dirty, disorganized, and lazy' and that they 'showed no initiative and relied on the Soviets to take care of them'.[33] Colonel-General I. I. Fediunsky called the Germans 'inefficient' and insisted that they 'stop sitting on their hands' or 'whining about their shortfalls'. At the same time the Soviets issued a flood of contradictory orders, making workers' lives miserable by 'dogging their every move and complaining about every misstep'; if Germans did not fulfil demands they faced 'anger, disdain, and derision from their Soviet bosses'. When railway officials dared to suggest that the hungry Germans might work harder if they were given better rations Major-General P. A. Kvashin, chief of SMAD's Transportation Administration, 'exploded, claiming that the problem was that they were lazy, inefficient, and indifferent, not poorly fed . . . the Germans took no initiative and left everything to Soviet officers'.[34] Another problem was confusion over the chain of command as 'just about every Soviet officer who was in the position to do so acted like a commandant, ordering Germans about under the assumption that Soviet ways were inherently better and that the Germans were always trying to shirk work and find excuses for why they could not deliver goods and services on time'. It was particularly difficult for German Communists loyal to Moscow to accept Soviet abuses such as confiscating grain earmarked for German workers and using it to make vodka for their troops.

Much of the dismantling of Berlin was done by the women of the city. Many who had started by clearing rubble were now rounded up and sent to dismantle factories; one recalled: 'Suddenly at about ten o'clock we heard a shout. A Russian voice: "Woman, come! Woman, come!" – words only too familiar to us. In an instant the women had scattered in all directions. They crept into doorways, cowered behind tubs and hills of rubble.' The women were not attacked but were taken to work in the grounds of a tool factory. 'German men were already loading the gigantic parts of a power press on to trucks while more men were unscrewing and dismantling the machines, lubricating them and dragging them away ... Outside on the factory track stood a long line of trucks, some of them already loaded high with machinery.' The women were ordered to collect everything made of brass or 'bright metal' and carry it in crates to one of the trucks. After working late into the evening they were given a kilo of bread and some sticky sweet green syrup and ordered to return the next day. The work was physically hard: one woman who had been washing filthy rags without soap was then made to move zinc bars and remembered the searing pain of the cold metal against her raw hands; others were forced to lift machine parts and equipment that was far too heavy for them.[35] This went on without respite for weeks on end and many of the women collapsed from malnutrition and exhaustion. Berliners were by now utterly dependent on Soviet supplies for their survival. A meagre rationing system was set up under Communist People's Committees and on 24 June all workers were issued with a 'Labour Book' – a ration and ID card which graded people according to their ability to work, their health and their age. The word 'unemployment' was officially banned.[36]

Throughout the months following capitulation Soviet soldiers continued to run riot and commanders were plagued by problems of discipline. Incidents ranged from armed robberies to desertion, from looting to drunkenness, which sometimes led to more serious incidents like accidental shootings and drownings; in 1946 alone there were 150 serious automobile accidents in the Soviet zone and 284 soldiers were killed or wounded in brawls. SMAD had to ban soldiers from swimming in the Berlin lakes because a number drowned after getting drunk.[37] Discipline often broke down again when new groups of soldiers moved into Berlin for occupation duty or shifted from summer camps to winter barracks as each new group was keen to experience the famous pleasures of Berlin. Once again, the women were often targeted, although it must be said that many Soviet soldiers behaved with dignity towards them. Regina Frankenfeld remembered the kindness of some, like the 'Stalin pupils' who spoke German and were nice to them, or the 'young Sasha' who helped her carry a heavy bag of potatoes home; but like so many others she also remembered the ever-present fear of molestation.[38] Once while returning from work she was stopped by a Russian who grabbed her by the elbow and said, 'Frau, komm.' Having already endured a number of rapes she recalled:

> I was so furious because I'd had it up to here ... he had me in such a clinch I couldn't free myself, so with my elbow I hit him in the pit of his stomach. That definitely hurt him, and he yelled, 'You, I shoot.' And he was brandishing this kind of machine gun around my nose and then I said, 'Then shoot.' Yelled it, yelled it just like he did. 'Then

shoot' ... Then he looked at me and let me go. *Ja.* You see, that happened, not once, a thousand times. The past is not *so* simple as one makes it out to be today, believe me.[39]

But for many women the threat of rape remained very real. Attacks continued throughout 1945 and the sadism which accompanied them was sometimes appalling. The building in the Kaiserstrasse which the US President Truman later used as an office had belonged to the renowned publisher Gustav Müller-Grote. In May Soviet troops broke in. The publisher and his young grandchildren were beaten and tied up in the main rooms while his daughters were repeatedly brought in, gang raped and tortured in front of them. This ordeal lasted for ten weeks. The liberal politician Ernst Lemmer wrote in his memoirs that when the Soviets occupied Friedrich Kayssler's house they shot the famous actor and then raped and slit open two young actresses they found there.[40] Co-operation was no guarantee against rape: one Soviet report documents how a senior lieutenant, 'R', invited a group of local German industrialists and their wives to a birthday party in Zittau to discuss the economic prospects of some firms. Instead of holding the meeting 'R' singled out one of the women and raped her in front of them. Another group of civilians watched as a Russian first lieutenant walked into a barber's shop, saw the twenty-one-year-old cashier and raped her on the sales table. There were also numerous cases of women KPD activists being raped, despite their links with the Soviet occupation forces.[41]

Some women complained to the Soviet authorities about the treatment but they had no recourse to the law. Unlike British and American forces there was no anti-fraternization order for Soviet soldiers and only a few, like Commandant Velisov, cared enough about maintaining order to distribute inkwells to German women and to send men with ink-stained uniforms back to the Soviet Union.[42] Normally, however, soldiers caught raping were merely turned over to Soviet military authorities, who rarely punished offenders. Michael Burtsev, the Soviet 'public relations officer' who was responsible for dealing with such complaints in the first years of the occupation, laughed loudly during a 1992 interview as he recalled the lines of Berlin women who had come to him for help; he was particularly amused by one who had complained 'not so much that she had been raped, but that it had been in a barn – she would have "preferred a bedroom" ... We called the soldier up. He shrugged and said "he could not hold on". That was life in the army!'[43] Some commanders like General Berzarin treated the population as if they were still at war long after hostilities had ceased: 'During my whole life I have seen nothing like the bestial way German officers and soldiers pursued the peaceful population [of Russia]. All of the destruction you have here in Germany is nothing by comparison.'[44] Others blamed German women themselves: Leonid Leonov wrote that 'Our patrols now stride through Berlin, and German ladies gaze in their eyes invitingly, ready to begin payment of "reparations" at once.'[45] It was only when the Soviets began to realize that public disapproval might in fact have political consequences that they began to rein in their troops. On 16 July 1947 a secret CPSU(b) communication called for a concerted effort to improve the 'honour and dignity' of Red Army officers and in January 1948 contact with foreigners, including German women, was outlawed and Marshal Sokolovsky confined soldiers to guarded posts and camps away from the German population. Finally, in 1949, an attempt was made, as Tiulpanov put it, to 'eliminate the unpleasant impression' left by the behaviour of Red Army soldiers when the Presidium of the Supreme Soviet issued a directive which gave those convicted of rape a mandatory sentence of ten to fifteen years in a labour camp.[46] Soldiers who had been encouraged to run riot in Berlin and had taken what they could from the city as payment for terrible years in battle were suddenly sent back to the Soviet Union not as heroes, but as prisoners. Stalin now feared that they would spread rumours of the great wealth of the west. Konstantin Simonov claimed that Stalin feared a new Decembrism – 'he had shown Ivan to Europe and Europe to Ivan, as Alexander I had done in 1813–1814' – and, at a time of terrible poverty and repression in Russia, felt the need to stifle all information of a better world abroad. Suddenly orders began to appear labelling those who fraternized with German women as politically unreliable. One 1948 directive stated: 'Recently it has been noticed that many Soviet officers have been yielding to bourgeois ideology thanks to their relations with the local population. This produces in them an anti-Soviet disposition and [can even turn them] into actual traitors to their country.'[47] To be labelled 'bourgeois' or a 'traitor' in the Soviet Union meant banishment to the Gulag at the very least; suddenly even syphilis was branded as a 'bourgeois' illness and could lead to a prison sentence. Stalin had over 100,000 Soviet officers and men who had served him loyally in Germany murdered between 1945 and 1948.[48]

Despite the gradual change in Soviet policy Berlin women continued to live with the consequences of rape. One of the results was a rampant spread in venereal disease, a problem completely ignored until the summer of 1945, when the situation became so extreme that the Soviets were forced to issue Order no. 25 of the Supreme Command 'On Measures to Combat Sexual Diseases in the Soviet Occupied Zone in Germany'. This included the provision of medical check-ups for women who had been raped or, as the 1 June 1945 order in Reinickendorf-Berlin delicately put it, 'who have been visited several times by soldiers of the Red Army'. The Soviets had little success in halting the spread of VD until the policy changes in 1948 because they stopped neither the rapes nor the rise in prostitution or semi-prostitution – the exchange of sex for food or cigarettes. Another consequence of rape was an increase in unwanted pregnancies. Abortion was still illegal under paragraph 218 of German law but many Berlin doctors waived this, particularly in the first six months of the Soviet occupation. Abortions cost around 1,000 marks and were performed without anaesthesia and with few supplies like disinfectant; nevertheless it has been estimated that around 2 million women in post-war Germany had abortions every year between 1945 and 1948; the majority took place in the Soviet zone. Many others tried to induce miscarriage and the chief SED health official Maxim Zetkin, son of the famous Berlin KPD activist Clara Zetkin, recorded that hundreds of mutilated, bleeding or poisoned women were brought into his local hospitals every month; 6,000 Berlin women died annually in the Soviet zone in the first years of the occupation from complications after botched abortions.[49] Some women kept their children and it has been estimated that between 150,000 and 200,000 'Russian babies' were born in the Soviet-occupied zone of Germany.[50]

Since the war many people have asked why the Soviet soldiers chose to commit rape on such an extraordinary scale, but as Norman Naimark has pointed out there were many contributing factors. First there was the widespread Soviet desire for revenge and the hatred of the Germans caused by the truly horrific crimes committed by the Germans in Russia and even by the high casualties suffered in the Battle of Berlin. Another factor was that in Russian patriarchal society the defilement of women was seen as an act of violence against the men as much as against the female victims. Russian soldiers had suffered terribly and many felt that all acts of violence against German civilians were justified. The writer Vsevolod Vishnevsky said in May 1945: 'Such a strange feeling that the war is all over and done with. There is *none* of that special atmosphere of triumph that we expected from the capture of Berlin, from victory. The war was too long and hard.'[51] But Berlin women, many of whom were unaware of the behaviour of their own soldiers on the eastern front, would never forget the rapes which they had been forced to endure, and even in the 1980s the heroic Red Army memorial at Treptow Park was quietly referred to as the 'Tomb of the Unknown Rapist' by a number of older women I met there.

Whatever the arguments for or against Soviet behaviour in Germany the systematic pillage, looting, oppression and rape led most Berliners to see the Russians not as liberators, but as brutal conquerors.[52] As such, their behaviour was counter-productive. In most parts of his empire Stalin had felt no need to concern himself with public opinion. He was free to impose his will on the captive populations of occupied countries from Ukraine and the Baltic States to Poland. Occupied Germany was different: here the people had direct contact with the western Allies and were able to make comparisons between the two systems of government. When it became clear that the Allies would insist on holding free democratic elections the Soviet legacy of violence made it virtually impossible for their German Communist representatives to win votes. Bernt von Kügelen, one of 'Stalin's Germans' who returned from Moscow in 1945, said that it would have been better 'if the war had ended before Red Army troops had entered Germany ... the behaviour of Soviet troops has had an adverse effect upon the Communist cause in Germany'.[53] Women consistently gave the Communists fewer votes than the men; Erich Gniffke was typical when he wrote to Pieck and Grotewohl complaining that it would be 'difficult to find a woman in Mecklenburg who was ready to vote for the SED', and in the run-up to the autumn 1946 elections the Soviet Lieutenant-Colonel G. Konstantinovsky reported back to Moscow that the SED was incapable of making gains amongst Berlin's female population and that if something was not done the party would face a humiliating electoral defeat; he suggested that 'experienced female Soviet propagandists and party veterans' be sent to Berlin to help deal with the 'deep antipathy' German women harboured for the SED. The Soviets noted that even in the big Berlin factories few women supported Communist organizations; by December 1948 only two out of 1,447 women workers at the Siemens factory were party members. Ruth Andreas-Friedrich, who had worked in the Gruppe Emil resistance in Berlin during the war, remembered that 'During the last months under the Nazis nearly all of us were pro-Russian. We waited for the light from the East. But it has burned too many. Too much has happened that cannot be understood. The dark streets still resonate every night with the piercing screams of women in distress. The plundering and shooting, the insecurity and violence aren't over yet.'[54] Despite the efforts of the Main Political Administration of the Red Army GlavPURKKA, and its Seventh Section for German Propaganda, which churned out articles and books and films portraying the Soviet victors as friendly and helpful, the people remembered what had really happened.

Stalin had made this error because he assumed that the western Allies would abandon continental Europe by 1948 and that he would then be able to take Germany for himself.[55] Public opinion had therefore meant nothing to him. In the first months of occupation he had co-operated with the west in order to obtain reparations and access to West German coal and mineral resources for the rebuilding of the decimated Soviet economy. Ultimately, however, Stalin was willing to see the establishment of a demilitarized, unified and neutral Germany because he genuinely believed that it would eventually come under Soviet control.[56] Foreign Minister Viacheslav Molotov admitted in a 1972 interview that by 1945 Stalin was trying to 'expand the limits of our Motherland as far as possible' and that he soon hoped to rule over Germany.[57] Stalin's adviser on Germany, Daniel Melnikov, remembered him saying in 1945: 'We need all of Germany, not part of Germany, all of Germany.' The Soviet President Kalinin said in August 1945 that they intended to 'overtake and surpass the most developed countries of Europe and the United States'.[58] Stalin could not use military force to achieve this as it might have provoked a war, but he did hope to set up a puppet government which would give him power 'legitimately'. Molotov admitted that 'our idea was to build socialism, but step by step so the people could not protest ... otherwise the people would rebel and we would have to use force'.[47] It was therefore vital for the Soviets to put German Communists in place – men who appeared to be independent but who were in fact controlled from Moscow.[48] Some had been recruited in the 1930s.

In the 1935 Seventh Conference of the Comintern Stalin had approved the recruitment of German Communists, who were to be trained to help set up a Soviet-backed Reich government after the defeat of Germany. Those who actually survived to 1945 were the fortunate ones. When Hitler took power in 1933 hundreds of German Communists had fled to the Soviet Union hoping to find refuge from the Nazis. A number had been taken in by Stalin and given quarters in Moscow, some at the splendid Hotel Luxe on Gorky Street (now Tverskaya). Despite the apparent hospitality they were in constant danger.[59] Stalin regarded all foreign Communists as potential traitors and the Great Purges, in which a staggering 9 million people were murdered, saw the liquidation of famous Communists like Hugo Eberlein, who had founded the German Communist Party, as well as four members of the German Polit-buro, ten from the Central Committee and dozens of other loyal party members. They joined those untold thousands who were awakened in the early hours of the morning, pushed into waiting bread vans and brought to the Lubyanka Prison, where they were shot in the courtyard or sent on to the Gulag. The German Communists suffered further losses when Stalin signed the Molotov–Ribbentrop Pact and handed a number of them back to Nazi Germany in an attempt to appease Hitler. These men were summarily executed by the Gestapo. It was only after the German invasion of the Soviet Union in 1941 that Stalin began to see the remaining Communists as indispensable in the future administration of Germany; their positions became more secure as victory approached and by 1944 'Stalin's Germans' had become the most important foreign Communist group in Moscow. The plot for the Soviet-backed German Communist takeover of the defeated nation was hatched in the art deco rooms of the Hotel Luxe. It was overseen by an icy Soviet apparatchik who had made his career by murdering Stalin's left-wing opponents during the Spanish Civil War.[60] His name was Walter Ulbricht.

On 27 April 1945 ten men of the 'Ulbricht Group' were told to prepare themselves for their mission in Germany. Three days later the agents, including Ulbricht, Wilhelm Pieck, Hans Mahle, Franz Dahlem, Otto Ackermann and Wolfgang Leonhard, left Moscow and were flown towards the Red Army front line. The Battle of Berlin was still raging and as they landed in the town of Bruchmühle they could see the burning Reich capital in the distance.

The men were debriefed by Zhukov's political staff and given orders to proceed immediately to Berlin and other cities, where they were to assist the Soviets in the setting up of a new, pro-Communist administrative system.[61] The Berlin group moved into the battered German capital on 1 May 1945. By June they had been put under the control of the infamous Soviet Military Administration in Germany, the SMAD, which would become the main instrument of Soviet policy in the occupied territory.[62]

SMAD was set up by Marshal Zhukov, Colonel-General V. D. Sokolovsky and Colonel-General I. A. Serov on 6 June 1945 and on 9 June Zhukov announced in Order No. 1 that its goals were: 1) to supervise the unconditional surrender of Germany, 2) to administer the Soviet zone of Germany, and 3) to see to the implementation of the most important Allied decisions on military, political and economic matters.[63] The next day the three fronts of the Red Army which had competed with one another so fiercely on the road to Berlin were reorganized into the Group of Soviet Occupation Forces in Germany, also under Zhukov. Sokolovsky took charge of the Group of Forces headquartered in Potsdam, while Serov was given 'leadership and control' of the administration of Germans in the zone, with its headquarters in Berlin-Karlshorst.[64] SMAD was a powerful force. It had 20,000 troops of its own and access to 20,000 security personnel attached to the MVD (Ministry of Internal Affairs) and MGB (Ministry for State Security).[65] According to Central Committee data there were 49,887 members of SMAD in twenty separate departments by 1946, each headed by a cognizant ministry or organization in Moscow. The appearance of German autonomy was a sham; all SMAD appointees had to be confirmed by the Council of People's Commissars and every important decision had to be approved in Moscow.[66]

The Soviet-backed 'Committee for a Free Germany' now worked under SMAD to establish a Communist infrastructure and military and civilian control in Germany. 'Stalin's Germans' were to be presented not as Russian puppets but as patriots who wished to 'fulfil the bourgeois-democratic revolution of 1848'.[67] They were not to mention their exile in Moscow and Zhukov expressly forbade the use of the word 'Communist'.[68] The transition was not without its problems; the 5,000 Communists who had survived in Berlin under the Nazis had long nurtured hopes of revolution and paraded around the city with red flags singing the *Internationale*.[69] The Soviets looked down on these ideologists with a mixture of patronizing amusement and utter contempt; Ulbricht referred to them as 'ultraradicals' who should be silenced for fear that they frighten off the bourgeoisie or scare 'average citizens'. Ulbricht quickly closed down their organizations, making it 'clear to the comrades that all energy must be concentrated in the city administration' set up by the Soviets. The new administration was divided into Political, Propaganda, Economy and Supply, Military Affairs and Security units; the Security sections were linked directly to the NKVD and were responsible for the procurement of German agents to carry out Soviet directives and for liaising with the People's Commissariat of Internal Affairs, which dealt with so-called 'terrorists, diversionaries, and other fascist elements' in Germany. In his book *Child of the Revolution* Wolfgang Leonhard noted the contrast between the naive and idealistic German Communists and the hardened NKVD operatives who were prepared to liquidate all those thought to be opponents of the Soviet occupation, whether they were Communists or not.[70] Even so, German Communists helped to identify both 'enemies of the people' – knowing full well the fate that awaited them – and Germans 'loyal to the Soviet occupation'. The latter were appointed as local supervisors or 'Obleute' in their districts. The Obleute system was a direct copy of the Nazi block system and employed wardens to watch over every street, every city block and every house; many were ex-Nazi wardens who were allowed to keep their old jobs if they professed support for the Soviet occupation forces.[71]

While the Obleute were being appointed Ulbricht created 'People's Committees' which were to 'go into various Berlin boroughs and select those anti-fascist elements who agree with the new German administration'.[72] Old working-class areas were to be given Communist mayors while bourgeois-democratic areas would be given pro-Soviet mayors who 'seemed acceptable' to the local population. Overt Communists and radicals were to be avoided, and Wolfgang Leonhard remembered the absurdity of being sent to find a 'pro-Communist yet bourgeois' mayor, preferably with a 'doctor title' to govern the well-to-do district of Wilmersdorf. Ulbricht told his operatives that the political takeover 'must look democratic, but we must have everything under our control'.[73] The Soviets quickly appointed mayors for all Berlin districts, forming the basis of the new Soviet-controlled Berlin government – the Magistrat. By 13 May General Zhukov had confirmed the new postings, effectively creating a Soviet-controlled government to replace the Nazi administrative system.[74]

Zhukov and General Berzarin did not stop there. Again using the German Communists and the 'Committee for a Free Germany' to mask their activities the Communists began to infiltrate every significant organization in Berlin. The Free German Trade Union Federation was forced to 'embrace all members of the working class' and on 15 June all pre-war trade unions which had regrouped immediately after the war were forced to merge under Soviet control. Factories were purged of anti-Communist workers. At the same time the Communists wooed the peasants with land reforms and the 'reconstruction of peasant holdings' out of seized estates. Anti-Fascist judges and advocates were told to set up a pro-Communist judicial system, which began to function on 20 May. By 31 May the Soviets had ordered the withdrawal of all licences held by 'Fascist' shopkeepers and disbanded all business associations, professional organizations and other economic bodies, which were immediately re-established under Communist direction.[75] The Finance and Taxation Department closed all banks except the Berlin Stadtbank, which became a public monopoly, while insurance could be issued only by the Communist-run VAB (Versicherungsanstalt) Berlin.

Those who refused to bow to this pressure were the first to feel the severity of the new Soviet occupation – many who opposed the Soviet-backed KPD and SPD were accused of being 'ex-Nazis' irrespective of their backgrounds, while many genuine ex-Nazis, grateful for the chance to hide their pasts, suddenly became loyal Communist employees.[76] The Communists were also quick to use high-ranking army officers and Junkers like Marshal von Paulus, who had been defeated at Stalingrad, and Bismarck's grandson Count Heinrich von Einsiedel, as well as clergymen and others to convince Berliners that these 'Anti-Fascist Committees' represented genuine German interests.[77] One of the most notorious of the 'new' Communists was Paul Markgraf, who had been taken prisoner by the Soviets in 1943 and had become an ardent Communist in captivity. He was appointed police president and immediately began to put Soviet sympathizers in charge of the precincts. Many of the new recruits had been in the Wehrmacht and some had even been Nazi storm troopers or members of the SS; others like Walter Mickinn and Erich Mielke were old Communists who had fled to Moscow under the Nazis. Markgraf proved to be a ruthless Soviet agent and would be responsible for the deaths of many anti-Communists in Berlin.[78]

No aspect of life was too trivial for Soviet attention. GlavPURKKA, the Main Political Administration of the Red Army, had overseen the political indoctrination of German POWs and Communists since 1941, and their operatives moved into Berlin in May 1945.[79] From October that year SMAD's Propaganda departments came under the control of Colonel Tiulpanov; they oversaw every aspect of culture from the distribution of films to guidelines for artists and set out to recruit artists and performers who would work in their service. The German Communist poet Johannes Becher was brought in from Moscow and on 4 July 1945 set up the Cultural League for the Democratic Renewal of Germany or Kulturbund to woo German intellectuals to their cause. Amongst other things he set up a canteen called Die Möwe (the Seagull) which offered artists a place to get warm and have a meal.[80] The Soviets quickly created a number of other cultural organizations in Berlin. The House of the Culture of the Soviet Union on Unter den Linden was soon staging exhibitions of poster art or the history of Soviet theatre; the Society for German–Soviet Friendship sponsored lectures on Russian topics like the importance of the Five Year Plan or the benefits of the Soviet education system, while the All-Union Society for Cultural Ties with Foreign Countries (VOKS) sponsored Soviet writers like Vsevolov Vishnevsky and Boris Gorbatov to lecture in Berlin.

The Soviet 'Cultural Officers' sent to Berlin in the first months of the occupation to work under Tiulpanov and Alexander Dymshits were often highly educated and sophisticated individuals who saw culture as possible propaganda. George Clare, a Viennese Jew, noted that in this regard the Russians

> seemed way ahead of their allies during the first year of the occupation. They had a lot going for them: Tiulpanov's power and single-mindedness, his understanding of the link between culture and politics, his officers' superior qualifications, the fact that they were unhampered by non-fraternization nonsense in their dealings with Germans, their ability to gild the Agitprop carrot with their Payok parcels, their familiarity with German customs . . . neither being nice to Germans nor cultural affairs ranked high on the western powers' original list of priorities.[81]

Initially the Soviets tried to 'make Germans again out of Germans' by staging traditional performances such as Beethoven's *Fidelio* at the State Opera, which was now located at the Admiralspalast, or stage productions like Lessing's *Nathan der Weise*, which was performed in September 1945. These productions were deeply moving for many Berliners for whom a night at the opera or the theatre was only a distant memory. Under the Performances Department of SMAD's propaganda section the operas, ballets and orchestras became showpieces of the Soviet sector. The Soviets also took over a number of Berlin theatres, including the Deutsches Theater, the Max Reinhardt Theatre and the Volksbühne; between 1945 and 1947 they staged over seventy plays in their zone. Despite the early emphasis on rescuing German culture Moscow became increasingly concerned that Germans were not being exposed to enough Soviet culture. After their victory in the war most Russians genuinely believed their culture to be superior to all others, and as the Soviet Union was said to have been at its cultural pinnacle in 1941, when the Germans attacked, all shortcomings could be blamed on them. To Berliners' annoyance, performances of Schiller and Mozart were gradually replaced by those of Russian artists from Pushkin and Gorky to Gogol, Chekhov, Rimsky-Korsakov, Tchaikovsky, and by officially acceptable artists like Chopin. The Germans were also exposed to ever more Bolshevik art, from paintings to agitprop such as Konstantin Simonov's anti-western play *The Russian Question*, which told the story of an American journalist who realized how much greater the peace-loving Soviet Union was than his own capitalist America; the western Allies protested at its overt anti-American message. Berliners also endured Soviet film productions from militaristic works like *The Fall of Berlin* with its score by Shostakovich, to dreary socialist realist propaganda like *The Stone Flower* and *Traktorist* (The Tractor Driver).[82]

German artists were expected to conform to Soviet socialist-realistic guidelines; those who persisted in creating Impressionist or Expressionist works or failed to show a 'positive view of the Soviet Union' were labelled 'rootless cosmopolitans' or 'lackeys of imperialism' and were purged. As a result, a number of important artists were forbidden to paint while talentless men like Fritz Duda and Horst Strempel, who produced suitable Communist scenes, were heralded as the great artists of a new age and received official commissions and honours. One of the problems faced by all artists was that the definition of what was 'acceptable' constantly changed, both in Germany and in the Soviet Union itself: plans by VOKS to promote the poetry of Anna Akhmatova in Berlin were quickly shelved in 1946 when she was labelled 'bourgeois'; Mayakovsky's plays, including *The Bedbug*, were banned and Ibsen's works were suddenly restricted. Even the toadying pro-Soviet poet Becher came under NKVD scrutiny until he redeemed himself by producing a series of poems in praise of 'the great Stalin'.[83] The NKVD was always present; George Clare remembered visiting the Theater des Westens in Kantstrasse, which despite being in the British sector was still 'firmly Russian held'. When Clare commented on a majestic-looking officer who passed by in lonely splendour his friend Corporal Tolliver said he was alone because of his 'smell': ' "What's the colour of the braid round his epaulettes?" "Light blue," I said. "Well, my boy, that's the colour of the MVD, formerly Cheka, OGPU, NKVD, which by any other name smells just as foul." '[84]

Propaganda was a vital element of Soviet control from the beginning and newspapers played an important role. The first newspaper of the Soviet sector, which was little more than a leaflet, appeared on 3 May 1945 and was called *Nachrichten für die deutsche Bevölkerung*. On 15 May the *Tägliche Rundschau*, a new German-language newspaper controlled by SMAD but sold as a paper 'for the German people', appeared in Berlin and offered co-operative writers and journalists the chance to 'participate in the reconstruction' of the German press. On 21 May the Soviet Kommandatura (the official organ of Allied government) in Berlin printed the first issue of the *Berliner Zeitung*, which was turned over to the city government a month later.[85] The Information Administration, successor to the GlavPURKKA, also started the *Deutsche Volkszeitung* and *Neues Deutschland*. The Dietz publishing house began publishing books by Marx, Engels, Lenin and Stalin in 1946, while Hans Mahle became head of radio with Mattheus Klein, the KPD functionary, in charge of recruitment. The Soviets also set up the Education Department (ONO) which controlled schools and the university, dictating the content of courses and purging anti-Communist teachers.[86] Those who did not conform were in constant danger. Teachers and lecturers were watched to make sure that they taught a pro-Soviet line; the report on the teacher Erich Reich was typical: he was criticized for being 'an individualist, [who] doesn't like criticism of his work [and] doesn't consult with democratic organizations about his work'. He was put under surveillance. By 1948 the Russians had grown impatient with 'anti-Communist' lecturers and Colonel Tiulpanov began to place Soviet officers within the administration in order to direct 'the ideological-political life of the university'.[87] Every important organization in every district of Berlin – including those ear-marked for American and British occupation – was now under Soviet control. Stalin's ambitious plans were threatened only by the impending arrival of the western powers. They were set to move into the zones of occupation which had been drawn up by the Allies long before the end of the war.

The geographical division of post-war Berlin had first been discussed in the winter of 1943, when the Allies realized that they would eventually win the war. At this point a tripartite body, the European Advisory Committee or EAC, had been set up to formulate joint Allied policy for the post-war control and occupation of Germany. At its second meeting on 18 February 1944 the Russian negotiator had eagerly accepted the generous zonal proposals submitted by the British representative Sir William Strange. These turned out to be greatly to Stalin's advantage. The Soviets were given almost 40 per cent of Germany's area, 36 per cent of the population and 33 per cent of productive resources. Berlin would now lie deep within the Soviet zone and 100 miles from the Anglo-American demarcation line. As the ex-German capital and the new centre of the joint Allied government it was to be divided into three zones. Lieutenant-General Morgan said later: 'I do not believe that anyone at the time could have realized the full and ultimate implications of the quartering decision – which in all probability was made by some minor official in the

War Office. But from it flowed all the rest.'[88] The 'implication' was that if the Soviets refused to co-operate with the west Berlin would be trapped deep inside hostile territory. In 1945, however, such thoughts were far from the minds of western negotiators.

In February 1945 the 'Big Three' had met at Yalta to discuss the imminent occupation of the Reich. On 11 February they had formally accepted the borders of their respective post-war zones, agreeing that France should receive a smaller zone carved out of the British and American sectors. The Allies concurred that each would have control over its own zone but they would have joint authority over Germany through the Allied Control Council. Berlin was to have a special role and would serve as the headquarters of both the Allied Control Council and the Kommandatura. For the first time since the Napoleonic Wars the city was to be governed not by Germans, but by external powers.

The western Allies were well meaning, but they were gullible when it came to dealing with Stalin and had agreed to all new borders on the assumption that the Soviets would co-operate with them and that they would be able to move swiftly into their own zones. Stalin had other plans. When the war was over he demanded that the United States immediately evacuate those Soviet areas 'illegally' occupied by American troops, while making no mention of the American right to move into its own zone, including its sector of Berlin. Churchill recognized the dangers of increased Soviet truculence in the east and repeatedly urged the Americans to take a stand against them using western-occupied territories designated for Soviet occupation as their bargaining chip. He was ignored.

The question of land was of prime importance, and restricting Soviet access would have sent a strong signal to Stalin not to push the west any further than he had already. The west held a sizeable area; indeed despite the fact that Eisenhower had decided against taking Berlin in 1945 the Americans had in fact occupied around one-third of the German territory earmarked for Soviet occupation, including the cities of Halle and Leipzig. Churchill urged President Truman to use this territory as leverage to force Stalin to fulfil the terms of Yalta and wrote to him suggesting that no western forces leave the Soviet zones until the Big Three could meet at Potsdam in July. He then wrote to Eden in San Francisco: the Allies should not retreat from the Soviet territory, he said, 'until we are satisfied about Poland and also about the temporary nature of the Russian occupation of Germany'.[89] Truman was still under the misguided impression that the Americans could co-operate with Stalin and he ignored Churchill's advice, retorting that postponement of the withdrawal of American forces would 'harm relations with Russia'. Churchill was forced to back down, and reluctantly prepared for the withdrawal of British troops from the east. Truman and Churchill wrote to Stalin on 14 and 15 June; Truman proposed that American troops should move out of the Soviet zone on 21 June while Churchill proposed the simultaneous movement of Anglo-American forces into Berlin. Both western leaders asked for free access to Berlin by air, rail and road. It was a grave error.

Stalin played for more time. He could not risk refusing the western Allies access to their zones in Berlin but he intended to delay the move so that he could continue to strip the city of 'reparations' and put Communist officials in place before they could reach the city. He concocted a number of excuses explaining why the western troops could not move in, insisting on one day that 'mine clearance operations were not yet complete' or claiming that all roads were blocked by the 're-deployment of Soviet troops' the next. He also avoided the issue of free access to Berlin.

It was only after increasing western pressure that Stalin eventually agreed to allow the Americans to carry out a survey of their zone. On 23 June a Preliminary Reconnaissance Party left for Berlin in high spirits with 100 vehicles and 500 people commanded by Colonel Frank L. Howley. To their astonishment the convoy was harassed by Russian troops as soon as it attempted to enter the Soviet zone at Dessau on the Elbe. After much wrangling Howley was permitted to cross the Elbe, but with only fifty vehicles. The convoy proceeded under Soviet escort to Babelsberg, where it was ordered to stop. Nobody was permitted to leave his vehicle. Finally the convoy was forced to return to the west with its mission unfulfilled.[90]

On 29 June Lieutenant-General Lucius Clay, representing General Eisenhower, and the British deputy military governor Lieutenant-General Sir Ronald Weeks flew to Berlin to discuss transit arrangements of their forces with Marshal Zhukov. Both were still unaware of Stalin's increasing determination to keep the western Allies out of Berlin. Without understanding the magnitude of the decision Clay accepted a verbal agreement which allowed the western Allies access via one main highway, a rail line and two air corridors. He assumed that the arrangement was temporary and reserved the right to reopen the question in the Allied Control Council. Later he wrote: 'I must admit that we did not then fully realize that the requirement of unanimous consent could enable a Soviet veto in the Allied Control Council to block all of our future efforts ... I think now that I was mistaken in not at this time making free access to Berlin a condition to our withdrawal into our occupation zone.'[91] In fact, with the exception of some small amendments for French access, Clay had unwittingly agreed to the establishment of the vulnerable corridors upon which the island city of West Berlin would depend for nearly half a century.

After Clay's meeting with Zhukov the Americans tried once again to bring troops to their zone. Colonel Howley set out from Halle on 1 July with a

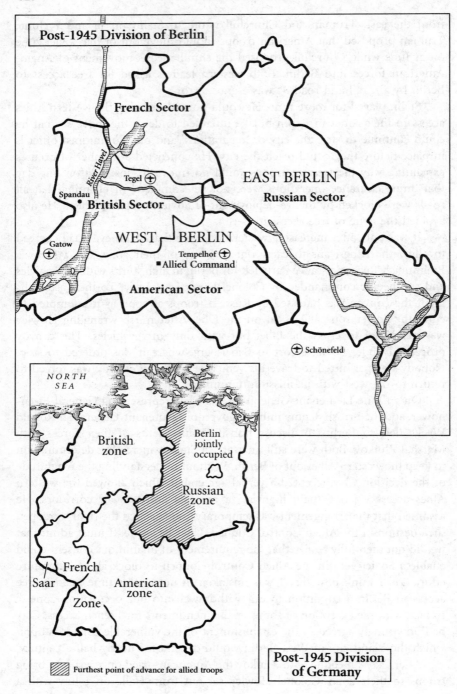

Post-1945 Division of Berlin

French Sector

River Havel

Tegel ✛

Spandau ●

British Sector

EAST BERLIN

Russian Sector

WEST BERLIN

Gatow ✛

Tempelhof ✛
■ Allied Command

American Sector

✛ Schönefeld

NORTH
SEA

British
zone

Berlin
jointly
occupied

Russian
zone

French
Saar

American
zone

Zone

▨ Furthest point of advance for allied troops

**Post-1945 Division
of Germany**

party of eighty-five officers and 136 armed men, pushing angrily past Soviet checkpoints. The Soviets resented having to move out of areas which they had occupied for months and when Howley's Military A1A1 Government Detachment (as the Berlin detachment was known) put up American procla- mations announcing their arrival the Russians ripped them down again. These antics stopped only after an exasperated Howley raised American flags through- out the district and posted armed guards to defend them against the Russian troops. The British were also experiencing problems in reaching Berlin. On 1 July the convoy leaders were told that the Magdeburg Bridge was 'closed' and that they would have to turn back. After many hours' delay they finally found an unguarded bridge and slipped into Berlin, but the Soviets continued to block troop transports, thereby preventing the western Allies from making their planned triumphal entry with their main occupation forces on 4 July, American Independence Day. It took weeks before the American forces were finally settled in Zehlendorf, Steglitz, Tempelhof, Neukölln, Schöneberg and Kreuzberg; the English in Spandau, Charlottenburg, Wilmersdorf and Tier- garten, and the French in Reinickendorf and Wedding. Only then was Berlin filled with the infamous signs in four languages warning of zonal boundaries. The most famous, which read YOU ARE NOW LEAVING THE AMERICAN SECTOR, went up by the Brandenburg Gate.

As the troops moved into Berlin the Allies prepared for the final conference of the Big Three at Potsdam. Code-named 'Terminal' it began on 17 July 1945 in the mock Tudor Cecilienhof at the southern end of Berlin. As if to emphasize their ownership of the area the Soviets planted a gigantic red star of geraniums in the garden. The Potsdam Conference was the last opportunity to rectify some of the mistakes made at Yalta, but the Allies were still convinced that four-power government was workable. As a result, Stalin got everything he wanted.

The conference started badly. Churchill, now awaiting the outcome of the elections which would remove him from power, balked at the Soviet arrogance in Berlin: 'we are in Berlin by right, on terms of absolute equality and not as guests of the Russians,' he protested. The Americans ignored him, not understanding that they too were subservient in a city dominated by the Soviets; even the train which brought the western representatives to Potsdam had been escorted by 17,000 crack NKVD troops and eight NKVD armoured trains – the same NKVD men who were otherwise engaged in bringing Berlin under Soviet control.

The conference confirmed the agreements made by the Big Three at Tehran and Yalta, including the vital agreements enshrining Soviet domination in east central Europe. The territory beyond the eastern Neisse was to remain under Polish occupation until a peace treaty was signed with Germany. German reparations were to be settled from each zone, although Russia was to be given 25 per cent of industrial goods from the western zones in return for the promise of raw materials and food. Reams of paper appeared covered with impressive plans under the heading of the 'five d's' – de-militarization, de-Nazification, de-industrialization, de-centralization, and democratization – but much would prove superfluous as it became clear that the Soviets would refuse to co-operate with the west and were indeed determined to cut the western zones off from the traditional food source in the east, starving them into submission.[92]

With the benefit of hindsight it is extraordinary to think that none of the dignitaries at Potsdam recognized the extreme seriousness of the Soviet threat.[93] Images of the heroic Red Army and 'Uncle Joe' still abounded, and the western powers deluded themselves that Stalin's aims were compatible with theirs and that he too stood for democracy and self-determination. Churchill was now no longer in power and other western leaders were unable to see their own vulnerability. The Alliance had been formed and held together for four years by one thing – the need to defeat Nazi Germany. Once Hitler had been crushed national interests began to take precedence over international goodwill. Stalin had no intention of sharing Berlin or Germany with the west, nor did he share the western vision of the eventual creation of a democratic, capitalist German state. He was delighted to learn that the Americans intended to withdraw from Europe in 1947. It would take two years for the western leaders to recognize their mistake. By then, they had very nearly lost Berlin.

The Potsdam Conference finished on 2 August 1945, and Gregori Klimov reported that Stalin 'regarded the decisions on Germany as a great victory for Soviet diplomacy'.[94] The Soviets believed that Potsdam had enshrined them as both the victors and as the permanent occupiers of Berlin, and they were keen to show off. At the international V-J Day parade General Zhukov's efforts to outshine the American General Patton reached absurd lengths. Brigadier-General Frank Howley recalled how Zhukov, dressed up in a bright blue uniform weighed down with enormous medals, planted himself conspicuously in the most important position at the front of the stand and jealously guarded it: 'each time Patton shifted his feet the Russian eyed him nervously, then moved nearer the front of the platform. When he did so, Patton inched up to him. In the end, Zhukov's rather expansive stomach was hanging indelicately over the rail while Patton stood, grim and soldier-like, beside him.' By the end of the parade the two men were openly insulting one another and two weeks later General Patton made overtly anti-Soviet comments at a press conference.[95] He was relieved of command of the Third Army. The Americans would not yet allow anyone to sour relations with Stalin.

This attitude extended to the Nuremberg trials, which began on 19 October 1945 – an attempt to bring to justice those responsible for the most heinous aspects of the Nazi regime. On the surface the Allies co-operated and meted out the death sentence to Göring and ten other Nazi leaders; others like Hess and Speer were sentenced to various terms in Spandau Prison. The trials were important, not least because they exposed to the world and to the Germans themselves the extent of Nazi criminality. Nevertheless they were fatally flawed, not least because they allowed men like Andrei Vishinsky, Stalin's erstwhile prosecutor during the Great Terror, to sit with the judges.[96] Interestingly it was his appointment as reporter of the trials for the KPD's radio service which marked the beginning of Markus Wolf's extraordinary career in the Soviet zone.[97] It would be decades before crimes committed by Stalin would be taken seriously by the west: at the time he was still seen as a great and trustworthy ally. It was precisely because of the general sense of goodwill that the western Allies received such a shock when they entered Berlin and discovered what the Soviets had done there.

The German capital was in a far worse condition than any of the western Allies had expected. They had seen bombed-out cities before but none which had endured months of Soviet occupation. Far from being put on its feet it had been stripped, ransacked and terrorized, and all who saw it were affected by the sight of the hideous wreckage and the grim, starving people who greeted them. Truman wrote: 'I thought of Carthage, Baalbek, Jerusalem, Rome, Atlantis, Peking . . . of Scipio, Ramses II, Sherman, Jenghiz Khan.' Churchill called it 'nothing but a chaos of ruins'. Far from treating the westerners as occupiers Berliners were relieved to see them; when Churchill visited the Reichstag and the Chancellery he was spontaneously applauded by German passers-by – something that would have been unthinkable had it been Stalin. Ten years later he wrote that although no advance notice had been given of his visit a large crowd had gathered there. 'I walked about among them; except for one old man who shook his head disapprovingly, they all began to cheer.' The troops were also surprised by the welcome they now received as liberators from the Russians. There was resentment against the 'occupation forces' but Richard Brett-Smith remembered many Berliners watching their arrival with expressions of relief on their faces, something which they had not encountered amongst western Germans who had not experienced Soviet occupation:

These hundreds of Germans are by no means sullen or resentful . . . they gaze fixedly, but many smile and some wave, a few almost cheer. It is indeed more like a sober liberation welcome than a triumphant entry into a conquered city, and for that, without doubt, we have the Russians to thank. Who could ever have foretold this, the most amazing irony of all, that when we entered Berlin we would come as liberators, not as tyrants, for the Germans.[98]

The western Allies were overwhelmed by the task which faced them. The provision of food and shelter for the destitute population soon took priority over everything else. One of the first British soldiers to enter the city, Colonel Byford-Jones, remembered

> Unter den Linden, now embankments of burnt-out buildings that were once stately palaces, the pavements littered with wreckage. Between these embankments, where the proud Wehrmacht had marched, were hundreds of ex-Wehrmacht prisoners, unshaven ... filthy, tattered, empty food tins tied to the string that girts their waists, their eyes empty. Like an army of zombies, they moved silently, their feet bound in sacking, as if propelled by some external power ... Rising in the heat of the day came a hideous smell of dampness, of charred remains, of thousands of putrefying bodies.[99]

Many of the 100,000 German civilians who had died in the Battle for Berlin still lay unburied; even the cool-headed General Clay described Berlin as a 'city of the dead'. The American Colonel H. G. Sheen, wrote: 'The bomb damage in the heart of the city is difficult to describe. In certain areas the stench of unburied dead is almost overpowering. From Tempelhof to the Wilhelmstrasse not one undamaged building is standing; roofs, floors and windows are gone, and in many cases the fragments of only one or two walls are standing.' It was in these shells of buildings that people struggled to eke out an existence. Hans Speier returned to Berlin in 1945 and was appalled at what he saw:

> anything human among these indescribable ruins must exist in an unknown form. There remains nothing human about it. The water is polluted, it smells of corpses, you see the most extraordinary shapes of ruins and more ruins and still more ruins; houses, streets, districts in ruins. All people in civilian clothes among these mountains of ruins appear merely to deepen the nightmare. Seeing them you almost *hope* that they are not human.[100]

George Clare, who had passed through the Nazi capital in 1938 on his way to exile in Britain, returned in 1945 as a Royal Artillery bombardier attached to the Control Commission. He was shocked by the transformation:

> 1938 Berlin had assaulted one's ears with lively and strident crescendo, harsh, atonal, high-decibel; a medley of blaring car horns, squeaking brakes, snorting buses, clanging trams, shouting newspaper sellers. But now – like slow eerie drum-beats of a *danse macabre* – each sound rose and remained alone, the clip-clop of often wooden-soled footsteps, the rattle of a handcart or an occasional tram, the chugging

of a wood-fuelled bus, the gear-clash of an allied army lorry. This absence of the constant roar of city life was more unsettling than the sight of bombed and shelled buildings, of jagged outlines of broken masonry framing bits of blue sky. I had been prepared for that, but not for a city hushed to a whisper. Yet Berlin was not a lifeless moonscape. It lived – albeit in something of a zombied trance – mirrored in the dazed looks of many of the people I passed, more often noticeable in men than women. But then the men were mostly old or elderly, bowed and bitter-faced; the few youngish ones who were about – emaciated shadows of the soldiers who had almost conquered an entire continent – looked pathetic and downtrodden in the tattered remains of their Wehrmacht uniforms. The women were of all ages and, with so many men killed and hundreds of thousands in prisoner-of-war camps, they, not as formerly the Prussian Male, dominated the scene.[101]

But Clare's experiences revealed the moral ambiguity of post-war Berlin – when he visited the house in which his mother's family had lived he found the old doorway still intact in front of a pile of rubble. The family name plate had been removed because, as Jews, they had been rounded up and sent to their deaths in 1943.

Despite such reminders it was difficult for many westerners to grasp that the filthy mutilated city had so recently been the nerve centre of Nazi terror. De-Nazification procedures were set up but three-quarters of the population was made up not of tough ex-Nazis but of destitute women and children. The absence of men was striking. Byford-Jones commented: 'Everywhere there were women alone, in pairs or groups, paying for their own drinks in cafés, cutting wood, moving debris, doing men's work. As the winter wore on every third woman or girl came out dressed in the trousers of her absent husband, brother or son.' Tom Pocock remembered watching the lines of women sorting rubble by hand: 'Sometimes we passed other lines of women carrying buckets, waiting outside the less ruined buildings, where the Allied troops had already been billeted, in the hope of being given a swill of the left-overs after the soldiers had eaten.'

De-Nazification and de-militarization policies were introduced with the intention of tracking down the worst Nazi criminals, but these proved inadequate and many thousands of important Nazis evaded justice.[102] The task was made more difficult by the fact that most Nazis simply 'disappeared' at the end of the war. Martha Brixius remembered: 'It was extremely embarrassing. No one was part of it any more. It happened very quickly. They suddenly were dressed differently, all uniforms were gone, no insignia at all, and they'd all been "forced" . . . The turnabout happened so fast, it was a joke. I never saw anything like it.'[103] Even the Communist Otto Ackermann complained that given the way the Germans carried on after the war 'one would think that 90 per cent of them had been in the resistance'.[104] All Berliners were expected to go through the de-Nazification process, which included filling out a *Fragebogen* or questionnaire. If they passed they were given a document referred to as a 'Persil' certificate (after the brand of soap), allowing them to work even in restricted professions like teaching. The system was often abused, with people doctoring their pasts or assuming false identities. Those who did come forward were often punished for their honesty: Ursula Meyer-Semlies, who registered with British occupation troops at the end of the war, openly stated that she had been a member of the Nazi Party and represented herself at her de-Nazification hearing. But as she recalled, 'Many other refugees were not as honest and maintained there had been no Nazi Party in their hometown, or that it had had no members.'[105] George Clare recalled,

Judging by the endless procession of 'anti-fascists' which passed through our office [Poppek] was the last Nazi alive in Germany. Everybody had always been against Hitler, had always believed in democracy, and Churchill clearly had more admirers in Germany than in Britain. Yet when questioned precisely about their activities during the previous twelve years most applicants had problems with their 'short-term' memories.

But Clare was concerned about having to make judgements on such flimsy evidence – had he made the right decision when he turned someone away who clearly needed help?

One day, facing such a cadaverous man, I began to wonder what he might have looked like when Germany was on top. Remembering that every German had to carry an identity card which . . . showed the holder's photograph, I suddenly said: 'Give me your identity card.' 'Yes sir, of course.' And with that pavlovian German reflex to obey immediately any order given by uniformed authority he handed it to me. I opened it and looked at his true face: double-chinned, hard-eyed, self-important, and in his left buttonhole – he had just told me how his local Nazi boss had persecuted him – there was the round swastika badge of the party member . . . Of course not all the people who passed through that glorified porter's lodge of ours were like that. Some were out of the ordinary and those I remember clearly after four decades. For instance, the young Waffen-SS soldier who had retained a conscience and the general's widow who had not lost her pride.[106]

There was much resentment at the de-Nazification procedure, not least because it was seen to be punishing the wrong people: 'They prosecuted the little ones and let the big ones run. Once again, they held high and worthy office. Doctors who perpetuated euthanasia were not forbidden from resuming their careers. But some small bureaucrat, they throw him *out*.'[107] A certificate was no guarantee of a genuine change of heart and many people still clung to old beliefs:

Before the war, many had no big careers or were nothing special themselves. Then they had careers as being true Party members. And in 1945 the career was over and they were only average citizens. Now they cling to this time. It was their golden age. They simply do not admit that they erred, or more carefully put, that they were seduced ... before the Third Reich they were nothing and after the Third Reich they were nothing, but during the Third Reich they thought they were a big deal.[108]

Even so ex-Nazis were in some cases used by the British, Americans and French, particularly if they had vital administrative or industrial skills.[109] This may seem strange from a distance of over fifty years, but at the time it was deemed a necessary evil.[110] Germany was in chaos, its cities smashed, its people starving, and it was felt that something had to be done to restore even the most basic services, even if it meant working with former enemies. The people were in a desperate state: 1945 and capitulation marked the beginning of the terrible 'Hunger Years' for Berliners.

The first task facing the Allies in the city was to distribute food and fuel, but this was made virtually impossible as the Soviets had severely limited access to the city. The British zone alone needed 600 tons of coal a day, all of which had to be brought in from the Ruhr, and food was required for 650,000 starving civilians. At the height of the first food crisis in October 1945 pathetic figures gathered nettles, scavenged in rubbish dumps and begged for food; the British took to putting starving children on 'Stork' flights to the west rather than try to care for them in the isolated city. By October the population was struggling to survive on 800 calories a day and by the New Year rations in the British sector dropped – in some cases to 400 calories. In the summer of 1945 the number of mouths was increasing by a staggering 20,000 per day following the expulsion of millions of Germans from the east. The first stop for most was Berlin and despite warnings to stay away from the city streams of war-ravaged people continued to arrive, adding to the unbearable strain on the slender resources of the city.

The refugee problem which overwhelmed Berlin was ultimately a result of the Potsdam Agreement, in which the Allies finally agreed to the massive westward shift of Europe's borders. The Soviet Union was now to cut deep into Polish territory, and Poland was to be given a vast chunk of Germany along the western Neisse as compensation. The Soviet plan required not only a transfer of land, but the mass expulsion of Poles from the new Soviet Union and of Germans from the Soviet-Polish and Czech zones. The human misery which resulted from these decisions was incalculable.[111]

When the notion of moving millions of Germans from the east was introduced at Potsdam Churchill objected, saying on 22 July: 'The British had grave moral scruples about vast movements of population ... a transfer of eight or nine million Germans, which was what the Polish request involved, was too many and would be entirely wrong.'[112] Nevertheless the western Allies did approve it in Article XIII of the Potsdam Protocol, with the proviso that the evacuations should take place in 'an orderly and humane manner'. They were neither orderly nor humane, and in the end hundreds of thousands of civilians died.[113] Most refugees from Czechoslovakia, Hungary and further south came to Germany via Bavaria, but despite attempts to restrict their entry into the city the first port of call for many of the 4,692,800 people expelled from former German territories east of the Oder–Neisse and the 346,800 ethnic Germans expelled from Poland was Berlin.[114] The effect of the human flood on the shattered capital was devastating. On 22 October 1945 Captain Marples informed the House of Commons that 'according to a recent report by the International Red Cross, protests against unorganized deportations of Germans by the Poles and Czechs have failed to have effect, and refugees are still streaming into Berlin, where thousands die in the streets'. The Joint Relief Commission of the International Red Cross attempted to help the pathetic expellees while Churchill told the House of Commons on 16 August 1945 that he was becoming increasingly worried about the disturbing news from Poland: 'I am particularly concerned, at this moment, with the reports reaching us of the conditions under which the expulsion and exodus of Germans from the new Poland are being carried out ... it is not impossible that tragedy on a prodigious scale is unfolding itself behind the iron curtain.'[115]

The expulsions continued. On 24 August 1945 Norman Clark described the terrible state of the civilians, who were given a few minutes to pack their belongings and were then pushed on to cattle trucks for the journey into Germany. Many were robbed, beaten and raped by gangs of Polish thugs who 'worked' the trains. At the Stettiner Bahnhof in Berlin he saw

hundreds who lay on bundles of belongings on the platform and in
the booking hall ... the dead and dying and starving flotsam left by
the tide of human misery that daily reaches Berlin ... Thousands
more – up to 25,000 in a day – trek on foot to the outskirts of
Berlin, where they are stopped and forbidden entry to the already
overcrowded city. Each day between fifty and 100 children – a total
of 5,000 already over a short period – who have lost both parents, or
have been abandoned, are collected from Berlin's stations and taken
to orphanages or found foster-mothers in Berlin. That is all that Berlin
charity can do.

On 10 September the Berlin correspondent for *The Times* wrote:

In the Robert Koch hospital here which I visited this morning, there
are more than sixty German women and children, many of whom
were summarily evicted from a hospital and an orphanage in Danzig
last month, and, without food and water or even straw to lie on, were
dispatched in cattle trucks to Germany. When the train arrived in
Berlin they said that of eighty-three persons crammed into two of the
trucks twenty were dead.[116]

Foreign Minister Ernest Bevin saw the expellees in Berlin and reported to the
House of Commons: 'It was a pathetic sight – the stream of perambulators
and small vehicles of one kind or another, and the people were nearly all
women and children, with very few men at all. One could not help saying,
"My God, this is the price of stupidity and war." It was the most awful sight
one could see.'[117] *Life* magazine reported that by 1 September 8 million refugees
had arrived in Berlin and that 2 million more were on the roads as they were
officially forbidden to remain in the city (although many of them did anyway);
Margaret Bourke-White and Robert Capa's photographs of the misery on the
streets of Berlin and Leonard McCombe's images of 'Blind mutilated soldiers,
homeless boys, grannies, starving verminous mothers, infants' at the crowded
train stations brought the problem home.[118] The Americans were equally concerned. Robert Murphy, the US political adviser for Germany, wrote to the
State Department on 12 October 1945:

In the Lehrter Rail Station in Berlin alone our medical authorities
state an average of ten have been dying daily from exhaustion, malnutrition and illness. In viewing the distress and despair of these
wretches, in smelling the odor of their filthy condition, the mind
reverts instantly to Dachau and Buchenwald. Here is retribution on
a large scale, but practised not on the *Parteibonzen*, but on women
and children, the poor, the infirm.[119]

Ruth Andreas-Friedrich recalled meeting a young woman refugee at the Hamburger Bahnhof; she had been raped eight times while crossing the border and had been left 'to bleed to death on her filthy mattress in the Red Cross bunker'.[120]

The refugees put an unbearable strain on Allied facilities. In the British sector forty-three out of forty-four hospitals had been destroyed or badly damaged, and American and British commanders were jointly responsible for feeding 1.5 million Berliners and the increasing numbers of refugees. It was at this crucial point that the Soviets announced that they would no longer allow food to be drawn from the Soviet zone. Stalin was clearly hoping that the western Allies would be overwhelmed by the task which faced them and simply move out of Berlin.[121]

The Soviet announcement came at the first meeting of the Kommandatura on 7 July 1945. The body was intended to represent the views of all the Allies but the Soviets dominated the proceedings. The first order of the four-power government of 11 July 1945 simply stated: 'The Inter-Allied Kommandatura has assumed control of the City of Berlin . . . Until special notice, all existing regulations and ordinances issued by the Commander of the Soviet Army Garrison and Military Commandant of the City of Berlin . . . shall remain in force.' As Colonel Howley recalled bitterly, they had in fact 'acquiesced to Russian control of Berlin'. After the first meeting it became virtually impossible to change any of the officials in the police, the judiciary, the arts, the city administration, even those working in western zones, as the Russians vetoed all western proposals. At the same time the Soviets began to place further restrictions on the western transports to Berlin.

By the beginning of 1946 the Soviets were allowing only sixteen trains per day into the British and American sectors and the food situation worsened. Manual workers were not replacing their energy and soon began to suffer chronic undernourishment. Production dropped dramatically and the incidence of illnesses such as tuberculosis shot up. Looking at the prosperous European city today it is difficult to believe that tens of thousands died of malnutrition and disease in the bleak years following the war. Twelve thousand Berliners perished during the bitterly cold winter of 1947 alone, when temperatures hovered around −30 degrees Celsius, and deaths outnumbered live births by more than two to one throughout the entire period. The misery and desperation fuelled the black market, and crime.[122]

Berlin had gone through defeat and destitution before, most notably in the years following the First World War, but it had never fallen as far as this. By 1947 it had become the undisputed crime capital of the world, an amoral, lawless place which made even the callous world captured by Georg Grosz and Otto Dix look civilized by comparison. Unscrupulous black marketeers of all kinds, both German and foreign, made fortunes dealing in everything from medical supplies to weapons, from drugs to fake de-Nazification certificates. There were on average 10,000 reported burglaries and forty to fifty murders every month. Terrible stories of crime and violence circulated through the city; one told of a man who went through the streets with a white cane asking destitute children for guidance. He would then lure them to the basement of his bombed-out house, murder them, and sell their bodies as meat. As one British soldier recalled, 'even if the story was not true, we all believed that in the Berlin of the day it *could* be true.' By this time Berliners were doing everything they could to get into the black market, from gathering and selling bits of wood to following Allied soldiers around hoping that they would drop their cigarette butts – seven could be turned into another cigarette. A Swiss visitor remembered Berliners in 1947 cramming into dirty trains in the hope of exchanging some household goods for scraps of food: 'The German goes hungry. He freezes. He sees his children die. He has become like a helpless, hunted animal.'

At the same time, a tough generation of entrepreneurs was coming of age amongst the ruins, young people who would soon fuel the 'economic miracle' of the 1950s. The nine-year-old Norbert Burkert was typical. He lived with his parents and a sister in two rooms in a Berlin cellar, his grandmother having already died in the first winter. The family was constantly hungry but like many older middle-class Germans his father refused to deal on the black market. The boy took no notice and went to the markets at the Brandenburg Gate, the Stresemannstrasse and the Potsdamer Platz. He stole coal and scavenged for wood and metal, which he sold to scrap dealers: 'We children organized ourselves in street bands. I belonged to the band at the Bendlerblock . . . a prime hunting ground for metal,' he remembered. These children soon controlled whole areas of the city. The black market quickly became an alternative underground economy in which the basic unit of exchange was the cigarette. Five cigarettes bought sex; twenty-five cartons bought a Leica camera. Many GIs made small fortunes in this way: the western soldiers were heavily involved in the black market despite official attempts to close it down.[123]

Although the city was commonly referred to by the Berlin garrison as the 'septic arsehole', soldiers stationed there often had a relatively pleasant life. Compared to civilians they were rich, powerful and privileged, and although there had been an official non-fraternization policy for US forces since 1944 it was being widely ignored by the time the troops reached Berlin.[124] The canteens and clubs such as the British Other Ranks Club on the Kurfürstendamm supplied western soldiers with what George Clare called 'The most effective aphrodisiac of the time: food'. Sex was cheap:

That man does not live by air alone was no problem in Berlin, where the desires of thousands of lonely soldiers were stilled by the many more thousands of lonely women whose husbands or boyfriends were either dead or dimming memories in prisoner-of-war camps dotting the globe from Iowa to Siberia. The non-fraternization order – a sop to British and American public opinion – banning any but strictly formal contacts between victors and vanquished was so universally disobeyed it had to be dropped ... All non-fraternization did was to give two now forgotten words to the English language: 'frat' for Tommys' or GIs' German girlfriends and 'fratting' for their relationship. Usually starting as soulless barter – sex for cigarettes, chocolates, nylons, food and other treasures from NAAFI or PX – it often developed into something deeper.[125]

It became quite common for GIs and Tommys to 'adopt' a Berlin woman; as the British Colonel Byford-Jones put it, 'of course quite a lot of us go to bed with the Fräulein. They are nice and they are so well developed physically by sport ... These girls will take any treatment and they treat you like a king – don't matter if you keep them waiting for half an hour – and they are thankful for little things, a bar of chocolate or a few fags! It's like giving these girls the moon.'

The view was somewhat different from the German perspective: Ursula Gray, a German refugee, remembered women prostituting themselves to get a few cigarettes or a can of coffee for the black market: 'I know very fine people who would have done anything,' she said. 'How could you blame a starving girl?' The 1948 film A Foreign Affair, which begins with devastating footage of the wrecked city, tried to tackle the complex relationship between victor and vanquished. Marlene Dietrich played Erika von Schlütow, the wife of an ex-Nazi now reduced to abject poverty and forced to make money by working as a cabaret singer in a sleazy nightspot reminiscent of the famous Blue Angel club. There she begins a cold-hearted affair with the American Captain John Pringle, played by John Lund, a relationship which revolves around cigarettes, nylons, sex and betrayal. The two most famous songs of the film, written by the great Friedrich Hollaender, were appropriately entitled Illusions and Black Market. It was not a flattering picture of the American liberators.[126] Ironically, however, the Allied presence began to change the face of Berlin. They may not have rivalled the sophisticated Soviet culture officers under Tiulpanov and Dymshits, but western troops brought not only food, cigarettes, stockings, and an insatiable demand for cheap sex, but also a certain kind of optimism and freedom which stood in stark contrast to the drudgery of the Soviet zone.[127] Berliners began to warm to them.

The easy-going attitude of the western Allies helped to fuel a brief cultural explosion in post-war Berlin, the extraordinary creativity of what became known there as the 'Golden Hunger Years'. Nightclubs and bars mushroomed in the well-hidden cellars of bombed-out buildings, offering a bizarre mixture of American jazz and German cabaret; they attracted GIs and German women wearing 'western' fashions pieced together out of old curtains and bits of fabric. Theatres began to open in all sectors of Berlin; the chiselled features of the young Horst Caspar graced the stage as Hamlet in 1945, while Gustaf Gründgens, Eduard von Winterstein and Karlheinz Martins contributed to more than 100 new productions staged in the first year. The Americans backed the Berlin Philharmonie, now housed in the Titania Palast. Artists like Bruno Bielefeld, who in *Chaos* painted a stark image of the Goddess of Victory in the twisted wreckage of Berlin, or Wolf Hoffmann, who painted *In Memoriam Berlin, 1945*, tried to come to terms with their ruined city, while the portraits of destitute men and women by artists like Heinrich Ehmsen or August Wilhelm Dressler were works of great poignancy. More book and newspaper publishers were given licences and by 1946 the 'Berlin newspaper forest' included thirteen papers produced under difficult conditions; the *Kurier* office was barely visible behind piles of old bricks and burnt-out walls in the Reinickendorfer Strasse. At the same time film studios began to prepare new productions; Billy Wilder was filming *A Foreign Affair* in 1947, the same year Roberto Rossellini came to the city to make *Anno Zero*. One of the most striking aspects was the resurgence of cabaret, which enjoyed a brief renaissance amidst the rubble. The most celebrated of the artists was Günter Neumann, who played at the Ulenspiel, capturing the desperate plight of post-war Berlin in his witty and cutting style. One Berliner remembered how this brilliant satirist 'drowned in waves of laughter floating on a sea of unwept tears: pain, hunger, cold, prostitution and the black market – the life one lived in Berlin'. Another recalled that although he had to tread very carefully so as not to offend the occupying powers he managed to show 'how poor we were, how hungry, how we longed for hope. But in such a way that we could laugh about it. He spelled out the truth without pity and yet he gave us consolation and new hope.' The brief surge of culture might well have continued, but it was soon overshadowed by political events. Once again, the changes were initiated by the Soviets.

On 4 June 1945 Stalin had called Walter Ulbricht and Wilhelm Pieck back to Moscow for a surprise meeting with Molotov and Zhdanov to lay the groundwork for the creation of political parties in the Soviet zone. The minutes were only discovered after the fall of the Berlin Wall in 1989.[128] Shortly afterwards, on 10 June, the Soviets had issued Order No. 2, which established four political parties: the KPD or Communist Party under Wilhelm Pieck, Becher, Paul Wander and Fred Oelssner; the Social Democrats (SPD), which had traditionally been the strongest party in Berlin; the Christian Democrats (CDU), and the Liberal Democrats (LDP). They were political fronts – free and independent political organizations were unthinkable in Soviet-occupied Germany. At this early stage, however, it was felt that the Communist KPD and the Social Democratic parties should remain separate: Stalin believed he could infiltrate and control the Social Democratic Party, while the KPD could be made into the true mass party of Germany. By late 1945, however, it had become clear that most Germans saw the Communists as little more than 'bullies and stooges whom the Soviet authorities manipulated for their own ends'.[129]

Stalin was now aware that a free election would almost certainly result in a victory for the western Social Democrats over the Soviet-backed Communists. 'Putting Communism on a German is like putting a saddle on a cow,' he complained. Instead of risking a lost election Stalin now decided to forcibly merge the Social Democratic and Communist parties and then go to the polls on the strength of Social Democratic support. Once in power, the Communists could literally kill off the SPD and take over 'legally', rather as Hitler had done in 1933. The merger was to 'secure the unity of Germany through a united party of the workers', to be called the 'Socialist Unity Party' or SED. Ulbricht returned to Berlin and called a meeting at the Communist club, the Café Rosa (which became the Liebezeit in eastern Berlin), to inform the Communists of the strategy. In October 1945 he suddenly announced that the SPD and the KPD had the 'same interests' and therefore had a 'sound basis' for unity. Dozens of meetings were held to encourage the union but many Social Democrats rejected the planned merger, protesting that they were not keen to be dictated to by the Russians; nor did they want their party to be associated with the 'unpleasantnesses' of the Soviet occupation. The KPD began to increase pressure on the Social Democratic Central Executive and the Soviets even gave Social Democratic leaders presents to try to win their support – Grotewohl, an amateur painter, was given art supplies and Zhukov worked to have his son released from a British POW camp. Those SPD members who resisted were already being rounded up and sent to prison.[130] In mid November 1945 the two workers' parties formed a sixty-man commission to plan the merger while the Soviets forcibly moved the SPD headquarters from the American to the Soviet zone; representatives of the Soviet-backed branch of the SPD and KPD decided on a common electoral programme not merely for the Soviet-occupied zone, but for all of Germany. The order to go ahead with the merger was spelled out to Ulbricht during another secret meeting in Moscow in February 1946. In the end, however, his plan was foiled – not by the western Allies, but by an anti-Soviet movement which arose in the city. It would prove to be one of the finest moments in Berlin history.

Throughout their long and troubled past Berliners have shown notoriously bad judgement in political matters, but only a year after the end of the war they acted with considerable courage and vision to defend democratic principles and the right to self-determination. It was an extraordinary transformation given that they had just emerged from the political wasteland of Hitler's Germany. Long before the western Allies realized the implications of Stalin's 'Unity Party' Berlin's legitimate Social Democrats had begun to resist the Communist plan. Many rank and file SPD members opposed their own pro-Soviet leaders and at the Party Congress on 1 March 1946 they refused to agree to a merger unless it was decided in a secret ballot. The Soviets feared the outcome and began to attack all those known to be against the Unity Party. Suddenly Social Democrats were stopped in the streets, beaten, arrested, and told to vote for the merger or face the consequences. The Americans were shocked by such behaviour and a week before the ballot General Clay declared that fusion would only be recognized by the American military government if it was agreed to by all party members. For the first time the Americans had agreed to defend Berliners against Soviet policy. This seemingly insignificant election marked the beginning of what came to be known as the Second Battle of Berlin. It also heralded the start of the Cold War.

On 31 March 1946 Social Democrats went to the polling booths to answer the question: 'Are you for or against an immediate union between the Social Democrats and the Communist Parties?' The Soviets, realizing that they could not win, suddenly stopped the election. Polling stations opened in two Soviet sector districts, Friedrichshain and Prenzlauer Berg, but Red Army soldiers closed them down at gunpoint and absconded with the ballot boxes. In the western zones the referendum was a landslide victory for the opponents of the merger – 19,529 voted against the Communists while only 2,937 voted for the merger, making this the first western victory in the political battle for Berlin. For the first time since the end of the war the Soviets had suffered a serious reversal in Germany. And it marked the beginning of a radical change in Soviet policy.[131]

The Soviets now ignored the election results, and on 22 April 1946 forcibly merged the KPD and the SPD in their zone. In a photograph which was later plastered over posters, placards and every East German history textbook, the Communist leader Wilhelm Pieck and the Communist Social Democratic leader Otto Grotewohl shook hands in front of over 1,000 party delegates. This marked the birth of the Socialist Unity Party. The stylized handshake was adopted as the official SED symbol and would later become part of East German iconography. Stalin would soon be able to test the popularity of his new party. Elections for the district and provincial assemblies were called under Allied jurisdiction for 20 October 1946.

Stalin must already have known that the SED, correctly seen as a mere extension of Soviet rule and known as 'the Russian party', had no chance of victory in a fair fight. But the election campaign was far from fair. The Soviets tried to disrupt the Social Democratic campaign at every turn. Free coal and food was handed out at SED meetings while the Social Democrats were forbidden to speak in the eastern zones. Copies of western newspapers like *Die neue Zeitung* and *Der Tagesspiegel*, in which Berliners had been given full editorial responsibility, were seized by Communist agents while the Soviets decreed a monopoly of news reporting in their zone. The elections had now come to stand for a clear choice between two opposing world views – the Soviet Union against the west. As such they were decisive in post-war history. If the SED had won, Berlin might well have been absorbed into the Soviet zone. It would prove to be the last free election in that zone.

On a cold autumn day on 20 October 1946 Berliners turned out to vote and patiently lined up outside the polling stations despite Soviet attempts to attack those not wearing Unity Party insignia. The atmosphere was tense. Ninety-two per cent of the electorate voted and, despite the harassment, the Social Democrats won a majority in every single borough in the Soviet zone, making them the undisputed victors with an overall return of 48 per cent. The SED received only 20 per cent. It was particularly difficult for the Soviets to accept these results in districts like 'Red Wedding', where in 1932 the KPD had received 60 per cent of the vote; in 1946, with the district now part of the British zone, the SED could muster only 29 per cent. The Soviets were astounded by the result and quickly held a special conference attended by a number of Central Committee members who flew in specially from Moscow. Throughout the two-day meeting the SED was largely blamed for the failure and Colonel Sergei Tiulpanov, who disliked Ulbricht, stated that the political future of their zone could not be left in the hands of the inept Germans; the Soviets must now transform the SED into an 'effective instrument' of Soviet policy. Tiulpanov admitted that the Berlin situation was unique because of the presence of the western Allies there but that the election results had been a disgrace; henceforth the Soviets would impose complete conformity on 'their' Germans; it would be 'necessary to forbid categorically even the slightest degree of disrespect toward the Soviet Union and Soviet occupation authorities'. 'Once and for all,' he said unconvincingly, 'this is not pre-electoral terror, but only quite normal order.' Nevertheless he would not allow opponents to 'spit in our face'; all anti-Soviet statements were to be controlled in the Russian zone – '*v nashei zone my po etoi linii khoziaeva*' (where we are the bosses).[132] It was the beginning of a new, harsh era of Soviet control.

To the annoyance of the Russians the new Berlin City Assembly met on 26 November 1946 and proceeded to elect an anti-Soviet Magistrat. The western Social Democrat Otto Suhr was made President and the Social Democrat Otto Ostrowski became the new Oberbürgermeister or lord mayor. At first Ostrowski tried to compromise with the Soviets but instead of being treated well he was dragged to their headquarters and an attempt was made to blackmail him into provoking a constitutional crisis. When the new Magistrat realized what was happening they called a motion of no-confidence and Ostrowski was forced to resign. The man who took his place proved to be one of Berlin's greatest leaders, a man who valiantly defended democracy in western Germany and who proved himself a powerful enemy of Soviet oppression. His name was Ernst Reuter.

Reuter was an unlikely hero. As a young man he had fought in the First World War and had been captured by the Russians in 1916; as a prisoner he came into contact with left-wing activists. After the Bolshevik Revolution he returned to Berlin an avid Communist. He took part in the doomed Spartacus Uprising, became the First Secretary of the Spartakusband, the First Secretary of the newly formed Berlin Communist Party, and in 1921 was appointed to one of the most important positions in the Communist hierarchy, Secretary General of the Berlin KPD. Reuter had been close to all the Berlin Communists – Rosa Luxemburg, Karl Liebknecht, Karl Radek – as well as Lenin, and it was widely assumed that he would have a great career in the KPD. Nevertheless, Reuter was first and foremost a German patriot and when Lenin began to push internationalism through the Comintern he foresaw the subjugation of the German working class under brutal Soviet domination. The murder of Erzberger revealed the growing danger of a Soviet *Putsch* and despite a personal appeal from Lenin Reuter left the Communist Party and was elected a lowly Social Democratic member of the Berlin City Assembly. It was there, during those grim Weimar years, that Reuter first encountered his arch-enemy Wilhelm Pieck, who was then busy collaborating with Goebbels to bring down the legitimate German government. When Hitler came to power Pieck was forced to flee to Moscow. Reuter was also targeted by the Nazis, and after being arrested and badly beaten he escaped to Turkey and spent the rest of the war in exile. After his experiences at the hands of both the Communists and the Nazis Reuter was determined to fight against all totalitarian threats to Germany, whether they came from the left or the right.

Reuter was finally permitted to return to Berlin in the bitter November of 1946 and was elected to the Magistrat as a Social Democratic representative. He was disturbed by Stalin's plans to dominate Germany and immediately began to make virulently anti-Communist statements. Ernst Reuter was a formidable opponent for the Soviets. Unlike capitalists or 'enemies of the people' he had actually known Lenin and had fought against Hitler; even Soviet propaganda could not convincingly portray him as an 'ex-Nazi'. Furthermore, he knew from long experience how the Soviets operated. When Ostrowski was forced out of power Reuter was chosen to stand as the new mayor of Berlin. The Soviets flatly refused to accept his appointment, and letters and documents delivered to him at the Red Rathaus were returned with 'no such person' scribbled across the front; in the interim period the fiery *Berlinerin* Louise Schröder was obliged to stand in as acting mayor. This remarkable woman, in frail health and constantly hectored by the Soviets, managed to guide the Magistrat through this troublesome period, an act which earned her the affectionate title 'Mother of Berlin'. Schroeder and Reuter began to rally Berliners against increasing Soviet aggression in Berlin. The Russian response was to further tighten their hold over the city, and to try to force the western Allies to leave.

The Russians began to disrupt life in Berlin wherever possible. They cut off electricity and water without warning while restricting movement around the city. When the western Allies protested in the Kommandatura the Soviets simply vetoed all western policies and issued orders through SMAD instead. They terrorized supporters of the western Allies, who would 'soon be forced to leave Berlin', threatening that anyone who had 'collaborated' with them would be punished. Twenty-five thousand workers and their families were suddenly rounded up and sent to the Soviet zone; they were told that it was safer to co-operate with the Russians than to be kidnapped or murdered – SPD reports of 1947 indicated that there were 400 Social Democrats in Zwickau prison and 900 in Dresden prison alone, while there were 597 documented cases of members of the CDU being arrested, the latest victims of the Soviet terror which now gripped the eastern zone.[133]

The west was first made aware of the new campaign of violence and kidnapping of pro-western Berliners in February 1946 when three non-Communist judges in Berlin simply disappeared. They were said to have 'refused to render judgement in accord with the expressed views of the German Communist leaders', and although two of them lived in the western sector all attempts to find them proved fruitless. General Clay knew that they had been taken by SMAD agents but nothing could be done to save them. Others managed to escape: Dr Ferdinand Friedensburg, co-founder of the Christian Democratic Party in the east, who refused to bow to the political dictats of the SED, only saved himself by fleeing to the west in 1947 while Jakob Kaiser, the head of the eastern CDU who had resisted the notion of political unity between the CDU and the Soviets, fled for his life on 18 March 1948.[134] By 1947 the American commandant had already documented over 1,600 kidnappings of employees and borough officials and it was known that thousands more had disappeared in other zones.[135] George Clare remembered watching in horror as the Soviets began to 'take out' political and human rights activists on the streets of Berlin:

> It was all over in seconds. A car screeched to a sudden halt, hefty men jumped out, grabbed their victim, bundled him into their vehicle and, before those who witnessed it could even begin to comprehend what had happened, they were racing off in the direction of the Soviet sector. There, of course, such dramatics were unnecessary – people just disappeared.[136]

The terror unleashed in the Soviet zone was overseen from Moscow by Lavrenti Beria, the People's Commissariat of Internal Affairs (NKVD/MVD). Berlin itself was run by the future Chairman of the KGB, General Serov, who moved to Germany in May 1945 to head the 'internal' NKVD/NKGB section of the Soviet Military Administration – which in 1946 was renamed the MVD (the Ministry of Internal Affairs) and the MGB (the Ministry for State Security).[137] The headquarters lay in an old German army engineer training centre and in the former St Antonius hospital in the south-east district of Karlshorst. They were from the beginning responsible only to Moscow. Serov's control of the zone was total. His *opergruppy* personnel reported on tens of thousands of people, from Germans employed in administrative units to Soviet military personnel who were spied on by Soviet counter-intelligence or SMERSH (an acronym for 'Death to Spies'), which was merged into the MGB in late 1946. The Soviets did not rely solely on Soviet agents; they also founded a new Soviet-backed German security service. The first step was taken in July 1946 when SMAD reorganized the police in the Soviet zone with the creation of a central Soviet-controlled organization called the Deutsche Verwaltung des Innern or DVdI. In August 1947 the Soviets increased the power of the police in the eastern zone further, renaming it the 'people's police' or Volkspolizei (commonly known as 'Vopos'), which was in turn divided into administrative, civil, railway, and criminal and intelligence sections as well as special border police and new units formed to guard interior administration buildings and the Information Department. The intelligence section, in effect the first German political police organization in the Soviet zone, was created by SMAD Order 201 and named Volkspolizei, Kommissariat-5 or K-5. This terrifying body was given the jurisdiction and equivalent power of the MVD/MGB in the Soviet Union and, under SMAD's watchful eye, carried out surveillance and wrote dossiers on hundreds of thousands of Germans; in 1948 the K-5 investigated 51,236 people in the province of Saxony alone, often under the cover of 'de-Nazification' procedures. K-5 was responsible for carrying out the thousands of kidnappings which plagued East Berlin in the post-war years. On 28 June 1948 the police force was itself purged of all those considered politically unreliable, including anyone who had been in a western POW camp or had had contact with relatives in the west; 10 per cent of the Berlin police was purged for alleged contacts with westerners.

Soviet control over the Berlin police intensified. Those who had proved their unquestioned loyalty to the Soviets were often rewarded by being asked to join one of the special departments – the 'Politkultur', for instance, whose job it was to guarantee the 'political loyalty' of Germans employed by the Soviets. Such officers were given special ideological training under the auspices of Major-General S. F. Gorokhov and Colonel A. M. Kropychev from SMAD Internal Affairs Administration, and by July 1948 there were 720 of these officers, one for every 100 regular policemen. The most prestigious group was known as the 'Alert Police', a paramilitary force trained for special missions which included Paul Markgraf and Richard Staimer, Pieck's son-in-law, amongst its members. American intelligence correctly saw this as the beginning of 'a cadre communist army' complete with tanks and armoured vehicles, important precisely because they could be used as a front for Soviet military personnel.[124] These recruits often tried to impress their Soviet bosses by the viciousness of their arrests and interrogations, using methods inherited from both the Gestapo and Stalin's secret police. By 1946 the Soviets had put in place a system of terror rivalled only by that in Russia itself.[138]

In his book *News from Soviet Germany* Fritz Löwenthal described some of the horrific murders which were taking place in and around Berlin in the post-war years, events which read like the early reports of Nazi crimes smuggled out of Germany in 1933. Even the place-names were the same: 'Bodies are frequently being found in mysterious circumstances in the Eastern Zone,' he reported. 'For instance, at the end of March 1947 labourers passing through the woods near Kottbus saw a human hand sticking out of the melting snow. The snow was cleared away to reveal the body, and several other corpses were found in the same place.' As usual, the Soviet Military Authority prevented investigation.

> On 10 April, farm labourers found nineteen male and one female body in a ditch on the Leipzig–Dessau road ... the cause of death in all cases was either a bullet in the nape of the skull or the beating in of the skull with some blunt instrument. No sooner had the bodies been taken to the nearest mortuary than they were seized by Lieutenant Volkhov and cremated. In July 1947 twenty male bodies were found but when the independent Berlin Press took up the matter no solution of the 'mystery' could be found.[139]

The Communist press insisted that the bodies were of men who had died during the war, but as they were not decomposed this was patently absurd. The western commandants sent protest notes to General Kotikov after every kidnapping, but the Soviets denied all knowledge of the abductions. Kotikov even had the gall to rebuke the Allies for failing to control 'bandits' in their zones. The kidnappings and sudden disappearances were made possible in part because of one of the perversions of the Stalinist regime: the reopening of Nazi concentration camps.

By the end of 1946 eleven infamous camps and a number of prisons, including Sachsenhausen, Buchenwald, Hohenschönhausen, Jamlitz, Forst, Roitsch-Bitterfeld, Mühlberg, Bautzen, Altenhain, Stern-Buchholz, Ketschendorf and Neubrandenburg were all operational. The ex-concentration camps were renamed *Spetslager* (special isolation camps) and were filled with tens of thousands of men and women, many of whom had been abducted in broad daylight on the streets of the city. They also created new camps in Frankfurt-an-der-Oder, Lieberose, Forst, Bitterfeld, Mühlberg, Altenhain, Stern-Buchholz, Beeskow and Berlin, while the old prisoner-of-war camp at Torgau was converted into a political prison.[140] One survivor from Sachsenhausen remembered:

> In the afternoon of October 30th, 1946, two Russian officers came up to me on the corner of Unter den Linden and the Friedrichstrasse and invited me to go with them to clear up a minor point. Without suspecting that anything very serious was wrong, I went with them. I was taken in a car belonging to the NKVD to Kupfergraben, where I was accused of having spied on behalf of the American military authorities. There was absolutely no basis for this charge, and I vigorously denied it. I was locked in a cellar and questioned for several nights in succession, during which I was held down on the floor and beaten with rubber truncheons whilst a wireless was on at full volume to drown my shouts. My head was bloody and I was unable to raise one arm. As I refused to 'confess', this went on for about a fortnight.[141]

Brunhilde Pomsel, who had worked at Goebbels's Propaganda Ministry, spent the period from November 1947 in East Berlin, where she built radios and sewed women's and men's suits.

> Just as unexpectedly as I arrived there one morning, I was sent away again. I was taken to Sachsenhausen . . . That was the worst part of the whole ordeal. In the meantime, the camps were thoroughly organized. The Russians had not only taken over the camps from the Germans, but they had also learned to run them with German perfection . . . The most difficult part was having to cope with not knowing why you were still being detained.[142]

Another prisoner from the Neubrandenburg camp reported how he and others had been arbitrarily arrested by the GPU (the Soviet security service):

> In January 1947 the first transports of prisoners were organized for labour in the east. Emaciated to a skeleton, with swollen legs and a long beard, I gave my age as forty-nine, although I was only thirty. No one doubted me; I looked every year of it. I drank soapy water in order to get into the lazaret with fever, for unless you have fever you are not sick for the Russians ... Almost all those who had been in camp with me were sent off to the east to labour camps.[143]

The death rates in the German camps were high; Lowenthal reported that of the 13,000 prisoners in Neubrandenburg only 6,000 were alive after six months, most having succumbed to spotted fever, dysentery and diphtheria. Executions by shooting were common, particularly in Bautzen.

Bautzen prison, which had been intended for 2,000 people, now held between 6,000 and 15,000 people at one time. Irmgard Höss, then a twenty-five-year-old, remembered hiding in the woods near her home in June 1945 and watching in horror as a group of Germans in prison uniform under the command of a Soviet officer shovelled twenty naked bodies into a shallow ditch. She had witnessed one of the daily trips of the Bautzen prison burial squad; about 16,000 Germans were executed in the prison yard and buried there. As in the Nazi period, the camps were ringed by three rows of guards, the first two of Russians, the third of German Communist members of the SED or Unity Party, who took over the jobs once carried out by the SS. The treatment of prisoners was brutal. One eye witness reported: 'One might the men were fetched by German police ... Sometimes the prisoners were left standing for hours in blinding searchlights. After many months they were transferred to different concentration camps. At Christmas 1946 there were 15,000 prisoners in Buchenwald camp alone.'[144] The old torture facilities at Buchenwald were used regularly, although the gas chambers and crematoria were not; instead, prisoners to be executed were either shot or shipped to the Gulag.

The numbers of people who disappeared alarmed the west but the Soviets continued to deny all knowledge of the abductions. When faced with names of victims they usually accused the suspect of being an ex-Nazi. Many genuine Nazi criminals were caught by the Soviets in 1945. Lothar Rühl remembered that after being arrested by the Russians in Berlin he was interrogated: 'a bored Russian officer said in broken German, "Take off your shirt." I had a good idea what they were after, so I held up my arms. I didn't have the SS tattoo giving my blood group.' In the first weeks of the occupation ex-SS men were executed or sent directly to the Soviet Union.[145] But to the dismay of the German Communists the persecution of Nazis soon stopped as the Soviets started to use them in the administration of their zone. Walter Ulbricht complained in vain that the commandant of the Berlin district of Friedenau had allowed the local administration to 'be dominated by ex-Nazis', and his attempts to prosecute the former Gauleiter of Saxony in order to publicize the horrors of Fascism were stopped because the Soviets argued that such trials would not be 'good politics' in their zone.[132] The KPD veteran Heinrich Fomferra was also disgusted by this use of ex-Nazis and complained to General Mickinn, chief of the Cadres Section, that except for a few Communists in charge, 'all the rest were, as far as I can tell, former military specialists from the Nazi army'.[133] Ex-Nazis were retained in the police force and when the chief of the Personnel Department of the DVdI complained about it he was sent to the Karl Marx Higher Party School for a six-month course – no doubt, as Norman Naimark has put it, 'to improve his understanding of the dialectics of using the talents of those who had fought for the Third Reich to build socialism in the zone'.[146] The Soviets also brought back the old Nazi administrators and heads of factories; at the Sachsenwerke in Dresden Viktor Abakumov wrote to Molotov in 1947 that 'of 1,800 workers and employees, 201 were former Nazis, 41 of those were in leading positions at the factory'.[147]

If the Soviets made use of ex-Nazis they also used the false charge of 'Nazism' to rid themselves of 'enemies of the state'. The NKVD were kept busy inventing false Nazi files and documents on potential Soviet targets and one anti-Soviet activist who was arrested for Nazi activities remembered: 'I never had anything to do with the Nazis ... But in August 1945 I was called to the GPU and told I was expected to volunteer for work in Russia. When I refused I was arrested, and for weeks I was questioned every night for hours ... I was sent to Buchenwald, where I was kept for a further year and released only when I was at the point of death.'[148] Others clearly innocent of Nazi crimes were caught up in the wave of arrests. One woman who had spent fourteen years in the Soviet Union and who had returned to Berlin to work with the Communists, struck up a conversation with a Soviet officer at an U-Bahn station. When the train arrived in the Russian sector he made her get out and took her to the nearest patrol, where he turned her in on suspicion of espionage. She only escaped deportation because someone at headquarters recognized her as a German Communist. The arrest of 'Nazis' became worse after the SMAD's de-Nazification initiative issued in December 1947 in Order No. 201, which put SMAD in charge of this matter; SMAD was now the ultimate authority and, as Erich Mielke put it, 'no other instructions are valid'.

The Soviets now became increasingly paranoid. Many groups were considered 'unreliable' and potential 'spies', from Jehovah's Witnesses to volunteers who distributed western CARE packages in the eastern zone to all those with connections with the west. Germans who had been in British or American POW camps and were sent back to the Russian zone after being processed were not permitted to go home but were forced to endure 'quarantine' and 're-education'. The majority were taken directly from the trains to Sachsenhausen, from where the healthiest were sent to forced labour camps in the Soviet Union; indeed in one case a trainload of 774 German POWs from England bound for East Germany were not even allowed to touch German soil but after passing through Frankfurt-an-der-Oder were sent directly to the Soviet Union.[149] Others were accused of spying even if they had merely wandered into the Soviet zone by mistake, like the dental mechanic Heinz Handke of Berlin-Charlottenburg who disappeared while trying to deliver a set of teeth. In 1947 the SPD reported that 800 of its members were languishing in Buchenwald alone, and in 1990 Bonn's Ministry for Intra-German Relations estimated that over 240,000 Berliners and eastern Germans passed through the *Spetslager* or special camps in the years following the war; an official American survey of 1947 put the number of political prisoners in the Soviet zone at 25,000. After the fall of the Berlin Wall a number of Soviet-era mass graves were found throughout eastern Germany. Fifty were discovered at Special Camp No. 7, Sachsenhausen, where it appears that around 12,500 Germans died. The official Soviet figures put the number of German deaths around 40,000; western estimates range around 100,000 but these figures do not take into account the untold number who died in the Soviet Union itself.[150] Bautzen, Buchenwald and Sachsenhausen remained open until early 1950, when the remaining prisoners were transferred to the Soviet Union; the burial battalions 'disappeared', probably so that they could not reveal the existence or location of the mass graves.[151] It must be remembered that the terror was not limited to vanquished Germany alone; over 1 million innocent people from east central Europe were killed by the Soviets between 1945 and 1953.[152]

Faced with this growing brutality the western Allies began to protect vulnerable Germans. Police were posted outside their doors and those in grave danger were flown to the western zone. Armed Russians who tried to seize Berliners in the western sectors were arrested; the British tended to disarm the Soviet thugs, beat them up, and dump them back in the eastern zone. A number were shot by American MPs. As Soviet persecution of Berliners continued and fear of the Russians intensified, the brief cultural renaissance of the 'Golden Hunger Years' began to fade in an atmosphere of suspicion and fear.

Another element in the growing conflict between the Soviets and the west came with the increasing tension over the Soviet race to get the bomb. At the

Potsdam Conference the Allies had agreed to share 'all past accomplishments and future developments of German science'. It was a sham. From the earliest days of the war the Allies had competed in the race to capture as many German scientists and as much equipment as possible. The extraordinary cat-and-mouse game only intensified as the war drew to a close. The American 'Operation Paperclip', the attempt to identify and recruit German scientists, was motivated above all by the desire to keep these specialists out of Soviet hands.[153] General Leslie Groves, the chief administrator of the American atomic bomb project, headed the 'Alsos Mission' to capture a prepared list of leading scientists, particularly atomic physicists.[154] He was extremely successful. In 1945 Groves found and held Werner Heisenberg in Bavaria and found Otto Hahn, Max von Laue, Karl Friedrich von Weizsäcker and Walter Gerlach; ten of the top German scientists were taken to Farm Hall in England for interrogation: the British secretly recorded their conversations, including their reactions to Hiroshima.[155] The Americans recovered German plans which proved that their scientists had lagged far behind in the construction of an atomic bomb; they found 1,200 tons of uranium which the Germans had stored in the salt mines near Stassfurt and captured the Peenemünde team, including Wernher von Braun and Walter Dornberger, who had developed the V-2 rocket. They captured the members of the Kaiser Wilhelm Institute for Physics, including Heisenberg and Hahn, who had been evacuated from Berlin to the west in 1943. The Americans also temporarily occupied parts of Saxony which were destined to become Soviet; the American Combined Intelligence Subcommittee (CIOS) teams removed vast amounts of equipment and, under the auspices of Operation Overcast, seized specialists, including Zeiss Jena employees and the parts for 100 rockets from the V-2 plant in Nordhausen; altogether the Americans evacuated around 5,000 German scientists and technicians and their families from the Soviet zone. But if the Americans took the elite, the Soviets took everything else.[156]

The overriding Soviet aim in early 1945 was to capture anyone and anything which might help in the development of their own atomic bomb, a mission headed by none other than the Commissar of Internal Affairs, Lavrenty Beria.[157] In reality Beria had been slow to understand the implications of American atomic research; he had long mistrusted Soviet scientists and did not believe intelligence reports which described American advances; L. R. Kvasnikov recounted how on one occasion when he was reporting on the latest intelligence data concerning the American atomic project in early 1945 Beria threatened him: 'If this is disinformation, I'll put you all in the cellar.'[158] On 16 July 1945 the Americans exploded an atomic bomb in the desert at Alamogordo in New Mexico; Truman informed Stalin at Potsdam on 24 July but Stalin was finally shocked out of his complacency when on 6 August 1945 the Americans exploded the bomb at Hiroshima. Henceforth Stalin would put all available resources into the Soviet atomic project.

Despite his initial scepticism Beria's representatives in Germany, Colonel-General I. S. Serov and Colonel-General A. P. Zaveniagin, had been active in the hunt for German scientists from the first days of the occupation. The operation came under the direct control of the NKVD/MVD so that the team which entered Germany in 1945 was completely independent and included around thirty scientists such as Kokoin, Flerov, Nemenov and Golovin, who wore the uniforms of NKVD lieutenant-colonels.[159] The Soviets found a number of German scientists still in their zone, including Manfred von Ardenne (who had designed a cyclotron and ran a private laboratory in Berlin-Lichterfelde), who was approached on 27 April and transferred to Russia on 21 May; and Gustav Hertz, who worked for the Siemens company, had received the Nobel Prize in 1925 for electron–atom collision experiments, and went to the Soviet Union along with his deputy Heinz Barwich.[160] Peter-Adolf Thiessen, a dedicated Nazi in charge of chemical research and development for the Third Reich, co-operated fully with the Soviets, as did Nikolaus Riehl, director of research at the Auer Company, which manufactured thorium and uranium metals and experimented with heavy water in Oranienburg. The Americans had long been aware that this installation would fall into the hands of the Soviets and had bombed it on 15 March 1945. They had failed to destroy several tons of rich uranium oxide; Riehl and his team were seized with the uranium and sent to Elekrostal east of Moscow along with the entire Auer lab, which was dismantled down to its washbasins and doorknobs; he would spend many years there producing pure uranium. The Russians took a number of other complete laboratories, including those from the institutes for Biology, Bio-chemistry, Chemistry, Anthropology and Silicate Research, and scoured the Berlin academic suburbs of Dahlem and Zehlendorf destined to be handed over to the Americans. Hundreds of scientists and technicians were seized, including physical chemist Max Volmer, the atomic physicist Robert Doepal, the chemist Wilhelm Eitel, and all the remaining scientists of the Kaiser Wilhelm Society in Berlin, the Institute for Physical Chemistry and Electrochemistry and the Kaiser Wilhelm Society Institute for Physics, including its head Ludwig Bewilogua. Many of those in the future American zone were offered presents like blocks of lard if they signed the Soviet contracts.[161] Others went willingly, believing that life working for the Soviets would be better than that promised by post-war Berlin; they included the physicist Max Steenbeck, who had been found starving in an internment camp.[162]

In some cases the Soviets reconstructed ex-Nazi sites, including the rocket facilities at Nordhausen and at Bleicherode. The Soviet Colonel Grigori Tokaev, who defected to the west in 1948, reported that although the Americans had taken a large amount of important equipment and personnel the Russians were able to painstakingly piece the facilities back together with the help of the German scientist Helmut Gröttrup and around 7,000 others. By 1946 a number of Berlin factories had been rebuilt, including EFEM, GEMA, AEG Kabelwerk Oberspree, Askania and Hermann Grau, and their scientists and researchers were encouraged to stay with promises of preferential treatment, good housing, access to restricted shops and gifts of large *payoks* or food and goods parcels. They seemed secure. But the Soviets were growing increasingly worried that these men might be enticed to the west at some future date, and they decided to act.

The Soviet counter measure was sudden. On 22 October 1946 an operation named *Osoaviakhim* and commanded by Beria's chief deputy in the zone, Colonel-General Serov, was launched to seize all scientific and top industrial personnel. NKVD and army units were stationed at bridges and crossing points throughout Berlin, private residences were surrounded and entire families detained while the contents of their homes were seized. Entire areas inhabited by factory workers like those at AEG Kabelwerk Oberspree were cordoned off and everyone taken; one eye witness reported that if there were 'employees of one of the aforementioned plants, they were politely asked to follow. In the dwellings of the families involved, the wardrobes were immediately nailed shut, and guards were posted until a Russian truck with several Russian soldiers arrived who loaded all the inventory and the family (from the grandfather to the baby) and took them to the railway stations of Köpenick or Friedrichshagen.'[163] The AEG plant alone lost 200 employees. Sometimes the kidnappings were more carefully planned; the rocket specialist Gröttrup and his colleagues were invited to a vodka and caviar party on the night of 21–22 October only to be told that they would soon be meeting their families at the train station to be moved east. While the party was underway the Gröttrups' apartment was surrounded by soldiers and when Gröttrup's wife managed to reach him on the telephone he told her that she must go with them: 'there is nothing I can do'.[164] In a matter of days Berlin was emptied of skilled workers. The Nordhausen and Bleicherode complexes were suddenly emptied and blown up. The scientists were sent to secret Soviet locations – the rocket scientists, for example, found themselves on the remote island of Gorodomlia in the middle of a huge lake in the Kalinin district. When the western Allies protested at the kidnappings Sokolovsky told Colonel Frank Howley that he had not interfered when the Americans took German scientists; 'I am not asking the Americans and British at what hour of the day or night they took their technicians. Why are you so concerned about the hour at which I took mine?'[165]

The fear of being targeted did not end in October 1946 and many others were to disappear in the coming months. Some were taken by force; others were asked to sign a paper declaring that they were leaving 'willingly'. The case of a Dr Ludwig who worked in the nylon industry was typical. On 1 November 1946 two Soviets in civilian clothes approached him with two contracts and demanded that he sign one of them. The first read: 'I agree to assist in the reconstruction of the Soviet Union' – for which he would be required to move for two years, although 'quarters with hard and soft furniture' would be provided; the other read that the undersigned 'herewith declared his unwillingness to assist in the reconstruction of the Soviet Union'.[166] Ludwig wisely signed the first. Scientists in the western zones were also approached but few agreed to leave because, as Heisenberg put it, 'The fox notices that many trails lead into the cave of the bear, but none come out.'[167] Both the British (under the code-name 'Scrum Half') and the Americans took steps to prevent Soviet contact with western scientists but we will never know how many were taken until Soviet Military Intelligence archives are finally opened.

There was one installation that could not be moved; it was destined to become the most infamous place in East German history – the Uranium mines around Wismut in the Erzgebirge.[168] These mines would soon supply most of the uranium for the Soviet atomic bomb project, but the cost in human lives would be high indeed.

Neither the Americans nor the Soviets were aware of the extent of the deposits in the region at the end of the war, but by 1946 the Soviets understood their value and by early 1947 the entire area had been cordoned off and the mines effectively turned into part of the Soviet system of labour camps.[169] Like the Gulag the mines' existence was officially denied despite the fact that the complex covered much of the Annaberg region of Saxony; when Brigadier-General Walter Hess of the US forces asked to see the mines Major-General Lavrentev of SMAD at Karlshorst answered: 'In reply to your letter of July 26 1947, containing a request for permission for you to visit the region of the uranium mines, Colonel General Malinin has instructed me to inform you that these mines are not under his jurisdiction and nothing is known of their existence.'[170]

The reality was quite different. The mines were enormous and workers from all of eastern Germany, including Berlin, were brought in to the recruitment centre at Aue, a town which came to be known as the 'Gate of Tears'. Around 30,000 workers were drafted in early 1947 but the Soviets demanded 75,000 more and soon tens of thousands of people were being rounded up to work as forced labourers.[171] The population of Aue swelled from 110,000 to 212,000 between 1946 and 1951 and included 'undesirable elements' from political prisoners to POWs returning from Russia who could be worked to death. There was no housing for the newcomers and many were forced to live in tents or makeshift barracks. Men and women shared the same quarters and it was estimated that of the 20,350 women forced to work in the mines around 80 per cent had venereal disease; one SED report stated that these women 'ended up morally and socially depraved'.[172] The work was particularly demanding as most recruits had no experience of mining and many were too weak for the backbreaking tasks expected of them. Most worked long hours knee deep in radioactive slime; conditions were extremely dangerous and in 1948 alone there were 574 recorded accidents in each of which on average a staggering ten or more people were killed. Workers died in their hundreds, not only from undernourishment and infection; as Dr Wildführ reported to the SED Central Secretariat: 'In addition to these effects [cancerlike lung diseases, tuberculosis from breathing in silicates], one must take into consideration that extended exposure to radioactive waves can lead to irreparable health damage.' He reported that the effects on miners included changes in the skin, 'bones that become decalcified and deformed or cancerlike deterioration in the blood, for example through the reduction of white corpuscles [leukaemia]'.[173] The mines did untold damage to the Soviets' reputation in Germany because, unlike the work camps in the Soviet far east and north, it was impossible to hide the exploitation of labourers and the high death rate. The conditions in the mines were widely known in the west, not least through works like David Dallin and Boris Nicolaevsky's *History of the Soviet Prison Camp System*, which maintained that the mines had in effect become part of the Soviet prison system. The Germans in the Soviet zone were terrified of being sent to the mines and many fled to the west for that reason. But the Russians were desperate for uranium and did not care how many people died in their attempt to obtain it, and the horror of the mines continued long after the Soviets exploded their first atomic bomb on 23 August 1949.

By 1947 it was becoming increasingly clear to the west that the war-time Alliance was over; George Kennan believed that the Soviets were now trying to strengthen their power base in Europe through 'the patient but deadly struggle for total destruction of a rival power, never in compacts and compromises with it'.[174] Those who had doubted Soviet expansionist aims in Germany could now look beyond Berlin to the annexation of the Baltic States and parts of Finland, Poland, Czechoslovakia, Romania and eastern Germany. In 1947 the Communist Party seized power in Hungary after forcing the resignation of the Nagy government. In Bulgaria Petkov, the leader of the opposition, was hanged; in Romania Maniu, leader of the Peasant Party, was condemned to life imprisonment, and in Poland Mikolajczyk, leader of the non-Communist opposition, was forced to flee to the west. By February 1948 a Soviet plot had brought about the capitulation of President Benes, who handed power to the Communists. The Soviets had been successful in eastern Europe largely because the west was unable or unwilling to act against them. Berlin was different. Unlike areas further east the city had not been given to the Soviets at Tehran, Yalta or Potsdam. When Stalin tried to take it the western Allies finally fought back.

In 1947 the American General Clay anticipated the eventual break-up of the Allied Control Council and warned Washington that the Soviets were certain to become increasingly aggressive.[175] He suggested that as a first step towards disassociation from the Soviet zone the west should decrease economic dependence on the Soviets by merging the western zones. On 1 January 1947 the Americans and British created a single economic area called 'Bizonia'. The Soviets responded by increasing the strength of the German Economic Commission or DKW, which was to create an economic plan for the Soviet zone, promoting a 'democratic economy' whose output 'would be centrally directed'.[176] They also responded with vicious anti-western propaganda and a new wave of arrests.

By early 1947 President Truman had at last realized that the greatest threat to peace came not from Germany but from the Soviet Union. In March 1947 he outlined the Truman Doctrine aimed at containing the spread of Communism and, with an eye on Greece and Turkey, extending the American policy of supporting free peoples who were resisting subjugation from 'foreign powers'. The second part of the Truman Doctrine dealt with the economic rebuilding of Europe. It was called the Marshall Plan.[177]

The US Secretary of State General Marshall was, like General Clay, part of the 'Berlin mafia' – Americans who had experienced Soviet belligerence in the German capital. Marshall had met Stalin on 17 April 1947 and became convinced that the Soviet dictator was 'obviously waiting for Europe, harassed and torn by war and in virtual ruins, to collapse and fall into the Communist orbit'. He ended his report, 'The patient is sinking while the doctors deliberate. So I believe that action cannot await compromise through exhaustion.'[178] Upon his return to Washington Marshall requested the Policy Planning staff in the State Department to draw up an aid programme for Europe which was revealed in his famous speech at Harvard on 5 June 1947. The American economic policy, bolstered by the findings of the President's Committee on Foreign Aid – the Harriman Committee – recommended substantial economic aid for the economic restoration of Europe – western Germany in particular. For the first time German recovery had been linked with European recovery. On 26 June 1947 the British and French Foreign Ministers called a meeting in Paris to discuss the Marshall Plan and make arrangements for the formal inauguration of the Organization for European Economic Co-operation (OEEC). The

Soviets had been invited to join but although Foreign Minister Molotov attended he had already denounced the plan as a capitalist plot. On 2 July he suddenly left the talks and forbade all east European countries to accept aid from the west. The political implications of this were clear: if the United States went ahead with the Marshall Plan it would mean the effective division of Europe along economic lines.

The introduction of the Truman Doctrine and the Marshall Plan soured already strained relations between the Soviets and the west. These were made worse by Stalin's blatant attempts to destabilize Berlin with increased violence and intimidation on the city streets. On 5 March 1948 General Clay warned Washington that a Third World War was now possible: 'For many months, based on logical analysis, I have felt and held that war was unlikely for at least two years. Within the last few weeks I have felt a subtle change in Soviet attitude which I cannot define but which now gives me a feeling that it may come with dramatic suddenness.' There was 'a feeling of a new tenseness in every Soviet individual with whom we have had official relations'. Clay was right. Stalin was determined to force a showdown over Berlin.[179] The old war-time Alliance deteriorated rapidly.

The western powers were increasingly alarmed at Soviet behaviour. On 6 March the West European Foreign Ministers met in London to discuss the possibility of forming a separate government for western Germany.[180] The Soviets were furious. On 20 March, at a meeting of the Allied Control Council in Berlin, Marshal Vassily Sokolovsky protested that the London Conference had been called without Russian approval. General Clay and General Sir Brian Robertson replied that the west was not obliged to 'seek approval' from the Russians. At this, Sokolovsky read a prepared statement stating that the British and American delegations were wrecking the basis of the four-power administration in Germany and had acted in a way which constituted 'one of the most serious violations' of four-power rule. With that he shouted, 'I see no sense in continuing this meeting and declare it adjourned,' swept up his papers and stormed out, followed by the entire Russian delegation. It was the last meeting of the Allied Control Council in Berlin. Four-power government was over.

The dramatic Soviet move encouraged the western Allies to continue with reforms in their own zone. One of the most urgent was the need to change the currency. The economic situation in Berlin and Germany was disastrous. Hitler's Reichsmarks were still in use and the chaotic exchange rates were crippling the struggling German economy, hindering investment, damaging export policy, isolating Germany from international markets and fuelling the black market. On 20 June 1948 the west replaced the old Reichsmark with the new Deutschmark. Berlin was initially excluded from the West German currency reform but as the Soviets imposed their own currency on the whole of Berlin two days later the western Allies had no choice but to issue West Marks in their sectors. On 25 June western currency stamped with a large 'B' was distributed in the city. The Berlin Magistrat agreed that both currencies should circulate and the western Allies immediately agreed to accept eastern notes for certain amenities such as rent, rationed food and utilities. The Soviets did not reciprocate and declared possession of West Marks a criminal offence.[181]

Despite Soviet threats the western Deutschmark soon became the dominant currency in Berlin and had a profound effect on life there. The stable currency wiped out the black market overnight and affected everything from prices to exchange rates to wages. The report of the military governor of 1948 reported proudly: 'No event since the capitulation of the German armies had such an impact upon every sector of German life as did the currency reform ... The foundation upon which normal ways of life could be re-established, had been erected.' Henry Wallich wrote,

> Currency reform transformed the German scene from one day to the next ... goods reappeared in the stores, money resumed its normal function, the black and grey markets reverted to a minor role, foraging trips to the country ceased, labour productivity increased, and output took off on its great upward surge. The spirit of the country changed overnight. The grey, hungry, dead-looking figures wandering about the streets in their everlasting search for food came to life as, pocketing their DM 40, they went out on their first spending spree.[182]

The currency reform showed Stalin that the west had no intention of leaving Berlin, but it provoked him into making one final, audacious attempt to force them out.[183] He blockaded Berlin.

Before the blockade many thought that the war-time Alliance might somehow be salvaged. By the time it was over the Alliance had given way to the Cold War.[184] The days of the Cuban missile crisis excepted, the world has never been closer to a Third World War than during the first tense months of the Berlin crisis. The blockade constituted a direct attack not only on the role of the west in Berlin, but on the American presence in Europe. Ironically, only three years after the demise of Hitler's Germania, Berlin had become an ally in the new battle with the Soviet Union, and had been elevated to the status of a symbol of freedom and democracy in the western world.

The Berlin blockade was introduced so gradually that the west was not initially aware of what was happening. The idea that the Soviets might try to strangle western Berlin was so bizarre and so outlandish that even the most cynical westerners could not believe that the traffic 'delays' or 'diversions' were

RIGHT On 7 November 1926, the twenty-nine-year-old Joseph Goebbels stepped from the train at the Anhalter Bahnhof. The new Gauführer of Berlin was determined to 'take the city' for Hitler despite the fact that the Nazis had fewer than 200 members in Berlin. This 1927 photograph shows Goebbels making a speech for the SA.

BELOW Goebbels in the NSDAP HQ in 1932. That year saw some 400 battles on the streets of the city, many carefully orchestrated from this office.

The Nazis were able to take advantage of the financial crisis and mass unemployment. By the end of 1932 one third of Berlin's labour force was out of work. Here, young men are given an evening meal in a shelter for the homeless in Charlottenburg.

Sign in a small Berlin shop, 1932, reads 'We are bankrupt – therefore closed.'

The Communists and the Nazis collaborated during the Weimar Republic to bring down their common enemy – the legitimate Social Democratic government. Many saw them as two sides of the same coin. Ernst Thälmann and Hermann Göring often joined forces in the Reichstag to undermine parliamentary procedure. So too during the rent strike in September 1932. The slogan in the picture reads 'First food – then rent', and hammers and sickles and swastikas hang side by side.

The trial of Marinus van der Lubbe, the young Dutch plasterer accused of setting the Reichstag alight on the night of 27 February 1933. Nobody is certain who masterminded the fire. The obvious advantages accrued from it led many to suspect Hitler's direct involvement; others see it as one in a series of accidents which he then ruthlessly exploited.

ABOVE A Nazi rally in the Lustgarten before the presidential elections, 4 April 1932. Hitler is being driven through the crowd; many greet him with the Nazi salute. On 30 January 1933, Hitler was made Chancellor of Germany.

RIGHT 'Actions' against the KPD began as soon as Hitler came to power. On 23 February 1933 the Nazis searched the Karl-Liebknecht-Haus, KPD headquarters. The Reichstag fire gave Hitler the excuse he needed to ban the Communists, Social Democrats and all other political parties, and to cancel civil liberties. Berlin cellars and prisons began to fill with 'enemies of the *Volk*'.

The majority of Berliners threw themselves into the new order with enthusiasm. The Olympic Games of 1936 were highly popular. Here a 'sporting sculpture' in the Nazi artistic style is exhibited in front of the Hotel Adlon.

For those considered 'acceptable' by the new regime, life continued much as before; here Goebbels, Wilhelm Weiss, Fran von Waldeck and Magda Goebbels enjoy the January 1939 Presseball – the event which replaced Ullstein's annual gala.

23 August 1939. The world is stunned when Stalin and Hitler sign a 'non-aggression treaty' – the Ribbentrop–Molotov Pact. It contained a secret protocol in which Germany and the Soviet Union agreed on borders in central Europe in the event of war. The agreement paved the way for Hitler's declaration of war on Poland. The photograph shows, from left to right, Under-Secretary Graus, (von) Ribbentrop, Stalin, Hilger, Molotov.

Berlin prepares for war: camouflage netting along the East–West Axis (now Strasse des 17 Juni), winter 1941.

In the early years of the war Berliners continued to live well. A rare photograph shows the Can Can dancers of the Kabarett der Komiker in March 1940, only days before the invasion of Norway and Denmark.

Berlin in the summer of 1941. At this moment Hitler's troops were over-running the Soviet Union.

Slowly, gradually, Jews lost their rights and Goebbels stepped up his bid to make the city '*Juden frei*'. In 1937, over 200 Jews were picked up in highly visible places such as cafes and restaurants, and in December 1938 the Berlin police chief Graf von Helldorf pushed through the *Ghettodekret* which forced Jews to move out of the government district and the affluent West End. This picture, taken in 1938 outside the Cafe Schön on Unter den Linden, shows Gestapo, SA and party functionaries co-operating in a raid; the men wait as their papers are checked.

RIGHT Berlin was the nerve centre of the Holocaust. The city contained thousands of bureaucrats who, although they did not commit acts of physical violence themselves, had the power 'to destroy a whole people by sitting at their desks'. This 1937 photograph was taken in the Rassenamt–SS, where information about people's racial characteristics was kept. Eye colour was one of the features that was used to distinguish 'Aryans' from 'inferior races'.

BELOW Sachsenhausen was built in July 1934, chosen for its proximity to Berlin and to SS headquarters. It was a labour camp, and the punishments meted out to prisoners were bestial. Medical experiments were also conducted there, including the testing of poison gas and the effects of hand grenade explosions on humans. There were some mass executions, as when 18,000 Russian prisoners were shot in September and October 1941.

The Reichsbank building on Werderscher Markt was built in 1940 as part of the scheme to turn Berlin into 'Germania - Capital of the Thousand-Year Reich'. As business carried on upstairs, the valuables belonging to the victims of the camps were delivered here and sorted: coins were sent off to the precious metals division, stocks and bonds to securities, jewellry was sent to the Berlin Pawnshop, the gold from fillings was sent to the Prussian State Mint. The building is to become Germany's new foreign office.

On 19 October 1942, unheated railcars filled with Berlin's Jews began to leave for a number of camps, including Theresienstadt and Auschwitz, from the Anhalter Bahnhof, Grunewald and Putlitzstrasse, shown here. By 11 March 1943, 35,738 of Berlin's remaining 66,000 Jews had been deported to Auschwitz in a total of 63 transports. On 19 May 1943, Goebbels declared Berlin 'Juden frei'. Only 6100 of Berlin Jews survived the Holocaust, most as partners in 'privileged mixed marriages'.

The treatment of Russian POWs was appalling and many were simply murdered or worked to death. Of the 5.7 million Soviet prisoners captured by the Germans, 3.3 million had died by 1945. This photograph, taken in the Baltic region in 1941, shows Russian POWs working for the Organization Todt.

The atmosphere in Berlin changed dramatically after Goebbels' call for Total War on 18 February 1943. The cafes and nightclubs closed, and the terror increased. Here, a soldier stands in front of the Romanisches Cafe, autumn 1944. The Gedächtniskirche is in the background.

On 18 November 1943, Arthur 'Bomber' Harris began the Battle of Berlin, a series of bombing raids which would leave Berlin a shattered ruin. The Allied bombing raids did not achieve their military objective of forcing a German surrender. Tens of thousands of civilians were killed, and 2690 bomber crew members died. This photograph was taken in February 1945 in front of the Anhalter Bahnhof.

leading to a full blockade. When in early 1948 Colonel Howley first mentioned his fear that the Soviets might try to isolate Berlin the French general Ganéval retorted that the Russians would never do 'such a cruel thing'.[185]

The first hint had come on 26 March 1948, when the Soviet Chief of Staff Lieutenant-General Lukyanchenko accused the western powers of aiding and abetting illegal traffic into Berlin; four days later he declared that steps would have to be taken to protect the inhabitants of the city against 'subversive and terrorist elements'. He never explained precisely what he meant. On 31 March, shortly after Sokolovsky had stormed out of the final Allied Control Council meeting, the Soviets announced that all western nationals travelling to Berlin via the Autobahn and railways would be required to show identification documents at Soviet control points and give their luggage over for inspection. New restrictions were also to be imposed on military freight, on parcel mail and on all waterway traffic. These measures were all in direct violation of Zhukov's oral agreement with General Clay of 29 June 1945.

Clay was authorized to counter the Soviet breach and he posted heavily armed guards on the American trains. Instead of confronting the American soldiers the Soviets simply shunted the trains on to sidings and forced them to remain there until they were backed out into the US zone.[186] After three American and two British trains had been treated in this humiliating manner Clay advocated sending in armed truck convoys instead, gambling that the Soviets would not risk escalation to war. The Soviets suddenly eased restrictions. The west hoped that the worst was over, but they were mistaken.

On 2 April 1948 the Soviets struck again. This time, cars travelling on the secondary routes from Hamburg and Frankfurt-am-Main found that their path had been blocked by Soviet barricades. All trains were suddenly diverted through Helmstedt. The western powers protested that the Soviets were denying unrestricted access to Berlin but the Russians argued that no such agreement existed. Technically they were right – the west had no 'legal' written agreement giving access to overland routes. When questioned about this in the House of Commons Ernest Bevin sheepishly admitted that 'the regulations for travel to and from Berlin are not so clearly specified . . . When the arrangements were made a good deal was taken on trust between the Allies.'[187]

On 5 April another serious incident occurred. A British transport plane was approaching the Berlin-Gatow airfield when a Soviet Yak-3 fighter pilot deliberately buzzed the plane, misjudged the turning for a second pass and smashed into the airliner, killing himself and fourteen British and American passengers and crew. When Sokolovsky was confronted he actually put the blame on the British for violating safety regulations. This disregard for those killed at Soviet hands sent shock waves around the world and did a great deal to steel the west's determination to stand up to Stalin. By the end of April

Berlin was in crisis. Civilians began to rebuild war shelters and stockpile food while General Clay contemplated evacuating Allied families. War seemed imminent.

The western Allies were in a very vulnerable situation, and they knew it. General Clay had only 6,500 troops in Berlin and the Americans only 60,000 men in the whole of Europe, whereas Stalin had 300 divisions – over 400,000 troops – within striking distance of Berlin. The Soviets had also encircled Berlin with no less than 10,000 officers from the Border Police, units which had been specially trained by the Soviets for this purpose. The Americans had the bomb but did not yet realize how terrified Stalin was of the new weapon; everyone understood that if the Soviets attacked, Berlin could not be defended.[188] The situation was salvaged by General Clay who, despite some opposition in Washington, decided to call Stalin's bluff.

On 10 April Clay was asked to outline his views on the situation in Berlin.

> Why are we in Europe? [he asked]. We have lost Czechoslovakia. We have lost Finland. Norway is threatened . . . After Berlin, will come western Germany and our strength there, relatively, is no greater and our position no more tenable than Berlin. If we mean that we are to hold Europe against Communism, we must not budge. We can take humilation and pressure short of war in Berlin without losing face. If we move, our position in Europe is threatened. If America does not know this, does not believe the issue is cast now, then it never will and Communism will run rampant. I believe the future of democracy requires us to stay here until forced out.

On 13 April he sent a telegram to Washington, stating: 'We are convinced that our remaining in Berlin is essential to our prestige in Germany and in Europe. Whether for good or bad, it has become a symbol of the American intent.'[189]

After the announcement of the currency reform on 23 June 1948 the situation worsened again. The next day the Soviets suddenly announced that the Elbe Autobahn bridge was in need of 'urgent repair' and that traffic would have to be 'diverted'. Later that day a long list of alleged technical problems were announced and all roads, canals and rail links leading from the western zones into Berlin were barricaded. The blockade which had been hinted at for so long had finally begun in earnest. When Berliners heard the news they were terrified. Few believed that the city could now hold out against the Soviet threat. Many wanted to flee, but this was now impossible.

By the last week in June the crisis had deepened. The western zones had only six weeks' supply of food and coal. Colonel Howley tried to reassure frightened Berliners that the Americans had no intention of being forced out and declared over the new RIAS (Radio in the American Sector) station: 'We are not getting out of Berlin ... The American people will not stand by and allow the German people to starve.' Clay said that the Soviets 'cannot drive us out by an action short of war as far as we are concerned', but the Americans feared that without road or rail transport they could not hold out for long. It was then that the US army Lieutenant-General Albert Wedemeyer suggested that the Americans should try to create an 'airbridge' to Berlin modelled on the flights which had supplied American and Chinese troops over the Himalayas during the war. The Berlin project would be on a much greater scale. Nobody knew if it would work.

General Clay was worried that the airlift would only be able to bring in minimal supplies – the trapped population might then be tempted to go over to the Soviets, who were now flooding their zone with generous rations. Before he would undertake such a risky venture he needed to be sure that Berliners would support the plan. He called Ernst Reuter, accompanied by his aide Willy Brandt, and said: 'Look, I am ready to try an Airlift. I can't guarantee it will work. I am sure that even at its best, people are going to be cold and people are going to be hungry. And if the people of Berlin won't stand that, it will fail. And I don't want to go into this unless I have your assurance that the people will be heavily in approval.' Reuter quickly assured Clay that Berliners would support the American plan no matter how generous the Soviets appeared to be; Brandt remembered Clay being 'visibly impressed by Reuter's frankness and his firm, unshakeable attitude' which 'won the sympathy of the American southerner, who instinctively saw a "red" in every Social Democrat'.[190] The airlift would go ahead.

The first plane landed in Berlin on Saturday 26 June at the Tempelhof Airport. General Clay hoped that this show of defiance coupled with the stationing of B-29s in Europe – planes which the Soviets believed could carry the bomb – might force Stalin to back down. He refused. War loomed closer.

The following weeks saw a series of terse exchanges between the Soviets and the west. On 17 July the war-time head of the American Office of Strategic Services declared at a press conference: 'The place to make a stand against the Russians is right here in Berlin.' The American press began to equate the Berlin crisis with the Munich crisis ten years before. On 21 July General Marshall declared that 'we are not going to be coerced'. On 22 July, following a meeting between Truman and the National Security Council, General Clay reported that the Americans would upgrade 'Operation Vittles' (called 'Plain Fare' in England) and increase the amount of food and fuel flown to Berlin to 4,500 tons per day.

The airlift started out as a haphazard affair but it was turned around after August 1948 by the extraordinary US air force transportation expert General William H. Tunner. 'My first overall impression was that the situation was just as I had anticipated – a real cowboy operation,' he recalled. 'Few people knew what they would be doing the next day. Neither flight crews nor ground crews knew how long they'd be there, or the schedules that they were working. Everything was temporary. I went out to Wiesbaden Air Base, looked round, then hopped a plane to Berlin. Confusion everywhere.' Berlin was a difficult place in which to stage such an operation. The weather was unpredictable, and Soviet restrictions coupled with the high buildings at Tempelhof made it dangerous to take off and land. These conditions caused numerous accidents and 'near misses': on a foggy 13 August, for example, Tunner watched as a huge C-54 Skymaster overshot the runway and caught fire; another landed too far down the runway so that the tyres blew. With the confusion on the runway planes began stacking up in the sky:

> As their planes bucked around like gray monsters in the murk the pilots filled the air with chatter, calling in constantly in near panic to find out what was going on. On the ground a traffic jam was building up as planes came off the unloading line to climb on the homeward-bound three minute conveyor belt, but were refused permission to take off for fear of collision with the planes milling round overhead.[191]

Tunner quickly imposed order. To avert a disaster planes would be allowed only one pass at the airstrip. If they could not land they were to turn over Berlin and head back to their base in western Germany without dropping their load. 'Conveyor belt' flying meant that planes could take off very quickly; when the pilots landed in Berlin they were met by a 'follow me' Jeep, which led them to a space on the ramp. The cargo was quickly unloaded by ten to fifteen German workers while the pilot and crew had sandwiches and coffee, brought to 'cheer up the men' by pretty Berlin girls working in moveable snack bars. After twenty minutes the plane taxied to its take-off position and was despatched by the tower at the unbelievable rate of three- or five-minute intervals.[192]

The logistics of the operation were staggering. It was the largest airlift in history, and everything – the supply of goods, planes and fuel, the maintenance of runways, and the loading and unloading of goods – had to run like clockwork. Tunner brought in everyone from top maintenance personnel to radio and radar operators, and from mechanics to meteorologists. The lessons learned in dealing with the sheer volume of planes later proved invaluable in setting up the international system of air traffic control. The aircraft themselves came from as far away as Alaska and Hawaii; British crews came from as far as New Zealand and South Africa. The assortment of planes was extraordinary and ranged from 170 Douglas C-47s to DC-3s (commonly known as 'Dakotas') to Avro Yorks, which could carry 10 tons. By late 1948 the Americans had started to replace C-47s with C-54s or DC-4s, which could also carry 10 tons; they also used the gigantic USAF C-97 Stratofreighters, which could carry 25 tons of heavy machinery. The British also brought in 103 civilian aircraft, one of which was flown by Freddie Laker who later founded his own airline. But despite the increased number of planes the airlift was still failing to deliver adequate supplies. The problem was not so much a shortage of planes as a lack of runways.

When the airlift began there were only two airfields in Berlin – Tempelhof in the US sector with its huge curved terminal building and its single grass runway, and Gatow in the British sector, also with only one runway. US army engineers tried to cover the grass at Tempelhof with a 12-foot-thick rubber base runway overlaid with pierced steel landing mats but before long the sheer number and enormous weight of the planes pounding on it broke the steel and cut deep grooves in its surface. Over 200 men were hired to rush out between landings to try to repair the runway but this was not a long-term solution. In early July 1948 the Americans began to build a new concrete runway and managed to complete it without interrupting airlift traffic; four months later a third Tempelhof runway was under construction.

Gatow was located in the south-west of Berlin on the western side of the Wannsee. In late June 1948 construction began to lengthen and improve the one existing area and on 16 July the new 1,800-metre concrete runway opened for service. Gatow was situated near Lake Havel, where the British began to bring in the famous Sunderland Flying Boats, each carrying over 4 tons of cargo. Their arrival resulted in some of the most bizarre scenes of the airlift. Berliners would wait for the planes to land and then gather *en masse* to greet the pilots with flowers and gifts looking, according to one observer, like a rather chilly Hawaiian welcoming party. In all the Sunderlands made over 1,000 round trips, bringing in 4,500 tons of food and taking 1,113 starving children to the west. The planes were particularly important because they were treated against corrosion and could carry bulk salt to Berlin.

Despite the new airstrips Berlin was still under supplied, and in the autumn of 1948 an extraordinary new airfield was planned on the site of an old Wehrmacht training ground in the French sector. The construction of Tegel Airport became a lasting symbol of Berliners' wholehearted support for the airlift and gave the people the chance to do something constructive and practical to help. Neither concrete nor labour could be brought in to the city, but when an emergency call went out over RIAS 17,000 Berliners responded immediately and work on the 5,500-foot runway began on 5 September. The task ahead was monumental: the 24-inch base required the laying of over 10 million bricks which had to be scavenged from the rubble. Berliners laboured around the

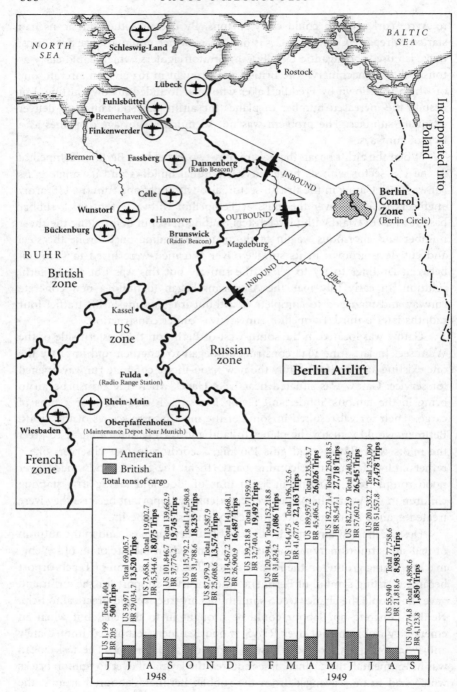

clock for three months under US army engineers and completed the airport two months ahead of schedule. The first C-34 landed on 5 November. There was only one problem: before the airfield could become fully operational a 200-foot radio tower, owned and operated by the Soviets for Radio Berlin, had to be removed. The French asked the Soviets to take it down but their messages were ignored. The French commandant General Jean Ganéval became so annoyed by Soviet intransigence that he ordered his men to attach explosives to its base and blow it up. The tower crumpled into a heap in a matter of seconds; when he heard about this, the new general Kotikov stormed up to Ganéval and demanded to know how he could have done such a thing – to which the general replied: 'With the help of dynamite and French sappers, my friend.' It did little to improve relations with the Soviets.

Within days of the opening of Tegel the airlift was exceeding all expectations. In July Berlin had received 69,000 tons of goods per month; by October it was up to 147,581 tons. The minimum of 4,500 tons per day had been revised up by 1948 to 5,620 tons per day; after January 1949 it was possible to actually stockpile food, and rations increased from 1,600 to 1,800 calories per day. Between February and April 1949 new tonnage records were set and by April had reached an extraordinary 7,845 tons a day. These figures were loudly broadcast to the Soviets via RIAS Berlin. On Easter Sunday, 16 April 1949, Berliners turned out to cheer as the Allies staged an Easter parade in which 1,398 flights roared continuously into Berlin every sixty-two seconds and carried in over 13,000 tons of coal. It was clear that the airlift could now continue indefinitely.

Despite their increasing success the missions remained difficult and dangerous. Crews were making two or more round trips every day and flying seven days a week in all weathers for tours of ninety or 180 days. They flew in old planes, many of which were in need of repair, and there were a number of tragic accidents. On 30 July 1948 the *Berlin Observer* reported 'The third accident and the second fatal crash of the 7,231 flights logged . . . occurred early Sunday morning, a C-47 crashed into the street in front of an apartment building in Berlin-Friedenau, pilot and co-pilot killed.' Another more sinister hazard came directly from the Soviets.

The Soviets had decided not to shoot directly at western planes flying to and from Berlin: this would almost certainly have led to a war which Stalin could not risk at this stage. Nevertheless they molested western planes whenever possible. Soviet Yak fighters would swoop and dive-bomb transport planes individually; others would fly at high speed along the corridors either singly or in formation, aiming directly at western planes and only pulling out sharply at the last minute; between August 1948 and May 1949 the Americans reported seventy-seven buzzing incidents and ninety-six which were described as 'close flying'. The Soviets also directed anti-aircraft fire near the western planes, blinded pilots with searchlights and tried to jam vital Allied radio frequencies. Some incidents caused the west to go on full alert – on 24 January 1949 a Dakota crashed in the Russian zone and it was assumed that the plane had been shot down. It later turned out to have been an accident, although the Soviets twisted the tragedy into crass propaganda with headlines like: ONE DAKOTA LESS – ONE LESSON MORE.

Berliners were aware of the dangers of the airlift and the pilots became the new heroes of the city. Captain Earl Overholser, an American public information officer, was assigned to Tempelhof to deal with

> all the grateful Berlin citizens who show up. Seems to me I've met every German in Berlin. They come down here, clutching extremely valuable heirlooms against their breasts, and want to make a little ceremony of giving the stuff to the pilots. Or some child will show up with flowers or a valued picture book. It's no act either. An old man so thin you could see through him showed up a few days ago with a watch that would have fed him for months on the black market. He insisted on giving it to an American. He called it 'a little token from an old and grateful heart'.[193]

The most celebrated pilot of the airlift was Lieutenant Gail S. Halversen, who had served in Africa and Italy during the war. When he came to Berlin he was amazed that the children did not beg for sweets despite the fact that they were hungry, so he decided to drop some from his plane. 'That night I tied some candy bars and gum in handkerchiefs and had my chief sling them out on a signal from me next day. Day by day the crowd of kids waiting for the drop got bigger, and day by day my supply of handkerchiefs, old shirts, GI sheets and old shorts, all of which I used for parachutes, gets smaller.' Word spread, and before long most crews were dropping loads of Hershey and Lyons chocolate bars, bubble gum and sweets for the children. The story was taken up by the press and 'Little Vittles' became a sentimental byword of the airlift throughout the western world.

The atmosphere in blockaded Berlin was a strange mixture of fear and hope, with the constant Soviet threat hanging over the city countered by the comforting drone of aeroplanes which lit up the sky like 'a row of pearls'. Most Berliners were grateful for the daring rescue of their city and began to revise their views of the occupying forces. By 1948 a large number had become actively pro-western. Unlike many Germans in the west who still resented the western Allies Berliners quickly took to American culture: they watched American films and learned American expressions; clubs and cafés featured American music. One of the reasons for the change in attitude was that

Berliners, unlike western Germans, could see the Soviet alternative. Their cutting humour was laced with reminders of what would happen to them if the Soviets won: when the Russians invaded in May 1945 women had dealt with rape by repeating the expression: 'Better a Russian on your tum than an Ami on your head' – which meant it was better to be raped than to die in a bombing raid. During the airlift it became: 'Better POM than "*Frau komm!*" ' – better American dried potatoes than something worse.

Another important American contribution to the spirit of Berlin was RIAS Radio in the American sector. It opened in September 1946; the Americans then installed a 20,000-watt station in July 1947 and allowed Berliners to broadcast for twenty-four hours a day from the studios on Kufsteiner Strasse. Programmes included everything from emergency information about food distribution and general news about the airlift to topical forums and round-table discussions which allowed people to voice their criticisms not only of the Soviets, but of the western Allies as well. By far the most popular programmes were the political satires – cabaret over the airwaves – which featured noted Berlin comedians poking fun at life in the cold, hungry, blockaded city and which helped to build morale. *Die Insulaner* (The Islanders) featured a cast of characters of 'typical Berliners' from housewives to Communist functionaries and black marketeers, all plotting and cheating their way through the post-war crisis.[194] Above all people listened to RIAS because unlike the Soviet-run Radio Berlin it allowed freedom of expression. For people emerging from twelve years of Nazi censorship such freedom was an extraordinary and welcome change. In a letter to the *Frankfurter Allgemeine Zeitung* in March 1995 the Berlin Professor Franz Ansprenger remarked,

> My generation of Berliners, growing up during 1945, learned a great deal about democracy through 'Radio in the American Sector'; free information delivered in an even-handed way, clear understanding of a political fight, humour (The Islanders) but without hatred, helped strengthen our will and our ability to withstand the strong, menacing [Soviet] opponent.[195]

By 1948 over 80 per cent of all Berliners were listening to RIAS, and General Clay would later comment: 'next to the airlift, RIAS was the strongest weapon in the Cold War.'[196]

If the city admired the western pilots there was a reciprocal sense of respect for Berliners, who persevered despite extreme hardship. In his book *Siege of Berlin* Mark Arnold-Foster wrote, 'The winter cold of 1948–49 was a severe experience . . . Western Berliners received a weekly ration of coal which they were able to take home in their shopping bags but a shopping bag half-full of coal does not suffice to keep a family warm for a week when it is snowing.'

Berliners carried on, accepting low rations, cold homes, severe cuts in power and water and the loss of their natural markets with good humour; the few manufactured goods produced in the city carried the defiant slogan MADE IN BLOCKADED BERLIN. Western Germans also supported the struggle. A special western 2-pfennig stamp for Berlin was issued and cities donated goods to the blockaded city: Hamburg sent medical supplies, Westphalia sent 10,000 candles; Schleswig-Holstein sent 2 million pine tree seedlings to replace those cut down for fuel.

The support was a welcome ray of hope as the Soviet repression continued: 5,413 Berliners had 'disappeared' and even western dignitaries were hounded.[197] John Sims, a British occupation officer, was arrested while investigating a hold-up of British-controlled barges at the Soviet–British sector border. He was seized by Russian troops, accused of spying and thrown into a filthy prison cell for four days. He was finally released after signing a statement issued by Marshal Sokolovsky stating that Britons were not permitted into the Soviet zone without an inter-zone pass. Even Colonel Frank Howley was followed, threatened over the telephone and intimidated in his own home. Much of the persecution originated at the Communist-backed police station under Paul Markgraf, who was still officially responsible for policing all Berlin and had free access to the western sectors. The situation was intolerable and the Americans decided to act.

Markgraf could not be dismissed from his post – this would have required Soviet approval – so the western powers decided to create an alternative police force to counter his influence. On 4 August Johannes Stumm was appointed and immediately called for all those police dissatisfied with Markgraf to report[198] to his office; 1,500 of the 2,000 Berlin police came over to the western force. For their part the Russians declared that any western policemen who set foot in the Soviet zone would face arrest. Although the borders between the zones were still technically open the creation of the new police force was a significant event. For the first time a city-wide administrative body was split into two. Berlin was beginning to divide along east–west lines.[199]

The cracks in the administration soon began to spread to the political sphere. On 29 July the democratically elected Magistrat met to demand that the Soviets lift the blockade but the Russians reciprocated by charging the members of the Magistrat with unspecified 'crimes against humanity'. Three weeks later Communist newspapers began to demand the removal of the existing representatives and called for a 'popularly elected Magistrat' – meaning a Magistrat backed by the SED. The Soviets could not force a new election but they had one trump card: the Magistrat still met in the Soviet sector. When the members tried to assemble at City Hall at the end of August 1948 they were stopped by 5,000 SED fighters who, like the Nazis on the eve of the Enabling Act, surrounded the building, bullied the delegates and managed to cancel this and a second attempted meeting. Social Democrats were beaten and told that their lives would be in danger if they returned to the Soviet zone but they were undaunted and arranged for a third meeting on 6 September. This time they were accompanied by fifty western policemen dressed in civilian clothes. The Communists again disrupted the meeting and when western police tried to help the Magistrat members they too were beaten up and arrested. Some took refuge in the American liaison office but Markgraf's men carried off twenty western policemen under the noses of the helpless Americans. The message was clear – the elected Berlin City Council could no longer risk going into the Soviet zone. They began to meet at the Technical University in the British sector, while the SED Communist faction members refused to accept the new venue and continued to meet in the east, in effect forming the basis of what would become the government of East Germany. Under the hum of planes bringing food and fuel to the western zones Berlin politics, like the city police force, had been split into two.

The vast majority of Berliners were appalled by the Soviet violence against the duly elected Magistrat and when Ernst Reuter called for a protest demonstration at the Brandenburg Gate they responded in their thousands. The anti-Soviet feeling in the city was reaching new heights. On the afternoon of 9 September nearly 300,000 Berliners gathered in the Platz der Republik in one of the largest voluntary meetings yet held in Berlin history. Even General Clay was shocked by the size of the crowd and wrote that the 'huge attendance was I am sure a great surprise even to the Germans'. Dozens of Berliners spoke against the Soviet threat to their liberty and Ernst Reuter gave one of the most moving speeches of his career, imploring the world to see 'what the Berlin people really stand for. We cannot be bartered, we cannot be negotiated, we cannot be sold ... People of the world. Look upon this city!' The demonstration was peaceful until the end, when youths climbed to the top of the Brandenburg Gate and ripped down the Soviet flags which had been there since 1945. The crowd tore them to pieces. Thanks to the presence of the western Allies and to the continuing airlift, the people of western Berlin became the first in central Europe to openly defy Soviet rule.

These developments in Berlin were a harsh blow to Stalin's plans to take Germany. He had not expected the airlift to succeed.[200] He had witnessed the failed Nazi attempt to supply Stalingrad and the hapless American and British food drops over Warsaw in 1944, and had assumed the Berlin operation would be equally disastrous. Ambassador Walter Bedell-Smith, who was in Moscow at the time, recalled: 'Neither Stalin nor Molotov believed that the airlift could supply Berlin. They must have felt sure that cold and hunger, and the depressingly short, gloomy days of the Berlin winter would destroy the morale of the Berlin population and create such a completely unmanageable situation that the Western Allies would have to capitulate and evacuate the city.'[201] Captain Tunner noted with pride that 'they didn't take [the airlift] seriously until it was too late'.[202] By late 1948, however, it had become clear that the planes could keep western Berliners alive despite the blockade. Stalin's extraordinary gamble had failed and the Kremlin had suffered a humiliating defeat. The Soviet leader, already looking to China as his next sphere of interest, needed a way out.

On 31 January, eleven days after Truman was inaugurated for a second term as President of the United States, Stalin held a press conference during which he was asked whether the Soviet Union would be prepared to lift the blockade if the western powers postponed the establishment of a separate West German state. Stalin answered that Soviet restrictions 'could' be removed. The Americans were curious. Dean Acheson sent Philip Jessup to ask Jaco Maki, the Soviet representative to the United Nations, what Stalin had meant by this comment. Through this covert channel the Americans learned that the Soviet Union would agree to lift the blockade if the Council of Foreign Ministers would convene 'to consider questions relating to Germany and problems arising out of the situation in Berlin, including the question of currency in Berlin'. An agreement was reached surprisingly quickly. On 4 May the four powers accepted that all traffic restrictions would be removed on 12 May 1949 in return for a meeting of Foreign Ministers to take place in Paris on 23 May 1949.

The atmosphere in Berlin on the day the blockade was due to end was a heady mixture of fear and excitement. Few believed that Stalin would keep his word. Then, shortly after midnight on Thursday 12 May 1949, Red Army troops began to pull down the now rusty barriers which blocked roads and railways around the city. The tension broke. A holiday was declared: factories, shops and schools closed for the day, and thousands flocked to the centre of town for the first celebration in eleven months. Lights began to come on over the entire western sector while Allied convoys, which had been lining up for hours in Western Germany, slowly began to cross the border and move towards Berlin under the gaze of glowering Soviet troops. Tens of thousands of Berliners gathered to cheer as the first vehicles began to roll into the city. Jeeps, private cars and buses excluded from Berlin for so long were wreathed with flowers and posters reading HURRAH – WE'RE STILL ALIVE! Over 200,000 people gathered in front of the Schöneberg town hall to thank those who had seen the city through such a terrible period: Ernst Reuter received rapturous applause when he declared: 'The attempt to force us to our knees has failed.'

Today the approach to the Tempelhof terminal building is enhanced by one of the only reminders of the extraordinary Allied airlift which saved Berlin from Soviet control. The soaring fan-shaped sculpture reaches to the sky with three gigantic arcs pointing west in the direction of the air corridors which supplied Berlin for over a year. It commemorates the fact that from 26 June 1948 the British and Americans brought an incredible 2,325,000 tons of food and supplies to Berlin on some 277,500 flights, with the 'Last Vittles Flight' leaving Rhein-Main air base on 30 September 1949 (the flights continued even after the Blockade was lifted). It had not been without cost: seventy-three Allied airmen and five Germans were killed, and their names are carved on the sculpture's surface.

The 1948 Berlin crisis was a milestone in history and marked a profound shift in virtually every aspect of the post-war world. When it began the Cold War was still a vague, undefined conflict; when it ended battle lines had been drawn across Europe, down the new line called the Iron Curtain. In four brief years Berliners had been transformed from a vanquished, disgraced enemy people into a new western ally. For their part Berliners no longer saw the western troops stationed in their city as arrogant occupiers, but as a 'protective force'. The western perception of the Soviet Union had changed dramatically as well; Stalin was no longer the benevolent, democratic 'Uncle Joe' of Yalta and Potsdam, but had become a symbol of tyranny and repression with his empire replacing Hitler's as the greatest threat to world peace. The Americans, who had so confidently expected to leave Europe by 1952, had come to realize that western Europe could not defend itself against the Soviet threat and they decided to remain. The continent was divided into two vast spheres of influence, between the two new entities called 'superpowers'. These giants rubbed against one another, like great seismic plates, at the 'flashpoint' – Berlin. As a result of the Berlin crisis of 1948 it became clear that Berlin would not be the capital of a united Germany as long as the division in Europe continued. The occupied city had become the ultimate symbol of the divisions of the Cold War.

XV

Flashpoint Berlin

Though there's still danger, Life and Liberty
are theirs alone who fight for them each day.

(*Faust*, Part II, Act 5)

THE BERLIN AIRLIFT MARKED the point at which the Cold War threatened
to turn 'hot'. For over a decade the city of Berlin was known as the 'Flashpoint
of the World'; it was widely assumed that war, perhaps even nuclear war,
might erupt here at any time. It remained a place consumed by tension,
suspicion and fear, a place where Soviet and American tanks could face one
another muzzle to muzzle over the sector boundary in a symbolic stand-off
between east and west. The new logic of the Cold War meant that Berlin
became the 'Spy Capital' of the world, the 'Filthy Swamp' which was home
to personnel from numerous agencies from the KGB to the Stasi, the CIA
to MI6. Berlin might have been a romantic backdrop to this world of thrillers
and spy fiction, but in reality it was a dirty and deadly business.

The division of Germany in 1949 had left Berliners uncertain about their
identity, and about their role in national life. As East Berlin was fashioned
into a Soviet imperial capital, West Berlin embarked on its often strained
relationship with the new Federal Republic of Germany. The creation of the
West German state was one of the defining moments of post-war history, but
it left Berlin in an ambiguous position.

The Federal Republic was born out of the ruins of the Second World
War, but above all it was the child of the Cold War and of Soviet belligerence.
Stalin had made it clear through the Berlin blockade that he had no intention
of allowing free democratic elections to take place in 'his' part of Germany
and that he would hold on to the Soviet zone at any cost rather than allow
Germany to unify as an independent and democratic state. When the Americans finally understood the Soviet position they abandoned plans for immediate reunification and opted for the creation of a free democratic state out of
the western zones.[1] This was the birth of West Germany. Dean Acheson told
the State Department Press Corps in May 1949: 'Our fundamental attitude is

to go ahead with the establishment of a Western government come hell or high water.' The Federal German Basic Law or constitution creating the second German democracy of the twentieth century was published on 23 May 1949, the very day that Stalin lifted the Berlin blockade.[2] The Soviets responded by creating the German Democratic Republic on 7 October.[3] The Iron Curtain, with its barbed wire, mine fields, 'no man's land', armed guards and attack dogs, had split Germany in two. Only Berlin remained physically undivided, an unstable enclave deep in the Soviet zone.

The future of the new West German state was far from certain in its first year but the path it chose was vital to the future of Berlin. After years of Nazism its guardians, the Americans, the British and the French, had no way of knowing if it would be peaceful, democratic, stable or even economically viable, so the first federal election of 14 August 1949 was critical. The election was fought between the two major parties led by two tough, opinionated, determined politicians: the Social Democrat Kurt Schumacher, and the Christian Democrat Konrad Adenauer. Both had fundamentally opposing views about the future of Germany. Kurt Schumacher was a stubborn West Prussian Protestant responsible for re-founding the Social Democratic Party after the collapse of the Third Reich. He was passionately opposed to the division of Germany and wanted the immediate resurrection of the state. He believed in the Bismarckian concept of a united Germany with Berlin at the centre of an all-powerful, centralized Prussian-style bureaucracy; he believed in nationalized industry and in government regulation. He was avidly anti-Communist and was well aware of the Soviet desire to dispose of him – when he travelled to Berlin he was always surrounded by British soldiers. Nevertheless he was an ardent German nationalist at a time when the concept had lost both its credibility and its feasibility, and although he mistrusted the Soviets he believed that unity could be bought by giving them concessions, including the promise of the removal of all foreign troops from German soil and the neutralization of Germany in return for the creation of a single German state. He was against the creation of a strong West Germany, stating: 'We must have a party which our people in the Soviet zone can trust, a party which does not have a West German complex.' In short, Kurt Schumacher appealed to those Germans who could not accept the division of their country.[4] Schumacher was opposed by one of the shrewdest politicians in German history, a man who presented a much more complex but – given Soviet ambitions in Germany – a much more workable vision of the future.[5]

Konrad Adenauer could not have been more different from his Social Democratic opponent. As a Catholic Rhinelander he had grown up in a part of western Germany infused with a traditional anti-Prussian bias and had served as the mayor of Cologne before being removed from office by Hitler.

He instinctively thought of Germany in terms of ancient principalities like Bavaria or Hessen and had an almost romantic view of the Holy Roman Empire. He had shed no tears over the loss of a centralized Germany, of Prussian might or the destruction of its traditional power base in Berlin.

Adenauer also disagreed with Schumacher over international affairs.[6] As early as 1946 he had warned that the Soviets would not give up their part of Germany in the immediate future and that the only hope was to make the western zones into a strong, stable democratic state irreversibly connected with the west, a state which might absorb the Soviet zone at some time in the distant future. Adenauer had few illusions about Stalin. He considered the Russians to be a vast barbaric horde illegally occupying 500,000 square miles of European land to which they had no right. He saw them as profoundly uncivilized and untrustworthy, a people who had broken forty-five out of the fifty-eight treaties they had signed with the west and who had sent over 1 million German soldiers and countless European civilians to the Gulag. He was willing to turn his back on the east, even if it meant sacrificing half of Germany and half of Berlin to the Soviets. Instead, he would anchor the new state in the west.[7]

Adenauer's commitment to the western Allies was total. Dean Acheson recalled that his ambition was to 'integrate Germany completely into Western Europe', giving this 'priority over the reunification of unhappily divided Germany'. The surrender of a whole German nation state was a price worth paying in return for the authority and power which accrued to the new West Germany when it became a member of supra-national bodies from the European Community to NATO. For him there was no question that 'West is best'.

Given the political situation and the unique position of their city Berliners faced an impossible choice in the August 1949 election. They could vote for Schumacher, which would mean that they might once again become the capital of Germany but in a neutral country vulnerable to Soviet domination. Or they could vote for Adenauer and be relegated to a marginal role in the new democratic West Germany, an impotent ex-capital locked deep in enemy territory. The campaign was heated and emotive, but in the end the seventy-two-year-old Konrad Adenauer was elected head of a coalition government by a single vote – his own – on 15 September. He was named the first federal Chancellor of West Germany on 15 September 1949. Germany was split down the middle. Unification now seemed unlikely, and Berlin remained in political limbo, under unworkable Allied control.[8]

The city retained its unique status in the newly divided Germany. It was still the official seat of four-power control and as such had a different status to other parts of Germany. Despite the divided government authorities and separate currencies in the eastern and western zones the city still functioned as something of a unified whole. Four-power Allied control sometimes worked smoothly: the four powers supervised the running of the vast Spandau Prison in West Berlin after the Nuremberg trials, when seven top Nazis were sentenced to imprisonment in 1946. Life was strangely normal in the divided city: trams and buses crossed from zone to zone; West Berliners went to the Soviet sector for cheap food and services and the theatre while East Berliners came west to attend films and exhibitions or to use the libraries or buy luxury goods. Telephones still connected the whole city and people could move from place to place without too much trouble. At the same time, the western zones began to benefit from the political and economic changes initiated in West Germany by the new Chancellor.

Adenauer immediately began to rebuild West Germany. He lobbied for full West German sovereignty and integration into the Atlantic Alliance while increasing co-operation with the United States, forging strong links with de Gaulle and reinforcing all aspects of political and economic solidarity with western Europe. West Germany was protected by NATO after 1949 and the outbreak of the Korean War and the world-wide panic about the spread of Communism gave Adenauer further opportunity to present the case for German integration in the international arena. In June 1950 Germany was permitted to make a contribution to the western defence system. On 10 March 1952 Stalin attempted to reverse the process of West Germany rearmament by offering to create a 'unified, democratic Germany' but the idea was rejected by Adenauer, who understood that a de-militarized Germany would be vulnerable to Sovietization.[9] In 1955, only ten years after the collapse of the Third Reich, West Germany was accepted as a full member of NATO.[10]

The 1950s saw the beginning of another defining aspect of West German life: the *Wirtschaftswunder* or Economic Miracle. Germans have always been known for their work ethic but they excelled themselves in rebuilding their shattered nation after the Second World War.[11] They were helped by the outbreak of the Korean War in 1951, which saw a massive increase in orders for German machinery and industrial goods, an upswing which was carefully nurtured by the Economics Minister between 1949 and 1963, Ludwig Erhard, who boldly introduced a free market economy to West Germany under the slogan '*Wohlstand für Alle*', prosperity for all. As he put it in a speech in 1948, 'Only when every German can freely choose what work he will do and where, and can freely decide what goods he will consume will our people be able to play an active part in the political life of their country.'[12] By mid 1951 West Germany was thriving. German producers were manufacturing high-quality goods and selling them cheaply on the world market helped by low labour costs, under-utilized capacity and helpful tax concessions. Gross National Product tripled between 1950 and 1960, export success brought increasing gold and currency reserves to the Bundesbank and by 1957 the Deutschmark had already become the strongest currency in Europe. Other Europeans watched enviously as West Germany emerged from the ashes of the Second World War but accusations that it had been given aid at the expense of other European countries were spurious; between 1949 and 1954 West Germany received $29 per capita of Marshall Aid money, whereas France and Britain received $72 and $77 respectively.[13] Now, in West Germany, there was a growing sense that identity lay not in traditional forms of nationalism but in the wholehearted pursuit of economic prosperity. The Deutschmark had replaced military conquest as the measure of national pride – a feeling which is still prevalent in Germany today.[14] The changes brought undisputed benefits to West Germans but they were a double-edged sword for Berlin. The more successful West Germany became, the less it needed its distant capital. The concepts of German unity and nationalism which had made Berlin powerful under Bismarck and Hitler were being swept away.

Berlin's growing importance in the nineteenth century had been based on Prussian might. The city had played a role during the confederation of 1815–66, but it was Bismarck's unification of Germany under Prussia which had made it the undisputed focal point of the new state. Hitler had further increased Berlin's dominance by eliminating regional autonomy in 1933 and creating a vast state with Berlin or 'Germania' as its colossal centre. And yet, despite decades of centralization, many Germans had retained a sense of regional loyalty and sentimental attachment to their *Heimat* and to their own cultures and customs, which could be traced back to the medieval Holy Roman Empire with its hundreds of principalities and city states. It was to this tradition that Adenauer appealed when he restored the idea of German federalism in West Germany. For the first time since 1871 regional governments from Bavaria to Hamburg would be given power which had previously been wielded from Berlin.[15] But the final blow in the diminution of its power was the designation of a new capital for the Federal Republic.

After 1949 it was clear that the West German state needed a capital of its own. Berlin was divided between four occupying powers and it could not resume its role until the 'German question' was resolved which might (and did) take decades. A number of cities were proposed but the final decision was made between Frankfurt and Bonn. Frankfurt would have made an impressive capital but it was rejected precisely because it was already too large and important. Bonn could not have been more different. This was a sleepy university town of 100,000 people known only as Beethoven's birthplace, and it was chosen because of its provincialism, because it was on the border of the north–south divide in Germany, because it could be seen as 'temporary' until the eventual unification of Germany, and – perhaps most significant – because

Adenauer preferred it. It was declared capital of the Federal Republic on 3 November 1950.

The announcement of the new capital city sent morale plummeting in Berlin. The city had lost its *raison d'être*, its historic purpose: it would be included in the legal, financial and economic system of the Federal Republic and would be permitted to send observers to the federal parliament, but given its unique status it could have no official political role in the new West German state. The western Allies could not permit the integration of the city into the federation for fear that the Soviets would use this as an excuse to reverse the Potsdam Agreement which granted the Allies the right to remain in Berlin. Worse still, Berliners faced a government in Bonn that was decidedly hostile towards them.

Adenauer made no secret of his hatred of Berlin. For him the city was 'Asiatic'; it symbolized decades of Prussian tyranny, of Nazi power and all that was wrong with German history.[16] He refused to visit Berlin for nearly a year after his election and when he finally flew in on 16 April 1950 he stayed for a mere forty-eight hours. His antipathy towards Berlin was quickly noted by the Americans: when John Foster Dulles, Eisenhower's Secretary of State, told him that the Americans would risk nuclear war if the Soviets pushed them too far he replied, '*Um Gottes Willen, nicht über Berlin!*' (For God's sake, not over Berlin!) Adenauer saw Berlin as little more than a financial drain on West Germany and refused to honour commitments of economic support until the western Allies, including General Howley, General Ganeval and the new British commandant General Bourne, forced him to declare it an 'emergency area' of the Federal Republic and give DM 60 million in aid. Its position was made worse by the creation in 1949 of a separate state out of the Soviet zone – the German Democratic Republic.

East Germany came into being on 7 October 1949 in response to the creation of West Germany. Despite its new constitution it was a Soviet puppet state with loyal Stalinist apparatchiks in all positions of power, including Wilhelm Pieck as President, Otto Grotewohl as Chancellor and Walter Ulbricht as Deputy Prime Minister. Whereas Adenauer was happy to disassociate West Germany from West Berlin it soon became clear that the Soviets intended to incorporate 'Pankow' (the derogatory term for the Soviet-run capital city of East Berlin) into the German Democratic Republic in direct contravention of the Potsdam Agreement. While West Berlin remained under American, British and French protection, the Soviets installed the official East German government in the heart of the old city, promising East Germans prosperity and a standard of living that would soon outstrip the west's. The new East German state was clearly meant to be a Soviet ally against the west, and in March 1949 Ulbricht announced:

> If the enemy in order to provoke a war carries out warlike aggression . . . against the Soviet Union, then as a German people we will do everything in our present power to support the Soviet Union . . . That means it is in our interests that aggression is defeated as quickly as possible, and thus it will not have the possibility to carry out warlike measures in the so-called West German areas . . . The gentlemen [of the west] should know that the distance from Berlin to the [English] Channel is not so far.[17]

Ulbricht clearly believed that East Germany would soon expand into West Germany – even going so far as to hint that it would be very easy to join the eastern economy with that of the west. He also stated that Germans in the western zone would soon be looking to the Soviet zone for leadership.[18]

In reality, there was no sign that West Germans would abandon their new state for the GDR. Life in the new East Germany was dreadful. From the day of its inception its people were repressed, its economic system was inefficient and its government highly unpopular. The Soviets forced East Germany into the Council for Mutual Economic Aid (COMECON) in 1950 but continued to strip it of its assets. The situation was made much worse by the Soviet policy of 'living off the land', which meant that East Germany was forced to support the Soviet army of occupation as well as its own population. Marshal Sokolovsky defended this, saying: 'If I ever went to Generalissimo Stalin and told him I am unable to make the troops and the German population under me live off the land . . . my fate would be quickly sealed. Stalin would order me to be shot on the spot and I could not help but think him right.' The results were disastrous for Berlin. The ownership of over 200 firms was transferred to Soviet control and plants were organized into inefficient combines whose sole purpose was to produce goods for the Soviet Union. All chemical, electrical and textile plants were nationalized, while armed men took over shops and businesses, arrested the owners and turned the property over to the state. Self-employed people had their ration cards ripped up and all manifestations of free enterprise were forbidden. While the inept leaders churned out propaganda most of the 17 million East Germans grew increasingly hostile to the Soviets and the privileged party elite. As one Soviet commander put it,

> The leaders of East Germany do not treat us too badly because we feed them, give them money, clothes, shoes, etc., but the ordinary East Germans hate us. If it comes to war, they will stone us, shoot us, start fires, commit all kinds of sabotage, etc. . . . many acts of

sabotage have been committed by German civilians who were sometimes permitted to do odd jobs at the Soviet military installations in
Germany. They drill holes in equipment, break vehicle parts, let out
the fuel. There was an instance when they drilled a hole in a missile
and the fuel leaked out.[19]

The anger was deepest in Berlin, where people could still simply walk into the
western zones and see the new western-style shops, fashions, neon lights and
cars for themselves. Many were so disgusted with life in the Soviet zone that
they simply walked to the western zone to start a new life.

Instead of responding to the needs of the people the East German leaders
tried to bully them into submission by increasing restrictions, raising work
norms and cutting the production of 'wasteful' consumer goods. As the austerity measures increased East Berlin agents reported an alarming increase in
hostility to the regime, but Ulbricht merely blamed the 'hornet's nest' of West
Berlin, launching bellicose propaganda against it. Attacks on West Berlin went
to absurd lengths. In 1950 Ulbricht's rival Gerhard Eisler tried to discredit
West Berlin by staging a 'coup', not with soldiers and tanks, but with crowds
of East German children of the Freie deutsche Jugend (FDJ) or Free German
Youth.

The idea was absurd. East Berlin children were to flood into West Berlin,
march through the streets, take over all official and government buildings and
call for the 'assistance' of the Volkspolizei – the East German police – who
would then cross the border and 'liberate' West Berlin. When news of the
plan leaked to the Americans they were alarmed enough to bring fighter planes
into Tempelhof and put their troops on full alert. When the Soviets realized
that the East German 'Children's Crusade' was in danger of turning into a
Third World War they tried to stop it, but the children had already started
towards the border. The East German leadership panicked, but when the
Americans and West Berliners saw the Vopos trying to stop the 'Crusaders'
they realized that the danger had passed and invited the children into shops,
giving them free presents and sweets; the city provided hot meals for hundreds
of young people, many of whom were so delighted by their 'day out' in West
Berlin that they refused to go home. The Children's Crusade was a disaster
for the East Germans. Newspapers tried to save face, claiming that the West
Berliners had orchestrated the whole thing; the Communist *Berliner Zeitung*
of 16 August 1950 claimed that the children had been abused by West Germans
and that the plan had been hatched by 'weapons magnates' in Bonn and
Washington. But Eisler's career was finished.[20]

By February 1953 it had become painfully clear that Ulbricht's attempt to
create a prosperous, wealthy East German state was failing. As Adenauer's

Germany grew more prosperous and West Berlin began to enjoy the fruits of the Economic Miracle shortages in the east became worse, bankruptcy loomed, and the Volkspolizei were forced to increase restrictions in order to keep the population under control. Thousands more East Germans began to walk across the border and register as refugees in the west; those who remained were increasingly restive. Then, late in the night of 5 March 1953, Stalin died. The news resulted in a surge of optimism for the millions of people trapped behind the Iron Curtain. News of his demise raised hopes that a new era might begin, and that the killing, the paranoia, the purges of Soviet rule would end. Their delight was short-lived. Stalin was succeeded not by a reformer, but by the terrifying Lavrenti Beria, the psychotic 'Bloody Dwarf' who had been head of Stalin's NKVD and had been personally responsible for the imprisonment, torture, show trials and deaths of millions of human beings.[21] His presence in the Kremlin had important consequences for the future of East Germany and East Berlin: the events now unfolding in East Germany would ultimately lead to his removal from power.

Ulbricht was not particularly disturbed by Beria's accession. At first he tried to impress his new master by increasing pressure on the East German population; spy-mania intensified and innocent people were plucked off the streets, accused of working for the Americans or the British; youth groups such as those linked to the Evangelical Church were declared 'illegal organizations', crude anti-western propaganda increased and the standard of living dropped again. Worse still, Ulbricht pressed on with his disastrous economic policy geared towards the improvement of heavy industry and the forced collectivization of agriculture. Beria was concerned enough to warn Ulbricht in a note in April, and to call him to Moscow twice, first in May and then on 2 June. As a result Ulbricht and the SED Politburo agreed to moderate reforms, which were outlined in an article published in *Neues Deutschland* on 11 June 1953. On 16 June, however, Ulbricht infuriated the German population by publishing another article in *Neues Deutschland* reversing some of the changes and informing them that the work norms were to be raised again after all.[22] This time the people reacted.

The workers' advocate Otto Lehmann published a bold article in the East Berlin trade union magazine *Tribune* entitled, 'Some Unfortunate Effects of the Raising of the Work Norms', which described the terrible burden placed on the shoulders of East German workers. The open attack sparked off a spontaneous wave of protest in a population worn out by long hours, low wages and terrible food. It was the start of the Berlin Uprising of June 1953 – the first anti-Soviet uprising in eastern Europe. It ended in tragedy.

The increase in production norms had hurt all East German workers but none more so than seasonal construction labourers in Berlin, who had only a few months in which to fulfil annual work quotas. At 9 a.m. on 16 June a group of eighty such workers located at Block 40 on the new building site on the Stalinallee decided that they had had enough, downed their tools and began a strike. One ripped down a propaganda banner reading, BLOCK 40 RAISES ITS NORMS TEN PER CENT and changed it to: WE DEMAND A LOWERING OF NORMS! The group began to move down the street and was joined by dozens of other disgruntled workers. Hundreds watching from houses and shops joined in the spontaneous protest. It is difficult to imagine the impact this had on East Berliners, who had lived with the ever-present fear of Soviet-backed secret police and prisons, concentration camps and show trials since 1945. A young East Berliner, Klaus Schütz, remembered the amazement in the city: 'Nobody thought that anything like this could be possible. These people had lived through twelve years of the Nazi regime and then seven years of Communist rule; they had never seen anything free and democratic so had thought a demonstration for freedom and democracy was not possible.'[23] Walter Ulbricht's first reaction to the news was to say, 'It's raining and people will go home.'[24] But the sight of crowds of demonstrators gave people courage and after an hour 5,000 people had gathered in the streets.

The demonstration soon took on a momentum of its own and people began to chant slogans calling for free elections and, most daring of all, for an end to Soviet domination. As they approached the House of the Ministries in Göring's ex-Luftwaffe building on the Leipziger Strasse they began to shout slogans against the hated East German puppet regime: 'Spitzbart, Bauch und Brille sind nicht des Volkes Wille' – which meant that neither the beard (Ulbricht), the stomach (Pieck) nor the glasses (Grotewohl) represented the will of the people. Ulbricht and Grotewohl began to panic but instead of going out to address the people they ordered that the great doors be slammed shut and iron bars lowered over the windows. They hid in the cellar and were spirited out of a side door some hours later. Another person in the building, the party activist and head of student affairs at Humboldt University, Robert Havemann, remembered the district party head Heinz Brandt being sent out into the crowd to announce that the government would discontinue the 10 per cent work production norm. It was too little, too late. The crowd shouted him down with: 'We are workers, not slaves!' and 'Get rid of the government.' Brandt was followed by the Minister of Mines, Fritz Selbmann, but he fared little better. Selbmann was a typical Communist functionary beloved of the Ulbricht government, able to sit through hours of SED speeches but incapable of understanding the people's grievances. Selbmann spread his arms in a gesture of paternalistic sympathy, and said: 'My dear colleagues. I, too, am only a worker.' With this the crowd burst into laughter and began to jeer. When a party van appeared a handful of men jumped on it, seized the loudspeaker and called for a general strike the next day. The groups of workers then dispersed peacefully.

The SED leadership was in turmoil. Ulbricht clearly believed that East Germany was on the verge of a revolution and loudly declared that 'no mob on the street' would be permitted to dictate policy. He was too frightened to see that the workers were badly organized and leaderless, and that the protest was little more than a spontaneous outburst of frustration and anger which might have been checked with the promise of some basic reforms. Instead of biding his time he appealed to the Russians for assistance. Beria flew to Berlin that night. Soviet troops were ordered into the city.[25]

By evening news of the general strike had spread beyond Berlin to dozens of towns and cities around East Germany. The Americans allowed West Berliners to broadcast news of the demonstration at three o'clock in the morning over RIAS. By contrast East German radio played endless operettas, a sure sign to anyone who has lived in a Communist country that something was wrong.[26] Not all Berliners supported the people; some privileged men openly backed the government – including Bertolt Brecht, who wrote a letter emphasizing his 'allegiance with the Socialist Unity Party of Germany' and 'Valued Comrade Ulbricht'.[27] The massive groundswell of support came from ordinary working people with nothing to lose.

In the pre-drawn gloom of a cold, rainy summer morning thousands of workers began to assemble in the main streets of Berlin. Ulbricht had banned all transportation to the city but 100,000 people had already gathered by daybreak and more continued to arrive from outlying areas, including 12,000 workers from the Hennigsdorf steel works and 16,000 people who had walked through the French sector from Velten. Over 400,000 East Germans gathered in over 250 other cities and towns in every corner of the country, from Erfurt to Leipzig, Magdeburg to Halle. Then, at ten o'clock, the mass of demonstrators began to march up Unter den Linden singing the old workers' song *Brother, to the Sun, to Freedom*. Some called for free elections, an end to Soviet rule and for the release of the thousands of prisoners still held in Russia. Fritz Schenk watched in amazement as the crowd suddenly stopped on Unter den Linden and began to sing the third verse of *Deutschland, Deutschland über Alles* calling for unity, law and freedom – the verse which had just been made the official anthem of West Germany but which had been banned in the east. It would not be heard there again until 1989.

The majority of those on strike were workers aged between twenty-five and forty – young men who saw no future in East Germany. When no government officials emerged to address the crowd the pent-up frustration and anger took hold: party members and those known to work for the secret police were searched out and beaten up; groups of young men overran the central East

German prison, releasing both criminal and political prisoners; at ten o'clock SED newspaper kiosks were set on fire and at eleven a group of youths clambered up the Brandenburg Gate and tore down the Soviet flag crying, 'We want freedom, we want bread, we will beat all Russians dead.' As the Volkspolizei appeared in increasing numbers the crowd became more unruly. Windows of government buildings were smashed, cars were burned, the Café Vaterland and the Columbushaus went up in flames, and the police barracks were set alight. A group of several hundred tried to storm the Economics Ministry but were pushed back by the Vopos. The group turned from the building and headed down towards the Potsdamer Platz. It was then that the Soviet commandant Major-General Dibrova gave the order to fire.

Unbeknownst to the East Berliners dozens of T-34 tanks – the same tanks which had taken the city eight years before – had been moving in towards the city centre. They reached Unter den Linden by noon. Twenty pushed past the crowds in the Lustgarten while others moved down towards Friedrichstrasse and the Potsdamer Platz. The first shots rang out just after midday on the Marx-Engels-Platz; a few minutes later the Russians shot a group of young men who had climbed on to a tank in Friedrichstrasse. Some Berliners began to hurl paving stones, bricks and pieces of iron at them; others rolled cars and debris on to the streets in a desperate attempt to stop the tanks. The Soviets responded by firing into the crowd, shooting salvoes near the sector boundary to prevent people from fleeing into West Berlin. A group of young men were shot at while trying to raise the West German flag. The Soviets positioned themselves around the perimeter of the city centre and the Volkspolizei moved in for the kill.

Most of the blood shed that day was the result of German, not Soviet, fire. The Volkspolizei showed no mercy to the trapped civilians but waded into the crowds, beating up protestors and even shooting people in the back if they tried to run away. Some Vopos were so disgusted by this that they dropped their weapons and joined the demonstrators but the majority ignored the pleas of the crowd. Violence raged on through the afternoon, continuing in other cities for days afterwards, but by evening the combination of Soviet armour and the brutality of the Volkspolizei had crushed the last pockets of resistance in Berlin. By evening the streets were deserted save for tanks and armoured cars on patrol and the Soviet troops, who had taken up positions on the tops of buildings and at street corners. Major-General Dibrova declared martial law, forbidding people to gather in groups of more than three and imposing a curfew between 9 p.m. and 5 a.m.; those who disobeyed would be tried by military court.

Berlin was in shock: 267 people had been killed throughout East Germany and 1,067 people were seriously injured; more would be summarily executed that night.[28] Soviet military tribunals and East German kangaroo courts were hastily set up and thousands of people 'disappeared'; even eminent SED members were targeted, including the East German Minister of Justice Max Fechner, who before the uprising had foolishly announced that the East German constitution guaranteed the right to strike, and 100 officers at the elite Juristische Hochschule near Berlin, who had joined the demonstrators against Ulbricht. Recently opened Stasi files record that over 4,000 people were arrested after the uprising, 200 were shot after show trials and 1,400 received life sentences, although one source suggests that 25,000 people were arrested.[29] A friend of mine, a young student at the time, had joined the demonstration on Unter den Linden. He escaped arrest that night but was taken some days later, probably after being betrayed by a colleague. He was sentenced to six years' hard labour and left for West Berlin immediately after his release. His deep sense of despair was, he claimed, shared by many Berliners on the night of 17 June 1953: 'All we had wanted was a voice,' he said. 'Suddenly we were being thrown in prison and our hopes were being dashed. The events really divided East Germans into those who could live with the regime and those who could stand it no longer.' Thousands of the latter decided to move to the west.[30]

One of the most famous testaments to the 1953 uprising was a poem written by Bertolt Brecht in response to an open letter by Kurt Bartel, the Secretary of the Writers' Union. In his letter Bartel thanked the Red Army for making the city safe but Brecht replied: 'Would it not be simpler if the Government dissolved the people and elected another?' Brecht appeared to be defiant but in fact he had sided against the workers as they were being mown down on the streets of 'his' city. According to his assistant Manfred Wekworth, Brecht had stood and watched the beginning of the uprising from a nearby building and when a high-ranking Soviet officer waved at him he had cheerfully waved back. Brecht did not join the fighting but had spent the rest of the day at the Berliner Ensemble ranting about the number of 'western *agents provocateurs*' in the crowd. The famous exculpation was written long after the event.[31]

The Berlin Uprising was a landmark in Cold War history. Not only did it precede the Hungarian Uprising and the Prague Spring as the first sign that the peoples of east central Europe wished to free themselves from the Soviet yoke; it had another, more immediate effect which remained shrouded in secrecy for decades. The Berlin Uprising was now used by Nikita Khrushchev as the excuse to remove Beria from power. As such, it was the catalyst which changed the course not only of East German, but of Soviet history as well.[32]

It is difficult to convey how terrifying a figure Lavrenti Beria, the head of State Security under Stalin, actually was. His grand residence is near my flat in Moscow and sends shivers down my spine when I walk home; the Tunisians, whose embassy it now is, recently discovered a number of skeletons buried in the garden, thought to be more of Beria's unidentified victims. Nobody, not even a member of the Politburo, was safe when he was around, and it is still sobering to watch the film footage of the stony-faced members of the Presidium standing around Stalin's coffin in 1953, and to notice how Molotov and Khrushchev, Bulganin and Malenkov move around the enormous bier, their eyes never meeting, their faces frozen.[33] All were keenly aware that they were in the presence of the most powerful and the most deadly man in Moscow. All knew that Beria had them under surveillance and that he had the power to move against any or all of them at any moment. They all wanted him dead, but they were too terrified to act for fear of denunciation or reprisal. It was the East Berlin Uprising which gave them the opportunity to kill him before they themselves were executed.

Beria had moved quickly to seize power after Stalin's death. One of his first tasks had been to merge the MGB (Ministry for State Security) and MVD (Ministry for Internal Affairs) to create the forerunner of the KGB. In the process he had recalled 800 MVD agents then working in East Berlin, throwing the complex intelligence network into chaos.[34] The Russians were aware of the worsening mood in East Germany as a result of Ulbricht's economic policy but the dearth of agents helps to explain how East German activists had been able to get access to forbidden goods like paper and printing presses so that articles opposing the regime could be published.[35] When the uprising began Beria realized the acute danger and had flown to Berlin to take charge of the situation himself, giving his enemies the chance to act. Hurried secret meetings were called back in Moscow between his arch rivals, including Nikita Khrushchev, the Minister of Defence Nikolai Bulganin, Marshal Zhukov, Georgi Malenkov and Beria's deputy Sergei Kruglov, men who would have found it difficult to meet had Beria been in the city. Beria became worried when he heard that a special Presidium meeting had been called in his absence and he hurried back to Moscow, allegedly to give an account of the situation in the GDR. Under normal circumstances nobody would have dared speak against him but he had given his enemies the chance they needed and for the first time he faced organized opposition and a barrage of criticism. According to Andrei Gromyko, who was present at the meeting, he began by giving a belligerent report on his mastery of the situation in East Germany: 'The GDR? What does it amount to, this GDR? It's not even a real state. It's only kept in being by Soviet troops, even if we do call it the German Democratic Republic.'[36] But then, according to Gromyko, the unthinkable happened. Molotov stood up and openly contradicted him, saying: 'I strongly object to such an attitude to a friendly country.' The others agreed. Beria had been openly attacked, and his days were numbered. On 26 June 1953, only nine days after the Berlin Uprising, he attended a special meeting of the Presidium, where he was suddenly detained on a pretext, stripped of office and arrested. A case was compiled against him accusing him of thousands of crimes and anti-state activities, including detailed evidence of his habit of driving around Moscow and kidnapping and raping pretty young girls. He was also criticized for his handling of the atomic bomb project in 1953.[37] The most bizarre of the thousands of charges was that he had secretly been working for the CIA; later Khrushchev would accuse him of having worked to dismantle the GDR. Beria's arrest was announced on 10 July 1953. He was murdered in prison.

Had Beria survived Walter Ulbricht might well have been liquidated and replaced by Beria's protégé, the head of internal security Wilhelm Zaisser.[38] When Khrushchev took power he retained Ulbricht despite the fact that his economic policies had done so much to provoke the 1953 uprising in the first place. He probably felt that to jettison Ulbricht would be seen as a sign of weakness in East Germany and might embolden those who had initiated the uprising in the first place, but it is also likely that he retained Ulbricht precisely because he had not been in Beria's favour. To help ensure that Ulbricht could maintain order the Soviets oversaw an increase in the size of the State Security Police – the Stasi – from 4,000 in 1952 to 10,000 in 1955. But if the uprising had helped to shape the history of East Germany and the Soviet Union, it would also have important consequences in the west.

West Berliners had watched in horror as fellow citizens had been mown down only a few metres away on Unter den Linden but they were helpless. When it was over 125,000 West Berliners gathered to honour the fallen victims of the uprising and a number of memorials were unveiled in West Berlin, including one to the Soviet soldiers and East German Volkspolizei who had refused to fire on the people. The avenue running from the Brandenburg Gate to the Siegessäule was renamed 'Strasse des 17 Juni' in honour of the victims and Adenauer wrote in his memoirs that the revolt had brought 'a wave of bitterness, of despair, encompassing the whole of the Soviet occupied zone'.[39] Rolf Lahr, a diplomat in the Foreign Ministry, wrote to his sister on 19 June that the uprising had shown the world 'that the Germans behind the Iron Curtain did not want this system'. But the uprising had a more important message. Although American, British and French forces had lined up along the inter-Berlin border they had stopped short of crossing to the Soviet zone despite their right to do so under the Potsdam Agreement. The Americans had sent no note of protest, nor had they introduced sanctions; indeed shortly after the uprising they had actually sent shipments of food to East Germany – a friend who was arrested remembered spending long nights loading American potatoes into sacks marked PRODUCT OF THE SOVIET UNION.[40] The uprising had led to a tacit agreement over the division of Berlin. All pretence at four-power status was fading and the city was now clearly being divided into two opposing camps which were in direct competition with one another. As Khrushchev worked to boost the prestige of the Soviet Union competition with the United States increased dramatically. Each side was desperate to learn what the other was about to do, thirsty for any information or knowledge which might give it an advantage over the other. The competition was at its most intense and visible in Berlin, where espionage rocketed.

Berlin became the centre of Soviet espionage directed against the west, with agents being recruited in POW camps, secretly re-educated and then told to 'escape' to the west, where they would either spy on specific targets or wait to receive further instructions. The western Allies were aware of this operation; Corporal Belling said to those interrogating Germans at British military government HQ: 'always listen carefully to people from the Soviet Zone. Pretend you send them to whatever department they want, but what you really do is send them up to Intelligence.'[41] Other Berlin operatives were chosen by Soviets like General Pavel Anatolevich Sudoplatov from the groups of experts who had carried out espionage, sabotage, assassination and guerrilla operations behind German lines during the war. On 1 January 1946 Sudoplatov was given command of Special Bureau (Spetsburo) No. 1, which was formed for the perpetration of peacetime sabotage and murder. He was utterly ruthless. When discussing the recruitment of agents he told an officer (who later defected):

> Go search for people who are hurt by fate or nature – the ugly, those suffering from an inferiority complex, craving power and influence but defeated by unfavourable circumstances . . . The sense of belonging to an influential, powerful organization will give them a feeling of superiority over the handsome and prosperous people around them . . . It is sad indeed, and humanly shallow – but we are obliged to profit from it.[42]

It is difficult to think of Cold War Berlin without imagining characters like Smiley, Quiller or Harry Palmer lurking around street corners or in seedy Berlin cafés; indeed many of the thriller writers did come close to capturing the atmosphere of the city when it was, as Le Carré put it, 'the world capital of the Cold War, when every crossing point from East to West had the tenseness of a major surgical operation'; where 'clusters of Berlin policemen and Allied soldiers used to gather under the arc lights, stamping their feet, cursing the cold, fidgeting their rifles from shoulder to shoulder'.[43] The real world of espionage was often stranger than fiction but it was far from romantic, and the information bought, sold and stolen could literally change the course of history.

Berlin was the natural centre of this dangerous and sleazy world. Whereas the rest of Europe was already divided by barbed wire and mine fields Berlin remained an open city, the only place where agents from the American CIA, the British Secret Intelligence Service (SIS) – commonly referred to as Military Intelligence Department Six (MI6) – the West German BND, the French SDECE, the Soviet NKVD-KGB, the East German Stasi and a host of others could meet without attracting undue attention. Over seventy agencies were based in Berlin in the 1950s and the city bristled with listening posts, drop zones, debriefing rooms, laboratories, forgery equipment, grimy interrogation rooms and safe houses; the British traitor George Blake once observed that espionage was much more exciting in Berlin before the Wall precisely because each operative had unique access to the enemy side. A character in *Smiley's People* said of Berlin that nothing was as it seemed: 'The place is a total minefield . . . even the damn cats are wired, no exaggeration.'[44] Berlin was made particularly dangerous by the presence of the largest foreign base of the most deadly spying organization in history – the Soviet KGB.

Of all the organizations based in 1950s Berlin the KGB (known as the NKVD until 1953) was the most effective. While the Americans pulled operatives out of Europe after 1945 the Soviets had worked to build up an extensive espionage network spanning not only east central Europe, but spreading over the globe from North America to the Middle East. It was an organization as paranoid as it was brutal. Its German base, set up by Beria himself in the old St Antonius Hospital complex in Berlin-Karlshorst in 1945, was meant to oversee the assimilation of Germany and the creation of a Communist government in Berlin, but its activities extended much further than that.[45] As far as Stalin was concerned the enemy had merely shifted from Hitler's Germany to the western Alliance after 1945 and he knew that control of Berlin would be fundamental to the struggle. The KGB was engaged in virtually every form of espionage in the 1950s; the Soviets had over 800 KGB operatives working in Berlin alone by 1953 and after the uprising the numbers increased again; the Soviet defector Aleksei Myagkov told West German intelligence debriefers in 1976 that from its Potsdam Directorate the KGB controlled 1,200 officers engaged solely in espionage against West Germany and that there were 10,000 spies or informers providing information to Communist controllers.[46] General Serov instructed Ulbricht to identify and exterminate 'western agents' in the GDR using any methods necessary. Nobody was above suspicion; telephones were tapped, letters were read and people were arrested at the slightest hint that they might work for the CIA or the SIS. Those suspected were not safe even if they fled to London or New York: the Stasi boasted that such people would be found, caught, brought back and either shot in the back of the neck or guillotined in prison. The Soviets and East Germans did capture western agents, but they also arrested hundreds of innocent people; in 1954 alone the Soviet high commissioner in Berlin told the Americans that the security forces of the GDR had recently arrested 'over 460 agents and "moles" smuggled into the country by American espionage centres in West Berlin; a further 100 or more had "come to regret" their actions and had "voluntarily" given themselves up along with lists of the names and addresses of other spies'.[47] The KGB's work was extremely damaging to the west and was made much more so by the Soviet use of East Germans.

The KGB were always quick to use native spies whenever possible and had recruited Germans long before the end of the war. The GDR had been given its own intelligence service under Ulbricht and Wilhelm Pieck in 1950, the MfS (Ministerium für Staatssicherheit or Ministry for State Security) – the Stasi – and in 1951 it was also given its own foreign intelligence service. This was called the Aussenpolitischer Nachrichtendienst (Foreign Political Intelligence Service) or APN, but it was best known by its disguises, the Institut für wirtschaftswissenschaftliche Forschung or IWF – literally the Institute for Economic Research – which posed as an east–west trade organization from its base in East Berlin-Pankow. The IWF was disbanded in 1953 after the uprising and incorporated in the Ministry for State Security as Hauptabteilung (Main Department) XV; in 1956 its name was changed again to Hauptverwaltung Aufklärung (Main Administration Reconnaissance) or HVA, the title it kept until it was disbanded in 1990.[48] Whatever its name it was a powerful organization which, although it reported to the Ministry of Foreign Affairs, was directly linked to the KGB – so much so that all information obtained by the HVA was sent in copy to the Soviets until 1990.[49]

One of the reasons for the extraordinary success of East German foreign intelligence was the appointment of Lieutenant-General Markus Johannes 'Mischa' Wolf in December 1952.[50] He was only thirty years old. The British foolishly dismissed him as an inept ex-Hitler Youth member, the French claimed he lacked the necessary academic background to be effective, while the Americans saw him as another opportunistic German who had made peace with the Soviets in order to advance his own career. What they failed to understand was that the Soviets trusted him completely, not least because he had lived in the Soviet Union, spoke Russian, and had no close family or other ties with the west.[51] He quickly became one of the greatest threats to western security. Wolf was young, aggressive and unencumbered by Stalinist baggage. He swept the HVA clean of tired operatives and replaced them with sophisticated agents capable of working in the new divided Germany. He oversaw the construction of the new prison in the Schumannstrasse, which contained torture facilities and specialized in NKVD techniques to prepare East Germans for show trials and to extract confessions of spying. His first task was to 'learn everything possible about NATO' by concentrating on the Federal Republic of Germany, but there were many departments for espionage abroad.[52] His approach was novel and highly effective. Wolf understood that even the most sensitive documents must at some point pass through the hands of office staff, and instead of targeting elite personnel he launched a comprehensive campaign to control the workforce in sensitive offices. Special schools were set up in East Berlin to train beautiful women in the art of the 'honeytrap' – the ploy to lure well-placed men into relationships; young and attractive men were also trained to seduce middle-aged single women employed in important West German offices. One of the most famous victims was Irmgard Römer, who gave her lover Carl Helmers, the 'Red Casanova', vital diplomatic secrets until his arrest in 1958, but there were many others. Dagmar Kahlig-Scheffler, a secretary in the Chancellor's office, had met a man on holiday in Bulgaria, had secretly married him in East Berlin, and had been persuaded by him to work for the East Germans. She was discovered in June 1976.[53] Another secretary, Inge Goliath, had been employed as a secretary for the Christian Democratic Union (CDU) from 1966; she disappeared on 9 March 1979, when it became clear she was about to be arrested for spying. Another highly sensitive case was that of Ingrid Barbe, secretary to a counsellor to NATO at the West German embassy, who was jailed for four years in 1980 for sending details of everything from troops strengths to contingency plans involving the neutron bomb to the East Germans.[54]

While flooding Germany with gigolos and secretaries – there were over sixty proven cases of secretaries caught working for the HVA – Wolf began to infiltrate at a higher level.[55] One of his most successful operatives was the West German intelligence employee Heinz Felfe, who became head of Soviet counter-intelligence in the BND (the West German Bundesnachrichtendienst). With Soviet help he built up a whole network of fake contacts in East Berlin and the Soviet Union; indeed the Soviets even supplied him with a detailed plan of the KGB headquarters at Karlshorst which greatly impressed both the SIS and the CIA. At the same time, Felfe was busy photographing confidential West German documents; over 15,000 frames of microfilm were duly delivered to Karlshorst in anything from cigarette packets to tins of baby food. His true identity was only revealed in 1961, a discovery which helped to topple the Adenauer government, and, as one CIA agent put it, compromised ten years of secret agent reports from Germany.[56] Wolf never ceased to cultivate men and women who might one day be close to possible leaders. One such figure was Günter Guillaume, the East German spy recruited by Wolf who became aide to Chancellor Willy Brandt and whose discovery later caused his downfall.[57] Felfe and Guillaume were merely Wolf's most spectacular successes; according to one HVA defector Wolf had placed over 500 penetration agents in West Berlin and had many more in training. In a 1990 interview in *Der Spiegel* Markus Wolf claimed that there were up to 10,000 MfS agents operating in West Germany in 1985.[58] In November 1991 the Ministry of the Interior estimated that there had been as many as 7,000 agents working in West Germany in 1989 alone, many of whom were highly trained and held important positions.[59] Ex-informants are still being discovered; in February 1995 another ex-aide to Willy Brandt, Karl Wienand, was arrested on suspicion of spying, while Egon Bahr, the architect of Willy Brandt's *Ostpolitik*, was suspected of having links with the KGB. Klaus Kuron, recently sentenced after being exposed as a double agent, said that at least twenty-five members in Bonn's parliament the year the Wall fell had been agents for East Germany during the Cold War, while Markus Wolf suggested in 1990 that there had in fact been between fifty and ninety agents closely linked to important West German politicians.[60] In the year to July 1993 a record 1,425 people were prosecuted in Germany for spying, of which almost half were accused of being former Stasi agents in West Germany.[61] Nevertheless when in 1990 the members of the Bundestag were asked if they would submit to investigation for possible connections with East German security only 315 of the 662 members agreed.[62]

The Soviets expended vast resources on espionage in Berlin and abroad and the west was slow to catch up. One of the first countries to understand the threat posed by the Soviets was Britain, and the SIS (MI6) was the first western body to establish itself in Berlin after the war. The Berlin SIS headquarters were located in a huge granite building which had been part of Hitler's Olympic Stadium complex, still ringed by gigantic Nazi statues. This incongruous setting became the largest SIS station in the world with over 100 agents being run from that office alone. Peter Lunn, then head of operations, focused on assessing Soviet capability and spying activities as well as recruiting anti-Soviet agents to work behind the Iron Curtain. At first the SIS recruited from the hundreds of anti-Soviets still languishing in refugee camps throughout Germany; later they took to approaching former high-ranking Nazis, including men like Klaus Barbie, to penetrate Communist groups in Germany and eastern Europe. Other agents like Bruce Lockhart spearheaded the drive to gather blackmail material against some of East Germany's top people and concentrated on the recruitment of Soviet officials. Despite its glamorous image the SIS experienced a period of 'continual and distressing failure' in the early 1950s. According to one commentator British intelligence was handicapped by personnel of varying quality who had been recruited by ludicrously insecure 'old boy' methods; many were incompetent, others merely eccentric and some undoubtedly effective spies – but for the wrong side. As a result, the SIS 'presided over a series of scandals and embarrassments' which limited its effectiveness, not least of which was the discovery of traitors at the highest level, including the Cambridge spies.[63] The SIS had hundreds of operatives, agents and informers in Berlin, but despite Markus Wolf's comment that British intelligence was 'probably the best in the world because it was the one about which he knew least' they were no match for the KGB.[64] By the late 1950s their position had been strengthened through partnership with the American Central Intelligence Agency.

The CIA was a product of the Cold War.[65] During the Second World War American espionage had been carried out by the Office of Strategic Services (OSS), which had combined spying, sabotage and military intelligence under 'Wild Bill' Donovan. On 1 October 1945, OSS intelligence and counter-intelligence were transferred to the War Department as the Strategic Services Unit (SSU). OSS then became the Berlin Operations Base (BOB), which was soon integrated into the new Central Intelligence Agency. From 1947 the CIA was working with the State Department, the Defense Department, the National Security Agency, the Military Intelligence Service and other bodies. Operations in West Berlin grew out of the State Department's Russian Department under General Lucius Clay, the US military governor.[66] Activity in Berlin was a priority. General Bedell-Smith, who directed operations between 1950 and 1953, had been US ambassador to Moscow from 1946 to 1949 and was as wary of the Soviets as his deputy Allen Dulles. Both encouraged anti-Soviet activity in Berlin; their main objectives were to infiltrate the KGB, to learn of possible Soviet military action against Berlin and elsewhere, to determine the military capability of the Red Army, to prevent the Communists from spreading further into western Europe, to provide support for anti-Communists in the east, to develop 'stay-behind' or 'retardation' networks to organize uprisings against the Soviets, and to organize counter-espionage. After the first difficult years the Americans became well established and although they managed to recruit only one of Markus Wolf's top agents, they were particularly successful at recruiting Soviet defectors. One of the first was Major Vladimir Popov of GRU, Soviet Military Intelligence, who 'turned' in 1952 and gave the Americans vital information, including a long list of Soviet agents operating in the west.[67] By far the most important Soviet defector of the era who worked both for the SIS and the CIA was Colonel Oleg Penkovsky or 'Alex', a Russian patriot who despaired of the Soviet system and feared Khrushchev might be foolish enough to start a nuclear war. For fourteen months during 1960–61 he passed film of 5,000 top secret papers from Moscow to the SIS, covering everything from nuclear capability to the identity of Soviet spies in the west. It was his information which indicated that Soviet missile sites in

Cuba were not yet operational, allowing Kennedy to stand up to Khrushchev during the 1962 Cuban missile crisis. Penkovsky was captured in 1961, tried, found guilty of high treason and executed in Moscow.

Like the KGB the British and Americans were quick to realize that they would be more effective if they used German agents in the fight against the Soviets, and locals were recruited as early as 1945. The most important German organization to be integrated with the west was run by the egregious General Gehlen.[68]

Gehlen had been Hitler's master spy and operative on the eastern front during the Second World War as colonel of the army department Fremde Heere Ost, and had spent years setting up an extraordinary anti-Soviet network throughout eastern Europe. As Hitler's Reich collapsed around him he prudently moved his massive collection of microfilm and files to a hideout in the Bavarian mountains, where the Americans found him in 1945. Despite his unsavoury past they were quick to take advantage of his information.

Gehlen's files contained a vast store of data about the Soviet Union. He had collected detailed information on the Red Army and NKVD personnel, including those Germans and other nationals who had worked for the Soviets; he had extensive contacts with pro-western agents behind the Iron Curtain, he controlled 'sleepers' in Russia, he kept tabs on partisans, and knew a great deal about the workings of the secretive NKVD.[69] In 1946 the Americans employed him along with fifty members of his old staff under Brigadier-General Edwin L. Silbert, who had now taken over all US intelligence and counter-espionage activity under Clay. In the early years his agents and sub-agents, whose identities were often unknown to Gehlen himself, were supplied with cigarettes, gold coins and other items with which to buy information in the Soviet zone. In December 1947 the CIA financed the move of Gehlen's organization to a renovated former SS estate at Pullach outside Munich, and in 1956 the status of the organization was normalized when Gehlen was made the first head of the BND, the West German Federal Intelligence Service.

The BND continued to work closely with the CIA and the SIS, providing invaluable information about KGB operations in Berlin. It was Gehlen who recruited Walter Gramsch, a member of East German intelligence who passed sensitive information about Soviet/East German military activity to the BND. Gramsch also unmasked several top KGB agents in the west and continued to work until 1953, when he noticed that he was being followed and was hurriedly removed to the west. Professor Hermann Kastner was another top-level agent working for the west. A liberal German who had been brought into the East German government for propaganda reasons, he rose to the rank of Deputy Prime Minister, all the while supplying West German intelligence with government papers. Information was couriered across the border by his wife, 'Frau Minister', who often entered West Berlin in a government car to 'visit her doctor'. They were detected by the KGB but rescued by the west in 1953.[70] Another of Gehlen's agents managed to steal plans and test-flight records of Russia's first jet plane, the MiG-15. Gehlen was the first to provide the west with the complete text of Khrushchev's Twentieth Soviet Congress speech in which Stalin was denounced, and it was he who predicted both the Hungarian Uprising and the subsequent Soviet invasion. The Soviets and the East Germans detested him; the East German chief of state security Ernst Wollweber put a price of DM1 million on his head, although Gehlen was never captured and died of natural causes in 1979.

The second West German intelligence organization was the Bundesamt für Verfassungsschutz (Office for the Protection of the Constitution) or BfV, founded in 1950 with the help of the British and based in Cologne. Its main purpose was to engage in counter-espionage against KGB and Stasi infiltration; its first director, Otto John, was kidnapped (or defected) in Berlin in 1954.[71] Although often at odds with Gehlen's organization, it too had dozens of operatives in Berlin.

Thanks primarily to the early use of Gehlen's information the British, Americans and West Germans had built up a formidable centre of espionage in Germany – above all in Berlin – by the mid 1950s.[72] The Soviets were furious at the challenge and were quick to denounce the western agencies. The Soviet diplomat Pyotr Abrasimov complained that West Berlin was being used chiefly for 'indirect forms of aggression' against the Soviet Union and that the Americans had 'turned West Berlin into a huge centre for espionage and agitation, making it a spy centre for the secret service activities of the United States, Great Britain and other NATO countries'.[73] He alleged that American spies had taken over the city, and denounced all western organizations, including the radio station RIAS Berlin, which regularly sent coded messages to western agents in East Berlin.[74] There were also frequent complaints against the BBC Berlin office. In 1953 the East Germans retaliated against the Gehlen organization for 'causing' the uprising by arresting around thirty people allegedly involved with it. This was followed by the arrest of twelve more alleged operatives in 'Operation Vermin'. In April 1954 Ernst Wollweber announced that his government had arrested '521 agents of the American and English secret services, of the Gehlen espionage organization as well as of the so-called "Task Force against Inhumanity", the so-called "Investigative Committee of Liberal Jurists", the RIAS, the Eastern offices of West Berlin parties and others'.[75]

The atmosphere in the 1950s city was tainted by the world of espionage and had become a landscape of spying with its 'telescopes and cameras, the directional microphones, all the useless hardware that was supposed to make the waiting easier; the crackle of the radios, the stink of coffee and tobacco'.[76]

Millions of dollars were pumped into operations in the only place in the world where agents from all sides could actually contact one another without having to cross a fortified border or draw undue attention to themselves. The secrets bought, sold, smuggled and betrayed in the city changed the history of the Cold War, and the atmosphere was blighted by the often sinister activities of the agents, the blackmailers, the pathological liars – operatives who did everything from recruit secretaries to exchange nuclear secrets. Contrary to popular belief spying was not limited to a tiny world of professionals; anyone who had access to power or information was considered fair game. By the 1950s Berlin was known as a city where nothing and nobody was what they seemed, where no innocent conversation or casual encounter could be taken at face value. Nobody in Berlin could really be trusted.

The escalation in recruitment of ordinary people in 1950s Berlin was sometimes taken to extremes. All sides relied on MICE – Money, Ideology, Compromise and Ego – as their standard tools but Berlin was unique for the sheer scale of the activity on both sides. The west was able to persuade many ordinary East Germans to work against their own system. The office worker Cäcilie Silberstein was typical; she was so disillusioned by life in East Berlin that she decided to work against her own government. She was recruited by West German intelligence to hand over industrial secrets, knowing full well that she would eventually be caught: 'It's the same thing as dying; but you cannot think about dying all the time. You know it will happen; but you hope it will not happen just now.' She was publicly denounced as a spy in 1959 but was fortunate enough to be exchanged later for a Soviet agent.[77] Another typical example was Hilde Halm, who was recruited during a visit to friends in West Berlin. An ex-Communist activist, she worked in the East German Ministry of State Security and managed to pass top-secret information from her office to West Berlin for six years until her arrest in April 1956, after which she was sentenced to life imprisonment. There were countless people who worked for the west in some way, often out of disgust with the Soviet system. But it was the KGB which remained the master of entrapment and blackmail.

When one passes the Kremlin in Moscow and heads east of Tverskaya past the Bolshoi Theatre one is suddenly confronted by a vast stone and stucco building, which rises up in front of a square where the gigantic statue of the founder of the Cheka, Felix Dzerzhinsky, stood until 1991.[78] Once the head office of the Rossiya Insurance Company, the building was taken over by the Cheka in 1918, and was turned into the infamous Lubyanka Prison. The Cheka, NKVD, KGB and now FSK (Federal Counter-Intelligence Service) were not confined to the prison itself but spread their organization throughout nearby buildings. It is now possible to enter some of these, including a special exhibition used by the KGB to educate recruits about the history of the service. The Museum of the Federal Counter-Intelligence Service offers a wealth of information on all aspects of intelligence, from the use of dead letter boxes to the development of hidden cameras, but it also includes a large section on work abroad, including Berlin. The exhibition underscores the fact that Soviet techniques were simple, but effective. Targets were carefully selected and researched before being approached. Some were simply offered money in exchange for information but it was more common for them to receive 'free' tickets to the opera, 'free' champagne at clubs and other more substantial gifts only to find that they could later be blackmailed for taking 'Red gold'. The KGB and the Stasi also favoured other forms of blackmail. Hundreds of victims in Berlin were set up by supposed waitresses, secretaries, or other attractive women whom they met 'by chance'. One such agent was Maria Knuth, a beautiful German actress who was set up by the Soviets as the manager of a charming antique shop frequented by foreigners. From there she would lure British and American officers to bed. Blackmail of homosexuals was also common; one of the most famous cases was that of John Vassall, who worked in the office of the British naval attaché in Moscow in 1954. A year after being invited to a party he 'was shown a box of photographs of myself at the party ... There I was, caught by the camera, enjoying every sexual activity.'[79] He was blackmailed into working for the KGB and used a Minox camera hidden inside a cigarette packet – there is a picture of him at the Lubyanka site. The use of sex as blackmail was very common in Berlin; IM or *Inoffizielle Mitarbeiter* (Stasi informers) were commonly used to entrap the unwary; one attractive young female lawyer code-named 'Micha', operated for nearly twenty years organizing both homosexual and heterosexual sex-parties for visiting churchmen.[80] The Soviets were also adept at massaging the egos of their targets. Journalists were sometimes given unbelievable 'scoops' by the East Berlin Disinformation Unit, and several prominent publications pursued false stories: *Der Spiegel*'s sensational anti-Strauss campaign had, according to ex-KGB agent Ilya Dzhirkvelov, been orchestrated by the KGB.[81] The exhibition at the Lubyanka is also interesting for what it leaves out, such as the KGB's use of old Nazi files as a source of blackmail material. The Soviets would comb through old Nazi police and military records, including those of the German police forces, the Gestapo, the SD, the RSHA and the Abwehr, and threaten to expose former Nazis in West Germany if they did not co-operate. They also identified women who still had fathers or husbands in Soviet prison camps: their release was promised in return for information – a particularly cruel form of blackmail in cases where the KGB were aware that the prisoner was already dead.

Espionage was a risky activity. Those caught by the west usually faced long prison sentences, with the possibility of eventual exchange back to East

Berlin. Those captured by the Soviets faced prison, with the hope of exchange, or death. The Soviets and East Germans had no qualms about torturing and murdering enemy agents at home, including important western agents like Frau Elli Barczatis, who was guillotined.[82] They also perfected novel forms of assassination for those who escaped to the west. Proof of laboratories reminiscent of those featured in James Bond films emerged in 1954 when the Soviet assassin Nikolai Kokhlov gave himself up to the CIA and informed his astounded audience of his attempt to kill Georgi Okolovich in Germany using a miniature electric gun, disguised as a packet of cigarettes, which silently fired bullets coated in potassium cyanide – these too are shown in Moscow. Three years later Kokhlov himself was poisoned by a Soviet agent who injected him with radioactive thallium, a substance which destroys human white blood cells.

As the thousands of individual agents bribed, blackmailed and betrayed their way through every level of Berlin society the agencies were also engaged in expensive and risky projects which sometimes involved hundreds of people. One of the most spectacular was the tunnel built by the CIA and the SIS to intercept Soviet telephone communications. 'Operation Gold' became a symbol of the Cold War city.[83]

The tunnel was an ingenious idea and was based on a successful British operation in Vienna in 1950, code-named 'Silver'. The plan was to dig a tunnel from the American sector to the Soviet sector and tap into telephone land lines which carried information to and from KGB headquarters at Karlshorst. The CIA were responsible for building the tunnel, while the SIS would supply wire-tapping equipment. It was kept completely secret, and Berliners were oblivious to the extraordinary events taking place beneath their city.[84]

After studying the Soviet sector boundaries the agencies decided that the best place to intercept the Soviet lines was in Alt Glienicke in south-east Berlin, where the American and Soviet sectors met next to the Schönefelder Chaussee. The tunnel would have to extend for at least 500 yards into the Soviet sector and it was feared that the work would be noticed, so the Americans set about building a radar station beside the sector boundary. This was ostensibly to monitor the nearby airfield at Johannisthal; in fact it hid the excavation work at the tunnel site.

Work began in August 1954. A hydraulically operated steel ring was pushed through the soil 20 feet below ground and the earth was removed in crates labelled 'radar equipment'. When the steel-lined tunnel was completed the British installed switch gear and 600 tape recorders; over 1,200 hours of material were recorded each day, and planes carrying crates of tapes flew out to England and the United States every week for decoding.[85]

The information was of vital importance. The west learned details of Soviet military and intelligence organizations, including the vast extent of the

KGB network in West Berlin and Germany. The information had wider implications; the CIA discovered that the Soviets did not intend to invade Tito's Yugoslavia, which meant that the United States could support the leader with no fear of armed conflict. The tap also recorded an extraordinary conversation between the wife of General Andrei Grechko, Red Army commander in Germany, and her daughter in Berlin, revealing Khrushchev's denunciation of Stalin. The conversation went: 'Your father met Marshal Bulganin at the Twentieth Party Congress. They had just heard Khrushchev denounce Stalin. It's a great secret but it's true. Amazing.' 'How did Father react?' 'He shat on the floor.'[86]

The Americans and British had always assumed that the tunnel had a finite life, and on 21 April 1956 East German telephone engineers dug up the cable 'for repairs' and 'discovered' the tunnel. At first the Soviets hoped to turn this into a propaganda coup, inviting the Berlin press corps to view the array of gleaming equipment and even publishing a guide to the installation, complete with maps and diagrams. Instead of denouncing western treachery, however, the papers called the venture a wonderful example of American ingenuity and the propaganda campaign was stopped. As with so many things in Cold War Berlin the 'discovery' of the tunnel was not what it had seemed. The Soviets had known about it all along but had kept silent in order to protect one of their top spies, the traitor in the SIS, George Blake.[87]

Blake was one of the Soviets' most important agents. Born in Holland, he had fled to Britain in 1943 and joined the Royal Navy. After the war he was recruited by the SIS, sent to Cambridge to read modern languages, and then joined the Far Eastern Department of the Foreign Office. From there he was sent to Seoul, where he was captured and taken to North Korea as a prisoner; there he volunteered to become a Soviet agent. Blake returned to London as a hero, his colleagues unaware that he had switched sides. He was posted to Berlin in January 1955 and given a highly sensitive post in the SIS Political Section, where his main task was to recruit KGB officers working in the city; under a separate directive code-named 'Operation Lyautey' he was sent to collect incriminating material for blackmail on all Soviet officials based in Berlin. The British believed him to be a double agent; in fact he was a triple agent and later admitted to giving the Soviets 'every secret that had crossed his desk'. Under the cover of his SIS job he held regular meetings with KGB operatives in East Berlin, where he passed the entire structure of the SIS Berlin operations to his KGB controller. The existence of the tunnel was only one of the many secrets he gave away. He betrayed over 400 people, including men like Lieutenant-General Robert Bialek of East German State Security, who had defected to the west in 1953 and lived in West Berlin under a false name. Blake revealed Bialek's new identity and one evening in 1956, as Bialek was walking his dog, a car screeched up beside him, he was pushed in, driven to SSD headquarters in East Berlin, and executed.[88] Blake probably also betrayed Lieutenant-Colonel Pyotr Popov, the CIA's first Soviet agent, who was arrested in 1958 and who, it was rumoured, was executed by being thrown into a furnace in the presence of GRU colleagues.[89] Blake crippled SIS operations in Berlin; those who might have been betrayed could no longer take the risk of working in the east, and had SOVBLOC RED stamped on their files. Blake was himself exposed by a Polish intelligence officer who defected to the west in 1960; Blake was sentenced to forty-two years' imprisonment but managed to escape from Wormwood Scrubs Prison after only six. He spent the rest of his life in Moscow.[90]

Blake was not the only westerner to defect to the Soviet side; indeed such betrayals had started in the 1940s and put all operations in Berlin at risk. The defection of Igor Gouzenko in Canada immediately after the war first revealed the shocking extent to which the Soviets were already operating in the west; it was he who exposed Dr Alan Nunn May, the British scientist who had passed on details of the first bomb tests and a sample of uranium to Soviet agents in Ottawa. There followed the exposure of the American network of Alger Hiss, David Greenglass and Harry Gold; the exposure of the British scientist Klaus Fuchs, who had witnessed the explosion of the first atomic bomb at Los Alamos and had revealed details about building atomic and plutonium bombs to the Soviets; and the exposure of the Rosenbergs, who also passed on atomic secrets. The worst was the discovery of KGB double agents high up in British intelligence. As early as 1938 and 1945 two Soviet defectors, Krivitsky and Volkov (both later murdered by the Soviets), had alerted the CIA to the fact that there was a mole in the SIS, and in 1951 the CIA identified him as Donald Maclean. Another of the Cambridge spies, Guy Burgess, fled with Maclean to Moscow. The third of the group, Kim Philby, was publicly exposed twenty years later, after which he too fled to Moscow. The damage wrought to western intelligence by the 'magnificent five' was immense; Philby in particular was responsible for the deaths of hundreds of agents, particularly of anti-Communists in Albania, the Baltic States and Ukraine.

The exposure of traitors within the SIS only served to heighten tension in Berlin and put even more pressure on operatives there. The Cold War city was becoming red-hot; this was the era of the 'bomber gap': in 1955 the Soviets duped the west into thinking they had a large fleet of long-range B-4 Bison bombers, which in turn prompted Eisenhower to build more B-52s. The myth of the 'bomber gap' was followed by the panic of the 'missile gap', sparked by the Soviets' successful launch of the first satellite, *Sputnik*, and by Khrushchev's boast that his country was producing missiles 'like sausages'. The

Americans retaliated in May 1956 with the first U-2 spy flights over the Soviet Union, which exposed a lack of Soviet military might, inter-continental ballistic missiles (ICBMs) and nuclear capability. Gary Powers's plane was shot down on 1 May 1960, after which he was tried for espionage in Moscow. He became the first spy to be exchanged over the Glienicke 'spy swap' Bridge in Berlin when he was traded for the Soviet Rudolph Abel on 10 February 1962.[91] It was precisely because of its vital importance to national and international security that so much effort and so many resources were pumped into Berlin espionage from both sides of the Iron Curtain. To some extent this covert world became self-perpetuating, with spies and counter-spies, agents and double agents collecting information on one another; indeed Khrushchev once joked to Allen Dulles that the Americans and Russians should cut down on the cancerous growth of espionage by exchanging their lists of spies, which would be largely duplicated anyway. Nevertheless both sides knew that spying was merely a symptom of the upheavals caused by the division of the world into two fiercely antagonistic blocs.

Espionage was not the only aspect of Cold War Berlin which reflected its role as the battleground between two opposing world views. Soviets and Americans competed for the very identity of the city, a struggle which affected every aspect of life from publishing newspapers to staging plays, from supporting new artists to putting on exhibitions extolling the virtues of one or other system. Nowhere was this struggle more visible than in the physical reconstruction of the two sides of the city. Suddenly, every memorial, new street, office block and housing development became a symbol of the 'glories of Communism' or the 'triumph of capitalism'.[92]

Of all the cities in the world, Berlin most powerfully represents the link between architecture and ideology. Over the centuries new styles have been developed to sweep away the old: the medieval brick town houses of the burghers were swept away by Hohenzollerns determined to make Berlin into a princely capital; the clean, neo-classical lines of the Prussian style were replaced by the bombastic buildings of Bismarck's Reich; the heavy imperial architecture gave way to the Bauhaus of Weimar; and during the Nazi period Albert Speer blasted acres of Berlin's past in the attempt to construct Hitler's Germania, which was itself destroyed in the flames of war. The situation in 1945 Berlin was unique. As in other bombed cities vast areas were little more than wasteland in need of redevelopment. The difference was that Berlin was at the centre of the struggle for the hearts and minds of its inhabitants. Nowhere was this more striking than in the creation of the 'showcase of capitalism' – West Berlin.

The creation of West Berlin started relatively late. No construction could take place during the airlift, and even in 1950 thousands of Berliners still lived in bombed-out buildings or makeshift shelters. Only a quarter of the rubble had been cleared and much had simply been dumped in adjacent bombed-out city blocks; indeed when Walter Gropius returned to Berlin in 1955 he said it was 'still a tragically shocking sight, much more behind than the western cities'.[93]

In May 1950 the Senate took the first step in the massive rebuilding of West Berlin by turning the old Wehrtechnische Fakultät in the northern part of Grunewald into the graveyard of old Berlin. Truckloads of rubble were dumped until a new feature began to rise out of the forest – the Teufelsberg, or Devil's Mountain. The artificial hill shoots 120 metres up out of the flat landscape and contains 18 million cubic metres of the old city, from staircases to lamps, from marble balustrades to tile ovens. As old Berlin vanished for ever groups of ambitious architects, town planners and politicians began to outline their vision of what the new Berlin should look like. They envisaged a new, exciting, modern city which would be timeless in its beauty and which would shine as a beacon of freedom and hope. Architecture was meant to teach a political lesson.

When one visits western Berlin today one is struck by the number of ugly post-war rectangular concrete and glass buildings which line street after street in the West End, in Zehlendorf, in Wedding and Charlottenburg. Few of these tall symmetrical buildings, with their flat roofs, large expanses of glass and curtain walls, give any sense that they rest on the bones of a historical European city. In the 1950s and 1960s, however, this rejection of traditional architecture was deliberate. In keeping with the *Stunde Null* or 'Zero Hour' mentality a line was to be drawn under Germany's past and the nation was to start afresh.[94] The concept was ludicrous, particularly in a city as scarred by recent events as Berlin, but it was embraced by many throughout the post-war world. Within months of the end of the war architects like Hans Scharoun, who worked from the Berlin Town Council, and Walter Moest, who represented the south-western residential suburb of Zehlendorf, had put forward their visions of the 'new Berlin'. The unifying theme was the destruction of all remnants of the past and their replacement with long rows of concrete and steel high-rises. Le Corbusier's plans were particularly worrying: he hoped to flatten vast swathes of the city so that it could be completely rebuilt on an east–west orientation, following the contours of the Havel valley and the Spree. Scharoun's new city was to be filled with modern offices and vast new residential developments which were, as he put it, to be 'divided into basic units for four thousand to five thousand inhabitants each'. These were to be 'fundamental cells that approximately correspond in size to the core of the Siemensstadt development . . . they reflect the unity of life, life as a coherent structure'.[95] In reality they represented little more than ugly rows of concrete and Berliners can be grateful that such attempts were thwarted by increasing tension between East and West Berlin. However, the architects were undaunted and continued to exert an influence over the rebuilding of Cold War Berlin. Under their supervision hundreds of partially damaged buildings which might have been saved were blown up and carted away to the Teufelsberg in an orgy of destruction only surpassed by the war itself; the lost treasures included everything from nineteenth-century town houses to that 'cathedral of industry' the Anhalter Bahnhof, which was destroyed even though it was still in working order. Only a small piece of the magnificent facade remains.[96] The loss to Berlin was immeasurable.

This destruction of historical buildings was promoted by the Germans' desire to cut themselves off from the Nazi past. 'Tainted' traditional styles were to be abandoned in favour of international modernism, which was considered politically correct as it had been developed in the United States primarily by German architects who had been forced to flee Nazi Germany. People genuinely believed that these buildings could help to teach Germans the meaning of freedom and democracy, and their introduction to post-war Germany was deliberate American policy; as early as 1947 the American military government was inviting architects like Martin Wagner, Erich Mendelsohn and Mies van der Rohe to travel around the country explaining the fundamentals of the new style. The requirement for an architectural break with the Nazi past often went to extremes and influenced not only the designs of buildings, but the building material itself. Traditional wood, brick or stone was rejected in favour of steel, glass and reinforced concrete in the mistaken belief that the Nazis had only used the former; when the boxy Allianzversicherung high-rise was built on the Kurfürstendamm in 1953 – one of the first post-war office buildings in Berlin – the architect was criticized not for creating a monstrous modern eyesore, but because he had used a kind of travertine cladding favoured by Albert Speer; architects were henceforth encouraged to use 'un-Nazi' tiles despite their tendency to fall off.

Given the mood of the times it is not surprising that West Berlin's first prestige project was a modernists' dream. It set the tone of development for over a decade. In 1956 the West Berlin Senate revealed plans to develop the once beautiful old diplomatic quarter at the southern edge of the Tiergarten, the Hansaviertel. Architects from around the world, including Alvar Aalto, the Brasilian Oscar Niemeyer, the Frenchman Pierre Vago, Walter Gropius and Le Corbusier, were asked to design a building for the site. It was given high priority in Berlin; when Walter Gropius was invited to speak about the project he noted that 'all Berlin' attended, and the American high commissioner James B. Conant told him that it would help the city to become the cultural capital and 'showcase' for West Germany.[97] When it was completed in 1958 the Hansaviertel was little more than a vast field dotted with enormous concrete buildings containing monotonous flats. The two churches, public library and restaurant did little to alleviate the boredom. Leonardo Benevelo called it a prime example of 'the indifference of modern European urban planning and design'[98] and even Gropius remarked: 'I am disappointed that so far the arrangement is more a chart of modern architecture than an organic setup from a community point of view.'[99] Despite its obvious flaws West Berliners applauded the project as a symbol of a 'new age' and it became the model for dozens of others such as the vast Otto Suhr Settlement in Kreuzberg, the hideous development at Falkenhagener Feld, which contains 10,000 drab apartments, and Le Corbusier's 1956 'Unité d'Habitation Typ Berlin', a residential 'machine' which squeezed 530 units on to seventeen floors.

The Hansaviertel was a quintessential project of 1950s West Berlin, invested with meaning in the Cold War competition with East Berlin. From the day of its inception it was consciously portrayed not only as an architectural experiment but as a rival to the vast East German development on the Stalinallee, which was going up only a few hundred metres away. It was made clear that, while the design of the Stalinallee project had been dictated from above, the Hansaviertel was the result of a 'free association of many architects', and while the Stalinallee was representative of totalitarianism the Hansaviertel 'epitomized the spirit' of the free and prosperous west.[100] The overt symbolism was extended to other projects, culminating in the competition 'Capital City Berlin' announced by the Senate in 1959. Architects were asked to submit 'visions of the unity and visual coherence of united Berlin as a capital city'. The plans were to extend from the Grosser Stern in the west to the Alexanderplatz well inside the Soviet zone in a defiant act which sought to prove to the East Germans that their state was illegitimate and that Berlin would soon be unified under western control, with western-style buildings dominating the Berlin skyline. One hundred and fifty designs were submitted and, in keeping with the mood of the times, virtually all advocated ripping down old Prussian landmarks around Unter den Linden; Le Corbusier wanted to flatten the entire city centre and replace it with gigantic rectangular skyscrapers. The grand plans were blocked only by the construction of the Wall in 1961, but some aspects survived, most notably in the construction of the notorious Kultur Forum in the eastern section of the Tiergarten, and in the vast Ernst-Reuter-Platz, which became little more than a traffic roundabout lined with impersonal high-rises and offices.[101] The attempt to create 'democratic' buildings was taken to extremes. Fritz Bornemann's hideous German Opera House on the Bismarckstrasse looks like a giant shoebox perched on a cube; the balconies and boxes in the spartan interior were arranged so that the seating was 'democratic and without rank'.

Despite their obvious ugliness Berliners applauded these new structures as symbols of progress. Many participated in the rebuilding programme; placards appeared everywhere showing the Berlin bear marching to work at slick new construction sites declaring: STEP BY STEP BERLIN MOVES FORWARD; *BERLIN BAUT AUF* or HELP FOR BERLIN THROUGH THE MARSHALL PLAN. Posters were accompanied by slogans like 'The Spree Still Flows through Berlin' or '*Berlin bleibt doch Berlin*' – Berlin remains Berlin.[102] The sense of optimism was due in part to prosperity and the increasing flow of western money into the new 'showcase'. In 1955 the Adenauer Foundation gave Berlin capital to improve the U-Bahn system and complete the city Autobahn, while dozens of department stores, cinemas and cafés were built by private investors. The area around the Zoo and the Kaiserdamm quickly filled with banks and insurance companies; the Zentrum am Zoo and Zoopalast Cinema and the Berliner Bank were finished in 1953, while the Telefunken Hochhaus, with its twenty-two floors, was finished in 1958. The new Deutschlandhalle, which Willy Brandt called proof of Berlin's 'will to live', was for a time the biggest sports stadium in Germany. Hotels were also considered important not because they recalled the grand hotel tradition of the past but because they implied that the city was once again an international travel destination – or 'worth a trip', as a new advertising slogan put it. The most prestigious of these was the 600-bed Berlin Hilton, designed by the Americans Pereira and Lucman at a cost of over $6 million. The 1958 opening was a highpoint of the year; people were impressed by the bevy of stars who flew in from New York and by the fact that the bell hops all carried American-made pocket radios.[103]

The number of American projects was startling but reflected West Berlin's importance as a Cold War symbol in the fight against Soviet Communism. The secret world of espionage had its public side and the US government donated over DM3,000 million worth of Marshall Plan aid to Berlin and financed the creation of landmarks to further German–American friendship, projects which still dot the Berlin landscape. One of the most original was the 1957 Kongresshalle, financed by the Benjamin Franklin Foundation, which looks like something out of a 1950s science fiction film. The vast curved white roof arches up like a giant shell (Berliners call it the 'pregnant oyster'), which is held up by pillars at either end, leaving the glass interior free to float as if in space. Unfortunately the faith in reinforced concrete was misplaced and the roof collapsed in 1980; by then the infatuation with America had waned and the building was not restored until 1987. Dozens of other modern glass and steel buildings were erected by the Americans; many included education as part of their official function. The Amerika Haus provided access to books, newspapers and films and funded lectures by luminaries including Gropius and Hindemith. Over 100,000 people visited the site in 1950 alone to be educated 'in the meaning of democracy and freedom'. In 1954 the gigantic American Memorial Library was opened on Blücherplatz in Kreuzberg with over 70,000 books, 1,000 newspapers and thousands of record albums. James Conant called it the 'most modern library in Europe' and a 'symbol of German–American friendship'. It was, he said, particularly important as it was 'only one hundred meters from East Berlin' and would be a beacon of democracy to those living in the east. Easterners were encouraged to come and use the facilities; when the Wall went up in 1961 the library lost thousands of volumes which the users suddenly could not return. Other American projects included the construction of much of the campus of the Free University of Berlin, which had been started in 1948 as a protest against Soviet restrictions on education; over a third of its students were from the GDR.[104] The American Henry Ford Foundation financed many of the buildings on the Gary-Strasse in Dahlem, including the main lecture theatre and the 1954 University Library, which costs $1.3 million. At the opening of the Foreign Ministry John Foster Dulles emphasized that 'as Berlin is a symbol of political freedom, so the Free University is a symbol of academic freedom of the world'.[105]

American influence extended not only into architecture and education, but to every aspect of cultural life. The emergence of the Soviet Union as the new enemy meant that de-Nazification was abandoned in favour of a broad acceptance of all but the most vile Nazi criminals. The difference in attitude was marked. In 1945 men like the conductor Wilhelm Furtwängler had submitted to lengthy de-Nazification procedures before being allowed back on the Berlin stage. He was better than most: he had not been a Nazi and had defended men like Hindemith, the Philharmonic's leader Simon Goldberg and a number of Jewish musicians in the orchestra; he had merely failed to understand that his very presence in Berlin had given the Nazis a cultural legitimacy that they would otherwise never have had. By the 1950s, however, Furtwängler's past had been put aside. He had been reinstated as director of the Berlin Philharmonic and became instrumental in its post-war revival. This was true of others who had remained in Berlin, including Karl Böhm, Eugen Jochum and Herbert von Karajan, some of whom had highly dubious Nazi pasts. Despite the fact that he had wholly embraced the Nazi Party by May 1933 Karajan was appointed 'Chief Conductor for Life' of the Berlin Philharmonic in 1954, a post he retained until his death in 1989.

The worst aspect of the sudden amnesia about Nazi Berlin was a sinister backlash against those who had left Nazi Germany and who now tried to come home. Refugees removed from their posts under the Nazis were not automatically reinstated if they returned to Berlin, and great musicians like Otto Klemperer, Erich Kleiber (who eventually died in Switzerland) and Fritz Busch (who died in London in 1951 after helping to establish Glyndebourne) were never really welcomed back to Berlin. Many of those who had spent the war in exile – like Thomas and Heinrich Mann – were openly referred to as 'traitors' by certain segments of Berlin society. The sudden arrival of the Cold War and the replacement of Nazi Germany by the Soviet Union as the great enemy of democracy and freedom meant that many individuals who should have been subjected to at least some censure in post-war West Berlin were now permitted to remain in their pre-1945 posts with little or no recrimination.[106]

Even though returning refugees were given a chilly welcome it was becoming increasingly clear by the 1950s that the cultural heart of Berlin had been ripped out between 1933 and 1945. Thousands of great film directors, playwrights and artists had either been forced into exile or murdered. But West Berliners now wanted to forget their past, and for most the future was not German – it was American. The revival in the 1950s owed more to prosperity than cultural innovation; architecture, sculpture and paintings did not question the past but reflected the longing for a brighter 'American-style' future in the face of the constant fear of invasion or war. There is an almost desperate quality to much of this work. Bleak post-war paintings gave way to exuberant but superficial visions of the new city like the busy street scenes in Hans Joachim Seidel's 1955 *Berlin am Zoo* with its shops, cafés and cars; Erhard Gross's 1956 painting of the slick new Gleisdreieck Bridge, or Peter Hanssen's 1959 view of the Kurfürstendamm with all its affluence on display. For all their liveliness the works were strangely lacking in conviction; perhaps the lurking fear that this was all a dream world, a tinsel town, was best captured by one of the most memorable paintings of the time, Wilhelm Götz-Knothe's 1958 *Trümmergrundstück am Ka De We* (Rubble Lot of the Ka De We). This showed not the familiar facade of the giant department store, but the bleak rubble field which still stretched out behind it. The painting captured the insecurity of these newly affluent West Berliners: the Ka De We stood for the glossy life now enjoyed by so many while the rubble field reminded them of a past which lay just below the surface.[107] The same was true of 1950s theatre, which offered foreign plays like *Waiting for Godot* but saw virtually nothing written in the post-war city itself. Even the new cabaret was stripped of its cutting wit, and titles like *Oh, You Wonderful Freedom!* at the Cabaret Stachelschweine could not hide the fact that even this had become little more than cheerful entertainment. The 1950s city was more at ease copying the latest trends from America than forging its own culture. The Deutschmark ruled.

The new obsession with material wealth quickly filled the gap left in a city floundering for an identity. The new culture of optimism took many forms, from glitzy shop displays and huge exhibitions of consumer goods to competitions to see who could down the largest quantity of beer and sausages in the new restaurants. The first National Football Championship was held in the Olympic Stadium in 1950, while the first Berlin Congress held in the Exhibition Centre that year saw a display of western technology from cars to washing machines; it was an enormous success and attracted over a million visitors, half from East Germany, and 1,000 prominent western guests, including Ludwig Erhard. In the same year Berlin held its first International Auto Exhibition at the Funkturm and thousands crammed in to see the new VW Beetle 1200 convertible and the latest from British Austin cars. The first 'International Green Week', with its garden show, was held on 3–10 February 1951, and on 29 May Anthony Eden opened a new English Garden by the Schloss Bellevue in the Tiergarten. Again over half the visitors were from the east. The GDR tried to stage its own exhibitions, but dull displays about the glories of socialism or the importance of the Free German Youth, with their stiff mannequins dressed in musty uniforms, could not compete with the dazzling wealth of the west. The idea of the 'showcase' was working.

Official exhibitions were only part of the attraction of West Berlin and by the mid 1950s it had become a Mecca of western culture and entertainment. The first department store to reopen was the Ka De We in 1950, and people queued for hours to catch a glimpse of the interior. The Kurfürstendamm was now crowded: the cafés and shops were packed with women in bright red lipstick, high heels and bad copies of the latest Dior and Chanel fashions from Paris; the streets were lined with the latest dream cars like VW Beetles, Opels and Borgwards, while teenagers took up the new craze for hula-hoops and motorbikes.[108] Luxury goods, from television sets to furs and jewellery, were displayed in huge glass cases, while kiosks sold American goods like Lucky Strike cigarettes and Coca-Cola.[109] At night the street was bathed in neon and the sound of jazz emanated from the clubs and cocktail bars. East Germans could come to the west and buy *Time, Life, Esquire* or the *National Geographic Magazine* as well as the new German publications based on their American counterparts like *Heute* and *Der Spiegel*. One of the most important Berlin publications was *Der Monat*, the quintessential Cold War magazine launched in 1948 to provide 'open discussion and debate on the basis of free speech'. The editor in chief, Melvin J. Lasky, worked with the CIA-sponsored Congress for Cultural Freedom to provide a forum for non-Communist intellectuals. Bookshops sold American Pocket Books by Faulkner, Hemingway and Norman Mailer for only 50 pfennigs each, while the theatres put on productions of *Death of a Salesman* and *A Streetcar Named Desire*.

The most successful import was film. The first Berlin Film Festival was held in the new Titania Palast in June 1951, with entries from twenty-one countries. The Swiss production *The Four in the Jeep* won the first ever Golden Bear, but American movies had long been favourites with the general public. In the early years of the Cold War the Americans had produced propaganda films for the German market such as the 1949 *Between East and West*, which recounted the story of growing American allegiance to Berlin in the years leading to the airlift. In 1952 the United States Information Service even sent a group of Hollywood writers and producers to Berlin to make films about the Communist menace; one, entitled *A Streetcar Called Freedom*, was about a tram which became so disgusted by life in East Berlin that it fled for the glitter of the Kurfürstendamm.[110] These crude attempts at propaganda were quickly eclipsed by popular films which did more to spread American culture and values than anything else; everyone wanted to see *Rebel without a Cause* or *Singin' in the Rain* or *High Noon*. Heinz Agosch said that West Germany was the most American country outside America, and that meeting teenagers 'in the American-made pin-table saloons, or skylarking on their noisy motor-bikes, you come across so many James Deans, Marlon Brandos and Marilyn Monroes that you scarcely know which country you are in!'[111]

By the end of the 1950s West Berlin had taken on the veneer of prosperity, glitz, optimism and wealth. People had no time for the sins of the past or for reflection about the horrors of Nazism; they might be worried about nuclear war but they were determined to live for the moment and enjoy the new prosperity while they could. East Berliners were also impressed by life in the west and became increasingly critical of the failings of the GDR. The Soviet representative in East Berlin, General Abrasimov, complained that West Berlin had undergone an 'artificial transmutation' into a 'shop-window of the West behind the Iron Curtain. Marshall Aid to the city was greatly increased,' he complained, 'both by the Western Powers and, especially, by the Federal German government in order to try and impress the people of the GDR with its superficial brilliance and dupe them into accepting the "superiority" of the capitalist system, thus making it more "attractive".' All this, he concluded, was only 'a smokescreen to conceal the principal role of West Berlin as a vital centre of intrigue and subversion for the Western Powers in the Cold War'.[112] The Soviets could complain, but there was little they could do to stem the tide of western culture. East Berliners were still free to cross to West Berlin and see the 'depraved western capital' for themselves. To the delight of the Americans and the West Germans, many began to pack up their bags and leave. A new crisis was about to erupt in East Berlin.

Compared to the west life in East Berlin had become intolerable. In 1951 Soviet-style collectivization had been forced through in the factories and in 1952 the collectivization of agriculture had been speeded up. When East German productivity fell the Russians blamed 'saboteurs', 'ex-Nazis' – indeed everything but the ridiculous system which they had put in place. Many East Berliners had hoped for improvements after the 1953 uprising but things had simply become worse. People continued to 'disappear' on suspicion of spying or other 'anti-state activities', and fear of arrest was a part of everyday life. Most people had no choice of job or profession, nor any say in where they lived or how much they earned. They endured constant shortages, bad food and a dull and oppressive culture. East Germans did work hard to rebuild their shattered lives but their successes were achieved in spite, and not because of, the Soviet economic system. People were willing to work hard, but to their chagrin they were now expected to produce goods for the Soviet Union and to build socialist-realist monuments to Stalin or the Red Army. If international modernism was the new face of West Berlin, socialist-realism was the only acceptable face of Stalin's empire. Projects were meant to serve as international advertising for the glories of Soviet Communism. Let the west build their modernist temples to freedom – the Soviet monuments would reflect only one thing: power.

The tone was set early with the creation of the vast Soviet War Memorial in Treptow Park out of the huge stone blocks from Hitler's Reich Chancellery; it was completed in 1948. Two huge flags made of tons of red marble flank the central memorial, 3,200 Soviet soldiers are buried under the trees nearby, and three enormous socialist-realist statues of Soviet soldiers in heroic poses tower above the park. This early symbol of Soviet Berlin became a necessary stop for all visiting eastern bloc dignitaries; Khrushchev made a point of paying his respects on 24 July 1955. The Soviets built other monuments to themselves, including their embassy on Unter den Linden, which spanned 400 feet and contained 320 rooms dripping with gold paint and red carpets. Nevertheless the first development planned as a direct challenge to western architects was the infamous housing project on the Stalinallee, instigated by the dictator himself. There was little doubt as to what it was to represent. The mile-long street was designed for military parades and was wide enough to accommodate anything from rows of Free German Youth members to Soviet tanks. It was lined by a collection of imperial, neo-classical, Stalinist wedding-cake buildings surrounded by gigantic statues, including a massive bronze of Stalin. Wilhelm Pieck described it as 'the greatest, widely visible symbol of our policy of peace and the improvement in conditions for all our population'. There was, however, a problem. No expense had been spared on the lavish decorations and the tile cladding and the cost ran well over budget. After Stalin's death Khrushchev ordered a change in building policy and Kurt Liebknecht, who had ironically been Stalin's chief architect, suddenly announced that it was 'not necessary to make a modern apartment building into a church or a museum'. Soviet client states did not need such luxury; architecture could be functional and cheap while still symbolizing the glories of Soviet Communism.

The new policy resulted in the construction of the ugliest buildings in Berlin's history.

The first principle of the new construction was standardization. Rules were laid down allowing no more than 9 square metres per person per flat, and all ground and floor plans were identical so that housing projects could be pieced together out of pre-fabricated concrete slabs and joined like so many pieces of Lego. The result was structures which were shoddy, ugly and poorly built; fittings were sub-standard, amenities did not work, windows fell out, and the rows of concrete were anonymous, monotonous and inhuman. The buildings conformed to the sixteen guidelines for the reconstruction of public areas of East Berlin, which had been issued by the East German Ministerial Council of the GDR. New streets and squares were to be created for 'political demonstrations, marches, and celebrations of national holidays', while buildings which had 'negative' links with the past were to be ripped down.[113] As in West Berlin, great treasures were lost, the most tragic being the great Berlin Schloss because of its imperial associations with the Second Reich. The only part saved was Andreas Schlüter's balcony, from which Liebknecht had proclaimed a 'Soviet Republic' in 1918 and which was incorporated into the front of the State Council Building on Marx-Engels-Platz. Ugly buildings replaced the historic masterpieces: Friedrich Ebert laid the groundstone for the ghastly complex between the Alexanderplatz and Strausberger Platz, which included a handful of six-storey apartment blocks, a cinema for 600 people and a tourist hotel. Fortunately the ruins which still lined Unter den Linden were regarded as too unimportant to tamper with, and they were left in place, only to be magnificently restored when the political climate changed in the 1970s and 80s.

The architecture and planning of East Berlin was only one aspect of life in the GDR; other arts were also centrally controlled and those who challenged official doctrine risked censure, arrest or worse. Soviet dictums banned anything 'cosmopolitan' from sexuality to bourgeois morality and the result was an extremely prudish and dull culture. Even great artists were censored. The poet Johannes Bobrowski, who had been taken prisoner on the eastern front and returned to East Berlin from Russia in 1949, wrote beautifully about the landscape near Memel in poems like *Schattenland Ströme*, but his novel *Litauische Klaviere* was published only in 1966 after much wrangling with the censors. The poet Erich Arendt, whose Communist credentials included work for the *Rote Signale* in 1931 and emigration in 1933, returned to East Berlin in 1948 but had difficulty publishing his volumes of poetry *Gesang der sieben Inseln* (1957) and *Unter den Hugen des Winds* (1966). When Brecht and Pohl staged a production of Goethe's *Urfaust* in 1952 which deliberately stressed all sexual references in the text the party had it banned, explaining that instead of questioning society the 'productions of our classics must help us to awaken the national strength of our *Volk*'. Caspar Neher wrote in 1952 that the kind of art promoted in East Berlin was like that 'in Goebbels's day'.[114] Artists regularly disappeared in the GDR: on 22 February 1953 the Stasi picked up Martin Pohl and threw him into an ex-SS jail; in 1957 the writer Erich Loest was arrested and charged as a 'revisionist and counter-revolutionary' and spent seven years in Bautzen prison for treason; the poet and painter Roger Loewig was arrested for 'anti-state agitation' because his work was 'critical of the DDR'; even Brecht feared for his life and tried to ingratiate himself with the East Germans by writing *The Herrenberger Report*, which advocated the reunification of Germany under Communist rule.

With important men like Brecht in danger from the state the lesser citizens felt increasingly vulnerable. They grew tired of the repression, appalling conditions, poor housing, and food which often consisted of little more than acid, coloured, fruit-flavoured drinks, bad meat and standard vegetables like potatoes and cabbage, while the party bosses enjoyed chauffeured limousines and special shops with luxurious goods hidden from public view. Furthermore the leaders took no responsibility for the disastrous economic situation; milk shortages were blamed not on an inefficient system but on Berliners, who were said to be secretly hiding their empty bottles. Even 'luxury' goods introduced after Stalin's death were dreadful; the clothes were unfashionable at best and even the state perfume produced by VEB Berlin Kosmetik was sickly – as was its shampoo, 'Poo-Exquisit'. Above all, East Berliners could still reach the west and each time there was a crisis, from the Berlin Uprising of 1953 to the crushing of the Hungarian Uprising in 1956, more people left the GDR permanently. As the political situation continued to worsen the numbers of refugees increased, and the flow of people reached epidemic proportions in 1958.[115]

The crisis of 1958 is not often remembered today but it marked one of the 'hottest' moments of the Cold War. Although the debate raged around the future of Berlin it raised the very real prospect of a nuclear world war. The crisis began on 10 November 1958, when Khrushchev gave a surprising speech in Moscow in which he suddenly demanded that the western powers leave West Berlin immediately: 'The time has evidently come for the power which signed the Potsdam Agreement to give up the remnants of the occupation regime in Berlin.' On 27 November the Soviets delivered an aggressive note to the western powers, accusing them of violating the Potsdam Agreement and claiming that the western presence in West Berlin was 'unlawful'. Khrushchev offered West Berlin the chance to become a 'Free City', and added that if the west did not accept the offer within six months East Germany would 'fully deal with questions concerning its space, i.e. exercise its sovereignty on land, water and in the air'. In short, if the west did not accept the Soviet offer, it faced a Third World War. At the time, the threat seemed very real.[116]

The ultimatum had come as a shock to the world and Berliners became increasingly nervous. The East Germans crossed into West Berlin, displaying their flag on the railway stations, which had officially remained under Soviet control after the war, and tried to restrict Allied flights in the corridors.[117] West Berlin braced itself for another blockade and perhaps an invasion. Fortunately the Americans held firm, retorting that if Khrushchev wanted to resolve the problem of Berlin he should withdraw his forces from eastern Europe and grant self-determination to the states there. Khrushchev backed down, but the crisis simmered for two difficult years, during which the flow of refugees continued to increase.[118] Then, in June 1961, it erupted again. This time it was sparked by the first summit meeting between Khrushchev and the newly elected American President John F. Kennedy in Vienna. It became one of the most infamous showdowns of the Cold War.[119]

Khrushchev was at his most arrogant – this was the belligerent leader who had taken his shoe off and pounded it on the podium in the United Nations, the leader who in 1957 had seen the Soviets launch *Sputnik* and had successfully tested an intercontinental ballistic missile, thereby achieving superpower status. Furthermore Khrushchev saw Kennedy as a weak and inexperienced leader disgraced by the recent Bay of Pigs disaster and the U-2 spy scandal. He genuinely believed that he could force the United States to give way in Berlin. Khrushchev made no secret of his plans. He referred to Berlin as 'the testicles of the West' which he had only to squeeze to 'make it scream'. It was time, he said, to 'lance the boil' of Berlin and to remove the source of western corruption from the Soviet zone.

Kennedy, a man who usually relied on personality to charm his opponents, quickly discovered that he had no leverage with the Soviet leader and he was deeply shaken by the first meeting. When he lamely warned the Soviet leader that 'miscalculation' between the two powers might lead to war Khrushchev literally screamed: 'All I ever hear from your people . . . is that damned word miscalculation. You ought to take that word and bury it . . . and never use it again. I am sick of it!' With that Khrushchev decreed that West Berlin should become a free city within six months. The meeting had grave repercussions for its future.

Upon his return to Washington Kennedy made a statement about the meeting: West Berlin, he said, was 'an integral part of the security of western Europe . . . We are determined to maintain those rights at all cost and thus to stand by our commitments to the people of West Berlin.' The speech seemed tough, but in fact it gave Khrushchev a huge concession. For the first time an American president had used the term 'West Berlin' instead of 'Berlin'. The draft upset the 'Berlin mafia' in Washington, who referred to it as the 'SLOB' speech – the Soft Line on Berlin – but when they tried to have it amended they were overruled by Kennedy himself. Karl Mautner in Intelligence and Research in the State Department remembered 'getting the "Oh my God" feeling of a government undercutting its own position'. Kennedy had just admitted that East Berlin was, *de facto*, a part of the Soviet sphere of influence. Worse still, he had made the statement at a crucial time in Berlin – at the height of the refugee crisis which threatened to destroy the GDR.

The movement of people from East Germany into West Berlin had continued unabated. As early as 1949 59,245 East Germans had left the GDR for the west. The numbers had increased steadily and in 1953, the year of the uprising, 331,390 had left East Germany. After the Soviet suppression of the Hungarian Uprising in 1956, a popular revolt which thousands of East Berliners had openly supported, 279,189 fled, and when Khrushchev threatened the west with the 1958 ultimatum the number rose to 100 people per day. Instead of trying to entice his people to stay the unimaginative Ulbricht continued to tighten restrictions, raise work norms, curb freedoms and increase propaganda.[120] More people were arrested on suspicion of espionage; schools were turned into *Alltagsschule*, where propaganda took up any 'free time'; Hollywood films were denounced as subversive and the quality of food and consumer goods grew steadily worse. Ulbricht denounced 'Flight from the Republic' as a crime; easterners caught in possession of western newspapers were given three years in prison, and the authorities exhorted the public to report those suspected of preparing to leave. Scare stories were published in *Neues Deutschland* warning of the pitfalls of moving to the west; one claimed that young men were being drafted and another asserted that West Berlin was in the grip of a dangerous polio epidemic. Erich Honecker, then a member of the SED Central Committee, accused 'West German monopolies' of sending saboteurs into East German factories to try to collect a skilled workforce for the west. The stories did nothing to stem the tide. Those wanting to leave needed only to pack a few belongings, travel two stops on the U-Bahn and emerge in West Berlin. From there they were directed to contact points, where all East German refugees were taken in without question. By the late 1950s the refugee centre at the Marienfelde barracks, with its huge banner reading THE FREE WORLD WELCOMES YOU!, was bursting at the steams. People were given food and a place to sleep; eventually they were housed in West Berlin, or were flown on regular scheduled flights to West Germany, where they were helped to find work and a place to live. The refugees were for the most part young skilled workers, professionals, new graduates, professors – the elite of East German youth – who could easily find work in *Wirtschaftswunder* West Germany. The GDR was slowly being bled dry.

Life for those who stayed behind became increasingly depressing. Women and pensioners were made to return to work to fill the empty places. Hospital wards were forced to close because so many nurses had left, entire factories stood empty, and the mass departure of bus and train drivers left parts of East Berlin paralysed. By 1961 over 5,000 doctors and dentists had left the GDR, as had hundreds of professors – including the entire Law Faculty of the University of Leipzig; over 2,000 scientists left, three-quarters of whom were under forty-five.[121] Thirty thousand students fled, many only days after receiving their diplomas. Some defections were particularly embarrassing: in 1961 the East German Miss Universe came to the west, followed by 4,000 members of the SED. Ironically not only East Germans, but Soviet soldiers also tried to flee through the gap to the west; Penkovsky recalled one commander complaining: 'Whenever possible, our soldiers try to escape to West Berlin or West Germany ... The soldier is told that if he is captured, he will be shot immediately. Even the East German police have been instructed to capture our soldiers.'[122] By 1961 it was clear that East Germany was facing collapse. East Berliners were gripped by *Torschlusspanik* – the rush to escape before something happened and the door slammed shut. In July 1961 30,415 people arrived in West Berlin, followed by 21,828 in the first week of August. Over half were under twenty-five years old. In all, 3 million East Germans had already registered and it was estimated that a further 430,000 escaped East Germany without informing the west. The west congratulated itself on its superior system. East Germans were voting with their feet.

As the crisis worsened Khrushchev became increasingly belligerent. He warned the west not to take advantage of the situation as it would lead to war. In response to an article in *Newsweek* which implied that the Americans were increasing their military presence in Berlin Khrushchev called the British ambassador Sir Frank Roberts into his box at the Bolshoi Theatre and informed him of the number of bombs needed to destroy Britain.[123] On 9 August he boasted that the Soviets could develop a 100-megaton bomb which would 'not be used for slicing sausages'. With each of these outbursts the number of refugees increased. The East German leadership were afraid that East Germany would collapse into anarchy. Something had to be done.

It was Walter Ulbricht who hit upon the solution to the refugee crisis, and it was he who persuaded the Soviets to allow him to act. On 3 August 1961 he flew to a secret meeting in Moscow for all First Secretaries of the Warsaw Pact countries. It was there that he was given permission to put his plan into action. A few days after the conference it was announced that Marshal Koniev was to be put in charge of twenty Soviet divisions in East Germany, despite the fact that he was far too senior for the post. Everybody feared that something was about to happen, but nobody knew what. Most western analysts predicted that the Soviets would once again try to blockade Berlin. Troops in the city were on full alert.

By 12 August the East Berliners were panicking; over 4,000 people had left by that Saturday evening and thousands more had packed their bags and prepared to follow on Sunday. The volunteers at the Marienfelde centre were preparing themselves for a massive influx of people the next day. But the people never came.[124] That night Ulbricht had given the order to seal the border between East and West Berlin. Early on the morning of 13 August the first phase of the Berlin Wall began to take shape. The old city was about to be sliced in two.

The operation to seal off the entire area of West Berlin from the Soviet zone was one of the best-guarded secrets in GDR history.[125] Hundreds of troops, armoured personnel carriers, equipment and workers had been brought into Berlin over the course of the week but nobody had been told the true reason for their presence. At four in the afternoon on 12 August Walter Ulbricht signed a paper giving Erich Honecker orders to commence, and at eleven o'clock that night Honecker, the Minister of State Security Erich Mielke and his staff gathered at Central Police headquarters in East Berlin. At midnight commanders throughout East Berlin were told to wake up their troops and to open the top-secret envelopes which they had been issued. Even senior personnel were shocked by what they read. The long document began with a denunciation of the United States, of NATO, of West Germany and of West Berlin, but it was only when they reached the end that officers learned that they were being ordered to divide their own city in half. Within two hours over 40,000 startled soldiers and policemen had been moved up to the sector boundary to form a line with their backs to the east. At precisely 1.11 on Sunday 13 August 1961 the East German news agency flashed a cryptic bulletin to the world: 'The present traffic situation on the borders of West Berlin is being used by ruling circles of [West Germany] and intelligence agencies of NATO countries to undermine the economy of the German Democratic Republic!' To stop this, 'reliable safeguards and effective controls' would be 'established around the whole territory of West Berlin'. By now workmen had begun to rip up asphalt and cobblestones, unloading piles of fencing and bales of barbed wire, which were quickly unrolled along the sector boundary. Soviet forces from the Sixth and Nineteenth motorized Rifle Divisions and the Tenth Guards Tank Division were deployed throughout East Berlin, but they remained in the background to give the illusion that this was an East German operation. Within hours, all of West Berlin had been encircled and sealed off.

The first place to be sealed was the symbolic Potsdamer Platz, which on 12 August had still been the busiest east–west crossing point in Berlin. By four o'clock in the morning it had been completely blocked off. Soon afterwards all the main streets in the city centre had been made impassable. Berliners were slow to respond. Only a few people had gathered to watch the proceedings in the early hours of the morning, but by six o'clock the first East Berlin workers were trying to cross the border to reach their jobs in the west. To their amazement, they were turned back. A few hours later the thousands who had planned to flee to West Berlin that day began to turn up at the Fried-richstrasse Station with their little bags and packages. They too were told that they could no longer travel. People begged police to be allowed to cross but were turned away; many broke down in tears when they realized that their chance of freedom had slipped away. One witness remembered the scenes at the station that morning:

> the hall – dimly lit and cavernous – seemed like the inside of a huge bunker. People of all ages, including small children, had gathered there. They carried packages and valises. Some sat on them. Their faces were marked by anguish and worry. Some were weeping. These were would-be refugees ... For them there was no doubt that the border closure was final, that the escape hatch was closed for good.[126]

The first hours of the division saw a kind of numb disbelief in Berlin. People could not grasp what was happening. The idea that the East Germans would seal off West Berlin, separating families and friends, dividing neighbourhood streets and local parks, was unimaginable. The new boundary looked so temporary, with its barbed wire and its line of soldiers. Berliners had no idea that plans were already afoot to turn this flimsy obstacle into one of the most heavily fortified strips of land in the world.

The failure to predict the building of the Wall ranks as one of the most spectacular blunders in the history of western intelligence.[127] Despite the number of agents and spies in Berlin not one could reveal what would happen in the early hours of the morning of 13 August 1961. The west was aware of Soviet and East German troop movements around the city but did not understand what they were for. Some would later claim that they knew about the Wall, but there is no evidence of this; CIA and West Berlin intelligence reports show western preparation for either a new blockade, a possible sealing-off of the entire city, or a repeat of the 1953 uprising; nobody predicted a wall. It was later recalled, with a sense of bitter irony, that at a press conference on 15 June Ulbricht had responded to a question about the refugee crisis by snapping: 'No one intends to build a Wall.' None of the journalists had taken the hint and western intelligence had dismissed the possibility as too outlandish to be taken seriously.[128] The failure was also due to precautions taken by Erich

Honecker, who had insisted on total secrecy coupled with a sophisticated disinformation campaign. As a result the west was left with no contingency plans. When they heard the news most analysts feared that the sealing of the border was merely the prelude to something much worse.

The first people to learn of the strange events at the inter-Berlin border were members of the Allied Kommandatura, who called an emergency meeting early on Sunday morning. Although they complained that the barbed wire barrier was 'a flagrant breach of Four Power status of Berlin' they did not respond. The first person to act was the new mayor of Berlin, Willy Brandt. On the night of 12 August he had been on a train near Hanover; at five o'clock the following morning he was woken with the news that something terrible was happening in Berlin. He immediately flew to Tempelhof and went directly to the Potsdamer Platz to talk to the crowds of people already gathering there. Although appalled at the action he wanted first and foremost to try to prevent West Berliners from mounting a protest, fearing that the Soviets would use this as an excuse to invade West Berlin. People he met were not aggressive, but simply asked, 'When will the Americans come?' The question was more ludicrous than they knew. As Willy Brandt walked amongst the crowds on that cold rainy morning President Kennedy was resting peacefully at Hyannis Port on the east coast of the United States. He did not yet know about the crisis.

The American response was inept. The United States army commander in Europe, General Bruce C. Clarke, learned of the disturbance in the early hours of the morning but decided to do nothing unless the Soviets actually started to blockade West Berlin. American communications continued through normal channels and Ambassador Walter C. Dowling spent much of the day watching a baseball game. It was not until noon on 13 August, sixteen hours after the news first broke, that the President of the United States was informed of events in Berlin.[129] Secretary of State Dean Rusk telephoned Kennedy in Hyannis Port but the two men agreed that the East German action did not seem to threaten Allied rights in West Berlin. He decided not to interfere. On the day the Berlin Wall went up the President of the United States went sailing.[130] When the British Prime Minister Macmillan was informed about the situation that day he said casually that 'Nobody is going to fight over Berlin,' and continued his golfing holiday in Scotland.[131]

Adenauer's response was little better. He refused to address the nation on television that Sunday, and he refused to go to Berlin. His behaviour reflected his hatred of the city; he was also in the midst of an electoral campaign against Willy Brandt for the Chancellorship. Elections had been scheduled for 17 September 1961 and Adenauer was loath to give Brandt any electoral advantage. When he addressed the nation on Monday he said that 'there is no reason to panic' and then launched into a personal attack against Brandt, even referring to his illegitimate birth and hinting that Ulbricht had staged this action simply to help Brandt at the polls.[132] Like the Americans, he failed to see the significance of events unfolding in the east. During the first hours and days Berliners faced the crisis alone.

By Monday morning all Berlin knew of the new barrier, and thousands streamed to the city centre to try to catch a glimpse of friends or relatives trapped in the east. People watched in silence as East Berliners were pushed back from the demarcation line. The telephones and mail service had already been cut between east and west so that the only way to communicate was by personal contact. Families and friends stood facing one another, trying to make themselves heard across the few metres separating them. Many were crying; many were trying to say goodbye. Some held up painted signs with messages to those on the other side. The journalist Norman Gelb remembered that

> There were poignant sights to be seen . . . An elderly East Berlin woman broke into a broad smile as she spotted her son west of the barrier, and then, almost instantly, dissolved in uncontrollable weeping at the realization that they could come no nearer. A man on the west side held up his wide-eyed bewildered baby for his parents in the East to see and coo at from too great a distance for the infant to notice. A young man and a young woman, separated by the wire, their faces masked by profound sadness, called out to each other.[133]

Some Berliners refused to accept the division and tried to run through the barrier to the west. A few of these heart-wrenching scenes were captured on film; in one case a little boy approached the barbed wire and begged one of the Vopos to let him through. The young man looked around, lifted the wire, and let him pass but was spotted by his superior and hauled away. Another famous piece of footage recorded the moment when the Vopo Peter Lieging, who was stationed at the corner of Ruppiner and Bernauer Strasse, looked cautiously around and then suddenly jumped over the barbed wire to the west. On that first day 800 people managed to escape, including many of the border guards, but the numbers were quickly reduced. Berliners' most common reaction, however, was sheer disbelief. A great city could not just be cut in two. Surely something would be done.

As the fact of the division began to sink in people became increasingly desperate. On Monday a crowd of 10,000 gathered at Hindenburgplatz on the west side of the Brandenburg Gate staring at the new barrier, uncertain what to do. Many began to suspect that the west was not going to come to their aid, and the demonstrations became more aggressive. Two thousand workers from the AEG turbine factory in Moabit marched to City Hall, tripling their number on the way. Brandt managed to control them by calling for a fifteen-minute pause so that West Berlin could demonstrate its solidarity with those in the east in silence, but the calm did not last and the crowd in front of the Brandenburg Gate grew increasingly violent. Young people began to throw stones at the East German guards and push at the barricades; the East Germans responded by spraying water cannon and lobbing tear gas over to the western side. Some Berliners began to push for action. Axel Springer, the newspaper magnate who owned the *Berliner Zeitung*, the *Berliner Morgenpost*, *Bild*, and *Die Welt*, held a conference at which he demanded that the west come in and tear down the barbed wire. The following morning West Berliners read in their Springer *Morgenpost*: WE APPEAL TO THE WORLD – PROTEST MARCHES – CONFERENCES – COUNTERMEASURES; the *BZ* said, ENOUGH OF THIS SLUGGISHNESS, while *Der Kurier* announced, BERLIN IS WAITING FOR COUNTERMEASURES. Border incidents increased; some East German Vopos actually jumped over the wire to beat up West Berlin youths; one teenager was dragged back to East Berlin and disappeared. The population was becoming increasingly angry. On Wednesday 16 August demonstrations began again. Springer printed headlines in bold red: THE WEST DOES NOTHING! The *Bild* complained: KENNEDY IS SILENT, MACMILLAN IS OUT HUNTING, ADENAUER SNEERS AT BRANDT. *Der Kurier* reported, incorrectly, that General Koniev had informed the Americans of the border closure and Berliners began to suspect that their city had been betrayed by the west – why else had the Americans, the British, the French and the West Germans not yet done anything?[134] Some feared that the Americans might be in the process of negotiating Berlin away; rumours circulated that the military was preparing to leave and that the American-run RIAS radio station was about to be closed down.[135] The city threatened to ignite in mass protests. Three-quarters of a million Berliners gathered at City Hall carrying placards reading: WHERE ARE THE AMERICANS?; PAPER PROTESTS DO NOT STOP TANKS; MUNICH 1938 – BERLIN 1961. Brandt again appealed for calm, this time announcing that he had written directly to President Kennedy requesting American support. It was a great political gamble.

The letter was one of the most controversial actions of Brandt's career. He wanted to inform Kennedy of his fears for Berlin if the Americans did not do something to boost morale in the western half of the city: 'The Soviet Union has used the People's Army to achieve half of its proposals for a "free city". Act Two is only a question of time. After Act Two we would find a Berlin which resembles a ghetto. Having lost not only its function as the refuge of freedom and the symbol of hope for reunification, it will also be cut off from the free section of Germany.' He appealed to Kennedy to show some support, to give West Berlin courage to face the months to come.

Brandt's letter was not well received in Washington. Kennedy was furious with the Berlin mayor for announcing its existence before it reached him: he did not want to be roped in to action in Berlin if he could avoid it.[136] Adenauer was even more angry that this 'mere mayor of Berlin' had bypassed him and gone directly to the American President. In the end, however, the document was significant. It helped Kennedy to see that the new barrier in Berlin was not a merely local problem but was indeed a challenge to vital American interests. Brandt made him realize that a crisis of confidence in West Berlin could lead to chaos, which could only tarnish America's claim to be the upholder of peace and freedom in the 'showcase Berlin' which they themselves had done so much to create.

Kennedy responded to Brandt's call by sending Vice President Lyndon B. Johnson and General Clay, the hero of the airlift, and announced he would increase the American presence in the city by 1,500 soldiers. The two men landed in Berlin six days after the crisis began, and the response of Berliners was overwhelming. Half a million people lined the streets to cheer Johnson as he drove from the airport to the city centre on Saturday afternoon, and a third of a million gave him a tremendous ovation at City Hall; General Clay was applauded rapturously when he said that 'Berlin will still be free'. Johnson, who had told Kennedy he did not want to go to Berlin at all because of the danger there, was deeply impressed by the welcome and insisted on walking amongst the crowds shaking hands and distributing ballpoint pens. The visit had the desired effect. It boosted morale in West Berlin and gave the people hope that they would not be sacrificed to the Soviets. It was also increasingly clear, however, that the city would remain divided. As Howard Trivers, the political adviser to the American United States Mission, put it, 'The United States government did not push for countermeasures because there were too many people at the top who espoused the view that [the barrier] might be "good" in the context of overall US–Soviet relationships.' Berliners did not understand that there was widespread relief in the rest of the world that the Soviet action had ended with the building of the Wall. The Americans had been concerned that it was part of a wider Soviet strategy to cut West Berlin off from West Germany completely; indeed in August 1961 Khrushchev implied that the Wall had been the first step in the destruction of West Berlin; the next step would be to attack the air corridors, which he claimed were being 'abused' by the western Allies. When Kennedy realized that the Soviets intended to take no further action after all he told his appointments secretary Kenneth O'Donnell that the Wall was Khrushchev's 'way out of his predicament. It's not a very nice solution, but . . . a hell of a lot better than a war.'[137]

The Soviets and the East Germans quickly realized that there would be no reaction to the barrier and proceeded with the second phase of construction. The barbed wire and fence posts were quickly replaced by large pre-fabricated concrete blocks. As the barrier rose would-be escapees were forced to look for other routes to cross to the west. Two young men swam across the Teltow Canal, arriving in Marienfelde in nothing but their underwear, but the East Germans blocked this route by stringing barbed wire through the water. A couple managed to squeeze through a drainage pipe with their young daughter but these routes were located and blocked off. Some people tried to escape through houses which straddled the east–west sector boundary, with their front doors in the east and their back doors in the west. The Vopos had already locked the eastern entrances but many people still managed to get into the buildings and escape through rear doors and windows. Detlef Kühn, then a student in West Berlin, watched people emerging from apartment blocks on the southern side of the Bernauer Strasse: 'The doors of these buildings were, of course, locked immediately on 13 August, but people who lived in these flats had a chance to escape by jumping from the windows ... I saw several people jump from the third or fourth floor into sheets held by the West Berlin Fire Brigade on the pavement outside.'[138]

The first person to die while trying to escape East Berlin was Rudolf Urban, who jumped out of his window at No. 1 Bernauer Strasse on 19 August 1961. On 25 September Olga Segler, an eighty-year-old grandmother who had waited until her daughter and three grandchildren had safely crossed the street before she jumped from the second floor, injured herself in the fall and died the following day. There were terrifying scenes as people trying to get out of these houses were suddenly dragged back from the windows by Vopos who had gone in after them. Some managed to break free and jump onto the mats held in place by the West Berlin fire brigade, but a number were hauled away into the shadows. The first person to be shot was an unknown young man who was trying to swim the Teltow Canal on 24 August, but many more soon followed. One of the most tragic cases was that of Peter Fechter, who tried to escape on 17 August 1962. He had almost scaled the cement at the Zimmerstrasse a few metres to the east of Checkpoint Charlie when he was shot by a border guard. He fell backwards, severely injured. Westerners threw cotton wool and bandages to him but could only watch helplessly as he struggled again and again to drag himself over the barrier. At one point he almost succeeded but fell backwards at the last moment and collapsed in a pool of blood. He was carried away by Vopos an hour later.[139] Another to die was Klaus Brüske, one of fourteen people who managed to break through in heavy vehicles before the Wall was fortified. Brüske was shot while trying to aim a lorry through a gap between cement blocks; although mortally wounded he still managed to drive his passengers to safety. In the early months some people successfully got to the east by racing through in small sportscars, by faking Soviet officers' uniforms or by hiding in cable or fuel drums, but as the East Germans grew more organized these methods were increasingly risky. Within months the Wall became virtually impenetrable.[140]

This first permanent Wall was a hideous blight on the Berlin landscape. It stood between 5 and 6 feet high and looked rough compared to the infamous structure which dominated the city in the 1980s. All access routes were sealed: U-Bahn stations were walled up, the canals were filled with deep fences and wire, and the dozens of houses straddling the border were ripped down. Blinds were erected to prevent people from waving to one another, and within a short time 231 look-out posts, 214 dog runs, sixty-three miles of anti-vehicle ditches, seventy-two miles of electrified fencing and seventy-one miles of patrol roads were in place; mine fields, fifty bunkers and hundreds of border guards encircled the entire city of West Berlin.

The construction of the Wall did not halt Soviet attempts to further infringe Allied rights in Berlin, and within weeks a border incident at the Wall was threatening to escalate into war. The event began when the Soviets tried to restrict the right of western Allied personnel to enter East Berlin without showing identification. The Americans had done nothing about the Wall but this was another direct infringement of Allied rights enshrined in the Potsdam Agreement. General Clay understood that if the Americans continued to allow themselves to be bullied by Khrushchev without fighting back they would soon be pushed out of Berlin. It was time to take a stand, as he had during the Berlin airlift.

The crisis began shortly after Johnson's morale-boosting visit to West Berlin. At that point the Soviets were still permitting Allied surface traffic to cross at Checkpoint Charlie ('Alpha' and 'Bravo' were at the East–West German border), but on the evening of 22 October an American diplomat who had set out with his wife to attend the opera in East Berlin was stopped at the Wall despite the fact that the car had American licence plates. The East Germans refused to allow him through unless he showed his passport but the American refused: to have done so would have been tantamount to recognizing the authority of the GDR over East Berlin. He demanded to see a Soviet officer, but his request was denied. General Clay was called in and decided to challenge this new East German 'rule'. Instead of trying to negotiate with the guards he simply ordered a platoon of American troops to the Wall. Within minutes a small group of men armed with M-14 rifles moved forward, surrounded the car and escorted it into East Berlin. The next day the Soviets issued an order that only military personnel in uniform could go through Checkpoint Charlie without showing their passports. Again this was in direct violation of Allied rights in Berlin. On Wednesday 25 October General Clay ordered ten American M-48 tanks to line up along the Wall, facing east. Dozens of jeeps, armoured personnel carriers and civilian vehicles were ordered to drive back and forth across Checkpoint Charlie. If Vopos tried to stop them the American jeeps would move in and escort them across. Clearly the Soviets could not stand for this, and early on the morning of Thursday 26 October thirty-three Soviet tanks rumbled down the streets of East Berlin. Ten moved up to the Wall. Berliners were understandably frightened, as Soviet tanks had not been seen there since the disastrous 1953 uprising. Photographs flashed around the world showing the American and Soviet tanks menacing each other muzzle to muzzle over the Wall while Soviet MiG fighter planes buzzed the city centre. Neither side was bluffing. The tank crews were ordered to load cannon shells into their gun racks, and the American machine guns atop the tanks were at half load. All forces in Berlin were put on full alert. The world held its breath; all knew that the slightest provocation might trigger a war. As the American commander at Checkpoint Charlie, Lieutenant-Colonel Thomas Tyree, put it, 'My major concern at the time . . . was to make sure something unexpected did not occur such as a nervous soldier accidentally discharging his weapons.'[141] The hours dragged by. Finally, on Saturday morning, Moscow gave the order for the Soviet tanks to withdraw. The Wall remained in place, but the Allied right of access was not withdrawn.[142] General Clay claimed a victory not only by safeguarding Allied rights in the city, but by proving that despite the facade, it was the Soviet Union, and not the East German government, which still controlled East Berlin. The Soviets and the Americans had achieved a stalemate in the divided city. Thanks to General Clay's action the Soviets had been sent a clear message that further infringement of Allied rights in Berlin would be met with force. Clay was not rewarded for his pains. When President Kennedy first heard of the border incident he misunderstood its significance and demanded to know why an American was going to the opera in East Berlin in the first place. General Clay was recalled to Washington shortly afterwards, but the 'truce' held.

The Soviet *volte face* in the autumn of 1961 begs one of the great questions of Berlin history: namely, what would have happened if the west had responded on 13 August 1961 and pushed down the Wall on the day of its inception? There is some evidence that the Soviets would have backed down; we now know that the East German troops who lined up along the boundary brandishing their weapons were not in fact armed, although the Soviets waiting behind the border were. We also know that Erich Honecker had planned to build the Wall out of concrete from the beginning, but the Soviets did not give final authorization for this permanent construction until 18 August in order to gauge the western response. American members of the 'Berlin mafia', including General Clay, believed that the Americans should have tried to do something and later insisted that if their jeeps had simply driven over the barbed wire on the first night the Wall would never have been built and the Soviets would have settled for tightening controls between East and West Berlin.[143] But the question of what might have been will never be answered. The west was not willing to risk antagonizing the Soviets over East Berlin, particularly as it was feared that any conflict might escalate to nuclear war. Whether they liked it or not Berliners had to come to terms with the new jagged barrier which cut through its centre. The city was undergoing its most radical metamorphosis yet, the creation of two distinct and competing identities out of one historic whole. The world had seen barriers and walls before, but it had never seen anything quite like this.

XVI

East Berlin

FAUST: 'Do you spend much of your free time in spying?'
MEPHISTOPHELES: 'I'm not omniscient yet– but I keep trying.'

(*Faust*, Part I)

THE BERLIN WALL SEALED OFF the last escape route from what had now become a giant 100,000-square-kilometre prison called the German Democratic Republic. The temporary border so hastily approved by the Allies during the Second World War had been turned first into a fortified barrier complete with a security no man's land surrounded by a 275-metre-wide mine field, a 500-metre-wide guarded 'death strip' and a 5-kilometre-wide restricted area along its western frontier, and was now completed by an impregnable cement wall which encircled all of West Berlin.

The construction of the Berlin Wall had come as a shock to all the German people, but none more so than those trapped in East Berlin. Suddenly they were barred from families and friends and from the tantalizing wealth of West Germany. All communication links were cut, West Berlin was blotted out on all new maps, and once bustling thoroughfares were left barren and empty. For the first time it seemed that the division of Germany and of Berlin was to be permanent and as the months went by people stranded in the eastern city were gripped by an overwhelming sense of sadness. The chance to escape had passed them by; they would now have to build their lives as best they could in the inhospitable climate of the GDR. Walter Ulbricht's gamble had been risky but it seemed to have paid off. The haemorrhage of people was stopped; there was no serious protest from the international community against the 'Anti-Fascist Protection Wall', and East Berlin soon began to settle into a decade of isolation, stagnation and repression.[1]

Ulbricht's post-Wall city was a grim and forbidding place. Despite attempts to reform the economy through the 1963 'New Economic System of Planning and Leadership', Ulbricht's strict centralized administration led to increased shortages and deprivation. People trudged off to uninspiring jobs in factories and offices knowing that they would end the day queuing for bread or meat, or for the few 'western-style' goods on sale in the East German 'boutiques'. East Germany quickly became a 'Party with a State', a system governed by a small cadre loyal to Moscow which aimed to control every aspect of people's lives. The state was all-powerful, determining where people could live, where they could go to school, what they could read, who they could have as friends, where they could travel, what they could eat, where they could work and how much they could earn. The ever-growing Stasi network of spies and informants meant that nobody was safe from the prying eyes of the party.[2] Ulbricht, ever fearful of a repeat of the 1953 uprising, demanded unquestioning loyalty and arrested anyone who spoke out against the state. All links between East and West Germany were cut and even priests who kept ties with colleagues in the West German Church were imprisoned.[3] People were forbidden all contact with westerners, including members of their own families; telephone calls, visits and letters were banned; West German radio was deemed 'harmful to the state', and watching western television was a criminal offence; children at school were asked to draw the most common television logo which they saw at home and if a western symbol appeared parents would be hauled in for questioning. Large red propaganda posters extolling the glories of Communism, Free German Youth rallies or the hideous prestige projects which sprang up in East Berlin, such as the concrete colossus around Alexanderplatz, provided no respite from the endless gloom.[4]

The citizens in the prison-state retained little sense of identity or pride in their country. From 1945 onward historians and propagandists had been expressly forbidden to link the GDR with German history; instead, they were instructed to find their heroes in the Soviet Union and the international Communist movement. German history was portrayed as an unbroken story of political and ideological desolation. This version of the past was known as the 'Misery Thesis' and it influenced East German national identity throughout the 1960s.

The Misery Thesis was introduced by the German Communists at the end of the war. Alexander Abusch, the East German Minister of Culture, outlined the approach in his 1946 *Der Irrweg einer Nation* – The Mistaken Path of a Nation – which demonstrated that the only thing East Germans had to be proud of was the fact that they had been liberated by the Soviet Union after the Second World War.[5] Historians like Wolfram von Hanstein explained that 'viewed in historical terms there is a direct line of continuity from Luther to the great medieval princes, to Frederick II and his successors, to Bismarck and the Wilhelmine era, and, finally, to Hitler'. Nazi historiography was merely turned on its head: two-dimensional Nazi heros became equally absurd cardboard villains. At the same time German culture was attacked; the SED ideologue Fred Oelssner was reprimanded for submitting a manuscript entitled

Hegel in Our Times which had showed that Marx and even Lenin had been influenced by the German philosopher. He was told that he had clearly not understood Marx, Lenin or indeed Stalin's superior view of the historical process, and that to suggest that Marx had been influenced by Hegel, a German from whom Hitler had taken his ideas, was objectionable.[6] The Soviets did allow the staging of Goethe celebrations in 1949 to commemorate the 200th anniversary of his birth but only because they treated him as the 'German Pushkin', arguing that where Pushkin had been the precursor of Lenin Goethe had similarly inspired Marx; even Thomas Mann was invited to Weimar for the event although he annoyed his hosts by remarking that the celebration shared 'fatal similarities with the Hitleresque'.[7] This relentless attack on all things German was a by-product of the war but it left very little with which the average person could identify. East Germans were isolated from their own past. Ironically this made it virtually impossible for Ulbricht to instil a sense of pride in the new GDR.

These problems were compounded by the international reaction to the building of the Wall. The country which had imprisoned its own people was treated like an outcast throughout the 1960s, particularly after the introduction of the West German Hallstein Doctrine, which threatened to cut off aid and break diplomatic relations with any state which recognized East Germany.[8] The Soviet bloc reacted by isolating the Federal Republic, and both were excluded from international bodies, including the Olympics and the United Nations. Ironically, Ulbricht was satisfied with the status quo. He saw West Germany as the greatest threat to the survival of the GDR; isolation was essential in order to protect his citizens from the destructive influences of the capitalist west. East Germany retained rigid Stalinism long after it had been abandoned elsewhere. West Berlin was still seen as the 'thorn to be extracted from East Germany', the illegitimate half-city filled with *Revanchists* and proto-Nazis. Cartoons still showed the ghosts of Hitler, Goebbels and Göring hovering over West Berlin, being pulled by strings from Washington and Bonn; the west was accused of everything from sabotaging East Berlin factories to importing destructive potato bugs to ruin East German crops; and the American flag was often depicted with a swastika in a corner instead of the blue and white stars, while cartoons of Adenauer often included a Hitler moustache painted under his nose. For nearly a decade Ulbricht kept East Germany in a socialist coma – isolated, backward and hated by much of the world. It was only when relations between the United States and the Soviet Union began to change that East Germany was dragged reluctantly into the era of détente.

Leonid Brezhnev took power in 1964 and his first priority was to make the Soviet Union a military superpower. He turned his attention to international power politics and reverted to the Stalinist model of manufacturing

armaments, increasing military spending in real terms by around 3 per cent
a year. As Soviet relations with China worsened and as it became clear that
American technology was outpacing the Soviet Union's – admirably demonstrated by the 20 July 1969 American moon landing – Brezhnev decided to
try to gain access to western technology and investment, preferably through
improved relations with West Germany. Furthermore, he hoped that closer
links with West Germany might drive a wedge into the western Alliance.

On 25 March 1969, at a conference to mark the fiftieth anniversary of the
Communist International, Brezhnev publicly signalled his desire to open up
to West Germany. By 28 April the Soviet Foreign Trade Minister had
announced the first West German–Soviet natural gas pipeline agreement and
on 3 July the Soviets and the West Germans resumed diplomatic exchanges
on renunciation of force agreements. This improvement in relations
eased tensions in western Europe but put immediate pressure on Walter
Ulbricht. After some hesitation the Americans agreed to support Brandt and
the Soviets began to encourage ties between the two Germanys; President
Johnson had referred to the need to 'build bridges' as early as May 1964
and in October 1966 had introduced the idea of 'peaceful engagement' with
the eastern bloc countries, while the NATO-approved Harmel Report of
December 1967 outlined the western desire 'to further a détente in east–
west relations'.[9]

The West Germans were happy to oblige in order to ease the crisis which
had been simmering around the 'German question' since 1945. The West
German Social Democrats had already made overtures to the East German
government in 1965, and in 1968 West Germany had restored diplomatic
relations with Yugoslavia and Romania, effectively ending the Hallstein Doctrine. In 1969 Willy Brandt formed a social–liberal coalition government and
launched his *Ostpolitik* initiative – an attempt to improve relations with eastern
Europe as far as would be tolerated by the Soviet Union.[10] Bonn made a
number of concessions to Moscow in order to facilitate co-operation between
the two Germanys, including signing the Nuclear Non-proliferation Treaty
renouncing any claim to nuclear weapons; supporting the Soviet Union's
proposal for a European security conference; approving closer economic and
technological ties; and above all accepting the 'real existing situation' in Europe,
including *de facto* ratification of the Oder–Neisse border.[11] Brandt recognized
the existence of the other German state, declaring shortly after he became
Chancellor that 'Even if two states in Germany exist they are none the less
not 'foreign countries'.[12] As Timothy Garton Ash has pointed out, it was in a
treaty with the Soviet Union, not with Ulbricht, that the Federal Republic first
expressed its recognition of the GDR.[13] Willy Brandt was accepting the 'results
of history'. Ulbricht, however, was not.

If Brandt's attempts to improve relations with the GDR were warmly welcomed in Moscow they received a decidedly frosty response in East Berlin. Although he longed for recognition of his fledgling state Ulbricht feared that closer ties with West Germany would undermine East German security and fuel German hopes for reunification. When Willy Brandt offered to visit East Germany Ulbricht stalled until Brezhnev forced him to co-operate. The visit confirmed his worst fears.

As Willy Brandt arrived in Erfurt in March 1970 for a meeting with the East German chairman of the Council of Ministers, Willi Stoph, huge crowds awaited him. Far from treating him as an enemy of the people they gathered under his hotel window chanting, 'Willy Brandt!' Brandt was in an impossible position and tried to calm the people, but the message to the GDR leadership was clear.[14] These were the largest spontaneous crowds seen in East Germany since 1953; it was an indication that Germans still regarded themselves as part of a single German nation. It was painfully obvious that Brandt, not Ulbricht, was the more popular of the two. Ulbricht was deeply shaken by this revelation and again resisted improving relations with the west. He became an embarrassing obstacle to Soviet aims, and Brezhnev was determined to do something about him.[15]

On 28 July 1970 the Soviet leader had a conversation with Ulbricht's 'close friend' Erich Honecker, complaining about Ulbricht's arrogance: 'I tell you quite openly,' he said, 'it will not be possible for [Ulbricht] to rule without us ... we have troops in your country.' Brezhnev then referred to the treaty which he was about to sign with West Germany: 'This will not solve all problems but the conclusion of this treaty will be a success for us. The GDR will gain from this treaty. Its international authority will be increased. Its frontiers, its existence will be confirmed for all the world to see, its inviolability. This will consolidate the position inside the GDR.'[16] Even so, he warned against over-friendly relations with West Germany; it 'must not come to a process of rapprochement between the FRG and the GDR'. The man chosen to steer the delicate course between Cold War and détente was Erich Honecker.

On 3 May 1971 Walter Ulbricht was ousted from power and replaced by Brezhnev's new man. Honecker's position was secured at the June SED Party Day, at which Brezhnev greeted him with a passionate godfather-like kiss in front of the entire Politburo. The dull, reedy-voiced First Secretary was a true product of the German Communist movement and had dedicated his life to a relentless climb to power. Born in the Saarland in 1912, he had spent his youth in Communist organizations, attending a Youth Cadre school in Moscow in 1930–31 and even spending time in the new industrial city of Magnitogorsk, where he became enamoured of Stalinist industrialization of the Soviet Union.[17] In 1935 he was captured by the Nazis and sent to Brandenburg prison, from which he was released in 1945. He always made much of his incarceration, ensuring that his Nazi mug shots appeared in the official version of history; he even released the dissident physicist Robert Havemann from house arrest so that the two could attend the celebration of the thirty-fifth anniversary of liberation from Brandenburg prison together, although the scientist was quickly locked up again after the ceremony.[18] Honecker was genuinely impressed by the Red Army's 'liberation' of Germany and the creation of the GDR; he was equally grateful for Brezhnev's backing. His first move was to reaffirm his state's commitment to the Soviets, revising the constitution in 1974 by adding that the GDR would be 'for ever and irreversibly allied with the Soviet Union'. He fully supported the Brezhnev Doctrine obliging the GDR to come to the aid of the USSR whenever Soviet Communism was threatened by a foreign country.[19] In 1976 the SED adopted a programme which ensured the 'development of all-round fraternal relations between the GDR and the USSR'. East Germany had become Moscow's most obedient ally, and its leader was only willing to co-operate with West Germany under the watchful eye of the Soviet Union.[10]

Honecker's stance meant that the first overtures between East and West Germany were initiated not through an internal treaty but through the 1971 Quadripartite Agreement on Berlin negotiated by Britain, France, the United States and the Soviet Union. It was a vague treaty, but for the first time the Soviets officially recognized West German links with West Berlin, guaranteeing traffic and communications between the two areas. (In reality, the Four-Power Agreement ended the Berlin crisis.)[20] It also facilitated talks between the two Germanys; these led to the 1972 Treaty on the Bases of Relations (the Basic Treaty), which opened up new areas of co-operation.[21] For the first time since the building of the Wall some of the severe restrictions on travel between the two Germanys were eased and the two states promised to build closer links in everything from the economy to science and technology, from legal relations to telecommunications, health, sports, environmental protection and postal services.[22] The German Democratic Republic was now to be treated *de facto* as a sovereign state: in September 1973 both East and West Germany were recognized by the United Nations; in 1972 twenty-four countries recognized the GDR; in 1973 forty-six others followed suit, and by 1974 eighty countries, including the United States, had recognized East Germany. Each successive diplomatic exchange was greeted with pompous ceremony and multi-page coverage in *Neues Deutschland*.[23] Honecker now worked with Willy Brandt to establish permanent missions each side of the border by increasing trade links and visits to the GDR by West German citizens.[24]

The new agreements resulted in a marked improvement in the lives of average Berliners. For the first time since the Wall was built West Berliners were permitted to visit relatives in the east; when the Traffic Agreement came into force in October 1972 thousands of West Berliners queued for hours to get a one-day visa so that they could visit friends and family for the first time in a decade. In November that year western journalists were permitted to set up offices in East Berlin; West German television reporters could travel to East Berlin and interview dissidents there. Life in divided Berlin was still tragic for those families and friends who were separated by the strip of concrete, but the threat of war or invasion had receded and people began to learn to live with the division.

The diplomatic changes were a welcome relief to Berliners on both sides of the Wall, but they posed an enormous problem for Erich Honecker. For over twenty years East German identity had been based on hatred of West Germany and West Berlin. As relations between the two Germanys began to normalize the very reason for the creation of the Wall seemed to be fading. Like Ulbricht before him Honecker feared that the sense of a common history, language and culture might move East Germans to demand reunification. His fear was backed up by intelligence reports indicating a deep resentment against the East German regime – kindled during the 1953 uprising and reignited during the 1968 invasion of Czechoslovakia, when thousands of SED members had handed in their party cards – which had once again been demonstrated by the spontaneous welcome accorded to Willy Brandt in Erfurt in 1970.[25] Research in East Berlin showed that over half the school children did not believe East German portrayals of the evils of the capitalist west; only 15 per cent believed that the Bonn government and West German Bundeswehr were the 'greatest enemies of the German people and a threat to all peace-loving people'.[26] The East German government could clearly attack 'electronic imperialism' and denounce the 'false but idyllic pictures of conditions in late capitalist society'; they could complain that the West German media was 'manipulating the masses, obscuring the realities of a capitalist order based on exploitation and spreading confusion on political issues', and they could create a special East German television programme called the Black Channel to 'correct the distortions' in West German news broadcasts. Nevertheless, Honecker knew that society at large was not anti-western and that if there had been no Wall they would have poured over the border as they had before 1961. Somehow, he had to dispel the resentment over the division of Germany; in its place he had to create a proud national identity for his rump state so that East Germans would be happy to live in the GDR and willing to sacrifice short-term material gains for the rewards of belonging to the world of 'Real Existing Socialism'.

Honecker's solution to this problem was bizarre. Brezhnev had told him not to make any further advances to West Germany but rather to 'concentrate everything on the all-sided strengthening of the GDR'.[27] So he decided to promote a new pride in the GDR, genuinely believing that this could be manufactured artificially. His dream was to inculcate a sense of identity in his citizens such that they would forget that they had ever had ties with their neighbour to the west, and would treat the Federal Republic like any other foreign country.

The first step in this aberrant experiment was *Abgrenzung*, the official declaration that the two German states were completely separate entities which historically had as much in common as Austria did with Italy or Spain did with Portugal. In July 1972 the Politburo member Albert Norden delivered a lecture at the Karl Marx Party College in East Berlin in which he said of the two Germanys: 'there are not two states in one nation but rather two nations in states with different social structures' – not only were East and West Germany to be considered two different states; they were also to be seen as two different nations. Germany had ceased to exist. In 1974 Erich Honecker codified this, changing the East German constitution to read that the GDR was no longer the 'Socialist State of the German Nation', but a 'Socialist State of Peasants and Workers'; at the same time East Berlin was severed from the history of united Berlin and declared the 'historic' capital of the East German state.[28] All references to 'Germany' were erased from history and replaced by the term 'German Democratic Republic'. All institutions and organizations which contained the word 'Germany' were renamed and workmen were sent out to chip away inscriptions and remove street signs, memorials and landmarks containing the forbidden name.[29] Even the prestigious old German Academy of Sciences became the 'Academy of Sciences of the GDR'. By far the most extraordinary result of *Abgrenzung* was the complete re-invention of German history – an invention which split the past into 'good' and 'evil'. Honecker now taught that East Germany had inherited all that was 'good and progressive, human and democratic in history'. This 'creative relationship with German history and with the world's history is an essential element of our Socialist national consciousness'.[30] History would now be 'created' to fit the needs of the SED.

The GDR was a totalitarian state. Like the Nazi regime before it, the Communist government was highly centralized and every aspect of cultural life was planned and directed from Berlin. Nobody could make a film, publish a book, write a newspaper article or exhibit a painting without the express approval of the relevant official in the city, and this control extended to the writing of history.[31] In 1971 Honecker instructed historians to follow a 'new course'; those who refused would lose their jobs. They were to cultivate the East German sense of identity, to foster individual initiatives and social engagement and love of the *Vaterland*.[32] This process would have been less extraordinary if East Germany had been a 'normal' eastern bloc country where pseudo-histories were being invented all the time. But German history was different. Reminders of Nazism were everywhere, particularly in Berlin; the very division of the city was a direct result of the Allied defeat of the Third Reich. Even East German historians could not completely deny that the Nazi period had happened. Instead they did the next best thing: they created a version of history which 'proved' that East Germans had not been involved in any of the terrible crimes of the Third Reich and that only those now in West Germany had any connection with Nazism. Of all the twentieth-century attempts to rewrite history, this one must stand alone as the most ludicrous.

On the face of it the argument put forward by the Politburo and taught by East German historians was perfectly logical. Nazism had been a form of capitalism; as there were still capitalists in proto-Fascist West Germany, there must also be Nazis. As there were no capitalists in East Germany, it could be declared 'Nazi-free'. This Orwellian-style 'Big Lie' became one of the fundamental pillars upon which East German identity was constructed.[33]

The purpose of this new history was to prove the innocence of all East Germans. As a result, the Nazi period became little more than a morality tale about the evils of capitalism.[34] Historians wrote that *Hitlerfascismus* had been a 'necessary historical step' on the road to the creation of socialism in Germany. There had been 'little difference' between Hitler's government and the Weimar period; in short, *Brüningfascismus* had been followed by *Papenfascismus* and *Schleicherfascismus*, which had led to *Hitlerfascismus*. Incidentally, the *Sozialfascismus* of the pre-war SPD had survived as the West German Social Democratic Party, led by such 'Fascists' as Willy Brandt and Helmut Schmidt.[35]

Significant aspects of Nazi Germany were ignored. Hitler's anti-Semitism, his use of national myths, his propaganda and his mesmerizing hold on the German public were all passed over. Hitler was described as nothing more than a capitalist puppet who had come to power not because of his broad appeal to most Germans, but because of scientifically proven historical laws; if there had been no Hitler, there would have been somebody else equally destructive. Individuals did not make history; economic forces did.

East Germans faced a more intractable dilemma when dealing with Berlin itself. The city had been the administrative and political centre of the Third Reich. East Berlin contained many Nazi buildings, including Hermann Göring's Air Ministry and the massive Reichsbank, where possessions stolen from camp victims had been sorted during the Holocaust. The East Germans simply ignored this dark legacy. Göring's building became the House of

Ministries, the Reichsbank became SED party headquarters. A visitor in the 1980s would have been forgiven for thinking that there had been no National Socialists in 1930s East Berlin. Pictures of the hundreds of thousands of Berliners cheering the goose-stepping soldiers at the news of the fall of France vanished completely, as did images of Hitler presiding over the Olympic Games and of Goebbels calling for total war in the Berlin Sportpalast. Instead, East Berlin was depicted as the heart of mass popular Communist resistance against the *Hitlerfascisten*.[36] As Erich Honecker put it, 'from the first days of the fascist dictator the KPD led a heroic courageous fight for his destruction, for the ending of the criminal war, and for the founding of a freedom loving German Democratic Republic'. Illegal cells of five people, the so-called Fünfergruppen, had 'operated in every neighbourhood, in every street, in every factory' throughout Berlin. I once asked an East German historian why there seemed to be so little tangible evidence of this 'mass Communist resistance'; he explained that new developments in shortwave radio had seen a shift in emphasis from the written to the spoken word, which is why there were so few traces for posterity.[37] Historical events were twisted at will. The 1932 Berlin transport strike was hailed by the East Germans as a massive anti-Nazi demonstration (Nazis and Communists had in fact collaborated in an attempt to bring down the legitimate democratically elected government). The image of East Berlin teeming with hundreds of Communist resistance fighters armed to the teeth bore almost no resemblance to the reality of Hitler's capital.[38]

Of all the lies printed in East Germany the most appalling concerned the re-invention of the Second World War itself. The fabrications ranged from a denial of any responsibility for the Holocaust to the castigation of the western Allies for abandoning the Red Army in its hour of need. According to the approved version of history, which appeared in every museum and school textbook, detailed 'scientific' studies showed how 'monopoly capitalists' had controlled Hitler and had forced him to start the war. Hitler had initiated the *Anschluss* not because of any dream of a greater Germany, but because AEG and Siemens, the Krupp concern and the Dresdner Bank had wanted control of Austria's economy and of raw materials like iron, lead, zinc, copper and coal.[39] Similarly the Sudetenland was seized because businessmen wanted 'its highly developed industry'. But it was not just German capitalists who were at fault; the British monopoly capitalists had also supported German aggression, as proved by the Munich Agreement of 1938. The problem with this argument was how to explain why, having agreed to the seizure of Czechoslovakia, the British had declared war on Germany after the invasion of Poland. The solution was novel. According to the new version war had only been declared by the British because the 'progressive impact of the masses' in England and France had 'forced Britain to promise to aid Poland'. A generation of East Germans grew up believing that hundreds of thousands of factory workers and miners had stormed Whitehall demanding that England come to the aid of struggling Polish workers. The British ruling classes had had to bow to the 'progressive forces' in their own society, but their desire to control the masses had led only to the 'Phoney War'.

The great hero, of course, was the Soviet Union, and even Stalin was still held in high esteem. Niggling problems like the famine in Ukraine or the Great Terror simply did not exist in East German texts, while Stalin's decision to sign the Ribbentrop–Molotov Pact with Hitler was also explained away. Stalin was said to have signed a 'non-aggression pact' with Germany as a 'ploy' to give the Soviets time to prepare for war with *Hitlerdeutschland*. East German histories invariably failed to mention the fact that the Ribbentrop–Molotov Pact also contained a secret protocol which sanctioned an aggressive attack by both parties on Poland, Bessarabia and the Baltic States, including parts of Finland. Far from 'preventing the Soviet Union from being encircled', it meant that for the first time in history Germany and the Soviet Union shared a common border – hardly a 'sound military decision' on Stalin's part. Furthermore, there was no mention of the numerous trade agreements between Germany and the Soviet Union or the exchange of technology and security information; nor was it disclosed that Stalin was so keen to appease Hitler, and indeed to rid himself of troublesome Communist exiles, that he denounced hundreds of German Communists to the Gestapo.[40]

The description of the war itself was equally absurd. *Hitlerdeutschland* was said to have invaded western Europe so that 'German monopoly capitalists could crush revolutionary working class movements and all other progressive forces there'.[41] The Allied efforts on the western front were entirely ignored. The 'real' war revolved around one thing: the attack on the Soviet Union, 'the greatest crime which the Nazis committed against both the USSR and the German people'. Battles in the Atlantic, western Europe, north Africa and the far east were passed over, as was the Holocaust, the euthanasia programme and the murder of hundreds of thousands of other innocent civilians. The only thing which 'counted' was the war in the east. Particular attention was paid to heroic Soviet victories like those at Kursk and Stalingrad.

The greatest absurdity of all was that the Second World War was presented almost as if it had been fought between the Soviet Union and East Germans on one hand, and the Nazis (who became West Germans), British, Americans and French on the other. German Communists were said to have assisted the Red Army by 'successfully' calling to German soldiers to 'halt their meaningless war' and surrender; photographs of Walter Ulbricht and Erich Weinart huddled in a trench 'calling by loudspeaker to German troops at Stalingrad' were dutifully reproduced in every school textbook, and it was claimed that 'a mass of German officers who did not wish to continue in the senseless war joined the side of the Communists'. This was another lie; there is no historical evidence that German soldiers surrendered *en masse* to the Soviets; indeed, the Germans staged a desperate last stand on the eastern front in a futile attempt to give the western Allies time to take Germany ahead of the Soviets. Like all East German lies, however, it was formulated with contemporary politics in mind. There were still hundreds of thousands of German ex-soldiers and their relatives living in the GDR, and if they were presented not as Nazi fighters but as closet Communists they could be absolved of guilt. The message was clear: Germans who had fled to the west after the war were ex-Nazis; those who had remained in East Germany had secretly been Communists all along, had assisted the liberation of their country and could not be guilty of war crimes.

When I first lived in East Germany in 1985 I was often asked about my background, and when it emerged that members of my British and Canadian families had fought in the war the atmosphere often became decidedly frosty. During the course of these conversations I was often asked why we had 'done it'; why we had wreaked such havoc on German cities. After being taken from one bomb site to another, whether in Dresden, Leipzig or East Berlin, I began to realize that many people genuinely saw themselves first and foremost as victims of the war. The official history had succeeded in portraying the British, Canadians, Americans and others as the villains. On one hand the western Allies were condemned for 'not coming to the aid of the Soviet Union' and for 'delaying the opening of a western front until 1944'; on the other they were criticized for resorting to the 'ineffectual and destructive' bombing raids which were an 'inadequate substitution for a second front'. The bombs, it was said, had been part of the Anglo-American effort to 'smash German production capability because they were unwilling to tolerate the predominance of German capitalists on the European continent'. The bombing of German cities was the result of 'the contest between rival groups of monopoly capitalists'. Descriptions of the bombing raids were emotional and often included photographs, eye-witness accounts and detailed lists of the treasures tragically lost to posterity. In East Berlin the raids were also used to highlight renovation work undertaken by the GDR; the SED guide to the thirty-fifth anniversary of the GDR contained twenty pages of 'before' and 'after' shots, comparing Berlin in 1945 with the eastern half in 1985; every bombed church, theatre or library had become a powerful propaganda weapon against the west. East Germans were not told of the appalling German crimes committed elsewhere; nor were they told that it was the Luftwaffe, not the RAF, which had started the bombing of innocent civilians. The bombing raids on German cities were indeed appalling, but East German historiography made it appear as if they had taken place in a historical vacuum, one in which only they had suffered.

In West Germany the history of Nazi atrocities was becoming increasingly well known, but the persecution and murder of 6 million European Jews were virtually ignored in the east, despite the fact that the Holocaust had been planned and directed from the very heart of Berlin.[42] This was in many ways a reflection on the pre-war KPD, who had been notoriously blind to the realities of Nazi anti-Semitism, viewing racial strife as a capitalist plot to divert workers away from the class struggle. In a skit written for the 1930 Reichstag elections the KPD satirist Georg Pijet had depicted a 'Jewish Capitalist' giving money to Hitler and applauding the Nazis, who called out 'Death to the Jews! Germany Awake!' at a party rally. In the production Pijet tried to show that this was mere Nazi rhetoric designed to fool workers into replacing the true revolutionary fight against capitalism with a sham fight against Jews. The sketch ended with Hitler stopping the Nazi thugs, who were trying to throw the Jewish capitalist out of the hall, and saying: 'Good Lord, you don't have to take everything so literally!'[43] Even Bertolt Brecht's 1932 analysis of Fascism, *The Roundheads and the Peakheads*, was in effect a denial of the Nazis' anti-Semitism.[44]

Reading the official East German history texts one got the impression that the relentless war against the Jews had not taken place at all: the war had been a class war 'waged by fascists and plutocrats against the People', not a racial war directed against specific groups. This meant that for East German historians Jews and gypsies were no different from other victims and counted only as members of a particular class. Capitalist Jews were as guilty of the war as Nazis, while Communist Jews deserved only as much sympathy as non-Jewish Communists. There was no analysis of the long history of anti-Semitism in Germany, nor was there discussion of Hitler's racial ideology or his use of the Jews as a universal scapegoat; nor was there any serious consideration of the murders committed by Einsatzgruppen or in the extermination camps of the east. The term Holocaust was not used in the GDR and the murder of Jews was referred to only as a financial crime which helped 'monopoly capitalists' to win power in Germany. The seizure of Jewish property was considered significant only because 'it allowed businessmen such as Krupp and Flick and the major banks' to take over more businesses. The Jews were not specifically named at memorials to the 'victims of Fascism'. Instead, displays at the concentration camps focused on Communist prisoners. Buchenwald, located in East Germany, was said to have been important not because of its role in the network of concentration and extermination camps set up throughout Europe but rather because Communists like Ernst Thälmann, chairman of the pre-war Communist Party, had been imprisoned there.[45] A visit to the camp, depressing

at best, was made almost intolerable by the potted East German history presented to the bus-loads of schoolchildren and factory workers brought in to
learn about their 'heritage' and their 'debt' to the resistance fighters of the
past. Ghastly monuments, films and photographs told the largely fictitious
story of the liberation of the camp by a group of Communists who had banded
together and fought the Nazis, supposedly 'preparing the way' for the Red
Army as they had at other camps like Mauthausen, and in areas like Greifswald,
Rostock and Neustrelitz. The fact that the camp had actually been liberated
by General Patton proved too embarrassing to warrant a mention. There was
of course no mention that the Soviets had re-opened Buchenwald and kept it
running until 1950, filled with Social Democrats and other opponents of the
Soviet regime; nor was there reference to the fact that the East Germans had
in fact hidden the identity of Franz Erich Giese, the deputy commandant at
Buchenwald, so that he could run a luxury hotel on their behalf, which he
did until his death in 1992.[46]

However ridiculous it was, the official version of history was fundamental
to the creation of East German identity and it was taken very seriously indeed.
All large factories, military bases and businesses had a *Traditionskabinett* or
'tradition room', which showed a brief history of the German workers' movement, the Communist anti-Fascist resistance, the liberation of Germany by
the Red Army and the foundation of the GDR. Dozens of museums kept the
message alive, from the Berlin-Karlshorst or 'Capitulation' Museum, which
described the heroic liberating work of the Red Army, to the Museum of
German History on Unter den Linden. Parades glorifying the past were held
in the streets of East Berlin every year and soldiers, schoolchildren and workers
were expected to take part; the official parade in 1987 contained a mock replay
of the Second World War, including images of heroic Communist resistance
fighters and the arrival of the liberating Red Army at the gates of Berlin. They
were followed by a large white plastic replica of the Berlin Wall complete with
a line of Volkspolizei armed with plastic rifles. This in turn was followed by
a gigantic plastic bear the size of a small building with a crown of bricks
perched on his head, representing the happy creation of the capital city Berlin.
The message was that if one lived in East Berlin there was no need to feel any
sense of responsibility for the war. British and Americans may have bombed
innocent people, sheltered Nazi war criminals and become heirs to *Hitlerfascismus*, but all East Germans were innocent by definition. The myth of the
Second World War set the stage for the next phase of the manipulation
of German history: the creation of a proud identity firmly rooted in the
past.

*   *   *

Erich Honecker was the first GDR leader to understand that East Germans needed an identity of their own, one that was based not on abstract Communist ideology but rooted in popular history. By removing all links between the GDR and the Nazi past Honecker had created a historical vacuum which he could fill as he saw fit, and he initiated a long, gradual rehabilitation of forbidden history. His attempt to build a national consciousness was one of the most extraordinary aspects of life in East Berlin.

Until the 1970s German history had been a taboo subject, mentioned only in the context of the Misery Thesis. All that changed in 1976, when the Politburo decided to use the past for their own ends. At the policy-setting speech at the East Berlin Museum of German History the Politburo member Kurt Hager declared that historians and other social scientists were now expected to change their approach to the past. The era of gloom was over; the new task was to show that 'the GDR continued the tradition of everything good . . . in German history'. The shining star of Marxist-Leninism would reveal 'positive socialist developments' in the most obscure subjects. Figures long derided as the embodiment of evil were to be resurrected. The whole of Germany's – and Berlin's – history was to be re-examined. Once again people would be told that they could be proud to be German – as long as they lived in the GDR.

The first famous figure from the past to undergo this treatment was Martin Luther, and his re-instatement after forty years was electrifying.[47] Since 1945 Martin Luther had been erased from history or mentioned only as an 'enemy of the people and traitor to the peasants; a groveller, a demagogue, and a lackey of princes'. Suddenly he was a 'great man', a 'figure of historical significance long misunderstood', and the 'precursor of Marx as surely as John the Baptist was of Christ'. Erich Honecker himself chaired the organizing committee for the grand celebration for him, to be held high up in Wartburg Castle, where Luther had translated the Bible into German. Copying a long forbidden ritual which harkened back to the Wars of Liberation and the Nazi period, thousands of torch-bearing East Germans wound their way up the steep path to the castle to attend ceremonies in Luther's honour; Erich Honecker later appeared on television to explain that Luther was important in the 'revolutionary process' because he had made the radical phase of the Reformation possible even if he had subsequently turned his back on it. He had a rightful place in East German history.[48]

The decision to resurrect Luther was a shrewd political move. Whereas Ulbricht had tried and failed to destroy the power of the Church in the GDR Honecker decided to harness it; as early as March 1978 he had tried to restore links with the 8 million Evangelical Christians in East Germany – in order not only to take advantage of the Church's social contribution, such as caring for the old and sick, but also to control its function as a focus for dissidents.[49]

He also understood that making concessions to the Church was a good publicity exercise both at home and abroad. To coincide with Luther's anniversary churches were reopened, religious artefacts put on display, and new links permitted with the West German Church. Honecker worked with that branch of the Church led by men like Albrecht Schönherr, bishop of Berlin-Brandenburg from 1972 to 1978, who was willing to sever links with the West German Church and create a *Kirche im Sozialismus*, a Church in Socialism, called the Bund der Evangelischen Kirchen, the Federation of Protestant Churches in the GDR, or the BEK.[50] Sadly it would later be revealed that a great many churchmen who advocated closer links with the SED were in fact working for the Stasi, including the leading East Berlin clergyman Günter Krusche and Dr Manfred Stolpe, Secretary of the BEK, who worked to undermine reform-minded clergy like Rainer Eppelmann, Wolfgang Thierse and Wolfgang Ullmann. Nevertheless as a result of the new spirit of co-operation the resurrection of Luther was a resounding success and encouraged bolder attempts to reclaim history.

The drive to claim all the 'good and the great' of the German past for East Germany went to extraordinary lengths: all 'great Germans' were shown to have been forerunners of the Communists, while all 'bad Germans' were precursors of the proto-Fascist West Germans. Goethe was East German, Hitler was West German; Beethoven was East German, although he had been born in Bonn and resided in Vienna, while Reinhard Heydrich, the architect of the SS, was 'West German' despite the fact that he had been born in Halle. East Germans claimed the great men as part of 'their' Germany, which had always been progressive, peace-loving and culturally rich. It was a strange twist on the much older *Dichter und Denker* myth which had supposedly divided the nation into the 'good' Germany of poets and thinkers and the 'bad' Germany of aggression and militarism. By using this past the GDR could preach Lessing's humanism and restore Goethe's house while in fact creating a police state which mirrored the very worst aspects of Wilhelmine and Nazi Germany. The desperation to find a past extended to efforts to publicize this abroad; I was able to live in the GDR in 1985 because I was studying the music of Johann Sebastian Bach, whose 300th anniversary it was that year – Bach was one of the 'good Germans' claimed by the East Germans and therefore it was deemed appropriate that foreign students should come to the GDR to see evidence of their Bach heritage.

Berlin was also part of the historical tug-of-war. Despite being split down the middle, 'their' Berlin, the East Germans insisted, was the 'true Berlin', heir to the greatest traditions of the capital city. East Berlin was the flagship of the GDR and as such the only rightful capital of Germany. With West Berlin erased from all East German street maps only East Berlin could claim to be the heir to that 'great historic, political, administrative, economic and cultural centre' which had grown into 'a centre of artistic and scientific excellence'. Old pictures and maps were carefully reproduced to show only the eastern side of the city, the most famous being the 1650 engraving by Merian which depicted the city boundary running where the Berlin Wall now stood. The East Germans claimed that men like Leibniz, the historian von Puffendorf, Arnold Nehring, Andreas Schlüter and Karl Friedrich Schinkel had lived and worked in 'their' Berlin – along with Prussian reformers like Freiherr Karl vom und zum Stein, whose statue was resurrected outside the Ministry for External Affairs, and Wilhelm von Humboldt, whose name was given to Berlin University. These men were the 'voice of their city' whose work was 'closely bound to the history of the capital of the GDR'. But there was one aspect of the past which had not yet been resurrected: the history of the state which had made Berlin so powerful – Prussia.

Prussia was the most despised of all German states. After the Second World War Churchill and Roosevelt shared the view that Prussia had formed the 'black heart' of German militarism and must be erased from the map. Stalin took up the call, eager to see Prussian territory carved up between the Soviet Union, Poland and East Germany, thereby extending Soviet influence further west.[51] In 1947 the Allies declared that the Prussian state, 'which from the early days had been a bearer of militarism and reaction in Germany, has de facto ceased to exist'.[52] In the early post-war years all positive references to Prussia were expressly forbidden in the GDR. Like their eastern neighbours East Germans zealously ripped down old Prussian landmarks, removed statues, changed street names and blew up buildings which evoked memories of Prussian history. They were taught that Prussian militarism had led directly to *Hitlerfascismus*: 'Frederick II begot Bismarck, begot William II, begot Hitler'. Prussia, the 'most militaristic state in German history', was the 'original sin' which had condemned Germany to Fascism. The Prussian curse had finally ended with the Soviet victory of 1945, but the ban on the mention of Prussian history continued.[53] Then, in 1976, everything changed.

The problem for Honecker was that a large section of what became East Germany had at one time been part of the Prussian state. Berlin had been its capital. There was no way East Germans could look to their own past without confronting Prussia; instead they had to find a way to make it respectable. Shortly after the resurrection of Luther an article appeared in *Einheit*, the organ of the SED Central Committee, entitled 'Prussia and German History'. It explained that there were two ways to look at the Prussian past: the wrong way and the East German way. According to the historian Ingrid Mittenzwei, head of the East German Academy of Sciences, 'Prussia is part of our history'; it was not merely a reactionary state which deserved blanket condemnation but a state whose ruling classes 'had contributed to progressive social developments' like industrialization and early social assistance for the Berlin working class.[54] When a large Prussian exhibition was held in West Berlin in 1981 it provoked a fierce reaction in East Berlin: the cry went up that *revanchist* West Germans were trying to claim Prussian history to which only the East German historians had 'rightful' access; only the Marxist-Leninist approach could provide the 'correct' interpretation of the past.[55] East and West Berliners were now competing for their own history.[56]

Shortly after the exhibition East Berlin embarked on a massive restoration of old Prussian memorials and buildings. The great equestrian statue of Frederick the Great was reinstated on Unter den Linden, money was earmarked for his palace, Sanssouci; the statues of Prussian reformers – including Scharnhorst, Gneisenau, Yorck von Wartenburg and Blücher – were not only restored but even illuminated at night, and millions of marks were poured into the refurbishment of buildings in the old city centre, including Schinkel's Schauspielhaus, which had lain in ruins since 1945.[57] The refurbishment of East Berlin continued throughout the 1980s and the ruins which had seemed such a liability in the post-war years had become an essential part of the political message. In preparation for the 750th anniversary celebrations Honecker sped up the refurbishment programme so that by 1987 the city centre had been virtually rebuilt: the historic Gendarmenmarkt, Academieplatz, the French and German cathedrals and the Nikolaiviertel were refurbished, the latter at a cost of $150 million.[58] Only a shell of the Nikolaikirche had survived war-time bombing but it too was rebuilt and surrounded by houses complete with gables, window frames and decorative arches. As one guidebook put it: 'What would our beautiful old Berlin be without the architecture of the highest forms which were erected under the reign of the Prussian kings?' East Berlin, not the glass and neon West, was now the 'true capital city Berlin'.[59] But by far the most daring rehabilitation was that of the Hohenzollern princes themselves, most notably Frederick the Great of Prussia.

For centuries Berliners have felt a strong traditional attachment to this most famous of the Prussian kings, who had already become a symbol of German unity by the time of the Napoleonic Wars and who was nothing less than an icon in nineteenth-century Berlin. Every young Berliner knew Anton Graff's portrait of the king with his piercing blue eyes and faded uniform; all had heard stories about his flute-playing, his friendship with Voltaire, his military victories, his passionate desire to civilize his backward Prussian state and to look after his poorest subjects, his land reforms, his introduction of the potato and his self-deprecating humour (when crowds were cheering him in Breslau he merely commented: 'Put an old monkey on a horse and they would cheer him the same'). For Berliners Frederick the Great had the stature of a George Washington in America or an Elizabeth I in England. It was the Nazis' use of Frederick which had made the East Germans so determined to erase his memory after 1945; similarly it was its association with Hitler's 'Day of National Awakening' which prompted Walter Ulbricht to blow up the Garrison Church in 1968. As a result Frederick was for decades depicted as a barbaric leader who had ruled the people of Prussia with an iron fist, skewing the 'correct' development of the German nation by impeding its progress from feudalism to capitalism; he had represented nothing less than the 'eighteenth century form of totalitarianism'. Then in 1979 the historian Ingrid Mittenzwei was permitted to publish a positive Marxist-Leninist biography of Frederick II, opening the floodgates to successive waves of Frederick-mania in East Berlin.

From one day to the next old history texts were scrapped and replaced with new ones in which the ruler was no longer portrayed as the enemy of the people but as their saviour. He was now said to have encouraged progress by fostering the rise of capitalism through the establishment of small businesses and increased power of the middle class. Now Frederick had created the Prussian bureaucracy whose officials were 'incorruptible' and exhibited 'great zeal' in serving the state – like their modern East German counterparts; it was he who had rebuilt Berlin after the devastation of the Seven Years War, creating the Opera House, the Royal Library, St Hedwig's Cathedral and Prince Henry's Palace. Far from repressing 'normal' economic development in Prussia he had promoted it; his crime, if anything, was that he made life too pleasant for the middle and working classes: they had not forged ahead towards the necessary revolution, as laid down by Marxist historical laws. Frederick's militarism was all but forgotten in the rush to praise his special abilities and accomplishments, his religious tolerance and his judicial reforms. This was the king who had turned a backward and provincial Prussia into a modern state accorded the international recognition which it had craved.

The rediscovery of Frederick was so overwhelming that anyone visiting East Berlin in the late 1980s might have been forgiven for thinking he had stepped back fifty years into Goebbels's Reich capital. Frederick was everywhere. He stared down from art gallery and museum walls, from the palace of Sanssouci and from every school textbook. The photographs, paintings and displays were precisely like those used by Goebbels, reflecting a nostalgic, sentimental view of the past which had survived the Second World War and forty years of silence. Some material was copied directly from old Nazi propaganda.[60]

The image of Prussia was useful to the SED in other ways. Although East Berlin was officially a 'pacifist' and 'anti-nuclear' 'city of peace', with images of Picasso's white dove plastered on buildings and placards, the reality was different. Indeed the SED sought to promote the militarism deeply ingrained in Prussian – and East German – culture. Present policy was justified by the revival of this tradition: as *Neues Deutschland* put it, the GDR had the right to demand 'from every male citizen . . . that he be ready at any time to perform his service' in 'the only German army deserving that name'.[61] Social institutions were required by law to 'prepare citizens for military service' and the military seeped into every aspect of life, from school education to patronage within local government. By 1987 the GDR was spending 6 per cent of GNP per capita on the army, second only to the USSR. The history of Prussian military service, with its sense of self-sacrifice and blind obedience, proved invaluable in Honecker's attempts to make his policies acceptable.

This rehabilitation was only possible because of the GDR's official denial of links to Hitler's Germany. It was this which led to bizarre sights like the goose-stepping guards parading on Unter den Linden. As Gordon Craig put it,

> the old Prussian style was submerged in that of the Wehrmacht in the traditional exercises that were now celebrated in front of the Neue Wache, the former military headquarters of Berlin, which now housed a memorial to the victims of Fascism and militarism. Here there were daily changing of the guard, effected with all the ceremonial of the Wilhelmine and Hitler armies, and, periodically, more elaborate reviews in which, *mit klingendem Spiel*, jackbooted and helmeted troopers moved, grim-faced and implacable, down Unter den Linden and, as they reached the Neue Wache, changed their pace to the old *Gänseschritt* [goose step], their legs rising in still precision and smashing back to the pavement, while their fellow citizens looked on, if not with satisfaction, at least with respect.[62]

When I questioned one East German about the association of goose-stepping with Nazi Germany he retorted that it was an old Prussian tradition and that people who associated it with the Nazis were simply ignorant. When asked about the East German uniform, which was similar to Hitler's Wehrmacht uniform, I was told that many such soldiers had joined the 'Free Germany' Communist Committees in 1945 to help the Red Army defeat *Hitlerfascismus* and that they had redeemed the uniform. Needless to say, historical evidence was not forthcoming.

By the late 1980s the list of 'acceptable' figures from the past had been extended to include other controversial Prussian monarchs and statesmen. The 'correct' interpretation of history was changing all the time; when I was living in East Berlin in 1987 East German guides at Sanssouci did not call Frederick 'the Great'; one year later it was common usage. In 1985 only privileged historians were permitted to talk about Bismarck; by the late 1980s he had been resurrected through a biography by Engelberg.[63] In 1985 there was no mention of non-Communist anti-Nazi resistance fighters; by 1989 small pictures of even the conservative 1944 plotters like Adam von Trott zu Solz and Helmuth-James von Moltke had appeared near those of hundreds of Communist resistance fighters in the Museum of German History. Even Nietzsche and Schopenhauer had been officially rehabilitated along with Freud, Kafka, and Günter Grass, while some of Rosa Luxemburg's articles in which she was critical of Lenin were reprinted for the first time in 1988.[64]

The attempt to 'create' an identity through history led to dramatic changes in perception, but these were still under the strict control of the state. To question the official line was a crime and any material which challenged it was forbidden in the GDR – as I discovered on my very first visit to East Berlin, when my copy of Gordon Craig's classic history, *Germany 1866–1945*, was confiscated by border guards. For all the revisionism in the 1980s there was nothing resembling open debate about the past; there was, after all, only one academic study of Frederick the Great and only one 'official' biography of Bismarck; there were still no balanced books on Kaiser William II and certainly nothing of substance about Hitler or Nazism. Only an elite group of academics and foreigners had access to West German history publications, which were kept locked up in the gloomy Department for Special Research Literature in the Prussian State Library – also referred to as the 'Poison Cabinet'. Despite its exotic name the room was disappointing and housed only a small collection of western history texts, journals and magazines, some West German newspapers and works by banned East German writers. In the 1980s some East German historians were allowed to attend selected historical seminars in the west, which gave the impression that East Germany was becoming more 'liberal'. In fact, those who did not have the connections of a Mittenzwei or an Engelberg were severely punished if they tried to study the past in a manner not approved by the state. One example was the case of Bernd Ettel and Christian Enzmann, two East Germans who in 1984 asked for permission to work with their West Berlin counterparts on the project to excavate the Gestapo headquarters just over the Wall from East Berlin. Instead of being granted permission they were arrested and interrogated, put into prison for two years, brought to trial, accused of 'defaming the architectural and peace policies of the GDR', and imprisoned again. Honecker might allow carefully screened biographies of Bismarck, but no historian was permitted to link East Germany with the Nazi past. By applying to study the Gestapo headquarters, Ettel and Enzmann had challenged one of the great taboos of the artificial East German state.

Honecker's attempt to use his historians to create a *sozialistisches Staatsbewusstsein* (socialist state identity) meant that they could not experience the cut and thrust of debate like their western counterparts. History became stale and lifeless; it had no relevance to people's lives – they might have been happy to see the old familiar faces of Luther or Frederick peering down at them from museum displays; they might have been proud of the old Prussian palaces and relieved at being able to mention Bismarck's name without fear of arrest, while academics, historians and museum curators enjoyed the greater scope for their work, but for most people that was as far as it went. The material was too sparse, the story too flimsy, to make this sterile view of the past attractive or to bolster the sense of identity which Honecker had tried so hard to create. The SED leaders had failed to understand that most East Germans, particularly the young, did not really care about official history. What they wanted was economic prosperity and the freedom to live without the constant interference of the state. By the late 1980s it was clear that the SED had been unable to offer the standard of living promised by 'real existing socialism'. East Germany remained the poor relation of the Federal Republic, and no amount of rewriting the past could change that fact. It would be the economy, not historiography, which would finally seal the fate of the GDR.

When Erich Honecker took power as Party Secretary in 1971 East Germans believed he heralded a new era of liberalization and, for a while, he seemed to live up to expectations. At the Eighth Party Conference in June that year he stated that the 'main task' of the party, the state and society, was to raise 'the material and cultural standard of living of the people'. Throughout the 1970s his reforms brought modest economic success, so much so that a World Bank report published in 1978 claimed that the GDR had a higher standard of living than Britain.[65] More consumer goods appeared in the shops, and privileged East Germans could sometimes buy chocolates, alcohol, television sets and jeans from the western currency Intershops.[66] At the same time Honecker launched a new social policy, increasing benefits for old people and invalids, social insurance for the sick, rental allowances for the disabled, loans to help young married couples and vacation leave with pay for working mothers. Women could have abortions on demand within twelve weeks, and for those who had children the state provided crèches and kindergartens, and allowed women leave from work if a child was ill.

Throughout the 1970s East German propaganda offered these improve-ments as evidence of the greatness of GDR socialism. East Germany was the 'German success story' which was already outstripping western countries and would soon overtake the Federal Republic. But the propaganda did not tell the whole story. Honecker might have introduced rigid social benefits but he had also created a highly restrictive, tightly controlled system which demanded total conformity in return for the guarantee of a very basic standard of living. People became dependent on their meagre benefits because there was no alternative. They could not escape the system by changing jobs or starting a small business or by leaving the country for a better life elsewhere; strikes, which had been permitted under the 1948 constitution, were made illegal in 1968.[67] Even the social system could not live up to the official image. One example of this discrepancy was the state's treatment of women in East Berlin. They were constantly told that they were 'equal' to men but few had high-ranking jobs in politics or institutions; although they made up one-third of SED members only twenty out of 156 of the Central Committee were women and there were none amongst the Politburo's eighteen full members.[68] (The only truly powerful woman in East Germany was Honecker's wife Margot, a member of the Council of Ministers and Minister of Education, who was responsible for indoctrinating the young and who spearheaded hideous pro-grammes which included the confiscation of over 12,000 children from 'politi-cally unreliable' parents and their forced adoption by 'acceptable' families.)[69] Instead, most working women worked in manufacturing or low-skilled jobs; others were expected to go into traditional fields like medicine and teaching. Not only did they earn less money than their male counterparts; they were expected to fit shopping, housekeeping, child-minding and other duties into a busy work schedule. As in other areas, no dissent was tolerated; even at the height of the feminist movement in the west it was made very clear that if women wanted to advance in the GDR they would have to do so by working with the party and not by pursuing 'western-style objectives'.[70] Women's groups were broken up by the Stasi, and feminists were frequently arrested and imprisoned. Women suspected of dangerous political tendencies were treated as harshly as men. One, Barbara Grosse, was arrested after visiting the Federal German embassy in Prague and its representation in East Berlin in an attempt to get permission to leave the GDR. After the collapse of the Wall she discovered that she had been spied on by at least seventeen 'friends' from work and in her neighbourhood. Another, Vera Wollenberger, discovered that both her husband and her lawyer had spied on her.[71] Other women deemed 'non-conformist' were targeted with equal vigour.

Despite the advances made during the 1970s the gap between the state propaganda and the realities of life was readily apparent in the GDR. East Germans were better off than they had been under Ulbricht, but they continued to live in a dreary, repressive state. Young people were taught that their 'basic right and basic duty' was to learn to be 'useful to society', to 'help form the developed Socialist society' and to further 'fraternal solidarity with the Soviet Union'.[72] To this end they were pushed through a relentless system which controlled everything from family life to schools, from clubs to job training.

The state saw young people as its most important – and malleable – resource, and it took control early. All children were funnelled through specially approved crèches and kindergartens, where political indoctrination began in earnest. From the ages of six to nine children were expected to join the Young Pioneers, where they were taught the basics of Communist ideology; from there over 95 per cent of East German children went into the Thälmann Pioneers, spanning the ages of ten to thirteen, where indoctrination continued. At the age of fourteen virtually every East German child took part in the *Jugendweihe*, a kind of pseudo-confirmation ceremony complete with suits or white dresses, flowers and stiff family dinners, which solemnly marked a child's progress from the Thälmann Pioneers into the Freie deutsche Jugend (FDJ).[73] Instead of Bibles the young people were given copies of Marx's *Das Kapital* and other such classics of Marxism-Leninism.[74]

The majority of East Germans between the ages of fourteen and twenty-five were expected to join the Free German Youth; with its bright blue uniforms and red scarves this was something of a bizarre cross between the Hitler Youth and the Soviet Young Pioneers. The FDJ had local organizations in all schools, factories and military units; its Ordnungsgruppen or Public Order Groups taught young people how to spy on parents, teachers and colleagues at work; those who shone at these tasks were seen as prime candidates for the Stasi.[75] Although official propaganda taught that GDR citizens were meant to 'eradicate militarism, racism, imperialism and ethnic prejudice', children were also told it was their duty to 'defend the Socialist *Vaterland*' and from a young age they took part in mock manoeuvres and complicated war games and visited military installations.[76] Like the Hitler Youth they were also expected to take part in 'make work' projects, which amounted to little more than cheap labour for the state; these included the 'FDJ Berlin Initiative', in which thousands of Berlin teenagers were expected to dedicate their summer holidays and weekends to working on the 377 projects in and around the city – such as planting the Havelfruit Orchards, converting abandoned open-pit mines into parkland, and building grotesque new East German housing projects like that in Marzahn.

Many young people resented the FDJ but those who wanted to go on to higher education had little choice but to conform: a clean FDJ record was an essential prerequisite for entry, and while official propaganda taught that universities had been transformed from 'institutes of the rich' into the training ground for the 'dictatorship of the proletariat' they were far from meritocratic. Admission was based not on academic ability but on party membership. Students would be accepted if their parents were loyal SED members and were descended from 'workers or peasants'; if they were known Church members, had fallen foul of the state or were part of an older social or academic elite their application would almost certainly be turned down. Above all, however, students should have demonstrated a deep commitment to the German Democratic Republic. Friends, teachers and informants were asked if they had shown a willingness to 'defend socialism' by volunteering for reserve officers' training or by doing extra work for the FDJ. If they had made anti-party comments (even at a pub or private dinner), if they had friends in dissident circles or contact with people in West Berlin they would probably lose their place. The final decision was made not by teachers or academics, but by the Ministry of Higher and Specialized Secondary Education, which was based in Berlin.[77]

The totalitarian system meant that parents lost control of their children early on. If a child was talented he would be made to go through a special education programme which, amongst other things, formed the foundation for the GDR's excellent record in sports. Like Hitler the Politburo recognized that sports events were a new mass spectacle which could bolster national pride.[78] Physical education was compulsory; those who excelled were identified by teachers and forced into one of nineteen special sports schools after approval from the bureaucrats in the Department of Sports in Berlin. These schools were often located far from the athlete's home, offered little in the way of conventional education and used extreme forms of punishment for those who faltered. The combination of social isolation, the use of steroids and other drugs, and the relentless pressure to win created sporting 'machines' and often led to tragedy, but society at large never heard about the failures. The schools churned out champions and the regime gloried in their victories; at a ceremony in 1982 Erich Honecker told a group of athletes: 'Your successes are a valuable contribution to strengthening our Workers' and Peasants' State and to its international reputation.' Full-page spreads of Olympic gold medal-winners appeared in *Neues Deutschland* and successful athletes were given privileges usually reserved for top party officials. East German athletic success startled the world, but for every champion there were dozens of young children who were abandoned by the schools with little education and few prospects; some were drug addicts, others suffered from severe depression, but they received little or no help if they were no longer deemed useful.

For those young people who were less conformist the GDR tried to create an 'alternative' youth culture with officially sponsored SED causes such as 'anti-Third World poverty' days or 'anti-nuclear' demonstrations. Rock music was another problem area. For thirty years the SED had banned all subversive 'western-style' rock music and had even denied its existence, but in practice this was virtually impossible in a city which had access to West Berlin radio stations. In 1982 the SED admitted that rock music did in fact exist and at a special conference in October the FDJ leader Hartmut König declared in typical SED party-speak that 'German Rock had its birthplace in the GDR' and that 'in the past 15 years we have seen developed dance music which is relevant, which captures our young people's feeling for life with which almost every young person in our country can identify and which has won international recognition'. With a few notable exceptions most East German rock music was dire and the official clubs had more in common with rural barn dances than the BIG CITY EXPERIENCE promised by the hand-painted placards outside. The official folk, rock and jazz bands lacked spirit precisely because they were expected to conform to state guidelines. The SED continued to push its artificial culture with the 'Rock for Peace' concerts or the 'Song Summer of the Free German Youth', but when East Berlin declared its 1988 'World Decade of Cultural Development' to 'bring peace to the world through art' local bands were sent notices detailing what they should write for the forthcoming state occasion. They would oblige or face a ban. A few good bands – like Die Puhdys – were given official decorations by Erich Honecker, while Karat, Silly, Pankow City and Enno consistently won the rock band 'song contests and talent shows' held by the Komitee für Unterhaltungskunst (Committee for the Entertaining Arts), which controlled the careers of over 9,000 performers.[79] When some of the more inventive musicians criticized the committee for stifling the spontaneity of rock music a spokesman retorted: 'the production of rock music is no more bureaucratically organized in the GDR than incomparably complex production units in the West such as EMI or CBS.' Indeed, because it was organized by the state GDR rock music was 'detached . . . from the give-and-take of the market place and is subordinate to the premises of socialist culture and youth policies'.[80]

The music was generally so bad that by the mid 1980s most young people were ignoring it altogether and spent their time trying to get hold of western albums and posters or strained to hear rock concerts held over the Wall in West Berlin. After years of pressure the state-owned record company VEB was finally permitted to reproduce a few western albums by specially approved artists such as Michael Jackson and Tina Turner as long as they were accompanied by long statements explaining why that particular artist had been considered 'acceptable' to GDR youth. When Bruce Springsteen's album *Born in the USA* appeared it was made clear that this

> does not represent the importation of bourgeois ideology – neither does it mean that the fans of Bruce Springsteen in the GDR would prefer to have been born in the USA, as the lyrics of the title track might suggest. Nor does this mean that we regard Bruce Springsteen as an advocate of Socialist ideology. And least of all should it be seen as an indication of a pragmatic surrender of socialist views.[81]

Furthermore, the roots of rock music, it was claimed, were not American at all but deeply rooted in East German culture. As one spokesman put it, 'the rhythm patterns and sound structures of rock music reflect a sensuousness, a sensuous relation to reality, which, irrespective of all commercial filters, has its social roots in our working class youth'.[82] First the state had claimed Beethoven; now it had Mick Jagger as well.

Despite all attempts to improve life in the GDR it was clear by the mid 1980s that the system was not working. Absurd attempts to claim rock music or to prove economic superiority over West Germany failed to convince. Honecker had made cosmetic changes to the system of central planning, with its Kombinats, fixed work norms and collectivization, hoping instead to keep the economy going by making people work more efficiently, by selling more to the west for hard currency and by building up his own 'high tech' industries.[83] These changes allowed him to carry on into the mid 1980s but it was now difficult to hide the general decline and increasing shabbiness of most people's lives. Erich Honecker's world was slowly falling apart.

Despite evidence of failure Günter Mittag, the architect of the centrally planned economy, resisted reform. When things became difficult his first response was to cut back on consumer goods and to increase hard currency sales to the west, without taking into account the effect this would have on the local population.[84] During the financial crisis of 1988 he suggested that East Germany stop importing expensive cattle fodder from western suppliers despite the fact that this would lead to a drastic reduction in the domestic food supply; the plan was halted only by the intervention of the agriculture minister Werner Felfe.[85] By the late 1980s the GDR owed the west over $10 billion; at a Politburo meeting on 8 June 1988 Kurt Hager presented a report criticizing the East German economy, calling investment 'inadequate' and pointing out 'serious shortcomings' in production. He was right. Industry was backward and inefficient. There was still too much emphasis on heavy industry; ridiculous manufacturing norms and schedules still led to the production of thousands of useless items like obsolete machine tools or large quantities of poor quality steel, while crucial items were unavailable.[86] The unwieldy centrally planned system meant that it took an inordinate length of time to do even the most menial tasks; hours were spent filling out forms and obtaining official stamps from well-paid bureaucrats while production lines remained idle. Machine parts were scarce, fuel was of poor quality, distribution networks were haphazard, quality control during the manufacturing process was non-existent and what economic success the GDR did achieve was purchased at great cost to the environment and to people's health. East German industry was filthy. Chemical and metal processing belched waste into the land, air and water; Bitterfeld, with its large chemical industry, became a byword for pollution, as did Eisleben: its Mansfeld metals complex created enormous slag heaps around the area. Eighty per cent of electricity was produced by sulphur-rich brown coal and as power plants had no filters and most homes were heated by coal-burning ovens, tons of sulphur dioxide and dust particles were constantly pumped into the air. East Germany had the worst air pollution in Europe, a fact instantly visible in the form of a greenish yellow layer oozing over the landscape. The renowned *Berliner Luft* was transformed in winter into a thick brown cloud which hung over the city, stinging the eyes and throat and causing frequent asthma alerts.[87] Water was also heavily polluted: half the rivers were too tainted to use as drinking water; only 75 per cent of the population was connected to a sewage system and far fewer to any kind of treatment plant. Only 1 per cent of lake water was suitable for drinking and the ground was contaminated by everything from toxic industrial waste to seepage from garbage dumps, residue from uranium mining and brown coal pits and the muck generated on the 280,000 hectares of Soviet-occupied bases – ecological nightmares complete with dumped fuel, discarded equipment, explosives and effluent.[88] Erich Honecker had tried to modernize the East German economy by promoting industries like engineering and optics, and industrial fairs were filled with the latest technological 'wonders', ranging from the gigantic RFT electronic calculators to the East German 'invention' – the helium-neon laser produced at Carl Zeiss Jena. It was telling that the official publication extolling the virtues of the 'East German designed laserchip as small as the eye of an ant' included an official photograph in which Günter Butzke, one of the members of the 'Collective of Technicians and Scientists', could just be seen clutching a copy of the basic English textbook *Handbook of Fibre Optics – Theory and Application*.[89] East German advances depended not so much on local research as on how much technology could be bought or stolen from the west. Despite the Promethean efforts of Erich Mielke's industrial espionage unit the gap between East German technology and that in the west in the age of Star Wars and Silicon Valley continued to grow rapidly. By 1988 it was clear that industrial espionage was no longer enough.[90]

The deficiencies in industry were revealed after the Wall came down.[91] When I worked in the former GDR in 1989 I interviewed a number of people who had worked at the Carl Zeiss Jena plant which, in the 1980s, had been the biggest research centre in East Germany and a symbol of national pride – not least because it supplied the Soviets with much of their equipment for the aeronautics industry. But even its most dedicated supporters had to admit it was falling behind the west. Electronics embargoes were having an effect and Zeiss engineers had to build their own computers; a great deal of time and talent was devoted to reinventing products which had been stolen from the west and were later portrayed as GDR inventions. As a result a large proportion of man hours was wasted on things already available on the world market; millions of Ost Marks were poured into the production of the 1-megabyte chip. Honecker greeted the news with delight, but although it was a coup for Zeiss and the first in the eastern bloc the chip was already being mass produced in the west.[92] Away from these glamour projects staff were faced with constant delays caused by suspicion and central planning, which only grew worse in the late 1980s. Scientists had to request any parts they might need two years in advance and their access to scientific knowledge was strictly controlled by the state: libraries in factories and research units held only vetted material while information about real scientific breakthroughs was locked away. Outspoken scientists were forbidden access to photocopiers, were denied any link with the west and were not even permitted to attend the show conferences in East Berlin. One prominent Zeiss scientist was married to a woman who had an uncle in West Germany; that fact alone excluded him from all business trips to the west: 'I refused to meet the condition that she should cut herself off from him,' he said; 'I could not accept that a person should have to break with an uncle or be struck off the "travel permit" list.'[93] These restrictions caused problems when work itself involved travel. One man from Zeiss was sent out to test new aerial cameras at Schönefeld Airport near West Berlin in 1988 but was told that because the authorities feared hijackings 'you can't go testing your equipment in a plane'.

The stuttering economy affected morale in the GDR. Although East Germans had the highest GDP per head in the eastern bloc the people measured their success not against Albania but against the images of West Germany projected into their homes every night via western radio and television. By comparison, East Germany looked poor. The people of the GDR worked hard, but how could they improve their lot when over half of their goods were exported to the Soviet Union while the rest went to West Germany for hard currency? Local people had to wait years for simple household appliances like washing machines and refrigerators; it sometimes took twenty years to get a telephone. The official waiting time for a Wartburg or a Trabant – the infamous two-stroke-engine fibreglass cars which belched out smoke and fumes – was seven years, although one East Berlin friend of mine waited eleven years and six months for his; even in the 1980s only nine households out of twenty had a car. When they finally had transportation East Germans drove on Hitler's Autobahns, which had been virtually untouched since the 1940s; most were still unfenced dual carriageways with 'rustic' granite bridges built by slave labourers in the 1930s, deep ruts in their surfaces and peeling road signs pointing not to Paris or Rome, but to Moscow and Leningrad.

The standard of living was still miserable. Food, clothing and other basics were difficult to obtain; foodstuffs like sausage and bread were cheap but of poor quality, while luxuries like the chocolates or alcohol available in the new Nikolaiviertel or in the hard currency Intershops were beyond the reach of most people. The central area of Berlin, deemed the 'Showpiece of Real Existing Socialism', was kept in good repair, but beyond the one grand street of restored Prussian buildings and well-maintained offices and flats reserved for party hacks and Stasi bosses lay the dispiriting, run-down working-class districts. The system did not reward individual initiative and people took little care of their surroundings: the *Hinterhof* in which I stayed was constantly shedding chunks of greenish concrete, its windows were broken and piles of rubbish filled the courtyards; indeed the back streets of East Berlin contained scenes of decay difficult to find in even the poorest and most neglected areas of West Berlin. In these hidden areas a flat cost only 5 per cent of a family's income but young couples had to wait for years before they could move into one. Some were put into the ghastly new pre-fab housing developments like that in Marzahn, where concrete towers stretching endlessly along the Alley of the Cosmonauts housed 170,000 people; if the inhabitants did not appreciate their good fortune they could always listen to the inane song composed for Erich Honecker in honour of the project which went: 'How wonderful to live in our newly constructed apartment in Marzahn! In Marzahn! In Marzahn!' Two-fifths of the housing stock was still pre-war. Most of these flats were without central heating; a third had no hot running water and a quarter of all East Berliners had to share an outside lavatory. My room on the top floor of a crumbling nineteenth-century building had a leaking roof and was heated by a cracked coal stove, but maintenance was centrally planned: in order to get leaking water taps or power failures fixed you had to apply to a central body. If your flat was not in a party building this could take weeks or even months but there was no alternative; you could not simply call a plumber or electrician as private businesses were forbidden and there were no DIY shops. In this sense East Germany was far from the 'Old Prussia' it sought to emulate; the Protestant work ethic and the values which had made the old state so efficient had been replaced by the Communist idea that fresh paint and manicured gardens were part of an unacceptable, decadent bourgeois world.

The inertia in the suburbs extended to a dreary cultural life in East Berlin, and with the exception of subsidized theatre and opera most entertainment was of a very low standard.[94] Painting and sculpture were generally uninspired.[95] A handful of clubs in the Friedrichstrasse area tried to emulate the 'cabaret' atmosphere of the Weimar era but most failed dismally. The table telephones at the Berlin Ballhaus no longer worked, and the tinselly revues at the Friedrichstadtpalast (built in 'only 35 months') offered little more than a few scantily dressed girls parading around with boas in the *leicht frivol*, which was said to evoke memories of the 'Tingel-tangel of the 1920s'. Most of these nightclubs were frequented by curious tourists and party members. The only relief was provided by a few daring political cabarets like the Distel, whose artists joked about current affairs and criticized the state only as far as the humourless Stasi would allow. For a supposedly wealthy country the restaurant food was appalling even in the modern Swedish-built hotels around Friedrichstrasse, which catered to foreign visitors and the party elite. One was invariably kept waiting by the surly head waiter until he felt like releasing a table, and the menus typically had half the dishes crossed off; meat was sold by weight, vegetables were soggy and tasteless, 'salad' was always the predictable eastern bloc bowl of grated carrot and cabbage swimming in sugar water, service was terrible and the atmosphere was always tainted by the knowledge that the only East Germans there were probably party or Stasi men. The quality dropped again beyond the city centre, and people ate out rarely and then only in the few pubs which served traditional soups or sausage. Shopping was difficult, food queues were common and meals often consisted of tinned sausages, bread, potatoes, pickled herring, beer, the worst Bulgarian wine and *ersatz* coffee. 'Luxuries' like bananas and pineapples – not to mention avocados, papayas and grapes – taken for granted only a few metres away, were unheard of.

Virtually everything about life in East Berlin was cheap and second rate. One felt it as soon as one reached the border and bought the mandatory 25 marks of tiny bills and featherweight coins which looked and felt like plastic. East Berlin was filled with GDR kitsch, from Berlin bear statuettes and ashtrays to cheap gold-painted jewellery and large plastic 'digital watches' which rarely worked. There was plastic everywhere – plastic replicas of the GDR television tower, plastic jackets, plastic curtains, plastic plates, milk which came in plastic bags. Everything for the mass market was of poor quality: cutlery bent the first time it was used, hinges broke, wheels fell off toys, 'Exquisit' boutique shampoos were unusable and the soap powder from the Walter Ulbricht detergent factory turned all my clothes greenish-grey. Comparisons with the west were telling: there were 3.7 million private cars in East Germany and 28.9 million in West; labour productivity was 51 per cent lower than in the Federal Republic;[96] only 7 per cent of households had telephones compared to virtually 100 per cent across the border; there were 5,600 new books published in East Germany in 1988 compared to nearly 51,000 in the FRG. East Berliners might not have known the statistics but they knew that they were badly off.[97] All this coupled with a repressive system meant that life for the majority of East Germans was dreary and uninspiring. Many resented the system and lived in a niche society of 'inner emigration', keeping quiet in public and opening up only with close friends and family at the local *Kneipe*, around the dinner table, or over a glass of beer in the allotment. The sense of anger and of 'missing out' was further fuelled by the lifestyle enjoyed by the SED elite.

The privileged few did not live by the same rules as the rest of society. Those at the top of the Socialist Unity Party, the government, the Stasi, the military, along with the most successful scientists, athletes and artists, lived in special suburbs on the outskirts of town or near their offices in the best apartments in the heart of East Berlin. These people had long since abandoned ideals of the dictatorship of the proletariat and equality for all. Their children always had access to university places, they could holiday in specially created beach resorts or country retreats, or even abroad. Members of the SED elite like Honecker and Erich Mielke could indulge in their favourite pastime of hunting in estates surrounded by guards and signs warning people off the 'military base'. Honecker in particular enjoyed tramping around the forests in his furry gumboots and suede jacket; at other times he could often be found in the heavily guarded suburb of Wandlitz watching Mickey Mouse videos or toasting his guests with bottles of Rotkäppchen sparkling wine. The leaders were shady, untouchable figures, rarely seen in public except at carefully staged events, and they were never exposed to journalists or anyone else who might challenge their authority. Many East Germans resented them but open criticism brought swift and severe punishment.

For all the propaganda, the reworking of history, the Olympic gold medals and the assurances that East Germans were living in the 'good' Germany, few people outside the charmed SED circle really believed that this was the paradise they had been promised. Most East Berliners regularly watched western television; some had western relatives or friends and knew that life elsewhere was different. Most wanted to travel just to 'see the west' before returning home like their Polish or Hungarian counterparts, but Erich Honecker feared that if he opened the border a flood of his brightest and best young people would leave in the sort of exodus which had led to the building of the Wall in the first place.[98] Unlike other citizens of the Soviet bloc, who could visit the west but could not stay, East Germans who reached West Germany did not need visas but became automatic citizens of the Federal Republic. The SED's greatest fear was that dissidents or activists might provoke another uprising like that of 1953. To prevent any hint of unrest they created the most efficient, most widespread police network in the eastern bloc.

By the 1980s the Stasi had almost complete control over the captive population of East Germany. Their extraordinary efficiency was due in part to their advanced recruitment, training, scientific and technical skills in the murky centre of espionage in East Berlin. But the Stasi were successful for another reason. In Poland, Czechoslovakia and Russia itself the secret police organizations faced problems, but here the Stasi were able to co-opt a very high percentage of the population into working with or for it. They took advantage of an unfortunate weakness which had been exhibited by Berliners time and again over the years: namely an acceptance of authority, and a willingness to help enforce this authority even if it meant informing on neighbours or family or friends.

It was impossible to visit East Berlin and remain unaware of the chilling influence of the Stasi. From the moment one approached the Wall one could sense the watchful eyes, the hidden microphones, the secret cameras and the other trappings of the police state which held East Berlin in its grip. The Stasi was established in February 1950 as the German arm of the KGB. Between 1957 and 1990 it was headed by Erich Mielke, whose position was virtually unassailable. He in turn was in charge of the *Kollegium* of thirteen generals who advised him, the most senior being Generaloberst Rudi Mittag.[99] The thuggish Egon Krenz was Secretary of the Central Committee responsible for security. From its first days the Stasi bore a striking resemblance to the Gestapo, and from small beginnings the 'Sword of the Party' grew exponentially, becoming more efficient and confident until it controlled every aspect of life in the GDR.

By 1980 every street, important building, café and theatre in central East Berlin had its informants and its hidden cameras and microphones. The Stasi had access to over 600 buildings, including over 200 furnished flats set up for clandestine meetings, many with two-way mirrors and bugging devices. The Stasi central office in the grey complex on the Magdalenenstrasse is still a terrifying place. An entire city block was taken over, the outside bristled with aerials and cameras, the entrances were made of thick steel and Volkspolizei patrolled the streets outside. It was a modern fortress. The thirty-eight buildings housed 3,000 offices and 33,000 employees. There was also a munitions bunker, a barracks, a canteen, a hospital, two copper-lined rooms to prevent satellite surveillance, and at the very centre the office of Minister Erich Mielke. The only sign on the building read THE OSCAR ZIETHEN KRANKENHAUS POLYKLINIK, the code-name for what East Germans called the 'House of One Thousand Eyes'.

The extent of the Stasi network was staggering. West German intelligence estimated that the Stasi employed 1,000,000 full-time and 500,000 part-time informers. It had 85,000 full-time, well-paid employees and over 100,000 collaborators placed in peace and environmental groups, in the churches and in universities and colleges. Assemblies of every kind, from seminars to gay bars, cycling clubs to church groups, had their Stasi contingent, who attended meetings to report on proceedings, tapped phones, followed 'suspects' and interfered in the most intimate aspects of people's lives. It was not surprising that the Stasi was the single largest employer in East Germany. It also took care of its own.

The Stasi elite lived in a separate world. Leading officials of the Stasi and the SED used a telephone network that could not be tapped. Mielke himself reported to the First and Second Secretaries of the SED, to the SED security chiefs, and to the heads of the police and the army. On serious matters he talked directly to Honecker. There was no question of parliamentary control over Stasi activities – how could there be when it did not officially exist? In order to keep its elite club going the Stasi had control over all appointments and ran security checks on anyone wanting to join the army, to work in industry or to go to university; in short anyone who applied for a position of any importance. The Stasi would consult their files and call on informers to check friends, colleagues, neighbours and family for inconsistencies in the record. They could make or break a career with a single phone call. Successful recruits were trained and given access to everything from false identity papers and passports to contacts in the SED and the military. They were taught the martial arts and the use of disguises; they learned how to follow suspects, how to search rooms, how to open mail and how to interrogate prisoners. If they were successful they could rise high in the system, and by GDR standards the rewards were immense. Employees earned OM2,000 a month (a very high wage); they had access to special shops; they could travel abroad; they could bring friends and relatives in from the west through a hidden door in Friedrichstrasse; they had access to western literature, magazines, newspapers and pornography; and they lived in the most luxurious apartments or villas. The Stasi could enjoy a vast entertainment and leisure network, which included twenty-three separate vacation spas, exclusive hospitals and sports complexes with swimming pools, modern gyms, tennis courts and saunas. Officials were given a Lada and a driver, while generals got sleek new Citroëns for official and private use and the Mielkes and Wolfs glided in and out of Berlin in their chauffeured Volvos. Some had yachts and motorcycles and shopped at the *Leiterladen* (special shops) for western jewellery, champagne and *haute couture*. The Stasi also had access to large amounts of stolen property; their warehouses were full of items taken from political prisoners and from tourists and visitors at the border. One building in East Berlin contained 20,000 items stolen from the post; another contained thousands of Cyrillic Bibles seized as a favour to Moscow. Stasi members had first pick of the goods; the rest were sold in state shops, but the Stasi bosses were also corrupt, dealing in everything from stolen antiques to diamonds. Alexander Schlack-Godolkowski's firm KoKo (Kommerzielle Koordinierung) had amassed 21.2 tons of gold ingots by 1988, a hoard financed in part by his arms- and drug-smuggling businesses. The elite were not adverse to spending this money on themselves; the Wandlitz government housing enclave, where Erich Honecker and other party bosses lived, received between OM6 and OM8 million worth of foreign exchange every year for new buildings, maintenance and personal funds for the residents. In 1989 the cost of the Stasi to the GDR was OM3.6 billion, money that the near bankrupt state could ill afford.

The extraordinary level of state control was readily apparent. For foreigners, crossing at Checkpoint Charlie was relatively painless but it was usually only possible in the company of Allied military personnel. One passed the sign announcing YOU ARE LEAVING THE AMERICAN SECTOR, drove past the forbidding barriers and cement pylons, crossed the Wall, and emerged on to the streets of East Berlin. The other route – the long trip through the Friedrichstrasse crossing point – revealed much more about the nature of East Berlin. One approached the station either by U-Bahn, passing 'ghost stations' which had been abandoned since 1961, or in rattling wooden S-Bahn carriages. In the latter one literally passed over the Wall and looked down on the 'death strip', the watch towers, the mine fields and the guards as if they were part of an eerie slow-motion film. Whenever I travelled to East Berlin I was always aware that this was a view very few East Germans my age had ever seen.

From the station one was forced to walk through a maze of filthy concrete tunnels in an area still out of bounds to East Germans, past dingy kiosks selling everything from duty free cigarettes to chocolate and alcohol. Then, finally, the visitor entered a large chamber lined with mustard and orange coloured tiles and was directed towards a cluster of grey steel and fake wood cubicles. After a long wait one would be called into one of these claustrophobic boxes, complete with mirrors positioned at an angle above one's head to expose all blind spots, to face a glass window from which an East German border guard demanded a passport. The document was taken, checked manually, held under ultraviolet light and the photograph studied at length; if one was fortunate it was stamped, the lock would be released with a loud buzzing sound and one was pushed along into another hall filled with currency forms, where one was obliged to buy OM25. After this came the gruelling customs check, during which bags and pockets were searched; all western books or newspapers were confiscated, all presents unwrapped and checked. The unwary traveller who had already changed money in the west was subjected to a strip search and a long wait in a guarded cubicle: a small amount led to a ban from entering the GDR; a large amount led to an immediate prison sentence. Even if one followed the rules to the letter one could suddenly be detained, questioned and searched for no reason. The experience was never pleasant. When I travelled frequently between East and West Berlin the guards would occasionally take my passport and make me stand in the customs hall, sometimes for over an hour, like a disgraced child, while other visitors were allowed to walk by. The guards were always surly and I was never told why I was being made to wait. The journey back to West Berlin was equally unpleasant and could be a mine field for the unwary traveller. The East Germans were not above entrapment or sheer harrassment. Once I was approached at the Humboldt University by an attractive young student who asked if I would take papers 'to his relative' in West Berlin. Naturally I refused, but on my way across the border later that day I was suddenly stopped and taken to a small room, where I was searched and questioned by an icy female guard: What was I working on at the university? Who did I know in East Berlin? Why did I travel so frequently between east and west? Had I ever published anything about the GDR? Since the collapse of the GDR it has become clear that a number of the academics I spoke to in East Berlin were themselves working for the Stasi; it has been estimated that a quarter of the staff at Humboldt University were employed by them. Westerners often had brushes with the Stasi: mail would disappear; or one might be detained without explanation. The effect of this unwelcome attention was not particularly serious; unless a foreign student or visitor was actually arrested for some real or imagined offence he could always leave the GDR, and the most obvious danger was that he would not be allowed back in. For East Germans trapped behind the Wall, however, the reality of Stasi oppression was quite different. People could not escape, and after forty years of intense Stasi activity fear had seeped into every aspect of life.

For those who have never lived in a police state it is difficult to imagine what it is like. It is not that one is afraid of committing a serious offence; one simply does not know whom to trust. It was difficult to remember that, for example, if someone approached me 'out of the blue' they might be curious civilians – in which case contact with me could prove dangerous for them – or they might be Stasi. I was warned before I went that even inviting East German friends back to my room could put them in danger as the official building informant, who betrayed his presence by a surreptitious parting of the net curtains when I walked by, would no doubt give their names to the officials. These precautions might have seemed trivial, but files were kept on over 6 million people, one-third of the population; 1,052 people were employed to listen to telephone conversations, 2,100 people opened letters and recorded their contents, 5,000 agents were on special surveillance and 16,000 were full-time spies.[100] It was a serious offence for GDR citizens to have 'unlawful contact' with westerners, and I remain grateful to those friends of mine willing to take the risk.

Amazingly the official paranoia actually increased during the 1980s, when changes in the USSR provoked Mielke to transform the Stasi into a paramilitary organization: 1985 saw the introduction of Mielke's Order No. 2, which directed the Stasi to 'prevent, discover and combat' underground political activities. Dissidents, critics and even moaners were all to be considered criminal and checked, followed and documented in files which were regularly updated. The object of Order No. 2 was 'total information'. By 1990 the Stasi was like a miniature army: it had 342 anti-aircraft guns, 3,537 anti-tank missiles, 4,499 machine guns, 76,592 machine pistols, 124,593 pistols and revolvers, 12,903 personnel carriers, 230 fast motorboats, 4,881 buses and trucks and four aircraft at its disposal. Every member kept a uniform and combat gear in his office and was given intensive military training. Agents were kept alert to the possibility of a western invasion and were taught to watch all foreigners and those with contacts in the west. It was a measure of the insecurity of Honecker's regime that Stasi activity actually increased after Gorbachev came to power and introduced his 'unwelcome' reforms.

One of the most horrific aspects of life in East Berlin was the sheer number of people who had become involved in spying, ranging from lowly dustmen to high-ranking officials. This was largely the result of Stasi recruitment policy. Every year each Stasi employee was asked to recruit twenty-five new people; if he failed he received a black mark on his file, which could mean demotion or a cut in benefits. Potential recruits came from all walks of life, but before an approach was made they were checked on a '101 point system' which documented their social position, hobbies, preferred reading matter, body language and accent, appearance and clothing sense, moods, intelligence, judgement, discretion, memorization skill, specialist knowledge (such as fluency in another language) or the ability to type, attitudes to the workplace, the army, the USSR and other socialist states, discrepancies between publicly expressed and privately held views, living conditions (including tidiness and personal habits), other contacts in the GDR, friends and relatives in the west, sexual behaviour and any other intimate details which might be useful. Nothing was too personal or too embarrassing for the Stasi. Many people were blackmailed into working for them; a past 'transgression' would be discovered and a punishment threatened. Some were bribed with everything from money or a new flat to a place at the university. Others were tricked into working 'just once', the transaction recorded and the victim locked into the system. If someone was caught having an affair he would be threatened with exposure unless he agreed to spy on his spouse; if a child was caught committing a minor crime he could escape punishment by spying on his parents; people even had important medication withheld if they did not co-operate. New recruits were forced to sign a form which read: 'I herewith pledge voluntarily to co-operate actively and with initiative with the Ministry for State Security of the German Democratic Republic. I have chosen the cover name of —.'[101]

Some informants were easy to spot: one knew that Intourist guides, hotel staff and bartenders, the semi-official prostitutes and others in the service industry in central Berlin were almost certainly on the payroll, but the rot went much deeper than that. The Stasi targeted everyone from miners to waitresses, from musicians to kindergarten teachers, but the number and spread of informants was astonishing.[102] There were IMs (unofficial collaborators), FIMs (unofficial collaborators running other unofficial collaborators), GMSes (low-level IMs), IMBs, IMEs, IMKs, or Mielke's IOBEs – officers on a special mission – placed in top areas of the army, the government and the party. All sent information to ZAIG, the Stasi's central processing group in Berlin, which lived by Mielke's dictum that 'everyone is a potential security risk'. The rest of the population learned to keep quiet in public, aware that a minor indiscretion could cost them their education or chance of promotion.

The Stasi moved swiftly against anyone it suspected of 'anti-state' activities. Most people were innocent of any real crime and did not realize they were being targeted, but victims had no rights whatsoever. Every postal room had a collection point for 'suspect' mail. In East Berlin the Postzollfahndung occupied an entire storey in the main railway station; here thousands of letters were steamed open by 600 operatives, their contents recorded and the envelopes resealed. If they were damaged during this process they were simply thrown away; control letters were sometimes placed in with ordinary post to check the reliability of the PFZ staff.[103] Hundreds of apartments were bugged, cameras were hidden all over the city, telephones were tapped (when the Wall fell 80,000 cassette tapes of recent telephone conversations were found in an East Berlin office), people were followed and data was handwritten as the Stasi distrusted computer files. There were 70 tons of forms and 100,000 tons of files in one East Berlin department alone in 1989. Information was often gathered by searching a victim's house or flat. The Stasi could ensure that everybody would be out of the building at a certain time: one target might suddenly get a long-awaited doctor's appointment; another would be called for a special meeting at his child's school. When everyone had gone the Stasi would move in. The door would be carefully unlocked and polaroids taken of the entire flat so that everything could be put back in place. Then the flat was searched. At this stage the agents looked for foreign currency, suspicious letters, work by foreigners or dissidents, religious information, posters of rock musicians, western products – anything which they saw as 'incriminating'. As most people had something 'suspicious' in their homes when judged by these criteria many were targeted again.[104] Even if the case was taken no further there were often signs that one had been a suspect: one's car might be confiscated, or a travel request turned down. One was never informed of the 'charges' and certainly had no right of appeal. Files were not destroyed and could turn up years later; a comment made in the 1950s could eventually result in the refusal of a travel permit or the denial of a university place for one's child. Everything from housing to work and income could be affected.

If a suspect was considered serious enough to be arrested rather than simply put on file he would usually be apprehended while at work: officials would ask him to come and clear up 'a small problem'. He would then be taken away for interrogation, and perhaps disappear for years. It was all part of the intimidation process; colleagues witnessing the arrest would be more likely to conform.

Once in prison the victim was in the hands of experts. The questioners were masters at humiliation and isolation. Interrogation and imprisonment could go on for months. The Stasi had time and might on their side; they were getting paid for doing their job and didn't care how long a suspect languished in prison. Many victims have said that interrogation was not usually violent, although torture and beatings were sometimes used; the Stasi favoured a favourite KGB trick of forcing the prisoner to stand for days under a blazing electric light bulb, unable to sit down or lean against the wall; when he collapsed he was woken and made to stand again. Psychological terror, like being exposed to the sounds of people being tortured down the hall, or being threatened with reprisals against family and friends on the outside, was much more common. The Stasi sought to wear a prisoner down and their techniques were so effective that few prisoners held out for more than six months. Shielded from all contact with the outside world or with other prisoners, the victim would eventually confide in his interrogator; most confessed out of sheer loneliness or fear, realizing that confession was the only way out. A conviction and a prison sentence would follow.

Conditions in the three Stasi prisons of East Berlin were harsh. The cells were 4-metre-square cubicles with no windows and only the bare necessities. The walls of some cells were wired so that touching them set off an alarm, and bullying, cruelty and sadism were common. Prison was regarded as an educational process. Political prisoners were mixed in with criminals, and the latter were encouraged to dominate and intimidate the former, often violently; the guards would not protect them. For more difficult prisoners the Stasi also used psychiatric clinics modelled on Soviet lines. Here the use of torture was commonplace. In the Waldheim psychiatric clinic in Hochschweitzschen patients were deprived of food, locked in dark cells for weeks and made to sit in ice water; white foam was sprayed in their eyes, they were injected with emetics and saline infusions to cause nausea, and both men and women were raped. The worst was Ward M1, 'the shelter', in which people were 'pumped' or made to lie on their stomachs with their legs pulled backward over their heads, a treatment uncovered by Amnesty International in Soviet psychiatric clinics. For the unfortunate men and women caught up in this nightmarish system of arrest, interrogation and torture there was little choice but to endure one's sentence and hope that one might be purchased by the West Germans. The Stasi had become so paranoid and yet so omnipotent that even now it is impossible to know how many people were falsely charged with crimes against the state. The East German regime was obsessed with dissidents, but their criteria for 'crimes' was so broad that virtually anybody targeted could be found 'guilty'; Mielke even kept a file on Erich Honecker. The attack on the population became a self-perpetuating system of oppression and violence. Even so, some dissidents warranted special state attention.

The internal security arm of the Stasi had actually been founded to counter the activities of *Gegner*, the 'opponents' or 'adversaries' of the state. Deep within the concentric circles of Stasi power was the very core of Erich Mielke's paranoid system, Division XX – the section in charge of dissidents. The centre had been essential to the survival of the GDR from the beginning, carefully weeding out (and initially murdering) Social Democrats, human rights activists, those in favour of unification, and those who disagreed with the system. With Stalin's death methods of dealing with dissidents became less severe – people were rarely executed outright – but the treatment of opponents was still brutal and included anything from house arrest to years of incarceration in an asylum, depending on the way in which the 'dissent' was classified; it did not necessarily mean active spying or open protest on the streets; it could also involve a chance comment against the regime, or the production of a work of art which seemed to be critical of the Workers' and Peasants' state.

The majority of writers and intellectuals in the GDR rose to prominence by producing work which slavishly adhered to the guidelines set out by the SED.[105] The others, like Bertolt Brecht, Anna Seghers and Stefan Heym, were already known before the war; they voluntarily returned to the GDR genuinely believing that socialism would finally triumph over the west. Unfortunately for the East German leaders many soon became disenchanted with Stalinist East Germany. Some, like the philosopher Ernst Bloch, Alfred Kantorowicz, professor of German literature at the Humboldt University, Theodor Plevier, author of *Stalingrad*, and Gerhard Zwerenz, who wrote *Casanova*, left for the west. Others, like the head of the Aufbau-Verlag Walther Janka, the editor of *Sonntag* Heinz Zögler and the writer Wolfgang Harich, actively campaigned for democratic change and were imprisoned; Harich got ten years' hard labour in 1957 for trying to pursue de-Stalinization beyond the limits set up by the party.

The SED was caught between two conflicting aims: on the one hand it feared that dissidents might inspire a popular uprising against the state; on the other it was keenly aware of the damage it was doing to the country's international reputation by imprisoning and torturing writers and others who merely questioned its authority. In 1959 the party tried to overcome the problem by creating a new, specifically East German elite. Brought together under the absurd slogan 'Greif zur Feder, Kumpel!' (Grab your pen, mate!) young writers were encouraged to become involved in society by spending time in a factory or on a farm before writing about their true-to-life experiences.[106] The initiative launched the careers of writers like Günter Kunert and Volker Braun, while a stint in a Halle railway-carriage factory prompted Christa Wolf to write Der geteilte Himmel (The Divided Heaven), one of the most famous works ever produced in the GDR. Despite these efforts, however, writers and intellectuals continued to criticize the state and the Eleventh SED Central Committee Plenum in December 1965 initiated another crack-down on writers who exhibited 'harmful tendencies'.[107]

When Honecker took over in 1971 he promised liberalization, declaring that if work was rooted in 'socialism' anything would be permitted; he even called the writing produced in the Ulbricht era 'boring' and promised that there would henceforth be 'no taboos'.[108] There were some improvements: Volker Braun was allowed to publish Das ungezwungene Leben Kasts, which was mildly critical of the 1968 invasion of Czechoslovakia, and Hermann Kant wrote Der Aula, which pointed to failures in East German socialism.[109] The most daring was Die neuen Leiden des jungen W. (The New Sufferings of Young W.) by Ulrich Plenzdorf, the story of a youth who could not cope with life in the GDR; a quintessential 1970s drop-out with long hair and jeans, he escaped from a ghastly factory job to live in a shack hidden on the outskirts of Berlin. At first the authorities allowed the novel largely because the story implied that the youthful protest was in vain, but young East Germans did not interpret it like this. The novel achieved cult status precisely because of its criticisms of the stifling drudgery of East Berlin life. It was quickly withdrawn from circulation.[110]

A number of other young people emerged as role models during the 1970s. The most important was Wolf Biermann, the satirical poet, songwriter and singer who, although born and raised in Hamburg, was a dedicated Communist and had volunteered to live in the GDR in 1953, initially working with Brecht's Berliner Ensemble in East Berlin. Although strictly pro-socialist, Biermann began to lace his lyrics with cutting comments about the bureaucracy, the party and the general ineptitude in the GDR.[111] This was too much for the SED; in November 1976, when he was performing at a cultural festival for the IG Metall Union in Cologne, the East German government suddenly withdrew his citizenship and marooned him in the west.[112]

The move backfired badly. Protests poured in from around the world and twelve eminent East German writers, including Stefan Heym, Christa Wolf,

Volker Braun and Stephan Hermlin, signed an open letter to the party criticizing the decision, although a number of others, including Anna Seghers, Hermann Kant, Peter Hacks and Konrad Wolf, applauded the measure.[113] Within a month over 100 others had signed the letter, but to no avail. Christa Wolf was expelled from the SED and the Berlin Committee of the Writers' Union, while Stefan Heym was charged with 'breaches of currency rules'.[114] In 1979 a new controversy stirred when a group of writers protested against the harassment of Stefan Heym and Robert Havemann, who had refused to break off contacts with the West Germans. Eight writers were expelled from the GDR, including Kurt Bartsch, Rolf Schneider, Dieter Schubert and Stefan Heym himself. The scientist Robert Havemann remained under house arrest. The economist Rudolph Bahro, who wrote a Marxist critique of the regime's shortcomings, was arrested and imprisoned for espionage, and many writers were spied on, their flats bugged and their offices searched. As this senseless harassment increased many leading writers, including Günter Kunert and Rainer Kunze, chose to leave. In 1978 at a GDR writers' congress the new head, Hermann Kant, made a speech against dissenters, saying: 'when you argue, do it with logic, sense and *Parteilichkeit*' (a proper feeling of party loyalty). Some authors continued to struggle against censorship but most were punished.

The writer Erich Loest, who had already spent seven years in Bautzen prison in the 1950s, was expelled from the GDR in 1981 for his *Es geht seinen Gang oder Mühen in unserer Ebene* (It Goes On As Usual or Efforts at Our Level), which was critical of the state. Joachim Schädlich, whose *Versuchte Nähe* had been published 'illegally' in the west, was expelled in 1977; his 1986 work *Tallhover* was a remarkable piece about a secret policeman who does not die, and who has served in Germany throughout history.[115] Unfortunately, those writers who stayed in East Germany invariably made concessions to the regime in order to remain in the Writers' Union and other professional bodies. If they wanted to publish in the GDR they were forced to compromise; much damaging information has emerged since 1989 about writers like Christa Wolf, who co-operated with the state rather than face arrest or deportation, and Heiner Müller, who defended his work for the Stasi after the fall of the Wall.[116] For other less well-known activists punishment was swift. Those arrested were taken to prison, where they were given a choice of a long sentence or immediate loss of East German citizenship and a transfer to the west, bought and paid for by the Federal Republic of Germany. Many reluctantly chose the latter. Ironically, West Germany's well-intentioned policy of relieving the suffering of political prisoners proved to be one of the East Germans' most potent weapons. Instead of making concessions to dissidents the GDR could simply push them out. Over 3,000 of its most daring, intelligent, questioning young people were shipped to West Germany every year; between 1963 and 1989 some 33,000 of the most troublesome political prisoners were bought by the west for between DM50,000 and DM100,000 each. At Christmas some human beings were swapped for oranges.

This constant drain on dissidents was one of the reasons why the GDR never developed a protest movement at universities, amongst intellectuals, amongst the workers or in the media; nor did it have anything resembling an 'alternative' civil society like that created by Solidarity in Poland. Dissent was spontaneous, haphazard and disorganized, which greatly reduced its effectiveness. It was based not on a sophisticated programme but relied on youthful outbursts against restrictions on travel to the west or on western consumer goods; these were easily quashed by the Stasi.

This situation might have continued for decades had it not been for one profound change which occurred in the Soviet Union in 1985. That year, Mikhail Gorbachev came to power. He was not the radical reformer people have since made him out to be. He was motivated primarily by a desire to retain the Soviet Union's superpower status and to maintain the rule of the Communist Party, but he knew that in order to achieve these things the USSR would have to reform. In the process he unwittingly unleashed a demand for profound change which he had not foreseen, which he did not want, and which he could not control. But despite the extraordinary events in Poland, Hungary and elsewhere Honecker refused to adapt. When revolution finally happened in eastern Europe it did not begin in East Berlin; indeed for all the myths which would evolve later Berlin did very little to push for change until the final months of 1989. Until then the SED, blinded by too many years in power, would insist that it could keep these forces under control. Nobody, least of all Erich Honecker, dreamed that within months his tightly controlled system would simply collapse. The entire post-war world order was changing. The artificial state and its artificial capital, which had survived on a diet of Stasi control, falsified history and oppression, was set to be destroyed in the extraordinary revolutions of 1989.

XVII

The Walled City – West Berlin

The upkeep needs money
and careful running, which makes for overheads.

(*Faust*, Part II, Act 4)

WEST BERLIN BECAME AN ISLAND CITY on 13 August 1961. It was, as the Dutch artist Armando put it, 'not a pretty town'.[1] The place which had so confidently projected itself as the 'bastion of freedom', the 'showcase of the west', was now a vulnerable enclave locked deep within the Soviet zone which could be reached from the west only by a handful of exposed transit routes running through East German territory. Before the Wall West Berlin had been a focus of world attention, a crisis point, an outpost which represented the struggle against Soviet oppression and the victory of capitalism over Communism. Not only was it now shorn of its economic, political, diplomatic, military and cultural roles; it had also lost its sense of identity, its post-war *raison d'être*. The composer György Ligeti called it a 'surrealist cage', a bizarre prison in which only those locked up inside were free.[2]

By the end of the first year West Berlin was in a precarious state. Morale was very low and many people – an average of 300 every day – were leaving despite offers of 'fear money' paid by the Federal Republic.[3] The Wall grew higher and more grimly fortified and the barrier became almost impossible to cross. As Egon Bahr put it, the sudden appearance of the Wall was 'like a terrible traffic accident' in which the patient wakes up to find one of his legs amputated, but is told by his friends to be grateful that he has not died.[4] West Berlin had not 'died', but it was fading fast. The Hilton Hotel, once filled with western businessmen, was now chronically underbooked, while the elegant tourist shops on the Kurfürstendamm remained empty. Even newspaper correspondents covering stories about further escapes over the Wall complained that the world's gaze had shifted elsewhere – not least to Cuba, which was then at the centre of the missile crisis. Even Konrad Adenauer began to worry that West Berlin would become 'neutralist' unless it was given encouragement from outside, and it was this which prompted him to ask President Kennedy to visit the city.

President Kennedy was not particularly keen to go. He saw the Wall as a monstrous manifestation of Communism, but he also knew that it represented a solution to the instability in Germany. As Arthur Schlesinger Jr put it, the Wall had stopped the flow of East Germans to the west and 'had secured the most immediate Soviet interest in Berlin ... Now the Wall, by achieving [Khrushchev's] minimum objective, released him from the necessity of forcing the issue to a showdown.'[5] In short, the Wall had given the Soviet leader a way out of his declared intention to annex West Berlin and risk nuclear war; it had stabilized the situation between East and West Germany, reduced the risk of a global conflict being sparked off in Berlin and was therefore consistent with the short-term interests of the United States. There has been much criticism of Kennedy's stance: some believed that his refusal to act when the Wall went up was tantamount to a betrayal of a loyal American ally; others, including General Clay, had contemplated tearing the Wall down and challenging the Soviets, who would surely back down. Whatever the merits of his case Kennedy was reluctant to go to the city. He was annoyed by Adenauer's 'alarmist' statements warning of defeatism in West Berlin and was convinced that the German Chancellor was using the crisis as a political weapon against his rival Willy Brandt. Although he was told that West Berliners had been deeply shaken by the erection of the Wall he refused to believe reports that they had been frightened into 'neutralism'.

Kennedy was finally persuaded to go by his own advisers, who warned that the lack of American action was causing Berliners to question US commitment; its image was suffering as a result. Ambassador Dowling told him from Bonn that if there was no overt response to the crisis West Germans might become hostile to the United States and turn eastward; Berliners had suffered a serious crisis of confidence, and if people continued to leave in such high numbers the half-city might collapse from within, which would in turn damage American interests and leave West Berlin open to the Soviets. As if to prove the point a group of West German students sent Kennedy a black umbrella similar to that used by Chamberlain at Munich.[6] After much debate he finally agreed to go.

Kennedy's plane touched down at Tegel Airport on 15 June 1963 to a twenty-one-gun salute and a rapturous welcome. Over three-quarters of the population had turned out on the streets to greet him. The President's motorcade made its way from the airport to the Wall and he made a point of walking through the crowds gathered at Checkpoint Charlie and at the Brandenburg Gate. The East Germans had clearly gone to a great deal of trouble over the presidential visit. For the first time in their short history they had obscured the view down Unter den Linden by unfolding enormous red banners between the columns of the Brandenburg Gate. They had even erected a gigantic sign accusing the United States of violating the Potsdam Agreement and asking: 'When will these pledges be fulfilled in West Germany and West Berlin, President Kennedy?' The encounter at the Wall was followed by a raucous ticker-tape parade, a trip to the Airlift Memorial and then to the Schöneberg Rathaus through hundreds of thousands of cheering, waving Berliners. The most moving tribute of the day was, by contrast, very quiet. When Kennedy climbed on to one of the wooden viewing platforms erected near the Wall he saw a small crowd of East Germans who, notwithstanding the immense danger to themselves, had gathered in a huddled group to salute the American leader. Kennedy was deeply stirred by this courageous gesture and this added poignancy and depth to the words he spoke later that day. His Berlin speech became one of the defining moments of the Cold War:

> There are many people in the world who really don't understand, or say they don't, what is the great issue between the free world and the Communist world. Let them come to Berlin. There are some who say that Communism is the wave of the future. Let them come to Berlin. And there are some who say in Europe and elsewhere we can work with the Communists. Let them come to Berlin. And there are even a few who say that it is true that Communism is an evil system, but it permits us to make economic progress. *Lasst sie nacht Berlin kommen!* Let them come to Berlin![7]

At this point over a million people who had gathered in the square below roared their approval. 'When all are free,' he continued, 'the people of West Berlin can take sober satisfaction in the fact that they were in the front lines for almost two decades.' And finally he uttered the famous words: 'All free men, wherever they may live, are citizens of Berlin and, therefore, as a free man, I take pride in the words *Ich bin ein Berliner!*' Ironically, the phrase was hastily scribbled down after Kennedy had experienced the warmth of the welcome and seen the silent East Germans standing alone beyond the Wall. As a non-German speaker he had had it rewritten phonetically as '*Ish bin ine Bear-LEAN-er!*' The crowd knew nothing of the changes but they were swept along by the emotion of the moment, even speculating that Kennedy's presence might mean that their city would soon be free. The clapping, cheering and yelling went on for over twenty minutes.

The mood inside the Rathaus was much more cynical. Adenauer had been appalled by the 'crowd mentality' of the Berliners and had blurted out to Dean Rusk: 'Does this mean Germany can one day have another Hitler?'[8] Kennedy was also disturbed by his reception and later commented that he feared that, had he told Berliners to go and 'tear down the Wall', they would have done so without question. In order to downplay the impact of his Rathaus speech he made a much less well known, but much calmer speech at the Free University that afternoon, during which he explained that unification would be a difficult and lengthy process. It made little difference. The overall impression of his visit was one of hope and optimism. In a mere eight hours John F. Kennedy had succeeded in boosting morale within the walled city and convincing its inhabitants that they would not be abandoned.

The memory of Kennedy's visit deepened the sadness, when less than half a year later, news came through that he had been assassinated in Dallas. West Berlin went into mourning, with tens of thousands lighting candles and holding public vigils and prayer meetings in his memory; Willy Brandt was invited to the funeral as a guest of honour. But Kennedy's death also heralded a gradual shift in Berliners' attitude towards the United States, and marked the end of the close bond so painstakingly established during the post-war years. Willy Brandt was also poised to make history through his proposal for a new approach to eastern Europe and the Soviet Union: *Ostpolitik*.

As mayor of West Berlin Willy Brandt had been horrified when the Wall went up and had advocated taking stern measures against the GDR. Nevertheless, when it became clear that the Wall would remain indefinitely he began to turn his attention to making life as easy as possible for Berliners. In many ways *Ostpolitik* was motivated by the desire to alleviate the suffering he had seen in the newly divided city. For Brandt, 'barbed wire Sunday' had been an admission of failure by the Communists, which meant that they might be willing to bargain with the west. As Brandt's *Ostpolitik* adviser Egon Bahr put it in his *Wandel durch Annäherung* (Change through Convergence) proposal introduced in 1963, aggression towards East Berlin was only hardening divisions between the two Germanys; the only way forward was to accept the existence of the Wall and gradually to move towards rapprochement. Berlin was to play a central role in this.[9]

Despite its humanitarian aims *Ostpolitik* was controversial from the beginning. It advocated a move away from the safety of Adenauer's Atlanticist policy, which had sought West German acceptance into the western Alliance. *Ostpolitik* shifted that emphasis in favour of new relations with the Soviet Union and the eastern bloc countries. Brandt was not against close links with the west but believed it was time to turn his attention eastward; by dealing with the Soviets he aimed to gain financial, technological and economic help for those trapped in East Germany while negotiating greater security for West Berlin. If Adenauer had used the Berlin crisis to strengthen ties between Bonn and Washington, Brandt wanted to help people in divided Germany and Berlin

– not by talking to the East Germans themselves, but by bargaining with Moscow.[10]

The *Ostpolitik* initiative resulted in the four-power talks, which on 3 September 1971 finalized the Quadripartite Agreement on Berlin, a document which officially recognized the status quo and ended the Cold War Berlin crisis in a single stroke. According to Henry Kissinger, *Ostpolitik* had given the United States the opportunity to end the permanent crisis over Berlin; he was convinced that it had been his insistence on linking *Ostpolitik* to free access to the city which had resulted in the successful agreement of 1972; as a result 'Berlin disappeared from the list of international crisis spots'.[11] For West Berlin the treaty became the single most important symbol of détente, fixing the shape of the city until the Wall fell in 1989. In the rather messy agreement the United States, the Soviet Union, Britain and France agreed that Berlin should officially remain under four-power rule and that earlier accords, including the Potsdam Agreement, should remain in place. This meant that West Berliners continued to be legally subject to draconian post-war laws: they could still be sentenced to death for carrying a kitchen knife. Spandau Prison, with its lone inmate Rudolf Hess, remained under four-power control, and it was forbidden to stop in front of the Soviet War Memorial on the Strasse des 17 Juni as the Soviets claimed that they feared 'molestation by the civil population'. At the local level Berlin retained its 1950 constitution; the Berlin parliament should have had 200 democratically elected members but only 144 seats were occupied as the rest were reserved for 'absent' East Berlin representatives. The parliament was permitted to pass legislation relating to Berlin, and elected the Berlin Senate, which consisted of the governing mayor, a deputy and sixteen senators. In addition each of the twelve West Berlin *Bezirke* or districts had an elected mayor and assembly for the administration of local issues.

For their part the Soviets agreed to allow unimpeded access to and from West Berlin from the Federal Republic and promised to give West Berliners permission to enter both East Berlin and East Germany (the latter had been closed to them since 1961). In return the western Allies agreed that West Berlin would remain under Allied control and would not become an integral part of West Germany. It would be permitted a West German 'liaison agency' and the Federal Republic could represent Berlin internationally but the city could not house any official government offices or host any functions associated with the Chancellor or with Bundestag committees. The result was a rather uneasy balance between the rights of the Allies and the rights of West Germans in West Berlin; Berliners were not West German citizens and could not vote in federal elections, and yet the federal parliament could enact legislation which influenced every aspect of their lives. Furthermore West Berliners had no right of appeal to the Karlsruhe Court, they had to be issued with special passports, and even the West German airline Lufthansa was not permitted to fly into their city.

The new status of West Berlin also had important implications for West Germany. The city remained vulnerable to pressure from East Germany and the Soviet Union, ultimately making West Germany weaker on the world stage. The ever-present Soviet threat and the resulting West German policy of appeasement meant that West German foreign policy was characterized throughout the 1970s and 1980s by a crippling lack of self-confidence.[12]

Ostpolitik was bitterly contested in West Germany, with conservative politicians and activists, including the newspaper magnate Axel Springer, accusing Brandt of selling out to the Communists by recognizing the continued division of Germany and the *de facto* legitimacy of the GDR. Nevertheless *Ostpolitik* did bring immediate benefits to Berliners: on 17 December 1971 Egon Bahr signed a Transit Agreement allowing the movement of traffic and goods between West Berlin and the Federal Republic; on 8 November 1972 East and West Germany signed the 'Basic Treaty' defining their future relationship and outlining areas of co-operation – from traffic and communications to culture and technology. West Berliners could now visit East Berlin for up to thirty days each year, a meagre postal service was restored, a handful of telephone lines were replaced and tensions between the two halves of the walled city eased. But these improvements could not make up for the rift caused by the Wall, and the distance between east and west grew wider with the passage of time as old business links, family ties and personal relationships slowly unravelled. Nearly 4 million West Germans visited the east between 1971 and 1972, but the number was less than 2 million five years later. The number of parcels sent east also dropped dramatically, from over 11 million in 1967 to less than 500,000 in 1980.[13]

By the late 1960s West Berlin had already become something of a quiet backwater. As the German writer Peter Bender wrote in 1981: 'The West Berliners accepted their lot so long as they were important, however much threatened, and so long as they had a clear mission to fulfil on behalf of German unity. Both of these conditions ... disappeared ... after the Wall was built in 1961, and still more since the Four-Power Agreement of 1971.'[14] Many feared that West Berlin would dwindle away. *Ostpolitik* had sought to bring West Berlin closer to the Federal Republic, but by normalizing the situation it had caused the two to drift apart. West Germans now talked about West Berlin as if it was a separate entity somewhere to the east of Helmstedt, and the term 'Federal Republic of Germany' no longer automatically included 'West Berlin' in people's minds. It was now common to talk about the flow of traffic from 'West Berlin to the Federal Republic'. The Cold War symbolism of the beleaguered capital struggling against Soviet oppression had been replaced in West Germany by a certain wariness of the alien half-city to their east. Even the journey from West Germany to West Berlin hindered contact, beginning as it did with long waits at the East German checkpoints, strict instructions to stay on the main Autobahn (failure to do so could result in a seven-year prison sentence for spying), and intimidation from East German police, who stopped western vehicles on the slightest pretext. I was stopped twice for speeding, although fortunately my car was equipped with a device which recorded its speed and proved the charge to be false. Harassment was often more serious: President Jimmy Carter's visit to West Berlin in 1978 was disrupted by sudden long delays on the Autobahn.[15] Train travel was equally unpleasant – the old wagons were often held at the checkpoints for long periods, during which the gruff border guards demanded passports and checked under the seats for stowaways. The sealed windows were a constant reminder that East Germans were forbidden to come near the train. The West Berlin SPD governing mayors were generally mediocre and uninspiring and had nothing to match Willy Brandt's innovative spirit, leading instead to an unhealthy dependency on West German federal subsidies. But West Berlin's problem was more serious than mere bad management. As many of the brightest and best-educated West Berliners left to make careers in the west Berlin began to face a demographic crisis.[16]

By the mid 1970s 15 per cent of the population of 2 million people was under fifteen years of age, while 22 per cent was over sixty-five. The number of pensioners was twice the average in the Federal Republic (many eked out an existence on meagre pensions in squalid pre-war conditions in the poorest districts, far removed from the tourist centres around the Kurfürstendamm), and after 1970 more young people left Berlin than moved in. Projections showed that the population could sink to below 1.7 million by the year 2000.[17] Young professionals only came to the city because they were sent there for a couple of years on a 'hardship posting' to further their career prospects in the west. There were dire warnings about increased unemployment and poverty and some predicted that West Berlin would not survive into the next millennium.

The situation was aggravated by the state of the economy. The uncertainty of the post-war period had made investors nervous and many businesses, including historical Berlin firms like Siemens and AEG, had moved their headquarters to the west; only a few, like the pharmaceutical giant Schering, remained. The Wall stymied production in Berlin not least because all materials had to enter along the expensive and unreliable transit routes, and many traditional industries, such as the manufacture of machines, electrical equipment and garments, continued to dwindle after 1961; the clothing industry employed 80 per cent fewer people in 1984 than it had in 1970.[18] Because of the proximity of East Germany the production of goods with even a marginal military significance was forbidden, hindering the development of the new 'high-tech' industries. Other cities began to outpace Berlin: Frankfurt became the undisputed financial centre of West Germany; Stuttgart of the car industry, Düsseldorf of insurance and advertising; the press were focused in Hamburg, electronics in Bavaria.

By the 1970s the once great economic powerhouse had been reduced to dependency on West German payments to meet its crippling budget deficit, but they kept the city alive. West Berlin now received millions of Deutschmarks in grants. These included payments for the improvement of transport and communications links, such as the Autobahn and the railway through East Germany. Schemes were concocted to lure businesses back to West Berlin: income tax, corporation tax and business tax rates were set at least 30 per cent below those in West Germany; businessmen were given credits for building commercial or industrial enterprises there, while products manufactured in West Germany but assembled in West Berlin benefited from a lower turnover tax so that truck- and bargeloads of nearly finished goods from West Germany were assembled and sent back to the Federal Republic with MADE IN WEST BERLIN stamped on them. The federal government also decreed that internal government orders, such as equipment for the West German postal service, should be manufactured in Berlin whenever possible. Workers were attracted to the city by huge subsidies: moving costs were covered if they agreed to stay for one year or more, and marriage loans were completely written off if the couple had three children in Berlin. During the 1970s over 40 per cent of the city budget was financed by the West German government and 50,000 people were employed in often superfluous jobs in the fifty federal government agencies located in the city. Despite all the assistance, however, the overall picture remained bleak. Capital investment continued to fall, and as late as 1987 15,000 more people were leaving per year than moved to the city. The population decline was hastened by 'Wall fever' – the claustrophobia which struck after people had been locked in the city for too long, heightened by the ever present fear that they might after all become trapped behind the Iron Curtain.[19]

West Berlin was not helped by its growing reputation for radicalism and violence, which began with the student riots of the late 1960s and continued throughout the 1970s and 1980s. Even before the 1971 agreements the city saw an influx of young people keen to study in a city increasingly known for its protest culture. It was perhaps inevitable that West Berlin would attract the most radical of German students in the protest years, and the 'most un-German city in Germany' became a magnet for young people who wanted to leave the 'bourgeois' life of *Wirtschaftswunder* West Germany. Some came to escape the draft, as West Berlin's four-power status meant that young men with a permanent residence certificate were exempt from military service; others were attracted by the rumours of a wild student life and the promise of freedom and counter-culture. West Berlin was a beacon to those who wanted to escape from their parents and from a stifling West Germany, with its narrow materialism and strict social hierarchy. Many students were attracted by the supposedly easy university life. They formed what would later be called the ' '68 generation' – young people who had grown up after the war and were able to enjoy a less rigid, more comfortable existence which was itself a product of the *Wirtschaftswunder* and of Germany's changing role in the international arena. Students were attracted to the *fainéant* atmosphere of West Berlin, making it ideal for long days of sit-ins, protests, riots and 'Happenings'; others survived on welfare and all took advantage of special laws restricting competition, which meant that small shops, cafés or factories producing crafts or health food could function as viable concerns. The main character Johann in Michael Kleeberg's novel *Der saubere Tod* was drawn to Berlin because he knew that within one year he could make enough money to afford a large old Berlin apartment and a sports car: 'One could either sell drugs or oneself. He was prepared for both.'[20] As the movement evolved young people began to reject traditional values and increasingly saw life in terms of confrontation with the existing political order.

The political counter-culture of the 1960s was intrinsically linked to changing perceptions of the United States after the erection of the Wall. For the generation of Berliners who had witnessed the Soviet occupation and lived through the Berlin airlift the Americans were still regarded as the guarantors of freedom, but for younger people that image had been badly damaged by the construction of the Wall. Kennedy's *'Ich bin ein Berliner'* speech might have been hailed as a milestone in history but it had quickly become obvious that the dramatic words would bring little real change.[21] The inaction had led to deep fears that the Americans might not defend the city in a future crisis – despite the fact that the Bonn government paid DM1.3 billion annually to keep the Allied forces in Berlin, that the Americans still kept 6,000 troops in West Berlin along with 3,000 French and 3,500 British personnel, and that the American commitment to the city was never really in doubt. Nevertheless the Americans were increasingly branded as 'occupiers' rather than Allies even though, with the exception of the military parades down the Strasse des 17 Juni to mark the 1953 uprising and the parties and barbecues at Tempelhof Airport or Doughboy City, they kept a low profile and left the running of the city to the elected Senate.[22] But it was precisely the diminution of the imminent Soviet threat as a result of détente and *Ostpolitik* which provided the younger generation with the sense of security in which a protest culture could evolve.[23] The very city which had been saved by the Berlin airlift and was thought of as the most pro-American place in Germany now became the centre of an anti-American storm which would soon sweep across western Europe. The catalyst which sparked off the protest was the Vietnam War.

The war became the 'great cause' of an entire generation.[24] Protests centred at the John F. Kennedy Institute, the Free University and the Technical University began in earnest in West Berlin in 1966, and Amerika Haus, with its library and cultural centre, was under constant siege for nearly a decade.[25] The United States was attacked for waging war, for controlling the world to its own advantage through its multinational corporations, and for dividing the globe between the 'First World' and 'Third World' or between 'north' and 'south'. Berlin became more extreme than any other West German city and by the mid 1960s protests against American (not Soviet) nuclear testing, against the western 'occupation' of Berlin, against 'Coca-Colonization' and against the American 'military industrial complex' had become commonplace.[26] A whole philosophy was evolved to attack western post-war values, and students and pseudo-intellectuals alike spouted various forms of Marxist rhetoric or slavishly followed the teachings of the radical-left Frankfurt School, headed by Max Horkheimer and Theodor Adorno and Karl Mannheim.[27] Some preached that modern civilization was so diseased that no reform could save it and that empiricism and positivism were so tainted that the only hope was 'critical theory', which could delve beyond mere facts to reveal the 'social genesis of knowledge'. At the same time journals published papers attacking all aspects of western capitalist culture and asked, in a twist on the familiar comment about art being impossible after Auschwitz: 'Can poetry be written about Vietnam?'[28] In his journal *Kursbuch* the poet Hans Magnus Enzensberger proclaimed the 'death of literature' in 1968; others decided that they were witnessing the 'death of history' and the 'death of the state'. Students used the Free Speech movement at Berkeley as a model for their own protests and fed off the increasingly hostile student movement in Paris. Milos Forman, the Czech film director, remembered his astonishment when he arrived in the west and found students demonstrating for Marxism at the time of the Prague Spring: 'when we were trying to take the red flag down, they were trying to put it up!' Nevertheless, the stage was set for further unrest.

The conflict which had been simmering in the universities finally erupted throughout West Berlin in April 1967, during a visit by the American Vice-President Hubert Humphrey. His reception could not have been more different from that which had greeted Kennedy only four years earlier. In place of the cheering crowds Berlin streets were filled with student protestors; some brought bags of dry flour to throw at the visitor, which the Springer Press mistakenly reported were bombs from East Germany; others chanted slogans and booed during Humphrey's speech. He left Berlin in disgust.

One month later, on 2 June 1967, the Shah of Iran, Mohammed Reza Pahlevi, and his wife visited the city. The Shah was seen as the epitome of an American-backed dictator and long before his arrival posters had gone up denouncing his visit and calling him ANOTHER HITLER.[29] One mimicked a WANTED poster, describing him as '1.70 metres tall, oval face, wears bullet proof vest under jacket covered with medals. Other distinguishing features: throne, golden telephone, 5,000 man bodyguard, eats from silver plates, has a taster to detect poison'.[30] Before his arrival Kommune 1 sold 10-pfennig stickers of his face which were to be stuck on to paper bags as masks. The next day crowds of demonstrators followed the party through the city, hurling abuse and insults. In the evening they gathered outside the Opera House, where the couple were being taken to see a performance of *The Magic Flute*. When the shah was safely inside the uniformed police officers, plain clothes men and Iranian security guards charged the demonstrators in an attempt to disperse the crowd. The attack backfired. The students refused to move and the police became increasingly heavy handed. When the fight was over forty-seven people had been seriously injured and one student, Benno Ohnesorg, had been killed by a police bullet.

This death radicalized the student movement in West Berlin: it was seized upon by student leaders as proof of the need to fight 'the system' with mass protests.[31] Seventy-one writers, including Günter Grass, signed a statement calling for a parliamentary inquiry into police behaviour but nothing was done. Street violence escalated throughout 1968. On 17 and 18 February over 5,000 students attended a Vietnam congress in the auditorium of the Technical University followed by a mass demonstration against the war, after which 12,000 students marched through the streets. The mood was made more tense by attacks by the Springer Press on the youth leader Rudi Dutschke, founder of the APO or Extra-Parliamentary Opposition Group which rejected western liberal democratic government and called for the overthrow of the Federal Republic in newspapers like the *Berliner Extra Dienst*. Springer labelled Dutschke's group *Radikalinskis*, Communist puppets and East German lackeys.[32] In one story a 'mug shot' of Dutschke was published implying that he was little more than a criminal. In a bizarre twist he was shot in the head as he walked down the Kurfürstendamm in a copy-cat assassination attempt following the Martin Luther King murder. Dutschke was badly wounded and the Springer Press was blamed for having caused the attempted murder with its inflammatory article. Once again the city exploded in ferocious riots and 10,000 policemen were put on the streets. Most had no training in crowd control and treated the demonstrators with undue violence. The students reacted in kind. One CDU spokesman said in despair: 'Stone throwing and stink bombs ... no longer have the peaceful character of a free exchange of ideas.'[33]

The focus of the new wave of attacks was the Springer building. In the early 1960s the tower, constructed within a few metres of the Wall, had been hailed as a symbol of western defiance against the Soviet Union. Now it was said to epitomize all the evils of modern society. On one occasion crowds of protesters gathered outside; some began to push past the barbed wire and the guards surrounding the building and set fires in the garages while others littered the streets with ripped copies of the *Morgenpost*. Over 400 people were arrested and 200 were injured, but the protests continued. By the end of 1968 things had become so anarchic that the *Spiegel* asked whether the world might not actually be witnessing the beginnings of a revolution akin to that of 1918.

The '1968 generation' had another focus for protest: the universities themselves and the older generation – universally labelled 'Nazis' irrespective of their pasts. German universities had been notoriously stuffy before the war and little had changed after 1945. They were over-hierarchical and ill-equipped to meet the demands of students in a modern, western democratic state, and it is true that some professors had managed to keep good jobs despite having been compromised during the Nazi period. One such example was Professor Werner Heyde, who had been a medical director of the euthanasia programme during the war. Although captured in 1945 he had escaped from prison and in 1947 purchased false identity papers on the black market in the name of 'Fritz Sawade'. As an experienced doctor he had set himself up as a sports physician and would have continued to practise had his wife – annoyed by the snubs of the spouses of other professors – not blurted out at a party: 'Don't you know who I am? I am not just a mere Frau Doktor, but, just so you know, Frau Professor Heyde!' Her husband was captured and committed suicide in 1964.[34] However, the students did not differentiate – all members of the older generation were instantly branded; on 7 November 1968 Beate Klarsfeld publicly slapped Chancellor Kiesinger on the face because he had been a member of the Nazi Party.[35]

Many professors retained a sense of superiority over the students, and when the latter began to agitate for change they were often dismissed out of hand. And there were grounds for change. The student population had grown exponentially during the post-war period and the student–teacher ratio was now so high so that some students never actually met their professors in person. Much of the teaching had been devolved to young and inexperienced *Assistenten*, who often joined students in the call to replace large lectures with smaller seminars. The students wanted a new governing body, dividing

responsibility between professors, academic staff and students, but these proposals were summarily dismissed by professors, who felt that their authority
was being challenged. When the older faculty members of the Free University
refused even to discuss the issues raised by Ohnesorge's death the campus
erupted in violence. A plethora of groups went on the attack, occupying offices,
disrupting lectures, throwing rubbish at professors and holding strikes in the
corridors. The campus was smothered in Vietcong, Ho Chi Minh and Che
Guevara banners and academic life ground to a halt. Again, all professors
were called 'Nazis', irrespective of their backgrounds, and student leaders
encouraged their followers to fight these 'fascists in modern form'. As the
extremist leader Gudrun Ensslin put it: 'This fascist state is organized to kill
us all. We must organize resistance. Violence can only be answered with
violence. They are the generation of Auschwitz – there is no point trying to
argue with them.'[36]

As the rift between the generations grew some groups began to preach
that mere protest was not enough and that only violence could destroy the
'Nazi Federal Republic'. The view was espoused by fringe organizations like
the K-Gruppen and the Autonome, Marxist-Leninist-Maoist groups whose
members advocated random violence and resistance to all forms of authority.
It has since been learned that many of the groups were financed and supported
by the East German or Soviet regime. Many of these ideas were published in
the infamous journal Konkret, edited by a young woman who was determined
to expose the evils of West German society. Her name was Ulrike Meinhof.[37]

Meinhof was profoundly shaped by her experiences in 1960s Berlin.
Although born in Jena she had moved to West Berlin in 1967 after divorcing
her publisher husband Klaus Rainer Röhl. From her rooms in the Kufsteiner
Strasse she wrote dozens of articles attacking all aspects of West German
government and politics; during the Shah's visit to Berlin she issued a searing
attack in the form of an open letter to his wife.[38] It was in these rooms in
West Berlin that Meinhof and a group of like-minded friends planned the
escape of another activist, Andreas Baader, who was being held at Tegel Prison
at the time. Meinhof's career as a terrorist began on 14 May 1970, when she,
Irene Goergens and three others donned wigs and hid guns in their briefcases.
They approached the detention centre, opened fire and freed Baader, killing
an innocent bystander in the process. The two now founded their terrorist
group known as the Red Army Faction, which issued the infamous 'Concept
City Guerrilla' Manifesto.[39] This outlined how they would set about destroying
West German society by whatever means necessary, including murder. The
allusion to the Royal Air Force (RAF) was deliberate; if the British had bombed
Germany from above, they argued, they could now explode it from within
by setting fire to the symbols of modern West Germany and by bombing

everything from military bases to government offices. In June 1970 Meinhof went to Jordan to undergo arms training and returned to West Berlin in August in order to oversee a spate of bank robberies. There followed a number of bombings at US army headquarters throughout Germany, the bombing of the Springer Press building in Hamburg, and increasingly violent attacks on a number of important West Germans. In 1972 a related group '2 Juni' kidnapped the West Berlin mayoral candidate Peter Lorenz, who was released only after imprisoned terrorists were freed and flown to South Yemen. The violence reached its peak in 1977. In April that year the head of public prosecution, Sigfried Buback, was shot dead. In June the chairman of the board of the Dresdner Bank, Jürgen Ponto, was murdered. In September the president of the West German Association of Employers, Hans-Martin Schleyer, was kidnapped in an attempt to blackmail the government into releasing 'comrades' then in prison. On 13 October a group of Palestinian terrorists hijacked a Lufthansa plane and held the passengers hostage in Mogadishu. The German government did not cave in but sent an elite unit of German border police who were advised by the SAS and who staged a spectacular rescue of the passengers; most of the hostages were killed. Sadly, Hans-Martin Schleyer was found murdered the next day.[40] Between 1970 and 1979 the RAF murdered twenty-nine innocent people in cold blood; they wounded ninety-three others and took a total of 162 people hostage. Ulrike Meinhof, who had been captured by West German police, committed suicide at the Stammheim maximum-security jail on 9 May 1976. She was buried in the Church of the Holy Trinity in Mariendorf, West Berlin. Four thousand West Berliners attended her funeral.

The RAF had a strong following amongst university radicals in the early years and spawned a number of deeply pessimistic Romantic anarchist groups, who tried to emulate its philosophy, if not its terrorism. By 1976, however, most student activists had become increasingly disgusted with the murders and mindless violence perpetrated by the group.[41] The mood at universities was changing. Students were fed up with the disruptions to their education. For their part the universities had tried to reach a compromise. As of 1969 the Free University decided that both its senate and the faculty boards should be made up in three equal parts of professors, junior lecturers and assistants, and students.[42] In reality the solution was unworkable. The Free University and the Technical University continued to decline; academic standards hit rock bottom and degrees from Berlin lost their credibility abroad. Further protest was also quashed by the *Radikalenerlass* or Radicals' Decree introduced by Willy Brandt in 1971. In this highly controversial move designed to curb student extremism he stipulated that young people would not be accepted by the civil service if they engaged in activities deemed anti-constitutional. Many students realized that they were jeopardizing their career prospects by engaging in protests at a time when the economic situation in Germany was changing and jobs were becoming more difficult to find.[43] The politicized movements of the 1968 generation began to disintegrate. Some activists advocated a 'long march through the institutions', particularly the SPD itself.[44] In other respects the '68ers' gave way to the new Ratlose Generation or 'lost generation', which was less overtly political and became increasingly concerned with universal causes ranging from feminism to nuclear energy and disarmament. The Alternative movement, the forerunner of the German Greens, had its roots in 1970s West Berlin.[45]

The counter-culture which developed in West Berlin in the 1970s made it a much more complex and interesting city than its bland West German counterparts. By the time I lived there the city contained a huge assortment of punks and gays, intellectuals and artists, communes and anarchist groups like the *Spontis*, who lived in self-contained ghettos shielded from the rest of the world. The city attracted artists and writers, playwrights and sculptors, who hung around alternative cafés and clubs discussing Walter Benjamin, going to the latest 'Happening' or listening to anarchic punk bands. The city often gave the impression of being caught in a time warp – rather like those little islands off the west coast of Canada settled by Americans who fled the Vietnam draft in the 1960s, where pottery wheels and the Grateful Dead are still *de rigueur*. The most interesting of the 'new lifestyles' sprang up around the Berlin communes known as *Wohngemeinschaften* or WGs. These were often located in derelict buildings or abandoned factories like the Merinhof. Typically they contained a collection of co-operatives, a health food depot, a crèche, workshops, artists' studios and small record or book stores. The ones I visited always struck me as being friendly, tolerant places, although amenities like private bathrooms or running hot water were considered unnecessary luxuries. One commune member described the life as decadent and carefree, with people moving in or out at will:

> The WG changed its members and the form of their relationships over time ... Most changes were provoked by heterosexual couples who wanted to move into private apartments. They were always replaced by singles, mostly students. The WG was large enough to offer a room to visiting guests ... Sexual partners, both male and female, were brought into the WG and members often had sex with each other, either in the context of an intensified relationship or in an orgy ...[46]

Dozens of these communities sprang up in the poorer districts of Berlin and they began to cause problems for the Berlin Senate. As the housing shortage grew worse, ever more young people became squatters. Attempts to stop the illegal settlements sparked off waves of protest and the streets became the setting for more violence. These housing riots were damaging to a city only just recovering from the turmoil of the late 1960s.

Squatting is common in all western industrial cities, but it was particularly prevalent in West Berlin in the late 1970s and early 1980s, when the shortage of cheap housing was acute. This was in part a consequence of the war-time destruction and the loss of the city's hinterland after the building of the Wall, but it was aggravated by a financial policy aimed at attracting investment. Immense tax write-offs encouraged speculators to buy old buildings and allow them to deteriorate; they would then have to be ripped down and replaced with expensive apartment or office blocks.[47] Not only did this deprive Berliners of cheap housing; it also meant that many historic buildings – of which there were precious few left – were systematically destroyed. Berlin activists began to identify derelict buildings and moved in as squatters. The first to be taken over was the Bethanien Hospital, a large complex which had survived the war but which was scheduled for demolition. Appeals to the housing authorities to save it had failed but the squatters refused to move. By the end of 1981 over 150 buildings in Kreuzberg and other areas were occupied by people claiming the right to domicile in their *Kietz* – a term originally applied to the small fishing villages in which the Wends had lived.[48] Clashes erupted, first with the property owners, and then with the police. The Berlin Senate had a legal obligation to protect the rights of landlords and retaliated by threatening the squatters – initially with fines and then with arrest. Most still refused to move. The situation became increasingly tense; around 80,000 people were looking for somewhere to live and many turned to the squats.[49] The new groups began to dig in for a fight, fortifying houses and even entire city blocks. The violence which had been simmering for months finally broke out towards the end of 1980. On 12 December the police tried to stop a group of squatters from occupying a house at the Kottbus Gate; as they moved in hundreds of young people charged at them. A lengthy battle ensued and over twenty people were arrested. That night the protesters demanded the immediate release of all those who had been put in prison or they would 'torch Berlin'. Their demands were ignored, and the city exploded.

The protesters decided not to remain in their own neighbourhoods but to move to the very heart of 'capitalist' West Berlin – the tourist and shopping area around the Kurfürstendamm. Thousands of young people gathered in the West End and rampaged through the city during Christmas week. Cars were overturned and set on fire, glass cases and windows were smashed, shops were looted and landmarks from the Gedächtniskirche to the Ka De We and the Café Kranzler were vandalized. Thirty-six people were arrested and 200 wounded but the riots persisted, moving back to Kreuzberg and Wedding in the New Year. The situation deteriorated over the following months; over 12,000 policemen were needed to patrol the streets and in the dozens of brawls which followed over 700 people were arrested; one was killed.

The escalation of violence caused a serious problem for the Senate and the city. Business confidence had only just started to return after the protests of the late 1960s but as television pictures of turbulent West Berlin flashed across the Federal Republic investment dropped again: businessmen claimed that they were afraid to put money into place where private property was not safe and where anarchy seemed to rule. Tourist numbers also dropped drastically. The Senate realized that something had to be done.

The government recognized that there was a serious housing shortage in the city and began to discuss options with the leaders of the protest movement. In the end squatters were given leases on apartments they had seized and even allowances to cover the cost of improvements made to the properties.[50] Landlords protested, but Berlin's sub-culture saw it as a stunning victory. Many of the smaller groups now merged into a coalition called the Alternative List (AL), which was set to become a political force in West Berlin.[51] Its offshoot, the Green Party, would mimic this success in the Federal Republic.

The rise of the Alternative List represented a clear shift away from the issues which had occupied the '68 generation towards a new agenda and a new approach to politics. The AL were still anti-nuclear but they also sought to create a new kind of society and a new grassroots approach to politics; increasingly they saw their responsibility as being to the 'planet' and to 'nature'. The AL and the early Green groups which evolved from it rejected the structures of industrial society, rejected the division of labour, rejected traditional patterns of work, rejected the nuclear family and rejected western democracy. According to their manifesto the word 'alternative' was 'synonymous with love of life and freedom . . . [which] preclude my oppressing others, especially weaker beings' like 'children, subordinates, wage-earners, women, disabled, old people and animals'. They embraced environmental protection, disarmament and greater social control over the means of production. Traditional Marxism was rejected in favour of an alternative society in a world which was over-industrialized and unhealthy, a new emphasis epitomized by Rudolf Bahro's move 'from Red to Green'.[52] The AL called for equality and wealth for all, for a world in which there was a 'classless society devoid of hierarchy, in which the distinctions between town and country, women and men, intellectual and manual work have been removed. There is no state, there are no wars or prisons.' At the same time they remained set against western foreign policy and even in the 1980s it was common to come across demonstrations against America's 'illegal occupation' of Berlin, complete with stink bombs and banners reading NO WAR or AMIS GO HOME.

The utopian project of the Alternative List generated many interesting ideas but by the 1980s these were sometimes being taken to extremes. Great emphasis was put on recycling and conserving energy, on animal rights and on helping the Third World, but the support for 'good causes' such as attempts to reduce factory waste was turned into an attack on all aspects of modern industrial society – from the use of private cars to the production of all industrial goods. Many members tried to recycle waste and grow their own food but it was virtually impossible to be self-sufficient in the centre of urban Berlin and the results were often preposterous. The radical feminists brought the subject of sex discrimination to the public arena, but instead of trying to help women to get better jobs or to juggle family and professional roles the debates often became bogged down in an indecipherable lingo which excluded the very women they were allegedly supporting; the dozens of feminist seminars held by earnest university students did little to support those eking out an existence in menial jobs.[53] There was also a tendency to interfere in the affairs of others if they did not conform to the 'alternative' view of the world; one centre I visited was surrounded by various bins and buckets for the collection of water and other recyclable items; my failure to use the recycled water sparingly enough resulted in a lecture on the importance of the environment; on another occasion I was offered a drink and asked for a cup of coffee, only to be told that many people in the Third World died picking coffee beans and that I should avoid the beverage in future.[54] The most striking thing about the new alternatives was their extraordinary lack of tolerance; in the late 1980s new cars parked outside houses in Kreuzberg were sometimes vandalized because they were considered to be 'too Yuppie'. Nevertheless the Alternative List became increasingly popular; a survey carried out in May 1981 revealed that 65 per cent of West Berliners believed that the Alternative List for Democracy and Preservation would get into parliament. The prediction was right. The Greens won their first victory in the 1980 election with 1.5 per cent of the vote, while the Alternative List won fifteen seats in the 1985 Berlin election.[55]

By 1980 it was estimated that there were over 100,000 people living in the infamous Berlin sub-cultures. Many were benign but there was also a self-destructive streak in the new city.[56] West Berlin became a centre for illegal drugs, with a higher estimated death rate for heroin users than anywhere else in Germany, not least because the East German customs officials allowed contraband in via Schönefeld Airport. Zoo Station became an infamous meeting point of petty criminals, child prostitutes, the homeless, illegal immigrants and teenage drug addicts so memorably portrayed in the harrowing film *Kristiane F.* This did little for Berlin's reputation in West Germany and abroad, and the city was often unfairly portrayed as little more than a dangerous collection of Communists, drug dealers, drop-outs and punks. It was also treated with suspicion because of its other distinguishing feature – the dramatic rise in the Turkish population. Germans are not noted for their acceptance of foreigners, particularly those who are racially different, and when West Berlin became the largest Turkish city in the world after Istanbul it was seen as another reason to avoid Germany's alternative city.

The new Turkish community was one of the most interesting features of 1970s West Berlin but it provoked both admiration and outrage. Many Germans resented the influx and tended to forget that the Turks had been invited into West Berlin to provide cheap labour and to do the menial jobs that locals would no longer deign to do themselves. The history of the so-called *Gastarbeiter* or 'guest workers' in Berlin can be traced to the construction of the Wall; in one night East Germans barred over 50,000 East German *Grenzgänger* from crossing to work in the west. West Berlin had been deprived of its pool of cheap, skilled workers. To ease the severe labour shortage the Federal Republic devised 'recruitment treaties' with a number of countries, including Italy, Spain, Greece, Turkey, Morocco, Portugal, Tunisia, Yugoslavia and, in 1970, South Korea. Over 500 recruitment centres were opened in these countries from 1961 onward. The drive was successful. In the 1950s less than 1 per cent of the population of West Germany was foreign; by 1973 the figure stood at 11.9 per cent.[57] Whereas in 1960 there were almost no foreign workers in West Berlin the numbers had risen to 10 per cent by 1975 and by 1982 every eighth West Berliner had been born abroad. Over half of these – 128,000 – were Turkish.[58]

Berlin likes to project itself as a city in which refugees have always found a safe haven, and indeed the history of the city has been profoundly shaped by immigrants, from the Huguenots to the Jews to Bohemian Protestants to the Polish and eastern German migrants who made up well over half the population in the late nineteenth century. But despite this rich history Berliners have usually been slow to accept newcomers. The French were scorned at first, eminent Jews like Moses Mendelssohn were forced to enter the city by a gate otherwise used for livestock, and in the late nineteenth century bourgeois Berliners were scathing about the Polish and Silesian peasants and *Ost Juden* flooding in from the east. Integration of the Turks proved equally sluggish. The Turkish writer Paul Zahl encountered discrimination when he first arrived and said in disgust that the only difference between West Berlin and Harlem was that instead of 'Niggers' West Berliners had 'Turks, pensioners, workers'.[59] The problems were exacerbated by government policy.

During the first years of immigration Berliners seemed tolerant enough. *Gastarbeiter* were removed from mainstream German society. They lived in isolated mass accommodation, they did menial work and they were seen as a temporary solution to a serious German problem. As long as their status was unambiguous and well defined there was little evidence of overt prejudice.[60] That changed in 1966. In that year a slight downturn in the German economy led to a fundamental shift in the treatment of the Berlin Turks. The situation was exacerbated when the *Bild* newspaper challenged German stereotypes of effortless superiority by claiming that the immigrants actually worked harder than the locals. When the economy went sour, xenophobia and racism began to surface.

The first serious change took place during 1973, when oil prices rocketed, currencies collapsed around the world, and West Germany faced its first serious recession. Unemployment rose from 1 per cent between 1961 and 1973 to 4.8 per cent between 1974 and 1978, not least because of the influx of the so-called 'baby boomers' on to the jobs market.[61] The changes coincided with the increased integration of Turks and other *Gastarbeiter*, who were now immigrants. The German government had not predicted that the people they had accepted as temporary workers would decide to stay, but throughout the 1960s and 70s Turks brought their families to West Berlin in order to settle there permanently. The government attempted to counter this; in 1973 they ruled that firms could only renew employment if no German applied for the job, but as few Germans wanted such menial work the law was hardly relevant.[62]

In short the Berlin Senate had tended to treat the Turks as temporary workers who would not actually settle in Berlin and had ignored the social consequences of the rapid influx of so many people. Little was done to educate Berliners, many of whom were rattled by the sight of tens of thousands of foreigners moving into districts like Neukölln or Kreuzberg. There were numerous incidents of racial abuse on the city streets; people wrote letters to local newspapers complaining about the smells of Turkish food or the strange religious practices going on in their midst. They were particularly upset when the Turks held large and noisy picnics in the normally quiet parks at weekends and it did not help that the majority of the immigrants were not part of the sophisticated elite from Istanbul but peasants from Anatolia who did not understand that tethering sheep on their staircases or slaughtering animals in their flats was simply unacceptable to local residents. It was years before the Senate and Berliners began to appreciate that the Turks were set to become an integral part of West Berlin, and it was only in the late 1970s that the government began to support some cultural initiatives, including projects to help Turkish women often cut off from the outside world, or Turkish children struggling with the German education system.[63] In 1978 the Office for the Integration of Foreign Workers was set up to act on behalf of foreigners. Turkish children were now educated with Germans their own age although they were able to take courses in their parents' language so that they would not lose touch with their own culture. By 1987 over 60 per cent of Turkish

children were finishing secondary school and many had started to outperform
their German peers. A sample of first generation Turkish immigrants taken
in 1988 showed that where 8.8 per cent had been skilled workers the figure
had risen to 23.1 per cent in the next generation; over 11 per cent had obtained
secondary level education.[64]

At the same time the Turks began to change the face of a number of
districts: Turkish businesses and mosques sprang up, a bustling street market
thrived on the Maybachufer on the Landwehr Canal, a Turkish bazaar was
established at the abandoned Bülowstrasse U-Bahn station, and Kreuzberg
became famous as 'little Istanbul'. The Turks contributed to West Berlin
cultural life through *Gastarbeiterliteratur*, which focused on the rewards and
difficulties of being an immigrant in Berlin.[65] One of the most interesting
authors was Aras Ören, who in 1969 moved to Kreuzberg – which had itself
been settled in the nineteenth century by eastern immigrants. For Ören, the
Berlin of their day had been a fast-paced, often terrifying city; now West Berlin
was a mere shadow of its former self, a grey and dreary 'provincial metropolis'.
Berlin, he wrote, was: 'horizon narrow, air polluted, clouds down to the
ground, ugly buildings grey and monstrous, no home and the streets broad
and ordered but without life'.[66] Other writers tried to promote mutual understanding between the two communities: on one occasion Günter Grass
exclaimed that the city needed a minaret, while the Grips Theatre tried to
challenge Berliners' xenophobia through productions like *Linie 1*, a play set
on the Kreuzberg U-Bahn which called for understanding between Turks and
Berliners. Despite these initiatives the acceptance of immigrants was slow and
Turks, Poles, East Germans, Romanians and others tended to stay within their
own communities, partly because of discrimination, but partly by choice: the
Turks fostered separatism, fearful that assimilation might mean the destruction
of their heritage and traditions.

In addition to the 'guest workers' there was a steady flow of illegal immigrants from Pakistan, Sri Lanka and elsewhere who were brought in by the
East Germans; the GDR charged illegal aliens a hefty sum to bring them into
Schönefeld Airport, after which they were quickly bundled into trains and
taken to West Berlin. The western authorities were aware of this traffic but
they could not stop it without setting up border checks at the Wall, thereby
recognizing it as an international boundary. By 1989 there were over 300,000
illegal immigrants in West Berlin. The East German strategy caused much
misery amongst the hapless immigrants pushed over the border at Friedrichstrasse, but it also made life more difficult for those who were there legally.
Tensions between newcomers and native Berliners increased, and unpleasant
examples of overt racial discrimination did little to enhance Berlin's image.
Many West Berliners remained hostile to immigrants, referring to the multi-

cultural city as *Niemandsland* or no man's land; as Amity Shlaes put it, Germans accepted the arrivals warily, and the moment 'foreign four-year-olds crowd their kindergartens or foreign workers fill jobs, citizens react with one phrase: Germany is not an immigration country.'[67] Others tried to play on the exoticism of the areas, bringing tourists to look at the strange settlements in Kreuzberg from the safety of their air-conditioned buses, much like the affluent nineteenth-century Germans who had caught a glimpse of the working-class slums by taking a ride on the new S-Bahn. For many West Germans, however, the transformation of Berlin into a 'city of foreigners' only made it seem more distant from the Federal Republic.

From the first days of the Wall it was clear that West Berlin had lost its dominant economic and political role in Germany. West Berlin needed a new role – one which would attract people and give the city a new international appeal without infringing four-power rule or reviving its old function as capital. The solution was to try to make it a 'world class' city of culture.[68] The next thirty years would see frenetic investment in everything from performance art to architecture. West Berlin would become known as a city 'whose business is culture'.[69]

The first plans were hatched in the spirit of the Cold War only days after the building of the Wall. At the time projects were meant to show the Soviets and the rest of the world that the west still believed in and was willing to invest in the city, and as a result they were highly ambitious. A third 'European' university was to be added to the existing Technical and Free Universities. Dozens of new schools were to be founded, including a secondary school for gifted students, the Deutsches Gymnasium Berlin. West Berlin was to be made into a 'world capital of learning'; the Deutsche Oper was to become a German National Opera to put Bayreuth or Munich to shame; cultural organizations and special bodies were to be set up to attract the best German and foreign artists to its door. But as the west realized that the city was not threatened by immediate collapse or invasion its attention turned to other parts of the world. None of these grandiose schemes was realized, and West Berlin was forced to re-invent itself. One of the points of departure for the creation of a new 'culture city' was to draw on the Golden Twenties, a time when it had been a truly great capital of European culture.

In political and economic terms the Weimar Republic was a disaster locked between the First World War and the rise of the Third Reich, but it was also the centre of a cultural explosion which had attracted some of the most innovative artists of the century. It was this era that Berliners now longed to re-create. By using Weimar as a role model West Berliners could simply focus on restoring cultural richness rather than dealing with more difficult aspects of the past; after all, it was Hitler who had banished Weimar culture from Germany, making it one of the few periods which could be celebrated without fear of appearing nationalistic or *revanchist*. As a result the world of Dix and Dietrich and Fritz Lang and cabaret was sanitized and reduced to a shallow image of the 1920s – purged of unpleasant reminders of the day. Politicians and artists alike now referred to Berlin's past role as the most 'modern city in Europe', the dynamic, vibrant 'Chicago on the Spree', and the word 'metropolis' was used *ad nauseam*.

From 1961 onward money was pumped into West Berlin in an attempt to recapture this lost world. The city was given a German Film and Television Academy, a centre of Comparative Music Studies, the Max Planck Society Institute for Education Research and a new National Gallery. Treasures which had been stored throughout West Germany during the war were returned to its museums – a courageous move at a time when Soviet invasion was still considered a possibility. The city was given a new Academy of Arts, a Kunstamt to promote local artists, and the Berlin College of Art. The Berlin Artists' programme, inaugurated in 1963 by the Ford Foundation and then taken over by the German Academic Exchange Service (DAAD), funded local talent and helped to give Berlin's artists international exposure.[70] Its founders – Joe Slater, later president of the Aspen Institute for Humanistic Studies, and Shepard Stone, who became director of Aspen Berlin – proposed the establishment not only of an artists-in-residence programme but also of an International Institute for Music Studies, the Berlin Literary Colloquium (LCB) and the Berlin Artists' Programme. West Berlin provided generous grants in an attempt to rejuvenate the artistic community, funding the dozens of self-help galleries run by and for artists – Grossgörschen 35, the Block Galleries, Raimund Kummer's Spaces 1979, and the 1/61 Gallery and KulturCentrumKreuzberg (KuKuCK) in Kreuzberg, which became a centre for art and alternative theatre and film. Even the squatters movement influenced the evolution of Berlin's art; Middendorf played rock music and Salomé performed at the Transformer Company, Matala and the Blue Moon clubs in support of the squatters, while projects like the 1978 Büro Berlin and the Charlottenburg Villa Schilla allowed struggling newcomers to meet and work with prominent contemporary artists like Joseph Beuys.[71] It was not long before West Berlin contained more artists than any other German city.

Art in Berlin has always mirrored politics, and the post-Wall period was no exception. The infamous debate 'for' or 'against' abstract art carried out between Karl Höfer and Will Grohmann in 1955 was magnified in the following years, when Berlin's increasing isolation marked a transition from the bleak post-war painting of Werner Heldt or the constructivist prison-like sculptures of Hans Uhlmann to something quite different. The Hochschule für bildene Künste (College of Visual Arts), established by Heinrich Ehmsen and Karl Höfer in 1945, now generated a series of new artistic movements in which many young artists reacted against formalist post-war European painting, particularly *l'art informel* and *tachisme*.[72] Nevertheless, rather than following the humorous, optimistic Pop artists and Nouveau Réalisme Berlin art mirrored life in the melancholy, claustrophobic, disturbed city. This was the beginning of the figurative, socially involved art which became the hallmark of post-war West Berlin.[73] Artists now tried to mirror the tensions arising from the anti-Vietnam protests and campus revolts sweeping the city and, like the students, were politically motivated and highly critical of West German society. Many genuinely believed that the world could be changed through politically relevant art and most of the work of the period contains a revolutionary message reminiscent of the Expressionists of the 1920s. The first significant event of the period took place in November 1961, when two young students at the college, Georg Baselitz and Eugen Schönebeck, published their first manifesto, *Pandämonium*, and organized an exhibition of their work in the Schaperstrasse. The work protested against the stiff academicism and prudishness of West Berlin post-war society, against materialism and the Deutschmark, against the United States, and against the *Wirtschaftswunder*. More specifically it was directed against the modern galleries and dealers who were becoming increasingly powerful in West Germany. Much of the work was considered too provocative, obscene and blasphemous to be displayed in public. Georg Baselitz's explicit paintings like *Die grosse Nacht im Eimer* (The Great Piss-Up), which depicted a young man masturbating his erect penis, and equally explicit *The Naked Man* were labelled obscene and confiscated from the Michael Werner–Benjamin Katz Gallery on the Kurfürstendamm, causing a riotous debate in West Berlin about the borders between 'art' and 'pornography'.[74] Art became increasingly political, and critical realists like Hans-Jürgen Diehl painted sinister images of the 'oppression' of the new West Germany: *Der umfunktionierte Student* (The Dysfunctional Student) shows a young man with square glasses giving a Nazi salute and flanked by the letters POL (probably short for 'Polizei'). Other artists were attracted by the politically charged atmosphere in Berlin; Wolf Vostell came to the city from Cologne in 1971 and influenced the development of political multi-media art. One of his more successful techniques was the mixing of press cuttings and paint as in *Wir waren so ein Art Museumsstück*, which combined images of (among others) the 1953 uprising, the building of the Wall, the Spiegel affair and a woman injured during an anti-American riot into an anti-establishment protest.[75] Such art was supposed to reflect 'experiences, history, humanity and inhumanity' and was to be seen in conjunction with other art forms like video, the performing arts, the 'Fluxus' movement, or politically aware Happenings.

'Fluxism' spread to Berlin from New York in 1964, although its most important characteristic was, as Robert Watts put it, that 'nobody knows what it is'.[76] Nam Jun Paik's *Kill Pop Manifesto* did little to clarify the situation, stating as it did that 'Opera with Aria – is banal; Opera without Aria – is boring; Karajan – is too busy; Callas – is too noisy . . .' One of the most famous performances by Paik and the cellist Charlotte Moorman took place on 15 May 1965: Moorman began to play Paik's *Swan of Toledo* (after Saint-Saëns), stopped halfway through, undressed, climbed into a barrel full of water, and finally clamped her cello between her wet thighs and proceeded to finish the piece.[77] The artists Henning Christiansen and Joseph Beuys were scheduled to give a performance at the Academy of Arts on 27 February 1969 – the day President Nixon secretly decided to visit West Berlin – but the stage was taken over by hecklers furious that the artists had not joined in the protests surrounding Nixon's visit and the accompanying 'police repression'. Christiansen was doused with water and sprayed with foam from fire extinguishers but struggled on to finish his *Sauerkraut Score*, played on a green violin from a music stand draped in pickled cabbage. Fluxus was condemned by the student activists that night as 'just one more instrument of repression in the hands of the ruling class, contributing nothing to the revolutionary cause'. René Block later chided himself for not realizing that 'these students wanted help, not concerts they couldn't understand but advice and assistance from Beuys. They wanted Happenings by artists, but with political purpose and content.'[78]

With the ending of the campus revolts a number of Berlin artists began to reject the notion that their work could actually influence politics. The Happenings and the Fluxus movement were abandoned as passé and Berlin moved into the post-modern world. Frank Dornseif used steel rods to create eerie outlines of figures in space, Raphael Rheinsberg used artefacts dug up from the ruins of bombed Berlin to create fascinating works like *Anhalt Station – Ruin or Temple*, or *Bricks from Condemned Berlin Buildings*, evoking memories of a lost city. His most moving work was *Botschaften*, translated both as 'Embassies' and 'Messages', in which he took photographs of the partially demolished Danish embassy building with its staircases, rails, first-aid kits and notice boards. Amongst the debris he found an issue of *Der Angriff* dated 19 September 1939, with the headline THE FÜHRER TO SPEAK AT 5:00 TODAY, and the file card of a Polish Jew whose name had been crossed out.[79] Critical realists like Peter Sorge and Klaus Vogelgesang now concentrated on the 'new issues' of the environment and nuclear energy, tracing the hideousness of childhood, adulthood and old age in the polluted, crime- and drug-ridden city. The most interesting of the new generation were the Berlin neo-Expressionists, including Rainer Fetting, Helmut Middendorf, Salomé and Bernd Zimmer, who co-founded the Galerie am Moritzplatz in Kreuzberg in 1977, a group which came to be known as the Neue Wilden – the new rebels – artists who had moved away from political activism into a world where the city and its tortuous history became a subject in itself.[80] They painted hard-edged city scenes of contemporary culture – discos and rock concerts, drag queens and desolate ruined architecture, lines of cars and lonely drug addicts. Helmut Middendorf's *Grossstadteingeborene II* (Born in the Big City) depicted the hard, aggressive, vibrant colours of nightlife in a Berlin disco; Dieter Hacker's 1984 *Gestapo* showed the ominous mound of rubble which covered the old secret police headquarters in West Berlin being passed by a sinister dark car in a scene reminiscent of a classic *film noir*. Salomé's *Self-Portrait*, which shows the artist naked except for vibrant make-up, high heels, stockings and bright red panties, with his legs ringed with barbed wire, became a Berlin icon. Non-figurative painting also emerged as a vibrant medium and artists like Fred Thieler openly attacked the politics of the past with his motto 'you cannot live with ideologies'; his student ter Hell captured the mood of his generation in his 1980 white canvas with '*Ich Bin's*' (It's Me) smeared across it in bright blood red reminiscent of graffiti on the Berlin Wall. A number of expressionists, including K. H. Hödicke, Markus Lüpertz and Bernd Koberling, helped found the Grossgörschen 35 Gallery, and Hödicke, originally a follower of Baselitz, emerged as the foremost painter of the city of Berlin. From his gallery near the Wall between Potsdamer Platz and the Anhalter Bahnhof he looked out over the devastated wasteland which had once been the city centre. His paintings questioned Berlin history. The 1977 *Kunstgewerbemuseum* depicts a dark, eerie landscape which juxtaposes the nineteenth-century Martin-Gropius-Bau with Göring's Air Ministry, bathed in the unnatural red light of the East German television tower; his *War Ministry* is a bleak depiction of a grim, soulless edifice, while in *Nocturne* (1983) the city of Berlin is itself shown as a large, cat-like beast stalking the dark streets and about to devour a car.[81]

Despite the plethora of artists who lived and worked in the city the West Berlin art world was a strange mixture of the exciting and the provincial. In any given year one could attend dozens of gallery openings from the tiny backroom squats in Kreuzberg to the Galerie René Block and the vast, white, spot-lit rooms in the West End, where the chain-smoking, black-clad cognoscenti admired everything from synchronized television screens showing shoddy pornography to bad copies of Beuys's work made out of lumps of fat and faeces.[82] The problem was that despite all this activity precious little work came up to the standard of the Neue Wilden or the critical realists, but because of the generous financial help and the 'laid back' attitude of the city virtually anybody could call him- or herself an 'artist'. The high level of patronage made it much easier for the talented to survive but it also sustained mediocrity;

many international critics dismissed much of the work done in West Berlin as self-important nonsense.[83] Even an extraordinary figure like Wolf Vostell wore the patience of some when he insisted on covering massive objects with concrete and lead. Dieter Hacker's first show in his own gallery, the 7. Produzentengalerie, was aptly called 'Everybody Could Be His Own Artist'. His reproduction of a George Stubbs painting was accompanied by the text: 'Art must claw to the neck of the bourgeois as the lion does at the horse', which was meant to be a 'comment on the tensions between bourgeois society's expectations of art and art's expectations of society'.[84] It was perhaps not surprising that the main exhibition and art-dealing centres remained firmly in Cologne and Düsseldorf, and for all the attempts to make West Berlin a world-class artistic community it was Munich which remained the undisputed centre of painting and sculpture.[85]

Painting was not the only art form to have suffered. Writers and playwrights were given large subsidies by the Ford Foundation and other bodies such as the LCB – the Berlin Literary Colloquium – but the attempt to recreate a time when Brecht, Mann, Döblin and hundreds of others lived within a few blocks of one another failed to produce any truly great works. Few writers came to Berlin. It was a new period of federalism, de-centralization and regionalism in Germany and the great post-war West German writers, poets and playwrights were dotted all around the country. This was exemplified by Gruppe 47, a loose discussion group founded by Hans Werner Richter and Alfred Andersch after the war which counted luminaries like Heinrich Böll, Siegfried Lenz, Gerd Kaiser, Wolfgang Hildesheimer, Günter Grass and the formidable critic Marcel Reich-Ranicki amongst its members.[86] The purpose of the group was to resurrect German literature and one of the recurrent themes was the need to examine the ways in which Nazism had changed people's lives. The writers tended to concentrate on regions they knew well: Böll wrote about Cologne in works like *The Clown*; Siegfried Lenz showed how a family in Schleswig was affected by dogmatic National Socialism in *The German Lesson*; Walter Kempowski wrote about the effect of Nazism in Rostock. The only great writer of that generation who worked in Berlin was Günter Grass, who had moved there in the 1960s. Grass wrote some works about the city, including the poem *Gleisdreieck* and the condemnation of Bertolt Brecht in *The Plebeians Rehearse an Uprising*, but the focus of his work remained Gdańsk and his best works, including *The Tin Drum*, were set there. If writers like Böll, Grass and Enzensberger had done little to resurrect Berlin as a centre of literature, their successors fared little better. The new 'experimental writers' like Robert Schnell, Günter Bruno and Rolf Hauf were dismissed by Grass as 'a chorus of small letter writers'.[87] During the 1960s and 1970s many foreign writers, such as Eugène Ionesco, John Dos Passos, Max Frisch and

Emmett Williams, came for a few months and Berlin became home to a handful of foreign-born writers, including Aras Ören and the Lebanese author Jusuf Naoum, who created *Gastarbeiterliteratur*, but as a whole the literary life was disappointing. As the novelist Robert Scholz pointed out, the city had a well organized literary life, but no organic one.[88]

Music was also heavily subsidized. The Berlin Philharmonic flourished under the egocentric maestro Herbert von Karajan, who took over in 1953 and forged it into one of the best orchestras in the world, while other groups from the Radio Symphony Orchestra to the Kreuzberg String Quartet ranked amongst the best in Germany. Some composers, including Igor Stravinsky, John Cage, Steven Reich and Krzysztof Penderecki, came as guests of the International Institute for Music Studies, but few stayed for long. The American composer Morton Feldman felt that his residence in Berlin was the most productive year of his life, not least because so much had been 'commissioned by various German radio and festival organizations'.[89] West Berlin excelled in some areas, particularly theatre. The outstanding and highly political Schaubühne was founded in the heyday of the 1960s and was later dominated by the daring and innovative Peter Stein, while the Grips Theatre staged productions from *Peer Gynt* to *Linie 1* and revived contemporary theatre. The city funded international concerts and festivals, and attracted performing artists and eminent soloists from around the world. Nevertheless it was clear that Berlin could not easily recover from the cultural decimation of the Nazi period when its greatest composers, artists and writers had been either forced into exile or murdered. Generous subsidies and exchange programmes helped to heal the wounds but even these were not always appreciated and many local Berlin artists attacked the influx of foreign artists, particularly as they were funded by the Americans. As Karl Ruhrberg put it, 'a latent anti-Americanism exacerbated by the Vietnam War had to be overcome, along with the suspicion that not cultural import but cultural imperialism, abetted by monstrous dollar-transfusions, was at the bottom of it all'.[90] Clearly not all shared Berlin critic Heinz Ohff's view of foreign talent that 'In the last analysis, artificially created rainfall is just as valuable as natural rain.'[91]

Berlin was also left out of the great post-war surge in film-making, a particularly harsh blow after the dominance of its cinema during the Weimar period. There were many attempts to revive the industry; the Deutsch Film-und Fernsehakademie (DFFB) was established in 1965 and nurtured the careers of a number of independent *Neues Kino* (New Cinema) film-makers from Clara Burckner, Regina Ziegler, Klaus Volkenborn and Ursula Ludwig. The documentary Chronos-Film and Journal-Film companies had access to private archives of historical footage and were responsible for films like Helga Reidemeister's 1987 *DrehOrt Berlin* (Film Location Berlin), which recorded aspects

of life on both sides of the Wall. The Filmförderung or Film Assistance Programme backed a number of projects, including Christian Ziewer's 1971 *Liebe
Mutter, mir geht es gut* (Dear Mother, I Am Well) about a group of cur-
mudgeonly Berlin workers, Ulrike Ottinger's 1970 *Bildnis einer Trinkerin* (Picture of a Woman Drinker), which follows a beautiful *haute couture*-clad lady
as she moves through Berlin determined to kill herself, Manfred Stelzer's 1985
Geschichten aus zwölf und einem Jahr (Tales of Twelve and One Years), which
tells the story of the Berlin squats at the Bethanien Hospital, and Helma
Sanders-Brahms's 1986 *Laputa* about the reunion of two lovers – one from
Warsaw and the other from Paris – in the transit city of West Berlin. But few
of these or any of the other hundreds of films produced in Berlin had any
real impact outside Germany.[92] The problem was due more to the quality of
the work than to a general shortage of German talent: 1960s and 1970s West
Germany produced a number of eminent directors, including Werner Herzog,
Edgar Reitz, Rainer Werner Fassbinder, Wim Wenders and Volker Schlöndorff,
but none were from Berlin: Herzog and Fassbinder were Bavarians; Reitz came
from the Hunsrück, an area made famous in his provocative film *Heimat*, and
Wenders was born in Düsseldorf. Only a handful of successful films had Berlin
as a subject, although they included works like Margarethe von Trotta's *The
Patience of Rosa L.* about Luxemburg's turbulent life during the revolution of
1919, *Stadt der verlorenen Seelen – Berlin Blues* (City of Lost Souls – Berlin
Blues) by Rosa von Praunheim (born Holger Mischwitsky), which went some
way to capturing a sense of the alternative lifestyle of drag artists in the 1980s
city, Fassbinder's overly long version of Döblin's *Berlin Alexanderplatz*, and
Wim Wenders's *Himmel über Berlin* (Wings of Desire), a touching portrayal
of isolation in the modern city.[93] Even so, most of the prizes awarded to
Germans at the annual Berlin Film Festival went to works produced in the
new German centre of film: Munich.[94]

Of all the art forms it was architecture which best reflected Berlin's desperate and failed attempt to create an identity after the construction of the
Wall. The bombed and shelled city was a pastiche of destroyed landscapes and
the Wall added to this by creating bleak new zones cut off from their previous
functions. The new border devastated city planning and architecture in West
Berlin; not only did it cut across its network of streets and U-Bahns but all
plans for the redevelopment of the city centre were put on hold. Ironically
this was perhaps the only positive consequence of the Wall, for it put a stop
to the destruction of the old city centre at a time when modernist skyscrapers
were at the height of architectural fashion.[95]

In the late 1950s Hans Scharoun and Berlin modernist architects had
mapped out a new future for the centre of Berlin – a 'new city' extending the
modernism of the 1920s to the post-war world. Despite the fact that Scharoun

had appealed to Otto Grotewohl to preserve the Berlin Schloss in 1946 the architects tended to see old ruins as something of a nuisance. Thankfully the construction of the Wall cut their building site in two. Nevertheless it still left great swathes of land to the west of the Wall open for redevelopment.

Few Berliners are aware of the scale of the original plans. The architects oversaw the destruction of dozens of salvageable old buildings, levelling what remained of old streets, neighbourhoods and landmarks which might have been saved in order to build the new 'Culture Forum'.[96] In many ways this development became a metaphor for West Berlin. It was impressive but always seemed out of place, stuck incongruously on an empty wasteland in the shadow of the Wall. Scharoun's daring buildings impressed fellow architects and critics alike but there was no infrastructure to support them or to soften their edges; people would drive to see Karajan at the Philharmonie and then drive home again. There were no houses or cafés or shops, and the development remained pristine and lifeless.

The buildings themselves remain Berlin landmarks. Scharoun's distinctive gold-coloured Philharmonic Hall was completed in 1963 and was quickly heralded as Berlin's greatest building. It was followed in 1967 by the massive Scharoun and Wisniewski Staatsbibliothek, by Mies van der Rohe's acclaimed 1968 National Gallery, which had in fact been designed for but never used by the Bacardi Rum Company in Cuba, and by the Kammermusikhall or chamber music hall, also by Scharoun and Wisniewski and done in the style of the Philharmonie. To be fair it was not Scharoun's fault that the area remained so barren: further development was to be delayed until Berlin was finally unified.[97] As a result, vast stretches of windswept land, once at the heart of the city, remained in ruins, untouched since the clean-up after the Second World War. I always found this one of the most interesting parts of the city. Few people ever went there, and one could walk around the abandoned gardens and fallen buildings and still find pieces of china or other remnants of old houses lying in the sand. There were startling reminders of the war hidden amongst the trees, from the ruin of Freisler's People's Court to the grandiose Japanese and Italian embassies built in the prestigious Tiergarten when those countries were Germany's closest allies, to the remains of the once great Hotel Esplanade on Bellevuestrasse. Unlike other West German cities Berlin had not yet been able to paper over its past; the scars of history were still visible in forgotten corners and desolate areas by the Wall as they were not in the pristine glass- and chrome-covered world which had taken over in western cities like Düsseldorf or Cologne.

With the old city centre still in ruins and further development around the Culture Forum prohibited, West Berlin was forced to shift its focus firmly to the West End. Of all the buildings which rose up in the 1960s only one

truly captured the imagination of the walled city: the Kaiser Wilhelm Gedächtniskirche. Many had called for the demolition of this burnt-out, jagged ruin
after the war but in 1961 the city government decided to turn it into a monument to peace. It became the new symbol of West Berlin.

The huge structure was dramatic as it stood, but the architect Egon Eier-
mann was hired to design five free-standing buildings to encircle the ruin.
These included two large towers on either side made of dark coloured glass
encased in honeycomb windows, which Berliners unceremoniously referred
to as the 'lipstick' and 'powder puff'; although they now look dated they did
capture the spirit of the time and were said to represent the 'new rising from
the old', the 'triumph of peace over war', the 'hope of the future of West
Berlin'. The strange memorial was situated in the heart of West Berlin's Kurfürstendamm shopping district and the juxtaposition of the massive old building
and the new towers surrounded by rows of featureless concrete and glass shops
and offices remained a poignant reminder of what West Berlin had lost in the
war.[98]

The memorial church was only one of many projects designed to boost
confidence in the city. In the first years after 1961 investment in West Berlin
had dropped sharply and there were fears that developers had left for good.
It was thanks to the generous tax breaks and the foresight of a number
of speculators and businessmen that a handful of vast developments were
constructed in the early 1960s. These became Berlin landmarks not because
they were beautiful – which they were not – but because they symbolized hope
in the future: if investors risked their money in West Berlin, perhaps others
could afford to follow. Of all these the most important was the Europa Centre,
built on a derelict bomb site just off the Kurfürstendamm, where the most
famous of Berlin cafés, the Romanischen, had once stood. The architects
Helmut Hentrich and Herbert Petschnigg were commissioned to design the
86-metre-high office building with an adjoining area filled with shops, restaurants and cafés. An enormous blue and white Mercedes star was erected
on the roof, ensuring that it would be clearly visible from East Berlin.

Other major developments followed in the wake of the Europa Centre.
The Springer Press high-rise was built hard against the Wall in the heart of
the old newspaper district, while a number of new office buildings were built
around the Kurfürstendamm. These buildings represented the future, and
Berliners were grateful for the investment. Nevertheless, the result was a collection of utilitarian and uninspiring lumps of concrete and glass dotted incongruously across some of Berlin's most historic ground. Eyesores like the
eighteen-storey Excelsior project near the Anhalter Bahnhof, built on the site
of one of Berlin's grand old railway hotels, epitomized the worst of 1970s
architecture in which planners made no attempt to fit their projects into

the old environment. The television centre for Senders Freies Berlin on the Theodor-Heuss-Platz towered above its surroundings; the residential complex on Schalengenbader Strasse consisted of an apartment house fifteen storeys high and a quarter of a mile long which dwarfed neighbouring houses and was so massive that it began to sink shortly after it was finished; Ral Shüler and Ursula Schüler-Wittes built a gigantic International Congress Centre between 1975 and 1979, which cost DM1,000 million and, with its silver anodised skin and huge metal body-within-a-body, looked like something out of *Star Trek*. Some Berliners began to resent the continued destruction of their heritage and protested against the wanton levelling of old Berlin in the name of 'modernism'. One of the most vocal was the publisher Wolf Jobst Siedler, who was so infuriated by the 1964 decision to go ahead with Gropius's hideous Märkisches Viertel, with its rows of concrete tower blocks, that he wrote a book called *Die gemordete Stadt* (The Assassinated City) in which he accused modern urban planners of the premeditated murder of Berlin.[99] Siedler made a poignant comparison between the old city and the modernist nightmare rising from its ashes, criticizing arrogant modern architects who had the audacity to rip apart buildings which had formed part of the historic city. The book was widely lambasted when it was published but by the 1980s many of the views had become accepted. The change came, at least in part, from an unlikely source: the Greens.

Urban renewal in West Berlin was born in the wake of the student protests, when young people had campaigned to save old houses and neighbourhoods from being torn down. Young architects took up the challenge and began to develop ways of integrating old buildings into a modern city setting. The West Berlin pioneer was the young architect Hardt-Waltherr Hämer, who lobbied to save old rental barracks and then transformed them by knocking down some of the oppressive back walls and adding new balconies, bathrooms and kitchens. The first model development was a group of salvaged houses on Putbusser Strasse in Wedding, which was completed in 1972 to great acclaim; its success led to dozens of similar projects like the Klausenerplatz in Charlottenburg, the Mariannenplatz in Kreuzberg, the Brunnenstrasse in Wedding and the area around the Nollendorfplatz in Schöneberg. By the 1980s this post-modernist mixture of old and new styles was going up everywhere: the International Bauausstellung (Architecture Exhibition) of 1984–7 rejected the previous model of the 1955 modernist Hansaviertel project and concentrated instead of renovating existing buildings in Kreuzberg; even the new structures built in the Tiergarten were not imposed on the landscape but echoed features of the pre-war villas which they were replacing. Now, old buildings were saved wherever possible. Ecological concerns began to creep into new designs; the Ökohaus was constructed from renewable resources; larger projects like the

PEP plant, designed to remove hydrophosphates from water, broke away from the ugly prefabricated factory style of the past and became attractive structures which nestled into the countryside. New apartment blocks like the 1988 project at Tegel Harbour brought housing down to a human scale; university buildings like the Gaudiesque Philosophical Institute in Dahlem broke from the rigid modern style and introduced frivolous cast-iron and glass work into the design. Sadly, the change came too late.[100] Much of West Berlin had already been destroyed and covered by concrete boxes so that, even with the new buildings, it looked shabby and uninspiring; its lack of continuity, its need for a real core and the instability of its post-war role were plain for all to see. The derelict Kaiser Wilhelm Gedächtniskirche might have been a powerful monument, but it was a strangely disjointed and depressing symbol in a city trying to appear confident and progressive. In reality, architecture revealed West Berlin for what it was; a provincial half-city isolated from its hinterland. It was likened to a patient in a coma, being kept alive only by the vital blood transfusions pumped in from the west – a place which was vulnerable and isolated, and lacked a real sense of identity.

This provincial atmosphere was evident to anyone who had spent time in Paris, New York or London, or had visited the thriving cities of Asia in the 1980s. Berliners wanted theirs to be a great and dynamic metropolis but such things cannot merely be created at will; all the investment in art, new architecture and shopping streets could not hide the fact that the city could not even begin to compete with its great rivals. The Polish writer and dramatist Witold Gombrowicz wrote in his diary that this 'liquidated place cries out for some novelty, on a grand scale ... But there's nothing but the telephone, activities, automobiles, offices and work, only this spider's web, spreading, all-encompassing ... here, mundanity and triviality are demonic.'[101] In some ways West Berliners were their own worst enemy; how could their city be a *Weltstadt* when its shops usually closed at 1 p.m. on Saturdays; when punks and drug addicts lined up for their social security cheques in front of neat offices, and when artists were paid in hard cash to bribe them to stay in the city and live a Bohemian lifestyle. When visitors came they did not search out the monuments or the museums or the shops. To Berliners' chagrin they came to see one thing: the Wall.

In the 1980s the Berlin Wall was the city's greatest attraction. Tourists flocked to the Brandenburg Gate in their thousands to stare at the 12-foot cement sides covered in graffiti and colourful murals and topped by the rounded tube to stop easterners from climbing over or throwing grapple hooks from the other side. After the obligatory photographs they would trek to the Haus am Checkpoint Charlie, which documented the history of escapes over the Wall, climb the platforms to stare over at East Berlin and try to catch a glimpse of the derelict Potsdamer Platz and the little mound of earth which was all that remained above ground of the Chancellery and Hitler's bunker.[102] The more adventurous trundled on a two-hour bus tour of East Berlin, which took in the Soviet War Memorial at Treptow Park and the Museum Island. Most tourists felt they had 'done' Berlin in three days.

West Berliners now ignored the Wall altogether and were baffled by the tourist interest. The majority lived very much like citizens of any ordinary West German town, enjoying the parks and forests, the lakes and pleasant suburbs on the outskirts of the city. In short, the city had settled down into a kind of dull provincialism punctuated by a much hyped, but not very interesting sub-culture.

By the 1980s the campus upheavals and the most violent squatter and anti-nuclear riots were over and the new CDU government entered into a fresh spirit of co-operation with the Alternatives, remaining critical of many of their ideas but willing to accept 'cultural input' from the radical fringe. The 1983 federal election saw the CDU under Helmut Kohl confirmed in power. Kohl's economic *Wende* or 'turning point' was to bring cuts in the civil service, deregulation and limited privatization – although it was not comparable to the Thatcherite revolution, not least because of the desire to retain low inflation and low unemployment.[103] Kohl brought a general increase in business confidence in the Federal Republic which spread to West Berlin. Both he and President Richard von Weizsäcker were dedicated to keeping West Berlin alive and persisted with Brandt's *Ostpolitik* in the hope of increasing contact with East Germany and further improving the life of those in West Berlin. Ironically this increased assistance to the GDR put West Berlin in a very difficult position.

Ostpolitik and the 'change through convergence' approach had led to some improvements in the quality of life in the divided city. The general acceptance of the status quo had reduced tensions and led to numerous agreements between the opposing blocs. Amongst other things the Soviets agreed to supply West Germany with natural gas via a spur line to West Berlin; they reopened the Teltow Canal, which had been closed to trading ships since 1945; they allowed West Berlin transport authorities to finally take over the S-Bahn system, which the Soviets had controlled since the war; transit routes between West Germany and West Berlin were improved, and Richard von Weizsäcker became the first governing mayor of West Berlin to meet Erich Honecker. By the 1980s, however, the costs of the policy were outweighing the benefits. *Ostpolitik* had originally been designed to bring the two Germanys closer together and in the early years it had been successful. But by the 1980s it was having the opposite effect. The policy had become not only redundant, but counter-productive.

Ostpolitik failed because of the misguided belief that East Germany was reformable. The theory of 'change through convergence' had been based on the assumption that increasing grants to the GDR would make the east more dependent on the west, would increase ties between Germans, and would make the GDR regime more susceptible to pressure from the west. The opposite now happened. The money pouring into the GDR did not make Erich Honecker more liberal in his outlook; indeed, he became more oppressive and reinforced the ideological battle lines between the two halves of Germany. It was ironic that, the less flexible he became, the more money he received from the west. The West German practitioners of *Ostpolitik* had lost sight of its original aim. The policy was failing, but nobody had the foresight or the courage to stop it.

The failure was important on a number of levels. First, it was expensive. The East German government appeared to make concessions to the west but in fact extracted a heavy price for the most trivial agreements. The GDR took 4 million cubic metres of rubbish annually from West Berlin but charged the city DM1.5 billion for the service; it treated West Berlin sewage and turned it into fertilizer but charged DM12 million; its population was told that pollution controls and other services had improved but in reality the West German taxpayers had paid for the changes. Second, the policy brought no improvement in the GDR's attitude to West Berlin. The SED continued to claim that West Berlin was a part of the GDR, continued to allow drugs and illegal immigrants across the border and continued to harass commuters on the transit routes. But, worst of all, the money from the west allowed Honecker to tighten the stranglehold over his own people.

The transfer of money to the east began to stimulate an invidious trade in human beings across the East–West Berlin border for East German profit. The original motive of the West Germans was clear: in the early years the Soviets and East Germans had treated political prisoners with Stalinist severity. Thousands had been killed or had vanished and many more had been given long prison sentences for alleged espionage or crimes against the state. The methods had become less brutal after Stalin's death but the state network of surveillance and prosecution meant that thousands of people were still arrested and imprisoned each year for real or imaginary crimes. During the 1960s the West Germans had started bargaining with the GDR to buy these people out; by the 1980s it was common practice.

The trade was facilitated by the East German lawyer Wolfgang Vogel, who for years lived a luxurious life on a small estate south of Berlin financed by these transactions. Vogel was one of Erich Honecker's confidants and represented East Germany in most of its high-profile 'humanitarian dealings'. His initial clients were the Cold War spies like the U-2 surveillance pilot Francis Gary Powers, who in 1962 became the first of many to be exchanged over the Glienicke Bridge, the infamous 'spy bridge' which later appeared in so many thrillers about the city. Vogel was involved in most of the important swaps after 1962; it was he who helped to organize the exchange of the British citizen Greville Wynne for the KGB agent Gordon Lonsdale and he was involved in the liberation of Anatoly Sharansky in February 1986, the first exchange to be filmed for the general public. Using the international spy swaps as a model he negotiated the trade of civilians and political prisoners between East and West Berlin. In the 1980s between 1,000 and 2,000 people were being released from East German prisons each year for between DM 90,000 and DM 100,000 per person. In all the trade cost Bonn around DM 400 million every year.[104] The GDR ransomed over 34,000 prisoners in a business which netted East Berlin over DM 1 billion. Vogel presented himself as a great humanitarian, but he was a loyal East German to the end; even when people were trying to escape to Prague following the opening of the Hungarian border in 1989 he could be seen amongst the crowds of refugees, trying to persuade them to return to the GDR. Markus Wolf recently stated that the 'most lucrative source of hard currency' for the GDR was the secret sale of its own citizens – a total of 215,000 people, for around DM 3.4 billion.[105]

In reality the policy of buying out dissidents became incompatible with the original aims of 'change through convergence'. What had begun as a humanitarian mission was now a self-perpetuating trade which did nothing to hasten change but propped up the status quo; West Germany bought dissidents out, and the East Germans simply arrested more. By giving Vogel money for prisoners the West Germans were essentially helping to finance the East German state and the Stasi. They did not seem to understand that draining East Germany of 'troublesome dissidents' only helped Honecker to rid himself of the very men and women who wanted fundamental change in the GDR. Many of East Germany's would-be reformers objected to the policy, knowing that they would be powerless to affect events in the GDR once they had been brought to the west, but the Bonn government refused to listen. Change in the GDR, the West Germans believed, could not be affected by these 'little people' but must come from above. Opponents to the SED were treated with more suspicion than members of the East German government itself.

Dissidents represented 'trouble' precisely because they threatened to disturb the carefully balanced policy towards the east – and in particular towards Moscow. It was for this reason that West Germans reacted so badly to the Solidarity movement in Poland; Helmut Schmidt continued to back the Jaruzelski government even when it engaged in the brutal oppression of Solidarity for fear that the equilibrium of *Ostpolitik* might be threatened. Rather than encourage the dissidents ministers in Bonn spoke of their fear of another Prague Spring, of potential streams of refugees trying to enter Germany, or of the danger of possible Soviet interference which might damage their step-by-step approach to German-German rapprochement. Those policy-makers who advocated 'keeping order at all costs' still wanted to see their nation unified but believed it could only be accomplished over a long period of time. They were wrong. East and West Germany would never have 'come together' if the Communists had remained in power in East Germany. The advocates of *Ostpolitik* were blind to the implacability of the SED and the Stasi.[106]

The desperate attempts to maintain the status quo in east–west relations were only too obvious in 1980s West Berlin. The Wall might have been a good backdrop for speeches during the Cold War but the era of détente had resulted in a muffled silence about the realities of life in the GDR. Even after the Helsinki Process of 1975 the West Germans veered further away from the original aims of *Ostpolitik* and closer to simple appeasement of the Soviet Union and its German ally, which meant avoiding hard-hitting criticism of any kind. The extraordinary blind spot to East German oppression continued in 1987: the co-operation declared between the SED and the SPD led to extraordinary moves – the SED was called a 'partner for peace', and SED and SPD historians met and were welcomed by Willy Brandt.[107] I always found it shocking when returning from East Berlin to realize how little West Berliners knew about what was happening to Germans just a few metres away. This persistent silence about the ghastly aspects of the GDR only bolstered Honecker's self-confidence, and he continued to treat West Berlin as his hostage, extracting high fees for every service and exerting pressure on West Germany not to publicly support dissidents in the GDR.

It would have been interesting to see what might have happened had the West Germans suddenly refused to continue with this insidious arrangement and demanded real changes for their money. It might indeed have had an effect. After a burst of growth in the 1970s the economy of the GDR had declined rapidly. By 1989 it had accumulated a debt of over $20 billion. The economy remained backward, there was little investment in industry, the entire system remained hobbled by inefficient central planning methods, and the GDR would have been highly vulnerable to economic pressure. But West Germans avoided demands for reform. The extent of the decline in the east was ignored. Honecker continued to publish exaggerated statistics about the economic performance of the GDR and bogus trade figures fooled many 'experts' in the west.

West Berlin was affected in other ways by this appeasement. While the walled city struggled for recognition East Berlin was able to present itself as an important capital city which overshadowed its western counterpart. Indeed East Berlin still looked and felt much more like a historic capital than West Berlin. It contained the historic city centre, the grand old museums, the massive cathedral, the Schinkel buildings and the spectacular Unter den Linden. Unlike West Berlin it had retained its function as a capital with administrative buildings, government offices, embassies and party headquarters, and it was still backed by nineteen Soviet divisions and by the East German military and Stasi. Its Marxist-Leninist philosophy allowed museum curators and historians to promulgate a self-righteous, propagandistic version of its history: not only could they gloss over the Nazi period but they also used the Prussian past to bolster a militaristic image. East Berlin was the show window of the eastern bloc and attracted tourists not just from Dresden and Leipzig, but from all Warsaw Pact countries. No expense was spared in the attempt to create an important centre which could both intimidate and outshine West Berlin. Both sides were locked in a competition over their identities but in the 1980s it seemed as if East Berlin was winning.

This competition had become increasingly intense after the construction of the Wall but it exploded into an open battle during the extraordinary celebrations to commemorate the 750th anniversary of the city in 1987, one of the most bizarre events ever to be held there. It was the largest historical festival ever held simultaneously in East and West Germany and saw the two parts of the same city competing over a common history, like two halves of one brain. The event became a tug-of-war between opposing sides for the right to show 'their' Berlin as the 'true' historical city.

The 750th celebrations had been discussed in West Berlin as early as 1984, in conjunction with the planning of a new museum of German history, a Deutsches Historische Museum, which was to go up near the Wall. From the day of its inception this giant 'Mammutmuseum' was the subject of heated debate; some accused Chancellor Kohl of ignoring the more difficult areas of history – in particular the Nazi past – in an attempt to create a sense of national pride and to counter East German claims to be the sole representative of all that was positive in German history.[108] It soon became clear that the museum would not be completed before 1987 and the city decided to mount temporary historical celebrations instead. At first the West Berliners hoped to involve East Germany in the scheme but Erich Honecker declared that the GDR would hold its own event and quickly published his nine historical *Theses*, which rejected West Berlin's role and restated his own hard-line Marxist-Leninist view of the past. As a result, the celebrations turned into out and out rivalry. Each half financed hundreds of displays, exhibitions, seminars, publications, cultural programmes, international visits, symposia and myriad other events throughout the year; both Germanys spent millions of marks on their separate events.[109] Erich Honecker was determined to present his half of the city as 'the true Berlin', calling it 'a city of progress, of history and of peace'. Workmen and restoration crews were brought in from all over the GDR to rebuild vast areas of the old city; the Nikolaiviertel alone was reconstructed at a cost of DM 400 million.

West Germany took the celebrations equally seriously, spending over DM 220 million on exhibitions alone. It also funded a substantial building programme. If East Berlin was a 'German capital', West Berlin was to be portrayed as a *Weltstadt* and an 'international centre of culture'; visitors that year included the Queen of England, Prince Charles and Princess Diana, President Mitterrand and President Reagan. As Helmet Kohl put it on 1 May 1987: 'Berlin was always a centre of German history and German culture, an *Umschlagplatz* for new ideas, a high mountain of creativity.' He added that 'Berlin is and remains a world city. This pulsating metropolis thrives today . . . it is full of atmosphere in which the traditional and modern meet.'[110] The exhibitions and cultural events in West Berlin were as impressive as those in the east and ranged from an extraordinary series of concerts to dozen of exhibitions examining aspects of Berlin history or culture.

Despite the displays, however, the West Berlin celebrations were marked by deep divisions on the symbolism of West Berlin and the way in which its controversial history should be portrayed. Unlike East Germans, whose view of history was limited to the official Marxist-Leninist line, West Germans could debate their past. The 750th celebrations soon turned into a squabble over the meaning of German history and identity. To further complicate matters they took place in the wake of the *Historikerstreit*, a peculiarly German historical debate which raged around the question of the uniqueness of Nazi crimes. The debate was sparked off on 6 June 1986, when the controversial historian Ernst Nolte wrote an article entitled 'The Past that Will Not Go Away' in the *Frankfurter Allgemeine Zeitung*, in which he argued that the mass murder of Jews should be put into historical perspective and claimed that Nazi atrocities 'lose their uniqueness against the larger record of the twentieth century'. Nolte's new book *Der europäische Bürgerkrieg 1945. Nationalsozialismus und Bolschewismus* (1987) compared Nazi genocide to Stalin's Gulag system and raised the question of whether there had been a '*kausaler Nexus*' in Hitler's mind between his and Stalin's crimes of mass murder. The view was controversial for many reasons, not least because it was feared that it might lead to a denial of the German people's collective responsibility for the Holocaust. A fierce debate erupted: Nolte was vehemently attacked in *Die Zeit* by Jürgen Habermas, who accused him of apologist tendencies and for defending the crimes of Auschwitz. Sadly the debate degenerated into a long-drawn-out battle between opposing factions and the very important questions raised about German national identity and the Nazi past were buried beneath sweeping condemnations and petty insults. In the end little new research or historical material emerged from these discussions but they further divided an already fractious group of historians. An uneasy truce was reached thanks, in part, to President Richard von Weizsäcker's speech on the fortieth anniversary of the Federal Republic, in which he stated, 'Auschwitz remains unique. It was perpetrated by Germans in the name of Germany. This truth is immutable and will not be forgotten.'[111]

The *Historikerstreit* was still raging when Berlin began to prepare for its 750th celebrations, splitting organizers into mutually antagonistic groups. As a result the presentation of history in West Berlin reflected not only the conflict with East Germany, but also the deep problems faced by West Germans attempting to come to terms with their past; as the composer György Ligeti put it, 'Two walls run through Berlin but only one of them is visible. The other is a time-wall, comprising the years 1933 to 1945.'[112] The problem of the Nazi past had as much to do with the future as it did with history, and represented nothing less than a fight over Berlin's identity and what the city should or should not stand for in the future.

While East Berlin basked in the security of its capital city status, West Berliners struggled to find a *raison d'être*, a sense of place in the future Germany. This went beyond the mere writing of history. Some were vehemently opposed to hints of nationalism, objecting to any references to Berlin as a national capital; others hankered after a distant past when Berlin had been at the centre of the Wilhelmine world. When *Stern* magazine asked leading politicians what they believed Berlin would look like in fifty years' time Eberhard Diepgen, the CDU governing mayor, said that he hoped his children would see a free and unified Berlin but that in the meantime Berlin must remain a cosmopolitan city: 'Berlin is and will remain the most extraordinary city in Europe, a metropolis with a human face.' Walther Momper, the SDP leader, saw the city as a 'double city in which there are two different social systems which cooperate on friendly terms, a bridge between East and West touristically, economically, scientifically and culturally'. Wolfgang Wieland, the leader of the Alternative List, said, 'We will not be celebrating in the manner of the cheap boasting bragging *Renomiershow* of this 750th Anniversary; Berlin will be a Greenzone.' These divisions were echoed throughout Berlin society. The publisher Wolf Jobst Siedler, who had served on Helmut Kohl's historical Committee of Experts in the 1980s, said that it was time to look to the future and to learn to appreciate the past. For him, Berlin had reached great heights after the First World War, when it became 'the spiritual capital of Europe', attracting everyone from

Giraudoux and Gide from Paris, Isherwood and Auden from London,
refugees from Petrograd and Moscow ... today Berlin must learn
from this example; it must remember the spiritual energy of those
years and not dwell on the negative things ... for decades Berlin
has searched for a new role, first the city was a bulwark [against
Communism], then a show window, then a dividing point. It must
look to its modern tradition to find its future.[113]

Rudolph J. Springer saw Berlin as 'self evidently the only German world city'
and hoped it would be celebrated as such.

In the main, conservatives tended towards the view that the history of
Berlin must not be seen solely in terms of the Nazi period and that young
Germans should be taught a more balanced approach to their past. Richard
von Weizsäcker put this view most sensibly when he stated that young Germans
'want to know and have to know who they are, where they come from and
who the others are with whom they are to shape and share this world ... For
their own lives they need an answer to the question of where we [their parents
and grandparents] were [between 1933 and 1945], what we did, what responsibility we assumed, and what responsibility we very much failed to live up
to.'[114] The study of history offered an opportunity for Germans to 'find themselves again' and, as Michael Stürmer put it, history could help them appreciate
'the identity of the German in the middle of Europe'.[115] Berlin's past was not
to be shown as an endless catalogue of mistakes and crimes but should also
contain those positive things which might help to make the city strong for
the future and to create a 'measure of patriotism', increasing, not diminishing,
the commitment to the floundering city.

The conservative view was challenged by social historians, who were critical
of conventional approaches to history and argued that one could not 'celebrate'
the past if one was serious about explaining the Nazi period. They tended to
focus on more critical historical exhibitions such as *Topographie des Terrors*
headed by Reinhard Rürup, an important exposé of the role of the SS headquarters in Berlin, or the most comprehensive exhibition of the year, *Berlin/
Berlin*, held in the recently restored Martin-Gropius-Bau, which presented an
even-handed view of all aspects of the past, including Berlin's role in the
Holocaust.

Berlin's Alternatives disagreed with the very concept of the 750th celebrations and in early 1987 the Alternative List Faction awarded Eberhard Diepgen
the *Grossen Gummi-Bären-Orden* (Great Jelly Bear Order) and criticized the
exhibitions for hankering after a dangerous dream to 'resurrect the lost function of a capital city'. For them, as for many in Berlin's alternative community,
the celebrations were a waste of time and money. The city had nothing to

celebrate, not least because 'the metropolitan character of Berlin is found only in its mass unemployment, its new poverty, and the corruption inherent in the present system'.[116] Throughout 1987 debates raged between those who believed that the history of West Berlin was so disgraceful that it should not be celebrated at all, and those who wanted to ignore the most difficult aspects of the past and make the anniversary into a joyful occasion. The divisions were reflected in the exhibitions. The Alternatives and Greens were highly critical of all official installations: exhibitors were missing the global issues of peace, the environment and disarmament, they said; there was too much history and not enough attention to contemporary problems like women's rights or racism. As one AL member put it, 'What kind of a city is this anyhow, in which tens of thousands can no longer find their birthplace today, because it has been torn down? What kind of a city is this in which one builds one museum after another, in order to show what one has lost?'[117] At the extremes there were fringe groups ranging from proto-Fascist skinheads, who wanted to deport all foreigners, to pro-Communists who advocated tearing down the Wall so that West Berlin could join the GDR.

Partly as a result of this in-fighting the variety of displays was immense – a veritable explosion of history and debate which was in itself the best advertisement for the western system, contrasting as it did with the stale, sanitized history being peddled in the east. Some exhibitions focused on medieval or Prussian history; others, like the *Topographie des Terrors* and the *Inszenierung der Macht*, looked at aspects of the Nazi period; others concentrated on positive aspects of Berlin history – *Die Reise nach Berlin* described the city's importance to the history of European travel but downplayed its central role in the transport system of the Third Reich. Not surprisingly in the 'city of culture', many concentrated on the positive influences of Weimar film, painting and sculpture on the modern technology of the 'German metropolis'.

The maze of interpretations of the past might have reflected West Berlin's democratic spirit and its post-war tolerance, but when the celebrations came to an end the city seemed no closer to understanding what it actually stood for. Even its role as 'European City of Culture' in 1988 did little to dispel the lingering sense of insecurity there. West Berlin had overcome the crisis of the construction of the Wall and had avoided complete collapse, but it had also become a strange, isolated place and, unlike smug East Berlin, lacked a proper place in the world. In 1988 there seemed no end in sight to this unhappy state of affairs. Many hoped that Communism might one day collapse and that Berlin might eventually be unified but few believed that they would actually walk freely under the Brandenburg Gate in the foreseeable future. By 1988, I had lived in and visited Berlin regularly for five years, but although I often looked at the Wall and hoped it would somehow vanish I never really believed I would be there to see it chipped away to nothing. And yet within one year the Berlin Wall would be gone and the city would once again be reinstated as the capital of a united Germany. East and West Berlin were about to disappear for ever.

XVIII

The New Capital

We all grow old – but who grows wise?
(*Faust*, Part II, Act 2)

FROM THE CHAOS OF WEIMAR to the violence of the Second World War and from the Soviet occupation to the building of the Wall, twentieth-century Berlin came to stand for a city tormented by its own history. All that changed in 1989. Within a few short months Berlin was engulfed in the sudden but peaceful revolution which brought about the demise of the Soviet system in eastern Europe. The most enduring symbol of that sweeping change – the image which has come to represent the end of the Cold War – was the sudden rupture of the Berlin Wall on 9 November 1989. The news astonished the world. Few of us who were there or who saw the television pictures of young Berliners rushing past the border guards to touch the forbidden western soil could have failed to be moved by the sheer outpouring of joy. Within hours the city's image had been transformed from one evoking grim repression to one which stood for hope and freedom. Today, in the bright new shopping district in the refurbished Friedrichstrasse, visitors cannot miss the Haus der Demokratie which has been opened as a reminder of the brave dissidents who rose up against the East German regime in 1989. Berlin is now portrayed as a hotbed of resistance against the authority of the Communist regime, leading East Germans to freedom and democracy. And yet behind the photographs and the breathless accounts and the new 'official' versions of that momentous evening there was another story to tell. Of all East German cities it was Berlin which would benefit most from the momentous events that year. The problem was that Berliners initially did very little to bring them about. The latest myths place Berlin at the centre of the demise of the German Democratic Republic and the collapse of Communism. The truth is very different.

A disappointed Lenin said that Berliners were incapable of sustaining a revolution, and despite the rebellious and anti-authoritarian image presented in endless tourist guidebooks Berliners have for centuries proved themselves to be, at best, politically naive. This was true of both East and West Berlin in the decade leading to the fall of the Wall. East Berlin in the 1980s was a bastion of proto-Stalinism and the most staunch advocate of 'real-existing socialism' outside Russia. It was not a great centre of dissidence; on the contrary it was the powerhouse of the party hierarchy, the Stasi, and many others who were dependent on the state for their special privileges.[1] It was they who had most to lose from change. Despite the courage of those dissidents in East Berlin, it was the people of Leipzig and Dresden who led the way in the Revolution of 1989.[2] The situation in West Berlin was even less auspicious. Although there was a cross-section of opinion in the western city, it had become known for its vocal protests against NATO and American policies even though they ultimately led to the breaching of the Wall. Until the very end the Berlin left continued to call for 'co-operation' and 'reconciliation' with the existing authorities in the Communist east and to oppose 'troublesome' dissidents in Poland and Czechoslovakia.[3] Instead of backing the western Alliance its representatives demanded nuclear disarmament, the recognition of the division of Germany, and closer links with the Honecker regime. If the political decisions leading to 1989 had rested with such Berliners the Wall would not have come down that year. In short, Berlin was freed because of the courage and the foresight of others. The destruction of the Wall was not simply a local event or even a European one; it was brought about by the changing relationship between the Soviet Union and the United States, and it is to this – not to Berlin mythology – that one must turn to understand the events of 1989.

By the 1970s the Berlin Wall seemed to most people like a permanent fixture on the map of Europe and the division of the world into superpower blocs seemed immutable. West Germany had continued to pursue its policy of *Ostpolitik* while American supported détente. But it had become clear that the American policy was not fulfilling its aims. For all the discussions and arms control agreements between the superpowers there had been no sign of Soviet retrenchment in the 1970s; on the contrary, the USSR had increased its defence expenditure by around 5 per cent per annum and had maintained its aggressive ideological stance, particularly against the Americans. Richard Pipes has pointed out that

> Détente was based on very faulty premises from the beginning. And that was the notion of building bridges to the Soviet system. They [the Soviets] always repeated that détente was irreversible. In other words, that we had to acquiesce in the kind of regime they were and in their conquests. The notion that through accommodation we can change them was faulty. To change them you needed a very hardline policy.[4]

In short, the détente of the 1970s had benefited the Soviets much more than it had the United States.[5] Far from becoming more co-operative towards the west they had become increasingly aggressive – a fact which was illustrated in 1977 when they suddenly deployed the SS-20 nuclear missiles with warheads targeted on western Europe, and again in 1979 when they invaded Afghanistan. This shattered any illusions the Americans might have had about détente. It also had serious implications for West Germany and for Berlin.

Until 1977 the Americans had enjoyed superiority in tactical battlefield nuclear weapons in Europe, although they had remained vastly inferior in conventional weapons. When the Soviets introduced the SS-20s to replace the outmoded SS-4s and SS-5s they gained a lead in both conventional and nuclear forces, leaving western Europe in a highly vulnerable position.[6] At the International Institute for Strategic Studies in London in 1977 the German Chancellor Helmut Schmidt asked NATO to take action against the new Soviet missiles, and it was decided that 108 1,800-km Pershing II ballistic missiles and 464 2,500-km cruise missiles should be stationed in West Germany if arms limitation talks with the Soviets failed.[7] The talks were already underway when Reagan became President on 4 November 1980.

At that time the US military had been in decline for nearly a decade. According to Caspar Weinberger, President Reagan's Defense Secretary from 1981 to 1987, the new administration was stunned by its relative weakness: 'When we took office in January of 1981, I believe the President – I certainly – was absolutely astounded at this gap that actually existed when we got our classified briefings. And it was growing in every way.'[8] Reagan set about changing this. He was determined to reverse the decline which had set in after the Vietnam War and, amongst other things, promised to deploy the cruise and Pershing II missiles in western Europe. The first German casualty was the man deemed responsible for the NATO decision there – Helmut Schmidt.[9]

The left wing of the Social Democratic Party was opposed to the new weapons and a group, including Egon Bahr, Oskar Lafontaine, Kärsten Voigt and Andreas von Bülow, spearheaded a move for a vote of no confidence against Schmidt.[10] The Chancellor lost and on 1 October 1982 his centre-left coalition government was disbanded. Schmidt was ousted from power.[11] Ironically, the SPD had opened the way for the Christian Democrat Helmut Kohl, and his accession to power marked the beginning of *Die Wende*, a new conservative approach in West German politics which would mirror changes taking place in the United States and Britain. Kohl's victory coincided with the decision to deploy the missiles in Germany. This in turn sparked the anti-nuclear peace movement which dominated the agenda in West Germany throughout the early 1980s. The anti-American demonstrations, marches and peace rallies now became one of the most pervasive features of West Berlin life.

For the Reagan administration the siting of the missiles in western Europe in 1983 was only one aspect of an overall policy. To the disgust of peace activists everywhere Reagan was determined to take a firm stand against the Soviets. Cold War rhetoric reappeared, the Soviet Union was branded an 'evil empire' and Reagan predicted that Communism would eventually collapse. The American Assistant Secretary of Defense between 1981 and 1987 observed that Reagan 'understood intuitively that the root of the Soviet problem, from the point of view of the Soviet leadership, was a lack of legitimacy in that society. They governed by force, by repressive measures; they would never have survived in an open election. And he understood that if you chipped away at that legitimacy, it would weaken the empire and, perhaps, even bring about its demise.'[12] One of Reagan's most controversial projects was the Strategic Defense Initiative or SDI, better known to the world as 'Star Wars', which was announced in March 1983. The importance of SDI was twofold. Its first aim was to create a system which would explode incoming ICBMs before they reached American soil: this would render them obsolete and, moreover, it meant that if the United States was attacked all-out nuclear war was no longer the only option. The secondary, although ultimately more significant aim was to stretch the Soviet economy to breaking point in its bid to copy such an advanced 'high tech' system. In the end the Americans failed to develop an effective anti-nuclear 'umbrella' but the very threat of SDI forced the Soviets to become more conciliatory.[13] The SDI initiative was severely criticized in both East and West Berlin and Ronald Reagan was portrayed as a dangerous radical.[14] At the same time, however, the Soviets were watching developments in the United States with increasing alarm. It was providential that the new American approach coincided with the death of General Secretary Konstantin Chernenko and the appointment of a new leader. The man chosen as CPSU General Secretary was only fifty-four years old, the youngest General Secretary since Stalin. His name was Mikhail Gorbachev.

When Gorbachev first came to power he seemed as tough as his predecessors, but he soon proved himself to be a dynamic and innovative leader. He was the first post-war Soviet leader to realize that for all its military hardware the Soviet Union had not kept up with the west and that if it did not change quickly its superpower status would be undermined. For him the Soviet system was fatally flawed. West Berlin hailed him as a great liberal reformer; in reality he was a Leninist, first because he believed in the supremacy of the Communist Party and the right of that party to govern the Soviet Union – his strategic goal was the maintenance of the one-party state, which should simply function better – and, secondly, because like Lenin he understood the need for tactical compromise. He was fully aware of the threat posed by American technical advancement and was willing to try a drastically new approach in order to improve the situation. It was for this reason that he introduced *perestroika* and *glasnost*, ultimately releasing a force which he could not control.[15] *Glasnost* meant the right to say the unsayable; it was not comparable to the freedom of speech enjoyed in western democracies but nevertheless represented a vast step forward for the USSR. Coupled with this was *perestroika*, or economic reform, which was an attempt to undo the damage done by the centrally planned economy and to make the Soviet Union a more dynamic and competitive place.[16] The dramatic reforms in Russia had a foreign policy angle as well. Gorbachev wanted to drive a wedge between western Europe and the United States. The offer of a 'common European home' coupled with the seemingly generous offers of arms reduction announced on 12 March 1985 appealed to those in West Germany already ill-disposed towards America. Germany began to divide into two opposing groups with different reactions to Gorbachev: those who believed that the Soviet Union was no longer a military threat, and those still wary of the vast empire to the east.[17]

The conservatives under Helmut Kohl belonged to the second category. They believed that the main threat to peace since 1945 had been the USSR and that a lasting peace depended on military power and the will to stand up to the Soviets from a position of strength. Kohl did not wish to abandon the Atlantic Alliance for some vague belief in Soviet goodwill and he was adamant that de-nuclearizing West German defence would leave western Europe open to a conventional attack by superior Soviet forces. After the 1986 Reykjavik Summit, in which Reagan and Gorbachev came close to removing all nuclear weapons in Europe (it was stopped only because Gorbachev demanded – and Reagan refused – a halt to the SDI initiative), Kohl hurried to Washington to try to persuade the Americans not to withdraw.[18] He was supported by the French Prime Minister Jacques Chirac and the British Prime Minister Margaret Thatcher.[19] But Gorbachev was beginning to persuade many Germans that they had a better chance of creating a lasting peace by co-operating with him than by relying on the Americans. Frederick Kempe wrote in the *Wall Street Journal*: 'What most strikes a frequent visitor to West Germany is the shift of its political right, once the guardian of the trans-Atlantic relationship, away from Washington . . .'[20] Those in the burgeoning West Berlin peace movement had turned their backs on their erstwhile protector.

At the same time the Americans and Soviets were engaging in arms control agreements to cut nuclear and conventional weapons in Europe. Just when West Germans had won the Pershing II and cruise missiles they were being bargained away. Worse still for Kohl, Washington decided to concentrate on the deployment in Germany of Lance missiles with a range of 500 kilometres.

These were highly unpopular in their host country as they could only reach German targets; the slogan 'the shorter the range, the deader the Germans' was heard throughout the Federal Republic. The resentment over the Lance missiles helped to convince even centre-right Germans that, as Foreign Minister Hans-Dietrich Genscher put it, one must 'take Gorbachev at his word'. The Americans were concerned about the change in attitude even amongst conservative Germans; Henry Kissinger noted that 'Genscherism' became a euphemism for being 'soft on the Russians' and for the nasty habit of portraying Washington and Moscow as moral equivalents. This perception was not helped by the increasingly vocal 'Gorby-mania' which swept through West Germany. Once again, West Berlin became the focal point of anti-American peace protests. The shift was confirmed in the city elections of 1989, when the CDU mayor Eberhard Diepgen was beaten by the SPD candidate Walther Momper, who formed a coalition with the West Berlin Greens and the 'Alternative List'.

The new government took its cue from the left wing of the Social Democratic Party under Egon Bahr, Kärsten Voigt and Andreas von Bülow, which called for the complete de-nuclearization of the West German defence system and the creation of an 'international nuclear-free zone' out of the two halves of Berlin. It maintained that the main threat to peace lay, as Bark and Gress have pointed out in their masterful study of the period, 'in the weapons and not in the policies of those who had the weapons . . . They saw little danger in Soviet power, but great danger in alleged American paranoia.'[21] Many argued that peace would result from negotiations with the Soviets and not from attempts to modernize NATO forces. They also continued to support illegitimate east European regimes rather than the dissidents who opposed them, ignoring the serious human rights abuses perpetrated against writers, poets, film-makers, journalists and many others under Communist rule.[22] Leaders like Erich Honecker and General Jaruzelski were accepted by the left as if they were democratically elected representatives of their people, and the voices of those who had been forced to live under Soviet occupation for half a century went unheard. The left-wing protestors in the west continued to insist that the Communist regimes of the east were now supported by 'the people'. As such they were completely unprepared for the desperate calls for freedom, democracy and unity which within the year would echo throughout eastern Europe and East Germany.

The left-wing Romantics of West Berlin fared little better in national politics. In keeping with the 'growing together' theme they believed that the time had come to accept the division of Germany. They objected to the conservative West German line which required all GDR citizens to be allowed into the Federal Republic with full rights and demanded instead the official recognition of GDR citizenship. They also believed that East Berlin should be recognized as the legitimate capital of the GDR, a move which they felt would reduce tensions and allow further co-operation between both 'systems'.[23] Eventually they hoped that Berlin would be demilitarized and turned into a 'bridge between east and west'. In 1982 the SPD had set up a Joint Commission of Fundamental Values to discuss these aims with Communists in East Germany; by 1988 this had turned into a forum in which West Germans met and entertained East German apparatchiks and Politburo members; as Elizabeth Pond has put it, the SPD's left wing and the Greens

> deplored the American nuclear presence in the Federal Republic as a victimization of Germany that was little better morally than Soviet hegemony in Eastern Europe. The party opened a dialogue with the SED as if the latter held no repressive monopoly on government but were a fellow party in a pluralist system, and signed joint appeals with the SED for various nuclear-and-chemical-weapons-free zones that ran counter to western alliance policy.[24]

The policies were outrageous, but they were popular. Bahr summed up the West Berlin view in his 1988 book *Zum europäischen Frieden*, in which he repeated that the division of Germany was permanent and that the first step to solving the lingering problem of European freedom was to settle the Berlin question.[25] They hoped to de-nuclearize Europe and create a 'collective European defence system' which would somehow result in the withdrawal of both Soviet and American troops from Germany, after which West Berlin would become a normal part of West Germany. These proposals bore a striking similarity to Khrushchev's 1958 ultimatum, which had also called for the de-militarization of West Berlin and the creation of a 'free city'.[26] Moreover, it was clear that Bahr and the Romantic idealists of the peace movement had not understood that the Soviet overture had been rejected two decades before precisely because it was they, and not the Americans, who had held Europe hostage and had forbidden self-determination through free elections. As long as there were hundreds of thousands of Soviet troops in eastern Europe and thousands of missiles just to the east any concept of a 'de-militarized' Berlin was a nonsense; even if the Soviets pulled their troops out of central Europe they would still be within a few hours of Berlin; if the Americans left, *they* would be an ocean away. Nevertheless this vision was very popular in West Berlin in the late 1980s and many West Germans, tired of American low-level flights and air crashes over their soil, were also beginning to support an American withdrawal.

Kohl was increasingly concerned about the change in attitude but was caught between the NATO Alliance and West German public opinion. In

February 1989 Bahr declared that if Helmut Kohl opted to modernize the Lance nuclear weapons he would 'certainly lose the elections scheduled for December 1990'.[27] Bahr was probably right. In early 1989 public opinion polls in West Germany indicated that 'as many as 80 per cent of West Germans now believe there is no longer a military threat from the East'. Eight out of ten West Germans, including West Berliners, wanted all nuclear weapons to be removed from Germany. This essentially pro-Soviet view was not altered by the shooting on 5 February 1989 of the twenty-year-old Chris Gueffroy at the Berlin Wall.[28] It seemed that Gorbachev's strategy was working. West Germany was turning away from the NATO Alliance and West Berlin was now overwhelmingly neutralist, pacifist and pro-Gorbachev. The only glimmer of hope for Helmut Kohl came from the United States, with the election of George Bush on 8 November 1988.

George Bush's role in the events of 1989 is often underrated but his staunch support for the American–German alliance gave Kohl the support he needed.[29] In May 1989 Bush called for a NATO summit in Brussels which proved vital in bolstering Kohl's position; not only did Bush diffuse criticism of the CDU by accepting Kohl's decision to postpone the modernization of the controversial Lance missiles; he also emphasized the importance of the American–German relationship and openly referred to West Germany as 'the political as well as the economic motor of Europe'. Bush helped to bring NATO together as a united alliance ready to face the dramatic upheavals now rumbling through central and eastern Europe. The new Secretary-General of NATO, the articulate and intelligent Manfred Wörner, captured the moment in early 1989: 'There is no doubt that Gorbachev is serious about his policy reforms,' he said. 'It is necessary to offer him co-operation on the way toward opening up and democratization of his social system . . . On the other hand we would be naive, if not to say stupid, if we overlooked the risks inherent in a change like the one that is currently taking place in the Soviet Union and in Eastern Europe.'[30] He concluded by saying that NATO should be cautiously optimistic about Gorbachev and should support positive change; however, it was essential to remember that the Soviet Union was still the greatest threat to the security of western Europe.

On its fortieth anniversary NATO had finally managed to provide a framework within which its members could confront the future. This was of vital importance in dealing both with the Soviets and with the events which led to the demise of the Wall. If Germany had followed the pacifist line or if the NATO Alliance had not been able to stand firm, the Wall might still be there. Had the Americans not abandoned détente or had Reagan not insisted on dealing with the Soviets from a position of strength by pursuing SDI, the Soviet Union would not have been forced to face up to its own weakness and

Gorbachev would not have needed to negotiate with Reagan over arms reduction or to change Soviet foreign policy with respect to eastern Europe. Nevertheless, from the beginning the American initiatives were ridiculed and criticized by the vocal peace movement, the Greens and the Social Democrats now in power in West Berlin.[31] The city itself had done little to prepare for the 'year of miracles'.

If West Berliners had missed the significance of events unfolding between the United States and the Soviet Union in the 1980s, they also failed to support the other great force for change: the development of opposition movements in eastern Europe. These were initiated through the courageous work of shipyard workers, intellectuals and dissidents in two countries: Hungary and Poland.

It was clear even in the mid 1980s that Hungary was not an ordinary eastern European country. When I first visited Budapest as a student in 1985 I was struck by the difference between the Hungarians and the East Germans; while the latter would not risk any act of defiance the Hungarians were already scathing about the Communist system, openly critical of Soviet rule and resentful of their behaviour during the 1956 uprising.[32] They longed for real freedom and for a western pluralistic democratic system, but they had already introduced some remarkable reforms. By the mid 1980s the Hungarian government had relaxed controls on the economy and was the first to take advantage of Moscow's 1986 Helsinki Declaration allowing greater economic freedom to its citizens. In 1988 the party itself tried to reform and its 'Social Democratic' wing under Károly Grósz agreed that political liberalization was a precondition for further economic reform. Official censorship was banned; there was talk of trying to emulate Austria's western-oriented neutralism, and pictures of the Emperor Franz Josef even appeared on postcards. Finally, the Communist Politburo member Imre Pozsgay secured the party's approval of the unthinkable – a plan for a multi-party system. By March 1989 the Hungarian Socialist Workers' Party was developing a new constitution which did not reserve a leading role for the Communists, and in April Pozsgay persuaded the Hungarian Politburo to allow further reforms.

The changes in Hungary happened quickly and would soon prove to be of vital importance to the revolution in East Germany, but they were undertaken largely from above. In the meantime, another eastern European country – Poland – had been longing for a different kind of reform: the creation of a civil society which would be an alternative to Communist power. Poland had never accepted the legitimacy of Soviet rule imposed on it so brutally in 1945 and by the 1980s the disaffection was obvious, reaching every level of·society, including those in the party cadres. Nobody paid any attention to notions of the 'dictatorship of the proletariat' any more and it was clear to most people that the party's only aim was to stay in power. This became increasingly difficult during the deepening economic crisis of the period up until 1980. Then the future of eastern Europe was changed for ever. On 13 August around 70,000 strikers took over the Lenin shipyard in Gdańsk demanding the creation of independent unions and the reinstatement of Lech Walesa, who had been dismissed in the 1970 riots; the strikes spread and on 22 September a new labour charter was drawn up in Gdańsk. The unions registered in a Warsaw court as a united group called Solidarity. Despite intimidation, arrests and repression Solidarity began to gather widespread support – not only from workers but from academics, journalists, artists, theatre directors, school teachers and intellectuals, all of whom operated with the co-operation of the Catholic Church. The declaration of Martial Law in 1981 only united the nation further and thousands of young people threw themselves into the creation of a genuine alternative civil society which would not so much fight the Communists as ignore them.[33] The Polish government only caused further anger when they viciously crushed workers' protests, imprisoned and tortured innocent people, and murdered sixty dissidents, including Father Jerzy Popieluszko. As the economy fell apart workers again staged strikes and in 1988 openly demanded that Solidarity be recognized. The Poles had lost their fear and the movement had become virtually uncontrollable – I remember how easy it was to purchase 'underground' literature published by courageous young people like Mirek Chojecki quite openly outside Warsaw University or to visit activists who were not afraid of harrassment or arrest.[34] In February 1989, after seven years of trying to crush the independent movement, General Jaruzelski suddenly entered into round-table negotiations with Lech Walesa and his advisers. In April Solidarity was legalized and semi-free elections were called. On 4 June and in the following run-off elections Solidarity won every single seat it was permitted to contest in the Sejm, the lower house, and ninety-nine out of 100 in the new Senate. By 5 June 1989 it was clear that Solidarity had done the unthinkable: it had fought and defeated an eastern European Communist Party in free elections.[35] Furthermore, when the Polish Communists reached a stalemate in their attempt to form a cabinet Walesa proposed that Solidarity form a government with two small parties – the United Peasant Party and the Democratic Party. To the astonishment of the world the Communists and the Soviets agreed. On 19 August 1989 Tadeusz Mazowiecki, an adviser to Walesa since the beginning of Solidarity, was named the new Chairman of the Council of Ministers. He became the first non-Communist to lead an east European government in forty years, making his election one of the most significant events of the post-war world.

The implications for all eastern European Communist leaders were profound. As Henry Kissinger put it, 'The Communists knew how to rule with the help of the secret police, but not with the secret ballot.' For the first time the puppet governments had to face the possibility that the Soviets would not come to their aid with tanks and guns. While these changes were sweeping through Hungary and Poland, however, East Germany seemed immune. Even in early 1989 it seemed that there was little hope of any real political change in the German Democratic Republic.

Erich Honecker had been appalled by the changes in Poland and Hungary, and by the fact that the new Soviet leader Mikhail Gorbachev had allowed them to happen. Honecker saw the world through the eyes of a man stuck firmly in the 1930s, when society was divided between 'good' Communists and 'bad' capitalist-Nazis. In his view the GDR had been a great success and there was no need to entertain thoughts of reform; the country had built itself up after the war and its people had enough to eat, adequate housing, basic clothing and health care; he could not imagine why anyone would want more. He was also keenly aware of the fact that East Germany had outperformed the Soviets by providing a higher standard of living for its citizens. There was a certain smugness in his approach to his Russian minders, and Honecker considered himself the 'elder statesman' of eastern Europe and an expert on West Germany; he did not like Gorbachev, whom he saw as a bumbling young fool, and consoled himself with the thought that he would no doubt soon be pushed from power.

The already tense relationship between the two men deteriorated in 1986 when Gorbachev forced Honecker to cancel his visit to West Germany. From that day East German Politburo members had to endure his long diatribes against the new Soviet leader and his reforms but they dutifully toed the line. Honecker refused to allow Gorbachev's reforms to 'infect' the GDR with the bacillus of reform and, as the ideologue Kurt Hager put it in 1987, 'If your neighbour put up new wallpaper would you feel obliged to do so too?' The SED repressed the new Soviet culture, forbidding people to see new film releases like Tengiz Abuladze's great work *Repentance* (1987), which criticized Stalinism and contained one of the most moving scenes in the history of film; in 1988 it took the extraordinary step of banning the Soviet magazines *Sputnik* and *Ogonyok* along with a list of films, plays and articles which were considered subversive.[36] The Stasi continued to fill East German prisons with political prisoners and kept vast internment camps with spaces for around 200,000 in case of serious unrest. East Germany never had any dissident leaders of the calibre of Václav Havel or Lech Walesa – partly because anyone who criticized Honecker's regime was arrested and sold to the west. Nevertheless, in the late 1980s a number of small groups inspired by Gorbachev's reforms had begun to demand modest changes. To Honecker's chagrin they used the one protective shield that the GDR could not completely disregard: the Soviet Union.

The popularity of Gorbachev's reforms put the East German regime in a very difficult position. In the past Honecker had always told his people to obey the Russians; criticism of the Soviet Union had been a punishable offence. Now Moscow was introducing changes which were hateful to the regime. Official culture could be used against the SED by ordinary Germans: on 17 January 1988 the official commemoration of the murders in 1919 of Karl Liebknecht and Rosa Luxemburg was disrupted by a brief protest. The official parade in front of the Palast der Republik was a typical SED set piece, complete with obligatory Free German Youth banners and boring speeches about the glories of peace-loving East Germany. I watched in amazement when this was suddenly interrupted by a group of over 200 young people who raced into its midst and began to unfurl banners emblazoned with Rosa Luxemburg's own words; one read: 'freedom remains freedom for those who think differently'.[37] The Volkspolizei quickly moved in to clear away the demonstrators, beating people and rounding up suspects: 120 people were taken away that night and within hours 100 of them had been expelled to the west. Others were in a more serious position. Genuine dissidents had no desire to be pushed westwards but wanted to stay in East Germany and work for reform at home. Eleven were put on trial and given sentences of between six months and a year for unlawful assembly while seven others were under investigation on the more serious charge of 'treasonous contacts with Western spies', which carried a minimum seven-year sentence. This group included the thirty-two-year-old singer-songwriter Stefan Krawczyck, who had become Wolf Biermann's successor after the latter had been barred from the country. When young people heard about the arrest of their hero they began to protest; over the next days hundreds of people gathered in Protestant churches in over twenty towns and cities in East Germany to pray for those in prison. Most I talked to were non-religious but saw churches as the only semi-legitimate places in which to assemble; over 2,000 people came together in East Berlin's Gethsemane Church the next weekend to listen to a moving plea from the Bishop of Berlin, Gottfried Forck, who demanded the release of the prisoners. The people wore expressions of stubborn resistance; many quietly clasped hands or hugged in a silent vigil before walking into the gaggle of Stasi agents waiting for them outside. Until then such defiance had been virtually unheard of in East Berlin, and the atmosphere was charged with emotion. The government were scared into expelling Krawczyck and his wife before they became local martyrs.

Krawczyck had initially refused to leave the GDR but was quickly given a choice: a twelve-year sentence for having 'treasonous contacts' or exile in the west. Under extreme pressure he and his wife chose the latter, although it was widely reported that they had gone 'of their own free will'. Nevertheless after this incident church meetings were suddenly filled with protestors and the names of dissidents like Bärbel Bohley became widely known. On 15 March 850 Stasi and regular policemen broke up one of the regular Monday afternoon prayer meetings held since 1983 at the Protestant Nikolaikirche in Leipzig. After the service the 3,000 worshippers were prevented from walking to the market place together, but for the first time in the history of East Germany a large group stood together and chanted, 'Stasi Out! Stasi Out!' It was a thrilling moment, although the people were quickly dispersed. Incidents like this under-lined the state's determination not to allow anyone to voice dissenting views, but they also illustrated the increasing power of the dissidents within the Church. The GDR Evangelical Church was still enormously cautious; it was riddled with Stasi agents and was determined not to provoke another 1950s-style clampdown by siding too openly with opponents of the state. Even so, it had become the only real forum for protest in East Germany, a role which had started with the 'swords into ploughshares' demonstrations in the early 1980s, when the famous proverb was used as an anti-government slogan before it was banned.[38] By the late 1980s the Church had become the most important centre for human rights activists, ecological groups and peace movements which campaigned against such things as air pollution or, in an extraordinary and courageous demonstration, the Soviet intervention in Afghanistan.[39] Some priests simply refused to co-operate with a regime which they considered to be evil and doggedly opposed the drive to create 'the Church in Socialism' which was, in fact, very much a successor to Hitler's 'National Church'. In 1988 the grassroots 'Church from Below' was established by people who rejected official co-operation with the government. Semi-legal organizations operated from church basements and halls, producing newsletters on environmental, disarmament and human rights issues.[40] In 1989 a number of groups inherently critical of the SED were founded in East Berlin, including the Christian Young Men's Association which provided support for conscientious objectors, who had no legal rights in East Germany. The centres were frequently raided and members were arrested upon leaving the church but their supporters continued to meet. When forty people were detained for using illegal printing equipment in March 1988 over 200 people gathered in East Berlin for a protest vigil against the state. In West Germany – or even, by then, in Budapest or Warsaw – this would have been considered a small group, but for East Berlin it was highly significant.

The Church did occasionally challenge the SED in more concrete ways – for example, in 1989 it attacked corrupt voting practices in the GDR. On 12 May that year the anti-Honecker pastor of the East Berlin Samaritan Church, Herr Rainer Eppelmann, openly questioned the official results of the previous weekend's elections in which the party had supposedly received a 98.85 per cent 'yes' vote for the government candidates. Eppelmann, who had participated in the vote-counting, claimed that in the Weissensee and Friedrichshain districts of East Berlin alone the number of 'no' votes was only a third of those declared in the presence of Church workers. This left over 3,000 voters unaccounted for. The Church then did the unthinkable by accusing the government of falsifying the voting figures by around 7 per cent. The government reacted angrily and Herr Kurt Loeffler, Minister of Religious Affairs, threatened to end the 'special understanding' between the Church and the SED. Although he was not arrested outright Pastor Eppelmann found three separate bugging devices in his flat within the next three weeks. For the first time dissidents in different cities began to communicate; 250 people braved arrest and filed complaints against the elections and small demonstrations followed, during which 120 people were arrested. Far from being silenced by these measures people came to special Leipzig prayer meetings held every Monday night in increasing numbers. By the end of May 1989 over 2,000 were attending.

The protests became more frequent when the East German government took the initiative in applauding the Chinese suppression of popular demonstrations in Tiananmen Square in June 1989. Honecker subtly blamed Gorbachev for the unrest, driving another wedge between the pro-Gorbachev East German people and their own backward-looking government. And the cracks were widening. People were getting tired of the nanny state. They no longer wanted to be told that they were unable to travel, to choose their employment or their friends, to buy basic western consumer goods or to criticize the endless diet of increasingly idiotic propaganda which was still churned out by teachers and journalists and historians. The discontent was aggravated by the western influences which reached the GDR via television and the growing exchange of visitors between east and west. The East German government had tried to portray the west as an evil land of heartless capitalists and Nazis waiting to take advantage of them, but most East Germans saw the west as a utopian land of plenty, a view which would only be challenged after 1989. Some ten years after the creation of Solidarity in Poland, a small number of East Germans began to organize and to agitate for change.

Gorbachev's response to the growing unrest in eastern Europe critically affected the course of events over the coming months. Rather than crush dissent as his predecessors had done he decided at some point in the 1980s that it would be better to disengage the Soviet Union from its troublesome charges in central Europe than to invade and control by force as it had in the past. Not only was he, as Kissinger put it, 'unsuited by temperament' to invade eastern

Europe; such a move would have undermined his entire foreign policy: 'the suppression of Eastern Europe would have solidified NATO and the Sino-American *de facto* coalition and intensified the arms race. Gorbachev was increasingly facing a choice between political suicide and the slow erosion of his political power.'[41] Gorbachev's solution came in the form of an astounding retreat from the Brezhnev Doctrine. This was first hinted at during the Communist Party Conference in June 1988, at which he asserted the principle of freedom of choice and renounced the use of military force to prop up the eastern bloc regimes, a policy described by his spokesman Gennady Gerasimov as the ('I Did It My Way') 'Sinatra Doctrine'. It was clarified when Gorbachev visited Bonn in June 1989. The welcome was rapturous. Tens of thousands of West Germans gathered, leading to the scenes of adulation not seen since Kennedy's visit to Berlin. Riotous crowds chanted 'Gor-by! Gor-by!' and cheered his every word. And what words they were. At a press conference he stated: 'The Wall can come down when the circumstances that led to its being built in the first place no longer apply.' Then, in July, Gorbachev finally repudiated the Brezhnev Doctrine for all of eastern Europe. To the amazement of the dignitaries assembled at the Council of Europe in Strasbourg he declared that the social and political order of European countries 'is entirely a matter for the people themselves and of their choosing'. He talked again about a 'common European home' and excluded the 'possibility of the use or threat of force, above all military force, by one alliance against another, within alliances, or anywhere else'.

Gorbachev's decision will remain one of the defining moments of the twentieth century, but although he would subsequently be portrayed as the great hero who had freed eastern Europe the changes he set in motion were largely unintended. Gorbachev's aim had been to allow eastern Europeans to rid themselves of hard-line leaders like Erich Honecker and replace them with 'reformers' who would still remain loyal to Moscow. In this Gorbachev made a massive error of judgement. He clearly had no real understanding of the deep hatred still harboured against the Soviet system in eastern Europe; he did not understand that once the people were given limited autonomy they would turn against their Soviet masters; he did not understand that it was impossible to reform Communism and that if people were really able to exercise their will in free elections no Communist leader would be able to control the outcome without the use of violence. The results were momentous.

The historical myths which had been used to underpin the Soviet system in central and eastern Europe began to unravel at breathtaking speed. The Polish Sejm and the Hungarian Communist leaders condemned their governments' participation in the crushing of the Prague Spring revolt of 1968. The Soviets admitted the existence of a secret protocol of the Ribbentrop-Molotov

Pact which had divided Poland and the Baltic States between Germany and the Soviet Union in 1939, and more than 1 million Lithuanian, Latvian and Estonian demonstrators linked hands and formed a 400-mile-long human chain to protest against the pact. The Soviets also admitted responsibility for the Katyn massacre – the mass murder of Polish officers which had provided Stalin with the excuse he needed to disown the Polish government-in-exile in London and to legitimize the Polish Communist regime; admitting to Katyn was tantamount to admitting that the Poles had been governed by an illegitimate Communist regime for over forty years. It was against this backdrop that on 2 May 1989 Hungarians decided to demonstrate their commitment to democratic change by cutting holes in their Austrian border. This coincided with George Bush's May 1989 visit to West Germany, during which he was given a piece of barbed wire from the Iron Curtain. Bush made a bold speech recognizing the extraordinary nature of the Hungarian decision and calling for more sweeping changes: 'Just as barriers are coming down in Hungary, so must they fall throughout all of Eastern Europe. Let Berlin be next . . . *Glasnost* may be a Russian word, but openness is a Western concept . . . bring *Glasnost* to East Berlin.'[42] Bush was more of a prophet than he knew. By punching the first ever hole in the Iron Curtain Hungary had provided East Germans with a legitimate escape route to West Germany, and for the first time since 1961 they began 'voting with their feet'.

Throughout the summer increasing numbers of East Germans made their way to Hungary for their 'holidays' in the hope of finding a way across the border. By 1 July 1989 25,000 had fled while thousands more began to seek refuge in the West German embassies of Prague and in Budapest.[43] The latter was finally closed on 13 August because of the massive influx of people. The West Berlin legation in East Berlin was also occupied and then closed. On 19 August 600 people broke through the Hungarian border into Austria, but the border guards allowed them to pass. Erich Honecker ignored the implications of this, still muttering that the Wall was destined to last 'one hundred years'. Then, on 10 September, Hungary went one step further on the border question. On a television programme, *The Week*, the presenter asked the Hungarian Minister of Foreign Affairs Gyula Horn about the situation: 'So, let us assume that tomorrow morning these 60,000 start out towards Austria – God forbid that I should give them ideas – then the Hungarian border guards will allow them through?' Horn retorted, 'They will allow them through without any further ado and I assume that the Austrians will let them in.'[44] The news flashed throughout the eastern bloc; the border was down, people were not being shot for breaking through the Iron Curtain. An amazing 22,000 East Germans fled in three days.

The Hungarian decision was a courageous one. The country did not want an open fight with the GDR but was ready to stand up for its new semi-independent foreign policy. Later the former British ambassador in Bonn, Sir Julian Bullard, would say of the revolutions in eastern Europe that 'the single most influential factor . . . was the Hungarian Government decision to subordinate its very clear obligations under an agreement with the GDR to its general duty under the Helsinki Final Act of 1976 – a decision which blew a hole in the sealed frontiers of the GDR and relegated to the past the comfortable slogans of the last three decades.'[45] It was true. The trickle of people now turned into a flood and the eastern European security system could not cope. The eastern bloc was beginning to break up.

All through September the countries in the region were trembling with the movement of people. Thousands of East Germans were quietly packing their bags, piling into their Trabbis, driving across the border and making for the West German embassies in Prague and Warsaw. To the consternation of the Communist Czech government and the delight of Czech dissidents East Germans continued to abandon their Trabbis – some with the keys still in the ignition – on the cobbled streets of Prague before running to the West German embassy at the beautiful Lobkovic Palace. By mid September the embassy grounds were packed: hundreds of people, many with young families, lived in the assorted tents and shelters dotted amongst the mud and rubbish. More than forty people arrived every hour, threw their small cases and packages over the high iron railings and climbed over into the mass of people already waiting below. The West Germans feared that the situation might lead to epidemics and Red Cross services were overstretched, but the people were adamant; they would not return to East Germany. The Czech Communists asked Honecker to do something about the hundreds of East Germans cluttering up the streets of Prague but he continued to pretend that nothing was happening. The East German Foreign Minister Oskar Fischer protested to the UN General Assembly that the states allowing in GDR citizens 'endangered the peace' but at Bonn's request the US Secretary of State James Baker spoke to the Czechs and Hungarians and on 30 September Hans-Dietrich Genscher flew to Prague and announced to the waiting crowds that the refugees would be allowed to emigrate. The only problem was that they would have to go via special trains back through the GDR, the very country from which they had escaped.

The train journey was Honecker's idea. It was intended as a propaganda lesson, in which he would publicly humiliate the escapees. The people were to be moved across the country in sealed carriages, have their GDR papers taken away en route and be publicly branded as 'expellees'. That, at least, was his plan. On 2 October the first group of people left Prague amidst tearful farewells and around 12,000 people were loaded on to eight trains. 'We are very happy to be leaving,' said one, 'but we are still afraid that our government could do something to us.'

The journey through the GDR was memorable but not for the reasons Honecker had hoped. Far from rejecting the refugees thousands of East Germans came out to watch them go by. They stood at crossings, in fields, and in village stations. Far from jeering they waved and shouted and wept; far from being humiliated the escapees were triumphant. As the trains pulled into Dresden the refugees, instead of guiltily handing over their papers, ripped them up and threw them out through cracks in the windows along with their worthless Ost Marks. More than 1,500 young people had gathered at the station and over 100 tried to get on the packed trains; the police tried to push them back – one man became trapped under the wheels of a carriage and had to have his legs amputated. As the trains pulled out those who remained began to fight with the police, and the station was wrecked. Meanwhile the 'freedom trains' made their way to the West German border and pulled into Hof in Bavaria, with the passengers chanting 'Freiheit! Freiheit!' They were met by hundreds of West Germans cheering and waving and welcomed with free food and drink and piles of donated clothing from children's jackets to Bavarian national costumes. After the initial round of hugs and tears they were taken by Red Cross volunteers to schools or colleges to be issued with West German papers and to receive food and shelter until they could be moved to other centres in West Germany. Although some locals voiced concerns that the refugees might take their jobs the overwhelming response in West Germany was positive. The pictures of the trainloads of delighted refugees being greeted by emotional West Germans flashed around the world and back into the GDR, making the journey seem all the more attractive. Within hours the grounds of the Prague embassy were filled again. Similar scenes took place in Warsaw, where by 1 October over 600 East Germans were waiting in the Wschodnia railway station for passage to West Germany. The exodus marked a point of no return: the East German regime could not stop the flood of people. If they stepped up the repression, it would simply mean a greater migration.

Honecker's response was laughable. Instead of addressing the issue he tried to blame the problem on Hungary and on the Federal Republic. The exodus, he said, had been masterminded by evil West Germans who were practising 'psychological warfare' on his people. Innocent East Germans were being 'blackmailed through enticements, promises and threats to renounce the basic principles and fundamental values of socialism'.[46] Those who were fleeing were called 'scum and ingrates' who were being 'aroused by the machinations of Western intelligence agencies or else drugged and shanghaied against their will'. Otto Reinhold, the repugnant rector of the Central Committee's

Academy of Social Sciences, added that there would be no reforms; such a step would compromise East Germany's *raison d'être*. Nevertheless the flood was having a profound effect on East German society. People became bolder. Fledgling dissident groups began to grow stronger and some activists called for people to stay in the GDR and to fight for fundamental reform at home. By the summer of 1989 the cities of Leipzig and Dresden had become engulfed by a popular protest movement. With the exception of a few individual activists, however, East Berlin remained quiet.

The protest movement was now firmly centred around the Protestant Church and although many in the hierarchy still opposed the dissidents some courageous activists openly fought the SED.[47] At the Eisenach Synod in mid September 1989 the Church demanded that East Germans be allowed to travel abroad and return home for visits if they chose to become citizens of the Federal Republic. They demanded free elections, a free press, the right to demonstrate without risking attack or arrest and the protection of the Geneva declaration on human rights, which had been signed by the GDR. On 16 September the Evangelical Church Federation in Dessau confirmed that the Church was prepared to risk a confrontation with the authorities, a reaction sparked after the Dresden Church weekly *Der Sonntag* was banned because it had publicly revealed that there were food queues in the GDR. A few months earlier such people would simply have been arrested but with the Hungarian border open the Honecker regime had to tread carefully. The Church's stance gave people courage to act, and small traditional Church gatherings now burgeoned into large demonstrations. Then, on 9 September, the first official protest group was formed. It was called New Forum.[48]

The old ramshackle flat of the forty-five-year-old artist Bärbel Bohley, located in the Prenzlauer district of East Berlin, became a focal point for reformers, who congregated there at all hours of the day and night to discuss the next move against the SED. In the following weeks a plethora of similar groups sprang up throughout the GDR, including Democracy Now, United Left, Democratic Awakening and the Social Democratic Party. All were banned but continued to meet in defiance of the SED. The protests began to spread beyond these small groups. Georg Sterzinsky, the new Roman Catholic bishop of Berlin-Brandenburg, called for reforms in the GDR; East German rock stars openly criticized the party and called teenagers on to the streets; the normally slavishly Communist East Berlin chapter of the Writers' Union suddenly reversed its old line and demanded freedom of expression; East Berlin's Bergmann Borsig factory workers refused to listen to any more pro-SED propaganda from the trades union chief. And yet, although there was increased dissident activity in the city, not very many Berliners were actually involved in the anti-SED movement.[49] Having spent most of my time in Berlin I was struck in October by the much higher level of activity in Leipzig. As East Berlin slumbered on the demonstrations on the streets of Leipzig became larger. On 2 October over 10,000 people gathered to protest at Honecker's lack of reforms, chanting slogans like 'Liberty, Equality, Fraternity', and 'We will stay HERE'. It was the largest demonstration on an East German street since 1953, but although there were some skirmishes with police there was no serious repression.

The situation became more tense as the GDR's fortieth anniversary loomed. Honecker was determined to make the celebrations – planned for 7 October – go smoothly, not least because Mikhail Gorbachev was to be the guest of honour. Honecker had planned an old-style Communist extravaganza but that was before the breaching of the Hungarian border, before the mass exodus of 100,000 East Germans and before the rise of the protest movement. He faced a highly unstable situation. Nobody knew how he would respond, and people feared violence.

The atmosphere on the streets of East German towns the night before the anniversary was very tense. Attempts were made to intimidate dissident leaders: Pastor Werner Kratschall, a Protestant leader, said that a senior government official had warned him that 'If your group wants to continue, please remember China' and Professor Jens Reich of the banned New Forum was also threatened. To their credit the people of Dresden and Leipzig again took to the streets. When Gorbachev arrived in East Berlin he was met by an ecstatic crowd and then treated to a vast torch-lit parade of 100,000 people, who were followed by lines of tanks and guns. He watched in silence.

The Soviet leader had been reluctant to visit East Germany but had been obliged to because of the anniversary celebration. He soon become visibly impatient with Honecker. According to Valeri Musatov discussions between the two men were disastrous: 'Gorbachev started to talk about *Perestroika*, political and economic reform but Honecker asked: "Has your population got enough food, bread, and butter?" He had visited the Soviet Union in the summer. And he asked Gorbachev, "Do you know how the population of the GDR live?" . . . And the discussion stopped.'[50] Gorbachev was not amused. On Saturday he met with the entire East German Politburo and hinted that Honecker should be eased from power: 'When we fall behind, life punishes us immediately,' he commented. Honecker seemed oblivious to the criticism and continued to boast of his own success and the prosperity of the GDR, which was 'among the top ten economies in the world'. At this point Gorbachev let out an audible snort. That night around the dinner table Egon Krenz, Honecker's 'Golden Boy' and heir apparent, quietly turned on his master and plotted with fellow Politburo members Günther Schabowski, Siegfried Lorenz and Erich Mielke to remove the old man from power. After dinner Krenz was able to indicate to Gorbachev that things were about to change.[51] Even so the demonstrations that night in Dresden and Leipzig were brutally put down by security forces. Many normal people feared that following the anniversary they faced increased repression. To their credit, they were undeterred.[52]

Despite the mounting fear amongst ordinary people a vast demonstration was planned for 9 October in Leipzig. It was a supreme act of defiance. All through the day rumours had circulated that 8,000 security police had been called into the city, that extra blood plasma had been delivered to Leipzig hospitals, that the regional army was on alert. Many feared a bloodbath, but even so over 70,000 demonstrators went on to the streets that night to call for the legalization of New Forum. The protest might well have become violent had it not been for the leadership shown by six Leipzigers, including Kurt Masur, the director of the Gewandhaus Orchestra who, although he had previously been a supporter of the regime, now appealed for calm.[53] The order to shoot never came. As it became clear that they were safe the people began to chant, 'Wir sind das Volk!' (We are the people), and even some security police joined in. That night in Leipzig marked a critical moment in the first successful revolution in Germany history. There had been no bloodshed, no violence, no repression. The people had won. It was only then, when it had become relatively safe, that mass demonstrations began in earnest in East Berlin.

East Germany now erupted in waves of protest marches which Egon Krenz used as the excuse to oust Honecker. On 18 October the Politburo confirmed Krenz as leader but when he appeared in public he was surprised to find that he was not hailed as the new hero of the GDR but was booed and jeered at. East Germans called him 'horse face' and 'the teeth' and compared him to the wolf in Red Riding Hood. The letters of his name EGON were used to taunt him in the chant: 'Er Geht Oock Noch' – (He'll be going too). Far from appeasing the people the appointment fuelled more demonstrations, and on 23 October 300,000 people marched against Krenz in Leipzig. On 30 October tens of thousands took to streets in cities all over the GDR to protest against the new government; more than 20,000 gathered at East Berlin's town hall to hear Günther Schabowski, the party chief, and to demand reform. On 31 October Krenz met Gorbachev and agreed to initiate perestroika and reform[54] in the GDR. It was too late.

On 4 November, one million East Germans gathered on the streets of their cities to demand genuine reforms and, in the largest march of the revolution, 500,000 people gathered in Berlin yelling, 'Allow New Forum!' and 'Free Elections!' The mood was electric and everyone there knew that something extraordinary was happening, something final – a revolution. Schabowski and Wolf came out to talk to the crowd and announced that East Germans could now drive directly through Czechoslovakia to Bavaria. Within hours the road was clogged with bumper-to-bumper Trabbis trying to reach the west. On 6 November people gathered again to demand free elections. On 7 November the government and Prime Minister Willi Stoph resigned; the contemptible Erich Mielke saw that the end had arrived and sent a secret directive to the Stasi ordering them to destroy all sensitive documents, particularly those which contained information about domestic informers. On 8 November the Politburo resigned. Egon Krenz seemed determined to hang on to power and even referred to the Wall as a 'bulwark' against the west. Nobody expected the momentous news which would greet them the next day.

The ninth of November dawned much like any other day of that extraordinary autumn; it seemed important only because it was the anniversary of both Kaiser William II's abdication and of *Kristallnacht*. There were more demonstrations throughout the GDR calling for free elections and the right to travel, but there was no dramatic news. When I walked around Berlin streets that day everything had seemed calm. That evening Günther Schabowski's regular press conference was even more predictable than usual – indeed some journalists and guests started to leave early. Then, at the very end of the meeting, he was asked about the new travel arrangements with Czechoslovakia. At 6.57 p.m. he blurted out that the Politburo had decided to issue passports and travel permits on demand so that people would no longer need to travel through other countries to get to the Federal Republic. East Germans would be permitted to use border crossings between the two Germanys. When asked by Tom Brokaw, of the American television network NBC, when this extraordinary development would come into force he replied, 'Immediately.'[55]

Nobody was quite sure what he meant. Did it really mean that East Germans could simply walk through the border into the west? And what of the Berlin Wall? Was the city somehow exempt from this new ruling? East Berliners were determined to find out for themselves. The announcement was broadcast on the evening news and within minutes the streets came alive as people began to rush to the Wall.[56] Everyone seemed to realize that something extraordinary was happening – something that they should witness for themselves. One waitress remembered hearing the news from a passer-by; she told her boss she was going to see for herself and left her station. A cabbie remembered his surprise at hearing loud shuffling and whispering in the middle of a performance of a musical at the Friedrichstadt Palast; at first he thought it must be a fire and only later did he realize what had been going on. Normally dour neighbours did most un-East German things like running down corridors banging on doors to spread the news.

The collection of humanity at the Wall was wonderful to behold – there were people carrying shopping, people carrying young children, people still dressed in their work clothes. Everyone was asking one another what was happening: Had anyone heard any news? Were they going to be arrested? They began to urge the bewildered guards to open the barriers. When nothing happened they began to get impatient and started chanting, 'Open the Gate! Open the Gate! The Wall must go! The Wall must go!' For three hours people surged up to the barred crossing points. By now West Berlin had also come alive; everyone knew that 'something' was happening at the Wall and rushed to chant in unison with East Berliners. Word reached the guards that they had permission to open the border. Then, at 20:30, the barrier at the Bornholmer Strasse was raised, followed quickly by those at Sannenallee and Invalidenstrasse. A loud cheer went up and people surged through, most touching West Berlin soil for the first time in their lives. The East German Interior Minister Friedrich Dicker confirmed that the Wall had been officially breached.[57] As people ran across the forbidden boundary they fell into the arms of waiting West Berliners, and the emotional scenes were indescribable. Complete strangers laughed, sang, sprayed one another with bottles of Sekt and beer, and hugged one another. They wept and kissed, they held hands and wept again.

I remember that night as a kind of dream; the atmosphere was one of giddy excitement and joy but also one of sheer disbelief. After nearly three decades people would be allowed the simple experience of walking from one district to another. The experience itself was quite banal – one simply walked a few metres past a large, ugly structure and into another district. But it meant so much. Delirious crowds continued to surge across – some in their nightclothes and bedroom slippers; everyone sensed that this was a moment that they would savour for the rest of their lives. Other border crossings were quickly opened and when the barrier at Checkpoint Charlie was folded back Trabbis began to chug past crowds, who cheered and pounded on their fibreglass roofs with delight. The little cars created massive traffic jams in West Berlin, particularly on the Strasse des 17 Juni. There was a loud honking of horns and cheering as they passed the detested Soviet War Memorial near the Reichstag. Before long people had begun to climb up on to the low, wide section of the Wall in front of the gate. The GDR authorities turned water cannon on the revellers but aimed over their heads so as not to cause any real damage – one person simply stood there in a raincoat like a latter-day Gene Kelly and the British even sent a brass band along to promote the holiday atmosphere. The party lasted well into the night; Radio Sender Freies Berlin said that more than 50,000 had crossed into West Berlin on that first night alone, people who had come 'just to see' before going home for the night.

Somehow, everyone seemed to sense that the Wall was now open for good.

The breaching of the Berlin Wall caused chaos in the GDR. Günther Schabowski would later say that 'we hadn't a clue that the opening of the Wall was the beginning of the end of the Republic. On the contrary, we expected a stabilization process.'[58] But if the East Germans were in turmoil the news was greeted with delight by the West German government. When the Bundestag first heard about the breach of the Wall its members spontaneously started to sing the national anthem.[59] Herr Rudolf Seiters, the Chancellery Minister speaking for Helmut Kohl, who was then on a state visit to Poland, said this was a step of 'outstanding meaning'. In Berlin the Social Democratic mayor Walter Momper – a staunch opponent of unification – conceded that 'This is a day of joy. An historic day. We will welcome the people with open arms. The border will no longer keep us apart.' Count Otto Lambsdorff, chairman of Helmut Kohl's Free Democratic allies, said that 'This is in effect the end of the Wall and the barbed wire' and that the East German leaders should tear down the Berlin Wall and fortifications as soon as possible. Volker Rühe, chairman of the Christian Democratic Union, called for the GDR to guarantee its people the right of self-determination through free elections.

World reaction was also overwhelmingly positive: President Bush said he was elated, it was a 'dramatic happening' and he hoped that reform in East Germany would follow. He also said that movement towards democracy in eastern Europe was 'irresistible', but that although he had predicted the eventual freeing of the eastern bloc countries he had not foreseen 'this development at this stage'. Bush also gave his crucial early support for a reunified Germany; at the same time US military facilities at three West German bases were made available to provide temporary shelter for 1,000 East German refugees.[60] The New York Times said although the Wall was still physically in place its 'capacity to divide a country and a continent seems at an end'. Margaret Thatcher called it 'a great day for liberty', although she quickly added that it was 'much too fast' to talk of German reunification. The Soviets were also positive; Mr Gennady Gerasimov, the Soviet Foreign Ministry spokesman who had first outlined the Sinatra Doctrine, said that 'It is their country, they know it better. What can we do?'[61] The Kremlin even hinted that it would not oppose the end of Communist power in Berlin provided that East Germany remained within the Warsaw Pact; Helmut Kohl and Gorbachev talked on the telephone the following day, with Kohl calming Soviet fears about the implications of the events in Berlin.[62] The Polish Solidarity paper Gazeta Wyborcza said that 'In Berlin, the heart of Europe has triumphed in the dispute between freedom and barbed wire.'

The next day the destruction of the Wall began in earnest: people with pickaxes began to take chunks out of its painted sides while more visitors climbed up on to the wide platform by the Brandenburg Gate. On the second day the infamous Glienicke Bridge was opened; East Germans began to come from beyond Berlin in their Trabbis. Tens of thousands crossed on the U- and S-Bahns, or simply walked over the border. On that first weekend over 800,000 East German shoppers and revellers crossed into West Berlin to go on an impromptu spending spree. They were given a tremendous welcome and everything from free hot soup, hamburgers, chocolate, fruit and Sekt, and the days were punctuated by small acts of generosity. I saw people handing out money to complete strangers and guiding them around the city; the Senate printed free street maps, there was free public transport, free beer, free football matches, free souvenirs and even free accommodation. East Germans collected their DM100 'welcome money' and snatched up everything from bananas to blue jeans and there were long queues outside discount stores with people eager to purchase radios and cameras, ski-jackets and colour televisions. Others avoided the shops and simply walked with friends or grandparents through old neighbourhoods or down once familiar streets. Within the first four days 4.3 million people – a quarter of the entire population of the GDR – had visited the west. In the meantime, the Wall was being pecked to pieces and cranes had begun to dismantle large sections. A week after the first crossings the once brutal and forbidding structure had begun to resemble a Swiss cheese.

The opening of the Wall was a momentous occasion in its own right but it also revived the dormant 'German question' for the first time since the advent of *Ostpolitik*. Furthermore, it raised the prospect of eventual German unification. Some groups, like the Social Democrats, rejected unification out of hand; when Walter Momper met East Berlin's lord mayor Erhard Krack on the border on 12 November he promised to co-operate with the east but to respect the autonomy of the GDR. Later he advocated giving the GDR huge cash injections to bribe its inhabitants into staying at home, a move rejected by Kohl unless the GDR government agreed to electoral reform. Günter Grass abhorred the idea of a united Germany and on 10 February 1990 said that neighbouring countries were 'right to mistrust us ... Even when they react hysterically, they are right ... If we think about Germany and the German future, we have to think about Auschwitz. It stands for everything which is hostile to the idea of European unity. It was the very expression of the anti-European spirit.'[63] Others, including New Forum and other East German groups, advocated the creation of a new East Germany which would find a 'Third Way' between Communism and capitalism. Nevertheless the majority of Germans, and particularly East Germans, advocated reunification. Willy Brandt had opposed the idea until he stood by the newly opened Wall; he then changed his mind, saying, 'What belongs together is now growing together.' Brandt's view was echoed by former governing mayor Richard von Weizsäcker, who said that he hoped Berlin would soon be reunited. But it was Chancellor Helmut Kohl who gave his wholehearted support for reunification. On 10 November he cut short his official visit to Poland and raced back to Berlin. Standing by the Wall he said: 'This is a great day for German history. We are and will remain one nation and we belong together. Step by step, we must find the way to our common future.'

Legally, Helmut Kohl was right. The preamble to the FRG's 1949 constitution advocated eventual German unity, stating that 'the entire German people is called upon to achieve in free self-determination the unity and freedom of Germany'. The problem was that by the 1990s few believed this would ever happen. Kohl's genius lay in his recognition of this brief chance to fulfil the dream and to complete the process begun by Adenauer after the Second World War. For Kohl, speed was imperative. Without consulting his NATO Allies he delivered a ten-point speech in the Bundestag on 28 November 1989 calling for the creation of a 'confederal structure' between East and West Germany:

> We are ... approaching the goal already set by the Atlantic Alliance in December 1967 – I quote: 'a final and stable settlement in Europe is not possible without a solution to the German Question, which forms the nucleus of the current tensions in Europe. Any settlement of that kind must remove the unnatural barriers between Eastern and Western Europe, which are manifested in the clearest and ugliest fashion in the division of Germany.'[364]

Nevertheless, the speech deeply upset his European neighbours.

It was natural that, given the legacy of the Second World War, other European states would be suspicious of unification and the resurrection of a mighty German state which might throw off the carefully constructed balance held in place by NATO and the European Community. Mrs Thatcher echoed the Belgian and Dutch views, saying that unification should be discussed in five or ten years.[65] President Mitterrand was worried that if Germany was unified it might turn eastward and threaten the German–French bond and thus France's power in Europe; according to Jacques Attali, Mitterrand said on 28 November 1989: 'He [Kohl] didn't tell me anything! Anything! I'll never forget this! Gorbachev will be furious; he won't let this pass, it's impossible. I don't have to do anything to stop it, the Soviets will do it for me. Just think. They will never allow this greater Germany just opposite them.'[66] Mitterrand even sped to Kiev in December 1989 to try to persuade Gorbachev to stall unification. Kohl argued that far from being contradictory a move towards the east and the promotion of joint operations between western EC members were complimentary; he even adopted the French pet idea of monetary union in order to appease his ally.[67] At a special EC summit in early December Kohl was treated with cool disdain by the British, French and other heads of state and on 26 January 1990 Margaret Thatcher said that if German unification went too fast it could have the disastrous effect of toppling Gorbachev; she also tried to resurrect the four-power Kommandatura in Berlin in an attempt to slow down the process.[68] The Polish President General Jaruzelski suggested that the Poles should be allowed to station troops on German territory. Gorbachev, too, suddenly seemed worried, and talked of 'Revanchism' and 'neo-Nazis'.[69] Helmut Kohl's drive for unity might have been stymied had it not been for the influence of two NATO countries: the United States and Canada.

Unlike the other western Allies both the Americans and the Canadians supported reunification from the beginning. Their memories of the Second World War were quite different from the memories of those who had endured German occupation and they had long treated the Soviet Union and not Germany as the real threat to peace in Europe. Both NATO countries believed in self-determination and had taken rhetoric about the Wall and the freeing of eastern Europe seriously. As a result, they saw German unification more as a symbolic end to the Cold War and a victory over Soviet Communism than as a threat to stability in Europe. As early as November 1989 both were referring to German unification as inevitable: there was no point in delaying it and possibly causing Versailles-like resentment in Germany.[70] But, as Elizabeth Pond has pointed out, it was George Bush who really facilitated unification, supporting it as a matter of principle, while reassuring Gorbachev that the Soviets would not be isolated after the event. Bush and Baker concluded that European stability was threatened more by caution than by impatience.[71] With Bush's tacit acceptance of German unification in the face of criticism from western Europe Kohl had the backing he needed to go ahead. If America had balked, it is unlikely that either the European Community or the Soviets would have accepted unification at such a pace; and if it had not been done quickly the opportunity might have been lost.[72]

Even with American support actual reunification was still a long way off and was still not inevitable. First, Kohl had to win the support of the East Germans themselves. As demonstrations continued to sweep the country Egon Krenz was forced to agree to free elections with multiple candidates and a secret ballot. Old political parties, including the Christian Democrats and the Liberals, were suddenly rejuvenated, substituting their Communist puppet leaders with real politicians. The once powerless Volkskammer began to exert real pressure after electing a new Presidium by secret ballot; twenty-five SED deputies, including Erich Honecker, were removed along with Erich Mielke, the head of the detested Stasi, who made an extraordinary valedictory speech. The man responsible for arrests, torture and repression in the GDR stood in front of the Volkskammer and said tearfully: 'We are the sons and daughters of the working class. We worked for you. I still love you all!'[73] Instead of applause the chamber filled with bitter laughter. On 17 November 1989 a new cabinet was elected in East Berlin and the new Prime Minister Hans Modrow promised sweeping reforms. The old SED was effectively dead.

As the old political parties began to reform they eclipsed the groups like New Forum and Democracy Now which had played such an important role in the lead-up to 9 November. These organizations had served their purpose, but their opposition to unification and support for a socialist 'Third Way' put them completely at odds with the aspirations of ordinary people. Furthermore, they hoped to fight an election without becoming political. Bärbel Bohley said of New Forum: 'let us not lose out on our traditional support by racing headlong into a party structure.' Neither she nor her colleagues had learned from Solidarity that in order to survive in a democracy one must organize politically. On 22 November the Communists proposed 'round table talks' with the opposition, but they were already redundant. People did not want any more socialist experiments; they were sick of being treated like political guinea pigs and longed for the instant wealth and prosperity which they naively believed unification would bring. After November the chant 'Wir sind das Volk' became 'Wir sind EIN Volk' – We are one people. They also called for Helmut Kohl: 'Helmut, du bist auch UNSERER Kanzler' and 'Neither brown nor red – Helmut Kohl is our bet!' became increasingly popular.[74]

Events continued to move quickly. On 3 December Egon Krenz resigned while Kohl continued to campaign for unity.[75] On 19 December he met Hans Modrow in Dresden and made a moving speech in front of the Frauenkirche, where he was drowned out by shouts for 'Unity' and 'Freedom' and 'Germany, United Fatherland'. He would later claim that it was at that moment that he first became aware of the depth of popular support for unification in East Germany. On 22 December he presided over the emotional opening of the Brandenburg Gate; despite the pouring rain masses of people flocked to watch as he stepped under the historic structure and into East Berlin for the first time to shake hands with Prime Minister Modrow. 'This is one of the most important moments in my life,' he said. 'Standing here I feel that we are in Germany, and that we will do everything in our power to achieve unity.' Once again, the Brandenburg Gate had become the symbol of German destiny. The new crossing point was a Christmas present to Berlin; church bells rang out, huge hot-air balloons floated above the city, people waved West German flags and the East German flag with the GDR logo cut out of the middle of it. The street party that night was overwhelmingly international, with revellers from New York and Prague, Warsaw and Paris and London commemorating not only the end of the Berlin Wall but the more recent events in the 'Velvet Revolution' which had unfolded only days before: on 10 November Zhivkov, the Bulgarian leader of thirty-five years, had been ousted; on 17 November 50,000 people had demonstrated in Wenceslas Square in Prague and on 24 November the Czechoslovak Presidium and Secretariat had resigned. Finally, amidst astounding scenes, Ceauşescu had been pushed from power in Romania on 23 December. Europe was reeling from these events. New Year's Eve under the Brandenburg Gate was a wake for the Cold War.

The momentum of the eastern European revolutions boosted Kohl's argument for unification and at Camp David on 26 February 1990 many of the last obstacles were overcome. Amongst other things Kohl and Bush agreed that the borders of Germany were inviolable, although Kohl maintained that they had finally to be settled by a freely elected parliament of both German states. This sent an understandable shiver through Poland, whose people feared that any delay might mean future German claims on their western territories, but Kohl snapped back that Germany had 'no intention of linking the question of national unity with changes of existing borders'.[76] Meanwhile, on 29 January 1990 Modrow formed a coalition government of all parties and brought forward East German elections to 18 March.[77] This would be the first free vote in East Germany since 1949; it was understood to be a referendum on the unity of Germany, and the unity of Berlin.

The election campaign was dominated by traditional parties who were now backed by their West German counterparts; as a result Willy Brandt campaigned for the East German Social Democrats while Helmut Kohl became the CDU's chief spokesman. And it was Kohl, so often ridiculed in the western media as a bumbling politician, who really shone during the campaign. He was passionate about his mission and argued for quick unification under Article 23 of the constitution. Travelling tirelessly from Rostock to Leipzig, from Magdeburg to Cottbus, he talked directly to nearly 1 million people. In his desperation to achieve unity he promised far too much to East Germans, painting a magical picture of instant wealth in which massive investment, entrepreneurs, safety nets and low unemployment would immediately bring them a better life. The message was warmly received in East Germany. Ironically, however, it was largely rejected in East Berlin.

East Berlin was not representative of East Germany as a whole; indeed, it was the last real bastion of the Communist elite. It had long been the centre of SED power and was seen as a 'reward' post for loyal party men from the provinces. It contained the largest concentration of Stasi employees, SED officials, bureaucrats, writers, academics and other state functionaries who were indebted to the old system. It was these people who had the most to lose from unification and they made their objections clear. Once again, Berlin was displaying that bizarre mixture of cynicism, self-interest, political naïveté and sheer petulance which has, throughout its entire history, stood in the way of clear-headed political decisions. Here was a chance for the eastern half of the city to make a statement for unity and for its own future. Sadly, the opportunity was rejected.

I spent the election campaign in East Berlin and the surrounding area, and the political divide between Berlin and elsewhere was clearly visible. On trips outside the city I met many ordinary people who quietly admitted that they intended to vote CDU; some even spoke of it as a long-awaited revenge on those *Knote* (rogues) in Berlin. One soft-spoken old lady showed me around the town of Potsdam, describing how the SED had ripped down the Garrison Church, how her son had been imprisoned for 'spying' in the 1950s, and how the Russians had taken her family house away in 1945; now she was going to vote for unity so that the Communists could never control her country again. Later that day I overheard an Intourist guide refer to Sanssouci as a palace built by 'Frederick II'; one of her tour group retorted swiftly: 'It's Frederick the Great, Miss.' This sort of behaviour towards a government employee would have been unheard of a few weeks before. But if the CDU were the popular favourites in the towns it was clear that they were disliked in Berlin itself; indeed Helmut Kohl's campaign team had decided against putting great resources into the city as it was assumed that the effort would be wasted.

As the CDU machine swept through East Germany on a promise of quick unity and instant prosperity the other parties struggled to find a voice in the East German capital. The opposition groups had faded from sight and the Social Democrats were hurt by their muddle over unification. The Communists under their new leader, the socialist lawyer Gregor Gysi, had renamed themselves the PDS (Party of Democratic Socialism) but Gysi's message was entirely negative; for him unification and capitalism would bring not a brave new world but would end in misery and unemployment and poverty for decades to come. His alternative was to remove 'socialism', and he mounted a thinly disguised call for a return to the old ways of the GDR. The general public did not yet know that Gysi was himself involved with the Stasi.[78]

The mood in Berlin in the days leading up to the election was agitated. Speeches and rallies became little more than mud-slinging matches and most parties offered outright bribes for support: the Social Democrats offered coffee, the German Social Union gave out bananas and Democratic Awakening imported Coca-Cola (its infuriated leader Rainer Eppelmann was dubbed the leader of the Coca-Cola Party). Hundreds of colourful posters went up around the city. Flashes of green, fluorescent pink and yellow paper could be seen even in the most remote nooks and crannies of dilapidated East Berlin and many contained witty jibes at their opponents; one anti-unification sign read: 23 . . . NO *ANSCHLUSS* UNDER THIS NUMBER, referring to Bill 23, designed to hasten East and West German unification, to the *Anschluss* of Austria and to the standard recorded telephone message for a wrong number. In the *Kneipen* of East Berlin the election was discussed, but I found most Berliners much more coy about revealing their choice than their compatriots in the countryside. They would hide behind cryptic remarks like, 'The election is being held between a murderer, a bank robber and a pickpocket – the most important thing is to prevent the murderer getting in.'

On the warm March evening before the election I stood on the once Stasi-infested Friedrichstrasse and watched Wartburgs and Trabants sputter up and down, their loudspeakers, perched precariously on their roofs, broadcasting election slogans. The area by the Wall itself was even more startling. Before November the vicinity had been blocked off, visible only from a distance across the empty Pariser Platz. Now one could walk up to the Brandenburg Gate and meet traders offering everything from party badges to SED membership books to plastic replicas of the television tower, from East German belts to Free German Youth posters and – for a mere US$30 – special badges cast in commemoration of the Stasi. Less than a year before a man had been shot dead trying to escape nearby; now dozens of people were sneaking back and forth through giant gaps in the Wall under the noses of the helpless border guards. I walked up to one of the men, still clad in his dreary green uniform, and asked him what he thought of the election. '*Na ja*,' he answered, '*es geht*' – it's happening. When I enquired how much a piece of the Wall cost he quipped, 'the Americans are buying whole slabs for 40,000 marks . . . What a waste! They could give me the 40,000 marks and I'll make them up a slab for a few pfennig!' Meanwhile one of his colleagues handed me a particularly colourful piece of the Wall; I did not refuse, for to be offered a piece by a border guard, the likes of whom had made past journeys to and from East Germany a misery – to be offered a piece of the Wall by such a man on the eve of the destruction of his state was too surreal an opportunity to pass up. Clearly the era of murder and oppression, of Wall sickness, mine fields, trip wires, seven-year prison sentences for fabricated 'crimes against the state', of the ever-vigilant security police and the despicable trade in human beings was finally drawing to a close.

The election results were a resounding vote for unity. Helmut Kohl's Alliance won over 48 per cent of the vote while the Social Democrats won only 22 per cent, the Communist PDS 16 per cent, the ex-dissidents with their unworkable 'Third Way' platform only 3 per cent; except in Berlin.[79]

Many East Berliners voted against unification. Thirty-five per cent voted for the 'traditional' Berlin party, the Social Democrats, while the Communist PDS scored a very high 24.8 per cent.[80] The results reflected the continuing power of the SED and the old ruling class in East Berlin. For other East Germans the result merely reinforced their view that Berlin was full of '*Bonzen* who think of themselves first and Germany second'. 'Berlin', they maintained, 'is and remains an island.'[81]

The Berlin result was particularly strange as it was Berlin which was set to gain the most from the unification of Germany. On 1 April the city's historic waterways were opened for unrestricted use for the first time since 1945. By 12 June huge cranes had been brought in to begin the official dismantling of the 1 million tonnes of the Wall, starting at the Bernauer Strasse, where dozens of people had jumped from the windows of their houses to escape the Vopos in August 1961. As the Wall disappeared old landmarks re-emerged. Potsdamer Platz, once the busiest intersection in the city, was opened once again, as was the eerie space around Hitler's bunker. On the other hand one of the most poignant symbols to disappear was Checkpoint Charlie. On 22 June James Baker, the American Secretary of State, Eduard Shevardnadze, the Soviet Foreign Minister, the Foreign Ministers of Germany, France, Britain and the US and two mayors of Berlin watched as the twenty-nine-year-old hut at the checkpoint was dismantled.[82] American, British and French flags were hoisted on a giant crane as the request 'Permission to close the Checkpoint Charlie control post' rang through the air. The command 'Formal dismissal of the attachment!' was barked back. The wooden hut was gently lifted, swayed in the air for a moment, and was taken away. According to James Baker, the Checkpoint 'now leads from the conflict of the past to the reconciliation of the future. As we raise the gate of history the spirit of liberty moves along this road to join this city, to unite this nation and to heal this continent.' Douglas Hurd said: 'We share the happiness of all Berliners and all Germans that the cruel division of decades is now over . . . At long last we are bringing Charlie in from the cold.' At the end of June President Weizsäcker became the first person to be named Freeman of the city of Berlin since 1946.

Despite the election results formal unification had to wait until the four war-time Allies could agree on a peace treaty which would finally bring the Second World War to a close. In the meantime Kohl worked hard to integrate the GDR into the West German system. One of the most important steps was the currency reform of 1 July 1990, which was set at the most generous rate of one : one – one Deutschmark for one Ost Mark. The reform was and continues to be a source of controversy. Some argued that without it thousands of East Germans would have felt alienated from West Germany or would simply have moved there to seek jobs. Others argued that a one-to-one rate would price inefficient East German goods and labour out of the market and impede recovery; the April 1990 issue of *The Economist* asked simply: 'Is this too generous?' However, the real reasons for its implementation were political.[84] The West Germans were purchasing unification and, as Helmut Kohl put it, the reform was a 'decisive step on the path toward German unity and an historic day for the German nation'. The Bundesbank accepted a one-to-one exchange rate reluctantly but its president, Karl Otto Pohl, warned East Germans to be cautious with their new-found wealth: 'There is certainly a temptation to spend the money but my advice is to be careful.' Few heeded his words.

East Berliners were excited by the currency reform. They knew that the Deutschmark was one of the great symbols of post-war West German success – the one thing which had filled the people of the angst-ridden Federal Republic with a sense of accomplishment. Now, after forty years, East Germans were to have a piece of the *Wirtschaftswunder*. There was widespread excitement as the large canvas bags filled with DM 25 billion in notes and coins printed by the Bundesbank were unloaded at banks around the city ready for distribution. Some makeshift banks had been set up in old army barracks and the Deutsche Bank opened its first East German branch on the Alexanderplatz. On the eve of the reform every East Berlin *Kneipe* was filled with a jolly 'end of currency' parties and as midnight approached the minutes were counted down to the sound of beer glasses and plastic Sekt tops popping. The Adlershof Palace of Culture, its walls no longer adorned with GDR propaganda murals but with bright cartoons poking fun at Erich Honecker and his cronies, held a 'Dance into the D-Mark' party late into the night and as the revellers went home at dawn they encountered early queues of people outside the banks with their old featherlight 'Aluchips' and monopoly-sized paper money. When the doors finally opened the banks were besieged. Savings could be exchanged at a one-to-one rate up to DM 40,000, salaries were to be paid in DM at parity and unemployment benefit was to be increased. East Germans were delighted. The millions of old Ost Marks were eventually buried in mine shafts, joining the old Reichsmarks which had been abandoned in 1948.

Other businesses also had to prepare for reform; on the night before the change-over the dreary East German shops, with their grey metal shelves and sub-standard goods, from cheap sausage to acid, coloured artificial 'fruit' juice, were transformed. Old produce was removed and the shelves were packed with brightly packaged West German food from chocolates and fruit to choice cuts of meat. The next day they were sold out in hours. People now refused to buy any East German goods: one old department store on the Alexanderplatz tried to shift 400,000 1950s-style polyester dresses and the like but nobody was interested. In an opinion poll carried out by the Dresdner Bank asking what East Germans would most like out of the currency reform around 82 per cent said they wanted to earn more money, 22 per cent said they wanted to own a telephone, 17 per cent said they wanted to buy a car and the same number said that they wanted to take a holiday abroad.[85] Most East Germans felt that they had 'arrived' and that the riches all around them would be theirs for the asking. That evening the city celebrated; there were fireworks and a huge party at the normally drab Alexanderplatz, and Mahler's 'Resurrection' Symphony was performed by a combined orchestra of East and West German musicians in the middle of the Potsdamer Platz. Few foresaw that the short-term legacy of the one-to-one currency reform would be factory closures, unemployment and bitterness which would descend on East Germany in the coming months.

It took a surprisingly long time for West Germans to realize exactly how backward the East German economy was. Before the currency reform the west had been flooded with optimistic reports about the inevitable improvement of the GDR economy. Walter Siepp, chairman of the management board at the Commerzbank, echoed a popular view when he said that East Germany's economy would be transformed into a market economy within two years, and would lead 'to an economic miracle of sorts'. By 29 March 1990, however, *The Financial Times* was already warning that 'East German industry is even more inefficient than feared, with output per head possibly as low as 30 per cent of West Germany's rather than the previous 50 per cent estimate'.[86] To help with the privatization of state-run groups, the restructuring of East German companies and the closure of factories deemed beyond hope the West Germans set up the Treuhandanstalt in July 1989.[87] The overall result was positive but in the short term huge cash infusions were poured into crumbling industries – payments which had already cost West Germans $200 billion by the end of 1994.[88] It was in this increasingly gloomy climate that the final negotiations took place between the war-time Allies to discuss the possibility of German unification.

By early 1990 the western Allies were reconciling themselves to the idea. The United States supported German unity, but there was still a degree of tension amongst Europeans. In March 1990, for example, Margaret Thatcher had held a secret seminar of academics at Chequers which was widely reported as an attack on unity. According to Timothy Garton Ash, who attended the meeting, the reports had been distorted: 'despite the inflamed headlines in London, Paris and Frankfurt there had not in fact been a list compiled or a collective view of "the German character" drawn up.'[89] Most British citizens were now in favour of German unity and supported the view summed up by Michael Howard, who said that 'for better or worse, the German question is a question for the Germans. Whatever our views about their past or apprehensions about the future, we can no longer deny the German people – East and

West – the right to work out their own destinies without foreign interference. The question at issue is not essentially about reunification. It is about self-determination.'[90] The French under François Mitterrand were less enthusiastic. Mitterrand had already snubbed Kohl on numerous occasions, declining an invitation to join the ceremony to open Berlin's Brandenburg Gate, but by March he had joined the 'realists' in accepting the inevitable.

The Soviet hurdle was more difficult but was cleared through co-operation between Bonn, Washington and Moscow. Once again George Bush played a crucial role. As early as December 1989 he had informed Gorbachev that he favoured the idea of German unification. He then sanctioned Kohl's meetings with Gorbachev – first in Moscow and then in Stavropol in the Caucasus in July 1990 – so that the two could come to some agreement on Soviet terms for withdrawal from the GDR.[91] The pictures of Helmut Kohl wrapped in his blue cardigan (later put in the House of German History in Bonn) and walking around the Stavropol countryside led to fears of another Rapallo but these were unfounded.[92] Gorbachev accepted that East Germany could be part of NATO as long as the joint German army after unification was reduced to a level of 370,000 and German NATO units would not be stationed in former East Germany until Soviet troops had been withdrawn. Voluntary Soviet withdrawal from East Germany – the 'Miracle of Moscow' – came about through Kohl's diplomatic skill, Hans-Dietrich Genscher's offers of financial aid to the Russians, George Bush's continued pressure on Moscow and Gorbachev's willingness to co-operate. With Soviet consent to unification the way was cleared for formal agreements between the Allies. Helmut Kohl persuaded the Americans and Russians to agree to a 'two plus four' formula, whereby the two Germanys plus the United States, the Soviets, the British and the French would meet as a body. Finally, on 12 September 1990 at a ceremony in Moscow, Germany was formally unified.

The 'Two Plus Four' Treaty formally ended the Second World War. It rescinded the rights of the victors of 1945 over Germany; it guaranteed German borders, including the Oder–Neisse Line with Poland, it reaffirmed Germany's commitment to peace, including the renunciation of nuclear, chemical and biological weapons; and it confirmed the phased withdrawal of Soviet troops from German soil. It was rightly seen as a personal triumph for Helmut Kohl, putting him beside Adenauer as one of the greatest German Chancellors in post-war history. For Berliners the results were momentous. Both East and West Berlin reverted to German control and the Allied armies, which had been in place since 1945, prepared to withdraw. Berlin's long period of crisis and occupation was over and it was fitting that the formal ceremony for the unification of Germany should take place in the city which had housed American, Russian, French and British troops for over forty years. This took place on 3 October 1990 but it was a strangely solemn affair – quite different from the stunning atmosphere of 9 November or the raucous celebrations on New Year's Eve – almost as if Berliners had suddenly become aware of the enormous responsibility being thrust upon them. They were now the focal point of a nation of 80 million people, but far from being proud or triumphant they seemed intimidated, even embarrassed by their new strength. The angst-ridden self-doubt was reflected in the agonized debates as to whether Berlin's church bells should be rung that day; political leaders filed into the Philharmonie to hear speeches warning against nationalism, and the general mood was sombre and restrained. It was only at midnight, when Helmut Kohl and President von Weizsäcker went to the Reichstag and watched as a giant flag was unfurled to the sound of the national anthem, that there was any sense of celebration.

The reaction to unification in the rest of the world was marked by cautious optimism: a *Sunday Telegraph* leader claimed that 'reunification was inevitable from the moment the Berlin Wall was breached, and the most sensible reaction to it is the joy honest men felt as they saw the prisoners from East Germany spilling out to the west . . . The gain for Europe and the world is immense.'[93] Others supported unity; Lord Weidenfeld wrote in January 1990 that 'those who still have a nightmarish vision of a Fourth Reich might banish their fears and put their trust in the enduring continuity of the moral standards set by such humane pragmatists as Adenauer and Heuss, Brandt and Weiszäcker, and in the younger generation of Germans of goodwill'.[94]

The impact of unification was most visible in Berlin. The disappearance of the Wall had already meant that the border checks, the transit corridors, the sealed trains and gruff guards had vanished; by 14 September 1990 the Berlin air corridor had ceased to exist and a British Airways plane became the last commercial airliner to fly along it. In April 1990 United States intelligence personnel had begun to dismantle the $1 billion worth of listening posts along the East German border, and the occupying forces prepared to leave the city for the last time. The Miracle of Moscow was coming true.

In 1989 there were 360,000 Soviet troops in East Germany, and it was not easy to persuade them to leave. Bonn had pledged DM 13 billion to cover the cost of their withdrawal, which included the construction of new housing for them in Russia. The money helped to buy Berlin's freedom and on 31 August 1994 the Russians marched through the city for the last time. The departure of a powerful army is always a highly emotive event but the peaceful retreat of the Red Army from Berlin was beyond compare. The Soviets had marched into the city in 1945 and there were still bitter memories of the raping, the looting and the imposition of the hated Stalinist regime there. Few people mourned their passing. General Matvei Burlakov, commander of the Western

Group of the Russian army, ensured that the departure was a solemn affair; he had drilled his men to perfection and they put on an extraordinary show, marching with mechanical precision through the city. In his speech Burlakov reminded the assembled crowd that although they were leaving, the Red Army had 'come to Berlin as victors', and the Russian writer Lev Kopelev was moved to say, 'These are moments when you hear the footsteps of history.' During the official ceremony Helmut Kohl tried to lighten the mood, declaring: 'You leave as partners, you leave as friends.' Boris Yeltsin threw his arms around Kohl, kissed him and said that the two countries 'will never wage war against each other again'; later that night there were parties complete with Cossack dancers, balalaikas and vodka.

But for all the noise the celebrations seemed forced. Old Soviet bases like Schönwalde were ecological disaster zones filled with unexploded ammunition, spilled fuel and dumped toxic waste. For their part the troops were unhappy to be leaving the relative prosperity of Berlin for a grim future in sub-standard army barracks in Russia. Few wanted to return and in 1990 Red Army desertions had risen dramatically, with 200 men going missing that year alone: some fifty-three asked Germany for asylum; others vanished into the country-side, begging for food and sleeping rough. Many had taken weapons with them to sell on the thriving black market; at the time a Kalashnikov brought around DM200 and, as the Moscow paper *Komsomolskaya Pravda* put it, the deserters had created an 'army mafia'. After his speech, General Burlakov turned away grim faced and clutched the Russian flag in both hands as he left for the military airport at Sperenburg. Most Berliners heaved a huge sigh of relief.

The joy in Berlin was not echoed in Moscow. During a visit there at the end of August I found that many older people felt that Russia had 'lost face'. The *Moskovsky Komsomolets* of 31 August 1994 claimed that although the Soviets were leaving Berlin 'we might have stayed ... Our last wish for the united Germans is that they live in such a way that our soldiers will never have reason to storm their capital a fourth time.' On 1 September *Sovietskaya Rossiy* published a little poem bemoaning the hasty withdrawal of troops: 'We who are leaving want to be good neighbours, but our hasty withdrawal seems more like retreat to me. In anguish I watch this defeat of our grandsons, and quietly ask myself: What would Marshal Zhukov say?' And on 1 September *Pravda* said, 'it is hard to agree with Yeltsin ... that "we can no longer think in terms of victors and vanquished" in that war. This opinion is not worthy of the achievements of the Soviet nation.' In an attempt to counter this negative impression the troops were welcomed in Moscow with an impressive ceremony at the Belorussky railway station followed by a march down Tverskaya Street to the Kremlin. It did little to dispel the gloom. There had been 546,000 Soviet staff and relatives in East Germany in addition to the soldiers. They had come home to an uncertain future.

The Soviet withdrawal from Berlin was quickly followed by the departure of the western Allies in September 1994. This was a much sadder occasion and despite the tense relations between Berlin and the US since the 1960s many people were genuinely sorry to see them go. The Americans were hailed by older people as saviours of West Berlin who had provided vital support in the grim post-war years: 'They bombed us during the Second World War but in 1948 they kept us alive,' said one seventy-six-year-old former engineer in the German air force.[95] Chancellor Helmut Kohl presided over the events of 9 September 1994 attended by President François Mitterrand, Prime Minister John Major and the American Secretary of State Warren Christopher. The salute was taken at the Luftbrücke (Airlift) Memorial at Tempelhof Airport, and at the official ceremony at the Schauspielhaus Kohl reminisced about his first visit to Berlin in 1947: 'I was 17 years old . . . the city lay in ruins, the future was uncertain. For almost half a century the three western Allies protected and defended freedom here in Berlin, in the heart of our continent.' The mood was solemn as the Allies took down their flags at bases all over the city. The British military mission in West Berlin merged with the embassy in East Berlin; the British headquarters, with its perfectly preserved Third Reich architecture, was handed over to the city, the American compound was turned into a museum, complete with a plane used in the Berlin airlift and one of the tanks which had nuzzled up against Soviet T-34s during the showdown at the Wall in 1961. When the last troops had finally gone Britain's chief diplomat in West Berlin, Michael Burton, said: 'Berlin is no longer under four-power authority, it is a free and democratic city.'

The unification of Germany and the planned departure of the Allied forces had put the issue of the German capital back on the political agenda. The question facing the nation was what to do with the city now that it was free; should it become the German capital and seat of government, or should Bonn retain its role? The issue was of vital importance for the newly united Germany for it was widely understood that the choice of capital would help to determine what kind of Germany would emerge from the fractured nation.

The debate about the German capital opened the day the Berlin Wall was first breached and reached its climax just before the official Bundestag vote on 20 June 1991. By then the conflict had degenerated into a mud-slinging match between advocates of each city, exposing a surprising level of chauvinism, prejudice and intolerance within the newly unified nation. In reality either city would have been adequate as a capital but Germans were passionate about the choice before them. It was much more than a decision about where the Bundestag would reside. It was a debate about history, about the burdens of the past, about the kind of future Germany wanted, about the way it would be treated by the rest of the world. Should Germany once again be a great power with a powerful capital? This might unite the nation but could it also lead to war. Should Germany adopt the western liberal democratic values represented by Bonn and continue to live in the safety of the post-war era, or should it risk confronting the ghosts of pre-1945 history which lingered in Berlin? Should Germany continue as a federal state with power diffused throughout the country or should it opt for a powerful centralized system based in the old capital? Did Germany even need a metropolis in which artists, bankers, politicians and entrepreneurs could meet? Was it not safer to do without such a strong centre, as it had since the war?

The debate about the German capital raged throughout 1990. Arguments were outlined on posters and billboards, they were aired in the press and on television; they were agonized over on talk shows and at public meetings; they appeared on bumper stickers and badges. The process was legitimate – after all, Germany was trying to come to terms with its own identity – but there was a strange urgency, as if the choice of capital would be the determining factor in Germany's future development. Advocates of each city set about rewriting history to 'prove' that theirs was the only one acceptable both to Germans and to the rest of the world. Berliners proved as capable of being selective about the past as Bonners. Prominent Berliners founded the 'Berlin as Capital' campaign; the Bonn publican Felix Drautzburg answered with 'Ja zu Bonn', which to his surprise quickly won him the signatures of 8,000 officials and politicians and the support of 15,000 civil servants whose jobs and homes were now threatened. The first round in the argument, however, went to the 'capital in waiting', Berlin.

When the Wall fell in 1989 most Berliners expected to automatically assume their previous role as the historic capital; the slogan 'We are the future capital of a united Germany' was already being used during the March 1990 election campaign. After all, in 1949 the new West German government had declared Berlin the 'natural German capital' and Bonn a temporary capital for the FRG. And, despite forty years of occupation and division, Berliners argued that the city still felt like a capital, with its wide imperial avenues, the Brandenburg Gate and the old Prussian administrative buildings. Berlin had been reduced to two small provincial enclaves by the Wall, but however run-down it now was it had once been a great metropolis – the only one in Germany that approached a Rome or a London; indeed it remained the largest city between Moscow and Paris. But Bonn supporters were not daunted.

Bonn claimed in its favour that it was not 'tainted' by the past and that it represented the only 'successful' German capital in modern history. It might have been the provisional capital of the Federal Republic but in forty years it had provided a sheltered environment and nurtured a stable democracy. Under Bonn's guidance West Germany had been accepted into the western community of nations and the city had been identified with Germany's entry into NATO and into the European Union. Bonners claimed that it was to their advantage that the city was not a traditional capital; it was not too powerful or too centralized and would be an ideal focal point for the new federal system. Bonn symbolized Germany's commitment to western values and the renunciation of the *Drang nach Osten*; it was balanced and predictable and rooted firmly in the safety of the recent past. As for Berlin, they argued, it had had its chance, and it had failed.

There were many powerful arguments levelled against Berlin. For Bonn advocates the old capital was a repressive, even terrifying place. It had been the centre of Prussian militarism, of Nazi terror and Stasi thugs; it had been home to the Gestapo and the SS and to those who had brought shame on the German nation; it should therefore be disqualified from the race. Countess Marion Dönhoff took up this line, saying that 'the legacy of Berlin as the seat of Nazi power makes it unsuitable to be the capital of a democratic Germany anxious to bed itself down in a unified Europe'. In *Die Zeit* of 6 May 1990 she wrote, 'The decision to make Berlin the capital would send out a false signal. It could tempt the Germans even without their intending it to embark on the way to becoming a nation state instead of keeping the European goal in mind.' Other luminaries also spoke out against Berlin on historical grounds: Golo Mann said that culturally Berlin was a fascinating city but that politically it had brought catastrophe: 'One thought of the murder of Karl Liebknecht and Rosa Luxemburg or of Walter Rathenau . . . and that the worst of German history politically was carried out from Berlin . . . and not from Munich or Stuttgart or Bonn.'[96] For these people, Berlin was condemned by its past.

Berliners quickly answered back. When members of the 'Berlin as Capital' campaign heard these arguments they were furious. How dare other Germans point to Berlin as the only place involved in Nazi crimes or in the Second World War? Were Bonn advocates claiming that there had been no Nazis in Bonn or Frankfurt or Bremen? How dare other Germans imply that the Third Reich had happened in a vacuum in the Mark Brandenburg? To counter this they wove their own rather melodramatic version of the past which depicted Berlin as the victim of German history rather than the perpetrator.

The arguments were extraordinary: everywhere one went in Berlin one heard about its alleged historic virtues: Berliners had always resisted authority with humour and resilience and the unique Berlin character had developed after years of oppression; Berlin had survived the sacking and massacre of the

The Reichstag in May 1945. It had been the supreme Soviet target in the Battle for Berlin, and the building was captured after fierce fighting on 1 May 1945. Two thousand two hundred Soviets and two thousand five hundred Germans died in the struggle for this building.

RIGHT Berlin – May 1945. German soldiers after capitulation on their way to the Gulag. Those in front were members of the *Volksturm*, the last-ditch defence of Berlin made up of boys under sixteen and men over fifty.

A German soldier hung for 'desertion'. The sign around his neck reads: 'So die all traitors to the Fatherland.' Hundreds of men were killed by the fanatical 'Werewolf' squads in the last days of the war.

Soviet soldiers storming a German position in Berlin, April 1945. A dead German soldier lies in the foreground. The Russians had to fight for the city street by street – they could not use their artillery, as it was blocked by the tall buildings, so they used mortars, rocket fire of the katyushi and hand-to-hand combat. Three hundred and four thousand Russians were killed or wounded in the fight for Berlin alone.

As the Soviets entered Germany they were told, 'Soldiers of the Red Army, the German women are yours!' Attacks on women were particularly brutal in the last days of April and in early May but they continued well into the occupation, and few Berlinerins were spared rape. Women meeting on the street or in food queues would begin a conversation with, 'How many times. . .?' Illegal abortion became common, although it was estimated that between 150,000 and 200,000 'Russian babies' were born in the Soviet zone. Russian behaviour towards the women of Berlin would have serious political repercussions later on. The photograph depicts two Russian soldiers harrassing a woman in 1945.

By May 1945 Berlin was dangerously short of food – not least because the SS had destroyed supplies so they would not fall into Soviet hands. Here two men cut up the cadaver of a horse in Tempelhof.

The Soviets reached the Führerbunker on 2 May 1945. This photograph, taken in August, shows a soldier in Hitler's conference room, in which he had married Eva Braun thirty hours before committing suicide at 15.30 on 30 April. The Soviets only found out about the Führerbunker – and Eva Braun – after Hitler's death, the details of which were pieced together by Hugh Trevor-Roper who was sent in by British Intelligence in September 1945. His work, *The Last Days of Hitler*, remains the definitive account of the event.

The black market flourished in post-war Berlin despite official attempts to stop the illegal trading. The most famous markets were at Potsdamer Platz and the Brandenburg Gate. The basic unit of exchange was the cigarette – five bought sex, twenty-five cartons bought a Leica camera. Many Allied soldiers made small fortunes in this way. Here (in 1945) a German offers an American soldier a camera.

The Soviets tried to control political life in all of Berlin, and when a non-Communist *Magistrat* was elected in October 1946, they tried to prevent it from meeting at all. This photograph captures the moment on 6 September 1948 when Soviets tried to block the delegates from entering the City Hall. The civilians fought back but it was clear that the *Magistrat* could not operate from the Soviet zone. Henceforth it met at the Technical University in the west, marking the split of Berlin government into two distinct 'blocs'.

ABOVE On 24 June 1948, Stalin blockaded Berlin in a final attempt to force the city into submission and the Western Allies to leave. On 9 September, 350,000 Berliners demonstrated against the Soviet action and Ernst Reuter appealed to the 'peoples of the world' to watch over Berlin.

INSET To Stalin's chagrin the Allies responded to the blockade with the Berlin airlift, which saw an astounding 2,325,000 tons of food and supplies brought to Berlin on some 277,500 flights. Stalin was forced to back down and the blockade was lifted on 12 May 1949. Here, Berliners celebrate the arrival of the first car over the Hannover–Berlin road. The sign reads: 'Hurrah! We're still alive.'

Tension often flared along the Soviet sector boundary and before the construction of the Wall everything from harassment to kidnapping had taken place along its length. This 1952 photograph captures a skirmish between an East German border guard and a civilian at the American–Soviet sector boundary.

The Berlin Wall was erected under a blanket of secrecy in the early hours of 13 August 1961. When people woke they found that over seventy-two miles of fencing now ringed West Berlin, cutting the city in two and dividing families and friends. This photograph, taken in September, shows a young couple holding up their new babies so that their grandparents in the east can catch a glimpse of them.

On 22 October 1961, the Soviets tried to restrict American access in Berlin and General Clay ordered ten M8 tanks to line up along the Wall at Checkpoint Charlie. The Soviets responded by sending thirty-three tanks into East Berlin. The world held its breath, knowing that one rash move could result in war. The Soviets backed down after three days.

The Allies promoted press freedom in their zones and Berlin produced thirteen newspapers by 1946. This 1948 kiosk displays local newspapers and magazines along with *Time* and *Newsweek*.

On 17 June 1953 East Germans rose up in the first large-scale anti-Soviet protest behind the Iron Curtain. Around 260 demonstrators were killed throughout the GDR; this cross was erected on the site where a Soviet Panzer had crushed a civilian. The uprising failed but set in motion the sequence of events which brought about Beria's downfall in Moscow.

With the end of the Airlift West Berlin was transformed into a 'Showcase of Capitalism' meant to prove the superiority of the West and to dazzle those in the Soviet zone. Here, in the Kurfürstendamm in 1953, Wirtschafts-wunder West Berlin is complete with cinemas, shop windows, Volkswagens and bright neon signs.

East and West Berlin competed with one another in architecture. In the 1950s and 1960s this took the form of seeing which side could build the most modern buildings. In the West these symbolized freedom and democracy and in the East projected the glories of Soviet Communism. Here, plans for the Spring Projekt in Kreuzburg are contrasted with the plans for Stalinallee in East Berlin.

Post-war Berlin developed into a centre of protest, beginning with the student anti-Vietnam demonstrations in 1968 and continuing with the anti-nuclear movement of the 1970s, the rise of the Green movement in the 1980s, and the virulent peace movement sparked off by the Pershing missiles also in the 1980s. Linking these together was an anti-American streak; bizarre in a city which had been protected by them since 1945. This demonstration on 13 September 1981 at the visit of Alexander Haig was typical.

CENTRE The end of the Wall: the night of 9/10 November 1989 saw the opening of the Berlin–Berlin border and riotous celebrations in the city. Here, people stand on the low Wall in front of the Brandenburg Gate.

INSET Although much maligned by West Berliners, the policies introduced by Ronald Reagan and continued by George Bush were largely responsible for setting in motion the events which led to the collapse of the Wall. President and Mrs Reagan stand by a gap chipped out of the Wall on 12 November 1990. The Berlin mayor Walther Momper – who opposed the idea of unification and on that very day promised to 'respect the integrity of the GDR' – stands behind them.

RIGHT 10 November 1989 – a traffic jam of Trabbis, as East Germans line up to drive from east to west through Checkpoint Charlie.

Thirty Years War, had weathered the street violence and hyper-inflation of the 1920s and had stood up to the Nazi dictatorship. Furthermore, it had suffered the worst of the Allied bombing, the brutal foreign occupation, the vicious Soviet blockade and the most terrible creation of the post-war world, the Berlin Wall. To those who claimed that Berlin was tainted because it had been the Nazi capital they retorted that Nazis had originated not in Berlin but in Austria and Munich and that the system had been forced on Berliners against their will; they were not to blame if their liberal city had been chosen as host to this parasite. Furthermore, they argued, they alone had been 'the city of resistance' and had saved 6,000 Jews at great risk to themselves within sight of Gestapo headquarters; as Konrad Kruis, a Karlsruhe Court judge, put it, Berlin had not only harboured the Nazis but contained the ashes of a 'better Germany', the Germany 'represented by Stauffenberg, Moltke, Delp, Wehrle and many others'.[97] There were foreign contributors as well. In *The Times* of 11 June 1991 Lord Annan wrote that those who called Berlin a symbol of Prussian militarism and Nazi brutality were wrong: 'Prussia was the first state to practise religious toleration and give refuge to the persecuted of every country. The Nazi party had its worst electoral results in Berlin, and it was there that in July 1944 Prussian aristocrats plotted against Hitler and paid for it with their lives.' Other Berliners argued that there had been proportionally as many Nazis elsewhere in Germany as in Berlin; one even told me that Berlin Nazis had 'come to the city from outside to further their careers' and that 'true Berliners' had been anti-Nazi.

Attention was directed to more recent history: even if Berliners had not behaved particularly well during the war they had surely redeemed themselves afterwards. It was East Berlin and not Bonn which had endured Red Army occupation in 1945, living under the Soviet yoke while West Germans grew fat on their economic miracle. In a letter to the *Frankfurter Allgemeine Zeitung* on 27 April Roland Hennicke reminded the nation of the bravery shown by Berliners during the blockade of 1948–9 and during the 1953 uprising. Lord Annan mentioned that perhaps the Germans did not realize

> what an affront to their Western allies to desert Berlin will be. In 1946 America and Britain helped the courageous Social Democrats, who risked abduction by Soviet hit squads, to oppose the compulsory amalgamation of their party with the Communist party ordered in the Soviet one. In 1948 the Allies spent millions organizing the airlift and several of their pilots were killed ... Berlin became the symbol of resistance to totalitarian rule.[98]

The barrage of emotionally charged half-truths did little to clarify the debate: Berlin had indeed been the Nazi capital and it had also acted as a centre of resistance; many high-ranking Nazis had come from outside Berlin and many had been locals; Berlin was the city in which the Holocaust was devised and more Jews had been saved there than in any other city – but did this prove anything? The fight over which city was 'more guilty' of the crimes of the Third Reich rather missed the point and was often offensive, as was the idea that the population of any single German city could be either blamed or excused from the legacy of the war. The fight over the capital became bogged down in historical arguments of dubious value.

Berlin advocates argued that East Germany would be successfully integrated only if their city was chosen as capital; East Germans might otherwise feel completely cut off from their new democracy. For decades the two halves of the nation had been separated and it was time for westerners to realize that Berlin had a historic place in the centre of Germany. East and West Germans would thus be brought together. President von Weizsäcker pointed out that Berlin was 'the one asset which East Germans could contribute to the unified state'. For him Berlin was pivotal in east–west European relations and he declared that he would not move to Berlin as 'a decoration for a so-called capital' if the government did not move with him. This sentiment was echoed by East Germans themselves: over 70 per cent declared their preference for Berlin. Many in the west were unmoved. They did not particularly care about the feelings of East Germans, most of whom were seen as 'ex-Stasi' or 'proto-Communists'.

Although it is an apparently unified nation state Germany still contains deep prejudices which were exposed by the Berlin/Bonn question. Some echo past conflicts rather like the nineteenth-century debate about the merits of Berlin over Vienna as the 'true' German capital. As before, southerners often described Berlin as the home of stiff northern Prussian Protestants who were unimaginative, cold, militaristic and generally unpleasant. Berliners dismissed the south as backward, weak, disorganized and Catholic. These divisions played an important if unspoken part in the fight, and fitted neatly into the new debate of the decade – between 'Ossies' (Prussian Protestant northerners) and 'Wessies' (southern *gemütlich* Catholics). These simplistic divisions were deepened by revelations about the poverty in the ex-GDR. West Germans knew that eastern Germany would eventually recover but they wanted to remain at a distance while it did so. François Mitterrand believed that 'East Germany is Prussia. It will never knuckle under to Bavaria',[99] and many others argued that to choose this 'eastern' capital would alienate West Germans; as one Municher put it to me, 'for Bavarians the idea of Berlin is unthinkable!' There were echoes of Adenauer's most vitriolic attacks against 'Asiatic' Berlin and for many southerners the city did indeed seem alien.

The geographical prejudice against Berlin ran deep. The city was seen as the 'wrong choice' because of its position in Europe, and because of its proximity to its eastern neighbours. This argument was a twist on the old German obsession with geographical determinism – the notion that situation somehow predetermines national behaviour. In the nineteenth century Germans were convinced that their place as the *Land der Mitte* had shaped their history; in the modern era Bonn was 'western' because it was 'in the west' and would keep unified Germany anchored there, while 'eastern' Berlin might draw it into the 'chaos' of Russia and central Europe. As the Munich satirist Konstantine Wecker put it, the most common objections to the move to Berlin were that the city was 'too left-wing, speaks a dialect equally impenetrable as that of Bavaria, and is almost in Poland'. The last was a highly contentious issue, for it touched on one of the most sensitive, if unspoken, issues in German history: the loss of Germany's eastern territories in 1945.

Before the border changes at the end of the Second World War Berlin had been virtually in the geographical centre of a Germany which stretched into Prussian lands which were now part of Poland and Russia. Post-war Berlin is only fifty miles from the Polish border. Some expressed the fear that if Berlin was chosen as capital it might re-open old wounds. The geographical argument cropped up everywhere; the *Neue Zürcher Zeitung* pointed out on 23 June 1991 that 'Bonn symbolizes Germany's western orientation', while Berlin now lay 'directly on the eastern border of the German territory'. Above all, however, the geographical argument hid a deep and lingering prejudice against Poland. Following 'unrest' in the east, Berlin, it was feared, would be flooded with refugees pouring in over the eastern border. The fear was fuelled by stories of Russian or Polish weapons merchants working in Berlin. Were Polish criminals not already stealing West German Mercedes and BMWs? Were not Polish craftsmen already undercutting German garden gnome manufacturers with their cheaper imitations? Berlin was not suitable as capital because it was next to a border which was 'too sensitive' at the present time. Berliners themselves had no problem with their geographical placement and countered that in 1949 the border with France had been equally precarious.

There was yet another, more mundane reason for the heated debate – greed. Bonners feared that the move to Berlin would cost too much (at the time it was estimated at DM90 billion) and predicted that their city would become a ghost town. They had a point. By the late 1980s one in every three jobs there was linked to its role as seat of government. The mayor of Bonn, Hans Daniels, argued that the government employed 100,000 people and that 'if diplomats and civil servants leave Bonn will die'. Count Otto Lambsdorff added helpfully that he had just bought a comfortable home there and saw no reason why he should move. Furthermore, after forty years as 'provisional

capital' Bonn had just spent around D M 2 billion on new government buildings
and civic projects which would now all go to waste.

This argument was linked to a more general question of lifestyle, and to
the traditional division between 'modernists' or 'cosmopolitans' on one hand,
and advocates of quiet, rural *Heimat* on the other. Some Bonners considered
Berlin a sprawling and ugly city while Berliners called the West German capital
the *Bundesdorf* (federal village), small and pretty but boring and provincial,
'half the size of Chicago's main cemetery and twice as dead'; even John le
Carré had dismissed it as a 'Small Town in Germany'. Bonners called their
city the 'Florence of the North' – it was, after all, Beethoven's birthplace –
but unkind Berliners pointed out that the great composer had left the little
town as soon as he could and that Berlin had more bridges than Bonn.
Some Bonn advocates ridiculed Berliners' obsession with their 'metropolis'
and argued that provincialism was Bonn's greatest asset: in an article in *Die
Zeit* of 21 June 1991 Günter Hofmann questioned the attacks on Bonn and
asked: 'What is wrong with provincialism? . . . It would not be so bad to have
a "*Hauptstadt* of *Gemütlichkeit*".' Ian Murray, another Bonn supporter, wrote:
'The Bundestag member in Berlin risks mugging as he looks for a taxi to take
him to his tiny flat or expensive hotel. The energetic Bundestag member in
Bonn can stroll home safely.'[100] The Labour Minister Norbert Blüm claimed
that 'Bonn will lose a great deal if it loses the Bundestag and the government,
Berlin on the other hand would win only problems: housing, rent, traffic and
environmental problems.' But Berliners would have none of it: Berlin was a
'natural' capital and could absorb the problems. As Hans Deutsch pointed out
in a letter to *Die Zeit* on 1 June 1991, Berlin already had 'all the elements for
a capital, with the exception of ministerial buildings. It has the social, artistic
and intellectual environment of a capital.' Others said that Berlin could easily
be reconverted; the restored Reichstag could become the Bundestag, the ex-East
German Volkskammer could be made into the Bundesrat or upper house, and
deputies could be put into the ex-Central Committee of S E D headquarters.

By the end the debate had become highly acrimonious. On 23 April 1991
Helmut Kohl declared for Berlin, saying that Germany would 'stand a better
chance of growing together if the decision were taken soon to move the
government from Bonn to Berlin'. His choice was based on 'personal relations
with the city' and 'respect for its achievements during the years of division';
Berlin 'deserved special trust'. As if to prove his point, twelve of the sixteen
German states, including all five of the new additions from eastern Germany,
spoke in favour of Berlin. Not all were convinced; Theo Waigel, the C D U
leader and Finance Minister, dismissed the Chancellor's support as nothing
but 'a decision by Bundestag member Kohl', who had only one vote. At the
same time the C S U, the Bavarian sister party of the C D U, rejected the idea

of Berlin outright. It was clear that the vote would be very close. The arguments about the capital city had sometimes been serious, sometimes farcical, sometimes insulting and sometimes xenophobic, but they had revealed a great deal about the German psyche in the aftermath of the events of 1989 and the nation's continuing uncertainty about its own identity.[101]

On 20 June 1991 a marathon eleven-hour debate was held in the Bundestag. There was no imposition of party discipline and the fight cut across ideological and geographical lines. The speakers in favour of Berlin included Helmut Kohl and Interior Minister Wolfgang Schäuble. Willy Brandt voted for Berlin and ruffled feathers when he compared Bonn to Vichy, the war-time French capital, claiming that 'In France no one would have thought of remaining in relatively idyllic Vichy when a foreign force no longer stood in the way of returning to the capital on the Seine.' Cornelia von Teichman reiterated the argument that East Germans needed to be included in united Germany: 'Symbols can create hope, and they can destroy hope . . . Today we have a chance to give a symbol of hope to all of Germany, a symbol that we support true co-operation between East and Western Germany.' But there were also important opponents to Berlin. Rita Süssmuth, Theo Waigel, Norbert Blüm and many others came down in favour of Bonn. In the end Berlin won, but it was an uncomfortable 337 votes for Berlin to 320 against.

Helmut Kohl was the first to react to the vote. 'The decision', he claimed, 'is of great importance for the future of Germany.' In an article for *Berliner Morgenpost* he said that no other city moved Germans as much as Berlin and, quoting Alan Bullock, that Berlin is the 'symbolic city of the Twentieth Century'. Many who had supported Bonn remained bitter: Theo Waigel warned that 'Not everything that is in Bonn must go to Berlin. I can tell you that in my budget projections through 1995 I don't have any money allotted for this.' The mayor of Bonn Hans Daniels admitted that the decision was 'a heavy blow for the city and area of Bonn'. Nevertheless, others were more positive. Berlin mayor Eberhard Diepgen was thrilled at the decision although he denied that Berlin had 'won' and merely said that the parliament had made 'an important political decision'. For Joachen Thies, managing editor of *Europa-Archiv*, 'The vote for Berlin is therefore a vote for the future of all of Europe. The German political class demonstrated that it has understood the importance of the moment.'

It was more surprising that international reaction was so positive. According to *Le Soir* Germany now faced a social, financial, material and psychological challenge but it had reached a great historical milestone. The French Prime Minister Edith Cresson said that she was pleased with the choice of Berlin: 'it is totally normal that a state has a large capital. Bonn was a city with a low profile. Now is the time for high profile.'[102] Other states lent their support.

The Polish paper *Zycie Warszawy* pointed out that 'the governmental centre of Germany will be nearer Poland. That means a close relationship.'[103] Americans, British, French and Russian politicians sent messages of goodwill.

When the news of the decision reached Berlin the city erupted into a giant street party. Hundreds walked up the Kurfürstendamm to the Brandenburg Gate waving red and white Berlin flags imprinted with their own symbol – the bear – and yelling, '*Hurra, hurra, hurra, wir sind wieder da!*' The city was filled with people and Beethoven's Ninth was piped out over the Alexanderplatz. Germany was formally united, and Berlin was capital. The city had been very lucky.

Berlin was now the united capital of a united Germany. The Wall was gone, the Allied forces had departed, and the government was destined to move back to the city by the year 2000. Now the city was expected to be the focus for a long-divided nation and to help overcome deep economic, cultural and political divisions. It would be a difficult task.

Despite its troubled past the choice of Berlin was ultimately the right one. It has brought new problems and great responsibilities but events bode well for the future. Like Goethe's Faust, Berlin had been given a 'second chance' to use its strengths for good.[104] In 1991 the city began the momentous task of becoming the capital for the first successful liberal, democratic, capitalist, united Germany in history. It was the beginning of a new era.

NOTES

INTRODUCTION

1 Goethe visited Potsdam and Berlin between 15 and 23 May 1778. At that time Prussia was in turmoil; there was threat of another war of succession due to the extinction of the main line of the Wittelsbach dynasty in Bavaria, and Frederick the Great was preparing to intervene to prevent Austria from seizing Bavaria. Goethe arrived in Berlin at the height of mobilization and was 'nauseated' by the way 'the great and lesser and the small figures behave among themselves', like something 'out of a circus'. See Richard Friedenthal, *Goethe: His Life and Times* (London, 1965), p. 277. It was this impression which found its way into Goethe's greatest work, as Faust's metropolis. The translations of *Faust* for the chapter headings throughout the book are taken from Johann Wolfgang Goethe, *Faust Parts I and II* (Birmingham, 1988), with the exception of the opening lines of the Introduction, which are from Johann Wolfgang von Goethe, *Faust*, trans. Walter Arndt (New York, 1976).

2 The Zitadelle is an extraordinary testimony to the skill of Italian architects. Built on the site of the old Slavic fortress, it was started in 1560, probably to the plans of Italian master builder Franciscus Chiaramelle de Gandino. It was completed by Rocush Guerrini in 1594. It served as a prison for centuries; many of the 1848 revolutionaries were imprisoned there and during the Second World War it was used as a laboratory for the creation of chemical weapons.

3 The Wannsee Conference of 20 January 1942, at which the Final Solution was formalized, was held in number 56–58. It was chaired by Reinhard Heydrich and attended by SS and government officials, including Adolf Eichmann and Roland Freisler. Protocol of the Wannsee Conference (Nuremberg: International Military Tribunal), Document NG 2586 F (6).

4 Elias Canetti, *Die Provinz des Menschen: Aufzeichnungen*, trans. Joachin Neugroschel as *The Human Province* (London, 1986), p. 37.

5 Friedrich Nietzsche, *Die fröliche Wissenschaft* (1882), trans. Walter Kaufmann as *The Gay Science* (New York, 1974), p. 344.

6 Maximilian Harden, *Die Zukunft*, vol. 37, 12 October 1901. This was written before the attempt on his life on 3 July 1922 which forced him to flee Berlin for Holland.

7 The Berlin production consisted of fragments of *Faust Part I* arranged by Prince Anton Henry Radziwill at Schloss Monbijou; the first complete performance of *Faust Part I* took place in Braunschweig on 19 January 1829. The Berlin production was performed to Prince Radziwill's own musical score, and it made theatrical history not least because of the sets designed by Karl Friedrich Schinkel;

this was the first time a room with three walls and a ceiling had ever been created on a stage. The famous set was the scene for Gretchen's room. See Helmut Börsch-Supan, *Karl Friedrich Schinkel: Bühnenentwürfe – Stage Designs* (Berlin, 1990); Athanasius Graf Raczynski, *Geschichte der neueren deutschen Kunst* (Berlin, 1841).

8 Anonymous, *Berlin für Kenner, Berlin – Wie dem Fremden Berlin gezeignet wird – Wie der Fremde sich Berlin ansehen soll*, reprinted in Jürgen Schutte and Peter Sprengel (eds.), *Die Berliner Moderne 1885–1914* (Stuttgart, 1987), p. 95.

9 'Die Bilanz des Jahrhunderts', *Berliner illustrirte Zeitung*, no. 52, 1899.

10 The legal change in Berlin's status is outlined in Presse- und Informationsamt des Landes Berlin, *Hauptstadt im Werden* (Berlin, 1966), pp. 15–25.

11 Dieter Hoffmann-Axthelm believes that Berlin's true 'essence' lies in its eighteenth-century block structure, which was destroyed not so much by the Second World War as by modernist developments in the twentieth century. It was this contempt for the past which saw the erasure of cultural landmarks, entire streets, parks and intimate spaces in favour of characterless housing estates and streets and parking lots. Dieter Hoffmann-Axthelm, 'Hinweise zur Entwicklung einer beschädigten Grossstadt', *Bauwelt*, 82, 1991, p. 565.

12 Eberhard Diepgen, 'Vortwort', in Berlin Press- und Informationsamt des Landes Berlin, *Berlin kurzgefasst* (Berlin, 1995), p. 1.

13 Georg Hermann, *Kubinke* (Berlin, 1910); Paul Scheerbart *Glasarchitektur* (Berlin, 1914); Conrad Alberti, *Wer ist der Stärkere?* (Berlin, 1888). Speer outlines Hitler's plans for Berlin in Albert Speer, *Inside the Third Reich* (London, 1970), pp. 195–266. See also Hans J. Reichardt and Wolfgang Schäche, *Von Berlin nach Germania: Über die Zerstörung der Reichshauptstadt durch Albert Speers Neugestaltungsplanungen* (Berlin, 1984).

14 The Adlon re-opened its doors on 23 August 1997; Bundespräsident Roman Herzog was the guest of honour at the extravagant celebrations.

15 Advertisement for the DB Projekt Knoten Berlin, Deutsche Bahn Gruppe, June 1997: 'Berlin hat den Bogen Raus – weiter geht's – 15 Juni–31 August 1997 – Schaustelle Berlin. Wenn eine Stadt neue Spannungsbögen bekommt, dann ist es Zeit, auf ArchitekTour zu gehen. Berlin bewegt. Verpassen Sie nichts.'

16 The *Financial Times*, 2 September 1994. The topping-out ceremony for the new dome took place on 18 September 1997; Sir Norman Foster and the President of the Bundestag Rita Süssmuth watched as the new cupola, trimmed with garlands and ribbons, was erected.

17 Daniel Libeskind became increasingly frustrated by Berlin's new planning regulations and moved his office from Berlin to Los Angeles. Alan Balfour (ed.), *World Cities: Berlin* (London, 1995), p. 113.

18 Wolf Thieme, who was a cook at the Weinhaus Huth on Potsdamer Platz from 1929 to 1939, provides an account of the historic significance of this area in Berlin's history. Wolf Thieme, *Das letzte Haus am Potsdamer Platz – Eine Berliner Chronik* (Hamburg, 1988).

19 Daniel Libeskind, in Balfour, *World Cities*, p. 113.

20 Jean-Paul Picaper, 'Berlin, le chantier du siècle', *Le Figaro*, 19 August 1997.

21 For the debate preceding the referendum to decide the Berlin–Brandenburg merger see Nicolaische Verlagsbuchhandlung, *Berlin und Brandenburg – ein Land?* (Berlin, 1996), a collection of essays with contributions by, amongst others, Wolf Jobst Siedler, Kerrin Gräfin Schwerin, Lothar de Maizière, Volker Schlöndorff and Matthias Koeppel.

22 *Spiegel Special,* no. 6, 1997. For an account of the growing antagonism between 'Ossis' and 'Wessis' after 1989 see Anne McElvoy, *The Saddled Cow. East Germany's Life and Legacy* (London, 1993), pp. 219–47.

23 *The Economist,* 21 May 1994.

24 Balfour, *World Cities,* p. 33.

25 Speech by Dr Wolfgang Schäuble, leader of the CDU/CSU, during the 'Capital City Debate' in the Bundestag, 20 June 1991.

26 Emnid poll of 24 May 1993; the poll also revealed that 71 per cent of Germans favoured delaying the move from Bonn to Berlin by ten years. Quoted in Michael Müller, 'Berlin – jeder zweite denkt dabei an Hauptstadt and Regierungssitz', *Berliner Morgenpost,* 25 February 1993. According to Jean-Paul Picaper, by August 1997 80 per cent of Germans remained hostile to the transfer. Picaper, 'Berlin, le chantier du siècle'.

27 Walter Benjamin, *Reflections,* trans. Edmund Jephcott (New York, 1978), p. 146.

28 Anonymous, 'Berlin, die Stimme Deutschlands?', *Die Grenzboten,* no. 51, 1892.

29 George L. Mosse, *The Crisis of German Ideology. The Intellectual Origins of the Third Reich* (New York, 1981), p. 23.

30 Heinz Knobloch, *Im Lustgarten* (Halle, 1989), p. 56.

31 Evelyn, Princess Blücher, *An English Wife in Berlin – A Private Memoir of Events, Politics, and Daily Life in Germany Throughout the War and the Social Revolution of 1918* (London, 1920), p. 229.

32 Walther Rathenau, *Impressionen* (Leipzig, 1902), 'Die schönste Stadt der Welt', p. 141.

33 Felix Huby, 'Ein Schwabe an der Spree', *Spiegel Special,* no. 6, 1997, p. 10.

34 Presse- und Informationsamt, *Hauptstadt im Werden,* p. 6.

35 Arnulf Baring (ed.), *Germany's New Position in Europe – Problems and Perspectives* (Oxford, 1994), p. 59.

36 Renata Fritsch-Bourazel, 'The French View', in Edwina Moreton (ed.), *Germany between East and West* (Cambridge, 1987), p. 74.

37 Ibid., p. 59. See also Diego A. Ruiz Palmer, 'French Strategic Options in the 1990s', *Adelphi Papers,* 260 (London, 1991); Ingo Kolboom, 'Die Vertreibung der Dämonen: Frankreich und das vereinte Deutschland', *Europa Archiv,* 25 August 1991, pp. 470–75.

38 Steve Crawshaw, 'Germany Looks East', *Prospect,* January 1997, p. 50. An opinion poll carried out in September 1997 by Bavarian Wickert Institutes revealed that nearly three out of four Germans feared that the Euro will be weaker than the Mark; only 17 per cent of 970 people interviewed did not share this view, while 42 per cent said they were not well enough informed to voice an opinion. Deborah Collcutt, 'Bonn shrugs off Kinkel doubts on budget target', *The Times,* 19 September 1997.

39 Before unification Helmut Kohl saw European unification as the way to over-

come German–German divisions. He concluded his 23 July 1983 address on the state of the nation with the words: 'We need European unification, just as the peoples of Europe need the elimination of the division of Germany.' Office of the Historian, Bureau of Public Affairs, *Documents on Germany 1944–1985* (Department of State Publications, Washington, DC, 1986), p. 1370.

40 In particular Conor Cruise O'Brien's infamous article in *The Times*, October 1989; see also Walter Russell Mead, 'The Once and Future Reich', *World Policy Journal*, vol. 7, autumn 1990, pp. 593–8.

41 *Business Central Europe*, December 1996/January 1997, p. 44.

42 Joachim Thies, 'Germany and Eastern Europe between Past and Future', in Baring, *Germany's New Position in Europe*, p. 74.

43 The declaration of reconciliation was less than both parties had hoped, with wrangling continuing between those Czechs who wanted compensation for the period of Nazi occupation, and the 2.3 million Sudeten Germans who underwent forced expulsion from Czechoslovakian territory at the end of the Second World War. *Prospect*, January 1997, p. 50; see also Anjana Shrivastava, 'Prague and Bonn Find (Some) Common Ground', *Wall Street Journal Europe*, 27 January 1997.

44 *Pod Jedna Korona. 300-lecie unii polsko-saskiej. Kultura i sztuka w czasach unii polsko-saskiej*, Zamek Królewski w Warszawie (Warsaw, 26 June–12 October 1997).

45 *Frankfurter Allgemeine Zeitung*, 26 June 1994; Marlies Jansen, 'Nachbarschaft mit Polen', *Deutschland Archiv*, no. 12, December 1990, pp. 1820–21.

46 CDU Bundestag Group, *Reflections on European Policy*, Novembeer 1994. See also Klaus Larres, 'Germany and the West: The "Rapallo Factor" in German Foreign Policy from the 1950s to the 1990s', in Klaus Larres and Panikos Panayi (eds.), *The Federal Republic of Germany since 1949: Politics, Society and Economy before and after Unification* (London, 1996), pp. 325–46.

47 The 1991 disaster was little more than an unskilled attempt to 'do something' in the face of mounting public pressure. Some would later accuse Germany of trying to re-establish the northern Balkans as a German sphere of influence, but in fact the fiasco revealed deep weaknesses in German foreign policy. See Christoph Bertram, 'The Power and the Past: Germany's New International Loneliness', in Baring, *Germany's New Position in Europe*, p. 98.

48 Henry Kissinger, 'The Beginning of the End of the Kohl Era', *Washington Post*, 22 October 1994.

49 Jacob Heilbrunn, 'Germany's New Right', *Foreign Affairs*, November/December 1996, p. 81. For an excellent analysis of the American role during German re-unification see Elizabeth Pond, *Beyond the Wall: Germany's Road to Unification* (Washington, DC, 1993).

50 The Polish economy grew between 5 and 7 per cent per year between 1991 and 1997. As early as March 1991 Marion Countess Dönhoff wrote in *Die Zeit* that the Poles were proving much better at adapting to the free market than the East Germans, despite the daunting problems they faced, ranging from a wage freeze to price rises, huge external and internal debts, lack of capital, backward agriculture and antiquated industry. And as Dan van der Vat put it in 1991,

'despite great hardships unmatched in eastern Germany the Poles, undiminished by years of political struggle which led the way to the liberation of Europe as a whole', seem to be regenerating with remarkable speed 'regardless of the sacrifices'. Dan van der Vat, *Freedom Was Never Like This – A Winter's Journey in East Germany* (London, 1991), p. 263.

The concept of Germany as the 'land in the middle' predates the twentieth century, but it was made popular again after the war through works such as Hellmuth Rössler, *Deutsche Geschichte. Schicksal des Volkes in Europas Mitte* (Gütersloh, 1961). For a critical view see Peter Bender, 'Mitteleuropa – Mode, Modell, oder Motiv', *Die neue Gesellschaft Frankfurter Hefte*, 34, April 1987, pp. 297–304.

51 *New York Review of Books*, 17 November 1994, p. 44.

52 Henry Kissinger, *Years of Upheaval* (London, 1982), p. 146.

53 Piotr Cywinski, 'Przeprowadzka stulecia', *WPROST*, 8 December 1996, p. 90.

54 Adolf Streckfuss's work was influential in shaping nineteenth- and twentieth-century views about the history of Berlin. Adolph Streckfuss, *500 Jahre Berliner Geschichte. Vom Fischerdorf zur Weltstadt* (Berlin, 1880); see also Oskar Schwebel, *Geschichte der Stadt Berlin* (Berlin, 1888).

55 Spiegel survey in which 10.1 per cent of those asked still connect Berlin with the Nazis, and 7.9 per cent consider it sullied by its role as the capital of the GDR; 3.9 per cent of Germans do not like Berlin because of its 'Prussian tradition'. 'Ungeliebte Hauptstadt', *Spiegel Special*, no. 6, 1997, p. 33.

56 G. W. F. Hegel, 'Vorlesungen über die Philosophie der Geschichte', in H. Glockner, ed., *Sämtliche Werke*, (1949), vol. 11, p. 43.

57 On the relationship between German politics and historiography see George G. Iggers, *The German Conception of History. The National Tradition of Historical Thought from Herder to the Present* (Middleton, Conn., 1968). See also Hans-Ulrich Wehler (ed.), *Deutsche Historiker*, 9 vols. (Göttingen, 1971–82); on Ranke's influence in Prussia see Ludwig Dehio, *Germany and World Politics in the Twentieth Century* (New York, 1967); on Mommsen see Alfred Heuss, *Theodor Mommsen und das 19. Jahrhundert* (Kiel, 1956); on Treitschke see Andreas Dorpalen, *Heinrich von Treitschke* (New Haven, Conn., 1957) – this transformation from liberal to Prussian nationalist can be seen in works such as Heinrich von Treitschke, *Zehn Jahre deutscher Kämpfe* (Berlin, 1874); on Droysen see Johann Gustav Droysen, *Politische Schriften*, ed. Felix Gilbert (Munich, 1933); on Sybel see Heinrich von Sybel, *Die deutsche Nation und das Kaiserreich* (Berlin, 1862).

58 On Weimar historiography see Bernd Faulenbach, *Ideologie des deutschen Weges: Die deutsche Geschichte in der Historiographie zwischen Kaiserreich and Nationalsozialismus* (Munich, 1980); on Nazi control of the historical profession see, for example, Helmut Heiber, *Walter Frank und sein Reichsinstitut, für Geschichte des neuen Deutschlands* (Stuttgart, 1966); Karl F. Werner, *Das NS-Geschichtsbild und die deutsche Geschichtswissenschaft* (Stuttgart, 1967). For an example of the Nazi exploitation of older Berlin myths see Horst Kube, *Die Berliner* (Berlin, 1935).

59 Fritz Ringer, *The Decline of the German Mandarins: The German Academic Community 1890–1933* (Cambridge, Mass., 1969).

60 These fabrications were evident in museums and school books, which were centrally controlled. See, for example, Zentralinstitut für Geschichte an der Akademie der Wissenschaften der DDR, Dr Florian Osburg (ed.), *Geschichte* (Berlin, 1985); Museum für Deutsche Geschichte, *Deutsche Geschichte 1789–1917* (Berlin, 1985); Museum für Deutsche Geschichte, *Sozialistisches Vaterland DDR – Entstehung und Entwicklung* (Berlin, 1985); Museum für Deutsche Geschichte, *Berlin 1871–1945 – Sonderausstellung des Museums für Deutsche Geschichte* (Berlin, 1987).

61 The Partei des Demokratischen Sozialismus, previously the Communist Sozialistische Einheitspartei Deutschlands or the SED. The all-Berlin city council elections of 2 December 1990 were part of this trend. The PDS won only 1.3 per cent of the vote in the districts of western Berlin, but 24.8 per cent in the eastern districts.

62 Brian Ladd, *The Ghosts of Berlin. Confronting German History in the Urban Landscape* (Chicago, 1997), p. 203. Ladd includes an excellent analysis of the debates on everything from the future of East German prison buildings to the changing of street names. It is interesting to compare the present arguments over Berlin's street signs with those of the last century. See, for example, Herrmann Vogt, 'Die Strassen-Namen Berlins', *Schriften des Vereins für die Geschichte der Stadt Berlin* (Berlin, 1885).

63 Many such works were displayed at a 1990 exhibition in Berlin. See Aktives Museums Faschismus und Widerstand in Berlin und der Gesellschaft für Bildende Kunst, *Erhalten – Zerstören – Verändern: Denkmäler der DDR in Ost-Berlin – Eine dokumentarische Ausstellung* (Berlin, 1990). See also Martin Schönfeld, *Gedenktafeln in Ost-Berlin* (Berlin, 1991).

64 The Soviet memorials are protected under the 1991 terms of German unification signed by Helmut Kohl and Boris Yeltsin. Despite similar agreements between the Soviets and the Poles, the gradiose Soviet war memorial in Torun was ripped down by indignant locals in August 1997. Many Poles, who were invaded and occupied both by the Nazis and by the Soviets, still rightly regard such memorials as symbols of oppression rather than of 'liberation'. Nevertheless the German case is different, and the Soviet memorials in Berlin should be preserved. For a discussion of street names in the GDR see Maoz Azaryahu, 'Street Names and Political Identity: The Case of East Berlin', *Journal of Contemporary History*, 21, 1986, pp. 581–605.

65 Hans-Joachim Maaz, *Der Gefühlsstau: Ein Psychogramm der DDR* (Berlin, 1990); see also Peter Schneider, *Extreme Mittellage: Eine Reise durch das deutsche Nationalgefühl* (Berlin, 1990).

66 Its official title is the Federal Authority for the Records of the State Security Service of the former German Democratic Republic. That it was opened at all was due in part to the campaign mounted by ex-GDR dissidents, including Wolf Biermann. For an interesting account of the inner workings of the 'Gauck' authority and the inherent dangers of relying completely on the information held within see Timothy Garton Ash, *The File. A Personal History* (London, 1997).

67 David Rose and Anthony Glees, 'Modern Germany: Death camps, torture,

experiments on children', *Observer*, 10 August 1997. Many of the deaths occurred when the Soviets re-opened Nazi concentration camps after 1945. See also Peter Bordihn, *Bittere Jahre am Polarkreis: Als Sozialdemokrat in Stalins Lagern* (Berlin, 1991).

68 Rose and Glees, 'Modern Germany'.

69 Hans Joachim Gauck, in response a public opinion survey which proved that 57 per cent of former East Germans favoured closing the Stasi secret police files. Quoted in David Tieman Doud, *Berlin 2000 – The Centre of Europe* (London, 1995), p. 71.

70 Aktives Museum, *Erhalten – Zerstören – Verändern*.

71 Doud, *Berlin 2000*, p. 71.

72 *Observer*, 10 August 1997.

73 For a discussion of the legal complexity involved in bringing former East Germans to justice see Ralf Altenhof, 'Die Toten an Mauer und Stacheldraht, *Deutschland Archiv*, 4, April 1992; Dieter Blumenwitz, 'Zur strafechtlichen Verfolgung Erich Honeckers: Staats und völkerrechtliche Fragen', *Deutschland Archiv*, 6, June 1992. On 25 August 1997 Egon Krenz, East Germany's last Communist leader, was jailed for six and a half years; two other members of the Politburo, Günter Schabowski, a propaganda specialist, and the economist Günter Kleiber, were imprisoned for three years. All were sentenced for manslaughter because of their roles in maintaining the Berlin Wall, where 263 people died. Roger Boyes was correct to point out that although Krenz rejects the charges, 'it would be rash to accept even a portion of Krenz's self-evaluation. The contrast between his life as a Politburo member – he was promoted in 1983 as a protégé of Erich Honecker – and the young men killed on the death strip shows who were the true Cold War martyrs.' Roger Boyes, 'Six years' jail for last East German boss', *The Times*, 26 August 1997.

74 Much of the official East German material for events such as the 750th anniversary celebrations in 1987 was taken directly from that published for the 700th anniversary celebrations ordered by Hitler in 1937; even the format of the celebration magazines was the same. East Germans would not have known this, as they had no access to libraries containing former Nazi propaganda. Compare, for example, *Berliner illustrirte Zeitung – Sonderheft zur 700-Jahr-Feier der Reichshauptstadt – Heimat Berlin* (Berlin, 1937) and *Neue Berliner illustrierte Sonderheft Berlin 750* (Berlin, 1987). Both begin with photographs of their respective leaders (Hitler and Erich Honecker) and contain almost identical articles (each keeping within their respective ideological constraints) about everything from Berlin history to the economy, from food and *Kneipen* to architecture.

75 Andrew Roberts, 'Hitler still occupies our minds', the *Sunday Times*, 27 July 1997.

76 *Frankfurter Allgemeine Zeitung*, 17 September 1994.

77 The Eichmann trial was followed by others, including the trials of the Treblinka camp guards. Franz Stangl, the commandant of Treblinka, was caught in Brazil in 1967 and was sentenced to life imprisonment in 1970. He died in prison.

78 For an analysis of the reception of the film in Germany see Anson Rabinbach and Jack Zipes (eds.), *Germans and Jews since the Holocaust* (New York, 1986).

79 Other film makers have tried to tackle the subject of the Holocaust; the best to date is Claude Lanzmann's extraordinary documentary *Shoah*. The Dutch artist Armando, who has lived in Berlin since 1979, complains about the tendency of the younger generation to blame their parents for not telling them about the Holocaust until the screening of the film: 'They could have known, because hundreds of books and films about the war have appeared since '45. They simply didn't care . . . In this respect they're exactly like their parents, who have also continued to claim they didn't know anything about it.' Armando, *From Berlin*, trans. Susan Massotty (London, 1996), p. 117. The book contains fascinating fragments of interviews with elderly Berliners who lived through the Second World War.

80 Ian Baruma, *The Wages of Guilt: Memories of War in Germany and Japan* (New York, 1994). Japan's reticence in facing its past was evident: events such as the Nanking massacre were censored or glossed over, 'comfort women' were forced to provide sex in Japanese imperial army brothels. Things are changing slowly; on 29 August 1997 the Japanese Professor Saburo Ienaga won a thirty-two-year-long struggle in the Supreme Court against the Education Ministry. The court ruled that the ministry was wrong to have changed his textbooks by deleting references to the infamous Unit 731 responsible for germ warfare which had conducted medical experiments on live prisoners in China. There is opposition to this, not least through the 'Committee to Produce New Textbooks', made up of historians and business leaders, who have demanded that the government stop this 'masochistic' history which 'slanders' Japan.

81 Ernst Nolte, 'Vergangenheit, die nicht vergehen will', *Frankfurter Allgemeine Zeitung*, 6 June 1986. Nolte has also argued that Chaim Weizmann's declaration of September 1939, stating that Jews would fight with the British against Germany, could have served as a plausible basis for treating the German Jews as 'prisoners of war'. This was rebutted by Saul Friedländer, who pointed out that Nolte's claim, also advanced by David Irving, derived from a pamphlet used by Goebbels himself. See Saul Friedländer, 'West Germany and the Burden of the Past: The Ongoing Debate', *Jerusalem Quarterly*, 42, spring 1987, p. 16.

82 Gordon Craig, 'The War of the German Historians', *New York Review of Books*, 15 January 1987, p. 18. The amount of material generated by the *Historikerstreit* was staggering; much was collected in the one-volume *Historikerstreit – Die Dokumentation der Kontroverse um die Einzigartigkeit der nationalsozialistischen Judenvernichtung* (Munich, 1987). See also Charles S. Maier, *The Unmasterable Past – History, Holocaust and German National Identity* (London, 1988); Richard J. Evans, *In Hitler's Shadow. West German Historians and the Attempt to Escape from the Nazi Past* (New York, 1989); Gina Thomas (ed.), *The Unresolved Past. A Debate in German History* (London, 1990); Kathy Harms, Lutz R. Reuter and Volker Dürr, *Coping with the Past. Germany and Austria after 1945* (Madison, 1990).

83 Office of the Historian, Bureau of Public Affairs, *Documents on Germany 1944–1985* (Department of State Publications, Washington, DC, 1986), p. 1397. For Weizsäcker's speeches on German history see Richard von Weizsäcker, President

of the Federal Republic of Germany, *A Voice from Germany*, trans. Karin von Abrams (London, 1986).

The many debates and events which took place in the 1970s and 1980s with reference to German history are too numerous to mention here. They include the development of new 'historical schools', particularly the Bielefeld School which concentrated on social rather than more traditional political history, and the staging of historical exhibitions such as the Staufen exhibition of 1977, which asked whether the existence of two German states was not more in keeping with German tradition than the longing for a unified state, and the 1981 Prussian exhibition in West Berlin, which challenged the post-war notion that Prussia was little more than the bastion of German militarism. Political events also provoked debate, ranging from Willy Brandt's moving gesture in front of the Warsaw Ghetto Uprising memorial, Helmut Kohl's January 1984 visit to Israel, the Bitburg debacle, as well as Richard von Weizsäcker's 8 May 1985 speech on the fortieth anniversary of the end of the war in Europe.

84 Klaus Behnken and Frank Wagner (eds.), *Inszenierung der Macht. Ästhetische Faszination im Faschismus* (Berlin, 1987). Some of the threatening letters were incorporated into the first part of the exhibition itself.

85 *The Times*, 22 January 1992.

86 The film starred Klaus Maria Brandauer and won the Oscar for Best Foreign Film in 1982. Mann was quite hard on his brother-in-law, but the fundamentals of the story are accurate.

87 Bundesarchiv Koblenz, R 58 (Reichssicherheitshauptamt) and BA NS 3 (SS-Wirtschafts-Verwaltungshauptamt). These files contain the information describing the important Gestapo and SS offices in Berlin and their official functions.

88 Informationszentrum Berlin, Gedenkstätte Deutscher Widerstand, *Plötzensee Memorial, Berlin* (Berlin, 1985).

89 In 1989 this memorial was expanded to include an exhibition about all resistance, including that mounted by conservatives, liberals, socialists and communists, Christians and Jews.

90 Reinhard Rürup (ed.), *Topographie des Terrors. Gestapo SS und Reichssicherheitshauptamt auf dem 'Prinz-Albrecht-Gelände'. Eine Dokumentation* (Berlin, 1987), p. 36.

91 The 1993 figure, quoted in Doud, *Berlin 2000*, p. 78n.

92 Ladd, *The Ghosts of Berlin*, p. 163. Gerhard Schoenberner is chairman of the 'Active Museum' organization.

93 Alfred Kernd'l, *Der Spiegel*, 17 April 1994; for his views on other buildings, particularly Hitler's Chancellery, see Alfred Kernd'l, *Zeugnisse der historischen Topographie auf dem Gelände der ehemaligen Reichskanzlei Berlin-Mitte* (Berlin, 1993).

94 Ulrike Puvogel (ed.), *Gedenkstätten für die Opfer des Nationalsozialismus: Eine Dokumentation* (Bonn, 1987).

95 A stream of orders, memos, reports and recommendations moved between Berlin and the Reich and occupied territories. There are thousands of examples: in November 1941 Heinrich Lohse, Reich Commissar for the 'Ostland' region of the Baltic, who had questioned the mass murder of Jews by Einsatzcommandos

not on moral but on economic grounds, was sent a letter from Berlin informing him that 'as a matter of principle, no economic factors are to be taken into consideration in the solution of the Jewish question. Letter, 18 November: Document P5-3663 (Nuremberg International Military Tribunal).

In the following example, translated by Claude Lanzmann in the film *Shoah* (1985), the Gruppenleiter of Gruppe II D – Technische Angelegenheiten, SS-Obersturmbannführer Walter Rauff, whose office was in the Reichssicherheitshauptamt in Berlin, is asked to approve changes to the vans used for the 'operation' at Kulmhof. Jews were brought to the camp in small groups, were herded into vans, and were gassed by carbon monoxide from the engine, which reached the cabin by way of a specially fitted pipe. When the people were dead the bodies were taken to the forest in the same van, and burned. Over 360,000 Jews were murdered in this way. But at each stage the 'technical problems' had to be ironed out and all changes approved by the bureaucrats in Berlin; the victims were referred to as 'pieces' or 'the load' or 'merchandise' to be 'processed', but the true meaning was clear:

Geheime Reichssache [Secret Reich Business]
Berlin 5 June 1942.
Changes for special vehicles now in service at Kulmhof [Chelmno] and for those now being built.

Since December 1941, 97,000 have been *verarbeitet* [processed] by the three vehicles in service with no major incidents. In the light of observations made so far, however, the following technical changes are needed.

First: The vans' normal load is usually 9 per square yard. In Saurer vehicles, which are very spacious, maximum use of space is impossible, not because of any possible overload, but because loading to full capacity would affect the vehicle's stability. So reduction of the load space seems necessary. It must absolutely be reduced by a yard, instead of trying to solve the problem as hitherto, by reducing the number of pieces loaded. Besides, this extends the operating time, as the empty void must also be filled with carbon monoxide. On the other hand, if the load space is reduced, and the vehicle is packed solid, the operating time can be considerably shortened. The manufacturers told us during a discussion that reducing the size of the van's rear would throw it badly off balance. The front axle, they claim, would be overloaded. In fact, the balance is automatically restored because the merchandise aboard displays during the operation a natural tendency to rush to the rear doors and is mainly found lying there at the end of the operation. So the front axle is not overloaded.

Second: The lighting must be better protected than now. The lamps must be enclosed in a steel grid to prevent their being damaged. Lights could be eliminated since they apparently are never used. However, it has been observed that when the doors are shut the load always presses hard against them [the doors] as soon as darkness sets in. This is because the load naturally rushes toward the light when darkness sets in, which makes closing the doors difficult. Also, because of the alarming nature of darkness screaming always occurs when the doors are closed. It would therefore be useful to light the lamp before and during the first moments of the operation.

Third: For easy cleaning of the vehicle there must be a sealed drain in the middle of the floor. The drainage hole's cover, 8 to 12 inches in diameter, would be equipped with a slanting trap, so that fluid liquids can drain off during the operation. During cleaning the drain can be used to evacuate large pieces of dirt.

The aforementioned technical changes are to be made to vehicles in service only when they come in for repairs. As for the 10 vehicles ordered from Saurer, they must be equipped with all innovation and changes shown by use and experience to be necessary.

Submitted for decision to Gruppenleiter II D SS-Obersturmbannführer Walter Rauff.

96 Excerpt from speech by Governor Hans Frank at a session of the General-gouvernement in Cracow, 16 October 1941, which began, 'But what should be done with the Jews? Do you think they will be settled in the Ostland, in villages?' He included the speech in his diary, which was used as evidence during the Nuremberg trials (Document PS-2233). From Cracow he ruled over Polish territory occupied by the Nazis but not incorporated directly in the Reich. He presided over an area in which over 3 million Jews and over 2 million Polish Catholics were killed. An extensive record of his activity in the Generalgouverne-ment is in the Bundesarchiv Koblenz, R52 II (Akten der Regierung des General-gouvernements).

97 See Wladyslaw T. Bartoszewski, 'Introduction', in Samuel Willenberg, *Surviving Treblinka* (Oxford, 1989).

98 See Wladyslaw T. Bartoszewski, *The Convent at Auschwitz* (London, 1991). The figures are from Martin Gilbert, *The Holocaust* (London, 1986), pp. 287, 853n.

99 James E. Young, *The Texture of Memory. Holocaust Memorials and Meaning* (New Haven, 1993), p. 53. See also Wulf E. Brebeck et al., *Zur Arbeit in Gedenkstätten für die Opfer des Nationalsozialismus: Ein internationaler Überblick* (Berlin, 1988).

100 The sign reads, 'Orte des Schreckens, die wir niemals vergessen dürfen'.

101 Before the war the Sonnenallee was the site of the German branch of the American firm the National Cash Register Company. Between 1942 and 1944 there were between 400 and 863 slave labourers there at any one time, mostly women from Poland, the Soviet Union and France. In August 1944 the barrack contained around 500 Jewish women, who had been marched there from Auschwitz; as the Red Army approached the women were moved back to Sachsenhausen. In 1945 the Soviets dismantled the factory; in the 1950s the Americans built a new factory and in the 1960s the site became a sports ground. Before Norbert Radermacher there was nothing on the site which hinted at its history.

Now, as one walks by, one trips a light trigger which switches on a slide projector. An image appears high up in the trees and slowly moves down until text appears on the pavement which recounts the story of the factory and the slave labourers. The artist Norbert Radermacher did not alter the site in any way; in his view the history of the place includes its present anonymity; 'its own forgetfulness, its own memory lapse'. Senatsverwaltung für Bau- und Wohnungswesen, *Gedenkstätte KZ-Aussenlager Sonnenallee Berlin-Neukölln: Bericht der Vorprüfung* (Berlin, 1989).

102 Ladd, *The Ghosts of Berlin*, p. 152.

103 Sachsenhausen was a concentration camp which was first built to hold German political prisoners; inmates included Jews herded there during the death marches at the end of the war; 20,000 people also died at Sachsenhausen under Soviet rule after 1945. Timothy Aeppel, 'Attack on Jewish Site Underscores Dilemma Facing Bonn 3 Years After Wall's Collapse', *Wall Street Journal*, 10 November 1992.

104 On 29 August 1997 the Tiergarten District Council in Berlin decided to use Marlene Dietrich's name for a square being built as part of the Potsdamer Platz. There had been opposition, particularly from older Germans who still reject her because she returned to Germany in 1945 in American uniform. It took five years to win approval for the idea. Her face also appeared on a German postage stamp in 1997.

105 On 20 July 1997 the German government announced that it may declare an amnesty for those convicted in Nazi courts, including those charged for conspiring against Hitler in 1944. Edzard Schmidt-Jortzig, the Justice Minister, explained that Germany would 'need a new law' to invalidate unjust Nazi convictions; the 1951 attempt to overturn sentences on men like Admiral Wilhelm Canaris, the former head of counter-intelligence, General Hans Oster, Captain Gehre, Judge Karl Sack, Hans von Dohnyani and Dietrich Bonhoeffer – all implicated in the plot against Hitler – failed, not least because to pardon them would mean pardoning those 30,000 soldiers who deserted from the Wehrmacht and who were sentenced to death by Nazi military courts for 'defeatism' or 'subversion of national defence', for 'denouncing Hitler' or for 'decrying the war'. Ironically, Claus Schenk von Stauffenberg, who actually planted the bomb to blow up Hitler, was executed without trial so there was no legal conviction to be overturned. Many Germans oppose any moves to pardon the deserters, fearing it would imply criticism of the soldiers who did stay and fight even if they did not agree with the regime. The process is complicated by divisions between various states. In Bavaria sentences against those convicted by Nazi courts were overturned in 1946. In Berlin, however, at least 200,000 cases of Nazi injustice are recorded, but those who wish their case to be heard must make a separate application to the courts before a sentence can be reversed. See Katerina von Waldersee, 'Bonn plans amnesty for Hitler's failed assassins', *Sunday Telegraph*, 20 July 1997.

106 Many Germans protested at the Ravensbrück plan from July 1991 and it was stopped – but not before a Kaiser grocery store was nearly completed a few hundred metres away from the memorial plaque to those who died.

107 For a view of racial problems and the place of Jews in post-1989 Berlin see Amity Shlaes, *Germany. The Empire Within* (London, 1991). See also Panikos Panayi, 'Racial Violence in the New Germany', *Contemporary European History*, 3, 1994; Cornelia Schmalz-Jacobsen et al., *Einwanderung und Dann? Perspektiven einer neuen Ausländerpolitik* (Munich, 1993).

108 Department of State, *Documents on Germany*, pp. 1403–10. See also Dennis L. Bark and David R. Gress, *A History of West Germany* (Oxford, 1993), vol. 2: *Democracy and Its Discontents 1963–1991*, p. 430.

109 Voltaire, *Oeuvres*, vol. I: *Première Lettre sur Oedipe* (Paris, 1785), p. 15n.

1: History, Myth and the Birth of Berlin

1 August Endell, who ran a school for applied arts in Berlin between 1904 and 1914, saw Berlin as both ugly and dynamic: 'despite its ugly buildings, despite the noise, despite everything for which it can be reproached, [the metropolis] is to one who has the desire to see, a miracle of beauty and poetry, a legend brighter, more colourful, more varied than anything a poet can evoke.' August Endell, *Die Schönheit der grossen Stadt* (Stuttgart, 1908), p. 41.

2 Karl Scheffler, *Berlin – Ein Stadtschicksal* (Berlin, 1910, rep. 1989), p. 219.

3 Paul Assmann, *Der geologische Aufbau der Gegend von Berlin* (Berlin, 1957), p. 32.

4 Wolfgang Ribbe and Jürgen Schmädeke, *Kleine Berlin-Geschichte* (Berlin, 1994), pp. 13–16. See also Adriaan von Müller and Alfred Kernd'l, *Ausgrabungen in Berlin. Forschungen und Funde zur Ur- und Frühgeschichte*, 8 vols. (Berlin, 1970–89); Adriaan von Müller, *Als Berlin noch in den Tropen lag. Von der Eiszeit bis zur mittelalterlichen Stadt* (Bergisch Gladbach, 1990).

5 Ribbe discusses the Roman attitude to the Semnonen in his excellent history of Berlin published for the 750th anniversary celebrations in 1987. For the reference to legate L. Domitius Ahenobarbus see Eberhard Bohm, 'Die Frühgeschichte des Berliner Raumes', in Wolfgang Ribbe (ed.), *Geschichte Berlins* (Munich, 1987), vol. 1: *Von der Frühgeschichte bis zur Industrialisierung*, p. 21.

6 Fergus Millar, *The Roman Empire and Its Neighbours* (London, 1996), p. 297.

7 Ptolemy placed the Semnonen around the middle Oder region in the heart of the Mark Brandenburg.

8 Velleius Paterculus' *Historia Romana*, written in AD 29, was particularly interesting as he had been an officer under Tiberius in AD 4–6 and wrote about the campaign along the river Elbe. Velleius Paterculus, *The Tiberian Narrative*, ed. A. J. Woodman (Cambridge, 1977).

9 Cornelius Tacitus, *The Agricola and the Germania*, trans. and ed. H. Mattingly (Harmondsworth, 1976).

10 In fact Emperor Trajan was still serving in Germany in 98–99 when Tacitus' book was published.

11 Tacitus, *The Agricola*, p. 27; Chapter 33, p. 129.

12 Tacitus, *The Agricola*, p. 136. At the time the river Oder was known as the Suebus, the Germans of the north and east as Suebi. The Semnonen around present-day Berlin believed that they possessed the sacred grove, true home to the god who was the origin of their race and who ruled over all things; as they held the grove, the Semnonen considered themselves to be the chief clan of the Suebi. Prudence Jones and Nigel Pennick, *A History of Pagan Europe* (London, 1995), p. 116. See also H. Schutz, *The Prehistory of Germanic Europe* (London, 1983).

13 Tacitus, *The Agricola*, p. 134.

14 Zui was later ousted by Wodan, the one-eyed god of victory, who was said to send down the Valkyries to carry warriors killed in battle off to Valhalla. Jan de Vries, *Altgermanische Religionsgeschichte* (Berlin, 1970), vol. 2, p. 32. For the excavation of sites in the region related to the sacrifice of animals and humans see Herbert Janhuhn, 'Archäologische Beobachtungen zu Tier- und Menschenopfern bei den Germanen in der römischen Kaiserzeit', *Nachrichten der Akademie der Wissenschaften in Göttingen* (Göttingen, 1962).

15 For an analysis of the archaeological finds in the Berlin area, including evidence of iron production in the first to fourth centuries, see Achim Leube, *Die römische Kaiserzeit im Oder-Spree-Gebiet* (Berlin, 1975), p. 54.

16 W. Kuhn, 'Die Siedlerzahlen der deutschen Ostsiedlung', *Studium Sociale*, 1963, p. 141; see also Eric Christiansen, 'How Europe Became Europe', *New York Review of Books*, 21 October 1993.

17 The Visigoths, who had settled on the banks of the river Don since the second century AD, were attacked in 376; in 410 the Gothic king Alaric sacked Rome and Gaul was left helpless when Roman troops were withdrawn for the defence of Constantinople. The Alemanni seized modern Alsace, the Franks took Belgium, the Saxons swept through Britain and the Lungobardi went into Lombardy. For the impact of the Burgundians on the Berlin area see Ribbe, *Geschichte Berlins*, vol. 1, p. 52. See also Adriaan von Müller, *Berlins Urgeschichte* (Berlin, 1977); Adriaan von Müller, *Mit dem Spaten in die Berliner Vergangenheit* (Berlin, 1981), and Achim Leube, 'Die Burgunden bis zum Untergang ihres Reiches auf der oberen Rhône im Jahre 534', in Bruno Krüger (ed.), *Die Germanen. Geschichte und Kulture der germanischen Stämme in Mitteluropa* (Berlin, 1983), pp. 367–70.

18 The demise of the Roman empire in the west was gradual but relentless. See R. H. C. Davis, *A History of Medieval Europe from Constantine to Saint Louis* (London, 1988), p. 24.

19 J. M. Roberts, *A History of Europe* (Oxford, 1996), p. 100.

20 The border was codified in the Treaty of Verdun of 843, in which Ludwig II was granted the eastern territories of Charlemagne's empire.

21 The last German grave in the area dates from 550 but some Germans survived in the area for longer. Ribbe, *Geschichte Berlins*, vol. 1, p. 57.

22 Fontane wrote a delightful poem incorporating many of the Slavic names of the area: 'All die lachenden Dörfer, ich zähle sie kaum:/ Linow, Lindow,/ Rhinow, Glindow,/ Beetz und Gatow,/ Dreetz und Flatow . . . Und zum Schluss in dem leuchtenden Kranz:/ Ketzin, Ketzür und Vehlefanz'. Theodor Fontane, *Sämtliche Werke. Wanderungen durch die Mark Brandenburg* (Munich, 1977), vol. 2, p. 11.

23 The word 'Berlin' implies quite different historical roots. If the name had been German it would have been combined with a place name such as Bärstadt (Bear Town), Bärwalde (Bear Forest) or Bärtal (Bear Valley). Reinhard E. Fischer, *Die Ortsnamen des Havellandes* (Weimar, 1976), p. 26. See also Ribbe, *Geschichte Berlins*, vol. I, pp. 4–10.

24 Pliny the Elder used the 'Venedi' term to describe settlers who lived east of the Vistula; Tacitus referred to them as 'Veneti'; Teutonic tribesmen called their

eastern neighbours the 'Wineda'; in King Alfred's *Orosius* the Anglo-Saxon designation of the Slavs south of the Baltic was 'Winedas' or 'Weonodas', and by the eleventh century the Scandinavians were calling them 'Vender'. The name 'Wend' has endured.

25 Two separate groups made their way towards the Berlin area – the Prager people, who came from the south-east, and the Sikow-Szeligi Group from the Warthe-Weichsel area. They divided the territory along the Spree and Havel rivers between themselves. Wolfgang H. Fritze and Klaus Zernack (eds.), *Grundlagen der geschichtlichen Beziehungen zwischen Deutschen, Polaben und Polen* (Berlin, 1976); Joachim Herrmann, *Germanen und Slawen in Mitteleuropa. Zur Neugestaltung der ethnischen Verhältnisse zu Beginn des Mittelalters* (Berlin, 1984), p. 21.

26 Ibrahim ibn Jacub, *Arabische Berichte von Gesandten an germanische Fürstenhöfe aus dem 9. und 10. Jahrhundert*, ed. Georg Jacob (Berlin, 1927), p. 11.

27 Ibn Khurradadhbeh, quoted by Bernard Lewis in *The Arabs in History* (London, 1954), p. 90.

28 The oldest Jewish gravestone in Spandau dates from 1244 although Jewish merchants traded there earlier. For a history of trade in the region see Kazimierz Slaski, 'Die Organisation der Schifffahrt bei den Ostseeslawen vom 10. bis zum 13. Jahrhunderts', in *Hansische Geschichtsblätter*, 91, 1973, pp. 1–11.

29 Clovis had subjugated his rival to become the king of the Franks; when he was baptized his people followed, making much of Gaul Christian by the time of his death in 511. For his importance to the foundation of France see E. James, *The Origins of France from Clovis to the Capetians, 500–1000* (London, 1982).

30 Conversions began through the efforts of missionaries; Saint Boniface of Crediton came to Frisia in 718 and established a number of monastic foundations in Hessen, Thuringia, Bavaria, Westphalia and Württemberg. But it was Charlemagne who invented the tradition of conquest in which massacre and conversion were combined; this forced conversion to Christianity would soon touch the area around Berlin. Jacques LeGoff, *Medieval Civilisation* trans. Julia Barrow (Oxford, 1988), p. 38.

31 Although this number is disputed it is still widely quoted. Ibid.

32 The phrase was coined by his son Otto I, who raised Magdeburg to an archbishopric in 968. Robert Bartlett, *The Making of Europe. Conquest, Colonization and Cultural Change 950–1350* (Harmondsworth, 1994), p. 8.

33 Widukind von Corvey, *Rerum Gestarum Saxonicarum, Libri Tres*, quoted in Davis, *A History of Medieval Europe*, p. 209.

34 At this point Otto's lands were divided into the great Trans-Elbian March conquered by Hermann Billung (whose family later became dukes of Saxony), which covered Holstein and Mecklenburg, and the Great March of Gero to the south, which was divided into smaller units after 965. On the tensions created between the Ottonians and the Slavs in the Marks see Herbert Ludat, *An Elbe und Oder um das Jahr 1000. Skizzen zur Politik des Ottonenreiches und der slawischen Mächte in Mitteleuropa* (Cologne, 1971).

35 See the catalogue for the exhibition held by the Museum für Vor- und Frühgeschichte Preussischer Kulturbesitz, the Archäologischen Landesamtes für

Bodendenkmalpflege and the Arbeitsgemeinschaft 'Germania Slavica' der Freien Universität Berlin. Dietrich Kurze, *Slawisches Heidentum und christliche Kirche zwischen Elbe und Oder. Vor 1000 Jahren: Der Slawenaufstand von 983* (Berlin, 1983), pp. 48–68.

36 Norman Davis, *God's Playground. A History of Poland* (New York, 1982), vol. I: *The Origins to 1795*, p. 62.

37 Stephen I of Hungary had adopted the same tactic, also bringing missionaries in from Bohemia and, in Stephen's case, from Byzantia. But by ultimately turning away from Germany Mieszko gained independence from the Ottonians. Ibid., p. 63.

38 Jacques Le Goff, *Medieval Civilisation* (Oxford, 1988), p. 51.

39 This independence was formalized in 1000, when Otto III granted Mieszko's successor Boleslaw Chobry an archibishopric at Gneizno which was subject directly to Rome rather than to Germany. Adan Zamoyski, *The Polish Way. A Thousand-Year History of the Poles and Their Culture* (London, 1987), p. 14.

40 The 'holy lance' was a symbol of the fight against the heathen. Andrea Schmidt-Rösler, *Polen von Mittelalter bis zur Gegenwart* (Regensburg, 1996), p. 16. The story of Adalbert and Poland is recounted in *Polytika*, June 1997; the text of the chronicler Gallus, who recounted the visit, is quoted in Zamoyski, *The Polish Way*, p. 13; the original text is published as Gallus Anonymous, 'Chronicon', in K. Maleczynski (ed.), *Monumentia Poloniae historica* (Cracow, 1952).

41 The outcome was that Boleslaw kept Moravia, Slovakia, Mielske and Lusitia but lost Bohemia and western Pomerania. Boleslaw Chobry was recognized as a semi-independent ruler of Poland although he did not receive the crown until 1024. After the coronation Boleslaw, who had himself spent seventeen years exiled in Thuringia, invited German Cistercians into his land, thereby continuing the long tradition of German settlement in lands under Polish rule. This did not change the fact that Polish and German interests were now in direct competition in the area between the Oder and the Elbe which affected the local populations. Joachim Herrmann, 'Herausbildung und Dynamik der germanisch-slawischen Siedlungsgrenze in Mitteleuropa', in Herwig Wolfram and Andreas Schwartz (eds.), *Die Bayern und Ihre Nachbarn* (Vienna, 1985), pp. 269–80. Hans-Dietrich Kahl, 'Slawen und Deutsche in der brandenburgischen Geschichte des zwölften Jahrhunderts. Die letzten Jahrzehnte des Landes Stodor', in *Mitteldeutsche Forschungen*, 30 (Cologne, 1964).

42 Henry II of Germany allied himself with pagan Slavs against Christian Poland, although he later atoned for this sin by founding a missionary bishopric at Bamberg. The Slav uprising against the Poles was eventually crushed but it did result in the relocation of the Polish capital to Cracow.

43 This point is made by Joachim Herrman in an article published for the Museum für Ur- und Frühgeschichte Potsdam, which emphasizes the independence of many of the settlements in the region. Joachim Herrmann, *Magdeburg – Lebus. Zur Geschichte einer Strasse und Ihrer Orte* (Berlin, 1963).

44 Ascania was a corrupted form of the name Aschersleben. For an excellent account of Albert the Bear's success in the Mark Brandenburg see Bartlett, *The Making of Europe*, pp. 33–6, 51–2. See also Eberhard Schmidt, *Die Mark*

Brandenburg unter den Askanien 1134–1320 (Cologne, 1973); Hans K. Schulze, 'Die Besiedlung der Mark Brandenburg im hohen und späten Mittelalter', *Jahrbuch für die Geschichte Mittel- und Ostdeutschlands*, 28, 1979, pp. 42–178.

45 One of the great medieval works, *La Chanson de Roland*, is a twelfth-century poem about the defeat of Charlemagne by the Basques. René Hague, *The Song of Roland* (London, 1937).

46 Bartlett, *The Making of Europe*, pp. 34–38.

47 For a time Albert even had the support of the Pole Boleslaw the Curly, whose daughter Judith was married off to Albert's son in 1147 – as a result Boleslav's brother Mieszko the Old joined Albert the Bear to fight the Slavs. The bishop was later known for having drawn up the first written version of the Magdeburg Law.

48 Bartlett, *The Making of Europe*, p. 137. The complete text is reproduced in Herbert Helbig and Lorenz Weinrich (eds.), *Urkunden und erzählende Quellen zur deutschen Ostsiedlung im Mittelalter* (Darmstadt, 1968–70), vol. 1, pp. 96–102.

49 The other coin from the Berlin area dating from the 1150s depicts Markgraf Albert the Bear. Herbert Ludat, *Slawen und Deutsche im Mittelalter. Ausgewählte Aufsätze* (Cologne, 1982), p. 34.

50 Bartlett, *The Making of Europe*, p. 34. The text is published as Heinrich von Antwerpen, 'Tractatus de captione urbis Brandenburg', in Oswald Holder-Egger (ed.), *Monumenta Germaniae historica Scriptores*, 25 (Hanover, 1800), pp. 482–4.

51 Johannes Schultze, 'Caput marcionatus Brandenburgensis', in Johannes Schultze (ed.), *Forschungen zur brandenburgischen und preussischen Geschicte. Ausgewählte Aufsätze* (Berlin, 1964), pp. 155–76.

52 The *Ostsiedlung* is described in Bartlett, *The Making of Europe*, pp. 111–32. See also Walter Kuhn, *Vergleichende Untersuchungen zur mittelalterlichen Ostsiedlung* (Cologne, 1973); Karl Leyser, *Medieval Germany and Its Neighbours* (London, 1982); Charles Higounet, *Die deutsche Ostsiedlung im Mittelalter* (Berlin, 1986); and the collection of essays including those by Adriaan von Müller and Stanislaw Trawkowski in Walter Schlesinger (ed.), *Die deutsche Ostsiedlung des Mittelalters als Problem der europäischen Geschichte* (Singmaringen, 1975).

53 Boso was bishop of Merseburg between 968 and 970. His comment was recorded in the 'Chronicon Theitmari Merseburgensis episcopi'. Davis, *A History of Medieval Europe*, p. 215n.

54 Richard W. Southern, *Western Society and the Church in the Middle Ages* (Harmondsworth, 1970), p. 254. For the Cistercians in the Berlin region see, for example, Willy Hoppe, *Kloster Zinna. Ein Beitrage zur Geschichte des ostdeutschen Koloniallandes und des Cistercienserordens* (Munich, 1914).

55 This was originally founded by Margrave Otto I in 1180; part of the original monastery is still standing. For a history of the Chorin monastery see Johannes A. Schmoll, *Das Kloster Chorin und die askanische Architektur in der Mark Brandenburg 1260–1320* (Berlin, 1961). For the history of the Franciscans in Berlin see Gerhard Bronisch, 'Die Franziskaner-Klosterkirche in Berlin', *Mitteilungen des Vereins für die Geschichte Berlins*, 50 (Berlin, 1933), pp. 89–142.

56 A. J. P. Taylor took this line when he traced German-Slav relations in the east: 'For a thousand years the Germans have been "converting" the Slavs from paganism, from Orthodox Christianity, from Bolshevism, or merely from being Slavs; their weapons have varied, their method has always been the same – extermination . . . No one can understand the Germans who does not appreciate their anxiety to learn from, and to imitate, the West; but equally no one can understand Germans who does not appreciate their determination to exterminate the East.' A. J. P. Taylor, *The Course of German History* (London, 1961), p. 3.

57 Michael Burleigh, *Prussian Society and the German Order. An Aristocratic Corporation in Crisis 1410–1466* (Cambridge, 1984), p. 6.

58 Bartlett, *The Making of Europe*, p. 56.

59 Some groups of Wends survived into the 1930s, when the Nazis decided, first to deny their unique history and then to eliminate them altogether. The report from a 1937 conference at the Ministry of the Interior stated: 'There is no *Wendei* and no self-contained area of settlement. The expression Wendish lingustic region is to be avoided. In case of need one should employ regional terms like Upper or Lower Lusatia or Spreewald.' Many were murdered during the war, and today there are only small groups of Sorbs left in Lausitz. Michael Burleigh, *Germany Turns Eastwards. A Study of 'Ostforschung' in the Third Reich* (Cambridge, 1988), p. 123; Walter Kuhn, 'Die Siedlerzahlen der deutschen Ostsiedlung', *Studium Sociale* (Cologne, 1963), pp. 131–54.

60 Helmold of Bosau, 'Slawenchronik', in Heinz Stoob (ed.), *Ausgewählte Quellen zur deutschen Geschichte des Mittelalters*, 19 (Darmstadt, 1973), p. 312. I have used Robert Bartlett's translation (*The Making of Europe*, p. 136).

61 Helmold of Bosau, 'Slawenchronik', in Stoob, *Ausgewählte Quellen*, p. 210. I have used Robert Bartlett's translation (*The Making of Europe*, p. 136).

62 'Cronica principum Saxonie', in Holder-Egger, *Monumenta Germaniae historica Scriptores*, 25, p. 478; quoted in Bartlett, *The Making of Europe*, p. 35.

63 For an excellent account of its foundation see Berthold Schulze, 'Berlins Gründung und erster Aufstieg. Sein Kampf mit der Territorialgewalt', in Richard Dietrich (ed.), *Berlin. Zehn Kapitel seiner Geschichte* (Berlin, 1981), pp. 51–79.

64 The East Germans chose to stress this early split as if this in some way justified the post-war division of the city. Berlin was typically referred to as 'Die mittelalterliche Doppelstadt', 'Berlin and Cölln' or 'B. and C.' for short. See, for example, Roland Bauer, *Berlin illustrierte Chronik bis 1870* (Berlin, 1988). Pomplun began a chapter in his 1985 Berlin handbook, 'Even the "Wendish Palace" is doubled in Berlin . . . we barely notice today that our city is divided because of political reasons . . .' Kurt Pomplun, *Pomplun's grosses Berlin Buch* (Berlin, 1985), 'Selbst das "Wendenschloss" gibt es doppelt in Berlin', p. 513.

65 Berlin and Cölln joined their administrations in 1307. Dozens of smaller German cities started in this way; Brandenburg did not unite until 1715; Potsdam, first documented when Emperor Otto III presented it to his aunt Abbess Mathilde von Quedlinburg on 3 July 993, had a Slavic castle on an island in the Havel and a Germanic settlement on the Nuthe. Willy Pastor, 'Berlin hinter Wall and Graben' in Horst Kube (ed.), *Das deutsche Volk – Die Berliner* (Berlin, 1935).

66 Berlin lay between the low plateaus of Barnim and Teltow, which were only five kilometres from each other, making it ideal for trade. T. H. Elkins, *Berlin. The Spatial Structure of a Divided City* (London, 1988), pp. 71–8; Winifried Schich, 'Stadtrandphänomene bei den Städten im Grossberliner Raum (Berlin-Cölln, Spandau and Köpenick) vom 13. bis zum 16 Jahrhundert', *Siedlungsforschung*, 1983, p. 70.

67 Eckhard Müller-Mertens, 'Berlin und die Hanse', in *Hansische Geschichtsblätter*, 80, 1962, pp. 1–25.

68 Old Lübeck started as the fortress of the Slavic kings of the Abodrites; it was sacked by rival Slavs in 1138 and taken in 1143 as part of the German occupation of eastern Holstein. The decisive change in its fortunes came in 1160, when it was taken by the duke of Saxony, Henry the Lion, who founded a bishopric near the old fortress, from which the trading city grew. The act including Berlin in the Hanseatic League was reprinted in *Die Recesse und andere Akten der Hansetage von 1256–1430* (Leipzig, 1870), vol. I. For Berlin's admission into the Hanseatic League see Ribbe, *Geschichte Berlins*, vol. I, p. 206.

69 For the growth of Berlin-Cölln in the fourteenth century see Adriaan von Müller, *Edelmann . . . Bürger, Bauer, Bettelmann. Berlin im Mittelalter* (Frankfurt-am-Main, 1970); Herbert Helbig, *Gesellschaft und Wirtschaft der Mark Brandenburg im Mittelalter* (New York, 1973); Ribbe, *Geschichte Berlins*, vol. 1, pp. 139–248. For a more general discussion of the medieval town see Fritz Rörig, *Mediaeval Cities*, trans. Don Bryant, (Princeton, 1925). Berliners also kept a chronicle of the city reprinted as Paul Clauswitz (ed.) *Berlinisches Stadtbuch* (Berlin, 1883).

70 Families like the Blankenfelds came from western Germany while the Reiches originated in the Low Countries. The name originated as Rikke and spellings have ranged from Ryke to Reiche – I use the anglicized form of Richie. For a hsitory of the family in Berlin see Carl Brecht, 'Die Familie Ryke', in *Berlinische Chronik, Vermischte Schriften im Anschluss an die Berlinische Chronik und an das Urkundenbuch* (Berlin, 1888), vol. 2.

71 Entry for 10 April 1288 in Clauswitz, *Berlinisches Stadtbuch*.

72 The man appointed to the position of Schultheiss was typically the *locator* who had helped the ruler to attract the most inhabitants to settle there. As a reward the *locators* received about six times the amount of land awarded to peasants. The first Berlin Schultheiss was called Marsilius, and was named in 1247. Georg Homsten, *Die Berlin-Chronik. Daten, Personen, Dokumente* (Düsseldorf, 1986), p. 25.

73 The first Berlin seal to portray bears was the second town seal dating from 1280 which showed two bears propping up a shield depicting an eagle. Werner Vogel, *Berlin und seine Wappen* (Berlin, 1987), p. 16.

74 There were several small trading towns in the Mark Brandenburg which rivalled Berlin: Kyritz was founded around 1200, Rheinsberg was settled by immigrants around 1300, Neurippen got its Stendal charter in 1256, Schwedt was founded in 1200 at the Oder crossing and the Berlin-Stettin, Prenzlau-Posen road junction, and Beeskow developed a thriving culture of guilds of merchants, shoe-makers, weavers, bakers, butchers, cloth makers and others who grew rich

because they were situated on the western trade route between Frankfurt and Leipzig. Schulze, 'Die Besiedlung der Mark Brandenburg', *Jahrbuch für die Geschichte Mittel- und Ostdeutschlands*, 28, 1979, pp. 42–178.

75 In fourteenth-century Germany only fifteen towns had more than 10,000 inhabitants.

76 Alfred Haverkamp, 'Die Judenverfolgungen zur Zeit des schwarzen Todes im Gesellschaftsgefüge deutscher Städte', in *Zur Geschichte der Juden im Deutschland des späten Mittelalters und der frühen Neuzeit* (Stuttgart, 1981), pp. 27–93.

77 Entries between the years 1391 and 1448 in Clauswitz, *Berlinisches Stadtbuch*.

78 Christoph Hinckeldey (ed.), *Strafjustiz in alter Zeit* (Heilsbronn, 1981), p. 141.

79 Clauswitz, *Berlinisches Stadtbuch*.

80 The letter from Dyderick van Quichow (Dietrich von Quitzow) to the 'Ratmannen von Berlin' of 31 July 1411 is reproduced in Klaus Weise, *Ein Dreivierteljahrtausend. Dokumente und Sachzeugen zur Geschichte Berlins* (Berlin, 1987), p. 21.

81 The 1485 *Totentanz* fresco in the Turmhalle of the St Marien-Kirche was only rediscovered in 1860. It is the most important late Gothic wall painting in Berlin. Erich Hühns, 'Der Berliner Totentanz', *Deutsches Jahrbuch für Volkskunde*, no. 14, 1968, p. 235. The chaos also had a religious dimension: as soon as the Askanien line died out, the town was at the centre of a dispute between the papacy and Emperor Ludwig of Bavaria. It resulted in the anti-clericalism which saw the murder by a mob of the Provost Nicholas of Bernau in 1324, which in turn led to a year-long papal ban; indeed, order was not restored until 1411 with the coming of the Hohenzollerns.

82 Berlin was first named a residence city in 1486 by the Hohenzollern Kurfürst von Brandenburg Johann-Cicero (1486–99).

83 Golo Mann, *The History of Germany since 1789* (London, 1974), p. 32.

84 Homer, *Iliad*, trans. Professor R. Lattimore (Oxford, 1980), p. 25.

85 *Von deutscher Art und Kunst*, a volume of essays by *Sturm und Drang* writers, published by J. G. Herder in 1773. Two were written by Herder, one by Goethe, one by Paolo Frisi and one by J. Möser.

86 Goethe gave the essay to Herder for publication in *Von deutscher Art and Kunst*, which in the 1770s had become the Bible of the early Romantic *Sturm und Drang* writers. These writers in turn, inspired by Rousseau and Herder, exalted freedom and nature, revelling in a cult of genius and anti-rationalism; they sought to find expression for the German spirit. The German Romantic movement, which reached its peak in the bitter wake of the Napoleonic occupation, took up the rediscovery of 'true German' culture with a vengeance. It would change the very nature of German historiography. Schiller, *Briefe zur Ästhetischen Erziehung des Menschen* (1795) and *Über naive und sentimentalische dichtung* (1795); Johann Wolfgang von Goethe, *Von deutscher Art und Kunst* (On German Character and Art) (1773), quoted in Carla Schulz-Hoffmann, *Studien zur Rezeption der deutschen romantischen Malerei in Kunstliteratur and Kunstgeschichte* (Munich, 1974), p. 30. See also Keith Hartley, *The Romantic Spirit in German Art 1790–1990* (London, 1994), p. 294.

87 This had an effect on architecture. For example, by the nineteenth century the

castle of the Grand Masters of Teutonic Order in Marienburg – which Frederick the Great had used as an ammunition dump – had fallen into ruin. It was set to be demolished around 1800 but the Berlin architect Friedrich Gilly argued for its preservation. From 1815 the first president of western Prussia Theodor von Schön set about having it restored in an attempt to transform it into a 'national monument', a 'Prussian Westminster'. At this point there was no reference to the Teutonic Order's policy of annexation; on the contrary, it was held up as the ideal state sought by the liberal reforms in Prussia after 1806. By the late nineteenth century, however, it had become the very symbol of German nationalism and would later become an important Nazi symbol of German cultural superiority in the east. Claude Keisch and Marie-Ursula Riemann-Reyher (eds.), *Adolph Menzel 1815–1905: Between Romanticism and Impressionism* (Yale, 1996), p. 191.

88 George Bernard Shaw, *The Perfect Wagnerite* (London, 1898).

89 By 1802 Hegel was predicting that a 'Theseus' would appear to enforce the unification of the Germans; in his lectures and pamphlets he claimed that the state was the predestined end of human organization and was endowed with 'saintly and inspiration virtues'. For him the German nation had been chosen to be the world's bearer of historical development. For a discussion of this and the increasing link between German *Volk* and *Kultur* see George L. Mosse, *The Crisis of German Ideology. The Intellectual Origins of the Third Reich* (New York, 1981), pp. 13–67.

90 Adolf Rapp, *Der deutsche Gedanke* (Bonn, 1920), p. 229; quoted in Mosse, *The Crisis of German Ideology*, p. 67n. See also Houston Stewart Chamberlain, *Die Grundlagen des 19. Jahrhunderts* (Munich, 1932). The revision of history was particularly sad in Berlin, where the Wends had at one time been accepted as an integral part of its past. In 1727, for example, Leibniz's friend at the Berlin Academy of Sciences had researched the history of the Wends, even publishing his findings in English. The work is in the British Library: Daniel Ernst Jablonski, *A letter . . . concerning the introduction of die Wendens, a nation in Brandenburgh that speaks the Sclavonick tongue* (London, 1727).

91 Adolph Streckfuss, *500 Jahre Berliner Geschichte. Vom Fischerdorf zur Weltstadt* (Berlin, 1880), vol. 1. For a discussion of his role in Berlin historiography see Ribbe, *Geschichte Berlins*, vol. 1, p. 4.

92 Pastor, 'Berlin hinter Wall and Graben', in Kube, *Das deutsche Volk*, pp. 4–9.

93 A classic example is the chapter 'Die Wendenzeit' (The Wendish Period) by the historian Albert Kiekebusch, in which he says: 'All that we know about Wendish culture . . . bears the stamp of wretchedness [*Armseligkeit*] . . . and serves only to demonstrate how suddenly the German culture sank down to the level of the Wends during the time of the movement of the peoples [*Völkerwanderungs-zeit*]. The Wends brought virtually nothing of value with them from their eastern home [*Heimat*].' Albert Kiekebusch, *Bilder aus der märkischen Vorzeit. Für Freunde der heimischen Altertumskund, insbesondere für die Jugend und ihre Lehrer* (Berlin, 1921), pp. 77–89. Wolfgang Ribbe points out that this treatment was already common at the turn of the century – for example, in works by Ernst Friedel and Robert Mielke: *Landeskunde der Provinz Brandenburg* (Berlin,

1912), vol. 3: *Die Volkskunde*, pp. 347–499. Ribbe, *Geschichte Berlins*, vol. I, pp. 3–4.

94 Friedrich Engels, 'The Magyar Struggle' (13 January 1849), in Karl Marx and Friedrich Engels, *Collected Works* (London, 1977), vol. 8, p. 238. See also Harold James, *A German Identity 1770–1990* (London, 1989), p. 52. The attempts by communities to use ancient history to legitimate present policies has long been widespread in many countries including Germany. As Benedict Anderson has put it, in the nineteenth century 'Romanovs ruled over Tatars and Letts, Germans and Armenians, Russians and Finns. Habsburgs were perched high over Magyars and Croats, Slovaks and Italians, Ukrainians and Austro-Germans. Hanoverians presided over Bengalis and Québecois, as well as Scots and Irish, English and Welsh. On the continent, furthermore, members of the same dynastic families often ruled in different, sometimes rivalrous, states.' This did not prevent the ruling houses from trying to use 'official nationalism' to legitimate their rule. Benedict Anderson, *Imagined Communities* (London, 1993), pp. 83–111.

95 The *Kulturkampf* or, in Rudolf Virchow's words, the 'fight for culture' began as a struggle between the German government and the Roman Catholic Church, which lasted from 1872 to 1878 and which amongst other things saw the abolition of the Roman Catholic office of the Prussian Ministry of Religion, the banning of the Jesuits, and other restrictions on clerical appointments; a law ordering the dissolution of the monasteries in Prussia was introduced in 1874. In 1872 education reform was introduced; religious schools were now overseen by state bureaucrats, and a government veto was introduced for the nomination of church officials. Most Roman Catholic bishops refused to obey and many clergymen were fined or imprisoned.

The *Kulturkampf* had an important effect on Prussian Poland, which was predominantly Roman Catholic. It led to further restrictions on Polish culture. It was motivated not only by religious but by national discrimination, which extended to a ban on teaching Polish at schools, and an attempt to restrict Polish ownership of land through control of the Prussian Colonization Commission. The measures were far reaching; in Posnan, for example, the Germans closed the theological seminary, the school of the Sisters of the Sacred Heart and the Ursulines, and imprisoned the Primate of Poland Ledochowski. The measures ultimately backfired, turning the Polish Catholic Church into a symbol of Polish national resistance against Prussia. Most of the measures were repealed by 1878 but the bitterness would linger in Polish memory for decades to come. For the influence of the *Kulturkampf* in Poland see Janusz Pajewski, *Historia Powszechna 1871–1918* (Warsaw, 1967), pp. 80–82. See also Lech Trzeciakowski, *The Kulturkampf in Prussian Poland*, trans. Katarzyna Kretkowska (New York, 1990).

96 L. Namier, *1848: The Revolution of the Intellectuals. The Raleigh Lecture* (London, 1946), p. 88; quoted in James, *A German Identity*, p. 53.

97 Wilhelm Unversagt, 'Zur Vorgeschichte des ostdeutschen Raumes', in Albert Brackmann and Karl Brandi (eds.), *Deutschland und Polen. Beiträge zu ihren geschichtlichen Beziehungen* (Munich, 1933), p. 4. See also Burleigh, *Germany*

Turns Eastwards, p. 66. This view of the superiority of the 'old Germans' was evident in scholarly works, including Heinrich Wesche, *Der althochdeutsche Wortschatz im Gebiete des Zaubers und der Weissagung* (Haale a.d. Saale, 1940), and Hermann Wirth, *Die Heilige Urschrift der Menschheit* (Leipzig, 1932–6).

98 Other publications for the anniversary dismissed the contribution of the Slavs. See Dr Hermann Rügler, 'Was der Berliner von der Geschichte Seiner Stadt wissen muss', *Sonderheft Berliner illustrirte Zeitung zur 700 Jahr-Feier der Reichshauptstadt. Heimat Berlin* (Berlin, 1937). Much of the work on the Slavic period and on ethnic Germans in the east was directed from the 'Nordost-Deutsche Forschungsgemeinschaft' (NODFG), founded on 19 December 1933 at the former Herrenhaus in Berlin. The activities of the institute are discussed in detail in Burleigh, *Germany Turns Eastwards*, p. 70. See also Wolfgang Wippermann, *Der Ordensstaat als Ideologie. Das Bild des deutschen Ordens in der deutschen Geschichtsschreibung und Publizistik* (Berlin, 1979).

99 This message underlay virtually all historical works of the time. The German mission in the east was explained in works like Erich Maschke, *Der deutscher Ordensstaat. Gestalten seiner grossen Meister* (Hamburg, 1936); Erich Keyser, *Geschichte des deutschen Weichsellandes* (Leipzig, 1940); and in a number of essays in Brackmann and Brandi, *Deutschland und Polen*. It would remain an important aspect of war propaganda. See, for example, Helmut Gauweiler, *Deutsches Vorfeld im Osten* (Cracow, 1941), p. 8, which began, 'It is important that the German *Volk* always keep the true meaning of the German re-building in the east before their eyes', a rebuilding of land which had been taken from Germany when the Reich was 'weak and torn apart'. In their 1941 book Heiner Kurzbein, Erwin Berghaus and Fred-Erich Uetrecht show German troops beside a group of houses during the invasion of Danzig under the heading 'Polennester im deutschen Danzig' (nest of Poles in German Danzig); after the victory the troops are saluted as 'Befreier volksdeutschen Landes' (liberators of German land of the *Volk*). The destruction in Warsaw is blamed on the 'guilty' Polish leadership who failed to surrender to Germany immediately in 1939, while a group of Warsaw Jews are shown being forced to clear rubble above the caption 'Zum erstenmal haben sie eine Schippe in der hand – und müssen aufräumen' (For the first time they have a shovel in their hands and must work), playing on the Nazi stereotype of Jews as 'incapable' of manual labour. Heiner Kurzbein, Erwin Berghaus and Fred-Erich Uetrecht, *Bilddokumente des Feldzugs in Polen* (Berlin, 1941), pp. 38, 60, 121.

100 Attempts by various communities to use ancient history to legitimate present boundaries have long been widespread. See Benedict Anderson, *Imagined Communities* (London, 1993), 'Census, Map, Museum', pp. 163–86.

2: The Capital of Absolutism

1 For a comparison of Europe's cities in the fifteenth century see Mark Girouard, *Cities and People* (Milan, 1985); on Rome see P. D. Partner, *Renaissance Rome 1500–1559* (Berkeley, 1976); on Florence see G. A. Bruckner, *Renaissance Florence*

(New York, 1969); on Paris see David Thomson, *Renaissance Paris: Architecture and Growth 1475–1600* (London, 1984).

2 Copernicus (1473–1543) was a student at Cracow University during the 'Golden Age of Poland'. At the time the university was introducing the Italian Renaissance into Poland, not least through the Cracow School of Painting and its teachings of religious tolerance; people like Conrad Celtis, Copernicus, the scholars of jurisprudence Paul Vlodowic and Jan Ostorok, and the greatest of Polish poets Jan Kochanowski lived and worked there. For a view of Poland at this time, and indeed for one of the best comparative studies of art and culture in central Europe see Thomas DaCosta Kaufmann, *Court, Cloister and City. The Art and Culture of Central Europe 1450–1800* (London, 1995), pp. 41, 50–73.

3 Karel van Mander wrote about Prague in the seventeenth century and called Rudolf II 'the greatest art patron in the world at the present time'. It was his German counterpart Joachim von Sandrart who called Prague the 'Parnassus of the arts'. Kaufmann, *Court, Cloister and City*, p. 185.

4 Frederick II (the Great) dismissed the politics and culture of Prussia before the reign of Johann Sigismund at the beginning of the seventeenth century as not worthy even of mention. In his history of Prussia he wrote: 'I have passed over Brandenburg's obscure beginnings and the reigns of the first Princes as they have little to offer of any interest ... Brandenburg's history only begins to get interesting during the time of Johann Sigismund with his acquisition of Prussia and the Cleves succession to which he was entitled by marriage. It is only from this point that the subject becomes meaty enough, as it were, for me to get my teeth into it.' Frederick the Great, 'Mémoires pour servir à l'histoire de la maison de Brandebourg', in Klaus Forster, (ed.), *Friedrich der Grosse, Denkwürdigkeiten zur Geschichte des Hauses Brandenburg* (Munich, 1963), p. 18.

5 *Joachim I, Nestor, Kurfürst von Brandenburg* (1529) by Lucas Cranach the Elder is in the Jagdschloss Grunewald in Berlin, as is *Joachim II, Hektor, Kurfürst von Brandenburg* (1551) by Lucas Cranach the Younger; *Henry VIII* (1536) by Hans Holbein the Younger is in the Thyssen-Bornemisza collection, Lugano.

6 Kaufmann, *Court, Cloister and City*, p. 229. Many courts, from Württemberg to Bamberg, from Bayreuth to Mergentheim, developed into magnificent centres of art and culture. For the development of the smaller courts see Adrien Fauchier-Magnan, *The Small German Courts in the 18th Century*, trans. Mervyn Savill (London, 1958).

7 The expression '*cuius regio, eius religiou*' meant that the religion of the governed should be the same as that of the territorial ruler, and that those subjects who did not wish to adapt to his religion should be permitted to emigrate.

8 There are hundreds of works on the Thirty Years War. I have relied primarily on Eberhard Faden, *Berlin im dreissigjährigen Kriege* (Berlin, 1927); Hans Jessen (ed.), *Der dreissigjährige Krieg in Augenzeugenberichten.* (Munich, 1963); Ricarda Huth, *Der dreissigjährige Krieg*, 2 vols. (Leipzig, 1957); Cicely Veronica Wedgwood, *The Thirty Years War* (London, 1992); Geoffrey Parker (ed.), *The Thirty Years War* (London, 1997); Moriz Ritter, *Deutsche Geschichte im Zeitalter der Gegenreformation und des dreissigjährigen Krieges, 1555–1648*, 3 vols. (Darmstadt, 1974); and Friedrich Nicolai, *Beschreibung der königlichen Residenzstädte Berlin*

and Potsdam aller daselbst befindliche Merkwürdigkeiten der umliegenden Gegend, 3 vols. (Berlin, 1786; rep. 1967). For Schwarzenberg in Berlin-Spandau, Felix Escher, 'Spandau im Schatten der Festung', in Wolfgang Ribbe (ed.), *Slawenberg, Landesfestung, Industriezentrum. Untersuchungen zur Geschichte von Stadt und Bezirk Spandau* (Berlin, 1983). For Gustavus Adolphus in the Berlin area, Michael Roberts, *Gustavus Adolphus and the Rise of Sweden* (London, 1973); Johannes Kretzschmar, *Gustav Adolfs Pläne und Ziele in Deutschland und die Herzöge zu Braunschweig und Lüneburg* (Hanover, 1904). And on propaganda, S. S. Tschop, *Heilsgeschichte und Deutungsmuster in der Publizistik des dreissigjährigen Krieges: pro- und anti-Schwedische Propaganda in Deutschland 1628 bis 1635* (Frankfurt-am-Main, 1991).

9 In recent decades many historians have criticized the 'myth of the destruction' of the Thirty Years War which grew up almost immediately after 1648. There are conflicting views both on the extent of devastation of the land and of the number of people killed. Geoffrey Parker suggests that the population of the Holy Roman Empire declined by around 20 per cent, but, as Mary Fulbrook has pointed out, overall figures do not take into account the fact that some areas were barely touched by the war and others (like the Berlin area) suffered great loss and deprivation. All historians agree that the war had a terrible effect on Germany both in terms of population and economy; the debate revolves around the extent and effect of the destruction. Parker, *The Thirty Years War*. See Mary Fulbrook, *A Concise History of Germany* (Cambridge, 1990), p. 65; Hans U. Rudolf (ed.), *Der dreissigjährige Krieg: Perspektiven und Strukturen* (Darmstadt, 1977); T. K. Rabb, 'The Effects of the Thirty Years War', in T. K. Rabb (ed.), *The Thirty Years War. Problems of Motive, Extent and Effect* (Lexington, 1964), pp. 41–51; Günther Frank, *Der dreissigjährige Krieg und das deutsche Volk. Untersuchungen zu Bevölkerungs- und Agrargeschichte* (New York, 1989).

10 On the attacks on the Jews see Stuart Cohen, *Germany* (Jerusalem, 1974), pp. 7–9; see also Friedrich Holtze, *Das Strafverfahren gegen die märkischen Juden 1510* (Berlin, 1884). The growing tension in Europe was reflected in Berlin through increasing attacks on money lenders and businessmen, many (but not all) of whom were Jewish. Several were accused of everything from racketeering to 'money clipping' following the introduction of new coins in 1621. In 1622 a mob in Spandau stormed the homes of 'racketeers'; sixteen people were killed and 200 injured. Georg Holmsten, *Die Berlin Chronik: Daten, Personen, Dokumente* (Düsseldorf, 1987), p. 123.

The sense of foreboding was only increased by the appearance of a comet in 1618, which was generally seen as a warning of coming violence and unrest; there was a flurry of literature predicting the end of the world or the coming of a new prophet, Elijah. Jakob Böhme, later associated with the rise of Pietism, wrote a tract called Aurora, emphasizing the importance of astrology. Jakob Böhme, *Aurora* (1612). The manuscript is in the Museum der Stadt Görlitz.

11 A poem published in a 1618 pamphlet entitled *The Way of the Present World* summed up the feelings of tension before the war: 'One wants this, the other that,/Thus terrible fighting and hate springs forth,/As each insists he is right,/Many a poor soul complains,/They who have nothing to ride,/But must walk

on foot through rain and snow,/The common man suffers,/If only there was a purpose to this suffering.' Herbert Langer, *Hortus Bellicus – Der dreissigjährige Krieg* (Leipzig, 1978), p. 20.

12 Electoral Prince Johann Sigismund had converted to Calvinism in 1613, to the chagrin of his Lutheran subjects. The alienation of the Hohenzollern rulers from their Lutheran subjects helped pave the way for absolutism. Rudolf von Thadden, *Prussia: The History of a Lost State*, trans. Angi Rutter (Cambridge, 1981), p. 3; Wedgwood, *The Thirty Years War*, p. 222.

13 Wallenstein was an extraordinary general who believed that his destiny had been determined by the stars. In 1608 he asked Kepler to create a horoscope for him; as it was the same as the powerful Grand Chancellor Jan Zamoyski of Poland and of Elizabeth I, he used it to justify his actions as a soldier. The prayer is quoted in Wedgwood, *The Thirty Years War*, p. 219.

14 This is the Ribbeckhaus on Breite Strasse, built for Electoral Kammerrat Hans Georg von Ribbeck in 1624. Peter Güttler et al. (eds.), *Berlin Brandenburg. Ein Architekturführer* (Berlin, 1990), p. 27.

15 Parker, *The Thirty Years War*, p. 193. Bernhard Stier and Wolfgang von Hippel stress that the very destruction of the war also led to economic and social restratification. Bernhard Stier and Wolfgang von Hippel, 'War, Economy, and Society', in Sheilagh Ogilvie (ed.), *Germany. A New Social and Economic History 1630–1800* (London, 1996), pp. 234–62.

16 Parker, *The Thirty Years War*, p. 173.

17 Wedgwood, *The Thirty Years War*, p. 87; F.S. Boas (ed.), *The Diary of Thomas Crosfield* (London, 1935), pp. 67–8.

18 For depictions of looting see, for example, the graphic painting of *Soldiers Brawling over the Division of the Spoils* by W. C. Duyster in the Staatliche Kunstsammlungen Dresden, or the etching of *Soldiers on the Rampage* by Johann Hulsmann in the Staatliche Graphische Sammlung Munich, which depicts a soldier carrying a sack of booty collected from corpses lying on the battlefield. On Holck see Parker, *The Thirty Years War*, p. 176.

19 A. Gindely, *Waldstein während seines ersten Generalats* (Prague, 1886), vol. 1, p. 348.

20 General Robert Monro, *Monro His Expedition with the Worthy Scots Regiment call'd Mackays* (London, 1637), vol. 2, p. 122; see also Parker, *The Thirty Years War*, p. 179. The attitude towards the Swedes was summed up in Böhme's *German Children's Song*: 'The Swedes have come,/Have taken everything,/Have broken windows,/Have taken the lead,/Have made bullets from it,/And have shot the peasants.'

21 Faden, *Berlin*, p. 194.

22 '*Vertendo stercorarium*' refers to an illness which was said to be caused by the retention of faeces in the starving; the faeces were thought to mix with the blood and then contaminate the body. Sir Thomas Roe, *Negotiations* (London, 1640), p. 37. See also E. A. Beller, 'The mission of Sir Thomas Roe to the conference at Hamburg, 1638–40', *English Historical Review*, XLI, 1926, pp. 61–77. In his work on war Newmayr von Ramsla wrote: 'In times of war it is the peasants who suffer. If it lasts long they slave their lives away; if it ends quickly

even the marrow is scraped from their bones.' Newmayr von Ramsla, *Vom Krieg* (1641).

23 The Plague swept through Berlin in 1626, 1630, 1631 and 1638; not only did the rich spend vast amounts on herbs and potions; those with money were encouraged to swallow pearls and sapphires. According to Friedrich Nicolai, who wrote a history of Berlin and Potsdam published in 1786, 2,066 people died in 1631, a quarter of the population; 840 died in 1637 and 1,395 died in 1638. Nicolai, *Beschreibung der königlichen Residenzstädte*, p. 215; see also Wedgwood, *The Thirty Years War*, p. 217.

24 Pfarrherrn Garcaeus, *Tägliche Aufzeichnungen des Pfarrherrn Garcaeus* (Brandenburg, 1894), p. 75.

25 Parker, *The Thirty Years War*, p. 193.

26 Martin Opitz was a fascinating figure. Born in the Silesian town of Bunzlau, he was influenced by the Dutch writer Daniel Heinsius to look to his own language for inspiration, completing the classic *Buch von der deutschen Poeterey* (1624) in a mere seven days. He moved frequently, leaving Silesia for Heidelberg, Leiden and then into the service of the imperial army under Karl von Dohna; he was accepted despite being a Protestant. After Dohna's death he worked for the Polish king Wladyslaw IV in his negotiations with the Swedes. Although he loved the German language he was no narrow nationalist; he was inspired by the refugees he met in Poland who had been drawn there because of its religious tolerance; as a result his work reflects a deep desire to break down the religious and national prejudices which had so blighted Europe during his lifetime.

His contemporary Andreas Gryphius was far less optimistic and his works mirror his sense of grief and his obsession with *Vanitas*. He spoke for a generation shaken by decades of senseless violence and destruction; for whom human beings were little more than 'Snow which soon melts and candles which quickly burn down'. Martin Opitz, 'Song'; Andreas Gryphius, 'Epitaph on Mariana Gryphius his Brother Paul's little Daughter'; 'Trauerklage des verwüsteten Deutschland' later called 'Tränen des Vaterlandes' (Tears of the Fatherland), in Leonard Forster (ed.), *The Penguin Book of German Verse* (Harmondsworth, 1959), pp. 104, 127, 131. See also Langer, *Hortus Bellicus*, p. 196; Ingrid Walsoe-Engel, *German Poetry from the Beginnings to 1750* (New York, 1992), pp. 218–28.

27 Kaspar Stieler, 'Lass die verstorbenen ruhen', in Forster, *The Penguin Book of German Verse*, p. 152. Violence to women was common, as seen in contemporary works such as Christian Richter's engraving of a soldier holding a sword against a woman with one hand and grabbing her hair with the other, forcing her to drop her child. Christian Richter, *A Soldier Attacks a Woman and Her Child* (copperplate engraving), Staatliche Graphische Sammlung Munich. It was also evident in the witch burnings of the period, documented in hundreds of gory engravings such as J. Michelet's sixteenth-century *Witch Torture* showing a woman in the stocks and another having her hand crushed; indeed Kepler's mother Katherina was accused of witchcraft and was saved from the stake only because of her son's position at court. One soldiers' song went: 'Watch out,

peasant, I am coming. Get yourself out of the way, quick. . . .Girl, come here,
Join me and the jug.' Quoted in Langer, *Hortus Bellicus*, pp. 99, 107; Michelet
is reprinted in Gunnar Heinssohn and Otto Steiger, *Die Vernichtung der Weisen
Frauen* (Herbstein, 1985), p. 133.

28 Even before the war leaflets were being produced in virtually every town in
northern Europe covering every subject from adultery and miracles to fashion;
many put words to the notes of well-known songs. During the war the emphasis
changed. Famous battles or well-known leaders were either glorified (Gustavus
Adolphus was treated as a god-like figure in the Berlin area) or relentlessly
attacked. Religious fervour was mirrored in scathing attacks on the papacy or
the Jesuits or the Protestants. Perceived 'enemies' were often belittled through
satire, filthy prose or highly detailed pornographic or gory illustrations. See G.
Rystad, *Kriegsnachrichten und Propaganda während des dreissigjährigen Krieges*
(Lund, 1960).

29 There has been much criticism of Grimmelshausen's work, not least because
he often embellished stories. He was also inaccurate; he claimed to have seen
the Battle of Wittstock in 1636 but in fact plagiarized the description from an
unrelated work, namely the 1629 edition of Sir Philip Sidney's *Arcadia*. Nevertheless, his accounts of soldiering and the effects of the all-consuming violence
remain important testimonies to life during the Thirty Years War. Another key
document was written by an anonymous soldier who served in Catholic regiments (with the exception of two years of service to the Swedes), and who
marched over 22,000 kilometres between 1625 and 1649. The work was published
in J. Peters (ed.), *Ein Söldnerleben im dreissigjährigen Krieg. Eine Quelle zur
Sozialgeschichte* (Berlin, 1933). See also Parker, *The Thirty Years War*, p. 269.

The Thirty Years War became a popular subject in German music as well
as literature; Carl Maria von Weber composed *Der Freischütz* in the years
following the war, while Richard Strauss wrote a *Festival Music in Living Scenes*,
based on events in the Thirty Years War. Alfred Döblin wrote *Wallenstein* and
August Strindberg wrote a historical drama about Gustavus Adolphus.

30 Joachim von Sandrart, *Teutsche Academie* (Nuremberg, 1675), quoted in Kaufmann, *Court, Cloister and City*, p. 235.

31 Jessen, *Der dreissigjährige Krieg*, 'Der dreiundzwanzigjährige Kurfürst von Brandenburg, Friedrich Wilhelm . . . schloss . . . mit den Schweden einen Neutralitäts-
vertrag', p. 388.

32 Parker, *The Thirty Years War*, p. 160.

33 Frederick the Great in a 1738 letter to the philosopher Christian Wolff, quoted
in Fauchier-Magnan, *The Small German Courts*, p. 22.

Many careers were made or broken at small courts like Württemberg,
Bamberg, Bayreuth and Mergentheim; in the 1670s my ancestors, the Hanover
branch of the von Moltke family, became Masters of the Hunt and Chancellors
of the Exchequer to Frederick William's rival, Ernst August von Hanover. The
most splendid courts were Heidelberg, Munich, Salzburg, Prague and Dresden,
which was soon to be graced by Pöppelmann's Zwinger Palace. See Hermann
Heckmann, *Matthäus Daniel Pöppelmann: Leben und Werk* (Berlin, 1972).

34 Frederick William and his heirs also gained the right to the title Elector of

Brandenburg and Duke of Prussia. He therefore joined the ranks of European rulers who were sovereign *de jure*. Junkers were ruling families of East Prussia but by 1653 he had brought them under control. In that year he summoned a full meeting of the Estates to Berlin which resulted in the celebrated constitutional document, the *Charter of July 1653*. The end result was that the elector gained control over his noble subjects through direct taxation, but the Junker nobility were otherwise left in control of the countryside. E. J. Feuchtwanger, *Prussia, Myth and Reality. The Role of Prussia in German History* (London, 1970), pp. 27–8.

35 Knut Schulz, 'Vom Herrschaftsantritt der Hohenzollern bis zum Ausbruch des dreissigjährigen Krieges (1411/12–1618)', in Wolfgang Ribbe (ed.), *Geschichte Berlins* (Munich, 1987), vol. 1: *Von der Frühgeschichte bis zur Industrialisierung*, p. 344.

36 For the magnificence of the court of Louis XIV see V. L. Tapié, *The Age of Grandeur, Baroque and Classicism in Europe* (London, 1960); see also J. B. Wolf, *Louis XIV* (London, 1968).

37 Many Berlin firms which had depended on trade were bankrupted by the war, including the Berlin trading company of Weiler and Essenbrücher, suppliers to Field Marshal Hans von Arnim during the war. Those cities which were lucky enough to be far from the centre of the conflict, or who were not forced to billet troops like Berlin typically fared much better; the turnover at the Frankfurt trade fairs actually increased between 1627 and 1632, from 15,000 to almost 38,000 imperial thalers. The profits were made in goods, from luxury articles to horses, butter, saltpetre and oxen. Langer, *Hortus Bellicus*, p. 149.

38 Gustav Schmoller (ed.), 'Das politische Testament Friedrich Wilhelm des Erstens von 1722', in *Deutsche Zeitschrift für Geschichtswissenschaft*, I, 1897, pp. 48–69. According to Adrien Fauchier–Magnan, the old French word Huguenot originates from the German *Eidgenossen* or confederates. Fauchier-Magnan, *The Small German Courts*, p. 25n. Frederick the Great said in *Considérations sur l'état présent du corps politique de l'Europe* that there were only two blots on the great reign of Louis XIV: 'to have authorised the burning of the Palatinate and to have revoked the Edict of Nantes'.

39 John Stoye, *Europe Unfolding 1646–1688* (London, 1988), p. 373.

40 Parker, *The Thirty Years War*, p. 20. For further examples see Wilmont Haacke, *Die politische Zeitschrift 1665–1965*, (Stuttgart, 1968), vol. 1.

41 Hajo Holborn, *A History of Modern Germany 1648–1840* (Princeton, 1964), p. 129.

42 By 1727 one fifth of the population of Brandenburg were immigrants. Rudolf Vierhaus, *Germany in the Age of Absolutism*, trans. Jonathan B. Knudsen (Cambridge, 1988), p. 15.

43 Eduard Muret, *Geschichte der französischen Kolonie in Brandenburg-Preussen, unter besonderer Berücksichtigung der Berliner Gemeinde* (Berlin, 1885), p. 310. For two contemporary accounts of the integration of the French in Berlin see Nicolai, *Beschreibung der königlichen Residenzstädte*, pp. 24–7; Johann Peter Sussmilch, *Der königlichen Residentz Berlin schneller Wachstum und Erbauung. In zweyen Abhandlungen erwieesen von J. P. Sussmilch* (Berlin, 1752).

44 Walter Hubatsch, *Frederick the Great: Absolutism and Administration* (London,

1975), p. 202. See also, H. I. Bach, *The German Jew. A Synthesis of Judaism and Western Civilisation* (Oxford, 1984), p. 30.

45 H. G. Adler, *The Jews in Germany. From the Enlightenment to National Socialism* (London, 1969), pp. 20–21.

46 David Sorkin, *The Transformation of German Jewry 1780–1840* (Oxford, 1987), pp. 5–8, and Section II, 'The Subculture', pp. 107–56.

47 For a sense of this lost culture see the section on Berlin in the catalogue of the 'Jüdische Lebenswelten' exhibition held at the Martin-Gropius-Bau in Berlin in 1991. Andreas Nachama and Gereon Sievernich (eds.), *Jüdische Lebenswelten Katalog* (Berlin, 1991), pp. 175–232.

48 L. F. Hartung, 'Die politischen Testamente der Hohenzollern', in O. Büsch and W. Neugebauer (eds.), *Moderne Preussische Geschichte 1648–1947* (Berlin, 1981), vol. 3, p. 1483.

49 Gerhard Oestreich, *Friedrich Wilhelm – Der Grosse Kurfürst* (Göttingen, 1971), p. 72. See also Kurt Jany, *Geschichte der königlich preussischen Armee bis zum Jahre 1807*, 3 vols. (Berlin, 1928). The Political Testaments are printed in Georg Küntzler and Martin Hass, *Die politischen Testamente der Hohenzollern* (Berlin, 1919).

50 Hans-Joachim Netzer et al. (eds.), *Preussen. Porträt einer politischen Kultur* (Munich, 1968), pp. 36–7.

51 West Prussia remained Polish, therefore he could not be called King 'of' Prussia. This was changed after the first partition of Poland in 1772, when Frederick the Great took over the territory, and became King of Prussia. On the acquisition of the title from the emperor by Frederick I see Holborn, *A History of Modern Germany*, p. 104.

52 Richard L. Gawthrop, *Pietism and the Making of Eighteenth-Century Prussia* (Cambridge, 1993), p. 66. See also Adler *The Jews in Germany*, p. 104.

53 Gawthrop, *Pietism*, p. 67; see also Ernst Klein, *Geschichte der öffentlichen Finanzen in Deutschland 1500–1870* (Wiesbaden, 1974), pp. 47–8.

54 On Sophia Charlotte see Holborn, *A History of Modern Germany*, p. 153. On the history of the Academy of Arts see the work celebrating its 200th anniversary, Hans Müller, *Zur Jubelfeier 1696–1896* (Berlin, 1896). On Leibniz's influence in Berlin see L. Keller *Gottfried Wilhelm Leibniz und die deutschen Sozietäten des 17. Jahrhunderts* (Berlin, 1903); Wilhelm Totok (ed.), *Leibniz* (Hanover, 1966).

55 Jan Chiapusso, *Bach's World* (Westport, Conn., 1968), pp. 8–48.

56 Schlüter had a great deal of bad luck in Berlin. The Münzturm (Mint Tower), built next to the Schloss, had to be demolished in 1706 as it was not supported by the Berlin sand and had started to crack. In 1707 he completed a hunting lodge for the king at Freienwalde but as the monarch approached a mud slide covered the entire building; the king did not return. Nicholas Powell, *From Baroque to Rococo* (London, 1959), pp. 44–5. See also Edwin Redslob, *Barock und Rokoko in den Schlössern von Berlin und Potsdam* (Munich, 1954), pp. 15–18; Heinz Ladendorf, *Der Bildhauer and Baumeister Andreas Schlüter: Beiträge zu seiner Biographie und zur Kunstgeschichte seiner Zeit* (Berlin, 1935).

57 The building was started by Nering and continued by Eosander after his death.

It was completed by Frederick the Great in 1740. Powell, *From Baroque to Rococo*, p. 44.

58 The church was endowed by Queen Sophie-Luise in 1712. The tower was not completed until 1732, although it was based on Schlüter's ill-fated Münzturm. The interior was refurbished in the neo-baroque style in 1892.

59 Lady Mary Montagu, *Letters and Works* (London, 1867), vol. 1, p. 41.

60 As Frederick William put it, 'Der liebe Gott hat Euch auf den Thron gesetzt, nicht zu faulenzen, sondern zu arbeiten und seine Länder zu regieren' (the dear Lord has put you on your throne not to loaf about but to work and to rule your country'. Hans-Joachim Schoeps, *Preussen. Geschichte eines Staates* (Berlin, 1966), p. 47.

61 This explains the dearth of art either commissioned or purchased during the years of his reign. 'See Helmut Börsch-Supan, *Die Kunst in Brandenburg-Preussen. Ihre Geschichte von der Renaissance bis zum Biedermeier dargestellt am Kunstbesitz der Berliner Schlösser* (Berlin, 1980).

62 The full title was General-Ober-Finanz-Kriegs-und-Domanen-Direktorium. Holborn, *History of Modern Germany*, p. 195. See also Otto Hintze, 'Der Beamtenstand', in *Gesammelte Abhandlungen* (Gottingen, 1967), vol. 2: *Soziologie und Geschichte*.

63 'The trial against Dorothea Steffin' (1760) in Georg Holmsten, *Die Berlin-Chronik. Daten, Personen, Dokumente* (Düsseldorf, 1987), p. 160.

64 Gawthrop, *Pietism*, p. 25.

65 Ibid., p. 265.

66 His obsession with the army was evident from an early age; when the duke of Marlborough came to Berlin in 1705 the prince was obviously embarrassed by the state of the Prussian forces, which had been run down by his father. Dr Carl Eduard Vehse noted many of the young man's militaristic pronouncements in his memoirs. Dr Carl Eduard Vehse, *Memoirs of the Court of Prussia*, trans. C. F. Demmler, (London, 1854).

67 The regiment was disbanded by Frederick the Great after his father's death – not least because it cost 300,000 thalers a year. On the story of its creation see J. R. Hutchinson, *The Romance of a Regiment: Being the True and Diverting Story of the Giant Grenadiers of Potsdam, How They Were Caught and Held in Captivity 1713–1740* (London, 1898).

68 Elézar de Mauvillon, *The Life of Frederick William I, late King of Prussia: Containing many Authentick Letters and Pieces*, trans. William Phelips (London, 1750), p. 524. This splendid volume is the source of many of the anecdotes surrounding the life of the dour 'Soldier King'. See also Werner Schwipps, *Die Garnisonkirchen von Berlin und Potsdam* (Berlin, 1964).

69 'War is the national industry of Prussia' attributed to Mirabeau by Albert Sorel, based on the introduction to *Monarchie prussienne*. Mirabeau continues: 'il est incontestable que l'énorme disproportion de l'armée à la population est un mal, un très grand mal; mais ce n'est pas la méthode du recrutement national que l'on en peut accuser; c'est le système politique de l'Europe, la périlleuse situation des provinces prussiennes, et le peu de contiguité des parties qui composent cette monarchie.' Honoré-Gabriel-Victor-Riquetti, comte de Mirabeau, *De la*

monarchie prussienne sous Frédéric le Grand, (Paris, 1788), vol. 1, p. 163. Napoleon would later add that Prussia had been 'hatched from a cannonball'.

70 The reaction in Berlin to his early reforms, including the banning of censorship and the abolition of torture, is outlined in G. B. Volz, *Friedrich der Grosse in Spiegel seiner Zeit*, (Berlin, 1901), vol. 1. The optimism was not limited to Prussia; a 1740 edition of the *Gentleman's Magazine* in London claimed that 'The present king of Prussia's accession to the throne hath given his subjects such an happy prospect of a mild, gracious and glorious reign.'

71 For the exchange of letters before the outbreak of war see Hans Jessen, *Friedrich der Grosse und Maria Theresa in Augenzeugen berichten* (Düsseldorf, 1965), pp. 125–8. See also Thomas Babington Macaulay, *Frederic the Great* (London, 1842) and, for another British view, Thomas Carlyle, *History of Frederick the Great of Prussia, called Frederick the Great* (centenary edition, London, 1899). See also Franz Theodor Kugler, *Life of Frederick the Great: Comprehending a Complete History of the Silesian Campaign and the Seven Years War*, trans. E. A. Moriarty (London, 1877).

72 Adam Zamoyski, *The Polish Way. A Thousand Year History of the Poles and Their Culture* (London, 1987), p. 228.

73 Horst Krüger, *Zur Geschichte der Manufakturen* (Berlin, 1958), pp. 476–8; Otto Hintze, 'Johann Ernst Gotkowsky', in *Historische und Politische Aufsätze* (Berlin, 1908), vol. 2, p. 109.

74 For the extraordinary contribution of the Huguenots to Berlin industry see Eckart Birnstiel and Andreas Reinke, 'Die Hugenotten in der Berliner Wirtschaft', in Stefi Jersch-Wenzel and Barbara John, *Von Zuwanderern zu Einheimischen. Hugenotten, Juden, Böhmen, Polen in Berlin* (Berlin, 1990), pp. 102–29; Conrad Grau, *Berlin. Französische Strasse. Auf den Spuren der Hugenotten* (Berlin, 1986), pp. 29–34; Rudolf von Thadden and Michelle Magdelaine (eds.), *Die Hugenotten 1685–1985*, 2 vols. (Munich, 1986).

75 Hubatsch, *Frederick the Great*, p. 72.

76 Ibid., p. 37.

77 The militaristic nature of the city was evident to everyone who visited: the surgeon John Moore, who was in the party of the Scottish duke of Hamilton, noted that there were 'soldiers parading and officers hurrying backwards and forwards. The town looked more like the cantonment of a great army, than the capital of a kingdom in the time of profound peace.' When watching regiments exercising in Berlin he noted that 'If the young recruit shows neglect or remissness, his attention is roused by the officer's cane, which is applied with augmenting energy, till he has acquired the full command of his firelock. He is taught steadiness under arms, and the immobility of a statue; he is informed, that all his members are to move only at the word of command, and not at his own pleasure: that speaking, coughing, sneezing, are all unpardonable crimes . . . that the smallest deficiency will be punished with rigour.' John Moore, *View of Society and Manners in France, Switzerland and Germany*, 2 vols. (London, 1789), quoted in Robert B. Asprey, *Frederick the Great. The Magnificent Enigma* (New York, 1986), pp. 607–8.

78 Montesquieu was so appalled by the cheap copies of Versailles throughout

Germany that he remarked, 'Versailles has ruined all of the princes of the German lands'. On the influence of French culture and the architecture of Versailles on the rest of Europe see M. S. Anderson, *Europe in the Eighteenth Century 1713–1783* (London, 1987), pp. 405–6.

79 Frederick the Great, quoted in Anthony Blunt, *Baroque and Rococo: Architecture and Decoration* (New York, 1978), p. 271.

80 Voltaire's memoirs about his time in Berlin are filled with wry observations about the city and Frederick the Great. François-Marie Arouet de Voltaire, *Mein Aufenthalt in Berlin*, ed. Hans Jacob (Munich, 1921). Saint-Simon and the anonymous French writer are quoted in Fauchier-Magnan, *The Small German Courts*, p. 35. See also Christoph Friedrich Nicolai, *Anekdoten von Friedrich dem Grossen*, ed. Emil Schaeffer (Leipzig, 1915). His obsession with France is clear from his own work, most of it written in French; see Johann David Erdmann Preuss (ed.), *Oeuvres de Frédéric le Grand*, 30 vols. (Berlin, 1846–57).

81 Nancy Mitford, *Frederick the Great* (London, 1973), p. 248.

82 Francis I of France reigned from 1515 to 1547; Frederick the Great's letter of 16 November 1746 to Voltaire is quoted in Kaufmann, *Court, Cloister and City*, p. 393.

83 Bach had perhaps hoped for a better position at Frederick's court; indeed his secretary was probably reflecting Bach's views when he wrote, 'at Berlin the golden age of music seemed to be inaugurated'. But Bach was not offered a position. Karl Geiringer, *Johann Sebastian Bach* (Oxford, 1967), p. 95.

84 For Knobelsdorff's influence on Frederick's taste in architecture see Anneliese Strichhan, *Knobelsdorff und das friderizianische Rokoko* (Magdeburg, 1932).

85 For two contemporary views of the architecture in Berlin, see Nicolai, *Beschreibung der königlichen Residenzstädte*, and John Daniel Friedrich Rumpf, *Beschreibung der äusseren und inneren Merkwürdigkeiten der königlichen Schlösser in Berlin, Charlottenburg, Schönhausen, in den bei Potsdam* (Berlin, 1794).

86 Frederick Pottle (ed.), *Boswell on the Grand Tour: Germany and Switzerland, 1764* (London, 1953), p. 110.

87 Germaine de Staël, *Über Deutschland*, trans. Robert Habs (Stuttgart, 1962), p. 127.

88 Sir Charles Hanbury Williams was the British envoy to Prussia. He fell into disfavour with Frederick the Great for criticizing him in public and was recalled to London in 1751. His writings, kept at the Lewis Walpole Library in Farmington, Connecticut (Hanbury Williams Papers), reflect this bitterness. This passage is quoted in Mitford, *Frederick the Great*, p. 169.

89 Hitler was obsessed with Frederick the Great. The *Die Woche* commemorative pamphlet for the 'Day of National Awakening' had Frederick the Great on the cover. 'Der Tag von Potsdam, zum 21 März 1933', *Die Woche*, Gedenksausgabe (Berlin, 1933). The 12 April 1933 edition was called 'Der Geist von Potsdam' (The Spirit of Potsdam).

90 Alexander S. Pushkin, *Mednyi vsadnik* (The Bronze Horseman), trans. B. Deutsch and A. Yarmolinsky (New York, 1958).

91 He was not alone. William Lee noted in June 1753, 'From Berlin I shall pass through Brunswick to Hanover. The roads they tell me are bad and the accommodations worse.' And of his journey from Magdeburg to Berlin he complained

that there was 'little to eat but bad sour hard heavy rye bread, and salt butter'. Henry Legge complained in 1748 of 'German extortion' in the inns, while a British newspaper of 1722 reported that 'In Germany . . . a man may travel many days and not find a bed to lie upon'. The threat of war also boded ill for the traveller; on 17 March 1785, as war between Austria and Prussia threatened, Sir Grey Cooper wrote to Sir Robert Murray Keith about his son's return journey from Vienna via Berlin and Hanover: 'the route by Berlin will not be so proper at the time of his return: There are I fear appearances which portend a storm.' Jeremy Black, *The Grand Tour in the Eighteenth Century* (Stroud, 1992), pp. 134, 139, 167.

92 Johann Wolfgang von Goethe, 'Brief an Charlotte von Stein – Reise nach Berlin, 17 Mai 1778', in Friedhelm Kemp, *Goethe. Leben und Welt in Briefen* (Munich, 1978), p. 171.

93 K. A. Mastiaux in a lecture on 2 December 1789 to his Bonn Reading Society. Richard van Dülmen, *Die Gesellschaft der Aufklärer: Zur bürgerlichen Emanzipation und aufklärerischen Kultur in Deutschland* (Frankfurt-am-Main, 1986), p. 89.

94 Ibid., p. 56. On the masons and the Enlightenment see Rudolf Vierhaus, *Das Vergangene und die Geschichte, Festschrift Wittram* (Göttingen, 1973), 'Aufklärung und Freimaurerei in Deutschland'; Heinrich Boos, *Geschichte der Freimaurerei. Ein Beitrag zur Kultur- und Literaturgeschichte des 18. Jahrhunderts* (Wiesbaden, 1969).

95 Norman Hampson, *The Enlightenment* (Harmondsworth, 1981), p. 105.

96 Ibid., p. 128. On the expense and complications surrounding the publication of the *Encyclopédie* see R. Darnton, *The Business of the Enlightenment: A Publishing History of the Encyclopédie, 1775–1800* (Cambridge, Mass., 1979).

97 Anderson, *Europe in the Eighteenth Century*, p. 429. On Montesquieu see M. Richter, *The Political Thought of Montesquieu* (Cambridge, 1977).

98 C. B. A. Behrens, *Society, Government and the Enlightenment. The Experiences of Eighteenth-Century France and Prussia* (London, 1985), p. 152. For a general look at the struggle between the Church and the Enlightenment thinkers see G. R. Cragg, *The Church and the Age of Reason, 1648–1789* (Harmondsworth, 1960).

99 Frederick's reasoning was simple: 'if a noble loses his honour he is ostracised by his family; whereas a commoner who has committed some fraud can continue to run his father's business'. Fauchier-Magnan, *The Small German Courts*, p. 52.

100 Sorkin, *The Transformation of German Jewry*, p. 18.

101 Behrens, *Society, Government and the Enlightenment*, p. 179.

102 Van Dülmen, *Die Gesellschaft der Aufklärer*, p. 93. On the early formation of societies see Karl F. Otto, *Die Sprachgesellschaften des 17. Jahrhunderts* (Stuttgart, 1972); Rolf Engelsing, *Der Bürger als Leser. Lesergeschichte in Deutschland 1500–1800* (Stuttgart, 1974); Martin Bircher and F. van Ingen (eds.), *Sprachgesellschaften, Sozietäten, Dichtergruppen* (Hamburg, 1978).

103 The Monday Club, or 'Berliner Montagsklub' was also known as the 'lachende Klub'. Its members met every Monday at 6 p.m. in a building in the Mohrenstrasse and it was here that Lessing met, amongst others, Frederick's flute teacher

Johann Quantz. Renate Klar and Kurt Wölfel, *Lessings Leben und Werk in Daten und Briefen* (Frankfurt-am-Main, 1967), p. 191.

104 Christian Wilhelm von Dohm, *Über die bürgerliche Verbesserung der Juden*, 2 vols. (Berlin, 1781–3); see also Sorkin's discussion of Dohm in Sorkin, *The Transformation of German Jewry*, pp. 23–8, and Horst Möller, 'Aufklärung, Judentum und Staat: Ursprung und Wirkung von Dohms Schrift über die bürgerliche Verbesserung der Juden', in Walter Grab (ed.), *Deutsche Aufklärung und Judenemanzipation* (Tel Aviv, 1980), pp. 119–48.

105 Van Dülmen, *Die Gesellschaft der Aufklärer*, p. 54n. On the lodges in Berlin see Carl Bröcker, *Die Freimaurerlogen Deutschlands von 1737 bis 1893* (Berlin, 1894); Albrecht Erlenmeier, *Die Namen der Freimaurerlogen, eine geschichtliche Untersuchung* (Leipzig, 1917).

106 Deborah Hertz, *Jewish High Society in Old Regime Berlin* (Yale, 1988), p. 21.

107 Ulrich im Hof, *The Enlightenment* (Oxford, 1994), p. 116.

108 James J. Sheehan, *German History 1770–1866* (Oxford, 1989), p. 158. The *Spectator* was the most important of English journals at the time and was influential in the creation of reading groups and 'friendship societies' (see, for example, *Spectator*, no. 68, 18 May 1711); see also im Hof., *The Enlightenment* (esp. Part IV – 'Champions of the Enlightenment'), pp. 105–54. For a study of the German journals see Wolfgang Martens, *Die Botschaft der Tugend. Die Aufklärung im Spiegel der deutschen moralischen Wochenschriften* (Stuttgart, 1968); Heinrich Wuttke, *Die deutschen Zeitschriften und die Entstehung der öffentlichen Meinung* (Leipzig, 1875); Rolf Engelsing, *Der Bürger als Leser. Lesergeschichte in Deutschland 1500–1800* (Stuttgart, 1974).

109 To their annoyance Goethe's and Schiller's satirical *Xenien* (1796), written in response to those who had attacked their monthly publication *Die Horen*, sold only 3,000 copies. They had targeted Friedrich Nicolai for having a 'narrow-minded' approach to culture. Kemp, *Goethe*, pp. 424–5.

110 Hertz, *Jewish High Society*, p. 51.

111 Gordon Craig, *The Germans* (Harmondsworth, 1982), p. 28. Lessing's letters to his 'Liebster Freund' Moses Mendelssohn are most touching. On 30 March 1761 he wrote: 'O schreiben Sie mir doch ja recht oft; aber mehr als blosse Vorwürfe über mein Stillschweigen. Ihre Briefe sind für mich ein wahres Almosen.' One of his last letters, written on 19 December 1780, eight weeks before his death, was to his old friend: 'Ach, lieber freund! die Szene ist aus! Gern möchte ich Sie freilich noch einmal sprechen!' Klar and Wölfel, *Lessings Leben und Werke*, pp. 97–8, 173.

112 Hertz, *Jewish High Society*, p. 36. Hertz's book is an excellent study of the Jewish salons in Berlin. For a more general view see Ingeborg Drewitz, *Berliner Salons: Gesellschaft und Literatur zwischen Aufklärung und Industriezeitalter* (Berlin, 1965).

113 H. I. Bach, *The German Jew. A Synthesis of Judaism and Western Civilisation 1730–1930* (Oxford, 1984), pp. 44–72; see also Sorkin, *The Transformation of German Jewry*, p. 20. One of the best general studies of Moses Mendelssohn is Alexander Altmann, *Moses Mendelssohn* (Alabama, 1973).

114 The porcelain quotas for Jews were determined by the 'Kabinettsordre' of 21

March 1769. These 'taxes', along with a list of other regulations, are outlined in Brigitte Scheiger, 'Juden in Berlin', in Jersch-Wenzel and John, *Von Zuwanderern zu Einheimischen*, pp. 185–91. See also Selma Stern, *Der preussische Staat und die Juden* (Tübingen, 1962–71), vol. 384, p. 511.

115 Frederick II, *De la littérature allemande* (1780), quoted in Fauchier-Magnan, *The Small German Courts*, p. 88. There was growing resentment against the French with the creation of the *Regie* in 1766. Although officially part of the General Directory in fact it largely controlled it. Furthermore, it was under the control of the consortium of French entrepreneurs. Ten per cent of its members – those in the most important positions – were French; as Johnson has put it, 'Frenchmen dominated positions of prestige and profit, while Germans occupied the humble posts of gatekeepers, inspectors, and collectors.' The resentment led to bitter feuds between Frenchmen and Germans but when the latter complained to Frederick about the behaviour of the French he retorted that they were to blame because of their 'own evil and dissolute way of life and economy since the war'. Hubert C. Johnson, *Frederick the Great and his Officials* (Yale, 1975), pp. 200–209.

116 Lessing wrote this in response to the king's burning of Voltaire's *Diatribe du Docteur Akakia* (1752), a satire attacking the king's friend Pierre-Louis Moreau de Maupertuis whom Voltaire disliked intensely. It was the publication of this work which caused Frederick the Great to expel Voltaire from Berlin. Gotthold Ephraim Lessing, in Heinz Steinberg, *Grosse Literatur in der grossen Stadt Berlin* (Berlin, 1995), p. 19.

117 Behrens, *Society, Government and the Enlightenment*, p. 153.

118 George Forster (1754–94), born in Danzig to English parents, went on Cook's second South Sea voyage (1772–5) and wrote an account, *A Voyage towards the South Pole and round the World*, in 1777. Winfried Ranke, *Preussen. Versuch einer Bilanz* (Berlin, 1981), p. 213.

119 Behrens, *Society, Government and the Enlightenment*, p. 185. See also Henri Braunschweig, *Gesellschaft und Romantik in Preussen im 18. Jahrhundert. Die Krise des preussischen Staates am Ende des 18. Jahrhunderts und die Entstehung der romantischen Mentalität* (Frankfurt-am-Main, 1976).

120 Hertz, *Jewish High Society*, p. 7.

121 Hannah Arendt, *Rahel Varnhagen: The Life of a Jewess* (New York, 1974), p. 99.

3: THE EMERGING GIANT

1 'Von hier und heute geht eine neue Epoche der Weltgeschichte aus,' Johann Wolfgang von Goethe said to friends at Valmy in 1793, 'und Ihr könnt sagen, Ihr seid dabei gewesen.' Nevertheless Goethe was not as enthusiastic about the revolution as his contemporaries, including Herder and Nicolai, and came to oppose it early on. His instinctive attachment to 'evolutionary' rather than 'revolutionary' politics was mirrored in his satirical allegory *Reise der Söhne Megaprazons* (1792).

2 Wordsworth wrote these lines in *French Revolution, as it appeared to Enthusiasts* (1808). For the German response see K. O. von Aretin and K. Härter (eds.), *Revolution und Konservatives Beharren. Das alte Reich und die französische Revolution* (Mainz, 1990); Dieter Borchmeyer, 'Weimar im Zeitalter der Revolution und der Napoleonischen Kriege', in Victor Zmegac (ed.), *Geschichte der deutschen Literatur vom 18. Jahrhundert bis zur Gegenwart*, (Königstein, 1984), vol. 1.

3 Friedrich Schiller, 8 February 1793, in F. Jonas (ed.), *Schillers Briefe* (Manchester, 1959), vol. 3: *Ausgewählte Briefe*, p. 333. For the reaction of intellectuals in Berlin to the revolution and its aftermath see Herbert Meschkowski, *Jeder nach seiner Facon. Berliner Geistesleben 1700–1810* (Munich, 1986).

4 Frances A. Yates, *The Rosicrucian Enlightenment* (London, 1986).

5 Before the royals left for Königsberg Queen Luise accompanied her cuirassier regiment as far as the Brandenburg Gate, wearing the regimental uniform, and became a symbol of the fighting spirit of Germany both in Berlin and abroad. On 8 October a Napoleonic bulletin stated, 'The Queen of Prussia is with the army dressed as an Amazon, and wearing the uniform of her dragoon regiment. She writes twenty letters a day to fan the flames in all directions.' French cartoons showed her as an 'unsexed Amazon' and a camp follower wearing an open hussar's jacket. Poultney Bigelow, *The History of the German Struggle for Liberty*, (New York, 1896–1903), vol. 1, p. 38.

6 The Napoleonic Wars would have a profound effect on the Jewish salons in Berlin; see Deborah Hertz, *Jewish High Society in Old Regime Berlin* (Yale, 1988), pp. 251–85; on the effect on salons in general see Rolf Strube (ed.), *Sie sassen und tranken am Teetisch. Anfänge und Blütezeit der Berliner Salons 1789–1871* (Munich, 1991).

7 The population watching the arrival of French troops could not believe that these men who were dressed in tattered uniforms and who smoked in the street had defeated them. See the eye-witness account of Richard George, 'Erinnerungen eines Preussen aus der Napoleonischen Zeit', reprinted in Ruth Köhler and Wolfgang Richter (eds.), *Berliner Leben, 1806–1847. Erinnerungen und Berichte* (Berlin, 1954), pp. 32–4.

8 As C. B. A. Behrens points out, the defeat and the extraction of payments were extremely damaging to Prussia and Berlin: 'Thousands of peasant holdings were ruined by the French requisitions. Thousands of businesses went bankrupt ... Of the 5,846 children born in Berlin [between 1806 and 1808], 4,300 died in infancy. The French plenipotentiary said on one occasion that no foreign occupation had ever pressed so heavily on any country.' As Clausewitz put it, 'The bankruptcies here are endless ... what was achieved in this sandy waste throughout centuries in the way of prosperity, culture and trade, will now be destroyed in perhaps a decade.' It was this very devastation which prompted the reform movement; things could not get worse than they already were. C. B. A. Behrens, *Society, Government and the Enlightenment. The Experiences of Eighteenth-Century France and Prussia* (London, 1985), p. 191; Carl von Clausewitz *Schriften, Aufsätze, Studien, Briefe*, ed. W. Hahlweg (Göttingen, 1966), vol. 1, p. 639.

9 Magnus Friedrich von Bassewitz, *Die Kurmarkt Brandenburg im Zusammenhang*

mit den Schicksalen des Gesamtstaats Preussen während der Zeit vom 22 Oktober 1806 bis zu Ende des Jahres 1808, (Leipzig, 1851–2), vol. 1, p. 154.

10 Nancy Mitford, *Frederick the Great* (London, 1973), p. 291. The visit took place on 25 October 1806. The scene was recorded in an engraving by J. F. Arnold after H. Dahling – a thoughtful, bare-headed Napoleon rests his hand on Frederick's coffin while his officers stand by, hats in hand. Napoleon may have been right; when Frederick the Great died the standing army numbered 171,000 well-trained, well-equipped men. Peter Paret, *Clausewitz and the State* (New York, 1967), p. 25.

11 On the Napoleonic period in general see the excellent volume by Thomas Nipperdey, *Germany from Napoleon to Bismarck, 1800–1866*, trans. Daniel Nolan, (Dublin, 1996); Stein's decision to go to war against France is discussed on p. 10. On Stein see Karl Freiherr vom Stein, *Briefe und amtliche Schriften*, ed. Erich Botzenhart and Walther Hubatsch (Stuttgart, 1957–74); Gerhard Ritter, *Stein: Eine politische Biographie* (Stuttgart, 1958).

12 He finishes with the exclamation: 'O my country, my *self-chosen* country!' quoted in J. R. Seeley, *Life and Times of Stein or Germany and Prussia in the Napoleonic Age* (New York, 1969), vol. 1, p. 393. See also the letters written in October–November 1806 in Karl Griewank (ed.), *Gneisenau. Ein Leben in Briefen* (Leipzig, 1939).

13 Heinrich von Bülow, July 1806, quoted in Seeley, *Life and Times of Stein*, p. 249.

14 Letter of March 1807. The most important of his documents outlining reform appeared in Hardenburg's *Reformdenkschrift Rigas* of 1807.

15 Stein wrote to the king, 'If his majesty does not resolve to adopt the proposed alterations, if he perseveres in acting under the influence of the Cabinet, it is to be expected that the Prussian State will either dissolve or lose its independence, and that the respect and love of the people will entirely depart from it.' It was a forceful argument and the king accepted his services reluctantly. Freiherr vom Stein, 'A Representation of the Faulty Organisation of the Cabinet, and the Necessity of Forming a Conference of Ministers', in Leopold von Ranke, *Hardenburg und die Geschichte des preussischen Staates 1793–1813* (Leipzig, 1875), vol. 2, p. 86.

16 Agatha Ramm, *Germany 1789–1919* (London, 1967), p. 71. Ramm includes a concise account of the Prussian reformers. See also Manfred Bozenhart, 'Von den preussischen Reformen zum Wiener Kongress', in Leo Just (ed.), *Handbuch der deutschen Geschichte* (Wiesbaden, 1980), vol. 3, pp. 546–9.

17 Ilja Mieck, 'Von der Reformzeit zur Revolution (1806–1847)', in Wolfgang Ribbe (ed.), *Geschichte Berlins* (Munich, 1987), vol. 1: *Von der Frühgeschichte bis zur Industrialisierung*, p. 448. See also Max Lenz, *Geschichte der königlichen Friedrich-Wilhelms-Universität zu Berlin*, 4 vols. (Halle, 1910).

18 Wilhelm von Humboldt, 'Über die innere and äussere Organisation der höheren wissenschaftlichen Anstalten in Berlin' (1810), in Andreas Flitner and Klaus Giel (eds.), *Werke in fünf Bänden* (Stuttgart, 1964), vol. 4, pp. 255–68. On Humboldt's influence on the reform process see Eduard Spranger, *Wilhelm von Humboldt und die Reform des Bildungswesens* (Tübingen, 1960); for a personal view see

Anna von Sydow (ed.), *Wilhelm und Caroline von Humboldt in ihren Briefen*, 3 vols. (1909). On the university see Helmut Klein (ed.), *Humboldt Universität zu Berlin 1810–1985*, 2 vols. (Berlin, 1985).

19 Golo Mann, *The History of Germany since 1789* (London, 1988), p. 66; see also Hubert Laitko (ed.), *Wissenschaft in Berlin. Von den Anfängen bis zum Neubeginn nach 1945* (Berlin, 1987). Even when discussing international politics Humboldt cannot resist references to the role of culture in the formation of national identity, but he also refers to the 'deeper ties' which supposedly bound Germans together; in his 'Memorandum concerning the German Constitution, December 1813' he explains that '. . . the feeling that Germany constitutes a whole cannot be erased from the German breast as it rests not merely on customs, language and a literature held in common . . . but on the memories of common laws and liberties, of glory and dangers overcome together, on the memories of the closer alliance which bound our fathers, and which lives on in the longing of their grandsons.' Flitner and Giel, *Werke in fünf Bänden*, vol. 4, p. 305.

20 Seeley, *Life and Times of Stein*, vol. 1, p. 371.

21 Ibid., vol. 2, p. 281.

22 The family's intense dislike of the French occupiers and indeed of Napoleon is evident in Gräfin Voss's memoir. Sophie Wilhelmine Gräfin von Voss, *69 Jahre am Preussischen Hof. Aus den Tagebüchern und Aufzeichnungen der Oberhofmeisterin von Voss* (Berlin, 1901).

23 The Rhine was itself only turned into a symbol of German nationalism when it was occupied by the French. The 'Rhine-song-movement' became a political force after 18 September 1840, when the poem by the unknown Nikolas Becker was published in the *Trierische Zeitung*; it concluded: 'They shall not have it/ Our free German Rhine/ Until its flood has buried/ The limbs of our last man!' The image of the Rhine as a symbol of German unity was largely the creation of Görres and Arndt. See Hagen Schulze, *The Course of German Nationalism. From Frederick the Great to Bismarck 1763–1867*, trans. Sarah Hanbury-Tenison, (Cambridge, 1991), p. 65; Koppel S. Pinson, *Modern Germany. Its History and Civilization* (New York, 1963), p. 36.

24 Adalbert von Chamisso, 'Reise um die Welt mit der Romanzoffischen Entdeckungs-Expedition in den Jahren 1815–1818', in Kurt Schleucher, *Adalbert von Chamisso* (Berlin, 1988), p. 129. See also W. Feudel, *Adalbert von Chamisso. Leben und Werke* (Leipzig, 1971).

25 Friedrich Maximilian Klinger, *Sturm und Drang* (1776); in fact the title had been suggested by Christoph Kaufmann. Gerhard Schulz, *Die deutsche Literatur zwischen französischer Revolution und Restauration* (Munich, 1983), p. 139.

26 For the importance of *The Robbers* to *Sturm und Drang* see Alan C. Leidner, 'Introduction', in Alan C. Leidner (ed.), *Sturm und Drang: The Soldier, The Childmurderess, Storm and Stress, and The Robbers* (New York, 1992), pp. ix–xiv, 181–297.

27 On Goethe see Johann Wolfgang von Goethe, *The Sufferings of Young Werther*, trans. Harry Steinhauer (New York, 1970).

28 Thomas K. Scherman and Louis Biancolli, *The Beethoven Companion* (New York, 1972), p. 388. For a fascinating discussion of Beethoven's views on Napoleon see

J. Hermand, 'Beethoven und Bonaparte. Biographisches und Autobiographisches in der "Eroica" ', in R. Grimm (ed.), *Vom Anderen und vom Selbst. Beiträge zu Fragen der Biographie und Autobiographie* (Königstein, 1982), pp. 183–97.

29 On the Romantic link between beauty and death see Mario Praz, *The Romantic Agony*, trans. Angus Davidson (Oxford, 1970), pp. 31–8.

30 James J. Sheehan, *German History 1770–1886* (Oxford, 1993), p. 327. Sheehan provides an excellent overview of the culture of the period: see 'Culture in the Revolutionary Era', pp. 324–71.

31 Franz Liszt and Princess Caroline von Wittgenstein, 'Berlioz and his "Harold" Symphony' (Berlin, 1855), in Donald Jay Grout and Claude V. Palisca, *A History of Western Music* (London, 1993), p. 661.

32 Craig includes a discussion of Romantic culture in Chapter 9, 'The Romantics', in Gordon Craig, *The Germans* (Harmondsworth, 1984), pp. 190–212. On the 'Black Ranger' see p. 193.

33 The inscription NATURE AND LIBERTY appears on his tomb near Geneva. On Rousseau's early journeys on foot see Matthew Josephson, 'Introduction', in Lowell Bair (trans.), *The Essential Rousseau*, pp. ix–xi. For his influence on the German Romantics, and links between France and the German Romantics see J. Droz, *Le romantisme allemand et l'État. Résistance et collaboration dans l'Allemagne napoléonienne* (Paris, 1966).

34 Friedrich Hölderlin, 'Brot und Wein', in Leonard Forster (ed.), *The Penguin Book of German Verse* (Harmondsworth, 1959), p. 293.

35 Bogumil Goltz, quoted in Craig, *The Germans*, p. 193.

36 Caspar David Friedrich, *Monk by the Sea* (1808–10), Staatliche Museen zu Berlin Preussischer Kulturbesitz, Nationalgalerie; *Wanderer above the Sea of Fog* (1818), Hamburger Kunsthalle; *Two Men Contemplating the Moon* (1819), Staatliche Kunstsammlungen Dresden, Gemäldegalerie Neue Meister.

37 Friedrich Hölderlin, 'Abendphantasie', in Forster, *The Penguin Book of German Verse*, p. 288.

38 Joseph von Eichendorff, 'Sehnsucht', in Forster, *The Penguin Book of German Verse*, p. 318.

39 Gotthilf Heinrich von Schubert, *Die Symbolik des Traumes* (Berlin, 1814). See also F. R. Merkel, *Der Naturphilosoph Gotthilf Schubert und die deutsche Romantik* (Munich, 1913).

40 Novalis, 'Hymnen an die Nacht', in Forster, *The Penguin Book of German Verse*, p. 304.

41 This expression in turn inspired Mahler's 'Resurrection' symphony.

42 Friedrich Schlegel, 'Fragmente (Ideen 131)', in Paul Kluckhohn (ed.), *Kunstanschauung der Frühromantik, Deutsche Literatur, Reihe Romantik* (Darmstadt, 1966), vol. 3, p. 137.

43 Ludwig Tieck's notes on Novalis's plans for *Heinrich von Ofterdingen*, quoted in Craig, *The Germans*, p. 196.

44 Joseph von Eichendorff, *Intimations and the Present* (1815), in Craig, *The Germans*, p. 197.

45 It was relatively easy for the Romantics to shift from radical individualism into the worship of the organic community of the *Volk*, with its rejection of

Enlightenment ideas and the doctrine of natural rights and the social contract. The state was a living thing, related by blood descent and history, an attitude first articulated by Adam Müller. See Pinson, *Modern Germany*, p. 43; Sheehan, *German History*, p. 374.

46 Johann Gottlieb Fichte, *Rede an die deutsche Nation* (Berlin, 1808). In his fourteenth lecture Fichte justifies his own role by claiming that all others had as yet refused to act: 'One of you should come forward and ask me: what gives you of all German men and writers the particular task, vocation and right to gather us together and browbeat us? ... I reply ... that I am the one to act is because none of them has done it before me; I would have kept silent if someone had come forward before me.' He then tells his audience that if they have the courage to act, 'You shall witness in spirit the German name raised by this race to the most glorious of all the peoples, you shall witness this nation as the renewing force and the restorer of the world.'

47 Heinrich von Kleist, quoted in Schulze, *The Course of German Nationalism*, p. 53. Schulze also quotes Brentano's poem rousing people to fight 'That no foe of Germany may survive!'

48 Ernst Moritz Arndt, *Geist der Zeit*, (Berlin, 1814), Part 3, p. 430. On Kleist see 'Das Grab am kleinen Wannsee', in Heinz Steinberg, *Grosse Literatur in der grossen Stadt Berlin* (Berlin, 1995), pp. 107–18. See also Sheehan, *German History*, p. 380.

49 Seeley, *Life and Times of Stein*, vol. 2, p. 77.

50 Ibid., vol. 3, p. 9.

51 The 'Federal Constitution' according to a statement by one of its members before a board of inquiry in connection with the 1821 'persecution of Demagogues', in Schulze, *The Course of German Nationalism*, p. 51n.

52 Lt H. A. Vossler, a soldier of the Grande Armée, wrote in his diary of the weather that August, noting that the days were terribly hot and the nights already cool: 'These sharp changes in temperature were beginning to affect our health and, to a much greater degree, that of the army as a whole. From Dogorobuzh onward we met many, sometimes very many, soldiers who had dropped by the roadside from sheer exhaustion and had died where they lay for lack of help.' A. Vossler, *With Napoleon in Russia 1812*, trans. Walter Wallich (London, 1969), p. 59.

53 Seeley, *Life and Times of Stein*, vol. 3, p. 32. Another soldier, Jakob Walter, recounted his horrific journey back from Moscow. At Dubrovna he could see the light of burning villages, 'and the shrieking, beating, and lamenting did not stop for a minute. Again and again people died, and sometimes froze to death; these were people who pressed toward the fire but were seldom permitted to get there; so they died away from the fire, and very often they were even converted into cushions in order that the living would not have to sit in the snow.' Jakob Walter, *The Diary of a Napoleonic Foot Soldier*, ed. Mark Raeff, (Moreton-in-Marsh, 1997), p. 72.

54 This was demonstrated in the model by the French engineer Charles Joseph Minard (1781–1870), who shows the terrible fate of Napoleon's army in Russia using six variables on the chart: the size of the army, its location on a two

dimensional surface, the direction of the army's movement, and the temperature on various dates during the retreat from Moscow. The portrayal of the reduction of the army from 50,000 to 28,000 men at the Berezina river, when the temperature fell to −20 degrees, or the reduction from 28,000 men at Berezina to 12,000 at Smorgoni, where the temperature was −30 degrees, is still shocking. Joseph Minard, *Carte figurative Russie 1812–1813*.

55 Ludwig Rellstab, *Aus meinem Leben* (Berlin, 1861), vol. 1, p. 165.

56 Gustav Parthey, *Jugenderinnerungen* (Berlin, 1907), vol. 1, p. 332.

57 Berlin's overall war losses as a result of the Napoleonic occupation and wars are recorded in Paul Schwartz, *Berlins Kriegsleiden in der Franzosenzeit. Ein zeitgemässes Kapitel aus der Vergangenheit* (Berlin, 1917).

58 Seeley, *Life and Times of Stein*, vol. 3, p. 382.

59 Ibid., p. 432.

60 He continues, 'It was only sixteen years ago, when we finally wanted to rid ourselves of the French that we discovered Germany everywhere.' Conversation between Goethe and Eckermann, 14 March 1830, quoted in Adrien Fauchier-Magnan, *The Small German Courts in the 18th Century* (London, 1958), p. 23.

61 The events were harmless enough; indeed it was only in 1881 that the Deutsche Burschenschaft began to push its own brand of rabid nationalism and anti-Semitism; at the time the group was of little significance.

62 Seeley, *Life and Times of Stein*, vol. 3, p. 430.

63 For an uncritical view of Biedermeier in Berlin see Paul Weiglin, *Berliner Biedermeier. Leben, Kunst und Kultur in Alt-Berlin zwischen 1815–1848* (Bielefeld, 1942). For a more general view see Marianne Bernhard, *Das Biedermeier. Kultur zwischen Wiener Kongress und Märzrevolution* (Düsseldorf, 1983).

64 Gerhard Krienke, 'Der schulische Aspekt der Kinderarbeit in Berlin 1825–1848. Zur Sozial- und Schulgeschichte der preussischen Hauptstadt', in *Der Bär von Berlin*, 18, 1969, pp. 94–121.

65 On the change in morality and the family see Nipperdey, *Germany from Napoleon to Bismarck*, pp. 109–11, 510.

66 Wilhelm von Humboldt, quoted in Dieter Vorsteher (ed.), *Die Reise nach Berlin* (Berlin, 1987), p. 235.

67 'The road from Greenwich to London was actually busier than the most popular streets in Berlin, so many people were to be encountered driving or walking,' he continued. Karl Philip Moritz, quoted in Roy Porter, *London. A Social History* (Harmondsworth, 1994), p. 165. See also Ernst Wickenberg (ed.), *Karl Philip Moritz* (Munich, 1987), p. 327.

68 On Schinkel see Michael Snodin (ed.), *Karl Friedrich Schinkel: A Universal Man* (London, 1991); Paul Ortwin Rave, *Berlin: Stadtbaupläne, Strassen, Brücken, Tore, Plätze* (Berlin, 1981).

69 Franz Grillparzer (1826), quoted in Vorsteher, *Die Reise nach Berlin*, p. 30.

70 Snodin, *Karl Friedrich Schinkel*, p. 131.

71 Ibid., p. 132.

72 Gothic was also coming back into fashion through the influence of the crown prince, who appeared to support German unification and equated Gothic buildings with this aim. It was he who commissioned the Friedrich-Werder-Kirche

in 1830. Johannes Sievers, *Bauten für den Prinzen von Preussen* (Berlin, 1985), pp. 45–6.

73 Gottfried Riemann, 'Schinkel's Buildings and Plans for Berlin', in Snodin, *Karl Friedrich Schinkel*, p. 23.

74 Heinrich Heine, *Reisebilder* (Frankfurt-am-Main, 1980), p. 235.

75 Heinrich Heine, in Marc Henry, *Trois villes: Vienne, Munich, Berlin* (Paris, 1917).

4: From Revolution to *Realpolitik*

1 Theodor Schieder, 'Partikularismus und Nationalbewusstsein', in Werner Conze, *Staat und Gesellschaft im deutschen Vormärz* (Stuttgart, 1962), pp. 15–23; see also Gustav Mayer, 'Die Anfänge des politischen Radikalismus im vormärzlichen Preussen', in Hans-Ulrich Wehler (ed.), *Radikalismus, Sozialismus und bürgerliche Demokratie* (Frankfurt-am-Main, 1969), pp. 7–107.

2 Wagner recalled that on 3 May 1831, after watching Polish troops leave to fight for their country, he was the only non-Pole invited to a banquet to celebrate the anniversary of the establishment of their constitution as a 'mark of special distinction and affection . . . throughout the evening a brass band from the city played Polish folksongs uninterruptedly, in which the entire company . . . joined in, jubilant and mournful in turn. The beautiful song, "The Third of May" aroused particularly uproarious enthusiasm. Tears and shouts of joy commingled in a tremendous tumult, until the group went out onto the garden grass in widely dispersed pairs of lovers whose extravagant endearments were keyed by the inexhaustible word "Oiczisna" (fatherland), the mantle of night finally enveloping this splendid debauch. The dreamlike evening later served me as the theme for an orchestral composition in the form of an overture with the title *Polonia*.' Richard Wagner, *My Life*, trans. Andrew Gray (New York, 1992), p. 61.

3 W. Hallgerten, *Studien über die deutsche Polenfreundschaft in der Periode der Märzrevolution* (Munich/Berlin, 1928). The Polish revolutionary Mieroslawski was a great favourite with Berlin ladies, and was later paraded through the streets after the release of political prisoners on 20 March 1848. The new March government in Berlin in 1848 would also be pro-Polish; the new Foreign Minister Count von Arnim wanted to restore the Polish state against the wishes of the Russians, but the French rejected the policy and the Prussian king lost interest. But Bismarck represented the views of the powerful conservative Junkers, writing after 1863: 'Restoring the Kingdom of Poland in any shape or form is tantamount to us creating an ally available to any enemy that might choose to attack us.' On Arnim see Thomas Nipperdey, *Germany from Napoleon to Bismarck 1800–1866*, trans. Daniel Nolan (Dublin, 1996), p. 556; Otto von Bismarck, *Die gesammelte Werke* (Berlin, 1924–35), vol. 4, p. 118.

4 James J. Sheehan, *German History, 1770–1866* (Oxford, 1993), p. 446. See also William Jacob, *A View of the Agriculture, Manufactures, Statistics, and State of Society of Germany and Parts of Holland and France* (London, 1820), p. 222.

5 Nipperdey, *Germany from Napoleon to Bismarck*, p. 268.

6 Not all papers supported the changes taking place in Berlin; some, such as the Catholic *Historisch-politische Blätter für das katholische Deutschland*, published in Munich, were deeply anti-Prussian. On the evolution of the German newspapers see Kurt Koszyk, *Deutsche Presse im 19. Jahrhundert* (Berlin, 1966).

7 Adolf Glassbrenner was one of the many liberal writers who challenged the censorship laws not least through his journal *Berlin, wie es ist und – trinkt*. He was friendly with Adalbert von Chamisso, Heinrich Heine and Willibald Alexis. Adolf Glassbrenner, *Berlin, wie es ist und – trinkt*, 32 vols. (Berlin 1832–50). See also Rainer Rosenberg, *Literaturverhältnisse im deutschen Vormärz* (Berlin, 1975); Ilja Mieck, 'Von der Reformzeit zur Revolution (1806–1847)', in Wolfgang Ribbe (ed.), *Geschichte Berlines* (Munich, 1987), vol. 1, *Von der Frühgeschichte bis zur Industrialisierung*, p. 537.

8 On the reception in Berlin to Frederick William IV's accession and early reforms see Bernt Engelman, *Berlin. Eine Stadt wie keine Andere* (Berlin, 1986), pp. 112–17. See also Wilhelm Schoof, *Die Gebrüder Grimm in Berlin* (Berlin, 1964).

9. William IV was well informed about the unrest throughout Europe: in an exchange of letters with Queen Victoria he reveals his fear that the revolution might threaten the crowned heads of Europe. 'Letter from Frederick William IV to Queen Victoria 27/28 February 1848', in Hans Jessen (ed.), *Die deutsche Revolution 1848/9 in Augenzeugen berichten* (Düsseldorf, 1968), p. 35.

10 The events of the 1848 Revolution in Berlin are related in Adolf Wolff, *Berliner Revolutions-Chronik. Darstellung der Berliner Bewegung im jahre 1848 nach politischen, socialien und literarischen Beziehungen* (Berlin, 1851). See also Eduard Bernstein, *Die Geschichte der Berliner Arbeiter-Bewegung. Ein Kapitel zur Geschichte der deutschen Sozialdemokratie* (Berlin, 1907); Günter Richter, 'Zwischen Revolution und Reichsgründung (1848–1870)', in Ribbe, *Geschichte Berlins*, vol. 2: *Von der Märzrevolution bis zur Gegenwart*, pp. 607–30.

11 The declaration is reprinted in Walter Grab (ed.), *Die Revolution von 1848* (Munich, 1980), p. 53.

12 Indeed, on 18 March he called General von Ditfurt, the Stadtkommandant of Berlin, and a number of others to discuss the placement of troops there. August von Schöler, 'Adjutantenjournal, 18 March', in Jessen, *Die deutsche Revolution*, p. 75.

13 Nipperdey, *Germany from Napoleon to Bismarck*, p. 531.

14 Veit Valentin, *1848. Chapters of German History* (London, 1965), p. 199.

15 The original document of 18/19 March is reprinted in Jessen, *Die deutsche Revolution*, p. 87–9.

16 Special maps were created for visitors so that they could identify the graves of their heroes; one of the most impressive was a lithograph which included the names of all 183 of the 'March Fallen'. *Plan vom Friedrichshaine bei Berlin (mit Anordnung der Gräber und den Namen der Märzgefallenen)* (lithograph), Berlin Staatsbibliothek, Handschriftenabteilung (YB 17141 gr).

17 Valentin, *1848*, pp. 214–15. This sense of goodwill was reflected in leaflets of the time which portrayed William IV in a positive light and spoke of 'brotherhood' and 'co-operation'. Sigrid Weigel, *Flugschriftliteratur 1848 in Berlin. Geschichte und Öffentlichkeit einer volkstümlichen Gattung* (Stuttgart, 1979), p. 20.

18 Nipperdey, *Germany from Napoleon to Bismarck*, p. 577. See also Manfred Botz-enhart, *Deutscher Parlamentarismus in der Revolutionszeit 1848–1850* (Düsseldorf, 1977), p. 183.

19 Bismarck always believed that it would be impossible to change the Prussian army; he told the opposition in 1850: 'Try as you will . . . you will never be able to turn the Prussian army . . . it will always be the army of the *King* and find honour in obedience!' Lothar Gall, *Bismarck. Der weisse Revolutionär* (Frankfurt-am-Main, 1980), p. 78.

20 Alexis de Tocqueville, *Oeuvres complètes. L'ancien régime et la Révolution* (Paris, 1952), vol. 2, p. 69. Bakunin echoed this when he chided the German eagle: 'Unter deinen Flügeln kann ich ruhig bügeln' (Beneath your wings I can quietly go about my ironing), quoted in Theodor von Laue, *Leopold Ranke. The Formative Years* (Princeton, 1950), p. 61.

21 Valentin, *1848*, p. 427; Nipperdey, *Germany from Napoleon to Bismarck*, p. 605.

22 A decree dated 13 November 1848 stated that henceforth the publications 'die Reform, die Zeitungshalle, die Locomotive, die Republik, die Volksblätter, die ewige Lampe, der Krakehler, Kladeradatsch' were to be 'suspended'. It was signed by von Wrangel. Koszyk, *Deutsche Presse*, pp. 120–26. See also Ursula Koch, *Der Teufel in Berlin. Von der Märzrevolution bis zu Bismarcks Entlassung. Illustrierte politische Witzblätter einer Metropole 1848–1890* (Cologne, 1990). When Marx's *Rheinische Zeitung* was banned, a cartoon was circulated in Berlin depicting him as Prometheus chained to a printing press and being pecked at by the Prussian eagle.

23 Werner Siemens had recalled the delight of the crowd when the reforms were first announced in March. Count Lichnowsky had climbed on to a table and had told the crowd at the palace that the king had sent the soldiers away and had granted reforms. 'When someone asked whether the reforms had really been granted he said, "Yes, gentlemen, everything!" "Smoking too?" asked another; "Yes smoking, too" came the response; "In de Dierjarten too?" the man persisted; "Yes, Gentlemen, smoking is allowed in the Tiergarten too." This did the trick.' The withdrawal of all rights except the right to smoke was seen by the 1848 activists as an insult. Werner von Siemens, *Lebenserinnerungen* (Berlin, 1901), p. 48. As Hajo Holborn has put it, 'The political reaction killed the liberal gains of the revolution practically all over Europe.' Holborn, *A History of Modern Germany. 1840–1945* (London, 1969), p. 112. Varnhagen's diaries remain one of the most important sources about the revolution and its aftermath. Karl August Varnhagen von Ense, *Tagebücher* (Leipzig, 1863).

24 'Schulung und Einsatz von Polizei und Schutzmannschaft – Der altpreussische Polizeigriff', reproduced in Gottfried Korff und Reinhard Rürup (eds.), *Berlin, Berlin. Die Ausstellung zur Geschichte der Stadt* (Berlin, 1987), p. 185.

25 On Hinckeldey's career see Richter, 'Zwischen Revolution und Reichsgründung', in Ribbe, *Geschichte Berlins*, vol. 2, pp. 647–54. See also Wolfram Siemann, *Deutschlands Ruhe, Sicherheit und Ordnung. Die Anfänge der politischen Polizei, 1806–1866* (Tübingen, 1985).

26 For a first-hand account of a duel and its ceremony see Otto Corvin, *Ein Leben voller Abenteuer* (Frankfurt-am-Main, 1934), vol. 1, p. 194. The ritual did not

die out until the late nineteenth century; on 17 June 1864 Bismarck shocked Berlin by challenging the liberal scientist Rudolf Virchow to a duel because he had questioned his veracity; only complex negotiations saw it called off. Fritz Stern, *Gold and Iron. Bismarck, Bleichröder, and the Building of the German Empire* (London, 1977), p. 55.

27 Some sources put the number as high as 100,000. Richter, 'Zwischen Revolution und Reichsgründung', in Ribbe, *Geschichte Berlins*, vol. 2, p. 650.

28 On the sudden 'powerful fascination' with Schopenhauer see Holborn, *A History of Modern Germany*, p. 121. On Wagner in Berlin see Adolf Weissmann, *Berlin als Musikstadt. Geschichte der Oper und des Konzerts von 1740 bis 1911* (Berlin, 1911).

29 The nobility accounted for 65 per cent of all Prussian army officers by 1865, but they held all top positions. This was reflected in a change in property ownership. In 1856 41.1 per cent of the 12,339 manors in Prussia were in the hands of the bourgeoisie, but this did not translate into an increase in their political power. Nipperdey, *Germany from Napoleon to Bismarck*, p. 140.

30 Ludwig August von Rochau, *Grundsätze der Realpolitik* (Berlin, 1853–69). See Harold James, *A German Identity 1770–1990* (London, 1989), pp. 62–3.

31 For an account of the creation of the Zollverein by one of its chief architects and champion of free trade see Rudolf Delbrück, *Lebenserinnerungen*, 2 vols. (Leipzig, 1905). On Friedrich List and his fight to abolish tolls see Paul Gehring, *Friedrich List und Deutschlands politisch-ökonomische Einheit* (Leipzig, 1956).

32 W. O. Henderson, *The Zollverein* (Cambridge, 1939). Henderson probably overstates the Zollverein's contribution to German unity; for a critique of this view see Sheehan, *German History*, p. 504.

33 Ilja Mieck, *Preussische Gewerbepolitik in Berlin 1806–1844* (Berlin, 1965), p. 129.

34 The atmosphere of the exhibition was captured in the diary of Heinrich Eduard Kochhann, who was particularly impressed by the Borsig display which won first prize 'after which his name was on everybody's lips'. He was proud of the fact that the exhibitions from Berlin outshone those from the Ruhr. Heinrich Eduard Kochhann, *Tagebücher* (Berlin, 1905–7), vol. 3, p. 47.

35 Walther Kiaulehn, *Berlin. Schicksal einer Weltstadt* (Munich, 1980), p. 140. On Beuth's support of Egells see Laurenz Dempts, 'Die Maschinenbauanstalt von Franz Anton Egells und die neue Berliner Eisengiesserei – ihre Bedeutung für die Industrialisierung Berlins', in *Berliner Geschichte. Dokumente, Beiträge, Informationen*, 1, 1980, p. 15.

36 Demps, 'Die Maschinenbauanstalt', in *Berliner Geschichte*, 1, 1980, p. 18.

37 As Peter Bley has put it, 'the transformation of Berlin into the capital of the German Reich and to the industrial metropolis of Germany is inextricably linked to the creation of a competitive rail transport'. Peter Bley, 'Eisenbahnknotenpunkt Berlin', in Jochen Boberg et al. (eds.), *Exerzierfeld der Moderne. Industriekultur in Berlin im 19. Jahrhundert* (Munich, 1984), p. 114. See also R. Fremdling, *Eisenbahnen und deutsches Wirtschaftswachstum 1840–1879* (Dortmund, 1979).

38 Helmut Maier, *Berlin Anhalter Bahnhof* (Berlin, 1987), pp. 238–40.

39 One witness who saw the departure of the first train between Fürth and Leipzig wrote that the platform and surrounding area was teeming with an 'immeasur-

able crowd' who cheered as the steam built up. When the locomotive began to move horses were startled and children began to cry. He considered it an extraordinary achievement: 'how much knowledge, experience, experiment, deduction, how much perception, genius and – luck must have worked together to think of such a machine, to construct it.' Friedrich Schulze, *Die ersten deutschen Eisenbahnen Nürnberg–Fürth und Leipzig* (Leipzig, 1917). For an account of one of the first train journeys between Berlin and Königsberg see Robert von Mohl, *Lebens Erinnerungen* (Stuttgart, 1902), vol. 2, p. 366.

40 August von der Heydt was the Prussian Minister of Commerce who promoted the building of railways during his fourteen years in office. See Friedrich Lütge, *Deutsche Sozial- und Wirtschaftsgeschichte* (Berlin, 1952), p. 367. Friedrich List enthused that now 'hundreds of thousands of strangers' could improve themselves by travelling throughout Germany. Friedrich List, *Schriften, Reden, Briefe* (Berlin, 1927–36), vol. 3, p. 161.

41 The new stations were celebrated in Berlin; see, for example, the *Illustrirte Zeitung*, 15 June 1880, which devoted much of the issue to the great stations of the city.

42 Heinz Jung and Wolfgang Kramer, 'Die Strassenbahn', in Boberg et al., *Exerzierfeld der Moderne*, p. 129; see also Peter Bley, *Berliner S-Bahn. 140 Jahre Technikgeschichte* (Düsseldorf, 1988); Sigurd Hilkenbach and Wolfgang Kramer, *125 Jahre Strassenbahnen in Berlin* (Düsseldorf, 1982). On Berlin canals see Werner Natzschka, *Berlin und seine Wasserstrassen* (Berlin, 1971), and Heinz Trost, *Zwischen Havel, Spree und Dahme. Aus der Geschichte der Berliner Fahrgast-Schifffahrt* (Hamburg, 1989).

43 Friedrich List was one of the most influential in illustrating the new potential of rail travel not only for economic development but in enabling Prussia to turn her central geographical position into a tactical advantage, as she would be able to move troops and supplies rapidly to any point along her border. List, *Schriften, Reden, Briefe*, vol. 3, pp. 155–270.

44 The tactical use of rail transport was pioneered by Helmuth von Moltke, Chief of the Prussian General Staff from 1857. As early as 1843 he wrote that every new development of railways 'is a military advantage'. See Graf Helmuth von Moltke, 'Welche Rücksichten kommen bei der Wahl der Richtung von Eisenbahnen in Betracht?', in *Vermischte Schriften des Grafen Helmuth von Moltke* (Berlin, 1892), vol. 2, p. 228.

45 E. M. Earle, *Makers of Modern Strategy* (Princeton, 1941), p. 150.

46 This was already evident in the literature of the day; pamphlets and stories appeared with titles like 'Rechts und links der Eisenbahn'; newspapers carried advertisements for the luxurious sleepers which now went from London to Berlin and on to Trieste; pictures showed elegant ladies and gentlemen enjoying breakfast 'Im Restaurationswagen der Berlin-Anhalter Eisenbahn'. Dieter Vorsteher (ed.), *Die Reise nach Berlin* (Berlin, 1987), pp. 81–92. See also Königl. Preuss. Ministers d. öffentlichen Arbeiten, *Berlin und seine Eisenbahnen 1846–1896*, 2 vols. (Berlin, 1896).

47 Pig iron production in the Zollverein grew from 24 million marks in 1848 to 66 million in 1857; coal production grew from 25 to 62 million, and iron ore

and coal mining went up from 45 to 135 million marks. Hans-Ulrich Wehler, *The German Empire 1871–1918*, trans. Kim Traynor (Leamington Spa, 1989), p. 16.

48 'Das Fest der tausendsten Locomotive', *Die Gartenlaube*, 1858, p. 54. See also Kurt Pierson, *Borsig – ein Name geht um die Welt* (Berlin, 1973); Dieter Vorsteher, *Eisengiesserei und Maschinenbauanstalt zu Berlin* (Berlin, 1983).

49 Albert Borsig intended the celebrations to be a tribute to his father August, who had died shortly after the production of the 500th locomotive. Dieter Vorsteher, 'Das Fest der 1000. Locomotive. Ein neues Sternbild über Moabit', in Tilmann Buddensieg and Henning Rogge (eds.), *Die nützlichen Künste* (Berlin, 1981), pp. 90–98; 'Das Fest der tausendsten Locomotive', *Die Gartenlaube*, 1858, p. 541.

50 Dieter Vorsteher, 'Mythos vom Dampf', in Boberg, *Exerzierfeld der Moderne* pp. 80–87.

51 On industrialization in Berlin see Gerhard Masur, *Imperial Berlin* (London, 1971), pp. 125–49. On Schering see Maria Borgmann, 'Die chemische Industrie', in Boberg, *Exerzierfeld der Moderne*, p. 344.

52 Newspapers reflected Berlin's growing cosmopolitanism; it was at this time that Rudolf Mosse, proprietor of the *Berliner Tageblatt*, could say: 'He who writes for Berlin writes for the civilised world.' Masur, *Imperial Berlin*, p. 70. See also Koszyk, *Deutsche Presse*, pp. 224–9.

53 The copying of photographs on to copper or zinc plates was pioneered in Berlin. It allowed for half tones and made printing faster and cheaper. Peter de Mendelssohn, *Zeitungsstadt Berlin* (Berlin, 1982), p. 138.

54 Georg von Siemens, *Geschichte des Hauses Siemens*, 3 vols. (Munich, 1947–52), vol. 1., p. 258. On the evolution of Siemensstadt in Berlin see Wolfgang Ribbe and Wolfgang Schäche, *Siemensstandort Nonnendamm. Industrielle Randwanderung und Industriebau in Berlin um die Jahrhundertwende* (Berlin, 1984).

55 Walther Rathenau, 'Gedächtnisrede für Emil Rathenau', in Walther Rathenau, *Gesemmalte Schriften* (Berlin, 1929), vol. 5: *Wirtschaft, Staat und Gesellschaft*, pp. 11–21. See also Ernst Robert Pinner, *Emil Rathenau und das elektrische Zeitalter* (Leipzig, 1918).

56 The contribution of Siemens and Rathenau, and the growth of the electrical industry in the city, is documented in the 1984 West Berlin volume *100 Jahre Strom für Berlin. 1884–1984. Ein Streifzug durch unsere Geschichte in Wort und Bild* (Berlin, 1984). For the spread of street lighting see the volume published by the Senator für Bau- und Wohnungswesen, West Berlin, *300 Jahre Strassenbeleuchtung in Berlin* (Berlin, 1988).

57 On the extraordinary growth of Berlin industry and the new districts created by the entrepreneurs see two volumes published under the auspices of the Historische Kommission zu Berlin (nos. 6 and 39): Ingrid Thienel, *Städtewachstum und Industrialisierungsprozess des 19. Jahrhunderts. Das Berliner Beispiel* (Berlin, 1971); Otto Büsch (ed.), *Untersuchungen zur Geschichte der drühen Industrialisierung, vornehmlich im Wirtschaftsraum Berlin/Brandenburg* (Berlin, 1971). See also Otto Wiedfeldt, *Statistische Studien zur Entwicklungsgeschichte der Berliner Industrie von 1720 bis 1890* (Liepzig, 1898).

58 Francis L. Carsten, 'The Court Jews. A Prelude to Emancipation', in *Yearbook of the Leo Baeck Institute*, 3, 1958, pp. 140–56; Heinrich Schnee, *Die Hoffinanz und der moderne Staat. Geschichte und System der Hoffaktoren an deutschen Fürstenhöfen im Zeitalter des Absolutismus*, 6 vols. (Berlin, 1953–7) – in particular vol. 1: *Die Institution des Hoffaktorentums in Brandenburg-Preussens*.

59 Daniel Itzig was granted general privileges in 1761. Berliner Historischen Kommission beim Friedrich-Meinecke-Institute der Freien Universität Berlin, *Die Judenbürgerbücher der Stadt Berlin 1809–1851* (Berlin, 1962), vol. 4, pp. 690–92.

60 W. E. Mosse, *Jews in the German Economy. The German-Jewish Economic Élite 1820–1935* (Oxford, 1987), p. 37.

61 Wehler, *The German Empire 1871–1918*, p. 184.

62 Ibid., p. 18.

63 Hermann Sudermann, *Sodoms Ende: Drama in 5 Akten* (Berlin, 1891). On Fürstenburg see Masur, *Imperial Berlin*, p. 148; Hans Fürstenburg, *Carl Fürstenburg. Die Lebensgeschichte eines deutschen Bankiers, 1870–1914* (Berlin, 1930). The Berlin banking district is described in Hans Weber, *Bankplatz Berlin*, (Cologne, 1957).

64 Helmut Böhme, *Prolegomena zu einer Sozial- und Wirtschaftsgeschichte Deutschlands* (Suhrkamp, 1972), p. 48. On the evolution of the Berlin stock exchange see Georg Buss, *Berliner Börse von 1685 bis 1913* (Berlin, 1913).

65 Non-hereditary titles were Kommerzienrat and Geheimer Kommerzienrat (Geheimrat) and were granted through the Kgl. Staatsminister für Handel, Gewerbe und öffentliche Arbeiten. See the excellent chapter in Mosse, *Jews in the German Economy*, pp. 69–95.

66 Jacob Toury compares the Jews' increasing role in Prussian industry with the rest of Germany. Jacob Toury, 'Der Eintritt der Juden ins deutsche Bürgertum', in Hans Liebeschütz and Arnold Paucker (eds.), *Das Judentum in der deutschen Umwelt, 1800–1850* (Tübingen, 1977), p. 230. See also Stefi Jersch-Wenzel, *Juden and 'Franzosen' in der Wirtschaft des Raumes Berlin/Brandenburg zur Zeit des Merkantilismus* (Berlin, 1978).

67 Mosse, *Jews in the German Economy*, p. 72.

5: THE RISE OF RED BERLIN

1 'Die zwei Himmel/ Auf der Reise nach Berlin im Wagen./ Die Berge ziehen, die Wälder fliehen./ Weg von dem sehnenden Blick Sie lassen keine Spur zurück.' Karl Marx, *Die zwei Himmel*, October 1836, in Karl Marx and Friedrich Engels, *Gesamtausgabe* (MEGA) (Berlin, 1975), vol. 1, p. 483. For Marx's arrival in Berlin see Fritz J. Raddatz, *Karl Marx. Eine politische Biographie* (Hamburg, 1975), p. 30.

2 On Marx's early life see Saul K. Padover, *The Man Marx* (New York, 1978); Isaiah Berlin, *Karl Marx: His Life and Environment* (Oxford, 1978); David McLellan, *Karl Marx: His Life and Thought* (New York, 1973).

3 On the Doktorklub see Richard Friedenthal, *Karl Marx. Sein Leben und seine*

Zeit (Munich, 1981), p. 153. On Heinrich Heine see Max Brod, *Heinrich Heine* (Amsterdam, 1934); Ludwig Börne was particularly critical of the 'cult' of Goethe because he had not used his position to change society, to 'oppose baseness'. He was also an ardent campaigner against anti-Semitism, writing, 'Some reproach me because I am a Jew; others excuse me for it; a third praises me for it. But all of them think of it . . .' Ludwig Börne, *Gesammelte Schriften* (Milwaukee, 1858), p. 31; on Arnold Ruge see *Sämtliche Werke*, 10 vols. (Mannheim, 1847–8).

4 Marx first studied Hegel whilst recovering from a lung infection near Berlin. He was so inspired that he rushed to Berlin wanting to throw his arms around all those poor people loafing around on street corners. On Hegel's influence on Marx see Sidney Hook, *From Hegel to Marx* (New York, 1935).

5 Will Durant, *The Story of Philosophy. The Lives and Opinions of the great Philosophers of the Western World* (New York, 1967), p. 233. Hegel's complete works are published as Georg Wilhelm Friedrich Hegel, *Werke*, 20 vols. (Frankfurt-am-Main, 1976).

6 Heinrich Floris Schopenhauer, *Parerga and Paralipomena*, trans. E. F. G. Payne (Oxford, 1974), vol. 1, p. 24.

7 Golo Mann, *The History of Germany since 1789* (Harmondsworth, 1987), p. 84.

8 Georg Wilhelm Friedrich Hegel, *Philosophy of History*, trans. T. Sibree (New York, 1956). See also Richard Norman and Sean Sayera, *Hegel, Marx and Dialectic* (Brighton, 1980), pp. 25–46.

9 On the 'Old Hegelians' see John Toews, 'Transformation of Hegelianism 1805–1846', in Frederick C. Beiser (ed.), *The Cambridge Companion to Hegel* (Cambridge, 1995), pp. 378–91.

10 David McLellan, *The Young Hegelians and Karl Marx* (London, 1980).

11 On Feuerbach see David McLellan, *The Young Hegelians*, 'Bruno Bauer', pp. 48–83; on Feuerbach see Eugene Kamenka, *The Philosophy of Ludwig Feuerbach* (London, 1970); Feuerbach, 'Ein Mann ist was er isst', in Koppel S. Pinson, *Modern Germany. Its History and Civilisation* (New York, 1963), p. 72.

12 Their friendship is evident in their letters; see, for example, letter from Bruno Bauer to Karl Marx, 12 April 1841 in Raddatz, *Karl Marx*, p. 48.

13 McLellan, *Karl Marx*, p. 33; McLellan, *The Young Hegel*, pp. 6–7.

14 See the poster by Paul Grulich, *Dämon Berlin. Aufzeichungen eines Obdachlosen* (Deutscher Verlag GmbH, 1907), in the Berlin Staatsbibliothek PK (Fb 4300).

15 In 1875, for example, of a total population of 964,539 only 41.2 per cent had been born in Berlin. The detailed figures of population growth in Berlin, including by district, are in Michael Erbe, 'Bevölkerungsentwicklung' in Wolfgang Ribbe (ed.), *Geschichte Berlins* (Munich, 1987), vol. 2: *Von der Märzrevolution bis zur Gegenwart*, pp. 693–9. For Polish immigration see Gottfried Hartmann, 'Polen in Berlin' (Demographische Entwicklung), in Stefi Jersch-Wenzel and Barbara John (eds.), *Von Zuwanderern zu Einheimischen. Hugenotten, Juden, Böhmen, Polen in Berlin* (Berlin, 1990), pp. 604–25. According to Hartmann over 53 per cent of non-German immigrants spoke Polish (including Masurian and Kusabian); the second largest group were the 9.9 per cent who spoke Russian.

16 Pinson, *Modern Germany*, p. 222. See also Werner Conze, 'Nationsbildung durch Trennung. Deutsche und Polen im preussischen Osten', in Otto Pflanze (ed.), *Innenpolitische Probleme des Bismarck-Reiches* (Munich, 1983), pp. 95–119.

17 Ingeborg Weber-Kellermann, *Landleben im 19. Jahrhundert* (Munich, 1987), p. 25.

18 Hans-Ulrich Wehler, *The German Empire 1871–1918*, trans. Kim Traynor (New York 1985), pp. 9–24; here p. 11. See also Klaus J. Bade (ed.), *Auswanderer-Wanderarbeiter-Gastarbeiter. Bevölkerung, Arbeitsmarkt und Wanderung in Deutschland seit der Mitte des 19. Jahrhunderts*, 2 vols. (Ostfildern, 1984); Jan Kazmierczak, *Polacy w Berlinie. Przyczynek do historii wychodzstawa polskiego w Berlinie i po prawym brzegu laby* (Inowroclaw, 1937).

19 Thomas Nipperdey, *Germany from Napoleon to Bismarck 1800–1866*, trans. Daniel Nolan (Dublin, 1986), p. 198.

20 Friedrich Kayssler, 'Die Weber. Soziales Drama. Auf Wunsch Sr. Durchlaucht von Serenissimus für eine Sondervorstellung bearbeitet fom Freiherrn von Kindermann', extracts in *Schall und Rauch*, 25 October 1901.

21 E. N. Anderson, *The Social and Political Conflict in Prussia, 1858–64* (Lincoln, 1954), p. 440; E. Klein, *Die Entwicklung der Landwirtschaft 1800–1930* (Würzburg, 1960). See also Max Weber, 'Die Varhältnisse der Landarbeiter im östlichen Deutschland', *Schriften des Vereins für Socialpolitik*, 55 (Leipzig, 1892).

22 On the 'potato revolution' in Berlin see Johann Friedrich Geist and Klaus Kürvers, *Das Berliner Mietshaus 1740–1862* (Munich, 1980), vol. 1, pp. 336–9.

23 Reinhart Koselleck, 'Staat und Gesellschaft in Preussen 1815–1848', in Werner Conze (ed.), *Staat und Gesellschaft im deutschen Vormärz 1815–1848* (Stuttgart, 1962), p. 102.

24 1,300,000 people came to Berlin in 1911 alone. Jürgen Schutte and Peter Sprengel (eds.), *Die Berliner Moderne 1885–1914* (Stuttgart, 1987), p. 96; Erbe, 'Bevölkerungsentwicklung' in Ribbe, *Geschichte Berlins*, vol. 2, p. 698.

25 There had been attempts to plan for housing growth, such as the 1853 *Die Fluchtlinie für Gebäude und bauliche Anlagen an Strassen und Plätzen wird von dem Polizeipräsident bestimmt*, but little was done and in the 1850s city planning degenerated into little more than a petty struggle between developers and those who wanted to improve transportation in the city. The general lack of action provoked Engels's fierce, and rather unfair, attack on housing policy in Prussia. Friedrich Engels, *Zur Wohnungsfrage* (Düsseldorf, 1882).

26 The most scathing book about the reforms is Werner Hegemann, *Das steinerne Berlin, die grösste Mietskasernestadt der Welt* (Berlin, 1930); see also Ingrid Thienel, 'Industrialisierung und Städtewachstum, die Wandel der Hauptsiedlungsformen in der Umgebung Berlins 1800–1850', in O. Busch (ed.), *Untersuchungen zur Geschichte der früheren Industrialisierung vornehmlich im Wirtschaftsraum Berlin/Brandenburg* (Berlin, 1971); E. Reich, *Der Wohnungsmarkt in Berlin von 1840–1910* (Munich, 1912), p. 59.

27 Following his exile in England Louis Napoleon sent a commission to study housing there in 1848; he also requested that the English architect Henry Roberts's *The Dwellings of the Labouring Classes* be published in 1850. 'Prop-

osition de M. de Melun (Nord) sur l'assainissement et l'interdiction des loge-
ments insalubres', *Annales de la Charité* (Paris, 1849), p. 445, quoted in Nicholas
Bullock and James Read, *The Movement for Housing Reform in Germany and
France 1840–1914* (Cambridge, 1985), pp. 295–7.

28 David H. Pinkney, *Napoleon III and the Rebuilding of Paris* (Princeton, 1958),
p. 25.

29 Haussmann's memoirs provide an extraordinary insight into his ambitions for
Paris; see Baron Haussmann, *Memoires du Baron Haussmann: Grand Travaux
de Paris*, 2 vols. (Paris, 1979). On Haussmann's influence see Mark Girouard,
Cities and People. A Social and Architectural History (Yale, 1985), pp. 285–300.

30 Hegemann, *Das steinerne Berlin*, p. 295.

31 On Hobrecht and Berlin see Ernst Heinrich, 'Der "Hobrechtplan"' in *Jahrbuch
für brandenburgische Landesgeschichte*, 13, 1962, p. 41.

32 Georg Simmel, 'Die Grossstädte und das Geistesleben', reprinted in Schutte and
Sprengel, *Die Berliner Moderne*, p. 125. On land development see Jutta Wietog,
'Der Wohnungsstandard der Unterschichten in Berlin. Eine Betrachtung anhand
des Mietsteurkatasters 1848–1871 und der Wohnungsaufnahme 1861–1871', in
Werner Conze and Ulrich Engelhard (eds.), *Arbeiterexistenz im 19. Jahrhundert.
Industrielle Welt*, 33 (Stuttgart, 1981), pp. 114–37.

33 As Gustav Schmoller expressed it in 1887, 'To put the psychological truth bluntly:
conditions are so horrific that it is to be wondered that the consequences are
not more terrible. It is only because a great part of the working classes are still
able to maintain in these vile dens a store of moral values, of religious conviction,
of decency left from earlier days, that the worst has not yet come to pass.' Gustav
Schmoller, 'Ein Mahnruf in der Wohnungsfrage', in *Jahrbuch für Gesetzgebung,
Verwaltung und Volkswirtschaft im deutschen Reich*, 1887, pp. 429–30, quoted in
Bullock and Read, *The Movement for Housing Reform*, p. 67.

34 The cellars really did 'glisten'; a survey conducted by the *Sanitätspolizei* in 1850
– not a particularly rainy year – found that one in ten of Berlin dwellings had
standing water up to a depth of 66 cm. E. Krieger, *Über die Kellerwohnungen
in Berlin* (Berlin, 1855). The Stadtmissionary Böckelmann described housing in
the early 1880s as deplorable. One tenement block was inhabited by '250 families
or groups . . . Overall things are so bad that they cannot get worse. In addition
the sheer filth of these dwellings must be mentioned. I find beds, if they can
be called that, which are jet black with dirt. I thought that in such a room as
I have just described there could be no room to sleep at all; on seeing a family
with five children and only one bed I wondered where they could all possibly
sleep. Four of them slept in one bed, the others on the floor, either on straw,
or on piles of old rags. Nor should you imagine that there is always just the
one family that lives in such a room; no! here and there, there are two, indeed
I even know of cases of three families living together in one room, who in
addition have four children amongst them, and of these, three are still forced
to live in their cradles.' Quoted in Bullock and Read, *The Movement for Housing
Reform*, p. 60. The figures for numbers per dwelling were collected from 1874
onwards in the *Statistisches Jahrbuch der Stadt Berlin*. See also Gerd Hohorst,
Jürgen Kocka and Gerhard A. Ritter (eds.), *Sozialgeschichtliches Arbeitsbuch*

(Munich, 1978), vol. 2: *Materialien zur Statistik des Kaiserreiches 1870–1914*, pp. 113–19; M. G. Daunton (ed.), *Housing the Workers: A Comparative History, 1850–1944* (Leicester, 1990), p. 30.

35 In 1875 alone 21 per cent of families in Berlin were taking in '*Schlafleute*'; in some districts 10 per cent of the population lived this way but the problem dated back to the housing shortages of the 1840s. Geist and Kürvers, *Das Berliner Mietshaus 1740–1862*, vol. 1, p. 441.

36 The child mortality rates in Berlin were published annually from 1874 in the *Statistisches Jahrbuch der Stadt Berlin*. See also Erbe, 'Bevölkerungsentwicklung', in Ribbe, *Geschichte Berlins*, vol 2, p. 698.

37 Kurt Pomplun, *Pomplun's grosses Berlin Buch* (Berlin, 1985), pp. 195–9.

38 This attitude was in stark contrast to liberal reformers like V. A. Huber, who in 1861 wrote, 'The present housing conditions of the worker, of the poor, of the great mass of the people, are already one of the greatest and most pressing social evils of the present, and, as the population increases, will become worse and worse unless this evil is immediately and effectively controlled by vigorous and far-reaching counter-measures.' V. A. Huber, 'Wohnungsfrage: die Hülfe', quoted in Bullock and Read, *The Movement for Housing Reform*, p. 43.

39 Rudolf Virchow, *Über die Kanalisation Berlins* (Berlin, 1868). For a general view of Virchow's contribution see A. Fischer, *Geschichte des deutschen Gesundheitswesens* (Hildesheim, 1965). On the effect of the 1866 cholera epidemic in Berlin see August Hirsch, 'Die Cholera-Epidemie des Jahres 1866 in Berlin. Vom Statistischen Standpunkte geschildert', *Berliner Stadt- und Gemeinde-Kalender und Städtisches Jahrbuch für 1867*, p. 309. Hirsch notes that women seemed to be much more at risk than men, not least because they were expected to clean the clothes and bedding of those already infected.

40 Rosa Luxemburg, *Gesammelte Werke* (Berlin, 1984), vol. 3: *Im Asyl*, p. 88.

41 Eduard Bernstein, *Die Geschichte der Berliner Arbeiterbewegung* (Berlin, 1928), vol. 1, p. 261.

42 Walther Kiaulehn, *Berlin. Schicksal einer Weltstadt* (Munich, 1980), p. 170.

43 Joachim Ringelnatz, quoted in Kiaulehn, *Berlin*, p. 505.

44 Alfred Döblin, 'Das märkische Ninive', *Der Sturm*, 10 March 1910, p. 5. For a general discussion of crime in the new industrial cities see Howard Zehr, *Crime and the development of modern society. Patterns of criminality in nineteenth-century Germany and France* (London, 1976); Vincent E. McHale and Eric A. Johnson, 'Urbanization, industrialization and crime in Imperial Germany', *Social Science History*, vol. 1, 1976–7, pp. 210–47.

45 The following clause was added to the Criminal Code: 'Whoever displays objects which are suited for obscene use in places which are accessible to the public, or who advertises or promotes such objects to the public will be punished with prison for up to one year and with fines up to 1000 Marks or with one of these penalties.' Ernst Huber, *Deutsche Verfassungsgeschichte seit 1789* (Stuttgart, 1969), vol. 4: *Struktur and Krisen des Kaiserreichs*, p. 284. As James Woyke has pointed out, contraceptives were affected by this because obscenity had already been defined by the *Reichsgericht* as 'anything which offends the public's sense of shame in a sexual sense'. James Woycke, *Birth Control in Germany 1871–1933*

(London, 1988), p. 51. On the Lex Heinze see Robin Lenman, 'Art, Society and the Law in Wilhelmine Germany: the Lex Heinze', *Oxford German Studies*, 8, 1973, pp. 86–113.

46 Hans Schneickert, 'Die gewerbsmässige Abtreibung und deren Bekämpfung', *Monatsschrift für Kriminal-Psychologie*, 2, 1906, p. 633.

47 *Kievskie vesti*, December 10 1907. See also Lynn Abrams, 'Prostitutes in Imperial Germany, 1870–1918: Working Girls or Social Outcasts?', in Richard J. Evans (ed.), *The German Underworld. Deviants and Outcasts in German History*, (London, 1988), p. 202.

48 Abraham Flexner reported that when prostitutes were asked whether or not they would register with the police, 'Nur die Dummen werden inscribiert!' (Only the stupid ones register). Abraham Flexner, *Prostitution in Europe* (New York, 1914), p. 157; Hans Ostwald, *Die Berlinerin. Kultur- und Sittengeschichte Berlins* (Berlin, 1921), p. 641. Ostwald and Flexner are quoted in Charles W. Haxthausen, '"A New Beauty": Ernst Ludwig Kirchner's Images of Berlin', in Charles W. Haxthausen and Heidrun Suhr (eds.), *Berlin Culture and Metropolis* (Minneapolis, 1990), p. 79. Friedrich Sass noted that in the 1840s it was not uncommon to see young girls of fourteen on the streets in Berlin. Friedrich Sass, *Berlin in seiner neuesten Zeit und Entwicklung* (Berlin, 1846), p. 171.

49 Nipperdey, *Germany from Napoleon to Bismarck*, p. 109.

50 Woycke, *Birth Control in Germany*, pp. 68–88.

51 Max Hirsch, 'Frauenerwerbsarbeit und Frauenkrankheit', *Monatsschrift für Geburtshilfe und Gynäkologie*, 38, 1913, Supplement, p. 319.

52 Other substances were commonly used to induce abortion; they included lead pills, mercury and arsenic. Berlinerins also relied on a book of herbal remedies by Johann Staricius, *Geheimnisvoller Heldenschats*, first published in 1616.

53 The Prussian Statistical Office estimated that of 60,000 female deaths in Prussia in 1927, when care had already improved, 3,500 could be considered 'hidden' abortion deaths – disguised under other headings. Together with known abortion deaths that totalled 5,000 possible deaths for Prussia. Woycke, *Birth Control in Germany*, p. 77.

54 The first German women's novel, which depicted a modern woman equal to men in rank, was Sophie von la Roche's *Geschichte Fräuleins von Sternheim* (The Story of Miss von Sternheim), published in 1771.

55 Gertrud Bäumer, 'Die Geschichte der Frauenbewegung in Deutschland', in Helene Lang and Gertrud Bäumer (eds.), *Handbuch der Frauenbewegung* (Berlin, 1901), Part 1, pp. 1–158. On Huch see Marie Baum, *Leuchtende Spur. Das Leben Ricarda Huchs* (Tübingen, 1950).

56 August Bebel, *Die Frau und der Sozialismus* (Zurich, 1879).

57 Gustav Rasch was horrified to find that it was the norm in the Berlin slums for children to be prevented from playing outside from the age of eight, when 'they must go into the factory and with their tiny delicate fingers wind thread' from 6 in the morning until 7 or 8 in the evening. He watched a shift returning home from the factory, the children 'pale, poorly dressed, boys and girls, many in rags, many without socks and shoes'. They did not behave like carefree young people but 'walked slowly and quietly like grown and mature people'.

When he questioned a local inspector about this he was told that nothing would change as the poor saw them as 'workers who can earn money'. Gustav Rasch, *Die dunklen Häuser von Berlin* (Wittenberg, 1863), p. 133. See also in Geist and Kürvers, *Das Berliner Mietshaus*, 'Die beruflich Zukunft der Kinder', p. 287.

58 During the first debate to bring the working day down to a maximum of ten hours Herr Schechard asked his fellow politicians if they could 'stand by while these poor young children must get up early in the morning at 5 o'clock in cold or miserable weather ... and be dragged by their mothers to a factory which is more like a prison; even your hearts would be broken'. Wolfgang Köllmann, *Die industrielle Revolution. Quellen zur Sozialgeschichte Grossbritanniens und Deutschlands im 19. Jahrhundert* (Stuttgart, 1961), p. 41.

59 Ottilie Baader, *Ein steiniger Weg. Lebenserinnerungen* (Berlin, 1921), p. 15.

60 Annemarie Lange, *Das wilhelminische Berlin* (Berlin, 1984), p. 42. See also Rosmarie Beier, *Frauenarbeit and Frauenalltag im deutschen Kaiserreich. Zur Lebenssituation Berliner Heimarbeiterinnen der Bekleidungsindustrie 1880–1914* (Frankfurt-am-Main, 1983). As Robyn Dasey wrote, 'Women and particularly married women were to be found amongst the lowest paid in the least hygienic and often most exhausting jobs such as brickyards, rag-and-bone sorting, laundries and hotel service. Industries employing very large numbers of women – textiles, clothing and food processing – were characterized by the lowest wages and longest hours, with married women commonly even more disadvantaged than their single counterparts.' Robyn Dasey, 'Women's Work and the Family: Women German Workers in Berlin and Hamburg before the First World War', in Richard J. Evans and W. R. Lee (eds.), *The German Family* (London, 1981), pp. 221–49.

61 Jay Winter and Jean-Louis Robert, *Capital Cities at War. London, Paris, Berlin* (Cambridge, 1997), p. 34.

62 Schmoller noted that 'These dwellings of the worker and the poor, the habitations of the greater part of the population of our present large industrial cities, are never visited by the civilised members of our society – apart that is from the constable, the bailiff, the almsgiver and the priest; the doctor hardly goes at all, as the poor cannot pay. The misery is never seen by the propertied and educated classes, indeed they do not wish to see it.' Schmoller, 'Ein Mahnruf in der Wohnungsfrage', in *Jahrbuch für Gesetzgebung*, pp. 429–30, quoted in Bullock and Read, *The Movement for Housing Reform*, p. 66.

63 *Berlin für Kenner. Ein Bärenführer bei Tag and Nacht* (Berlin, 1912).

64 Franz Held, 'Auf der Weidendammer Brücke', in *Trotz Alledem! Einiges aus meinem Schatzhaus* (Berlin, 1894), p. 115.

65 Bettina von Arnim, *Dies Buch gehört dem König* (Berlin, 1921); see also 'Die Entstehung des "Königsbuchs"', in Geist and Kürvers, *Das Berliner Mietshaus* , pp. 214–31.

66 Lina Morgenstern, 'Gedenkblatt zum 25 jährigen Jubiläum des Kinderschutzvereins', Berlin, 1894, in Berlin Staatsbibliothek P K (Fd 10831).

67 Nipperdey, *Germany from Napoleon to Bismarck*, pp. 552, 654–67. On liberal women see Dorothea Frandsen, 'Die deutsche Frauenbewegung bis 1914: Die

Liberalen', in Liselotte Funcke (ed.), *Die Liberalen. Frei sein, um andere frei zu machen* (Stuttgart, 1984), pp. 27–56; D. Fricke et al (eds.), *Die bürgerlichen Parteien in Deutschland. Handbuch der Geschichte der bürgerlichen Parteien und andere bürgerlicher Interessenorganisationen vom Vormärz bis zum Jahre 1945* (Leipzig, 1970), vol. 2, pp. 285–95.

68 Hermann Schulze-Delitzsch, 'Die Kulturaufgabe der Menschheit erfordert die Kräfte aller und die gemeinsame Arbeit gibt das gemeinsame Recht', in *Schriften und Reden* (Berlin, 1909–1913), vol. 4, p. 7.

69 Rita Aldenhoff, *Schulze-Delitzsch. Ein Beitrag zur Geschichte des Liberalismus zwischen Revolution und Reichsgründung* (Baden-Baden, 1984).

70 Shlomo Náaman, *Lassalle* (Hanover, 1970). His life was the inspiration for George Meredith's novel *The Tragic Comedians*.

71 Marx now referred to Lassalle as that 'judische Nigger Lassalle'. See Raddatz, pp. 256–91.

72 Ferdinand Lassalle, *Reden und Schriften*, ed. Ludwig Maenner (Berlin, 1926), p. 211.

73 Bernstein, *Geschichte der Arbeiterbewegung*, vol. 1, p. 261.

74 Bismarck was also responding to Lassalle's programme of radical democratic measures. Bismarck introduced the 'State socialist' programme of compulsory insurance legislation for old age sickness and accidents between 1883 and 1890 but he combined this with the anti-socialist legislation of 19 October 1878. K. E. Born, 'Sozialpolitische Probleme und Bestrebungen von 1848 bis zur Bismarkischen Sozialgesetzgebung', in *Vierteljahrschrift für Sozial- und Wirtschaftsgeschichte*, 46, 1959, pp. 29–44.

75 On Liebknecht's and Bebel's combined fight against the Lassalleans see Ursula Herrman et al., *August Bebel. Eine Biographie* (Berlin, 1989), p. 85.

76 Karl Marx, 'Critique of the Gotha Programme', in David Michellan (ed.), *Marx and Engels. Selected Works* (Moscow, 1955), vol. 2, p. 33.

77 On Bismarck's response to Nobiling's assassination attempt see Walter Henry Nelson, *The Soldier Kings. The House of Hohenzollern* (New York, 1970), pp. 319–22; on Bebel see Herrman et al., *August Bebel*, p. 186. On the enforcement of the anti-socialist laws in Berlin see Werner Pöls, 'Staat und Sozialdemokratie im Bismarck-Reich. Die Tätigkeit der Politischen Polizei beim Polizeipräsidenten in Berlin in der Zeit des Sozialistengesetzes', in *Jahrbuch für die Geschichte Mittel- und Ostdeutschlands*, 14, 1965; pp. 200–221.

78 Julius Bruhns, *Es klingt im Sturm ein altes Lied: Aus der Jugendzeit der Sozialdemokratie* (Berlin, 1921). See also Alex Hall, 'By other means: the legal struggle against the SPD in Wilhelmine Germany 1890–1900', *Historical Journal*, vol. 17, 1974, pp. 322–4. On the creation of the myth of the 'heroic years' see Michael Schneider, 'Gewerkschaften und Emanzipation. Methodologische Probleme der Gewerkschaftsgeschichtsschreibung', in *Archiv für Sozialgeschichte*, 17, 1977, pp. 404–44.

79 Heinrich von Treitschke, 'Sozialismus und seine Gönner', in Andreas Dorpalen, *Heinrich von Treitschke* (New Haven, 1957), p. 198.

80 James J. Sheehan, *German Liberalism in the Nineteenth Century* (Chicago, 1978), p. 143.

81 Reinhard Höhn, *Die Vaterlandslosen Gesellen* (Cologne-Opladen, 1964), quoted in Gerhard Masur, *Imperial Berlin* (London, 1971), p. 105.

82 Samuel Lublinski, *Die Bilanz der Moderne* (Berlin, 1904), p. 3. William increased his control by refusing to allow the academy to choose its own appointments. In 1908, for example, he vetoed the appointment of Anders Zorn and Albert Besnard as he disliked their work. See the report of 19 June 1908 in the Archiv der Akademie der Künste, 'Friedensklasse des Ordens *Pour le merite*', section 3, no. 7. On Cassirer's extraordinary contribution to Berlin art see Paul Cassirer, *X. Jahrgang: Ausstellung 1–10* (Berlin, 1907–8) and the discussion in Peter Paret, *The Berlin Secession. Modernism and Its Enemies in Imperial Germany* (Cambridge, Mass., 1980), pp. 93–6.

83 Heinrich and Julius Hart, *Kritischen Jahrbuch* (Leipzig, 1889), vol. 1, p. 3.

84 Eugen Wolff, 'Die jüngste deutsche Literaturströmung und das Princip der Moderne', in *Die literarische Moderne. Dokumente zum Selbstverständnis der Literatur um die Jahrhundertwende* (Frankfurt-am-Main, 1971), p. 37.

85 Erwin Bauer, *Die 'Modernen' in Berlin und München*, in Jürgen Schutte and Peter Sprengel (eds.), *Die Berliner Moderne 1885–1914* (Stuttgart, 1987), p. 208.

86 Otto Brahm, 'Zum Beginn', in *Freie Bühne für modernes Leben*, vol. 1, 29 January 1890, p. 1.

87 A. von Hanstein, *Das jüngste Deutschland* (Leipzig, 1905), p. 172; see also Alfred Dreyfuss, *Deutsches Theater Berlin* (Berlin, 1987), p. 118.

88 Chlodwig zu Hohenlohe-Schillingsfürst, *Denkwürdigkeiten* (Stuttgart, 1907), vol. 2, p. 507.

89 The relationship between socialism and artists was a complex one. In 1924 the art historian Julius Meier-Graefe admitted that despite their interest in the lives of the workers artists had generally remained aloof from their world: 'it provided us with models for our paintings and stories; other than that it was a necessary evil – like a bus or a postage stamp – towards which one remained as passive as possible. We wrote social dramas, but never gave a thought to socialism.' Julius Meier-Graefe, 'Einleitung', in *Die doppelte Kurve* (Berlin, 1924), pp. 9–10; see also Masur, *Imperial Berlin*, p. 247; Paret, *The Berlin Secession*, p. 159.

90 Wilhelm Liebknecht, 'Brief aus Berlin', *Neue Zeit*, 9, 1890/91, vol. 1, pp. 709–11.

91 On the history of Berlin cabaret see the excellent history: Peter Jelavich, *Berlin Cabaret* (Harvard, 1993), pp. 30–35. For the image of the 'typical Berliner' see, for example, Hans Meyer, *Der richtige Berliner* (Berlin, 1911).

92 Franz Servaes, 'Moderne Monumentalmalerei', in *Neuen deutsche Rundschau*, 1896, p. 541.

93 Lovis Corinth, *Das Leben Walter Leistikows. Ein Stück Berliner Kulturgeschichte* (Berlin, 1910), 'Die Bilder aus der Mark und die Gründung der Berliners Sezession', p. 55. On the Munch exhibition see the article written by Leistikow under a pseudonym, Walter Selber, 'Die Affaire Munch', *Freie Bühne*, 3, 1892, p. 1297.

94 The first secession had sixty-eight members. Max Liebermann was president, Walter Leistikow was first secretary, and the other members of the executive committee were painters Ludwig Dettmann, Otto Engel, Oscar Frenzel and Curt Herrmann, and the sculptor Fritz Klumsch. The minutes of the executive

committee covering the period from 18 January to 25 March 1899 were published as 'Protokol Buch der Vorstand Sitzungen der "Berliner Sezession"'. See also Paret, *The Berlin Secession*, p. 59.

95 Kiaulehn, *Berlin*, p. 310. See also Peter Selz, *German Expressionist Painting* (Berkeley, 1974).

96 It was the introduction of this culture which, in Peter Gay's words, transformed all aspects of culture and 'compelled Western civilization to alter its angle of vision, and to adopt a new aesthetic sensibility, a new philosophical style, a new mode of understanding social life and human nature'. Peter Gay, *Freud, Jews and Other Germans* (New York, 1978), p. 22.

97 Zille is best known for his caricatures about the Berlin slums but he was also an accomplished photographer. See Winfried Ranke, *Heinrich Zille. Photographien Berlin 1890–1910* (Munich, 1925). For his social criticism see Winfried Ranke, *Heinrich Zille vom Milljöh ins Milieu. Heinrich Zilles Aufstieg in der Berliner Gesellschaft* (Berlin, 1979), pp. 166–91.

98 When Kollwitz was proposed in 1897 the Minister of Culture Robert Bosse said in his report to William II, 'The suggested prize for the etcher Käthe Kollwitz gives me cause for concern. This artist has exhibited a cycle of rather small etchings and lithographs, which she has entitled "Revolt of the Weavers". They depict the misery of the weavers and of their families ... The technical competence of the work, as well as its forceful, energetic expressiveness may seem to justify the decision of the jury from a purely artistic standpoint. But in view of the subject of the work ... I do not believe I can recommend it for explicit recognition by the state.' Minister Robert Bosse to William II, 23 May 1897, Merseburg, Königliches Geheimes Civil-Cabinett, Rep. 2.2.a, Nr 20564, pp. 200–202. See Paret, *The Berlin Secession*, pp. 21–2; Hans Kollwitz, (ed.), *Ich sah die Welt mit lebevollen Blicken. Käthe Kollwitz. Ein Leben in Selbst Zeugnissen* (Wiesbaden, 1979).

99 Herwarth Walden, 'Lexikon der deutschen Kunstkritik. Zusammengestellt aus Zeitungsberichten über den Herbstsalon', in *Der Sturm*, nos. 182–3, October, 1913, p. 115. Walden quoted over fifty insulting phrases taken from reviews. They included; 'Neuigkeitsjäger', 'Bunthäutige Tölpel', 'Neger im Frack', 'Hottentotten im Oberhemd', 'Horde farbespritzender Brüllaffen', 'Tollwütige Pinselein', 'Scheusslicher und Lächerlicher Klumpen', 'Bastardtalente', 'Bluff', 'Neue Wahnsinnsuniformen'. Nikolaus Pevsner, on the other hand, has called the 'acceptable' artists 'A proletariat of artists, including lots of mediocre men ...' Nikolaus Pevsner, *Academies of Art, Past and Present* (New York, 1973), p. 223.

6: IMPERIAL BERLIN

1 Gerhart Hauptmann, 'Neue Tragikomödie', in Hans-Egon Hass et al. (eds.), *Gerhart Hauptmann. Sämtliche Werke*, 11 vols. (Frankfurt-am-Main/Berlin, 1962–1974), vol. 9, p. 382.

2 Menzel also painted a brown ink and gouache entitled *Painters Preparing a Transparent Panel* (1871), showing various artists adding finishing touches to

one of the giant portraits already hanging on the side of a building. Berlin, Kupferstichkabinett (SZ Menzel N 1180).

3 Sebastian Hensel, *Ein Lebensbild aus Deutschlands Lehrjahren* (Berlin, 1903), p. 298.

4 Hans-Ulrich Wehler, *The German Empire 1871–1918* trans. Kim Traynor, (Leamington Spa, 1989), p. 149.

5 There are hundreds of studies of Bismarck. The most revealing view can be found in his correspondence, diaries, speeches and memoirs. See Otto von Bismarck, *Die gesammelte Werke* (the 'Friedrichsruh Edition') (Berlin, 1924–35), vol. 15; Horst Kohl (ed.), *Bismarck-Jahrbuch*, 6 vols. (Berlin, 1894–9); Horst Kohl (ed.), *Die politische Reden des Fürsten Bismarck*, 13 vols. (Stuttgart/Berlin, 1920); Hans Rothfels (ed.), *Otto von Bismarck, Briefe* (Göttingen, 1955). Useful biographies include Erich Eyck, *Bismarck. Leben und Werke*, 3 vols. (Zürich, 1941–4); Arnold Oskar Meyer, *Bismarck: Der Mensch und der Staatsmann* (Stuttgart, 1949), and Lothar Gall, *Bismarck der weisse Revolutionär* (Frankfurt-am-Main, 1980). Gall includes references to important documents which were either edited or omitted from the collected works.

6 Although not particularly warm towards his mother, he would later say that she had wanted him to 'learn a lot and achieve a lot'. Bismarck, *Die gesammelte Werke*, vol. 14, p. 66.

7 Bismarck made it clear that he put Prussia first and maintained that he would never tolerate the great kingdom of Prussia to be 'destroyed in a stinking brew of cosy southern German sentimentality'. Friedrich Meinecke, *Weltbürgertum und Nationalstaat* (Berlin, 1908), p. 360.

8 Wehler, *The German Empire*, p. 22. See also Julius Heyderhoff and Paul Wentzcke (eds.), *Deutscher Liberalismus im Zeitalter Bismarcks. Eine politische Briefsammlung*, 2 vols. (Bonn, 1925–6).

9 Kohl, *Die politische Reden des Fürsten Bismarck*, vol. 2, p. 38.

10 Gerhard Ritter, *Die preussischen Konservativen und Bismarcks deutsche Politik, 1858–76* (Heidelberg, 1913), p. 75.

11 Arnold Ruge, 'Deutschland und Österreich', *Das Jahrhundert*, 1859, quoted in Koppel S. Pinson, *Modern Germany. Its History and Civilisation* (New York, 1963), p. 118.

12 P. J. Grant, *Europe in the Nineteenth Century* (London, 1927), p. 321.

13 Wilhelm Oncken, *Das Zeitalter des Kaisers Wilhelm*, vol. 1 (Berlin, 1890), p. 517.

14 For an analysis of the battle and a re-evaluation of the Prussian mythology which grew up around it see Gordon Craig, *The Battle of Königgrätz. Prussia's Victory over Austria, 1866* (London, 1964). On the reaction in Europe where 'all expectations had been overturned' see Thomas Nipperdey, *Germany from Napoleon to Bismarck, 1800–1866*, trans. Daniel Nolan (Dublin, 1966), p. 700.

15 Gustav Mevissen, quoted in Pinson, *Modern Germany*, pp. 140–41.

16 Helmuth von Moltke, letter to J. K. Bluntschli, 11 December 1880, in Feldmarschall Helmuth Graf von Moltke, *Erinnerungen, Briefe, Dokumente* (Stuttgart, 1922).

17 The documents relating to the question of the Hohenzollerns and the Spanish succession are reproduced in Charles Bonnin (ed.), *Bismarck and the Hohenzol-*

lern Candidature for the Spanish Throne: The Documents in the German Diplomatic Archives, trans. Isabella M. Massey (London, 1957).

18 Even so, as Michael Howard has pointed out in the excellent study of the Franco-Prussian War, conflict between France and Germany was seen by most Europeans in the 1860s as more or less inevitable. Michael Howard, *The Franco-Prussian War. The German Invasion of France, 1870–1871* (London, 1979), pp. 40–42.

19 Otto Eduard Prinz von Bismarck-Schönhausen, *Bismarck: Die gesammelten Werke* (Berlin, 1924–32), vol. 6, p. 1597.

20 The telegram is quoted in Bismarck, *Die gesammelte Werke*, vol. 6b, pp. 368–71; see also Robert H. Lord, *Origins of the Franco-Prussian War* (London, 1924), p. 111; Count Benedetti gives his own version of the events in Count Benedetti, *Ma Mission en Prusse* (Paris, 1871), p. 87.

21 Howard, *The Franco-Prussian War*, p. 55; Alfred, Graf von Waldersee *Denkwüdigkeiten*, ed. H. O. Meissner (Stuttgart, 1922–5), vol. 1, p. 79.

22 Claude Keisch and Marie-Ursula Riemann-Reyher (eds.), *Adolph Menzel 1815–1905: Between Romanticism and Impressionism* (Yale, 1996), p. 345. Menzel is referring to Schlüter's sculptures of dying warriors on the Arsenal in central Berlin.

23 Frederick III, Kaiser, *Das Kriegstagebuch von 1870–1*, ed. H. O. Meissner (Berlin, 1926), p. 240.

24 On the attitude of the Prussian army see above all Gordon Craig, *The Politics of the Prussian Army 1640–1945* (Oxford, 1955), pp. 205–15; Fritz Honig, *Gefechtsbilder aus dem Kriege, 1870–71* (Berlin, 1891–4); Helmuth Carl Bernhard Graf von Moltke, *Militärische Korrespondenz. Aus den Dienstschriften des Krieges 1870–1871* (Berlin, 1897).

25 Prince Otto of Bavaria, quoted in Fritz Stern, *Gold and Iron, Bismarck, Bleichröder, and the Building of the German Empire* (London, 1977), p. 146. Sir Robert Morier wrote to Baron Stockmar from Berlin, that far from being a force for the good the victory and the 'unparalleled successes as those which have attended the German arms, and the consequent absolute power which the German nation has acquired over Europe, will tend especially to modify the German character, and that not necessarily for the better. Arrogance and overbearingness are the qualities likely to be developed in a Teutonic race under such conditions...' Sir Robert Morier, *Memoirs and Letters of the Right Hon. Sir Robert Morier, G.C.B. from 1826 to 1876*, ed. Rosslyn Wemyss (London, 1911), vol. 2, p. 243. See also Howard, *The Franco-Prussian War*, pp. 455–6.

26 The extraordinary nature of the relationship between Bismarck and William I is captured in their correspondence; see William I, German Emperor and King of Prussia, *The Correspondence of William I and Bismarck, with other letters from and to Prince Bismarck*, trans. J. A. Ford (London, 1915). For the typical nineteenth century Prussian view of the foundation of the Reich and its consequences see Heinrich von Sybel, *Die Begründung des deutschen Reiches durch Wilhelm I*, 5 vols. (Munich, 1890).

27 On the transformation of German liberalism from the 1860s see F. C. Sell, *Die Tragödie des deutschen Liberalismus* (Stuttgart, 1953); Otto Klein-Hattingen,

Geschichte des deutschen Liberalismus, 2 vols. (Berlin, 1911), and the collection of letters by political figures of the day in Heyderhoff and Wentzcke, *Deutscher Liberalismus im Zeitalter Bismarcks.*

28 The belief that Germany followed a *Sonderweg* and 'failed' to develop into a western liberal democratic state when it was 'supposed to' was in effect a reversal of the nineteenth-century view that Germany had developed in a different but 'better' way than western democracies. Although it is true that Germany became a modern economic industrial nation without ridding itself of its old agrarian aristocratic-based power structure, and that much interesting research has been done on the 'social' consequences of this, the idea that a nation's development can follow a 'correct' or an 'incorrect' path is based on somewhat simplistic notions of historical determinism. Sadly, the critique then offered by 'social' historians that German history could only be understood when looked at 'from below' through the experiences of ordinary people was also one sided. None seemed to think that the best history could in fact be one which tries to combine all these perspectives – social and cultural history with more 'conventional' military and diplomatic history. The debate was important in German historiography, particularly in the 1970s and 1980s. For an excellent summary see Georg G. Iggers, 'Introduction' in Georg G. Iggers, *The Social Politics of History* (Leamington Spa, 1985), pp. 1–48; see also Georg G. Iggers, *The German Conception of History. The National Tradition of Historical Thought from Herder to the Present* (Middletown, 1968); Hans-Ulrich Wehler (ed.), *Deutsche Historiker*, 9 vols. (Göttingen, 1971–82); Robert G. Moeller, 'The Kaiserreich Recast? Continuity and Changes in Modern German Historiography', *Journal of Social History*, 17, 1983–4, pp. 655–82. For a critical view see James J. Sheehan, 'What is German History? Reflections on the Role of the *Nation* in Germany History and Historiography', *Journal of Modern History*, 53, 1981, pp. 1–23.

29 For the election results between 1871 and 1912 see Michael Erbe, 'Berlin im Kaiserreich (1871–1918)', in Wolfgang Ribbe, *Geschichte Berlins* (Munich, 1987) vol. 2: *Von der Märzrevolution bis zur Gegenwart*, pp. 772–3, and the annual statistics collected in the *Statistisches Jahrbuch der Stadt Berlin.* For a contemporary critique of the system see Eduard Bernstein, *Die Berliner Arbeiterbewegung von 1890 bis 1905* (Berlin, 1924).

30 Wermuth wrote about his long and interesting career as mayor of Berlin in his memoirs: Adolph Wermuth, *Ein Beamtenleben* (Berlin, 1922).

31 Felix Philippi, *Alt Berlin* (Berlin, 1913–15), pp. 25–6, quoted in and translated by Gordon Craig, *Germany, 1866–1945* (Oxford, 1984), p. 81.

32 The empress insisted that he be cared for by Sir Morell Mackenzie, who misdiagnosed his cancer. Sir Morell Mackenzie, *The Fatal Illness of Frederick the Noble* (London, 1888); see also R. S. Stevenson, *Morell Mackenzie: The Story of a Victorian Tragedy* (London, 1946); Michael Freund, *Das Drama der 99 Tage: Krankheit und Tod Friedrichs III* (Cologne, 1966).

33 On the empress's view of Bismarck, whom she detested, see her introduction in Rennell Rodd, *Frederick, Crown Prince and Emperor: A Biographical Sketch Dedicated to His Memory, with an Introduction by Her Majesty the Empress Frederick* (London, 1888).

34 For general works on William II see, for example, Wilhelm Schlüssler, *Kaiser Wilhelm II, Schicksal und Schuld* (Göttingen, 1962); Lawrence Wilson, *The Incredible Kaiser: A Portrait of William II* (London, 1963); Anton Ritthaler, *Kaiser Wilhelm II: Herrscher in einer Zeitwende* (Cologne, 1958). See also William II, German Emperor and King of Prussia, *The Emperor's Speeches: Being a Selection from the Speeches, Edicts, Letters and Telegrams of the Emperor William II*, trans. L. Elkind, (London, 1904); Wilhelm II, Kaiser, *Ereignisse und Gestalten aus den jahren 1878–1918* (Leipzig, 1922).

35 His childhood was made all the more grim by the bullying of his tutor Hinzpeter, who wrote a self-congratulatory memoir of his influence on the Kaiser. See Georg Hinzpeter, *Kaiser Wilhelm II: Eine Skizze nach der Natur gezeichnet* (Bielefeld, 1888).

36 Count Robert Zedlitz-Trützschler, Controller of the Household of William II from 1903 to 1915, noted that although the Kaiser exhibited childlike delight when he killed a stag, he could also be extremely rude to his guests. On one occasion the Kaiser decided that the Minister of Agriculture, Victor von Podbielski, had not donated enough to the Romintern Domain. The emperor attacked him after dinner 'with such biting sarcasm, that he was driven into a corner. Finally, when the Emperor's tone became impressive and serious, there was no escape for him, he could only murmur: "As your majesty commands." For a man such as a Prussian Minister is generally supposed to be, it was a very humiliating and pitiful position.' Count Robert Zedlitz-Trützschler, *Twelve Years at the Imperial German Court* (London, 1924), p. 32.

37 Letter from Queen Victoria to the Crown Princess, 25 February 1859, quoted in Alan Palmer, *The Kaiser, Warlord of the Second Reich* (London, 1978), p. 39.

38 Craig, *The Politics of the Prussian Army*, pp. 236–40.

39 Wehler, *The German Empire*, 'The Army', pp. 146–55, here p. 148.

40 Imperial Chancellors were expected to wear military uniforms when in the Reichstag; at royal functions Chancellor Bethmann Hollweg, a mere major, was seated at the lower end of the table beyond the colonels and generals. Wehler, *The German Empire*, pp. 156–60, here p. 160. See also Karl Demeter, *The German Officer Corps in State and Society, 1650–1945* (London, 1965). Between 1885 and 1914 no Jews were promoted to the rank of reserve officer in the Prussian army and the discrimination in the officer corps encouraged anti-Semitism throughout the ranks. On increasing anti-Semitism in the army in the late nineteenth century see Werner T. Angress, 'Prussia's Army and the Jewish Reserve Officer Controversy Before World War I', *Leo Baeck Institute Yearbook*, 17, 1972, pp. 19–42.

41 Albrecht Graf von Roon, *Denkwürdigkeiten* (Berlin, 1905), vol. 1, p. 154.

42 The Convention of Tauroggen signed by General Yorck in defiance of the king on December 1812 opened the border to the tsar's army, allowing the two to pursue the French into Prussia together. It led to the Prussian defeat of France in the Wars of Liberation.

43 James W. Gerard, *My Four Years in Germany* (London, 1917), p. 46.

44 Wolfgang Heidelmeyer (ed.), *Der Fall Köpenick* (Frankfurt-am-Main, 1968). In 1906 the bust of the 'Berlin character Voigt', the 'Hauptmann von Köpenick',

was put into the Castans Panoptikum in Berlin; the original is now in the Museum der Stadt Wien (175.711.S).

45 Jules Laforgue, *Berlin, la Cour et la Ville* (Paris, 1887), trans. Anneliese Botond as *Berlin: Der Hof und die Stadt* (Frankfurt-am-Main, 1970). Laforgue also wrote numerous articles about Berlin, several about artistic life of the 1880s, which were printed in newspapers including the *Gazette des Beaux-Arts* and *Chronique des arts et de curiosité*.

46 Laforgue, *Berlin: Der Hof und die Stadt*, p. 66.

47 Klaus Vondung, 'Zur Lage der Gebildeten in der wilhelminischen Zeit', in Klaus Vondung (ed.), *Das wilhelminische Bildungsbürgertum. Zur Sozialgeschichte seiner Ideen* (Göttingen, 1976), pp. 20–33.

48 Rudolf Martin calculated that there were already 747 millionaires in Prussia by 1908. Rudolf Martin, *Jahrbuch des Vermögens und Einkommens der Millionäre in Preussen* (Berlin, 1912), p. xii. See also Erich Achterberg, *Berliner Hochfinanz. Kaiser–Fürsten–Millionäre um 1900* (Frankfurt-am-Main, 1965).

49 Gerard, *My Four Years in Germany*, p. 78.

50 Ibid., p. 82.

51 *Beati Possidentes* (Happy Owners) by Adolph Menzel (1888), Georg Schäfer Collection, Euerbach. See Peter-Klaus Schuster, 'Menzel's Modernity', in Keisch and Riemann-Reyher, *Adolph Menzel*, p. 155.

52 Maximilian Harden, 'Die Krisis', in *Die Zukunft*, 37, 12 October 1901, p. 51.

53 Georg Hermann, *Werke* (Stuttgart, 1922), vol. 2, p. 7.

54 The closest the 'official' culture came was the Wilhelmine 'römischen Barock', although there were some interesting advances in industrial and institutional architecture; see Erbe, 'Berlin im Kaiserreich', in Ribbe, *Geschichte Berlins*, vol. 2, p. 762; see also Julius Posener, *Berlin auf dem Wege zu einer neuen Architektur. Das Zeitalter Wilhelms II* (Munich, 1979).

55 Walther Rathenau, quoted in Jürgen Schutte and Peter Sprengel (eds.), *Die Berliner Moderne 1885–1914* (Stuttgart, 1987), p. 64.

56 Christian Morgenstern, 'Die Bierkirche – Eine Berliner Szene', in *Jubiläumsausgabe in vier Bänden* (Munich, 1979), vol. 1, pp. 230.

57 Adolf Behne, 'Bruno Taut', *Der Sturm*, 4, no. 198/199, Februar 1914, p. 184.

58 Stephen Spender, *World within World* (London, 1977), p. 121.

59 Charles Dickens, *Our Mutual Friend* (New York, 1964), p. 20; see also Stern, *Gold and Iron*, p. 159.

60 Goerd Peschken, 'Wohnen in der Metropole', in Jochen Boberg et al. (eds.) *Exerzierfeld der Moderne. Industriekultur in Berlin im 19. Jahrhundert* (Munich, 1984), pp. 208–19.

61 On the Berlin markets see Richard Schachner, *Märkte und Markthallen für Lebensmittel* (Berlin, 1914).

62 Kaufhaus des Westens (Ka De We), built by Johann Emil Schaudt. Peter Güttler et al. (eds.), *Berlin Brandenburg. Ein Architekturführer* (Berlin, 1990), p. 73.

63 Walther Kiaulehn, *Berlin, Schicksal einer Weltstadt* (Munich, 1980), p. 31.

64 Harden, 'Die Krisis', p. 53.

65 Laforgue, *Berlin: Der Hof und die Stadt*, p. 107.

66 Most eighteenth-century visitors went to Berlin because they were interested in

some aspect of the military or the 'art of war'. Berlin became a 'tourist destination' only in the nineteenth century. B. I. Krasnobaev (ed.), *Reisen und Reisebeschreibungen im 18. und 19. Jahrhundert als Quellen der Kulturbeziehungsforschung* (Berlin, 1980).

67 The first two large hotels in Berlin were the Hôtel de Rôme and the Hôtel d'Angleterre, followed by the König von Portugal and the Hôtel de Brandebourg. The first Grand Hotel, built between 1873 and 1875, which cost the enormous sum of 165,000 Marks, was burnt to the ground shortly after its opening on 10 October 1875. It was re-opened a year later but had already been overtaken by the new Bristol. Bodo-Michael Baumunk, 'Grand Hotel', in Dieter Vorsteher (ed.), *Die Reise nach Berlin* (Berlin, 1987), pp. 192–8. See also 'Das Grand Hotel', in Gottfried Korff and Reinhard Rürup (eds.), *Berlin, Berlin. Die Ausstellung zur Geschichte der Stadt* (Berlin, 1987), pp. 204–11.

68 Vicky Baum, *Menschen im Hotel* (Berlin, 1928). On the film starring Greta Garbo, which was set in the Adlon Hotel, see Korff Rürup, *Berlin, Berlin,* p. 462.

69 One critic complained that the Adlon was so ornate as to be in bad taste. Maximilian Rapsilber, *Hotel Adlon* (Berlin, 1908), p. 10.

70 Kiaulehn, *Berlin,* p. 216.

71 Conrad Alberti, *Wer ist der Stärkere? Ein sozialer Roman aus dem modernen Berlin* (Leipzig, 1888), vol. 1, p. 82.

72 Kaiser William II, quoted in Hans Herzfeld, *Das Hauptstadtproblem in der Geschichte. Festgabe zum 90. Geburtstag Friedrich Meineckes Jahrbuch für Geschichte des deutschen Osten* (Tübingen, 1952), 'Berlin als Kaiserstadt und Reichshauptstadt', vol. 1, p. 168. See also Gerhard Masur, *Imperial Berlin* (London, 1971) p. 126.

73 For a contemporary view see Richard Bormann, *Die Bau- und Kunstdenkmäler von Berlin. Mit einer geschichtlichen Einleitung von P. Clausewitz* (Berlin, 1893).

74 For an interesting study of the relationship between the two capitals see Pierre Paul Sagave, *Berlin and Frankreich 1685–1871* (Berlin, 1980).

75 'Siegessäule' by Johann Heinrich Strack, 1873. See Güttler, *Berlin Brandenburg,* p. 63.

76 Dieter Hildebrandt, *Unter den Linden* (Berlin, 1981).

77 On William's rivalry with London see Robert K. Massie, *Dreadnought. Britain, Germany, and the Coming of the Great War* (London, 1992).

78 The Kaiser's outburst is recorded in Michael S. Cullen, *Der Reichstag. Die Geschichte eines Monuments* (Berlin, 1983), p. 246.

79 In the seventeenth-century Philipp Spener and August Wilhelm Francke taught that a true Christian did not need elaborate services but should spend his life trying to understand God through prayer.

80 Craig, *Germany,* p. 72.

81 These measures were counter-productive as they brought Catholics together and elicited much sympathy from many non-Catholics in Germany; Bismarck reversed the *Kulturkampf* in the late 1870s.

82 The East Germans also claimed the Dom for themselves; for a rather one-sided view of the building of the Dom see Karl-Heinz Klingenburg, *Der Berliner Dom. Bauten, Ideen und Projekte vom 15. Jahrhundert bis zur Gegenwart* (Berlin, 1987).

83 Masur, *Imperial Berlin*. See also Vera Frowein-Ziroff, *Die Kaiser-Wilhelm-Gedächtniskirche. Entstehung und Bedeutung* (Berlin, 1982).

84 Masur, *Imperial Berlin*, p. 141.

85 Twenty-five old Berlin houses were ripped down to make way for the Rathaus; the building cost 8 million marks. The festival to mark its opening in 1871 cost the city a further half a million marks. Günter Richter, 'Zwischen Revolution und Reichsgründung (1848–1870), in Ribbe, *Geschichte Berlins*, vol. 2, p. 684.

86 Walther Rathenau, *Impressionen* (Leipzig, 1902), 'Die schönste Stadt der Welt', p. 148.

87 Kaiser William noted that if Germany was to 'remain a model for other nations' the entire nation must foster proper art based on classical values: 'That can be done only if art holds out its hand to raise the people up, instead of descending into the gutter.' Kaiser Wilhelm II, Speech of 18 December 1901, in Johannes Penzler (ed.), *Die Reden Kaiser Wilhelms II* (Leipzig, 1907), vol. 3, p. 62. Jacob Burckhardt, letter to Eduard Schauenburg, 5 December 1846, in Jacob Burckhardt, *Briefe*, ed. Max Burckhardt (Basle, 1955), vol. 3, p. 41.

88 The eleven Berlin novels are *Vor dem Sturm, Schach von Wuthenow, L'Adultera, Cécile, Irrungen, Wirrungen, Stine, Frau Jenny Treibel, Effi Briest, Die Poggenpuhls, Mathilde Möhring*, and *Der Stechlin*. Henry Garland, *The Berlin Novels of Theodor Fontane* (Oxford, 1980). On his early life see Conrad Wandrey, *Theodor Fontane* (Munich, 1919). See also Gordon A. Craig, *Über Fontane* (Munich, 1997).

89 Theodor Fontane, letter to Georg Friedländer, 21 December 1884, quoted in Hans-Heinrich Reuter, *Fontane* (Munich, 1968), vol. 1, p. 499.

90 Peter Jelavich, *Berlin Cabaret* (Harvard, 1993), p. 109.

91 Kaiser William maintained that when art showed only misery and ugliness, 'art commits a sin against the German people'. Kaiser Wilhelm II, Speech of 18 December 1901, in Penzler, *Die Reden Kaiser Wilhelms II*, vol. 3. On William's views on art in Berlin see Masur, *Imperial Berlin*, 'Berlin and the Arts', pp. 203–53.

92 Letter from Felix Mendelssohn Bartholdy to Karl Klingsman, 15 July 1841, in Rudolf Elvers, *Die Mendelssohns in Berlin* (Berlin, 1983), p. 38.

93 Walther Kiaulehn, *Berlin*, p. 272.

94 Nipperdey, *Germany from Napoleon to Bismarck*, p. 468.

95 Emil Ludwig, *Kaiser Wilhelm II*, trans. Ethel Colburn Mayne (London, 1926), p. 349. Strauss was often criticized by those in the Kaiser's circle; the sculptor Fritz Klimsch recalled an evening at Anton von Werner's house at which Richard Strauss was invited to play the piano in the performance of a trio. At the end of the performance Werner said to Strauss that he would be 'better to stick to Beethoven' than to compose such strange music; apparently Strauss merely smiled at him. Fritz Klimsch, *Erinnerungen und Gedanken eines Bildhauers* (Berlin, 1952), p. 37.

96 Peter Paret, *The Berlin Secession. Modernism and Its Enemies in Imperial Germany* (Cambridge, Mass., 1980), p. 107.

97 In a speech of 18 December 1901 Kaiser William II announced that 'When faced with the magnificent remnants of classical antiquity we are overwhelmed with

the same emotion: here too an eternal constant law dominates, the law of beauty and harmony, the law of aesthetics ... we are proud when a particularly fine achievement is praised with the words: "That is virtually as good as the art done 1900 years ago."' Kaiser Wilhelm II, Speech of 18 December 1901, in Penzler, *Die Reden Kaiser Wilhelms II*, vol. 3, p. 60.

98 This attitude was shared by many; in 1893 Alfred Lichtwark, the director of the Hamburg Kunsthalle, said after visiting the Berlin salon that 'I do not want to disgust you with a comprehensive report of the exhibition. It seems to me more pitiful than ever. Berlin is ruled by a brutal variant of academic art, whose colours are more vulgar than reality, and whose portraits more commonplace than their models.' Alfred Lichtwark, 'Briefe an die Kommission für die Verwaltung der Kunsthalle', *Kunst und Künstler*, 21, 1922–3, pp. 48–9, quoted in Paret, *The Berlin Secession*, p. 12.

99 On Lovis Corinth see the catalogue for the 1996 exhibition of his work at the Nationalgalerie, Berlin, 2 August–20 October 1996. Peter-Klaus Schuster, Christoph Vitalie and Barbara Butts (eds.), *Lovis Corinth* (Munich, 1996).

100 Count Harry Kessler also complained about official taste and its limiting effects on exhibitions. In July 1904 he travelled to London to contribute to a select committee of the House of Lords investigating the public funding of the arts. He exclaimed that the German tendency to use the Kaiser's bureaucrats to determine what and who should appear meant that 'the artists who really worked were pushed out either by amateurs or by people who, somehow or other, had got a great power in the Association'. 'Select Committee on the Chantrye Trust', *Parliamentary Papers*, vol. 1 (*Reports*, 5, February–August 1904), p. 179. The report was reproduced in Count Harry Kessler, *Der deutsche Künstlerbund* (Berlin, 1904), p. 13. See also Paret, *The Berlin Secession*, pp. 135–6.

101 Hans Rosenhagen, 'Die nationale Kunst in Berlin', *Die Zukunft*, 20, 1897, p. 430. On Werner see Paret, *The Berlin Secession*, pp. 12–20; Anton von Werner, *Erlebnisse und Eindrücke, 1870–1890* (Berlin, 1913).

102 Theodor Fontane to Georg Friedländer, 21 December 1884, quoted in Reuter, *Fontane*, vol. 1, p. 499.

103 Gerhart Hauptmann, *Tagebuch 1892–1894*, ed. Martin Machatzke (Berlin, 1985), p. 243.

104 Max Liebermann, *Gesammelte Schriften* (Berlin, 1921), p. 122.

105 This view was challenged in the superb exhibition of Menzel's work held at the Musée d'Orsay, the National Gallery in Washington, DC, and the Nationalgalerie in Berlin organized by Claude Keisch, curator of the Nationalgalerie in Berlin, and Marie-Ursula Riemann-Reyher, curator of the department of prints and drawings at the State Museum of Berlin. See the outstanding catalogue Keisch and Riemann-Reyher, *Adolph Menzel*.

106 Françoise Forster-Hahn, 'Adolph Menzel: Readings between Nationalism and Modernity' in Keisch and Riemann-Reyher, *Adolph Menzel*, p. 103.

107 On Bode see his autobiography, Wilhelm von Bode, *Mein Leben*, 2 vols. (Berlin, 1930); on Tschudi see Hugo von Tschudi, *Gesammelte Schriften zur neueren Kunst*, ed. D. Schwedeler-Meyer (Munich, 1912).

108 For an account of Bode see Kiaulehn, *Berlin*, 'Bode und seine Sammler', pp. 313–

33. The Bode Museum (renamed the Kaiser-Friedrich-Museum in 1956) is on the Museum-Insel. For its development see Renate Petras, *Die Bauten der Berliner Museumsinsel* (Berlin, 1987).

109 See, for example, the catalogue for the Deutsche Kolonial-Ausstellung complete with elephant tusks and rifles mixed up with drums, spears and shields; *Deutsche Kolonial-Ausstellung im Rahmen der Gewerbe-Ausstellung im Treptower Park* (Berlin, 1896), in Landesarchiv Berlin, Rep. 250 Acc.1623; see also the wooden carvings of figures and other artefacts taken from the Congo or Angola and stored in the Museum für Völkerkunde, for example wooden figures in SMPK, Abt. Afrika (III).

110 In 1884 Alfred Messel (who had designed Wertheim's department store) was commissioned to design a new 'Museum für Original-Sculpturen und Gipsabguesse, Pergamon-Museum. Museum für Abguesse nach den Antiken Sculpturen, Olympia-Museum'. The result was the Pergamonmuseum am Kupfergraaben, designed by Messel and Ludwig Hoffmann, and completed between 1912 and 1930. It now contains the west side of the Pergamon altar dating from the second century BC. The original plans are at TUB Plansammlung der Universitäts-bibliothek (15661).

111 Richard Muther, 'Wilhelm II und die Kunst', *Aufsätze über bildende Kunst*, vol. 2 (Berlin, 1914), p. 198.

112 Kaiser Wilhelm II, 'Die wahre Kunst: Ansprüche an die bei der Ausgestaltung der Siegesallee beteiligten Künstler, gehalten beim Frestmahl im Königlichen Schloss aus Anlass der Enthüllung der letzten Denkmalsgruppe am 18. Dezember 1901'. Ernst Johann (ed.), *Reden des Kaisers. Ansprachen, Predigten und Trinksprüche Wilhelms II*, quoted in Schutte and Sprengel, *Die Berliner Moderne*, p. 572.

113 Kaiser Wilhelm II, *Reden Kaiser Wilhelms II*, ed. Axel Matthes (Munich, 1976), p. 12.

114 Oscar Bie, 'Sezession', *Neue deutsche Rundschau* (Berlin, 1900), vol. 2, p. 658.

115 Karl Baedeker, *Berlin und Umgebung* (Leipzig, 1906), p. 54.

116 *Berliner illustrirte Zeitung*, 'Die Bilanz des Jahrhunderts', 1898.

7: THE ROAD TO THE FIRST WORLD WAR

1 Hans Rosenberg (ed.), *Grosse Depression und Bismarckzeit. Wirtschaftsablauf, Gesellschaft und Politik in Mitteleuropa* (Berlin, 1967).

2 On the change in the German economy throughout the late nineteenth century see Walther E. Hoffmann, *Das Wachstum der deutschen Wirtschaft seit der Mitte des 19. Jahrhundert* (Berlin, 1965).

3 Walther Kiaulehn, *Berlin. Schicksal einer Weltstadt* (Munich, 1980), pp. 149–50. For an autobiographical account of his business dealings written after his bankruptcy see Henry Bethel Strousberg, *Dr Strousberg und sein Wirken* (Berlin, 1876).

4 Gordon R. Mork, 'The Prussian Railway Scandal of 1873: Economics and Politics in the German Empire', *European Studies Review*, 1, 1971, pp. 35–48. See also

Heinrich Steubel, *Das Verhältnis zwischen Staat und Banken auf dem Gebiete des Preussischen Anleihewesens von 1871–1913* (Berlin, 1935).

5 Günter Richter, 'Zwischen Revolution und Reichsgründung', in Wolfgang Ribbe (ed.), *Geschichte Berlins* (Munich, 1987), vol. 2: *Von der Märzrevolution bis zur Gegenwart*, p. 682. Hans Blum was the son of the democratic martyr of the 1848 revolution, Robert Blum, and wrote *Die deutsche Revolution 1848–49* (Leipzig, 1898).

6 Peter Pulzer, *The Rise of Political Anti-Semitism in Germany and Austria* (London, 1988), p. 21.

7 On the effects of the Depression see Rosenberg, *Gross Depression und Bismarckzeit*, p. 187.

8 This was criticized by Friedrich Naumann, who in *Demokratie* accused them of 'pretending to be frightened [of the red menace] in order to further their own interests'; quoted in Hans-Ulrich Wehler, *The German Empire 1871–1918*, trans. Kim Traynor (Leamington Spa, 1989), p. 75. See also H. H. Herlemann, 'Vom Ursprung des deutschen Agrarprotektionismus', in E. Gerhardt and P. Kuhlmann (eds.), *Agrarwirtschaft und Agrarpolitik* (Cologne, 1969), pp. 188–92; see also Hans-Jurgen Puhle, *Agrarische Interessenpolitik und preussischer Konservatismus im Wilhelminischen Reich, 1893–1914* (Bonn, 1975).

9 Between 1763 and 1786 Frederick the Great had introduced tariffs supporting new commercial and industrial projects like canals and roads. The memory of this appealed to many. See, for example, Shulamit Volkov, *The Rise of Popular Antimodernism in Germany. The Case of the Urban Master Artisans, 1873–1896* (Princeton, 1978), pp. 10–12.

10 The wealth of literature against 'capitalism' and 'modernism' was extraordinary; one notable exception was written by one of the great developers of the period who tried to inform Berliners about the positive changes brought to the city by the influx of capital; see Georg Haberland, *Aus meinem Leben* (Berlin, 1931).

11 Later, after the First World War, Alfred Döblin would urge Berliners already looking back with nostalgia to the imperial period not to forget '. . . the conservative terrorism in the Prussian Chamber. Of the sovereign might of the *Junker* provincial councillors. Of the farce of the Reichstag. Of the special farce of the Black-Blue bloc. Of the worshipping of the officer.' Alfred Döblin, 'Republik', *Die neue Rundshau*, 1, 1920, p. 79.

12 Fritz Stern, *Gold and Iron. Bismarck, Bleichröder, and the Building of the German Empire* (London, 1977), p. 160.

13 Theodor Fontane, *Briefe an seine Familie* (Berlin, 1924), vol. 2, p. 302, quoted in Stern, *Gold and Iron*, p. 227.

14 Friedrich Nietzsche, *Gesammelte Werke* (1920–29), vol. 3, p. 23.

15 Isaiah Berlin, *The Crooked Timber of Humanity* (London, 1990): 'The Apotheosis of the Romantic Will', p. 207.

16 Peter the Great also failed to 'westernize' Russia but the rejection of the west was not determined by geography; despite being nestled between Germany and Russia, Poland has typically looked to and tried to emulate the west. On the backlash against the west in Russia in the nineteenth century T. N. Granovsky

wrote angrily to A. I. Herzen in 1854: 'To you, who are cut off from Russia, Peter cannot be so close or so understandable. Looking at the sins of the West, you incline towards the Slavs and are ready to offer them your hand. If you lived here, you would speak differently . . .'; quoted in Hugh Seton-Watson, *The Russian Empire 1801–1917* (Oxford, 1989), p. 279.

17 Isaiah Berlin, *The Age of the Enlightenment. The Eighteenth-Century Philosophers* (Oxford, 1978): 'Johann Georg Hamann', p. 271.

18 Ludwig van Beethoven, *Symphony No. 3 in E Flat, Op. 55*. The dedication was changed to read: *'Sinfonia eroica, composta per festiggiare il souvenire di un grand' uomo.'* (Heroic symphony to celebrate the memory of a great man.)

19 On the rise of nationalism see, for example, John C. G. Röhl, *Germany without Bismarck: The Crisis of Government in the Second Reich, 1890–1900* (London, 1967); G. W. F. Hallgarten, *Imperialismus vor 1919* (Munich, 1951); and for the reaction in Berlin to the economic changes, the volume first published in 1879, Henry Vizetelly, *Berlin Under the New Empire*, 2 vols. (New York, 1968).

20 These themes formed the basis of the *Heimatroman* and the *Bauernroman* of the era, which later developed into the *Blut und Boden* literature of the Third Reich. One of the first works of this type was written by Wilhelm Heinrich Riehl; he maintained that the culture of a *Volk* developed from the very soil on which it was found. He also claimed that German cities destroyed the natural harmony of the *Volk*. Wilhelm Heinrich Riehl, *Land und Leute* (Stuttgart, 1867).

21 Spengler, like German Romantics before him, saw culture as an outward expression of history's hidden qualities, but he made the distinction between superior 'culture' and mere 'civilization' much wider. For him those with *Kultur* also had a 'soul', while civilization was 'the most external and artificial state of which . . . humanity . . . is capable'. George L. Mosse, *The Culture of Western Europe. The Nineteenth and Twentieth Centuries* (London, 1988), p. 1.

22 Karl Scheffler, *Berlin: Ein Stadtschicksal* (Berlin, 1910, rep. 1989), p. 200.

23 Karl Baedeker, *Berlin and Its Environs: Handbook for Travellers* (Leipzig, 1903), p. 50.

24 Klaus Bergmann, *Agrarromantik und Grossstadtfeindschaft* (Meisenheim-am-Glan, 1970), pp. 23–5.

25 George Simmel, 'The Metropolis and Mental Life', in Donald N. Levine (ed.), *On Individuality and Social Forms: Selected Writings* (Chicago, 1971), p. 325.

26 On the rise of *völkisch* nationalism and racial anti-Semitism see in particular George L. Mosse, *The Crisis of German Ideology. Intellectual Origins of the Third Reich* (New York, 1981), pp. 13–126. See also Fritz Stern, *The Politics of Cultural Despair: A Study in the Rise of Germanic Ideology* (Berkeley, 1961).

27 On Chamberlain see Mosse, *The Crisis of German Ideology*, pp. 93–7; see also Houston Stewart Chamberlain, *Die Grundlagen des XIX. Jahrhunderts*, 2 vols. (Munich, 1932). On Lagarde see Ludwig Schemann, *Paul de Lagarde* (Leipzig, 1919); Paul de Lagarde, *Deutsche Schriften* (Göttingen, 1910), pp. 10–18.

28 Julius Langbehn, *Rembrandt als Erzieher* (Leipzig, 1900); see also Mosse, *The Crisis of German Ideology*, pp. 39–46.

29 On Wilhelm Förster's 'Ethische Gesellschaft' of 1892 see Mosse, *The Crisis of*

German Ideology, p. 46. On Egidy see Heinrich Driesmans, *Moritz von Egidy, Sein Leben und Werk* (Dresden, 1900), vol. 2, pp. 86–112.

30 This 'truly German' way of life was increasingly identified with notions of medieval rural society. The big modern city, particularly Berlin, was increasingly held up as the very antithesis of their ideal. See, for example, Riehl, *Land und Leute*, pp. 98–101.

31 The society was founded in 1910 – the Nazis took up *Fraktur* but it has hardly been used since 1945.

32 As Peter Gay has put it, the value-laden epithet 'Aryan' 'conjured up a tall, fair-haired, blue-eyed, loyal, family-loving but warlike race, its manly – and womanly – members sharply contrasting with the Semites, who threatened to subvert civilization with their unhealthy offspring, mercantile outlook, and decadent modernism.' Peter Gay, *The Cultivation of Hatred. The Bourgeois Experience: Victoria to Freud* (London, 1995), p. 77.

33 Lech Trzeciakowski, *The Kulturkampf in Prussian Poland* (New York, 1990), pp. 115–40.

34 Gottfried Korff and Reinhard Rürup (eds.), *Berlin, Berlin. Die Ausstellung zur Geschichte der Stadt* (Berlin, 1987), p. 257; Hermann Simon, *Die neue Synagoge Berlin. Geschichte, Gegenwart, Zukunft* (Berlin, 1991), pp. 9–14.

35 Alfred Etzold et al., *Jüdische Friedhöfe in Berlin* (Berlin, 1987), pp. 75–82.

36 Stern, *Gold and Iron*, p. xix.

37 Reinhard Rürup, 'The Tortuous and Thorny Path to Legal Equality, "Jew Laws" and Emancipatory Legislation in Germany from the Late Eighteenth Century', *Leo Baeck Institute Yearbook*, 31, 1986, p. 6.

38 Shephard Thomas Taylor, *Reminiscences of Berlin during the Franco-German War of 1870–71* (London, 1885), p. 238, quoted in Stern, *Gold and Iron*, p. 466–7.

39 Berlin's anti-Semitism prompted Walther Rathenau to say that 'Der Jude ist als Bürger zweiter Klasse in die Welt getreten' (the Jew has come into the world as a second-class citizen). Hildegard Baronin Spitzemberg noted of the young Jewish banker Albert von Goldschmidt-Rothschild that he was treated in 'shifts', at one moment being grandly fêted, the next treated in a most humiliating way. Hildegard von Spitzemberg, *Das Tagebuch der Baronin Spitzemberg geb. Freiin von Vernbüler, Aufzeichnungen aus der Hofgesellschaft des Hohenzollernreiches*, ed. Rudolf Vierhaus (Göttingen, 1960), p. 57.

40 Bleichröder's story is told in Stern's remarkable book, *Gold and Iron*; this incident is recorded in Gerhard Masur, *Imperial Berlin* (London, 1971), p. 88.

41 Comte Paul Vasili, *La Société de Berlin* (Paris, 1884), pp. 152–3. Fritz Stern explains that Comte Paul Vasili is a pseudonym for Princess Catherine Radziwill. Stern, *Gold and Iron*, p. 463.

42 Stern, *Gold and Iron*, p. 183n.

43 Otto Glagau, 'The Social Question is the Jewish Question', in Harold James, *A German Identity 1770–1990* (London, 1989), p. 101.

44 Constantin Frantz, *Der Fäderalismus als das leitende Prinzip für die soziale, staatliche und internationale Organisation unter besonderer Bezugnahme auf Deutschland* (Mainz, 1879), p. 267.

45 Stern, *Gold and Iron*, p. xviii.

46 Friedrich Nietzsche, *Menschliches, all zu Menschliches* (1878), trans. R. J. Hollingdale as *Human, All Too Human* (Cambridge, 1986), p. 175.

47 Ibid.

48 Friedrich Nietzsche, *Der Antichrist* (1888), trans. R. J. Hollingdale as *The Antichrist; Twilight* (Harmondsworth, 1968), p. 98.

49 On the anti-Semitism of intellectuals, including Paul de Lagarde and Konstantin Frantz, see Stern, *The Politics of Cultural Despair*.

50 Daniel Jonah Goldhagen, *Hitler's Willing Executioners. Ordinary Germans and the Holocaust* (London, 1996), p. 65.

51 As Adolf Stöcker, the leader of the Christian-Social movement, wrote in a pamphlet of 1881, 'I have emphasized that the social revolution has to be overcome by healthy social reform, built on a Christian foundation . . . I do not want culture that is not Germanic and Christian. That is why I am fighting against Jewish supremacy.' Seven years later he organized the Christian Social Workers' party. Koppel S. Pinson, *Modern Germany. Its History and Civilisation* (New York, 1963), p. 167.

52 Goldhagen, *Hitler's Willing Executioners*, p. 74n.

53 Eleonore Sterling pointed to the spreading of anti-Semitic views 'through innumerable leaflets, posters, and newspaper articles. In the streets and in the taverns "rabble-rousers" deliver hateful speeches and distribute inflammatory petitions among the population . . . the agitation continues to be conducted not only by street and tavern orators, but even by those who fancy themselves to be the most Christian.' Eleonore Sterling, quoted in Goldhagen, *Hitler's Willing Executioners*, p. 64n.

54 On overt anti-Semitism in Berlin see Michael Erbe, 'Berlin im Kaiserreich (1871–1918)', in Ribbe, *Geschichte Berlins*, vol. 2, p. 767.

55 Mosse, *The Crisis of German Ideology*, pp. 149–235.

56 On increasing nationalism in Wilhelmine schools see the fascinating study of school texts, Erich Weymar, *Das Selbstverständnis der Deutschen* (Stuttgart, 1961). And, as Fritz Stern has pointed out, these ideas did not wane in the coming years; indeed 'a thousand teachers in republican Germany who in their youth had worshipped Lagarde or Langbehn were just as important in the triumph of National Socialism . . .' Stern, *The Politics of Cultural Despair*, p. 291.

57 Walter Z. Laqueur, *Young Germany. A History of the German Youth Movement* (London, 1961); Hans Blüher, *Wandervogel, Geschichte einer Jugendbewegung* (Berlin, 1916); Friedrich Bärwald, *Das Erlebnis des Staates in der deutschen Jugendbewegung* (Berlin, 1921). Interesting material is to be found in the Archiv der deutschen Jugendbewegung, Burg Ludwigstein, Witzenhauen, including numerous posters and pamphlets encouraging young Berliners to join, and copies of their magazine *Der Wandervogel*.

58 See, for example, Amalie Altmann-Reich, 'Evas Rückkehr ins Paradies', *Berliner illustrirte Zeitung*, no. 28, 12 June 1903, p. 436; Hugo Höppener, 'Kalenderblatt des deutschen Bundes der Vereine für naturgemässe Lebens- und Heilweise', *Findus* (Berlin, 1928). Material on the naturist movement is in the Berlinische Galerie, Findus Archiv.

59 Bernhard vom Brocke, 'Hochschul- und Wissenschaftspolitik in Preussen und im deutschem Reich 1882–1907', in Peter Baumgart, (ed.), *Bildungspolitik in Preussen zur Zeit des Kaiserreichs* (Stuttgart, 1980), pp. 1–118; see also Erbe, 'Berlin im Kaiserreich, in Ribbe, *Geschichte Berlins*, vol. 2, pp. 778–82.

60 Leonore Koschnick, 'Zentrum der Wissenschaften', in Korff and Rürup, *Berlin, Berlin*, pp. 290–302. See also Max Lenz, *Geschichte der königlichen Friedrich-Wilhelms-Universität zu Berlin*, 4 vols. (Halle, 1910).

61 See, for example, Fritz K. Ringer, *The Decline of the German Mandarins: The German Academic Community, 1890–1933* (Cambridge, Mass., 1969).

62 Gordon Craig, *Germany, 1866–1945* (Oxford, 1984), p. 201.

63 On Arons see Annemarie Lange, *Das wilhelminische Berlin* (Berlin, 1984), p. 407.

64 Craig, *Germany*, p. 194.

65 On the primacy of the Prussian state see Leopold von Ranke, *Zwölf Bücher preussischer Geschichte*, ed. Georg Küntzel, 3 vols. (Munich, 1930).

66 Friedrich Naumann, *Mitteleuropa* (Berlin, 1915), p. 61. See also Theodor Heuss, *Friedrich Naumann* (Berlin, 1937).

67 The Kaiser reflected this in his speech at the unveiling of the Siegessäule. If German art constituted an ideal force in life, 'We Germans have permanently acquired these great ideals, while other peoples have generally lost them. Only the Germans remain, and are above all others called upon to guard these great ideals, to nurture and perpetuate them . . .' Kaiser Wilhelm II, Speech of 18 December 1901 in Johannes Penzler (ed.), *Die Reden Kaiser Wilhelms II* (Leipzig, 1907), vol. 3, p. 61.

68 The most infamous was the 'Berlin Anti-Semitism Debate' which was sparked when the historian Heinrich von Treitschke published an article in the *Preus-sische Jahrbücher* called 'Unsere Aussichten', claiming that there was a 'Jewish problem' in Germany. It included the fateful words, 'The Jews are our misfor-tune.' A number of industrialists, politicians and academics, including Theodor Mommsen, responded by writing a declaration calling the article a 'disgrace'. The angry exchanges are reprinted in Walter Boehlich, *Der Berliner Antisemi-tismusstreit* (Frankfurt-am-Main, 1965); see Masur, *Imperial Berlin*, pp. 113–14; see also Pulzer, *The Rise of Political Anti-Semitism*, pp. 337–8. As a result of his pronouncements Treitschke helped to make racial anti-Semitism acceptable in Berlin.

69 Roger Chickering, *We Men Who Feel Most German: A Cultural Study of the Pan-German League 1886–1914* (London, 1984), p. 10.

70 For Heinrich Class's own self-congratulatory view of the Pan-German League see Heinrich Class, *Wider den Strom* (Leipzig, 1922).

71 Stöcker, in Walter Frank, *Hofprediger Adolf Stoecker und die christlichsoziale Bewegung* (Hamburg, 1935), p. 183; Waldersee is quoted in Otto von Bismarck, *Gedanken und Erinnerungen*, ed. Robert Lucius von Ballhausen (Berlin, 1920), vol. 3, p. 35.

72 Otto von Bismarck, *Gesammelte Werke* (1924–35), vol. 15, p. 493.

73 The tsar wrote that he was 'un garçon mal élevé et de mauvais foi'. J. Alden Nichols, *Germany after Bismarck: The Caprivi Era, 1890–1894* (Cambridge, Mass., 1958), p. 24.

74 'Dropping the Pilot', *Punch*, 22 March 1889.

75 On Bismarck's departure from Berlin see Robert K. Massie, *Dreadnought. Britain, Germany, and the Coming of the Great War* (London, 1992), pp. 97–100. Bismarck continued to vent his anger against William's rule and his 'popular absolutism'; see Bismarck, *Gesammelte Werke*, vol. 15, p. 640.

76 The British were, however, not particularly eager to come to an agreement either. On British intransigence and the failure of the Hague Conference see G. P. Gooch and H. Temperley (eds.), *British Documents on the Origins of the War* (London, 1930), vol. 6, pp. 67–70; see also Viscount Grey of Falloden, *Twenty-Five Years* (London, 1925), vol. 1, p. 148.

77 August Bebel, in Jonathan Steinberg, *Yesterday's Deterrent: Tirpitz and the Birth of the German Battle Fleet* (New York, 1965), p. 195.

78 See Volker R. Berghahn, *Germany and the Approach of War in 1914* (London, 1973), p. 42; see also Imanuel Geiss, *Der lange Weg in die Katastrophe. Die Vorgeschichte des ersten Weltkrieges 1815–1914* (Munich, 1990).

79 Friedrich von Holstein, *The Holstein Papers: The Memoirs, Diaries and Correspondence of Friedrich von Holstein*, ed. Norman Rich and M. H. Fischer (New York, 1955); Joachim von Jürenberg, *His Excellency the Spectre: The Life of Fritz von Holstein* (London, 1933). On Bülow's relations with Holstein see Prince Bernhard von Bülow, *Memoirs*, 4 vols. (Boston, 1931–2), in particular vol. 4.

80 On Holstein's hostility to the treaty see Holstein, *The Holstein Papers*, vol. 2, p. 271–2; on Russia's attempts to reverse the decision see H. L. von Schweidnitz, *Denkwüdigkeiten*, ed. W. von Schweidnitz (Berlin, 1927), vol. 2, pp. 435–8.

81 Quoted in Bülow, *Memoirs*, vol. 4, p. 639. Even Fontane reflects the new hostility to Russia in his novel *Die Poggenpuhls*, written between 1891 and 1895 after the dropping of the 'Rückversicherungsvertrag'. In the book the girls state that Leo will be covered in glory in the 'next great Russian battle'. Theodor Fontane, *Die Poggenpuhls*, in W. Keitel and H. Nurnberger (eds.), *Werke, Shriften und Briefe* (Dušseldorf, 1970), p. 485.

82 Tirpitz long tried to convince the Kaiser of the need for battleships rather than cruisers; on 3 January 1896, for example, he wrote to him that 'Even the greatest sea-state in Europe would be more conciliatory towards us if we had two or three highly trained squadrons to add to the political scales'; in June he declared that 'The military situation in England demands battleships in as great a number as possible'. Quoted in Jonathan Steinberg, *Yesterday's Deterrent: Tirpitz and the Birth of the German Battle Fleet* (New York, 1965), p. 230.

83 Quoted in Holger H. Herwig, *The German Naval Officer Corps* (Oxford, 1973), p. 18. On the tax increase see Volker Berghahn, *Der Tirpitz-Plan* (Düsseldorf, 1971), p. 248.

84 William II to Nicholas II, 2 January 1896, in N. F. Grant (ed.), *The Kaiser's Letters to the Tsar* (London, 1920), p. 30.

85 On Bülow's relations with Holstein see Bülow, *Memoirs*, vol. 1, p. 418; see also Richard O'Connor, *The Spirit Soldiers: A Historical Narrative of the Boxer Rebellion* (New York, 1973), p. 84.

86 Count Waldersee, quoted in Massie, *Dreadnought*, p. 285. Massie notes that Waldersee himself 'went everywhere wearing his cordon of the Order of the

Black Eagle and carrying his Field Marshal's baton'. Waldersee's own version of events is recorded in Count Alfred von Waldersee, *A Field Marshal's Memoirs* (London, 1924), pp. 208–11.

87 Increased tension between the two countries was reflected in a wave of fear in 1904 in which Germans became convinced that Britain was planning a preemptive strike on Germany to curb her naval build-up. G. W. Monger, *The End of Isolation: British Foreign Policy 1900–1907* (London, 1963), p. 73.

88 Winston S. Churchill, *The World Crisis 1911–1918* (London, 1922), vol. 1, p. 67.

89 It was only the German stance in the Balkans in the war of 1912–13 and the conciliatory German response to British concerns over the Berlin–Baghdad railway which led to a temporary improvement in relations between the two countries. On this, and for an interesting look at the origins of the First World War see Niall Ferguson, 'The Kaiser's European Union', in Niall Ferguson, *Virtual History. Alternatives and Counterfactuals* (London, 1997), p. 240. See also John B. Wolf, *The Diplomatic History of the Baghdad Railway* (Columbus, 1936).

90 Berghahn, *Germany and the Approach of War*, p. 59. See also J. S. Steinberg, 'Diplomatie als Wille und Vorstellung: Die Berliner Mission Lord Haldanes im Februar 1912', in H. Scottelius and W. Diest (eds.), *Marine und Marinepolitik im kaiserlichen Deutschland* (Düsseldorf, 1972).

91 The 'war council' was cited by Fritz Fischer in *Krieg der Illusionen* as that which determined German policy from that time forward. This was challenged by a number of academics who believed that Fischer had overstated the case of German war aims. See Wolfgang J. Mommsen, *Central European History*, 6, no. 1, March 1973; see also Craig, *Germany*, p. 332.

92 For a discussion of German preparations for war see Geiss, *Der lange Weg in die Katastrophe*; see also James Joll, *The Origins of the First World War* (London, 1984), p. 186.

93 Paul Meuriot, 'Le Reichstag impérial, 1871–1912, étude de démographie politique', *Journal de la société de statistiques de Paris*, 1914, p. 72.

94 For all its success Berlin's middle class was still comparatively small when compared with the burgeoning working class – only 5.5 per cent of the population earned over 3,000 marks in 1914. Dieter Groh, *Negative Integration und revolutionärer Attentismus: Die deutsche Sozialdemokratie am Vorabend des ersten Weltkrieges* (Frankfurt-am-Main, 1973), p. 315.

95 On Harden's career see Bjoern Uwe Weller, *Maximilian Harden und die 'Zukunft'* (Bremen, 1970).

96 Once, when commuting a death sentence imposed on a cavalryman found to have committed sodomy with his horse, an unruffled Frederick II had simply ordered: 'Transfer to the infantry!' Walter Henry Nelson, *The Soldier Kings. The House of Hohenzollern* (New York, 1970), p. 206.

97 For an account of his life, and of homosexuality in nineteenth-century Germany, see William Manchester, *The Arms of Krupp 1587 – 1968* (Boston, 1968), pp. 206–32.

98 'Krupp auf Capri', *Vorwärts*, no. 268, 15 November 1902.

99 'Barbarismus', *Der Tag*, 27 November 1902.

100 The affair, as the court marshal put it, was really most remarkable. 'They assembled after dinner in the stately hall of the magnificent castle, an orchestra playing on the staircase landing. Sudden Count Hülsen-Haeseler appeared, dressed as a ballerina ... and began to dance. Everyone was vastly delighted for the Count's dancing is quite superb, and there was something quite out of the common in seeing the Chief of the Military Cabinet, got up as a woman, perform a *pas-seul*.' After his death they 'hastily transformed him from a ballerina into a soldier'. The saga is recounted in Emil Ludwig, *Kaiser Wilhelm II*, trans. Ethel Colburn Mayne (London, 1926), pp. 348–9.

101 Norman Rich, *Friedrich von Holstein. Politics and Diplomacy in the Era of Bismarck and William II* (Cambridge, 1956), vol. 2, p. 790.

102 Holstein, *The Holstein Papers*, vol. 1, pp. 203–6.

103 Lord Grey, quoted in Massie, *Dreadnought*, p. 685.

104 The Zabern affair led to a vote of no-confidence against Bethmann-Hollweg. Hans-Ulrich Wehler, 'Der Fall Zabern. Rückblick auf eine Verfassungskrise des wilhelminischen Kaiserreiches', *Die Welt als Geschichte*, 1963, pp. 23–36; see also Erwin Schenk, *Der Fall Zabern* (Stuttgart, 1927).

105 Marsden Hartley, *Portrait of a German Officer* (1914), Metropolitan Museum of Art, Alfred Stieglitz Collection; *Painting No. 48, Berlin* (1913), Brooklyn Museum, New York. See also Marsden Hartley, 'Tribal Ethics', *Dial*, November 1916.

106 Friedrich Meinecke, who was in the process of moving from Freiburg to Berlin, commented on 'war fever' in the city. See Friedrich Meinecke, 'Strassburg/Freiberg/Berlin, 1901–1919, Erinnerungen', in Eberhard Kessel (ed.) *Autobiographische Schriften* (Stuttgart, 1969), vol. 8, pp. 220–25.

107 According to Princess Blücher, one English woman who visited her in August 1914 recounted how 'she had just seen a spy caught in the street. He had been dressed as a woman, and had been hooted by the mob to the police station, had made one last desperate struggle to escape, and was shot. I cannot help wondering myself if all these "spies" that are being persecuted in the streets are not often the most innocent people in the world. All the inherent qualities of cruelty and ferocity seem to be aroused simply by the word war.' Evelyn, Princess Blücher, *An English Wife in Berlin. A Private Memoir of Events, Politics, and Daily Life in Germany Throughout the War and the Social Revolution of 1918* (London, 1920), p. 13.

108 On recruitment see *Histories of two hundred and fifty-one divisions of the German army which participated in the war (1914–1918) compiled from the records of the intelligence section of the general staff, American Expeditionary Forces* (Chaumont, 1919).

109 Tilla Durieux, *Meine ersten neunzig Jahre* (Berlin, 1971), pp. 212–13.

110 Wehler, *The German Empire*, p. 152. On Schlieffen see Generalfeldmarschall Graf Alfred Schlieffen, *Briefe* (Göttingen, 1958); Gerhard Ritter, *Der Schlieffenplan, Kritik eines Mythos* (Munich, 1956). The enduring mythology surrounding the Schlieffen Plan was hinted at in the bizarre exchange of letters in the *Spectator* in 1987.

111 The obsession with 'encirclement' had not waned; upon hearing the news of 30 July 1914 William exclaimed that 'England, France and Russia have conspired

... to fight together for our annihilation ... The dead Edward VII is stronger than the living I'. Kaiser Wilhelm II, quoted in Ludwig, *Kaiser Wilhelm II*, p. 394.

112 The invasion of Belgium is described in Barbara W. Tuchman, *The Guns of August* (New York, 1962), pp. 137–61.

113 Blücher, *An English Wife in Berlin*, p. 24.

114 Asquith's cabinet of nineteen was still deeply divided on 31 July: the three groups were those who favoured neutrality, (Morely, Burns, Simon, Beauchamp and Hobhouse), those in favour of intervention (Grey and Churchill) and those undecided (Crewe, McKenna, Haldan and Samuel but according to Ferguson also Lloyd George and Harcourt and Asquith). The violation of the neutrality of Belgium – and Moltke's decision to go through the whole of Belgium rather than just a small corner – was cited as the reason that the cabinet changed its mind. In effect, this action saved the Liberal government. Niall Ferguson, 'The Kaiser's European Union', in Niall Ferguson (ed.), *Virtual History*, p. 275.

115 Blücher, *An English Wife in Berlin*, p. 5.

116 On the reaction in Berlin to the outbreak of war see James W. Gerard, *My Four Years in Germany* (London, 1917), pp. 107–53.

117 The most important post war German analysis of the problem of German responsibility for war in 1914 are Fritz Fischer, *Germany's Aims in the First World War*; Fritz Fischer, *War of Illusions: German Policies from 1911 to 1914* (London, 1975).

118 Friedrich Meinecke wrote to his friend Alfred Dove in September 1914 that 'Our Opponents ascribe to us military plans for the conquest of a new Roman empire – but trees don't grow up to heaven all at once. It is true that one hears of all kinds of continental appetites these days – Tirpitz is said to consider Antwerp indispensable and they say that Belgium is to be divided into four parts (one for us, one for Holland, one for France, which they want to spare, and one for Luxemburg) – which doesn't please me. The compactness and unity of our national state, upon which our present strength depends, ought not to be hurt by resistant appendages. Of course, we must at last beat England down to the point where it recognizes us as a world Power of equal rights, and I believe that our strength will be sufficient – despite the momentary squeeze in northern France – to achieve that purpose.' Friedrich Meinicke, *Briefwechsel* to A. Dove 25 September 1914, p. 47. The correspondence is translated by Craig, *Germany*, p. 341.

119 Helmut Kuhn et al. (eds.) *Die deutsche Universität im dritten Reich* (Munich, 1966), p. 26.

120 The Battle of Tannenburg, fought 27–29 August 1914, followed by the Battle of the Masurian Lakes a few days later, saw the decimation of the Russian Army by Ludendorff's Eighth Army. For the German view of the Battle of Tannenburg see Chef des Stabes der I Division von Reichenau, *Schlachtfelder in Ostpreussen* (Königsberg, 1916), pp. 62–7. See also Norman Stone, *The Eastern Front, 1914–1917* (London, 1975).

121 The number of workers to return to Berlin in the *Zurückstellung* was 700 in 1914, 21,400 in 1915, 24,900 in 1916, 27,600 in 1917, 18,900 in 1918. Pr.Br.Pre. 30

Berlin C, *Jahresberichte der Gewerbe-Aufsicht*, n. 1958, Brandenburg, Landeshauptarchiv.

122 Gerhard Hecker, *Walther Rathenau und sein Verhältnis zu Militär und Krieg* (Boppard, 1983), pp. 201–68.

123 Jay Winter and Jean-Louis Robert, *Capital Cities at War: London, Paris, Berlin 1914–1919* (Cambridge, 1997), p. 174–5.

124 *Reichsarbeitsblatt* (Berlin, 1916), vol. 14, p. 974; see also Winter and Robert, *Capital Cities at War*, pp. 174–5.

125 The problem of the black market was a subject of much discussion in war-time Berlin; the newspaper *Berliner Lokal-Anzeiger* carried out a campaign against the black marketeering of coal by calling for customer lists; these were adopted only in March 1918.

126 Jürgen Kuczynski, *Geschichte des Alltags des deutschen Volkes, 1600 bis 1945* (Berlin, 1982), vol. 4, p. 450.

127 *Vorwärts*, vol. 34, no. 339, 11 December 1917. This despite the plethora of organizations set up to solve the problem including the Reichskommissar für die Kohlenverteilung (Imperial Commissioner for Coal Distribution) founded in February 1917: *Kohlenstelle Gross-Berlin* (Greater Berlin Coal Office), the Kohlenverband Gross-Berlin (Greater Berlin Coal Association) founded in August 1917, *Deputation für die Kohlenversorgung* (Berlin Coal Supply Department) as well as the private firm *Berliner Brennstoffbeschaffungsgesellschaft GmbH)* (Berlin Supply Company for Combustible Fuels).

128 Jürgen Kocka, *Facing Total War: German Society 1914–1918* (Warwick, 1984), p. 123.

129 Pr.Br.Rep. 30 Berlin C no. 1466: *Jahresberichte der Gewerbe-Aufsicht*, no. 1958, in the Brandenburg Landeshauptarchiv (LHA), pp. 269–75; see also Winter and Robert, *Capital Cities at War*, p. 190.

130 Georg Grosz, *The Autobiography of Georg Grosz. A Small Yes and a Big No*, trans. Arnold J. Pomerans (New York, 1982), p. 80.

131 Siegfried Knappe and Ted Brusaw, *Soldat. Reflections of a German Soldier 1936–1949* (New York, 1992), p. 140.

132 Much of this extraordinary work, including paintings by Ernst Barlach, Max Beckmann, Otto Dix, Konrad Felixmüller, Georg Grosz, Erich Heckel, Willy Jaeckel, Ernst Ludwig Kirchner, Käthe Kollwitz, Will Küpper, Wilhelm Lehmbruck, Ludwig Meidner, Max Pechstein, Josef Scharl, Max Slevogt, and Albert Weisgerber, who died at Ypres in 1915, was gathered for an exhibition at the Barbican Gallery in London in 1994, and is reproduced in the catalogue. See Richard Cork, *A Bitter Truth: Avant-Garde Art and the Great War* (London, 1994).

133 See, for example, the tragic photographs in the Berlin Bildarchiv PK of war cripples doing 'exercises' in Korff and Rürup, *Berlin, Berlin*, p. 361.

134 The Rudolf Virchow hospital treated over 200,000 men and the military hospital at Busch treated 30,000 men during the war – there were around 5,000 injured men in Berlin at any one time; by comparison London had beds for 36,664, of which 20,000 were used for officers and soldiers.

135 Grosz, *Autobiography*, p. 89.

136 General Henry Thoresby Hughes, quoted in 'Report of the Special Committee, Fourth Session, Thirteenth Parliament, 1920', in the Canadian Battlefields Memorials Commission, *Canadian Battlefield Memorials* (Ottawa, 1929), p. 76.
137 Walther Rathenau, *Walther Rathenau. Industrialist, Banker, Intellectual and Politician. Notes and Diaries 1907–1922*, ed. Hartmut Pogge von Strandmann (Oxford, 1985), p. 228.

8: The Bitter Aftermath of War

1 Political divisions and regional rivalries also blocked efforts to create a national monument to honour the nation's war dead. The lack of consensus over the meaning of the war and the politicization of the war experience was also revealed in squabbles over the nature and symbolic content of local war memorials. Was the war to be memorialized as a glorious chapter in the nation's history, or as a disaster? James M. Diehl, *The Thanks of the Fatherland. German Veterans after the Second World War* (Chapel Hill, 1993), p. 18. See also Wolfgang Ribbe, 'Flaggenstreit und Heiliger Hain. Bemerkungen zur nationalen Symbolik in der Weimarer Republik', in *Aus Theorie und Praxis der Geschichtswissenschaft. Festschrift für Hanz Herzfeld zum 80. Geburtstag* (Berlin, 1982), pp. 181–7; Meinhold Lurz, *Kriegerdenkmäler in Deutschland* (Heidelberg, 1985), vol. 4: *Weimarer Republik.*
2 On differing approaches to the commemoration of war see Alan Borg, *War Memorials. From Antiquity to the Present* (London, 1991).
3 *Pall Mall Gazette*, 2 September 1918.
4 George L. Mosse, *Fallen Soldiers. Reshaping the Memory of the World Wars* (Oxford, 1990), pp. 7–8.
5 In 1916 the Kaiser declared that the king of Belgium would not be permitted back to his country at the end of the war, and that 'the coast of Flanders must belong to us'; in July 1915 a group of 1,347 intellectuals signed a petition defending expansionist war aims. There are dozens of such examples, as cited in Fritz Fischer, *Griff nach der Weltmacht: Die Kriegszielpolitik des kaiserlichen Deutschland 1914–1918* (Düsseldorf, 1964), p. 198.
6 Reginald Isaacs, *Gropius. An Illustrated Biography of the Creator of the Bauhaus* (London, 1991), p. 58.
7 On propaganda and the popular view of inevitable victory see Ludwig von Knesebeck, *Die Wahrheit über die Propagandafeldzug und Deutschlands Zusammenbruch* (Munich, 1927); Harold D. Lasswell, *Propaganda Technique in the World War* (New York, 1927).
8 The delusion was in part to do with Ludendorff's tendency to lie to his own government, refusing to give Chancellor Hertling, Vice Chancellor Payer or Foreign Minister Hintze an honest account of the deterioration on the front. General Oldershausen returned from Berlin to inform Ludendorff that 'the people in Berlin, indeed in the leading positions, judged the situation in general as much too favourable' and had no idea of the actual military situation. Robert

B. Asprey, *The German High Command at War. Hindenburg and Ludendorff and the First World War* (London, 1994), pp. 462–3.

9 Even in August 1918 Ludendorff was claiming that he could win the war: 'I had to move troops back on five occasions during this war but in the end I beat the enemy. Why should this not happen for a sixth time?' he asked. K. Graf von Hertling, *Ein Jahr in der Reichskanzlei. Erinnerungen an die Kanzlerschaft meines Vaters* (Freiburg, 1919), pp. 145–6.

10 It was extraordinary that even at this point Hindenburg was stating that Germany should still try to retain the Longwy and Briey areas in France under any peace agreement. He was told by Paul von Hintze that Germany was in no position to dictate terms. Erich Eyck, 'The Generals and the Downfall of the German Monarchy 1917–1918', *Transactions of the Royal Historical Society*, vol. 2, 1952, p. 63; Asprey, *The German High Command*, p. 468. See also Gerhard Schultze-Pfaelzer, *Hindenburg: Peace, War, Aftermath*, trans. C. R. Turner (London, 1931).

11 Olga Djakova (ed.), *Leitfaden für Russen in Berlin* (Berlin, 1922), pp. 28–30.

12 For an excellent overview of the period see the catalogue to the exhibition held in 1996 in the Martin-Gropius-Bau, Berlin, and the Pushkin Museum, Moscow. Irina Antonova and Jörn Merkert (eds.), *Berlin–Moscow/Moscow–Berlin 1900–1950* (Munich, 1995), pp. 89–125.

13 Klaus Kändler et al. (eds.), *Berliner Begegnungen. Ausländische Künstler in Berlin 1918 bis 1933* (Berlin, 1987), p. 47.

14 Ilya Ehrenburg, *Menschen Jahre Leben,* (Munich, 1965), vol. 2, p. 515.

15 Roman Gul, *Russland in Deutschland* (New York, 1978), pp. 75–80; Alfred Döblin, *Ein Kerl muss eine Meinung haben. Berichte und Kritiken 1921–1924* (Munich, 1976), p. 32.

16 Alfred Dölling, *Das Schicksal des russischen Emigranten – Stationen des Exils – Konstantinopel – Paris – Berlin – zurück nach Russland* (Berlin, 1924); Andrej Belyj, *Eine der Wohnstätten des Schattenreichs*, trans. Birgit Veit (Leningrad, 1924).

17 Z. A. Zeman, *Germany and the Revolution in Russia 1915–1918* (London, 1950), p. 44–5.

18 Norman Stone, *Europe Transformed 1878–1919* (London, 1983), pp. 218–19.

19 James W. Gerard, *My Four Years in Germany* (London, 1917), pp. 301–2.

20 On German support of Lenin see Richard Pipes, *The Russian Revolution 1899–1918* (London, 1990), pp. 389–95.

21 Count von Brockdorff-Rantzau, German Ambassador in Copenhagen, to the Ministry of Foreign Affairs (Top Secret), 2 April 1917, reprinted in Alexander Solzhenitsyn, *Lenin in Zürich*, trans. H. T. Willetts (London, 1975).

22 For Lenin's relations with Germany I have drawn on Richard Pipes, *Russia under the Bolshevik Regime 1919–1924* (London, 1994), esp. pp. 166–92; Richard M. Watt, *The Kings Depart. The Tragedy of Germany: Versailles and the German Revolution* (London, 1968).

23 Message from Assistant Secretary of State von Stumm to Ambassador Romberg in Berlin, 31 March 1917, reprinted in Solzhenitsyn, *Lenin in Zürich*, p. 221.

24 Eduard Bernstein, *Die deutsche Revolution* (Berlin, 1921), vol. I, p. 187–8.

25 For the attitudes of the German General Staff to Brest-Litovsk see Winfried Baumgart, *Von Brest-Litovsk zur deutschen Novemberrevolution* (Göttingen, 1971), and Winfried Baumgart, *Deutsche Ostpolitik 1918* (Munich, 1966). See also John W. Wheeler-Bennett, *Brest-Litovsk. The Forgotten Peace* (London, 1938).

26 A. J. P. Taylor, *The Course of German History* (London, 1985), pp. 203–4.

27 Irrespective of Rathenau's reforms, the German army was still short of equipment and, above all, manpower. Tying up troops in the east was disastrous for the war in France. Gerald D. Feldman, *Army, Industry and Labor in German 1914–1918* (Princeton, 1966), pp. 91–3.

28 Again, in the speech to the Communist Party on 7 March 1918, Lenin announced that 'it is an absolute truth that we will sink without a German revolution'. W. I. Lenin, *Ausgewählte Werke* (Berlin, 1925), p. 493.

29 The Supplementary Treaty called for under the terms of Brest-Litovsk was signed by the Central Powers on 27 August 1918. Wheeler-Bennett, *The Forgotten Peace*.

30 Letter from Lenin to Y. A. Berzin, 14 August 1918, reprinted in Richard Pipes, *The Unknown Lenin* (Yale, 1996), p. 53.

31 Margarete Buber-Neumann, *Kriegsschauplätze der Weltrevolution. Ein Bericht aus der Praxis der Komintern 1919–1943* (Frankfurt-am-Main, 1973), p. 9.

32 Silvia Rodgers, *Red Saint, Pink Daughter. A Communist Childhood in Berlin and London* (London, 1996), p. 10.

33 The workers were becoming increasingly despondent. The Reichstag member Conrad Hausmann noted that 'the public no longer reads the army communiqués . . . People are concerned more and more only with food and clothing shortages'. Asprey, *The German High Command*, p. 403.

34 Jay Winter and Jean-Louis Robert, *Capital Cities at War. London, Paris, Berlin 1914–1919* (Cambridge, 1997), p. 101.

35 The Berlin metal workers were the first to ignore their party and trade union and support Spartacus. Ralph H. Lutz, *Fall of the German Empire 1914–1918* (Palo Alto, 1932) vol. 2, p. 233. For a participant's view see R. Müller, *Vom Kaiserreich zur Republik: Ein Beitrag zur Geschichte der revolutionären Arbeiterbewegung während des Weltkrieges*, 2 vol, (Berlin, 1924).

36 This was at least a factor, although the overriding concern was of course the fear that he had to attack before the Americans arrived in large numbers. Watt, *The Kings Depart*, p. 142. For a sympathetic view of the strikes see Annemarie Lange, *Das wilhelminische Berlin* (Berlin, 1967), pp. 732–3.

37 Max Hoffmann left an extraordinary record of the First World War in his diaries. Max Hoffmann, *Diaries and Other Papers*, ed. Karl Novak, trans. Eric Sutton (London, 1929).

38 Karl Liebknecht's speeches and samples of the Spartacus Letters are published as Karl Liebknecht, *The Future Belongs to the People* (New York, 1918), p. 85.

39 Isaacs, *Gropius*, p. 55.

40 On the devastating effect of the influenza pandemic see the figures compiled in the *Tabellen über die Bevölkerungsvorgänge Berlins* (Berlin, 1918).

41 Jürgen Kocka, *Klassengesellschaft im Krieg. Deutsche Sozialgeschichte 1914–1918* (Göttingen, 1973), p. 147.

42 Lutz, *Fall of the German Empire*, vol. 2, p. 382.

43 Charles Vidil, *Les Mutineries de la marine allemande* (Paris, 1931), p. 151.

44 The seaman Stumpf was on the battleship *Helgoland* in Kiel and wrote of the revolution in his diary. Daniel Horn, *Private War of Seaman Stumpf* (London, 1969), pp. 211–15. On the plans to attack the British fleet (Operation Plan 19) see H. E. H. von Waldeyer-Hartz, *Admiral von Hipper* (Berlin, 1933), p. 237.

45 On 30 October William had complained to Hindenburg that 'Prince Max's government is trying to throw me out!' and on 1 November he declared to an emissary from Berlin: 'I wouldn't dream of abandoning the throne because of a few hundred Jews and a thousand workers. Tell that to your masters in Berlin.' Alan Palmer, *The Kaiser. Warlord of the Second Reich* (London, 1978), p. 209. The Wolff Press agency statement was issued on 9 November 1918. See Prince Max von Baden, *Memoirs*, (London, 1928), vol. 1, pp. 198–200.

46 Lutz, *Fall of the German Empire*, vol. 2, p. 473.

47 Theodor Wolff, *Through Two Decades* (London, 1936), p. 122.

48 After 9 November, Scheidemann noted, it was 'impossible' for the Kaiser to carry on. Philipp Scheidemann, *Der Zusammenbruch* (Berlin, 1921), p. 210.

49 Count Kuno von Westarp, *Das Ende der Monarchie am 9 November 1918* (Berlin, 1952), pp. 61–3; G. R. Halkett, *The Dear Monster* (London, 1939), p. 107; General Wilhelm Groener, *Lebenserinnerungen* (Göttingen, 1957), p. 485–6.

50 Carl Zuckmayer, *A Part of Myself* (London, 1970), p. 178.

51 Philipp Scheidemann, *Memoiren* (Dresden, 1928), vol. 2, pp. 522–3. The events are described in Alex de Jonge, *The Weimar Chronicle. Prelude to Hitler* (London, 1978), pp. 25–49.

52 Liebknecht's declaration is described in Ruth Fischer, *Stalin and German Communism. A Study in the Origins of the State Party* (Cambridge, Mass., 1948), p. 60. See also Gerhard A. Ritter and Susanne Miller (eds.), *Die deutsche Revolution 1918–1919, Dokumente* (Hamburg, 1975).

53 Ernst Troeltsch, *Spektator-Briefe. Aufsätze über die deutsche Revolution und die Weltpolitik 1918–1922* (Tübingen, 1924), p. 33. See also Koppel S. Pinson, *Modern Germany. It's History and Civilization* (New York, 1963), p. 365.

54 The report of the adjutant is reprinted in de Jonge, *The Weimar Chronicle*, p. 31.

55 Klaus Dettmer, *Arbeitslose in Berlin. Zur politischen Geschichte der Arbeitslosenbewegung zwischen 1918 und 1923* (dissertation, Freie Universität Berlin, 1977), pp. 51–7. See also Richard Geary and Dick Geary (eds.), *The German Unemployed, experiences and consequences of mass unemployment from the Weimar Republic to the Third Reich* (London, 1987).

56 Winter and Robert, *Capital Cities at War*, p. 217.

57 The leaders also published a 'Spartacus Manifesto' calling on the people to fight: 'Proletarians of all countries! This must be the last war! We owe that to the twelve million murdered victims; we owe that to our children; we owe that to humanity.' The manifesto was published in the *New York Times*, 29 November 1918.

58 Pipes, *Russia under the Bolshevik Regime*, p. 168; for the opposite view see Klaus Mammach, *Der Einfluss der russischen Februarrevolution und der grossen*

sozialistischen Oktoberrevolution auf die deutsche Arbeiterklasse, Februar 1917–Oktober 1918 (Berlin, 1955).

59 Georg Grosz, *The Autobiography of Georg Grosz. A Small Yes and a Big No*, trans. Arnold J. Pomerans, (London, 1982), p. 95.

60 Robert Scholz, 'Ein unruhiges Jahrzehnte: Lebensmittelunruhe, Massenstreiks und Arbeitslosenkrawalle in Berlin 1914–1923', in Manfred Gailus (ed.), *Pöbelexzesse und Volkstumulte in Berlin. Zur Sozialgeschichte der Strasse (1830–1980)* (Berlin, 1984), pp. 79–122.

61 Liebknecht had tried to rally support for Eichhorn on 21 November but the march was stopped by Otto Wels. The 7 December rally at the Siegesallee was much more effective. A. J. Ryder, *The German Revolution of 1918–1919* (Cambridge, 1967), p. 184.

62 The constitution, written by a group of jurists led by Hugo Preuss, named Germany a republic. It was to be led by a President who was to be elected by the people every seven years; he was given the power of nominating the Chancellor, appointing public officials and commanding the armed forces. He was also given emergency powers to deal with domestic insurrection and seize state governments in turmoil. The men who drafted the constitution believed that the Chancellor and the Reichstag would dominate German politics but, as Paul Bookbinder has pointed out, they should have listened to the jurist Carl Schmitt, who believed that in reality the constitution gave primary power to the President, and who wrote, 'Whoever decides in the exceptional case is sovereign.' The constitution combined elements of the British parliamentary system, Soviet workers' councils and the American presidential system. Above all it was created in the name of the people: 'The German people, united in their racial elements and impelled by the will to renew and strengthen their Reich in freedom and justice, to serve the ends of peace at home and abroad and to further social progress, have established this Constitution,' see Carl Schmitt, *Die Diktatur – von den Anfängen der modernen Souveränität bis zum proletarischen Klassenkampf* (Munich, 1938), p. 180; Paul Bookbinder, *Weimar Germany* (New York, 1996), p. 43.

63 Groener, *Lebenserinnerungen*, pp. 473–6; see also de Jonge, *The Weimar Chronicle*, p. 28; John Wheeler-Bennett, *The Nemesis of Power: The German Army in Politics 1918–1945* (London, 1953), pp. 21–2.

64 Noske's and Ebert's visit to Zossen is described by Maercker in Ludwig R. von Maercker, *Vom Kaiserheer zur Reichswehr* (Leipzig, 1921), p. 64. See also Gustav Noske, *Von Kiel bis Kapp* (Berlin, 1920), pp. 61–70.

65 Winter and Robert, *Capital Cities at War*, pp. 59–60. The confusion in the figures stems from the distinction between Berlin before and after 1920, when the city was expanded to include suburban areas.

66 Robert G. L. Waite, *Vanguard of Nazism. The Free Corps Movement in Post-War Germany, 1918–1923* (Cambridge, Mass., 1952), pp. 22–30.

67 Noske referred with pride to those 'monarchists' and former officers he had recruited who had already been 'beaten and spat upon'. Noske, *Von Kiel bis Kapp*, p. 70. In fact Noske wrote *Von Kiel bis Kapp* to legitimate his actions before the Social Democratic Party Congress of 1919.

68 The battle is vividly described in Werner T. Angress, *Stillborn Revolution. The*

Communist Bid for Power in Germany, 1919–1923 (Princeton, 1963); see also Watt, *The Kings Depart*, pp. 240–74.

69 Karl Heinz Luther, 'Die nachrevolutionären Machtkämpfe in Berlin. November 1918 bis März 1919' in *Jahrbuch für die Geschichte Mittel- und Ostdeutschlands*, 8, 1959, pp. 187–221.

70 Despite later Communist versions of events Spartacus had not succeeded in becoming representative of Berlin workers. For the East German view see, for example, 'Die Gründung der Spartacusgruppe', in Dr Wolfgang Büttner (ed.), *Geschichte* (Berlin, 1985), pp. 222–3. See also K. Retzlaw, *Spartacus. Aufsteig und Niedergang eines Parteiarbeiters* (Frankfurt-am-Main, 1972), p. 64; Eberhardt Kolb, *Die Arbeiterräte in der deutsche Innenpolitik 1918–19* (Frankfurt-am-Main, 1978), p. 48.

71 For Luxemburg's comments on Radek see J. P. Nettl, *Rosa Luxemburg* (London, 1966), vol. 2, p. 471.

72 Karl Radek, 'Erinnerungen', trans. O. E. Schüddekopf, in *Archiv für Sozialgeschichte*, vol. 2, 1962, p. 95; for an interesting fictional account of his life see Stefan Heym, *Radek* (Munich, 1995).

73 The investigation into the murders of Karl Liebknecht and Rosa Luxemburg was published as *Der Mord an Karl Liebknecht und Rosa Luxemburg. Zusammenfassende Darstellung des gesamten Untersuchungsmaterials mit ausführlichem Prozessbericht* (Berlin, 1920).

74 The Prussian Investigating Commission reported that, in all, 196 people had been killed during the January riots and that 1,175 had died in the March insurrection. The statistics were published in *Vorwärts*, 9 April 1919.

75 The elections to the National Assembly took place on 19 January 1919. The Volkspartei received 16.4 million votes, the SPD 11.4, although in Berlin the vote went to the left. Christian Engelii and Wolfgang Haus (eds.), *Quellen zum modernen Gemeindeverfassungsrecht in Deutschland* (Stuttgart, 1975), p. 579–600.

76 Count Harry Kessler, *Tagebücher 1918–1937* (Frankfurt-am-Main, 1961), p. 27. For a description of the street fighting see Watt, *The Kings Depart*, pp. 203–73.

77 See, for example, Max Beckmann's *The Night* (1918–19) – Kunstsammlung Nordrhein-Westfalen, Düsseldorf – which depicts the sadistic treatment meted out to a family, perhaps of revolutionaries. A man is being tortured and strangled; the woman at the front of the painting has been stripped and raped before being tied to a window frame; see also Max Ernst, *The Bellowing of a Savage Soldier* (1919), Arturo Schwarz, Milan; Otto Dix, *The Cry* (1919), Kunstgalerie, Gera, Saxony.

78 *Tabellen über die Bevölkerungsvorgänge Berlins* (Berlin, 1918). See also F. Bumm (ed.), *Deutschlands Gesundheitsverhältnisse unter dem Einfluss des Weltkrieges*, (Stuttgart, 1928), vol. 1; Winter and Robert, *Capital Cities at War*, pp. 480–85.

79 Ernst Jünger, *Der Kampf als Inneres Erlebnis* (Berlin, 1922).

80 Klabund, 'Ich baumle mit de Beene', in Dorothea Gotfurt, *While I'm Sitting on the Fence* (London, 1967), p. 47.

81 Walther Mehring, 'Die Kartenhexe'; Erich Kästner, 'Wir sitzen all im gleichen Zug', both reprinted in Gotfurt, *While I'm Sitting on the Fence*, pp. 57–65.

82 Peter Jelavich, *Berlin Cabaret* (London, 1996), p. 144.

83 For an overview of the Dadaists in the city see Karl Riha (ed.), *Dada Berlin: Texte, Manifeste, Aktionen* (Stuttgart, 1977); see also Walther Mehring, *Berlin Dada: Eine Chronik* (Zurich, 1959).

84 Käthe Kollwitz, *Die Lebenden dem Toten. Erinnerung an den 15. Januar 1919*, (Gedenkblatt für Karl Liebknecht), Kassel, Arbeitsgemeinschaft Friedhof und Denkmal, Stiftung Zentralinstitut und Museum für Sepulkralkultur; Conrad Felixmuller also did a lithograph of Karl Liebknecht and Rosa Luxemburg, *Menschen über der Welt*, Museum Wiesbaden.

85 See, for exmaple, his *Skin Graft*, in which a soldier is shown sitting in bed: one side of his face is unscathed but on the other his nose has been broken and pushed towards his cheek, which is in turn ripped away to reveal a row of teeth. The top part of his head is a mound of flesh while the skin on his forehead has been torn off. Otto Dix, *Skin Graft* (1924), British Museum, London.

86 On Versailles see Eberhard Kolb, *Die Weimarer Republik* (Munich, 1984), pp. 28–33; on the 'War Guilt' Clause 231 see Alma Luckau, *The German Delegation at the Paris Peace Conference* (New York, 1941), p. 242.

87 Ulrich Heinemann, *Die verdrängte Niederlage. Politische Offentlichkeit und Kriegsschuldfrage in der Weimarer Republik* (Göttingen, 1983).

88 An article about the assassination of Rathenau and the Feme murders stated that 'The assassination of Dr Walther Rathenau is the 378th political murder in Germany since the formation of the Republic, and some press dispatches point out that in 353 cases the guilty persons either escaped or were acquitted by reactionary courts.' 'The German Republic's Trail of Blood', *Literary Digest*, 8 July 1922.

89 Heinrich Hannover and Elisabeth Hannover, *Politische Justiz 1918–1933* (Frankfurt-am-Main, 1966), pp. 60–78.

90 *Vossische Zeitung*, no. 154, 24 March 1920.

91 Walter Gropius, Denkmal der Märzgefallenen (1921), which stands in the old Weimar cemetery. In a letter to Donald Egbert on 14 October 1948 he wrote that 'The concrete memorial in Weimar was not designed for working men but for people of different circles of the population who fell in the upheaval of the *kapputsch* [sic]. It was ordered by a Staatsrat in the Weimar Ministry who was a social democrat.'

92 Harold James, *The German Slump. Politics and Economics 1924–1936* (Oxford, 1987), p. 41; Gustav Stolper, *German Economy 1870–1940* (New York, 1940), pp. 355–67.

93 W. Aubin and H. Zorn (eds.), *Handbuch der deutschen Wirtschafts- und Sozialgeschichte* (Stuttgart, 1976), vol. 2, p. 700.

94 Those who advocated a policy of reconciliation and reconstruction faced a thankless task. On 7 July 1921 Walther Rathenau delivered a speech to the Reichstag stating, 'I am convinced that the world does not consist one hundred per cent of chauvinists, nor does it consist of 150 million enemies; it also contains a large number of objective people. The millions of eyes of such people turn to Germany and enquire: What will Germany do? Will it lead a life of reconciliation and fulfilment or not? Not enslavement; none of us want that; but it is in keeping with the dignity of a debtor to pay.' But Rathenau was detested by

those who already believed in the 'stab-in-the-back' legend and a particularly virulent wave of anti-Semitism swept Berlin; on 24 June 1922 Rathenau was assassinated by a group of nationalists. Rathenau, quoted in Pinson, *Modern Germany*, p. 429. On his negotiations with the Reparations Commission in Paris see *Walther Rathenau. Industrialist, Banker, Intellectual and Politician. Notes and Diaries 1907–1922*, ed. Hartmut Pogge von Strandmann (Oxford, 1985), pp. 288–90.

95 On the strike and its consequences see Oskar Rusch, *Der Streik in der Berliner Metallindustrie im Jahre 1919* (Berlin, 1920).

96 For the effects of the inflation see H. A. Winkler, *Von der Revolution zur Stabilisierung. Arbeiter und Arbeiterbewegung in der Weimarer Republik 1918 bis 1924* (Berlin, 1984).

97 Hans Oswald, *Sittengeschichte der Inflation. Ein Kulturdokument aus den Jahren des Marksturzes* (Berlin, 1931), pp 30–32.

98 The contempt for those who came through the war unscathed and with vast wealth is evident in Hubertus Maria Davringhausen's painting *The Profiteer* (1920). The subject sits at his desk in a pristine modern office block, a telephone off the hook beside a glass of wine and a case of cigars. Kunstmuseum, Düsseldorf.

99 Grosz, *Autobiography*, p. 95.

100 Ibid., p. 115.

101 Winter and Robert, *Capital Cities at War*, p. 458.

102 Stefan Zweig, *Meisternovellen* (Frankfurt-am-Main, 1970). Erich Maria Remarque, *Der schwarze Obelisk: Geschichte einer verspäteten Jugend* (Cologne, 1971).

9: THE GOLDEN TWENTIES

1 On Weimar culture see, above all, Peter Gay, *Weimar Culture. The Outsider As Insider* (Harmondsworth, 1988). See also J. Hermand and F. Trommler, *Die Kultur der Weimarer Republik* (Munich, 1978); Walter Laqueur, *Weimar. A Cultural History, 1918–1933* (London, 1974).

2 Gay, *Weimar Culture*, p. 138.

3 As Volker Berghahn has put it, 'the roots of this postwar militarism are to be found not only in the intensive mobilization of the population . . . but also in the defeat which broad sections of the nation flatly refused to accept.' Volker R. Berghahn, *Militarism. The History of an International Debate 1861–1979* (Leamington Spa, 1981), p. 33.

4 This was particularly true of the para-military organizations from the Stahlhelm to the Jungdeutscher Orden and the Rotfrontkämpferbund, but their views were widely accepted. Volker R. Berghahn, *Der Stahlhelm, Bund der Frontsoldaten, 1918–1935* (Düsseldorf, 1966), pp. 91–4.

5 Radek's visitors included Finance Minister Wirth, General von Seeckt, and Ago von Maltzan, head of the Russian desk in the Foreign Ministry. 'Radek's "Political Salon" in Berlin 1919', *Soviet Studies*, 3, 1951–2, pp. 411–30.

6 Seeckt wanted nothing less than action by the two powers Russia and Germany to erase Poland from the map and restore the 1914 frontier, a view which he made clear on numerous occasions. His memorandum of 11 September 1922 and other documents reveal a deep hatred for Poland. Hans Meier-Welcker, *Seeckt* (Frankfurt-am-Main, 1967), pp. 343–4. See also *Deutsch-sowjetische Beziehungen von den Verhandlungen in Brest-Litovsk bis zum Abschluss des Rapallo-Vertrages* (Berlin Ost, 1967–71), vol. 2; H. L. Dyck, *Weimar Germany and Soviet Russia 1926–1933* (New York, 1966).

7 Friedrich von Rabenau, *Seeckt. Aus seinem Leben 1918–1936* (Leipzig, 1940), p. 194. See also Wipert von Blücher, *Deutschlands Weg nach Rapallo* (Wiesbaden, 1951), p. 152; Reginald H. Phelps, 'Aus den Seekt-Dokumentation: Die Verabschiedung Seeckts 1926', *Deutsche Rundschau*, September 1952.

8 Count von Brockdorff-Rantzau, who was made German ambassador to Moscow after the signing of Rapallo, referred to Lenin and his government as 'mere criminals', but this did not prevent him from implementing the treaty in Germany's favour. In 1919 he had said that Germany should 'play down the extent of military defeat' so that 'in the final battle we shall be the victors'. A treaty with Soviet Russia was part of this strategy. G. W. Hallgarten, 'General Hans von Seeckt and Russia, 1920–1922', *Journal of Modern History*, xxxi, 1949, pp. 28–34. See also Gustav Hilger and Alfred C. Meyer, *The Incompatible Allies* (New York, 1953), p. 91.

9 For his part Lenin said of the war that the overthrow of Poland offered a unique opportunity to liquidate the entire Versailles settlement. 'By destroying the Polish army we are destroying the Versailles Treaty ... Had Poland become Soviet ... the whole international system arising from the victories over Germany would have been destroyed.' Only the Soviet failure stymied these plans. Richard Pipes, *Russia Under the Bolshevik Regime 1919–1924* (London, 1994), pp. 182, 425–8.

10 This echoed the Social Democrat Scheidemann's equally bizarre slogan in defence of the Kaiser at the outbreak of the First World War, in which he said: 'We are defending the fatherland in order to conquer it.' Gerhard Masur, *Imperial Berlin* (London, 1971), p. 267.

11 On the evolution of Rapallo and Rathenau's involvement see David Felix, *Walther Rathenau and the Weimar Republic. The Politics of Reparations* (London, 1971), pp. 127–47. On the industrial advantages for Germany see H. Pogge von Strandmann, 'Grossindustrie und Rapallopolitik. Deutsch-sowjetisch Handelsbeziehungen in der Weimarer Republik', in *Historische Zeitschrift*, vol. 222, 1976, pp. 265–341; see also H. Heilbig, *Die Träger der Rapallo-Politik* (Göttingen, 1958); Theodor Schieder, 'Die Entstehungsgeschichte des Rapallo-Vertrates', *Historische Zeitschrift*, 204, 1967.

12 In fact the negotiations had been less than cordial. On Wilson see Ray Stannard Baker, *Woodrow Wilson and World Settleemnt* (Gloucester, Mass., 1930), vol. 3, pp. 460–68.

13 André François-Poncet, *Der Weg von Versailles biz Potsdam. Die Geschichte der Jahre 1919 bis 1945* (Mainz/Berlin, 1964), pp. 68–9.

14 The Americans later refused to ratify the treaty. Ferdinand Czernin, *Versailles*

1919. *The Forces, Events and Personalities that Shaped the Treaty* (New York, 1964), pp. 397–421.

15 Erich Eyck, *Geschichte der Weimarer Republik (Zürich/Stuttgart, 1957)*, vol. I: *Vom zusammenbruch des Kaisertums bis zur Wahl Hindenburgs*, p. 255.

16 This is revealed in the diary of Viscount d'Abernon, British ambassador to Berlin from 1920 to 1926. On his friendship with Stresemann see Edgar Viscount d'Abernon, *An Ambassador of Peace: Pages from the Diary of Viscount d'Abernon* (London, 1929–30), vol. I, p. 290.

17 Nationalists objected to the Dawes Plan on the basis that the payment of any reparations was an affront to the German nation. Stresemann was bitterly attacked and compared his situation to that of a condemned man who will be spared if he teaches the king's horse to fly. One could not refuse to try 'because the king, the horse or I may die', and you never know, 'the horse may even learn to fly'. Anneliese Thimme, *Gustav Stresemann, eine politische Biographie zur Geschichte der Weimarer Republik* (Frankfurt-am-Main, 1957), p. 70.

18 Hugh Quigley and R. T. Clark, *Republican Germany: A Political and Economic Study* (London, 1928), p. 119.

19 On the importance of the German merchant marine to the recovery see Henry Meyer (ed.), *The Long Generation. Germany from Empire to Ruin, 1913–1945* (New York, 1973), p. 12. See also Ferdinand Friedensburg, *Die Weimarer Republik* (Frankfurt-am-Main, 1957), p. 211.

20 Many nationalists objected because although the agreement guaranteed Germany's western frontier it accepted the loss of Alsace-Lorraine. On the eve of the conference preparations were marred by 'a persistent rumor that German Nationalists have planned to assassinate Dr Stresemann rather than permit him to conclude with the Allies a compact for the security of Europe laid within the terms of the Treaty of Versailles. Discovery of the plot by the Berlin police is responsible, it is understood, for the strange action of Dr Stresemann and Dr Luther in leaving the special German delegation train at Bellinzona and motoring to Locarno after dark last night.' *New York Times*, 5 October 1925. See also Jon Jacobson, *Locarno Diplomacy. Germany and the West, 1925–1929* (Princeton, NJ, 1972); see also W. Link, *Die amerikanische Stabiliserungspolitik in Deutschland 1921-1932* (Düsseldorf, 1970).

21 This was shattered by the severe depression at the end of the 1920s and gave 'spectacular justification for the Nazi regime'. Harold James, *The German Slump. Politics and Economics 1924–1936* (Oxford, 1987), p. 7. See also John W. Wheeler-Bennett, *Information on the Reparation Settlement, Being the Background and History of the Young Plan and the Hague Agreements, 1929–1930* (London, 1930).

22 Gay, *Weimar Culture*, p. 139.

23 The unification formally took place on 27 April 1920 under the jurisdiction of Oberbürgermeister Wermuth, but it was his successor Oberbürgermeister Böss who was responsible for implementing the policy. On the contributions of the two appointees see Henning Köhler, 'Die Schaffung von Gross-Berlin und der Sturz Wermuth' and 'Politik und Verwaltung: Die 'Ara Boss', in Wolfgang Ribbe (ed.), *Geschichte Berlins* (Munich, 1987), vol. 2: *Von der Märzrevolution bis zur*

Gegenwart, pp. 815–75. See also Christian Engeli, *Gustav Böss. Oberbürgermeister von Berlin 1921–1930* (Stuttgart, 1971).

24 After the war government expenditure as a proportion of national income rose from 14.5 per cent (1910–13) to 24 per cent (1925–9). Furthermore, a greater part of government expenditure was controlled by the central state. Reich expenditure was just over 40 per cent of all government spending in 1913 but by 1925 it represented 45 per cent. Where before the war most Reich spending had been military by 1925 it accounted for only 9 per cent of the Reich's total. James, *The German Slump*, p. 39.

25 Otto Büsch, *Die Berliner Kommunalwirtschaft in der Weimarer Epoche* (Berlin, 1960).

26 Carl Zuckmayer, 'Warum den Weinen . . .', in *Als wär's ein Stück von mir. Horen der Freundschaft* (Frankfurt-am-Main, 1976), vol. 2, p. 325.

27 On the artists in other cities, including Dresden, Munich, Karlsruhe, Cologne, Düsseldorf and Hanover, see Sergiusz Michalski, *Neue Sachlichkeit. Malerei, Graphik und Photographie in Deutschland 1919–1933* (Cologne, 1992).

28 Gay, *Weimar Culture*, p. 135; see also Willy Haas, *Erinnerungen* (Berlin, 1960); Willy Haas, *Sitten und Kultur in Nachkriegsdeutschland* (Berlin, 1932).

29 Gay, *Weimar Culture*, p. 135.

30 Siegfried Kracauer, *Das Ornament der Masse* (Frankfurt-am-Main, 1977), p. 93.

31 Max Weber, *Gesammelte Aufsätze zur Wissenschaftslehre* (Tübingen, 1951), p. 526.

32 Hans Gotthard Vierhuff, *Die neue Sachlichkeit. Malerie und Fotografie* (Cologne, 1980), p. 9.

33 See, for example, Boris Pasternak, 'Briefe aus Berlin'; Andrei Bely, 'Wie schön es in Berlin ist', in Fritz Mierau (ed.), *Russen in Berlin, 1918–1933* (Leipzig, 1988), pp. 69–74, 56–68. See also Sergei Tretjakov, *Gesichter der Avantgarde. Porträts – Essays – Briefe* (Berlin, 1985); Vladimir Nabokov, *Laughter in the Dark* (Harmondsworth, 1963); Erich Bucholz, 'Begegnung mit osteuropäischen Künstlern', in *Avantgarde Osteuropa 1910 bis 1930* (Berlin, 1967); Klaus Kändler et al. (eds.), *Berliner Begegnungen. Ausländische Künstler in Berlin 1918–1933* (Berlin, 1987).

34 Igor Sewerianin Mayakovsky, *Berlin Heute* (Berlin, 1923), p. 55; see also Kynaston McShine, *Berlinart 1961–1987* (New York, 1987), p. 52.

35 There is a huge literature on the Bauhaus; see, for example, Marcel Franciscono, *Walter Gropius and the Creation of the Bauhaus at Weimar* (University of Illinois, 1971); H. M. Wingler, *The Bauhaus* (Cambridge, Mass., 1962); Karl-Heinz Hüter, *Das Bauhaus in Weimar* (Berlin, 1976). On the Bauhaus in Berlin see Peter Hahn (ed.), *Bauhaus Berlin. Auflösung Dessau 1932, Schliessung Berlin 1933* (Berlin, 1985).

36 Gropius outlines the basic principles, from 'standardization' to 'rationalization', in Walter Gropius, *Die neue Architektur und das Bauhaus – Grundzüge und Entwicklung. Einer Konzeption* (Mainz/Berlin, 1965).

37 On the contemporary view of the housing problem see Martin Wagner (ed.), *Das neue Berlin. Grosstadtprobleme* (Berlin, 1929). Wagner was in charge of construction in the district of Schöneberg; in 1924 he worked for the Deutsche Wohnungsfürsorge AG (DEWOG) and with Bruno Taut planned the Hufeisensiedlung in Britz.

38 'Siedlungsbau', in Norbert Huse, *Neues Bauen' – 1918 bis 1933. Moderne Architektur in der Weimarer Republik* (Munich, 1975), pp. 91–103.

39 Barbara Miller Lane, *Architecture and Politics in Germany 1918–1945* (Cambridge, Mass., 1968), 'The New Architecture and the Vision of a New Society', pp. 41–69.

40 John Willet, *The New Sobriety. Art and Politics in the Weimar Period 1917–1933* (London, 1987), p. 79.

41 Georg Simmel, *The Philosophy of Money*, trans. Tom Bottomore and David Frisby (Boston, 1978).

42 'Der Linden lang! Galopp! Galopp!/ Zu Fuss, zu Pferd, zu Zweit!/ Mit der Uhr in der Hand, mit'm Hut auf'm Kopp/ Keine Zeit! Keine Zeit! Keine Zeit!' Walther Mehring, *Heimat Berlin* (Berlin, 1920).

43 August Endell, *Die Schönheit der grossen Stadt* (Stuttgart, 1908), p. 23.

44 Jerzy Toeplitz, *Geschichte des Films 1895–1928* (Berlin, 1992), vol. 1, p. 21; see also Michael Hanisch, *Auf dem Spuren des Filmgeschichte* (Berlin, 1991); Uta Berg-Ganschow and Wolfgang Jacobsen, *... Film ... Stadt ... Kino ... Berlin ...* (Berlin, 1987). Many original film posters are stored at the Stiftung Deutsche Kinemathek, Berlin.

45 Many of these items are collected at the Siemens Museum in Munich, and at the Berliner Kraft- und Licht (Bewag) – AG Gerätesammlung, Berlin. See also Rosmarie Beier, 'Rationalisierung der Arbeit', in Gottfried Korff and Reinhard Rürup (eds.), *Berlin, Berlin. Die Ausstellung zur Geschichte der Stadt* (Berlin, 1987), pp. 401–10.

46 One of the symbols of the age was the Kraftwerk Rummelsburg, the Rummelsburg power plant. Started in 1925 by AEG it was constructed to a plan by Gustav Klingenberg and by 1927 was producing 270,000 kilowatts. Berliners were proud of the fact that it contained the 'largest turbines in the world' and had one of the most modern control centres yet built.

47 Mischa Spoliansky and Marcellus Schiffer had less success with their other 'department store' production called *Rufen Sie Herrn Plim!* (Get Mr Plim!), a critique of consumerism in which the main character, the manager of a large store, is tormented by a series of angry customers. In 'Schaufensterreklame' Sergei Tretyakov called Berlin a city made for consumerism, all 'asphalted, glassed in, polished like a mirror'. Sergei Tretyakov, 'Nu kupite zh!' *Krasnaja riva*, 1931, no. 27, p. 7.

48 On the fascination with America and modernism in Weimar Berlin see Botho-Michael Baumunk, 'Die schnellste Stadt der Welt', in Korff and Rürup, *Berlin, Berlin*, pp. 459–512.

49 Christian Morgenstern, *Melancholie. Gedichte.* (Berlin, 1906), 'Berlin', p. 37.

50 Paul Lincke had originally written the song 'Glühwürmschen, Glühwürmschen flimmre' for his 1902 operetta *Lysistrata*.

51 Alex de Jong, *The Weimar Chronicle. Prelude to Hitler* (London, 1978), p. 130; see also Sefton Delmer, *Weimar Germany* (London, 1972).

52 Kästner was generally critical of Weimar Berlin in keeping with the value of the Neue Sachlichkeit writers. In his cutting 1931 novel *Fabian* about the depression, he called Berlin a huge city of stone which was rotten to the core:

'Crime resides in the east, chicanery in the centre, poverty in the north, depravity in the west and decadence in any direciton you can name.' Erich Kästner, *Fabian. Die Geschichte eines Moralisten*, (Munich, 1989), p. 98. The work is reprinted in a volume which also contains autobiographical fragments, including an essay describing Kästner's first impressions of Berlin. See Erich Kästner, 'Meine sonnige Jugend', Rodolf Walter Leonhardt (ed.), *Kästner für Erwachsene* (Cologne, 1966).

53 Joan Weinstein, *The End of Expressionism. Art and the November Revolution in Germany 1918–19* (Chicago, 1990), p. 242.

54 Christian Schad, *Selbstbildnis mit Modell* (1927), private collection; *Zwei Freundinnen* (1928), private collection; Rudolf Schlichter, *Treffen der Fetischisten* (1921), private collection, reprinted in Michalski, *Neue Sachlichkeit*, pp. 24–51.

55 For early radio programmes see 'Funkstunde Berlin AG. Rund um den Rundfunk', in Bärbel Schrader and Jürgen Schebera, *Kunst-Metropole Berlin 1918–1933* (Berlin, 1987), pp. 176–96.

56 There was still hostility to the new art. On 4 June 1929 Schoenberg wrote to Wilhelm Furtwängler complaining about changes to a programme: 'Dear Herr Doktor . . . I am somewhat disappointed that you didn't do my orchestral pieces again after the scenes in Berlin, considering, after all, that the hissing was of oafish impertinence to you as much as to me.' Catherine Lorenz (ed.), *Arnold Schönberg 1874–1951. Lebensgeschichte in Begegnungen* (Vienna, 1992), p. 121.

57 Günther Rühle, *Theater für die Republik im Spiegel der Kritik* (Frankfurt-am-Main, 1998), vol. 1, pp. 24–5.

58 Indeed Oliver Sayler claims that it was Max Reinhardt who made Berlin into a theatre city again after the First World War. Oliver M. Sayler, *Max Reinhardt and His Theater*, trans. Mariele S. Gudernatsch, (New York, 1968), p. 37.

59 Erwin Piscator, *Das politische Theater* (Hamburg, 1963), pp. 44–51.

60 On Brecht's first visit to Berlin on 21 February 1920 see Werner Mittenzwei, *Das Leben des Bertolt Brecht oder Der Umgang mit den Welträtseln* (Berlin, 1987), pp. 154–8.

61 Alfred Kerr did, however, praise Lotte Lenya's performance. Count Harry Kessler wrote that it was a 'Gripping production, Piscatoresque, primitive and proletarian'. Graf Harry Kessler, *Tagebücher, 1918–1937* (Frankfurt-am-Main, 1961), p. 349.

62 Robert Walser, *Aufsätze* (Frankfurt-am-Main, 1985), p. 87.

63 For him such behaviour was tantamount to a betrayal of the ideals of 1918; see Alfred Döblin, *Verratenes Volk* (Munich, 1948).

64 For a sentimental portrait of café life see Jürgen Schebera, *Damals in Romanischen Café* . . . (Berlin, 1988). See also Peter Hielscher, 'Das Gedränge der Namen', in Korff and Rürup, *Berlin, Berlin*, pp. 431–42.

65 Eberhard Roters, 'Café und Cabaret', in Eberhard Roters and Bernhard Schulz (eds.), *Ich und die Stadt. Mensch und Grosstadt in der deutschen Kunst des 20. Jahrhunderts* (Berlin, 1987), pp. 109–30.

66 In a letter to Josef Ponten of 29 March 1919 he had written, 'I prefer not to start on politics . . . Communism, as I understand it, contains much that is good and human. Its goal is ultimately the total dissolution of the state (which

will always be dedicated to power), the humanization and purification of the world by de-politicizing it. At bottom, who would be against that?' Thomas Mann, *The Letters of Thomas Mann, 1889–1955*, ed. Richard Winston (London, 1970), vol. 1, pp. 92–3.

67 Thomas Mann, *Reflections of a Nonpolitical Man* (New York, 1983); see also M. Swales, 'In Defence of Weimar: Thomas Mann and the Politics of Republicanism', in A. Bance (ed.), *Writer and Society in the Weimar Republic* (Edinburgh, 1982), pp. 1–12.

68 But, as Golo Mann points out, '*The Magic Mountain* was the representative novel of the Stresemann years, a work which provided stimulus and first-class entertainment but did not tell people what to think and why.' Golo Mann, *The History of Germany since 1789* (London, 1988), p. 611.

69 Kurt Tucholsky, *Gesammelte Werke*, (eds.) Mary Gerold-Tucholsky and Fritz J. Raddatz (Hamburg, 1962), vol. 2, p. 790.

70 Raoul Hausmann (1919), quoted in Peter Jelavich, *Berlin Cabaret* (Harvard, 1993), p. 144.

71 M. Stark, *Deutsche Intellektuelle 1910–1933* (Heidelberg, 1984), p. 275.

72 A recording of the sketch was made by Paul Morgan in 1930; the complete text was printed in 'Zeitungsparodie', *Frechheit* September 1929. Jelavich, *Berlin Cabaret*, p. 200.

73 Jelavich, *Berlin Cabaret*, p. 198; Kurt Robitschek, '5 Jahre Kabarett der Komiker', *Frechheit*, September 1929. In 1926 he went so far as to say that the 'art form has died out'. Alan Lareau, *The Wild Stage: Literary Cabarets of the Weimar Republic* (Columbia, 1995), p. 184–5.

74 Lacqueur, *Weimar*, p. 710.

75 See for example, Friedrich Holländer's song 'Der Spuk persönlich', in *Spuk in der Villa Stern* (Berlin, 1931). On the *Weltbühne* debacle see Gay, *Weimar Culture*, p. 78; Martin Broszat, *Der Staat Hitlers* (Munich, 1969), p. 94; Istvan Deak, *Weimar Germany's Left-Wing Intellectuals. A Political History of the Weltbühne and Its Circle* (Berkeley, 1968).

76 Dorothy Rowe, 'Desiring Berlin. Gender and Modernity in Weimar Germany', in Marsha Meskimmon and Shearer West (eds.), *Visions of the 'Neue Frau'. Women and the Visual Arts in Weimar Germany* (Aldershot, 1995), pp. 143–4.

77 On the vote see Gabrielle Bremme, *Die politische Rolle der Frau in Deutschland* (Göttingen, 1956); see also Clare Mende, 'Darf die Frau ihr Wahlrecht wieder aufgeben?', *Deutsche Stimmen*, xxxvii, no. 2, January 1925, pp. 28–32.

78 Kracauer, *Das Ornament der Masse*, p. 46.

79 *The Blue Angel* was set in a sailor's dive in Hamburg, but is commonly associated with Berlin. On the making of the film see Thierry de Navacelle, *Sublime Marlene*, trans. Carey L. Smith (London, 1984), pp. 30–35. For a critique of the Weimar industry see Siegfried Kracauer, *From Caligari to Hitler: A Psychological History of the German Film* (Princeton, 1947).

80 On the evolution of the genre see S. S. Prawer, *Caligari's Children. The Film as Tale of Terror* (Oxford, 1980) p. 8; see also John D. Barlow, *German Expressionist Film* (Boston, 1992).

81 On Piscator's use of film in the theatre see Piscator, *Das politische Theater*, p. 81.

82 The film was banned for a short time, resulting in fierce protests by the left-wing press, whose pundits referred to it as one of the greatest German films ever made. Heinz Lüdecke, in *Magazin für Alle*, June 1933. For a sympathetic view of Münzenberg see Gertraude Kühn et al., *Film und revolutionäre Arbeiterbewegung in Deutschland 1918–1932* (Berlin, 1975), vol. 2, pp. 93–128.

83 On the 'screen couple' see Max Cichocki and Ingeborg Jessulat, *Du warst mein schönsten Liebestraum. Lilian Harvey, Willy Fritsch. Das klassische Liebespaar* (Berlin, 1973).

84 Wolf Von Eckardt and Sander L. Gilman, *Bertolt Brecht's Berlin. A Scrapbook of the Twenties* (London, 1993), pp. 96–7.

85 Klaus Budzinski, *Die Muse mit der scharfen Zunge – Von Cabaret zum Kabarett* (Munich, 1961), pp. 104–26, 182–7.

86 For an overview of Berlin cabaret see 'Von A (dmiralspalast) bis Z(illeball). Das Reich der Unterhaltung', in Schrader and Schebera, *Kunst–Metropole Berlin*, pp. 108–75.

87 Waldoff later claimed that she fell 'passionately in love with Berlin' within minutes of her arrival. Franke Deizzner-Jenssen, *Die zehnte Muse Kabarettisten erzählen* (Berlin, 1982), p. 167. See also Jelavich, *Berlin Cabaret*, pp. 100–104; Claire Waldoff, *Weesste noch . . . !* (Düsseldorf, 1953).

88 Jelavich, *Berlin Cabaret*, p. 118; Kurt Tucholsky, quoted on p. 135.

89 Ibid., p. 135. Kurt Tucholsky, 'Politische Couplets' letter to Hans Erich Blaich, 6 March 1920, in Kurt Tucholsky, *Ausgewählte Briefe 1913–1935* (Reinbek, 1962), p. 76.

90 Performers like Willi Schaeffers, who sung Tucholsky's songs in the Weimar period, would go on to become great stars under the Nazis; others like Claire Waldoff were still popular. On cabaret under the Nazis see Volker Kühn (ed.), *Deutschlands erwachen: Kabarett unterm Hakenkreuz 1933–1945* (Weinheim, 1989).

91 Günter Berghaus, 'Girlkultur – Feminism, Americanism and Popular Culture in Weimar Germany', *Journal of Design History*, 1, 1988, pp. 193–219.

92 The review *Drunter und Drüber* opened at the Theater am Nollendorfplatz in September 1923. One reviewer called it a 'monstrous offering of people, costumes and nudity' with hundreds of scantily dressed 'show-girls'. The review did contain a song by Walter Kollo which was to become something of an anthem for Berlin: 'Solang noch Untern Linden die alten Bäume blühn, kann uns nichts überwinden – Berlin bleibt doch Berlin'. Otto Schneidereit, *Berlin. Wie es Weint und Lacht. Spaziergänge durch Berlins Operettengeschichte* (Berlin, 1976), p. 232.

93 Fritz Giese, *Girlkultur: Vergleiche zwischen amerikanischen und europäischen Rhythmus und Lebensgefühl* (Munich, 1925).

94 Alfred Polgar, 'Girls' (1926), in *Auswahl: Prosa aus vier Jahrzehnten* (Reinbek, 1968), p. 186.

95 Walter Benjamin and Bernhard Reich, 'Revue oder Theater', *Querschnitt*, 1925, p. 1043.

96 Jelavich, *Berlin Cabaret*, p. 157.

97 Police Report of 16 May 1921 in Brandenburgisches Landeshauptarchiv (Th 1504

f); Police Report of 9 August 1926, Brandenburgisches Landeshauptarchiv (Th 1504), quoted in Jelavich, *Berlin Cabaret*, p. 164.

98 Lotte H. Eisner, *Eldorado. Homosexuelle Frauen und Männer in Berlin 1850– 1950* (Berlin, 1984).

99 This song, featured in *Es liegt in der Luft*, described how two girlfriends, dissatisfied with their husbands, spend their time on a shopping trip. Peter Jelavich notes that the text makes it clear they are having a lesbian affair. Jelavich, *Berlin Cabaret*, p. 192. The text appears in Mischal Spoliansky and Marcellus Schiffer, *Es liegt in der Luft: 5 Haupt Schlager* (Berlin, 1928).

100 Felix Gilbert, *A European Past. Memoirs 1905–1945* (New York, 1988), p. 67.

101 The wax bust of 'Madame Dimanche, die gehörnte Frau aus Paris' is in Vienna, Museen der Stadt Wien (175.711/4). On the Panoptikum and the Luna Park see Bodo-Michael Baumunk, 'Luna-Park und Metropol', in Korff and Rürup, *Berlin*, pp. 411–30.

102 On the 'Haus Vaterland' see Inge von Wangenheim, *Mein Haus Vaterland. Erinnerungen einer jungen Frau* (Berlin, 1950).

103 On his life in Weimar Berlin, including friendships with Brecht, Grosz and Dietrich, see Max Schmeling, *Erinnerungen* (Frankfurt-am-Main/Berlin, 1977), pp. 47–197.

104 Hagen Schulze, *Die Weimarer Republik* (Berlin, 1982), p. 125.

105 For her explanation of the move see Marlene Dietrich, *Nehmt nur mein Leben* (Munich, 1979), pp. 105–7.

106 De Navacelle, *Sublime Marlene*, pp. 38–71.

107 Paul Erich Marcus, *Heimweh nach dem Kurfürstendamm. Aus Berlins glanzvollsten Tagen und Nächten* (Berlin, 1952), p. 14; see also Anton Gill, *A Dance between Flames. Berlin between the wars* (London, 1993), pp. 108–9; Lothar Fischer, *Anita Berber* (Berlin, 1984).

10: The Betrayal of Weimar

1 Düsterberg was soon 'neutralized' by the Nazis when it was shown that he had a Jewish grandmother. See Theodor Düsterberg, *Der Stahlhelm und Hitler* (London, 1949).

2 Goebbels radio broadcast, 30 January 1933, reprinted in Joseph Wulf, *Presse und Funk im dritten Reich: Eine Dokumentation* (Frankfurt-am-Main, 1983), p. 291.

3 Gottfried Korff and Reinhard Rürup (eds.), *Berlin, Berlin. Die Ausstellung Zur Geschichte der Stadt* (Berlin, 1987), p. 529.

4 On Hitler's appeal see Eberhard Kolb, *The Weimar Republic*, trans. P. S. Falla, (London, 1988), pp. 110–26: Dick Geary, 'Employers, Workers, and the Collapse of the Weimar Republic', in Ian Kershaw, *Weimar: Why Did German Democracy Fail?* (London, 1990), pp. 92–119.

5 On Ossietzky see Raimund Koplin, *Carl von Ossietzky als politischer Publizist* (Berlin, 1964).

6 Hitler believed that 'It is between the ages of ten and seventeen that youth exhibits both the greatest enthusiasm and the greatest idealism, and it is for

this period of their lives that we must provide them with the best possible instructors and leaders.' Martin Bormann (ed.), *Hitler's Table Talk, 1941–1944*, intro. Hugh Trevor-Roper (Oxford, 1988), p. 524.

7 Gitta Sereny, *Albert Speer: His Battle with Truth* (London, 1995), p. 77.

8 Groups like the Silesian Society for the Preservation of the Native Land were opposed to the mass production of Iron Crosses or headstones as they did not reflect the values of pre-industrial society. George L. Mosse, *Fallen Soldiers. Reshaping the Memory of the World Wars* (Oxford, 1990), p. 90.

9 The paper *Deutsches Volkstum*, edited by Wilhelm Stapel and Albrecht Erich Günter, was not a Nazi publication, although it advocated the destruction of the 'effete', 'weak' parliamentary democracy and welcomed the Nazi rise to power. On the glorification of militarism see M. Golbach, *Die Wiederkehr des Weltkrieges in der Literatur. Zu den Frontsromanen der späten zwanziger Jahre* (Kronberg am Taunus, 1978).

10 Ernst Jünger's appeal to educated youth made him dangerous as he attracted those who might otherwise have shunned the Nazi programme. For a sympathetic account see Thomas Nevin, *Ernst Jünger and Germany. Into the Abyss 1914–1945* (London, 1997); see also Dagmar Barnouw, *Weimar Intellectuals and the Threat of Modernity* (Bloomington, 1988), 'The Magic Spaces of Terror', pp. 194–230.

11 Klaus Theweleit reproduces a number of memoirs of Freikorps fighters which reflected the relationship between the cult of violence which emerged after the First World War and the rise of Nazism. See Klaus Theweleit, *Männerphantasien* (Reinbek, 1980). Theodore Abel, who travelled to Berlin in 1936 to interview Germans who had decided to support the Nazis, wrote of one Freikorps member: 'Fighting had become our life purpose and goal; any battle, any sacifice for the might and glory of our country.' Theodore Abel, *Why Hitler Came to Power* (Englewood Cliffs, NJ, 1936), p. 45. For another contemporary account see F. W. Heinz, *Die Nation greift an* (Berlin, 1933). See also Robert G. L. Waite, *Vanguard of Nazism. The Free Corps Movement in Postwar Germany 1918–1923* (Cambridge, Mass., 1952).

12 'The German tradition has gone to the Devil,' he fumed. 'In England one can do something, and as a Russian and as an American and perhaps even as a Frenchman, but in Germany an upstanding man can only comply and manage, that is what has happened!' Hans Grimm, *Volk ohne Raum* (Munich, 1926), p. 1009.

13 Ibid., p. 1353.

14 Interview with Ellen Frey in Alison Owings, *Frauen. German Women Recall the Third Reich* (Harmondsworth, 1993), p. 184.

15 R. Walther Darré, *Neudel aus Blut und Boden* (Munich, 1930); *Landvolk in Not und Seine Rettung durch Adolf Hitler* (Munich, 1931); *Das Bauterntum als Lebensquell der nordischen Rasse* (Munich, 1933). On Darré see also Peter Zimmermann, 'Kampf um den Lebensraum. Ein Mythos der Kolonial- und der Blut und Boden-Literatur', in Horst Denkler and Karl Prümm (eds.), *Die deutsche Literatur im dritten Reich. Theme, Traditionen, Wirkungen* (Stuttgart, 1976), pp. 168–71.

16 Johannes Lange, *Verbrechen als Schicksal* (Leipzig, 1928).

17 On the creation of 'enemies of the *Volk*' in literature and the link to Nazi ideology see George L. Mosse, *The Crisis of German Ideology. The Intellectual Origins of the Third Reich* (New York, 1981); see also Gerhard Ritter, *The Third Reich* (London, 1955): 'Historical Foundations of the Rise of National Socialism'; Fritz Stern, *The Politics of Cultural Despair: A Study in the Rise of Germanic Ideology* (Berkeley, 1961).

18 On his early influence on the *Auf Gut Deutsch* see Albert Reich, *Dietrich Eckart* (Munich, 1933). On his influence on Hitler see Mosse, *The Crisis of German Ideology*, pp. 296–8. Arthur Moeller van den Bruck, *Das dritte Reich* (Hamburg, 1931).

19 Albert Speer, *Inside the Third Reich* (New York, 1993), p. 41. As Spengler wrote, 'We no longer believe in the power of reason over life. We know that life rules reason.' Oswald Spengler, *Der Untergang des Abendlandes* (Munich, 1972).

20 Hans Blüher, *Merkworte für den Freideutschen Stand* (Hamburg, 1919); Hans Friedrich Blunck, *Deutsche Heldensagen* (Berlin, 1938). See also I. Jens, *Dichter zwischen rechtes und links. Die Geschichte der Sektion für Dichtkunst der preussischen Akademie der Künste* (Munich, 1971), pp. 92–140; Jost Hermand, *Der alte Traum vom neuen Reich. Völkische Utopien und Nationalsozialismus* (Frankfurt-am-Main, 1988), pp. 182–95.

  On Rosenberg see Alfred Rosenberg, *Der Mythus des 20. Jahrhunderts. Eine Wertung der seelisch-geistigen Gestaltenkämpfe unserer Zeit* (Munich, 1930); Alfred Rosenberg, *Das politische Tagebuch Alfred Rosenbergs aus den Jahren 1934–5 und 1939–40. Nach der photographischen Wiedergabe der Handschrift aus den Nürnberger Akten*, ed. Hans-Gunther Seraphim (Berlin, 1956); Robert Cecil, *The Myth of the Master Race: Alfred Rosenberg and Nazi Ideology* (London, 1972).

21 Hans Kohn, *The Mind of Germany* (London, 1961), p. 309.

22 Graf Harry Kessler, *Tagebücher*, ed. Wolfgang Pfeiffer-Belli (Frankfurt-am-Main, 1982), p. 362; on the universities see Mosse, *The Crisis of German Ideology*, pp. 190–203. Ironically both Hauptmann and Richard Strauss were given lavish birthday celebrations by Gauleiter von Schirach in Vienna. Henrietta von Schirach, *The Price of Glory* (London, 1960), p. 163.

23 Koppel S. Pinson, *Modern Germany. Its History and Civilization* (New York, 1963), pp. 500–504.

24 Felix Gilbert, *A European Past. Memoirs 1905–1945* (New York, 1988), p. 83.

25 Speer, *Inside the Third Reich*, p. 43.

26 Ibid., p. 45.

27 Hitler reflected this view when he declared on 22 February 1942 that 'The discovery of the Jewish virus is one of the greatest revolutions that has taken place in the world. The battle in which we are engaged today is of the same sort as the battle waged, during the last century, by Pasteur and Koch. How many diseases have their origin in the Jewish virus! . . . We shall regain our health only by eliminating the Jew. Everything has a cause, nothing comes by chance.' Bormann, *Hitler's Table Talk*, p. 332.

28 Ludwig Ferdinand Clauss's *Die nordische Seele* (1930) was only one such work. More influential was Hans F. K. Günther, whose 1921 work *Ritter, Tod und*

Teufel predicted the coming of a German 'heroic saviour' and whose 1922 book *Rassenkunde des deutschen Volkes* created a 'scientific' racial hierarchy which placed Aryans at the top and Jews at the bottom. His pseudo-scientific designation of the 'Jewish stereotype', backed by 'research' supported by endless footnotes provided the reader with a list, not only of the 'racial' Jewish appearance (Jews had bent shoulders as opposed to Germans, who stood upright, for example) but also character traits (Jews were apparently racially predisposed to be obsessed by money). This nonsense was henceforth treated as scientific 'fact'. Mosse, *The Crisis of German Ideology*, pp. 302–5. Hitler was greatly influenced by the ideas of racial 'purity'. For him, anything of value, even in other cultures, could usually be traced to Aryans, or to those who still had Aryan blood in their veins. On 2 November 1941, for example, he said, 'Here and there one meets amongst the Arabs men with fair hair and blue eyes . . . They're the descendants of the Vandals who occupied North Africa. The same phenomenon in Castile and Croatia. The blood doesn't disappear.' Bormann, *Hitler's Table Talk*, p. 110.

29 Hitler would later say, 'Jesus was most certainly not a Jew . . . It is quite probable that a large number of the descendants of the Roman legionaries, mostly Gauls, were living in Galilee, and Jesus was probably one of them . . . Jesus fought against the materialism of His age, and, therefore, against the Jews.' *Hitler's Table Talk*, p. 721. See also Hermand, *Der alte Traum vom neuen Reich*, Ibid., p. 229.

30 For Max von Gruber's testimony see Joachim C. Fest. *The Face of the Third Reich*, trans. Michael Bullock (London, 1988), pp. 57–8. For Richter's analysis of Hitler and other Nazi leaders see Alfred Richter, *Unsere Führer im Lichte der Rassenfrage und Charakterologie. Eine rassenmässige und charakterologische Beurteilung von Männern des dritten Reiches* (Leipzig, 1933).

31 Walter Z. Laqueur, 'Hitler and Russia, 1919–1923', *Survey 44/45* (London, 1962), p. 110. On 5 November 1941 Hitler explained, 'The Jew totally lacks any interest in things of the spirit. If he has pretended in Germany to have a bent for literature and the arts, that's only out of snobbery, or from a liking for speculation. He has no feeling for art, and no sensibility.' Bormann, *Hitler's Table Talk*, p. 117.

32 For an account of anti-Semitism in Germany during the First World War see W. E. Mosse (ed.), *Deutsches Judentum in Krieg und Revolution 1916–1923* (Tübingen, 1971). Hitler nurtured the myth, stating that 'During the First World War, I didn't wear my Iron Cross, First Class, because I saw how it was awarded. We had in my regiment a Jew named Guttmann, who was the most terrible coward. He had the Iron Cross, First Class. It was revolting.' Bormann, *Hitler's Table Talk*, p. 119.

33 Mosse, *Fallen Soldiers*, p. 176. In 1935 Goebbels issued a decree that the names of fallen Jewish soldiers were not to be inscribed on any memorial erected in Germany from then on. Saul Friedländer, *Nazi Germany and the Jews* (London, 1997), vol. 1: *The Years of Persecution 1933–39*, p. 292, n. 84.

34 Wolters would say after the war, 'Thanks to the insane hate of the leadership [of Einstein and 'Jewish physics'] we allowed ourselves to lose a weapon of

decisive importance. If, instead of backing the – in the final analysis – ineffective rockets with hundreds of millions, we had devoted them to supporting atom research from the start, it would have been more useful for the war.' Rudolf Wolters to Albert Speer, Spandau 1953 (Wolters Archive at Federal Archive in Koblenz NL7-NL11), in Sereny, *Albert Speer*, p. 318.

35 On the rise of the occult and related movements see Ulrich Linse, *Barfüssige Propheten. Erlöser der zwanziger Jahre* (Berlin, 1983).

36 Guido von List, *Die Armanenschaft der Ario-Germanen* (Vienna, 1911), vol. 2; Rosmarie Beier, 'Die Befreiung des Körpers', in Korff and Rürup, *Berlin, Berlin*, pp. 387–400.

37 It is interesting to compare the two autobiographical works: Leni Riefenstahl, *Hinter den Kulissen des Reichsparteitages* (Munich, 1935); Leni Riefenstahl, *A Memoir* (New York, 1997). Neither is particularly self-critical.

38 In 1906 Dr Fedor Fuchs founded the 'Deutsche Luftbadegesellschaft' in Rixdorf. Korff and Rürup, *Berlin, Berlin*, p. 358.

39 One article, entitled 'The Moral', was a story of two children playing 'Adam and Eve' in a Berlin garden and accompanied by graphic photographs. It ended with one adult convincing the other that the children's behaviour was both natural and healthy. Felix Solterer, 'Die Moral', in *Die Schönheit Lebens-erneuerungsheft*, XXIII 2 (Berlin, 1925), p. 37.

40 Ibid., p. 21.

41 Stephen Spender, *World within World* (London, 1977), pp. 109, 116.

42 Walter Z. Laqueur, *Young Germany. A History of the German Youth Movement* (London, 1961); A. Klimert and H. P. Bleuel, *Deutsche Studenten auf dem Weg ins dritte Reich* (Gütersloh, 1967); for a fascinating contemporary account see Hans Blüher, *Wandervogel, Geschichte einer Jugendbewegung* (Berlin, 1912). See also the periodical *Wandervogel*, published in Berlin from 1905.

43 Peter Gay, *Weimar Culture. The Outsider As Insider* (Harmondsworth, 1988), pp. 48–72; see also Franz Schonauer (ed.), *Stefan George in Selbstzeugnissen und Bilddokumenten* (Hamburg, 1960).

44 Louis Hagen, *Follow My Leader* (London, 1951), p. 261.

45 Klaus Völker, *Bertolt Brecht: Eine Biographie* (Munich, 1976), p. 60.

46 'Address at the Closing Ceremony of First Tutorial Week of the German Academy of Education', *Morning Post*, 30 July 1935; see also Richard Grunberger, *A Social History of the Third Reich* (Harmondsworth, 1991), p. 392.

47 Sereny, *Albert Speer*, p. 323.

48 Heinrich Himmler, speech at Gauleiter Conference in Posen, 6 October 1943. The notion that the 'soil' helped to shape human beings was fundamental to the ideology. Hitler said on 5 November 1941: 'In Bavaria, the race is handsome in fertile regions. On the other hand, one finds stunted beings in certain remote valleys.' In German forests 'one meets only idiots, whilst all around, on the plain of the Rhine, one meets the finest specimens of humanity. I realised that the Germanic conquerors had driven the aboriginals into the mountainy bush in order to settle in their place on the fertile lands.' Bormann, *Hitler's Table Talk*, pp. 115–16.

49 'The brown shirt would probably not have existed without the black shirt. The

March on Rome, in 1922, was one of the turning-points of history. The mere fact that anything of the sort could be attempted, and could succeed, gave us an impetus . . .' Ibid., p. 10. Kurt Hesse believed that a leader would soon appear similar to the 'German heroes' Ludendorff and Hindenburg. Kurt Hesse, *Der Feldherr Psychologos. Ein Suchen nach dem Führer der deutschen Zukunft* (1922); Wilhelm Gellert, founder and leader of the group called 'Der deutsche Ring', held similar views. See Wilhelm Gellert, *Tragödie dreier Weltteile. Deutschlands Erhebung. Der 'Sturmvogel', seine Taten und Fahrten im Kampf um den fernen Osten* (1922).

50 On Joseph Goebbels and the rise of the Nazis in Berlin I have drawn on Joseph Goebbels, *Kampf um Berlin* (Munich, 1934); Joseph Goebbels, *Das Tagebuch von Joseph Goebbels 1925–1926*, ed. Helmut Heiber (Stuttgart, 1960); Joseph Goebbels, *Die Tagebücher von Joseph Goebbels: Sämtliche Fragmente*, ed. Elke Fröhlich (New York, 1987); Joseph Goebbels, *Vom Kaiserhof zur Reichskanzlei* (Munich, 1934); Joseph Goebbels, *The Goebbels Diaries: The Last Days*, ed. Hugh Trevor-Roper (London, 1979); Heinrich Fraenkel and Roger Manvell, *Goebbels. Eine Biographie* (Cologne/Berlin, 1960); Viktor Reimann, *Dr Joseph Goebbels* (Munich, 1971); and the excellent biography by Ralf Georg Reuth, *Goebbels* (London, 1993). See also Herbert Michaelis and Ernst Schraepler (eds.), *Ursachen und Folgen: Vom deutschen Zusammenbruch 1918 und 1945 bis zur staatlichen Neuordnung Deutschlands in der Gegenwart. Eine Urkunden- und Dokumentensammlung zur Zeitgeschichte*, (Berlin, 1965), vol. 10: *Das dritte Reich: Die Errichtung des Führerstaates. Die Abwendung vom System der kollektiven Sicherheit.*

51 Reuth, *Goebbels*, p. 14.

52 Ibid., p. 37, n 84; on Friedrich Gundolf see Fraenkel and Manvell, *Goebbels*, p. 42.

53 The academic record of top Nazis was dismal, not least because the key to success was based on the length of membership of the party rather than on traditional measures of ability or education. Of thirty Gauleiter in the Reich, twenty-three had only elementary education; only three had university degrees and Goebbels was without question the best educated of the elite. Michael Kater, *The Nazi Party. A Social Profile of Members and Leaders 1919–1945* (Oxford, 1983).

54 Sereny, *Albert Speer*, p. 322.

55 Gordon Craig, 'Man of the People?', in *New York Review of Books*, vol. XLIV, no. 18, 20 November 1997, p. 21.

56 Hitler said of Versailles that 'The attitude of our rulers after the collapse of 1918 was truly inconceivable' and claimed that even afterwards Germany should have evaded elements of the '*diktat*': 'There's no doubt that at this moment the spirit of treachery was rampant in Germany.' Bormann, *Hitler's Table Talk*, p. 406.

57 As Gordon Craig has noted, 'It took the war, in which Hitler served from its first to last day, and Germany's defeat to awaken his political consciousness. It took the experience of the Munich Soviet in 1919 and his discovery in its aftermath that he was able to make public speeches, and, more important, that he could persuade people, to make him decide to go into politics.' Craig, 'Man of the People?' *New York Review of Books*, 20 November 1997, p. 21. See also

John Lukacs, *The Hitler of History* (New York, 1997), the subject of Craig's review.

58 Rudolf Diels, *Lucifer ante Portas: Zwischen Severing und Heydrich* (Stuttgart, 1950), p. 48.

59 See, for example, Joachim Fest, *Hitler. Eine Biographie* (Frankfurt-am-Main, 1973); Alan Bullock, *Hitler. A Study in Tyranny* (London, 1960); Lukacs, *The Hitler of History*.

60 Adolf Hitler, *Mein Kampf*, trans. James Murphy (London, 1939); see also *Der Hitler-Prozess. Bericht über die Verhandlungen des Volksgerichthofs in München 1924* (Munich, 1924).

61 Reuth, *Goebbels*, p. 57; Goebbels wrote about the *Weimar* party congress in his diary entries for 19 and 20 August 1924.

62 Hitler said of Goebbels on 24 June 1942 that 'From the time I started to organise the Party, I made it a rule never to fill an appointment until I had found the right man for it. I applied this principle to the post of Berlin Gauleiter. Even when the older members of the Party bombarded me with complaints over the Party leadership in Berlin, I refrained from coming to their assistance, until I could promise them that in Dr Goebbels I had found the man I was seeking. For Dr Goebbels possesses two attributes, without which no one could master the conditions in Berlin: he has intelligence and the gift of oratory . . .' Bormann, *Hitler's Table Talk*, p. 532. On Goebbels's struggle with Strasser see Reuth, *Goebbels*, p. 119; for Strasser's view see his *Hitler und Ich* (Konstanz, 1948), pp. 128–31.

63 On Goebbels's arrival in Berlin, and his quick change of heart see Reuth, *Goebbels*, pp. 75–6. He described his first impressions of Berlin in his diaries: 27 and 28 April and 1, 3, 7 and 17 May 1928.

64 Goebbels, *Kampf um Berlin*, p. 28.

65 Ibid., p. 84. See also Reuth, *Goebbels*, pp. 78–96; Fraenkel and Manvell, *Goebbels*, pp. 108–47.

66 Horst Wessel, in Reuth, *Goebbels*, pp. 82–113; Reimann, *Dr Joseph Goebbels*, pp. 131–4. On Wessel see Thomas Oertel, *Horst Wessel: Untersuchung einer Legende* (Cologne, 1988); on Wessel's death see diary, 1 March 1930.

67 Moeller van den Bruck, *The Third Reich*; see the discussion of Moeller van den Bruck in Stern, *The Politics of Cultural Despair*.

68 Berlin was the headquarters of the secret agency, the Soviet Western European Secretariat (WES), which operated until Hitler seized power. The first head was Lenin's personal representative Yakov Reich, who also had Felix Dzerzhinsky's blessing. The operation was funded by treasure stolen from their victims by the Bolsheviks in Russia – indeed Yakov arrived in Berlin with 25 million in cash and 37 million marks worth of valuables taken from stacks of treasure kept by the Cheka in the Palace of Justice in Moscow. The WES operated independently from the KPD and reported directly to Moscow, and it was key to the Communists in everything from providing money to creating false identities and passports through their *Pass-Apparat* headed by Georgi Dimitrov. David Childs and Richard Popplewell, *The Stasi. The East German Intelligence and Security Service* (London, 1996), pp. 4–10.

69 Helmut Heiber, *Joseph Goebbels* (Berlin, 1962), pp. 63–4.

70 Report of February 1927 in Martin Broszat, 'Die Anfänge der Berliner, NSDAP 1926–7', in *Vierteljahrheft für Zeitgeschichte*, 8, 1960, pp. 102–3.

71 A. Tyrell, *Führer befiehl . . . Selbstzeugnisse aus der 'Kampfzeit' der NSDAP. Dokumentation und Analyse* (Düsseldorf, 1969), pp. 235–6.

72 *Der Angriff* was in direct competition with Gregor Strasser's *Berliner Arbeiter-Zeitung*. Strasser was furious when in 1927 his rival Goebbels arranged for party information to be withheld from his paper; indeed Strasser complained to the Reichsleitung in Munich that Goebbels had arranged for the Monday edition of *Der Angriff* to publish the complete calendar of party events for the week, thereby forcing people to buy the paper. Strasser's protests were in vain; by 1930 Goebbels's *Angriff* had become the official Gau organ. After 1933 Hitler forced all newspapers to become 'property of the party'. See Oron J. Hale, *The Captive Press in the Third Reich* (Princeton, 1973), p. 48. See also Walter Hagemann, *Publizistik im dritten Reich. Ein Beitrag zur Methodik der Massenführung* (Hamburg, 1948); Martin Löffler, *Presserecht – Kommentar* (Munich, 1955). For a contemporary account of the evolution of Nazi newspapers see Adolf Dresler, *Geschichte des 'Völkischen Beobachters' und des Zentral-Verlags der NSDAP* (Munich, 1937).

73 On his increasing anti-Semitism see Reuth, *Goebbels*, pp. 182–3, 228, 233–4.

74 Goebbels had referred to Maximilian Harden, editor of *Die Zukunft*, as 'Isador' in 1924, and when he died on 30 October 1927 Goebbel's wrote in *Der Angriff* that his death had robbed him of the chance to settle the score using their 'own methods'. He used other 'Jewish' names like 'Levy' and 'Cohn' to eminent Berliners including his nemesis Theodor Wolff, who had refused to give him a job on the *Berliner Tageblatt* in 1923. See Goebbels diaries, 27 June 1924. On the Nazi abuse of names in anti-Semitic propaganda see Dietz Bering, *Der Name als Stigma* (Stuttgart, 1987).

75 Harold James, *The German Slump. Politics and Economics 1924–1936* (Oxford, 1987), pp. 283–342.

76 Henning Köhler, 'Politik und Verwaltung: Die Ära Boss', in Wolfgang Ribbe (ed.), *Geschichte Berlins* (Munich, 1987), vol. 2: *Von der Märzrevolution bis zur Gegenwart*, pp. 868–75.

77 A literature developed attacking profiteers and playing on local prejudices; see, for example, Alfred Mühr, *Kulturbankrott des Bürgertums* (Dresden, 1928). The tradition continued into the 1930s in works such as Anton Mayer, *Finanz-Katastrophen und Spekulanten* (Leipzig, 1938).

78 Martin Broszat (ed.), 'Die Anfänge der Berliner NSDAP', in *Vossische Zeitung*, 8, 1960, pp. 85–128.

79 *Kuhle Wampe* was made into Slatan Dudow's 1932 KPD film of the same name scripted by Bertolt Brecht.

80 Alex de Jonge, *The Weimar Chronicle. Prelude to Hitler* (London, 1978), p. 205.

81 Interview with Karma Rauhut, in Owings, *Frauen*, p. 343.

82 Spender, *World within World*, p. 129.

83 Goebbels, 'Kütemeyer', *Der Angriff*, 26 November 1928.

84 Putzi Hanfstaengl claimed that Horst Wessel had stolen the tune from Franz

Wedekind. Putzi Hanfstaengl, *The Missing Years* (London, 1957) p. 149; see also Reuth, *Goebbels*, p. 113. According to R. H. Bruce Lockhart, the British agent who had lived in Berlin throughout the Wessel saga, 'doubtful' Nazis 'include Horst Wessel, the composer of the song which ranks with *Deutschland Ueber Alles* as the Nazi national anthem. The son of a well-known Protestant preacher, he was a good-looking blond, who, left poorly off at the end of the war, led for several years a hand-to-mouth and disreputable existence. He had a job as a taxi-driver. But mostly he was known as a frequenter of low night-haunts. His mistress was a girl taken off the streets of Berlin. Then he was converted to Nazi-ism by Dr Goebbels. He took over an SA troop and waged a semi-gangster war against the Communists. In the end the Reds got him. Eight of them entered his flat and shot him down in cold blood. Even Nazi supporters admit, although they dare not say so openly, that apart from his services to Nazi-ism Wessel was little better than a degenerate. But his martyrdom has washed away all the stain of a doubtful past, and to-day he is enshrined as the Rouget de Lisle of Nazi Germany.' R. H. Bruce Lockhart, *Guns or Butter. War Countries of Europe Revisited* (London, 1938), p. 356.

85 Spender, *World within World*, p. 130.

86 Hitler praised Goebbels for 'taking Berlin': 'I have never regretted giving him the powers he asked for. When he started, he found nothing particularly efficient as a political organisation to help him; nevertheless, in the literal sense of the word, he captured Berlin. He worked like an ox, regardless of all the stresses and strains to which the latent opposition of people like Stinnes must have exposed him.' Bormann, *Hitler's Table Talk*, p. 533; Hanfstaengl, *The Missing Years*, p. 182.

87 Putzi Hanfstaengl claimed that after Wessel's death Goebbels flew to the Brown House in Munich to try to pursuade Hitler to attend the funeral but that Göring intervened, saying, 'If anything goes wrong it will be a catastrophe . . . if Hitler comes to Berlin it will be a red rag to the Communist bulls and we cannot afford to take the consequences.' Hanfstaengl, *The Missing Years*, p. 149.

88 Martin Broszat, *The Hitler State: The Foundation and Development of the Internal Structure of the Third Reich* (London, 1981), pp. 17–54.

89 Gregor Strasser was Hitler's only potential rival within the party. Hitler had elevated Goebbels above him in Berlin and put the press under his control. He would later say: 'It is only by means of the concentration of the whole machinery of press and propaganda in one single organisation that a unified direction of the press can be assured . . . only a unified press is free from those contradictions of news items, of political, cultural and such-like communications, which . . . rob it of any prestige as a purveyor of truth and of any value as an instrument for the education of public opinion.' Bormann, *Hitler's Table Talk*, p. 526.

90 Hitler would later say that the early speeches were marred by the poor quality of the loudspeakers: 'Once, at the Sports Palace in Berlin, there was such a cacophony that I had to cut the connection and go on speaking for nearly an hour, forcing my voice. I stopped when I realised that I was about to fall down from exhaustion . . . It was only gradually that we learnt the necessity of distributing the loud-speakers through the hall. One needs about a hundred –

and not just one, placed behind the platform which was what we had at the Sports Palace. Every word was heard twice: once from my mouth, and then echoed by the loud-speaker.' Ibid., p. 176.

91 Speer, *Inside the Third Reich*, p. 47.

92 Hanfstaengl, *The Missing Years*, p. 192.

93 Spender, *World within World*, p. 131.

94 The *New York Times* reported: 'The Berlin theatre showing the German version of the motion picture 'All Quiet on the Western Front', where Fascists recently broke up a performance by shouting and releasing white mice, was the scene of another demonstration tonight . . . Crowds of Fascists collected in the square opposite the building and shouted, "Germany awake" until they were dispersed by the police.' *New York Times*, 8 December 1930, p. 6.

95 Interview with Karma Rauhut, Owings, *Frauen*, p. 344.

96 Carl von Ossietzky, 'Remarque Film', *Weltbühne*, 11 December 1930.

97 Peter Jelavich, *Berlin Cabaret* (Harvard, 1993), p. 203.

98 The text was printed in Berlin in 1931 as Friedrich Holländer, 'An allem sind die Juden schuld!', *Spuk in der Villa Stern* (Berlin, 1931).

99 Jelavich, *Berlin Cabaret*, pp 207–9.

100 Hitler would later say that Berlin 'played a part in our rise to power', and although it was 'different' from Munich he was very grateful to Berlin, saying: 'It's at Berlin and Württemberg that I got our financial backing, and not in Munich, where the little bourgeois hold the crown of the road.' Bormann, *Hitler's Table Talk*, p. 81.

101 Goebbels diaries, 23 February 1932.

102 In a typical outburst Hitler would blame the Jews for having caused him to make various forced landings: 'at that time Lufthansa was infested by Jews. They let me fly when it was forbidden to fly all over Reich territory. They obviously had only one wish – that I should end my career in an aircraft accident,' Bormann, *Hitler's Table Talk*, p. 196. Putzi Hanfstaengl described the journeys as 'like accompanying a musical artist on a concert tour'. Hitler would 'give his performance, have his bags packed, and be off to the next town . . .' Hansfstaengl, *The Missing Years*, pp. 176–81.

103 Edgar Ansel Mowrer, *Germany Puts the Clock Back* (New York, 1939), p. 36.

104 Eve Rosenhaft, *Beating the Fascists? The German Communists and Political Violence, 1929–1933* (Cambridge, 1983), p. 12.

105 The first show trial took place on 20 May 1928, during which *Shakhtintsy* or 'wreckers' of the Donbass mines were arrested. Fifty-three engineers were called before the court. The Kulaks, the intelligentsia, and before long everyone else would be in danger in the Soviet Union. Edvard Radzinsky, *Stalin* (London, 1996), p. 236.

106 Silvia Rodgers, *Red Saint, Pink Daughter. A Communist Childhood in Berlin and London* (London, 1996), p. 41.

107 Erich Weinert, *Das rote Sprachrohr* (June 1929).

108 Jelavich, *Berlin Cabaret*, pp. 219–21.

109 Walter Däumig's speech at the Agitprop conference in Hamburg on 16 September 1932, as reported to the police. 'Bericht des westeuropäischen Büros des

IATB', Geheimes Staatsarchiv Preussischer Kulturbesitz, cited in Jelavich, *Berlin Cabaret*, p. 225.

110 Rodgers, *Red Saint, Pink Daughter*, p. 97.

111 Paul Simmel captured this in a cartoon. Two men meet on a Berlin street. One points to a large badge on the other's coat and asks 'What kind of insignia is that you're wearing?' The other replies, 'Yes, a Soviet star and a Swastika – you never know which direction the Putsch will come from!' Paul Simmel, 'Humor', reprinted in Christian Ferber (ed.), *Berliner illustrirte Zeitung. Zeitbild, Chronik, Moritat für jedermann 1892–1945* (Berlin, 1987), p. 228.

112 Kolb, *The Weimar Republic*, pp. 194–5.

113 Upon being offered the Vice-Chancellery Hitler said to Papen: 'A Vice-Chancellor never becomes active except when the Chancellor is ill. If I am the Vice-Chancellor, you will never be ill. So I refuse the Vice-Chancellery.' Bormann, *Hitler's Table Talk*, p. 239.

114 On 18 January 1942 Hitler would reveal his true feelings on the matter: 'We owe a debt of gratitude to Papen, by the way, for it was he who opened the first breach in the sacred constitution. It's obvious one couldn't expect more from him than that.' Ibid., p. 223.

115 Friedrich Hussong, *Kurfürstendamm* (Berlin, 1933), p. 62.

11: Nazi Berlin – Life Before the Storm

1 On 8 June 1942 Hitler declared that he intended to encourage all 'Germanic peoples of continental Europe into the German channel of thought'. He continued, 'I really believe that by renaming Berlin the capital of our Reich "Germania", we would give very considerable impetus to the movement. The name Germania for the capital of the Reich in its new representative form would be very appropriate, for it would give to every member of the German community, however far away from the capital he may be, a feeling of unity and closer membership. There would be no technical difficulty about re-naming Berlin, as we can see from the Germanisation of Gdynia into Gotenhafen and the changing of the name of Lodz into Litzmannstadt.' Martin Bormann (ed.), *Hitler's Table Talk, 1941–1944*, Hugh Trevor-Roper (Oxford, 2988), p. 523.

2 Hitler claimed that he was 'fond' of the city, not least because of its 'Germanic' roots. On 1 September 1942 he said of Vienna, 'I myself have never succumbed to the magic of Vienna, because I have been adamantly true to my German sentiments . . . Berlin, of course, is a city vibrating with energy; it has all the faults of youth, but it will soon learn.' Ibid., p. 680.

3 Hitler did not attempt to turn Berlin into a provincial town. 'Do you know anything more ridiculous than than a Berliner in leather shorts? . . . anyone in Berlin who put on a Tyrol costume would give the impression that he was going to Carnival.' Ibid., p. 317. Hitler may have had negligible technical intelligence but as Dagmar Barnouw has put it, 'he understood extremely well certain dynamics of mass technocracy. With his palpable modern love for cars, high-

ways, and planes he demonstrated the taming of potentially dangerous technological forces which would now be prepared to serve the German everyman as
Volksgenosse, that is, the individual German as member of the body of the *Volk*.
In the late twenties and early thirties the deep pleasures of blood and soil and
rich promises of technology did not cancel each other out but rather combined
to redirect Weimar technocracy so that it would support a brutal atavistic
totalitarian regime.' Dagmar Barnouw, *Weimar Intellectuals and the Threat of
Modernity*, (Bloomington, 1988), p. 228. According to Otto Dietrich the Führer
was dedicated to technological and scientific progress which would be used in
the service of the *Volk*. Otto Dietrich, *Das Wirtschaftsdenken im dritten Reich*
(Munich, 1936), pp. 25ff.

4 Berliners' post-war attempts to prove how Hitler disliked their city ring hollow
when one reads Hitler's words on the subject: 'I have always been fond of
Berlin. If I'm vexed by the fact that some of the things in it are not beautiful,
it's precisely because I'm so much attached to the city. During the First World
War, I twice had ten days' leave. I never dreamt of spending those leaves in
Munich. My pleasure would have been spoilt by the sight of all those priests.
On both occasions, I came to Berlin, and that's how I began to be familiar with
the museums of the capital . . . What is ugly in Berlin, we shall suppress. Nothing
will be too good for the beautification of Berlin.' Bormann, *Hitler's Table Talk*,
p. 88.

5 Hitler argued that Germany must have a single capital to which all Germans
would be loyal. In old Austria the provinces had hated Vienna because of its
power, but 'No such sentiment, in a similar form, was ever expressed against
Berlin.' On another occasion he told Bormann, 'I will not tolerate any rivalry
between Vienna and Berlin. Berlin is the capital of the Reich, and will remain
the capital of the Reich' and maintained that 'Treitschke once said: "Germany
has cities, but she possesses no capital." To that I will add that she must, and
she shall, have one. I shall take care that no town in the Reich can rival the
capital.' Ibid., pp. 47, 709–12.

6 Dr Hermann Rügler, 'Was der Berliner von der Geschichte seiner Stadt wissen
Muss', in *Sonderheft Berliner illustrirte Zeitung für 700 Jahr-Feier der Reichshauptstadt. Heimat Berlin* (Berlin, 1937), p. 13.

7 Hitler later justified this by saying that the 5 February 'Law for the Protection
of the German People' and the raid on the Liebknecht Haus had 'resulted in a
tremendous loss of prestige for the Communist Party and caused great indignation in Berlin'. Bormann, *Hitler's Table Talk*, p. 497.

8 The excuse was manufactured by Goebbels and released by the Prussian Press
Bureau on 28 February 1933. It read, 'The police inquiry has revealed that
inflammable material had been laid throughout the entire building from the
ground floor to the dome . . . A policeman saw people carrying torches moving
about in the dark building . . . In the hundreds of tons of pamphlets found by
the police in the Karl Liebknecht House were instructions for carrying out a
Communist terror after the Bolshevist pattern . . . government buildings, castles,
museums and vitally important factories were to be set on fire . . . women and
children, and wherever possible the wives and children of policemen, were to

be used as cover by the Communists ... The burning of the Reichstag was intended to serve as the signal for bloodshed and civil war.' Prussian Press Bureau release, 28 February 1933, in K. Heiden, *A History of National Socialism* (London, 1934), pp. 220–21.

9 Putzi Hanfstaengl, *The Missing Years* (London, 1957), pp. 201–3. Hitler called the Reichstag a 'monstrosity' although he did concede the fact that it was 'well and truly built was proved at the time of the great fire'. Bormann, *Hitler's Table Talk*, p. 705.

10 Sefton Delmer witnessed the Reichstag fire, although his account of events changed over the years and it is not clear if he actually spoke to Göring or saw Hitler. The official press release stated, 'The Reich Commissar for the Prussian Ministry of the Interior Reich Minister Göring, on arriving at the scene of the fire, immediately took charge of operations and issued the necessary orders. On receiving the news of the fire Chancellor Adolf Hitler and Vice-Chancellor Papen at once betook themselves to the scene', but the release was not reliable. Prussian Press Bureau release, 28 February 1933.

11 The Prosecutor at the Nuremberg trials summed up the Enabling Act, pointing out that 'On 24 March 1933 only 535 out of the regular 747 deputies of the Reichstag were present. The absence of some was unexcused; they were in protective custody in concentration camps. Subject to the full weight of the Nazi pressure and terror, the Reichstag passed an enabling act known as the "Law for the Protection of the People and the State" with a vote of 441 in favour. This law marks the real seizure of political control by the conspirators.' Prosecutor's speech, *Trial of German Major War Criminals* (HMSO. London, 1946), vol. 1, p. 109.

12 Hitler later explained the 'difficulty' he had in persuading the 'Old Gentleman' of the 'necessity of curtailing the liberty of the press'. 'I played a little trick on him ... and developed the argument that in the Army criticism from below was never permitted ... This the Old Gentleman admitted and without further ado approved of my policy, saying: "You are quite right, only superiors have the right to criticise!" And with these words the freedom of the press was doomed.' Bormann, *Hitler's Table Talk*, p. 550.

13 Detlev J. K. Peukert, *Inside Nazi Germany. Conformity, Opposition and Racism in Everyday Life*, trans. Richard Deveson (London, 1993), p. 105. Carl Severing remembered that none of his fellow Social Democrats was ready to take responsibility for active resistance against the regime; no one dared to be 'courageous at the comrades' expense'. Carl Severing, *Mein Lebensweg* (Cologne, 1950), vol. 2, p. 347.

14 Silvia Rodgers, *Red Saint, Pink Daughter. A Communist Childhood in Berlin and London* (London, 1996), p. 100. See also Susanne Millter and Heinrich Potthoff *A History of German Social Democracy From 1848 to the Present*, trans. J. A. Underwood, (New York, 1986), pp. 118–19.

15 Hitler believed that even 'second-rate criminals' should 'either be sent to a concentration camp for life or suffer the death penalty'. Bormann, *Hitler's Table Talk*, p. 303.

16 'As concerns Jews', *New York Times*, 27 March 1933. On this and the increase

of violence in Berlin see the excellent collection compiled by Philip Metcalfe, *1933* (Reading, 1990).

17 For an account of the beating stations and 'wild' concentration camps in Berlin see Hans-Norbert Burkert, Klaus Matussek and Wolfgang Wippermann, '*Macht-ergreifung' Berlin 1933. Stätten der Geschichte Berlins in Zusammenarbeit mit dem Pädagogischen Zentrum Berlin* (Berlin, 1982), pp. 20–94. The spread of these 'wild' camps was not limited to Berlin; see, for example, Lawrence D. Stokes, 'Zur Geschichte des "wilden" Konzentrationslagers Eutin', in *Vierteljahreshefte für Zeitgeschichte*, 27, 1979, pp. 570–625.

18 Diels himself admitted to a British embassy official, 'after a number of instances of unnecessary flogging and meaningless cruelty I tumbled to the fact that my organization had been attracting all the sadists in Germany and Austria without my knowledge for some time past. It had also been attracting unconscious sadists, i.e. men who did not know themselves that they had sadist leanings until they took part in a flogging. And finally it had been actually creating sadists. For it seems that corporal chastisement ultimately arouses sadistic leanings in apparently normal men and women . . .' Diels' conversation recorded at the British embassy, Berlin, 25 April 1934. Foreign Office 371/17706 XP 3367, Public Record Office.

19 Reinhard Rürup (ed.), *Topographie des Terrors. Gestapo, SS und Reichssicher-heitshauptamt auf dem 'Prinz-Albrecht-Gelände'. Eine Dokumentation* (Berlin, 1987), p. 89; Johannes Tuchel and Reinold Schattenfroh, *Zentrale des Terrors Prinz-Albrecht-Strasse: Hauptquartier der Gestapo* (Berlin, 1987), pp. 197–9.

20 The SS prison was located in one of the most modern buildings in Berlin, Erich Mendelssohn's Columbus Haus, which had housed the Woolworth store on the Potsdamer Platz. The prison was on the top six floors and held between 400 and 600 prisoners, although the basement was also used. Ironically it was its modern wide open spaces, which could be filled with tailor-made equipment and rooms, that recommended it to the Nazis. And, while the beatings and tortures took place above, the second floor was occupied by a German travel agency which was filled with posters for the Winter Olympics. The bunkers in the Hedemann and Voss Strassen became hellish torture chambers; even so the worst was the SS Columbia prison (Columbus Haus). By the end of April 1933 10,000 Berliners had been arrested. Between 1934 and 1940 the SPD in exile was able to gather information from informants throughout the Reich. This information was delivered to Prague and later to Paris – at great risk to their agents – and collected in the *Deutschland-Berichte* or German Reports. See Klaus Behnken (ed.), *Deutschland-Berichte der Sozialdemokratischen Partei Deutsch-lands (SOPADE) 1934–1940*, 7 vols. (Frankfurt-am-Main, 1980).

21 Litten's terrible fate is recounted by his widow in Irmgard Litten, *Beyond Tears* (London, 1940). On his 'confession' see p. 42.

22 Karl Billinger, *Fatherland* (New York, 1935), quoted in Duff Hart-Davis, *Hitler's Games. The 1936 Olympics* (London, 1986), p. 19.

23 Kurt Hiller, *Leben gegen die Zeit* (Reinbek, 1967); see also Metcalfe, *1933*, p. 255.

24 Rürup, *Topographie des Terrors*, p. 50.

25 Much research has been done on the views of ordinary Germans about these events, although many were concerned the general picture that emerges of Berlin at the time is of a population willing to turn a blind eye to Nazi crimes because of the benefits they were thought to be bringing to Germany. See, for example, Hans Kohn, *The Mind of Germany* (New York, 1951); Richard Grunberger, *A Social History of the Third Reich* (Harmondsworth, 1991); Ian Kershaw, *The 'Hitler Myth'. Image and Reality of the Third Reich* (Oxford, 1987); David Schoenbaum, *Hitler's Social Revolution* (New York, 1966); Jill Stephenson, *Women in Nazi Germany* (London, 1975); Peukert, *Inside Nazi Germany*; Marlis Steinert, *Hitler's War and the Germans* (Athens, Ohio, 1977); Bernhard Vollmer, *Volks-opposition im Polizeistaat* (Stuttgart, 1957).

26 There were attempts to alert the world about the first concentration camp, Oranienburg. In 1934 Gerhart Seger, a Social Democrat politician who had been a Reichstag representative in the Weimar Republic, had been imprisoned in Oranienburg. He escaped from Berlin to Prague, where he wrote a pamphlet, with an introduction by Heinrich Mann. Seger managed to reach London, where Lady Astor campaigned to have his wife released from prison. Despite the fact that he sold over 200,000 copies in the west, Seger's reports of Nazi brutality were largely ignored. Gerhart Seger, *Oranienburg – Erster authentischer Bericht eines aus dem Konzentrationslager Geflüchteten* (Karlsbad, 1934). The American ambassador was also concerned, but when he talked to the Foreign Minister, von Neurath, he was told, 'The SA men are so uncontrollable that I am afraid we cannot stop them'. W. E. Dodd Jr and M. Dodd (eds.), *Ambassador Dodd's Diary 1933–38* (London, 1933–8), p. 57.

27 Hanfstaengl, *The Missing Years*, p. 213.

28 On 15 September 1941, for example, Hitler complained that the revolution had been possible in Germany in 1918 because the revolutionaries had not been rounded up and executed. To avoid the same fate he had 'ordered Himmler, in the event of there being some day reason to fear trouble back at home, to liquidate everything he finds in the concentration camps. Thus at a stroke the revolution would be deprived of its leaders.' Bormann, *Hitler's Table Talk*, p. 29.

29 *Der Tag von Potsdam. Die Woche*, 21 March 1933.

30 This ceremony helped to damn the names of Frederick II, Bismarck – indeed of Prussia – for decades to come. This was the foundation of the 'misery thesis' of the GDR, which taught that Luther–Frederick – Bismarck led inevitably to Hitler. See, for example, Alexander Abusch, *Der Irrweg einer Nation* (Berlin, 1946).

31 Otto Wels ended his address with the words: 'We salute the persecuted and oppressed. We salute our friends in the Reich. Their resoluteness and faithfulness are worthy of our admiration. The courage of their dedication and their unwavering confidence point to a brighter future.' Shortly afterwards Wels fled to Prague. Otto Wels, Final Reichstag Address, 23 March 1933, in Germany, Reichstag, *Stenographische Berichte VIII*, V Wahlperiode, 1933, 457, pp. 32–4.

32 According to Goebbels, 'Berlin does not dream of going to rest, and in unison with this huge city the entire Reich is yet thrilling with joy and emotion, and

is conscious of the great hour that compasses the junction of two eras, the past and the future.' Joseph Goebbels, *My Part in Germany's Fight* (London, 1935), pp. 251–3.

33 Goebbels diary, 1 May 1933.

34 Richard Löwenthal and Patrik von zur Mühlen (eds.), *Widerstand und Verweigerung in Deutschland 1933–1945* (Bonn, 1982).

35 Hanfstaengl, *The Missing Years*, p. 155. Rohm had been provocative, telling Hermann Rauschning that 'Adolph is a swine ... He only associates with the reactionaries now. His old friends aren't good enough for him ... Are we revolutionaries or aren't we? ... If we're not, then we'll go to the dogs. We've got to produce something new, don't you see?' Hermann Rauschning, *Hitler Speaks* (London, 1939), p. 145.

36 After the Night of the Long Knives Hitler justified the murders, claiming that only 'ruthless and bloody intervention' would stifle 'the revolt'; 'If anyone reproaches me and asks why I did not resort to the regular courts of justice ... then all that I can say to him is this: in this hour I was responsible for the fate of the German people, and thereby I became the supreme Justice of the German people!' Speech to the Reichstag, 13 July 1934, in N. Baynes (ed.), *The Speeches of Adolf Hitler 1922–1939* (London, 1942), vol. 1, p. 320. See also Max Gallo, *The Night of the Long Knives*, trans. L. Emmet (New York, 1972); Kershaw, *The 'Hitler Myth'*, pp. 84–104.

37 See Hans Buchheim et al., *Anatomie des SS-Staates*, 2 vols. (Olten, 1965); Robert Lewis Koehl, *The Black Corps: The Structure and Power Struggles of the Nazi SS* (Madison, 1983). On Heydrich see Shlomo Aronson, *Reinhard Heydrich und die Frühgeschichte von Gestapo und SD* (Stuttgart, 1971).

38 On 3 January 1943 Hitler summed up Himmler's contribution to the SS: 'Being convinced that there are always circumstances in which elite troops are called for, in 1922–23 I created the "Adolf Hitler Shock Troops". They were made up of men who were ready for revolution and knew that one day or another things would come to hard knocks ... It was Maurice, Schreck and Heyden who formed in Munich the first group of "tough'uns", and were thus the origin of the SS. But it was with Himmler that the SS became that extraordinary body of men, devoted to an idea, loyal until death. I see in Himmler our Ignatius de Loyola. With intelligence and obstinacy, against wind and tide, he forged this instrument. The heads of the SA, for their part, didn't succeed in giving their troops a soul. At the present time we have had it confirmed that every division of the SS is aware of its responsibility.' Bormann, *Hitler's Table Talk*, p. 167.

39 Heinz Höhne, *The Order of the Death's Head: The Story of Hitler's SS*, trans. R. Barry, (London, 1972).

40 This was the subject of Rolf Hochhuth's *Eine Liebe in Deutschland* (Reinbek, 1980). See also Ulrich Herbert, *Hitler's Foreign Workers. Enforced Foreign Labour in Germany under the Third Reich* (Cambridge, 1997), pp. 64–9.

41 On informers and popular opinion see, for example, Ian Kershaw, *Popular Opinion and Political Dissent in the Third Reich* (Oxford, 1983). On Gestapo informers see Robert Gellately, *The Gestapo and German Society. Enforcing Racial*

Policy 1933–1945 (Oxford, 1990), pp. 62–4; Robert Gellately, 'The Gestapo and German Society: Political Denunciation in the Gestapo Case Files', *Journal of Modern History*, 60, 1988; Walter Otto Weyrauch, 'Gestapo Informants: Facts and Theory of Undercover Operations', *Columbia Journal of Transnational Law*, 24, 1986. There were also documented cases of KPD members being forced to spy; on the case of Bremen see, for example, Inge Marssolek and René Ott, *Bremen im dritten Reich: Anpassung, Widerstand, Verfolgung* (Bremen, 1986), p. 183. For an early view see E. K. Bramstedt, *Dictatorship and Political Police: The Technique of Control by Fear* (New York, 1945).

42 On Lammers see Lutz Graf Schwerin von Krosigk, *Es geschah in Deutschland* (Tübingen/Stuttgart, 1951), p. 203.

43 Interview with Karma Rauhut, in Alison Owings, *Frauen. German Women Recall the Third Reich* (Harmondsworth, 1993), p. 347.

44 Most Berliners were unwilling to challenge the regime; as Walter Laqueur has said, they avoided the issue which had by now become 'an unpleasant topic, speculation was unprofitable, discussions of the fate of the Jews were discouraged. Consideration of this question was pushed aside, blotted out for the duration.' Walter Laqueur, *The Terrible Secret* (London, 1980), p. 201.

45 Hanns Peter Herz, in Johannes Steinhoff, Peter Pechel and Dennis Showalter (eds.), *Voices from the Third Reich. An Oral History* (New York, 1994), p. 48.

46 Shirer was in no doubt that Berliners were aware of the violence; on 2 September 1934 he was walking down the Friedrichstrasse with a friend who 'pointed out a building where a year ago for days on end, he said, you could hear the yells of Jews being tortured'. William L. Shirer, *Berlin Diary. The Journal of a Foreign Correspondent 1934–1941* (New York, 1984), p. 15.

47 Hans Albers was an actor who had supporting roles in *The Blue Angel* and *Metropolis*. Gottfried Korff and Reinhard Rürup, (eds.), *Berlin, Berlin. Die Ausstellung zur Geschichte der Stadt* (Berlin, 1987), p. 472.

48 Tuchel and Schattenfroh, *Zentrale des Terrors*, pp. 156–60.

49 Heinrich Fraenkel and Roger Manvell, *Goebbels. Eine Biographie* (Cologne/Berlin, 1960), p. 187.

50 Bella Fromm, *Blood and Banquets: A Berlin Social Diary* (New York, 1944), pp. 99–100. The importance of Ullstein before the Nazi takeover was mirrored in his fantastic building, the 'Ullsteinhaus' on the Mariendorfer Damm, which survived the war. Built by Eugen Schmohl in 1925–6, it was to be, in Ullstein's words, 'a prestigious home for the largest publisher of newspapers and magazines in Europe, whose building is intended to be a striking symbol of the greatness and cultural significance of the house'. Peter Güttler, et. al., *Berlin Brandenburg. Ein Architekturführer* (Berlin, 1990), p. 125.

51 Anonymous, *Why I Left Germany by a German Scientist*, trans. Margaret Goldsmith, p. 123. See also 'The hour of 10 Saturday', *New York Evening Post*, 1 April 1933.

52 Hitler believed that Jews were 'damned' by their race irrespective of their contribution to society. On 23 January 1942 Hitler rejected their achievements, including those of 'philanthropists' who 'endow foundations'. 'When a Jew does that, the thing is particularly noticed – for it's known that they're dirty dogs. As a

rule, it's the most rascally of them who do that sort of thing. And then you'll hear these poor Aryan boobies telling you: "You see, there *are* good Jews!" ' Bormann, *Hitler's Table Talk*, p. 236.

53 Interview with Rita Kuhn, in Owings, *Frauen*, p. 457. On the housing orders see Saul Friedländer, *Nazi Germany and the Jews* (London, 1997), vol. 1: *The Years of Persecution 1933–39*, pp. 292–3.

54 Hitler called Amann a genius and stated: 'He's the greatest newspaper proprietor in the world. Despite his great discretion, which explains why it's not generally known, I declare that Rothermere and Beaverbrook are mere dwarfs compared to him. Today the *Zentral Verlag* owns from 70 per cent to 80 per cent of the German press. Amann achieved all that without the least ostentation . . . Amann makes a point of preserving the individual personality of each of his newspapers.' Bormann, *Hitler's Table Talk*, p. 331. On Amann see Oron J. Hale, *The Captive Press in the Third Reich* (Princeton, 1964), pp. 122–31.

55 David Marsh, *Germany at the Crossroads* (London, 1989), pp. 208–9. See also Jörg Friedrich, *Die kalte Amnestie. NS-Täter in der Bundersrepublik* (Frankfurt-am-Main, 1984); Helmut Genschel, *Die Verdrängung der Juden aus der Wirtschaft im dritten Reich* (Göttingen, 1966).

56 Count von Helldorf was an old friend of Goebbels and was head of the Berlin SA. In July 1935 the Berlin police commissioner Magnus von Levetzow had annoyed Goebbels by not rounding up a group of protestors agitating outside an anti-Semitic film. Goebbels knew Helldorf was in financial trouble, not least because he supported a large group of SA men on his estate, and saw him as an ideal candidate because of his anti-Semitism. Helldorf would later be implicated in the July 1944 plot against Hitler and was sentenced to death. Rolf Georg Reuth, *Goebbels* (London, 1993), p. 205: Goebbels diaries, 9–15 December. See also Friedländer, *Nazi Germany and the Jews*, vol. 1, p. 261.

57 On the Nüremberg Laws see Friedländer, *Nazi Germany and the Jews*, vol. 1, pp. 141–4; see also Otto Dov Kulka, 'Die Nürnberger Rassengesetze und die deutsche Bevölkerung in Lichte Geheimer NS-Lage- und Stimmungsberichte', *Vierteljahresheft für Zeitgeschichte*, 32, 1984; Karl A. Schleunes, *The Twisted Road to Auschwitz: Nazi Policy towards German Jews 1933–1939* (Urbana, 1970).

58 As Saul Friedländer has pointed out, Hitler and Goebbels took great pains to make this appear like a 'spontaneous' outburst. Friedländer, *Nazi Germany and the Jews*, vol. I, p. 270.

59 SOPADE report November 1938, vol. 5, p. 1205.

60 Peukert, *Inside Nazi Germany*, p. 60; Friedländer, *Nazi Germany and the Jews*, vol. 1, pp. 294–5. See also Hermann Graml, *Der 9 November 1938: 'Reichskris-tallnacht'* (Bonn, 1956); Hermann Greive, *Geschichte des modernen Antisemi-tismus in Deutschland* (Darmstadt, 1983); Leonard Gross, *The Last Jews in Berlin* (Toronto, 1983).

61 The conversation took place at Sonnenberg camp, eighty miles north of Berlin. For him the SA youths guarding the camps were the scum of Germany, the product of years of catastrophe, unemployment and violence, who lived accord-ing to the dictum 'kill or be killed'. It was there that he met the former editor of the *Weltbühne* Carl von Ossietzky and other well-known doctors, lawyers

and statesmen dressed in prison uniform. Under the watchful eyes of the guards, Ossietzky asked if Lochner might send him some books, commenting wryly that 'medieval history' would be appropriate. Louis P. Lochner, *What About Germany?* (Toronto, 1942), p. 52.

62 For birth-rate figures in Germany during the Nazi period see *Statistisches Handbuch für Deutschland 1928–1944* (Munich, 1949), p. 53.

63 On the Nazi economy after 1933 see Harold James, *The German Slump. Politics and Economics 1924–1936* (Oxford, 1987). On economic reform see J. Noakes and G. Pridham (eds.), *Nazism. A History in Documents and Eyewitness Accounts 1919–1945*, (New York, 1984), vol. 1, pp. 277–300; see also Richard Overy, *The Nazi Economic Recovery 1932–1938* (London, 1982).

64 As Peter Labyani has pointed out, concentration camp prisoners were literally worked to death in quarries to meet the huge demands for natural stone. Without this ruthless exploitation of labour the projects 'could never have been carried out'. Peter Labyani, 'Images of Fascism: Visualization and Aestheticization in the Third Reich', in Michael Kaffan (ed.), *The Burden of German History 1919–1945* (London, 1988), p. 167.

65 Hitler even insisted that the new Chancellery should have 'permanently at its disposal two hundred of the finest motor-cars. The chauffeurs can perform a secondary function as footmen.' Bormann, *Hitler's Table Talk*, p. 80.

66 Albert Speer, *Fragments of Life*, quoted in Gitta Sereny, *Albert Speer. His Battle with Truth* (London, 1997), p. 27.

67 On 18 January 1942 Hitler recalled his meeting with the British ambassador in 1933, when he told him that he would not honour Germany's debts: 'His reply was: "You mean to say that the new Germany does not recognise the obligations of preceding governments?" I replied: "Freely negotiated agreements, yes! But blackmail, no! Everything that comes under the heading of *Treaty of Versailles* I regard as extortion." "Well, I never!" he said. "I shall immediately inform my Government of that."' Bormann, *Hitler's Table Talk*, p. 224.

68 Rudolf Hess, in the *Völkischer Beobachter*, 13 October 1936.

69 'Inflation is not caused by increasing the fiduciary circulation. It begins on the day when the purchaser is obliged to pay, for the same goods, a higher sum than that asked the day before. At one point one must intervene. Even to Sahacht, I had to begin by explaining this elementary truth: that the essential cause of the stability of our currency was to be sought for in our concentration camps. The currency remains stable when the speculators are put under lock and key . . .'; later, 'When I demanded three thousand millions for rearmament I again met this objection of what we owed abroad. I replied: "You want to give this money to foreigners? Let's rather use it in our own country!"' Bormann, *Hitler's Table Talk*, pp 65, 84–5.

70 For an account of the industrialists' view of the labour movement see Reinhard Neebe, *Grossindustrie, Staat und NSDAP 1930–1933* (Göttingen, 1981).

71 In 1938 the Sicherheitsdienst (Security Service), known by the initials SD, began to compile detailed reports on public opinion. Although they wanted to create a favourable impression they provided an invaluable insight both into the workings of the SD and into views of ordinary Germans. These are published

as Heinz Boberach (ed.), *Meldungen aus dem Reich 1938–1945. Die geheimen Lageberichte des Sicherheitsdienstes der SS*, 17 vols. (Herrsching, 1984). On Berlin's armaments industry see Hans-Erich Volkmann, 'Politik, Wirtschaft und Aufrüstung unter dem Nationalsozialismus', in Manfred Funke (ed.), *Hitler, Deutschland und die Mächte* (Düsseldorf, 1978), pp. 273–91.

72 Interview with Frau Charlotte Müller, in Owings, *Frauen*, p. 159.

73 As Speer noted, 'The public credited Hitler and no one else with the achievements in economics and foreign policy'. Albert Speer, *Inside the Third Reich* (London, 1993), p. 110.

74 Martin Broszat, 'Zur Struktur der NS-Massenbewegung', *Vierteljahresheft für Zeitgeschichte*, 31, 1983, pp. 52–76.

75 *Völkischer Beobachter*, 1 September 1935. See also Grunberger, *A Social History of the Third Reich*, pp. 70–72.

76 Peukert, *Inside Nazi Germany*, p. 69; see also Friedrich Forstmeier and Hans-Erich Volkmann (eds.), *Wirtschaft und Rüstung am Vorabend des zweiten Weltkrieges* (Düsseldorf, 1975).

77 On Ley and the DAF see Helga Grebing, *The History of the German Labour Movement*, trans. Edith Körner, (Leamington Spa, 1985), pp. 140–42.

78 for discussion of workers' attitudes to the Nazi regime see SOPADE reports of April – May 1934. These divided German workers into three categories:

1 *Previously indifferent* These have gone over into the NSBO [National Socialist Works Cells Organisation] because they were told that that is where the fight against the 'red' bosses would be waged. Now they are becoming increasingly disenchanted because they have to pay more than they did when they were in unions and, instead of 'red' bosses, they have got 'brown' ones.

2 *Our previous people* They are still as solid as ever. The total inability of the new people to run a trade union has seen to this, as well as the fact that the labour Front subscriptions are higher than the old ones without producing anything to show for it. (Top subscription: 7Mk a month.)

3 *The old NSBO people* Are angriest, because they are terribly disappointed. Reams of letters of protest are arriving at the NSBO head office demanding information, particularly about the way subscription money is being used.

See also Peukert, *Inside Nazi Germany*, p. 108.

79 Ludolf Herbst, 'Die Krise des nationalsozialistischen Regimes am Vorabend des zweiten Weltkriegs und die forcierte Aufrüstung', *Vierteljahresheft für Zeitgeschichte*, 26, no. 3, pp 347–93.

80 Hitler noted on 24 June 1942 that Berlin was a city of hard work: 'In Berlin, I think, people work harder than anywhere else. I know of no other city in which it would have been possible to complete the construction of the Reich Chancellery in nine months. The Berlin workman is unique as a swift and efficient craftsman. There is nothing to touch him in Munich or Vienna, where the infusion of foreign blood – Polish, Czech, Slav, Italian – still has influence.' Bormann, *Hitler's Table Talk*, p. 532.

81 On the KdF perks see Hans Peter Bleuel, *Strength Through Joy. Sex and Society in Nazi Germany*, ed. Heinrich Fraenhel (London, 1973), pp. 86–92. For all that

has been written about workers' opposition and resistance in the Third Reich there was very little the workers could – or would – do to protest against it. As Tim Mason has put it, 'The behaviour of the German population, civilian and military, from early 1943 to May 1945 remains to me in the end incomprehensible. In circumstances in which the war was obviously lost and the "Hitler Myth" was crumbling, there was obviously much room for given-and-take between the regime and the people . . . there should have been more acts of resistance, especially by the workers, than there in fact were . . .' Tim W. Mason, *Social Policy in the Third Reich* (London, 1993), p. 277.

82 Hitler admired American production methods and hoped to emulate them in Berlin: 'It was reading Ford's books that opened my eyes to these matters . . . In America everything is machine-made, so that they can employ the most utter cretins in their factories.' Bormann, *Hitler's Table Talk*, p. 279.

83 Hitler referred to Dr Porsche as 'the greatest engineering genius in Germany today . . . His experiments made during the war concerning the resistance of materials will enable us continually to improve our Volkswagen.' Ibid., p. 326. Michael Pinto-Duchinsky, 'Can the Beetle live down its terrible past?', *The Times*, 25 August 1997.

84 Grunberger, *A Social History of the Third Reich*, p. 478.

85 Jeffrey Herf, *Reactionary Modernism: Technology, Culture and Politics in Weimar and the Third Reich* (Cambridge, 1984), p. 105.

86 On the official image see for example, 'Mutter, Kind und Staat', *NS-Frauen-Warte*, vol. 8, 1933–4; W. Gross, 'Du bist nichts, Dein Volk ist alles!', *NS-Frauen-Warte*, vol. 6, 1934–5; H. Braun, 'Familie und Volk', *NS-Frauen-Warte*, vol. 7, 1933–4. On the role of women in the Third Reich see Annette Kuhn and Gerhard Schneider (eds.), *Frauen in der Geschichte* (Düsseldorf, 1979); C. Witrock, *Weiblichkeitsmythen. Das Frauenbild im Faschismus und seine Vorläufer in der Frauenbewegung der 20er Jahre* (Frankfurt-am-Main, 1983).

87 Hitler said: 'The essential thing for the future is to have lots of children. Everybody should be persuaded that a family's life is assured only when it has upwards of four children – I should even say, four sons.' Later he would say, 'Nature wants a woman to be fertile. Many women go slightly off their heads when they don't bear children. Everybody says, of a childless woman: 'What a hysterical creature!' Bormann, *Hitler's Table Talk*, pp. 74, 92.

88 *Berliner illustrirte Zeitung*, 4 March 1936.

89 On Goebbels's views about German women see Josef Goebbels, 'Deutschen Frauentum', *Ders: Signale der neuen Zeit* (Munich, 1934), p. 122–30; see also Grunberger, *A Social History of the Third Reich*, p. 73. Restrictions on women working were dropped altogether after Stalingrad in January 1943; by 1944 over 14 million women were working in virtually every field, including the armaments factories, although slave labour was used for the worst jobs.

90 On the Nazi use of jazz and other forms of popular music see Horst J. P. Bergmeier and Rainer E. Lotz, *Hitler's Airwaves. The Inside Story of Nazi Radio Broadcasting and Propaganda Swing* (Yale, 1997), pp. 136–77.

91 George K. Glaser, *Geheimnis und Gewalt* (Stuttgart, 1953), p. 510. Of course Hitler knew about and ordered the looting of art treasures. During a conversation on

17 December 1941, for example, he could joke that his colleague Liebel did not yet know 'that I've found the *Goblet* by Jamnitzeer for him. He supposes it's still at the Hermitage ... I bought it back in Holland at the same time as the objects of the Mannheimer collection. *The Festival of the Rosary* by Albrecht Dürer is still in Prague. So Liebel never misses an opportunity of reminding me that he possesses the frame of this picture.' Bormann, *Hitler's Table Talk*, p. 148.

92 For a discussion of the corruption amongst members of the Nazi elite see, above all, Grunberger, *A Social History of the Third Reich*, pp. 123–44. On Göring see also Joachim Fest, *The Face of the Third Reich*, trans. Michael Bullock (London, 1988), pp. 113–29.

93 Hanfstaengl, *The Missing Years*, p. 229.

94 On Goebbels's indiscretions see 'Joseph Goebbels: The unscratchable itch', in Bleuel, *Strength Through Joy*, pp. 69–73. Streicher's *Der Stürmer* was the most base of Nazi anti-Semitic smear sheets, although Hitler would say: 'Streicher is reproached for his *Stürmer*. The truth is the opposite of what people say: he *idealised* the Jew. The Jew is baser, fiercer, more diabolical than Streicher depicted him.' Bormann, *Hitler's Table Talk*, p. 154.

95 Grunberger, *A Social History of the Third Reich*, p. 89. In his excellent study Grunberger points out that many of the Gauleiter and other party functionaries were, for all the rhetoric about a *völkisch* and classless society, extraordinarily deferential when dealing with nobility: '... one must remember the small-town petit-bourgeois origins of the leadership – as an inclination towards *parvenu* attitudes of deference and emulation *vis-à-vis* hierarchical figures', (pp. 87–8).

96 Saul Friedländer recounts Elberstadt SA leader Adolf Heinrich Frey's visit to the old Jewish widow Susannah Stern's house on 10 November 1938. 'When the lady answered the door in her nightclothes Frey ordered her to dress and go with them. When she refused Frey took his pistol and shot her in the chest: "At the first shot, Stern collapsed on the sofa. She leaned backward and put her hands on her chest. I immediately fired the second shot, this time aiming at the head" ... Proceedings against Frey were dismissed ...' Friedländer, *Nazi Germany and the Jews*, vol. 1, p. 269.

97 Typical propaganda was printed in the catalogue for the Deutschland Ausstellung. A caption pasted over a picture of an Autobahn, a group of German KdF tourists in Norway and a collection tin for the Winterhilfe read: 'Reich motor roads – labour service – holiday trips for all workers – the winter relief work – evidence of the will to reconstruction and the unity of the German people.' Catalogue, *Deutschland Ausstellung 18 Juli bis 16 August 1936* (Berlin, 1936), p. 20. On the status of the block wardens, who kept 'the residents of a particular tenement block under the closest surveillance and ... thrust the Party's collecting tins under their noses on every occasion', see Grunberger, *A Social History of the Third Reich*, p. 96.

98 Joseph Goebbels, 'Rund um die Gedächtniskirche' (23 January 1928), in *Der Angriff: Aufsätze aus der Kampfzeit* (Munich, 1936), p. 338. On the rise of the 'March violets' see David Schoenbaum, *Hitler's Social Revolution* (London, 1967), pp. 235–6.

99 All school and university texts were now 'cleansed'. The British agent Bruce Lockhart said, 'while I was in Berlin, I bought a collection of the new Nazi text-books for schools and universities ... they are written in accordance with the explicit instructions laid down in the handbook of the Reich and Prussian Ministry of Education. They therefore conform to one standard pattern. The central date in Germany's new historical life is the 30th of January, 1933. Everything that happened in Germany before that date leads up to Adolf Hitler. Everything that has happened since 1933 is Adolf Hitler ... The glorification of racial superiority and of the armed might of National Socialism stands out on every page ... Every German who has ever had a liberal idea is either neglected or vilified.' R. H. Bruce Lockhart, *Guns or Butter. War Countries and Peace Countries of Europe Revisited* (London, 1938), pp. 356–7.

100 Borries von Münchhausen, in *Die neue Literatur*, 9 September 1935, p. 599.

101 Hitler had strong views on painting, detesting most art of the Weimar period, when 'the worst rubbish in painting became the expression of the height of artistic accomplishment ... When I visit an exhibition, I never fail to have all the daubs pitilessly withdrawn from it. It will be admitted that whoever visits the House of German Art today will not find any work there that isn't worthy of its place.' Bormann, *Hitler's Table Talk*, p. 371. See also Joseph Wulf (ed.), *Die bildenden Künste im dritten Reich Eine Dokumentation* (Gütersloh, 1963).

102 Some works caused problems for the Nazi censors. One of Lovis Corinth's landscapes was declared 'half acceptable, half degenerate' and the censors were at first not certain how to deal with his work. Peter-Klaus Schuster, Christoph Vitali and Barbara Butts, *Lovis Corinth* (New York, 1996), p. 91.

103 On the exhibition see Peter-Klaus Schuster, *Die 'Kunststadt' München 1937. Nationalsozialismus und 'Entartete Kunst'* (Munich, 1988). For a discussion of painting in Nazi Germany see Berthold Hinz, *Die Malerei im Deutschen Faschismus. Kunst und Konterrevolution* (Frankfurt-am-Main, 1977). Hitler's own views were rather muddled. On 15 June 1943 he defended 'kitsch', claiming that 'the admiration for what we sometimes call chocolate-box beauty is not of itself vicious; it gives evidence, at least, of artistic feeling, which may well become later the basis for real taste. Permanent injury is done only by real depravity in art.' Bormann, *Hitler's Table Talk*, p. 707.

104 Hitler complained that these works were making 'top dollar' on the international art market. See Charles de Jaeger, *The Linz File. Hitler's Plunder of Europe's Art* (Exeter, 1981); Hildegard Brenner, *Kunstpolitik des National Sozialismus* (Hamburg, 1963).

105 Hinz, *Die Malerei im Deutschen Faschismus*; Gabriele Huster, 'Die Verdrängung der Femme Fatale und ihrer Schwestern. Nachdenken über das Frauenbild des Nationalsozialismus', in Klaus Behnken and Frank Wagner (eds.), *Inszenierung der Macht. Asthetische Faszination im Faschismus* (Berlin, 1987), pp. 143–50.

106 On Breker see Wolfgang Fritz Haug, 'Ästhetik der Normalität-Vorstellung und Vorbild. Die Faschisierung des männlichen Akts bei Arno Breker', in Behnken and Wagner, *Inszenierung der Macht*, pp. 79–102. On 18 October 1941 Hitler emphasized the importance of creating heroic sculpture and monuments of

enormous size for posterity: 'If time were to blot out our soldiers' deeds, the monuments I shall have set up in Berlin will continue to proclaim their glory a thousand years from to-day. The Arc de Triomphe, the Pantheon of the Army, the Pantheon of the German people.' Bormann *Hitler's Table Talk*, p. 72.

107 'Partei und Wehrmacht schützen den Frieden des Reiches', *Berliner illustrirte Zeitung*, no. 16, 1939.

108 German works from the Nazi period were not exhibited until 1974 in an exhibition in Frankfurt, which was then shown in other German cities, but this generated much controversy. The catalogue was reissued as *Kunst im 3. Reich. Dokumente der Unterwerfung* (Frankfurt-am-Main, 1979). See the catalogue for the 1978 exhibition sponsored by the Akademie der Künste, *Zwischen Widerstand und Anpassung. Kunst in Deutschland 1933–1945*. Many Nazi works were shown at the exhibition *Inszenierung der Macht* by the Neue Gesellschaft für Bildende Kunst in the Kunstquartier Ackerstrasse, Berlin-Wedding, 1 April – 17 May 1987. In the catalogue see in particular Silke Wenk, 'Aufgerichtete weibliche Körper – Zur allegorischen Skulptur im deutschen Faschismus', in Behnken and Wagner, *Inszenierung der Macht*, p. 104.

109 Hitler stated that his second great contribution to the world was that he had given German supremacy 'a solid cultural foundation. In fact, the power we today enjoy cannot be justified, in my eyes, except by the establishment and expansion of a mighty culture. To achieve this must be the law of our existence ... I wish to be a builder.' Bormann, *Hitler's Table Talk*, p. 82.

110 Indeed, Hitler attacked Rosenberg's *The Myth of the Twentieth Century*, insisting that the book 'is not to be regarded as an expression of the official doctrine of the Party'. Ibid., p. 422.

111 Hitler once criticized Gauleiter Mutschmann in Dresden for hiring poor quality musicians although they were National Socialists: 'After Krauss and Furtwängler, Busch would have become the greatest German conductor, but Mutschmann wanted to force on him old Party comrades for his orchestra, so that this orchestra should be inspired by a good National-Socialist spirit.' Nevertheless he also spat that 'The Jew has brought off the same trick upon music. He has created a new inversion of values and replaced the loveliness of music by noises.' Ibid., p. 325. On music in the Third Reich see Grunberger, *A Social History of the Third Reich*, pp. 512–29; Joseph Wulf (ed.), *Musik im dritten Reich. Eine Dokumentation* (Gütersloh, 1963).

112 On Furtwängler and 'de-Nazification' see George Clare, *Berlin Days 1946–1947* (London, 1989), pp. 74–91.

113 Hitler suggested to Bormann that rather than being subjected to tedious diplomatic protocol important visitors to Berlin should simply be left in the company of the city's charming actresses. As for their appeal to the British, Bruce Lockhart noted that 'To the Germans Shakespeare has long been a German and is already half-a-Nazi.' Lockhart, *Guns or Butter*, p. 365.

114 On the use of film in the euthanasia project see Michael Burleigh, *Death and Deliverance. 'Euthanasia' in Germany 1900–1945* (Cambridge, 1994), 'Selling Murder: The Killing Films of the Third Reich', pp. 183–219.

115 There were memorable scenes of conflict between the 'hopeless' older generation and vigorous youth. When the Hitler Youth leader meets the Communist father he asks where he was born. The father replies, 'In Berlin.' 'And where's that?' 'On the Spree.' The Hitler Youth leader then asks: 'On the Spree – yes of course. But where? What country?' The father responds: 'Oh don't be ridiculous. In Germany, of course.' The Hitler Youth leader retorts: 'Yes, of course, in Germany. In OUR Germany. Now, you'd better think about that.' The entire script is reproduced in Helmut Lessing and Manfred Liebel, *Wilde Cliquen* (Bensheim, 1981), p. 153.

116 A book based on the film, *Wir beginnen das Wunschkonzert für die Wehrmacht*, sold 200,000 copies in Germany. Marc Silbermann, 'The Fascist Discourse in Cinema: A Reading of Eduard von Bursody's "Wunschkonzert"', in Ingeborg Hoestery and Ulrich Weisstein (eds.), *Intertextuality: German Literature and Visual Arts from the Renaissance to the Twentieth Century* (Columbia, 1993). The lead actress in the film published an autobiography which includes discussion of the film. Ilse Werner, *So wird's nie wieder sein. Ein leben mit Pfiff* (Bayreuth, 1982).

117 Joseph Wulf, *Theater und Film im dritten Reich. Eine Dokumentation* (Gütersloh, 1984); Julian Petley, *Capital and Culture. German Cinema 1933–45* (London, 1945), p. 6.

118 Peter Jelavich, *Berlin Cabaret* (Harvard, 1993), p. 252.

119 Ibid., p. 253.

120 The Nazi newspaper *Das schwarze Korps* used pictures of women taken at a Scala to illustrate degrading and 'negative' images of women. To his credit the director Will Schaeffers bravely introduced the performance the next day with the words: 'We left our nude dancer at home today, since I have no desire to appear a second time in *Das schwarze Korps*. I don't know if you saw that – apparently not. That just proves that the paper doesn't have the circulation that its editors think it does.' A number of SS walked out at that point and Schaeffers was put under great pressure to apologize, which he did in a grovelling letter to *Das schwarze Korps*. See also Jelavich, *Berlin Cabaret*, p. 253.

121 Those forced to leave included some of the most memorable writers and performers of the Weimar cabaret, including Kurt Gerron, Valeska Gert, Paul Fraetz, Fritz Brünbaum, Annemarie Hase, Friedrich Holländer, Margo Lion, Walther Mehring, Paul Morgan, Rudolf Nelson, Kurt Robitschek and Mischa Spoliansky. Paul Nikolaus wrote a tragic note before committing suicide in Lucerne, in which he said: 'For once, no joke: I am taking my own life. Why? I could not return to Germany without taking it there. I cannot work there now, I do not want to work there now, and yet unfortunately I have fallen in love with my fatherland. I cannot live in these times.' A number of others who had escaped Nazi Germany were eventually captured as other countries were occupied. Kurt Gerron, the Berlin star of the 1920s, turned down Marlene Dietrich's offer to get him from Holland to the United States; he was sent to Theresienstadt, where he helped set up the cabaret *Karussell*. He died in Auschwitz. Willy Rosen, Max Ehrlich and Erich Ziegler were three of the many thousands of German Jews who were captured in Holland and sent to Theresien-

stadt; Ehrlich and Rosen were murdered in Auschwitz; Ziegler survived. On the fate of these extraordinary artists see Jelavich, *Berlin Cabaret*, p. 231. See also Will Meisel, *Willy Rosen: 'Text und Musik von mir'* (Berlin, 1967); Zdenek Lederer, *Ghetto Theresienstadt* (New York, 1983); H. G. Adler, *Theresienstadt 1941–1945: Das Antlitz einer Zwangsgemeinschaft* (Tübingen, 1955).

122 Erwin Lowinsky, 'Von der Jägerstrasse zum Kurfürstendamm erzählen', in Frauke Deissner-Jennsen (ed.), *Die zehnte Muse: Kabarettisten erzählen* (Berlin, 1986), p. 266.

123 The distinction made by the Gestapo during trials for such behaviour was between 'popular opposition' or *Volksopposition* and 'malicious offences' or *Heimtückedelikte* – the latter could mean the death sentence. See Peukert, *Inside Nazi Germany*, p. 52.

124 Hitler announced that Berlin was a simple and dignified city until the epoch of the nineteenth course, after which there was 'a surfeit of bad food indifferently cooked, the era of Wilhelm II and the bad taste which was its hallmark! A happy hunting-ground for the upstart, a vicious and degenerate Society, and a Court life that was a ridiculous as it was undignified. A woman like the wife of General Litzmann had not the entrée to the Court, but any old rich Jewess, or the daughter of any old Chicago pork king, was most welcome.' It was his task 'to see that the Berlin of the future is worthy of the capital of the world; not a city of feasting and carousing, but a city beauteous and gracious to live in.' Bormann, *Hitler's Table Talk*, pp. 679–80.

125 'Hundreds of windows are mirrored in the Landwehr Canal. One of the greatest office buildings to lend its image to the Tirpitz-Ufer.' *Berliner illustrirte Zeitung*, March 1937, p. 17.

126 Hart-Davis, *Hitler's Games*, p. 13.

127 Hitler said on 12 April 1942 that 'the Olympic Games afforded us a unique opportunity to amass foreign credits, and at the same time a splendid chance of enhancing our prestige abroad. I can still see the faces of my colleagues when I said that I proposed to make a preliminary grant of twenty-eight million marks for the construction of the Berlin stadium!' Bormann, *Hitler's Table Talk*, p. 426. See also Werner March, *Bauwerk Reichssportfeld* (Berlin, 1936), pp. 16–17.

128 Hart-Davis, *Hitler's Games*, pp. 105–16. Christian Engeli and Wolfgang Ribbe, 'Berlin in der NS-Zeit (1933–1945)', in Wolfgang Ribbe (ed.), *Geschichte Berlins* (Munich, 1987), vol. 2: *Von der Märzrevolution bis zur Gegenwart*, p. 972.

129 This is evident in the Olympic Committee reports: *Bulletins of the International Olympic Committee, 1926–1936* (Anvers, 1937); see also Arnd Krüger, 'Die Olympischen Spiele 1936 und die Weltmeinung', in *Sportwissenschaftliche Arbieten*, 7 (Berlin, 1972), pp. 42–54.

130 E. L. Woodward, in Hart-Davis, *Hitler's Games*, pp. 115–16.

131 The official Olympic reports substantiated this view. *The XIth Olympic Games: Berlin, 1936* (Berlin, 1937).

132 'Türme der Wissenschaft, Hochburgen der Wirtschaft', *Berliner illustrirte Zeitung. Zur 700 Jahr-Feier der Reichshauptstadt, Heimat Berlin*, March 1937, pp. 16–17.

133 Hitler revealed that he had once toyed with the idea of moving the capital to Lake Müritz in Mecklenburg; 'Speer persuaded me to abandon the idea, because the soil there is bad, from the building point of view, as it is in Berlin. I shall see to it that Berlin acquires all the characteristics of a great capital. But none of this is based on a sentimental preference. I do not like the Berliners more than I like the Viennese. I feel equally at home anywhere in the Reich, and my love for all Germans is equal, as long as they do not range themselves against the interests of the Reich, of which I am the guardian.' Bormann, *Hitler's Table Talk*, pp. 709–10.

134 Sereny, *Albert Speer*, p. 153.

135 Ibid., p. 149.

136 Hitler claimed that he had wanted to rebuild Berlin since his youth: 'I lived in palaces of the imagination, and it was precisely at that time that I conceived the plans for the new Berlin.' Bormann, *Hitler's Table Talk*, p. 45.

137 On Hitler's plans for his new Chancellery see Speer, *Inside the Third Reich*, p. 202. Hitler also believed that 'The heroic deeds of our troops will turn pale, one day . . . But the monuments we shall have built will defy the challenge of time. The Coliseum at Rome has survived all passing events. Here, in Germany, the cathedrals have done the same . . . To accomplish my work as a builder, I have recourse especially to men of the South – I install in Berlin my greatest architect . . . My acts are always based upon a political mode of thinking . . . Berlin will one day be the capital of the world.' Bormann, *Hitler's Table Talk*, p. 82.

138 'One will arrive there along wide avenues containing the Triumphal Arch, the Pantheon of the Army, the Square of the People – things to take your breath away!' Ibid., p. 81. According to Speer, the buildings were meant to 'serve chiefly for purposes of prestige, not for the housing of the bureaucratic apparatus'. Speer, *Inside the Third Reich*, p. 200.

139 Hitler insisted that 'we shall succeed in eclipsing our only rival in the world, Rome. Let it be built on such a scale that St. Peter's and its Square will seem like toys in comparison.' Bormann, *Hitler's Table Talk*, p. 81; Speer, *Inside the Third Reich*, p. 203.

140 'For material we'll use granite. The vestiges of the German past, which are found on the plains to the North, are scarcely time-worn. Granite will ensure that our monuments last for ever. In ten thousand years they'll be still standing, just as they are, unless meanwhile the sea has again covered our plains.' Bormann, *Hitler's Table Talk*, p. 81.

141 The grandeur was consciously designed for intimidation; for control of Russians he noted on 9 August 1941 that 'Once a year we shall lead a troop of Kirghizes through the capital of the Reich, in order to strike their imaginations with the size of our monuments.' Ibid., p. 24.

142 Ibid., p. 41.

143 On the first Berlin raid see Max Hastings, *Bomber Command* (London, 1992), pp. 104–5.

144 Hitler became increasingly ambitious for Berlin; in March 1942 he said 'Berlin, as a world capital, can make one think only of ancient Egypt, it can be compared

only to Babylon or Rome. In comparison with this capital, what will London stand for, or Paris?' Bormann, *Hitler's Table Talk*, p. 361.
145 Interview with Frau Margarete Fischer, in Owings, *Frauen*, p. 1.

12: THE SECOND WORLD WAR

1 The Berlin beaucracy created by the Nazis was disliked by other Germans; as Hitler said, 'I'm not surprised that the country is full of hatred for Berlin. Ministries ought to direct from above, not interfere with details of execution. The Civil Service has reached the point of being only a blind machine.' Later he would say: 'The Berlin bureaucracies confuse central administration, whose proper task is to indicate broad lines and to intervene when help is required, with a species of unitarianism, which lays a cold and lethal hand on activity throughout the country. The danger is a very real one, because during the last twenty years the ministerial bureaucracies have grown and expanded . . . If we allow the bureaucrats to continue in their present ways, in a few years we shall find that the nation has lost all faith in the administration.' Martin Bormann (ed.), *Hitler's Table Talk, 1941–1944*, intro. Hugh Trevor-Roper (Oxford, 1988), p. 104.
2 Hitler clearly intended Berlin to be not a cultural centre but rather a place which would project German strength and German militarism. On 3 May 1942 he announced that 'Brilliant city though Berlin undoubtedly is, I doubt whether we can make of it a metropolis of the Arts. As a metropolis of political and military power, it is ideal, as I realised on the occasion of the procession organised for my last birthday.' Even so there was no reason to allow 'any other town to gain the stature of Berlin'. Ibid., p. 458.
3 I have drawn on a number of sources in the general discussion of the war; see the documents of the German Foreign Ministry archives published as *Akten zur deutschen auswärtigen Politik 1918–1945*, part of which has been translated into English as *Germany. Auswärtiges Amt, Documents on German Foreign Policy*, Series D (Washington, DC, 1949); *Trials of the Major War Criminals before the International Military Tribunal* (Nuremberg) and Military History Research Office of the German Federal Republic, *Das deutsche Reich und der zweite Weltkrieg*, 6 vols.; P. Schramm, *Kriegstagebuch des OKW der Wehrmacht*, 8 vols., (Munich, 1963). I have used a number of general histories, including Peter Calvocoressi, Guy Wint and John Pritchard, *Total War. The Causes and Courses of the Second World War* (Harmondsworth, 1989); Gordon Wright, *The Ordeal of Total War, 1939–1945* (London, 1954); John Keegan, *The Second World War* (London, 1989); Janusz Piekalkiewicz, *Der zweite Welktkrieg* (Düsseldorf, 1985); Hans-Adolf Jacobsen and Hands Dollinger, *Der zweite Weltkreig in Bildern und Dokumenten*, 3 vols. (Wiesbaden, 1963); Norman Rich, *Hitler's War Aims: Ideology, the Nazi State and the Course of Expansion* (New York, 1974).
4 'The Ukraine, and then the Volga basin, will one day be the granaries of Europe. We shall reap much more than what actually grows from the soil. It must not be forgotten that, from the time of the Tsars, Russia with her hundred and

seventry million people, has never suffered from famine. We shall also keep
Europe supplied with iron ... We'll get it from Russia'; and again, 'We'll supply
grain to all in Europe who need it. The Crimea will give us its citrus fruits,
cotton and rubber (100,000 acres of plantation would be enough to ensure our
independence). The Pripet marshes will keep us supplied with reeds. We'll
supply the Ukrainians with scarves, glass beads and everything that colonial
people like.' Bormann, *Hitler's Table Talk*, pp. 28, 34.

5 The Hossbach Memorandum did not specifically mention war in the east but
did talk of the 'right to a greater living space'. Most important was that Hitler
expressly set out his foreign policy aims, rearmament and commitment to war,
to 'Anschluss' with Austria, and the destruction of Czechoslovakia. Friedrich
Hossbach, *Zwischen Wehrmacht und Hitler 1934–1938* (Wolfenbüttel-Hanover,
1965), pp. 190–91. The memorandum is in *Germany. Auswärtiges Amt, Documents on German Foreign Policy*, vol. I: pp. 38–9.

6 Göring informed the Austrian Seyss-Inquart that if the Nazi demands were not
met, 'then an invasion by the troops already mobilized on the border will follow
tonight and that will be the end of Austria ... The invasion will only be stopped
and the troops remain at the border if we hear by 7.30 that Miklas has handed
over the Chancellorship to you ... and you must let the National Socialists
loose throughout the whole country. They are now to be allowed to go on the
streets everywhere ...' Field Marshall Göring to Seyss-Inquart, 11 March 1938,
Vienna – Berlin, 17:26–17:31, quoted in J. Noakes and G. Pridham, *Nazism* (New
York, 1984), vol. 2, p. 704.

7 William Shirer recalled arriving at his house on the Ploesslgasse in Vienna on
19 March; like all other houses in the street, it was guarded by SS men. ' "Where
can I find your commandant?" I asked. "In the Rothschild palace" ... As we
entered we almost collided with some SS officers who were carting up silver
and other loot from the basement. One had a gold-framed picture under his
arm. One was the commandant. His arms were loaded with silver knives and
forks, but he was not embarrassed.' Three days later Shirer wrote: 'On the streets
today gangs of Jews, with jeering storm troopers standing over them and taunting
crowds around them, on their hands and knees scrubbing the Schuschnigg signs
off the sidewalks. Many Jews killing themselves. All sorts of reports of Nazi
sadism and from the Austrians it surprises me. Jewish men *and* women made
to clean latrines. Hundreds of them just picked up at random off the streets to
clean the toilets of the Nazi boys.' William L. Shirer, *Berlin Diary. The Journal
of a Foreign Correspondent 1934–1941* (New York, 1984), pp. 109–11.

8 John Weitz, *Hitler's Diplomat. The Life and Times of Joachim von Ribbentrop*
(New York, 1992), p. 183.

9 Neville Chamberlain gave in to Hitler's demands. Calvocoressi noted that
whereas the aim of appeasement to Weimar Germany in the 1920s was 'justice',
the aim of appeasement to Nazi Germany in the thirties was 'safety'; the price
of the latter was 'turning a blind eye to German ambitions and what these cost
other people (primarily Czechoslovakia). Munich, where Czechoslovakia was
sacrificed, became synonymous with betrayal, as Canossa with a similar kind
of abasement.' Calvocoressi et al., *Total War*, p. 82. As Wheeler-Bennett has

put it, 'Had Mr Chamberlain returned to London, not with garlands but in sackcloth, and urged Britain to embark upon a policy of "blood, sweat, toil and tears" our national record would have been cleaner and we should have been the better prepared, both morally and materially, for the ultimate conflict.' John W. Wheeler-Bennett, *Munich, Prologue to Tragedy* (London, 1948), p. 293.

10 Reinhard Spitzy, *So Haben wir das Reich verspielt. Bekentnisse eines Illegalen* (Munich, 1988), p. 320.

11 Winston Churchill, in *House of Commons Debates*, 5 October 1938, col. 367–8. Hitler's annoyance at Chamberlain's 'interference' was given in evidence by Schacht before the International Military Tribunal at Nuremberg on 2 May 1946 (Part 13, p. 4). On Churchill and the war see above all, Winston S. Churchill, *The Second World War*, 6 vols. (London, 1948–53); Martin Gilbert, *Winston S. Churchill*, (London, 1983–6), vol. 6: *Finest Hour*, and vol. 7: *Road to Victory*; Martin Gilbert, *Churchill: A Life* (London, 1991). See also William Manchester, *The Last Lion: Winston Spencer Churchill* (Boston, 1988), vol. 2: *Alone, 1932–1940*, p. 303.

12 This account is given in Dr Paul Schmidt, *Statist auf diplomatischer Bühne, 1923–1945* (Bonn, 1951), p. 190. Ribbentrop merely noted that 'At night Hacha was received at the Reich Chancellery, where Hitler announced his intention to occupy Bohemia and Moravia,' Joachim von Ribbentrop, *The Ribbentrop Memoirs* (London, 1954), pp. 94–5.

13 Sir Neville Henderson, *Failure of a Mission: Berlin 1937–1939* (New York, 1940), p. 60.

14 Newsreel no. 451, 20 April 1939.

15 Stalin's telegram to Hitler on 21 August 1939 read: 'To the Chancellor of the German Reich, Herr A. Hitler. I thank you for your letter. I hope that the German–Soviet non-aggression pact will bring a great turn for the better in the political relations between our two countries . . . The Soviet govenment has instructed me to inform you that it agrees to Herr von Ribbentrop's arriving in Moscow on 23 August. J. Stalin.' *Documents on German Foreign Policy*, Series D, vols. IV–XII (HMSO). See also R. J. Sonntag and J. S. Beddie (eds.), *Nazi–Soviet Relations, 1939–41; Documents from the Archives of the German Foreign Office* (Washington, DC, 1948), p. 78. On the international response to the pact see Wolfgang Leonhard, *Betrayal. The Hitler–Stalin Pact of 1939*, trans. D. Bosley (New York, 1989), pp. 73–172.

16 His views are reflected in a brief selection of his words to Bormann: 'The Slavs are a mass of born slaves, who feel the need of a master'; 'The Russian space is our India. Like the English we shall rule this empire with a handful of men'; or 'I am not a partisan, either, of a university at Kiev. It's better not to teach them to read . . . We'll find amongst them the human material that's indispensable for tilling the soil'; 'This Russian desert, we shall populate it . . . We'll take away its character of an Asiatic steppe, we'll Europeanise it'; 'Our guiding principle must be that these people have but one justification for existence – to be of use to us economically. We must concentrate on extracting from these territories everything that it is possible to extract'. Subject peoples would receive no education, culture or health care: 'In the field of public health there is no need

whatsoever to extend to the subject races the benefits of our own knowledge. This would result only in an enormous increase in local populations, and I absolutely forbid the organisation of any sort of hygiene or cleanliness crusades in these territories.' Bormann, *Hitler's Table Talk*, pp. 33, 34, 68, 424, 425.

17 Ibid., pp. 35-42.

18 Schmidt, *Statist auf diplomatischer Bühne*, p. 445.

19 Sonntag and Beddie, *Nazi–Soviet Relations, 1939–41*, p. 78.

20 Interview with Frau Mathilde Mundt, in Alison Owings, *Frauen: German Women Recall the Third Reich*, (Harmondsworth, 1993), p. 97.

21 Interview with Irene Burchert, ibid., p. 142.

22 Shirer wrote this after witnessing Berliners' response to *Der Führer*, headlines: 'WARSAW THREATENS BOMBARDMENT OF DANZIG – UNBELIEVABLE AGITATION OF THE POLISH ARCH-MADNESS [POLNISCHEN GRÖSSEN-WAHNS]!' Shirer, *Berlin Diary*, p. 173. On Nazi radio propaganda see C. Schubiger, *La guerre des ondes* (Geneva, 1941).

23 Gitta Sereny, *Albert Speer: His Battle with Truth* (London, 1995), p. 207.

24 Interview with Irene Burchert, in Owings, *Frauen*, p. 143.

25 Hitler believed that the Germans had practised a misguided 'policy of kindness' toward Poles in the Second Empire, in which 'kindly Germans of the interior – who suppose, for their part, that kindliness is the way to win these foreign hearts for Germany, had only inflamed Polish nationalism'. The only way to prevent such nationalism was to be completely brutal. Bormann, *Hitler's Table Talk*, p. 234.

26 Paul Schmidt, *Hitler's Interpreter* (New York, 1950), pp. 157–8.

27 Ibid., p. 158.

28 Henderson, *Failure of a Mission*, p. 87.

29 Even so, Shirer noted on 3 September: 'In 1914, I believe, the excitement in Berlin on the first day of the World War was tremendous. Today, no excitement, no hurrahs, no cheering, no throwing of flowers, no war fever, no war hysteria.' Shirer, *Berlin Diary*, p. 210.

30 On 5 April 1942 Hitler explained his bizarre notion that Poles who had shown any bravery in battle 'were actually of German descent'. Intermarriage should be banned so that no more of this 'good German blood' would mix with Polish blood and be used against Germany: 'It's very important for the future that the Germans don't mingle with the Poles, so that the new Germanic blood may not be transmitted to the Polish ruling class. Himmler is right when he says that the Polish generals who genuinely put up a serious resistance in 1939 were, so to speak, exclusively of German descent.' Bormann, *Hitler's Table Talk*, p. 405.

31 On 5 April 1942 Hitler once again stated that Poles must be kept under control by being 'outnumbered by the German elements. It was agreed with Frank, the Governor-General of occupied Poland, that the Cracow district (with its purely German capital) and also the Lublin district should be peopled by Germans. Once these two weak spots have been strengthened it should be possible to drive the Poles slowly back.' Ibid., p. 405.

32 Wladyslaw Bartoszewski was imprisoned by Stalin after the war. His publications include *Warsaw Death Ring* (1972) and *The Warsaw Ghetto As It Really Was*

(1983). In 1990 he was voted the Chairman of the International Council of the Museum at Auschwitz; between 1990 and 1995 he was Polish ambassador to Vienna; he was made Polish Foreign Minister in 1995 and elected to the Senate in 1997. F. Ryszka pointed out that the Germans meant to create a 'psychosis of fear' and to 'humiliate Poles . . . and completely to disregard their personal dignity and feelings'. F. Ryszka, *Państwo stanu wyjatkowego. Rzecz o systemie państwa i prawa w Trzeciej Rzeszy* (Wroclaw, 1974), pp. 302–5.

33 Professor Voss, diary extract, 15 June 1941, quoted in Michael Burleigh, *Germany Turns Eastward* (Cambridge, 1988), p. 294. For further extracts from Voss's diary see Götz Aly, Peter Chroust, H. D. Heilmann and H. Langbein, *Beiträge zur nationalsozialistischen Gesundheits- und Sozialpolitik* (Berlin, 1987), pp. 15–18.

34 Howard K. Smith, *Last Train from Berlin* (London, 1942), p. 38.

35 Ibid., p. 67.

36 Ferdinand Krones, in Johannes Steinoff, Peter Pechel and Dennis Showalter (eds.), *Voices from the Third Reich. An Oral History* (New York, 1994), p. 77.

37 Werner Bartels, ibid., p. 78.

38 When von Kluge asked him his impressions of Paris, Hitler replied, 'The old part of Paris gives a feeling of complete distinction. The great vistas are imposing. Over a period of years I sent my colleagues to Paris so as to accustom them to grandeur – against the time when we would undertake, on new bases, the re-making and development of Berlin. At present Berlin doesn't exist, but one day she'll be more beautiful than Paris.' Bormann, *Hitler's Table Talk*, p. 98; Albert Speer, *Inside the Third Reich* (New York, 1993), p. 249.

39 Shirer, *Berlin Diary*, p. 451.

40 Ibid., p. 452.

41 Alexsander Bregmann, *Najlepszy sujusznik Hitlera* (London, 1980), pp. 104–5.

42 Józef Garlinski, *Poland in the Second World War* (London, 1985), p. 38.

43 Molotov described his meetings with Hitler in *Sto Sorok Besed s Molotvym* (Moscow, 1991). For the English translation see Albert Resis (ed.), *Molotov Remembers. Inside Kremlin Politics. Conversations with Felix Chuev* (Chicago, 1991), pp. 14–20.

44 Speer, *Inside the Third Reich*, p. 317.

45 Operation Sealion: 'Preparations for a landing operation against England', *DGFP*, Series D, vol. X, pp 226-8.

46 On the Battle of Britain see Keegan, *The Second World War*, p. 88–102.

47 On 26 October 1941 Hitler stated that it would now be in Britain's own interest to join with Germany against Russia: 'If the English are clever, they will seize the psychological moment to make an about-turn – and they will march on our side. By getting out of the war now, the English would succeed in putting their principal competitor – the United States – out of the game for thirty years . . . At present England no longer interests me. I am interested only in what's behind her.' Bormann, *Hitler's Table Talk*, pp. 92–3.

48 Erich Kuby, *Die Russen in Berlin, 1945* (Munich, 1965), p. 118.

49 Peter Jelavich, *Berlin Cabaret* (Harvard, 1993), p. 256.

50 Richard Grunberger, *A Social History of the Third Reich* (Harmondsworth, 1991), p. 58.

51 As Ian Kershaw has noted, 'The Führer had become like a drug for the people, needed for reassurance whenever doubts, worries and uncertainties began to mount.' Ian Kershaw, *The 'Hitler' Myth. Image and Reality in the Third Reich* (Oxford, 1987), p. 158.

52 On 7 January 1942 Hitler even tried to convince himself that Churchill was unpopular there: 'The opposition to Churchill is in the process of gaining strength in England . . . If a nation were to quit the war before the end of the war, I seriously think it might be England.' Bormann, *Hitler's Table Talk*, pp. 187–8.

53 Goebbels diaries, 16 June 1941.

54 On 17 September Hitler said of the decision not to publish propaganda against the Soviets, 'I couldn't start a campaign of propaganda to create a climate favourable for the reverse situation; and innumerable lives were saved by the fact that no newspaper or magazine article ever contained a word that could have let anyone guess what we were preparing . . . there were many people amongst us who might have reflected that we had, after all, a pact of friendship with the Russians.' Bormann, *Hitler's Table Talk*, p. 31.

55 Smith, *Last Train from Berlin*, p. 47. On Hitler's plans to invade the Soviet Union see Helmuth Greiner, *Die oberste Wehrmachtführung 1939–43* (Wiesbaden, 1951).

56 One of the problems was that there was no communication between the two and that 'Neither of the dictators was by nature a cooperator. They lacked – indeed despised – the habits of intercourse and interchange which are the everyday experience of democratic politicians.' On the disastrous results for Hitler see Calvocoressi et al., *Total War*, pp. 168–85.

57 Franz Halder, *Diary* (Nuremberg: Office of Chief of Counsel for War Crimes, 1946), vi. 42 (entry for 30 March 1941).

58 Those sycophantic generals, including Keitel and Jodl, did not question the order to attack. Admiral Raeder, Commander-in-Chief of the German navy, openly cirticized it, saying that Germany should win the war against Britain before turning on the Soviet Union. General Halder was sceptical, and General von Brauchitsch noted that the risk in the west 'must not be underestimated'. Alexander Dallin, *German Rule in Russia 1941-1945. A Study of Occupation Policies* (London, 1988), pp. 15–16.

59 Karl Rupp, in Steinhoff et al., *Voices from the Third Reich*, p. 127.

60 Many were also worried about the outbreak of war on two fronts; indeed Rudolf Hess's flight to Scotland on 10 May was thought to be a strange attempt to make peace in the west so that Germany could turn against Russia without having to worry about the western front. And yet, although a number of Hitler's generals from von Hassel to Beck, from Popitz to Oster, were critical of the invasion, they did nothing to act against Hitler. Ulrich von Hassel, *The Von Hassell Diaries* (Garden City, New York, 1967), pp. 197–9.

61 Chadayev was with Stalin at the time and noted the dictator's disbelief and shock at the news; indeed for a time he 'hated everybody and everything for the error he had made'. Edvard Radzinsky, *Stalin*, trans. Harry Willets, (London, 1997), p. 447–50. See also Dmitri Volkogonov, *Stalin: Triumph and Tragedy*, ed. and trans. Harry Shukman (London, 1991).

62 On the purges see Robert Conquest, *Stalin. Breaker of Nations* (London, 1991),

pp. 171–235; on Stalin's response to the declaration of war see pp. 236–9.

63 Hitler contradicted this later in the war, when he stated that 'what confirmed me in my decision to attack [Russia] without delay was the information brought by a German mission lately returned from Russia, that a single Russian factory was producing by itself more tanks than all our factories together.' Even so, he claimed that the Russian soldiers had not improved since 1914: 'One can even say that the Russian's fought better during the First World War,' Bormann, *Hitler's Table Talk*, pp. 182, 172.

64 This was not surprising given Soviet treatment of ethnic groups under their control, not least the orchestrated famine accompanied by deceit on an extraordinary scale which Pasternak called 'the inhuman power of the lie'; see, for example, Robert Conquest, *Harvest of Sorrow* (London, 1988). Ukrainians had hoped for German support in plans for reunification and independence. Dallin, *German Rule in Russia*, p. 107.

65 Calvocoressi et al., *Total War*, pp. 192–5.

66 Harry W. Flannery, *Assignment to Berlin* (London, 1942), p. 259.

67 Peter Pechel, in Steinhoff et al., *Voices from the Third Reich*, p. 131.

68 Karl Rupp, ibid., p. 129.

69 Willi Nolden, ibid., p. 142.

70 Hitler noted, 'We've forgotten the bitter tenacity with which the Russians fought us during the First World War ... We knew ... a type of Russian combatant who was more good-natured than cruel. Nowadays, this type no longer exists. Bolshevism has completely wiped it out.' Bormann, *Hitler's Table Talk*, p. 41.

71 Hugo Volkheimer, in Steinhoff et al., *Voices from the Third Reich*, p. 147.

72 Hitler admitted to this collection of fur coats on 6 January 1942 when he said, 'It's really moving to observe what is happening just now about the collection of wool for the Russian front. Civilians deprive themselves of their most precious possessions. But they must have the conviction that everything is being put through without the slightest fraud, and that every object will reach its proper destination. Let anyone beware, therefore, who might try to interfere with the proper channels and intercept, for example, such-and-such a sumptuous fur, which will be worn perhaps by the simplest of our soldiers.' Bormann, *Hitler's Table Talk*, p. 185. See also Hugo Volkheimer, in Steinhoff et al., *Voices from the Third Reich*, p. 146.

73 Sereny, *Albert Speer*, p. 238.

74 Michael Burleigh, 'Nazi Europe', in Niall Ferguson (ed.), *Virtual History. Alternatives and Counterfactuals* (London, 1997), p. 323.

75 Karl Rupp, in Steinhoff et al., *Voices from the Third Reich*, p. 129.

76 The stone has since been used to face the buildings along Tverskaya, one of Moscow's grandest streets, and was largely put in place by German prisoners of war.

77 On Stalin's extraordinary conduct during the war see Adam B. Ulam, *Stalin. The Man and His Era* (London, 1989), pp. 536–615.

78 Richard Sorge, one of the early members of the German Communist Party headed a spy ring in Japan for the GRU from the mid 1930s until his arrest in 1941. Although he did transmit information about Japan's decision to move

south against Indo-China rather than north against the Soviet Union, there is increasing evidence that Stalin had already decided to move some troops before Sorge's message reached Moscow. His loyal service did not stop Stalin from excuting him in 1944. See Robert Whymant, *Stalin's Spy. Richard Sorge and the Tokyo Espionage Ring* (London, 1996).

79 Peter Pechel, in Steinhoff et al., *Voices from the Third Reich*, p. 132.

80 Sereny, *Albert Speer*, p. 269.

81 Hitler had nothing but contempt for the Americans and did not understand the significance of his declaration of war. On 4 January, shortly after the American entry into the war, he said of Roosevelt, 'there's no doubt about it, he's a sick brain. The noise he made at his press conference was typically Hebraic. There's nobody stupider than the Americans.' And on 5 January 1941, 'I'll never believe that an American soldier can fight like a hero'; on 7 January, 'I don't see much future for the Americans. In my view, it's a decayed country.' Bormann, *Hitler's Table Talk*, pp. 179, 188.

82 Hitler was blunt: 'As for the natives, we'll have to screen them carefully. The Jew, who destroyed, we shall drive out. As far as the population is concerned, I get a better impression in White Russia than in Ukraine. We shan't settle in the Russian towns, and we'll let them fall to pieces without intervening. And, above all, no remorse on this subject! We're not going to play at children's nurses; we're absolutely without obligations as far as these people are concerned ... For the rest, let them know just enough to understand our highway signs, so that they won't get themselves run over by our vehicles ... In this business I shall go straight ahead, cold-bloodedly. What they may think about me, at this juncture, is to me a matter of complete indifference ... Everything that resembles civilisation, the Bolsheviks have suppressed it, and I have no feelings about the idea of wiping out Kiev, Moscow or St. Petersburg.' Ibid., pp. 69–71. See, above all, Dallin, *German Rule in Russia*; Christian Striet, *Keine Kameraden: Die Wehrmacht und die sowjetischen kriegsgefangenen 1941–1945*. (Stuttgart, 1978); Omer Bartov, *German Troops and the Barbarization of Warfare* (New York, 1985).

83 On the Active Museum of Fascism and Resistance in Berlin see Brian Ladd, *The Ghosts of Berlin. Confronting German History in the Urban Landscape* (Chicago, 1997), pp. 169–70.

84 Himmler was proud of his ability to record everything. On 24 January 1942 he told Hitler, 'I've arranged that each of my subordinates shall sign everything that issues from our offices, with his own name and in a legible fashion. Thus one always knows with whom one is dealing, and nobody can take refuge behind abstractions.' Bormann, *Hitler's Table Talk*, p. 240.

85 Hitler said of Russia on 22 February 1942, 'We'll get our hands on the finest land, and we'll guarantee for ourselves the control of the vital points. We'll know how to keep the population in order. There won't be any question of our arriving there with kid gloves and dancing-masters.' Ibid., p. 327.

86 Peter Peterson, in Steinhoff et al., *Voices from the Third Reich*, p. 9.

87 Dallin, *German Rule in Russia*, pp. 409–27; Martin Gilbert rightly points out that the story of the mass murder of Russian prisoners of war in German hands

'is one of the least known atrocity stories of the Second World War', and notes that of a total of 5,700,000 Russian soldiers captured in the Second World War, 2,500,000 died in captivity. Of them, it is estimated that one million were shot by the Einsatzgruppen and that the rest died from hunger, cold and disease in camps where they were often denied even the rudiments of shelter and medical attention.' Sites of the murder of Russian prisoners of war in the area of post-1945 Poland are listed in *Obozy hitlerowskie na ziemiach polskich 1939–45: Informator encyclopedyczny* (Warsaw, 1979). Martin Gilbert, *The Holocaust. The Jewish Tragedy*, (London, 1986), p. 845, nn. 12, 13.

88 Lothar Loewe, in Steinhoff et al., *Voices from the Third Reich*, p. 474.

89 Hitler sanctioned this; on 29 December 1941 he stated, 'A Russian is not so stupid, after all, that he can't work in a mine . . . With the help of this colossal human material – I estimate the employable Russian labour at two and a half millions – we'll succeed in producing the machine tools we need'; 'I'm in favour of great public works (building of tunnels, etc.) being carried out for the duration of hostilities by prisoners-of-war. Any fool can be put in charge of them. It would be wasting German labour to impose such tasks on it.' Bormann, *Hitler's Table Talk*, pp. 158, 163.

90 The historians now began to justify the 'historical right' of the Germanic race to remove or exterminate the local populations and re-settle the land; it was now claimed that 'even in pre-Christian times, proto-Teutons had lived in southern Russia'. Dallin, *German Rule in Russia*, p. 68.

91 Excerpt from a speech by Governor Hans Frank at a session of the Government-General in Cracow, 16 October 1941; see also Bundesarchiv Koblenz, R52 II (Atken der Regierung des Generalgouvernements). Hans Frank, *Im Angesicht des Galgens. Deutung Hitlers und seiner Zeit auf Grund eigener Erlebnisse und Erkenntnisse* (Neuhaus, 1955).

92 The text was handed to General Jodl. See Walter Warlimont, 'Vortragsnotiz', 12 May 1941, Document 884–PS. *Trial of the Major War Criminals* (Nuremberg, 1947–9), xxvi, pp 406–8.

93 OKH, 'Behandlung feindlicher Landeseinwohner', 6 May 1941. Document 877–PS, *Trial of the Major War Criminals*, xxvi, pp. 403–6.

94 Von Hassell, *The Von Hassell Diaries*, pp. 198–9.

95 Ibid., p. 207.

96 Einsatzgruppen commander Otto Ohlendorf's testimony, 30 September 1946. Ohlendorf Testimony, *Trial of the Major War Criminals*, iv, pp. 312–37. See also Dallin, *German Rule in Russia*, p. 73.

97 Erlass des Chefs des OKW, 16 September 1941. Document 389–PS, *Trial of the Major War Criminals*, xxv, p. 531.

98 Walter von Reichenau, 'Verhalten der Truppe im Ostraum', 10 October 1941, Document 411-D, *Trial of the Major War Criminals*, p. 85.

99 Bormann, *Hitler's Table Talk*, p. 44. 'Leningrad soll vernichtet werden', *Völkischer Beobachter*, 16 September 1941.

100 I have drawn, above all, on Raul Hilberg, *The Destruction of the European Jews*, 3 vols. (New York, 1985). Hilberg's research on the bureaucratic and the administrative aspects of the Holocaust has been invaluable. See also Jürgen

Rohwer and Eberhard Jäckel (eds.), *Der Mord an den Juden im zweiten Weltkrieg:
Entschlussbildung und Verwirklichung* (Stuttgart, 1985); Martin Gilbert, *The Holo-
caust. The Jewish Tragedy* (London, 1986); Saul Friedländer, *Nazi Germany and
the Jews*, 2 vols. (London, 1997); Gerald Fleming, *Hitler and the Final Solution*
(Berkeley, 1987); Robert M. W. Kempner, *Der Mord an 35,000 Berliner Juden*
(Heidelberg, 1970).

101 The debates between 'intentionalists' – those who believe that the Holocaust
was planned before Hitler came to power and implemented by him step-by-step
after 1933 – and 'functionalists', who believe that decisions were linked function-
ally to one another and did not follow a preconceived master plan, continues
today. For a summary of the debate see Saul Friedländer, Introduction, in
Fleming, *Hitler and the Final Solution*, pp. vii–xxxiii.

102 There is no written evidence that Hitler gave the order(s) to begin the 'Final
Solution' but it is inconceivable that he did not know about or sanction or
approve the mass murder of the European Jews. His tacit approval is revealed
in many of his own statements, conversations, speeches and actions. On 25
October 1941, for example, Hitler said,' From the rostrum of the Reichstag I
prophesied to Jewry that, in the event of war's proving inevitable, the Jew would
disappear from Europe. That race of criminals has on its conscience the two
million dead of the First World War, and now already hundreds of thousands
more. Let nobody tell me that all the same we can't park them in the marshy
parts of Russia! Who's worrying about our troops? It's not a bad idea, by the
way, that public rumour attributes to us a plan to exterminate the Jews. Terror
is a salutary thing'; again, on 3 February 1942 he declared, 'But this time, the
Jews will disappear from Europe. The world will breathe freely and recover its
sense of joy, when this weight is no longer crushing its shoulders.' On 23 January
1942, when the extermination of Jews was underway, he exclaimed: 'One must
act radically . . . The Jew must clear out of Europe . . . It's the Jew who prevents
everything. When I think about it, I realise that I'm extraordinarily humane.
At the time of the rule of the Popes, the Jews were mistreated in Rome. Until
1830, eight Jews mounted on donkeys were led once a year through the streets
of Rome. For my part, I restrict myself to telling them they must go away. If
they break their pipes on the journey, I can't do anything about it. But if they
refuse to go voluntarily, I see no other solution but extermination. Why should
I look at a Jew through other eyes than if he were a Russian prisoner-of-war?'
Bormann, *Hitler's Table Talk* pp. 87, 235, 288.

103 Eugen Fischer was a physical anthropologist who legitimated Nazi racial policies
through his pseudo-scientific work, including his *Deutsche Rassenkunde*. Dr
Walter Gross of the Race Policy Bureau was informed about the RFSS memorandum by Karl Wolf on 29 November 1940. Himmler's pre-dated memorandum
from the summer of 1940, about the 'treatment of foreign nationals in the
East' read: 'I hope to see the concept of Jew completely eradicated, through a
large-scale deportation of the entire Jewish population to Africa, or else to
some colony.' (10 a Js 39/60, pp. 90–91); Fleming, *Hitler and the Final Solution*,
p. 44.

104 'Geheime Reichssache! Berlin, den 17 July 1941 Amt I V', reprinted in Reinhard

Rürup (ed.), *Topographie des Terrors. Gestapo, SS und Reichsicherheitshauptamt auf dem 'Prinz-Albrecht-Gelände'. Eine Dokumentation* (Berlin, 1987), p. 134–5. On the Einsatzgruppen see Helmut Krausnick, Hans Buchheim, Martin Broszat and Hans-Adolf Jacobsen, *Hitlers Einsatzgruppen. Die Truppen des Weltanschauungskrieges 1936–1942* (Frankfurt-am-Main, 1985).

105 Rudolf Christoph von Gersdorff, quoted in Weitz, *Hitler's Diplomat*, p. 278.

106 Interview with Karma Rauhut, in Owings, *Frauen*, p. 353.

107 Bericht des Einsatzkommandos 3 der Einsatzgruppe A vom 1. Dezember 1941: 'Der Befehlshaber der Sicherheitspolizei und des SD. Einsatzkommando 3, Geheime Reichssache! Kauen, am 1. Dezember 1941.' Privatbesitz Wolfgang Scheffler.

108 The SS elite were meant to be killers; on 3 January 1942 Hitler had said, 'The SS shouldn't extend its recruiting too much . . . People must know that troops like the SS have to pay the butcher's bill more heavily than anyone else – so as to keep away the young fellows who only want to show off'. Bormann, *Hitler's Table Talk*, p. 166.

109 Moltke maintained that the situation was worse than he had imagined because 'the tyranny, the terror, the loss of values of all kinds, is greater than I could have believed . . .' Helmuth James Graf von Moltke, *A German of the Resistance. The Last Letters of Count Helmuth James von Moltke* (Oxford, 1948). See also Helmuth James von Moltke, *Briefe an Freya 1939–1945*, ed. Beate Ruhm von Oppen (Munich, 1988). Many Germans would have heard rumours and snippets of information from returning soldiers about crimes committed by Germans on the eastern front (the Scholls of the 'White Rose' group were one notable example). Missie Vassiltchikov recalled the 'first-hand accounts of German atrocities' which she heard in Berlin and which left her with no 'illusions'; the views of others changed 'as the brutal stupidity of German policy in the occupied territories became known, and the tide of victims mounted both there and inside the Russian POW camps'. Marie 'Missie' Vassiltchikov, *The Berlin Diaries 1940–1945* (London, 1985), p. 81. In the autumn of 1941 Christabel Bielenberg remembered listening to her friend Dr Langbehn about the behaviour of the SS in the east: 'I remembered too that if it had not been Langbehn speaking, quietly, soberly without emotion, I would not have been able to believe what he had to say about the SS, what he called a State within the State . . . one which had no legal conscience, where the word "liquidate" had replaced any conception of legality. It would be useless to appeal to their consciences – they had none.' Christabel Bielenberg, *The Past is Myself* (London, 1989), p. 86.

110 Protocol of the Wannsee Conference (International Military Tribunal, Nuremberg).

111 Eichmann admitted that the specific topic of the conference was 'killing, elimination, and annihilation'. Eichmann Trial, session 107, 24 July 1961, E1/RV.

112 There were built-in gas chambers in the euthanasia institutes in Brandenburg, Bensburg, Grafeneck, Hartheim, Hadamar, Sonnenstein and Eichberg, which had been created by the T-4 scientists based in Berlin. By the autumn of 1941 'T-4 personnel were en route to Riga and Lublin . . . to construct gassing vans,

[Viktor Brack was] on loan to Odilo Globocnik, the organiser of "Aktion Reinhard". They were going there to deal with the millions of Jewish people deemed to lack labour value. The "euthanasia" programme was not halted because of some local difficulties with a handful of bishops, but because its team of practised murderers were needed to carry out the infinitely vaster enormity in the East that the regime's leaders were actively considering.' Michael Burleigh, *Death and Deliverance. 'Euthanasia' in Germany 1900–1945* (Cambridge, 1994), p. 180.

113 Detlev J. K. Peukert, *Inside Nazi Germany. Conformity, Opposition and Racism in Everyday Life*, trans. Richard Deveson (London, 1993), p. 212.

114 After his first day at Buchenwald, during which he had been sending people to be gassed, he wrote to her: 'Home again, my little mouseykins! The first working day at Buchenwald is over . . . So, my dearest mummykins, now you'll receive soooooooooo many lovely kisses again, and be embraced so strongly in anticipation of your coming, you eensy-teensy mouse – from your loyal Pa.' Shortly afterwards his wife did visit him to admire his handiwork. He was quite explicit about what he was doing; for example, on 29 November 1941 he wrote that he had just 'done' eighty-nine himself, although he had 'another 1038' to go; he referred to his victims as 'pats' or 'portions'. On this extraordinary exchange of letters see Burleigh, *Death and Deliverance*, pp. 221–9; see also Peter Chroust, 'Ärzteschaft und "Euthanasie" – unter besonderer Berücksichtigung Friedrich Menneckes', in Landeswohlfahrtsverbandes Hessen, *Euthanasie in Hadamar. Die nationalsozialistische Vernichtungspolitik in hessischen Anstalten* (Kassel, 1991), pp. 123–33; Ute Deichmann, *Biologists Under Hitler*, trans. Thomas Dunlap, (Harvard, 1996); Benno Müller-Hill, *Murderous Science. Elimination by Scientific Selection of Jews, Gypsies, and Others. Germany 1933–1945*, trans. George R. Fraser, (Oxford, 1988).

115 Zyklon B was used at Auschwitz; at Kulmhof people were gassed in the backs of vans which drove around with the exhaust pipe emptying into the cabin, and at Treblinka people were gassed by carbon monoxide produced by a tank engine and pumped into a concrete room. On the development of Zyklon B through Eichmann's attempts to 'try and find a gas that was in ready supply and would not entail special installations for its use' see Rudolf Höss, *Commandant in Auschwitz*, ed. Martin Broszat (Cleveland, 1959), p. 206–7.

116 In August small groups of political prisoners were sent to Auschwitz by the Gestapo and were selected for liquidation. Höss wrote that 'In accordance with a secret order issued by Hitler, these Russian *politruks* . . . were brought to Auschwitz for liquidation . . . While I was away on duty, my deputy, Fritzsch, the Protective Custody Commander, first tried gas for these killings. It was a preparation of prussic acid, called Zyklon B . . .' Höss, *Commandant in Auschwitz*, pp. 125–8.

117 Ibid., p. 126–7.

118 Hilberg, *The Destruction of the European Jews*, vol. 3, p. 889.

119 Goebbels diaries, 10 October 1939. On 18 October 1941 the first RSHA convoy of Jews left Berlin; Kempner, *Der Mord an 35,000 Berliner Juden*, p. 185; 'Listen der Berliner Deportationen', in Hans Gert Sellenthin, *Geschichte der Juden in*

Berlin und des Gebäudes Fasanenstrasse 79/80. Festschrift anlässlich der Einweihung des Jüdischen Gemeindehauses (Berlin, 1959), pp. 83–5.

120 On the film see Ralf Georg Reuth, *Goebbels* (London, 1993), p. 262; see also Hans-Adolf Jacobsen, *Nationalsozialistische Aussenpolitik* (Frankfurt-am-Main/ Berlin, 1959), pp. 83–5.

121 The Jüdische Gemeinde zu Berlin still has bolts of 60 cm-wide yellow cloth stamped with printed stars which were to be distributed after 19 September 1941. Berlin Jews had to pay 10 Pfennig for the 'privilege' of having the star; failure to wear it or to display it prominently could lead to immediate arrest and deportation. Gottfried Korff and Reinhard Rürup (eds.), *Berlin, Berlin. Austellung zur Geschichte der Stadt* (Berlin, 1987), p. 566.

122 Smith, *Last Train from Berlin*, p. 138.

123 Wolters kept a 'Chronik', an official record of Speer's activities from January 1940 to September 1944. CHRONIK Wolters Archive Koblenz (r3 1662), quoted in Sereny, *Albert Speer*, p. 225.

124 Smith, *Last Train from Berlin*, p. 141.

125 Goebbels diaries, 2 November 1939.

126 The lists of the arrivals in Auschwitz on transports from Berlin are in Archiwum Panstwowego Muzeum w Oswiecimiu – Archive of the State Auschwitz Museum D-Aul-3a/65ff., Labour Deployment. Schwarz's letter of 5 march was sent to the Wirtschafts-Verwaltungshauptamt, the department which dealt with financial and administrative issues for the SS. Danuta Czech, *Auschwitz Chronicle 1939– 1945* (London, 1990), pp. 334, 346–7.' Reimund Schnabel, *Macht ohne Moral: Eine Dokumentation über die SS* (Frankfurt-am-Main, 1957), Document 182, p. 514.

127 Interview with Frau Doktor Margret Blersch, in Owings, *Frauen*, p. 385.

128 Interview with Rita Kuhn, ibid., p. 465. Wolfgang Wippermann, *Die Berliner Gruppe Baum und der jüdische Widerstand* (Berlin, 1981).

129 Nathan Stoltzfus, *Resistance of the Heart: Intermarriage and the Rosenstrasse Protest in Nazi Germany* (London, 1995).

130 There were some extraordinary incidents – for example, the love affair between Lilly, an apparently model Nazi mother of four, and twenty-one-year-old Felice, one of the city's Jews who had gone underground to avoid arrest. The two women lived together in Berlin, Lilly's pro-Nazi record acting as something of a cover. Nevertheless the two women were betrayed, and Felice was arrested in August 1944. 'Love Story', *BBC 2 Timewatch* (London, 1996).

131 Hilberg, *The Destruction of the European Jews*, vol. 3, p. 1024.

132 Ibid., vol. 2, pp. 407–16.

133 The extraction of gold fillings from the mouths of prisoners who died in concentration camps was ordered by Himmler on 23 September 1940. The extermination camps like Sobibor and Treblinka and Auschwitz yielded large quantities of precious metal which was sent to Berlin. Prisoners admitted to Auschwitz had their dental work examined and recorded; the presence of false teeth was noted and these were removed after the prisoner's death. At first the extraction of precious metals was carried out by SS dentists but by 1943 the work was done by imprisoned dentists known as *Goldarbeiter* or by Sonderkommandos

who worked at the gas chambers and crematoria. Metal teeth were extracted with dental pincers, chisels or crowbars, and in the summer of 1944 at least forty prisoners carried out this work. Once removed, the teeth were soaked in muriatic acid to remove scraps of tissue and bone and the gold was melted and cast into ingots of 0.5 to 1 kg, or into discs of 140 g. The gold was initially sent to the Sanitation Department to be used by the German dental service but the supply was so great (they had 50 kg by 8 October 1942) that no more was needed; from November 1942 the gold was sent to the Reichsbank. Nuremberg Document NO-2305, quoted in Andrzej Strzelecki, 'The Plunder of Victims and Their Corpses', in Yisrael Gutman and Michael Berenbaum (eds.) *Anatomy of the Auschwitz Death Camp* (Washington, DC, 1994), p. 259. Miklos Myiszli claims that there was a room in Crematorium III which had a 'melting pot' for gold teeth. Miklos Myiszli, *Auschwitz: A Doctor's Eyewitness Account* (New York, 1960), p. 72.

134 'The United States Holocaust Memorial Museum tested several bars of soap reported to be composed of human fat but no such fat was found.' Gutman and Berenbaum, *Anatomy of the Auschwitz Death Camp*, p. 80.

135 Sereny, *Albert Speer*, p. 310.

136 On the competition for trains see Hilberg, *The Destruction of the European Jews*, p. 414.

137 Testimony by Streicher, XII, p. 384; testimony by Schacht, XXII, p. 389; testimony by von Schirach, XII, p. 508, *Trial of the Major War Criminals*: Hilberg, *The Destruction of the European Jews*, pp. 1068–75.

138 Hans Boberach, *Meldungen aus dem Reich* (Neuwied, 1965), p. 239.

139 On Stalingrad see Louis C. Rotundo (ed.), *Battle for Stalingrad: The 1943 Soviet General Staff Study* (Washington, DC, 1989); Manfred Kehrig, *Stalingrad: Analyse und Dokumentation einer Schlacht* (Stuttgart, 1972); Earl F. Ziemke, *Moscow to Stalingrad: Decision in the East* (Washington, DC 1987); John Erickson, *The Road to Stalingrad* (London, 1975). Ziemke points out that before the Battle of Kursk around 3 million Germans, along with 350,000 Romanians and Hungarians with around 2,000 tanks faced almost 6 million Soviet soldiers equipped with more than 8,000 tanks. Ziemke, *Moscow to Stalingrad*, p. 144.

140 Count Friedrich Ernst von Solms, in Steinhoff et al., *Voices from the Third Reich*, p. 173.

141 Jesco von Puttkamer, ibid., p. 170.

142 Josef Kayser, ibid., p. 164.

143 Heinz Pfennig, captured at Stalingrad 1943, remained in Russian captivity until 1955. Heinz Pfennig, ibid., p. 153.

144 Hitler had made von Paulus a field marshal knowing that none had ever been captured alive and that it would be his duty to commit suicide. His gamble failed and von Paulus was captured. He died in Germany in 1957. Jesco von Puttkamer, ibid., p. 170.

145 Speer said: 'Stalingrad had shaken us – not only the tragedy of the Sixth Army's soldiers, but even more, perhaps, the question of how such a diaster could have taken place under Hitler's orders. For hitherto there had always been a success to offset every setback; hitherto there had been a new triumph to compensate

for all losses or at least make everyone forget them. Now for the first time we had suffered a defeat for which there was no compensation.' Speer, *Inside the Third Reich*, p. 351.

146 On the reaction to Stalingrad in Germany see Kershaw, *The 'Hitler Myth'*, pp. 190–94.

147 Hitler claimed to miss the capital, saying on 25 February 1942, 'Here in the Wolfschanze, I feel like a prisoner in these dugouts, and my spirit can't escape ... Ah, if we were at least in Berlin!' Bormann, *Hitler's Table Talk*, p. 340. On Goebbels's growing awareness of the consequences of Hitler's decision not to talk to the population see W. A. Boelcke (ed.), *'Wollt ihr den totalen Krieg?' Die geheimen Goebbels-Konferenzen 1939–1943* (Munich, 1968).

148 Speer hints at the motivation behind Goebbels's new propaganda drive. According to him, Goebbels had noted the 'uneasiness and disssatisifaction' amongst the population. 'The populace was actually demanding a ban on all luxuries, which did not help the national struggle. In general, Goebbels said, he could sense a great readiness among the people to exert themselves to the utmost. In fact, significant restrictions were a real necessity if only to revive popular confidence in the leadership.' Speer, *Inside the Third Reich*, p. 352.

149 Harry W. Flannery, *Assignment to Berlin* (London, 1942), p. 268.

150 Ibid., p. 269–71.

151 Ibid., p. 264.

152 Solomon Slowes, *The Road to Katyn*, ed. Wladyslaw T. Bartoszewski (Oxford, 1991). Reuth, *Goebbels*, p. 319.

153 The worst of the Berlin prisons was Plötzensee or 'die Plötze', described in terrifying detail by the prison pastor Harald Poelchau. Poelchau describes his ghastly 'education' in the prison, from the shock of seeing his first execution – the beheading of a petty thief – to the terrible ordeal experienced by those condemned to execution by firing squad. The delays and petty regulations meant that by the time the condemned person was killed by a bullet he had already 'died a thousand deaths'. Poelchau also recorded the testimonies of the tragic figures of the Kreisau Circle after the doomed plot of 20 July 1944. Harald Poelchau, *Die letzten Stunden: Erinnerungen eines Gefängnispfarrers*, ed. Graf Alexander Steinbock-Fermor (Cologne, 1987).

154 Interview with Frau Rosa Chlupaty in Vienna, April 1965, in Grunberger, *A Social History of the Third Reich*, p. 59.

155 This story was recounted to Wolf-Jobst Siedler while he was in prison in Wilhelmshaven after being court martialled and sentenced to nine months for 'defeatism' at the age of seventeen. According to Siedler there were 'constant' executions there: one victim was a drunken sailor who had said, 'If things go wrong here, the bigwigs will surely have planes ready to fly them off to their villas in Switzerland; nothing will happen to them.' Wolf-Jobst Siedler, in Steinhoff et al., *Voices from the Third Reich*, p. 357–8.

156 Christine Weihs, in Owings, *Frauen*, p. 425.

157 Interview with Emmi Heinrich, ibid., p. 310.

158 Hitler always assumed that there would be attempts to overthrow him, as there had been in 1918. On 7 April 1942 he stated, 'If the slightest attempt at a riot

were to break out at this moment anywhere in the whole Reich, I'd take immediate measures against it. Here's what I'd do: (a) on the same day, all the leaders of the opposition, including the leaders of the Catholic party, would be arrested and executed; (b) all the occupants of the concentration camps would be shot within three days; (c) all the criminals in our lists – and it would make little difference whether they were in prison or at liberty – would be shot within the same period. The extermination of these few hundreds of thousands of people would make other measures superfluous.' Bormann, *Hitler's Table Talk*, p. 409.

159 On the bombing see the authorized biography of 'Bomber' Harris, Dudley Saward, *'Bomber' Harris: The Story of Marshal of the Royal Air Force Sir Arthur Harris* (Garden City, NY, 1985); Noble Frankland, *The Bombing Offensive Against Germany* (London, 1965); Sir Charles Webster and Noble Frankland, *The Strategic Air Offensive Against Germany*, vols. 1–4, (HMSO, 1961); Norman Longmore, *The Bombers: The RAF Offensive Against Germany 1939–1945* (London, 1983); John Terrain, *A Time for Courage: The Royal Air Force in World War II* (New York, 1985); Max Hastings, *Bomber Command* (London, 1993); Basil Collier, *A History of Air Power* (London, 1974); Alan J. Levine, *The Strategic Bombing of Germany, 1940–1945* (London, 1992); Conrad C. Crane, *Bombs, Cities, and Civilians: American Airpower Strategy in World War II* (Lawrence, 1993); Richard J. Overy, *The Air War, 1939–1945* (London, 1980).

160 Peukert, *Inside Nazi Germany*, p. 51.

161 Noel Annan, *Changing Enemies. The Defeat and Regeneration of Germany* (London, 1995), p. 82; Hans Rumpf, *Das war der Bombenkrieg* (Oldenburg, 1961), pp. 75–7.

162 Sir Arthur Harris to Sir William Portal, 12 August 1943, in Hastings, *Bomber Command*, p. 256. See also Arthur Harris, *Bomber Offensive* (London, 1947).

163 Annan, *Changing Enemies*, p. 83.

164 Kurt Pritzkoleit, *Berlin* (Düsseldorf, 1962), p. 55.

165 In a total of 207 raids between 1940 and 1945, with 23,407 planes, the British and American forces dropped 52,055 tons of explosives and damaged 125, 775 buildings in Berlin; between 1943 and 1945 alone 15,148 buildings were obliterated. Between 28,000 and 29,000 Berliners and others trapped in the city were killed in the bombing raids. Hartwig Beseler and Niels Gutschow, *Kriegsschicksale deutscher Architektur. Verlust – Schäden – Wiederaufbau. Eine Dokumentation für das Gebiet der Bundesrepublik Deutschland* (Neumünster, 1988), vol. 1, p. 135.

166 Leo Welt, in Steinhoff et al., *Voices from the Third Reich*, p. 436. Others had terrifying experiences during the raids; one schoolgirl believed she would suffocate in her cellar. 'Schulaufsatz aus einer Mädchen-Oberschule Prenzlauer Berg, January 1946', *Stadtarchiv Berlin*, Rep. 134, Nr. 230. The sheer number of dead led to problems with the disposal of bodies, and rumours circulated in Berlin that corpses were being collected and disposed of in the Crematorium Baumschulenweg instead of being buried. On 26 March 1945 Jacob Kronika recorded a conversation in his diary between a group of women in a Neukölln bomb shelter. One stated that they were being 'swindled' out of their bodies, and that

'incorrect things' were being done with them; she had noticed that the coffin in which people were supposedly to be buried was in fact empty during the ceremony and that every time she was at Baumschulenweg she saw precisely the same coffin used for different corpses. She suspected that the bodies 'were being burned en masse without a coffin and without ceremony'. Another woman said that this was logical as there were so many dead in Berlin, but the first woman retorted: 'There are limits. We can't in the end throw everything aside.' Jacob Kronika, *Berlins Undergang* (Copenhagen, 1945), pp. 73–4.

167 Simon Wiesenthal's estimate, 1996.

168 Detlev Peukert has suggested that 12 million foreigners were incorporated into the labour force in Germany during the war, of which around 7.5 million were in Germany by May 1945. In 1944 this consisted of around 2 million Soviet civilian workers, 2.5 million Soviet prisoners of war, 1.7 million Poles, 300,000 Czechs, 200,000 Belgians and 270,000 from the Netherlands, as well as nationals from most other conquered countries. Peukert, *Inside Nazi Germany*, p. 128. See also Hans Pfahlmann, *Fremdarbeiter und Kriegsgefangene in der deutschen Kriegswirtschaft 1939–1945* (Darmstadt, 1968). For Soviet prisoners see Streit, *Keine Kameraden.*

169 'Numbers of arrests recorded in daily reports by State Police (Gestapo) Stations and Central Stations, December 1941'; 'Meldungen wichtiger staatspolizeilicher Ereignisse', Reichssicherheitshauptamt, Bundesarchiv Koblenz (R 58). See also Peukert, *Inside the Third Reich*, p. 266.

170 Berliners did come into contact with these prisoners; indeed one spy noted in his report on 2 April 1945 how a group of Soviet prisoners of war were being moved through Berlin by being pushed into a section of an already over-filled S-Bahn. An old lady stood nearby but when another passenger tried to force a prisoner to move for her she declined, saying that these people 'are also human beings and we must not be so raw and hard'. The spy put this behaviour down to the fact that people feared that the war would soon be over which made them behave better towards foreigners and prisoners of war. *Bericht über den 'Sondereinsatz Berlin' für die Zeit von 30.3–7.4.1945* (Bundesarchiv-Militärgeschichte Freiburg RW/4, vorl. 266), 2 April 1945.

171 'Foreign workers were exposed to the bombing raids to a far greater degree than the German population.' Ulrich Herbert, *Hitler's Foreign Workers. Enforced Foreign Labour in Germany under the Third Reich*, trans. William Templer (Cambridge, 1997), p. 317.

172 Speer was ambiguous about this in his memoirs; after the Hamburg raid he told Hitler that six more attacks like that on Hamburg and armament production would be brought to a standstill. He later said that 'luckily for us, the RAF didn't follow it up with similar raids on other cities and the Americans, who two weeks later tried and failed to destroy our ball-bearing plants at Schweinfurt, made similar tactical mistakes. If they hadn't, we would have been finished, Hitler's confidence in me notwithstanding.' But Speer must have known that Hamburg was a unique event which could not be repeated in Berlin. Sereny, *Albert Speer*, p. 385; Annan, *Changing Enemies*, p. 85.

173 Interview with Ursula Meyer-Semlies, in Owings, *Frauen*, p. 65.

174   Speer, *Inside the Third Reich*, p. 381.

175   Ibid., p. 390.

176   'I can't believe that in November 1918 this city saw a revolt. That would be impossible under my leadership . . . The workers greet me here with enthusiasm that is difficult to describe. This was once known as Red Wedding around the Ackerstrasse . . .' Heinrich Fraenkel and Roger Manvell, *Goebbels. Eine Biographie* (Cologne/Berlin, 1960), p. 286.

177   Von Moltke, *Briefe an Freya*, p. 368.

178   Goebbels diaries, 8 April 1944; Reuth, *Goebbels*, p. 325.

179   Letter from Air Vice-Marshal F. F. Inglis, Assistant Chief of Air Staff (Intelligence) to Sir Charles Portal, 5 November 1943, quoted in Hastings, *Bomber Command*, p. 258. As Calvocoressi has written, 'British independence, which had been saved by Fighter Command in 1940, was symbolized thereafter by Bomber Command.' Calvoressi et al., *Total War*, p. 516.

180   The American P51 or Mustang allowed the B17s to resume their offensive, and it was that combination of both which overcame German defences. German fighters were eliminated from battle by fighters and American and British bombers were able to undertake round-the-clock bombing of Germany. Calvocoressi et al., *Total War*, p. 522; Webster and Frankland, *The Strategic Air Offensive against Germany*, vol. 2, p. 142.

181   Annan, *Changing Enemies*, p. 100. As Peter Calvocoressi puts it, 'Speer's evidence after the war was that precision bombing could do crucial damage; but until the last phase the allies were not able to carry out effective precision bombing operations. Area bombing, to which they resorted instead, paid only a small dividend and one which those who bring ethics into the equation may well regard as too small.' Calvocoressi et al., *Total War*, p. 532.

182   The Germans also forgot what Hitler himself had intended to do: on 9 February 1942 he had said that the Germans should put more effort into bombing in order to produce 200 bombers of 500 kilograms: 'With two hundred bombers fulfilling these conditions, and continuing to fly for six months, I'll annihilate the enemy . . .' Bormann, *Hitler's Table Talk*, p. 307. Martin Gilbert, *Second World War* (London, 1989), p. 495.

183   On 5 April 1942 Hitler said that one of the officers to whom he had recently awarded the Oak Leaves had told him that 'famine has already reduced the population of Leningrad to two millions. If one thinks that, according to the report of the Turkish Ambassador in Russia, the city of the diplomats itself no longer offers anything decent to eat; and if one knows, too, that the Russians are continuing to eat the meat of broken-down horses, it's not difficult to imagine that the population of Leningrad will rapidly diminish. The bombs and artillery fire have contributed their share to the city's destruction.' Bormann, *Hitler's Table Talk*, p. 401. See also Sereny, *Albert Speer*, p. 490.

184   The Nazi elite were always aware of possible resistance on the 'home front'. On 24 July Hitler said, 'For an élite force, like our SS, it's great luck to have suffered comparatively heavy losses. In this way, it's assured of the necessary prestige to intervene, if need be, on the home front – which, of course, won't be necessary. But it's good to know that one disposes of a force that could show itself capable

of doing so, on occasion . . . if I'd been Reich Chancellor at the period, in three months' time I'd have cut the throat of all obstruction, and I'd have reasserted our power.' Bormann, *Hitler's Table Talk*, pp. 13–14.

185 On 14 October 1941 Hitler said, 'So it's not opportune to hurl ourselves now into a struggle with the Churches. The best thing is to let Christianity die a natural death. A slow death has something comforting about it. The dogma of Christianity gets worn away before the advances of science. Religion will have to make more and more concessions. Gradually the myth crumbles.' Ibid., p. 61.

186 Otto Ogierman, *Bis zum letzten Atemzug. Der Prozess gegen Bernhard Lichtenberg, Dompropst an St. Hedwig in Berlin* (Leipzig, 1968); Walter Adolph, *Geheime Aufzeichnungen aus dem nationalsozialistischen Kirchenkampf 1935–1945* (Mainz, 1979); Hilberg, *The Destruction of the European Jews*, vol. 2, p. 471.

187 Martin Niemöller, *Exile in the Fatherland. Martin Niemöller's Letters from Moabit Prison*, ed. Herbert G. Locke, trans. Ernst Kaemke et al., (Grand Rapids, 1986); Dietrich Bonhoeffer, and Maria von Wedemeyer, *Love Letters from Cell 92. Dietrich Bonhoeffer, Maria von Wedemeyer 1943–1945*, ed. Ruth-Alice von Bismarck and Ulrich Kabitz, trans. John Brownjohn. (London, 1992); on the church in general see Klaus Gotto, Konrad Repgen (eds.), *Kirche, Katholiken und Nationalsozialismus* (Mainz, 1980); Richard Gutteridge, *Open thy Mouth for the Dumb: The German Evangelical Church and the Jews 1870–1950* (Oxford, 1976); Ernst Christian Helmreich, *The German Churches under Hitler: Background, Struggle, and Epilogue* (Detroit, 1979); Ulrich von Hehl (ed.), *Priester unter Hitlers Terror: Eine biographische und statistische Erhebung* (Mainz, 1985).

188 The international situation was a factor in the timing of the 1944 attempt on Hitler's life. As Peter Hoffman has noted, 'About the turn of the year 1942–43 something like a sense of catastrophe spread through Germany and in some cases to the front. Stalingrad and the annihilation of Sixth Army were fearful blows, from which the German Army never recovered. At the same time the demand for "unconditional surrender" was announced from Casablanca, implying the abolition not only of the Nazi regime, which was more or less detested in any case, but of German sovereignty as a nation.' Peter Hoffmann, *The History of the German Resistance*, trans. Peter Barry, (London, 1977); see also Joachim Fest, *Plotting Hitler's Death. The German Resistance to Hitler 1933– 1945*, trans. Bruce Little (London, 1996).

189 There is still uncertainty about his exact words; some sources claim that he said, 'Es lebe das heilige Deutschland!' (Long live sacred Germany!); others claim it was, 'Es lebe das geheime Deutschland!' (Long live secret Germany!). Timothy Garton Ash, *The File. A Personal History* (London, 1997), p. 39.

190 Sereny, *Albert Speer*, p. 455.

191 Vassiltchikov, *The Berlin Diaries*, p. 231.

192 On 20 July 1997 the German government announced that it may declare an amnesty for those convicted in Nazi courts, including those charged for conspiring against Hitler in 1944; see Introduction note 102. Katerina von Waldersee, 'Bonn plans amnesty for Hitler's failed assassins', *Sunday Telegraph*, 20 July 1997.

193 One cannot take such reports at face value, given the fear of speaking one's

mind; nevertheless the overwhelming picture is of a nation relieved that Hitler had not died. Kershaw, *The Hitler Myth*, pp. 217–18. Hoffman was right to say that 'the heritage and lineage of the resistance to Hitler lives on, however, not only in the families of those who gave their lives, but wherever their sacrifices and sufferings are remembered.' Peter Hoffmann, *The History of the German Resistance 1933–1945*, p. 534.

194 Sereny, *Albert Speer*, p. 214.

13: THE FALL OF BERLIN

1 Max Hastings, *Overlord: D-Day and the Battle for Normandy* (London, 1984), pp. 24–26; Dieter Ose, *Entscheidung im Westen, 1944: Der Oberbefehlshaber West und die Abwehr der allierten Invasion* (Stuttgart, 1982); Peter Calvocoressi, Guy Wint and John Pritchard, *Total War. The Causes and Courses of the Second World War* (Harmondsworth, 1989), pp. 533–46. On Tehran see Keith Sainsbury, *The Turning Point. Roosevelt, Stalin, Churchill, and Chiang Kai-shek, 1943. The Moscow, Cairo, and Teheran Conferences* (Oxford, 1986).

2 This was the view of General Sir Bernard Law Montgomery, 'Monty', hero of El Alamein and Tunisia, who had been accused of moving too slowly against Rommel and too slowly in Normandy, and who now believed Berlin should be reached as quickly as possible even at the expense of other targets. Noel Annan, *Changing Enemies. The Defeat and Regeneration of Germany* (London, 1995), p. 113. The view was shared by Patton, but not by Eisenhower, who was concerned about logistics such as supply lines, and aware of Roosevelt's political agenda which lent itself to the 'broad front' strategy. Arthur Bryant, *Triumph in the West 1943–1946* (London, 1986), p. 242.

3 Anglo-American tensions were already showing by 1943; see Keith Sainsbury, *Churchill and Roosevelt at War* (New York, 1994); Ann Lane and Howard Temperley (eds.), *The rise and fall of the Grand Alliance, 1941–1945* (London, 1995); George McJimsey, *Harry Hopkins* (Cambridge, Mass., 1987); Ted Morgan, *FDR: A Biography* (London, 1986); Joseph P. Lash, *Roosevelt and Churchill, 1939–1941: The Partnership That Saved the West* (New York, 1976).

4 Chester Wilmot, *The Struggle for Europe* (London, 1952), p. 489. This was ironic given the fact that at the Quebec Conference in November 1943 Roosevelt had said that he wanted to get to Berlin as quickly as the Russians, and had predicted a 'race for Berlin' while on board the USS *Iowa* on his way to the Big Three meeting at Tehran; he had reviewed the Hopkins plans for the invasion of Europe, which resulted in tensions between the American cross-Channel strategy and the British Mediterranean strategy. Robert Sherwood, *Roosevelt and Hopkins* (New York, 1950), p. 714; see also Eric Larrabee, *Commander in Chief: Franklin Delano Roosevelt, His Lieutenants and Their War* (New York, 1987).

5 B. L. Liddell-Hart, *The Other Side of the Hill* (London, 1948), p. 591.

6 On the Ardennes see Hugh M. Cole, *The Ardennes: Battle of the Bulge* (Washington, DC 1965); Bernard Law, Viscount Montgomery of Alamein, *The Memoirs of Field-Marshal the Viscount Montgomery of Alamein, K. G.* (London, 1958),

pp. 299–315. David Eisenhower, *Eisenhower at War, 1943–1945* (New York, 1986), pp. 562–90.

7 Ralph Bennett, himself a veteran of Bletchley, notes that both SHAEF and the 21st Army Group had numerous indications that German forces were concentrating in the area; their failure was one of analysis, brought on by their own preoccupations. Hew Strachan, 'How the War was Waged', *The Times Literary Supplement*, 5 May 1995, p. 30. See also I. C. B. Dear and M. R. D. Foot (eds.) *The Oxford Companion to the Second World War* (Oxford, 1995); Robin Neillands, *The Conquest of the Reich. From D-Day to VE-Day: A Soldier's History* (London, 1995).

8 It was then, under SS-commander Colonel Peiper, that the Nazis committed the worst single atrocity against American forces – the murder in cold blood of eighty-four American prisoners of war in the woods near the town of Malmedy. James J. Weingartner, *Crossroads of Death: The Story of the Malmedy Massacre and Trial* (Berkeley, 1973).

9 Goebbels diary, 27 March 1945.

10 Ibid., 31 March 1945.

11 Robert Capa, *Slightly out of Focus* (New York, 1947), p. 236.

12 Strachan, 'How the War was Waged', *Times Literary Supplement*, 5 May 1995, p. 31. Wehrmacht intelligence reports in Berlin indicated that people hoped the city would fall to the western Allies: 'Very often the wish is spoken aloud that the Anglo-Americans come to Berlin before the Soviets. Here and there one hears delight at the American successes. And there are those who hope that one can stop the war in the west and together with the Anglo-Americans march against the Soviets.' *Bericht über den 'Sondereinsatz Berlin' für die Zeit vom 30.3.– 7.4.1945* (Bundesarchiv-Militärarchiv Freiburg RW 4/ vorl. 266).

13 As Dmitiri Volkogonov wrote, Stalin was 'more concerned about governments than borders' and believed that whoever occupied a territory by force of arms had the right to impose his own social system. Dmitri Volkogonov, *Stalin* (Moscow, 1989), p. 489. On his treatment of civilians in Soviet-occupied territory see, for example, Keith Sword, *Deportation and Exile. Poles in the Soviet Union, 1939–48* (London, 1996); A. Halpern, *Liberation – Russian Style* (London, 1945); Robert Conquest, *The Nation Killers. The Soviet Deportation of Nationalities* (London, 1970). On Stalin's treatment of Russia's ethnic Germans see Ingebord Fleischhauer and Benjamin Pinkus, *The Soviet Germans, Past and Present* (London, 1986), pp. 103–52. According to G. F. Krivosheyev, the Soviets captured 3,486,206 prisoners from seventeen countries between 22 June 1941 and 9 September 1945 alone. G. F. Krivosheyev (ed.), *Without Seal of Secrecy: The Losses of the Soviet Armed Forces in Wars, Military Campaigns, and Conflicts. A Statistical Research* (Moscow, 1993), p. 390.

14 Omar N. Bradley, *A Soldier's Story* (London, 1951), p. 62; see also David Eisenhower, *Eisenhower at War*.

15 The Ninth Army commander later recalled that he was so shocked he was unable to 'even remember half of the things Brad said from then on . . . I got back on the plane in a kind of daze. All I could think of was, How am I going to tell my staff, my corps commanders and my troops? Above all, How am I

going to tell my troops?' quoted in D. M. Giangreco and Robert E. Griffin, *Airbridge to Berlin. The Berlin Crisis of 1948. Its Origins and Aftermath* (Novato, 1988), pp. 3–4. See also Bradley, *A Soldier's Story*.

16 Churchill, quoted in Martin Gilbert, *The Road to Victory* (London, 1986), pp. 1273–5.

17 Ibid., p. 1275.

18 Bradley, quoted in Robert Nisbet, *Roosevelt and Stalin. The Failed Courtship* (London, 1989), p. 86. Willy Brandt wrote in his memoirs, 'In April 1945 the Americans had stopped at the Elbe; if they had marched on they would have saved themselves a good deal of trouble and given the world a different face. But they left the triumph of marching into Hitler's capital to the Russians. One reason was that General Eisenhower, the Supreme Allied Commander, no longer considered Berlin an especially important objective. He failed to understand the symbolic value of the place, regarding the German capital as merely a point on the map. At the end of the 1950s, when I broached the subject with Eisenhower, then President of the United States, he freely admitted that he had not foreseen the consequences of his order not to advance on Berlin.' Willy Brandt, *My Life in Politics* (London, 1992), pp. 13–14.

20 That Stalin still considered Berlin of the utmost importance was made clear in his order of 1 May 1945, when he boasted that the Red Army had swept through Germany and had 'taken the most important districts of the capital city of Germany, Berlin'. Now the flag of their victory 'shines over Berlin'. Josef W. Stalin, *Über den grossen vaterländischen Krieg der Sowjetunion* (Berlin, 1951), p. 215. On Yalta see Diane Clemens, *Yalta* (Oxford, 1970); on Roosevelt's fateful comments consigning Berlin to Stalin see Nisbet, *Roosevelt and Stalin*, pp. 83–4.

21 Wolfgang Stresemann, in Johannes Steinhoff, Peter Pechel and Dennis Showalter (eds.), *Voices from the Third Reich. An Oral History* (New York, 1994), p. 35.

22 This pro-Stalin stance was coupled with a growing anti-British feeling; Roosevelt saw the Britsh empire as an anachronism and believed that after the war the world could be ruled peacefully and in a climate of co-operation by the two non-imperialist powers, the United States and Russia. For the letter of 18 March 1942 see Warren F. Kimball, *Churchill and Roosevelt. The Complete Correspondence*, (Princeton, 1984), vol. 1: *Alliance Emerging*, p. 421; see also Ministry of Foreign Affairs of the USSR, *Stalin's Correspondence with Roosevelt and Truman, 1941–45* (New York, 1965); Steven Merritt Miner, *Between Churchill and Stalin. The Soviet Union, Great Britain, and the Origins of the Grand Alliance* (London, 1988). On Roosevelt's suggestion that General Eisenhower communicate directly with the Soviet staff rather than through the Chiefs of Staff in London and Washington see United States Department of State, 'Malta and Yalta', *Foreign Relations of the United States* pp. 570–71.

23 For the Soviet push westward and the Battle of Berlin see S. M. Schtemenko, *The Last Six Months* (New York, 1977); S. M. Schtemenko, *Im Generalstab* (Berlin, 1983); Georgi K. Zhukov, *Erinnerungen und Gedanken* (Berlin, 1983), vol. 2; I. S. Koniev, *Year of Victory* (Moscow, 1969); V. I. Chuikov, *The End of the Third Reich* (Moscow, 1978); I. A. Tolkonjuk, *Berlinski epilog* (Novosibirsk,

1970); A. N. Bassarab, *Panzer im Visier* (Berlin, 1975). See also John Erickson, *The Road to Berlin* (London, 1983); Anthony Read and David Fisher, *The Fall of Berlin* (London, 1992); R. C. Raack, *Stalin's Drive to the West, 1938–1945* (Stanford, 1995).

24 An imposing equestrian statue of Zhukov was erected in front of the Kremlin in Moscow in 1991. On the need to 'crush opposition in Poland, Czechoslovakia, Hungary and Austria' and on his decision to concentrate on the Warsaw – Berlin line see Zhukov, *Erinnerungen und Gedanken*, vol. 2, pp. 280–85.

25 Koniev wrote of the battle, 'I had never seen, and never again saw, such a vast number of corpses in such a small area.' Harold Shukman (ed.), *Stalin's Generals* (London, 1993), p. 97.

26 Gitta Sereny, *Albert Speer: His Battle with Truth* (London, 1995), p. 433.

27 Lord Ismay, *Memoirs* (London, 1960), p. 72.

28 On the Warsaw Uprising see Wladyslaw Bartoszewski, *Dni Walczacej Stolicy. Kronika Powstania Warszawskiego* (London, 1984); *1859 Days of Warsaw* (Warsaw, 1974); *The Warsaw Death Ring 1939–1944* (Warsaw, 1970); Janusz K. Zawodny, *The Story of the Uprising in Warsaw 1944* (London, 1962). Ehrenburg consciously incited the Red Army soldiers to ferocious acts of violence and revenge; on his view of the sweep west see Ilya Ehrenburg, *The War: 1941–1945*, trans. Tatiana Shebunina, (Cleveland, 1967). For the view from Moscow see the history by the American correspondent there during the war, Alexander Werth, *Russia at War* (New York, 1964). Stalin's meeting with his generals to determine the timing of the offensive is recorded in Zhukov, *Erinnerungen und Gedanken*, vol. 2, pp. 315–17.

29 According to the Soviet figures the offensive on the Oder–Neisse began with the Soviets of the First and Second Belorussian and First Ukrainian Fronts, with 2,500,000 troops facing 1,000,000 German troops of the 'Weichsel' and the Fourth Panzerarmee, a ratio of 2.5 to 1. *Institut für Marxismus-Leninismus beim ZL der KPdSU, Geschichte des grossen vaterländischen Krieges der Sowjetunion* (Berlin, 1967), vol. 5, p. 302.

30 The Waffen-SS leader Leon Degrelle tried to justify the German failure, saying: 'The Russians were used to that weather. Their skis, their dogs, their sleighs, their high-strung ponies helped them.' But fear of the Soviets was evident as Degrelle recalled how 'they carried out a monstrous man hunt, wheeling around the isbas, amusing themselves by crushing our comrades one by one, whether they were unharmed or wounded or dead. We realized perfectly well that we were going to be surrounded and pulverized in our turn by those mastodons . . .' Leon Degrelle, *Campaign in Russia. The Waffen SS on the Eastern Front* (Newport Beach, 1992), p. 52; James Lucas, *World War Two through German Eyes* (London, 1987), p. 161.

31 Dimitri Shchegolev, 'Military Council Representative (An Officer's Notes),' in V. Sevruk (ed.), *How Wars End: Eyewitness Accounts of the Fall of Berlin* (Moscow, 1974), p. 299.

32 Erikson, *The Road to Berlin*, p. 682.

33 Alexander Solzhenitsyn, *Prussian Nights*, trans. Robert Conquest (New York, 1983), p. ix.

34 Alfred M. deZayas, *Nemesis at Potsdam. The Expulsion of the Germans from the East.* (London, 1989), p. 72.

35 A Wehrmacht intelligence report of March 1945 noted, 'The news about the *Grueltaten der Bolschewisten* is still not being taken seriously by some Berliners ... Above all virtually everyone believes that the Anglo-Americans are not as dangerous.' *Bericht über den 'Sondereinsatz Berlin' für die Zeit vom 23.3.–29.3.1945* (Bundesarchiv-Militärarchiv Freiburg RW 4/vorl. 266).

Generaloberst Heinz Guderian, Chef des Generalstabes des Heeres, also tried to whip up fear of the advancing Red Army, saying that all must work to 'liberate German land in the east from the bloodstained claws of the Bolsheviks'. *Völkischer Beobachter*, 7 March 1945.

36 For Hitler's last days, the best account remains Hugh Trevor-Roper, *The Last Days of Hitler* (London, 1995).

37 Hitler had long been obsessed by Frederick the Great; on 28 January 1942, for example, he had said, 'When one reflects that Frederick the Great held out against forces twelve times greater than his, one gets the impression: "What a grand fellow he must have been!"' Martin Bormann (ed.), *Hitler's Table Talk*, 1941–1944, intro. Hugh Trevor-Roper (Oxford, 1988), p. 260.

38 Albert Speer, *Inside the Third Reich*, (New York, 1993), p. 631.

39 Even now intelligence reports note that although wary the people longed to hear Hitler speak; 'The trust in the leadership has generally fallen. However the wish is often expressed that the Führer would speak once more. He spoke in the good times, now in the hour of greatest need people want to hear his voice, particularly if he would say something to give them courage. Or Dr Goebbels should at least speak about the most fundamental problems and stop spouting "Propaganda".' *Bericht über den 'Sondereinsatz Berlin' für die Zeit vom 30.3.–7.4.1945* (Bundesarchiv-Militärarchiv Freiburg RW 4/vorl. 266.) (This material was also kept in the *Zentrales Staatsarchiv Potsdam*, Film Nr. 42930).

40 Siegfried Knappe and Ted Brusaw, *Soldat. Reflections of a German Soldier 1936–1949* (New York, 1992), pp. 44–5.

41 Trevor-Roper, *The Last Days of Hitler*, p. 89.

24 Speer, *Inside the Third Reich*, p. 631–2.

43 Sereny, *Albert Speer*, p. 506.

44 Ibid., p. 507.

45 Interview with Rita Kuhn, in Alison Owings, *Frauen: German Women Recall the Third Reich* (Harmondsworth, 1993), p. 464. Even now Berliners hoped that there would be no full-scale attack on the city; on 10 April Jacob Kronika noted that 'the main theme of the morning newspapers ... is the "*Schlacht um Berlin*". People do not believe what is before their eyes but the gazettes explain ... that the "*Schlacht um die Reichshauptstadt*" will be one of the great turning-points of the war!' Jacob Kronika, *Berlins Undergang* (Copenhagen, 1945), p. 99.

46 Knappe and Brusaw, *Soldat*, p. 45.

47 Speer, *Inside the Third Reich*, pp. 605–6.

48 Hitler showed callous disregard of the high casualties, saying in January 1942 that 'if this war costs us two hundred and fifty thousand dead and a hundred

thousand disabled, these losses are already made good by the increase in births in Germany since our seizure of power . . . All life is paid for with blood.' Bormann, *Hitler's Table Talk*, p. 261.

49 Speer, *Inside the Third Reich*, p. 588.

50 Jakob Kronika noted on 22 April that people had started to 'go wild' because of the shortage of food and that despite Goebbels's orders long lines continued to grow in front of shops in which one might find some sugar or some meat: 'The shop keepers are terrified of violence and plundering.' He also noted that the Nazi leadership had suddenly decided to distribute some coffee: 'They have promised us thirty grams per person.' Kronika, *Berlins Undergang*, p. 134. The situation was made worse by Hitler's order to destroy all 'military, transportation, information, industry and public utilities' within the Reich territory to prevent them falling into the hands of the enemy. (Nuremberg Process 1949, vol. 41, p. 430, Dok. Speer-25).

51 Margaret Boveri, *Tage des Überlebens. Berlin 1945* (Munich, 1968), p. 89; interview with Erna Dubnack, in Owings, *Frauen*, p. 446.

52 The propaganda continued to whip up fear and hatred of the Bolsehviks: 'The deadly Jewish-Bolshevik enemy has attacked us for the last time. He has tried to destroy Germany and massacre our people . . . This time the Bolshevik will experience the old destiny of Asia: he must and will bleed in front of the capital city of the German Reich . . .' *Völkischer Beobachter*, 17 April 1945.

53 Raul Hilberg, *The Destruction of the European Jews* (New York, 1985), vol. 3, p. 983.

54 Daniel Jonah Goldhagen, *Hitler's Willing Executioners. Ordinary Germans and the Holocaust* (London, 1996), p. 75.

55 Ibid., p. 363; see also Elie Wiesel, *Night* (New York, 1969), pp. 91–3; Martin Gilbert, *The Holocaust. The Jewish Tragedy* (London, 1986), pp. 767–83.

56 Martin Broszat, 'The Concentration Camps', in Helmut Krausnick et al., *Anatomy of the SS State* (London, 1968), p. 248.

57 Goldhagen, *Hitler's Willing Executioners*, p. 356.

58 Interview with Frau Erna Tietz, in Owings, *Frauen*, p. 271.

59 Degrelle, *Campaign in Russia*, p. 315. For eye-witness accounts of life in Berlin in the final days of the Reich see Peter Gosztony, *Der Kampf um Berlin 1945 in Augenzeugen berichten* (Düsseldorf, 1970); Anthony Read and David Fisher, *The Fall of Berlin* (London, 1992); Helmut Altner, *Totentanz Berlin. Tagebuchblätter eines Achtzehnjährigen* (Offenbach-am-Main, 1947); Theodor Busse, 'Die letzte Schlacht der 9. Armee', in *Wehrwissenschafliche Rundshau*, no. 4, 1955 (Darmstadt); Theo Findahl, *Letzter Akt – Berlin 1939–1945* (Hamburg, 1946); Heinrich Grüber, *Erinnerungen aus sieben Jahrzehnten* (Cologne, 1968); Karl Friedrich Borée, *Frühling 45. Chronik einer Berliner Familie* (Darmstadt, 1954); Jakob Kronika, *Berlin's Undergang* (Flensburg, 1946); Matthias Menzel, *Die Stadt ohne Tod. Berliner Tagebuch 1943–5* (Berlin, 1946).

60 Interview with Erma Semlies, in Owings, *Frauen*, p. 67. Jakob Kronika noted on 10 April 1945 that 'boys and girls, far too young to be in uniform, swarm around the crowded Zoo bunker, interested only in sex and in a 'coarse eroticism.' Kronika, *Berlins Undergang*, p. 98.

61 Goebbels diaries, 29 March 1945. But getting to the city would soon not be possible. Hans von Luck, *Panzer Commander. The Memoirs of Colonel Hans von Luck* (New York, 1989), pp. 262–5.

62 Michael Guss also describes this part of Berlin on 2 May 1945. Michael Guss, 'Aus dem Tagebuch eines Berichterstatters', in *Tägliche Rundschau*, 3 May 1946. The order for the defence of the Reich capital was given by Generalleutnant Hellmuth Reymann, *Grundsätzlichen Befehl für die Vorbereitungen zur Verteidigung der Reichshauptstadt*, 9 March 1945. Degrelle noted that the Russians already surrounded the city, and that the barricades were pathetic: 'always the six largest, most beautiful, oldest trees on opposite sides of the road were cut down and laid over the street . . . Older men shake their heads when they see them . . . a few hundred years ago such barricades might have been of some use. But now?' Emilie Karoline Gersternberg, entry for 28 April 1945, in *Die Schlussphase der russischen Eroberung Berlins 1945. Ein Westender Tagebuch* (Munich, 1965), p. 16. Furthermore, on 23 March Hitler ordered that the East–West Axis be turned into a runway.

63 Degrelle, *Campaign in Russia*, p. 319.

64 Margaret Boveri noted the strange sights on Berlin streets and the terrible condition of the men who trundled into the city on 'Panzers, guns, lorries, horse-drawn carts; the soldiers cooked where they were, slept there, flirted with women, exchanged goods. Nobody spoke about the war . . .' Boveri, *Tage des Uberlebens*, p. 85.

65 Anonymous, *A Woman in Berlin*, trans. James Stern (London, 1955), p. 31.

66 The eighteen-year-old Robert Milter noted that of the 300 men gathered on 20 April for recruitment into the *Volkssturm* 'at least twenty were fourteen years old, and fifty were over sixty years old'. Robert Milter, Report collected while a Soviet prisoner of war, in the former Institut für Marxismus-Leninismus beim ZK der SED, *Zentrales parteiarchiv* (NL 36/590).

67 Isa Vermehren, *Reise durch den letzten Akt. Ein Bericht* (Hamburg, 1947), p. 146; Hugo Stehkämper, in Steinhoff et al., *Voices from the Third Reich*, p. 490; Horst Lange, *Tagebücher aus dem Zweiten Weltkrieg*, ed. H. D. Schäfer, (Mainz, 1979) p. 198.

68 In one of the most appalling of his decisions Stalin later had many ex-Soviet prisoners of war murdered. Stalin's note of 11 May 1945 to the commanders of the First and Second Belorussian Fronts, the First, Second, Third and Fourth Ukrainian Fronts and to comrades Beria, Merkulov, Abakumov and others, called for the establishment of holding camps for recaptured Soviet POWs in which they were to be interrogated. See Dmitiri Volkogonov, *Triumf i Tragediia* (Moscow, 1989), p. 394; David E. Murphy, Sergei A. Kondraschev and George Bailey, *Battleground Berlin. CIA vs. KGB in the Cold War* (Yale, 1987), p. 460. Many were sent to the Gulag. The fate of those repatriated by the western Allies after the war, some but by no means all of whom had fought against Stalin, was even worse and many were killed outright. Lieutenant-Colonel H. E. N. Bredin recalled the Cossacks who were sent back to the Soviet Union: 'I spoke to people who had seen prisoners being shot and I think there was clear evidence that shootings took place.' According to Colonel Horatio Rogers, those prisoners

who did talk 'said they did not wish to return to Russia because they knew they would be shot . . . In some instances their families have been killed or deported and they would rather commit suicide than return.' This did not stop the disgraceful repatriations. Nicholas Bethell, *The Last Secret. Forcible Repatriation to Russia 1944–7* (London, 1974), pp. 150, 169; see also Vyacheslav Naumenko, *The Great Betrayal* (New York, 1970), vol. 2, pp. 250–82.

69 The fourteen-year-old Herbert Neuber was also recruited to 'defend' Germany and noted seeing various 'Vaterlandsverräter' who had been hanged. *Stadtarchiv Berlin* (Rep. 134, Nr. 137). The reports collected throughout Berlin (in cellars, restaurants, food lines, etc.) by Oberstleutnant Wasserfall in conjunction with the Reich Propaganda Ministry are an invaluable source, revealing much of the decline in morale as the Russians approached Berlin and young boys and old men were recruited to fight. An entry recounting conversations with unnamed sources on 10 April 1945 reads: 'People are inceasingly sceptical about the press and the propaganda. Too many predictions have not come true. Many ask, where is the new weapon which Dr Goebbels went on about, which he went on about in his article in the *Reich*? Where are these new weapons anyway?' *Berichte über den 'Sondereinsatz Berlin' October 1944 – April 1945*, (Bundesarchiv-Militärarchiv Freiburg RW4/ vorl. 266).

70 Lothar Rühl, in Steinhoff et al., *Voices from the Third Reich*, p. 433; Emilie Karoline Gerstenberg remembered Goebbels's 22 April 1945 broadcast over the radio, stating that 'anyone who lives in a house outside which a white flag has been hung will be shot immediately and the house destroyed. One must stop any such bacillus from infecting the city!' Gerstenberg, *Die Schlussphase der russischen Eroberung Berlins*, p. 12.

71 The most infamous case of execution occurred at a ravine near the Olympic Stadium where over 100 people were shot for desertion. Leo Welt, in Steinhoff et al., *Voices from the Third Reich*, p. 437.

72 On 22 April 1945 Hitler had ordered that anyone who in any way 'weakens the strength of our resistance . . . is a traitor. He is to be immediately shot or hung!' These actions were to be carried out 'in the name of the Führer'. *Der Panzerbär*, 23 April 1945. See also Lothar Loewe, in Steinhoff et al., *Voices from the Third Reich*, p. 470.

73 On the battle from the Soviet perspective see W. I. Kasakow, 'Die sowjetische Artillerie im Endkampf um Berlin'; F. J. Bokow, 'Sieg und Befreiung. Erinnerung an den Frühling des Jahres 1945', in *Mitteilungsblatt der Arbeitsgemeinschaft ehemaliger Offiziere* H.5, 1971; Lev Besymenski, 'In jenen Tagen bei Berlin', *Horizont*, no. 19, 1970; A. N. Bassarab, *Panzer im Visier* (Berlin, 1975); Ivgeni Domatovski, 'Gedanken am Brandenburger Tor', *Wochenpost*, no. 38, 1961; Tolkonjuk, *Berlinski epilog*. The memoirs of the Soviet generals are invaluable: see Zhukov, *Erinnerungen und Gedanken*; I. S. Koniev, *Year of Victory* (Moscow, 1969); Simonov, *Aus den Kriegstagebüchern*; Chuikov, *The End of the Third Reich*.

74 Chuikov, *The End of the Third Reich*, pp 213-25.

75 Jürgen Graf, in Steinhoff et al., *Voices from the Third Reich*, p. 429.

76 Norman M. Naimark, *The Russians in Germany. A History of the Soviet Zone of Occupation, 1945–1949* (Cambridge, 1995), p. 75.

77 Brunhilde Pomsel, in Steinhoff et al., *Voices from the Third Reich*, p. 432.

78 Peter Bloch, *Zwischen Hoffnung und Resignation: Als CDU-Politiker in Brandenburg, 1945–1950* (Cologne, 1986), p. 31.

79 Regina Frankenfeld, in Owings, *Frauen*, p. 407.

80 Hedwig Sass, in Steinhoff et al., *Voices from the Third Reich*, p. 457.

81 Interview with Frau Rita Kuhn, in Owings, *Frauen*, p. 466.

82 Interview with Erna Dubnack, ibid., p. 448.

83 Leo Welt, in Steinhoff et al., *Voices from the Third Reich*, p. 437.

84 Naimark, *The Russians in Berlin*, p. 82.

85 Hanna Gerlitz, in Steinhoff et al., *Voices from the Third Reich*, p. 459.

86 Interview with Frau Margarete Fischer, in Owings, *Frauen*, p. 10.

87 Anonymous, *A Woman in Berlin*, p. 89.

88 Interview with Walter Killian, acting Bürgermeister of Charlottenburg, in Naimark, *The Russians in Germany*, p. 81.

89 The Soviets did not limit their attacks to Germans, although these were by far the most severe: the women of Hungary, Romania, Slovakia, Yugoslavia and others were also attacked. Milovan Djilas, *Conversations with Stalin* (New York, 1962), p. 88.

90 Wolfgang Leonhard, *Child of the Revolution*, trans. C. M. Woodhouse, (London, 1957), p. 366.

91 Max Schnetzer, 'Tagebuch der Abenteuer: Endkampf um Berlin, Reise durch Russland', pp. 154–7, quoted in Naimark, *The Russians in Germany*, p. 80.

92 Knappe and Brusaw, *Soldat*, p. 259.

93 Marshal G. Zhukov, quoted in Tony le Tissier, *Berlin Then and Now* (London, 1992), p. 218.

94 Müncheberg Panzer diary, in Jürgen Thorwald, *Das Ende an der Elbe* (Stuttgart, 1950), p. 178.

95 Leutant Jürgen Koch also saw the flooded tunnels and noted that 'many people who had sought shelter there have drowned'. Jürgen Koch, 'Das letzte Kapitel des Todeskampfes', in *Berliner Zeitung*, 7 June 1957.

96 Le Tissier, *Berlin Then and Now*, p. 226.

97 The Zoo had been bombed by the Russians from 22 April but had continued to hold out; Jacob Kronika noted that it was known as 'Berlin's strongest defensive position' and that the streets around it, from the East–West Axis to the Tiergartenstrasse, had been turned into a 'regular field camp'. Kronika, *Berlins Undergang*, p. 133. Leo Welt, in Steinhoff et al., *Voices from the Third Reich*, p. 436.

98 Müncheberg Panzer diary, in Thorwald, *Das Ende an der Elbe*, pp. 201–2.

99 As construction continued in Berlin in the late 1990s more decorated bunkers and other reminders of the last days of the war have been found, sparking off further debate as to whether they should be preserved out of historical interest or destoyed because of their links to Nazism. In the case of the Potsdamer Platz bunker the head of the municipal archaeology office, Alfred Kernd'l, attempted to save it, arguing that to destroy it would play into the hands of the very right-wing elements the destruction was allegedly meant to stop. At the time of writing the fate of the bunker is still undecided. See Brian Ladd, *The Ghosts*

of Berlin. Confronting German History in the Urban Landscape (Chicago, 1997), p. 132.

100 Oberst F. M. Sintschenko, Kommandeur des 756. Schützregiments der 150 Schützdivision der 3. Stossarmee der 1. Byelorussian Front, 'Fjodor Matwejew-itsch, wo bleibt die rote Fahne?', *Volksarmee*, Nr. 23, 1965. At the same time the Soviets were ripping the swastika flags off the Red Rathaus and replacing them with the red flag. Generalleutnant F. J. Bokow, 'Sieg und Befreiung', *Mitteilungs-blatt der Arbeitsgemeinschaft ehemaliger Offiziere* H.7, 1970, p. 3.

101 It has recently been shown that the photograph was contrived by the Ukrainian war photographer Yevgeni Khaldei and was taken not on 1 but on 2 May 1945. Before he died on 7 October 1997 he revealed that when the Russians reached Berlin in late April 1945 there were no red flags large enough for the picture he wanted. He was able to collect large red tablecloths in Moscow from Tass's head Grisha Lubinsky and bring them to Berlin; on 2 May Khaldei led several soldiers on to the roof of the Reichstag, where he took the famous picture. The official story was that a Georgian infantryman called Kaldaria held the flag aloft, 'But it was not true. The actual soldier holding the flag was called Aleksei Kovalyov. The soldier hanging onto his legs to stop him falling off was a guy from Dagestan, whose name I never got.' Khaldei fell from favour with Stalin for taking pictures of Marshal Tito, and was fired by Tass. *The Times*, 13 October 1997. The Reichstag had remained the primary target throughout; it was known as 'Object No. 105' on the Soviet plans. Tokonjuk, *Berlinski epilog*, p. 26.

102 Knappe and Brusaw, *Soldat*, p. 26.

103 Joachim C. Fest, *The Face of the Third Reich*, trans. Michael Bullock (London, 1988), p. 189.

104 Hitler sent General Keitel and General Jodl to join Admiral Dönitz in the north and his personal adjutant Schaub to the Berghof. Everyone was authorized to go on 22 April except Generals Krebs, Burgdorf and Mohnke, with their adjutants; Admiral Voss, the liaison to the Naval Command, SS Brigadeführer Rat-tenhuber, head of Führer security, and his deputy Axmann, head of the Hitler Youth; Captain Baur, Hitler's personal pilot, Press Chief Heinz Lorenz, the military adjutants Below and Hohannmeier; Hitler's personal aide Günsche and two surgeons Stumpfeggaer and Haase, who looked after wounded soldiers in a neighbouring bunker. Linge stayed, as did Traudl Junge, Hitler's chauffeur Kempka, three orderlies, the kitchen personnel and telephone operator Rochus Misch, chief engineer and electrician Henschel. Le Tissier, *Berlin Then and Now*, pp. 263–7; Trevor-Roper, *The Last Days of Hitler*, pp. 175-203.

105 Sereny, *Albert Speer*, p. 536.

106 Traudl Junge, Magda Goebbels, SS General Burgdorf, Hewel, Axmann, Below, Gerda Christian, Hitler's valet Linge and his aide Otto Günsche were present. Pierre Galante and Eugene Silianoff, *Last Witness in the Bunker* (London, 1989), p. 142.

107 Sereny, *Albert Speer*, p. 539.

108 Linge then asked SS-Brigadeführer Johann Rattenhuber, Chef der Leibwache, to help him carry the bodies to the garden. For his account, taken by the Soviets while he was a prisoner of war, see Johann Rattenhuber, 'Aussage Rattenhubers

vom 20.5.1945 in Moscau', in Lew Besymenski, 'Ein Schuss, der nie fiel', *Horizont*, Nr.2, 1969, p. 32. There were many different reactions to Hitler's death in Berlin; some loyal followers committed suicide, others were relieved. Karla Höcker remembered sitting in her cellar on 1 May 1945 when a man in a black leather coat, 'Nazi Blockwarden or something. Not liked', came to the door and said in a cold voice: 'The Führer is said to be dead.' The woman in charge of the cellar simply muttered: 'Na, denn ist ja jut' (So, then it's OK). 'Thin laughter. We couldn't sleep and got up. The awesome truth faced us: that this man was finally dead. Murdered, fallen, committed suicide?' Karla Höcker, *Die letzten und die ersten Tage. Berliner Aufzeichnungen 1945* (Berlin, 1966), p. 30.

109   In May 1989 the sixty-seven-year-old Martin Bormann Jr agreed to DNA testing to establish the identity of the corpse which the German police had identified as Bormann's in 1973. The tests were carried out by the forensic scientists and geneticists under the auspices of the Federal Criminal Agency in Wiesbaden. *The Times*, 7 May 1997.

110   On the surrender see Le Tissier, *Berlin Then and Now*, pp. 284–5.

111   Zhukov, *Erinnerungen und Gedanken*, vol. 1, pp. 624–6.

14: THE BERLIN CRISIS AND THE COLD WAR

1   John Lewis Gaddis, *The United States and the Origins of the Cold War, 1941– 1947* (New York, 1972); Michael Charlton, *The Eagle and the Small Birds. Crisis in the Soviet Empire from Yalta to Solidarity* (London, 1984), pp. 11–52; Wolfgang Benz, *Potsdam 1945: Besatzungsherrschaft und Neuaufbau im Vier-Zonen-Deutschland* (Munich, 1986); Robert Nisbet, *Roosevelt and Stalin. The Failed Courtship* (London, 1989), pp. 69–90; Daniel J. Nelson, *Wartime Origins of the Berlin Dilemma* (University of Alabama, 1978).

2   According to Koniev, 134,000 soldiers and officers had been taken prisoner by 2 May 1945. I. S. Koniev, *Das Jahr Fünfundvierzig* (Berlin, 1982), p. 176. Some testimonies were recorded from prisoners in the Soviet Union, including that of General Weidling who had surrendered the city of Berlin to the Soviets. *Bulletin des Arbeitskrisis 'Zweiter Weltkrieg'* H.2/1965. Aussage in sowjetischer Kriegsgefangenschaft.

3   Konstantin Simonov, *Kriegstagebüchern* (Berlin, 1979), vol. 2. Simonov wrote extensively for *Krasnaia zvezda* during the war. See also V. Sevruk (ed.), *How Wars End: Eyewitness Accounts of the Fall of Berlin* (Moscow, 1974).

4   Simonov, *Kriegstagebüchern*, vol. 2, p. 687.

5   Oberstleutnant Ivan Klimenko reported on 3 May 1945 that the male corpse was of someone of small build with a club foot; he saw a damaged metal prosthesis over which lay the remnants of a burned NSDAP party uniform and a gold party badge. Report of 3 May 1945 regarding the discovery of two corpses (Joseph Goebbels and his wife). Lew Besymenski, 'Ein Schuss, der nie fiel', *Horizont*, no. 8, 1968, p. 32.

6   Ada Petrova and Peter Watson, *The Death of Hitler* (New York, 1995), p. 127. In a typical twist of Soviet historical writing the confusion was blamed on

'Hitlerfascist' propaganda: 'Hitler committed suicide on 30 April . . . The Last Nazi announcement of his "hero's death" was an attempt even in the hour of defeat to create a legend out of history.' Klaus Scheel (ed.), *Die Befreiung Berlins 1945* (Berlin, 1985), p. 24.

7 Simonov, *Kriegstagebüchern*, vol. 2, p. 690.

8 Theo Findhal, *Undergang. Berlin 1939–1945* (Oslo, 1945), p. 190. Theo Findahl was Berlin correspondent for the Norwegian daily *Aftenposten* during the war and lived through the Soviet offensive.

9 The musician and music journalist Karla Höcker, who lived through the fall of Berlin and for whom 'death grinned over every shoulder', wrote of her neighbourhood on 4 May: 'Hubertusallee, Humboldt-, Kaspar-Theyss-Strasse. All houses bear traces of heavy fighting . . . slit-up red bedding hangs from a window . . . All the unburied dead are like material, like dolls, like wax figures. The mystery of death is gone.' Diary entry for 4 May 1945, Karla Höcker, *Die letzten und die ersten Tage. Berliner Aufzeichnungen 1945* (Berlin, 1966), p. 31.

10 Wolfgang Leonhard, *Child of the Revolution*, trans. C. M. Woodhouse (London, 1957), p. 41.

11 Willy Brandt, quoted in Terence Pritte, *Willy Brandt. Biography* (Frankfurt-am-Main, 1943), pp. 139–40.

12 Life in the ruins was surreal. When she returned to her house at Lindenallee 38, Karla Höcker found that the ceilings and walls were hanging like 'old gloves'. Suddenly she heard over the radio that 'Lindley Frazer from the BBC was reporting about the situation of Russian troops in Alexanderplatz!' Katharina Heinroth noted that 'the war removed every sense of trust in others; it meant the end of civilisation'. Höcker, *Die letzten und die ersten Tage*, p. 22; Katharina Heinroth, *Mit Faltern begann's. Mein Leben mit Tieren in Breslau, München und Berlin* (Munich, 1979), p. 140.

13 Karla Höcker noted that finding wood was not a problem because of the destruction: 'There is wood everywhere in the ruins, one must merely break it into small pieces . . .' (3 May 1945). Höcker, *Die letzten und die ersten Tage*, p. 29.

14 Berliners had little or no accurate information about the state of affairs. Karla Höcker wrote that the great question of the day was 'what is going on?' Everybody wanted to know, 'Where is Goebbels. Where is Göring? Who is telling Dönitz what to do? Who capitulated for Berlin? We know nothing' (3 May 1945). Höcker, *Die letzten und die ersten Tage*, p. 29.

15 One Soviet report claimed that 'The situation of the people is very bad. Many eat the cadavers of horses. In the centre of the city the distribution of bread is not yet regulated. The problem of water is noticeable. Hundreds of citizens stand at the pumps and fountains all day long just to get two pots of water.' 'Meldung der 1. Byelorussian Front an die politische Hauptverwaltung der Roten Armee 3 May 1945', in the former Institut für Marxismus-Leninismus beim ZK der SED, Zentrales Parteiarchiv, NL 36/590.

16 See G. K. Zhukov, *Erinnerungen und Gedanken* (Berlin, 1983), vol. 2, p. 300. This despite comforting articles which stated that the 'Sovietkommando Marshal Zhukov . . . has taken in hand the task to organise a normal life in the city

occupied by the Red Army.' A. I. Mikojan, 'Berlin wird versorgt', *Freis Deutschland*, 24 May 1945.

17 I have drawn on Norman M. Naimark's excellent book *The Russians in Germany. A History of the Soviet Zone of Occupation, 1945–1949* (Cambridge, 1995). Much of the material on the Soviet occupation, including the Soviet hunt for German scientists and the nuclear problem, has been invaluable; it was also useful in directing me to sources in Moscow. As Naimark has pointed out, until the KGB and Ministry of Internal Affairs of the Soviet Union archives and Presidential Archives are opened, many of the questions concerning the Soviet occupation will remain unanswered; Naimark was able to gain access to the SVAG (Soviet Military Administration in Germany) files at GARF – the Gosudarstvennyi Arkhiv Rossiiskii Federatsii (State Archives of the Russian Federation), which have since been closed. AVPRF – Arkhiv Vneshnoi Politiki Rossiiskii Federatsii (Foreign Policy Archives of the Russian Federation) – which contains files on 'Germany' and on the 'Internal history of Four-Power Occupation', esp. f.48 'Z' – (internal history of the four-power occupation). The RTsKhIDNI – Rossiiskii Tsentr Khraneniia i Izucheniia Dokumentov Noveishei Istorii (Russian Centre for the Preservation and Study of Documents of Contemporary History) – and the TsGALI – Tsentralnyi gosudarstvennyi aarkhiv literatura i iskusstva Rossii (Central State Archive of Literature and Art) – are still accessible. I have also drawn on Martin Broszat and Hermann Weber (eds.), *SBZ Handbuch* (Munich, 1990); David Pike, *The Politics of Culture in Soviet-Occupied Germany* (Stanford, 1992); W. Sandford, *From Hitler to Ulbricht: The Communist Reconstruction of East Germany, 1945–46* (Princeton, 1983); Vojtech Mastny, *Russia's Road to the Cold War: Diplomacy, Warfare and the Politics of Communism, 1941–1945* (New York, 1979).

18 Anonymous, *A Woman in Berlin*, trans. James Stern (London, 1955), p. 232.

19 On 6 November 1945 the American army officer Walter Farmer was given strict orders from Washington to ship 202 pictures, including works by Rembrandt, Dürer and Botticelli, to the United States from the Thuringian mine. He was appalled by the sequestration of art treasures under the guise of 'keeping them safe' and called a protest meeting of fellow officers with responsibility for fine arts. On 7 November thirty-two of the thirty-five officers signed the 'Wiesbaden Manifesto', which ended: 'We wish to state that from our own knowledge, no historical grievance will rankle so long, or be the cause of so much justified bitterness, as the removal, for any reason, of a part of the heritage of any nation, even if that heritage be interpreted as a prize of war. And though this removal may be done with every intention of altruism, we are none the less convinced that it is our duty, individually and collectively, to protest against it, and state that though our obligations are to the nation to which we owe allegiance, there are yet further obligations to common justice, decency and the establishment of the power of right not might, among civilised nations.' The paintings were shipped to the United States but none of the officers was court-martialled and the publication of the manifesto fomented nationwide opposition to the policy of taking German art works; in 1948 President Truman reversed it and in 1948–9 the pictures were returned to Germany. In 1996 the German government

presented Farmer with the Commander's Cross of the Federal Order of Merit.

20 Hitler had ambitious plans for treasure looted from the rest of Europe; on 15 January 1942, for example, he said, 'I must do something for Königsberg. With the money Funk has given me, I shall build a museum in which we shall assemble all we've found in Russia.'

21 According to Akinsha and Kozlov, the Soviets looted over 2,500,000 paintings, pieces of furniture, sculptures, books, documents and other objects of which over 1 million remain in Russia. For their fascinating account of the search for the stolen treasure, and a history of how it came to be there see Konstantin Akinsha and Grigorii Kozlov, *Stolen Treasure. The Hunt for the World's Lost Masterpieces* (London, 1985). The Schliemann treasure is discussed on pp. 7–10.

22 Indeed, Stalin intended to build a gigantic Socialist Realist building near the Pushkin Museum on the site of a cathedral which he had recently blown up, which would house a museum of 'world art'. When the Rubens was found along with others in the Gross Cotta mine, Stalin sent a personal telegram to Koniev reading: 'Give necessary help in transportation to Moscow of the cargo prepared by the brigade of Colonel Rotoayev. Remember that the cargo is of state importance, provide the necessary security, report the accomplishment. Stalin.' Akinsha and Kozlov, *Stolen Treasure*, p. 127.

23 There were 593 paintings in the Gemäldegalerie and 852 paintings from the Nationalgalerie; over 400, including Rubens's *Bacchanalia*, were destroyed by a fire which started mysteriously while the Soviets were packing the crates; they also emptied the enormous storage facility on the third level of the Zoo flak tower under the eyes of the Americans. Their most spectacular coup was to dismantle and remove the great Pergamon Altar; the American MFAA officer Richard Howard later commented, 'Their most spectacular job in Berlin was the Pergamon Altar ... The friezes were ripped anew from their walls, loaded upon flat cars, and were never seen again. About a hundred other first class Greek sculptures and architectural pieces, from Olympia, from Samos, from Priene and Miletos, from Didyma and Baalbek, brought by the devoted labour of archaeologists to Berlin, went with them ...' Richard Howard, quoted in Akinsha and Kozlov, *Stolen Treasure*, p. 82.

24 Many of the works were destroyed or damaged by the Soviets. This did not stop Soviet propaganda explaining how they had carefully removed and saved them. The East German writer Ruth Seydewitz wrote that '... the valuable treasures of the Dresden Picture Gallery were saved from destruction because Soviet officers and soldiers, brought up in a spirit of humanism and proletarian internationalism, were full of respect and profound understanding for the irreplaceable works of art, even at a time when – as army General P. Y. Petrov expressed it – "they were still touched by the breath of battle".' Manfred Gerstäcker and Boris Koslov (eds.), *Yesterday and Today. Contemporaries Report on the Progress of German–Soviet Friendship* (Dresden and Moscow, 1967), pp. 117–18.

25 For the Soviet view see, for example, the article by the director of the Pushkin Museum who also helped to unload the crates in 1945 and who organized the

'Twice Saved' exhibition. Irina Antonova, 'Miy nikomu nichevo de dolzhni', *Nezavisimaya Gazeta*, 5 March 1995.

26 Major General L. M. Gaidukov, chief of the Soviet rocket project in Germany, traced the archives of the German rocket industry to a thirty-car train near Prague and asked Malenkov to transport the whole collection back to the USSR. Naimark, *The Russians in Germany*, p. 177.

27 The Soviets also plundered art and archives from other nations; the Prague archives of the Russian emigration were sent to Moscow, as were valuable archives and works of art from Poland, Ukraine and the Baltic States to Hungary, Czechoslovakia and beyond. Naimark, *The Russians in Germany*, p. 178; Akinsha and Kozlov, *Stolen Treasure*, p. 146; the latter also include an extraordinary photograph showing vast piles of old leather-bound books mouldering in the secret depository of the Uzkoe church in Moscow (p. 105).

28 On 23 August 1946 Stalin was informed that Zhukov had sent seven train-carriage loads of furniture to Moscow. On the night of 8 January 1948 his dacha was searched, revealing crates of objects from German palaces, including silverware, porcelain, crystal, 4,000 metres of expensive cloth, hundreds of furs, forty-four excellent carpets and piles of other 'trophies'. His rival Abakumov put in his report that 'it is hard to imagine that you are not in Germany but close to Moscow' when you see this house. The revelations would eventually be used by Stalin, who had Zhukov exiled to Odessa. *Voennie arkhivi Rossii* (Military Archives of Russia), no. 1, 1993, p. 190.

29 Naimark, *The Russians in Germany*, p. 176.

30 On 13 May 1997 Russia's Federation Council voted to declare over 300,000 works of art taken from Germany the property of the Russian Federation, vetoing President Boris Yeltsin's proposal which would have allowed the return of selected works. (Yeltsin was concerned that more than DM1 billion or $1.7 billion of German loan credits intended to support Russian reform might be at risk if the art works are not returned.) In April 1997 Yeltsin returned a token piece of art during a visit to Helmut Kohl, and Presidential Press Secretary Sergei Yastrzhembsky confirmed that nearly 2 million works of art and 3 million archive documents were returned to Germany between 1958 and 1969. These included Raphael's Sistine Madonna and the collection from Berlin's National Gallery. However, works by Rembrandt, Cézanne, Degas and Goya still remain in Russia. 'Yeltsin's Veto on Trophy Art Overturned', *Moscow Tribune*, 14 May 1997.

31 Naimark, *The Russians in Germany*, p. 181; Philip Windsor, *City on Leave. A History of Berlin 1945–1962* (London, 1963), p. 37.

32 The Americans were alerted to the mass removal of equipment when their agents at the Berlin Operations Base (BOB), the successor in Berlin to the Office of Strategic Services (OSS), procured the minutes of a 26–27 September meeting between the Central Administration for Industry and Soviet officials during which industrial conditions in the zone were reviewed; BOB also tracked shipments of dismantled industrial equipment by covering the Soviet collection point at Berlin-Lichtenberg. David E. Murphy, Sergei A. Kondraschev and George Bailey, *Battleground Berlin. CIA vs. KGB in the Cold War* (Yale, 1987),

p. 8. On the football field incident see Naimark, *The Russians in Germany*, p. 180.

33 In a speech to the Magistrat on 21 May 1945 Bersarin warned Berliners that they must 'work good and hard' if they were 'to gain freedom and *Entspannung* (relaxation)'. *Berliner Zeitung*, 21 May 1945.

34 Major General P. A. Kvashin, chief of SMAD's Transportation Administration, quoted in Naimark, *The Russians in Germany*, p. 62.

35 Anonymous, *A Woman in Berlin*, pp. 235–6.

36 By mid May 2.6 million Berliners had been given ration cards. One typical example of May 1945, called a 'Lebensmittelkarte für Deutsche', allows adults 200 grams of bread per day, 25 grams of meat, 400 grams of potatoes, 10 grams of sugar, 2 grams of coffee and 10 grams of salt. Much was later made in East German historiography of Soviet efforts to 'feed Berlin'; see, for example, Horst Schützler, *Die Unterstützung und Hilfe der Sowjetunion für die demokratischen Kräfte Berlins in ihrem Kampf um eine friedliche und demokratische Stadt (April/ Mai 1945 bis Oktober 1946,* (Phil. Diss. Humboldt University, Berlin, 1964).

37 Naimark, *The Russians in Germany*, p. 34.

38 Much propaganda was written to support this view; according to Corporal Josef Kilimnik of the First Polish Army, on 30 April 1945 a woman had approached him and demanded some bread. Far from turning against her, he claimed, 'I gave her my ration ... In 1939 the Germans didn't even give our prisoners a turnip, but as victors in Berlin we gave the Germans bread. That is the extraordinary thing about this war.' Josef Kilimnik, *Wojsko Polskie pod Brama Brandenburska* (Warsaw, 1972), p. 56.

39 Regina Frenkenfeld interview, in Alison Owings, *Frauen: German Women Recall the Third Reich* (Harmondsworth, 1993), p. 406.

40 Ernst Lemmer, *Manches war doch anders: Erinnerungen eines deutschen Demokraten* (Frankfurt-am-Main, 1968), p. 255.

41 This incident occurred in Weimar in October 1945. The first lieutenant was stopped only when two Russian officers were called in from the street. Naimark, *The Russians in Germany*, p. 85. The Soviets were surprised by the numbers of Berliners who now claimed to have been members of the KPD: a report issued by the First Byelorussian Front on 26 April 1945 noted that 'the closer the Red Army gets the more Communists appear. Some show old KPD membership books, others tell of abuse in prison or concentration camps. Some describe their illegal war against Fascism ... Many prisoners-of-war claim that the Nazis forced them to take false papers and assume false identities.' The document is in the former Institut für Marxismus-Leninismus beim ZK der SED, Zentrales Parteiarchiv (NL 36/590).

42 Naimark, *The Russians in Germany*, p. 117.

43 Interview with M. I. Burtsev, in C. Barraclough, *Russian Connection* (Pacem Productions, 1992). The programme was broadcast on BBC television in 1995.

44 Naimark, *The Russians in Germany*, p. 108.

45 Leonod Leonov, quoted in ibid., p. 108.

46 Ibid., p. 97.

47 This top-secret order no. 009 of 23 May 1947 for the Soviet forces in Austria

signed by Major General Kurasov was printed in the west by an émigré newspaper under 'Glavnyi shtab tsentralnoi gruppy sil', 25 May 1947, Prikaz no. 009, *Za svobodu Rossii*, no. 10, 1948, pp. 47–9, quoted in Naimark, *The Russians in Germany*, p. 95; Robert Conquest, *Stalin. Breaker of Nations* (London, 1991), p. 271.

48 Conquest, *Stalin*, p. 271; Alexander I. Solzhenitsyn, *The Gulag Archipelago, 1918– 1956*, 2 vols. (New York, 1974). On the forced repatriations to Russia of prisoners of war see Nicholas Bethell, *The Last Secret. Forcible Repatriation to Russia 1944–7* (London, 1974).

49 *Die Welt*, 17 August 1948.

50 Klaus-Jörg Ruhl (ed.), *Unsere verlorenen Jahre – Frauenalltag in Kriegs- und Nachkriegszeit, 1939–1949* (Darmstadt, 1985), p. 184.

51 There were virtually no (reported) incidences of homosexual rape. Naimark, *The Russians in Germany*, p. 109.

52 In December 1946 a meeting took place between Marshal Vasily Kololovsky and the SED leaders, including Wilhelm Pieck, Walter Ulbricht, Otto Grotewohl and Max Fechner. The official memorandum of the conversations was found in SVR archives. It reveals the extent to which the German leaders were concerned about Soviet behaviour in their zone, including rape and the dismantling of factories, and the extent to which they felt it might damage their electoral chances in the coming election. Murphy et al., *Battleground Berlin*, pp. 401–5.

53 Naimark, *The Russians in Germany*, p. 120.

54 Diary entry for 29 May 1945, Ruth Andreas-Friedrich, *Schauplatz Berlin: Tagebuchaufzeichnungen 1945–1948* (Frankfurt-am-Main, 1984), p. 36.

55 In his order to the Red Army on 1 May 1945 Stalin had stated that 'Poland, Hungary, much of Czechoslovakia, an important part of Austria and the capital of Austria, Vienna, have been liberated', together with East Prussia, Pomerania, most of Brandenburg and Berlin. It soon became clear that 'liberation' was little more than a euphemism for brutal subjugation. Josef Stalin, *Über den grossen vaterländischen Krieg der Sowjetunion* (Berlin, 1951), p. 215.

56 At this point the Soviets did not have an overall plan for the political development of the zone similar to that issued by the Americans for their zone in the form of 'JCS 1067', but they did not need one as all Soviets had shared the experiences of bolshevization, of collectivization, of economic five-year plans and of the purging of 'enemies of the people'.

   During his victory message of 9 May 1945 Stalin had announced that Russia had 'no intention' of dismembering Germany and in the first year after the war the relationship between the Americans and the Soviets was quite harmonious. And, as Avi Shlaim has pointed out, the conventional notion that Stalin operated according to one master plan is inaccurate, as he pursued a number of policies, some of which were contradictory. Avi Shlaim, *The United States and the Berlin Blockade, 1948–1949. A Study in Crisis Decision Making* (Berkeley, 1983), pp. 19– 21. See also Windsor, *City on Leave*, p. 23; John H. Backer, *The Decision to Divide Germany: American Foreign Policy in Transition* (Durham, NC, 1978).

57 This despite the fact that Molotov had said to James F. Byrnes at Yalta that Russia wanted to participate in four-power government of Germany. Shlaim,

The United States, p. 24. See also James F. Byrnes, *Speaking Frankly* (London, 1947), p. 174.

58 Kalinin also stressed the Soviet desire to continue the 'satellization' of eastern Europe through the increased 'cooperation between the peace-loving Socialist powers'. Anthony Nutting, *Europe Will Not Wait* (London, 1960), p. 8.

59 Now the Hotel Tsentralnaya on Tverskaya.

60 It is striking how many of Stalin's top men in the security services of the Soviet zone had not only spent time in Moscow, but had fought in the Spanish Civil War. Aside from Ulbricht they included Kurt Fischer, who became head of the notorious People's Police, and Wilhelm Zaisser, who had fought under the name 'Gomez' and who was made Deputy Minister of the DVdI in 1948. On Ulbricht in Moscow see Carola Stern, *Ulbricht. Eine politische Biographie* (Berlin/Cologne, 1963), pp. 94–120.

61 Ackermann's group linked with the First Ukrainian Front and moved into Dresden on 1 May under Koniev; Gustav Sobottka's group linked up with the Second Byelorussian Front on 6 May and moved north into Rostock and Schwerin.

62 Despite the carefully laid plans the first phase of the occupation was chaotic. Stalin had dithered and issued contradictory orders, which became evident in the lack of a coherent administration in the Soviet zone. Various units, including the army, vied with one another for control of the region. Eventually commandants who set up local headquarters or *kommandaturas* created the first functional units of administrative authority in occupied Germany. These were eventually brought under the control of SMAD but not without conflict, particularly from local commandants, many of whom had set up fiefdoms for themselves.

63 Order no. 1 was presented in East Berlin as 'Befehl Nr. 01 des Stadtkommandanten Generaloberst N. E. Bersarin, mitunterzeichnet vom Stabschef Generalmajor Kuschtschow, über die Sicherung der medizinischen Betreuung der Berliner vom 2 Mai 1945'.

64 Colonel General Ivan Aleksandrovich Serov from Poland was officially merely Marshal Zhukov's deputy for civil affairs. In reality he was the personnel representative of the People's Commissar of Internal Affairs (NKVD) with the Group of Soviet Occupation Forces; in short, he supervised the police, the guards, the prisons, the surveillance in the Soviet zone; indeed even Zhukov was reported on by him and by Vyshinsky. Serov was responsible for the creation of the *Spetslager*, the prison camps which would contain over 10,000 people sentenced as ex-Nazis or as dangerous elements who opposed the Soviet regime. Achim Killian, *Einweisen zur völligen Isolierung: NKWD-Speziallage Muehlberg/Elbe, 1945–48* (Leipzig, 1993).

65 The MGB, the Ministry of State Security, evolved from the NKGB. On this metamorphosis see Murphy et al., *Battleground Berlin*, p. 34.

66 Naimark, *The Russians in Germany*, pp. 21–4.

67 One of Stalin's Germans, Otto Winzer, was at pains to make it clear to his fellow citizens that, despite having lived in Moscow, Berlin was his home, 'ist meine Vaterstadt'. See Otto Winzer, 'Für die neue Macht des Volkes', *Neues*

Deutschland, 29 June 1963. Soviet propaganda had echoed Stalin's propaganda, which maintained that although 'Hitlers come and go the German people remain' or, as one poster in the Karlhorst Museum put it, that the destruction of Hitler should not mean the end of the German people but rather 'die Rettung aus der faschistischen Sklaverei und vor der Ausrottung des deutschen Volkes in diesem sinnlosen Krieg' (the salvation from fascist slavery and from the destruction of the German people in this meaningless war). One typical newspaper article stated that it was time to begin the 'peaceful rebuilding and *Wiedergutmachung* [making good again] . . . so that Germany can once again take her place in the peaceful *Völkerfamilie* [family of peoples]'. *Berliner Zeitung*, 22 May 1945. See also Wilhelm Pieck's comforting first speech to the German people on 4 May 1945 which concentrated on the benefits to be gained from Soviet–German co-operation. Wilhelm Pieck, *Reden und Aufsätze. Auswahl aus den Jahren 1908–1950* (Berlin, 1954), vol. 1, p. 423.

68 Theo Findahl felt that the Russians were 'disappointed' by the German communists, who had not done enough against Hitler: 'the resistance against Hitler had not been carried out by workers and petty bourgeoise but much more by circles of German aristocrats, the Catholic Church and the Confessing Church!' (11 May 1945). Findahl, *Undergang*, p. 194.

69 Even so it is somewhat difficult to believe in the account by the NKVD functionary Bernhard Bechler, who wrote of the sudden outpouring of joy and the spontaneous demonstrations by 'working class women with red headscarves and red flags' who raced from the wreckage of their homes in Wittenau to greet the Red Army. According to him they listened to news about 'W. Pieck, W. Ulbricht and E. Weinert . . . with tears in their eyes as they had not believed that these workers' functionaries still lived'. Now they knew that 'the Party would continue its role as leader of the working class'. Bernhard Bechler, 'Aus der Arbeit des Nationalkomitees "Freies Deutschland" bei der 2. Byelorussian Front im Jahre 1945', in Historischen Institut der Ernst-Moritz-Arndt-Universität, *Befreiung und Neubeginn* (Berlin, 1966), p. 129.

70 Leonhard, *Child of the Revolution*, p. 41. Leonhard lived in exile in Moscow during the war, returned to Berlin in 1945, and fled from the Soviet zone in 1948. His works include *Die Revolution entlässt ihre Kinder* (Cologne, 1955), and *Das kurze leben der DDR. Berichte und Kommentäre aus vier Jahrzehnten* (Stuttgart, 1990). For decades he was the only available source about the creation of the Soviet system in East Germany; new research has shown something of the complexity and confusion amongst the Russian victors about what to do in Germany after the defeat.

71 On the block warden system see Hans Herzfeld, 'Berlin und das Berlinproblem vom Zusammenbruch bis zu den Stadtverordnetenwahlen des 20 Oktober 1946', in Berlin Senat, *Kampf um Freiheit und Selbstverwaltung, 1945–46* (Berlin, 1957), pp. 15–17. The Soviets encouraged this 'democratic' recruitment (i.e. the recruitment of ex-Nazis and others who would be sympathetic to the new regime); Kurt Steffen, member of the KPD in Weissensee, described how on 23 April 1945 he was told to recruit 'around twenty members of the KPD' for his district, but was praised for having 'bonded' with many 'anti-Fascists' when he brought

in '. . . Social Democrats and citizens of no party' who have 'close connections to the entire population'. Kurt Steffen, 'Sie stellten 1945 die Weichen in Weissensee', *Tribune*, 7 May 1945.

72 The sycophancy of Kurt Schöps, a KPD member appointed by the Soviets to help in the creation of a new police force in Weissensee, was typical: 'The Soviet officers and soldiers have helped both in practical and in ideological ways to find solutions to our problems in the spirit of internationalism.' Kurt Schöps, *Wie Weissensee aus Ruinen auferstand* (Berlin, 1965), p. 34. See also the memoirs of Johannes Kupke, who was made mayor of Niederschönhausen in April 1945. Johannes Kupke, *Im Besitz des herausgebers* (Berlin, 1965).

73 The new mayor of Weissensee, for example, took the task of imparting Soviet values to his district very seriously. On 2 May 1945 he ordered that every factory and organization was to submit a plan of action which 'must have his signature'. 'The mayor has complete control over the entire population of Weissensee,' he continued. Above all, the administration was 'to co-operate fully with the Kommandatur'. 'Protokoll der Besprechung des Bürgermeister von Weissensee mit seinen Mitarbeitern vom 2 Mai 1945' (Stadtarchiv Berlin, Rep. 148, Nr. 201).

74 The list of mayors and other key posts was published along with a thinly veiled order to Berliners to give 'the newly created Magistrat active assistance' and to allow it to 'fulfil the obligations demanded by the military command of the Red Army'. *Tägliche Rundschau*, 18 May 1945.

75 A 1946 report noted that a number of functioning businesses included 372 out of 1,829 chemists, 800 out of 1,650 radio and electrical shops and around 200 out of 600 furniture stores. All were seized by the state. Magistrats der Stadt Berlin, *Das erste Jahr. Berlin im Neuaufbau. Ein Rechenschaftsbericht des Magistrats der Stadt Berlin* (Berlin, 1946).

76 Theo Findahl noted wryly how quickly 'Nazis' had 'become Communists' after the surrender. By 11 May 1945 white and red flags had sprouted at Berlin's windows. A white flag meant simply that 'non-Nazis live there' while 'the red indicate that a Communist lives there'. The irony was that these red flags appeared at the windows of 'the most beautiful apartments in which Nazis lived . . . The "red" Germans are organised in the same "cells" as their "brown" counterparts . . . the change is far from revolutionary.' Diary entry for 11 May 1945, Findahl, *Undergang*, p. 194.

77 Over 300 such pro-Communist German POWs were indoctrinated by GlavPURKKA, which was founded shortly after the German invasion of the Soviet Union. In the war years its 'Seventh Section' was responsible for propaganda and counter-propaganda. It was this group which combed German POW camps for potential Communist sympathizers, which put them through special training schools for the 'Movement of a Free Germany' and sent them to Germany in 1946. One of the recruits was Count Heinrich von Einsiedel, born in 1921. He was shot down in Stalingrad and taken to a Soviet POW camp, where he became active in the National Committee for a Free Germany. In a recent interview Einsiedel recalled that the camp commander 'called upon me to ask that I write a declaration committing myself to collaborate with the Soviet Union in its fight against Hitler. I saw no reason at all to hesitate in making

such a statement . . . I must admit that I had totally succumbed to the Communist ideology . . . On January 1, 1945, I left Moscow to go to Germany with the Red Army. I witnessed some horrendous crimes committed by the Red Army. As it marched into Germany I was ordered to tell the German members of the National Committee that what I saw were really German soldiers dressed in Russian uniforms committing the atrocities. Of course I didn't give in to such madness, which resulted in my falling out of grace in the Soviet Union. I was ordered to return to the Committee's headquarters. This is why I wasn't released from Russian imprisonment until 1947.' Another leading member of the Committee for a Free Germany remembered that many of those who joined were recruited in POW camps after Stalingrad: 'For Stalingrad veterans, the oath [to Hitler] usually wasn't important.' Johannes Steinhoff, Peter Pechel and Dennis Showalter (eds.), *Voices from the Third Reich. An Oral History* (New York, 1994), pp. 158–61.

78 Naimark, *The Russians in Germany*, p. 355; Windsor, *City on Leave*, p. 56. On the East Berlin police involvement in kidnappings and in the forced transfer of Berlin workers see Hans Herzfeld, *Berlin in der Weltpolitik 1945–1970* (Berlin, 1973), p. 67.

79 Dimitrov and A. S. Paniushkin recommended to Molotov and G. M. Malenkov that the GlavPURKKA take over all propaganda in Germany, which included the founding of newspapers which were to have 'some kind of national title', leading to the creation of the *Deutsche Volkszeitung* and *Neues Deutschland*, amongst others. The organization printed propaganda sheets, used loudspeaker trucks for propaganda broadcasts and oversaw the radio stations. By 1947 GlavPURKKA activities were taken over by the Propaganda and Censorship Department (later the Information Administration). Naimark, *The Russians in Germany*, p. 20. On the creation of a Stalinist culture in East Germany see Ilse Spittmann and Gisela Helwig (eds.), *DDR Lesebuch. Von der SBZ zur DDR 1945–1949* (Berlin, 1989), pp. 207–29.

80 George Clare, *Berlin Days 1946–1947* (London, 1989), p. 66. For an excellent overview of the creation of a new culture in the GDR see Manfred Jäger, *Kultur und Politik in der DDR. 1945–1990* (Cologne, 1995), pp. 5–68; Johannes R. Becher is cited on pp. 34–5.

81 Clare, *Berlin Days*, p. 65. On Dymshits see Alexander Dymshits, *Ein unvergesslicher Frühling* (Berlin-Ost, 1970); on Tulpanov see Sergei Tulpanov, 'Zeit des Neubeginns', *Neue deutsche Literatur*, i, 1979, pp. 42–57.

82 By 14 May 1945 the Soviets could boast that there were cinemas in Berlin and that all were oversubscribed, including the two in Weissensee which catered for 600 people. According to one report: 'At the box offices people stand in lines for two to three hours before the projection and the tickets are soon sold out. The prices have stayed the same. Berliners watch Soviet films with great interest.' Former Institut für Marxismus-Leninismus beim ZK der SED, Zentrales Parteiarchiv, NL 36/590.

83 A work could be banned on Dymshits's whim; in 1947, for example, he wrote an article explaining why he did not like Jean-Paul Sartre's *Fliegen*, calling his theory that 'good is false and dangerous' harmful to revolutionary consciousness.

Alexander Dymshits, 'Warum mir das nicht gefällt – Jean-Paul Sartres "Flie-gen"', *Tägliche Rundshau*, 30 September 1947. Life for artists banned by the Soviets was dangerous; Isaiah Berlin visited the poet Anna Akhmatova in January 1946 and spoke to her on the telephone during a visit to Russia in 1956 during which she told him 'something of her experience as a condemned writer: of the turning-away of some whom she had considered faithful friends, of the nobility and courage of others'. When they met in Oxford in 1965 she told him that Stalin was 'personally enraged' that she had met a foreign visitor without official approval and that this had contributed to her being banned. Isaiah Berlin, *Personal Impressions* (Oxford, 1980), pp. 190–96. On Becher see Spittmann and Helwig, *DDR Lesebuch*, p. 211.

84 Clare, *Berlin Days*, p. 45.

85 On the 'Berliner Zeitung' see Konrad Wolf, 'Auf den Tag vor 20 Jahren', in *Berliner Zeitung*, 8 May 1965; see also A. W. Kirsamow, 'Der erste Monat', in *Berliner Zeitung*, 21 May 1965. On 9 May 1945 the newspaper *Freies Deutschland* was proud to print a speech by Heinrich Mann, signed by Alexander Abusch, Ludwig Renn, Anna Seghers, Kurt Stern and Bodo Uhse, congratulating those who were building a new Berlin.

86 The first children's books were published in the Mitte district on 15 May.

87 Naimark, *The Russians in Germany*, p. 66.

88 On Strang and the EAC see Ann and John Tusa, *The Berlin Blockade* (London, 1988), pp. 10–15. On the EAC agreement issued on 12 September and 14 November 1944 see Dennis L. Bark and David R. Gress, *From Shadow to Substance, 1945–1963* (Oxford, 1993), vol. 1, p. 25.

89 Churchill had warned of Stalin's hunger for land as early as May 1945. See Lord Ismay, *NATO, The First Five Years 1949–1954* (Paris, 1954), p. 4.

90 Frank Howley, *Berlin Command* (New York, 1950), pp. 146–8.

91 Lucius D. Clay, *Decision in Germany* (New York, 1950), p. 15.

92 Soviet propaganda defended the policy by claiming that they were trying to prevent the western allies from taking over Germany in the name of 'capitalist imperialism'. See, for example, Joachim Piskol, *Konzeptionell Pläne und Massnahmen der deutschen Monopolbourgeoisie für den Übergang von imperial-istischen Krieg zum imperialistischen Frieden und zur Rettung ihrer Machtgrund-lagen aus der faschistischen Niederlage (1943–1945)*, (Diss. Humbolt University, Berlin, 1972).

93 See Klaus Larres, *Politik der Illusionen: Churchill, Eisenhower und die deutsche Frage 1945–1955* (Göttingen, 1995).

94 Gregory Klimov, *The Terror Machine: The Inside Story of the Soviet Adminis-tration in Germany*, trans. H. C. Stevens (London, 1953), p. 146.

95 Howley, *Berlin Command*, p. 140.

96 The trials were thwarted by the Soviet presence; as Robert Conquest has pointed out, it was ironic that one of the states passing judgement over Nazi Germany had been expelled as a belligerent from the League of Nations six years before. Furthermore, the Soviet judge Nikitchenko had been a judge in the faked Zinoviev trial and other show trials while one of the Soviet prosecutors, Lev Sheinin, had been head of the prosecution 'Section Investigating Important

Cases' in Moscow and was responsible for almost all the main frame-ups. Conquest also points to the fact that the Katyn massacre was one of the charges made against the Germans at Nuremberg. The presence of such charges and such men 'made nonsense of Nuremberg'. Gina Thomas (ed.), *The Unresolved Past – A Debate in German History* (London, 1990) p. 49. See also International Military Tribunal, Nuremberg, *The Trial of German Major War Criminals: Documents and Proceedings*, ed. L. D. Egbert (Nuremberg, 1947–9), vols 1–13; Airey Neave, *Nuremberg: A Personal Record* (London, 1978), pp. 73–85; International Military Tribunal, Nuremberg, *Speeches of the Chief Prosecutors* (London, 1946); R. K. Woetzel, *The Nuremberg Trials in International Law* (New York, 1962); A. and J. Tusa, *The Nuremberg Trial* (London, 1983).

97 Markus Wolf, *In eigenem Auftrag. Bekenntnisse und Einsichten* (Munich, 1991). His story is repeated in Markus Wolf (with Anne McElvoy), *Man Without a Face. The Memoirs of a Spymaster* (London, 1997), pp. 41–2.

98 Howley, *Berlin Command*, p. 137.

99 Hans Speier, *From the Ashes of Disgrace: A Journal From Germany 1945–1955* (Amherst, 1981), p. 26. See also Dagmar Barnouw, *Germany 1945* (Bloomington, 1996), p. 139.

100 Clare, *Berlin Days*, p. 16.

101 It has been estimated that around 245,000 people had been arrested in all four zones of occupation in connection with suspected past Nazi activity; this figure includes dubious Soviet statistics. See Wolfgang Eisert, *Die Waldheimer Prozesse. Der stalinistische Terror 1950* (Munich, 1993), p. 32.

102 Brixius lived in Marburg, but her experiences were shared by many women in the Soviet zone. Interview with Frau Martha Brixius, in Owings, *Frauen*, p. 210.

103 'Stenogramma soobshchenii', 7 June 1945, Rossiiskii Tsentr Khraneniia i Izucheniia Dokumentov Noveishei Istorii (Russian Centre for the Preservation and Study of Documents of Contemporary History) Central Committee, op. 128, Otdel mezhdunarodnoi informatsii Ts VKP (b) d 750 1.166; Naimark, *The Russians in Germany*, p. 259.

104 Interview with Frau Ursula Meyer-Semlies, in Owings, *Frauen*, p. 67.

105 The rapid transformation of identity from Nazi to anti-Nazi was particularly common amongst DPs or 'displaced persons' whose true backgrounds were difficult to trace. Clare, *Berlin Days*, p. 39.

106 Interview with Verena Groth, in Owings, *Frauen*, p. 112.

107 Interview with Verena Groth. Martha Brixius recalled how the Americans took over their house, threw possessions out, and when they went back they had done obnoxious things like leaving used toilet paper in all their cooking pots and filling juice containers with urine. Owings, *Frauen*, pp. 101, 211.

108 Some ex-Nazis achieved important positions in the Federal Republic. One of the most controversial was Hans Globke, who had been an important figure in Hitler's Ministry of the Interior but who nevertheless became Adenauer's chief aide from 1950 to 1963. His appointment was of particular concern as he had been a civil servant under Hitler and had written the official commentary of the Nuremberg Laws which deprived Jews of many basic rights. Other important

figures included Kurt Georg Kiesinger, who became Federal Chancellor; Professor Karl Schiller, who became the Minister of Economics; Karl Carstens, who became Federal President, and a number of important members of the judiciary, armed services, public administration, universities and diplomatic service. It must be said, however, that this was not comparable to the use of ex-Nazis in the Soviet zone in what became the German Democratic Republic, where thousands of top Nazis were employed in important posts – not least the infamous SS-Obersturmbannführer Franz Erich Giese, who had been the deputy commandant at Buchenwald. He called himself Erich Gust and ran a top Stasi hotel in Heimathof; his past was deliberately hidden by the Stasi. It has been estimated, that in 1963 fifty-three of the 500 members of the Volkskammer were former Nazi party members. See David Childs and Richard Popplewell, *The Stasi. The East German Intelligence and Security Service* (London, 1996), p. 146; see also Louis Hagen, *Der heimliche Krieg auf deutschen Boden seit 1945* (Düsseldorf, 1969); Eugene Davidson, *The Trial of the Germans* (New York, 1966).

109 In some cases the appointments were highly dubious and Jörg Friedrich has estimated that around 4,000 of Himmler's officials from the SS or SD were employed in significant positions after the war. Jörg Friedrich, *Die kalte Amnestie NS-Tater in der Bundesrepublik* (Berlin, 1965), p. 6.

110 For documentation and photographs of the German expulsions see: *Die Flucht und Vertreibung. Eine Bilddokumentation vom Schicksal der Deutschen aus Ostpreussen, Oberschlesien, Niederschlesien, Danzig, Westpreussen, Ost–Pommern, Ost-Brandenburg u.a. und dem Sudetenland* (Bad Nauheim, 1966); Douglas Botting, *From the Ruins of the Reich* (New York, 1985); Martin K. Sorge, *The Other Price of Hitler's War: German Military and Civilian Losses Resulting from World War II* (New York, 1985); Manfred Malzahn, *Germany 1945–1949: A Sourcebook* (London, 1991).

111 Winston Churchill, *Triumph and Tragedy* (London, 1953), p. 658; see also Alfred M. de Zayas, *Nemesis at Potsdam. The Expulsion of the Germans from the East* (London, 1988), p. 87.

112 One estimate puts the figure at 2 million people although this is almost certainly too high. Wolfgang Benz, 'Fremde in der Heimat: Flucht–Vertriebung–Integration', in Klaus J. Bade (ed.), *Deutsche im Ausland – Fremde in Deutschland. Migration in Geschichte und Gegenwart* (Munich, 1992), p. 381.

113 According to the Office of the United States High Commission, the population movement of Germans was 4,692,800 from former German territories east of the Oder-Neisse; 346,800 ethnic Germans from Poland, 1,970,600 ethnic Germans from Czechoslovakia, 203,600 ethnic Germans from Hungary, 123,700 ethnic Germans from Romania, 138,700 ethnic Germans from Yugoslavia, 398,900 ethnic Germans from other countries. Office of the US High Commission, *Fifth Quarterly Report* (Washington, 1950).

114 *Time*, 27 August 1945, p. 4.

115 Norman Clark, *News Chronicle*, 24 August 1945, quoted in de Zayas, *Nemesis at Potsdam*, p. 111.

116 *The Times*, 27 October 1945.

117 A selection was published in Robert Capa, *Sommertage, Friedenstage. Berlin*

1945 (Berlin, 1986). Leonard McCombe's photographs were published in the 22 September 1945 issue of *Illustrated*. See also Bill Richardson and Leonard McCombe, *Menschen erleiden Geschichte. Das Gesicht Europas von der Themse bis zur Weichsel 1943–1946* (Zurich, 1948).

118 Botting, *From the Ruins of the Reich*, p. 180.

119 Diary entry, 14 February 1947, in Andreas-Friedrich, *Schauplatz Berlin*, p. 163.

120 As Michael Howard has pointed out, the Soviets actually 'held all the cards' for achieving their foreign policy aims in Germany and Berlin in 1945, but their antagonistic behaviour destroyed any western goodwill towards them and lost them the opportunity to influence events to their own advantage. See Michael Howard, Introduction, in Olav Riste (ed.), *Western Security: The Formative Years. European and Atlantic Defence 1947–1953* (New York, 1985), p. 15.

121 For descriptions of Berlin in the immediate aftermath of war see B. Byford-Jones, *Berlin Twilight* (London, 1946); Andreas-Friedrich, *Schauplatz Berlin*.

122 When Gertrude Stein travelled to Germany in 1945 she saw American soldiers proudly showing off their newly acquired possessions: 'Where they had acquired, what they had acquired, better not know. There are three million American soldiers there and each of them has to have at least six souvenirs. Dear me. They call these objects liberated. This is a liberated camera. Liberated they are.' Gertrude Stein, 'Off We All Went to See Germany', *Life*, 6 August 1954. In his 'Diary of an Inspection Trip to Europe in October–December 1945' Navy Captain H. E. Saunders noted: 'Although one is not supposed to take private property, an American in the American zone of Germany can walk off with almost anything he finds in the way of military or naval equipment, scientific apparatus, instruments, and records, commercial property, and public property. After a few weeks of filling our pockets and car with loot, what is to keep our sense of right and wrong from being dulled . . . ?' H. E. Saunders, Behnke Papers, Hoover Institution Archive, Stanford, quoted in Barnouw, *Germany 1945*, p. 99. The photographer Margaret Bourke-White admitted to having engaged in the practice: 'In other countries through which the war carried me, looting never became the big-time obsession it was in Germany. But now we were in the country of the enemy, the enemy from whom we had suffered so much and who had stolen so much from other vanquished countries.' Margaret Bourke-White, *Portrait of Myself* (New York, 1963), p. 261. American involvement in the black market was explored in the article 'Black Markets Boom in Berlin', with photographs by Frank Capa, *Life*, 10 September 1945.

123 The non-fraternization order was issued in September 1944 when American troops occupied the Aachen region and photographs appeared in the press showing American soldiers with German women and children. General Marshall transmitted a message from President Roosevelt to General Eisenhower on 22 September 1944 alerting him to the 'objectionable' photographs. Americans were henceforth not to eat in the same restaurants, not to go to German homes, indeed not to mix with the population in any way; fraternization was to be 'suppressed completely' and offenders were to face a fine of $65. The Civil Affairs Division *Pocket Guide to Germany* warned troops, 'There must be no

fraternization! This is absolute!' But the average soldier paid little attention to the order and friendships, particularly between GIs and German women, were increasingly common. Earl Ziemke, *The US Army in the Occupation of Germany 1944–1946* (Washington, DC, 1975), p. 98.

124 Clare, *Berlin Days*, p. 74. On 26 April 1945 the Joint Chiefs of Staff issued the directive JCS 1067, which was to guide the American occupation of Germany. Among other things it forbade fraternization between Americans and Germans; its emphasis on agriculture and the banning of American aid in the industrial reconstruction of Germany belied Morgenthau's influence. It remained in force until July 1947. Bark and Gress, *From Shadow to Substance*, vol. 1, pp. 25–7.

125 Some Americans attacked the behaviour of their compatriots; in his memoirs George Kennan savaged those employed by the American Office of the Military Government, feeling 'the sheer horror at the spectacle of this horde of my compatriots and their dependants camping in luxury amid the ruins of a shattered national community, ignorant of the past, oblivious to the abundant evidences of present tragedy all around them, inhabiting the very same sequestrated villas that the Gestapo and the SS had just abandoned, and enjoying the same privileges, flouting their silly supermarket luxuries in the face of a veritable ocean of deprivation, hunger and wretchedness . . .' George F. Kennan, *Memoirs 1925–1950* (Boston, 1967), p. 428.

126 On the increasing influence of the Americans in the zones of occupation, including Berlin, see Botting, *From the Ruins of the Reich*; Alan S. Milward, *The Reconstruction of Western Europe, 1945–1951* (Berkeley, 1984); Roger P. Morgan, *The United States and West Germany, 1945–1973* (London, 1974); Karl Heinz Rothenberger, *Die Hungerjahre nach dem zweiten Weltkrieg* (Boppard, 1980).

127 *Frankfurter Allgemeine Zeitung*, 30 March 1990.

128 History in East Germany was later rewritten to imply that the union had been inevitable. In an article recounting how the new KPD government took hold in the district of Lichtenberg, Gerda and Erwin Reisler said, 'We know that the Central Committee of the KDP, the Ulbricht Group . . . want to build an anti-fascist, democratic Germany together with all anti-fascist, democratic power . . . Some comrades wish to increase the bond with the Social Democratic Party of Germany.' Gerda and Erwin Reisler, 'Als die Freiheit anbrach. Berlin in den letzten Tagen des zweiten Weltkrieges', *Neues Deutschland*, 7 May 1963.

129 Naimark, *The Russians in Germany*, pp. 112, 279.

130 One of the victims of the political failure was General Zhukov. False charges were brought against him and although he miraculously escaped liquidation he was nevertheless removed from command of SMAD in Berlin and demoted to head the Odessa Military District. Zhukov recalled that while he was there 'Abakumov, on Beria's orders, prepared an entire case of a military conspiracy. They sank to such obscene and disgusting depths as to accuse me of masterminding a military plot against Stalin. But I was told by people who were present at the meeting that Stalin, when Beria called for my arrest, said: "No. I won't let you arrest Zhukov." It was left to me only to thank Stalin mentally for not throwing me to Beria.' SMAD was then taken over by Sokolovsky, who bolstered the party organization at the expense of Red Army control. See Marshala

G. K. Zhukova, 'Kak lomali', *Voenno-istoricheskii zhurnal*, no. 12, 1992, p. 87; Harold Shukman (ed.), *Stalin's Generals* (London, 1993), p. 358.

131 Naimark, *The Russians in Germany*, p. 332. This was in part responsible for the wave of arrests throughout 1946. Murphy et al., *Battleground Berlin*, p. 17.

132 This figure is for the CDU arrests between 1948 and 1950, although such arrests occurred earlier. Childs and Poppelwell point out that most of these CDU prisoners would have been taken directly to the Soviet Union rather than being imprisoned in the Soviet zone of Germany. Childs and Poppelwell, *The Stasi*, p. 39. Soviet reports from Kovalchuk to Abakumov show that in the first half of December 1946 alone 487 people had been arrested, of whom 432 were Germans; thirty-seven were arrested for espionage and 191 were 'ex-Nazis'. No reason was given for the arrest of the 200 others but they were almost certainly targeted for political opposition. The report is in the archives of Sluzhba vneshnei razvedki (SVRA), file 60345, vol. 2, Report by 'VCh' from Kovalchuk to Abakumov, 19 December 1946, no. 0167, in Murphy et al., *Battleground Berlin*, p. 38.

133 Kidnappings of well-known opponents of the Soviet Union and 'subversive organizations' in West Berlin, including figures on the Free Jurists' Committee, were increasingly common. Walter Linse, who worked on problems of expropriation of property without compensation and on workers' rights, was kidnapped on 8 July 1952. The report of his interrogation states that 'arrests of exposed agents continue' and that the Soviets would continue to send agents to West Berlin under 'cover' as 'refugees'. On 18 December 1952 an MGB report stated proudly that 'Linse's kidnapping made it possible to carry out a large-scale operation to liquidate the espionage nets of the Committee in the GDR, which led to the arrest of eighty-four agents who had been employed in positions in the state apparatus of the GDR, in large factories and mills, and also in design bureaux'. Murphy et al., *Battleground Berlin*, pp. 117–18. See also Johann B. Gradl, *Anfang unter dem Sowjetstern: Die CDU 1945–1948 in der sowjetischen Besatzungszone Deutschlands* (Cologne, 1981).

134 The arrests began in earnest in the autumn of 1946 when Soviet security services began rounding up both western agents and anyone suspected of espionage. Until then American BOB agents had worked in 'chains' where many knew one another; it soon became clear that these groups had been infiltrated. The Soviets arrested anyone merely suspected of opposing their policies. Murphy et al., *Battleground Berlin*, p. 19.

135 Clare, *Berlin Days*, p. 177.

136 Shukman, *Stalin's Generals*, p. 151.

137 David J. Dallin, *Soviet Espionage* (New Haven, 1955) p. 331–2; see also Klimov, *The Terror Machine*.

138 Fritz Löwenthal, *News from Soviet Germany*, trans. Edward Fitzgerald (London, 1950), p. 254. See also Erich Mielke, 'Gangster und Mörder im Kampf gegen unsere Republik', *Neues Deutschland*, 28 January 1950.

139 The *Spetslager* were set up by Colonel General Ivan Aleksandrovich Serov on 27 July 1945. Serov was the head of the NKVD. Spittmann and Helwig, *DDR Lesebuch*, p. 48.

140 Löwenthal, *News from Soviet Germany*, p. 256.

141 Phil Davidson, 'Death in the forests: Stalin's final solution', *Independent on Sunday*, 22 April 1990.

142 Interview with Lothar Rühl in Steinhoff et al., *Voices from the Third Reich*, p. 433.

143 Naimark, *The Russians in Germany*, pp. 44, 372. Robert Bialek was removed as head of the police section of the Central Secretariat of the SED for the same reason.

144 In some cases the acceptance of Nazis was recorded; one report of a meeting on 20 November 1945 noted that '253 colleagues' had joined to create a new union for S-Bahn workers. One employee, a 'Herr Pg.', had been 'an SA-Sturmführer' and was told that he could now 'help rebuild what was destroyed'. Report of 20 November 1945, in VEB Kombinat Berliner Verkehrsbetriebe, Kombinatsarchiv, no. 3013/1. Abakumov, a rival of Beria's, was arrested by Stalin, imprisoned and executed in December 1954.

145 Löwenthal, *News from Soviet Germany*, p. 259.

146 Naimark, *The Russians in Germany*, p. 385; Naimark quotes the document: 'Rearrest in the Soviet Zone of German Prisoners of War Released by the Western Powers', December 1947, PRO Germany 1947 file 1009, 64472.

147 'Spravka o nalichii i dvizhenii zakliuchennykh, soderzhashchikhsia v spetslageriakh, MVD SSSR', A. N. Dugin, 'Niezvestnyi Gulag: Dokumenty i fakty', pp. 50–51, quoted in Naimark, *The Russians in Germany*, p. 377. According to recent figures 122,671 Germans were sent to the camps between 1945 and 1952, of whom 45,262 were eventually freed, 42,889 died of illness, 756 were actually sentenced to death by a court and 12,770 were taken to the Soviet Union. Spittmann and Helwig, *DDR Lesebuch. Stalinisierung*, p. 46.

148 For a general account of the camps in the Soviet zone see Jan Fiocken and Michael Klonivsky, *Stalin's Lager in Deutschland 1945–1950, Zeugen-berichte* (Berlin, 1991).

149 Naimark, *The Russians in Germany*, p. 387. Many groups were deported in appalling conditions, including the Chechens, Crimeans, the Volga Germans, Balts, Ukrainians, Poles and many others. Keith Sword, *Deportation and Exile. Poles in the Soviet Union, 1939–48* (London, 1996), pp. 163–73.

150 See Clarence G. Lasby, *Project Paperclip: German Scientists and the Cold War* (New York, 1971); Tom Bower, *The Paperclip Conspiracy: The Hunt for the Nazi Scientists* (Boston, 1987).

151 Leslie Groves, *Now It Can Be Told: The Story of the Manhattan Project* (New York, 1962).

152 Sir Charles Frank, *Operation Epsilon: The Farm Hall Transcripts* (Berkeley, 1993), pp. 70–94.

153 On the Soviet hunt for German scientists and the nuclear project see Naimark's excellent chapter, 'The Soviet Use of German Science', in *The Russians in Germany*, pp. 205–50. The Americans discovered the progression of the Soviet atomic bomb project through the Soviets themselves; Yevgeny Petrovich Pitovranov, a senior KGB official, has spoken of intelligence leaks regarding the shipments of ore from Wismut; the information about the shipments was trans-

mitted by enciphered messages sent over land to Novosibirsk, but from there they were transmitted by radio which was intercepted by the Americans, alerting them to the shipments of uranium. Murphy et al., *Battleground Berlin*, pp. 14–15.

154 Beria maintained his position as head of the nuclear project even when he exchanged his position as the head of the NKVD in March 1946 and became a full member of the Politburo. On Beria's involvement in the Soviet bomb project see Amy Knight, *Beria. Stalin's First Lieutenant* (Princeton, 1993), pp. 132–45.

155 David Holloway, *Stalin and the Bomb. The Soviet Union and Atomic Energy 1939–1956* (Yale, 1994), p. 115.

156 Holloway, *Stalin and the Bomb*, p. 109.

157 Gustav Hertz is said to have died while testing one of his nuclear devices in 1951. Department of State Message, F790010-1449, 5 July 1951, National Archives, no. 761.5611/7–551, RG 59, box 694; Amy Knight, *Beria*, p. 262.

158 V. L. Sokolov, *Soviet Use of German Science and Technology, 1945–1946* (New York, 1955), p. 8. See also Naimark, *The Russians in Germany*, p. 209.

159 Heinz and Elfi Barwich, *Das rote Atom* (Munich, 1967), p. 34.

160 Naimark, *The Russians in Germany*, p. 221, n. 62.

161 Helmut Gröttrup, *Die Besessenen und die Mächtigen: Im Schatten der roten Rakete* (Stuttgart, 1958), p. 16.

162 Not all sensitive industries were destroyed or moved; the I. G. Farben plant at Bitterfeld, which made distilled calcium, was kept because of its importance in the production of uranium 235; indeed this calcium was used at the Yelektrostal atomic facility near Moscow. The Tewa plant in Neustadt, which produced very fine copper mesh also used in the production of uranium, remained intact. Naimark, *The Russians in Germany*, p. 226, n. 84; Henry S. Lowenhaupt, 'On the Soviet Nuclear Scent', *Studies in Intelligence*, 2, Fall 1967; Murphy et al., *Battleground Berlin*, p. 14.

163 Naimark, *The Russians in Germany*, p. 229.

164 Ibid., p. 230.

165 The mines lay just across the border from the Czechoslovakian mine at Jachymov. See Naimark, *The Russians in Germany*, pp. 235–50; Holloway, *Stalin and the Bomb*, p. 177.

166 Jan Fiocken and Michael Klonivsky, *Stalin's Lager in Deutschland 1945–1950*; Karl Wilhelm Fricke, *Die DDR-Staatssicherheit* (Cologne, 1989), p. 25.

167 General Malinin was at the time the head of the MGB in East Berlin. Letter from Lavrenev to Hess, 1 August 1947, in National Archives Record Group 260 OMGUS Office of the Military Government – Adjutant General Top Secret, Box 645. Nevertheless General Lucius Clay did know about the operations at Wismut, writing in his autobiography that 'A Soviet corporation was formed to mine uranium ores . . .'; he also noted that they were using 'forced labor in this work'. Clay, *Decision in Germany*, p. 158; Naimark, *The Russians in Germany*, p. 238.

168 The recruitment was overseen by Beria's assistant, Major General A. M. Maltsev, who supervised the mining and processing of the ore until 1950. Nikolai Grishin,

'The Saxony Mining Operation ("Vismut")', in Robert Slusser, *Soviet Economic Policy* (New York, 1953), pp. 127–53.

169 Naimark, *The Russians in Germany*, p. 246, n. 183.

170 Letter from Wildführ to Buchwitz, 27 May 1947, quoted in Naimark, *The Russians in Germany*, p. 242.

171 *Foreign Relations of the United States*, 1946, vol. 6, p. 699.

172 Jean Edward Smith (ed.), *The Papers of General Lucius D. Clay: Germany, 1945–1949* (Bloomington, 1974), vol. 2, p. 563. See also Daniel J. Nelson, *Wartime Origins of the Berlin Dilemma* (University of Alabama, 1978).

173 John Foster Dulles, *War or Peace* (New York, 1950), pp. 101–6.

174 John Gimbel, *The American Occupation of Germany. Politics and the Military 1945–1949* (Stanford, 1968), p. 151; Albert Z. Carr, *Truman, Stalin and Peace* (New York, 1950).

175 George C. Marshall, quoted in Earl F. Ziemke, 'The Formulation and Initial Implementation of US Occupation Policy in Germany', in Hans A. Schmitt (ed.), *US Occupation in Europe after World War II* (Lawrence, 1978), p. 39. An excellent analysis of the American response to the threat is in Schlaim, *The United States and the Berlin Blockade*.

176 Stalin genuinely believed that he could force the Allies out of Berlin. Newspapers in the Soviet zone had already begun questioning the need for four-power occupation of Berlin and the American embassy in Moscow predicted a 'noisy campaign to scare us out'. On 22 December 1947 the CIA reported that 'there was a possibility of steps being taken in Berlin by the Soviet authorities to force the other occupying powers to remove [their forces] from Berlin'. The CIA report is referred to in a memorandum, DCI to the president, 16 March 1948, Harry S. Truman Library, Papers of Harry S. Truman, President's Secretary's Files, in Murphy et al., *Battleground Berlin*, p. 52, n. 2. Clay's cable is reprinted in Smith, *The Papers of General Lucius D. Clay*, vol. 2, p. 568.

177 Kennan, *Memoirs*, pp. 401–2; Dean Acheson, *Present at the Creation* (New York, 1969).

178 This led to a strike in June 1949 by railway workers, who complained at the percentage of wages paid in eastern currency; it ended on 28 June when the Soviet railway administration agreed to pay 60 per cent of their wages in West Marks. The Soviets also used the strike as an excuse to extend their claim over land belonging to the railways, even if it was located in West Berlin. Murphy et al., *Battleground Berlin*, p. 74.

179 Office of the Military Governor for Germany, United States, *Monthly Report*, no. 37, July 1948, p. 2.

180 Stalin's decision was not helped by the terrible results for the SED and the Soviet-backed Free German Federation of Unions in the March 1948 union and factory council elections which once again proved that the Germans would not support the Communists if given a free choice.

181 The blockade also marked the point at which Stalin accepted the 'East German option' – that is, the acceptance of a divided Germany. In January 1948 Stalin told Djilas that 'the West will make West Germany their own and we shall make East Germany ours'. Milovan Djilas, *Conversations with Stalin* (New York,

1962), p. 153. On the consequences of Stalin's gamble, particularly in China, see Adam B. Ulam, *Stalin, The Man and His Era* (London, 1989), pp. 686–96.

182 Howley, *Berlin Command*, p. 170.

183 Clay, *Decision in Germany*, p. 359.

184 Ibid., p. 27. See also Tony Sharp, *The Wartime Alliance and the Zonal Division of Germany* (Oxford, 1975); Michael Balfour and John Mair, *Four-Power Control in Germany and Austria, 1945–1946* (London, 1956).

185 Andrei Gromyko later stated that he believed that Stalin 'embarked on that affair in the certain knowledge that the American administration was not run by frivolous people who would start a nuclear war over such a situation', while Donald Maclean noted that Stalin 'behaved cautiously, and in the end he was willing to forgo his goals in the interests of avoiding war'. Andrei Gromyko, *Memoirs* (New York, 1989), p. 391; Holloway, *Stalin and the Bomb*, p. 260.

186 Smith, *The Papers of General Lucius D. Clay*, vol. 2, pp. 621–3.

187 Willy Brandt, *My Road to Berlin* (London, 1960), p. 186; Shlaim, *The United States and the Berlin Blockade*, p. 204; Fred L. Hadsel, 'Reflections of the US Commanders in Germany and Austria', in Schmitt, *US Occupation in Europe*, pp. 156–7.

188 Lt. Gen. William Turner, *Over the Hump* (New York, 1964), p. 161.

189 Even the Soviets were impressed by this; an intelligence report written by one of Sokolovsky's staff officers described the planes flying over Karlshorst: 'One would appear overhead, another would disappear over the horizon, and a third emerge, one after another without interruption, like a conveyor belt!' Askold Vsevolodovich Lebedev, quoted in Murphy et al., *Battleground Berlin*, pp. 67–9.

190 W. Phillips Davidson, *The Berlin Blockade: A Study in Cold War Politics* (Princeton, 1958), p. 364.

191 The pilots also had their own brand of humour, best represented in the bawdy cartoons by Jake Schuffert in the *Task Force Times*.

192 *Frankfurter Allgemeine Zeitung*, 16 March 1995.

193 The Soviets attacked RIAS and in 1952 mounted a campaign to arrest those who listened to the radio station; the warning was printed in GDR newspapers together with cartoons depicting neighbours listening through the walls and turning one another in. See, for example, 'ZACHARIAS', *Frischer Wind*, 5, 1953; *Volksstimme*, 28 August 1952. Pyotr Abrasimov, who became Soviet ambassador to the GDR in 1962, stated that 'Films, newspapers, radio and other mass media were playing their part in the cold war. One of the most important was the radio station Sender Freies Berlin (SFB). More important as a propaganda instrument was the radio station RIAS (Rundfunk im Amerikanischen Sektor), an organ of the United States Information Agency . . . Behind its name lurks one of the worst and most aggressive sources of subversive activity against the Soviet Union, the GDR and other socialist states – a true centre for spies and *agents-provocateurs*. Not only that, it is also directly responsible for organizing espionage, as is clear from documents.' Pyotr Abrasimov, *Zapadny Berlin – vchera i segodnya* (Moscow, 1980), p. 23.

194 For the November 1947 figures see Georg Homsten, *Die Berlin Chronik* (Düssel-

dorf, 1987), p. 406. A report submitted to MGB Minister Viktor Abakumov, MGB head in Germany. Nikolai Kovalchuk stated that '549 people had been arrested for espionage in Germany during the first half of 1948'. Murphy et al., *Battleground Berlin*, p. 415.

195 As a result, Soviet propaganda claimed that 'Over one third of the West Berlin police force consisted of former SS men or members of the Nazi Party. All these men were out to ensure that West Berlin fulfilled its role as a "front-line city" and that a corresponding "front-line spirit" should prevail.' Abrasimov, *Zapadny Berlin*, p. 29.

196 By 1949 Markgraf was considered by the Soviets to be politically unreliable and was dismissed in favour of more 'ideologically sound' operatives. Murphy et al., *Battleground Berlin*, p. 59.

197 Amazingly, Soviet intelligence sources had not anticipated an airlift and continued to encourage Stalin in the belief that a blockade would force the western allies to abandon Berlin. As David Murphy, Sergei Kondrashev and George Bailey have put it, KI (Committee of Information, USSR) reporting during the Berlin blockade was often startlingly misleading. 'No better example can be found of how Cold War reporting from well-placed Soviet sources was filtered and revised until a report was fashioned that was sure to appease Stalin ... The reports prolonged the blockade by underestimating both Western resolve and how apprehension in the West caused by the blockade led to efforts to enlist West Germany in European defense.' See the excellent analysis in Murphy et al., *Battleground Berlin*, pp. 62–74.

198 Walter Bedell Smith, *Moscow Mission, 1946–1949* (London, 1950), p. 244; see also Murphy et al., *Battleground Berlin*, pp. 57–8.

199 Tunner, *Over the Hump*, p. 43.

15: FLASHPOINT BERLIN

1 The Soviets tried to prevent the creation of a separate West German state in May 1949 by proposing the creation of a 'National Front' which was meant to allow the East German SED to pose as the advocates of national unity in contrast to the 'splitters' in the west. These plans failed to have any effect, not least because the western Allies now saw the future West German state as a potential bulwark against the further spread of Communism, particularly into France and Italy. Karl-Dietrich Bracher et al. (eds.), *Geschichte der Bundesrepublik Deutschland* (Stuttgart, 1981), vol. 1; John Gimbel, *The American Occupation of Germany: Politics and the Military, 1945–1949* (Stanford, 1968); John Lewis Gaddis, *The United States and the Origins of the Cold War, 1941–1947* (New York, 1972); Hermann Graml, *Die Allierten und die Teilung Deutschlands: Konflikte und Entscheidungen 1941–1948* (Frankfurt-am-Main, 1981).

2 The authors of the Basic Law of the Federal Republic of Germany were deeply influenced by Germany's recent past; in order to prevent a disastrous repeat of the instability of the Weimar Republic, the power of the President was diminished in favour of the Chancellor – in future it would, for example, be impossible

for the President to dismiss the Chancellor without an absolute majority in the
Bundestag. Stability was also promoted by the introduction of the 'five per cent
clause', which meant that only parties which had passed this hurdle could be
represented in the Bundestag. The desire to avoid any recurrence of Nazi criminality encouraged the authors of the constitution to give over the first nineteen
articles to issues of human and civil rights.

3 The SED had intensified its campaign for the National Front while making it
clear to the Soviets that it was time to form a government in the east. As
Wilhelm Pieck said, the situation in the west made it imperative that a German
government be formed in the Soviet zone. To campaign effectively against the
West German government the people (the SED) needed their own German
government, 'and as quickly as possible'. On 8 October 1949 three formal actions
confirmed the creation of the German Democratic Republic. SMAD agreed to
the list of senior officials and requested confirmation from Moscow, while on
the same day Andrei Gromyko passed on to the Central Committee of the
CPSU his recommendation that a German government be formed. On 11
October the newly formed Landkammer met the Volkskammer and elected
Wilhelm Pieck as the first President of the GDR. On 12 October Otto Grotewohl
was confirmed as Prime Minister. Norman Naimark, *The Russians in Germany.
A History of the Soviet Zone of Occupation, 1945–1949* (Cambridge, Mass., 1995),
pp. 58–61; David Childs, *The GDR: Moscow's German Ally* (London, 1983),
pp. 22–5.

4 Kurt Schumacher, *Reden–Schriften–Korrespondenzen 1945–1952*, ed. Willy
Albrecht (Berlin, 1985), p. 134.

5 Konrad Adenauer, *Erinnerungen* (Stuttgart, 1984), vols. 1 and 2; see also Henning
Köhler, *Adenauer: Eine politische Biographie* (Frankfurt-am-Main, 1994).

6 For an analysis of Adenauer's foreign policy see Werner Weidenfeld, *Konrad
Adenauer und Europa: Die geistigen Grundlagen der westeuropäischen Inte-
grationspolitik des ersten Bonner Bundeskanzlers* (Bonn, 1976).

7 There are a number of excellent studies of Adenauer's views on integration with
western Europe. See, above all, Adenauer, *Erinnerungen*, vols. 1 and 2; see also
Kurt von Schubert, *Wiederbewaffnung und Westintegration. Die innere Auseinandersetzung um die militärische und aussenpolitische Orientierung der Bundesrepublik* (Stuttgart, 1970); Weidenfeld, *Konrad Adenauer und Europa;* John Gillingham,
*Coal, Steel and the Rebirth of Europe, 1945–1955: The Germans and French from
Ruhr Conflict to Economic Community* (Cambridge, 1991).

8 For Schumacher's reaction to the result see Schumacher, *Reden–Schriften–
Korrespondenzen*, p. 147.

9 This caused great resentment amongst those more positively disposed to the
Soviet Union and Adenauer was criticized for 'missing' an opportunity to unify
Germany, criticism which abated only after the 17 June 1953 uprising in East
Germany. See Gerhard Wettig, 'Stalin and German Reunification: Archival Evi-
dence on Soviet Foreign Policy in Spring 1952', *Historical Journal*, 57, no. 2,
1994, pp. 411–19; Hermann Graml, 'Die Legende von der verpassten Gelegenheit.
Zur sowjetischen Notenkampagne des Jahres 1952', *Vierteljahreshefte für Zeitge-
schichte*, 29, 1981, pp. 307–41; Boris Meissner, *Russland, die Westmächte und*

Deutschland: Die sowjetische Deutschlandpolitik 1943–1953 (Munich, 1984); Rolf Steininger, *Eine Chance zur Wiedervereinigung? Die Stalin-Note vom 10 März 1952* (Bonn, 1985).

10 Before its entry into NATO West Germany had been a member of the European Defence Community or EDC, not least because the Americans wanted Germany to contribute to the defence of Europe, particularly after western vulnerability had been exposed during the Berlin blockade. The EDC was created to quell British and French fears of too great a West German contribution to defence in Europe, but it faltered in 1954 when the French were forced to admit defeat in Vietnam. After this Germany was permitted to contribute to European defence by becoming a member of NATO. The Soviets had railed against West Germany joining NATO; an article of 30 August said that 'the Anglo-American bloc regards German militarists as their allies . . . The heart of the Atlantic Pact is a military alliance of the two aggressive forces of the post-war period.' M. M. Marinin, *Pravda*, 29 March 1949. See also Gerhard Wettig, *Entmilitarisierung und Wiederbewaffnung in Deutschland, 1943–1955* (Munich, 1967).

11 The 'Economic Miracle' is something of a misnomer. True, much of German industrial potential had been destroyed in the war, and the Germans were prohibited from producing radios, ball bearings, ships and other products seen to have a possible military application. Nevertheless, labour was plentiful and inexpensive, many machines had been saved despite the bombing, and in 1949 manufacturing industry was still operating at only 63 per cent of its capacity. The decisive change was brought about by the 1948 currency reform which encouraged investment, wiped out debts, and led to stable wages and prices; by 1951 most trade restrictions had been lifted. See Richard Overy, 'The Economy of the Federal Republic since 1949', in Klaus Larres and Panikos Panayi (eds.), *The Federal Republic of Germany since 1949. Politics, Society and Economy before and after Unification* (London, 1996), p. 5; see also A. Kramer, *The West German Economy 1945–1955* (Oxford, 1991), p. 168; Werner Abelshauser, *Wirtschaftsgeschichte der Bundesrepublic Deutschland 1945–1980* (Frankfurt-am-Main, 1983); Anthony J. Nicholls, *Freedom with Responsibility: the Social Market Economy in Germany 1918–1963* (Oxford, 1964); Volker R. Berghahn, *The Americanisation of West German Industry, 1945–1973* (Leamington Spa, 1986).

12 Ludwig Erhard helped to create a social market economy which although encouraging a trade boom underpinned it with stable price levels, low wage increases and high levels of productive investment. As Richard Overy has put it, 'high export growth, price stability and exceptional levels of domestic investment turned the German economy in ten years back to the trajectory of high growth interrupted in 1914.' Overy, 'The Economy of the Federal Republic', in Larres and Panayi, *The Federal Republic of Germany*, pp. 9, 34.

13 Ibid., p. 7; Overy quotes M. Knapp's estimate that the total of all aid granted to Germany after the war was $3.157 billion, of which one third had been paid back to the United States by 1966. M. Knapp, 'Reconstruction and West-Integration: The Impact of the Marshall Plan on Germany', *Zeitschrift für die gesamte Staatswissenschaft*, 137, pp. 421–4.

14 On the relationship between German nation-building and economic success see

Harold James, *A German Identity 1770–1990* (London, 1989), pp. 177–209.

15 For an insight into Allied fears of the creation of a centralized German state see Hans-Jürgen Grabbe, 'Die deutsch-allierte Kontroverse um den Grundgesetz-entwurf im Frühjahr 1949', *Vierteljahreshefte für Zeitgeschichte*, 26, 1978, pp. 393–418.

16 Even when he was forced to travel to Berlin as head of the Prussian Staatsrat during the Weimar Republic, he would draw the curtains of his train carriage when he crossed the river Elbe and mutter, 'We are entering the land of the heathen.' On the other hand, he remained decidedly pro-French throughout his term in office, and respected western values, including the rights of the individual in a democracy. Konrad Adenauer, *Memoirs 1945–1953* (London, 1965), p. 165; see also Kurt Sontheimer, *Die Adenauer-Ära. Grundlegung der Bundesrepublik* (Munich, 1991).

17 Ulbricht's speech of March 1949 in Dresden is quoted in Naimark, *The Russians in Germany*, p. 56.

18 Ibid., p. 56; Carola Stern, *Ulbricht. Eine politische Biographie* (Berlin/Cologne, 1963), pp. 220–21. Ulbricht spoke constantly about 'economic and political crises' which were about to destroy the Federal Republic and push it into the arms of the GDR. See, for example, the *Protokol des IV. Parteitages der SED* (Berlin, 1954), p. 44; Walter Ulbricht, speech to the 24th Central Committee printed in a brochure as *24 ZK-Tagung im Juni 1955* (Berlin, 1955), p. 28; and his speech 'Jahre der Wende', *Neues Deutschland*, 1 January 1959, in which he predicted the imminent collapse of the West German government through 'civil war'.

19 Oleg Penkovsky, *The Penkovsky Papers* (London, 1988), p. 257.

20 Western intelligence sources noted that the rally, involving a planned 600,000 youths from the GDR and other countries, was a cover to 'overthrow the legal West Berlin government'. With its failure Eisler was put under surveillance and by early 1953 a purge was being planned against him and some of his colleagues. David E. Murphy, Sergei A. Kondrashev and George Bailey, *Battleground Berlin. CIA vs. KGB in the Cold War* (Yale, 1987), p. 106, n. 10. See also Armin Mitter, 'Die Ereignisse im Juni und Juli 1953 in der DDR', *Aus Politik und Zeitgeschichte*, B5/91, 25 January 1991, pp. 31–41.

21 In theory Stalin was succeeded by Malenkov and the Soviet Union was to be ruled collectively. But in practice Lavrenti Beria was the most powerful man in Russia, having built his power base on the strength of the KGB. See Amy Knight, *Beria. Stalin's First Lieutenant* (Princeton, 1993). Ulbricht's eulogy to Stalin was published in *Neues Deutschland*, 8 March 1953; Johannes R. Becher's sycophantic poem to him began with the lines, 'All of Germany will thank Stalin, whose monument stands in every town . . .' Johannes R. Becher, 'Danksagung', in *Sonntag*, no. 11, 15 March 1953. Despite the propaganda, many rejoiced at Stalin's death; Peter Bordihn, a German sent to Siberia after being labelled a 'Social Democrat' in 1949, heard the news of Stalin's death and recalled that although work went on as normal someone near him cried: 'he lived far too long, that dog . . .' Peter Bordihn, 'Streik im Gulag', in Ilse Spittmann and Gisela Helwig (eds.), *DDR Lesebuch. Stalinisierung 1949–1955* (Berlin, 1989), p. 226.

22 *Neues Deutschland*, 11 June 1953; *Neues Deutschland*, 16 June 1953.

23 Gabriel Partos, *The World That Came In from the Cold* (London, 1993), p. 37.

24 David Childs and Richard Popplewell, *The Stasi. The East German Intelligence and Security Service* (London, 1996), p. 51. For a 'factional' account of the 1953 uprising see Stefan Heym, *5 Days in June. A Novel* (London, 1977); for events of 16 June see pp. 139–255. See also Cold War International History Project (introduced by Christian F. Ostermann), 'New Documents on the East German Uprising of 1953', *Bulletin*, no. 5, spring 1995.

25 Roy Medvedev, *Khrushchev* (Garden City, NY, 1983), p. 60. This version of events is endorsed by Christopher Andrew and Oleg Gordievsky in *KGB. The Inside Story of Its Foreign Operations from Lenin to Gorbachev* (London, 1991). Some, including David Childs and Richard Popplewell, have questioned it, claiming that neither Rudolf Herrnstadt nor Wilhelm Zaisser mention a visit to Beria after the beginning of the uprising; Vladislav Zubok and Constantine Pleshakov also claim that Beria did not flee to Berlin but remained in Moscow throughout the crisis. See Vladislav Zubok and Constantine Pleshakov, *Inside the Kremlin's Cold War. From Stalin to Khrushchev* (Harvard, 1996), p. 162. Nevertheless, Molotov backs the Medvedev version, stating in an interview with Felix Chuev that shortly before his arrest 'Beria had been dispatched to Berlin to suppress the unfolding revolt there. He was excellent in cases like that. We had passed a decision to use tanks. We had approved the use of drastic measures to put down the revolt, the most ruthless measures. Let the Germans rise up against us?! Everything would have turned shaky, the imperialists would have taken action. There would have been a total collapse. As soon as reports of the events in the GDR started to come in, Beria was among the first to say, "We must act! Unhesitatingly! Ruthlessly! Most urgently!"' Albert Resis (ed.), *Molotov Remembers. Inside Kremlin Politics. Conversations with Felix Chuev* (Chicago, 1993), p. 346. On Herrnstadt's view of the 1953 uprising and his antipathy to Ulbricht see Nadja Stulz-Herrnstadt (ed.), *Rudolf Herrnstadt – Das Herrnstadt-Dokument: Das Politburo der SED und die Geschichte des 17. Juni 1953* (Hamburg, 1990), pp. 73–4.

26 This habit persisted for decades; even during the Yeltsin coup in 1992 the only thing played on Russian television was the national anthem and many relied on the information broadcast by the BBC World Service.

27 John Fuegi, *The Life and Lies of Bertolt Brecht* (London, 1994), pp. 542–5; see also Martin Esslin, *Brecht: The Man and His Work* (New York, 1971), p. 195.

28 Those killed included eighteen Soviet soldiers and 116 East German officials and Volkspolizei. See Bruno Leuschner's account of the violence in the city centre in Michael Richter et al., *Geschichte der DDR* (Bonn, 1991), p. 60. On the death penalties meted out after the uprising see Manfred Hagen, *DDR Juni '53. Die erste Volkserhebung im Stalinismus* (Stuttgart, 1992), p. 175.

29 The East German State Security was itself purged following the uprising; around thirty state officers were arrested in July 1953. Childs and Popplewell, *The Stasi*, p. 51.

30 The figures for refugees are recorded in the information published by the

Federal Ministry for All-German Questions; for 1953 the number was 331,390. Bundesministerium für gesamtdeutsche Fragen, *A bis Z. Ein Taschen- und Nachschlagebuch über den anderen Teil Deutschlands* (Bonn, 1969), p. 212.

31 Timothy Garton Ash describes his reaction to 1953 as 'perhaps the most controversial moment in Brecht's political career'. Timothy Garton Ash, *The Uses of Adversity* (London, 1989), p. 32.

32 According to David E. Murphy et al., 'Beria's determination to re-assert control over the security and intelligence apparatus . . . led to his downfall.' Murphy et al., *Battleground Berlin*, pp. 151–63. On the treatment of Beria's allies at Karlshorst, including Amaiak Kobulov, see Pavel Sudoplatov et al., *Secret Tasks* (Boston, 1994), pp. 389–92.

33 The terrifying scene is described in Andrew and Gordievsky, *KGB*, p. 426; Resis, *Molotov Remembers*, pp. 234–9.

34 Pyotr Deryabin later claimed that around 800 MVD agents were recalled from the GDR alone. Andrew and Gordievsky, *KGB*, p. 426. Sergei Romanovich Savchenko stated that 'Beria's simultaneous recall of all of our residents and operational staff under the pretext of examining their work and considering measures for improving it was . . . dangerous for intelligence work'; David Murphy et al. have found 'substantial evidence that Beria virtually dismantled both the field and headquarters elements of the German department of the service'. The issue is discussed at length in Murphy et al., *Battleground Berlin*, pp. 159–63.

35 For a general discussion of the 1953 Uprising in relation to the role of the East German MfS, the Ministerium für Staatssicherheit (Ministry for State Security), the MVD and the roles of Beria, Herrnstadt and Zaisser see Childs and Popplewell, *The Stasi*, pp. 50–59.

36 Andrei Gromyko, quoted in Andrew and Gordievsky, *KGB*, p. 428.

37 See D. M. Stickle (ed.), *The Beria Affair: The Secret Transcripts of the Meetings Signalling the End of Stalinism*, trans. Jean Farrow (New York, 1992); see also Knight, *Beria*, pp. 198–9.

38 It is likely that Beria would have toppled Ulbricht had he remained in power. He had been critical of Ulbricht's economic policy in East Germany even before the uprising and had given Ulbricht an informal warning to introduce reforms when Ulbricht was in Moscow for Stalin's funeral; when nothing was done he sent an official note of warning in April and ordered him to visit Moscow twice, once in April and once on 2 June, when he was berated by Beria. Furthermore, Beria had long supported his rival, Zaisser, personally ordering his release from prison in 1939 and approving his appointment as his counterpart in East Germany, the first ever Minister for State Security there on 8 February 1950. Beria's concise plans for the future of the GDR are as yet unknown and some, including Childs and Popplewell, assert that no evidence has come to light which supports the conclusion that Beria was Zaisser's patron. Childs and Popplewell, *The Stasi*, p. 57; see also Helmut Müller-Enbergs, *Der Fall Rudolf Herrnstadt. Tauwetterpolitik vor dem 17. Juni* (Berlin 1991). For a contrasting view see Knight, *Beria*, p. 191.

39 Adenauer, *Erinnerungen 1953–1955* (Stuttgart, 1984), vol. 2, p. 220.

40 The potatoes were one of the products sent to the east under the auspices of

the 'American food package program' launched on 10 July by President Eisenhower. It was sent directly to East Germany where, by mid-August, 75 per cent of the East Berlin population had received food packages. The East German state security service was called to disrupt the programme. Murphy et al., *Battleground Berlin*, p. 179.

41 George Clare, *Berlin Days 1946–1947* (London, 1989), p. 38.

42 Very little had changed by the 1980s; see their chapter on 'Agent Recruitment' in Christopher Andrew and Oleg Gordievsky, *Instructions from the Centre. Top Secret Files on KGB Foreign Operations 1975–1985* (London, 1993), pp. 55–92; see also Sudoplatov, *Secret Tasks*, p. 392.

43 Len Deighton's portrayal of post-war Berlin was similar: 'This side of Checkpoint Charlie had not changed. There never was much there; just one small hut and some signs warning you about leaving the Western sector. But the East German side had grown far more elaborate. Walls and fences, gates and barriers, endless white lines to mark out the traffic lanes . . .' Len Deighton, *Berlin Game* (London, 1986), p. 9.

44 John le Carré, *Smiley's People* (London, 1980), p. 329.

45 This vast complex was located near SMAD headquarters, but unlike that organization it would remain in place until 1991. It was a high security area and access was restricted to all but security personnel. The KGB's senior officers lived in the compound. The military intelligence operations of the GRU in the Soviet zone were based in a separate headquarters alongside the Red Army's General Staff in Wünsdorf and Zossen, fifteen miles south of Berlin. Childs and Popplewell, *The Stasi*, p. 34. For an excellent account of the growth of the various often competing bodies that constituted Soviet intelligence in East Berlin after 1945 see Murphy et al., *Battleground Berlin*, pp. 24–50.

46 Andrew and Gordievsky, *KGB*, p. 72.

47 Pyotr Abrasomov, *Zapadny Berlin – vehera i segodnya* (Moscow, 1980), p. 25.

48 This was in turn divided into a number of departments, including political and military espionage, economic espionage, central evaluation of all intelligence and general administration, counter-intelligence and personnel. Childs and Popplewell, *The Stasi*, p. 120.

49 The very creation of the IWF might have been the result of 'a disagreement between the Soviet MGB in Berlin and the KI Berlin residency over the use of different sources for intelligence collection. In any case, KI was under pressure to develop an East German foreign intelligence capability, and fast.' Murphy et al., *Battleground Berlin*, p. 135.

50 Markus Wolf, *In eigenem Auftrag. Bekenntnisse und Einsichten* (Munich, 1991); Markus Wolf (with Anne McElvoy), *Man Without a Face. The Memoirs of a Spymaster* (London, 1997); Irene Runge and Uwe Stelbrink, *Markus Wolf. 'Ich bin kein Spion'* (Berlin, 1990); Alexander Reichenbach, *Chef der Spione. Die Markus Wolf Story* (Stuttgart, 1992).

51 Runge and Stelbrink, *Markus Wolf*, p. 15.

52 The HVA had fifteen operational departments, three of which concentrated specifically on West Germany (I for the West German State Apparatus, II for Parties and Social Organizations, IV for West German Military and Strategic

Intelligence). Department III was responsible for HVA agents in the west; Department XII was specifically for espionage against NATO; Department XI for work against North America (including sections responsible for the US embassy in Bonn, and the recruitment of US citizens travelling in the GDR as well as the training of cadres in Canada, Mexico and the United States). Reichenbach, *Chef der Spione*, p. 151.

53 *Der Spiegel*, 4 September 1978.
54 Childs and Popplewell, *The Stasi*, p. 159.
55 Reichenbach, *Chef der Spione*, p. 60.
56 Andrew and Gordievsky, *KGB*, p. 453. For their interview with Felfe see Murphy et al., *Battleground Berlin*, pp. 435–9.
57 Willy Brandt, *My Life in Politics* (New York, 1992), p. 294. See also Günter Guillaume, *Die Aussage Wie Es Wirklich War* (Munich, 1990).
58 *Der Spiegel*, 2 July 1990.
59 *Woche im Bundestag*, 13 November 1991, p. 7; see also Karl Wilhelm Fricke, *Die DDR-Staatssicherheit* (Cologne, 1989).
60 Markus Wolf, interview in *Der Spiegel*, 2 July 1990.
61 *The Sunday Times*, 18 July 1993.
62 Childs and Popplewell, *The Stasi*, p. 195.
63 Tom Bower, 'The Perfect English Spy', *The Times Literary Supplement*, 12 May 1995. See also Jeffrey T. Richelson, *A Century of Spies: Intelligence in the Twentieth Century* (New York, 1995).
64 Childs and Popplewell, *The Stasi*, p. 130.
65 The CIA has published its own account of its first years, in Arthur B. Darling, *The Central Intelligence Agency: An Instrument of Government, to 1950* (University Park, Penn., 1990). Darling demonstrates the crucial role played by, amongst others, George Kennan in the creation of an agency to run covert operations, provoked largely by the increasing threat to Berlin in 1948. See also Evan Thomas. *The Very Best Men: Four Who Dared: The Early Years of the CIA* (New York, 1995).
66 OSS flew a team into Berlin on 4 July 1945, the first day the Soviets would allow the Americans into the city. Allen Dulles chose a building on the Foehrenweg in Dahlem, thinking that the OSS would become little more than a peacetime service. This idea was soon shattered and on 1 October OSS intelligence and counter-intelligence was transferred to the War Department as the Strategic Service Unit SSU. Dulles's successors Richard Helms and, in particular, Dana Durand oversaw the transition of BOB from the Strategic Services Unit (SSU) to the Central Intelligence Group (CIG) and finally, on 18 September 1947, to the Central Intelligence Agency (CIA). Murphy et al., *Battleground Berlin*, pp. 8–10; see also Anthony Cave Brown, *The Last Hero: Wild Bill Donovan* (New York, 1982).
67 Murphy et al., *Battleground Berlin*, pp. 267–8.
68 See Richard Gehlen, *Der Dienst. Erinnerungen, 1942–1971* (Mainz, 1971); Mary Ellen Reese, *General Reinhard Gehlen: The CIA Connection* (Fairfax, 1990).
69 For an account of Gehlen's use of former Nazi personnel see E. H. Cookridge, *Gehlen: Spy of the Century* (London, 1972), p. 185. See also Hermann Zolling

and Heinz Höhne, *The General Was a Spy: The Truth About General Gehlen and His Spy Ring* (New York, 1972).

70 Gehlen, *Der Dienst*, p. 202.

71 Evidence which came to light after the collapse of the GDR seemed to indicate that John had been kidnapped, taken to East Berlin and drugged. *Der Spiegel*, 20 September 1993. A more thorough analysis is given in Murphy et al., *Battleground Berlin*, pp. 183–203.

72 See, for example, the document written on 10 April 1953 from Richard Helms to Allen Dulles, director of Central Intelligence. Helms recounts the 'roll-up' of a Soviet-controlled intelligence net in West Germany: 'The roll-up began today, and has already resulted in the arrest of at least thirty-four persons. More arrests are expected ... The Soviet Zone intelligence service, with the cover name Institut für Wirtschaftswissenschaftliche Forschung and offices in Berlin, was set up a year and a half ago for the purpose of conducting political, scientific, military, and economic espionage against Western Germany. Staffed with trusted SED men, controlled by Russian advisors, and headed for a time by Anton Ackermann, SED-stalwart, the IWF has assessed hundreds of people in East and West Germany as possible agent material and has dispatched a number of agents to Western Germany ... For the past year, Berlin Operations Base has run a penetration of the IWF at a good level and collected voluminous documentary information on its aims, staffing, methods, training, and agent personnel ...' The CIA document is reprinted in Murphy et al., *Battleground Berlin*, p. 141.

73 Abrasomov, *Zapadny Berlin*, p. 21.

74 Ibid., p. 23; Wilfried Rogasch, 'Ätherkrieg über Berlin. Der Rundfunk als Instrument politischer Propaganda im Kalten Krieg 1945–1961', in Christoph Stölzl (ed.), *Deutschland im Kalten Krieg 1945–1963* (Berlin, 1992), pp. 69–83.

75 Childs and Popplewell, *The Stasi*, pp. 60–61. See also Jan von Flocken and Michael F. Scholz, *Ernst Wollweber. Saboteur–Minister–Unperson* (Berlin, 1994).

76 Le Carré, *Smiley's People*.

77 Partos, *The World that Came In from the Cold*, p. 188.

78 It is not surprising that busts of Felix Dzerzhinsky also decorated the offices of the grim Stasi headquarters on the Normannenstrasse, together with portraits of Lenin and witty little desk ornaments reading: 'Jeder Dritte, der meckert, wird erschossen! Zwei waren schon hier!' (Every third person who complains will be shot! Two have already been here!) Johannes Beleites et al. (eds.), *Stasi intern. Macht und Banalität* (Leipzig, 1991), pp. 14–18.

79 Andrew and Gordievsky, *KGB*, p. 443.

80 *Der Spiegel*, 21 September 1992.

81 Ilya Dzhirkvelov, *Secret Servant. My Life with the KGB and the Soviet Elite* (London, 1987), p. 301. See also Thomas Ellwein, *Krisen und Reform: Die Bundesrepublik seit den sechziger Jahren* (Munich, 1989), pp. 33–7.

82 Frau Elli Barczatis, 'Daisy', had been a Gehlen operative while working as private secretary to the DDR head of government Otto Grotewohl. Childs and Popplewell, *The Stasi*, p. 150.

83 On the tunnel and 'Operation Gold' see the excellent chapter 'The Berlin Tunnel:

Fact and Fiction', in Murphy et al., *Battleground Berlin*, pp. 205–37. The authors include transcripts of the voice and telephone circuits recorded up to the moment the tap cables were cut on 22 April. They cite 'The Berlin Tunnel Operation', Clandestine Services History (CSHP-150), CIA-HRP. See also David Martin, *Wilderness of Mirrors* (New York, 1981); Joseph C. Evans, 'Berlin Tunnel Intelligence; A bumbling KGB', *International Journal of Intelligence and Counterintelligence*, 9, no. 1, spring 1996.

84 Cookridge, *Gehlen*, p. 283.

85 In all 443,000 conversations were fully transcribed from voice reels, of which 368,000 were Soviet and 75,000 East German. The value to western intelligence of the information collected was immense. Through it the west learned, amongst other things, about the creation of an East German National People's Army based on the existing paramilitary alert police in the GDR, about the Soviet nuclear programme and other vital issues regarding Soviet intelligence and security in West Berlin. Murphy et al., *Battleground Berlin*, pp. 423–8.

86 Tom Bower, *The Perfect English Spy. Sir Dick White and the Secret War 1935–1990* (London, 1995), p. 182.

87 On Blake's view of the tunnel see George Blake, *No Other Choice: An Autobiography* (London, 1990); see also Tony le Tissier, *Berlin: Then and Now* (London, 1994), pp. 372–3.

88 Andrew and Gordievsky, *KGB*, p. 442. Harry Nunwick, who had worked at the Berlin MI6 station when George Blake was there, wrote of the shock of discovering who had betrayed his colleagues: 'Now I knew who the mole was. He had been six doors away from my office on the same floor, behind the top security barrier . . . This chap was one of the recipients of copies of every report I made and all were highly classified. You can imagine my feelings towards this chap, knowing that he had also been responsible for the disappearance of more than forty brave men, some of whom I knew of by the output of their work.' Tony Geraghty, *Beyond the Frontline* (London, 1996), pp. 92–3.

89 On 12–16 March 1957 the Soviet Minister of Defence Marshal Georgi Zhukov visited East Germany. A Central Intelligence Agency Teletyped Information Report of 29 March 1957 quoted him as saying that the international situation was 'a manifestation of tensions and the sharpening of relations between the camps of capitalism and socialism as well as between individual countries, including certain NATO nations'. The KGB deduced that Popov was the source of the report; he was soon to be executed as a spy. Murphy et al., *Battleground Berlin*, p. 271.

90 Andrew and Gordievsky, *KGB*, p. 461.

91 Michael R. Beschloss, *Mayday: Eisenhower, Khrushchev and the U-2 Affair* (London, 1986).

92 For a general overview of post-war architecture see J. M. Diefendorf, *In the Wake of War: The Reconstruction of German Cities after World War II* (New York, 1993); Hermann Glaser, *Kulturgeschichte der Bundesrepublik Deutschland* (Munich, 1986), vol. 2. Thomas Sieverts makes the point that immediately after the war a number of architects who had worked under the Nazis continued to work in Germany, although they did make some concessions to the new style.

Thomas Sieverts, 'From the Task Force of Albert Speer for the Reconstruction of the Destroyed Cities to the International Building Exhibition *Emscher Park* – Cultures of Planning in Germany from 1943–1994', in Reiner Pommerin (ed.), *Culture in the Federal Republic of Germany 1945–1995* (Oxford, 1996), p. 96.

93 Walter Gropius, letter to Ise Gropius, Berlin, 23 September 1955, in Reginald Isaacs, *Walter Gropius. An Illustrated Biography of the Creator of the Bauhaus* (London, 1993), p. 288.

94 The term was widely used; on its use in Berlin see Rolf Italiaander, Arnold Bauer and Herbert Krafft, *Berlins Stunde Null 1945* (Düsseldorf, 1983), p. 9; John Lukacs, *1945: Year Zero* (New York, 1978). For a comprehensive account of those buildings destroyed during the war see Hartwig Beseler and Niels Gutschow, *Kriegsschicksale deutscher Architektur*, pp. 135–99.

95 Le Corbusier believed that the great architect could shape society, for who else 'possesses a complete awareness of man, who has abandoned illusionary designs, and who, judiciously adapting the means to the desired ends, will create an order that bears within it a poetry of its own? The answer is, the architect!' Le Corbusier, *Charte d'Athènes* (New York, 1973), p. 101. His design for Hauptstadt Berlin would have eliminated all vestiges of the old city because, as he saw it, 'The demolition had been performed by airplanes and nothing was left standing in the centre of Berlin.' He was furious at not being awarded the contract for the Hauptstadt Berlin project. Alan Balfour, *Berlin. The Politics of Order 1737– 1989* (New York, 1990), p. 173.

On Scharoun see Peter Pfankuch, *Scharoun Hans: Bauten, Entwürfe, Texte* (Berlin, 1974), p. 256. Scharoun disagreed with Le Corbusier's and Gropius's belief that one could impose a vast geometrical order on a city and was more inclined to the creation of a more 'organic' area. See, for example, Hans Scharoun, 'Gropius als Gast der Technischen Universität Berlin', *Neue Bauwelt*, 1947, p. 583.

96 Helmut Maier, *Berlin Anhalter Bahnhof* (Berlin, 1987), pp. 293–4. On the growing opposition to this destruction see, for example, H. Bodenschats, V. Heise and J. Korfmacher, *Schluss mit der Zerstörung* (Berlin, 1983), pp. 17–113.

97 Isaacs, *Walter Gropius*, p. 288. On the influence of architects returning from exile in the United States see Klaus von Beyme, *Die Wiederaufbau. Architektur und Städtebaupolitik in beiden deutschen Staaten* (Munich, 1987), pp. 67–70. Hans Scharoun was the only major modernist architect who had remained in Berlin during the Nazi period despite having been named a 'cultural Bolshevik'.

98 Josef Paul Kleihues, 'From the Destruction to the Critical Reconstruction of the City: Urban Design in Berlin after 1945', in Josef Paul Kleihues and Christina Rathgeber, *Berlin – New York. Like and Unlike. Essays on Architecture and Art from 1870 to the Present* (New York, 1993), p. 399.

99 Isaacs, *Walter Gropius*, p. 287.

100 Kleihues, 'From the Destruction to the Critical Reconstruction of the City', in Kleihues and Rathgeber, *Berlin – New York*, pp. 399–403.

101 Theodor Heuss attacked the widespread destruction, stating that political idiocy in Berlin had led to the destruction of precious landmarks on a scale unheard of in any other German city, destruction which was prompted by 'stupidity and

maliciousness'. Theodor Heuss, quoted in the catalogue of the International Buildings Exhibition, *Interbau Berlin 1957* (Berlin, 1957).

102 See, for example, Ludwig Erhard, 'Mit Mut and Kraft in die Zukunft' (Speech at the Opening of the 'German Industrial Exhibition in Berlin', 1 October 1950), in Ludwig Erhard, *Deutsche Wirtschaftspolitik. Der Weg der sozialen Marktwirtschaft* (Düsseldorf, 1962), pp. 134–7.

103 Brandt worked hard to improve Berlin's image in the eyes of the world, stating that 'Berlin itself was credited, unduly, with much of what should really have been laid at the door of Nazi rule (and the Kaiser's Germany before it) . . . In the West they called Berlin a "heathen city" and in the south it was said that the new capital should stand among vineyards, not potato fields. I may claim some of the credit for helping to restore the image of Berlin.' Brandt, *My Life in Politics*, p. 7. On the new architecture see Hermann Glaser, *Kulturgeschichte der Bundesrepublik Deutschland. Zwischen Grundgesetz and grosser Koalition 1949–1967* (Munich, 1986), vol. 2, pp. 140–44.

104 On the history of the Free University see James F. Tents, *Free University of Berlin* (University of Indiana, 1988).

105 Detlef Falken, *Dulles und Deutschland: Die amerikanische Deutschlandpolitik, 1953–1959* (Bonn, 1993); Richard H. Immerman (ed.), *John Foster Dulles and the Diplomacy of the Cold War* (Princeton, 1990). See also Bericht von Professor Walter Gropius für General Lucius D. Clay, den Militärgouverneur für Deutschland (US Zone), *Baurundshau*, 1948, vol. 9/10, p. 80.

106 As Robert C. Bachmann has written, 'Karajan discarded the twelve years of National Socialist ideology as if they were a dirty and no longer fashionable shirt. Mourning, understanding, heartfelt and inner regret for everything that had happened during the Third Reich – there is no sign of any of this.' Robert C. Bachmann, *Karajan. Notes on a Career*, trans. Shaun Whiteside (London, 1990), p. 145.

107 On the Berlin paintings of this period see Carola Jüllig, 'Zwischen Ruinen und Wiederaufbau. Zur kunstlerischen Verarbeitung des Stadtbildes nach dem Zweiten Weltkrieg', in Dominik Bartmann et al., *Stadtbilder. Berlin in der Malerei vom 17. Jahrhundert bis zur Gegenwart* (Berlin, 1987), pp. 365–411. Wilhelm Götz-Knothe, *Trümmergrundstück am KaDeWe* (1958), is reproduced on p. 406.

108 See, for example, Hans Rosenthal, 'Unterhaltsames im Wirtschaftswunderland', in Dieter Franck (ed.), *Die fünfzigern Jahre. Als das Leben wieder anfing* (Munich, 1981), pp. 146–69; W. Nelson, *Small Wonder: The Amazing story of the Volkswagen* (London, 1967); Glaser, *Kulturgeschichte der Bundesrepublik Deutschland*, vol. 2, pp. 145–52.

109 On the 'Americanization' of Berlin see Ralph Willett, *The Americanization of Germany 1945–1949* (London, 1992), pp. 1–16; see also Edward N. Petersen, *Retreat to Victory: The American Occupation of Germany* (Detroit, 1978); Berghahn, *The Americanization of West German Industry*; S. Reich, *The Fruits of Fascism: Postwar Prosperity in Historical Perspective* (London, 1990); Albert Norman, *Our German Policy: Propaganda and Culture* (New York, 1951).

110 On the US information films see Willett, *The Americanization of Germany,*

p. 27. See also Henry P. Pilgert, *The History of the Development of Information Services through Information Centers and Documentary Films* (Berlin, 1951).

111 Heinz Abosch, *The Menace of the Miracle: Germany From Hitler to Adenauer* (New York, 1963), p. 109; Willett, *The Americanization of Germany*, p. 122. Walter Laqueur was also struck by the abandonment of German culture in favour the American import. See Walter Laqueur, *Germany Today: A Personal Report* (London, 1985), p. 27.

112 Abrasimov, *Zapadny Berlin*, p. 24.

113 Kleihues, 'From the Destruction to the Critical Reconstruction of the City', in Kleihues and Rathgeber, *Berlin – New York*, p. 399. The centre of East Berlin was rebuilt according to the 'Schweitzer Proposal' developed in the spring of 1961 to become the basis of a five-year construction programme centred around the Marx-Engels-Platz. The plan is reproduced in Balfour, *Berlin. The Politics of Order*, p. 180.

114 Caspar Neher, cited in Fuegi, *The Life and Lies of Bertolt Brecht*, p. 537, n. 25.

115 The refugees (including expellees and returning prisoners of war) who crossed from the east into the Federal Republic between 1953 and 1958 numbered 2.2 million. Statistisches Bundesamt, *Die Wanderungen im Jahr 1958* (Stuttgart, 1959), p. 20.

116 On Khrushchev's threat and the Berlin crisis of 1958–1961 see George D. Embree (ed.), *The Soviet Union and the German Question: September 1958–June 1961* (The Hague, 1963). For the Berlin perspective see K. A. Aanderud, *Die eingemauerte Stadt. Die Geschichte der Berliner Mauer* (Recklinghausen, 1991); Penkovsky, *The Penkovsky Papers*, p. 163.

117 From January travel along the transit routes had become increasingly unpleasant. Americans on military trains from Berlin arrived at Marienborn at around midnight; here the train commander would give the Soviets passengers' documents to check. Each identity document number had to conform exactly to the travel order or the train would be delayed. 'More than once, a Nazi swastika drawn in the dust of the side of a passenger car furnished an excuse for a delay. Because American passengers could not leave their cars during the trip – by Soviet order, even the window shades of each compartment had to be lowered – it was a mystery who had drawn the forbidden emblems. A passenger who raised the shade while stopped at the Marienborn checkpoint risked staring down the barrel of a Soviet submachine gun ... Although most people tried to appear calm, the atmosphere among the American military and intelligence communities was becoming very tense.' Murphy et al., *Battleground Berlin*, p. 308.

118 The people of the GDR were subjected to increasingly hysterical propaganda against the west; Khrushchev was portrayed as a peace-loving ruler who merely wanted to unify Germany and rid the world of nuclear weapons; the western leaders were portrayed as everything from revanchist war-mongers to neo-Nazis. The propaganda was equally virulent in Moscow itself, particularly in newspapers like *Pravda* and *Izvestia*; see, for example, 'Yuri Zhukov, 'Atlantic Pact, European Defence – Caution! Aggressor is Hiding Under Water', *Current Digest of the Soviet Press*, XV.6, 6 March 1963, pp. 26–7. See also Dietrich Geyer (ed.),

Osteuropa-Handbuch. Sowjetunion: Aussenpolitik: 1955–73 (Cologne, 1976).

119 For an account of this see Adrian W. Schertz, *Die Deutschlandpolitik Kennedys und Johnsons* (Cologne, 1992); Richard Crockatt, *The Fifty Years War: The United States and the Soviet Union in World Politics, 1941–1991* (London, 1995). See also Richard J. Walton, *Cold War and Counter-Revolution: The Foreign Policy of John F. Kennedy* (Baltimore, 1973).

120 This was ordered by Stalin as he now believed that the west had determined unification could not happen without free all-German elections, which his party would have lost. 'Stalin directed Ulbricht to embark on a harsh program of forced socialization in East Germany. It was another major miscalculation by Stalin.' Murphy et al., *Battleground Berlin*, p. 146.

121 Between 1952 and 1962, 3,948 doctors and nurses left East Germany for the Federal Republic. Bundesministerium für gesamtdeutsche Fragen, *A bis Z*, p. 214; see also Gerhart Binder, *Deutschland seit 1945. Eine dokumentierte gesamtdeutsche Geschichte in der Zeit der Teilung* (Stuttgart, 1969), pp. 463–6.

122 Penkovsky, *The Penkovsky Papers*, p. 257.

123 Philip Windsor, *City on Leave. A History of Berlin 1945–1962* (London, 1963), p. 238.

124 Federal Ministry for All-German Questions, *The Flights from the Soviet Zone and the Sealing-off Measures of the Communist Regime of 13th August 1961 in Berlin* (Bonn/Berlin, 1962).

125 On the building of the Wall see Ann Tusa, *The Last Division. Berlin and the Wall* (London, 1996), pp. 259–342; Jack M. Schick, *The Berlin Crisis 1958–62* (University of Pennsylvania, 1971); Geoffrey McDermott, *Berlin: Success of a Mission?* (London, 1963); Honoré M. Catudal Jr., *Kennedy and the Berlin Wall Crisis 1961: A Case Study in US Decision Making* (London, 1978); Curtis Cate, *The Ides of August: The Berlin Wall Crisis 1961* (London, 1978); Michael R. Beschloss, *The Crisis Years: Kennedy and Khrushchev 1960–63* (New York, 1991); Brandt, *My Life in Politics*; Norman Gelb, *The Berlin Wall* (New York, 1990); Richard L. Merritt and Anna J. Merritt (eds.), *Living with the Wall. West Berlin, 1961–1985* (Duke University, 1985).

126 Gelb, *The Berlin Wall*, p. 162.

127 As Theodore Sorensen noted, 'Our contingency plans had been prepared for interference with our access to West Berlin, not emigration from the east.' Theodore S. Sorensen, *Kennedy* (New York, 1965), p. 594.

128 *Neues Deutschland*, 16 June 1961, p. 4.

129 This series of events is described by John C. Ausland, the duty officer of the State Department Operations Centre, in Catudal, *Kennedy and the Berlin Wall Crisis*, pp. 22–23.

130 Tusa, *The Last Division*, p. 279.

131 The British Minister in Berlin, Geoffrey McDermott, was critical both of his government and of British intelligence, commenting that with hindsight 'it is now clear that our intelligence was not too good'. McDermott, *Berlin: Success of a Mission?*, pp. 28–31.

132 It is generally thought that Adenauer did not visit Berlin when the Wall was built primarily because he was loath to be seen with Willy Brandt. Adenauer

would later claim that it was because he had not wanted to increase the tension there. Köhler, *Adenauer*, p. 1090. See also Walther Stützle, *Kennedy und Adenauer in der Berlin-Krise 1961–1962* (Bonn, 1973).

133　Gelb, *The Berlin Wall*, p. 199.

134　Richard L. Merritt, 'A Transformed Crisis: The Berlin Wall', in Merritt and Merritt, *Living with the Wall*, p. 26.

135　Walter Steigner (ed.), *Berlin 13. August. Die Spaltung einer Stadt. Das Echo auf die Sonderberichterstattung des SFB* (Berlin, 1961), p. 2.

136　It did not help that the letter was printed across the front page of the *Frankfurter Allgemeine Zeitung* on 19 August 1961. Willy Brandt, *Begegnungen mit Kennedy* (Munich, 1964), pp. 71–2.

137　Gelb, *The Berlin Wall*, p. 213.

138　These scenes were photographed; see, for example, Dr Rainer Hildebrandt, *Es Geschah an der Mauer* (Berlin, 1981), pp. 13–14; Jürgen Petschull, *Die Mauer. August 1961. Zwölf Tage zwischen Krieg und Frieden* (Hamburg, 1981), pp. 90–92.

139　Willy Brandt was moved by the death of a young man whom 'we were unable – forbidden – to help . . . His death had far-reaching consequences; indignation ran high. There were demonstrations of grief and anger.' Brandt, *My Life in Politics*, p. 5. See also Hildebrandt, *Es Geschah an der Mauer*, pp. 50–52; Federal Ministry for All-German Questions, *Violations of Human Rights, Illegal Acts and Incidents at the Sector Border in Berlin since the Building of the Wall (13 August 1961–15 August 1962)* (Bonn/Berlin, 1962).

140　On the various ingenious escape attempts see, for example, Hildebrandt, *Es Geschah an der Mauer*, pp. 38–76.

141　Gelb, *The Berlin Wall*, p. 256.

142　Khrushchev told the West German ambassador to the Soviet Union, Hans Kroll, that he had ordered Koniev to withdraw the tanks because the Americans' 'prestige' would preclude them moving first and that he wanted 'to make the beginning'. Hans Kroll, *Lebenserinnerungen eines Botschafters* (Cologne/Berlin, 1967), p. 514.

143　Sorensen later maintained that Clay had not meant this seriously, as no 'responsible official – in this country, in West Berlin, West Germany or Western Europe – suggested that Allied forces should march into East German territory and tear the wall down. For the Communists, as General Lucius Clay later pointed out, could have built another, ten or twenty or five hundred yards back, and then another, unless the West was prepared to fight a war over extending its area of vital interest into East Berlin.' Sorensen, *Kennedy*, p. 594.

16: EAST BERLIN

1　Ulbricht was able to consolidate his position in the GDR after Beria's death at the Central Committee Meeting on 24–26 July 1953. Nadja Stulz-Herrnstadt (ed.), *Das Herrnstadt-Dokument* (Reinbek, 1990), pp. 262–6. See also Carola Stern, *Ulbricht. Eine politische Biographie* (Berlin/Cologne, 1963), p. 232.

2 Henry Krisch, *The German Democratic Republic. The Search for Identity* (London, 1985), p. 18.

3 New restrictions were outlined in a speech by Otto Grotewohl on 10 June 1953 and published in the *Kirchliches Jahrbuch* (Gütersloh, 1953), p. 178. On Church protests against the first 'Jugendweihe-Gelöbnis' in 1955 see Hans-Gerhard Koch, *Neue Erde ohne Himmel* (Stuttgart, 1963), p. 136.

4 The FDJ was to create loyalty to the GDR and a militaristic spirit through sport; from May 1953 FDJ leaders were expected to teach young men and women how to shoot. 'Militarisierung durch Sport', *Junge Welt*, 26 May 1956.

5 Alexander Abusch, *Irrweg einer Nation* (Berlin, 1951). For an overview of East German historiography see Andreas Dorpalen, *German History in Marxist Perspective. The East German Approach* (London, 1985), pp. 24–61.

6 The East Germans believed in the Marxist-Leninist view of history and criticized Hegel for attributing change to 'ideas and theories' and to individuals or 'great men' who were 'propelled by their subjective motives within this framework of ideologies, religions, or some undefinable world spirit'. *Grundlagen des Marxismus-Leninismus: Lehrbuch* (Berlin-Ost, 1960), p. 141.

7 Mann was not particularly critical, however, and noted with pride that the East Germans 'are extremely eager to make my life work accessible to the people and especially to the youth, to expose them as much as possible to its "critical realism" and its "humanism" . . . Among the Communist functionaries of the German East Zone there are of course some lickspittle, self-serving and power-hungry despots. But I have looked into other faces and seen resolute good will and pure idealism – the faces of people who work eighteen hours a day and sacrifice themselves to make a reality of what they believe to be truth.' Thomas Mann, letter to Paul Olberg, 27 August 1949, in Richard and Clara Winston (trans.), *Letters of Thomas Mann 1889–1955* (London, 1970), vol. 2, pp. 581–2.

8 The Hallstein Doctrine declared that 'the recognition of the German Democratic Republic would mean international recognition of the partition of Germany into two separate states . . . The Federal Government . . . will feel compelled in future to regard the establishment of diplomatic relations as an unfriendly act calculated to intensify and aggravate the partition of Germany.' C. C. Schweitzer et al., *Politics and Government in the Federal Republic of Germany: Basic Documents* (Leamington Spa, 1984), pp. 298–301.

9 Klaus Larres, 'Germany and the West: the "Rapallo Factor" in German Foreign Policy from the 1950s to the 1990s', in Klaus Larres and Panikos Panayi, *The Federal Republic of Germany since 1949: Politics, Society and Economy before and after Unification* (London, 1996), p. 302. See also Richard W. Stevenson, *The Rise and Fall of Détente: Relaxations of Tension in US–Soviet Relations, 1953–1984* (Basingstoke, 1985).

10 For an excellent analysis see Timothy Garton Ash, *In Europe's Name: Germany and the Divided Continent* (London, 1993); see also William E. Griffith, *The Ostpolitik of the Federal Republic of Germany* (Cambridge, Mass., 1978); Adrian W. Schertz, *Die Deutschlandpolitik Kennedys und Johnsons* (Cologne, 1992).

11 Some Americans, notably Henry Kissinger but also Dean Acheson, John McCloy, Lucius Clay and Kenneth Rush (the American ambassador to Bonn), were

initially sceptical of Brandt's initiative and feared that Bonn was pursuing a German nationalist policy which might ultimately lead to a more 'neutralist Germany' and thereby upset the international status quo. In *Years of Upheaval*, Kissinger stated that in order to forestall the revival of German nationalism each of Brandt's colleagues, including Nixon, 'sought to preempt Germany by conducting an active détente policy of its own. In this sense Ostpolitik had effects far beyond those intended. It contributed to a race to Moscow and over time heightened mutual suspicions among the allies.' Eventually, however, Washington accepted Brandt's initiatives, not least because they hoped to avoid the risk of cutting the Federal Republic loose from the bonds of NATO and the restaints of the European Community. Henry Kissinger, *Years of Upheaval* (London, 1982), p. 409.

12 In his memoirs Brandt recounts how in Moscow in 1970 he and Brezhnev were concerned with 'the transition to a new period in European post-war history. At the same time I had an opportunity to set the parameters for settling certain practical questions. In the first place, there was Berlin: I said we would ratify the Moscow Treaty only when the Four Powers had concluded their negotiations on Berlin satisfactorily. If we wanted détente, Berlin could not remain a factor in the Cold War; it must play a part in peaceful co-operation instead of being an apple of discord.' Willy Brandt, *My Life in Politics* (New York, 1992), pp. 189–90.

13 Garton Ash, *In Europe's Name*, p. 67; particularly Chapter 3, 'Bonn–Moscow–Berlin', pp. 48–125.

14 Willy Brandt recalled that day as one 'charged with emotion . . . the road was lined with people waving, although the People's Police were supposed to have stopped them . . . A large crowd outside the hotel was expressing its pleasure with shouts of welcome . . . I was moved, and felt these were one people with me.' Brandt, *My Life in Politics*, p. 211.

15 Ulbricht still refused to allow formal links between the Federal Republic and the German Democratic Republic until the latter left NATO. Mike Dennis, *The German Democratic Republic. Politics, Economics and Society* (London, 1988), p. 36.

16 Note from Brezhnev to Erich Honecker, 28 July 1970, quoted in Garton Ash, *In Europe's Name*, p. 77.

17 Honecker's loyalty to the Soviet Union was not in question: 'I had always taken a lively interest in the land of Red October,' he wrote in his memoirs; 'the country of Lenin was my fatherland, its party my party, its youth organisation my youth organisation.' Indeed, it was precisely his conviction that he knew the 'true' Russia of Lenin better than younger leaders which would bring him into conflict with Gorbachev in the 1980s. Erich Honecker, *From My Life* (Oxford, 1981), p. 38.

18 Havemann was appointed to a chair of physical chemistry at the Humboldt University in East Berlin, which he occupied until his dismissal in 1964. Despite having been awarded the National Prize of the GDR in 1959 and having worked for the Stasi in the same period, Robert Havemann became an outspoken critic of aspects of the political system in the GDR; he openly sympathized with the

Prague Spring and his continued criticism led to his being placed under indefinite house arrest in 1976; this order was lifted in 1979, although he was fined for allowing his work to be published in the west that year. Havemann died in 1982. See David Childs and Richard Popplewell, *The Stasi. The East German Intelligence and Security Service* (London, 1996), p. 99.

19 Honecker affirmed his links to the Soviet Union in his speech to the VIII Parteitag; see Dieter Borkowski, *Erich Honecker. Statthalter Moskaus oder deutscher Patriot?* (Munich, 1987), p. 282.

20 Jonathan Dean, 'The Quadripartite Agreement on Berlin in the Context of Past and Future East–West Relations', in Richard L. Merritt and Anna J. Merritt (eds.), *Living with the Wall. West Berlin, 1961–1985* (Duke University, 1985), pp. 79–85.

21 The treaty is reprinted in Department of State, *Documents on Germany, 1944–1985* (Washington, DC, 1986), pp. 1124–7, 1135–43.

22 The number of visits by citizens of the FRG to the GDR for stays of one day or more went from 1,423,378 in 1967 to 2,278,989 in 1973, and to a high of 3,123,941 in 1976. There were 9.7 million telephone calls from West to East Germany in 1975 but this jumped to over 23 million calls by 1980; in 1975 there were 80 million letters from West to East, and 140 million from East to West. 'The SED and Ostpolitik and Glasnost', in David Childs, Thomas A. Baylis and Marilyn Rueschemeyer (eds.), *East Germany in Comparative Perspective* (London, 1989), pp. 6–7.

23 This was still common practice in the 1980s when visits by even minor officials of small countries would be reported on at length in the East German press. Michael Simmons, *The Unloved Country. A Portrait of East Germany Today* (London, 1989), p. 109.

24 On the changing relationship between East and West Berliners see John Borneman, *Belonging in the Two Berlins. Kin, State, Nation* (Cambridge, 1992).

25 In contrast to other eastern European capitals, there was little visible reaction to the 1956 Soviet invasion of Hungary in the GDR, probably because of the memories of the failure of 1953 and the increased role of the Stasi in controlling potential unrest. Jan von Flocken and Michael F. Scholz, *Ernst Wollweber. Saboteur – Minister – Unperson* (Berlin, 1994), p. 168.

26 Roger Woods, *Opposition in the GDR Under Honecker 1971–1985* (London, 1986), p. 11; Marc Fisher, *After the Wall. Germany, The Germans and the Burdens of History* (New York, 1995), p. 108.

27 Brezhnev to Honecker, quoted in Garton Ash, *In Europe's Name*, p. 78.

28 The approach was summed up in the East German phrase for 'defence education', meant to encourage East Germans to shoot at West Germans should the need arise: 'perhaps my brother but . . . my enemy'. Garton Ash, *In Europe's Name*, p. 190; see also Thilo Vogelsang, *Das geteilte Deutschland* (Nordlingen, 1966), p. 324.

29 The constitution of 1974 defined East Germany as a 'socialist state of workers and peasants' and deliberately omitted reference to reunification. Article 1 also stated that the capital of the GDR was Berlin. D. Müller-Römer (ed.), *Die neue Verfassung der DDR* (Cologne, 1974), p. 78ff. The removal of the word 'German'

extended even to registration letters for East German vehicles, which were changed from 'D' for Deutschland, to 'DDR' and to the abandonment of the national anthem.

30 As Kurt Hager put it, the very history of the GDR had to be written to demonstrate that it, not West Germany, was the German state in which 'all great progressive and revolutionary traditions of our people are being preserved'. Dorpalen, *German History in Marxist Perspective*, p. 58; see also Irma Hanke, 'Sozialistischer Neohistorismus? Aspekte der Identitätsdebatte in der DDR', in *Deutschland Archiv*, September 1988, p. 980.

31 The teaching of the Marxist view was rigously enforced; as one Stasi document stated, anyone who called for the 'abandonment of the "claim to totality" of the Marxist-Leninist world view as a valid doctrine and practice in all educational facilities' was to be punished. Stasi report on the East German opposition, 1 June 1989, in A. Mitter and S. Wolle (eds.), *Ich liebe euch doch alle! Befehle und Lageberichte des MfS* (Berlin, 1990), pp. 46–8.

32 The link between culture and politics was taken very seriously and the writing of history was always considered a political task as it was meant to instruct GDR citizens about their own political responsibilities. The party would often intervene to demonstrate to historians how events such as the 1848 revolution or the role of the Communists during the Second World War was to be portrayed to the general public, and the lessons which should be drawn from them. As Ernst Engelberg, Dean of German Historians wrote, 'the political struggle is of particular importance to the historian'. Ernst Engelberg (ed.), *Probleme der marxistischen Geschichtswissenschaft* (Cologne, 1972); Hermann Weber, 'Geschichte als Instrument der Politik. Zu den Thesen des ZK der SED "Zum 70. Jahrestag der Gründung der KPD"', in *Zeitschrift für Fragen der DDR und der Deutschlandpolitik*, no. 21, January 1988, p. 863–72.

33 This version was found in every modern history text; see, for example, Ernst Diehl et al., *Klassenkampf, Tradition, Sozialismus: Von den Anfängen der Geschichte des deutschen Volkes bis zur Gestaltung der entwickelten sozialistischen Gesellschaft in der deutschen demokratischen Republik Grundriss* (Berlin, 1978), p. 503ff.

34 'Capitalism' remained the main villain even in later works; see, for example, Joachim Petzold, 'Die deutsche Grossbourgeoisie und die Errichtung der faschistischen Diktatur', *Zeitschrift für Geschichtswissenschaft*, vol. 31, no. 3, pp. 214–32. For the historical roots of *Hitlerfascismus* see W. Ruge, 'Zur Taktik der deutschen Monopolbourgeoisie im Frühjahr und Sommer 1919', in *Zeitschrift für Geschichtswissenschaft*, no. 13, 1963, p. 1090ff.

35 Dietrich Eichholtz and Kurt Gossweiler (eds.), *Faschismusforschung: Positionen, Probleme, Polemik* (Berlin, 1980). See also Walter Ulbricht, *Der faschistische deutsche Imperialismus* (Berlin, 1956), pp. 91–2.

36 The version was repeated in the 676-page textbook *History of the Socialist Unity Party*, which was required reading in every school. It contained a collection of party documents and 'proof' of the SED's primary role in the fight against *Hitlerfascismus*. See also Walter A. Schmidt, *Damit Deutschland lebe. Ein Quellenwerk über den deutschen antifaschistischen Widerstandskampf 1933–1945*

(Berlin, 1959); Alexander Balnk and Julius Mader, *Rote Kapelle gegen Hitler* (Berlin, 1979); Werner Herden, *Wege zur Volksfront: Schriftsteller im antifaschistischen Bündnis* (Berlin, 1978); Jürgen Stroech, *Die illegale Presse – eine Waffe im Kampf gegen den deutschen Faschismus: Ein Beitrag zur Geschichte und Bibliographie der illegalen antifaschistischen Presse 1933–1939* (Leipzig, 1979); Kurt Laser et al., *Berlin 1871–1945* (Berlin, 1987), pp. 78–96; Luise Kraushaar, *Berliner Kommunisten im Kampf gegen den Faschismus 1936–1942* (Berlin, 1981); Margot Pikarski, *Jugend im Berliner Widerstand. Herbert Baum und Kampfgefährten* (Berlin, 1978). See also the series of pamphlets about each Berlin district financed by the GDR for West German consumption: Verband der Antifaschisten Westberlin, *Antifaschistischer Stadtplan* (Berlin, 1987).

37 The speed of the utter collapse of German Communism in 1933 was a source of humiliation and disturbed the future East German leaders. Communist propaganda could say little in praise of the KPD's performance in 1933 but they were able to create a much repeated and believed myth of resistance to the Nazis. According to the myth, after 1933 the KPD quickly reorganized itself at the grass-roots level, with German workers heroically rallying to the cause and forming resistance cells of five people or *Fünfergruppen*. The myth was particularly effective as the *Fünfergruppen* had been organized on a 'need to know' basis, with only the leader knowing the names of the other members. After the war it was easy to claim that a much more extensive network had existed than was actually the case. The fact that these Communist cells failed to carry out a single act of resistance of any military significance throughout the Second World War was simply ignored. Childs and Popplewell, *The Stasi*, pp. 20–21.

38 For a critique of the GDR version see Dorpalen, *German History in Marxist Perspective*, pp. 367–92.

39 Diehl, *Klassenkampf, Tradition, Sozialismus*, pp. 430–58.

40 There was no mention of the secret protocol, nor was there mention of the hundreds of German Communists and elite members of the KPD who had fled to the Soviet Union when Hitler came to power and were murdered by Stalin in the Great Purges or handed over to Hitler in 1939. In reality the Hitler–Stalin Pact resulted in German Communists being dragged out of the labour camps and handed over to the SS in exchange for Russian émigrés and Ukrainians who had tried to find refuge in Germany and Poland. Josef Garlinski, *Poland in the Second World War* (London, 1985), p. 38; see also Norman Davis, *God's Playground: A History of Poland* (Oxford, 1982), vol. 2, p. 433; Anthony Read and David Fisher, *The Deadly Embrace: Hitler, Stalin and the Nazi–Soviet pact 1939–1941* (London, 1988), p. 432.

41 Laser, *Berlin 1871–1945*, pp. 75–6.

42 If the Holocaust was mentioned at all, it was referred to merely as an 'extreme side-effect' of capitalism. Fisher, *After the Wall*, p. 122.

43 Georg Pijet, 'Wenn die Firma verkrachte . . .', *Das rote Sprachrohr*, August–September 1930, pp. 17–18; Peter Jelavich, *Berlin Cabaret* (Harvard, 1993), p. 227.

44 The play *Die Rundköpfe und die Spitzköpfe* was loosely based on Shakespeare's *Measure for Measure* and was a parable for the rise of Hitler from a Marxist

perspective. In this the roundhead tenant farmers are seduced by the notion that they may no longer have to pay rent to sharp-headed landlords and therefore forget their need for solidarity with sharp-headed tenants. Brecht maintains that international capital was simply fomenting anti-Semitism in order to deflect energy from the true class struggle – a line upheld in the GDR. Ronald Hayman, *Brecht* (London, 1983), pp. 163–4.

45 Klaus Drobisch (et al.), *Juden unterm Hakenkreuz* (Frankfurt-am-Main, 1973); for a critical view see Franz Loeser, 'Ehrlicher Sinneswandel?', in *Deutschland Archiv* (September 1988), pp. 960–61; Nora Goldenbogen, 'Juden in der DDR. Erwartungen – Realitäten – Wandlungen', in Günther B. Ginzel (ed.), *Der Anfang nach dem Ende. Jüdisches Leben in Deutschland 1945 bis heute* (Düsseldorf, 1996), pp. 123–49.

46 Childs and Popplewell, *The Stasi*, p. 146.

47 Goethe had been given a modest anniversary but he had never been defamed by the Soviets in the same way. Luther's rehabilitation was interesting precisely because he had formerly been seen as one of the precursors of militarism. See Robert F. Goeckel, 'The Luther Anniversary in East Germany', *World Politics*, 37, October 1984, pp. 112–33.

48 The text of Erich Honecker's founding speech of the state Luther Committee was published in *Neues Deutschland*, 14–15 June 1980; all the speeches were collected in the volume *Martin Luther und unsere Zeit* (Berlin, 1980). See also Johannes Kuppe, 'Die Geschichtsschreibung der SED im Umbruch', *Deutschland Archiv*, vol. 18, no. 3, 1985, pp. 278–94.

49 As Mark Brayne saw it, the move was entirely cynical, not least because the Church was seen as a 'potentially great source of foreign currency . . . worth some 100 million West German marks a year to the East German state'. Mark Brayne, 'Luther: One of the Greatest Sons of the German People', in *GDR Monitor*, no. 3, summer 1980, p. 40.

50 On the Honecker–Schönherr meeting see Reinhard Henkys, 'Church–State–Society', in Reinhard Henkys (ed.), *Die evangelischen Kirchen in der DDR* (Munich, 1982), pp. 11–61.

51 In his order to the Red Army on 1 May 1945, Stalin announced that they had conquered Ostpreussen, the 'Brutstätte des deutschen Imperialismus'. Josef Stalin, *Über den Grossen vaterländischen Krieg der Sowjetunion* (Berlin, 1951), p. 215. This view was repeated in post-war GDR history; see, for example, Wolfram von Hanstein, *Vom Luther bis Hitler, ein wichtiger Abriss deutscher Geschichte* (Berlin, 1947).

52 *Abolition of the State of Prussia.* The Prussian State which from early days has been a bearer of militarism and reaction in Germany has *de facto* ceased to exist. Guided by the interests of preservation of peace and security of peoples and with the desire to assure further reconstruction of the political life of Germany on a democratic basis, the Control Council enacts as follows: Article I. The Prussian State together with its central government and all its agencies is abolished. *Law No. 46 of the Allied Control Council*, 25 February 1947.

53 Günter Heydemann, 'Geschichtswissenschaft und Geschichtsverständnis in der DDR seit 1945', *Politik und Zeitgeschichte*, 1987, p. 15.

54 Ingrid Mittenzwei, *Friedrich II von Preussen* (Cologne, 1980); see also Horst Bartel and Ingrid Mittenzwei, 'Prussia and German History', in *Einheit*, no. 3, 1981, p. 272.

55 The West Berlin exhibition was entitled *Preussen. Versuch einer Bilanz. Eine Austellung der Berliner Festspiele GmbH.* It was held between 15 August and 15 November 1981 in the Gropius-Bau. On the new interest in Prussia of the west see, for example, Otto Büsch (ed.), *Das Preussenbild in der Geschichte. Protokoll eines Symposions* (Berlin, 1981); Hans-Jürgen Puhle and Hans-Ulrich Wehler, 'Preussen in Rückblick', *Geschichte und Gesellschaft*, Sonderheft 6, 1980. See also I. R. Martin, 'The Changing Image of Prussia in the German Democratic Republic', *German Life and Letters*, vol. XXXVII, no. 1, pp. 57–70.

56 Johannes Kuppe, 'Die Geschichtsschreibung der SED in Umbruch', in *Deutschland Archiv*, vol. 3, 1985, pp. 278–94; Walter Schmidt, 'Zur Entwicklung des Erbe- und Traditionsverständnisses in der Geschichtsschreibung der DDR', in *Zeitschrift für Geschichtswissenschaft*, no. 33, 1985, pp. 338–47. For an example of the change see Siegfried Schmidt, 'Junkertum und Genesis des deutschen Konservatismus im 19. Jahrhundert', *Zeitschrift für Geschichtswissenschaft*, no. 27, 1979, p. 1058.

57 Frederick II's statue was replaced in 1980; during the dedication Erich Honecker referred to him as 'Frederick the Great' although he was still referred to as 'Frederick II' in history texts.

58 Günter Stahn, *Das Nikolaiviertel am Marx-Engels-Forum. Ursprung. Gründungsort und Stadtkern Berlins. Ein Beitrag zur Stadtentwicklung* (Berlin, 1985).

59 The programme was outlined in Komitee der Deutschen Demokratischen Republik zum 750 jährigen Bestehen von Berlin, *750 Jahre Berlin. Das Buch zum Fest* (Leipzig, 1986); for photographs of the building work see pp. 12–80.

60 See, for example, *Neue Berliner Illustrierte. Sonderheft Berlin 750* (Berlin, 1987). This was not surprising as important members of the GDR elite, including Hans Bentzien (Minister of Culture), Kurt Blecha (head of the government press office), and Professor Ernst Giessmann (Minister for Higher Education), had been members of the NSDAP.

61 German students and servicemen were 'trained in hatred' towards every form of capitalist 'exploitation and aggression'. Thomas M. Forster, *The East German Army: The Second Power in the Warsaw Pact*, trans. Deryck Viney (London, 1980); see also Krisch, *The German Democratic Republic*, p. 48.

62 Gordon Craig, *The Germans* (Harmondsworth, 1984), p. 250.

63 Ernst Engelberg, *Bismarck. Urpreusse und Reichsgründer* (Berlin, 1985).

64 There was great reluctance to rehabilitate Nietzsche because his philosophy maintained that history is an eternal cyclical recurrence. This contradicted the Marxist vision of progress or, as Stephan Hermlin said in 1979, the notion that the GDR is 'like a bow whose arrow is speeding on ahead'. J. H. Reid, *Writing Without Taboos, The New East German Literature* (New York, 1990), p. 198.

65 David Childs, *The GDR: Moscow's German Ally* (London, 1988), p. 147.

66 By 1985 each inhabitant of the GDR was spending 567 Marks a month on goods. Half went on food, beverages and tobacco, the rest on industrial goods, including clothing, and furniture. Maria Elisabeth Ruban, 'The Retail Trade',

in Eileen Martin, *GDR and Eastern Europe – A Handbook* (Aldershot, 1989), p. 134.

67 The new constitution of 1968 was more restrictive than that of 1948. See Dietrich Müller-Römer (ed.), *Ulbrichts Grundgesetz. Die sozialistische Verfassung der DDR* (Cologne, 1968).

68 Marilyn Rueschemeyer, 'Women in the GDR and Hungary', in Childs, *East Germany in Comparative Perspective*, p. 91; the figures are from Christiane Lemke, 'Women and Politics in East Germany', *Socialist Review*, no. 15, 1985, p. 123.

69 Margot Honecker was directly involved in the control of education and the crushing of dissent in schools. In the late 1980s Soviet journals such as *Literaturnaya Gazeta* and *Sputnik* were becoming increasingly critical of Soviet Communism as a result of Gorbachev's reforms. When some of the teachers at the Carl Ossietzky school in Pankow questioned why their subscription to *Sputnik* had been cancelled, Margot Honecker sent three of her senior officials to take charge. Annerose Gerecke, the school's deputy director said: 'They said we were not qualified to lead the school politically. The supervisors were here every day from 7 a.m. to 8 p.m. They took Herr Forner by the hand every step of the way. They said he had to be helped. They said we were politically negligent even to listen to opposing views.' Fisher, *After the Wall*, p. 110.

70 See 'Frauen, Familie, Alte', in Christoph Klessmann and George Wagner (eds.), Das gespaltene Land. Leben in Deutschland 1945 bis 1990. Texte und Dokumente (Munich, 1993), pp. 441–55.

71 Childs and Popplewell, *The Stasi*, p. 110.

72 Krisch, *The German Democratic Republic*, p. 153.

73 Ilse Spittmann (ed.), *Die SED in Geschichte und Gegenwart* (Cologne, 1987), p. 208.

74 On the conflict between church and state see Richard L. Merritt, 'East Berlin as a Metropolis', in Mergy Gerber (ed.), *Studies in GDR Culture and Society 8* (London, 1988), pp. 16–21.

75 Youth leaders were expected to maintain an 'optimistic duty oriented atmosphere' in all their activities. They were to recruit new members and organize their free time so they did productive work beneficial to the GDR. FDJ-Sekretär, *Junge Generation*, vol. 7, 1984. See also Arnold Freiburg and Christa Mahrad, *FDJ: Der sozialistische Jugendverband der DDR* (Opladen, 1982), and for a GDR view Martin Herzig, *Youth at Work, at Leisure and in Politics* (Berlin, 1977); Peter Voss (ed.), *Die Freizeit der Jugend* (Berlin, 1981).

76 School texts warned of western plans to invade the GDR: one included a map of Europe showing large black arrows representing western forces making their way from the 'west' towards Berlin (on day one), Stettin (on day two) and Warsaw (on day three). The caption read: 'This is how the Bundeswehr generals plan their Aggression.' The map appeared with a photograph of Generaloberst Willi Stoph reviewing the first regiment of the National Volksarmee. Rudolf Lau et al., *Geschichte. Lehrbuch für Klasse 10* (Berlin, 1984), pp. 160–61.

77 Barbara Hille, 'Zum aktuellen Forschungsstand über die Jugendlichen in der DDR', *Deutsche Studien*, vol. 19, no. 76, pp. 332–45. See also Gabriele Husner, *Studenten und Studium in der DDR* (Cologne, 1985). For the official GDR view

see, for example, Kelmut Klein and Ulrich Zückert, *Learning for Living. Education in the GDR* (Berlin, 1979).

78 See the GDR publication by Wolfgang Gitter and Bernhard Wilk, *Fun–Health–Fitness* (Berlin, 1974).

79 Werner Filmer and Heribert Schwan (eds.), *Alltag im anderen Deutschland* (Düsseldorf, 1985), p. 154.

80 Peter Wicke, 'Rock Music and Everyday Culture in the GDR', in Gerber, *Studies in GDR Culture and Society 8*, p. 177.

81 Ibid., p. 173.

82 On GDR rock music see Jürgen Balitzki, *Rock aus erster Hand* (Berlin, 1985); Stefan Lasch, *PS: Rockmusic* (Berlin, 1980).

83 The foreign debt of the GDR increased throughout the 1970s, reaching $710 per capita in 1984 compared with a Comecon average of $230, due in part to its dependency on foreign sources of energy (the GDR mined its last coal in 1977 although it continued to produce lignite). Its economy was also badly affected by the OPEC price rises of 1973–4 and 1979–80, by recession in the west between 1980 and 1983, by increasing competition from South-East Asia and by the widening technology gap between it and the west. The end result was stagnation, and increasing public disenchantment. Ian Derbyshire, *Politics in Germany. From Division to Unification* (Edinburgh, 1991), pp. 122–3.

84 See Philipp J. Bryson, *The Consumer under Socialist Planning: The East German Case* (New York, 1984); see also Gert-Joachim Glaessner, *Die andere deutsche Republik. Gesellschaft und Politik in der DDR* (Opladen, 1989), pp. 274–8.

85 *Eastern Europe Newsletter*, 15 June 1988.

86 There were improvements after Honecker's 1986 reform but as he was unwilling to scrap central planning they had only modest success. Phillip J. Bryson, 'Enterprise and Association in Soviet Planning: Comparisons with the East German Experience', in Childs, *East Germany in Comparative Perspective*, pp. 163–89.

87 The GDR's annual emissions of sulphur dioxide from lignite were 40 tonnes per square kilometre. Michael von Berg, 'Zum Umweltschutz in Deutschland', *Deutschland Archiv*, vol. 17, no. 4, 1984, p. 374; Dennis, *The German Democratic Republic*, p. 181.

88 *Financial Times*, 12 February 1992.

89 Ursula Bergmann, 'Laserchips aus Berlin, Lichtfabrik en miniature. Weltspitzerzeugnis durch Forschungskooperation', *Neue Berliner Illustrierte. Berlin 750 Sonderheft*, p. 51.

90 As Phillip Bryson put it, 'The East Germans combine an intrinsic Soviet-type disinclination to rely on market mechanisms with a willingness to pursue orthodox Soviet-style central planning ... From the termination of the 1960 reform era to the 1986 reform legislation, both countries exhibited a strong antipathy to reform.' Furthermore, 'the reforms introduced by Honecker did not embrace the market mechanism'. Bryson, 'Enterprise and Association in Soviet Planning', in Childs, *East Germany in Comparative Perspective*, pp. 174–5.

91 The attempt to create a computer industry was not helped by Politburo members like Kurt Hager, who warned that the obsession with computers was going so far that 'the language of a particular scientific specialty might become the

political language of the Party', and that the party would then cease to be a Marxist-Leninist party. Gary Geipel, 'Politics and Computers in the German Democratic Republic: The Robotron Combine', in Gerber, *Studies in GDR Culture and Society 8*, p. 87.

92 Honecker was convinced that he could turn East Germany into another Silicon Valley. In 1986 he said that 'We will have to succeed in this [technology] race against time, leading the field in key areas to achieve major economic and social changes', but although the GDR could produce goods they were of poor quality and lagged far behind the west in terms of technological advancement. Erich Honecker, *Report of the Central Committee* (Dresden, 1986), p. 59. In the Five Year Plan Act of 1986 it was stated that the GDR would have to produce 'at least 170,000 office and personal computers, 1950 minicomputers and 670 mainframes . . . and 80,000 industrial robots'. See *Five Year Plan Act* (Dresden, 1986), p. 52; *Mit qualitativ neuen schritten zu höchsten Leistungen. Seminar des Zentralkomitees der SED mit den Generaldirektoren der Kombinate und den Parteiorganisatoren des ZK* (Berlin, 1986), p. 26.

93 Karl-Heinz Wessali, Karl-Zeiss Jena, interview, May 1990.

94 Even in these areas the stifling atmosphere prevailed: 'plays are simply not being written; new dramatists do not break onto the scene. If anything the relative stagnation of contemporary drama seen at the turn of this decade seems to continue.' H. G. Huettich, *Theater in the Planned Society. Contemporary Drama in the German Democratic Republic in Its Historical, Political and Cultural Context* (Chapel Hill, 1978), p. 152.

95 For an overview of GDR painting see Monika Flacke, *Auftrags Kunst der DDR* (Berlin, 1995).

96 *The Financial Times*, 4 May 1992; the figures quoted were for the year 1988.

97 *Economist: A Survey of the New Germany*, 30 June 1990.

98 The hundreds of bitter jokes about attempts to obtain a travel permit, or the destinations people were allowed to visit in the eastern bloc revealed the intense frustration about the travel restrictions. One young East German said in 1984 that when he died he wanted to be cremated and his ashes scattered in the Sahara so that at least he would have made one long journey 'once in my life'. Filmer and Schwan, *Alltag im anderen Deutschland*, p. 157.

99 The most important men in the Stasi network reported directly to Mielke. The Kollegium included Generalleutnant Dr Gerhard Neiber, Generalleutnant Dr Wolfgang Schwanitz, and Generaloberst Werner Grossman. At the same time Mielke presided over the Arbeitsgruppe des Ministers (AGM), led by Generalmajor Erich Rümmler, which had 700 Stasi members attached to it. This was responsible for everything from planning the arrests and imprisonment of victims to organizing Mielke's hunting parties. He also presided over Generalmajor Manfred Döhring, head of the Guard Regiment Geliks E. Dzerzynski, an army within the Stasi with 10,211 troops; Generalleutnant Günter Wolf, head of the Hauptabteilung Personenschutz, with 3,772 full-time operatives to guard the SED elite; Generalleutnant Dr Werner Imler, head of the Zentrale Auswertungs und Informationsgruppe, or ZAIG, which was responsible for collecting and analysing information on everything from foreign media reports to church

and youth problems; Generalleutnant Dr Günther Kratsch, who headed Haupt-abteilung II, with 1,408 operatives engaged in counter-espionage, covering foreign embassies and controlling foreign mail; and Generalmajor Heinz Pommer, head of the Stasi's own football team. Mielke also presided over the Abteilung Finanzen (the Finance Department). Childs and Popplewell, *The Stasi*, pp. 71–5; see also Ken Smith, *Berlin. Coming in From the Cold* (London, 1990), pp. 196–224.

100 *Welt am Sonntag*, 10 April 1994. For a fascinating account of confronting this past see Timothy Garton Ash, *The File. A Personal History* (London, 1997).

101 Johannes Beleites et al., *Stasi intern. Macht und Banalität* (Leipzig, 1991), pp. 10–11.

102 'Stasi-Richtlinien zur Bekämpfung "feindlicher Gruppen"', *Frankfurter Allgemeine Zeitung*, 3 September 1990.

103 Nancy Travis Wolfe, *Policing a Socialist Society. The German Democratic Republic* (New York, 1992), p. 75.

104 This process is described in detail in Beleites, *Stasi intern*, pp. 100–45.

105 Culture played an 'essential part in developing the personality and instilling a socialist lifestyle, in releasing people's creative talents and contributing to the general well-being'. Anything which did not help to integrate citizens into the socio-political system, or which was in any way critical of the achievements of the workers' and farmers' state, was banned. *Cultural Life in the GDR* (Berlin, 1982), p. 7; Dennis, *The German Democratic Republic*, p. 173.

106 The 'Bitterfeld Path' was meant to encourage interaction between factory workers, farmers, construction workers and others with writers so that they could all overcome the barrier between art and life. Dennis, *The German Democratic Republic*, p. 174; Childs, *The GDR*, p. 209.

107 In the 1980s *Sinn und Form*, a respected East German journal of the East Berlin Academy of Arts under the editor Max Walter Schulz, came under increasing pressure to conform. In May 1984, for example, Schulz was forced to reject the memoirs of Trude Richter, one of the victims of Stalin's purges, because as Kurt Hager and Erich Honecker made clear, 'there is to be no discussion of education, the army or labour camps'. Stephen Parker, 'Re-establishing an all-German identity. "Sinn und Form" and German unification', in Osman Durrani, Colin Good and Kevin Hilliard (eds.), *The New Germany. Literature and Society after Unification* (Sheffield, 1995), p. 16.

108 On the changes in GDR literature see J. H. Reid, *Writing Without Taboos, The New East German Literature* (New York, 1990); on the novel see Dennis Tate, *The East German Novel: Identity, Community, Continuity* (Bath, 1984).

109 Stefan Heym's critique of Stalinism, *The King David Report*, and Brigitte Reimann's attack on bureaucracy, *Franziska Linkerhand*, were also published after Kurt Hager's 1972 speech. Wolf Emmerich, *Kleine Literaturgeschichte der DDR* (Darmstadt, 1984), p. 19. Hermann Kant's work did not prevent him from becoming the President of the Writers' Union or from giving a key speech in that capacity on 20 September 1984, proudly proclaiming that over the past thirty-five years the East Germans had 'created a *Heimat*'. Erich Honecker's speech noted that the 'most important task' of the union was to 'make fast our

brotherly bond with the Soviet Union and to continue to anchor the GDR in the group of socialist states'. Erich Honecker, 'Reiche Kultur – vom Volke für das Volk geschaffen', and Hermann Kant, 'Erfahrung Heimat', in *Reiche Kultur – vom Volke für das Volk geschaffen. Treffen Erich Honeckers mit Kunst- und Kulturschaffenden der DDR am 20. September 1984* (Berlin, 1984), pp. 11, 41.

110 On 'dissident' literature see Thomas C. Fox, *Border Crossings. An Introduction to East German Prose* (University of Michigan, 1993).

111 His lyrics are collected in Wolf Biermann, *Poems and Ballads*, trans. Steve Gooch (London, 1977).

112 Dennis, *The German Democratic Republic*, p. 122.

113 Kunze wrote a song in defence of Biermann and critical of the GDR leadership. 'Song: The Biermann Cometh. Biermann is their man? What pus! A man's a man beer is beer/Biermann came from there to here/You did not want to drink'. Fox, *Border Crossings*, p. 151.

114 Erich Honecker reacted quickly. At the Eleventh Party Congress in 1986 he stated that 'the only valid stance [of an GDR artist] is as a fellow-fighter or fervent protagonist who spreads the ideas of peace and socialism amongst the masses with his or her special tools.' Erich Honecker, *Report of the Central Committee* (Berlin, 1986), p. 25.

115 Childs and Popplewell, *The Stasi*, p. 103.

116 *Der Spiegel*, 13 June 1994; Eric Hansen, 'The Writer whom the Wall No Longer Protects', *The European*, 3–5 August 1990.

17: THE WALLED CITY – WEST BERLIN

1 'Berlin may not be a beautiful city,' he wrote later, 'but it is exciting. What makes it exciting is the occasionally unbearable tension between a seemingly carefree present and an oppressive past.' Armando, *From Berlin*, trans. Susan Mossotty (London, 1996), p. 12.

2 György Ligeti, *10 Jahre Berliner Künstlerprogramm* (Berlin, 1975).

3 Klaus Schütz, who worked on Willy Brandt's campaign for chancellorship, remembered the demoralization in West Berlin after August 1961 and recalled Chancellor Adenauer paying one hundred Marks of 'jitters money' to each West Berliner. One of his tasks as a member of the Berlin Senat after December 1961 was a daily review, a file marked 'secret' which contained the latest emigration figures. The 'alarming data . . . was underscored by the sight, which was there for all to see, of columns of furniture vans leaving the city.' Klaus Schütz, 'The Wall and West Berlin's Development', in Richard L. Merritt and Anna J. Merritt (eds.), *Living with the Wall. West Berlin 1961–1985* (Duke University, 1985), pp. 37, 225.

4 Egon Bahr, quoted in Norman Gelb, *The Berlin Wall* (New York, 1990), p. 237.

5 John Kenneth Galbraith echoed these sentiments in an infamous interview in which he said: 'I think the Wall is a good thing. At any rate, it has preserved peace.' *Die Zeit*, 5 July 1968, in Dennis L. Bark and David R. Gress, *A History of West Germany* (Oxford, 1986), vol. 1: 'From Shadow to Substance 1945–1963,'

pp. 470–2. Willy Brandt said bitterly that years later he learned Khrushchev
had stipulated that no wall should be built until western reactions had been
tested but that once it was built 'Counter measures that might have been effective
were not demanded of the Western powers . . . objectively speaking, this terrible
day for the people of Berlin brought relief to the Western governments: their
rights in West Berlin remained untouched, and the dreaded danger of war had
been averted.' Willy Brandt, *My Life in Politics* (New York, 1992), p. 48.

6 Gelb, *The Berlin Wall*, p. 220.

7 Department of State, *Documents on Germany 1944–1985* (pub. no. 9446), 1986,
pp. 849–50. Brandt remembered Kennedy 'laughingly' rehearsing the words just
before his speech. According to him the idea was thought up by Ted Sorensen.
Brandt, *My Life in Politics*, p. 60.

8 Brandt was critical of Adenauer and felt that he 'did not really trust his own
people. He did not believe they could find their way to moderation and a central
position, and so he thought Germany must be protected against itself.' When
de Gaulle visited Germany to much acclaim, Adenauer said to Brandt, 'The
Germans easily lose their balance.' Ibid., p. 34.

9 As Brandt put it, 'I was convinced that the unnaturally tense situation in a
divided Germany had to be eased, for the sake of peace and the human beings
affected.' Ibid., p. 7.

10 For Brandt's role in the creation of *Ostpolitik* see Timothy Garton Ash, *In
Europe's Name: Germany and the Divided Continent* (London, 1993), pp. 59–83.

11 Henry Kissinger, *Diplomacy* (London, 1994), p. 317.

12 Bart and Gress, *From Shadow to Substance*, vol. 1, p. 490.

13 Figures from the Landespostdirektion Berlin, quoted in Richard L. Merritt,
'Interpersonal Transactions across the Wall', in Merritt and Merritt, *Living with
the Wall*, p. 180.

14 Peter Bender, 'Die Absurdität Berlin', *Der Spiegel*, 11 May 1981.

15 The tension was exacerbated by the introduction of the 'shoot-to-kill' policy
along the inter-zonal border. See Kurt L. Shell, *Bedrohung and Bewährung.
Führung and Bevölkerung in der Berlin-Krise* (Cologne, 1965), p. 339.

16 Hans Herzfeld, *Berlin in der Weltpolitik, 1945–1970* (Berlin, 1973), p. 495.

17 Wolfgang Watter, 'The West Berlin Economy', in Merritt and Merritt, *Living
with the Wall*, p. 138.

18 For an analysis of Berlin's economy after the Wall see Joachim Mawrocki,
Berliner Wirtschaft: Waschstum auf begrenztem Raum, in Dieter Baumeister,
Berlin Fibel. Berichte zur Lage der Stadt (Berlin, 1975), pp. 269–71.

19 Richard L. Merritt, 'Living with the Wall', in Merritt and Merritt, *Living with
the Wall*, p. 195.

20 Michael Kleeberg, *Der saubere Tod* (Munich, 1987), p. 13.

21 'The Wall created widespread disappointment about the Western allies, especially the United States – indeed the criticism focused on the United States – and
doubt about their reliability and even their ability to honor their promises.'
Dieter Mahncke, 'From the Wall to the Quadripartite Agreement: Some Underlying Trends', in Merritt and Merritt, *Living with the Wall*, p. 99.

22 John Ardagh, *Germany and the Germans* (Harmondsworth, 1990), p. 52.

23 On the evolution of the peace movements see David Gress, *Peace and Survival: West Germany, the Peace Movement and European Security* (Stanford, 1985), pp. 129–50.

24 *Eugon Kogon, Die restaurative Republik. Zur Geschichte der Bundesrepublik Deutschland* (Berlin, 1996), p. 266. Jürgen Habermas saw the first goal of the radical students as 'the transformation of the precarious four-power status of Berlin and the establishment of an open city. Campaigns against the Springer Company ... serve as the means of mobilization.' There was a new conflict between the 'politicized sections of the student body and the population and Senate of the city of Berlin. In particular, Vietnam protests have made this conflict break out into the open ... All organs of the government, the police, administration of justice, house of representatives, and the mayor himself distinguished and compromised themselves by foolish prejudice and repression: illegal prohibitions of demonstrations, dubious confiscations and problematic arrests, indefensible court proceedings, open police terror, and a mayor who even thanked the police after Ohnesorg was shot.' Jürgen Habermas, *Towards a Rational Society. Student Protest, Science and Politics*, trans. Jeremy J. Shapiro (Frankfurt-am-Main, 1970), pp. 18–19.

25 Wolfgang Ribbe, 'Berlin zwischen Ost und West (1945 bis zur Gegenwart)', in Wolfgang Ribbe (ed.), *Geschichte Berlins* (Munich, 1987), vol. 2: *Von der Märzrevolution bis zur Gegenwart*; see also Klaus Schroeder, 'Die Krise (1964–1967)', in *Freie Universität Berlin 1948–1973.* (Berlin, 1983), Part 4: *Hochschule im Umbruch*, ed. Klaus Schroeder.

26 Bahro's views on disarmament were typical: 'The German peace movement has the right to articulate its demands ... Disarmament East and West ... Let's begin in Germany. And there are good reasons for this, because it is precisely here in Germany that the bloc confrontation is most acute. It was no accident that the discussion of a pact-free policy, containing the perspective of reunification [of a neutral Germany], began in Berlin.' Rudolf Bahro, *From Red to Green. Interviews with the New Left Review*, trans. Gus Fagan and Richard Hurst (London, 1984), pp. 193–4.

27 The division between political groups over the disarmament issue was clear; in 1982 Werner Filmer and Heribert Schwan conducted interviews with over 100 West Germans who were asked 'what peace means to me'. Petra Kelly answered that first and foremost peace meant having no obvious enemies – 'ohne Feindbilder' and advocated a neutral demilitarized Germany. Helmut Kohl responded: 'even if the weapons are removed, will it lead to freedom?' For Kohl peace was not an end in itself; on the contrary, 'with peace goes freedom, human rights, and self-determination. Peace without freedom and without self-determination, both from within and externally, is not freedom, at least not that which we understand in the west.' Werner Filmer and Heribert Schwan (eds.), *Was heisst für mich Frieden?* (Oldenburg, 1982), pp. 148, 153. For an analysis of the neutralist propositions see Gress, *Peace and Survival*, pp. 173–88.

28 This was a play on Theodor W. Adorno's statement: 'To write a poem after Auschwitz is barbaric.' In fact Adorno had meant to expose the failure of lyric poetry to respond to the shock and trauma, to the poetic spirit of the experience

of the extermination camp. Wolfgang Beutin, *A History of German Literature*, trans. Clare Krojzl (London, 1993), p. 676; Peter Härtling, *Monat*, May 1987. See also Keith Bullivant (ed.), *After the Death of Literature. West German Writing of the 1970s* (Oxford, 1989).

29 Imanuel Geiss, 'The Federal Republic of Germany in International Politics Before and After Unification', in Klaus Larres and Panikos Panayi (eds.), *The Federal Republic of Germany since 1949. Politics, Society and Economy before and after Unification* (London 1996), p. 153.

30 Petra Goldmann, '2 Juni 67', in Ulrich Baehr et al., *Mythos Berlin* (Berlin, 1987), p. 272.

31 Jürgen Habermas wrote of his death that '. . . the Free University is the Berkeley of West Germany. Yet the activism of the students of Berlin is echoed at the other West German universities. This has become clear since June 2 of this year. The outrage over the death of Benno Ohnesorg . . . touched every university in West Germany. Nowhere, to be sure, did these conflicts attain the extent and the constancy of the student protests in Berlin, which have been going on since the spring of 1965 and whose end is not yet in sight.' Habermas, *Towards a Rational Society*, p. 15. See also Knut Nevermann, *Der 2. Juni 1967. Studenten zwischen Notstand und Demokratie. Zu den Ereignissen anlässlich des Schahbesuchs* (Cologne, 1967); Richard Löwenthal, *Studenten und demokratische Öffentlichkeit* (Berlin, 1967).

32 For his part, Habermas said that the Berlin press was 'monopolized by the anti-intellectual and *ressentiment*-filled newspapers of the Springer Company'. Habermas, *Towards a Rational Society*, p. 20. See also Reinhard Rürup, 'Stadt der Widersprüche', in Gottfried Korff and Reinhard Rürup (eds.), *Berlin, Berlin. Die Ausstellung zur Geschichte der Stadt* (Berlin, 1987), p. 632.

33 Jürgen Rühle, 'Rudi Dutschke – eine deutsche Utopie', in *Deutschland Archiv*, 1980, pp. 133–5; Uwe Bergmann, Rudi Dutschke, Wolfgang Lefevre and Bernd Rahehl, *Die Rebellion der Studenten oder die neue Opposition* (Reinbek, 1968).

34 On this, and for an excellent analysis of euthanasia in Germany see Michael Burleigh, *Death and Deliverance. 'Euthanasia' in Germany 1900–1945* (Cambridge, 1994), p. 282.

35 According to Klarsfeld, the hall was filled with people, and Chancellor Kiesinger, Ludwig Erhard, Bruno Heck and Gerhard Schröder were on the stage. She sneaked on to the podium. 'Kiesinger sensed my presence . . . Shouting "Nazi! Nazi!" at the top of my lungs, I slapped him.' Beate Klarsfeld, *Wherever They May Be* (New York, 1975). See also Thomas Ellwein, *Krisen und Reform: Die Bundesrepublik seit den sechziger Jahren* (Munich, 1989), p. 20.

36 Stefan Aust, *Der Baader-Meinhof Komplex* (Munich, 1989), p. 54.

37 Eckhard Jesse, 'Linksextremismus in der Bundesrepublik Deutschland', *Aus Politik und Zeitgeschichte*, B-34, 10 January 1992. See also Mathias Siekmeier and Klaus Larres, 'Domestic Political Developments II: 1969–90', in Larres and Panayi, *The Federal Republic of Germany*, p. 116.

38 Ulrike Marie Meinhof, 'Offener Brief an Farah Diba', in Baehr, *Mythos Berlin* (Berlin, 1987), pp. 273–5.

39 On the RAF see Hans Josef Horchem, 'Der Verfall der Roten Armee Faktion',

Aus Politik und Zeitgeschichte, B46/90, 9 November 1990, pp. 54–61; Jillian Becker, *Hitler's Children: The Story of the Baader-Meinhof Terrorist Gang* (Philadelphia, 1977). For a personal view see Ian Walker, *Zoo Station. Adventures in East and West Berlin* (London, 1988), pp. 48–69.

40 Siekmeier and Larres, 'Domestic Political Developments II ', in Larres and Panayi, *The Federal Republic of Germany*, p. 116; see also U. Backes and E. Jesse, *Politischer Extremismus in der Bundesrepublik Deutschland* (Bonn, 1990); Aust, *Der Baader-Meinhof Komplex*.

41 'Eine pervers Kombination', *Der Spiegel*, no. 25, 1990.

42 Torsten Oppeland, 'Domestic Political Developments I. 1949–69', in Larres and Panayi, *The Federal Republic of Germany*, p. 97. See also Arnulf Baring, *Machtwechsel: Die Ära Brandt-Scheel* (Stuttgart, 1982), pp. 793–4.

43 Despite fears to the contrary these measures were not taken to extremes. One reason which has been suggested was that one of its most powerful advocates, the Prime Minister of Baden-Württemberg Hans Filbinger, had an incriminating Nazi history. Gordon Craig, *The Germans* (Harmondsworth, 1984), pp. 184–9. See also Ulrich Chaussy, 'Jugend', in Wolfgang Benz (ed.), *Die Bundesrepublik Deutschland. Geschichte in drei Bänden* (Frankfurt-am-Main, 1983), vol. 2, p. 47.

44 *Die SPD: Klassenpartie–Volkspartei–Quotenpartei. Zur Entwicklung der Sozialdemokratie von Weimar bis zum deutschen Vereinigung* (Darmstadt, 1992), pp. 132–4.

45 Gerd Langguth, *Protestbewegung: Entwicklung, Niedergang, Renaissance* (Cologne, 1983); see also Gerd Langguth, *Der Grüne Faktor: Von der Bewegung zur Partei?* (Osnabrück, 1984); Elim Papadakis, *The Green Movement in West Germany* (Croom Helm, 1984).

46 John Borneman, *Belonging in the Two Berlins* (Cambridge, 1992), p. 249; see also Hannelore Brunhöber, 'Wohnen', in Benz, *Die Bundesrepublik Deutschland*, pp. 202–3.

47 H. Bodenschatz, V. Heise and J. Korfmacher, *Schluss mit der Zerstörung?* (Berlin, 1983), p. 30. See also Renate Petzinger and Marlo Riege, *Die neue Wohnungsnot – Wohnungswunder Bundesrepublik* (Hamburg, 1981).

48 Eberhard Roters, *Im Westen nichts Neues* (Lucerne, 1982), 'Einleitung', p. 83. See also Bernd Sonnewald and Jürgen Raabe-Zimmermann, 'Die "Berliner Linie" und die Hausbesetzer Szene', in *Politische Studien*, 27 (Berlin, 1983).

49 As one pamphlet asked, 'What is going on in this city? . . . Senate, police and legal system, Springer and Co., the building contractors and the demolition firms, or the squatters, the Kreuzbergers, the Alternatives and the left-wingers – who has flipped out? . . . In Berlin 80,000 people are looking for somewhere to live . . . The truth is, Hübner and his police troops provoke with their blue lights, tear gas and batons, practise at making a police state and appease the Senate and Springer . . . But when the Senate cries "stop the plunderers" then we ask you to please pose this question: WHO precisely is plundering WHOM?' AL demonstration pamphlet, '1, 2, 3, – lasst die Leute frei!', 20 December 1980.

50 On aid for housing see 'Beschluss des Senats von Berlin Nr. 2309/78, 4 April 1978', in Berliner Bauhandbuch, *Das Milliarden-Modernisierungsprogramm von*

1978 (Berlin, 1979), p. 28. See also Hermann Glaser, *Kulturgeschichte der Bundes-republik Deutschland. Zwischen Protest und Anpassung 1968–1989* (Munich, 1989), pp. 289–98.

51 On the creation of the AL in October 1978 see 'Gründerungserklärung der "Alternative Liste für Umweltschutz und Demokratie" ', in Michael Bühnemann, Michael Wendt and Jürgen Wituschek (eds.), *AL. Die Alternative Liste Berlin. Entstehung, Entwicklung, Positionen* (Berlin, 1984), pp. 80–82. On early conflicts between the Greens and the AL see Rebekka Schmidt, 'Die Grünen lehnen Beitrage mit der AL ab', *Stachel*, September 1983. In November 1983 the Greens and the AL agreed to co-operate on questions of 'the Economy, Environment, the Third World, Women, Europe and the Peace Movement (East and West), Democratic Rights and Foreigners', although the AL would continue to field independent candidates.

52 The call for a neutral Germany led to a tendency to downplay problems in the GDR and to heap criticism on the western powers, in particular the United States. Rudolf Bahro said of the GDR, 'If I had to make a comparison, I would say that the average person lives better in the GDR than in Italy. It has been said that living standards in the GDR are some twenty-five percent below those in West Germany. But since the Federal Republic is one of the richest countries in the world, the GDR must also be comparatively wealthy. There is sometimes a problem of quality, but the bulk of material goods are in adequate supply . . . Already quite a number of people even have a little cottage in the country as well as their town flat . . .' Bahro, *From Red to Green*, p. 102.

53 See, for example, Rita Hermanns, 'Die Hälfte des Himmels? Über alternative Frauen, Frauen und die Alternative Liste, Frauen in der Alternativen Liste', in Bühnemann, *AL*, pp. 99–120.

54 This rather self-righteous approach was not limited to Berlin. My father, out walking through his Canadian forest with our dachshund Bella, was once startled by a Green, visiting for the first time, who came up to him and told him to put the dog on a leash because she might 'frighten the animals'.

55 Th. Poguntke, *Alternative Politics: the German Green Party* (Edinburgh, 1993); E. G. Frankland and D. Schoonmaker, *Between Protest and Power: the Green Party in Germany* (Boulder, 1992); M. Dittmers, *The Green Party in West Germany: Who Are They and What Do They Really Want?* (Buckingham, 1988); Werner Hülberg, *The German Greens. A Social and Political Profile* (London, 1988).

56 Ardagh, *Germany and the Germans*, p. 59.

57 For an overview of immigration and the Federal Republic see Hartmut Berghoff, 'Population Change and Its Repercussions on the Social History of the Federal Republic', in Larres and Panayi, *The Federal Republic of Germany*, pp. 51–73; see also Wolfgang Benz, 'Fremde in der Heimat: Flucht–Verbreibung–Integration', in Klaus J. Bade (ed.), *Deutsche im Ausland – Fremde in Deutschland. Migration in Geschichte und Gegenwart* (Munich, 1992), p. 381; Klaus J. Bade (ed.), *Auswanderer, Wanderarbeiter, Gastarbeiter. Bevölkerung, Arbeitsmarkt und Wanderung in Deutschland seit der Mitte des 19. Jahrhunderts* (Ostfildern, 1984), vol. 2, pp. 625–9.

58 Merritt, 'Living with the Wall', in Merritt and Merritt, *Living with the Wall*, p. 202. See also Hartmut Esser, 'Gastarbeiter', in Benz, *Die Bundesrepublik Deutschland*, vol. 2, p. 133.

59 Peter Paul Zahl, 'Kreuzberg, Bruder, ist Westberlins Harlem', in Ingrid Krüger and Eike Schmitz (eds.), *Berlin, du deutsche Frau* (Darmstadt, 1985), p. 170.

60 Berghoff, 'Population Change and Its Repercussions', in Larres and Panayi, *The Federal Republic of Germany*, p. 56. See also Klaus J. Bade, *Vom Auswanderrungsland zum Einwanderungsland? Deutschland 1880–1980* (Berlin, 1983); Ray C. Rist, *Guestworkers in Germany. The Prospects for Pluralism* (New York, 1978); Klaus F. Zimmermann (ed.), *Migration and Economic Development* (Berlin, 1992).

61 The German workforce was growing for demographic reasons. Between 1975 and 1985 there was an increased need for 80,000 new jobs each year to handle Germans coming of age. Berghoff, 'Population Change and Its Repercussions', in Larres and Panayi, *The Federal Republic of Germany*, pp. 51–67.

62 Ibid., pp. 60–62.

63 *Der Spiegel*, no. 38, 15 October 1984, pp. 45–94.

64 In 1990–91 there were 14,500 Turkish students in German universities (0.8 per cent of the university population), although as E. Kürsat-Ahlers has pointed out, 'even the best educated young Turks in Germany continue to be penalised because of the background of their parents'. Elcin Kürsat-Ahlers, 'The Turkish Minority in German Society', in David Horrocks and Eva Kolinsky (eds.), *Turkish Culture in German Society Today* (Oxford, 1996), p. 131.

· 65 Heidrun Suhr, 'The Outsider's View from the Inside', in Charles W. Haxthausen and Heidrun Suhr (eds.), *Berlin. Culture and Metropolis* (University of Minnesota, 1991), pp. 234–8; Kürsat-Ahlers, 'The Turkish Minority in German Society', in Horrocks and Kolinsky, *Turkish Culture*, pp. 117–35.

66 Aras Ören, *Gefühllosigkeiten: Reisen von Berlin nach Berlin* (Frankfurt-am-Main, 1986), p. 16; see also Suhr, 'The Outsider's View from the Inside', in Haxthausen and Suhr, *Berlin*, pp. 225–34.

67 Amity Shlaes, *Germany. The Empire Within* (London, 1991), p. 4.

68 Berlin's precarious position and the need to invest in the 'city of culture' was recognized as the only hope of survival. Walter Schmieding wrote in 1969 that West Berlin had lost its function as a capital but, because of the other problems the city faced, 'the loss of the real functions of a capital has only been felt very moderately. Today, however, nearly a quarter of a century after the break-down of the old "capital of the Reich", this loss is becoming distressingly evident and calls for compensation in one way or another. West Berlin is no longer the "capital of Germany", but should it not at least be the "cultural centre of Germany"?' Walter Schmieding, 'Cultural centre Berlin', in Hermann Kiessling (ed.), *Kunst in Berlin* (Berlin, 1969), p. 8.

69 Thomas Steinfeld, 'Afterword: Writing about Berlin', in Haxthausen and Suhr, *Berlin*, p. 254.

70 The DAAD – German Academic Exchange Service – was founded in 1925; it resumed work in 1950 after closing down during the Second World War. It is an organization of German universities and colleges meant to promote international relations in the field of higher education, particularly through exchanges in all

disciplines and from most countries. Its central office is in Bad Godesberg but it established a presence in Berlin in 1950.

71 On Beuys see Heiner Stachelhaus, *Joseph Beuys* (Düsseldorf, 1988); Klaus Staeck (ed.), *Ohne die Rose tun wir's nicht. Für Joseph Beuys* (Heidelberg, 1986).

72 Abstract Expressionism was represented in the 1950s by Fred Thieler and Hann Trier; see Georg Nothelfer (ed.), *Fred Thieler zum 70. Geburtstag, Berlin, 17 März, 1968* (Berlin, 1986); Wolfgang Zemter (ed.), *Fred Thieler* (Bonn, 1979).

73 Kynaston McShine (ed.), *Berlinart 1961–1967* (New York, 1987), p. 13.

74 Diane Waldman, 'Georg Baselitz. Kunst auf der Kippe', in Sibylle Gross et al., *Georg Baselitz* (Berlin, 1995), pp. 20–23.

75 Toni Stoss and Wolf Vostell, *Vostell und Berlin: Leben und Werk, 1964–1976* (Berlin, 1982); see also David Schoenbaum, *The Spiegel Affair* (New York, 1968).

76 René Block, 'Fluxus and Fluxism in Berlin 1964–1976', in McShine, *Berlinart*, p. 66. See also Jürgen Becker and Wolf Vostell (eds.), *Happenings – Fluxus, Pop Art, Nouveau Realisme. Eine Dokumentation* (Hamburg, 1965); Wolf Vostell, *Aktionen: Happenings und Demonstrationen zeit 1965: Eine Dokumentation* (Reinbek, 1970); Wolf Vostell, *Edition* (Berlin, 1969).

77 The Berlin performance was allowed to continue, although a few months later Paik and Moorman were arrested during a performance of the *Opera Sextronique*. Block, 'Fluxus and Fluxism in Berlin', in McShine, *Berlinart*, p. 70.

78 Ibid., p. 75.

79 Raffael Rheinsberg, *Botschaften. Archäologie des Krieges* (Berlin, 1982), p. 11.

80 Peter Hans Göpfert, 'Die Indianer im Gropius-Bau', in Eckhart Gillen et al. (eds.), *Kunst in Berlin von 1870 bis heute* (Berlin 1987), pp. 229–38. See also Heinrich Klotz, *Die Neuen Wilden in Berlin* (Stuttgart, 1984).

81 Eckhart Gillen, 'Comeback der Aussenwelt. Berliner Realisten der sechziger und siebziger Jahre', in Gillen, *Kunst in Berlin*, p. 203. Karl Horst Hödicke, *Nocturno* (1983), is in the Gallery Bmyrek, Düsseldorf; Karl Horst Hödicke, *War Ministry (Kriegsministerium)* (1977), is in the Berlinische Galerie, Berlin.

82 The Galerie René Block was famous not least because it introduced Joseph Beuys to Berlin in 1964 with the performance *The Chief.* See René Block, *Grafik des kapitalistischen Realismus: KP Brehmer, Hödicke, Lueg, Polke, Richter, Vostell: Werkverzeichnisse bis 1971* (Berlin, 1971).

83 Karl Schwarz, 'Die Metropolen wollen, Berlin als Metropole wollen', in Karl Schwarz (ed.), *Die Zukunft der Metropolen: Paris, London, New York, Berlin* (Berlin, 1984), vol. 1, p. 12.

84 Dieter Hacker, Helga Retzer and Toni Stooss (eds.), *Die politische Arbeit des Künstlers beginnt bei seiner Arbeit: 7. Produzentengalerie, Dieter Hacker: Zwischenbericht, 1971–1981* (Berlin, 1981).

85 One of the more outspoken critics called art produced in Berlin in the early 1990s 'a range of conflicting styles, much dross', which mixed 'contraptions of the present with the painting and sculpture of the past'. Brian Sewell, 'Hang Them All on the Wilder Shores', *Evening Standard*, 10 August 1995.

86 On Gruppe 47 see Friedhelm Kröll, *Die Gruppe 47. Soziale Lage und gesellschaftliches Bewusstsein literarischer Intelligenze in der Bundesrepublik* (Stuttgart,

1979). See also Heinrich Vormweg, 'Literatur', in Benz, *Die Bundesrepublik Deutschland*, vol. 3, pp. 52–7; K. Stuart Parkes, *Writers and Politics in West Germany* (London, 1986); Werner Ross, *Mit der linken Hand geschrieben . . .: Der deutsche Literaturbetrieb* (Zürich, 1984).

87 Harald Hartung, 'Lyric Poetry in Berlin since 1961', in Haxthausen and Suhr, *Berlin*, p. 189.

88 Robert Scholz, *Am Grünen Strand der Spree* (Berlin, 1968).

89 Karl Ruhrberg and Thomas Deecke, *DAAD Berlin Artists Program: 10 Jahre Berliner Künstlerprogramm* (Berlin, 1975).

90 Karl Ruhrberg, 'Visitors to a City in Exile', in McShine, *Berlinart*, p. 57.

91 Heinz Ohff, 'Die Muse küsst den widerstrebenden Bären', *Magazin Kunst*, 3 (Berlin, 1976).

92 Cynthia Beatt and Silvia Voser (eds.), *Berlin im Film 1965–1985* (Berlin, 1985); Hubert Ortkemper (ed.), *Film in Berlin. 5 Jahre Berliner Filmförderung* (Berlin, 1983).

93 Wim Wenders and Peter Handke, *Der Himmel über Berlin – Ein Filmbuch* (Frankfurt-am-Main, 1987).

94 Another element of Berlin cinema was the establishment of small private cinemas like the Arsenal and the Kino Eiszeit in a converted Kreuzberg loft, one of twelve places dedicated to video and super-8 films. See Keith J. Sanborn, *Super-8/Berlin. The Architecture of Division* (Buffalo, 1983).

95 On the 'myth of ruins' and the destruction of Berlin's architectural heritage after 1945 see Wolfgang Schäche and Wolfgang J. Streich, 'Wiederaufbau oder Neuaufbau – über die Legende der "total zerstörten Stadt"', in Wolfgang Schäche and Wolfgang J. Streich (eds), *IFP Stadtentwicklung nach 1945* (Berlin, 1984), pp. 36–55.

96 Frank Werner, 'Die vollendente Unvollendete', in Mathias Schreiber, *40 Jahre Moderne in der Bundesrepublik. Deutsche Architektur nach 1945* (Stuttgart, 1986), pp. 56–9.

97 Manfred Throll et al., *Kulturforum und zentraler Bereich Berlin. Zur Auseinandersetzung zwischen Moderne und Postmoderne im Zentrum Berlins* (Berlin, 1986).

98 Eberhard Schulz, 'Kontrapunkt des Kurfürstendamms', in Schreiber, *40 Jahre Moderne in der Bundesrepublik*, pp. 53–5.

99 Wolf Jobst Siedler and Elisabeth Niggemeyer, *Die gemordete Stadt* (Berlin/Munich, 1978).

100 Rüdiger Lutz, 'Zwischen Technopolis und Ökopolis – die Zukunft', in Joachim Winter and Jürgen Mach (eds.), *Herausforderung Stadt. Aspekte einer Humanökologie* (Frankfurt-am-Main/Berlin, 1988), pp. 124–39.

101 Witold Gombrowicz, *Die Tagebücher* (Pfullingen, 1970), vol. 3, p. 47.

102 Hitler's bunker still existed underground until largely demolished by the East Germans in the 1980s. Brian Ladd, *The Ghosts of Berlin. Confronting German History in the Urban Landscape* (Chicago, 1997), p. 133.

103 Siekmeier and Larres, 'Domestic Political Developments II: 1969–90', in Larres and Panayi, *The Federal Republic of Germany*, pp. 122–36.

104 David Marsh, *The New Germany at the Crossroads* (London, 1989), p. 322.

105 Robert Harris, 'I, Spy. The curious career of East Germany's Markus Wolf',

New Yorker, 9 June 1997, p. 98. See also Markus Wolf (with Anne McElvoy), *Man Without a Face: The Memoirs of a Spymaster* (London, 1997).

106 Timothy Garton Ash states that there were two basic mistakes in the second *Ostpolitik*: 'The first was to believe that, as Bahr expressed it, "security is the key to everything" . . . And two years later he observed: "My real mistake was, as I see now, that in the last thirty-five years I have believed: since the heart of the matter is the security question, the power question, one must make sure that wars are no longer possible. Then politics and everything else will follow. Including German unity, including the overcoming of the East–West division in Europe. That was wrong. Politics have overtaken the security question." The second basic mistake concerned politics. This was the belief that political change in Eastern Europe could only come from those who already held power, through reform from above – and the concomitant neglect of the individuals, groups and movements working for change from below.' Garton Ash, *In Europe's Name*, p. 340. Bahr's quote appeared in *Die Zeit*, 13 March 1992.

107 The historians met in Bonn ostensibly to 'discuss the history of the Weimar Republic', but, as the East Germans refused to make any fundamental changes in their Marxist line, the unfortunate appearance was of a tacit western acceptance of their highly distorted view of the past. See Susanne Miller and Malte Ristau (eds.), *Erben deutscher Geschichte. DDR-BRD: Protokolle einer historischen Gegenung* (Reinbek, 1988).

108 Hans Mommsen, 'Such nach der "verlorenen Geschichte"? Bemerkungen zum historischen Selbstverständnis der Bundesrepublik', *Merkur*, 9/10, September/October 1986; Gisela Völger, '36,000 qm Geschichte', *Die Zeit*, 30 October 1987.

109 For West Berlin see Ulrich Eckhardt (ed.), *750 Jahre Berlin Stadt der Gegenwart. Lese- und Programmbuch zum Stadtjubiläum* (Berlin, 1986); for East Berlin see Komitee der Deutschen Demokratischen Republik zum 750 jährigen Bestehen von Berlin (eds.), *750 Jahre Berlin. Das Buch zum Fest* (Berlin, 1986).

110 *Berliner Morgenpost*, 6 January 1987.

111 On the *Historikerstreit* see 'Introduction' above. See also 'Facing the Mirror of German History', *New York Times*, 22 October 1988; Josef Joffe, 'The Battle of the Historians', *Encounter*, June 1987, pp. 72–7; Charles S. Maier, *The Unmasterable Past: History, Holocaust, and German National Identity* (Harvard, 1988); Richard J. Evans, *In Hitler's Shadow. West German Historians and the Attempt to Escape from the Nazi Past* (New York, 1989); R. Piper (ed.), '*Historikerstreit': Die Dokumentation der Kontroverse um die Einzigartigkeit der nationalsozialistischen Judenvernichtung* (Munich, 1987).

112 György Ligeti, in Ruhrberg and Deecke, *DAAD Berlin Artists Program*.

113 Wolf-Jobst Siedler, speech in the Hebbel-Theater Berlin, 14 August 1987.

114 Gordon Craig, 'Facing Up to the Nazis', *New York Review of Books*, 2 February 1989, pp. 10–15.

115 Gordon Craig, 'The War of the German Historians', *New York Review of Books*, 15 January 1987, p. 18.

116 'Zum Geburtstag spendiert Bonn Reichstag die Kuppel', *Berliner Volksblatt*, 30 April 1987.

117 Karl Heinz Krüger, 'Wat de kriegen kannst, det nimmste', *Der Spiegel*, 5 January

1987, pp. 55–66. See also Gerhard Weiss, 'Panem et Circenses', in Haxthausen and Suhr, *Berlin*, pp. 243–52.

18: THE NEW CAPITAL

1 Gerhart Hoffmeister and Frederic C. Tubach, *Germany: 2000 Years. From the Nazi Era to German Unification* (New York, 1992), vol. 3, p. 258; Hans Herbert Götz, *Honecker – und was dann? 40 Jahre DDR* (Herford, 1989), p. 263. The people of Dresden and Leipzig were proud of their accomplishments; see Hartmut Zwahr, *Ende einer Selbstzerstörung. Leipzig und die Revolution in der DDR* (Göttingen, 1993), pp. 9–10.

2 Despite the presence of many courageous individuals it took longer for the people of East Berlin to organize against the regime than those in other cities, notably Dresden and Leipzig. The reasons for the relative lack of action in East Berlin are complex and have to do not only with the high percentage of SED functionaries keen to block change but with the strength of the Stasi and the military. Stasi documents reveal how dissidents, including Pastors Eppelmann, Tschiche and Wonneberger, and Gerd and Ulrike Poppe, Bärbel Bohley and Werner Fischer were monitored throughout this period. See Armin Mitter and Stefan Wolle (eds.), *Ich liebe euch doch alle! Befehle und Lageberichte des MfS Januar–November 1989* (Berlin, 1990), p. 10.

3 David Gress refers to as this as the 'New Ostpolitik', the approach by those who saw European division as a necessary condition of stability rather than as a threat or a problem, and who believed in the fundamental compatibility of Soviet security needs with those of the west. In the mid-1980s the new *Ostpolitik* was represented by the overwhelming majority of the SPD but also had strong support in the FDP and in certain groups within the CDU. 'Because their primary aim was East–West stability, they tended to give the Soviet Union and its communist allies the benefit of the doubt when judging such actions as the invasion of Afghanistan or the suppression of democratic movements in Poland.' In short, they defended Martial Law 'because it improved stability'. David Gress, *Peace and Survival. West Germany, the Peace Movement and European Security* (Stanford, 1985), p. 74.

4 The notion that one could defuse tensions between the Soviet Union and the west by simply demonstrating good will to the Soviets was naive in the extreme; nevertheless it dominated thinking in 1980s West Berlin. Richard Pipes, quoted in Gabriel Partos, *The World That Came In from the Cold* (London, 1993), p. 208.

5 Zbigniew Brzezinski urged the Carter administration to adopt a more forceful approach towards the Soviets. He and others argued that what might deter the west would not necessarily deter the Soviets, and that it was misleading to judge the Soviet Union by values or standards understood or accepted by the west. And, as Adam Ulam pointed out, only a show of strength would persuade the Soviets to modify their position. See, for example, the list of recommendations drawn up in May 1979 regarding Soviet–US relations in Zbigniew Brzezinski, *Power and Principle. Memoirs of the National Security Advisor, 1977–1981* (New

York, 1983), p. 335; see also Adam B. Ulam, *Dangerous Relations* (Oxford, 1982).

6 By early 1984 the Soviets had deployed 378 SS-20 launchers, each capable of firing three 150-kiloton warheads with a range of over 5,000 kilometres. Gress, *Peace and Survival*, p. 70. See also London Institute for Strategic Studies, *The Military Balance 1984–85* (1984), pp. 134–8.

7 Elizabeth Pond, *Beyond the Wall. Germany's Road to Unification* (New York, 1993), p. 38.

8 Caspar Weinberger, quoted in Partos, *The World That Came In from the Cold*, p. 226.

9 On Schmidt's support of the American decision see Helmut Schmidt, *Menschen und Mächte* (Berlin, 1987), p. 338–9; see also Herbert Dittgen, *Deutsch– amerikanische Sicherheitsbeziehungen in der Ära Helmut Schmidt: Vorgeschichte und Folgen des NATO-Doppelbeschlusses* (Munich, 1991).

10 Lafontaine advocated, amongst other things, the German withdrawal from NATO. On his vision for the future see Oskar Lafontaine, *Angst vor den Freunden* (Reinbek, 1983).

11 Jochen Thies, *Helmut Schmidt's Rückzug von der Macht. Das Ende der Ära Schmidt aus nächster Nähe* (Stuttgart, 1988), pp. 11–29.

12 Richard Perle, American Assistant Secretary of Defense 1981–7, quoted in Partos, *The World That Came In from the Cold*, p. 227. See also Richard N. Perle, *Reshaping Western Society: The United States Faces a United Europe* (Washington, DC, 1991).

13 On the introduction of the SDI initiative see George P. Schultz, *Turmoil and Triumph. My Years as Secretary of State* (Oxford, 1993), pp. 246–64. On SDI technology see the United States Office of Technology Assessment, *SDI: Technology, Survivability, and Software*, May 1988.

14 The project was supported by Helmut Kohl; see Dennis L. Bark and David Gress, *A History of West Germany* (Oxford, 1993), vol. 2: *Democracy and Its Discontents 1963–1991*, pp. 465–7. See also Th. Benien, *Der SDI-Entscheidungsprozess in der Regierung Kohl/Genscher (1983–1986): Eine Fallstudie über Einflussfaktoren sicherheitspolitischer Entscheidungsfindung unter den Bedingungen strategischer Abhängigkeit* (Munich, 1991).

15 Ernst Kux maintains that Gorbachev did not simply grant freedom to the Soviet colonies; on the contrary, his reforms prompted developments in eastern Europe which he could not control. The revolutions occurred not because of the success but rather because of the failure of *perestroika*; 'the failure of the "revolution from above" to satisfy the desires which it awakened provoked the "revolution from below" in Poland, Hungary, Leipzig, Prague, Sofia and Bucharest'. Ernst Kux, 'Revolution in Eastern Europe – Revolution in the West?', in *Problems of Communism*, 40, May–June 1991, pp. 1-13.

16 Mikhail Gorbachev, *Perestroika: New Thinking for Our Country and the World* (New York, 1987). See also Michel Tatu, *Gorbatchev* (Paris, 1987), pp. 254–9.

17 On the differing views on SDI and the debate as to which approach 'won the Cold War' see Timothy Garton Ash, *In Europe's Name: Germany and the Divided Continent* (London, 1993), pp. 119–25.

18 According to George Shulz, Gorbachev 'referred to the many concessions he

had made and said he wanted only one concession in return, SDI. I felt that Gorbachev had instructions or had agreed – perhaps with the Politburo – that he had to get the scalp of SDI.' Shulz, *Turmoil and Triumph*, p. 772.

19 Josef Joffe, *The Limited Partnership: Europe, the United States, and the Burdens of Alliance* (Cambridge, Mass., 1987), pp. 85–6.

20 Frederick Kempe, *Wall Street Journal*, 13 March 1989.

21 On the relationship between Germany, NATO and the Soviets see Bark and Gress. *A History of West Germany*, vol. 2, pp. 452–567; here p. 472.

22 The policies practised by leading Social Democrats, including Willy Brandt, Egon Bahr, Günter Gaus and Oskar Lafontaine, 'have come to mean the maintenance of relations with Eastern governments rather than the support of human rights in Eastern Europe. Their success in these, limited, terms, then necessarily becomes hostage to the good will of the very Eastern regimes who are themselves the principal obstacles to peace and democracy in Europe, and they thus become self-defeating.' Gress, *Peace and Survival*, p. 70.

23 As early as 1985 David Gress could write that 'one of the most significant changes in West German public opinion since approximately the mid-1970s has been the loss of confidence in transatlantic cooperation and in the importance of American strength for peace and security'. Ibid., p. 71. See also Lawrence Freedman, *The Evolution of Nuclear Strategy* (London, 1981).

24 Pond, *Beyond the Wall*, p. 204. See also Wolfgang Brinkel (ed.), *Das SPD: SED-Papier. Der Streit der Ideologien und die gemeinsame Sicherheit* (Freiburg i. Br., 1988), p. 204.

25 Egon Bahr, *Zum europäischen Frieden. Eine Antwort an Gorbatschow* (Berlin, 1988).

26 They also echoed Hellmut Diwald's view that Germany was being treated as a football between the superpowers. In his *Geschichte der Deutschen* (History of the Germans) Diwald had asked, 'what does Germany, what do the Germans, have to do with the motives, arguments, and interests of the two rivals?' He conveniently failed to mention that the division of Germany had ultimately been caused by Hitler's aggression and that it had then come about because of Stalin's refusal to allow the people of the GDR self-determination. Diwald preferred to blame the west, and the Americans in particular, for the situation. He gave academic credibility to the notion that unity could be achieved in a neutral demilitarized state. Hellmut Diwald, *Geschichte der Deutschen* (Berlin, 1978), p. 59; see also Gress, *Peace and Survival*, pp. 58–9.

27 *The Week in Germany*, 24 February 1989, quoted in Bark and Gress, *A History of West Germany*, vol. 2, p. 543. On the Lance continuing see also Christoph Bertram, *Die Zeit*, 14 April 1989.

28 Ingo Heinrich, the border guard who killed Gueffroy, fired at his chest from 37 metres away, making the shooting 'akin to an execution'. He was given a three-and-a-half-year prison sentence. Anne Mc Elvoy, *The Saddled Cow. East Germany's Life and Legacy* (London, 1993), pp. 132–4.

29 The best account of Bush's foreign policy and German unification was written by two Bush administration officials who recorded the diplomatic events taking place behind the scenes; their study is made better through their access to East

German and Soviet state archives, including documents prepared for the Soviet Politburo. Philip Zelikow and Condoleezza Rice, *Germany Unified and Europe Transformed: A Study in Statecraft* (Cambridge, Mass., 1955).

30 Manfred Wörners speech was reprinted in *Die Welt*, 25 May 1989.

31 Preparations for a rally to coincide with Ronald Reagan's visit included plans to blare taped messages about world peace out of windows. Michael Bühnemann, Michael Wendt and Jürgen Wituschek (eds.), *AL. Die Alternative Liste Berlin. Enstehung, Entwicklung, Positionen* (Berlin, 1984), pp. 163–4. Willy Brandt was also critical of Reagan. When asked why he did not comment on Reagan's speech to Gorbachev on 13 August 1986 in which Reagan had challenged them to 'tear down the Wall', he replied that strong words were 'no use' and that even then 'in negotiations with his Russian opposite number he laid the emphasis elsewhere, and he did not question the division of Germany established at Yalta in 1945. This was why I would not enter into discussion with him.' Willy Brandt, *My Life in Politics* (New York, 1992), p. 45.

32 Timothy Garton Ash, 'A Hungarian Lesson', in Timothy Garton Ash, *The Uses of Adversity* (Harmondsworth, 1989), pp. 130–41.

33 Zbigniew Brzezinski, *The Grand Failure. The Birth and Death of Communism in the Twentieth Century* (London, 1989), pp. 114–19.

34 Mirek Chojecki, who ran the biggest clandestine publishing and printing house in Poland, published books as well as pamphlets and newspapers in the late 1970s and early 1980s. Many young Warsawians, including my husband, Wladyslaw Bartoszewski, worked avidly against the Communist system, doing everything from writing articles and obtaining paper to distributing material and safeguarding illegal printing presses.

35 John Tagliabue, 'Big Solidarity Victory Seen in Poland', *New York Times*, 4 June 1989.

36 The film *Repentance* (USSR, 1987), directed by Tengiz Abuladz and starring Avttandil Makhardadze, Ily Ninidze and Zeinab Botsvadze, tells the story of a tyrannical city mayor – unmistakably Stalin – whose corpse continues to show up in the town despite the official burial. The scene to which I refer is based on fact. Stalin's Gulag included camps in which prisoners were forced to work cutting down trees. They would sometimes carve their names on the tree trunks in the hope that someone might see them when the trunks were floated downstream for later collection. The film depicts the mother and daughter climbing over vast piles of logs along with another group of women, in the desperate search for a name or some other sign from their loved ones.

37 David Childs, 'The SED and Ostpolitik and Glasnost', in David Childs, Thomas A. Baylis and Marilyn Rueschemeyer (eds.), *East Germany in Comparative Perspective* (London, 1989), p. 15.

38 Joyce Marie Mushaben, 'Swords into Ploughshares', *Studies in Comparative Communism*, no. 33, July–August 1984, pp. 44–56.

39 For an overview see Wolfgang Büscher and Peter Wensierski (eds.), *Friedensbewegung in der DDR. Texte 1978–1982* (Hattingen, 1982).

40 These included a group of homosexuals, who approached the Church in the quest for social respect in a hostile system. See for example, Matthias Hartmann,

'Als abartig verdammt – zur Ordination berufen?', *Kirche im Sozialismus* 11, no. 3, June 1985. On the Church and the environmental movement see Hubertus Knabe, *Umweltprobleme und Umweltbewusstsein in der DDR* (Cologne, 1985), 'Gesellschaftlicher Wissens in Wandel. Ökologische Diskussion und Umweltbewusstengagement in der DDR', pp. 42–8. See also Robert F. Goeckel, 'Is the GDR the future of Hungary and the Baltics? Dissent and the Lutheran Church in Eastern Europe', in Childs et al., *East Germany in Comparative Perspective*, pp. 123–8.

41 Henry Kissinger, *Diplomacy* (London, 1985), p. 793.

42 George Bush's speech is reprinted in *Jahresbericht des Koordinators für die deutsch-amerikanische zwischengesellschaftliche, kultur- und informationspolitische Zusammenarbeit 1989* (Bonn, 1990); see also Bark and Gress, *A History of West Germany*, vol. 2, p. 580.

43 Marlies Menge, *'Ohne und läuft nichts mehr'. Die Revolution in der DDR* (Stuttgart, 1990), p. 106.

44 Gyula Horn, *Freiheit, die ich meine* (Hamburg, 1991), p. 311; Henry Kamm, 'East Germans Put Hungary in a Bind', *New York Times*, 1 September 1989.

45 *Guardian*, 11 November 1989.

46 *International Affairs*, 13 September 1989; *Neues Deutschland*, 11 September 1989.

47 Hans-Jürgen Buntrock, 'Die Kirche von Unten', in Ferdinand Kroh (ed.), *'Freiheit ist immer Freiheit . . .' Die Andersdenkenden in der DDR* (Frankfurt-am-Main/Berlin, 1988), pp. 181–209.

48 'Declaration of New Forum on the Fortieth Anniversary of the GDR. Appeal to All Members of the SED', reprinted in Harold James and Marla Stone (eds.), *When the Wall Came Down. Reactions to German Unification* (New York, 1992), p. 124.

49 On East Berlin dissident activity see Ulrike Bresch et al. (eds.), *Oktober 1989 – Wieder den Schlaf der Vernunft* (Berlin, 1989), p. 43.

50 Günter Schabowski, *Der Absturz* (Berlin, 1991), pp. 211–15. See also 'Ich hab' an den geglaubt', *Der Spiegel*, 14 September 1991.

51 In a 1994 interview with David Childs, Krenz admitted to having made the decision to move against Erich Honecker on 9 October 1989. David Childs and Richard Popplewell, *The Stasi. The East German Intelligence and Security Service* (London, 1996), p. 190.

52 'In East Berlin, Dresden, Leipzig and elsewhere, the police beat back defiant protesters, swinging riot sticks and menacing them with water cannon. In East Berlin tonight, a candlelight vigil was broken up by the security police, who set upon some of the nearly 1,500 people there as the protesters shouted, "No violence"!' Serge Schmemann, 'Security Forces Storm Protesters in East Germany', *New York Times*, 8 October 1989.

53 Cornelia Heins, *The Wall Falls: An Oral History of the Reunification of the Two Germanies* (London, 1994), p. 230.

54 The numbers of those on the streets outside Berlin are revealing: on 30 October 1989, 200,000 people marched in Leipzig, 50,000 in Halle, 40,000 in Schwerin, 20,000 in Cottbus, and 20,000 in Karl-Marx-Stadt. On 4 November there were demonstrations in Magdeburg, Rostock, Altenburg, Potsdam, Lauscha, Suhl

Plauen, Schwerin, Dresden and Arnstadt. Karl Bruckmeier, 'Die Bürgerbewegung der DDR in Herbst 1989', in Gerda Haufe and Karl Bruckmeier (eds.), *Die Bürgerbewegungen in der DDR und in den Ostdeutschen Ländern* (Berlin, 1992), p. 30.

55 Schabowski's conference ended at 19:00:54. After a question about GDR citizens' rights to travel across the East German borders NBC's Tom Brockaw asked him: 'Is it possible for them to go through the Wall at some point?' According to the NBC News Archives Schabowski responded at 19:01:47 with the words, 'It is possible for them to go through the border.' The news was relayed to New York by NBC but had also been recorded by an SFB news team, who broadcast it within West Germany just after 19:00 hours. The signal was picked up throughout both East and West Berlin. See Hans-Hermann Hertle, *Chronik des Mauerfalls. Die dramatischen Ereignisse um den 9. November 1989* (Berlin, 1996), pp. 141–8.

56 Hundreds of eye-witness accounts have recorded the mixture of disbelief and excitement on that night; one Helga Hahnemann said, 'My 9 November: I have said "Thank God" a hundred times!' *Berliner illustrirte Zeitung*, 9 November 1989; another admitted that she was 'still wearing her nightclothes under her coat'. See the collection of articles in Hedda Angermann et al., *Aufbrüche. Dokumentation zur Wende in der DDR (Oktober bis März 1990)* (Munich, 1991). For other eye-witness accounts see McElvoy, *The Saddled Cow*, pp. 206–9; Timothy Garton Ash, *We the People. The Revolution of 89 Witnessed in Warsaw, Budapest, Berlin and Prague* (Cambridge, 1990), pp. 61–77; Peter Millar, *Tomorrow Belongs to Me. Germany through the Extraordinary Lives of Ordinary People* (London, 1992), pp. 164–80.

57 By 20:00 the area around the Bornholmer Strasse was packed with thousands of people. Oberstleutnant Harald Jäger, who had worked at the Bornholmer Strasse border post for twenty-five years, did not know what to do. When people began yelling that he might open the border immediately he recalled: 'Ich dachte: Das ist doch Quatsch. Ab sofert?' (I thought, that is rubbish. At once?) People continued to arrive, and the crowd yelled, 'Tor auf! Tor auf!' The Bornholmer Strasse barrier was lifted at 20:30, and thousands of people rushed through into West Berlin. Hertle, *Chronik des Mauerfalls*, pp. 159–66.

58 Günter Schabowski, *Das Politbüro: Ende eines Mythos* (Reinbek, 1990), p. 139.

59 Helmut Herles and Ewald Rose, *Parliaments-Szenen einer deutschen Revolution. Bundestag und Volkskammer im November 1989* (Bonn, 1990), p. 18.

60 On 24 October 1989, sixteen days before the Wall fell, George Bush had said, 'I don't share the concern that some European countries have about a reunified Germany.' On Bush's crucial role in German unification see Pond, *Beyond the Wall*, pp. 161–9.

61 *The Times*, 10 November 1989.

62 Moscow had been informed about events as they unfolded on 9 November; see Melvin J. Lasky, *Wortmeldung zu einer Revolution* (Frankfurt-em-Main, 1991), p. 74.

63 *Die Zeit*, 10 February 1990.

64 Speech by Chancellor Dr Helmut Kohl to the Bundestag on 28 November 1989,

on his 10-Point Plan towards German Unification (unofficial translation). The text was published in *Die Zeit*, 24 November 1989.

65 Margaret Thatcher, *The Downing Street Years* (London, 1993), pp. 797–8.

66 Julian Nundy, 'Jacques Attali Verbatim III', *Sunday Telegraph*, 15 October 1995.

67 Pond, *Beyond the Wall*, p. 156–61; see also Horst Teltschik, *329 Tage: Innenansichten der Einigung* (Berlin, 1991), p. 60.

68 Attali recalled that 'Margaret Thatcher sent François Mitterrand a copy of her letter to Mikhail Gorbachev which expressed her anxiety at developments in East Germany and in all the countries of Eastern Europe. She too considers that the speed of the recent changes contains a risk of instability ... "Mrs T" as her aides call her is more and more determined to set up a coalition of the Four – Paris, London, Moscow, Washington – to counter Kohl's ambitions. Nundy,' 'Jacques Attali Verbatim III', *Sunday Telegraph*, 15 October 1995.

69 'Genscher bekräftigt die Unverletzlichkeit der Grenzen in Europa', *Frankfurter Allgemeine Zeitung*, 27 September 1989.

70 Pond, *Beyond the Wall*, p. 161; see also Stephen F. Szabo, *The Diplomacy of German Unification* (New York, 1992).

71 Gerald R. Kleinfeld, 'Partners in Leadership? The Future of German–American Relations', in Peter H. Merkl (ed.), *The Federal Republic of Germany at Forty-Five* (New York, 1995), p. 61.

72 Gerald R. Kleinfeld, 'Die Verwirklichung des Unwahrscheinlichen: Amerikanische Aussenpolitik und deutsche Wiedervereinigung', in Wolfgang-Uwe Friedrich (ed.), *Die USA und die deutsche Frage 1945–1990* (Frankfurt-am-Main, 1991).

73 Childs and Popplewell, *The Stasi*, p. 191.

74 Jens Reich, *Abschied von den Lebenslügen. Die Intelligenz und die Macht* (Berlin, 1992), p. 21.

75 In his *Wenn Mauern fallen* (When Walls Fall) Egon Krenz describes himself as the man who benevolently opened the Berlin Wall. Honecker spat back on 12 March 1990 that he had simply driven the GDR into the arms of West Germany after he had 'lamed, discredited and finally destroyed' the Communist party. Egon Krenz, *Wenn Mauern fallen. Die friedliche Revolution: Vorgeschichte–Ablauf–Auswirkungen* (Vienna, 1990).

76 *Wall Street Journal*, 2 March 1991.

77 Karl Bruckmeier, 'Die allgemeine Situation in Herbst 1989' in Haufe and Bruckmeier, *Die Bürgerbewegungen in der DDR*, pp. 29–31.

78 Gregor Gysi opposed unification; when asked what effects unification had had on the consciousness of East German citizens he responded: 'Catastrophic. After the fall of 1989, the people had already lost faith in themselves, and they have already come to reject the possibility of approaching unification in an impartial fashion.' Interview with Gregor Gysi, 'Germany United and Divided', in James and Stone, *When the Wall Came Down*, p. 150. On his links with the Stasi see *Der Spiegel*, 29 May 1995.

79 On the advocates of the 'Third Way' see Hubertus Knabe (ed.), *Aufbruch in eine andere DDR* (Hamburg, 1989).

80 The election results are listed in Brigitte Walz, Anke Notle and Uwe Prell (eds.),

Berlin Handbuch. Das Lexikon der Bundeshaupstadt (Berlin, 1993), p. 1342.

81 Reinhard Weisshuhn, 'Nach der Wahlen', in Haufe and Bruckmeier, *Die Burger-bewegungen in der DDR*, pp. 160–2.

82 On his role in the unification process see Eduard Shevardnadze, *The Future Belongs to Freedom*, trans. Catherine A. Fitzpatrick (New York, 1991).

83 Leslie Lipschitz and Donogh McDonald (eds.), *German Unification: Economic Issues* (Washington, DC, 1990); Ullrich Heilemann and Reimut Jochimsen, *Christmas in July? The Political Economy of German Unification Reconsidered* (Washington, DC, 1993).

84 Hans-Werner Sinn, *Jumpstart: The Economic Unification of Germany* (Cambridge, Mass., 1992), pp. 19–27. See also Klaus Larres, 'Germany and the West: the "Rapallo Factor" in German Foreign Policy from the 1950s to the 1990s', in Larres and Panayi, *The Federal Republic of Germany*, p. 320.

85 *The Times*, 2 July 1990.

86 *The Financial Times*, 29 March 1990.

87 'Wer hört die Signale?', *Die Zeit*, 6 January 1995; '500 Milliarden DM im Osten investiert', *Frankfurter Allgemeine Zeitung*, 19 January 1995; Treuhandanstalt, *Informationen*, 21 December 1994.

88 On some of the problems encountered by the organization see Karl H. Kahrs, 'Treuhand: The privatisation of a Planned Economy', in Merkl, *The Federal Republic of Germany*, pp. 168–83.

89 Timothy Garton Ash, 'The Chequers Affair', *New York Review of Books*, 27 September 1990.

90 Michael Howard, 'After 44 Years Let Us at Last Talk Peace', *The Times*, 15 November 1989.

91 Hans Klein, *Es begann im Kaukasus. Der entscheidende Schritt in die Einheit Deutschlands* (Berlin, 1991).

92 Helmut Kohl, *Ich wollte Deutschlands Einheit*, ed. Kai Diekmann and Ralf Georg Reuth, Hamburg, 1996), pp. 421–44.

93 *Sunday Telegraph*, 30 September 1990.

94 In this vein see, for example, Helmut Kohl's speech of 2 October 1990, which ended with the words 'Gott segne unser Vaterland' – God bless our Fatherland. *Dokumentation zum 3. Oktober 1990. Reden zur deutschen Einheit* (Bonn, 1990), p. 9.

95 *The Financial Times*, 9 September 1994.

96 *Die Welt*, 22 June 1991.

97 *Frankfurter Allgemeine Zeitung*, 27 April 1991.

98 *The Times*, 11 June 1991.

99 Nundy, 'Jacques Attali Verbatim III', *Sunday Telegraph*, 15 October 1995.

100 *Die Zeit*, 21 June 1991.

101 Helmut Herles (ed.), *Die Hauptstadtdebatte* (Bonn/Berlin, 1991).

102 *Die Welt*, 24 June 1991.

103 Schamirs Ben-Aharon said that each state had the right to choose its capital, and there was no reason to think that Germany would slip backwards into history. See *Frankfurter Allgemeine Zeitung*, 22 June 1991.

104 *Washington Post*, 29 July 1989.

INDEX